Direct Social Work Practice

Theory and Skills

Sixth Edition

Dean H. Hepworth
Professor Emeritus, University of Utah
and Arizona State University

Ronald H. Rooney
University of Minnesota

Jo Ann Larsen
Private Practice
Salt Lake City

BROOKS/COLE

THOMSON LEARNING

Australia • Canada • Mexico • Singapore • Spain • United Kindgom • United States

BROOKS/COLE

THOMSON LEARNING

Executive Editor: *Lisa Gebo*
Editorial Assistant: *Sheila Walsh*
Marketing: *Caroline Concilla/Megan Hansen*
Assistant Editor: *Jennifer Wilkinson/Alma Dea Michelena*
Project Editor: *Kim Svetich-Will*
Production: *TSI Graphics*
Manuscript Editor: *Suzanne Davidson*

Permissions Editor: *Karyn Morrison*
Interior Design: *TSI Graphics*
Cover Design: *Laurie Albrecht*
Print Buyer: *Vena Dyer*
Compositor: *TSI Graphics*
Cover Printing: *R.R. Donnelley, Crawfordsville*
Printing and Binding: *R.R. Donnelley, Crawfordsville*

For more information about this or any other Brooks/Cole product, contact:
BROOKS/COLE
511 Forest Lodge Road
Pacific Grove, CA 93950 USA
www.brookscole.com
1-800-423-0563 (Thomson Learning Academic Resource Center)

Printed in the United States of America

10   9   8   7   6   5   4   3   2   1

Library of Congress Cataloging-in-Publication Data

Hepworth, Dean H.
  Direct social work practice : theory and skills/Dean H.
Hepworth, Ronald H. Rooney, Jo Ann Larsen. — 6th ed.
        p.   cm.
  Includes bibliographical references and index.
  ISBN 0-534-36838-7
  1. Social service.   I. Rooney, Ronald H., [date].   II. Larsen, Jo Ann.   III. Title.
HV40 . H53   2001
361.3'2—dc21   2001037317

Brief Contents

Contents

CHAPTER 7
ELIMINATING COUNTERPRODUCTIVE COMMUNICATION PATTERNS   171

CHAPTER 8
MULTIDIMENSIONAL ASSESSMENT   187

CHAPTER 9
ASSESSING INTRAPERSONAL AND ENVIRONMENTAL SYSTEMS   219

PART 3
THE CHANGE-ORIENTED PHASE   357

CHAPTER 13
PLANNING AND IMPLEMENTING CHANGE-ORIENTED STRATEGIES   359

CHAPTER 14
ENHANCING CLIENTS' PROBLEM SOLVING, SOCIAL, ASSERTIVENESS, AND STRESS MANAGEMENT SKILLS   399

CHAPTER 18
ADDITIVE EMPATHY, INTERPRETATION, AND CONFRONTATION   543

CHAPTER 19
MANAGING INDIVIDUAL AND FAMILY BARRIERS TO CHANGE   565

PART 4
THE TERMINATION PHASE   589

CHAPTER 20
THE FINAL PHASE: TERMINATION   591

REFERENCES   R1
AUTHOR INDEX   A1
SUBJECT INDEX   S1

About the authors

Dean H. Hepworth is Professor Emeritus at the School of Social Work, Arizona State University, Tempe Arizona, and the University of Utah. Dean has extensive practice experience in individual psychotherapy, and marriage and family therapy. Dean was the lead author and active in the production of the first four editions, and he is the co-author of *Improving Therapeutic Communication*. He is now retired and lives in Phoenix, Arizona.

Ronald H. Rooney is Professor, School of Social Work, University of Minnesota, Twin Cities. Ron revised the 5th edition and 6th edition, with the assistance of the contributors. Ron's practice background is primarily in public and private child welfare, including work with involuntary clients, about which he does training and consultation. Ron is the author of *Strategies for Work with Involuntary Clients*.

Jo Ann Larsen is in private practice in Salt Lake City, Utah, and was formerly a faculty member at the School of Social Work, University of Utah. Jo Ann was active in the preparation of the first four editions of the book. Jo Ann has extensive experience in psychotherapy with individuals, families, and groups. Jo Ann is the author of four books on women's issues.

About the contributors

Glenda Dewberry Rooney is an Associate Professor at Augsburg College and currently a Visiting Professor at the School of Social Work, University of Minnesota, Twin Cities. She has taught both graduate and undergraduate practice courses using earlier editions of Hepworth, Rooney and Larsen. Her experience in education, training and consulting with community agencies concerned with children, youth and families is reflected in the five chapters she revised and edited for this edition (chapters 10, 12, 13, 15,16).

Kim Strom-Gottfried is an Associate Professor and Acting Dean of the School of Social Work, University of North Carolina at Chapel Hill. Kim revised and edited four chapters of this edition (chapters 4, 8, 9, and 20). Kim has extensive experience in direct service, administration and planning in mental health. She provides training and consultation and research related to private practice, ethics and managed care. Kim is the editor of *Social Work Practice: Cases, Activities and Exercises*.

Preface

We are proud of the legacy of the first five editions of *Direct Social Work Practice* and are anxious to share with you what we have retained and what we have changed in the 6th edition. Ron worked with Glenda and Kim as a team in planning this edition and drew from their past experience teaching social work practice courses using earlier editions of this text. That experience about what worked best for their students led them to five main goals for this edition.

Goals for the 6th Edition

1. A great strength of previous editions has been guidance and modeling for social work students in how to implement practice skills. The 6th edition now contains specific guides to assessing certain problems such as potential for suicide and includes full examples of written assessments. In addition, we now include several detailed case studies in Chapter 15 on macro social work practice, describing what social workers have actually done to promote social justice with their clients.

2. *Update and streamline the theory and knowledge base of the book.* Over the course of its first five editions, the text has reflected the models and theories that were current in their day. The edition includes extensive updating of references in all chapters. We have chosen to streamline the book, maintaining focus on the helping process with illustrative examples from a variety of fields and settings. However, we have eliminated many sections on specific problems and settings as we felt that they tended to sidetrack students from learning about intervention skills and quickly became dated.

3. *Continue to enhance diversity in the book.* In addition to including references to the most recent publications, we have consciously used case examples in the book to exemplify our commitment to honoring diversity in multiple forms. Hence, case examples and dialogues were chosen to reflect this commitment to diversity.

4. *Place practice skills in current social and policy context.* This edition reflects changes in social policy including welfare and work programs, child welfare laws, and the growing influence of managed care. This context is then reflected in case examples, dialogues, and settings for learning practice skills.

5. *We incorporate technology into your learning of direct practice skills as well as within the skills we teach.* To facilitate your learning about Internet resources, each chapter includes a new section entitled *Internet Resources* containing URLs for useful sites. Because you have purchased this book, you are also entitled to a four-month free membership in InfoTrac®, an Internet information retrieval service, that will permit you to read the full text of relevant articles and print them on your home printer. As InfoTrac® contains articles from many academic and professional fields, each chapter will contain guidelines for entering useful key words and a listing of some of the more pertinent articles you can directly access. We will also explore issues related to operating groups via the Internet, e-mail and telephone in Chapter 17. By the very dynamic nature of the Web, URLs are subject to change. Therefore, while weblinks in this text were selected with care, please note that some links that were active the time of publication may no longer be functional.

Theoretical Orientation

We address human problems in this text from an ecological systems framework. A major feature of the book is the inclusion of material germane to various systems and subsystems typically implicated in problems encountered by social workers. They include individuals, couples, families, groups, and various environmental systems.

To equip students with a broad range of skills, we present a systematic-eclectic (pluralistic) perspective of practice. Both demanding and rigorous, this perspective enables practitioners to choose from various theories, practice models, and interventions those that best match the unique needs of each client. In selecting intervention models, interventions, and techniques, we are strongly influenced by those that are most empirically grounded. Those approaches include Task-Centered, Solution Focused and Cognitive Behavioral, as well as Strengths-Oriented and Empowerment-Based influences. Moreover, we have included interventions and techniques applicable to modifying environments, improving interpersonal relationships, and enhancing individuals' biophysical, cognitive, emotional, and behavioral functioning. The text thus has a multidimensional approach to both assessment and interventions.

Structural Organization

This edition of the book has four parts. The first part introduces the reader to the profession and to direct practice and provides an overview of the helping process. In the first chapter, the knowledge base of social work and the influence of systems theory have been expanded to include new content on nonlinear applications. The second chapter presents roles and domain of the field within a more current context of policy and practice. Chapter 3 presents an overview of the helping process. Part I concludes with Chapter 4, which is concerned with the cardinal values of social work and how they are operationalized in practice. This chapter includes greatly enhanced materials on confidentiality, ethical decision-making and boundaries.

Part 2, which is devoted to the beginning phase of the helping process, opens with Chapter 5, which focuses on relationship-building skills in the context of socialization to roles. Examples in Chapter 5 have been updated for currency as well as references and more recent research on relationship building. Chapter 6 shifts the focus to theory and skills entailed in eliciting information from clients, exploring problems in depth, and providing direction, focus, and continuity to sessions. The chapter now includes examples of skills in settings beyond direct practice such as communication with managed care utilization reviewers. Chapter 7 addresses barriers to communication and now includes positive alternatives to counterproductive communication patterns.

Chapters 8–12 are concerned with assessing the problems and strengths of individuals, families, and groups; forming groups; enhancing motivation; and formulating goals and negotiating contracts. Chapter 8 has been streamlined and focused on the process and content of assessment, as well as elaborating on tests and including examples of written assessments. Chapter 9 addresses the assessment of intrapersonal and environmental systems and includes assessment questions relating to drug and alcohol use, assessment of suicidality, updated references to DSM-IV and symptoms of possible drug abuse. Chapter 10 focuses on family assessment and includes both cultural- and family-variant content including current information on family stressors. That content is now imbedded in more recent theory including many ethnic groups and immigrant populations. Chapter 11 includes updated content and references on beginning and assessing groups. Chapter 12 is substantially expanded with new materials on contracting and goal setting, a new case study, a form for tracking goals and tasks, a new section on qualitative measures and an example using an eco-map as a measure of change.

Part 3 is devoted to the middle phase (goal attainment) of the helping process. It begins with Chapter 13, which is concerned with planning and implementing change-oriented strategies, including the task-centered approach, crisis intervention, and cognitive restructuring. The chapter now links change-oriented strategies to the helping process and includes many new references, updated language in dialogues, and new examples. Chapter 14 delineates numerous interventions and skills, including teaching independent problem-solving skills, social skills, assertiveness, and stress management, including new information about the use of technology to enhance client support.

In Chapter 15, the focus shifts to modifying environments, developing resources, empowering clients, serving as case managers, employing advocacy, and engaging in social planning. The chapter includes a major revision and updating of references and theory base, and an updated focus on empowerment in a current social and policy context. It includes five new case studies of supplementing resources, of developing supports and networks, advocacy and social action, class advocacy, and efforts to improve an organizational environment. It also includes a case and figure related to service fragmentation and duplication,

Chapter 16 deals at length with methods of enhancing family relationships. Concepts, strategies, and techniques have been linked to specific family approaches and models from which they arose. The cultural, racial, and gender content was enhanced and includes cautions and concerns of immigrant families. Cultural concepts and dimensions to be used when exploring the importance of race and culture with families were expanded, including dialogues to reflect adding racial/cultural issues and an explanation of dynamics.

Chapter 17 focuses on theory and skills entailed in work with social work groups and now has updated material on the stages of group development including variations for gender and other variables. Chapter 18 is concerned with the implementation of additive empathy, interpretation, and confrontation. The chapter now includes a substantially revised section on confrontation incorporating a stages-of-change model. Part 3 concludes with Chapter 19, which discusses manifestations and methods of dealing with relational reactions and other obstacles to change, methods of coping with opposition to change, and strategies for dealing with them in the context of individuals and families. Chapter 19 includes a new section on over- and underinvolvement of the social worker with clients.

Part 4 consists of Chapter 20, which deals with the terminal phase of the helping process. This chapter includes content on the evaluation of practice and on the termination process. This edition includes reactions to termination and adds examples of time-limited groups, solution-focused and brief intermittent therapy across the life cycle to a task-centered approach as examples of terminations determined by the interventive model. The chapter includes a section on termination celebrations and rituals.

Key Changes to the 6th Edition

Chapter 15 now incorporates content on organizational barriers to change that were previously in Chapter 19. Consequently, Chapter 19 now focuses on individual and family barriers to change. Phase III and Chapter 20 have been retitled "Termination" rather than "Termination and Evaluation" to reflect that evaluation is a step within the termination phase. A figure depicting the helping process that was formerly in Chapter 3 is now included on the inside cover as a handy reference throughout your use of the book.

Acknowledgments

We would like to thank the following colleagues for their help in providing useful comments and suggestions. We have been supported by members of two writers' groups which have included: Priscilla Gibson and Terry Lum (from the University of Minnesota), Tony Bibus, Su Min Hsieh and Maria Dinis (from Augsburg College), Michael Chovanec and Carol Kuechler (from the College of St. Thomas). We also wish to thank Kyoungho Kim for her careful work on references and indexing.

We are very grateful to the reviewers of this edition, whose constructive criticisms and suggestions have been extremely helpful. They are Delores Macey, University of South Carolina; Rachelle Zuckerman, UCLA; Louise Skolnik, Adelphi University; Bruce Friedman, Michigan State University; Mikal Rasheed, Aurora University; Lacey Cox, Arizona State University; and Sharon Collins, Anderson University.

Finally, this edition could not have been developed without the support, challenge, and inspiration of our families including George Gottfried, and Chris and Pat Rooney.

Dean H. Hepworth
Ronald H. Rooney
Jo Ann Larsen

PART 1

Introduction

Part 1 of this book provides you with a background of concepts, values, historical perspectives, and information about systems that prepares the way for you to learn specific direct practice skills in Part 2.

Chapter 1 introduces you to the social work profession, its mission, purposes, and values, and the guiding role of systems perspectives in assisting us in conceptualizing our work.

Chapter 2 elaborates roles played by social workers, including distinctions between clinical and direct social work practice, and it includes a philosophy of direct practice.

We move next in Chapter 3 to an overview of the helping process including exploration, implementation, and termination.

Finally, in Chapter 4, cardinal values and ethical concerns are introduced.

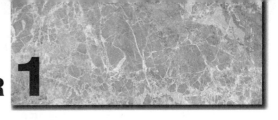

CHAPTER 1

The Challenges of Social Work

CHAPTER OVERVIEW

Chapter 1 introduces the mission of social work and the purposes of social work services, illustrates the roles played by social workers within the organizational context for such services, and identifies the value perspectives that guide social workers. Social workers attempt to understand the interactions of individuals and families with their environment through the lenses of ecology and systems. This chapter also introduces systems concepts useful to that understanding. These topics are introduced and exemplified through the following case example.

CASE EXAMPLE

Jane Percy, 39, the single-parent mother of Jerald, 13, telephoned The Arch, a social service agency that works with runaway and homeless youth as well as "throwaways" (children banished from the home). The Arch provides brief out-of-home placements of children with the goal of reuniting children with their families as soon as possible. Agency services usually include time-limited, in-home counseling in which resources and problems are identified and follow-up services after reunification are developed.

Ms. Percy told the intake worker that she was very upset and needed help with Jerald, who was getting into trouble. Most recently Jerald had been throwing rocks from an overpass onto cars on the expressway near the housing project in which they lived. Ms.

Percy had attempted to keep Jerald at home after school and out of trouble. He had stayed away from the home for several nights in the past month, though he was currently at home. Jerald is biracial, with an African American father, whom he does not see, and a Caucasian mother. The housing development included a higher percentage of African American families than the surrounding communities. Ms. Percy was dating a Caucasian man who made comments about Jerald that she described as racist. She reported that they felt like excluded minorities and that Jerald had been hanging out with a group of African American boys at school.

During the intake worker's initial assessment, she found that Ms. Percy's apartment in the housing development offered the benefit of low rent, but public transportation was infrequent and inconvenient for getting to shopping centers and for buying groceries. Frequent bus services were available for commuters to and from the central city, but few routes were available within Ms. Percy's community. Consequently, she rode a bicycle to work and took cabs for groceries.

Social workers advocate for poor, disadvantaged, disenfranchised, and oppressed people (Barber, 1995a). Hence, social workers are likely to work with many persons like Jane Percy and her neighbors. Social work's domain has steadily expanded, and social workers serve in such diverse settings as governmental agencies, schools, health care centers, family and child welfare agencies, mental health centers, business and industry, correctional settings, and private practice. Social workers work with people of all ages, races, ethnic groups, socioeconomic levels, religions, sexual orientations, and abilities (see Table 1-1).

Social workers themselves variously describe their work as rewarding, frustrating, satisfying, discouraging, stressful, and, most of all, challenging. Consider, for example, the difficulties suggested by the Percy family example. You might take a couple of minutes to list the potential problems and concerns raised by her situation. List also the possible strengths and resources that could be explored.

PROBLEMS AND CONCERNS:

POTENTIAL STRENGTHS AND RESOURCES:

Ms. Percy asked for help in reducing her stress, and guidance in parenting her son Jerald, including dealing with his absenting from the home. During the intake worker's initial assessment, several additional potential issues have emerged that may or may not be Ms. Percy's concerns or require action. For example, Ms. Percy and her neighbors lack adequate transportation for shopping; she may be interested in groups for biracial children, single parents, or parents of biracial children; there may be a lack of recreation opportunities or access to them; and Ms. Percy's male friend seems to have a racist attitude toward Jerald. Meanwhile, Jerald may have concerns related to making friends and having access to recreation. Social work assessments frequently include (1) exploration of multiple concerns expressed by potential clients, (2) circumstances that might involve legally mandated intervention or concerns about health or safety,

and (3) other potential problems that emerge from the assessment. Such assessments also include strengths and potential resources. The fact that Ms. Percy was employed, coping with the many pressures of single parenthood, and seeking help were considered potential strengths.

Table 1-1 Groups of people served by social workers

- Persons who are homeless
- Families that have problems of child neglect or sexual, physical, or spousal abuse
- Couples that have serious marital conflicts
- Families, including single-parent families, that have serious conflicts manifested by runaways, delinquency, or violence
- People afflicted with AIDS and their families
- Individuals and families whose lives have been disrupted by punishment for violations of the law
- Unwed, pregnant teenagers
- Persons who are gay, lesbian, or bisexual who face personal or family difficulties
- Individuals or families whose lives are disrupted by physical or mental illness or disability
- Persons who abuse drugs or alcohol and their families
- Foster parents, and children whose parents are deceased or who have been unable to safely care for them
- Immigrants and persons from oppressed groups who lack essential resources
- Persons with several physical or developmental disabilities and their families
- Aging persons no longer able to care for themselves adequately
- Persons who are migrants and transients who lack essential resources
- Children (and their families) who have school-related difficulties
- Persons who experience high stresses related to traumatic events or to major life transitions such as retirement, death of loved ones, children who leave home, or coming out for gay, lesbian, and bisexual persons

THE MISSION OF SOCIAL WORK

The perspectives taken by social workers in their professional roles will influence how Ms. Percy's concerns are conceptualized and addressed. According to the National Association of Social Workers (NASW), "the primary mission of the social work profession is to enhance human well-being and help meet basic human needs, with particular attention to the needs of vulnerable, oppressed, and poor people" (NASW, 1996). Similarly, the Council on Social Work Education (CSWE), the organization that accredits undergraduate and master's degree social work programs, describes the social work profession as "committed to the enhancement of human well-being and to the alleviation of poverty and oppression" (CSWE, 1995). These statements place social work as a helping profession to enhance human well-being, but do so with a special focus on the alleviation of poverty and oppression and on service to vulnerable people.

We shall delineate core elements that lie at the heart of social work wherever it is practiced. These core elements can be subsumed under the following four dimensions:

1. The purposes of the profession
2. Values and ethics
3. Knowledge base of direct practice
4. Methods and processes employed

In this chapter, we consider each of the first three dimensions. The fourth dimension is discussed in Chapter 3 in order to draw the big picture of the helping process and to set the stage for the remainder of the book.

PURPOSES OF SOCIAL WORK

Social work practitioners serve clients toward specific objectives while the means of accomplishing those objectives vary according to the unique circumstances of each problematic situation. The activities of all practitioners share common goals that constitute the purpose and objectives of the profession. These goals unify the profession and assist members in avoiding the development of perspectives limited to particular practice settings. To accomplish the purpose of the profession, practitioners must be willing to assume responsibilities and engage in actions that go beyond the functions of specific social agencies and their designated individual roles as staff members. For example, staff at The Arch may assist Ms. Percy with problems such as transportation and recreation programs for Jerald that are not directly related to the agency's function of providing counseling and brief, out-of-home care.

CSWE describes the social work profession as receiving its sanction from public and private auspices, as the primary profession in the provision of social services, and as practiced in a wide range of settings (CSWE, 1995, p. 135). CSWE describes social work as having four purposes.

1. "The promotion, restoration, maintenance, and enhancement of the social functioning of individuals, families, groups, organizations, and communities by helping them to accomplish tasks, prevent and alleviate distress, and use resources" (p.135). This purpose suggests that Ms. Percy and Jerald might be assisted in restoring and maintaining their relationship, including nurturing and discipline, guidance, and protection. Also, Ms. Percy can help him navigate the development of his identity, friendships, school, and growing up without hurting himself or others. The family might receive help to accomplish such tasks and alleviate their distress through resources both within the agency and without. As social workers work with multiple client systems, the client system may evolve from Ms. Percy as client to the family unit including Jerald as client, to work with either or both through groups and to work with the community around expressed needs.

Social workers perform preventive, restorative, and remedial functions in pursuit of this purpose. *Prevention* involves the timely provision of services to vulnerable persons, promoting social functioning before problems develop, and includes programs and activities such as family planning, well-baby clinics, parent education, premarital and preretirement counseling, and marital enrichment programs. For example, Ms. Percy might be linked to ongoing support groups for single parents or parents of biracial children, a Big Brothers program, or a peer group for Jerald. *Restoration* is aimed at assisting clients in the restoration of functioning that has been impaired by physical or mental difficulties. Included in this group of clients are those with varying degrees of paralysis caused by severe spinal injury, people afflicted with severe mental illness, persons with developmental disabilities, persons with deficient educational backgrounds, and people with many other types of disability. *Remediation* entails the elimination or amelioration of existing social problems. Clients in need of remedial services form the largest group served by social workers and include all the groups listed in Table 1-1 as well as many others. Many of the potential clients in this category are not like Ms. Percy; they have not applied for a service, but they may be referred by others such as family members, neighbors, and doctors who have perceived a need, or they may be legally mandated to receive services (R. H. Rooney, 1992).

Enhancing social functioning involves addressing common human needs that must be adequately met to enable individuals to achieve a reasonable degree of fulfillment and to function as productive and contributing members of society. Essential resources and opportunities must be available to meet human needs, and social workers are vitally involved in resource utilization and development. Rosenfeld (1983) defines the domain of social work practice as constituted by incongruities or discrepancies between needs and resources that various systems and social institutions have not dealt with adequately. Social workers aim "to match resources with needs to increase the 'goodness of fit' between them, largely by harnessing potential provider systems to perform this function" (p. 187). Tapping re-

sources essential to meeting human needs generally involves enhancing transactions between people and their social or physical environments. To further clarify the transactions between individual needs and environmental resources, social workers consider certain basic needs and the loci of resources that correspond to those needs. These interactions are graphically demonstrated in Table 1-2, showing that human beings are extremely dependent on the environment for the fulfillment of basic needs. Social work practice thus is directed to the interface between people and their environments.

Problems at the interface between people and these environments are not exclusively caused by environmental deficiencies. Many clients whom practitioners serve have difficulties that impair their ability to utilize available resources. For example, recreation and socialization programs may be available for Ms. Percy and Jerald, but they may lack knowledge of these resources or how to gain access to them. Practitioners, therefore, often must focus their efforts on helping clients to gain interpersonal skills to reduce the mismatch between their clients' needs and environmental resources (see Table 1-2).

2. "The planning, formulation and implementation of social policies, services, resources, and programs needed to meet basic human needs and support the development of human capacities" (CSWE, 1995, p. 135). This purpose suggests that although some social workers provide direct services to clients such as Ms. Percy and Jerald, others act indirectly to influence the environments supporting the client, developing and maintaining the social infrastructure that assists clients in meeting their needs.

3. "The pursuit of policies, services, resources, and programs through organizational or administrative advocacy and social or political action, to empower groups at risk and to promote social and economic justice." This purpose is also reflected in the second value in the social work Code of Ethics: "Social workers challenge social injustice"

Table 1-2 Human needs and related loci of resources

HUMAN NEEDS	LOCI OF RESOURCES
Positive self-concept: Identity Self-esteem Self-confidence	Nurturance, acceptance, love and positive feedback provided by significant others (parents, relatives, teachers, peer group)
Emotional: Feeling needed and valued by others Companionship Sense of belonging	Parents, marital partner, friends, siblings, cultural reference groups, social networks
Personal fulfillment: Education Recreation Accomplishment Aesthetic satisfaction Religion	Educational, recreational, religious, employment, and other social institutions
Physical needs: Food, clothing, housing Health care Safety Protection	Economic, legal, and health care institutions; formal social welfare systems, law enforcement, and disaster relief organizations

(NASW, 1996, p. 5). This value points social workers to the pursuit of social change on behalf of vulnerable or oppressed people on the basis of poverty, discrimination, and other forms of injustice. The focus of efforts on populations at risk should increase the power of such persons to influence their own lives.

The curriculum policy statement of CSWE also requires that social work education programs "provide an understanding of the dynamics and consequences of social and economic justice, including all forms of human oppression and discrimination. . . . [and include] strategies of intervention for achieving social and economic justice and for combating the causes and effects of institutionalized forms of oppression" (CSWE, 1995, p. 140). If resources and opportunities are to be available to all members of society, laws,

governmental policies, and social programs must assure equal access of citizens to resources and opportunities. Social workers promote social justice by advocating for clients who have been denied services, resources, or goods to which they are entitled. Social workers also actively engage in efforts to combat racism, sexism, and other forms of discrimination that block equal access of clients to resources to which they are entitled. For example, racism and lack of political and economic power may be reasons that Ms. Percy and her neighbors do not have adequate access to transportation.

The preceding purpose focuses social work efforts also on populations at risk. Social work educational programs "must present theoretical and practice content about patterns, dynamics, and consequences of discrimination, economic deprivation, and oppression. The curriculum must provide content about people of color, women, and gay and lesbian persons. Such content must emphasize the impact of discrimination, economic deprivation and oppression on these groups. Each program must include content about populations at risk that are particularly relevant to its mission. In addition to those mandated above, such groups include but are not limited to those distinguished by age, ethnicity, culture, class, religion, and physical or mental ability" (CSWE, 1995, p. 140).

In promoting social and economic justice with populations at risk, social workers in direct practice join with other social workers and groups to promote social action and legislation that redress wrongs resulting from unfair decisions and dysfunctional policies and practices. Moreover, they advocate for programs and resources to increase opportunities and enhance the welfare of disadvantaged people; they advocate especially for groups of people who are unable to effectively advocate for themselves, such as persons with developmental disabilities or severe mental illness. For example, the social workers at The Arch joined with other local groups including clients and consumers of service in advocating for more accessible services for the residents of Ms. Percy's neighborhood.

The objective of promoting social and economic justice merits a renewed commitment by social workers in view of more conservative trends in the political climate over the past three decades (Specht & Courtney, 1994). Most recently the radical restructuring of governmental approaches to poverty of women and children in the form of Pub. L. No. 104–193, the Personal Responsibility and Work Opportunity Reconciliation Act of 1996, "ended welfare as we know it" (Hagen, 1998). Specifically, work requirements were increased without a guarantee of child care support. In addition, educational assistance was decreased and the specific circumstances of women who tend to work in the part-time, low-wage, low-benefit service sector were not addressed. In essence, the law increased the accountability demands on recipients of aid without requiring a comparable accountability of the state and federal governments about types of employment attained and income levels (Hagen, 1998). Social workers need to advocate for the welfare of low-income families and children and monitor whether sufficient services and supports are created to in fact reduce poverty and improve the welfare of children.

4. "The development and testing of professional knowledge and skills related to these purposes" (CSWE, 1995, p. 140). The social work profession engages in ongoing efforts to expand the knowledge base to assist clients such as Ms. Percy and Jerald and others so as to provide services that are efficient, ethical, and effective. This purpose is also reflected in the sixth value in the NASW Code of Ethics: "Social workers practice within their areas of competence and develop and enhance their professional expertise" (NASW, 1996). This value commits individual social work practitioners to continually increase their professional knowledge and skills and "aspire to contribute to the knowledge base of the profession."

SOCIAL WORK VALUES

All professions have value preferences that give purpose and direction to their practitioners. Indeed, the purpose and objectives of social work and other professions emanate from their respective value systems. Professional values, however, are not separate from societal values. Rather, professions espouse selected societal values, and society in turn gives sanction to professions through supportive legislation, funding, delegation of responsibility for certain societal functions, and mechanisms for ensuring that those functions are adequately discharged. Because a profession is linked to certain societal values, it tends to serve as society's conscience with respect to those particular values.

Values represent strongly held beliefs about how the world should be, about how people should normally behave, and about preferred conditions of life. Broad societal values in the United states are reflected in the Declaration of Independence, the Constitution, and the laws of the land, which declare and ensure certain rights of the people. Societal values are also reflected in governmental entities and programs designed to safeguard the rights of people and to promote the common good. Interpretations of values and rights, however, are not always uniform, as reflected, for example, in heated national controversies over the right of women to have abortions, rights of gays and lesbians, and conflicts between advocates of gun control and those espousing individual rights.

The values of the profession of social work similarly refer to strongly held beliefs about the rights of people to free choice and opportunity. They also refer to the preferred conditions of life that enhance people's welfare, how members of the profession should view and treat people, preferred goals for people, and how those goals should be reached. In the following sections, we consider the five values and purposes that guide social work education. The values are italicized and the content that follows each is our commentary.

1. *Social workers' professional relationships are built on regard for individual worth and dignity, and are advanced by mutual participation, acceptance, confidentiality, honesty, and responsible handling of conflict* (CSWE, 1994, p. 139). This value is also reflected in several parts of the Code of Ethics. The first value of the code states: "Social workers' primary goal is to serve" (NASW, 1996, p. 5). This means that service to others is elevated above self-interest and that social workers use their knowledge, values, and skills to help people in need and to address social problems. The second value states that they serve others in a fashion such that "social workers respect the inherent dignity and worth of the person." Every person is unique and has inherent worth; therefore, social worker interactions with people as they pursue and utilize resources should enhance their dignity and individuality, enlarge their competence, and increase their problem-solving and coping abilities. People who employ social work services are often overwhelmed by their difficulties and have exhausted their coping resources. Many, such as Jane Percy, come to services feeling stressed by a multitude of problems. In addition to attempting to help clients such as Ms. Percy reduce stress, practitioners provide service to clients in a variety of ways: assist them to view their difficulties from a fresh perspective, consider various remedial alternatives, foster awareness of strengths, mobilize both active and latent coping resources, enhance self-awareness, and teach problem-solving strategies and interpersonal skills.

Social workers perform these functions while recognizing "the central importance of human relationships" (NASW, 1996, p. 5). This principle suggests that social workers engage people as partners in purposeful efforts to promote, restore, maintain, and enhance client well-being. Finally, this value is also reflected in the Code of Ethics

principle that "social workers behave in a trustworthy manner" (p. 6). This principle suggests that social workers practice consistently with the profession's mission, values, and ethical standards, and promote ethical practices in the organizations with which they are affiliated (p. 6).

2. *Social workers respect the individual's right to make independent decisions and to participate actively in the helping process* (p. 139). People have a right to freedom insofar as they do not infringe on the rights of others; therefore, transactions with people in the course of seeking and utilizing resources should enhance their independence and self-determination. Too often in the past, social workers and other helping professionals have focused on "deficit, disease and dysfunction" (Cowger, 1994). The current emphasis on empowerment and strengths leads us to attempt to assist clients in increasing their personal potential and political power such that clients can improve their life situation (Gutierrez, Parsons & Cox, 1990; Saleeby, 1997). Consistent with this value, we present in this book an empowerment and strength-oriented perspective for working with clients. We have further devoted Chapter 14 to a modality that enhances clients' problem-solving capacities and have included in this and other chapters content that delineates ways of assisting clients to expand their interpersonal and other coping skills.

3. *Social workers are committed to assisting client systems to obtain needed resources.* People should have access to the resources they need to meet life's challenges and difficulties as well as access to opportunities to realize their potentialities throughout their lives. Our commitment to client self-determination and empowerment is hollow if clients lack access to the resources necessary to achieve their goals (Hartman, 1993). People often know little about available resources, so practitioners often perform the role of broker in referring people to resource systems such as public

legal services, health care agencies, child welfare divisions, mental health centers, centers for elderly persons, and family counseling agencies. Some individual clients or families may require goods and services from many different providers and may lack the language facility, physical or mental capacity, experience, or skill in availing themselves of essential goods and services. Practitioners then may assume the role of case manager, which involves not only providing direct services but also assuming responsibility for linking the client to diverse resources and ensuring that the client receives needed services in a timely fashion. Both the broker and case manager roles are discussed in the next chapter and in Chapter 15. The Arch assisted Jane Percy by providing her information about their own counseling and support programs for herself and Jerald, as well as those provided by other agencies. Clients sometimes need resource systems that are not available, and in these cases, practitioners must carry out the role of program developer by assisting in creating and organizing new resource systems. Examples of such efforts include the following: working with citizens and public officials to arrange transportation to health care agencies for the elderly, persons with disabilities, and indigent people; developing neighborhood organizations to campaign for better educational and recreational programs; organizing tenants to assert rights to landlords and housing authorities for improved housing and sanitation; and organizing support groups, skill development groups, and self-help groups to assist people in coping with difficult problems of living. In the Percys' case, a supervisor at The Arch became part of a task force that advocated for increased bus services to support the many persons in the housing project who did not have cars.

Social workers also frequently pursue this goal by facilitating access to resources. Social workers perform the role of facilitator or enabler in carrying out the following functions: enhancing communication among family members; coordinating efforts of teachers, school counselors, and social workers in assisting troubled students; assisting

groups to provide maximal support to members; opening channels of communication between coworkers; including patients or inmates in the governance of institutions; facilitating teamwork among members of different disciplines in hospitals and mental health centers; and providing for consumer input into agency policy-making boards. Later chapters deal specifically with content intended to assist students and practitioners in accomplishing this objective. The Arch specifically attempted to assist Ms. Percy and Jerald in improving their relationship. In assisting her with providing male role models for Jerald, they helped her make contact with Jerald's father and family. In addition, they helped Ms. Percy consider the implications of her own and her male friend's attitudes toward people of color for Jerald's developing identity as a multiracial person considered African American by others.

4. *Social workers strive to make social institutions more humane and responsive to human needs.* Although direct practitioners work primarily in providing direct service, they also have a responsibility to work toward improving the quality of life by promoting policies and legislation that enhance physical and social environments. Problems of individuals, families, groups, and neighborhoods can often be prevented or ameliorated by laws and policies that prohibit contamination of the physical environment and enrich both physical and social environments. Therefore, direct social workers would not limit themselves to remedial activities but should also seek to discover environmental causes of problems and to sponsor or support efforts aimed at enhancing people's environments. We discuss this topic at greater length in Chapters 15 and 19.

Social workers also enact this value when they assume the role of expediter or troubleshooter by scrutinizing the policies and procedures of their own and other organizations to determine if clients have ready access to resources and if services are delivered in ways that enhance the dignity of clients. Complex application procedures, needless delays in providing resources and services, discriminatory policies, inaccessible agency sites, inconvenient service delivery hours, dehumanizing procedures or staff behaviors—these and other factors may deter clients from utilizing resources or subject them to demeaning experiences. Systematically obtaining input from consumers is a method of monitoring an organization's responsiveness to clients. Advocacy actions with and on behalf of clients are sometimes required to secure services and resources to which clients are entitled (see elaboration in Chapters 15 and 19). The Arch made a short-term decision in light of the transportation problems in the housing project to make an agency van available to assist clients in getting to appointments and shopping for groceries.

Social workers additionally support this value through performing the roles of coordinator, mediator, or disseminator of information. For example, as a case manager, a social worker may coordinate medical, educational, mental health, and rehabilitative services provided a given family by multiple resource systems. A mediator may be required to resolve conflicts between agencies, minority and majority groups, and neighborhood groups. The social worker may disseminate information regarding legislation or the availability of new funding sources that potentially affect the relationships between public and private agencies to strengthen interactions between these resource systems.

Social workers must also maintain liaison with key organizations to facilitate mutual awareness of changes in policies and procedures that affect ongoing relationships and the availability of resources.

5. *Social workers demonstrate respect for and acceptance of the unique characteristics of diverse populations.* This value acknowledges the fact that social workers perform their services with populations characterized by great diversity, including "groups distinguished by race, ethnicity, culture, class, gender, sexual orientation, religion, physical or mental ability, age, and national origin" (CSWE, 1995, p. 140). The value suggests that social workers must be informed about and respectful of differences. They must educate themselves over time as a part of lifelong learning because there can be no "how-to" manual that will guide the practitioner in understanding all aspects of diversity. The value suggests that the practitioner must continually update his or her knowledge about the strengths and resources associated with individuals from such groups to increase the sensitivity and effectiveness of services.

Value and Ethics

Realization of the foregoing values should be the mutual responsibility of individual citizens and of society. Society should foster conditions and provide opportunities for citizens to participate in the policy-determining processes of society. Citizens should fulfill their responsibilities to society by actively participating in those processes.

Considered individually, the preceding values and mission are not unique to social work. Their unique combination, however, differentiates social work from other professions. Considered in their entirety, these ingredients make it clear that social work's identity derives from its connection with the institution of social welfare, which, according to Gilbert (1977), represents a special helping mechanism devised to aid those who suffer from the variety of ills found in industrial society. "Whenever other major institutions, be they familial, religious, economic, or educational in nature, fall short in their helping and resource-providing functions, social welfare spans the gap" (p. 402).

These five values represent the ultimate values or prized ideals of the profession and, as such, are stated at high levels of abstraction. As Siporin (1975) and C. Levy (1973) have noted, however, there are different levels of professional values. At an intermediate level, values pertain to various segments of society, as for example, characteristics of a strong community. At a third level, values are more operational, referring to preferred behaviors.

For example, the ideal social work practitioner is a warm, caring, open, and responsible person who safeguards the confidentiality of information disclosed by clients. Because you, the reader, have chosen social work, it is probable that most of your personal values coincide with the cardinal values espoused by the majority of social work practitioners. However, at the intermediate and third levels of values, you may not always be in harmony with specific value positions taken by the majority of social workers. During the Vietnam War, the majority of social workers favored withdrawal from Vietnam, but support of that position by members of the profession was by no means unanimous. The same might be said of other controversial issues, such as the legalization of marijuana, tax-supported abortion, and capital punishment. Currently, social workers insist on access to adequate child care, job training, and job opportunities for participants in state welfare-to-work programs (Hagen, 1998).

Self-determination refers to the right of people to exercise freedom of choice in making decisions. Issues such as those above may pose value dilemmas for individual practitioners because of conflicts between personal and professional values. In addition, conflicts between two professional values and/or principles are common. For example, when considered in relationship to the issue of legalized marijuana, the value of the right to self-determination collides with the concept that it is good to promote the health and well-being of others. Public positions taken by the profession that emanate from its values also sometimes stand in opposition to attitudes of a large segment of society. For example, professional support for universal health coverage has not been endorsed by Congress (Webber, 1995).

With respect to diverse value preferences among social workers, we advocate the value that social workers should be sufficiently flexible to listen to many differing value positions on most moral and political issues. Different value positions do not necessarily reflect divergence among social workers on the five values delineated earlier. Rather, such differences reflect that there are many possible means of achieving given ends, and rigid assumptions about preferred means to an end often crumble when put to the test of hard experience. Consistent with our value preference for flexibility, we reaffirm our commitment to the value that social workers, whatever their beliefs, should assert them in a forum of professional organizations such as NASW (the National Association of Social Workers). We maintain further that social workers should accord colleagues who differ on certain value positions the same respect, dignity, and right to self-determination that would be accorded clients. Differences on issues may be frankly expressed. Those issues can be clarified and cohesiveness among professionals fostered by debate conducted in a climate of openness and mutual respect.

Conflicts between personal and/or professional values and the personal values of a client or group sometimes occur. Not infrequently, students (and even seasoned practitioners) experience conflict over value-laden, problematic situations such as incest, infidelity, rape, child neglect or abuse, spouse abuse, and criminal behavior. Because direct practitioners encounter these and other problems typically viewed by the public as appalling, and because personal values inherently shape attitudes, perceptions, feelings, and responses to clients, it is vital that you be flexible and nonjudgmental in your work. It is equally vital that you be aware of your own values, how they fit with the profession's values, and the impact they may have on clients whose values differ from your own or whose behavior offends you.

Because values are critical determinants of behavior in interaction with clients and other professional persons, we have devoted Chapter 4 to practice situations involving potential value dilemmas, including exercises to assist you in expanding your awareness of your personal values. Chapter 4 also deals at length with the relationship-enhancing dimension of respect and contains exercises to assist you in responding respectfully to value-laden situations that are potentially painful for both you and your clients.

Social Work's Code of Ethics

An essential attribute of legitimate professions is a code of ethics consisting of principles that define expectations of its members. A code of ethics specifies rules of conduct to which members must adhere to remain in good standing within a professional organization. It thus defines expected responsibilities and behaviors as well as prescribed behaviors. Central to the purposes of a code of ethics is its function as a formalized expression of accountability of (1) the profession to the society that gives it sanction, (2) constituent practitioners to consumers who utilize their services, and (3) practitioners to their profession. By promoting accountability, a code of ethics serves additional vital purposes, including the following:

1. Safeguards the reputation of a professional by providing explicit criteria that can be employed to regulate the behavior of members
2. Furthers competent and responsible practice by its members
3. Protects the public from exploitation by unscrupulous or incompetent practitioners

Most states now have licensing boards that certify social workers for practice and review allegations of unethical conduct (Land, 1988; De Angelis, 2000). Similarly, local and state chapters of the National Association of Social Workers establish committees of inquiry to investigate alleged violations of the profession's Code of Ethics, and national committees provide consultation to local committees and consider appeals of decisions made by local chapters. We have blended the values in the code of ethics above in our presentation of the five values stated by CSWE.

KNOWLEDGE BASE OF SOCIAL WORK PRACTICE

One of the core elements of social work practice is its undergirding knowledge base. Although much of the knowledge base is borrowed from other disciplines in the social and behavioral sciences, that knowledge is assembled in unique ways. Moreover, many of the profession's basic concepts are unique to social work. The profession's universe of knowledge can be subsumed under the following five categories, which are regarded as core curriculum areas by the Council on Social Work Education.

1. *Human behavior and the social environment.* Knowledge about "human bio-psycho-social development, including theories about the range of social systems in which individuals live (families, groups, organizations, and communities) (CSWE 1995, pp. 139–140) is required to function effectively as a social worker. Such knowledge, including human growth and development with particular emphasis on the life tasks encountered by individuals during different developmental stages, is essential to practitioners. To assess and to work with human problems, practitioners must be aware of needs and resources associated with each developmental phase. They must also become aware of how these needs are identified and met in different cultures. Knowledge of ecological systems theory, which we discuss later in this chapter, is also essential, as is knowledge about the forces that motivate behavior in groups and organizations. Because of its mission in enhancing the social functioning of people, social work is particularly concerned with the knowledge of factors that contribute to developmental difficulties. Knowledge of these factors, which commonly involve inadequate physical and emotional resources, is essential to planning and implementing effective preventive and remedial programs. Social work's focus on the person in a situation is reflected in "the ways in which systems promote or deter people in the maintaining or achieving optimal health and well-being" (p. 141).

2. *Social welfare policy and services.* Content in this curriculum area "must be presented

about the political and organizational processes used to influence policy, the process of policy formulation, and the frameworks for analyzing social policies in light of principles of social and economic justice (p. 141). Social work's emphasis on knowledge concerned with social policy most sharply differentiates social work curricula from those of related disciplines. This broad body of knowledge embodies the complex factors involved in the formulation of social policies that shape and guide planning of human service systems at all levels of government and in the private sector as well. To practice in full accordance with the mission and ethics of the profession, social workers have a responsibility to participate in developing and utilizing social policies that enhance the social functioning of individuals, families, groups, and communities. The study of social welfare policy and services must occur in the context of the profession's commitment to social and economic justice. Social work must address the consequences of oppressed conditions (Longres, 1991). Knowledge of inequities in the distribution of opportunities, resources, goods, and services in America and the impact of these inequities on minority and disadvantaged groups, are essential to social work practitioners (Brill, 1990).

3. *Social work practice methods.* These methods "emphasize mutuality, collaboration, and respect for the client system. . . . Content on practice assessment focuses on the examination of client strengths and problems in the interactions among individuals and between people and their environments . . . to enhance the well-being of people and to ameliorate the environmental conditions that affect people adversely . . . [in] practice with clients from differing social, cultural, racial, religious, spiritual, and class backgrounds, and with systems of all sizes (CSWE, 1995, p. 141).

To accomplish the mission and objectives of the profession, practitioners need knowledge and practice skills that enable them to enhance the social functioning of clients. Knowledge of and skills in practice methods vary according to the level of client system served by practitioners. The levels have been designated as *micro, mezzo,* and *macro.* Effective practice requires knowledge related to all three levels of practice, but schools of social work commonly offer "concentrations" in either micro or macro practice and require less preparation in the other methods. Curricula vary, of course, and some schools have generalist practice curricula, which require students to achieve balanced preparation in all three levels of practice. Undergraduate programs and the first year of graduate programs have generalist practice curricula, which are aimed at preparing students for working with all levels of client systems. The practice methods that correspond to the three levels of practice are as follows:

- *Micro level practice.* At this level, the population served by practitioners includes various client systems, including individuals, couples, and families. Practice at this level is designated as direct (or clinical) practice because practitioners deliver services directly to clients in face-to-face contact. Direct practice, however, is by no means limited to such face-to-face contact, as we discuss in Chapter 2.

- *Mezzo level practice.* The second level is defined as "interpersonal relations that are less intimate than those associated with family life; more meaningful than among organizational and institutional representatives; [including] relationships between individuals in a self-help or therapy group, among peers at school or work or among neighbors" (Sheafor, Horejsi, & Horejsi, 1994, pp. 9–10). Mezzo events are "the interface where the individual and those most immediate and important to him/her meet" (Zastrow & Kirst-Ashman, 1990, p. 11). Mezzo intervention is hence designed to change the systems that directly affect clients, such as the family, peer group, or classroom.

• *Macro level practice.* Still further removed from face-to-face delivery of services, macro practice involves the processes of social planning and community organization. On this level, social workers serve as professional change agents who assist community action systems composed of individuals, groups, or organizations to deal with social problems. Practitioners at this level may work with citizen groups or with private, public, or governmental organizations. Activities of practitioners at this level include the following: (1) development of and work with community groups and organizations; (2) program planning and development; and (3) implementation administration, and evaluation of programs (Meenaghan, 1987).

Administration entails assuming leadership in human service organizations directed to enabling the effective delivery of services in accordance with the values and laws of society. Definitions of administration vary, but according to Sarri (1987):

"administration is the sum of all the processes involved in:
1. *Formulation of policy and its translation into operative goals.*
2. *Program design and implementation.*
3. *Funding and resource allocation.*
4. *Management of internal and interorganizational operations.*
5. *Personnel direction and supervision.*
6. *Organizational representation and public relations.*
7. *Community education.*
8. *Monitoring, evaluation, and innovation to improve organizational productivity."*
(pp. 29–30)

Direct practitioners are necessarily involved to some degree in administrative activities, as we discuss in the next chapter. Further, many master's degree direct practitioners become supervisors or administrators later in their professional careers. Knowledge of administration, therefore, is vital to direct practitioners at the master's degree level, and courses in administration are frequently part of the required master's degree curriculum in so-

cial work. Although many direct practitioners engage in little or no macro level practice, those who work in rural areas where practitioners are few and specialists in social planning are not available may work in concert with concerned citizens and community leaders in planning and developing resources to prevent or combat social problems.[1]

4. *Research.* "The research curriculum must provide an understanding and appreciation of a scientific, analytic approach to building knowledge for practice and to evaluating service delivery in all areas of practice" (CSWE, 1995, p. 108). Knowledge of research is indispensable to scientific and scholarly inquiry, which in turn is the driving force behind advancement of knowledge. To keep abreast of knowledge, practitioners must be able to utilize information gained from research studies. This requires knowledge of research designs and the ability to discriminate between conclusions based on empirical data and others that are unwarranted. Moreover, direct service practitioners require knowledge of appropriate research designs to be able to evaluate the effectiveness of their own practice from time to time. In addition, they are often involved in agency outcome and process evaluations.

5. *Field practicum.* "The field practicum is an integral component of the curriculum in social work education. It engages the student in supervised social work practice and provides opportunities to apply classroom learning in the field setting" (CSWE, 1995, p. 142). Graduates of social work programs consistently report that their experiences in the field practicum are integral to their learning how to practice as responsible professionals. Your learning of content in your classroom courses and from this book will be greatly enhanced by the opportunity to apply your knowledge, values, and skills in the field and receive modeling and appropriate feedback from your field instructor.

PRACTICING COMPETENTLY: AN ETHICAL REQUIREMENT

As reflected in the earlier section on the profession's Code of Ethics, "social workers practice within their areas of competence and develop and enhance their professional expertise" (NASW, 1996). Consequently, attaining and maintaining competence in practice is an ethical requirement of social workers. To meet this requirement, aspiring social workers must achieve proficiency in a broad range of activities. The rationale for this requirement is compelling because much is at stake for consumers of social work services. Furthermore, who would question that clients have the right to expect competent services from those who represent themselves to the public as experts in their field of practice? Some have argued that clients should be assured of competent treatment and hence that practitioners should deliver empirically supported interventions (Myers & Thyer, 1997). Competent practice is defined as "fitting, suitable for the purpose; adequate; properly qualified; having legal capacity or qualification." Hence competence is somewhat more broadly defined than empirically supported. Others argue that this requirement suggests that clients be informed of different viewpoints about the problem at hand (Raw, 1998; S. L. Witkin, 1998). To assess professional competency, however, is far from simple because competency in practice embodies knowledge, values, skills, and attitudes essential to fulfill one's professional role skillfully. Ingredients essential to perform one's role adequately vary according to the demands of each situation. A practitioner may thus be competent in providing certain types of service, such as marital or family therapy, and not in others, such as correctional services or protective services to children who have been abused or neglected. Furthermore, the elements of competent practice in various settings evolve as a result of expanding knowledge, emerging skills, and the changing demands of practice. Competency must thus be viewed within a temporal context, for a practi-

tioner may achieve competence at one time only to suffer steady erosion of that competence by failing to keep abreast of ever-expanding knowledge and skills.

Because of the broad scope of social work activities embodied in the three levels of practice, it is highly doubtful that, without extensive study beyond the master's level, practitioners can achieve advanced expertise in all levels of practice. This reality is reflected in the curricula of schools of social work, which typically require master's level students to select one level of practice or "concentration" for intensive study. Our primary aim in writing this book was to assist students and practitioners to achieve and to advance their professional competence. This is not a modest objective, as social work practice theory has been in a state of vigorous ferment for the past 30 years.

This ferment has resulted from three major sources: (1) analyses of earlier research studies that cast doubt on the effectiveness of traditional social work interventions (Mullen & Dumpson, 1972); (2) emerging theories and empirically proven interventions; and (3) ever-constricting sources of funding for social work programs that has produced strident demands for accountability and cost-effectiveness of services. The knowledge base of social work practice has expanded rapidly, and empirical research has infused the profession with welcome stimulation and scientific vitality. Whereas students of the 1970s entered the profession during a time when earlier research findings had cast serious doubt on the efficacy of social work interventions, subsequent research studies have provided more support for the effectiveness of social work practice in helping clients (W. Reid & Hanrahan, 1982; A. Rubin, 1985; Thomlison, 1984; Gorey, Thyer, & Pawluck, 1998). Moreover, practitioners can employ an ever-widening array of interventions for many different human problems. Our objective of assisting students and practitioners to achieve competence presented a formidable challenge. We responded by including principles of effective practice identified by prominent theoreticians, researchers, and educators. Our task was further complicated by the fact that competence embodies much more than possessing knowledge of practice theory; competent practitioners must be able to transform that knowledge into action. Social work educators have been increasingly occupied with identifying and defining competencies (skills) in explicit terms and with developing technologies for assisting students to master these skills. We have incorporated these technologies in this book.

Evolving Theory and Competence

Possessing skills alone does not ensure competence, for without an undergirding knowledge base a practitioner would be little more than a technician. To analyze problems, persons, and situations, to plan remedial interventions, and to implement appropriate techniques requires an adequate grasp of practice theory and knowledge about human behavior in the social environment. The social work practitioner uses skills to understand the systems and contexts in which problems take place. Direct practice theory involves a complex domain within which rapid expansion in recent years has supplied much needed vigor, but not without troublesome growing pains. Much of the new theory has not expanded the margins of preexisting theory but has tended to be incompatible with and replace the older theory. Incorporating new theory, therefore, has posed some challenging dilemmas to schools of social work, responses to which are discussed in the following section.

Trend Toward Integrating Practice Models

Because human beings present a broad array of problems of living, no single approach or practice model is sufficiently comprehensive to adequately address them all. Moreover, techniques associated with one practice model may be applied equally effectively by practitioners who espouse other models. Indeed, although some practitioners identify largely with only one practice model, few limit themselves to interventions and techniques from a single practice model. Single-model practitioners do a disservice to themselves and their clients by attempting to fit all clients and problems into their chosen model. Practitioners should select interventions and techniques that best fit certain types of problems and clients (Berlin & Marsh, 1993).

Practice theories vary widely in their worldviews, targets of intervention, specifications of techniques, methods of assessment, length of intervention, and other important dimensions. Some interventions are thus more relevant to and cost-effective for certain problems than are others. Moreover, except for a limited number of problems, no single theory has proven to be more effective than other practice theories, although some interventions have proven to be effective and others ineffective in treating certain problems. All theories may thus be viewed as possessing some part of the universe of truth.

The proliferation of theories in the social sciences, social work, and allied disciplines has ushered in a new era that offers practitioners specific interventions proven effective for specific problem situations. To achieve this potential presents a formidable challenge, however, since available knowledge is often fragmented. To integrate the many theories and interventions, a generic framework capable of encompassing such theories and interventions is essential. Fortunately, such a unifying framework, the ecological systems model, is available (Germain, 1979, 1981; Meyer, 1983; Pincus & Minahan, 1973; Siporin, 1980).

Ecological Systems Model

Adaptations of this model, originating in biology, make a close conceptual fit with the "person-in-environment" perspective that was dominant in social work until the mid-1970s. Although that perspective recognized the impact of environmental factors upon human functioning, internal factors had received an inordinate emphasis in assessing human problems. In addition, a perception of the environment as constraining the individual did not sufficiently acknowledge the individual's actions to affect the environment. This heavy emphasis, which resulted from the prominence and wide acceptance of Freud's theories in the 1920s and 1930s, reached its zenith in the 1940s and 1950s. With the emergence of ego psychology, systems theory, theories of family therapy, expanded awareness of the importance of ethnocultural factors, and emphasis on ecological factors in the 1960s and 1970s, increasing importance was accorded to environmental factors and to understanding ways in which people interact with their environments.

Systems models were first created in the natural sciences. Meanwhile, ecological theory developed from the environmental movement in biology. Ecological systems theory in social work adapted concepts from systems and ecological theories. Two concepts of ecological theory that are especially relevant to social workers are habitat and niche. *Habitat* refers to the places where organisms live and, in the case of humans, consists of the physical and social settings within particular cultural contexts. When habitats are rich in resources required for growth and development, human beings tend to thrive. When habitats are deficient in vital resources, physical, social, and emotional development and ongoing functioning may be adversely affected. For example, a substantial body of research indicates that supportive social networks of friends, relatives, neighbors, work and church associates, and pets mitigate the damaging effects of painful life stresses. By contrast, people with deficient social networks may respond to life stresses by becoming severely depressed, resorting to abuse of drugs or alcohol, engaging in violent behavior, or coping in other dysfunctional ways.

The concept of *niche* refers to statuses or roles occupied by members of the community. One of the tasks in the course of human maturation is to find one's niche in society, which is essential to achieving self-respect and a stable sense of identity. Being able to locate one's niche, however, presumes that opportunities congruent with human needs exist in society. That presumption may not be valid for members of society who lack equal opportunities because of race, ethnicity, gender, poverty, age, disability, sexual identity, and other like factors.

An objective of social work, as noted earlier, is to promote social justice in order to expand opportunities for people to create appropriate niches for themselves. Ecological systems theory posits that individuals are engaged in constant transactions with other human beings and with other systems in the environment and that these various persons and systems reciprocally influence each other.

Further, each system is unique, varying in characteristics and ways of interacting (e.g., no two individuals, families, groups, or neighborhoods are the same). People thus do not merely react to environmental forces. Rather, they act on their environments, thereby shaping the responses of other people, groups, institutions, and even the physical environment. For example, people make choices about where to live, whether to upgrade or to neglect their living arrangements, and whether or not to initiate or support policies that combat urban decay, safeguard the quality of air and water, provide adequate housing for the elderly poor, and the like.

Adequate assessments of human problems and plans of interventions, therefore, must consider the reciprocal impact of people and environmental systems. The importance of considering the reciprocal interaction between people and their environments in formulating assessments has been reflected in changing views of various human problems over the past decade. Disability, for example, is now defined in psychosocial terms rather than in medical or economic terms, as had previously been the case. As Roth (1987) has clarified, "What is significant can be revealed only by the ecological framework in which the disabled person exists, by the interactions through which society engages a disability, by the attitudes others hold, and by the architecture, means of transportation, and social organization constructed by the able-bodied" (p. 434). Disability is thus minimized by goodness of fit between needs of people with physical or mental limitations and environmental resources that correspond to their special needs (e.g., rehabilitation programs, special physical accommodations, education, and social support systems).[2]

It is clear from the ecological systems perspective that the satisfaction of human needs and mastery of developmental tasks require adequate resources in the environment and positive transactions between persons and their environments. For example, effective learning by a student requires adequate schools, competent teachers, parental support, adequate perception and intellectual ability, motivation to learn, and positive relationships between teachers and students. Gaps in the environmental resources, limitations of individuals who need or utilize these resources, or dysfunctional transactions between individuals and environmental systems block the fulfillment of human needs and lead to stress or impaired functioning. To reduce or remove the stress requires coping efforts aimed at gratifying the needs or, stated another way, achieving adaptive fit between person and environment. People, however, often do not have access to adequate resources, or they lack effective coping methods. Social work involves assisting such people to find ways to meet their needs by linking them with or developing essential resources. Social work could also include enhancing their capacities to utilize resources or cope with environmental forces.

Assessment from an ecological systems perspective obviously requires knowledge of the diverse systems involved in interactions between people and their environments. These systems include the following: subsystems of the individual (biophysical, cognitive, emotional, behavioral, motivational); interpersonal systems (parent-child, marital, family, kin, friends, neighbors, cultural reference groups, spiritual belief systems, and others in people's social networks); organizations, institutions, and communities; and the physical environment (housing, neighborhood environment, buildings, other artificial creations, water, and

weather and climate). These various systems and their interactions are considered in Chapters 8–11.

A major advantage of the ecological systems model is its broad scope. Typical human problems involving health care, family relations, inadequate income, mental health difficulties, conflicts with law enforcement agencies, unemployment, educational difficulties, and so on can all be subsumed under this model, enabling the practitioner to analyze the complex variables involved in such problems. Assessing the sources of problems and determining the focuses of interventions are the first steps in applying the ecological systems model.

Pincus and Minahan have adapted systems models to social work practice, suggesting that a *client system* includes those persons who are requesting a change, sanction it, are expected to benefit from it, and contract to receive it (Pincus & Minahan, 1973; Compton & Galaway, 1999). Jane Percy fits the first part of this definition, because she requested a change. Potential clients who request a change are described as *applicants*. Her son Jerald has not requested a service, though he might be expected to benefit from it. Many persons like Jerald come into contact with social workers without requesting a service. Additional terms are needed for potential clients related to their various routes in social work contact. *Referrals* are persons who are referred by other professionals and family members. Jerald is a referral, referred by his mother. Contacted persons are approached through an outreach effort (Compton & Galaway, 1999). Some referred and contacted persons may not experience pressure from that contact, which was not sought out. Others experience the contact as pressure, though not legally binding, and may be considered *nonvoluntary clients* (Rooney, 1992). Still others have contact with a practitioner through current or impending legal pressure and might be considered *legally mandated clients*. Rather than immediately bestow the label client on all persons who have contact with a social worker, it is better to consider them potential clients and be aware of their route to such contact and their response to that contact.

The next step is to determine what is to be done vis-à-vis the pertinent systems involved in the problem situation. In this step, the practitioner surveys the broad spectrum of available practice theories and interventions. To be maximally effective, interventions, of course, must be directed to all systems that are critical in a given problem system. The *target system* represents people and problems that must be influenced to reach goals (Compton & Galaway, 1999, p. 33). When a client desires assistance on a personal problem, the target and client systems overlap. Frequently, however, clients request assistance with a problem outside themselves. In such instances, that problem becomes the center of a target system. For example, if part of the contract with Ms. Percy entails assessment of conditions and her responses to them, which have produced stress, the client system and target system would overlap. Even when there is overlap, it is important to focus on *the problem* that is the overlap rather than on the entire person as the target. Focusing on a person as the target system objectifies that person and diminishes the respect for individuality to which each person is entitled. Frequently, the target system relates to problems outside the person. For example, the lack of recreational opportunities for Jerald suggests inclusion of the YMCA and possible school and scouting programs. The *action systems* refers to those persons with whom the practitioner needs to cooperate to accomplish a purpose. Meanwhile, the *agency system* includes the practitioners and service systems involved in work on the agreed upon problems (Compton & Galaway, 1999).

Social systems also vary in the degree to which they are open and closed to new information or feedback. Closed systems have relatively rigid *boundaries* preventing the input or export of information, while open systems have relatively permeable boundaries permitting more free exchange. Thus families may vary from being predominantly closed to new information to excessively open. In fact, all families and human systems exhibit a tension between trying to maintain stability and boundaries in some areas while seeking and responding to change in others. For example, at this point the boundary linking Ms. Percy and Jerald as a family is tenuous while Ms. Percy's part of the system is open in seeking solutions to their problems. Systems theorists also suggest that change in one part of a system often affects other parts of the system. For example, work with Ms. Percy on the problem she identified—high stress—may affect her parenting of Jerald. The principle of *equifinality* suggests that the same outcome can be achieved from different starting places. For example, starting on any problem that motivates both Ms. Percy and Jerald, no matter what the problem, may eventuate in better relations between them. Meanwhile, the principle of *multifinality* suggests that beginning from the same starting points may end in different outcomes. For example, starting on work with Ms. Percy's difficulties in parenting Jerald may enhance her coping ability more generally and lead to a variety of additional targets for change, such as parenting, support, transportation, returning for more education and training, and recreation.

Nonlinear applications of systems theory. Traditional systems theory as described above suggests that systems or organizations are characterized by order, rationality, and stability (Warren, Franklin, & Streeter, 1998). Hence, the emphasis on such concepts as boundaries, homeostasis, and equilibrium. In addition to ordered circumstances, systems theory can also be useful for consideration of nonlinear systems. Systems in the process of change can be very sensitive to initial events and feedback to those events. For example, a nonlinear change would be the circumstance in which an adolescent's voice changes by 1 decibel of loudness resulting in a change of 10 decibels in an adult (Warren et al.). Minor incidents in the past can reverberate in a system. Some have suggested this as support for the notion that family systems can make significant changes as a result of a key intervention that reverberates and is reinforced in a system. Such nonlinear circumstances emphasize the concept of multifinality in the sense of viewing how the same initial conditions can lead to quite varied outcomes. Among the implications of the above are the possibility of considering chaos not as a lack of order but as an opportunity for flexibility and change.

Limitations of Systems Theories. While system models are often seen as useful in providing concepts for describing person-situation interactions, others have suggested that they have limitations in providing the basis for specific intervention prescriptions (Whittaker & Tracy, 1989). Similarly, Wakefield (1996a, 1996b) has argued that systems concepts do not add much to domain specific knowledge. Others argue that, however faulty or inadequate, systems theory continues to provide useful metaphors for conceptualizing the relations between complex organizations. Perhaps we should not overextend our expectations for it (Gitterman, 1996). We take the view that systems theory provides useful metaphors for conceptualizing the varied levels of phenomena social workers must recognize. They are insufficient alone to guide practice. Concepts such as equifinality and multifinality can not be rigidly applied in all human and social systems.

Systematic eclecticism. To make judicious choices and to implement chosen interventions skillfully requires knowledge of numerous practice theories and techniques and a rigorous approach to selecting those that are most appropriate for a given client (F. J. Turner, 1996). Systematic eclecticism (Beutler, 1983; Beutler & Clarkin, 1990; Fischer, 1978; Siporin, 1979) is such a rigorous approach to practice. A systematic eclectic practitioner adheres to no single theory exclusively but rather selects models and theories that best match a given problem situation and accords highest priority to techniques that have been empirically demonstrated to be effective and efficient.

Systematic eclecticism requires the practitioner to keep abreast of emerging theories and research findings. In our judgment, this approach to practice holds the highest promise of being effective with a broad range of clients and problems. The theoretical base of this book, therefore, is systematic eclecticism practiced under the umbrella of ecological systems theory. The systematic eclectic approach to practice would be fairly straightforward if clear guidelines for selecting theories and interventions were available, but the state of the art in social work has not reached that level of sophistication. However, significant progress was made in the early 1990s (Beutler & Clarkin, 1990; Burman & Allen-Meares, 1991), and in Chapter 13 we discuss pertinent criteria that have been identified.

Six general criteria also exist to guide social workers in deciding which theories and interventions to study in depth.

1. The extent to which a given theory has been supported by empirical research is an important criterion. Those theories whose tenets have been affirmed through research and whose efficacy has likewise been established are preferable to theories that have not been subjected to rigorous empirical testing. A number of writers have stressed the importance of basing direct practice upon empirical research. This has prompted controversy over a period of several years, with other writers cautioning that adherents of empirically based practice have taken an extreme position that discounts the importance of other approaches to expanding knowledge (S. L. Witkin, 1998).

2. When two interventions both have been proven effective, the intervention that produces results with less expenditure of time, money, and effort is the more efficient and is preferable.

3. Interventions and techniques subsumed under the theory should be specifically delineated. Theories that are largely composed of abstractions fail to inform practitioners how

to implement theory in actual practice situations and therefore have limited value. Psychoanalytic theory has been criticized for that reason. Behavior modification, by contrast, is characterized by the high degree of specificity with which its procedures are delineated.

4. Ethical and value implications of interventions play a role. Practitioners should avoid interventions that subject the client to emotional trauma or humiliation, that violate confidentiality, or that otherwise conflict with the profession's Code of Ethics. Assessing whether the information source emphasizes health and strengths versus pathology relates to the value emphasis on strengths in social work. A similar value leads to preference for methods that emphasize collaborative work with clients versus practitioner manipulation. Hence, how power is viewed in the approach and the role of practitioner and client or consumer is an important criterion (Laird, 1993).

5. The practitioner must have knowledge and skill with respect to given interventions. It is vital that the practitioner be well grounded in knowledge of interventions, including the rationale of an intervention, indications and contraindications for employing it, cautions to be observed, guidelines for appropriate timing, and specific procedures for implementing it. Interventions are best learned under careful supervision, and practitioners have an ethical responsibility not to apply them in a haphazard manner or to subject clients to the risk of trial-and-error learning.

6. The intervention should lend itself to ethnocultural sensitivity or appropriateness. That is, models have some assumptions that can match or be congruent with cultural beliefs while other assumptions may be inconsistent.

7. The recognition of both a personal and a societal context within materials from outside the field selected as sources is consistent with the person-situation focus of social work (Compton & Galaway, 1999).

Because this book rests on a systematic eclectic approach to direct practice, we have drawn from and integrated numerous behavioral theories and models of practice extant in social work and other helping professions. These theories and models include the task-centered system, cognitive therapy, behavior modification, client-centered therapy, ego psychology, role theory, social learning theory, decision theory, crisis intervention, existential theory, solution-oriented therapy, and several models of family therapy. We refer to these theories and models in the book, and you will study some of them in depth during your professional education.

Summary

This chapter has introduced social work as a profession marked by a specific mission and values. As social workers and their clients operate in many different kinds and levels of environments, ecological and systems concepts are useful metaphors for conceptualizing what social workers and clients must deal with. Chapter 2 will take us further into specifying direct practice and the roles that social workers play.

Internet Resources

Social workers and their clients increasingly make use of the Internet to gather information to form solutions to problems. Each chapter will include Internet sites you can use to further your knowledge. You may also choose to use InfoTrac® with the free 4-month subscription you received upon purchasing this book. Enter the URL as follows: *http://www.infotrac-college.com*. You will then be asked to provide the passcode that was included with your purchase. After providing identifying information, you can then enter key words or subjects for a review of articles available on this subject. For example, if you enter the key words "involuntary clients," you can access a useful article as follows: O'Hare, T. (1996). Court-ordered versus voluntary clients: Problem differences and readiness for change. *Social Work, 41* (4), 417–422. If you enter the key words "social work values," you will receive a listing of 14 or more articles (the service is updated frequently). For example, you can read Cohen, B. (1999). Intervention and supervision in strength-based social work practice. *Families in Society, 80* (5), 450–459. Outside of Infotrac, you can also begin to browse several souces that you should find useful by accessing one of the following sites. For opportunities to chat with social workers, review job listings, and find other social work links, access: *http://www.socialworker.com/*. For a general resource on many social work areas, access: *http://www.nyu.edu/socialwork/wwwrsw/*.

Internet Exercise

You might also try the following exercise on the Internet to enrich your classroom learning. Let's assume that you are acting as a social work field student in a hospital setting and are assigned to work with a Hmong client for the first time. Further, this client is scheduled to have a blood transfusion, and you have heard that this might be a problem for some Hmong clients. You can find a useful resource to assist you in answering your question related to use of blood transfusions at *http://www.hmongnet.org/faq/blood.html/*. You can then discuss with classmates and your instructor your conclusions about how you would approach work with this client related to the blood transfusion.

Notes

1. For a brief but informative overview of social planning and community organization, see the article by Gilbert and Specht (1987), the source of the foregoing information.
2. In this regard, the critical importance of environmental resources to rehabilitation of patients with major paralysis caused by severe spinal cord injuries has been illustrated and documented in a study reported by Mackelprang and Hepworth (1987).

CHAPTER 2

Direct Practice: Domain, Philosophy, and Roles

CHAPTER OVERVIEW

This chapter presents a context for direct practice, including definitions of direct and clinical practice, a philosophy for direct practice, and descriptions of the varied roles played by direct practitioners.

DOMAIN

Prior to 1970, social work practice was defined by methodologies or by fields of practice. Social workers were thus variously identified as caseworkers, group workers, community organizers, child welfare workers, psychiatric social workers, school social workers, medical social workers, and so on. The terms *direct practice* and *clinical practice* are relatively new in social work nomenclature. The profession was unified in 1955 by the creation of the National Association of Social Workers (NASW) and, with the inauguration of the journal *Social Work*, the gradual transformation from more narrow views of practice to the current broader view was under way. This transformation accelerated during the 1960s and 1970s when social unrest in the United States led to challenges and criticisms of all institutions, including social work. Minority groups, organized

groups of poor people, and other oppressed groups accused the profession of being irrelevant to their pressing needs. These accusations were often justified because many social workers were engaged in narrowly focused and therapeutically oriented activities that did not address the social problems of concern to oppressed groups (Specht & Courtney, 1994).

Casework had been the predominant social work method during this period. Casework involved activities in widely varying settings, aimed at assisting individuals, couples, or families to cope more effectively with problems that impaired social functioning. Group work had also evolved as a practice method, and group workers were practicing in settlement houses and neighborhoods, on the streets with youth gangs, in hospitals and correctional institutions, and in other settings. Although the target units served by group workers were larger, their objectives did not address broad social problems. It was clear that urgent needs for broadly defined social services could not be met through the narrowly defined remedial (therapeutic) efforts of the casework and group work methods.

The efforts of W. Gordon (1965) and Bartlett (1970) to formulate a framework or common base for social work practice composed of purpose, values, sanction, knowledge, and common skills resulted in a broadened perspective of social work. This new perspective was not oriented to methods of practice and fostered the use of the presently employed generic term *social work practice*.

GENERALIST PRACTICE

The Council on Social Work Education responded by adopting a curriculum policy statement stipulating that to meet accreditation standards, social work educational programs must have a curriculum containing foundation courses that embody the common knowledge base of social work practice. Both undergraduate (BSW) and graduate (MSW) programs embody such foundation courses and thus prepare students for generalist practice. BSW curricula, however, are designed primarily to prepare generalist social workers and avoid specialization in practice methods.

The rationale for generalist programs, as we discussed in Chapter 1, is that practitioners should view problems holistically and be prepared to plan interventions aimed at multiple levels of systems related to client concerns. Similarly, client goals and needs should suggest appropriate interventions rather than be led by interventions into exploring compatible goals. Client systems range from micro systems (individuals, couples, families, and groups) to mezzo to macro systems (organizations, institutions, communities, regions, and nations).

Connecting client systems to resource systems that can provide needed goods and services is a paramount function of BSW social workers. Many BSW programs, in fact, are oriented to preparing students to assume the role of case manager, a role that focuses on linking clients to resource systems. We alluded to this role in Chapter 1 and discuss it briefly again later in this chapter and more extensively in Chapter 15.

The first year (foundation year) of MSW programs also prepares graduate students for generalist practice. Although a few MSW programs are oriented to preparing students for "advanced

generalist practice," the large majority of second-year curricula in the MSW programs are designed to permit students to select specializations or "concentrations" that may be in methods of practice or in fields of practice (e.g., substance abuse, aging, child welfare, work with families, health care, or mental health) (Raymond, Teare, & Atherton, 1996). Methods of practice typically are denoted as *micro* or *macro*, the former referring to direct practice and the latter to social policy, community organization, and planning to bring about social and economic justice. MSW students thus are prepared for both generalist and specialized practice.

Both similarities in orientation and differences in function between BSW and MSW social workers and the importance of having practitioners at both levels are highlighted in the following case example, in which the different levels of practice are indicated by initials that correspond to BSW and MSW levels. Please note also that similarities and differences exist on a continuum such that some MSW social workers perform some of the tasks described as related to the BSW practitioner and vice versa. Similarly, there may also be differences according to region, field of practice, and availability of MSW trained practitioners.

CASE EXAMPLE

Mrs. C, a recipient of AFDC public assistance, called her social worker, Ms. BSW, to report that she felt she was "falling apart" and needed to talk. Ms. BSW made a home visit the following day and found Mrs. C in a highly agitated state. Mrs. C reported that three days before she had been visiting with a neighbor who had been attending a group for adult women who were sexually abused as children. The neighbor had related the "horror stories" of several group participants as well as her own. The day following the visit with her neighbor, Mrs. C found herself flooded with memories of being sexually abused by her stepfather during her childhood. Experiencing the memories for the first time was extremely painful, and Mrs. C began feeling worthless and depressed, and having thoughts of taking her life. She wondered if she should be hospitalized but didn't know what she would do with her three children if she were to go to the hospital. She was apprehensive that being hospitalized would be traumatic to her children, especially to her 7-year-old son, Joe, who had been doing poorly in school and had been clinging to her since her divorce from her husband 6 months ago.

Ms. BSW listened carefully and, after exploring further Mrs. C's feelings of depression and thoughts of suicide, explained that she would contact the mental health center regarding alternatives for treatment. She also inquired about Mrs. C's insurance coverage. Ms. BSW assured her that they would plan together for assistance with her children and offered to contact Joe's school regarding his poor performance, if that were agreeable with Mrs. C, who gratefully assented.

Interventions Ms. BSW phoned the mental health center and talked with Ms. MSW, a social worker assigned to the inpatient unit. Ms. MSW arranged for an appointment with Mrs. C the same day and explored her troubling thoughts, depression, and suicidal impulses. In consulting with the psychiatrist in charge and reviewing reimbursement guidelines from Mrs. C's health plan, she determined that Mrs. C did not meet the criteria of imminent danger required for hospitalization but might be helped quickly through participation in an outpatient group (K. Strom, 1992).

Part of Mrs. C's treatment would consist of participating in an outpatient therapy group led by Ms. MSW for women sexually abused as children. Previous experience indicated Mrs. C would benefit by expressing her troubling feelings in a supportive environment provided by the group to regain her equanimity. Moreover, this experience would bolster her damaged self-esteem. Further, Ms. MSW helped Mrs. C see that her seeking help in this time of need was evidence of coping strength. Ms. MSW shared the same holistic orientation to problem assessment and an emphasis on strengths as Ms. BSW from similar training in her first year of graduate school. Consequently, they consulted about how best to support and assist in empowering Mrs. C and her family while she was a part of the outpatient group.

Other types of intervention were discussed with Mrs. C, including having a friend or relative stay with her for a few days or for her to stay with the friend with child care arranged. Mrs. C preferred to have a friend stay with her. Ms. MSW taught Mrs. C some coping skills for handling thoughts of suicide and a plan for addressing them should they rise again. Home visits and regular calls were also planned to help her get through the crisis period.

Ms. BSW contacted the school the following day and talked with the school social worker, Mr. MSW, regarding Joe's difficulties in school. She explained that the school difficulties and Joe's clinging behavior appeared temporally associated with Mrs. C's divorce. Mr. MSW said he would explain the situation to the teacher and would recommend that Joe be given special attention. He also explained that he was leading a group of children from families in transition and would include Joe in the group.

DIRECT PRACTICE

Direct practice includes work with individuals, couples, families, and groups. Direct practitioners perform many roles besides delivering face-to-face service; they work in collaboration with other professionals, organizations, and institutions, and act to advocate with landlords, agency administrators, policy-making boards, and legislatures, among others.

The term *clinical practice* is commonly used interchangeably with direct practice, but the terms may have different meanings for different people. Proponents of the term have emphasized that clinical social work entails liberating, supporting, and enhancing people's adaptive capacities and increasing the responsiveness of physical and social environments to people's needs. Swenson suggests that "clinical social workers work with clients to bring about social psychological change and to increase access to social and economic resources (Swenson, 1995, p. 503). Some people think of clinical practice as limited to psychotherapy done in mental health settings, independent practice settings, or similar settings. Opponents of the term suggest that it has connoted a focus on disease and pathology rather than health and strengths. Direct practice encompasses a full range of roles, including acting as a psychotherapist. Subsequently in this book, we use the terms *direct practice* or *clinical practice* in the broad sense to refer to practice done in any of the diverse settings in which micro services are delivered. Services delivered by direct practitioners may be addressed to most of the troubling situations encountered by human beings and may be delivered in any of the diverse settings listed at the beginning of Chapter 1.

Central to assisting people with difficulties is knowledge of and skill in problem solving. Problem solving requires knowledge and skills in assessing human problems and in locating, developing, or utilizing appropriate resource systems. Skills in engaging clients, mutually planning relevant goals, and defining roles of the participants are also integral parts of the problem-solving process. Similarly, the practitioner must possess knowledge of interventions and skills in implementing them. A more extensive review of the helping process is contained in the next chapter, and the entire book is devoted to explicating theory and skills related to direct practice with clients.

Direct practitioners of social work must be knowledgeable and skilled in interviewing and in assessing and intervening in problematic interactions involving individuals, couples, families, and groups. Knowledge related to group process and skill in leading groups are also essential, as are skills in forming natural helping networks, functioning as a member of an interdisciplinary team, and negotiating within and between systems. The negotiating function entails skills in mediating conflicts and advocating and obtaining resources, both of which embody high levels of interpersonal skills.

Questions as to whether direct practitioners do or should engage in psychotherapy are still raised by some who regard psychotherapy as the exclusive province of psychologists, psychiatrists, and specially trained social workers. These individuals argue that only psychoanalysts are trained to work with the unconscious mind and that social workers should limit their function to casework or counseling. Others have questioned whether engaging in psychotherapy is appropriate for a profession whose mission focuses on social justice (Specht & Courtney, 1994). However, Jerome Wakefield argues that social work is distinguished as a profession by its goal of pursuing minimum distributive justice for its clients and that social workers can appropriately utilize psychotherapy as a method in pursuit of this goal (Wakefield, 1996 a & b). Similarly, Swenson (1998) has argued that clinical work that draws on client strengths, is mindful of social positions and power relationships, and attempts to counter oppression is consistent with a social justice perspective. In our opinion these debates are moot. Currently many practitioners in social work and other helping professions practice psychotherapy that draws on additional theory bases such as behavioral and family systems models; hence the emphasis on work with the unconscious, which presumes a psychoanalytic theory, is less relevant. In fact, more social workers are employed in mental health centers (which deal in psychotherapy) than members of any other core helping profession (Taube & Barrett, 1983; Timberlake, Sababatino, & Martin, 1997).

A PHILOSOPHY OF DIRECT PRACTICE

As a profession evolves, its knowledge base expands and practitioners gain experience in applying abstract values and knowledge to specific practice situations. Instrumental values thus gradually evolve, and as they are adopted, they become principles or guidelines to practice. Such principles express preferred beliefs about the nature and causes of human problems. They also describe perspectives about people's capacity to deal with problems, desirable goals, and valued qualities in helping relationships. Finally, those principles include beliefs about vital elements of the helping process, roles of the practitioner and client, characteristics of effective group leaders, the nature of the human growth process, and so on.

Over many years, we have evolved a philosophy of practice from a synthesis of principles gained from sources too diverse to acknowledge, including our own value preferences. We thus offer as our philosophy of direct practice the following principles (see Figure 2-1):

ROLES OF DIRECT PRACTITIONERS

During recent years, increasing attention has been devoted to the various roles that direct practitioners perform in discharging their responsibilities. In Chapter 1, we referred to a number of these roles. In this section, we summarize these and other roles and refer to sections of the book where we discuss certain roles at greater length. We have categorized the roles based in part on a schema presented by Lister (1987) (see Figure 2-2).

A PHILOSOPHY OF DIRECT PRACTICE

1. The problems experienced by social work clients stem from lack of resources, knowledge, and skills (societal, systemic, and personal sources), either alone or in combination.

2. As social work clients are often afflicted with poverty, racism, sexism, heterosexism, discrimination, and lack of resources, social workers negotiate systems and advocate for change to ensure clients access to rights, resources, and treatment with dignity.

3. People are capable of making their own choices and decisions. Although controlled to some extent by their environment, they are able to direct their environment more than they realize. Social workers aim to assist in the empowerment of their clients by helping them gain the ability to make decisions that affect their lives and increase their working toward changing environmental influences that adversely affect them individually and as members of groups.

4. As social service systems are often funded on the basis of individual dysfunctions, social workers often play an educational function in sensitizing service delivery systems to more systemic approaches to problems emphasizing health, strengths, and natural support systems.

5. Frequently, social workers deal with persons who are reluctant to receive services under referrals pressured by others or through the threat of legal sanctions. While people have a right to their own

values and beliefs, sometimes their behaviors violate the rights of others, and the social worker assists these clients in facing these aspects of their difficulties. Since reluctant or involuntary clients are often not seeking a helping relationship but rather wishing to escape one, negotiation is frequently called for.

6. Some clients apply for service and wish to experience change through a social worker's assistance. Such clients are often helped by having an accepting relationship, with appropriate self-disclosure, which will allow them to seek greater self-awareness and to live more fully in the reality of the moment.

7. All clients, whether voluntary or involuntary, are entitled to be treated with respect and dignity, and to have choices facilitated.

8. Client behavior is goal directed, although these goals are often not readily discernible. Clients are, however, capable of learning new skills, knowledge, and approaches to resolving difficulties. Helping professionals are responsible for helping clients discover their strengths and affirming their capacity for growth and change.

9. While current problems are often influenced by past relationships and concerns, and though limited focus on the past is sometimes beneficial, most difficulties can be alleviated by focusing on present choices and by mobilizing strengths and coping patterns.

Figure 2-1 Principles of a Philosophy of Direct Practice

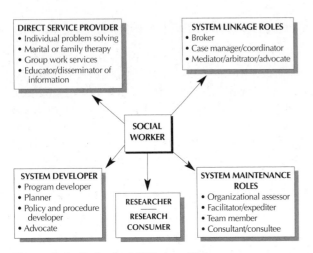

Figure 2-2   Roles Social Workers Play

Direct Provision of Services

Roles subsumed under this category are those in which social workers meet face to face with clients or consumer groups in providing services. These include the following:

- *Individual casework or counseling.*
- *Marital and family therapy* (may include sessions with individuals, conjoint sessions, and group sessions).
- *Group work services* (may include support groups, therapy groups, self-help groups, task groups, and skill development groups).
- *Educator/disseminator of information.* The social worker may provide essential information in individual, conjoint, or group sessions or may make educational presentations to consumer groups or to the public. For example, practitioners may conduct educative sessions concerned with parenting skills, marital enrichment, stress management, or various aspects of mental health or health care (Dore, 1993).

The above roles are primary in the work of most direct service social workers. Because this book is aimed at preparing social workers to provide such direct services, we shall not elaborate on these roles in this section.

System Linkage Roles

Because clients often need resources not provided by a given social agency and lack knowledge of or ability to utilize other available resources, social workers often perform roles in linking people to other resources. System linkage roles include the following:

- *Broker.* To perform the role of broker (i.e., an intermediary who assists in connecting people with resources), social workers must have a thorough knowledge of community resources so that they can make appropriate referrals. Familiarity with the policies of resource systems and working relationships with key contact persons are essential to successful referrals. The preceding case example of Mrs. C being referred by Ms. BSW to the mental health center was an example of performing the broker role. Before some people are able to avail themselves of resources, they may require the practitioner's assistance in overcoming fears and misconceptions. Social workers also have responsibilities in developing simple and effective referral mechanisms and ways of monitoring whether clients actually follow through on referrals. To assist you in gaining skills in referring clients to needed resources, we present relevant guidelines in Chapter 3.

- *Case manager/coordinator.* Some clients lack the ability, skills, knowledge, or resources to follow through on referrals to other systems. In such instances, the social worker may serve as *case manager,* a person designated to assume primary responsibility for assessing the needs of a client and arranging and coordinating the delivery of essential goods and services provided by other resources. Case managers also work directly with the client to ensure that the goods and services are provided in a timely manner. Case managers must maintain close contact with clients (including sometimes acting to provide direct casework services) and with other service providers to ensure that plans for service delivery are in place and are subsequently delivered as planned. It is noteworthy that in the case manager role, practitioners function at the interface between the client and the environment more than in any other role. Because of dramatic increases in recent years in the numbers of people needing case management services (e.g., homeless, elderly, and chronically mentally disabled people), numerous articles have appeared in the literature concerned with those who need such services, issues related to case management, and various functions of case managers. Because we discuss these topics at some length in Chapter 15, we defer discussion of them to that chapter.

- *Mediator/arbitrator.* Occasionally breakdowns occur between clients and service providers so that clients do not receive needed services to which they are entitled. For example, clients may be seeking a resource to which they believe they are entitled by their health insurance. In other cases, participants in workfare programs may find themselves sanctioned for failure to meet program expectations (Withorn, 1998). Service may be denied, because clients did not adequately represent their eligibility for services, or because of strains that sometimes develop between clients and service providers that precipitate withdrawals of requests for services by clients or withholding of services by providers.

In such instances, practitioners may serve as mediators with the goal of eliminating obstacles to service delivery. *Mediation* is a process that "provides a neutral forum in which disputants are encouraged to find a mutually satisfactory resolution to their problems" (Chandler, 1985, p. 346). In serving as a mediator, you must carefully listen to and draw out facts and feelings from both parties to determine the cause of the breakdown. It is important not to take sides with either party until you are confident that you have accurate and complete information. When you have determined the nature of the breakdown, you can plan appropriate remedial action aimed at removing barriers, clarifying possible misunderstandings, and working through negative feelings that have impeded service delivery. This process entails the use of communication skills that are delineated in subsequent chapters of this book.

In recent years, knowledge of mediation skills has evolved to a high level of sophistication, and a small but increasing number of practitioners are working independently or in tandem with attorneys to mediate conflicts between divorcing partners regarding child custody, visitation rights, and property settlements. These same skills can be used to mediate personnel disputes, labor-management conflicts, and victim-offender situations (Umbreit, 1993).

- *Client advocate.* Social workers have assumed the role of advocate for a client or group of clients since the inception of the profession. The obligation to assume this role has been reaffirmed most recently in the NASW Code of Ethics, which includes advocacy among the activities performed by social workers in pursuit of the professional mission (NASW, 1996, p. 2). With respect to linking clients with resources, advocacy is the process of working with and/or on behalf of clients to obtain services and resources that would not otherwise be provided. We discuss circumstances under which this might occur and appropriate remedial measures at length in Chapter 19. We also discuss skills involved in advocacy (including social action for groups of clients) in Chapter 15.

System Maintenance and Enhancement

As staff members of social agencies, social workers bear responsibility for evaluating structures, policies, and functional relationships within agencies that impair effectiveness in service delivery. Roles that relate to fulfilling this responsibility include:

- *Organizational analyst.* Discharging the role of organizational analyst[1] entails pinpointing factors in agency structure, policy, and procedures that have a negative impact on service delivery. Knowledge of organizational and administrative theory is essential to performing this role effectively. We focus on this role in Chapter 15 in the section "Organizational Resistance." You will also learn more about organizational dynamics in courses concerned with organizational theory.

- *Facilitator/expediter.* After pinpointing factors that impede service delivery, social workers have a responsibility to plan and implement ways of enhancing service delivery. This may involve providing relevant input to agency boards and administrators, recommending staff meetings to address problems, working collaboratively with other staff members to bring pressure to bear on resistant administrators, encouraging and participating in essential inservice training sessions, and other similar activities. In Chapter 1, we saw how the social worker from The Arch working with Ms. Percy was able to convince agency administrators to make the agency van available to clients to bring them to appointments and to facilitate their shopping for groceries.

- *Team member.* In many agency and institutional settings (e.g., mental health, health care, rehabilitation, and education settings), practitioners function as members of clinical teams that collaborate in assessing clients' problems and delivering services (Sands, 1989; Sands, Stafford, & McClelland, 1990). Teams commonly consist of a psychiatrist or physician, psychologist, a social worker, a nurse, and perhaps a rehabilitation counselor, occupational therapist, educator, and/or a recreational therapist, depending on the setting. Members of the team have varying types of expertise that are tapped in formulating assessments and planning and implementing therapeutic interventions. As team members, social work practitioners often contribute knowledge related to family dynamics and engage in therapeutic work with family members. B.O. Dane and Simon (1991) note that social workers in host settings, where the mission and decision making are dominated by non-social workers, often experience a discrepancy between their professional mission and the values of the employing institution. They can act, however, to sensitize team members to strengths and a more holistic approach while exercising their knowledge of resources and expertise in linking clients with resources. Social workers also are expected to apply their knowledge of community resources in planning for the discharge of patients and facilitating their reentry into the community following periods of hospitalization. In so doing, social workers bring their systems and strengths perspectives to teams that are sometimes more deficit focused. Social workers are also increasingly involved in collaborative work across systems such as schools and child welfare, which require knowledge of ability to work in several systems (Bailey-Dempsey, & Reid 1995). As team members, social workers also often serve as case managers in coordinating discharge planning for patients (Dane & Simon 1991; Kadushin & Kulys, 1993).

- *Consultant/consultee.* Consultation is a process whereby an expert enables a consultee to deliver services more effectively to a client by increasing, developing, modifying, or freeing the consultee's knowledge, skills, attitudes, or behavior with respect to the problem at hand (Kadushin, 1977). Although social workers both provide and receive consultation, there has been a trend over the past decade for MSW social workers to serve less as consumers of consultation and more as providers. BSW social workers may provide consultation regarding the availability of specific community resources but more often are consumers of consultation when they need information about how to work effectively in problem solving that entails complex situations and behaviors. Social workers assume the consultee role when in need of expert knowledge from doctors and nurses, psychiatrists, psychologists, and other social workers who possess high levels of expertise related to certain types of problems (e.g., substance abuse, child mal-treatment, sexual problems, and other issues that require advanced knowledge).

Social workers serve as consultants to members of other professions and to other social workers in need of their special expertise, including the role of supervisor. For example, they may provide consultation to school personnel who need assistance in understanding and coping with problem students; to health care providers who seek assistance in understanding a patient's family or ethnic and cultural factors; to court staff regarding matters that bear on child custody decisions and decisions about parole and probation; and in many other similar situations.[2]

Researcher/Research Consumer

Practitioners face responsibilities in both public and private settings to select interventions that can be evaluated, to evaluate the effectiveness of their interventions, and to systematically monitor the progress of their clients. Implementing these processes requires practitioners to conduct and make use of research.

Actual research conducted by direct practitioners sometimes involves single-subject (also denoted as single-system) designs. This type of research design enables practitioners to obtain measures of the extent (frequency and severity) of problem behaviors before implementing interventions aimed at eliminating or reducing the problem behaviors or increasing the frequency of behaviors that are insufficient (e.g., doing homework, engaging in prosocial behaviors, setting realistic and consistent limits with children, sending positive messages, abstaining from drinking). These measures provide a baseline against which the results of implementing interventions can be assessed by applying the same measures periodically during the course of the interventions, at termination, and at follow-up (J. Reid, 1994). perhaps more frequently, practitioners use some form of Goal Attainment Scaling that calls for rating goal achievement on a scale with points designated in

advance (Corcoran & Vandiver, 1996). Unless practitioners employ such designs to evaluate their practice, they place too much reliance on clinical judgment. Assessing progress through repeated measures, by contrast, enables both client and practitioner to discern small changes that might otherwise be underestimated or to determine that interventions are not producing the desired changes and a different approach is indicated.

System Development

Direct practitioners sometimes have opportunities to improve or to expand agency services based on assessment of unmet client needs, gaps in service, needs for preventive services, or findings of one's own or other research studies that indicate more promising results achieved by interventions other than those currently employed. Roles that relate to system development include:

- *Program developer.* As we noted earlier, practitioners often have opportunities to develop services in response to emerging needs of clients. Such services may include educational programs (e.g., for immigrants or unwed pregnant teenagers), support groups (e.g., for rape victims, adult children of alcoholics, and victims of incest), and skill development programs (e.g., stress management, parenting, and assertiveness training groups).

- *Planner.* In small communities and rural areas that lack access to community planners, direct practitioners may need to assume a planning role, usually in concert with community leaders. In this role, the practitioner works both formally and informally with influential people to plan programs in response to unmet and emerging needs. Varying from one area to another, such needs may include child care programs, transportation for elderly and disabled persons, and recreational and health care programs, to name just a few.

- *Policy and procedure developer.* Participation of direct practitioners in formulating policies and procedures typically is limited to agencies in which they provide direct services to clients. This degree of participation is largely determined by the style of administration with a given agency. Able administrators generally solicit and invite input from professional staff as to how the agency can more effectively respond to consumers of services. Because practitioners serve in the "front lines" they are in a strategic position to evaluate clients' needs and how policies and procedures serve or fail to serve the best interests of clients. It is important, therefore, that social workers seek to be actively involved in decision-making processes related to policies and procedure. In rural areas and small communities, direct practitioners often partici-

pate in policy development concerned with the needs of a broad community rather than the needs of a circumscribed target group. In such instances, social workers must draw from knowledge and skills gained in courses in social welfare policy and services and community planning.

- *Advocate.* Just as social workers may advocate for an individual client, they may also join client groups, other social workers, and allied professionals in advocating for legislation and social policies aimed at providing needed resources and enhancing social justice. We discuss skills in advocacy and social action in Chapter 15.

Summary

Direct social work practice is characterized by performance of multiple roles. Those roles are performed at varied system levels depending on the level of the concerns addresses. As we have indicated previously, knowledge and skills related to some of the foregoing roles are taught in segments of the curriculum that lie outside direct practice courses. To do justice in one volume to the knowledge and skills entailed in all these roles is impossible; consequently, we have limited our focus primarily to the roles subsumed under Figure 2-2, providing direct service.

Internet Resources

You can access a copy of the Code of Ethics of NASW (the National Association of Social Workers) by entering the URL: *http://www.naswdc.org/ code.htm*. Using InfoTrac®, you can search keywords "mediation," "program planning," and "consulting." Additional resources on

clinical social work are available at *http://www.cswf.org/ ethframe.htm*. Resources on populations at risk are available at *http://webdb.nyu.edu/sociallinks/menu. cgi?cid=438*. At the website for the National Associaton of Social Workers (NASW), *http:// www.naswdc.org*, you can access standards for the clinical practice of social work. By selecting "practice issues" you can access information about on-line therapy and the clinical social worker, telecommunications and the clinical social worker, and an HIV/AIDS fact sheet for social workers.

Notes

1. We have adapted this term from Weissman, Epstein, and Savage (1987).
2. The principles and skills involved in consultation are beyond the scope of this book. Those interested in pursuing this topic further will find Dougherty's 1990 book informative. A quarterly journal, *Consultation: An International Journal,* published by Human Sciences Press, is also an excellent reference.

CHAPTER 3

Overview of the Helping Process

CHAPTER OVERVIEW

This chapter provides an overview of the three phases of the helping process: exploration, implementation, and termination. The helping process is related to problem solving with social work clients in a variety of settings. Hence, the process is presented with the larger systems context in mind. That context includes potential clients who are at varied levels of initial voluntarism ranging from required or mandated, to referred, to voluntary.

COMMON ELEMENTS AMONG DIVERSE THEORISTS AND SOCIAL WORKERS

Direct social workers working with individuals, couples, families, groups, and other systems draw on contrasting theories of human behavior, use different models of practice, implement diverse interventions, and serve widely varying clients. Despite these varied factors, all direct social workers work to assist clients in coping more effectively with problems of living and improving the quality of their lives. People are impelled by either internal or external sources to secure social work services because current solutions are not working in their lives. Some persons are hence *applicants* who request services of a social worker to deal with these internal or external problems (Alcabes & Jones, 1985). In many other instances, the need for help has been identified by teachers, doctors, employers, or family members, and people who initiate contact at the behest of these others. Such persons might be best considered *referrals* because they are not applicants (Compton & Galaway, 1999). There is variation, then, among referrals, as some perceive pressure to seek help while others perceive assistance in finding the appropriate help. Still others are at least initially involuntary clients and could be considered *respondents*, because they are responding to requests or perceived requirements to seek help as a result of pressure from other persons or legal sources (Reid, 1978). Persons who begin their contact as applicants, referrals, or respondents are all potential clients if they can negotiate a contract addressed to some of their concerns. However potential clients begin their contact, they are facing a situation of disequilibrium in which there is potential to achieve growth in problem-solving ability by developing new resources or employing untapped resources in ways that reduce tension and achieve mastery over problems.

Whatever their approach to assisting clients, most direct social workers employ a problem-solving process. That is, social workers need to assist clients in assessing the concerns that they perceive or that their environment presses upon them, making decisions about fruitful ways to identify and prioritize those concerns. Next, they identify together possible approaches to reducing the concerns and make decisions about which ones to pursue. Involuntary clients face situations in which some of these concerns are not of their choice and some of the approaches to reducing concerns may be mandated. Even in these circumstances, clients have the power to make at least constrained choices in the way they address these concerns or in addressing additional concerns beyond those that are mandated. After approaches are identified and selected, they are implemented and together the client and social worker assess the success of their efforts and make revised plans. Social workers use communication skills to implement the problem-solving process with different systems involved in clients' problems.

The first portion of this chapter is devoted to an overview of the helping process and its three distinct phases, and subsequent portions of the book are organized to correspond to these phases. The latter part of this chapter focuses on the structure and processes involved in interviewing. Later chapters deal with the structure, processes, and skills involved in modifying the processes of families and groups.

THE HELPING PROCESS

Virtually all social work theorists agree that the helping process consists of three major phases. Each has distinct objectives, and the helping process generally proceeds successively through them. These phases, however, are not sharply demarcated by the activities and skills employed. The activities and skills of the three phases differ more in frequency and intensity that in kind. The processes of exploration and assessment, for example, are central during Phase I, but these processes continue in somewhat diminished significance during subsequent phases of the helping process. The three major phases are:

• Phase I Exploration, engagement, assessment, and planning
• Phase II Implementation and goal attainment
• Phase III Termination

Phase I. Exploration, Engagement, Assessment, and Planning

The first phase lays the groundwork for subsequent implementation of interventions and strategies aimed at resolving clients' problems and promoting problem-solving skills. The phase is implemented in helping relationships of any duration and setting, from crisis intervention and discharge planning to long-term and institutional care. Processes involved and tasks to be accomplished during Phase I include the following:

1. Exploring clients' problems by eliciting comprehensive data about the person(s), the problem, and environmental factors including forces influencing the referral for contact

2. Establishing rapport and enhancing motivation

3. Formulating a multidimensional assessment of the problem, identifying systems that play a significant role in the difficulties, and identifying relevant resources that can be tapped or must be developed

4. Mutually negotiating goals to be accomplished in remedying or alleviating the problem and formulating a contract

5. Making referrals

We briefly discuss each of these five processes in the following sections and refer to portions of the book that include extensive discussions of these processes.

1. *Exploring clients' problems by eliciting comprehensive data about the person(s), the problem, and environmental factors including forces influencing the referral for contact.* Contact begins with an initial exploration of the circumstances that have led to contact. Because self-referred persons are the minority of clients served in many settings, and even those who self-refer often do so at the suggestion or pressure of others, one should not assume that potential clients at this stage are really applicants or voluntary clients (Cingolani, 1984). Further, they may be anxious about the prospect of seeking help and lack knowledge about what to

expect. For many, the social worker will have information from an intake form or referral source about the circumstances that have brought them into contact.

These many possibilities can be explored by asking *"What brings you here? How can we help you?"* These questions should elicit a beginning elaboration of the concern or pressures that the potential client sees as relating to his or her contact. The social worker can hence begin to determine to what extent the motivation for contact was initiated by the potential client and to what extent the motivation is in response to external forces.

The social worker should also give a clear, brief description of his or her own view of the purpose of this first contact and encourage an exploration of how the social worker can be helpful.

2. *Establishing rapport and enhancing motivation.* Effective communication in the helping relationship is crucial, for unless social workers succeed in engaging clients, the clients may be guarded in revealing vital information and feelings and, even worse, may not return after the initial session. Engaging clients successfully means establishing rapport, which involves reducing the level of threat and gaining the trust of clients in the social worker's intent to be helpful. A condition of rapport is that clients perceive a social worker as understanding and genuinely interested in their well-being. To create such a positive perception among clients whose race or ethnicity differs from the social worker's, the social worker must attend to relevant cultural factors and vary interviewing techniques accordingly, as we discuss later in this chapter and throughout the book. Further, when potential clients have been referred by others, they will need to be assured that their wishes are important and that they do not have to necessarily work on the concerns seen by the referral source.

Potential clients who are not applicants or genuinely self-referred frequently have misgivings about the helping process. They don't perceive themselves as having a problem and often attribute the source of difficulties to another person or to untoward circumstances. Such clients confront social workers with the challenging task of (1) neutralizing negative feelings, (2) attempting to help potential clients understand problems attributed by others and assessing the advantages and disadvantages of dealing with those concerns, and (3) creating an incentive to work on acknowledged problems. Skillful social workers often succeed in tapping into the motivation of such involuntary clients, thus affirming the principle from systems theory that motivation is substantially influenced by the interaction between clients and social workers.

In still other instances, clients freely acknowledge problems and do not lack incentive for change but assume a passive role, expecting social workers to magically work out their difficulties for them. Social workers must be able to avoid taking on the impossible role that some clients would ascribe to them. Instead they should impart a belief in clients' abilities to work as partners in searching for remedial courses of action and mobilize clients' energies in implementing tasks essential to successful problem resolution.

Very useful in the helping process are acknowledgment of a problem and adequate client motivation to actively work toward its solution. Potential clients do not lack motivation; they sometimes lack motivation to work on the problems and goals perceived by others. In addition, motivation relates to a person's past experience that leads him or her to expect that behaviors will be successful or will fail in attempting to reach goals. Hence, those with limited expectations for success often appear to lack motivation. The work of social workers is then often directed to attempting to increase motivation by assisting clients to discover that their actions can be effective in reaching their goals (Gold, 1990).

Social workers, therefore, must possess skills for tapping into client motivation and assisting those who readily acknowledge a problem but are reluctant to expend the required effort or to bear the discomfort generally involved in effecting essential change. A major task in this process is then to provide information to the potential client about what to expect from a helping process. This socialization process includes identifying the kinds of concerns the social worker and agency can help with, client rights including confidentiality and circumstances in which it might be abridged, and information about what behavior to expect from the social worker and client (Videka-Sherman, 1988).

The task for clients in groups is twofold, for they must develop trust not only in the social worker but in other group members as well. If group members vary in race, ethnicity, or social class, the group leader must be sensitive to such cultural determinants of behaviors and assume a facilitative role in breaking down related barriers to rapport not only between himself or herself and individual group members but also among group members. Developing group norms and mutual expectations together assists in the creation of a group cohesiveness that helps groups become successful.

Establishing rapport requires that social workers manifest (1) a nonjudgmental attitude; (2) acceptance; (3) respect for clients' right of self-determination; and (4) respect for clients' worth and dignity, uniqueness and individuality, and problem-solving capacities (discussed at length in Chapter 4). Finally, social workers foster rapport when they relate with empathy and authenticity. Both skills are considered in later chapters of this book.

3. *Formulating a multidimensional assessment of the problem, identifying systems that play a significant role in the difficulties, and identifying relevant resources that can be tapped or must be developed.* Establishing rapport and exploring clients' problems are processes that social workers implement concurrently. Moreover, these processes are mutually reinforcing. Astute exploration not only yields rich data but also cultivates rapport by inspiring confidence in the social worker.

Similarly, empathic communication not only conveys understanding and fosters rapport but also elicits expanded expressions of feelings, enabling social workers to evaluate the role clients' emotions play in their difficulties. Certain responses thus serve dual functions, and the processes of re-

lationship building and problem exploration not only proceed concurrently but also overlap.

Problem exploration is a critical process, for comprehensive information must be gathered before all the dimensions of a problem and their interaction can be understood. Exploration begins by attending to the emotional states and immediate concerns manifested by clients. Gradually, the social worker broadens the exploration to encompass relevant systems (individual, interpersonal, and environmental) and explores in depth aspects of the problem that appear most critical. During the process of exploration, the social worker is also alert to and highlights client strengths, realizing that these strengths represent a vital resource to be identified and tapped later during the goal attainment phase.

Skills that are employed in the exploratory process with individuals, couples, families, and groups are delineated later in this chapter and at length in subsequent chapters. To explore problematic situations thoroughly, social workers must also be knowledgeable about the various systems commonly involved in human difficulties, topics considered at length in Chapters 8–11.

Problem exploration skills are put into use as part of the assessment process that begins from the first contact with clients and continues throughout the helping relationship. During interviews, social workers weigh the significance of clients' behavior, thoughts, beliefs, emotions, and, of course, information revealed. These moment-by-moment assessments guide the social worker in deciding what aspects of the problem to explore in depth, when to explore emotions more deeply, and so on, as we discuss at greater length later in this chapter. In addition to this ongoing process of assessment, the social worker must formulate a working assessment from which flow the goals and contract upon which Phase II of the problem-solving process is based.

An adequate assessment includes analysis of the problem, the person(s), and the ecological context. Since there are many possible areas that can be explored and limited time to explore them, focus in assessment is critical. Focus is promoted by conducting assessment in layers. At the first layer, you must focus your attention on issues of client safety, legal mandates, and the client's wishes for service. The rationale for this threefold set of priorities is that client wishes should take precedence in circumstances in which legal mandates do not impinge on choices or in which no dangers to self or others exist.

Analysis of the problem specifies that nature of the difficulties. These may involve inadequate resources; decisions about a crucial aspect of one's life; difficulties in individual, interpersonal, or societal systems; or interactions between any of the preceding factors. Analysis of the problem also involves judgments about the duration and severity of a problem as well as the extent to which the problem is susceptible to change, given the client's potential coping capacity and the ability of the problematic situation to change. In considering the nature and severity of problems, social workers must also weigh these factors against their own competencies and the types of services provided by the agency. If the problems call for services that are beyond the agency's function, such as prescribing medication or rendering speech therapy, referral to another professional or agency may be indicated.

Analysis of the individual system includes assessment of the client's wants and needs, coping capacity, strengths and limitations, and motivation to work on the problem(s). In evaluating the first two dimensions, the social worker must assess such factors as flexibility, judgment, emotional characteristics, degree of responsibility, capacity to tolerate stress, ability to reason critically, and interpersonal skills. These factors, which are critical in selecting appropriate and attainable goals, are discussed at length in Chapter 9.

Assessment of ecological factors entails consideration of the adequacy or deficiency, success or failure, and strengths or weaknesses of salient systems in the environment that bear on the client's problem. Ecological assessment thus is aimed at identifying systems that must be strengthened, mobilized, or developed in response to the client's unmet needs. Systems that often bear on clients'

needs include marital, family, and social support systems (e.g., kin, friends, neighbors, co-workers, peer groups, and ethnic reference groups); spiritual belief systems, child care, health care, and employment systems; various institutions; and the physical environment.

Cultural factors are also vital in ecological assessment, for personal and social needs and the means of satisfying them vary widely from culture to culture. Moreover, the resources that can be tapped to meet clients' needs also vary according to cultural contexts. Some cultures have indigenous helping persons, such as folk healers, religious leaders, and relatives from extended family units who have been invested with authority to assist clients in times of crisis. These persons can often provide valuable assistance to social workers and their clients.

Assessment of the client's situational context further involves consideration of the circumstances as well as actions and reactions of participants in problematic interaction. Knowledge of circumstances and specific behavior of participants before, during, and after troubling events is crucial to understanding the forces that shape and maintain problematic behavior. Assessment, therefore, requires that social workers elicit detailed information about actual transactions between people.

Whether making assessments of individuals per se or of individuals as subsets of marital dyads, families, or groups, it is important to assess the functioning of these larger systems. These systems have unique properties including power distribution, role definitions, rules, norms, channels of communication, and repetitive interactional patterns. Such systems also manifest both strengths and problems that strongly affect and shape the behavior of constituent members. It follows that individual difficulties tend to be related to systemic dysfunction, and interventions must therefore be directed to the system as well as to the individual.

Assessments of systems are based on varied data-gathering procedures. With couples and families, social workers may or may not conduct individual interviews, depending on their theoretical biases, practice styles, agency practices, and impressions gained during preliminary contacts with family members. If exploration and assessment are implemented exclusively in conjoint sessions, the processes are similar to those of individual interviews except that interaction between the participants assumes major significance. Whereas information gained in individual interviews is limited to reports and descriptions by clients, requiring the social worker to make inferences about actual interaction within relevant systems, social workers view interaction directly in conjoint interviews and group sessions. The social worker is alert to strengths and dysfunction in communication and interaction and to the properties of the system (see Chapters 10 and 11). Assessment therefore focuses heavily on styles of communication employed by individual participants, interactional patterns among members, and the impact of individual members on processes that occur in the system. These factors are weighed in selecting interventions aimed at enhancing functioning at these different levels of the larger systems.

Finally, a working assessment involves synthesizing all relevant information gained in the exploration process. To enhance the validity of the assessment, it is desirable to involve clients in the process by soliciting their perceptions and assisting them in gathering data about their perceived difficulties. Share impressions with them and invite affirmation or disconfirmation of those impressions. It is also beneficial to further highlight their strengths and to identify other relevant resource systems that can be tapped or need to be developed to accomplish remediation of the difficulties. When the social worker and client(s) reach agreement about the nature of the problems involved, they are ready to enter the process of negotiating goals, assuming that clients are adequately motivated to advance to Phase II of the helping process.

4. *Mutually negotiating goals to be accomplished in remedying or alleviating the problem and formulating a contract.* If the social worker and the individual client, couple, family, or group have reached agreement concerning the nature of the

difficulties and the systems that are involved, the participants are ready to negotiate individual and/or group goals. This is a mutual process aimed at identifying what needs to be changed and what related actions need to be taken to resolve or ameliorate the problematic situation. We briefly discuss the process of goal selection in this chapter and at length in Chapter 13. If agreement is not reached about the appropriateness of services or clients choose not to continue, then services may be terminated. In some situations, then, services are finished when the assessment is completed. In the case of involuntary clients, some may continue under pressure even if agreement is not reached about the appropriateness of services or if problems are not acknowledged.

After goals have been negotiated, participants undertake the final task of Phase I: formulating a contract. The contract (see Chapter 12), which is also mutually negotiated, consists of a formal agreement or understanding between the social worker and client that specifies the goals to be accomplished, relevant strategies to be implemented, roles and responsibilities of participants, practical arrangements, and other factors. When the client system is a couple, family, or group, the contract also specifies group goals that tend to accelerate group movement and to facilitate accomplishment of group goals.

Mutually formulating a contract is a vital process because it demystifies the helping process and clarifies for clients what they may realistically expect from the social worker and what is expected of them; what they will mutually be seeking to accomplish and in what ways; and what the problem-solving process entails. While most straightforward with voluntary clients or applicants, developing contracts that are voluntary, at least in part, is also a feasible goal for involuntary clients.

5. *Making referrals.* Exploration of clients' problems often reveals that resources or services beyond those provided by the agency are needed to remedy or ameliorate presenting difficulties. This is especially true of clients who present a broad

array of needs. In such instances, referrals to other resource and service providers may be necessary. Moreover, clients may lack the knowledge, skills, or resources needed to avail themselves of resources that are badly needed. Social workers may assume the role of case manager in such instances (e.g., for persons with severe and persistent mental illness, developmental and physical disabilities, foster children, and infirm elderly clients).

Linking clients to other resource systems requires careful handling if clients are to follow through in seeking and obtaining essential resources.

Phase II: Implementation and Goal Attainment

After mutually formulating a contract, the social worker and client(s) enter the heart of the problem-solving process—the implementation and goal attainment phase, also denoted as the action-oriented or change-oriented phase (terms that are used interchangeably in this book). Phase II involves translating plans formulated between the social worker and individual clients, couples, families, or groups into actions. The participants thus combine their efforts in working toward the goal accorded highest priority. This process begins by dissecting the goal into general tasks that identify general strategies to be employed in pursuit of the goal. These general tasks are then subdivided into specific tasks that designate what the client and social worker plan to do between one session and the next (Epstein, 1988; Reid, 1992; Robinson, 1930; Taft, 1937).[1] Tasks may relate to the individual's personal functioning or to interaction with others in the client's environment, or they may involve interaction with other resource systems, such as schools, hospitals, or law enforcement agencies. The processes of negotiating goals and tasks are discussed in Chapter 12.

After mutually formulating goals with clients, social workers select and implement interventions designed to assist clients in accomplishing their goals and subsidiary tasks. Interventions should directly relate to the problems and to the consequent goals that were mutually negotiated with

clients and derived from accurate assessment. Helping efforts often fail when social workers employ global interventions without considering clients' views of their problems and without attending to the uniqueness of such problems.

Enhancing Self-Efficacy

Research findings (Bandura, 1977; Kazdin, 1979; Lane, Daugherty, & Nyman, 1998) have strongly indicated that a major source of gain in the helping process is an increased sense of self-efficacy on the part of clients. Self-efficacy refers to an expectation or belief that one can successfully accomplish tasks or perform behaviors associated with specified goals. Note that the concept also overlaps with notions of individual empowerment. The most powerful means for enhancing self-efficacy is to assist clients in actually performing certain behaviors prerequisite to accomplishing their goals. Another potent technique is to make clients aware of their strengths and to recognize incremental progress of clients toward goal attainment. Moreover, family and group members represent potent resources for enhancing self-efficacy. Social workers can develop and tap these resources by assisting families and groups to accomplish tasks that involve perceiving and accrediting strengths and progress of group and family members. We consider other sources of self-efficacy and relevant techniques in Chapter 14 and to a lesser extent in other chapters.

Monitoring Progress

As work toward goal attainment proceeds, it is important to monitor progress on a regular basis. The reasons for this are fourfold:

1. *To evaluate the effectiveness of change strategies and interventions.* Social workers are increasingly required to document the efficacy of services to satisfy third-party funders of services in a system of managed care. If an approach or intervention is not producing desired effects, social workers should determine the reasons for this and/or consider negotiating a different approach.

2. *To guide clients' efforts toward goal attainment* (Corcoran & Vandiver, 1996). Evaluating movement toward goals enhances continuity of focus and efforts and promotes efficient use of time.

3. *To keep abreast of clients' reactions to progress or lack of progress.* When they believe they are not progressing, clients tend to become discouraged and may lose confidence in the helping process. By evaluating progress periodically, social workers will be alerted to negative client reactions that might otherwise undermine progress.

4. *To concentrate on goal attainment and evaluate progress.* These will tend to sustain clients' motivation to work on their problems.

Methods of evaluating progress vary from eliciting subjective opinions to using various types of measurement. These and other matters related to evaluating progress on an ongoing basis are discussed in Chapter 12.

Barriers to Goal Accomplishment

As clients strive to accomplish goals and related tasks, progress is rarely smooth and uneventful. Rather, clients encounter obstacles and experience anxiety, uncertainties, fears, and other untoward reactions as they struggle to solve problems. Furthermore, family or group members or other significant persons may undermine clients' efforts to change by opposing such changes, by ridiculing the client for seeing a social worker, by making derisive comments about the social worker, or by otherwise making change even more difficult for the client. (For this reason, it is vital to involve significant others in the problem-solving process whenever feasible.) Because of the potency of barriers to change, social workers must be perceptive to manifestations of clients' struggles and skillful in assisting them to surmount these obstacles.

Barriers to goal accomplishment are frequently encountered in work with families and groups. Such barriers include personality factors that limit participation of certain group members, problematic behaviors of group members, or processes within the group that impede progress. Such barriers also include impediments in the family's environment. These matters are addressed in later chapters.

Still other barriers may involve organizational opposition to change within systems whose resources are essential to goal accomplishment. Denial of resources or services (e.g., health care, rehabilitation services, and public assistance) by organizations, or policies and procedures that unduly restrict clients' access to resources, may require the social worker to assume the role of mediator or advocate. A portion of Chapter 15 in Part 3 of this book is devoted to ways of overcoming organizational opposition.

Relational Reactions

As social workers and clients work together in solving problems, emotional reactions on the part of either party toward the other may impair the effectiveness of the working partnership and pose an obstacle to goal accomplishment. Clients, for example, may have unrealistic expectations or may misperceive the intent of the social worker. Consequently, clients may experience disappointment, discouragement, hurt, anger, rejection, longings for closeness, or many other possible emotional reactions that may seriously impede progress toward goals. Marital partners, parents, and group members may also experience relational reactions to other members of these larger client systems, resulting in problematic interactional patterns within these systems. Not uncommonly, such relational reactions are manifestations of inappropriate attitudes and beliefs learned from relationships with parents or significant others. In many other instances, however, the social worker or members of clients' systems may unknowingly behave in ways that understandably foster unfavorable relational reactions by individuals or family or group members. In either event, it is critical to explore and resolve the relational reactions. Otherwise, clients' efforts may be diverted from working toward goal accomplishment, or even worse, clients may prematurely withdraw from the helping process.

Social workers are also susceptible to relational reactions. Social workers who relate in an authentic manner provide clients with experience that is transferable to the real world of the client's social environment. They communicate that they are human beings not immune to making blunders and experiencing emotions and desires in relationships with clients. It is vital that social workers be aware of unfavorable reactions to clients and be knowledgeable about how to manage them. Otherwise, they may be working on their own problems rather than the client's, placing the helping process in severe jeopardy. Chapter 18 is designed to assist social workers in coping with potential relational reactions residing with the client(s), the social worker, or both.

Enhancing Clients' Self-Awareness

As clients interact in a novel relationship with a social worker and risk new interpersonal behaviors in marital, family, or group contacts, they commonly experience emotions (or physical manifestations of emotions) that may be pleasing, frightening, confusing, and even overwhelming. Though managing such emotional reactions may require a temporary detour from goal attainment activities, such activities frequently represent rich opportunities for growth in self-awareness. Self-awareness is the first step to self-realization. Many voluntary clients wish to understand themselves more fully, and they can benefit from being more aware of feelings that have previously been buried or denied expression. Social workers can facilitate the process of self-discovery by employing additive empathic responses during the goal attainment phase. Additive empathic responses focus on deeper feelings than do reciprocal empathic responses (referred to earlier in the discussion of Phase I). This technique can be appropriately applied in individual and conjoint interviews as well as in group sessions. Additive empathy, explicated at length in Chapter 18, is of particular value in assisting clients to get in touch with their emotions and to express them clearly to significant other persons.

Another technique that can be employed in fostering self-awareness is confrontation, a major topic of Chapter 18. This technique is employed to assist clients in becoming aware of growth-defeating discrepancies in perceptions, feelings, communications, behavior, values, and attitudes, and to examine such discrepancies in relation to stated goals. It is also used in circumstances when clients act to violate laws or threaten their own safety or that of others. Confrontation must be offered in the context of goodwill, and it requires high skill.

Use of Self

As helping relationships become strong during the implementation and goal attainment phase, social workers increasingly use themselves as tools to facilitate growth and accomplishment. Relating spontaneously and appropriately disclosing one's feelings, views, and experiences provide for clients an encounter with an open and authentic human being. Modeling authentic behavior encourages clients to reciprocate by risking authentic behavior themselves, thereby achieving significant growth in self-realization and in interpersonal relations. Indeed, when *group leaders* model authentic behavior in groups, members often follow suit by assuming like behavior. Social workers who relate in an authentic manner provide clients with experience that is transferable to the real world of the clients' social relationships. A contrived, detached, and sterile "professional" relationship, by contrast, lacks transferability to other relationships. Obviously these factors should also be covered in the training process for social workers.

Assertiveness involves dealing tactfully but firmly with problematic behaviors that impinge on the helping relationship or impede progress toward goal attainment. For example, when clients' actions are contrary to their goals or potentially harmful to themselves or others, the social worker must deal with these situations. Further, social workers must relate assertively to larger client systems at times; for example, to focus on the behavior of group members that hinders the accomplishment of goals. To passively permit dysfunctional behavior to continue is tantamount to contributing to that same behavior. Using oneself to relate authentically and assertively is a major focus of Chapter 5.

Phase III: Termination

The terminal phase of the helping process involves 3 major aspects: (1) assessing when individual and group goals have been satisfactorily attained and planning termination accordingly, (2) effecting successful termination of the helping relationship, (3) planning for maintenance of change and continued growth following termination, and evaluating the results of the helping process. Deciding when to terminate is relatively straightforward when time limits are specified in advance as part of the initial contact, as is done with the task-centered approach. Decisions about when to terminate are also simple when individual or group goals are clear-cut (e.g., to get a job, obtain a prosthetic device, arrange for nursing care, secure tutoring for a child, implement a specific group activity, or hold a public meeting).

In other instances, however, goals *involve* growth or changes that have no limits, and judgments must be mutually made about when a satisfactory degree of change has been attained. Examples of such goals include increasing self-esteem, communicating more effectively, becoming more outgoing in social situations, and resolving conflicts more effectively. Actually, judgments about termination that involve such goals are much less difficult when goals have been explicitly specified in terms of behavioral indexes of desired levels of growth, a matter discussed in Chapters 12 and 20. It is increasingly the case that decisions about termination and extension involve third parties, because managed care funders must be consulted in decisions about how much service is enough (Corcoran & Vandiver, 1996).

Evaluating Results

Evaluation of results helps social workers, clients, and interested parties such as funders determine whether termination is called for. By evaluating results, social workers are able to test the efficiency of interventions employed and monitor their own successes, failures, and progress in achieving favorable outcomes.

Until recent years, social workers were unable to evaluate outcomes because research studies required large numbers of clients, substantial expense, and sophistication in both research design and statistical analysis. Moreover, group research designs are of little value in assessing individual outcomes. Single-subject design has evolved in recent years, making it feasible for social workers to go far beyond subjective evaluation of outcomes. Single-subject research is convenient, involves little or no expense, appeals to most clients, and can be employed with minimal research expertise. In addition, social workers can now access a variety of standardized outcome measurement instruments that are often useful. A discussion of single-subject research and outcome measurement is included in Chapter 12.

Ideally, evaluation should not end with termination. Planning for follow-up sessions not only makes it possible to evaluate the durability of results but also facilitates the termination process by indicating the social worker's continuing interest in clients, a matter we discuss in Chapter 20.

Successfully Terminating Helping Relationships

Social workers and clients often respond positively to termination, reflecting pride and accomplishment from both (Fortune, Pearlingi, & Rochelle, 1992). Clients who were required or otherwise pressured to see the social worker may experience a sense of relief at getting rid of pressure or outside scrutiny. Because voluntary clients share personal problems and are accompanied through rough emotional terrain by a caring social worker, they often feel close to the social worker. Consequently, termination tends to produce mixed feelings for clients. They are likely to feel strong gratitude to the social worker. They are also likely to experience a sense of relief over no longer having to go through the discomfort associated with exploring problems and making changes (not to mention the relief from paying fees when fees are charged). Although clients are usually optimistic about the prospects of confronting future challenges independently, they sometimes experience a sense of loss over terminating the working relationship. Moreover, uncertainty about their ability to cope independently often is mixed with their optimism.

When engaged in the helping process over a lengthy period of time, clients sometimes develop a strong attachment to a social worker, especially if the social worker has fostered dependency. For such individuals, termination involves a painful process of letting go of a relationship that has met significant emotional needs. Moreover, these clients often experience apprehension about facing the future without the reassuring strength represented by the social worker. Group members often similarly experience painful reactions as they face the loss of supportive relationships with the social worker and group members as well as a valued resource that has assisted them to cope with their problems. To effect termination with individuals or groups and minimize psychological stress requires both perceptiveness to manifestations of emotional reactions and skills in helping clients to work through such reactions. This subject is discussed in Chapter 20.

Planning Change Maintenance Strategies

In recent years, social workers have been increasingly concerned over the need to develop strategies that maintain change and continue growth after formal service is terminated (Rzepnicki, 1991). These concerns have been prompted by disconcerting findings to the effect that a significant portion of clients revert to previous dysfunctional behavior patterns following termination. Consequently, strategies for maintaining change are receiving increasing attention (see Chapter 20).

INTERVIEWING PROCESS: STRUCTURE AND SKILLS

Direct social workers employ interviewing as the primary vehicle of influence, although administrators and social planners also rely heavily on interviewing skills to accomplish their objectives. Interviews vary according to purpose, types of setting, characteristics, and number of participants. For example, interviews may involve interaction between a social worker and individuals, couples, and family units. Interviews are conducted in offices, homes, hospitals, prisons, automobiles, and other diverse settings. Despite the numerous variables that affect interviews, certain factors are essential to all effective interviews. The following discussion identifies and discusses these essential factors and highlights relevant skills.

Physical Conditions

Interviews sometimes occur in office or interview settings that the social worker has some control over. Other interviews in a client's home, of course, are more subject to the client's or family's preferences. The physical climate in which an interview is conducted determines in part the attitudes, feelings, and degree of cooperation and responsiveness of people during interviews. Conditions conducive to productive interviews include:

1. Adequate ventilation and light
2. Comfortable room temperature
3. Ample space (to avoid a sense of being confined or crowded)
4. Attractive furnishings and decor
5. Chairs that adequately support the back
6. Privacy appropriate to the cultural beliefs of the client
7. Freedom from distraction
8. Open space between participants

The first five items obviously are concerned with providing a pleasant and comfortable environment and need no elaboration. Privacy is vital, of course, because people are likely to be guarded in revealing personal information and expressing feelings if other people can see or hear them. Interviewers also find it awkward and have difficulty in concentrating or expressing themselves when others can hear them. Settings vary in the extent to which social workers can control these conditions. In some settings, it may be impossible to ensure complete privacy. Even when interviewing a patient in a hospital bed, however, privacy can be maximized by closing doors, drawing curtains that separate beds, and requesting nursing staff to avoid nonessential interruptions. Privacy during home interviews may be even more difficult to arrange, but people will often take measures to reduce unnecessary intrusions or distractions if interviewers stress that privacy enhances the productivity of sessions. Similarly, social workers in public social service settings often work in cubicle offices. They can conduct client interviews in special interview rooms.

Because interviews often involve intense emotional involvement by participants, freedom from distraction is a critical requirement. Telephone calls, knocks on the door, and external noises can impair concentration and disrupt important dialogue. Moreover, clients are unlikely to feel important and valued if social workers permit avoidable intrusions. Still other sources of distraction are crying, attention seeking, and restless behavior of clients' infants or children. Small children, of course, cannot be expected to sit quietly for more than short periods of time. It is advisable to encourage parents to make arrangements for the care of children during interviews (except when it is important to observe interaction between parents and their children). Because requiring such arrangements can create a barrier to service utilization, many social workers and agencies maintain a supply of toys for such occasions.

Having a desk between an interviewer and interviewee(s) emphasizes the authority of the social worker. In some Asian cultures, emphasizing the authority or position of the social worker may be a useful way to indicate that the worker occupies a formal, appropriate position. With many others, having a desk dividing social worker and client creates a barrier that is not conducive to open communication. If safety of the social worker is an issue, then a desk barrier can be useful. In addition, there may be instances in which an interviewer believes that maximizing authority through a desk barrier will promote his or her service objectives. In most circumstances, social workers strive to foster a sense of equality. Hence, they arrange their desks so that they can rotate their chairs to a position where there is open space between them and their clients. Others prefer to leave their desks entirely and use other chairs in the room when interviewing.

The Structure of Interviews

Interviews in social work have purpose, structure, direction, and focus. The purpose is to exchange information systematically with a view toward illuminating and solving problems, promoting growth, or planning strategies or actions aimed at improving the quality of life for people. The structure of interviews varies somewhat from setting to setting, from client to client, and from one phase of the helping process to another. Indeed, skillful interviews adapt flexibly both to different contexts and to the ebb and flow of each individual session. Thus, each interview is unique. Still, effective interviews conform to a general structure, manifest certain properties, and reflect use of certain basic skills by interviewers. In considering these basic factors, we shall begin by focusing on the structure and processes involved in initial interviews.

Establishing Rapport

Before discussing how to begin exploring clients' difficulties, it is important to focus on achieving rapport. Rapport with clients fosters open and free communication, the hallmark of effective interviews. Achieving rapport enables clients to gain trust in the helpful intent and goodwill of the social worker to the extent they are willing to risk revealing personal and sometimes painful feelings and information. Some clients readily achieve trust and confidence in a social worker, particularly when they have the capacity to form relationships easily. Voluntary clients often want to know "Who am I and why am I in this situation?" whereas involuntary clients have less reason to be initially trusting and want to know "Who are you and when will you leave?" (R. H. Rooney, 1992).

Establishing rapport begins by greeting the client(s) warmly and introducing oneself. If the client system is a family, you should introduce yourself to each family member. In making introductions and addressing clients, it is important to extend the courtesy of asking clients how they prefer to be addressed; doing so conveys your respect and desire to use the title they prefer. Although some clients prefer the informality involved in using first names, social workers should be discreet in using first-name introductions with all clients because of their diverse ethnic and social backgrounds. For example, some adult African Americans and members of other groups as well interpret being addressed by their first names as indicative of a lack of respect (Edwards, 1982; McNeely & Badami, 1984).

With many clients, social workers must surmount formidable barriers before establishing rapport. It is important to bear in mind that the majority of clients have had little or no experience with social work agencies and enter initial interviews or group sessions with uncertainty and apprehension. Many did not seek help initially; they may view having to seek assistance with their problems as evidence of failure, weakness, or inadequacy. Moreover, revealing personal problems is embarrassing and even humiliating for some people, especially those who have difficulty with confiding in others.

Cultural factors and language differences compound potential barriers to rapport even further. For example, Asian Americans who retain strong ties to cultural traditions have been conditioned not to discuss personal or family problems with outsiders. Revealing problems to others may be perceived as a reflection of personal inadequacy and as a stigma upon an entire family. The resultant fear of shame may thus impede the development of rapport with clients from this ethnic group (Kumabe, Nishida, & Hepworth, 1985; Lum, 1996; Tsui & Schultz, 1985). African Americans, Native Americans, and Latinos may also experience difficulty in developing rapport because of distrust that derives from a history of being exploited or discriminated against by other ethnic groups (Longres, 1991; Proctor & Davis, 1994).

Clients' difficulties in communicating openly tend to be even more severe when their problems involve allegations of socially unacceptable behavior, such as child abuse, moral infractions, or criminal behavior. In groups, the pain is further compounded by having to expose one's difficulties to other group members, especially in early sessions when the reactions of other members represent the threat of the unknown.

One means of fostering rapport with clients is to employ a "warm-up" period. This is particularly important with ethnic minority clients for whom such openings are the cultural norm, including Native Americans, persons with strong roots in the cultures of Asia and the Pacific Basin, and Latinos. Aguilar (1972), for example, has stressed the importance of warm-up periods in work with Mexican Americans.

When Mexican Americans meet to negotiate or arrange affairs, the first step is to set the climate or ambiance. A preliminary period of warm, informal, personal conversation precedes the discussions of the concerns that brought them together. Jumping into the middle of serious and controversial affairs—as many people in the United States are inclined to do—seems confusing and even discourteous to most Mexican Americans. (Aguilar 1972, p. 67)

Native Hawaiians and Samoans also typically expect to begin new contacts with outside persons by engaging in "talk story," which also involves warm, informal, and light personal conversation similar to that described by Aguilar. To plunge into discussion of serious problems without a period of talk story would be regarded by members of these cultural groups as rude and intrusive. Social workers who neglect to engage in a warm-up period are likely to encounter passive-resistant behavior from members of these cultural groups.

A warm-up period and a generally slower tempo are also critically important with Native Americans, as Hull (1982) has emphasized: "The social worker who is all business and who attempts to deal with an Indian family as she or he might with a non-Indian family may be rebuffed, since forcing or hurrying relationships with Native Americans does not work. A variety of casual behaviors including small talk, comments addressed to all family members regardless of age, and patience are important if the Indian is to feel comfortable with the worker" (p. 346).[2] Consistent with this recommendation, Palmer and Pablo (1978) suggest that social workers who are most successful with Native Americans are low-key, nondirective individuals.

Warm-up periods are also important in gaining rapport with adolescents, many of whom are in a stage of emancipating themselves from adults and who are also frequently referred by those adults. Consequently, they may be wary of social workers, and this is a particularly strong tendency among those who are delinquent or who are otherwise openly rebelling against authority. Moreover, adolescents who have had little or no experience with social workers have an extremely limited grasp of their roles. Many adolescents, at least initially, are involuntary clients and perceive social workers as adversaries, fearing that their role is to punish or to exercise power over them.

With the majority of clients, a brief warm-up period is usually sufficient. When the preceding barriers do not apply, introductions and a brief discussion of a timely topic (unusual weather, a widely discussed local or national event, or a topic of known interest to the client) adequately foster a climate conducive to exploring clients' concerns. Most clients, in fact, expect to plunge into discussion of their problems early on, and their anxiety level heightens if social workers delay getting to the business at hand. This is particularly true with involuntary clients who did not seek the contact. With these clients, rapport often develops rapidly if social workers respond sensitively to their feelings and skillfully give direction to the process of exploration by sharing the circumstances of the referral, thus defusing the global sense of threat experienced by many.

Respect for clients is critical to establishing rapport. Early in this chapter and in Chapter 1, we stressed the importance of respecting clients' dignity and worth, uniqueness, capacities to solve problems, and other factors. An additional aspect of respect is common courtesy. Being punctual, attending to clients' comfort, listening attentively, remembering clients' names, and assisting clients who have limited mobility convey the message that the social worker values the client and esteems the client's dignity and worth. Courtesy should never be taken lightly.

Verbal and nonverbal messages from social workers that convey understanding and acceptance of clients' feelings and views also facilitate the development of rapport. This does not mean agreeing with or condoning clients' views or problems but rather apprehending and affirming clients' rights to their own views, attitudes, and feelings. Attentiveness to feelings that clients manifest both verbally and nonverbally and empathic responses to these feelings convey understanding in a form that clients readily discern. Empathic responses clearly convey the message, "I am with you. I understand what you are saying and experiencing." The "workhorse" of successful helping persons, empathic responding is important not only in Phase I but in subsequent phases as well. Mastery of this vital skill (discussed extensively in Chapter 5) requires consistent and sustained practice.

Authenticity, or genuineness, is still another social worker quality that facilitates rapport. Being authentic during Phase I of the helping process involves relating as a genuine person rather than assuming a contrived and sterile professional role. Authentic behavior by social workers also models openness, the effect of which is to encourage clients to reciprocate by lowering their defenses and relating more openly (Doster & Nesbitt, 1979). Further, encounters with authentic social workers provide clients with a relationship experience that more closely approximates relationships in the real world than do relationships with people who conceal their real selves behind a professional facade.

A moderate level of authenticity or genuineness during early interviews fosters openness most effectively (Giannandrea & Murphy, 1973; Mann & Murphy, 1975; Simonson, 1976). At this level, the social worker is spontaneous and relates openly to the extent of being nondefensive and congruent. The social worker's behavior and responses match her or his inner experiencing. Being authentic also permits the constructive use of humor. Relating with a moderate level of authenticity, however, precludes a high level of self-disclosure. Rather, the focus is on the client, and the social worker reveals personal information or shares personal experiences judiciously. During the change-oriented phase of the helping process, however, social workers engage in self-disclosure when they believe that doing so may facilitate the growth of clients. Self-disclosure is discussed at length in Chapter 5.

Rapport is also fostered by not employing certain types of responses that block communication. To avoid responses that hinder communication, social workers must be knowledgeable about such types of responses and must eliminate them from their communication repertoires. Toward this end, we have devoted Chapter 7 to identifying various types of responses and interviewing patterns that inhibit communication and to describing strategies for eliminating them.

Beginning social workers often fear that they will forget something, fail to observe something crucial in the interview that will lead to dire consequences, freeze up with tongue tied, or talk endlessly to reduce their anxiety (Epstein, 1985). Practice interviews such as those presented in subsequent chapters will assist in reducing this fear. It helps to be aware that referred clients need to know the circumstances of the referral and clarify choices, rights, and expectations before they are likely to wish to have rapport with the social worker.

Starting Where the Client Is

Social work researchers have suggested that motivational congruence or the fit between client motivation and what the social worker attempts to provide is a major factor in explaining more successful findings in studies of social work effectiveness (Reid & Hanrahan, 1982). Starting with client motivation helps social workers in establishing and sustaining rapport and in maintaining psychological contact with clients. If, for example, a client appears to be in emotional distress at the beginning of an initial interview, the social worker focuses attention on the client's distress before proceeding to explore the client's problematic situation. An example of an appropriate focusing response would be "I can sense you're having a difficult time. Could you share with me what you're experiencing at this moment?" Discussion of the client's emotions and related factors tends to reduce the distress, which might otherwise impede the process of exploration. Moreover, responding sensitively to clients' emotions fosters rapport as clients begin to regard social workers as concerned, perceptive, and understanding persons.

Beginning social workers sometimes have difficulty in starting where the client is because they are worried they will not present quickly and clearly the services of the agency, thus neglecting or delaying exploration of client concerns. Practice will allow them to relax and recognize that they can meet the expectations of their supervisors and others by focusing on client concerns while sharing content about the circumstances of referrals and their agency's services.

Starting where the client is has critical significance with involuntary clients. Because these clients are compelled by external sources to see social workers, they often enter initial interviews with negative, hostile feelings. Social workers, therefore, should begin by eliciting these feelings and focusing on them until they have subsided. By responding empathically to negative feelings and conveying understanding and acceptance of them, skillful social workers often succeed in neutralizing these feelings, which enhances clients' receptivity to exploring their problem situations. Such feelings can often be reduced by clarifying choices available to the involuntary client. If social workers fail to deal with clients' negativism, they are likely to encounter persistent opposition responses. These responses are frequently labeled as resistance, opposition to change, and lack of motivation. It is useful to reframe these responses by choosing not to interpret them with deficit labels and replacing them with expectations that these attitudes and behavior are normal when something an individual values is threatened (R. H. Rooney, 1992).

Language also poses a barrier with many ethnic minority clients who may have a limited grasp of the English language, which could cause difficulty in understanding even commonplace expressions. With ethnic minority clients and others whose educational backgrounds have been limited, social workers must slow down the pace of communication and be especially sensitive to nonverbal indications that clients are confused. To avoid embarrassment, ethnic minority clients sometimes indicate that they understand messages when, in fact, they are perplexed.

Using Interpreters

When ethnic minority clients have virtually no command of the English language, effective communication requires the use of an interpreter of the same ethnicity as the client, making it possible to bridge both cultural value differences and language differences. To work effectively together, however, both the social worker and interpreter must possess special skills. Interpreters must be carefully selected and trained to understand the importance of the interview and their role in the process, and to interpret cultural nuances to the social worker. Skilled interpreters thus assist social workers by translating far more than verbal content: nonverbal communication, cultural attitudes and beliefs, subtle expressions, emotional reactions, and expectations of clients. To achieve rapport it is also essential for social workers to convey empathy and establish an emotional connection with the ethnic minority client. The interpreter thus "must have the capacity to act exactly as the interviewer acts—express the same feelings, use the same intonations to the extent possible in another language, and through verbal and nonverbal means convey what the interviewer expresses on several levels" (Freed, 1988, p. 316).[3]

The social worker should explain the interpreter's role to the client and ensure the client of neutrality and confidentiality on the part of both the social worker and the interpreter. Obviously these factors should also be covered in the training process for interpreters.

Successful transcultural work through an interpreter requires that the social worker be acquainted with the history and culture of the client's and the interpreter's country of origin. Social workers must also adapt to the slower pace of interviews. When social workers and interpreters are skilled in working together in interviews, effective working relationships can evolve, and many clients experience the process as beneficial and therapeutic. As implied in this brief discussion, interviewing through an interpreter is a complex process requiring careful preparation of interviewers and interpreters.

Exploration Process and Skills

When clients indicate that they are ready to discuss their problem situations, it is appropriate to begin the process of problem exploration. Messages typically employed to initiate the process are:

- "Could you tell me about your situation?"
- "I'm interested in hearing about what brought you here."
- "Tell me about the difficulties you've been having, and we can think about them together."

Clients will generally respond by beginning to relate their problems. The social worker's role at this point is to draw out the client(s), to respond in ways that convey understanding, and to seek elaboration of information needed to gain a clear picture of factors involved in clients' difficulties. Some clients, particularly applicants, spontaneously provide rich information with little assistance. Others, especially referred and involuntary clients, may be hesitant; many struggle with their emotions; and many have difficulty finding words to express themselves.

Because referred clients may perceive that they were brought in by the concerns of others, they often respond by recounting those external pressures. The social worker can assist in this process by sharing his or her information about the circumstances of the referral.

To facilitate the process of exploration, social workers employ a number of skills, often blending two or more in a single response. One type of skill, furthering responses, encourages clients to continue verbalizing. Furthering responses include minimal prompts (both verbal and nonverbal) and accent responses. Furthering responses, which convey attention, interest, and an expectation that the client continue verbalizing, are discussed in Chapter 6.

Other responses facilitate communication (and rapport) by providing immediate feedback that assures clients that social workers have not only heard but also understood their messages. Paraphrasing is employed to provide feedback that the social worker has grasped the content of a client's message. In using paraphrasing, the interviewer rephrases (with different words) what the client has expressed. Empathic responding, by contrast, provides feedback that the social worker is aware of emotions the client has experienced or is currently experiencing.

Both paraphrasing and empathic responding, which are discussed in Chapters 5 and 6, are especially crucial with clients who have limited language facility, including ethnic minority and developmentally disabled clients. When language barriers exist, social workers should be careful not to assume that they correctly understand the client or that the client understands the social worker. Further, with ethnic clients who have been culturally conditioned not to discuss personal or family problems with outsiders, social workers need to make special efforts to grasp intended meanings. Many of these clients are not accustomed to participating in interviews and tend not to discuss their concerns openly. Rather, they may send covert (hidden) messages and expect social workers to discern their problems by reading between the liens. Social workers thus need to use feedback more extensively with these clients to determine if their perceptions of intended meanings are on target. Using feedback to ascertain that the social worker has understood the client's intended meaning and vice versa can avoid unnecessary misunderstandings. Further, clients generally appreciate efforts of social workers to reach shared understanding, and they interpret patience and persistence in seeking to understand as evidence that the social worker respects and values them. It is not the ethnic minority client's responsibility, however, to educate the social worker.[4]

On the other hand, what the social worker thinks he or she knows about the minority client's culture may be an inappropriate stereotype, because individuals and families vary on a continuum of assimilation and acculturation with majority culture norms (Congress, 1994). Based on a common Latino value, the social worker might say, "Can you call on other family members for assistance?"

Exploring Expectations

Before exploring problems, it is important to determine clients' expectations, which vary considerably and are influenced by socioeconomic level, cultural background, level of sophistication, and previous experience with helping professionals. In fact, socialization that includes clarifying expectations about the roles of clients and social workers has been found to be associated with more successful outcomes, especially with involuntary clients (R. H. Rooney, 1992; Videka-Sherman, 1988). In some instances, clients' expectations diverge markedly from what social workers can realistically provide. Unless social workers are aware of and deal successfully with such unrealistic expectations, clients may be keenly disappointed and disinclined to continue beyond the initial interview. In other instances, referred clients may have mistaken impressions about whether they can choose to work on concerns as they see them as opposed to the views of referral sources such as family members. By exploring expectations, however, social workers create an opportunity to clarify the nature of the helping process and to work through clients' feelings of disappointment. Being aware of clients' expectations also assists social workers to vary their approaches and interventions according to clients' needs and expectations, a matter discussed at greater length in Chapter 5.

Eliciting Essential Information

During the exploration process, social workers assess the significance of information revealed as clients discuss problems and interact with the social worker, group members, or significant others. Indeed, judgments about the meaning and significance of fragments of information guide social workers in deciding which aspects of a problem are salient and warrant further exploration, how ready a client is to explore certain facets of a problem more deeply, what patterned behaviors of the client or system interfere with effective functioning, when and when not to draw out intense emotions, and so on.

The direction of problem exploration proceeds from general to specific. Clients' initial accounts of their problems are typically general in nature ("We fight over everything," "I don't seem to be able to make friends," "We just don't know how to cope with Scott. He won't do anything we ask," or "Child protection says I don't care for my children"). Clients' problems, however, typically have many facets, and accurate understanding requires careful assessment of each one. Whereas open-ended responses, such as those illustrated earlier, are effective in launching problem explorations, other types of responses are used to probe for the detailed information needed to identify and unravel the various factors and systems that contribute to and maintain the problem. Responses that seek concreteness are employed to elicit such detailed information. There are many different types of such responses, each of which is considered at length in Chapter 6. Another type of response needed to elicit detailed factual information (also discussed in Chapter 6) is the closed-ended question.

Focusing in Depth

In addition to possessing discrete skills to elicit detailed information, social workers must be able to maintain focus on problems until they have elicited comprehensive information. Adequate assessment of problems is not possible until a social worker possesses sufficient information concerning the various forces (involving individual, interpersonal, and environmental systems) that interact to produce the problems. Focusing skills (discussed at length in Chapter 6) involve blending the various skills identified thus far as well as summarizing responses.

During the course of exploration, social workers should elicit information that will enable them to answer numerous questions, the answers to which are crucial in understanding various factors that bear on the clients' problems, including ecological factors. These questions (discussed in Chapter 8) serve as guideposts to social workers and provide direction to interviews.

Employing Outlines

In addition to answering questions that are relevant to virtually all interviews, social workers may need to collect information that will answer questions pertinent to the function of specific practice settings. Outlines that embody essential questions to be answered, for given situation or problem, can be extremely helpful to beginning social workers. It is important, however, to use outlines flexibly and to focus on the client, not the outline. Examples of outlines and suggestions for using them are contained in Chapter 6.

Assessing Emotional Functioning

During the process of exploration, social workers must be keenly sensitive to clients' moment-to-moment emotional reactions and to the part that emotional patterns (e.g., inadequate anger control, depression, and widely fluctuating moods) play in their difficulties. Emotional reactions during the interview (e.g., crying, intense anxiety, anger, and hurt feelings) often impede problem exploration and require detours aimed at assisting clients to regain equanimity. It must be noted that anxiety and anger exhibited by involuntary clients may be as much influenced by the circumstances of involuntary contact as by more enduring emotional patterns.

Emotional patterns that powerfully influence behavior in other contexts may also be problems in and of themselves that warrant careful exploration. Depression, for example, is a prevalent problem in our society and one that responds well to proper treatment. When clients manifest symptoms of depression, the depth of the depression and risk of suicide should be carefully explored. Empathic communication is a major skill employed to explore emotional patterns.

Factors to be considered, instruments that assess depression and suicidal risk, and relevant skills are discussed in Chapter 9.

Exploring Cognitive Functioning

Because thought patterns, beliefs, and attitudes are powerful determinants of behavior, it is important to explore clients' opinions and interpretations of circumstances and events deemed salient to their difficulties. Often, careful exploration reveals that misinformation, distorted meaning attributions, mistaken beliefs, and dysfunctional patterns of thought (such as rigid, dogmatic thinking) play a major role in clients' difficulties. Messages commonly employed to explore clients' thinking include the following:

1. How did you come to that conclusion?
2. What meaning do you make of _____?
3. How do you explain what happened?
4. What are your views (or beliefs) about that?

The significance of cognitive functioning and other relevant assessment skills are discussed further in Chapter 9.

Exploring Substance Abuse, Violence, and Sexual Abuse

Because of the prevalence and magnitude of problems associated with substance abuse (including alcohol), violence, and sexual abuse in our society, the possibility that these problems contribute to or are the primary source of clients' difficulties should be routinely explored. Because of the significance of these problematic behaviors, we devote a major section of Chapter 9 to their assessment.

Negotiating Goals and a Contract

When social workers and clients believe they have adequately explored the problems, they are ready to enter the process of planning. By this point (if not sooner), it should be apparent whether other resources and/or services are needed. If it appears other resources are needed or are more appropriate, the social worker may initiate the process of referring clients elsewhere. If clients' problems match the function of the agency and clients express readiness to proceed further in the helping process, it is appropriate to begin negotiating a contract. When involuntary clients are unwilling to participate in a helping process, their options should be clarified at this point. For example, they can choose to return to court, choose not to comply and risk legal consequences, choose to comply minimally, or choose to work with the social worker on problems as they see them in addition to legal mandates (R. H. Rooney, 1992).

Goals specify the end results that will be attained if the problem-solving efforts are successful. Generally, after participating together in the process of exploration, social workers and clients share common views as to results or changes that are desirable or essential. In some instances, however, social workers may recognize the importance of accomplishing certain goals that clients have overlooked and vice versa. Social workers introduce the process of negotiating goals by explaining the rationale for formulating them. If formulated in explicit terms, goals give direction to the problem-solving process and serve as progress guideposts and as outcome criteria for the helping efforts. To employ goals effectively, social workers need skills in involving clients in selecting attainable goals, in formulating general task plans for reaching these goals, and in developing specific task plans to guide social worker and client efforts between sessions.

When more than one goal is entailed in resolving a problematic situation, as is usually the case, social workers assist clients in assigning priorities to goals so that immediate efforts can be directed to the most burdensome aspects of the problem. Giving clients major responsibility for selecting goals enhances their commitment to actively participate in the problem-solving process by ensuring that goals are of maximal relevance. Even involuntary clients can often choose the order of goals to be addressed or participate in the process of that choice. Essential elements of the goal selection process are delineated in Chapter 12.

Ending Interviews

Both initial interviews and the contracting process conclude with a discussion of "housekeeping" arrangements and an agreement about next steps. During this final portion, social workers should describe the length and frequency of sessions, who will participate, the means of accomplishing goals, the duration of the helping period, fees, date and time of next appointment, pertinent agency policies and procedures, and other relevant matters. The contracting process is discussed at length in Chapter 12.

When you have completed these interview processes, or when the time allocated for the interview has elapsed, it is appropriate to conclude the interview. Messages appropriate for ending interviews include the following:

1. "I see our time for today is nearly at an end. Let's stop here and we'll begin next time by reviewing our experience in carrying out the tasks we discussed."

2. "Our time is running out, and there are still some areas we need to explore. Let's arrange another session when we can finish our exploration and think about where you'd like to go from there."

3. "We have just a few minutes left. Let's summarize what we accomplished today and what you and I are going to work on before our next session."

Goal Attainment

During Phase II of the helping process, interviewing skills are used to help clients accomplish their goals. Much of the focus during this phase is on identifying and carrying out actions or tasks clients must implement to accomplish their goals. Preparing clients to carry out actions is crucial to successful implementation. Fortunately, effective strategies of preparation are available (see Chapter 14).

As clients undertake the challenging process of making changes, it is important that they maintain focus on a few selected priority goals until they have made sufficient progress to warrant shifting to other goals. Otherwise, they may jump from one concern to another, dissipating their energies without achieving significant progress. The burden, therefore, falls on the social worker to provide structure for and direction to the client. Toward this end, skills in maintaining focus during single sessions and continuity between sessions are critical (see Chapter 6).

As noted earlier, barriers to goal attainment commonly occur during the helping process. Typical individual barriers include fears associated with change and/or behavior and thought patterns that are highly resistant to change efforts because they serve a protective function (usually at great psychological cost to the individual). With couples and families, barriers include entrenched interactional patterns that resist change because they perpetuate power or dependence, maintain safe psychological distance, or foster independence (at the cost of intimacy). In groups, common barriers involve dysfunctional processes that persist despite repeated efforts by leaders to replace these patterns with others that are conducive to group goals and to group maturation.

Additive empathy, a skill referred to earlier, is used with individuals, couples, and groups to recognize and to resolve emotional barriers that are blocking growth and progress. Confrontation is a high-risk skill used to assist clients in recognizing and resolving resistant patterns of thought and behavior. Because of the sophistication involved in using these techniques effectively, we have devoted Chapter 18 to them and have provided relevant skill development exercises. Additional techniques for managing barriers to change (including relational reactions) are discussed in Chapter 19.

Termination

Evaluating results (outcomes) also has assumed increasing importance, as we discussed in earlier chapters. Measuring progress at termination by using the same instruments or strategies employed in obtaining baseline data is thus an integral part of the termination process. Determining the durability of gains achieved at one or more follow-up points is also part of effective evaluation.

During the final phase of the helping process, the focus shifts to consolidating gains achieved by clients, planning maintenance strategies, managing emotional reactions to the impending separation, and evaluating results. Each of these processes is discussed in Chapter 20.

Because relapse is high with certain client groups, most notably in cases involving substance abuse, marital difficulties, chronic mental illness, and overeating, developing maintenance strategies is of critical importance. Increasing attention has been accorded to developing and testing such strategies, which we discuss in Chapter 20.

Summary

In this chapter, we have viewed the three phases of the helping process from a global perspective and have briefly considered the structure and processes involved in interviewing. The inside cover of the book depicts in summary form constituent parts of the helping process and their interrelationships with various interviewing processes.

The remaining parts of the book focus in detail on the three phases of the helping process and on various subsidiary interviewing   skills and interventions.

Internet Resources

 Two useful books that can orient you toward use of the Internet and World Wide Web are: Vernon, R., & Lynch, D. (2000). *Social work and the Web.* Belmont, CA: Wadsworth; Kardas, E. (1999). *Psychology resources on the World Wide Web.* Pacific Grove, CA: Brooks/Cole; Grant, G. B., & Grobman, L. M. (1998). *The social worker's Internet handbook.* A useful site for many social work sources is SWAN: Social work access network at *http://www.sc.edu/swan/.* You can also explore social work from an international perspective by accessing the website for the International Federation of Social Workers: *http://www.ifsw.org.* At that site, you can access an international definition of social work practice and a policy statement on peace and social justice. You can also find a useful source on prevention at *http://www.uky.edu/RGS/PreventionResearch/* and on diversity at *http://webdb.nyu.edu/sociallinks/menu.cgi?cid=387.* Using InfoTrac®, you can find more about the experience of interpreters by downloading this article: Karttunen, F. (1996). Between worlds: Interpreters, guides and survivors. *Frontiers, 17, 3.*

Notes

1. The idea of specific phases and their accompanying tasks in structuring casework was originally developed by Jessie Taft and Virginia Robinson and the Functional School. They were later elaborated by W. J. Reid (1992) and L. Epstein (1988) in the task-centered approach.

2. An interesting model of developing rapport through sharing tribal backgrounds is depicted in the instructional videotape *Ethnic sensitive practice with involuntary Native American client.* (Available from INSIGHT–MEDIA.com under psychology resources.)

3. We recommend Freed's (1988) article, which addresses the complexities and cites many useful references.

4. Lila George, Department of Social Work, University of Minnesota-Duluth (personal communication, 1993).

CHAPTER 4

Operationalizing the Cardinal Social Work Values

Revised and edited by Kim Strom-Gottfried

CHAPTER OVERVIEW

As we noted in Chapter 1, social work practice is guided by knowledge, skills, and values. This chapter addresses the last of those three areas. We will introduce you to the cardinal values of the profession and the ethical obligations that arise from those values. Because, in practice, values can clash and ethical principles may conflict with each other, the chapter also describes some of these dilemmas and offers guidance about resolving them. As you read this chapter, you will have opportunities to place yourself in complex situations that challenge you to analyze your values and to assess their compatibility with social work values.

THE INTERACTION BETWEEN PERSONAL AND PROFESSIONAL VALUES

Values are "preferred conceptions," or beliefs about how things ought to be. All of us have values—a sense of what things are important or proper that guides our actions and decisions. The profession of social work has values, too. These values indicate what is important to social workers and guide the practice of the profession. Social workers must be attuned to their personal values and be aware of when those values mesh or clash

with those of the profession. It is not enough to be attuned only to our own values and those of the social work profession. Our clients also have personal values that shape their beliefs and actions, and these may conflict with our values or with those of the profession. Further, the society in which we work has values that are articulated through policies and laws. These can also conflict with our own beliefs, our clients', or our profession's.

Self-awareness is the first step in sorting out all these possibilities for difficulty. The following sections describe the cardinal values of the profession, provide opportunities to become aware of personal values, and describe the difficulties that can occur when social workers impose their own beliefs on clients.

THE CARDINAL VALUES OF SOCIAL WORK

The cardinal values of the social work profession can be summarized as follows:

1. All human beings deserve access to the resources they need to deal with life's problems and to develop their potentialities.

2. All human beings have intrinsic worth and dignity.

3. The uniqueness and individuality of each person is of value.

4. Given appropriate resources, human beings are capable of growth and change and should be supported in increasing their choices in solving their problems and directing their lives.

What do these values mean? What difficulties can arise in putting them into practice? How can they conflict with workers', clients', and society's values? The following sections describe each of the values and situations in which conflicts can occur. Skill-building exercises at the end of the chapter will assist you in identifying and working through value conflicts.

1. *All human beings deserve access to the resources they need to deal with life's problems and to develop their potentialities.* A historic and defining feature of social work is the profession's focus on individual well-being in a social context. Attending to the environmental forces that create, contribute to, and address problems in living is a fundamental part of social work theory and practice (NASW, 1996, p. 2). Implementing this value means believing that people have the right to resources. It also means that you are committed to securing these resources, and that you are willing to develop and implement policies and programs to fill unmet needs.

Social workers generally express a firm commitment to this value. Yet when applied to certain situations, that commitment sometimes dwindles because of conflicting beliefs and personal biases. To enhance your awareness of the situations in which you might experience difficulty with this value, we have listed a range of challenging situations. Imagine yourself in interviews with the clients involved in each of the following situations. Try to picture yourself and your client as vividly as possible. Imagine the client making the request for the resource described and think of the response you would make. Be aware of your feelings and of possible discomfort or conflict. Next, contemplate how your response is or is not consistent with the social work value in question. If the client has not requested a resource, but the need for one is apparent, consider what resource might be developed and how you might go about developing it.

Situation 1 You are a practitioner in a public assistance agency that has limited, special funds available to assist clients to purchase essential eyeglasses, dentures, hearing aids, and other prosthetic items. Your client, Mr. Y, who lives in a large apartment complex for single persons, is disabled by a chronic psychiatric disorder. He requests special aid in purchasing new glasses. He says he accidentally dropped his old glasses and they were stepped on by a person passing by. However, you know from talking to his landlord and his previous worker that due to his confusion, Mr. Y regularly loses his glasses and has received emergency funds for glasses several times in the last year alone.

Situation 2 During a home visit to a large, impoverished family in the central city, you observe Eddy, a teenage boy, drawing pictures of animals. The quality of the drawings reveals an exceptional talent. When you compliment him, he appears shy, but his faint smile expresses his delight over your approval. Eddy's mother then complains that he spends most of his time drawing, which she thinks is a waste of time. Eddy's face registers pain and discouragement at her remarks.

Situation 3 During a routine visit to an elderly couple who are recipients of public assistance, you discover that the roof on their home leaks. They have had small repairs on several occasions, but the roof is old and worn out. They have had bids for reroofing, and the lowest bid was over $2,500. They ask if your agency can assist them with funding. State policies permit expenditures for such repairs under exceptional circumstances, but much red tape is involved, including securing special approval from the county director of social services, the county advisory board, and the state director of social services.

Situation 4 A number of low-income families in your community have been forced to move to very expensive housing because real estate development companies have demolished their older apartment houses to construct high-rise condominiums. In the last session of the state legislature, a bill to provide low-interest mortgage funds for low-income families was defeated by a narrow margin. The legislature will be convening next month.

Situation 5 Mr. M sustained a severe heart attack 3 months ago. His medical report indicates that he must limit future physical activities to light work. Mr. M has worked as a freight handler for trucking firms and has no other special skills. Not working, he feels useless and worried about how he can provide adequately for his wife and three children.

Situation 6 During the course of an interview with Laurie, a teenage girl in foster care, you learn that her younger sister, age 15, has been having serious difficulties with her parents and has confided in Laurie that she plans to run away and support herself through prostitution. An older male has promised to set her up in an apartment and refer customers to her.

The preceding vignettes depict situations in which clients need resources or opportunities to develop their skills or potential or to ensure their safety and quality of life. Possible obstacles to responding positively to these needs, according to the sequence of the vignettes, are as follows:

1. judgmental attitude by a practitioner,
2. failure of significant others or of a practitioner to recognize a potential that might be developed,
3. unwillingness to support a request because of the effort and red tape involved,
4. unwillingness by social workers and others to actively support needed legislation,
5. ignorance of both social worker and client of potential rehabilitation services, and
6. judgmental attitude or failure to intervene assertively in a timely manner.

As you read the vignettes, you may have experienced some of these reactions or additional ones. Such reactions, which are not uncommon among learners, may result from personal values that you have not scrutinized. Don't be alarmed if you experienced negative reactions to these situations; these reactions indicate your need for expanded self-awareness and additional experience.

2. *All human beings have intrinsic worth and dignity.* This value is reflected in both the NASW Code of Ethics and Council on Social Work Education accreditation guidelines. This cardinal value means that social workers believe that all human beings have intrinsic worth, whatever their past or present behavior, beliefs, lifestyle, or status in life. It also recognizes that respect is an essential element of the helping process. Throughout their work, practitioners should affirm the dignity and self-worth of those whom they serve. Universally accepted among the helping professions, this value embodies several related concepts, variously referred to as "unconditional positive regard," "nonpossessive warmth," "acceptance," and "respect."

Although this value derives largely from Judeo-Christian and humanistic moral beliefs, it also has pragmatic implications associated with the helping process. Before people will risk sharing personal problems and expressing deep emotions, they must first feel fully accepted and experience the goodwill and helpful intent of practitioners. Keep in mind that many people feel highly vulnerable in requesting or accepting assistance, fearing they may be perceived as inadequate or as failures. Vulnerability is even greater when clients' alleged behavior involves moral infractions, cruelty, child neglect, dishonesty, and other behaviors generally violating societal norms. Such allegations often coincide with involuntary status, so that potential clients enter helping relationships with their antennas finely attuned to possible condemning reactions by practitioners. Usually these clients have been criticized, rebuked, and condemned previously by others, and their anticipation and fear of being judged by the practitioner are readily understandable.

The social worker's role is not to judge but to seek to understand clients and their difficulties and to assist them to search for solutions. The role of judging falls under the purview of legal and ecclesiastical authorities. Social workers thus should avoid making judgments as to whether clients are good, bad, evil, worthy, guilty, or innocent. Similarly, it is inappropriate for social workers to determine the extent to which clients are to blame for their difficulties.

Sometimes, the ability to embrace this value comes with increased experience and exposure to a range of clients. Seasoned practitioners have learned that acceptance comes through understanding the life experience of others, not by criticizing or judging their actions. As you work with clients, therefore, seek to view them as persons in distress and avoid perceiving them according to labels, such as "lazy," "irresponsible," "delinquent," "dysfunctional," or "promiscuous." As you learn more about your clients, you will find that many of them have suffered various forms of deprivation and have themselves been victims of abusive, rejecting, or exploitative behavior. Remember also that many clients lacked sustained love and approval during critical periods of development, the result of which is a diminished sense of self-worth. Consistent respect and acceptance on your part is vital in helping them gain the self-esteem that is essential to change and to sound mental health.

Withholding judgments does not mean that social workers condone or approve of illegal, immoral, abusive, exploitative, or irresponsible behavior. Like other persons, social workers have their own values and moral codes and are offended by child neglect, rape, brutal crimes, and other such behaviors. Moreover, social work as a profession and social workers as individuals have responsibilities to assist people to live according to the laws of society.

The objective of not blaming people for their difficulties should not be construed to mean that social workers avoid assisting clients to take responsibility for the part they play in their difficulties. Indeed, change is possible in many instances only as clients gain awareness of the effect of their decisions and seek to modify their behavior accordingly. The difference between blaming and defining ownership of responsibilities lies in the fact that the former tends to be punitive, whereas the latter emanates from positive intentions to be helpful and to assist clients in change.

The implication of the preceding discussion is that you as a practitioner are confronted with the challenge of maintaining your own values (except those that hinder relating effectively to people) without imposing them on others. A first step in this is addressing your own judgmental tendencies. Still another challenge is to develop composure, so that you don't reveal embarrassment or dismay when people discuss problems associated with socially unacceptable behavior.

Let's use the value clarification exercises that follow to identify particular areas of vulnerability. In each situation, imagine yourself in an interview or group session with the client(s). If appropriate, you can role-play the situation with a fellow student, changing roles so that you can benefit by playing the client's role as well. As you imagine or role-play the situation, be aware of your feelings, attitudes, and behavior. After each situation, contemplate or discuss the following:

1. What feelings and attitudes did you experience? Were they based on what actually occurred or did they emanate from preconceived beliefs about such clients?

2. Were you comfortable or uneasy with the client? What were your partner's perceptions of your attitudes as reflected in your behavior?

3. Did any of the situations disturb you more than others? What values were reflected in your feelings, attitudes, and behavior?

Situation 1 Your client is a 35-year-old married male who was sentenced by the court to a secure mental health facility following his arrest for peering in the windows at a women's dorm at your college. He appears uncomfortable and blushes as you introduce yourself.

Situation 2 You are assigned to do a home study for a family interested in adoption. When you arrive at the home for the first interview, you realize that the couple interested in the adoption are gay males.

Situation 3 You are a child welfare worker, and your client is a 36-year-old stepfather whose 13-year-old stepdaughter ran away from home after he had sexual intercourse with her on several occasions during the past 2 months. In your first meeting, he states that he "doesn't know what the big deal is . . . it's not like we're related or anything."

Situation 4 Your 68-year-old client has been receiving chemotherapy for terminal cancer at your hospital for the past month. Appearing drawn and dramatically more emaciated than last month, she reports she has been increasingly suffering with pain and believes her best course of action is to take an overdose of sleeping pills.

Situation 5 You are a probation officer, and the judge has ordered you to complete a presentence investigation of a woman arrested for befriending elderly and mentally retarded individuals, then stealing their monthly disability checks.

Situation 6 You have been working for 8 weeks with an 8-year-old who has had behavioral difficulties at school. During play therapy he demonstrates with toys how he has set fire to or cut up several cats and dogs in his neighborhood.

Situation 7 Your client, Mrs. O, was admitted to a domestic violence shelter following an attack by her husband in which she sustained a broken collarbone and arm injuries. This is the eighth time she has contacted or been admitted to the shelter. Each previous time she has returned home or allowed her husband to move back into the home with her.

Situation 8 A low-income family with whom you have been working recently received a substantial check as part of a settlement with their former landlord. During a visit in which you plan to help the family budget the funds to pay their past due bills, you find the settlement money is gone—spent on a large television and lost in gambling at a local casino.

If you experienced discomfort or negative feelings as you read or role-played any of the above situations, your reactions were not unusual. Most people (even social work students) are repulsed by some of the problematic behaviors embodied in the situations described. It can be challenging to look beyond appalling behaviors to see clients as individuals in distress. However, by focusing selectively on the person rather than the behavior, you can gradually overcome inclinations to label people negatively and learn to see them in full perspective.

How does this acceptance play itself out in practice? Acceptance is conveyed by listening attentively; by responding sensitively to feelings manifested by the client; by using facial expressions, voice intonations, and gestures that convey interest and concern; and by extending courtesies and attending to the client's comfort. These skills are discussed and demonstrated in Chapter 6 and in exercises at the end of this chapter.

On the other hand, if you are unable to be open and accepting of people whose behavior runs counter to your values, your effectiveness in helping them will be diminished, for it is difficult if not impossible to conceal negative feelings toward others. Even if you are able to mask negative feelings toward certain clients, you are likely to be unsuccessful in helping them, for clients can be quick to detect insincerity. To expand your capacity for openness and acceptance, it may be helpful to view association with others whose beliefs, lifestyles, and behaviors differ strikingly from your own as an opportunity to enrich yourself as you experience their uniqueness. Truly open people relish such opportunities, viewing differentness as refreshing and stimulating. Furthermore, gaining understanding of the forces that motivate people can also be intriguing and enlightening. By prizing the opportunity to relate to all types of people and by seeking to understand them, you will gain a deeper appreciation of the diversity and complexity of human beings. In so doing, you will be less likely to pass judgments and you will achieve personal growth in the process. It may also be helpful to talk with other social workers who have been in the field for some time. How do they manage value conflicts? Are they still able to treat clients with respect, even while disdaining their actions?

3. *The uniqueness and individuality of each person is of value.* Intertwined with acceptance and nonjudgmental attitude is the equally important value that every person is unique and that social workers

should affirm the individuality of those whom they serve. Human beings, of course, are endowed with widely differing physical and mental characteristics; moreover, their life experiences are infinitely diverse. Consequently, people differ from one another in appearance, beliefs, physiological functioning, interests, talents, motivation, goals, values, emotional and behavioral patterns, and many other factors.

To affirm the uniqueness of another person, you must be committed to the value just discussed and also enter the other person's world, endeavoring to understand how that person experiences life. Only through attempting to walk in the shoes of another person can you gain a full appreciation of the rich and complex individuality of that person. Affirming the individuality of another, of course, goes far beyond gaining an appreciation of the other person's manifold perspectives of life. One must be able to convey awareness of what the other is experiencing moment by moment and affirm the validity of that experience.

Affirming the validity of another's experience does not mean agreeing with or condoning that person's views and feelings. Part of your role as a practitioner is to help people to disentangle their confusing, conflicting thoughts and feelings; to align distorted perceptions with reality; and to differentiate irrational reactions from reality. To fulfill this role, you must retain your own separateness and individuality. Otherwise, you may overidentify with clients, thereby losing your potential for providing fresh input. Affirming the experiences of another person, then, means validating those experiences, thus fostering that person's sense of personal identity and self-esteem.

Appreciation for uniqueness goes beyond individual characteristics to include those that occur through membership in a group. As CSWE suggests, "Social workers demonstrate respect for and acceptance of the unique characteristics of diverse populations" (1995, p. 140). Those populations include, but are not limited to, "groups distinguished by race, ethnicity, culture, class, gender, sexual orientation, religion, physical or mental

ability, age, and national origin" (1995, p. 140). Further, the NASW Code of Ethics includes as evidence of culturally competent practice that practitioners "have a knowledge base of their clients' cultures and be able to demonstrate competence in the provision of services that are sensitive to clients' culture and to differences among people and cultural groups" (NASW, 1996, p. 9).

Opportunities for affirming individuality and sense of self-worth are lost when practitioners are blinded to the uniqueness of clients by prejudices and stereotyped perceptions of the groups to which they belong. Although prejudices may be either favorable or unfavorable, in either case they act to blind the practitioner to unique characteristics of the individual. Such prejudices generally are associated with misconceptions caused by limited and inaccurate information and little or no interaction with members of a particular group. We have observed various social work students, for example, who manifest irrational fears of talking with "delinquents," "old people," or "mental patients," perceiving them as strange, different, or otherwise vaguely threatening. Interestingly, social workers themselves have been the objects of stereotyping, being labeled by some people as "do-gooders" or "baby snatchers."

Prejudices tend to diminish or to disappear when people have frequent personal contacts with members of a particular group. As they are subjected to the test of actual experience, supposed or even real differences among people tend to shrink due in large measure to the fact that people become more aware of how much greater are their similarities than their differences.

A danger of unexamined prejudices is that they may lead social workers to stereotypical perceptions of persons or groups. Working from these stereotypes, practitioners may fail to effectively engage with clients; they may overlook strengths and capacities and as a result, their assessments, goals, and interventions are distorted. The consequences of such practice are troubling. Imagine an elderly client whose reversible health problems (associated with inadequate nutrition or need for medication) are dismissed as merely symptomatic of advanced age! Visualize the developmentally disabled client who is interested in learning about sexuality and contraceptives, but whose worker fails to address those issues, considering them irrelevant for this population! What about the terminally ill patient who is more concerned about allowing her lesbian partner to make her end-of-life decisions than she is about her illness and impending death? Avoiding presumptions and prejudices is central to effective social work practice.

The following exercises will assist you in expanding your awareness of prejudices or stereotypes that could impair your effectiveness in working with certain clients. In each situation, imagine yourself in an interview or group session with the client(s). Try to picture the client as vividly as possible and try to be aware of your feelings, attitudes, and behavior. After each situation, contemplate or discuss the following:

1. What feelings and attitudes did you experience?

2. What assumptions did you make about the needs of the clients in each vignette?

3. What actions would you take (or what information would you seek) to move beyond stereotypes in understanding your client(s)?

Situation 1 You are seeing a couple in their mid-twenties who have requested help in resolving difficulties in their relationship. One complains that the other is jealous and overly possessive. The other replies that her partner is insensitive to her needs and feelings. They have lived together in a lesbian relationship for two years.

Situation 2 You are asked to work with a Laotian family. The parents report increasing difficulties with their children, who are disrespectful and disobedient.

Situation 3 You are a hospital social worker who is asked to facilitate a postsurgical adjustment group for transgendered persons.

Situation 4 You are an African American outreach worker. One Caucasian client has expressed appreciation for the help you have provided, yet tells you repeatedly that she is "afraid living in this area with so many coloreds."

Situation 5 A 69-year-old widow is a new resident at an assisted living facility. One day during activity group, she screams about the crafts, the meals, and the other residents and insists on leaving the facility. Several staff members have commented on her resistance to treatment and asked you to work with her to help her become more cooperative.

Situation 6 You are working with a high school senior, the eldest girl in a large family from a fundamentalist religious background. Your client wants desperately to attend college but has been told by her parents that she is needed to care for her younger siblings and assist in her family's ministry.

Becoming aware of our discomfort and assumptions is the first step in overcoming prejudices. Some practitioners mistakenly pride themselves on possessing no biases, but their naïveté in this regard limits their openness to experiencing themselves, let alone other people. Still others perceive themselves as champions of victims of discrimination and, blinded by their zeal, erroneously attribute problems rooted in other sources to the effects of discrimination. Such zeal often emanates from unconscious overcompensation for guilt about living in a racist society. Overcompensation and overidentification with the oppressed can result in offering special privileges and relaxing standards of behavior beneath those expected by minorities themselves. As such, overidentification can impair effective work as much as prejudices and stereotypes.

4. *Given appropriate resources, human beings are capable of growth and change and should be supported in increasing their choices in solving their problems and directing their lives.* This value embodies the beliefs that clients have the capacity to grow and change and to develop solutions to their difficulties, as well as the right and capacity to exercise free choice responsibly. These values are magnified when practitioners adopt a strengths-oriented perspective,

looking for positive qualities and undeveloped potential rather than limitations and past mistakes (Cowger, 1994; Saleeby, 1997). Such a positive perspective engenders hope and courage on the client's part and nurtures self-esteem as well. These factors, in turn, enhance the client's motivation, which is indispensable to a successful outcome.

Belief in the capacity of others to change is critically needed, for people's perceptions of themselves and their problems are strongly influenced by feedback from others. If you view clients positively and express the belief that they can work out their problems, they are likely to adopt a similar outlook. Of course, your view must be realistic, assuming that the client's situation is susceptible to change and that he or she possesses the capacity to implement whatever actions are required. Otherwise you may engender false hope that ultimately will lead to discouragement and perhaps to justifiable resentment toward you. Most problem situations can be remedied to some extent, however, and the large majority of clients have the capacity to take constructive actions on their problems.

Another challenge in carrying out this value is the temptation to resolve clients' problems for them, or to impose the worker's values on the clients. Several problems result when workers impose solutions or beliefs on clients.

1. Coercing clients to behave in a way that is contrary to deeply held values may create intense feelings of guilt.

CASE EXAMPLE

Mr. R, a single man, age 35, who lived with his aging parents and was very devoted to them, sought counseling because of conflicts between his personal needs and those of his parents. He had recently become interested in a widow but could tell that his parents were hurt because of the amount of time he was spending with her. They had said nothing, as was typical, but they related coolly to him. He didn't wish to hurt them but felt they should understand that he needed

to live his own life. The practitioner appropriately supported his thrust for independence but, in addition, pushed Mr. R to confront his parents directly with their unrealistic expectations and to express his intentions of living his own life. The practitioner further indicated that, in devoting himself to his parents, Mr. R had done himself a strong injustice, and the practitioner suggested it was high time he rectified the situation. Upon the strong urging of the practitioner, Mr. R agreed to confront his parents, although he was apprehensive. His parents responded with unexpected understanding to the confrontation. Mr. R could sense their hurt and disappointment, however, and felt extremely guilty. Attempts to relive his guilt failed, and he rapidly became depressed and preoccupied with thoughts that life was not worth living.

2. Many clients resent and oppose attempts to impose values upon them—some to the extent that they discontinue seeing a practitioner.

CASE EXAMPLE

Mrs. W, a widow, had sought professional help for depression that had persisted following her husband's death 1 year earlier. In this, the fifth interview, Mrs. W expressed a deep sense of loss associated with her husband's death. She said that she and Mr. W had been very close and had enjoyed a mutually fulfilling sexual relationship. She missed their sexual relationship and was frustrated because she believed only married people should engage in sexual relations. She had dated several men, most of whom had made sexual overtures. She was inclined to respond positively on a few occasions but believed to do so would be wrong. The practitioner responded that she was an adult and that there was nothing wrong with sex between consenting adults. The practitioner further suggested she needed to discard her outmoded ideas and enjoy herself more. Mrs. W hesitantly replied that she wasn't sure she could or wanted to do that. She subsequently canceled her next appointment and did not return for additional interviews.

3. Practitioners who rush in with advice may prohibit clients from making their own decisions. People who are struggling can benefit from exploring their situation, analyzing the issues and weighing the consequences involved in various courses of action from their own value preferences. This isn't to say that practitioners may not point out issues or consequences that the client is overlooking. In this case, the practitioner's motivation is constructive, for it is based on the client's needs. By contrast, attempting to convert clients to one's values because of a conviction that these values are right meets the needs of the practitioner, not the client.

CASE EXAMPLE

Selena, a college student, was distressed to find that she was pregnant following a "one-night stand" over Christmas break. She tearfully discussed her situation with Amy, a social work student placed at the college student health center. Amy's strong beliefs against abortion led her to press Selena to choose to keep the baby or to make plans for adoption. Selena, too, thought adoption might be a good option, but felt pressured and rushed in making her decision.

4. The final ramification is that the practitioner may sometimes represent organizational or cultural values that are in conflict with a client's culture.

CASE EXAMPLE

Mrs. D, 75, a Navajo woman, was released from a hospital with a chronic kidney condition, but otherwise in good health. While making a home visit, the social worker found that Mrs. D lived in a one-room home with a dirt floor and no indoor plumbing. The walk to the outhouse was several hundred feet away. There was, however, a

house with indoor plumbing on the property that the Bureau of Indian Affairs had built for her several years earlier. The worker could not understand why she was not living there. Was this evidence that she was incapable of making rational decisions about her well-being?

A culturally competent worker might know that she was choosing to live in a traditional fashion and the dirt floor had spiritual meaning for her, not unlike the cross hanging over the bed of a Catholic. Mrs. D considered the walk to the outhouse good exercise rather than a problem, and had lived in these conditions her entire life. She was well cared for by extended family and fully capable of making her own decisions. While she appreciated the government housing, she was not comfortable there and chose to use it as a storage area for the pottery she made.

In our presentation of the four cardinal values of the social work profession, you've seen numerous situations and cases that highlight the potential for value conflicts. We've suggested that self-awareness, openness to new persons and events, and increasing practice experience are all elements in overcoming value conflicts. But what if you've done these things and values still conflict? Social workers occasionally encounter situations in which they cannot conform to the profession's values or where a client's behaviors or goals evoke such negative reactions that a positive helping relationship cannot be attained. For example, practitioners who have personal experience with child abuse or who are intensely opposed to abortions may find it difficult to accept a pedophile as a client or to offer help to a person with an unintended pregnancy. In such instances, it is important to acknowledge such feelings and to explore them through supervision or therapy. It may be feasible to help the worker overcome these difficulties to be more fully available as a helping person. If this is not possible, or the situation is exceptional, the worker and supervisor should explore transferring the case to another practitioner who can accept both the client and the goals. When a transfer is possible, it is vital to clarify for clients that the reason for transfer is not personal rejection of them but that they deserve the best service possible and that the practitioner cannot provide that service because of value conflicts. Such an explanation conveys goodwill and safeguards the self-esteem of clients. Frequently such a transfer is not possible, and the social worker is responsible for being up front with the client about the difficulties while committing to carrying out ethical and professional responsibilities. When practitioners frequently encounter difficulties in accepting clients, they owe it to themselves and to future clients to seriously consider whether they have chosen the appropriate profession.

Ethics

Codes of ethics are the embodiment of a profession's values. They set forth principles and standards for behavior of those in the profession. In social work, the primary Code of Ethics is promulgated by the National Association of Social Workers (NASW). The code addresses a range of responsibilities social workers have to their clients, their colleagues, their employers, their profession, and to society as a whole. In this section we will address primary areas of ethical responsibility: self-determination, informed consent, the maintenance of client-worker boundaries, and confidentiality. We will begin, though, by discussing the way that ethics are related to legal responsibilities and malpractice risks, and we will conclude by discussing the resources and processes available for resolving ethical dilemmas.

The Intersection of Laws and Ethics

The practice of social work is governed by an array of policies, laws, and regulations. Whether established by court cases, Congress or state legislatures, licensure boards, or regulatory agencies, these rules affect social workers' decisions and actions. For example, state mandatory reporting laws require social workers to report instances where child abuse is suspected. Health department rules may require social workers

to divulge the names of HIV+ clients to public health authorities. In other states, similar rules may forbid the sharing of patient's names or HIV status. Licensure board regulations may forbid social work practice by persons with felony convictions. Federal court cases may extend evidential privilege to communications with social workers. Federal laws may prohibit the provision of certain benefits to undocumented immigrants. Good social work requires practitioners to be aware of the laws and regulations that govern the profession and apply to their area of practice. But knowing the laws is not enough. Consider the following case:

CASE EXAMPLE

Alice is a 38-year-old woman who has presented for treatment, racked with guilt as the result of a brief extramarital affair. In her third session, she discloses to you that she is HIV+, but unwilling to tell her husband of her status because then the affair would be revealed and she fears losing him and her two young daughters. You are concerned about the danger to her husband's health and press her to tell him or to allow you to do so. Alice responds that if you do, you will be breaking confidentiality and violating her privacy. She implies that she would sue you or report you to your licensing board and to your profession's ethics committee.

This case neatly captures the clash of ethics, laws, and regulations and illustrates the stakes for workers who make the "wrong" decision. In times like these the social worker just wants a clear answer from a lawyer or supervisor who will tell him or her exactly what to do. Unfortunately, it's not that easy. Good practice requires knowledge of both the applicable ethical principles and the relevant laws. Even with this knowledge, dilemmas may persist. In this case, the ethical principles of self-determination and confidentiality are pitted against the principle to protect others from harm, which itself is derived from a court case (Reamer, 1995). The particular state or setting where the case takes place may have laws or regulations that govern the worker's actions. Finally, the threat of litigation looms large, even when the worker's actions are thoughtful, careful, ethical, and legal.

When you think about the intersection of laws and ethics, it may be helpful to think of a Venn diagram, in which two circles overlap (see Figure 4-1). In the center are areas common to both ethics and laws, but within each circle there are items that are exclusive to laws and ethics. Some standards contained in the Code of Ethics are not addressed by laws and regulations. Similarly, some areas of the law are not covered by the Code of Ethics. Where the two intersect there can be areas of agreement as well as areas of discord. As the NASW Code itself notes, "Social workers' primary responsibility is to promote the well-being of clients. In general, clients' interests are primary. However, social workers' responsibility to the larger society or specific legal obligations may on limited occasions supersede the loyalty owed clients and clients should be so advised" (1996, p. 7). Also, "Instances may arise when social workers' ethical obligations conflict with agency policies or relevant laws or regulations. When such conflicts occur, social workers must make a responsible effort to resolve the conflict in a manner that is consistent with the values, principles, and standards expressed in this Code. If a reasonable resolution of the conflict does not appear possible, social workers should seek proper consultation before making a decision" (1996, p. 3).

The processes for ethical decision making are addressed later in this chapter. For now, though, it is important to acknowledge that social workers must know both the law and ethical principles in order to practice effectively. Workers must also know that at times there will be conflicts between and among ethical and legal imperatives. Thoughtful examination, consultation, and skillful application of the principles will serve as guides when conflicts and dilemmas arise.

Key Ethical Principles

Self-Determination

Biestek (1957) has defined self-determination as "the practical recognition of the right and need of clients to freedom in making their own choices and decisions" (p. 103). Self-determination is central to the social worker's ethical responsibility to clients: "Social workers respect and promote the right of clients to self-determination and assist clients in their efforts to identify and clarify their goals. Social workers may limit clients' right to self-determination when, in their professional judgment, clients' actions or potential actions pose a serious, foreseeable, and imminent risk to themselves or others" (NASW, 1996, p. 7).

The extent to which you affirm self-determination rests in large measure on your perceptions of the helping role and of the helping process. If you consider your major role to be that of providing solutions or dispensing advice freely, you may foster dependency, demean clients by failing to recognize and affirm their strengths, and relegate them to a position of passive cooperation (or passive resistance, as often occurs under such circumstances).[1] Such domineering behavior is counterproductive. Not only does it discourage open communication but, equally important, it denies clients the opportunity to gain strength and self-respect as they actively struggle with their difficulties. Fostering dependency generally leaves people weaker rather than stronger and is a disservice to clients.

The type of relationship that affirms self-determination and fosters growth is a partnership

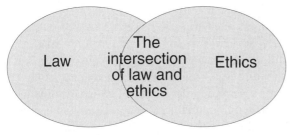

Figure 4-1   The Relationship of Law and Ethics

wherein practitioner and client (whether individual, couple, or group) are joined in a mutual effort to search for solutions to problems or to promote growth. As enablers of change, practitioners assist clients to view their problems realistically, to consider various solutions and their consequences, to implement change-oriented strategies, to understand themselves and others more fully, to gain awareness of previously unrecognized strengths and opportunities for growth, and to resolve obstacles to change and growth. As helpful as these steps are, however, ultimately the responsibility for pursuing these options rests with the client.

Just as fostering self-determination enhances client autonomy, paternalism (i.e., preventing self-determination based on a judgment of the client's own good) infringes on autonomy. Linzer (1999) refers to paternalism as "the overriding of a person's wishes or actions through coercion, deception or nondisclosure of information, or for the welfare of others" (p. 137). A similar concept is paternalistic beneficence, wherein protective interventions are used to enhance the client's quality of life, even if done, at times, despite the client's objections (Abramson, 1985; Murdach, 1996, 1998).

Under what conditions might it be acceptable for a social worker to override a client's autonomy? Paternalism may be acceptable when a client is young or mentally incompetent, when an irreversible act such as suicide can be prevented, or when the interference with the client's decisions or actions ensures other freedoms or liberties, such as by preventing a serious crime (Abramson, 1985; Reamer, 1983, 1989). Murdach suggests three gradations of beneficent actions, which vary in their level of intrusiveness depending on the degree of risk and the client's decision-making capacity. Yet, even under these circumstances, social workers must weigh the basis for their decisions and the impact of their actions. For example, if a psychiatric patient refuses medication, some would argue that the client lacks competence to make such a decision, and that forcing him or her to take the medication would be "for his or her own good." Yet diagnosis or placement is not a

sufficient basis for overriding the client's autonomy. For this reason, states have elaborate administrative and judicial processes that must be pursued before hospitalizing or medicating a patient against his or her will.

Even when clients have reduced capacity for exercising self-determination, social workers should act to ensure that they exercise their capacities to the fullest feasible extent. For example, based on research findings, Abramson (1988) concluded that discharge planning for hospitalized elderly patients who are severely ill or have mild senile dementia should include the patient whenever possible. These findings indicated that some patients afflicted with mild dementia still manifested capacity to participate in decision making, although moderate or severe dementia seriously impeded participation. Depression also did not appear to limit participation of elderly patients in planning their posthospital arrangements.

Self-determination can be extended to individuals who are terminally ill when they are educated about their options and encouraged to articulate their desires through advance directives, which provide instructions to health care personnel regarding what medical interventions are acceptable. These directives become operative when the patient's condition precludes decision-making capacity. Advance directives can take the form of living wills or authorizing an individual to act with durable power of attorney. The latter procedure is broader in scope and more powerful than a living will. The person designated to have durable power of attorney or medical power of attorney is authorized to make decisions as if he or she were the patient when grave illness or accident has obliterated the patient's autonomy.

Operationalizing clients' rights to self-determination sometimes can pose perplexing challenges. Adding to the complexity is the reality that in certain instances, higher-order principles such as safety supersede the right to self-determination. To challenge your thinking about how you might affirm the value of self-determination in practical situations, we have provided exercises that consist of problematic situations actually encountered by the authors or colleagues. As you read each scenario, analyze alternative courses of action that are available. Consider how you would work with the client to maximize self-determination, taking care also to promote the best interests of the client. You may also wish to raise these issues for group discussion in class.

Situation 1 In your work for the state welfare department, you oversee the care of numerous group home residents whose expenses are funded by the state. Two of your clients, both in their twenties, reside in the same home and have told you that they are eager to get married. The administrator of the home strenuously protests that the two are retarded and, if they marry, might produce a child they could not properly care for. Further, she has stressed that she has no private room for a couple and that if the two marry, they will have to leave the group home.

Situation 2 A runaway 15-year-old adolescent who is 4 months pregnant has contacted you several times in regard to planning for her child. In her last visit, she confided to you that she is habituated to heroin. You have expressed your concern that the drug may damage her unborn child, but she does not seem worried nor does she want to give up use of the drug. You also know that she obtains money for heroin through prostitution and is not attending school.

Situation 3 While making a visit to Mr. and Mrs. F, an elderly couple living in their home on their own savings, you discover that they have hired several home health aides who have stolen from them and provided such poor care that their health and nutrition are endangered. When you discuss with them your concern about the adequacy of their care, they firmly state that they can handle their own problems and do not want to be put in a nursing home.

Situation 4 As a rehabilitation worker, you have arranged for a young woman to receive training as a beautician in a local technical college, a vocation in which she expressed intense interest. Although initially enthusiastic, she now tells you that she wants to discontinue the program and go into nursing, indicating that her supervisor at the college is highly critical of her work and that the other trainees tease her and talk about her behind her back. You are torn about what to do, knowing that your client tends to antagonize other people with her quick and barbed remarks. You wonder if, rather than change programs, your client needs to learn more appropriate ways of communicating and relating to her supervisor and co-workers.

Situation 5 A middle-aged client with cancer has found herself so debilitated by the latest round of chemotherapy that she has decided to refuse further treatment. Her physician states that her age, her general health, and the stage of her cancer all argue for continuing her treatments, with the likelihood of a successful outcome. Her family is upset at seeing her in pain and supports her decision.

Providing Informed Consent

Six principles in the NASW Code of Ethics address facets of informed consent. At its essence, though, informed consent requires that social workers "use clear and understandable language to inform clients of the purpose of the services, risks related to the services, limits to services because of the requirements of a third-party payer, relevant costs, reasonable alternatives, clients' right to refuse or withdraw consent, and the time frame covered by the consent. Social workers should provide clients with an opportunity to ask questions" (1996, pp. 7–8). The Code also indicates that clients should be informed when their services are being provided by a student!

Some workers view informed consent as a formality to be disposed of at the first interview or a legalistic form to have clients sign and then file away. In fact, informed consent should be an active and ongoing part of the helping process. With the tension and uncertainty that can accompany a first session, clients may not realize the significance of the information they are provided. Therefore, it makes sense to revisit the parameters of service and invite questions throughout the helping process.

Having a "fact sheet" with relevant policies and answers to commonly asked questions can also help clients by giving them something to refer to between meetings, should questions arise (Houston-Vega, Nuehring, & Daguio, 1997).

To facilitate informed consent for persons with hearing, literacy, or language difficulties, social workers should utilize interpreters, translators, and multiple communication methods. When clients are temporarily or permanently incapable of providing informed consent, "social workers should protect clients' interests by seeking permission from an appropriate third party, informing clients consistent with the client's level of understanding" and "seek to ensure that the third party acts in a manner consistent with the client's wishes and interests" (NASW, 1996, p. 8). Even clients who are receiving services involuntarily are entitled to know the nature of the services they will be receiving and about their right to refuse service.

Preserving Professional Boundaries

Boundaries refer to clear lines of difference that are maintained between the social worker and client so that the working relationship is preserved. In part, boundaries help clarify that the relationship is not a social one, and though it may involve a high degree of trust and client self-disclosure, it is not an intimate one, as might be experienced with a friend, partner, or family member. When clients can trust that boundaries exist and will be maintained by the worker, they are more able to focus on the issues for which they are seeking help. They can freely share of themselves and trust that the worker's reactions and statements, whether of support, confrontation, or empathy, are artifacts of the working relationship, not social or sexual overtures or personal reactions as might arise when friends disagree.

Sometimes social workers and other helping professionals have a difficult time with the notion of boundaries, feeling that boundaries establish a hierarchical relationship in which the client is "less worthy" than the social worker. Some professionals may also feel that to establish such boundaries is

cold and clinical, treating the client as an object instead of a fellow human deserving of warmth and compassion (Lazarus, 1994). Our viewpoint is that the two positions are not mutually exclusive. Social workers *can* have relationships with clients that are characterized by collaborative problem solving and mutuality, and can react to clients authentically without blurring the boundaries of their relationship or obscuring the purpose of their work.

The NASW Code of Ethics addresses boundaries through six provisions.

- "Social workers should not take unfair advantage of any professional relationship or exploit others to further their personal, religious, political, or business interests" (1996, p. 9).

- "Social workers should not engage in dual or multiple relationships with clients or former clients in which there is a risk of exploitation or potential harm to the client. In instances when dual or multiple relationships are unavoidable, social workers should take steps to protect clients and are responsible for setting clear, appropriate, and culturally sensitive boundaries. (Dual or multiple relationships occur when social workers relate to clients in more than one relationship, whether professional, social, or business. Dual or multiple relationships can occur simultaneously or consecutively.)" (1996, pp. 9–10).

- "Social workers should not engage in physical contact with clients when there is a possibility of psychological harm to the client as a result of the contact (such as cradling or caressing clients) . . . " (1996, p. 13).

- "Social workers should under no circumstances engage in sexual activities or sexual contact with current clients, whether such contact is consensual or forced" (1996, p. 13).

- "Social workers should not engage in sexual activities or sexual contact with clients' relatives or other individuals with whom clients maintain a close personal relationship when there is a risk of exploitation or potential harm to the client.

Sexual activity or sexual contact with clients' relatives or other individuals with whom clients maintain a personal relationship has the potential to be harmful to the client and may make it difficult for the social worker and client to maintain appropriate professional boundaries. Social workers—not their clients, their clients' relatives, or other individuals with whom the client maintains a personal relationship—assume the full burden for setting clear, appropriate, and culturally sensitive boundaries" (1996, p. 13).

- "Social workers should not engage in sexual activities or sexual contact with former clients because of the potential for harm to the client . . . " (1996, p. 13).

Although these standards of practice may seem self-evident, they are an area of considerable difficulty within the profession. Research on ethics complaints indicates that in NASW-adjudicated cases, boundary violations accounted for more than half of the cases in which there were violations (Strom-Gottfried, 1999). Similarly, in research on the frequency of malpractice claims against social workers for the period 1961 to 1990, Reamer (1995) found that sexual violations were the second most common area of claim, and the most expensive in terms of money paid out. Most social workers cannot imagine developing sexual relationships with their clients, and yet, this is often the culmination of a "slippery slope" of boundary problems that may include excessive self-disclosure on the part of the worker, the exchange of gifts, socializing or meeting for meals outside the office, and asking the client to perform office and household chores or other favors (Borys & Pope, 1989; R. S. Epstein, Simon, & Kay, 1992; Gabbard, 1996; Gartrell, 1992). It is not uncommon to have feelings of sexual attraction for clients. When such feelings arise, however, it is crucial to raise them with faculty or supervisors so they can be acknowledged and examined. Such discussion normalizes and neutralizes such feelings and decreases the likelihood that the worker will

act on the attraction (Pope, Keith-Spiegel, & Tabachnick, 1986). These issues will be discussed further in Chapter 19 on relational reactions.

Other boundary issues can be both subtle and complex. For example, you may meet a neighbor in the agency waiting room or run into a client while doing your grocery shopping. You may decide to buy a car and find that the salesperson is a former client. You may visit a relative in the hospital and find that her roommate is a current or former client. Friends in need of social work services may ask to be assigned to your caseload, because you already know them so well. A client may ask you to attend a "family" event, such as a graduation or wedding. You may resonate with a particular client and think what a great friend he or she could be. The possibilities are endless, and addressing them involves other ethical principles, such as maintaining confidentiality and avoiding conflicts of interest. The key is to be alert to dual relationships, to discuss troubling situations with colleagues and a supervisor, and to take care that in questionable boundary situations, the primacy of the helping relationship is preserved. It is incumbent on the social worker to make sure that clients are not taken advantage of and that their services are not obscured or affected detrimentally when boundaries must be crossed.

Safeguarding Confidentiality

From a practical standpoint, confidentiality is a sine qua non of the helping process, for without assurance of confidentiality, it is unlikely that clients would risk disclosing private aspects of their lives that, if revealed, could damage their reputations. This is especially true when clients' problems involve marital infidelity, deviant sexual practices, illicit activities, child abuse, and the like. Implied confidentiality, if not explicitly requested by clients, is an assurance that the practitioner will never reveal such personal matters to others.

Social workers are bound by the NASW Code of Ethics to safeguard confidentiality. Numerous standards operationalize this principle, but in essence, social workers are expected to respect clients' privacy, to gather information only for the purpose of providing effective services, and to disclose information only with clients' consent. The disclosure of information without the client's permission should be done only for compelling reasons, and even under these circumstances, there are limits on what information can be shared and with whom. These exceptions to confidentially will be addressed later in this section.

An unjustified breach of confidentiality is a violation of justice and is tantamount to theft of a secret with which one has been entrusted (Biestek, 1957). Kutchins notes further that if social workers "ignore these ethical mandates, the law governing fiduciary relationships can make them pay dearly" (1991, p. 107). Maintaining strict confidentiality requires a strong commitment and constant vigilance, for clients sometimes reveal information that is shocking, humorous, bizarre, or "juicy." To fulfill your responsibility in maintaining confidentiality, it is vital to guard against disclosing information in inappropriate situations. Examples are discussing details of your work with family and friends, having gossip sessions with colleagues, dictating within the listening range of others, discussing client situations within earshot of other staff, and making remarks about clients in elevators or other public places. The emergence of technology for the electronic collection, transfer, and storage of information raises new complexities for maintaining client privacy. When you leave a voice mail for a client, are you certain only the client will receive the message? When a colleague sends you a fax on a case, can you be sure that others won't see that information before you retrieve the document? As authors such as Davidson & Davidson (1996) have noted, these technological advances have emerged at the same time that insurance companies and others who fund services are demanding more and more detailed information about cases in order to approve services. As a result, clients should be well informed about the limits of confidentiality and the potential risks of information shared for insurance claims (Corcoran & Winslade, 1994).

What Are the Limits on Confidentiality?
Supervision and Consultation
The right to confidentiality is not absolute, for case situations are sometimes discussed with supervisors and consultants and may be presented at staff conferences. Disclosing information in these instances, however, is for the purpose of enhancing service to clients, who will generally consent to these uses when the purposes are clarified. The client has a right to be informed that such disclosures may occur, and practitioners have a responsibility to conceal the identity of the client to the fullest extent possible and also to reveal no more personal information than is absolutely necessary.

Other persons such as administrators, volunteers, clerical staff, consultants, board members, researchers, legal counsel, and outside persons who may review records for purposes of quality assurance, peer review, or accreditation may have access to files or case information. The access to information should be for the purposes of better serving the client, and these individuals should sign binding agreements not to misuse confidential information. Further, it is essential that social workers promote policies and norms that protect confidentiality and assure that case information is treated carefully and respectfully.

Client Waivers of Confidentiality
Social workers are often asked by other professionals or agencies to provide confidential information about the nature of their client's difficulties or the services provided. Sometimes, these requests can come with such authority that the recipient is caught off guard, inadvertently acknowledging a particular person as a client or providing the information requested about the case. In these instances, it is important that such information be provided only with the written, informed consent of clients, which releases the practitioner and agency from liability in disclosing the requested information. Even when informed consent is obtained, however, it is important to reveal informa-

tion selectively according to the essential needs of the other party.

There are exceptions when information can be revealed without informed consent, such as a bona fide emergency in which a client's life appears to be at stake or when the social worker is legally compelled, as in the reporting of child abuse. In other instances, however, it is prudent to obtain supervisory and legal input before disclosing confidential information without a written consent for release of information.

A final example of the client's waiver of confidentiality occurs if the client files a malpractice action against the social worker. Such an action would "terminate the patient or client privilege" (Dickson, 1998, p. 48) and free the practitioner to share publicly such information as is necessary to defend against the lawsuit.

Danger to Self or Others

In certain instances, the client's right to confidentiality may be less compelling than the rights of other people who could be severely harmed or damaged by actions planned by the client and confided to the practitioner. For example, if a client plans to commit kidnapping, injury, or murder, the practitioner is obligated to disclose these intentions to the intended victim and to law enforcement officials so that timely preventative action can be implemented. Indeed, if practitioners fail to make appropriate disclosure under these circumstances, they may be liable to civil prosecution for negligence. The fundamental case in this area is the *Tarasoff* case (Reamer, 1994). In it, a young man seeing a psychologist at a university health service threatened his girlfriend, Tatiana Tarasoff. The therapist notified university police, who after interviewing the young man determined he was not a danger. Some weeks later he murdered Ms. Tarasoff, and her family filed a lawsuit alleging that she should have been warned. Ultimately the court ruled that mental health professionals have an obligation to protect intended victims. In the court's words, "The protective privilege ends where the public peril begins" (Reamer, 1995).

This court decision has led to varying interpretations in subsequent cases and in resulting state laws (Dickson, 1998; Houston-Vega, et al., 1997), but two principles resulting from it are consistent. If the worker perceives a *foreseeable and imminent threat* to an *identifiable potential victim,* the social worker should act to warn that victim or take other precautions (such as notifying police or placing the client in a secure facility) to protect others from harm.

Another application of the duty to protect personal safety involves intervening to prevent a client's suicide. Typically, lawsuits focused on the breach of confidentiality to protect suicidal clients are not successful (VandeCreek, Knapp, & Herzog, 1988). Conversely, "liability for wrongful death can be established if appropriate and sufficient action to prevent suicide is not taken (Houston-Vega, et al., 1997, p. 105). Knowing when the risk is sufficient to warrant breaking a client's confidence is both a clinical and an ethical matter. Chapter 8 will offer you guidelines to use when determining the risk of lethality in suicidal threats or in client aggression.

Suspicion of Child or Elder Abuse

The rights of others also take precedence over the right to confidentiality in instances of child abuse and/or neglect. In fact, all 50 states now have statutes making it mandatory for professionals to report suspected or known child abuse. Moreover, statutes governing the mandatory reporting of child abuse may contain criminal clauses for the failure to report. It is noteworthy that practitioners are protected from both civil and criminal liability for breach of confidentiality resulting from the legal mandate to report (Butz, 1985). Some states have similar provisions for reporting the suspected abuse of the elderly or other vulnerable adults (G. Corey, Corey, & Callanan, 1998; Dickson, 1998).

Although afforded immunity from prosecution for reporting, practitioners are still confronted with the difficult challenge of preserving the helping relationship after having breached confidentiality.[2] One way of managing this tension is through informed consent. As noted earlier, clients should know at the outset of service what the "ground rules" for service are and what limits exist on what the worker can hold as confidential. When clients understand that the worker must report suspected child abuse, such a report may not be as damaging to the worker-client relationship. Similarly, the Code indicates, "Social workers should inform clients, to the extent possible, about the disclosure of confidential information and the potential consequences, when feasible before the disclosure is made . . . " (1996, p. 10). With informed consent, and careful processing of the decision to file a child abuse report, feelings of betrayal can be diminished and the helping relationship preserved.

The decision to comply with mandated reporting requirements may not always be straightforward, however. As K. A. Long (1986) reports, "On Indian reservations and in small rural towns it is often impossible to prevent community awareness of abuse victims, abuse perpetrators, and abuse informants. Despite the best efforts of health care professionals involved, abuse perpetrators may learn of an informant through informal channels or through tribal court procedures" (p. 133). Further, the sense of loyalty to one's clan members may take precedence over the commitment to protect an informant and the need to protect an abused child. Consequently, tribal sanctions may be more severe in relation to the informant than to the abuser. Definitions of abuse also differ from culture to culture, and within certain subcultures even severe abuse (according to common standards) may not be considered a problem by the victim or other family members.

Subcultural differences are by no means limited to members of ethnic minority groups. Long provides additional documentation of how closely knit Anglo health care practitioners discounted reports of child abuse perpetrated by a colleague and hindered effective intervention. Clearly, professional and social class loyalties have shielded abusers and hampered efforts to protect the child.

What course of action should practitioners take when community or subcultural definitions of child abuse diverge from generally accepted standards, and when loyalties may result in punishment to informants and victims rather than perpetrators? We concur with Long's (1986) recommendations that we "must look beyond legal guidelines and discipline-specific prescriptions" (p. 136). If professionals are to be both genuinely helpful and realistically effective, there is often a need to make compromises related to treatment ideals. Thoughtful evaluation is required to allow for treatment strategies that can fit and be useful within a given subcultural context, and still maintain the ethical and legal principles.

Subpoenas and Privileged Communication

Still another constraint on clients' rights to confidentiality is the fact that this right does not necessarily extend into courts of law. Unless social workers are practicing in one of the states that grant privileged communication, they may be compelled by courts to reveal confidential information and to produce confidential records. "Privileged communication" refers to communications made within a "legally protected relationship," which "cannot be introduced into court without the consent of the person making the communication," typically the patient or client (Dickson, 1998, p. 32).

Yet determining the presence and applicability of privilege can be complicated. As Dickson notes, "Privilege laws can vary with the profession of the individual receiving the communication, the material communicated, the purpose of the communication, whether the proceeding is criminal or civil, and whether the professional is employed by the state or is in private practice, among other factors" (1998, p. 33). On the federal level, the U.S. Supreme Court in *Jaffee v. Redmond* upheld client communications as privileged and specifically extended "that privilege to licensed social workers" ("Therapy privilege upheld," 1996, p. 7).

Despite the apparent clarity that this ruling brings to the federal courts, the ambiguity and variability on the state level means that social workers must understand their state laws and regulations and assure that clients are fully informed about the limits to confidentiality should records be subpoenaed or testimony required. B. Bernstein (1977) suggests that practitioners explain to clients that they may be "subpoenaed in court, records in hand, and forced under penalty of contempt to testify under oath, as to what was said between the parties and what was recorded concerning such exchanges" (p. 264).[3] Bernstein further recommends that clients sign a document verifying this understanding and that the document be kept in the client's case file.

It is important to note that laws recognizing privileged communication are created for the protection of the *client;* thus the privilege belongs to the client and not to the professional (Schwartz, 1989). In other words, if the practitioner were called on to take the witness stand, the attorney for the client could invoke the privilege to prohibit testimony of the practitioner (Bernstein, 1977). The client's attorney can also waive this privilege, in which case the practitioner would be obligated to disclose information as requested by the court.

Another important factor regarding privileged communication is that the client's right is not absolute (Levick, 1981). If, in a court's judgment, disclosure of confidential information would produce benefits that outweigh the injury that might be incurred by revealing that information, the presiding judge may waive the privilege. Occasionally, the privilege is waived in instances of legitimate criminal investigations, because the need for information is deemed more compelling than the need to safeguard confidentiality (Schwartz, 1989). In the final analysis, then, courts make decisions on privilege on a case-by-case basis.

Because subpoenas, whether for records or testimony, are orders of the court, they cannot be ignored. Still, subpoenas may be issued for irrelevant or immaterial information. Therefore, social workers should be wary about submitting privileged materials. Careful review of the subpoena, consultation with the client, and legal guidance can help the social worker determine whether or how to respond. The following sources provide helpful information to social workers contending with subpoenas: Austin, Moline, and Williams (1990), Dickson (1998), Houston-Vega et al. (1997), and Polowy and Gilbertson (1997).

Confidentiality in Various Types of Recording

Because case records can be subpoenaed and because clients and other personnel have access to them, it is essential that practitioners work toward the development and implementation of policies and practices that provide maximal confidentiality. To this end, social workers should observe the following:

1. Record no more than is essential to the functions of the agency. Identify observed facts and distinguish them from opinions.

2. Omit details of clients' intimate lives from case records; describe intimate problems in general terms.

3. Do not include verbatim or process recordings in case files.

4. Employ private and soundproof dictation facilities.

5. Keep case records in locked files and issue keys only to those who require frequent access to the files. Use similar precautions for the protection of electronically stored data.

6. Do not remove case files from the agency except under extraordinary circumstances with special authorization.

7. Do not leave case files on desks where others might have access to them or keep case information on computer screens where it may be observed by others.

8. Take precautions, whenever possible, to ensure that information transmitted through the use of computers, electronic mail, facsimile machines, voice mail, answering machines, and other technology is secure, and that identifying information is not conveyed.

9. Use in-service training sessions to stress confidentiality and to monitor observance of

agency policies and practices instituted to safeguard confidentiality.

Accreditation standards, funding sources, state and federal laws—all may dictate how agencies maintain record-keeping systems. The guidelines that follow all help to protect the privacy of clients and assure the appropriate use of case records:

1. Maintain only information relevant and necessary to the agency's purposes.

2. Collect as much information as possible from the client directly.

3. Inform clients of the agency's authority to gather information, whether disclosure is mandatory or voluntary, the principal purpose of the use of the information, and the routine uses and effects, if any, of not providing part or all of the information.

4. Maintain and update records to assure accuracy, relevancy, timeliness, and completeness.

5. Notify clients of the release of records owing to compulsory legal actions.

6. Establish procedures to inform clients of the existence of their records, including special measures if necessary for disclosure of medical and psychological records and a review of requests to amend or correct the records. (Schrier, 1980, p. 453)

The NASW Code of Ethics (1996) reflects most of these provisions, stating that "social workers should provide clients with reasonable access to records concerning the clients" (p. 12). It further notes that the social worker should provide "assistance in interpreting the records and consultation with the client . . . " (p. 12) in situations where the worker is concerned about misunderstandings or harm arising from seeing the records. Access to records should be limited "only in exceptional circumstances when there is compelling evidence that such access would cause serious harm to the client" (p. 12).

Given the importance and uses of case records, Freed (1978) recommends that practitioners carefully distinguish objective from subjective information, use descriptive terms rather than professional jargon, and avoid using psychiatric and medical diagnoses that have not been verified. Further, information gained in confidence from other sources should not be made a part of the record unless permission is obtained from parties who provided the information. Finally, if there is reason to believe the client may be harmed by knowing what is in the record, the social worker is obligated to share this opinion with the client. In our opinion, the trend toward client access to records has enhanced the rights of clients by avoiding misuse of records and has compelled practitioners to be more prudent, rigorous, and scientific in keeping case records.

Social workers sometimes record live interviews or group sessions so that they can later analyze interactional patterns or group process as well as scrutinize their own performance with a view toward improving skills and techniques. Recording is also used extensively for instructional sessions between students and practicum instructors. Still another use of recordings is to provide firsthand feedback to clients by having them listen to or view their actual behavior in live sessions.

Before recording sessions for any of the preceding purposes, practitioners should obtain written consent from clients on a form that explicitly specifies how the recording will be used, who will listen to or view the recording, and when it will be erased. In no instance should a recording be made without the knowledge and consent of the client. Clients vary widely in their receptivity to having sessions recorded, and if they indicate reluctance, their wishes should be respected. Yet, the chances of gaining consent are enhanced by discussing the matter openly and honestly, taking care to explain the client's right to decline. If approached properly, the majority of clients consent to taping. Indeed, it has been our experience that students are more uncomfortable with taping than are clients.

Social workers who tape sessions assume a heavy burden of responsibility in safeguarding confidentiality, for live sessions are extremely revealing. Such recordings should be guarded to ensure that copies cannot be made and that unauthorized persons do not have access to them. When they have served their designated purpose, tapes should be promptly erased. Failure to heed these guidelines may constitute a breach of professional ethics.

Managing Ethical Dilemmas

Social workers sometimes experience quandaries in deciding which of two values or ethical principles should take precedence when a conflict exists. In the foregoing discussions of self-determination and confidentiality, for example, we cited examples of how these rights of clients and ethical obligations of social workers are sometimes superseded by higher-order values (e.g., the right to life, safety, and well-being). Thus, clients' right to confidentiality must yield when they confide that they have physically or sexually abused a child or otherwise reveal intentions or plans to engage in harmful acts that would jeopardize the health or safety of other persons. Moreover, in your practice you may find certain policies or practices of your employing agency that seem detrimental to clients. You may be conflicted about your ethical obligations to advocate for changes because doing so may jeopardize your employment or pose a threat to relationships with certain staff members.

Situations such as these present social workers with agonizingly difficult decisions. Reamer (1989), however, has presented general guidelines that can assist you in making these decisions. Here we present our versions of certain of these guidelines and illustrate instances of their application.

1. The right to life, health, well-being, and necessities of life takes precedence over rights to confidentiality and opportunities for additive "goods" such as wealth, education, and recreation. We have previously alluded to the application of this principle in instances of child abuse or plans to do physical harm to another person. In such instances the rights of both children and adults to health and well-being take precedence over clients' rights to confidentiality. Similarly, a neglected child's

rights to health and well-being take precedence over parents' rights to confidentiality and self-determination.

2. An individual's basic right to well-being takes precedence over another person's right to privacy, freedom, or self-determination. Put another way, in the language of the courts (which have consistently upheld this principle), individual rights end when the public peril begins. The rights and needs of infants and children to receive medical treatments thus supersede parents' rights to withhold medical treatment because of religious beliefs. Similarly, several states have adopted rules that stipulate "the duty to warn," requiring professionals to warn potential victims and to inform law enforcement officials when clients reveal plans to do physical harm to others.

3. People's right to self-determination takes precedence over their right to basic well-being. This principle asserts the right of people to carry out actions that appear contrary to their best interests, provided they are competent to make an informed and voluntary decision with consideration of relevant knowledge, and as long as the consequences of their decisions do not threaten the well-being of others. This principle affirms the cherished value of freedom to choose and protects the rights of people to make mistakes and to fail.

It is important to recognize that this principle must yield to principle when an individual's decision might result in either his or her death or severe damage to his or her physical or mental health. For example, when a client is at high risk of committing suicide, a social worker has an ethical (and legal) obligation to take preventative action. Otherwise, the social worker is vulnerable to a malpractice suit.

4. A person's rights to well-being may override laws, policies, and arrangements of organizations. Ordinarily, social workers are obligated to comply with the laws, policies, and procedures of social work agencies, other organizations, and voluntary associations. When a policy is unjust or otherwise harms the well-being of clients or social workers,

however, violation of the laws, policies, or procedures may be justified.

Examples of this principle include policies or practices that discriminate against or exploit certain persons or groups. An agency, for example, might employ clients (or social workers for that matter) on a part-time, hourly, or other basis to avoid having to pay for Social Security or unemployment benefits. Reamer (1989) also cites the example of a consortium of private agencies that might conspire to create a monopoly on services provided a certain group of clients, thus stifling competition and inflating the cost of services. In these and similar situations the well-being of affected groups takes precedence over compliance with the laws, policies, and arrangements at issue. Ethical social work involves advocacy for effective change in policies that are unfair or unethical. For example, in regard to the ethical challenges posed by managed care, Sunley (1997) suggests engaging in both "case advocacy" and "cause advocacy" to help both individual clients and groups of clients who may be disadvantaged by particular policies or practices. Chapter 15 of this text should be useful in helping you develop skills and strategies to employ when your organization's practices pose ethical dilemmas.

Although Reamer's guidelines are a valuable resource in resolving value dilemmas, applying them to the myriad situations that social workers encounter still involves uncertainties and ambigui-ties, a reality that practitioners must accept. What steps should you take as you find yourself confronted with ethical dilemmas? Corey, Corey, and Callanan (1998) suggest eight steps, including:

1. Identifying the problem or dilemma, gathering as much information from as many perspectives as possible, about the situation

2. Identifying the potential issues involved, determining the core principles and the competing issues

3. Reviewing the relevant codes of ethics

4. Reviewing the applicable laws and regulations

5. Obtaining consultation from colleagues, supervisors, or legal experts

6. Considering the possible and probable courses of action

7. Examining the consequences of various options

8. Deciding on a particular course of action, weighing the information you have and the impact of your other choices

Remember that these procedures need not be followed in the order listed. Yet engaging in each of these tasks is important for prompting a thorough and thoughtful examination of the issues and options in play in your ethical dilemma. Beyond these steps, you should also be sure to document carefully the input and considerations involved at each phase of the decision-making process.

Summary

In this chapter, you have been introduced to the ethics and values that undergird the social work profession. You have been provided guidelines for respecting confidentiality, obtaining informed consent, and approaching ethical dilemmas. In Chapter 5, we will move toward putting these professional values into action as you learn begin-ning skills for effective communication with and on behalf of clients.

Internet Resources

 In Chapter 1 we introduced a collection of social work resources at *http://www.nyu.edu/socialwork/wwwrsw/*. By choosing "social work" as the area you

wish to explore and selecting "ethics," you can gain access to the following useful resources pertinent to content in this chapter. A resources center on self-determination is available at *http://www.ohsu.edu/selfdetermination/*. You can compare the NASW Code of Ethics developed in the United States, *http://www.naswdc.org/code.htm/* (or see the following for an overview of the Code: *http://www.socialworkers.org/CODE.HTM/*), with the International Social Work Code of Ethics: *http://www.ifsw.org/Publications/4.4.pub.html#standards/*.

Using Infotrac®, you can search keywords "social work ethics," "self-determination," "privileged communication," and "beneficence" to read and/or download useful articles related to social work values and ethics such as: Murdach, A. (1996). Beneficence re-examined: Protective intervention in mental health. *Social Work, 41,* 26–32. Wesley, C. A. (1996). Social work and end-of-life decisions: Self-determination and the common good. *Health and Social Work, 21* (2), 115–121. Galambos, C. M. (1998). Preserving end-of-life autonomy: The Patient Self-Determination Act and the Uniform Health Care Decisions Act. *Health and Social Work, 23* (4). Reamer, F. G. (1998b). The evolution of social work ethics. *Social Work, 43* (6).

SKILL DEVELOPMENT EXERCISES IN MANAGING ETHICAL DILEMMAS

The following exercises will give you practice in applying ethics concepts and ethical decision making to specific practice situations. These situations include some of the most difficult ones that we and our colleagues have encountered in practice. You will note that in few of the situations is the appropriate response or course of action cut and dried. After reading each situation, consider the following:

1. What conflicting principles and feelings are in play in the case?
2. What are the pros and cons of various courses of action?
3. What guidelines are applicable in resolving this dilemma?

4. What resources could you consult to help you decide on an ethical course of action?

Situation 1 A male client confided in an individual marital therapy session several weeks ago that he is gay, although his wife does not know this. The client's wife, whom you have also seen conjointly with him, calls you today troubled over the lack of progress in solving marital problems and asks you point-blank whether you think her husband could be gay.

Situation 2 You are forming a youth group in a state correctional facility. You know from past experience that youths sometimes make references in the group to previous offenses that they have committed without being apprehended. You also know that they may talk about plans to run from the institution or about indiscretions or misdemeanors they (or others) may have committed or plan to commit within the institution, such as smoking marijuana or stealing institutional supplies or property from peers or staff. Are you required to share all the information you learn in the group? How can you encourage trust and sharing if there are limits to confidentiality?

Situation 3 In conducting an intake interview with a client in a family agency, you observe that both of her young children are withdrawn. Further, one of the children is badly bruised, and the other, an infant, appears malnourished. Throughout the interview, the client seems defensive and suspicious and also ambivalent about having come for the interview. At one point, she states that she feels overwhelmed with her parenting responsibilities and is having difficulty in coping with her children. She also alludes to her fear that she may hurt them but then abruptly changes the subject. As you encourage her to return to the discussion of her problems with the children, your client says she has changed her mind about wanting help, takes her children in hand, and leaves the office.

Situation 4 You have seen a husband and wife and their adolescent daughter twice regarding relationship problems between the parents and the girl. The parents are both extremely negative and blaming in their attitudes toward their daughter, believing their troubles would be over if she would just "shape up." Today, during an individual interview with the girl, she breaks into tears and tells you that she is pregnant and plans to "go somewhere" with her boyfriend this weekend to get an abortion. She pleads with you not to tell her parents; she feels they would be extremely angry if they knew.

Situation 5 In a mental health agency, you have been working with a male client who has a history, when angered, of becoming violent and physically abusive. He has been under extreme psychological pressure lately because of problems relating to a recent separation from his wife. In an interview today, he is extremely angry, clenching his fists as he tells you that he has heard that his wife has initiated divorce proceedings and plans to move to another state. "If this is true," he loudly protests, "she is doing it to take the kids away from me, and I'll kill her rather than let her do that."

Situation 6 Some of your clients in your private practice rely on their health insurance to pay for their counseling. One client is addressing sensitive issues and is very concerned about anyone else knowing about his situation, especially his employer. Recent experiences have increased the severity of his condition, and you must share this with the care manager at the insurance company to get further treatment sessions approved. You have concerns about sharing the information with his insurer, especially via their voice mail system. The insurance company representative replies that this is the organizational policy and, if you cannot abide by it, you are unlikely to get approval for continuing treatment and unlikely to receive further referrals from them.

Situation 7 You and your spouse are advertising for a housekeeper to clean your home once a week. One of the applicants is a former client. In her letter she states that she needs the work very badly and hopes you won't discriminate against her just because she formerly saw you for service.

Situation 8 You are a social work student beginning your first field placement. At orientation, your supervisor informs you that you are not to let clients know that you are a student. She acknowledges that the school wants you to inform clients of your status as a social worker in training

but states that it is her opinion and agency policy that clients not be told. She feels it undermines their confidence in the services they are getting and raises problems in collecting fees for services.

Situation 9 You are a social worker in a high school that has strict rules about student health and safety. Specifically, the rules state that you cannot tell students about contraceptives or safe sex practices, even if asked, nor can you refer them to someone who is likely to tell them of such options. You are instructed to refer students with such problems or questions only to their parents or their family physician.

SKILL DEVELOPMENT EXERCISES IN OPERATIONALIZING CARDINAL VALUES

To assist you in developing skill in operationalizing the cardinal values in specific practice situations, we have provided a number of exercises with modeled responses. As you read each one, note which of the values is (are) germane to the situation and whether one of the six threats to acceptance and respect is involved in the client's messages. To refresh your memory, the values are as follows:

1. All human beings deserve access to the resources that they need to deal with life's problems and to develop their potentialities.
2. All human beings have intrinsic worth and dignity.
3. The uniqueness and individuality of each person are of value.
4. Given appropriate resources, human beings are capable of growth and change and should be supported in increasing choices in solving their problems and directing their lives.

Next, assume you are the client's practitioner and formulate a response that implements the relevant social work value. After completing each exercise, compare your response with the modeled response that follows the exercises. Bearing in mind that the modeled response is *only one of many* possible acceptable responses, analyze it and compare it with your own. By carefully completing these exercises, you will improve your competence in operationalizing the cardinal values in the varied and challenging situations encountered in direct social work practice.

Client Statements

1. *Group member [in first group session]:* Before I really open up and talk about myself, I need to be sure what I say isn't blabbed around to other people. *[Turning to practitioner]* How can I be sure that won't happen?

2. *Rural mother [living in dilapidated but neatly kept home; her children are shabbily dressed but appear healthy]:* You city folk don't seem to understand that you don't have to have a fancy home and a lot of luxuries to have a good life and raise healthy kids.

3. *Adolescent in correctional institution [after practitioner introduces self]:* So you want to help me, huh? I'll tell you how you can help. You can get me out of this damn place—that's how!

4. *Female client, age 21 [to mental health practitioner]:* Yeah, I know that kicking the habit was a victory of sorts. But I look at my life and I wonder what's there to live for. I've turned my family against me. I've sold my body to more rotten guys than I can count—just to get a fix. I've had VD three times. What do I have to offer anyone? I feel like my life has been one big cesspool.

5. *Teenage male [in a group session in a correctional setting]: [Takes off shoes and sprawls in his chair. His feet give off a foul odor; other members hold noses and make derisive comments. He responds defensively.]* Hey, get off my back, you creeps. What's the big deal about taking off my shoes?

6. *Female [initial interview in family counseling center]:* Before I talk about my marital problems, I need to let you know I'm a Seventh Day Adventist. Do you know anything about my church? I'm asking because a lot of our marital problems involve my religion.

7. *Client [as interview ends and time of next appointment is discussed]:* Oh, just work me into your schedule where it's convenient for you.

Just let me know when you want me to come, and I'll get here somehow.

8. *Female client [sixth interview]:* Maybe it sounds crazy, but I've been thinking this last week that you're not really interested in me as a person. I have the feeling I'm just someone for you to analyze or to write about. . . .

9. *Mexican American male client [in fifth group session, the members of which are largely Anglos]:* I have the feeling that you people look down on my people. It really pisses me off.

10. *Teenage female [caught with contraband in her possession by supervisor-counselor in a residential treatment center]:* Please don't report this, Mrs. Wilson. I've been doing better lately, and I've learned my lesson. You won't need to worry about me. I won't mess with drugs anymore.

11. *Client [observing practitioner taking notes during initial interview]:* I'm dying to know what you're writing down about me. But I guess I'm afraid, too—wondering if you think I'm a nut. Can I take a copy of your notes with me when we're done?

12. *Single female client, age 29 [in mental health center]:* I just heard about a job that opened up on the outskirts of town. It'd be right up my alley, but I'd have to drive because there's no bus service that comes within three miles. I don't drive, and I don't want to learn. I've always been afraid I might have an accident and kill someone. Everyone tells me I should learn to drive.

13. *Male parolee, age 27, who has a reputation as a con artist [in mandatory weekly visit to parole officer]:* Man, you've really got it made. Your office is really cool. I admire your taste in furnishing it. But then you deserve what you've got. You've probably got a terrific wife and kids, too. Is that their picture over there?

14. *Female client, age 34 [in third interview]:* I'm really uptight right now. I've got this tight feeling I get in my chest when I'm nervous. *[Pause]* Well, I guess I'll have to tell you if I expect to get anything out of this. *[Hesitant]* You know the marital problems we've talked about. Well, Jack doesn't know this, but I'm a lesbian. *[Blushes]* I've tried—I've really tried, but Jack doesn't turn me on.

I can't even tolerate sex unless I'm thinking about other women. Jack thinks something's wrong with him, but it's not his fault. *[Chin quivers.]*

15. ***Female, age 68*** *[to geriatric worker in county-sponsored housing complex]:* It's been hard since Ralph died a year ago. I didn't know how many things I depended on him for . . . even just for conversation and socializing. I just feel like I'm chained down now because I don't have any outside activities. Ralph always prodded me to learn to paint, because I've always been interested in watercolors. Do you think I'm too old to learn? I'm no kid, you know, and I might not have the time left in me to get good at it.

16. ***Black male probationer*** *[to white therapist]:* You're so damn smug. You say you want to help me, but I don't buy that crap. You don't know the first thing about black people. Man, I grew up where it's an accomplishment just to survive. What do you know about life in my world?

Modeled Responses

1. "Ginny raises a good point that concerns all of you. So that you can feel more comfortable about sharing personal feelings and experiences with the group, we need an understanding that each of you will keep what is shared in the strictest confidence. I can assure you that I'll keep information confidential myself, but I am interested in hearing from the rest of you regarding the question that Ginny is asking."

2. "It sounds like you're concerned I might look down on you because I'm from the city. I agree with you that luxuries aren't so important in raising children, and I can tell it's important to you to take good care of your children."

3. "I guess that's what I'd want also if I were in your situation. As a matter of fact, that's what I want for you, too. But we both know the review board won't release you until they feel you're prepared to make it on the outside. I can't get you out, but with your cooperation I can help you to make changes that will get you ready for release."

4. "I can see you're really down on yourself and feel pretty worthless. Even though you've done a lot that you feel bad about, it's important not to let your past ruin your future. I'm impressed at what it's taken to get and stay clean. That's a giant step in the right direction. I really think you can gradually rebuild your life, and with that you'll feel a lot better about yourself."

5. "I think we need to look as a group at how we can give Jim some helpful feedback rather than making fun of him. Let's talk about what just happened. Maybe you could begin, Jim, by sharing with the group what you're feeling just now."

6. "I have to confess I know just a little bit about your religion, which may make you wonder if I can appreciate your problems. I can assure you I'll do my best to understand if you're willing to take a chance with me. You might have to educate me a little bit, but I'm a willing learner. The most important thing, though, is your feelings about it. How do you feel about sharing your problems with me under these circumstances?"

7. "I appreciate that, but your time's important too. Let's see if we can find a mutually convenient time. I have openings at two and four. Would any of those times be convenient for you?"

8. "That sounds like a painful feeling—that I'm not personally concerned with you as an individual. I'd like to explore that with you further because that's not at all how I feel about you, and I'm uncomfortable being seen that way. I'd like to understand more how I've come across to you and how you've reached that conclusion."

9. "Arturo, I'm pleased you could share these feelings because I've noticed you've been pretty quiet in our sessions and I have wondered why. I'd like to know more about you as a person. Perhaps you could tell the group a little more about what you've been experiencing."

10. "I'm sorry you're still involved with drugs, Joy, because of the trouble it's caused you. I don't like to see you get into trouble but I have no choice. I have to report this. If I didn't, I'd be

breaking a rule myself by not reporting you. That wouldn't help you in the long run. Frankly, I'm going to keep worrying about you until I'm satisfied you're really sticking to the rules."

11. [Chuckling] "So you're wondering what I think of you. Well, you surely don't come across as a nut. Actually what I'm writing down is what we're talking about. What you tell me is important, and notes help to refresh my memory. You're welcome to look at my notes if you like. Actually, I would be interested in hearing a little more about your thoughts regarding what I might think of you."

12. "I can understand your desire not to harm anyone, but it sounds as though you have to pass up some choice opportunities because of your fear. I respect your right to decide for yourself about learning to drive. But it strikes me that you're letting yourself be at the mercy of that fear. Fears like that can be mastered, and if you're inclined to work on your fear of driving, I'd be happy to explore it with you."

13. "As a matter of fact it is, and I think they're pretty terrific. But we're here to talk about you, Rex. I'd like to hear how your job interview went."

14. "This has been very painful for you, sharing this problem with me. You've kept this inside for a long time, and I gather you've been afraid I'd condemn you. I'm pleased you brought it up so that we can work on it together. And rest assured I won't sit in judgment. It took some real courage on your part to talk about this, and I respect you for that."

15. "If you have the determination, I see no reason why you couldn't learn. There are some excellent instructors available in the adult education program. To be honest, I'm delighted you're considering it. You'd feel more independent, and it would open up a lot of possibilities. But what you feel is most important. What goes on inside you when you think about it?"

16. "I'd be phony if I said I understood all about being black and living in your neighborhood . . . and I'm sorry if it seems I'm being smug. I am interested in you, and I'd like to understand more about your life. How have you come to the conclusion that I can't help you?"

Notes

1. After goals have been mutually identified and roles in helping the relationship clarified, practitioners need not be hesitant to offer advice, for their expertise and input give impetus and direction to change efforts. Our point is that giving advice should not be the primary means of assisting clients.

2. Butz (1985) discusses related issues at length and makes a number of recommendations. To do justice to his discussion, however, would exceed space limitations, and we therefore refer you to his article.

3. Privileged communication is a legal right that protects clients from having a confidence revealed publicly from the witness stand during legal proceedings. Statutes that recognize privileged communication exempt certain professions from being legally compelled to reveal content disclosed in the context of a confidential relationship.

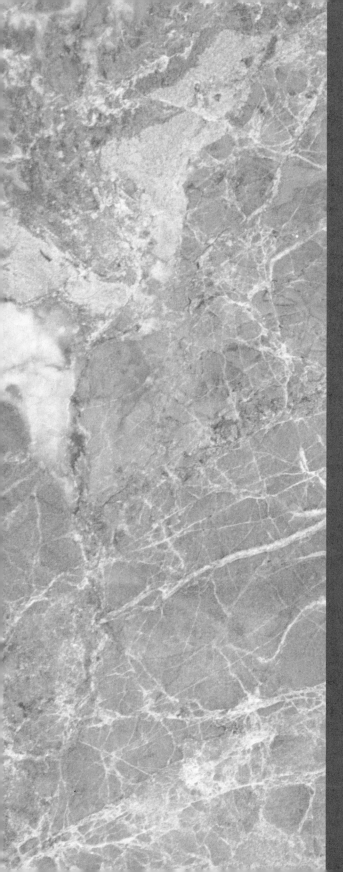

PART 2

Exploring, Assessing, and Planning

Part 2 of this book deals with processes and skills involved in the first phase of the helping process. We introduce this part by focusing in this chapter on setting the context and developing skills for building effective working relationships with clients, one of the two major objectives of initial interviews. We shift our focus in Chapter 6 to skills entailed in accomplishing the second major objective: to thoroughly explore clients' difficulties. In Chapter 7, we identify verbal and nonverbal patterns of communication that impede the development of effective working relationships.

In Chapters 8 and 9, we focus specifically on the process of assessment, dealing in Chapter 8 with explaining the process, sources of information, delineation of clients' problems, and questions to be addressed during the process. In Chapter 9, we focus on the multidimensionality of ecological assessment, delineating the intrapersonal, interpersonal, cultural, and environmental systems and how they reciprocally interact to produce and maintain problems.

In Chapter 10, the focus narrows to an examination of family systems. We discuss various types of family structures and consider the various dimensions of family systems that must be addressed in assessing family functioning, including the cultural context of families.

In Chapter 11, the focus changes to groups. We discuss purposes of groups, selection of group members, arrangements to be made, and how to begin group process. We then focus on various factors to be considered in assessing the functioning of groups.

Part 2 concludes with Chapter 12, which deals with negotiating goals and contracts with both voluntary and involuntary clients. Included in this chapter are theory, skills, and guidelines that address these processes, which lay the foundation for the process of goal attainment.

CHAPTER 5

Relationship-Building Skills: Communicating with Empathy and Authenticity

CHAPTER OVERVIEW

Social work relationships occur in a context. Potential clients have contact with a social worker usually through an agency setting, public or private. An important step in beginning to develop such a relationship is to clarify what the potential client can expect from the contact. The chapter continues by presenting the facilitative conditions and applying them in learning how to respond empathically. Additional guidelines are presented to assist you in acting with appropriate authenticity, self-disclosure, and assertiveness. The chapter contains many exercises to assist you in that learning.

ROLES OF THE PARTICIPANTS

Clients often have little understanding of the helping process and may have expectations that are discrepant from those of the social worker, which may impair the helping process. The findings of two classic research studies (Aronson & Overall, 1966; Mayer & Timms, 1969) revealed that unacknowledged discrepancies in expectations produced dissatisfactions and higher rates of discontinuance from therapy of lower-class clients as compared with middle-class clients. Moreover, H. Perlman (1968) found that she and two other social workers were able to lower the drop-out rate

of clients during the intake process by concentrating on eliciting clients' conceptions and expectations of the helping process and by clarifying discrepancies between expectations and what realistically could be offered. Equally important, Perlman found that the rate of return could be predicted more accurately when it was determined whether or not clarity of expectation and mutual agreement were achieved in the interviews. The potency of using a "role induction interview" to increase the continuance of clients beyond the initial interview has been demonstrated by Hoehn-Saric et al. (1964). Clients prepared by role induction continued contact at a higher rate and fared better in treatment than control clients who received no special preparation. Similar findings have been reported by Zwick and Atkinson (1985), who used a videotape for "pretherapy orientation." More recently, in a study of a group program for low-income abusive mothers, socialization of the mothers to group norms was enhanced by pregroup induction procedures (Lovell, Reid, & Richey, 1992). Kooden has described how a gay male therapist can serve as a model for socialization of gay adolescents through self-disclosure (Kooden, 1994). Finally, socialization takes on an even more significant role in work with mentally retarded clients who are in the process of deinstitutionalization (C. Whitman, 1995). The following guidelines will assist you to achieve similar positive results in role clarification.

1. *Determine the clients' expectations.* The varied expectations that clients bring to initial sessions include lectures, magical solutions, advice giving, changing other family members, and so on. In the previously cited study conducted by Perlman, only 6 of the 26 clients had realistic expectations of what the social worker might do with or for them. With minority clients, especially those who are inexperienced with professional helping relationships, sensitively exploring expectations and modifying one's role when indicated are critical.

Clients sometimes convey their expectations without prompting from a social worker. For example, after reciting the difficulties created by her son, a mother declared, "We were hoping you could talk with him and help him understand how much he is hurting us." Notice that the mother's "hope" involved a request for specific action by the social worker. When clients thus express their expectations spontaneously, you have the opportunity to deal with those that are unrealistic. Frequently, however, clients do not openly express their expectations, and you will need to elicit them. It is important not to probe too far into expectations until you have established rapport, because the client's request often turns out to be a most intimate revelation. Seeking disclosure too soon thus may put clients on the defensive. The social worker thus should seek to weave exploration of clients' expectations into the natural flow of the session sometime after clients have had ample opportunity to report their difficulties and to discern the sensitive understanding and goodwill of the social worker.

If voluntary clients have not spontaneously revealed their requests and timing appears appropriate, you can elicit their requests by asking a question similar to one of the following:

- "How do you hope (or wish) I (or the agency) can assist (or help) you?"

- "As you thought about coming, what were your ideas as to the nature of help you wanted?"

For potential clients who were referred or mandated for service, such requests may be elicited by saying:

- "We have explored the reasons why you were referred/required to seek our service. But I would like to know what *you* hope to gain from this process."

2. *Briefly explain the nature of the helping process, and define your relationship as partners seeking a solution to their difficulties.* Clients commonly hope that social workers will give them advice that they can implement and thereby quickly remedy their problematic situations. They will relinquish these unrealistic expectations with a minimum of disappointment and discouragement in favor of a more realistic understanding if you clarify how you can actually be of help and why it would be less useful to approach their problems in the manner they expected. It is very important to convey your intent to help clients find the best possible solution and to clarify that offering advice prematurely would likely be a disservice to them. In the absence of such an explanation, clients may erroneously conclude you are unwilling to meet their expectations because of a lack of concern for them. In this regard, Mayer and Timms (1969) found that clients who were dissatisfied with service for interpersonal problems reasoned that the counselor's failure to give concrete advice stemmed from a lack of interest and desire to help. Taking the time to explore expectations and to clarify how you can help thus prevents clients from drawing unwarranted negative conclusions that may result in discontinuance.

At this point, it is important to clarify that we are not arguing against the value of advice. Our point is that to be effective, advice must be based on adequate knowledge of the dynamics of a problem and of the participants in it. Such a grasp is unlikely to be achieved in an initial session. You can assist many clients to modify unrealistic expectations and clarify your respective roles through a message similar to the following:

- "I can sense the urgency you feel in wanting to solve your problems. I wish I could give advice that would lead to solving them. You've probably already had plenty of advice, because most people offer advice freely. It has been my experience, though, that what works for one person (couple or family) may not work at all for another."

- "As I see it, our task is to work together in considering a number of possible options so that you can decide what solution fits best for you and your situation. In the long run, that's what will work best for you. But it takes some time and a lot of thought."

Notice that the preceding role clarification embodies the following essential elements referred to earlier: (1) acknowledging and empathizing with the client's unrealistic expectation and sense of urgency, (2) expressing helpful intent, (3) explaining why the client's unrealistic expectation cannot be fulfilled, and (4) as part of the social worker's expertise, clarifying the helping process and defining a working partnership that places responsibility on the client for actively participating and ultimately making choices as to the courses of action to be taken in solving problems.

When couples seek help for relationship problems, they commonly view the partner as the source of difficulties and have the unrealistic expectation that the couples counselor will influence the partner to shape up. Because this expectation is so pervasive, we often elicit partners' expectations early in the initial session (individual or conjoint) and clarify the helping role, thereby setting the stage for more productive use of the exploration to follow. Clarifying the process early in the session tends to diminish mutual blaming and competing. Moreover, partners are less likely to respond defensively when the social worker refuses to be drawn into the "blame game" and focuses instead on assisting each person to become aware of his or her part in the difficulties. The following excerpt of an actual session typifies our approach to role clarification with couples.

Social worker: How much understanding do you have about how couples counseling works?

First partner: Not very much, really. We just know we need help because we're fighting all the time. [*Second partner in agreement.*]

Social worker: Perhaps it would be helpful if I took just a few minutes to explain how I work with couples. Would that be agreeable with you?

Both partners [*nod affirmatively*]: Yes, we'd like that.

Social worker: OK, then, I'll explain it as best I can and give you a chance to ask any questions. It's important that all three of us have the same understanding about what we're going to be doing. [*Partners nod in understanding.*] As I see it, my role is to help each of you to better understand yourself and your partner.

Marital problems usually are caused by the fact that the needs of one or both partners aren't being met adequately. Lots of factors can block the meeting of important needs, and when they do, problems in relationships develop. My job is to help each of you to understand your partner's needs better and to be more aware of your own needs so that you can express them clearly to your partner. Accomplishing that means you have to communicate in such a way that you really understand each other better. So another part of my job is to help you to communicate more effectively.

Second partner: Good! We need that. Our communication is really bad. We can't seem to talk without getting into a fight.

Social worker: Well, we'll need to work on that. Part of my job will be to help you see what's going wrong in your communication and to help you get back on track by learning new ways of communicating. In some ways, that means I'll function much as a teacher at times.

First partner: That's OK. If it will help, I'm willing to learn.

Social worker: That willingness will be a real asset. Another thing that's important to understand is that I can't help by getting involved in assigning blame to one of you or the other. It's been my experience that most partners in a relationship believe the other person is causing the difficulties, and many of their struggles involve blaming each other. Usually it isn't one or the other who's at fault. Both partners contribute to the difficulties, and my task is to assist each of you to see the part you play in them. It's important that you understand this. Otherwise, you might think I'm siding with your partner when I focus on your part. I won't be taking sides, but if it feels to you like I am, please let me know. Otherwise, you're likely to resent me, and I won't even be aware of it. To work effectively together we'll have to be open with each other. I'll be open with you, but I have to expect the same of you. [*Pause*]

Further clarification of the roles of the participants will occur later in the session as the participants negotiate goals and formulate a contract.

Implied in the above excerpt is another aspect of the client's role—to be open in sharing feelings, thoughts, and events. By explaining the rationale for openness and by expressing your intent to communicate openly, you enhance clients' receptiveness to this factor. The following illustrates one way of explaining this aspect of the client's role:

• "For you to benefit to the fullest, you will need to be as open as possible with me. That means not holding back troubling feelings, thoughts, or events that are important. I can understand you and your difficulties only if you're open and honest with me. Only you know what you think and feel; I can know only as you share with me. Sometimes it's painful to share certain thoughts and feelings, but often those are the very feelings that trouble us the most. If you do hold back, you'll need to remind yourself you may be letting yourself down. If you're finding it difficult to share certain things, let me know. Discussing what's happening inside you—why it's difficult—may make it easier to discuss those painful things."

• "I'll be open and honest with you, too. If you have any questions or would like to know more about me, please ask. I'll be frank with you. I may not answer every question, but I'll explain why if I don't."

To enhance clients' participation in the helping process, it is also important to emphasize that they can accelerate their progress by working on their difficulties between appointments. Some clients mistakenly believe that change will result largely from what occurs in sessions. In actuality, the content of sessions is far less significant than how clients apply information gained. The following excerpt illustrates clarifying this aspect of a client's responsibility:

• "We'll want to progress toward your goals as rapidly as possible. One way you can hasten your progress is by working hard between our sessions. That means carrying out tasks you've agreed to, applying what we talk about in your daily life, and making mental notes or actually writing down thoughts, feelings, and events that relate to your problems so we can consider them in your next session. Actually, what you do between sessions is more important in accomplishing your goals than the session itself. We'll be together only a brief time each week. The rest of the week you have opportunities to apply what we talk about and plan together."

Still another aspect of the client's role involves keeping appointments. This factor is obvious, but discussing it emphasizes clients' responsibilities and prepares them to cope constructively with obstacles that may cause them to fail or to cancel appointments. The following is an example of a message that clarifies this aspect of the client's role:

• "As we work together, it will be most important for you to keep your appointments. Unforeseen things such as illness happen occasionally, of course, and we can change appointments when this happens. At times, however, you may find yourself feeling discouraged or doubting if coming here really helps. It's also possible you may feel upset over something I've said or done and find yourself not wanting to see me. I won't knowingly say or do anything to offend you, but you may have some troubling feelings toward me anyway. The important thing is that you not miss your appointment, because when you're discouraged or upset we need to talk about it. I know that may not be easy, but it will help you to work out your troubled feelings. If you miss your appointment, you may find it even harder to return."

A final factor conveys that difficulties are inherent in the process of making change. Clarifying this reality further prepares clients for the inevitable mixed feelings they will experience. By anticipating these difficulties, clients are enabled to conceive of feelings and experiences as natural obstacles that must be surmounted, rather than yield to them or feel defeated. An explanation about these predictable difficulties similar to the following clarifies the vicissitudes of the change process:

• "We've talked about goals you want to achieve. Accomplishing them won't be easy. Making changes is seldom accomplished without a difficult and sometimes painful struggle. People usually have ups and downs as they seek to make changes. If you understand this, you won't become so discouraged and feel like throwing in the towel. I don't mean to paint a grim picture. In fact, I feel very hopeful about the prospects of your attaining your goals. At the same time, it won't be easy, and I don't want to mislead you. The important thing is that you share your feelings so that we can keep on top of them."

Over the years, numerous clients have reported retrospectively that they appreciated explanations similar to the preceding. When the going became rough and they began to waver in pursuing their goals, they recalled that such discouragement was natural and, rather than discontinuing, mustered the determination to persevere.

In addition to clarifying the client's role, it is vital to clarify your own role. Again, it is desirable to stress you will be a partner in helping clients to understand their difficulties more fully. Because you have an outside vantage point, you may be able to assist them to see their difficulties in a new perspective and to consider solutions they may have overlooked. We recommend that you clarify further that although you will be an active partner in considering possible remedial actions, the final decisions rest with them. You will help them to

weigh alternatives, but your desire is to see them develop their strengths and to exercise their capacities for independent action to the fullest possible extent. It is also important to emphasize that one of your functions is to assist them in focusing on strengths and the incremental growth they achieve. Stress that although you will actively assume this function in the initial stage of the helping process, you will be encouraging them to learn to recognize their own strengths and growth independently.

Another aspect of the helping role that you should clarify for clients is that you will assist them in anticipating obstacles they will encounter in striving to attain their goals and will help them formulate strategies to surmount these obstacles. Clarifying this facet of your role further reinforces the reality that change is difficult but you will be with and behind them in offering support and direction. You might share that each family has its own situation and values and it will be your job to get to know them from their point of view in order to help them plan what makes sense for them to do.

There are special hurdles in developing productive working relationships between social workers and potential clients in mandated settings, because the mandated client did not seek the contact and often perceives it as contrary to his or her interests. Notice how, in the following dialogue, the social worker begins to develop expectations about a collaborative relationship.

Client: I didn't like the earlier workers because they came into my house telling me what I can do and can't do. One thing I don't like is someone telling me what I can do with my kids and what I can't.

Social worker: It sounds like you have had a negative experience with earlier workers.

Client: Yeah, I did. I did not like it at all because they were telling me what I should do.

Social worker: I'm going to have a different approach with you because I don't feel that I know it all; you know best about the situation occurring in your own family and in your own life. I will want you to tell me about the problems you are concerned about and how we can best resolve those together.

Client: OK.

Social worker: So my job will be to develop a case plan with you. I won't be the one to say, "This is what you need to do." I want you to have input in that and to say, "Well, I feel I can do this." I will be willing to share ideas with you as we decide what to work on and how to do it. I will need to include any court-mandated requirements, such as our need to be meeting together, in the agreement. However, I want you to have a lot of say in determining what we work on and how.

THE FACILITATIVE CONDITIONS

The social worker uses communication skills as building blocks to assist in the development of a productive working relationship. The present chapter is concerned with two of the three skills embodied in what have been variously referred to as the facilitative conditions or core conditions in helping relationships. These conditions or skills were originally denoted by Carl Rogers (1957) as empathy, unconditional positive regard, and congruence. Other terms have since evolved, and we shall refer to the conditions as empathy, respect or nonpossessive warmth, and authenticity or genuineness. Because we addressed nonpossessive warmth or respect at length in Chapter 4, we limit our focus in this chapter to empathy and authenticity.

Research (primarily in psychology) has documented that the conditions are associated with positive outcomes. One important study by a social worker (Nugent, 1992) has further documented the effectiveness of these conditions in facilitating positive helping relationships. It is thus vital that social workers master these skills. While they are particularly useful in treatment situations with voluntary clients, we will describe ways that such skills

can be building blocks in both involuntary relationships and other situations such as discharge planning that do not have therapy as the primary focus (Bennett, Legon, & Zilberfein, 1989).

EMPATHIC COMMUNICATION

Empathic communication involves the ability of the social worker to perceive accurately and sensitively the inner feelings of the client and to communicate understanding of these feelings in language attuned to the client's experiencing of the moment. The first dimension of empathy, that of empathic recognition, is a precondition of the second dimension, that is, demonstrating through accurate reflection of feelings that the social worker comprehends the client's inner experiencing.

Empathic communication plays a vital role in nurturing and sustaining the helping relationship and providing the vehicle through which the social worker becomes emotionally significant and influential in the client's life. In mandated circumstances in which involuntary clients are not seeking a helping relationship, conveying empathic understanding reduces threat and defensiveness, conveys interest and helpful intent, and creates an atmosphere conducive to behavior change. In addition, many clients live in environments that constrict resources and opportunities. Social worker empathy with the social and economic context of problems is an important adjunct to empathy with personal experiencing (Keefe, 1978).

In responding to clients' feelings, social workers must avoid being misled by conventional facades used to conceal emotions. Thus, the empathic communicator responds to feelings that underlie such messages as "Oh, no, it doesn't really matter," or "I don't care what he does!" These messages often mask disappointment or hurt, as do such messages as "I don't need anyone" when experiencing painful loneliness, or "I don't let anyone hurt me" when one is finding rejection hard to bear. To enter the client's private world of practical experience, the social worker must also avoid making personal interpretations and judgments of the client's private logic and feelings that, in superficial contacts, might appear as weak, foolish, or undesirable.

Being empathically attuned involves not only grasping the client's immediately evident feelings but, in a mutually shared, exploratory process, identifying underlying emotions and discovering the meaning and personal significance of feelings and behavior. In getting in touch with camouflaged feelings and meanings, the social worker must tune in not only to verbal messages but to more subtle cues, including facial expressions, tone of voice, tempo of speech, and postural cues and gestures that amplify and sometimes contradict verbal meanings. Such nonverbal cues as blushing, crying, pausing, stammering, changing voice intonation, clenching jaws or fists, pursing the lips, lowering the head, or shifting the posture often reveal the presence of distressing feelings and thoughts.

Empathic communication also involves "stepping into the shoes of another," in the sense of attempting to perceive the world of experience of the other person. When clients feel pressure from an involuntary referral, such empathy includes conveying that the social worker understands and is aware of that pressure and how it feels. The listener, however, must remain outside and avoid being overwhelmed by the fears, anger, joys, and hurts of that person, though deeply sensing the meaning and significance of these feelings for the other. "Being with" the client involves the social worker's focusing intensely on the client's affective state without losing perspective or taking on the emotions experienced by the client.

A person who experiences feelings in common with another person and is similarly affected by whatever the other person is experiencing usually responds sympathetically rather than empathically. Sympathetic responding, which depends on emotional and intellectual accord, involves supporting and condoning the other person's feelings (e.g., "I'd feel the same way you do if I were in your position" or "I think you're right"), whereas empathic responding involves understanding the other person's feelings and circumstances without taking that person's position (e.g., "I sense you're feeling . . . " or "You seem to be saying . . . "). When social workers support clients' feelings, clients may feel no need to examine their behavior or circumstances and may not engage in the process of self-exploration so vital to growth and change. In such instances, clients look to the social worker to change the behavior of other persons who play a significant role in their problems. Retaining separateness and objectivity thus is a critical dimension in the helping process, for when social workers assume the client's feelings and positions, they lose not only vital perspective but the ability to be helpful as well.

Being empathic involves more than recognizing clients' feelings. Social workers must also respond verbally and nonverbally in ways that affirm their understanding of clients' inner experiencing. It is not unusual for a person to experience empathic feelings for another without conveying them in any way to the second party. High-level empathy requires skill in verbally and nonverbally demonstrating understanding. A common mistake made by social workers is to tell the client, "I understand how you feel." Rather than produce a sense of being understood, such a response often creates doubts in the client's mind about the social worker's perceptiveness because specific demonstration of understanding is lacking. Indeed, use of this response may mean that the social worker has not explored the client's feelings sufficiently to fully grasp the significance of the problematic situation. To convey unmistakably, "I am with you; I understand," the social worker must respond empathically. Use of this skill creates an ambience of acceptance and understanding in which the client is more likely to risk sharing deeper and more personal feelings.

Later in the chapter, we present theory and exercises for developing skill in empathic responding. Initially, we provide a list of affective words and phrases to assist you in expanding your vocabulary so that you can meet the challenge of responding to the wide range of emotions experienced by clients. We also provide exercises to help you to refine your ability to perceive the feelings of others—a prerequisite to the mastery of empathic communication. To assist you to discern levels of empathy, we include a rating scale for empathic responding, accompanied by examples of varying levels of social worker responses and exercises. These exercises will help you to gain mastery of empathic communication at an effective working level.

DEVELOPING PERCEPTIVENESS TO FEELINGS

A vital and universal aspect of human experiencing, feelings or emotions exert a powerful influence on behavior and often play a central role in the problems of clients. Applicants or voluntary clients often seek the helping relationship with openness and hope that they will explore both their concerns and their related feelings. Involuntary clients experience strong feelings but have not sought a helping relationship for dealing with them (Cingolani, 1984). Hence, use of the skills sometimes takes a slightly different course with them, as a goal is to express empathy with the *situation* the involuntary client experiences and the feelings related to them.

To respond to the broad spectrum of emotions and feeling states presented by clients, the social worker must be fully aware of the diversity of human emotion. Further, the social worker needs a rich vocabulary of words and expressions that not only reflect client feelings accurately but also capture the intensity of those feelings. For example, there are dozens of descriptive feeling words to express anger, including *furious, aggravated, vexed, provoked, put out, irritated, impatient*—all of which express different shades and intensities of this feeling. When used judiciously, such words serve to give sharp and exact focus to the feelings of clients.

Possessing and utilizing a rich vocabulary of affective words and phrases that accurately reflect client feelings is a skill that often is not developed by even experienced social workers. It is important to realize that high-level empathic responding involves first a thinking process and, second, a responding process. A deficient vocabulary of feelings limits social workers' ability to conceptualize and hence to reflect the full intensity and range of feelings experienced by clients.

It has been our experience that beginning social workers have a limited range of feeling words from which to draw in conveying empathy. Although there are literally hundreds of words that may be used to capture feelings, learners often limit themselves to, and use to excess, a few terms, such as *upset* or *frustrated,* losing much of the richness of client messages in the process.

The accompanying lists illustrate the wide range of expressions available for social workers' use in responding to clients' feelings. It must be noted that using feeling words in a discriminating fashion is not only important in empathic responding but indispensable in relating authentically as well. Becoming a competent professional involves a maturing process whereby social workers develop not only the capacity to deeply share the inner experiencing of others, but also a way to express their own personal feelings constructively.

AFFECTIVE WORDS AND PHRASES
Competence/Strength

convinced you can	confident
sense of mastery	powerful
potent	courageous
resolute	determined
strong	influential
brave	impressive
forceful	inspired
successful	secure
in charge	in control
well-equipped	committed
sense of accomplishment	daring
feeling one's oats	effective
sure	sense of conviction
trust in yourself	self-reliant
sharp	able
adequate	firm
capable	on top of it
can cope	important

Competence/Strength (continued)

up to it	ready
equal to it	skillful

Happiness/Satisfaction

elated	superb
ecstatic	on cloud nine
on top of the world	organized
fantastic	splendid
exhilarated	jubilant
terrific	euphoric
delighted	marvelous
excited	enthusiastic
thrilled	great
super	in high spirits
joyful	cheerful
elevated	happy
lighthearted	wonderful
glowing	jolly
neat	glad
fine	pleased
good	contented
hopeful	mellow
satisfied	gratified
fulfilled	tranquil
serene	calm
at ease	

Caring/Love

adore	loving
infatuated	enamored
cherish	idolize
worship	attached to
devoted to	tenderness toward
affection for	hold dear
prize	caring
fond of	regard
respect	admire
concern for	taken with
turned on	trust
close	esteem
hit it off	value
warm toward	friendly
like	positive toward
accept	

Depression/Discouragement

anguished	in despair

Depression/Discouragement (continued)

dreadful	miserable
dejected	disheartened
rotten	awful
horrible	terrible
hopeless	gloomy
dismal	bleak
depressed	despondent
grieved	grim
brokenhearted	forlorn
distressed	downcast
sorrowful	demoralized
pessimistic	tearful
weepy	down in the dumps
deflated	blue
lost	melancholy
in the doldrums	lousy
kaput	unhappy
down	low
bad	blah
disappointed	sad
below par	

Inadequacy/Helplessness

utterly	worthless
good for nothing	washed up
powerless	helpless
impotent	crippled
inferior	emasculated
useless	finished
like a failure	impaired
inadequate	whipped
defeated	stupid
incompetent	puny
inept	clumsy
overwhelmed	ineffective
like a klutz	lacking
awkward	deficient
unable	incapable
small	insignificant
like a wimp	unimportant
over the hill	incomplete
immobilized	like a puppet
at the mercy of	inhibited
insecure	lacking confidence
unsure of self	uncertain
weak	inefficient
unfit	

Anxiety/Tension

terrified	frightened
intimidated	horrified
desperate	panicky
terror-stricken	paralyzed
frantic	stunned
shocked	threatened
afraid	scared
stage fright	dread
vulnerable	fearful
apprehensive	jumpy
shaky	distrustful
butterflies	awkward
defensive	uptight
tied in knots	rattled
tense	fidgety
jittery	on edge
nervous	anxious
unsure	hesitant
timid	shy
worried	uneasy
bashful	embarrassed
ill at ease	doubtful
uncomfortable	self-conscious
insecure	alarmed
restless	

Rejection/Offensive

crushed	destroyed
ruined	pained
wounded	devastated
tortured	cast off
betrayed	discarded
knifed in the back	hurt
belittled	abused
depreciated	criticized
censured	discredited
disparaged	laughed at
maligned	mistreated
ridiculed	devalued
scorned	mocked
scoffed at	used
exploited	debased
slammed	slandered
impugned	cheapened
mistreated	put down
slighted	neglected
overlooked	minimized
let down	disappointed
unappreciated	taken for granted
taken lightly	underestimated
degraded	discounted
shot down	

Confusion/Troubledness

bewildered	puzzled
tormented by	baffled
perplexed	overwhelmed
trapped	confounded
in a dilemma	befuddled
in a quandary	at loose ends
going around in circles	mixed-up
disorganized	in a fog
troubled	adrift
lost	disconcerted
frustrated	floored
flustered	in a bind
torn	ambivalent
disturbed	conflicted
stumped	feeling pulled apart
mixed feelings about	uncertain
unsure	uncomfortable
bothered	uneasy
undecided	

Anger/Resentment

furious	enraged
livid	seething
could chew nails	fighting mad
burned up	hateful
bitter	galled
vengeful	resentful
indignant	irritated
hostile	pissed off
have hackles up	had it with
upset with	bent out of shape
agitated	annoyed
got dander up	bristle
dismayed	uptight
disgusted	bugged
turned off	put out
miffed	ruffled
irked	perturbed
ticked off	teed off
chagrined	griped

Anger/Resentment (continued)

cross	impatient
infuriated	violent

Loneliness

all alone in the universe	isolated
abandoned	totally alone
forsaken	forlorn
lonely	alienated
estranged	rejected
remote	alone
apart from others	shut out
left out	excluded
lonesome	distant
aloof	cut off

Guilt/Embarrassment

sick at heart	unforgivable
humiliated	disgraced
degraded	horrible
mortified	exposed
branded	could crawl in a hole
like two cents	ashamed
guilty	remorseful
crummy	really rotten
lost face	demeaned
foolish	ridiculous
silly	stupid
egg on face	regretful
wrong	embarrassed
at fault	in error
responsible for	goofed
lament	blew it

Use of the Lists of Affective Words and Phrases

The lists of affective words and phrases may be used with the exercises at the end of the chapter to formulate responses that capture the nature of feelings expressed by clients. Note that involuntary clients are more likely to initially experience the emotions of anger, resentment, guilt, embarrassment, rejection, confusion, tension, inadequacy, helplessness, depression, and discouragement. After you have initially responded to "feeling messages," check the lists to determine if there are other words and phrases that might more accurately capture the client's feelings. Also, scan the lists to see if the client's message involves feelings in addition to those you identified. The lists may similarly assist you in checking out the accuracy of your reflective responses as you review taped sessions.

We suggest you read the lists aloud several times to aid you in making the feeling words and phrases part of your working vocabulary. We further recommend that you memorize five or six words or phrases in each category to further your mastery of feeling language. Developing an alertness to affective words used in the communication media, in conversations with acquaintances, or in reading material and repeating them to yourself will also assist you in expanding your feeling vocabulary. You will increasingly employ words that you rarely, if ever, used before. As you broaden your vocabulary you will experience growing confidence in your ability to formulate feeling responses in sessions. A further benefit will be that your feeling responses will assist your clients to experience their emotions more keenly, thereby pinpointing some of the distress they are feeling.

Acquisition of a wider range of emotional vocabulary is a step toward expressing greater empathy for clients. You are conveying your understanding and compassion for what they are experiencing. Since many clients want to change their situations as well as their feelings about it, conveying empathy is the first step toward helping them work on those concerns.

Although the lists of affective words and phrases are not exhaustive, they encompass many of the feelings and emotions frequently encountered in the helping process. Feeling words are subsumed under 11 categories, running the gamut of emotions from intense anguish and pain, such as grieved, terrified, bewildered, enraged, and powerless, to positive feeling states such as joy, elation, ecstasy, bliss, and pride in accomplishment. Given our emphasis on clients' strengths in this book, we have taken care to include a grouping of terms to assist social workers in capturing clients' feelings related to growth, strengths, and competence.

Feeling words in each category are roughly graduated by intensity, with words conveying strong intensity grouped toward the beginning of each category and words of moderate to mild intensity toward the end. In responding to client messages, the social worker should choose feeling words that accurately match the intensity of the feelings the client is experiencing. To illustrate, picture an African American client in a drug aftercare program who has returned to work as a meter reader. He reports that when he knocked on the door in a largely white suburb intending to read the meter, the elderly white woman would not let him in, despite his wearing his picture identification name tag on his uniform. "I was so low down and depressed. What can you do? I am doing my thing to keep straight and I can't even do my job because I'm black." Such a response appropriately calls for an intense response by the social worker: "Sounds like you felt demeaned and humiliated that you couldn't do your job because of this woman's fear of black people. You felt discriminated against, disrespected, yet you did not let these humiliating feelings carry you back to drug use—you kept your head on course, keeping straight, and not being stopped by other people's perceptions."

In addition to using words that accurately reflect the intensity of the client's feelings, it is important to respond with a tone of voice and nonverbal gestures and expressions that similarly reflect the intensity of feelings conveyed by the verbal response. Further, the proper intensity of affect may also be conveyed by using appropriate qualifying words. For example, "You feel (somewhat) (quite) (very) (extremely) discouraged by your low performance on the entrance test."

Clients' messages may also contain multiple feelings. Consider, for instance, the following client message: "I don't know what to do about my teenage daughter. I know that she's on drugs, but she shuts me out and won't talk to me. All she wants is to be out with her friends, to be left alone. There are times when I think she really dislikes me."

Feeling words that would capture the various facets of this message include *confused, bewildered,*

alarmed, troubled, overwhelmed, lost, desperate, worried, frightened, alienated, rejected, and *hurt.* A response that included all of these feeling words would be extremely lengthy and overwhelming to the client. However, a well-rounded empathic response should embody at least several of the surface feelings, such as worried and confused, and with appropriate timing. The social worker might also bring deeper-level feelings into focus, as explained in the following paragraphs.

Notice in the preceding client message that many feelings were implied but not explicitly expressed by the client. Some of these emotions would likely be just beyond the client's level of awareness but could easily be recognized if they were drawn to the client's attention. For example, the client might emphatically confirm a social worker response that sensitively identifies the hurt, rejection, and even anger inherent in the client's message. Yet without the social worker's assistance, the client might not develop full awareness of those deeper-level feelings.

In responding to client messages, you must be able to distinguish between readily apparent feelings and probable deeper feelings. In the early phase of the helping process, the social worker's objectives of developing a working relationship and creating a climate of understanding are best accomplished by using a reciprocal level of empathy—that is, focusing on the client's immediately evident feelings. As the client perceives your genuine effort and commitment to understand, that experience of being "empathically received" gradually creates a low-threat environment that obviates the need for self-protection.

Note, however, that clients from oppressed groups, such as the African American client in the previous situation, may rightly both feel better understood by the social worker and continue to feel disillusioned by an alien environment. It is important to acknowledge those feelings about the environment. Cingolani writes of the "negotiated relationship" with such clients in place of the "helping relationship" (Cingolani, 1984). But even in negotiated relationships, increased trust is essential. That trust may be gained, however, by actions outside the session that indicate that the social worker is trustworthy and has the client's best interest at heart, as well as verbal conveyance of empathy in the session. Similarly, Ivanoff, Blythe, and Tripodi (1994) suggest that too much emphasis on empathy can feel manipulative to involuntary clients (p. 21).

With voluntary clients, the resultant climate of trust sets the stage for self-exploration, a prerequisite to self-understanding, which in turn facilitates behavior change. This positive ambience prepares the way for the use of "additive" or "expanded" levels of empathy to reach for underlying feelings, as well as hidden meanings and goals of behavior. However, attempting to explore underlying feelings during the early phase of the helping process is counterproductive. Uncovering feelings beyond the client's awareness before a working relationship is firmly established tends to mobilize opposition and may precipitate premature termination. Involuntary clients in a negotiated relationship may never desire such uncovering of deeper feelings and may find exploration for them to be intrusive (p. 21).

EXERCISES IN IDENTIFYING SURFACE AND UNDERLYING FEELINGS

In the following exercise, identify both the apparent surface feelings and the probable underlying feelings embodied in the client's message. Remember that most of the feelings in the messages are only implied, as clients often do not use feeling words. As you complete the exercise, read each message and write down the feelings involved. Then scan the lists of affective words and phrases to see if you can improve your response. After you have responded to all four messages, check the feeling words and phrases you identified with those given by the authors at the end of the chapter. If the feelings you identified were similar in meaning to those of the authors, consider your responses accurate. If they were not, review the

client messages to see if you can identify clues about the client's feelings that you overlooked.

CLIENT STATEMENTS

1. *Elderly client:* I know my children have busy lives. It is hard for them to have time to call me.

   Apparent feelings:

   Probable deeper feelings:

2. *Client:* I don't know if my husband loves me or not. He says he cares, but he doesn't pay much attention to me, particularly when we're with other people. Sometimes he even seems ashamed of me.

   Apparent feelings:

   Probable deeper feelings:

3. *Client:* When I was a teenager, I thought that when I was married and had my own children, I would never yell at them like my mother yelled at me. Yet, here I am doing the same things with Sonny. [*Tearful*]

   Apparent feelings:

   Probable deeper feelings:

4. *African American client in child welfare system:* The system is against people like me. People think that we drink, beat our kids, lay up on welfare, and take drugs.

   Apparent feelings:

   Probable deeper feelings:

Exercises at the end of this chapter for formulating reciprocal empathic responses will also assist you in increasing your perceptiveness to feelings.

ACCURATELY CONVEYING EMPATHY

Empathic responding is a fundamental yet complex skill that requires systematic practice and extensive effort to achieve competency. Skill in empathic communication has no limit or ceiling; rather, this sill is always in the process of "becoming." In listening to their taped sessions, even highly skilled professionals discover feelings they overlooked. Many social workers, however, do not fully utilize or selectively employ empathic responding. They fail to grasp the versatility of this skill and its potency in influencing clients and fostering growth in moment-by-moment transactions. In fact, some social workers dismiss the need for training in empathic responding, mistakenly believing themselves to be empathic in contacts with clients.

Research findings indicate that beginning social work students relate at empathic levels considerably lower than the levels necessary to work effectively with clients (Fischer, 1978; Larsen, 1975). These findings are not totally unexpected, for comparatively few people are inherently helpful in the sense of relating naturally with high levels of empathy or any of the other core conditions.

Although people achieve varying degrees of empathy, respect, and genuineness through life experiences, to attain high levels of these skills appears to require rigorous training.

Research scales that operationalize empathy conditions have been developed and validated in extensive research studies (Truax & Carkhuff, 1967). These scales, which specify levels of empathy along a continuum ranging from high- to low-level skills, represented a major breakthrough not only in operationalizing essential social worker skills but also in establishing a relationship between these skills and successful outcomes in therapy.

The empathic communication scale has been particularly helpful to social work educators in assessing pre- and post-levels of empathy of trainees in laboratory classes (Larsen & Hepworth, 1978; R. Wells, 1975). The scale has been further employed to help students distinguish between high- and low-level empathic responses and has been used by peers and instructors in group training to assess levels of students' responses. Students then receive guidance in reformulating low-level responses to bring them to higher levels.

The Carkhuff (1969) empathy scale, which consists of nine levels, has been widely used in

training and research, and similar versions of this scale can be found in the literature. Although we have found nine-point scales valuable as training aids, they have proven somewhat confusing to students, who have difficulty in making the fine distinctions between levels. For this reason, we have adapted the nine-level scale described by Hammond, Hepworth, and Smith (1977) by collapsing it to the five-level scale reproduced in the next section.

On the following empathic communication scale, level 1 responses are generally made by social workers who are preoccupied with their own rather than the client's frame of reference and as such completely fail to match the client's feelings. At this low level of responding, social workers' responses are usually characterized by the ineffective communication styles identified in Chapter 7. Responses at level 2 convey an effort to understand but are partially inaccurate or incomplete. At level 3, the midpoint, social workers' responses are essentially interchangeable in affect with the surface feelings and expressions of the client. This midpoint, widely referred to as "interchangeable" or "reciprocal" responding in the literature, is considered the "minimally facilitative level" at which an effective and viable process of helping can take place. Above the midpoint, the social worker's responses add noticeably to the surface feelings and, at the highest level, add significantly to client expressions. At these higher levels of empathic responding, the social worker accurately responds to clients' full range of feelings at their exact intensity and is "with" clients in their deepest moments. Level 4 and 5 empathic responses, which require the social worker to infer underlying feelings, involve mild to moderate interpretations.

Empathic Communication Scale

Client statement [*African American male to child welfare worker*]: I don't trust you people. You do everything you can to keep me from getting back my son. I have done everything I am supposed to do and you people always come up with something else.

Level 1: Low Level of Empathic Responding

At this level, the social worker communicates little or no awareness or understanding of even the most conspicuous of the client's feelings; the social worker's responses are irrelevant and often abrasive, hindering rather than facilitating communication. Operating from a personal frame of reference, the social worker changes the subject, argues, gives advice prematurely, lectures, or uses other ineffective styles that block communication, often diverting clients from their problems and fragmenting the helping process. Furthermore, the social worker's nonverbal responses are not appropriate to the mood and content of the client's statement.

When social workers relate at this low level, clients often become confused or defensive, reacting by discussing superficialities, arguing, disagreeing, changing the subject, or withdrawing into silence. Thus, the client's energies are diverted from exploration and/or work on problems.

LEVEL 1 RESPONSES

- "Just carry out the case plan and you are likely to succeed." (*Giving advice.*)

- "Just think what would have happened if you had devoted more energy in the last year to carrying out your case plan: You would have been further along." (*Persuading with logical argument; negatively evaluating client's actions.*)

- "How did you get along with your last social worker?" (*Changing the subject.*)

- "Don't you think it will all work out in time?" (*Leading question, untimely reassurance.*)

- "Why, that's kind of an exaggeration. If you just work along with me, before you know it things will be better." (*Reassuring, consoling, giving advice.*)

The preceding examples illustrate various ineffective styles of communication used at this low level. Notice that messages reflect the social worker's own formulations concerning the client's problem rather than capture the client's inner experiencing. Such responses stymie clients, blocking their flow of thought and producing negative feelings toward the social worker.

Level 2: Moderately Low Level of Empathic Responding

The social worker responds to the surface message of the client but erroneously omits feelings or factual aspects of the message. At this level, the social worker may also inappropriately qualify feelings (e.g., "somewhat," "a little bit," "kind of") or may inaccurately interpret feelings (e.g., "angry" for "hurt," "tense" for "scared"). Responses may also emanate from the social worker's own conceptual formulations, which may be diagnostically accurate but not empathically attuned to the client's expressions. Although level 2 responses are only partially accurate, they do convey an effort to understand and, for this reason, do not completely block the client's communication or work on problems.

LEVEL 2 RESPONSES

- "You'll just have to be patient. I can see you're upset." The word *upset* only vaguely defines the client's feelings, whereas feeling words such as *angry, furious, discounted* more accurately reflect the inner experiencing of the client.

- "You feel angry because your case plan has not been more successful to date. Maybe you are expecting too much too soon; there is a lot of time yet." In this case, the listener begins to accurately capture the client's feelings but then moves to an evaluative interpretation ("you expect too much too soon") and inappropriate reassurance.

- "You aren't pleased with your progress so far?" This response focuses on external, factual circumstances to the exclusion of the client's feelings or perceptions regarding the event in question.

- "You feel like things aren't going too well." This response contains no reference to the client's immediately apparent feelings. Beginning social workers often use the lead-in phrase "You feel like . . ." without noticing that, in employing it, they have not captured the client's feelings.

- "You're disappointed because you haven't gotten your son back?" This response, although
partially accurate, fails to capture the client's
anger and distrust of the system, wondering
whether any of his efforts are likely to succeed.

- "I can see you are angry and disappointed because your efforts haven't been more successful
so far, but I think you may be expecting the system to work too quickly."

Although the message has a strong beginning,
the empathic nature of the response is negated by
the listener's explanation of the reason for the
client's difficulties. This response represents a
form of taking sides, that is, justifying the actions
of the child welfare system by suggesting that too
much is expected of it.

The preceding responses illustrate many of the
common errors made by social workers in responding empathically to client messages. Although some
part of the messages may be accurate or helpful,
notice that all the responses in some way ignore or
subtract from what the client is experiencing.

Level 3: Interchangeable or Reciprocal Level of Empathic Responding

The social worker's verbal and nonverbal responses
at this level convey understanding and are essentially interchangeable with the obvious expressions
of the client, accurately reflecting factual aspects of
the client's messages and surface feelings or state
of being. Reciprocal responses do not appreciably
add affect or reach beyond the surface feelings, nor
do they subtract from the feeling and tone expressed. Factual content of the client's message,
though desirable, is not required; if included, this
aspect of the message must be accurate. Level 3 responses facilitate further exploratory and problem-
focused responses by the client. The beginner does
well in achieving skill in reciprocal empathic responding, which is an effective working level.

LEVEL 3 RESPONSES

- "You're really angry about the slow progress in
your case and are wondering if your efforts are
likely to succeed."

- "I can tell you feel very let down and are asking
yourself, will I ever get my son back?"

Essentially interchangeable, these responses express accurately the immediately apparent emotions in the client's message. The content of the
responses is also accurate, but deeper feelings and
meanings are not added. The second also illustrates a technique for conveying empathy that involves changing the reflection from the third to
the first person, and speaking as if the social worker
were the client.

Level 4: Moderately High Level of Empathic Responding

Responses at this level are somewhat additive, accurately identifying implicit underlying feelings
and/or aspects of the problem. The social worker's
response illuminates subtle or veiled facets of the
client's message, enabling the client to get in touch
with somewhat deeper feelings and unexplored
meanings and purposes of behavior. Level 4 responses thus are aimed at enhancing self-awareness.

LEVEL 4 RESPONSES

- "You feel very frustrated with the lack of
progress in getting your son back. You wonder
if there is any hope in working with a new
worker and this system, which you feel hasn't
been helping you."

This response not only conveys immediately
apparent feelings and content but also is noticeably additive in reflecting the client's deeper feelings of suspicion of institutional racism.

Level 5: High Level of Empathic Responding

Reflecting each emotional nuance, and using
voice and intensity of expressions finely attuned to
the client's moment-by-moment experiencing,
the social worker accurately responds to the full
range and intensity of both surface and underlying
feelings and meanings. The social worker may
connect current feelings and experiencing to previously expressed experiences or feelings, or may
accurately identify implicit patterns, themes, or
purposes. Responses may also identify implicit

goals embodied in the client's message, which point the direction for personal growth and pave the way for action.

Responding empathically at this high level facilitates the client's exploration of feelings and problems in much greater breadth and depth than at lower levels.

LEVEL 5 RESPONSES

• "Not succeeding in getting custody of your son by now has angered and frustrated you very much. I'm sensing that you're unsure of whether any efforts will succeed and maybe thinking 'the system is stacked against me.' You want to be able to trust that your efforts are likely to succeed and that I and this child welfare system will do all we can to assist you."

Significantly additive, this response goes well beyond the surface feelings in reflecting the keen disappointment of the client and his underlying fear that he may never regain custody of his son. In addition, the latter part of the response includes an action or goal statement that paves the way for further exploration of the problem. The latter is critical. Client suspicions of institutional racism and the lack of responsiveness of the system are not alleviated exlusively or even primarily by empathic statements, however well formed. The key to engaging client motivation would be demonstrating that the social worker and agency will respond in a reliable, trustworthy fashion.

EXERCISES TO DISCRIMINATE LEVELS OF EMPATHIC RESPONDING

The following exercises in rating varied responses for their level of empathy are designed to assist you in refining your ability to determine the helpfulness of responses. These exercises will prepare you for subsequent practice in formulating empathic messages. Three client statements are given, followed by a number of possible responses. Using the empathic scale, rate each response. Rating

messages will be less difficult if, using the list of affective words and phrases, you first identify the feelings contained in the client's message. After you have rated each response, compare your rating with those of the authors at the end of the chapter. Referring to the rating scale, analyze the responses you rated inaccurately, trying to pinpoint the reason for the authors' ratings.

Client Statements

1. *Single woman, age 80* [*to social worker concerning her request to move to an independent living complex provided for ambulatory elderly persons*]: Goodness, the more I think of moving, the more scared I get. I have neighbors here who look after me, and I won't know a soul there. I'm afraid I'll be all alone.

LEVEL RESPONSES

1. "It's pretty scary to you, leaving your neighbors and familiar surroundings. But there will be a lot of friendly people there and things to do. Besides, they fix one hot meal for you every day."

2. "Don't worry, you'll make friends in no time, and you'll wish you'd moved sooner."

3. "Did you sign those application papers I left with you a few days ago?"

4. "Just thinking about moving worries you because you'll be leaving your own neighborhood and friends. Even though your life would be much easier, you're unsure you'll be better off in other ways."

5. "So I gather in some ways you'd rather stay right where you are rather than gamble on a change."

6. "Lots of other people in the new apartments were just as scared as you before they moved, but I don't know a single one who's sorry now."

7. "It sounds as though you have some pretty mixed feelings about moving. Part of you wants to go because you could live more comfortably, but another part of you is afraid

you'll feel alone and lost and wants to cling to people you know care about you."

8. "Are you saying we just ought to forget the whole thing?"

2. *Male, age 16* [*in weekly visit to social work probation officer*]: I don't see the sense in having to come here every lousy week. I haven't been in any trouble now since I went to court a month ago. You should know by now you can trust me.

LEVEL RESPONSES

1. "A month isn't very long, you know. And how can I be sure you're staying out of trouble?"

2. "I gather you'd rather not have to see me. I can understand that, but the judge ordered it and you'd be in trouble with him if you didn't meet the conditions of your probation."

3. "Has it been a month since you went to court? I didn't think that it had been that long."

4. "You'd prefer not coming here and feel you've earned my trust."

5. "Having to come here each week gripes you, and I gather you're irritated with me for encouraging you to follow the judge's order."

6. "Look, you got yourself into this mess so don't complain to me if you don't like it. Maybe you'd like to talk the judge into changing his mind."

7. "It irritates you to have to come here each week. You'd like to get me off your back."

8. "You're confused about why you have to come here and wish you didn't have to."

3. *Group member* [*in hesitant, quiet voice*]: It's really hard for me to say what I want to say in this group. When I do start to talk, I get tongue-tied, and my heart starts beating faster and faster. I feel like some of you are critical of me.

LEVEL RESPONSES
(BY GROUP MEMBERS OR GROUP LEADER)

1. "Yeah, I feel that same way sometimes, too."

2. "It is frightening to you to try to share your feelings with the group. Sounds like you find yourself at a loss for words and wonder what others are thinking of you."

3. "I know you're timid, but I think it's important that you make more of an effort to talk in the group, just like you're doing now. It's actually one of the responsibilities of being a group member."

4. "You get scared when you try to talk in the group."

5. "I sense that you're probably feeling pretty tense and tied up inside right now as you talk about the fear you've had in expressing yourself. Although you've been frightened of exposing yourself, I gather there's a part of you that wants to overcome that fear and become more actively involved with the rest of the group."

6. "What makes you think we're critical of you? You come across as a bit self-conscious, but that's no big deal."

7. "You remind me of the way I felt the first time I was in a group. I was so scared, I just looked at the floor most of the time."

8. "I wonder if we've done anything that came across as being critical of you."

DEVELOPING SKILL IN RESPONDING WITH RECIPROCAL EMPATHY

Reciprocal or interchangeable empathic responding (level 3) is a basic skill used throughout the helping process to acknowledge client messages and to encourage exploration of problems. In the initial phase, empathic responding serves the vital purpose in individual, conjoint, and group sessions of facilitating the development of a working relationship and fostering the climate of understanding necessary to communication and self-disclosure. It thereby sets the stage for deeper exploration of feelings during subsequent phases. Additive empathic responses, that is, those rated as a 4 or 5 on the empathic scale, exceed the level of feelings and meanings expressed by clients and are thus reserved, in large part, for the later phases of the helping process.

Since reciprocal responding is an essential skill used frequently to meet the objectives of the first phase of the helping process, we recommend you first seek beginning mastery of responding at level 3. Extended practice of this skill should significantly increase your effectiveness in establishing viable helping relationships, interviewing, and gathering data. In the remainder of this chapter, we provide guidelines and practice exercises that will help you in mastering reciprocal responding. Although responding at additive levels is an extension of the skill of reciprocal responding, the former is an advanced skill that can be used in varied ways to achieve specific objectives. For this reason, it has been grouped with other change-oriented or "action" skills presented in Part 3 of the book.

Constructing Reciprocal Responses

To reach level 3 on the empathic scale, you must be able to formulate responses that accurately capture the content and the surface feelings in the client message. It is also important to frame the message so that you do not merely restate the client's message. The following paradigm, which identifies the various elements of an empathic or reflective message, has proven useful for conceptualizing and mastering the skill of empathic responding:

about or
You feel _____ because _____.
(Accurately   (Accurately
identifies   describes situa-
feelings of   tion or event
client)   referred to
                       by client)

As shown, the response focuses exclusively on the client's message and does not reflect the social worker's conceptualizations. The following excerpt from a session involving a social worker and a 17-year-old female illustrates the use of the preceding paradigm in constructing an empathic response:

Client: I can't talk to my father without feeling scared and crying. I'd like to be able to express myself and to disagree with him, but I just can't.

Social worker: Sounds as though you just feel panicky when you try to talk to your father. I gather you're discouraged because you'd like to feel comfortable with your dad and able to talk openly with him without falling apart.

Many times, client messages contain conflicting or contrasting emotions, such as the following: "I like taking drugs, but sometimes I worry about what they might do to me."

In such cases, each contrasting feeling should be highlighted:

• You feel _____, yet you also feel _____.

• I sense that you feel torn because while you find taking drugs enjoyable, you have nagging thoughts that they might be harmful to you.

Remember that in order to respond empathically at a reciprocal level, you must use language clients will readily understand. Abstract, intellectualized language and professional jargon are barriers to communication that should be avoided. It is also important to vary the language you use in responding. Many professionals tend to respond with stereotyped, repetitive speech patterns, commonly using a limited variety of communication leads to begin their empathic responses. Such leads as "You feel . . ." and "I hear you saying . . ." repeated over and over not only are distracting to the client but also seem phony and contrived. Such stereotyped responding draws more attention to technique than to message.

The list of varied introductory phrases will help you expand your repertoire of possible responses. We encourage you to read the list aloud several times and to review the list frequently while practicing the empathic communication training exercises in this chapter and in Chapter 18 on additive empathic responding. The reciprocal empathic response format ("You feel _____ because _____") is merely a training aid to assist you in focusing on the affect and content of client messages. The leads list will help you respond more naturally.

LEADS FOR EMPATHIC RESPONSES

Could it be that . . .

I wonder if . . .

What I guess I'm hearing is . . .

Correct me if I'm wrong, but I'm sensing . . .

Perhaps you're feeling . . .

Sometimes you think . . .

Maybe this is a longshot, but . . .

I'm not certain I understand; you're feeling . . .

As I hear it, you . . .

Is that the way you feel?

Let me see if I'm with you; you . . .

The message I'm getting is that . . .

If I'm hearing you correctly . . .

So, you're feeling . . .

You feel . . .

It sounds as though you are saying . . .

I hear you saying . . .

So, from where you sit . . .

I sense that you're feeling . . .

Your message seems to be . . .

I gather you're feeling . . .

If I'm catching what you say . . .

What you're saying comes across to me as . . .

You're feeling . . .

I'm not sure if I'm with you but . . .

You appear to be feeling . . .

It appears you feel . . .

Maybe you feel . . .

Do you feel . . .

I'm not sure that I'm with you; do you mean . . .

It seems that you . . .

Is that what you mean?

What I think I'm hearing is . . .

I get the impression that . . .

As I get it, you felt that . . .

To me it's almost like

you are saying . . .

So, as you see it . . .

I'm picking up that you . . .

I wonder if you're saying . . .

So, it seems to you . . .

Right now you're feeling . . .

You must have felt . . .

Listening to you, it seems as if . . .

You convey a sense of . . .

As I think about what you say, it occurs to me you're feeling . . .

From what you say, I gather you're feeling . . .

Exercises designed to help you to respond to clients with level 3 reciprocal empathic responses are found at the end of the chapter. Contained in the exercises are a variety of client statements taken from actual work with individuals, groups, couples, and families in diverse settings.

In addition to completing the skill development exercises, we also recommend that you keep a record of the number of empathic responses you employ in sessions over several weeks to determine the extent to which you are applying this skill. We also suggest that either you or a knowledgeable associate rate your responses and determine the mean level of empathic responding for each session. If you find (as most beginning social workers do) that you are underutilizing empathic responses or responding at low levels, you may wish to set a goal to improve your skill.

Employing Empathic Responding

In early sessions, empathic responding should be used frequently as a method of developing rapport and "staying in touch" with the client. Responses should be couched in a tentative manner to allow for inaccuracies in the social worker's perception. Further, checking out the accuracy of responses with appropriate lead-in phrases, such as "Let me see if I understand . . ." or "Did I hear you right?" is helpful in communicating a desire to understand and a willingness to correct misperceptions.

In initially using empathic responses, learners are often leery of the flood of emotions that sometimes occurs as the client, experiencing none of the usual barriers to communication, releases feelings often pent up for months or years. It is important to understand that empathic responses have not "caused" such feelings but rather have facilitated their expression, thus clearing the way for the client to explore and to consider such feelings more rationally and objectively.

You may worry, as do many beginning social workers, about whether you will "damage" the client or the helping relationship if your empathic responses do not always accurately reflect the client's feelings. Perhaps even more important than accuracy, however, is the "commitment" to understand conveyed by genuine efforts to perceive the client's experience. If you consistently demonstrate your goodwill and intent to help through attentive verbal and nonverbal responding, occasional lack of understanding or faulty timing will not damage the relationship. In fact, efforts to clarify the client's message will usually enhance rather than detract from the helping process, particularly if you respond to corrective feedback in an open, nondefensive, and empathic manner.

MULTIPLE USES OF EMPATHIC COMMUNICATION

Earlier in the chapter, we referred to the versatility of empathic communication. In this section, we delineate a number of ways in which you can employ reciprocal empathic responding.

1. *Establishing relationships with clients in initial sessions.* As discussed previously, the use of empathic responding actively demonstrates the social worker's keen awareness of clients' feelings and creates an atmosphere wherein the latter will risk and explore personal thoughts and feelings. Numerous researchers have established that when social workers relate empathically, clients are more likely to continue contact that when little empathy is conveyed.

Over a span of many years, many studies have emphasized the critical nature of empathic com-

munication to successful work with virtually every type of client. For example, W. R. Miller (1983) has stressed the vital nature of empathy in work with problem drinkers, and Zingale (1985) has focused on the importance of empathy with a broad spectrum of clients.

Research studies (e.g., Banks, Berenson, & Carkhuff, 1967; Cimbolic, 1972; Santa Cruz & Hepworth, 1975) also indicate that empathic communication, along with respect and genuineness, facilitate the development of effective working relationships when social workers and clients are from different ethnic or cultural backgrounds. These findings are particularly meaningful in view of the fact that social workers typically work with diverse populations that include ethnic minorities and clients from low socioeconomic backgrounds. To employ empathy with maximal effectiveness to transcultural relationships, social workers must be aware of and sensitive to cultural factors.

The importance of knowledge of cultural factors was documented almost 40 years ago by the research findings of Mayer and Timms (1969), who studied clashes of perspectives between clients and social workers. Based on their findings they concluded: "It seems that social workers start where the client is psychodynamically but they are insufficiently empathic in regard to cultural components" (p. 38).

Although empathic communication is important in bridging cultural gaps, it can be used to excess with many Asian Americans and Native Americans. Many members of these groups tend to be lower in emotional expressiveness than other client groups and may react with discomfort and confusion if a social worker relies heavily on empathic communication. Still, it is important to "read between the lines" and to sensitively respond to troubling emotions that these clients do not usually express directly. Like other clients, they are likely to appreciate a social worker's sensitive awareness to painful emotions associated with their difficulties.

We again emphasize the importance of assuming a more directive, active, and structured stance with some Asian Americans. As Tsui and Schultz (1985) have clarified, "A purely empathetic, passive, nondirective approach serves only to confuse and alienate the [Asian] client" (p. 568). The same can be said of many Native American clients according to their levels of acculturation.

2. *Staying in touch with clients.* Reciprocal empathic responding operationalizes the social work principle of "starting where the client is" and keeps social workers attuned to clients' current feelings. Although employing many other skills and techniques, the social worker utilizes and returns to empathic responding to keep in touch with the client. In that sense, empathic communication is a fundamental intervention prerequisite to the use of other interventions. Writing to this point, Gendlin (1974) uses the analogy of driving a car to refer to the vital role of empathy in keeping in touch with clients. Driving involves much more than watching the road. A driver does many things, including steering, braking, signaling, and watching signs. One may glance at the scenery, visit with others, and think private thoughts, but watching the road must be accorded highest priority. When visibility becomes limited or hazards appear, all other activities must cease and one must attend exclusively to observing the road and conditions that may pose hazards. Just as some drivers fail to maintain proper lookout and become involved in accidents, some social workers also fail to attend sufficiently to cultural differences and changes in clients' moods and reactions, mistakenly assuming they know their frame of mind. As a consequence, social workers may fail to discern important feelings of clients, who may perceive them as disinterested or insensitive and subsequently disengage from the helping process.

3. *Accurately assessing client problems.* Extensive evidence indicates that the levels of empathy offered by social workers correlate with levels of self-exploration by clients. High-level empathic responding thus increases clients' exploration of self and problems. As the social worker moves "with" clients by frequently using empathic responses in

initial sessions, clients begin to unfold their problems and to reveal events and relevant data. Figuratively speaking, clients then take social workers where they need to go by providing information crucial to making an accurate assessment. Such an approach contrasts sharply with sessions in which history-taking is emphasized and where social workers, following their own agendas rather than the clients', spend unnecessary time asking hit-or-miss questions and gathering information often extraneous to the problem.

4. *Responding to the nonverbal messages of clients.* Clients often convey through their facial features, gestures, and body postures feelings they do not express verbally. In the course of a session, for instance, a client may become pensive, or show puzzlement, pain, or discomfort. In such instances, the social worker may convey understanding of the client's feeling state and verbalize the feeling explicitly through a reflective response that attends to the emotion suggested in the client's nonverbal expressions. For instance, in response to a client who has been sitting dejectedly with her head down for several minutes after having reported some bad grades, a social worker might say: "At this moment you seem to be feeling very sad and discouraged, perhaps even defeated." Further, in group or conjoint sessions, the social worker might reflect the nonverbal messages of several, or all, of the members—for example: "I sense some restlessness today, and we're having a hard time staying on our topic. I'm wondering if you're saying, 'We're not sure we want to deal with this problem today.' Am I reading the group correctly?" Empathic responses that accurately tune into clients' nonverbal experiencing will usually prompt clients to begin exploring feelings they have been experiencing. Making explicit the nonverbal messages of clients is an important skill discussed in several chapters in the book.

5. *Making confrontations more palatable.* Confrontation is employed in the change-oriented phase to expand clients' awareness and to motivate them to action. They are most appropriate when

clients are contemplating actions that are unlawful, or dangerous to themselves or others. They are also appropriate when such actions conflict with goals and values a client has chosen for himself or herself. However, even well-timed confrontations may be met with varying degrees of receptivity. Concern as well as prudence dictate that the social worker determine the impact of confrontations upon clients and implement a process of making these interventions more palatable. This may be accomplished by employing empathic responses attuned to client reactions immediately following confrontations. As social workers listen attentively and sensitively to client expressions, defensiveness abates, and clients often begin to engage in processing new information and thinking through and testing the validity of ideas, embracing those that fit and rejecting others that seem inapplicable. Blending confrontation and empathic responses is a particularly potent technique for managing group processes when the social worker must deal with a controversial issue or distractive behavior that is interfering with the work of the group.

6. *Handling obstacles presented by clients.* Client opposition to what is happening in a session is sometimes healthy. What is often interpreted as unconscious resistance may be a negative reaction to poor interviewing and intervention techniques or to client confusion, misunderstanding, or even inertia. It is thus important to carefully monitor client reactions and to deal directly and sensitively with their related feelings. Clients' verbal or nonverbal actions may comment indirectly on what is occurring in the helping process. For instance, the client may look at her watch and ask how long the session is going to take, shift body position away from the social worker, begin tapping a foot, or stare out the window. In such cases, when it appears the client is disengaging from the session, an empathic response that reflects the client's verbal and/or nonverbal message may be used effectively to initiate discussion of what is occurring. Shifting to what is happening in the here-and-now is an important skill that we further elaborate in later chapters.

Social workers are also often confronted with excessively verbal clients who talk rapidly and move quickly from one topic to another. Overly verbal clients present a particular challenge to beginning social workers, who must often overcome the misconception that interrupting clients is rude. Because of this misconception, novice interviewers sometimes spend most of an initial session listening passively to verbal clients without providing any form or direction to the helping process. Further, beginning social workers may also allow clients to talk incessantly because they mistakenly view this as constructive work on problems. Quite the contrary, verbosity often keeps the session on a superficial level and interferes with problem identification and exploration. It may also be an indication of a more serious affective mental health problem.

It is important that social workers provide structure and direction, thereby conveying an expectation that specific topics will be considered in depth. Much more will be said about this in later chapters. However, for the present, it is important to underscore the necessity of using empathic responses with verbal clients as a preliminary effort to slow the process and to provide some depth to the discussion. For example, a social worker might interject or intervene with: "I'd like to interrupt to check if I'm understanding what you mean. As I get it, you're feeling . . ." or "Before you get into talking about that, I would like to make sure I'm with you. You seem to be saying . . ." or "Could we hold off discussing that for just a minute? I'd like to be sure I understand what you mean. Would you expand on the point you were just making?"

7. *Managing anger and patterns of violence.* During individual or group sessions, clients (especially those who were not self-referred and may be involuntary) often experience surges of intense and conflicting feelings, such as anger, hurt, or disappointment. In such instances, empathic responding is a key tool for assisting them to work through those feelings. As empathic responses facilitate expanded expression of these feelings, clients engage in a process of ventilating, clarifying, and experiencing different feelings,

gradually achieving a mellowing of emotions and a more rational and thoughtful state of being. Employed to focus sharply on clients' feelings, empathic responding thus efficiently manages and modifies strong emotions that represent obstacles to progress. As the social worker successfully handles such moments and clients experience increased self-awareness and cathartic benefits, the helping relationship is strengthened.

Empathic responding is particularly helpful in dealing with hostile clients and is indispensable when clients are angry with the social worker, as illustrated in the following example: "What you're doing to help me with my problems doesn't seem to be doing me any good. I don't know why I keep coming."

At such moments, the social worker must resist the temptation to react defensively, for such responses further antagonize the client and exacerbate the situation. Responding by challenging the client's perception, for instance, would be destructive to the helping relationship. The purpose of the social worker's responses should be to understand the client's experiencing and feelings and to engage the client in fully exploring those feelings. Keeping this in mind, consider the impact of the following reciprocal empathic response: "You're very disappointed that things aren't better, and are irritated with me, feeling that I should have been more helpful to you."

This response accurately and nondefensively acknowledges the client's frustration with the situation and with the social worker. By itself, the preceding response would not be sufficient to mellow the client's ire and to free the client to consider the problem more fully and rationally. Carefully following feelings and remaining sensitively attuned to the client's experiencing by employing empathic responses for several minutes usually assists both the social worker and client to understand more clearly the strong feelings that prompted the client's message and to adequately assess the source of those feelings. Attending to the emotions expressed does not mean that the content is discounted. The social worker can follow the empathic response above by saying, "I'd like to explore more with you about the parts of our work that have not felt worthwhile to you."

When faced with angry clients in group and conjoint sessions, it is critical that the social worker empathically reflect not only the negative feelings and positions of the clients who are manifesting the anger but also reach for and reflect the feelings or observations of members who may be experiencing the situation differently. Utilizing empathic responses in this manner assists the social worker to gather information that will elucidate the problem, help angry members air and examine their feelings, and put other points of view before the group for consideration. Further, employing empathic responding at such moments also encourages a more rational discussion of issues involved in the problem and thus sets the stage for possible problem solving.

The principles just discussed also apply to clients who are prone to violent behavior. Such clients often come to the attention of social workers because they have abused their children and/or spouses. People who engage in violence often do so because of underlying feelings of helplessness and frustration and because they lack skills and experience in coping with troubling situations in more constructive ways.

Some have short fuses and weak emotional controls, often coming from backgrounds in which they vicariously learned violence as a mechanism of coping. Using empathy to defuse their intense anger and to tune in to their frustrations is an important first step in work with such clients (Lane, 1986). Other clients have difficulties with anger and express it only when under the influence of alcohol or other substances. Assisting them to experience and to ventilate anger when sober and in control is a major approach employed to assist such clients to learn constructive ways of coping with anger (Potter-Efron & Potter-Efron, 1992). Assisting clients to control anger, of course, involves use of other interventions, as we discuss in later chapters.

8. *Utilizing empathic responses to facilitate group discussions.* Social workers may facilitate discussion of specific issues in conjoint or group sessions by first identifying a desired topic and then utilizing empathic (or paraphrasing) responses to reflect the observations of various group members in relation to that topic. The social worker may also reach for responses from members who have not contributed and then employ empathic responses (or paraphrases) to acknowledge their observations. Utilized frequently in this manner, empathic responding encourages (and reinforces) clients' participation in group discussions.

Teaching Clients to Respond Empathically

Clients often have difficulties in relationships because their styles of communication include many barriers that prevent them from accurately hearing messages or conveying understanding to others. An important task of the social worker thus involves teaching clients to respond empathically, a task accomplished in part by modeling, which is generally recognized as a potent technique for promoting client change and growth. People who manifest problems associated with distorting or ignoring messages of others (as frequently occurs in marital, family, and other close relationships) vicariously benefit by observing the social worker listen effectively and respond empathically. Moreover, clients who are hard to reach or who have difficulties in expressing themselves gradually learn to recognize their own emotions and to express themselves more fully as a result of the social worker's empathic responding.

Teaching clients empathic communication skills also can entail assuming an educative role. A number of approaches to assisting mates (married or otherwise) who are having serious conflicts embody teaching them to gain and to express empathy for each other. A similar approach has been employed in Parent Effectiveness Training (T. Gordon, 1970). Still another approach to increasing empathy for children by parents at risk for child abuse has

successfully employed a cognitive component designed to assist these parents to attribute less negative meanings to behaviors otherwise perceived by the parents as deliberately provocative (Whiteman, Fanshel, & Grundy, 1987).

Social workers' roles as educators require them to intervene actively at opportune moments to enable clients to respond empathically, particularly when they have ignored, discounted, or attacked the contributions of others in a session. With respect to this role, we suggest that social workers consider taking the following actions:

1. Teach clients the paradigm for empathic responding introduced in the chapter. If appropriate, ask them to engage briefly in a paired practice exercise similar to the one recommended for beginning social workers at the end of the chapter. Utilizing topics neutral to the relationship, have each person in turn carefully listen to the other for several minutes, and afterwards evaluate with participants the impact of the exercise on them.

2. Introduce clients to the list of affective words and phrases and to the leads list contained in this chapter. If appropriate, you may wish to have clients assume tasks during the week to broaden their feeling vocabulary similar to those recommended for beginning social workers.

3. Intervene in sessions when clients ignore or fail to validate messages, a situation that occurs frequently in work with couples, families, and groups. At those moments, facilitatively interrupt the process to ask the sender to repeat the message and the receiver to paraphrase or capture the essence of the former's message with fresh words, as illustrated in the following example:

16-year-old daughter: I don't like going to school. The teachers are a bunch of jerks, and most of the kids just laugh and make fun of me.

Mother: But you've got to go. If you'd just buckle down and study, school wouldn't be half so hard for you. I think . . .

Social worker [*interrupting and speaking to mother*]: I can see that you have some real concerns about Janet's not going to school, but for a moment, I'm going to ask you to get in touch with what she just said to you by repeating it back to her.

Mother [*looking at social worker*]: She said she doesn't like school.

Social worker: That's close, but turn and talk to Janet. See if you can identify what she's feeling.

Mother [*turning to daughter*]: I guess it's pretty painful for you to go to school. And you don't like your teachers and you feel shut out and ridiculed by the kids.

Janet [*tearfully*]: Yeah, that's it . . . it's really hard.

Notice that the mother did not respond empathically to her daughter's feelings until the social worker intervened and coached her. This example thus illustrates the importance of persevering in teaching clients to "hear" the messages of others, a point we cannot overemphasize. Clients often have considerable trouble mastering listening skills because habitual dysfunctional responses are difficult to discard. This is true even when clients are highly motivated to communicate more effectively and when social workers actively intervene to assist them.

4. Give positive feedback when you observe clients listening to each other or, as in the preceding example, when they respond to your coaching. In the example cited, for instance, the social worker might have responded to the mother as follows: "I liked the way you responded because your message accurately reflected what your daughter was experiencing. I think she felt you really understood what she was trying to say." It is also helpful to ask participants to discuss what they experienced during the exchange and to highlight positive feelings and observations.

AUTHENTICITY

Although theoreticians generally agree that empathy and respect are vital to developing effective working relationships, they do not agree about the amount of openness or self-disclosure practitioners should offer. Theorists who espouse traditional psychoanalytically oriented theory have advocated that social workers should relate to clients in a professionally detached manner, although one psychoanalyst, Bernstein (1972), contends that psychoanalysts have gone to an undesirable extreme in emotionally detaching themselves from their patients. He adds, "if an analyst is a healthy, mature, gentle human being, his human response to the expression of a need for help . . . is a feeling of compassion" (p. 163). The findings of a study by Grunebaum (1986) further indicate that emotional detachment by social workers can actually be harmful to clients. In a study of 47 patients who believed they had been harmed by psychotherapy, 18 attributed the harm to coldness, distance, and rigidity by the therapist. It is noteworthy that the patients in this study were all mental health professionals who had sought psychotherapy for themselves.

Taking an opposing position to the traditional view, humanistic writers maintain that social workers should relate openly and authentically as "real" persons. These writers argue that relating in a prescribed "professional" role presents clients with a sterile, contrived relationship that fails to model openness and authenticity, inhibits clients' growth, and fails to provide clients with an experience in relating that is transferable to the real world.

With respect to empirical evidence, numerous research studies cited by Truax and Mitchell (1971) and Gurman (1977) indicated that empathy, respect, and genuineness were correlated with positive outcomes. Critical analyses of these studies and conflicting findings from other research studies have led experts to question these earlier findings and to conclude that "a more complex association exists between outcome and therapist 'skills' than originally hypothesized" (Parloff, Waskow, &

Wolfe, 1978, p. 251). However, authenticity or genuineness and the other facilitative conditions are still viewed as central to the helping process.

Authenticity is defined as the sharing of self by relating in a natural, sincere, spontaneous, open, and genuine manner. Being authentic, or genuine, involves relating personally so that expressions are spontaneous rather than contrived. Social workers' verbalizations are also congruent with their actual feelings and thoughts. Authentic social workers thus relate as real persons, expressing their feelings and assuming responsibility for them rather than denying the feelings or blaming the client for causing them. Authenticity also involves being nondefensive and human enough to admit errors to clients. Realizing that they expect clients to lower their defenses and to relate openly (thereby increasing their vulnerability), social workers themselves must model humanness and openness and avoid hiding behind a mask of "professionalism."

Relating authentically does not mean that social workers indiscriminately disclose feelings. Indeed, authentic expressions can be abrasive and destructive. Yalom and Lieberman (1971), for example, found in a study of encounter groups that attacks or rejections of group members by leaders or other members produce many psychological casualties. Social workers should thus relate authentically only when doing so is likely to further therapeutic objectives. This qualification provides considerable latitude and is only intended to constrain social workers from (1) relating abrasively (even though the social worker may be expressing genuine feelings) and (2) meeting their own needs by focusing on personal experiences and feelings rather than those of the client.

With respect to the first constraint, social workers must avoid misconstruing authenticity as granting free license to do whatever they wish, especially with respect to expressing hostility. The second constraint reiterates the importance of social workers' responding to clients' needs rather than their own. Moreover, when social workers share their feelings or experiences for a therapeutic purpose, they should immediately shift the focus back on the clients. Keep in mind that the purpose of relating authentically, whether with individuals, families, or groups, is to facilitate growth of clients, not to demonstrate one's own honesty or authenticity.

Types of Self-Disclosure

The aspect of authenticity denoted as self-disclosure has been variously defined by different authors (Chelune, 1979). For this discussion we define it as the conscious and intentional revelation of information about oneself through both verbal expressions and nonverbal behaviors (e.g., smiling, grimacing, or shaking one's head in disbelief). Viewed from a therapeutic perspective, self-disclosure encourages clients to reciprocate with trust and openness. In fact, numerous studies (Doster & Nesbitt, 1979) document that client self-disclosure is correlated with social worker self-disclosure.

Danish, D'Augelli, and Hauer (1980) have identified two types of self-disclosure, *self-involving statements* and *personal self-disclosing*. The former type includes messages that express the social worker's personal reaction to the client during the course of a session. Examples of this type would be:

- "I'm impressed with the progress you've made this past week. You applied what we discussed last week and have made another step toward learning to control angry feelings."

- "I want to share my reaction to what you just said. I found myself feeling sad for you because you put yourself down unmercifully. I see you so differently from how you see yourself and find myself wishing I could somehow spare you the torment you inflict on yourself."

- "You know, as I think about the losses you've experienced this past year, I marvel you've done as well as you have. I'm not at all sure I'd have held together as well as you have."

Personal self-disclosure messages, by contrast, center on struggles or problems the social worker is currently experiencing or has experienced that are similar to the client's problems. The following are examples of this type of self-disclosure:

- [*To couple*] "As you talk about your problems with your children, it reminds me of similar difficulties I had with mine when they were that same age" (goes on to relate his experience).

- [*To individual client*] "I think all of us struggle with that same fear to some degree. Earlier this week I . . ." (goes on to relate events in which she experienced similar fears).

Research findings comparing the effects of different types of self-disclosure have been mixed (Dowd & Boroto, 1982; McCarty & Betz, 1978; Reynolds & Fischer, 1983). Given the sparse and inconclusive findings, social workers should use personal self-disclosure judiciously. They should also recognize cultural variations that may suggest that some relatively low-level self-disclosure may be necessary early in the helping process. Logic suggests that self-disclosures of current problems may undermine the confidence of clients, who may well wonder how social workers can presume to help others when they haven't successfully resolved their own problems. Moreover, focusing on the social worker's problems diverts attention from the client, who may conclude that the social worker prefers to focus on his/her own problems. Self-involving disclosures, by contrast, appear to be low risk and relevant to the helping process.

Timing and Intensity of Self-Disclosure

Still another aspect of self-disclosure involves timing and level of intensity, ranging from superficial to highly personal statements. Giannandrea and Murphy (1973) found that moderate self-disclosing by social workers, rather than high or low levels, resulted in clients' higher rate of return for second interviews. Simonson (1976) has reported similar findings. It is thus logical to assume that social workers should avoid sharing personal feelings and experiences until rapport and trust have been achieved and clients have demonstrated readiness to engage on a more personal level. The danger in premature self-disclosure is that such responses can threaten clients and lead to emotional retreat at the

very time when it is vital to reduce threat and defensiveness. The danger is especially great with clients from other cultures who are unaccustomed to relating on an intense personal basis. For example, in a study comparing the reactions of American and Mexican undergraduate students to self-disclosure, Cherbosque (1987) found that the Mexican students perceived counselors who did not engage in self-disclosure as more trustworthy and expert than those who did. This researcher concluded, therefore, that social workers who work with Mexican Americans need to maintain a degree of formality that is unnecessary with Anglo clients. We believe that this caution is also applicable to Native American clients. Formality, however, should not preclude honesty, for Gomez, Zurcher, Farris, and Becker (1985) have reported that manifesting honesty and respect and communicating genuine concern were positively correlated with satisfaction levels of Latino clients treated as outpatients in a mental health system.

With respect to Asian Americans, Tsui and Schultz (1985) indicate that self-disclosure by social workers may facilitate the development of rapport:

Personal disclosure and an appropriate level of emotional expressiveness are often the most effective ways to put Asian clients at ease. Considering the generally low level of emotional expressiveness in Asian families, the therapist is, in effect, role modeling for the client and showing the client how the appropriate expression of emotion facilitates the treatment process. (p. 568)

Asian American families, of course, vary as their members range in acculturation and familiarity with values such as self-disclosure.

As clients manifest trust, social workers can appropriately relate with increased openness and spontaneity, assuming, of course, that authentic responses are relevant to clients' needs and do not shift the focus from the client for more than brief periods. Even when trust is strong, social workers should exercise moderate self-disclosure, for beyond a certain level authentic responses no longer facilitate the helping process (Truax & Carkhuff, 1964). Social workers must exercise discretion in employing self-disclosure with severely mentally ill clients. Shimkunas (1972) and Doster, Surratt, and Webster (1975) report higher levels of symptomatic behavior (e.g., delusional ideation) by paranoid schizophrenic patients following personal self-disclosure by social workers. Superficial self-disclosure, by contrast, did not produce increases in disturbed behavior.

With respect to social workers' actual use of self-disclosures, it is heartening to note that a recent study (Anderson & Mandell, 1989) indicated that self-disclosure gained increased acceptance by social workers between 1978 and 1989. Moreover, they were adhering to the guidelines advocated in this and other relevant references. As expected, however, psychodynamically oriented social workers were less likely to use self-disclosure than were other social workers.

A Paradigm for Responding Authentically

Beginning social workers (and clients) learn the skill of relating authentically more readily if they have a paradigm for formulating effective messages. Note in the following paradigm that there are four elements of an authentic message:

(1) "I" ( )	About	Because
(2) Specific feeling or wants	(3) Neutral description of event	(4) Impact of situation upon sender or others

The following example (Larsen, 1980), involving a social work student intern's response to a message from an institutionalized youth, illustrates the use of the paradigm. The student describes the situation: "Don and I had a tough go of it last week. I entered the living unit only to find that he was angry with me for some reason, and he proceeded to abuse me verbally all night long. This week, Don approached me to apologize."

Don: I'm really sorry about what happened the other night, I didn't mean nothing by it. You probably don't want nothing more to do with me.

Student: Well, you know, Don, I'm sorry it happened, too. I was really hurt and puzzled that night because I didn't understand where all your anger was coming from. You wouldn't talk to me about it, so I felt frustrated and I didn't quite know what to do or make of it. And you know, one of my real fears that night was that this was going to get in the way of our getting to know each other. I didn't really want to see that happen.

In the preceding message, note that the student uses all the elements of the paradigm, identifying specific feelings (hurt, puzzlement, frustration, fear), describing the events that occurred in a neutral, nonblaming manner, and identifying the impact she feared these events might have upon their relationship.

As you consider the paradigm, note that we are not recommending that you use it in a mechanistic and undeviating "I-feel-this-way-about . . ." response pattern. Rather, we suggest you learn and combine the elements of the paradigm in various ways as you practice constructing authentic messages. Later, as you incorporate authentic relating within your natural conversational repertoire, you will no longer need to refer to the paradigm.

This paradigm is also applicable in teaching clients to respond authentically. We suggest that you present the paradigm to clients and guide them through several practice messages, assisting them to include all the elements of the paradigm in their responses. For example:

Specific "I" Feelings	Description of Event	Impact
I get frustrated	when you keep reading the paper while I'm speaking	because I feel discounted and very unimportant to you.

It is important to stress with clients the need to use conversational language when they express authentic messages. Also emphasize, however, that they should talk about their own feelings and opinions. Otherwise, they may slip into accusatory forms of communication as they vary their messages.

Guidelines for Responding Authentically

As you practice authentic responding and teach clients to respond authentically in their encounters with others, we suggest you keep in mind the following guidelines that relate to the four elements of an authentic message.

1. *Personalize messages by using the pronoun "I."* When attempting to respond authentically, both social workers and clients commonly make the mistake of starting their statements with "You." This introduction tends to focus a response on the other person rather than on the sender's experiencing. Beginning messages with "I," however, encourages senders to own responsibility for their feelings and to personalize their statements.

Efforts by social workers to employ "I" statements when responding can profoundly affect the quality of group processes, increasing the specificity of communications and the frequency of "I" statements by clients. As a general rule, groups (including couples and families) are likely to follow a social worker's communication style.

Just as groups tend to follow suit when social workers frequently use "I" messages, they also imitate counterproductive behaviors of the social worker, including communicating in broad generalities, focusing on issues external to the individual, or relating to the group in an interrogative or confrontational manner.

The behavior of social workers thus may not necessarily be a good model for clients to emulate in real life. Social workers must be careful to model the skills they wish clients to acquire. Social workers should master relating authentically to the extent that they automatically personalize their messages and constructively share their inner experiencing with clients. To facilitate personalizing messages, social workers can negotiate an agreement with individuals or groups specifying that clients will endeavor to incorporate the use of "I" statements in their conversational repertoires. Thereafter, it is critical to intervene consistently to assist clients to personalize their messages when they have not done so.

2. *Share feelings that lie at varying depths.* To achieve this, social workers must reach for feelings that underlie their immediate experiencing. Doing so is particularly vital when social workers experience strong negative feelings (dislike, anger, repulsion, disgust, boredom) toward a client, for an examination of the deeper aspects of feelings often discloses more positive feelings toward the client. Expressing these feelings preserves the client's self-esteem, whereas expressing superficial negative feelings often poses a threat to the client, creating defensiveness and anger. In expressing anger (and perhaps disgust) toward a client who is chronically late for appointments, the social worker may first connect his feelings of anger to feeling inconvenienced. In reaching for deeper feelings, the social worker may discover that the annoyance derives from disappointment that the client is not fully committed to the helping process. At an even deeper level may lie hurt in not being more important to the client. Further introspection may also discover a concern that the client may be manifesting similar behavior in other areas of life that could adversely affect relationships with others.

Utilizing an example of boredom, Gendlin (1967) illustrates the process a social worker might go through to analyze feelings toward a client and to discover positive aspects of this experiencing that can be safely and beneficially shared with the client. Rather than just blurting out, "You bore me" or "Why do you never say anything important?" Gendlin recommends that social workers advance their own experiencing for a few moments in a chain of "content mutation and explication": "I am bored . . . This isn't helping him . . . I wish I could help . . . I'd like to hear something more personal . . . I really would welcome him . . . I have more welcome on my hands for him than he lets me use . . . but I don't want to push away what he does express . . . ." The resulting therapist expression now will make a personal interaction, even if the client says nothing in return. The therapist will say something like "You know, I've been thinking the last few minutes, I wish I'd hear more from you, more of how you really feel inside. I know you might not want to say, but whenever you can or want, I would like it" (p. 90).

By employing the process just described, the social worker may discover multiple (and sometimes conflicting) feelings that may be beneficially shared with the client, as illustrated in the following message:

- [*To mother*] "I've been experiencing some feelings in the session I want to share with you because it may shed some light on what others may experience with you. I was wanting to tell you that it appears you often come to Robert's [*son's*] rescue in the session and that at times you seem to protect him from the consequences of his own actions, but I held back and began to feel a slight knotting in my stomach. Then it hit me that I was afraid you'd be hurt and offended and that it might have a negative impact on our relationship. As I think about it just now, I'm aware that sometimes I feel I'm walking on eggshells with you, and I don't like that because it puts distance between us. Another reason I don't like it is because I think I'm underestimating your ability to handle constructive feedback. I think you're stronger than you come across at times. [*Slight pause.*] Could you share what you're feeling just now about what I said?"

Sharing multiple emotions also assists social workers to manage situations in which they experience frustration or anger with clients. Dyer (1969) cites an example of feeling extremely angry with a client and simultaneously feeling guilty about having that feeling. Rather than share just the anger, Dyer shared the multiple emotions he was experiencing, including his wish not to feel angry and his desire to discuss and resolve his feelings. In such instances, a social worker could also express underlying caring for the client and highlight the importance of understanding the dynamics involved so that both might learn from the situation. It is critical, of course, to analyze what

changes need to be made by the client and/or social worker to prevent future recurrences.

Like prospective social workers, clients are prone to focus on one aspect of their experiencing to the exclusion of deeper and more complex emotions. Clients often have difficulty, in fact, pinpointing any feelings they are experiencing. In either case, social workers should persevere to help clients broaden their awareness of their emotions and to express them openly, as illustrated in the following excerpt. The social worker speaks to the husband:

Social worker: When you told your wife you didn't want to take her to a movie and she said you were a "bump on a log"—that you never seemed to want to do anything with her—what feelings did you experience?[1]

Husband: I decided that if that's what she thought of me, that's what I'd be.

Social worker: Can you get in touch with what you were feeling? You told me a little bit about what you thought, but what about what's happening inside? Try to use feeling words to describe what you're experiencing.

Husband [*pause*]: I felt that if she was going to get on my back . . .

Social worker [*gently interrupting*]: Can you use a feeling word like "bad," or "hurt," or "put down"? What did you feel?

Husband: OK. I felt annoyed.

Social worker: So you experienced a sense of irritation. Good. I'm pleased you could get in touch with that feeling. Now see if you can get to an even more basic feeling. Remember, as we've talked about before, anger is usually a surface feeling that camouflages other feelings. What was under your annoyance?

Husband: Uhhh, I'd say frustrated. I just didn't want to sit there and listen to her harp at me. She never quits.

Social worker: I would like to check out something with you. Right now, as you're talking about this, it seems you're experiencing a real sense of discouragement and perhaps even hopelessness about things ever changing. It's as though you've given up. Maybe that's part of what you were feeling Saturday.

Husband: Yeah, I just turn myself off. Doesn't seem to be anything I can do to make her happy.

Social worker: I'm glad that you can recognize the sense of despair you're feeling. I also appreciate your hanging in there with me for a minute to get in touch with some of your feelings. You seem to be a person whose feelings run deep, and at times expressing them may come hard for you. I'm wondering how you view yourself in that regard.

In the preceding excerpt, the social worker engaged in extensive coaching to assist the client to get in touch with his underlying feelings. Deeper than the feelings of annoyance and frustration the client identified lay the more basic emotions of hurt and being unimportant to his wife. By providing other spontaneous "training sessions," the social worker can help him to identify his feelings more readily, to find the feeling words to express them, and to begin formulating "I" statements.

3. *Describe the situation or targeted behavior in neutral or descriptive terms.* In their messages, clients often omit reference or make only vague reference to situations that prompted their responses. Moreover, they may convey their messages in a blaming manner, engendering defensiveness that overshadows other aspects of self-disclosure. In either event, self-disclosure is minimal and respondents do not receive information that could otherwise be of considerable value. Consider, for example, the low yield of information in the following messages:

- "You're a neat person."
- "You should be more conscientious."
- "You're progressing well in your work."
- "You have a bad attitude."

All the preceding messages lack supporting information that respondents need to identify

specific aspects of their behavior that is competent and warrants recognition or is substandard or dysfunctional. Social workers should thus assist parents, spouses, or others to provide higher-yield feedback by including behavioral references. Examples of such messages are as follows (parent talking to 6-year-old girl):

- "I've really appreciated all that you've done tonight by yourself. You picked up your toys, washed your hands before dinner, and ate dinner without dawdling. I'm so pleased."
- "I'm very disappointed with your behavior right now. You didn't change your clothes when you came home from school; you didn't feed the dog; and you haven't started your homework."

Note in the last example that the parent sent an "I" message and owned the feelings of disappointment rather than attack the child for being undependable.

When responding authentically, social workers should also carefully describe specific events that prompted their responses, particularly when they wish to bring clients' attention to some aspect of their behavior or to a situation of which they may not be fully aware. The following social worker's message illustrates this point:

- "I need to share something with you that concerns me. Just a moment ago, I gave you feedback regarding the positive way I thought you handled a situation with your husband. [*Refers to specific behaviors manifested by client.*] When I did that, you seemed to discount my response by [*mentions specific behaviors*]. Actually, this is not the first time I have seen this happen. It appears to me that it is difficult for you to give yourself credit for the positive things you do and the progress you are making. This, in fact, may be one of the reasons that you get so discouraged at times. I wonder how you view your behavior in this regard."

Social workers constantly need to assess the specificity of their responses to ensure that they give clients the benefit of behaviorally specific feedback and provide positive modeling experiences for them. It is also vital to coach clients in giving specific feedback whenever they make sweeping generalizations and do not document the relationship between their responses and specific situations.

4. *Identify the specific impact of the problem situation or behavior on others.* Authentic messages often stop short of identifying the specific impact of the situation upon the sender or others, even though such information would be very appropriate and helpful. This element of an "I" message also increases the likelihood that the receiver will adjust or make changes, particularly if the sender demonstrates that the receiver's behavior is having a tangible effect on him or her. Consider a social worker's authentic response to a male member of an adult group:

• "Sometimes I sense some impatience on your part to move on to other topics. [*Describes situation that just occurred, documenting specific messages and behavior.*] At times I find myself torn between responding to your urging us 'to get on with it' or staying with a discussion that seems beneficial to the group. It may be that others in the group are experiencing similar mixed feelings and some of the pressure I feel."

Note that the social worker first clarifies the tangible effects of the client's behavior upon himself and then suggests that others may experience the behavior similarly. Given the social worker's approach, it is likely that others in the group will also give feedback. The client is then free to draw his own conclusions about the cause-effect relationship between his behaviors and the reactions of others and to decide whether he wishes to alter his way of relating in the group.

Social workers can identify how specific client behavior negatively impacts not only the social worker but also the clients themselves (e.g., "I'm concerned about [*specific behavior*] because it keeps you from achieving your goal"). Further, they may document the impact of a client's behavior on others (e.g., wife) or the relationship between the client and another person (e.g., "It appears that your behavior creates distance between you and your son").

Clients often have difficulty in clarifying the impact of others' behavior on themselves. A mother's message to her child, "I want you to play someplace else," establishes no reason for the request nor does it specify the negative impact of the behavior on her. If the mother responds in the following authentic manner, she clearly identifies the tangible effect of her child's behavior: "I'm having a hard time getting through the hallway because I keep stumbling over toys and having to go around you. I've almost fallen several times, and others might also. I'm worried that someone might get hurt, so I'm asking you to move your toys to your room."

The preceding illustration underscores our point that when clients clarify how a situation affects them, their requests do not appear arbitrary and are more persuasive; hence, others are likely to make appropriate accommodations. We suspect that an important reason why many clients have not changed certain self-defeating behaviors before entering the helping process is that others have previously attacked or pressured them to change, rather than authentically and unabrasively imparting information that highlights how the clients' behavior strikes them. Others have also often attempted to prescribe behavioral changes that appear to be self-serving (e.g., "Come on, stop that sulking") instead of relating their feelings (e.g., "I'm concerned that you're down and unhappy. I'd like to help but I'm not sure how"). Such responses do not strike a responsive chord in clients, who may equate making changes with putting themselves under the control of others (by following their directives), thereby losing their autonomy.

In the following excerpt, note how the social worker assists Carolyn, a group member, to personalize her statements and to clarify her reaction to the behavior of another member who has been consistently silent throughout the first two sessions:

Carolyn: We've talked about needing to add new guidelines for the group as we go along. I think we ought to have a guideline that everyone should talk in the group. [*Observe that the member has not personalized her message but has proposed a solution to meet a need she has not identified.*]

Social worker [*to Carolyn*]: The group may want to consider this guideline, but for a minute, can you get in touch with what you're experiencing and put it in the form of an "I" statement?

Carolyn: Well, all right. Janet hasn't talked at all for two solid weeks, and it's beginning to really irritate me.

Social worker: I'm wondering what else you may be experiencing besides irritation? [*Assists member to identify feelings besides mild anger.*]

Carolyn: I guess I'm a little uneasy because I don't know where Janet stands. Maybe I'm afraid she's sitting in judgment of us—I mean, me. And I guess I feel cheated because I'd like to get to know her better, and right now I feel shut out by her.

Social worker: That response helps us to begin to get to the heart of the matter. Would you now express yourself directly to Janet? Tell her what you are experiencing and, particularly, how her silence is affecting you.

Carolyn [*to Janet*]: I did wonder what you thought about me since I really opened up last week. And I do want to get to know you better. But, you know, underneath all this, I'm concerned about you. You seem unhappy and alone, and that makes me uncomfortable—I don't like to think of your feeling that way. Frankly, I'd like to know how you feel about being in this group, and if you're uneasy about it, as you seem to be, I'd like to help you feel better somehow.

In the preceding example, the social worker assisted Carolyn to experience a broader range of feelings and to identify her reaction to Janet's silence. In response to the social worker's intervention, Carolyn also expressed more positive feelings than were evident in her initial message—a not infrequent occurrence when social workers encourage clients to explore deeper-level emotions.

Engaging one member in identifying specific reactions to the behavior of others provides a learning experience for the entire group, and members often expand their conversational repertoires to incorporate such facilitative responding. In fact, there is a correlation between the extent to which social workers assist clients to acquire specific skills and the extent to which clients acquire those same skills.

Cues for Authentic Responding

The impetus for social workers to respond authentically may emanate from (1) clients' messages that request self-disclosure or (2) social workers' decisions to share perceptions and reactions they believe will be helpful. In the following section, we consider authentic responding that emanates from these two sources.

Authentic Responding Stimulated by Clients' Messages

Requests from Clients for Personal Information Clients often confront students and social workers with questions aimed at soliciting personal information such as "How old are you?" "Do you have any children?" "What is your religion?" "Do you and your wife ever fight?" and "Are you a student?" It is natural for clients to be curious and to ask questions about a social worker in whom they are confiding, especially when their well-being and future are at stake.

Self-disclosing responses may or may not be appropriate, depending on the social worker's assessment of the client's motivation for asking a particular question. When questions appear to be prompted by a natural desire for information, such responses are often very appropriate. Seemingly innocuous questions, however, may camouflage deep concerns or troubling feelings. In such instances, providing an immediate answer may be countertherapeutic because doing so may close the door to exploring and resolving clients' concerns and feelings. Clients are thus left to struggle with their feelings alone, which may seriously impair progress or cause premature termination. To illustrate, consider the following excerpt taken from an initial session involving a 23-year-old student and a 43-year-old woman who requested help for marital problems:

Client: Are you married?

Student: No, but I'm engaged. Why do you ask?

Client: Oh, I don't know. I just wondered.

Given the context of an older adult with a much younger student, the client's question was likely motivated by the concern that the student might lack life experience essential to understand her marital difficulties or the competence needed to assist her in resolving them. In this instance, immediate authentic disclosure by the student was inappropriate because it did not facilitate exploration of the feelings underlying the client's inquiry.

An exchange such as the preceding may yield information vital to the helping process if the social worker avoids premature self-disclosure. It is sometimes very difficult to distinguish whether the questions of clients are motivated by a natural desire for information or by hidden concerns or feelings. As a rule of thumb, when you have questions about clients' motivation for making personal inquiries, *precede disclosures of views or feelings with either open-ended or empathic responses.* Responding in this manner significantly increases the probability that clients will reveal their real concerns. Notice what happens when the social worker utilizes an empathic response before responding authentically:

Client: Are you married?

Student: I gather you're wondering if I can understand and help you with your difficulties in light of the fact that I'm much younger than you.

Client: Well, I guess I was thinking that. I hope that doesn't offend you.

Student: To the contrary—I appreciate your frankness. It's natural that you want to have confidence in your counselor. I know there's a lot at stake for you. Tell me more about your concerns.

In this excerpt the student responded to the probable concern of the client and struck pay dirt.

Such astuteness tends to foster confidence in clients and greatly facilitates the development of a therapeutic partnership. The fact that the student "leans into" the situation by inviting further exploration rather than skirt the issue may also be read by the client as an indicator of the student's own confidence in his or her ability to help. After fully exploring the client's concerns, the student can respond with an authentic response identifying personal qualifications, as illustrated in the following message:

• "I do want you to know that I believe I can be helpful to you. I have studied marriage counseling at some length, and I have counseled other clients whose difficulties were similar to your own. I also consult with my supervisor regularly. However, the final judgment of my competence will rest with you. It will be important for us to discuss any feelings you may still have at the end of the interview as you make a decision about returning for future sessions."

Questions That Solicit the Social Worker's Perceptions Clients may also pose questions that solicit the social worker's opinions, views, or feelings. Typical questions include, "How do I compare to your other clients?" "Do you think I need help?" "Am I crazy?" or "Do you think there's any hope for me?" Such questions can be challenging, and social workers must again consider the motivation behind the question and judge whether to disclose their views or feelings immediately or to employ either an empathic or open-ended response. As social workers do disclose their perceptions, however, their responses must be congruent with their inner experiencing. In response to the question "Do you think there's any hope for me?" the social worker may congruently respond with a message that blends elements of empathy and authenticity:

• "Your question tells me you're probably afraid you're beyond help. Although you do have some difficult problems, I'm optimistic that if we work hard together things can improve. You've shown a number of strengths that should help you make changes, including [*reviews strengths*]. A lot, of course, will depend on whether you're able and willing to commit to making changes you think would improve your situation and to invest the time and effort necessary to achieve your goals. In that respect, you're in control of the situation and whether things change for the better. That fact is something that many people find encouraging to know."

It is not necessary to answer all questions of clients in the service of authenticity. If you feel uncomfortable about answering a personal question or deem it inadvisable to do so, you should feel free to decline answering. In so doing, it is important to explain your reason for not answering directly, again utilizing an authentic response. If a teenage client, for example, asks whether the social worker had sexual relations before she married, the social worker may respond as follows:

- "I would rather not reveal that information to you since that is a very private part of my life. Asking me took some risk on your part. I have an idea that your question probably has to do with a struggle you're having, although I could be wrong. I would appreciate your sharing your thoughts about what sparked your question."

The social worker should then utilize empathic responding and open-ended questions to explore the client's reaction and motivation for asking her question.

Authentic Responding Initiated by Social Workers

Authentic responding initiated by social workers may take several forms, which are considered separately in the following sections.

Disclosing Past Experiences As we previously indicated, such responses should be sparingly used, brief, relevant to the client's concerns, and well timed. In relating to a particular client's struggle, a social worker may indicate, "I remember I felt very much like that when I was struggling with . . ." Social workers may also cite personal perceptions or experiences as reference points for clients, as, for example, "I think that is very normal behavior for a child. For instance, my five-year-old . . ." A fundamental guideline that applies to such situations is that social workers should be certain they are focusing on themselves to meet the therapeutic needs of clients.

Sharing Perceptions, Ideas, Reactions, and Formulations A key role of the social worker in the change-oriented phase of the helping process is to act as a "candid feedback system" by revealing personal thoughts and perceptions relevant to client problems (Hammond et al., 1977). The function of such responding is to further the change process in one or more of the following ways:

1. To heighten clients' awareness of dynamics that may play an important part in problems

2. To offer a different perspective regarding issues and events

3. To aid clients in conceptualizing the purposes of their behavior and feelings

4. To enlighten clients on how they affect others (including the social worker)

5. To bring clients' attention to cognitive and behavioral patterns (both functional and dysfunctional) that operate at either an individual or group level

6. To share here-and-now affective and physical reactions of the social worker to clients' behavior or to processes that occur in the helping relationship

7. To share positive feedback concerning clients' strengths and growth.

After responding authentically to achieve any of these purposes, it is vital to invite clients to express their own views and draw their own conclusions. *Owning* perceptions rather than using under-the-table methods to influence clients to adopt particular views or to change in ways deemed desirable by the social worker (e.g., "Don't you think you ought to consider...") relieves clients of the need to behave deviously or to defend themselves from the tyranny of views with which they do not agree.

Sharing perceptions with clients involves some risk that clients may misinterpret the social worker's motives and thus feel criticized, put down, or rebuked. Clarifying helpful intent before responding diminishes the risk somewhat. Nevertheless, it is vital to be observant of clients' reactions that may indicate a response has struck an exposed nerve.

To avoid damaging the relationship (or to repair it), the social worker should be empathically attuned to the client's reaction to candid feedback, shifting the focus back to the client to determine the impact of the self-disclosure. If the client appears to have been emotionally wounded by the social worker's authentic response, the social worker can use empathic skills to elicit troubled feelings and to guide subsequent responses aimed at restoring the relationship's equilibrium. Expressions of concern and clarification of the goodwill intended by the response are also usually facilitative: "I can see that what I shared with you hit you pretty hard—and that you're feeling put down right now. [*Client nods but avoids eye contact.*] I feel bad about that because the last thing I'd want is to hurt you. Please tell me what you're feeling."

Openly (and Tactfully) Sharing Reactions When Put on the Spot   Clients sometimes create situations that put social workers under considerable pressure to respond to messages that bear directly on the relationship, such as when they accuse a social worker of being uninterested, unfeeling, irritated, displeased, critical, inappropriate, or incompetent. Clients may also ask pointed questions (sometimes before the relationship has been firmly established) that require immediate responses. The first statement of one female client in an initial interview, for example, was, "I'm gay. Does that make any difference to you?" In the opening moments of another session, a pregnant client asked the social worker, "How do you feel about abortion?"

Over the years, students have reported numerous such situations that sorely tested their ability to respond facilitatively. In one instance, a male member of a group asked a female student leader for her photograph. In another, an adolescent boy kept taking his shoes off and putting his feet (which smelled very bad) on the social worker's desk. By reflecting on your practice experience, you too can no doubt pinpoint instances in which the behavior of clients caused you to squirm or produced butterflies in your stomach. Experiencing discomfort in sessions (sometimes *intense* discomfort) may be an indication that something is going awry and needs to be addressed. It is thus important to reflect on your discomfort, seeking to identify events that seem to be causing or exacerbating that discomfort (e.g., "I'm feeling very uneasy because I don't know how to respond when my client says things like, 'You seem to be too busy to see me,' or 'I'm not sure I'm worth your trouble.'") After privately exploring the reason for the discomfort, the social worker might respond:

- "I'd like to share some impressions about several things you've said in the last two sessions. [*Identifies client's statements.*] I sense you're feeling pretty unimportant—as though you don't count for much—and that perhaps you're imposing on me just by being here. I want you to know that I'm pleased you had the courage to seek help in the face of all the opposition from your family. It's also important to me that you know that I want to be helpful to you. I am concerned, however, that you feel you're imposing on me. Could you share more of those feelings with me?"

Notice that in the preceding response the social worker specifically identifies the self-defeating thoughts and feelings and blends elements of empathy and authenticity in the response.

Situations that put social workers on the spot also include clients' angry attacks, as we discuss later in the chapter. Social workers must learn to respond authentically in such situations. Consider a situation in which an adolescent attacks a social worker in an initial interview, protesting, "I don't want to be here. You counselors are all losers." In such instances, social workers should share their reactions, as illustrated in the following:

- "It sounds as though you're really ticked off about having to see me and that your previous experiences with counselors have been bummers. I respect your feelings and don't want to pressure you to work with me. I am concerned and uncomfortable, however, because you apparently have lumped all counselors together and that makes me a loser in your eyes. If you close your mind to the possibility that we might accomplish something together, then the chances are pretty slim I can be helpful. I want you to know that I am interested in you and that I would like to know what you're up against."

Interwining empathic and authentic responses in this manner often defuses clients' anger and encourages them to think more rationally about a situation.

Sharing Feelings When Clients' Behavior Is Unreasonable or Distressing Although social workers should be able to take most client behaviors in stride, there are times when they experience justifiable feelings of frustration, anger, or even hurt. In one case, a client acquired a social worker's home phone number from another source and began calling frequently about daily crisis situations, although discussions of these events could easily have waited until the next session. In another instance, a tipsy client called the social worker in the middle of the night "just to talk." In yet another case, an adolescent client let the air out of a social worker's automobile tires. In such situations, social workers should share their feelings with clients—*if they believe they can do so constructively.* In the following recorded case example, note that the student interweaves authentic and empathic responses in confronting a Latino youth in a correctional institution who had maintained he was innocent of hiding drugs that staff had found in his room. Believing the youth's story, the student went to bat for him, only to find

out later that he had lied. Somewhat uneasy at her first real confrontation, the student tries to formulate an authentic response; ironically, the youth helps her to be "up-front" with him:

Student: There's something I wanted to talk to you about, Randy...[*Stops to search for the right words.*]

Randy: Well, come out with it, then just lay it out for me.

Student: Well, remember last week when you got that incident report? You know, I really believed you were innocent. I was ready to go to the hearing and tell staff I was sure you were innocent and that the charge should be dropped. I guess I'm feeling kind of bad because when I talked to you, you told me you were innocent, and, well, that's not exactly the way it turned out.

Randy: You mean I lied to you. Go ahead and say it.

Student: Well, yes, I guess I felt kind of hurt because I was hoping that maybe you had more trust in me than that.

Randy: Well, Susan, let me tell you something. Where I come from, that's not lying, that's what we call survival. Personally, I don't consider myself a liar. I just do what I need to do to get by. That's an old trick, but it just didn't work.

Student: I hear you, Randy. I guess you're saying we're from two different cultures, and maybe we both define the same thing in different ways. I guess that with me being Anglo, you can't really expect me to understand what life has been like for you.

Several minutes later in the session, after the student has further explored the client's feelings, the following interchange occurs:

Student: You know, Randy, I want you to know. One is that when social workers work with clients, they have what they call confidentiality, so I won't be sharing what we talk about without your permission in most cases. An exception to this relates to rule or law violations. I can't keep that confidential. The other thing is that I don't expect you to share everything with me. I know there are certain things you don't want to tell me, so rather than lying about something that I ask you about, maybe you can just tell me you don't want to tell me. Would you consider that?

Randy: Yeah, that's OK. [*Pause.*] Listen, Susan, I don't want you to go around thinking I'm a liar now. I'll tell you this, and you can take it for what it's worth, but this is the truth. That's the first time I've ever lied to you. But you may not believe that.

Student: I do believe you, Randy. [*He seems a little relieved and there is a silence.*]

Randy: Well, Susan, that's a deal, then. I won't lie to you again, but if there's something I don't want to say, I'll tell you I don't want to say it.

Student: Sounds good to me. [*Both start walking away.*] You know, Randy, I really want to see you get through this program and get out as fast as you can. I know it's hard starting over because of the incident with the drugs, but I think we can get you through. [*This seemed to have more impact on Randy than anything I had said to him in a long time. The pleasure was visible on his face, and he broke into a big smile.*]

Noteworthy in this exchange is that the social worker relied almost exclusively on the skills of authenticity and empathy to bring the incident to a positive conclusion. Ignoring her feelings would have impaired the student's ability to relate facilitatively to the client and would have been destructive to the relationship; focusing on the situation, on the other hand, was beneficial for both.

Sharing Feelings When Clients Give Positive Feedback Social workers sometimes have difficulty responding receptively to clients' positive feedback about their own attributes and/or performance. We suggest that social workers model the same receptivity to positive feedback they ask clients to demonstrate in their own lives, as illustrated in the following exchange between a client and a social worker:

Client: I don't know what I would have done without you. I'm just not sure I would have made it if you hadn't been there when I needed you. You've made such a difference in my life.

Social worker: I can sense your appreciation. I'm touched by your gratitude and pleased you are feeling so much more capable of coping with your situation. I want you to know, too, that even though I was there to help, your efforts have been the deciding factor in your growth.

Positive Feedback: A Form of Authentic Responding

Because positive feedback plays such a vital role in the change process, we have allocated this separate section to do justice to the topic. Social workers often employ (or should employ) this skill in supplying information to clients about positive attributes or specific areas in which they manifest strengths, effective coping mechanisms, and incremental growth. In so doing, social workers enhance motivation to change and foster hope for the future. Many opportune moments occur in the helping process when social workers experience warm or positive feelings toward clients because of the latter's actions or progress. When appropriate, social workers should share such feelings spontaneously with clients, as illustrated in the following messages:

- "I'm pleased you have what I consider exceptional ability to 'self-observe' your own behavior and to analyze the part you play in relationships. I think this strength will serve you well in solving the problems you've identified."

- "I've been touched several times in the group when I've noticed that, despite your grief over the loss of your husband, you've reached out to other members who needed support."

- [*To newly formed group*]: "In contrast to our first session, I've noticed that this week we haven't had trouble getting down to business and staying on task. I've been pleased as I've watched you develop group guidelines for the past twenty minutes with minimal assistance from me, and I had the thought, This group is really moving."

The first two messages accredit strengths of individuals, and the third lauds a behavioral change the social worker has observed in a group process. Both types of messages sharply focus clients' attention on specific behaviors that facilitate the change process, ultimately increasing the frequency of such behaviors. Given consistently, positive messages also have the long-range effect of helping clients who have low self-esteem to develop a more positive image of self. When positive feedback is utilized to document the cause-effect relationship between their efforts and positive outcomes, clients also experience satisfaction, accomplishment, and control over their situation. Positive feedback can have the further effect of increasing clients' confidence in their ability to cope. We have occasionally had experiences with clients who were on the verge of falling apart when they came to a session but left feeling able to manage their problems for a while longer. We attribute their increased ability to function in part to authentic responses that documented and highlighted areas in which they were coping and successfully managing problems.

Taped sessions of students and social workers often reflect a dearth of authentic responses that underscore clients' strengths or incremental growth, which is unfortunate because, in our experience, clients' rates of change often correlate with the extent to which social workers focus on these two vital areas. As social workers consistently focus on clients' assets and the subtle positive changes that often occur in early sessions, clients invest more effort in the change process. As the rate of change accelerates, social workers can focus more extensively on clients' successes, identifying and reinforcing their strengths and functional coping behaviors.

Social workers face several challenges in accrediting clients' strengths and growth, including enhancing their ability to recognize and express fleeting positive feelings when clients manifest strengths

or progress. Social workers must also learn to document events so that they can provide information about specific positive behaviors. Still another challenge and responsibility is to teach clients to give positive feedback to each other, strategies which we discuss in Chapter 16.

To increase your ability to discern client strengths, we recommend you and your clients construct a profile of their resources. This may be done with individuals, couples, families, or groups, preferably early in the helping process. In individual sessions, the social worker should ask the client to identify and list all the strengths she or he can think of. The social worker also shares observations of the client's strengths, adding them to the list, which is kept for ongoing review to add further strengths as they are discovered.

With families, couples, or groups, social workers may follow a similar procedure in assessing the strengths of individual members, but they should ask other group members to share their perceptions of strengths with each member. The social worker may also wish to ask couples, families, or groups to identify the strengths and incremental growth of the group per se periodically throughout the helping process. After clients have identified their strengths or those of the group, the social worker should elicit observations regarding their reactions to the experience. Often they may mutually conclude that clients have many more strengths than they have realized. The social worker should also explore discomfort experienced by clients as they identify strengths, with the goal of having them acknowledge more comfortably their positive attributes and personal resources.

We further suggest that you carefully observe processes early on in sessions and note subtle manifestations of strengths and positive behavioral changes, systematically recording these in your progress records. The following observations are taken from the progress records of a social worker regarding the strengths of several members of a group formed for young adults with cerebral palsy:

- *Lorraine:* Expresses caring and concern for feelings of other members; acts as "interpreter" between members with difficult speech patterns and myself; speaks for herself when appropriate; exhibits leadership in the group; can carry out tasks both in the group and outside; open to change.

- *Ken:* Accepts his physical limitations; is concerned for members' feelings and problems; expresses love and affection freely; has many friends; gets along remarkably well with father and sister; is patient and easy going; sense of humor; encourages group members to participate; actively involved in every session; listens attentively.

- *Dale:* Helps keep group on designated topic when one member strays or focuses too much on self; expresses opinion and feelings somewhat openly and freely; can present positive aspects of situations, sometimes in a different light than others; can be persistent, even patient; is able to "hear" another's honest, sincere response to his behavior (positive and negative); at times can be very open and nondefensive; can admit to mistakes and has the ability to keep to tasks when he wants to accomplish things.

In your progress records, note not only the strengths and incremental growth of clients but also whether you (or group members) focused on those changes. Keep in mind that changes often occur very subtly within a single session. For instance, clients may begin to discuss problems more openly during the later part of a session, tentatively commit to work on a problem they refused to tackle earlier, show growing trust in the social worker by confiding high-risk information about themselves, or own responsibility for the first time for their part in problems. Groups and families may likewise manifest growth within short periods of time. It is thus vital to keep your antenna finely attuned to such changes so that you do not overlook clients' progress.

RELATING ASSERTIVELY TO CLIENTS

Still another aspect of relating authentically entails relating assertively to clients when a situation warrants such behavior. Reasons for relating assertively are manifold. To inspire confidence and influence clients to follow their lead, social workers must relate in a manner that projects competence. This is especially important in the initial phase of the helping process in which clients usually covertly test or check out social workers to determine whether they can understand their problems and appear competent to help them.

In conjoint or group sessions, clients may also entertain the question of whether the social worker is strong enough to protect them from destructive interactional processes that may occur in sessions. (Family or group members, in fact, generally will not fully share, risk, or commit to the helping process until they have answered this question affirmatively through consistent observation of assertive actions by the social worker.) If social workers are relaxed and demonstrate through decisive behavior that they are fully capable of handling clients' problems and of providing the necessary protection and structure to control potentially chaotic or volatile processes, clients generally relax, muster hope, and begin to work on problems. If the social worker appears incapable of curtailing or circumventing dysfunctional processes that render clients vulnerable, clients will have justifiable doubts as to the advisability of placing themselves in jeopardy and, consequently, may disengage from the helping process.

Skill in relating assertively is also prerequisite to implementing confrontation, a major technique that social workers employ to surmount opposition to change. But social workers must employ confrontation with sensitivity and finesse, as the risk of alienating clients by using this technique is high. All forms of assertiveness, in fact, must be conveyed in a context of goodwill and empathic regard for clients' feelings and self-esteem.

In the following discussion, we identify guidelines that can help you to intervene assertively with clients.

Making Requests and Giving Directives To assist clients to relate more facilitatively and to solve problems, social workers frequently must make requests of them, some of which involve relating in new ways during sessions. These requests may include asking clients to do any of the following:

1. Speak directly to each other rather than through the social worker.
2. Give feedback to others in the session.
3. Respond by checking out meanings of others' messages, take a listening stance, or personalize messages.
4. Change the arrangement of chairs.
5. Role-play.
6. Make requests of others.
7. Assume tasks to respond in specified ways within sessions.
8. Agree to carry out defined tasks during the week.
9. Identify strengths or incremental growth of themselves or others in the group or family.

In making requests, it is important to express them firmly and decisively and to deliver them with assertive nonverbal behavior. Social workers often err by couching their requests in tentative language, thus conveying doubt to clients as to whether they expect them to comply with requests.

The contrast between messages couched in tentative language and those couched in firm language can be observed in the illustrations that follow.

Many times social workers' requests of clients are actually *directives,* as are those under the column "Firm Requests." In essence, directives are declarative statements that place the burden on clients to object if they are uncomfortable, as the following message illustrates: "Before you answer that question, please turn your chair toward your wife. [*Social worker leans over and helps client to adjust chair. To wife.*] Will you please turn your chair, also, so that you can speak directly to your

TENTATIVE REQUESTS	FIRM REQUESTS
Would you mind if I interrupted . . .	I would like to pause for a moment . . .
Is it OK if we role-play?	I'd like you to role-play with me for a moment.
Excuse me, but don't you think you are getting off track?	I think we are getting off track. I'd like to return to the subject we were discussing just a minute ago.
Could we talk about something Kathy just said?	Let's go back to something Kathy just said. I think it is very important.

husband? Thank you. It's important that you be in full contact with each other while we talk."

If the social worker had given clients a choice (e.g., "Would you like to change your chairs?"), they might not have responded affirmatively. We thus suggest that when you want clients to behave differently in sessions, you simply state what you would like them to do. If clients verbally object to directives or manifest nonverbal behavior that may indicate reservations, it is vital to respond empathically and to explore the basis of their opposition. Such exploration often resolves fears or misgivings, freeing clients to engage in requested behavior.

Maintaining Focus and Managing Interruptions Maintaining focus is a vital task that takes considerable skill and assertiveness on the social worker's part. It is often essential to intervene verbally to focus or refocus processes when interruptions or distractions occur. At times, social workers also respond assertively on a nonverbal level to prevent members from interrupting important processes that may need to be brought to positive conclusion, as illustrated in the following excerpt from a family session:

Kim, age 14 [*In tears, talking angrily to her mother*]: You hardly ever listen. At home, you just always yell at us and go to your bedroom.

Mrs. R: I thought I was doing better than that . . .

Mr. R [*interrupting his wife to speak to social worker*]: I think it's hard for my wife because . . .

Social worker [*holds up hand to father in a "halt" position, while continuing to maintain eye contact with mother and daughter. To Kim*]: I would like to stay with your statement for a moment. Kim, please tell your mother what you're experiencing right now.

Interrupting Dysfunctional Processes Unseasoned social workers often permit dysfunctional processes to continue for long periods either because they lack knowledge of how to intervene or because they think they should wait until clients have completed a series of exchanges. In such instances, social workers fail to fulfill one of their major responsibilities, that is, to *guide and direct* processes and to influence participants to interact in more facilitative ways. Remember that clients often seek help because they cannot manage their destructive interactional processes, and permitting them to engage at length in their usual patterns of arguing, cajoling, threatening, blaming, criticizing, and labeling each other only exacerbates their problems. Rather, the social worker should intervene, teaching them more facilitative behaviors and guiding them to implement such behaviors in subsequent interactions.

If you decide to interrupt ongoing processes, do so decisively so that clients listen to you or heed your directive. If you intervene nonassertively, your potential to influence clients (particularly aggressive clients) will suffer, because being able to interrupt a discussion successfully manifests your power or influence in the relationship (Parlee, 1979). If you permit clients to ignore or to circumvent your intrreventions to arrest dysfunctional processes, you yield control and assume a "cone-down" position in relationship to the client.

With respect to interrupting or intervening in processes, we are advocating assertive, not aggressive, behavior. You must be sensitive to vested interests of clients, for even though you may regard certain processes as unproductive or destructive, clients may not. The timing of interruptions is thus vital. If it is not critical to draw clients' attention to what is happening immediately, you can wait for a natural pause. If such a pause does not occur shortly, you should then interrupt. You should *not* delay interrupting destructive interactional processes, however, as illustrated in the following excerpt:

Wife [*to social worker*]: I feel the children need to mind me, but every time I ask them to do something, he [*husband*] says they don't have to do it. I think we're just ruining our kids, and it's mostly his fault.

Husband: Oh—well—that shows how dumb you are.

Social worker: I'm going to interrupt you because finding fault with each other will only lead to mutual resentment.

Observe that the social worker intervenes to refocus the discussion after only two dysfunctional responses on the clients' part. If participants do not disengage immediately, the social worker will need to use body movements that interfere with communication pathways or, in extreme instances, an exclamation such as "time out!" to interrupt behavior. When social workers have demonstrated their intent to intervene quickly and decisively, clients will usually comply immediately when asked to disengage.

"Leaning into" Clients' Anger We cannot overstate the importance of openly addressing clients' anger and complaints. Unless social workers are able to handle themselves assertively and competently in the face of such anger, they lose the respect of most clients and thus their ability to help them. Further, clients may use their anger to manipulate social workers just as they have done with others. To help you respond assertively in managing clients' anger, we offer the following suggestions:

- Respond empathically to reflect clients' anger and, if possible, other underlying feelings (e.g., "I sense you're angry at me for _____ and perhaps disappointed about _____").

- Continue to explore the situation and the feelings of participants until you understand the nature of the events that have caused the angry feelings. As you do so, you may find that anger toward you dissipates and that clients begin to focus on themselves, assuming appropriate responsibility for their part in the situation at hand. The "real problem," as often happens, may not directly involve you.

- As you explore clients' anger, authentically express your feelings and reactions if it appears appropriate (e.g., "I didn't know you felt that way . . . I want to hear how I might have contributed to this situation. There may be some adjustments I'll want to make in my style of relating . . . I'm pleased that you shared your feelings with me").

- Apply a problem-solving approach (if appropriate) so that all concerned make adjustments to avoid similar occurrences or situations in the future. If a particular client expresses anger frequently and in a dysfunctional manner, you may also focus on the client's style of expressing anger, identify problems this may cause him or her in relationships with others, and negotiate a goal of modifying this response pattern.

Saying No and Setting Limits

Some social worker tasks are quite appropriate; for example, negotiating for clients and conferring with other parties and potential resources to supplement and facilitate client action (L. Epstein, 1992, p. 208). In contracting with clients, social workers must occasionally decline requests or set limits. This is sometimes difficult for beginning social workers, who may be zealous in their desires to render service and to demonstrate willingness to help others. Commitment to helping others is a desirable quality, but it must be tempered with judgment as to when acceding to clients' requests is in the best interests of both social worker and client. Certain clients may have had past experiences that lead them to believe that social workers will do most of the work required out of sessions. Clients are often more likely to become empowered by increasing their scope of actions than by social workers doing things for them that they can learn to

do for themselves. Consequently, if social workers unthinkingly agree to take on responsibilities that the client can now or could in the future perform, they may reinforce passive client behavior.

Setting limits has special implications when social workers work with involuntary clients. Cingolani (1984) has noted that social workers engage in negotiated relationships with such clients in which roles of compromiser and mediator and enforcer are called for in addition to the more comfortable counselor role. For example, when an involuntary client requests a "break" related to performance of a court order, the social worker must be clear about the choices and consequences of those choices that the client may make as well as clarify what to expect from the social worker.

Rory [*member of domestic violence group*]: I don't think that it is fair that you report that I didn't meet for eight of the ten group sessions. I could not get off work for some of those sessions. I did all I could do.

Social worker: You did attend seven of the sessions, Rory, and made efforts to attend others. However, the contract you signed which was presented in court stated that you must complete eight sessions in order to be certified as completing the group. I do not have the power to change that court order. Should you decide to comply with the court order, I am willing to speak with your employer to urge him to work with you to arrange your schedule so that you can meet the court order.

Note that in this response the social worker made clear that he would not evade the court order, that if Rory chose to comply with it, he would be willing to act as a mediator to assist him with difficulties in scheduling with the employer.

Being tactfully assertive is no easier for social workers who have excessive needs to please others than it is for clients. These social workers have difficulty declining requests or setting limits when doing so is in the best interests of clients. We therefore recommend that such social workers engage in introspection and study carefully the section of Chapter 14 that deals with cognitive factors involved in nonassertive behavior. Further, such social workers may benefit by setting tasks for themselves related to increasing their assertiveness. Participating in an assertiveness training group and delving into the popular literature on assertiveness may also be highly beneficial.

Following are a few of the many situations in which you may need to decline requests of clients:

1. When clients invite you to participate with them socially

2. When clients ask you to grant them preferential status (e.g., set lower fees than specified by policy)

3. When clients request physical intimacy

4. When clients ask you to intercede in a situation they should handle themselves

5. When clients request a special appointment after having broken a regular appointment for an invalid reason

6. When clients make requests to borrow money

7. When clients request that you conceal information about violations of probation, parole, or institutional policy

8. When spouses request that you withhold information from their partners

9. When clients disclose plans to commit crimes or acts of violence against others

10. When clients ask you to report false information to an employer or other party

In addition to declining requests, you may need to set limits with clients in situations such as the following:

- Making excessive telephone calls to you at home or the office

- Canceling appointments without advance notice

- Expressing emotions in abusive or violent ways

- Habitually seeking to go beyond designated ending points of sessions

- Continuing to fail to abide by contracts (e.g., not paying fees or missing appointments excessively)

- Making sexual overtures toward you or other staff members

- Coming to sessions when intoxicated

Part of maturing professionally involves being able to decline requests, set limits, and feel comfortable in so doing. As you gain experience, you will realize increasingly that in holding clients to reasonable expectations you help as much as when you provide a concrete action for them. Modeled responses for refusing requests and for saying no to clients are found among the exercises to assist social workers to relate authentically and assertively.

Situations also occur in which it is important that social workers assert themselves with other social workers and members of other professions. Lacking experience and sometimes confidence, beginning social workers often tend to be in awe of physicians, lawyers, psychologists, and more experienced social workers. Consequently, they may relate passively or may acquiesce in plans or demands that appear unsound or unreasonable. Although it is critical to be open to ideas of other professionals, beginning social workers should also risk expressing their own views and asserting their own rights. Otherwise, they may know more about a given client than other professionals but fail to contribute valuable information in joint case planning.

Beginning social workers should also set limits and assert their rights in refusing to accept unreasonable referrals and inappropriate assignments.

Assertiveness may also be required when other professionals deny resources to which clients are entitled, refer to clients with demeaning labels, or engage in unethical conduct. Assertiveness, indeed, is critical in assuming the role of client advocate, a role we discuss at length in Chapter 15.

Summary

This chapter has prepared the way for you to communicate with clients and other persons on behalf of clients with appropriate empathy, assertiveness, and self-disclosure. The next chapter will build on these skills by developing your abilities in listening, focusing, and exploring. Before that chapter begins, you can practice your new skills in the following exercises.

Internet Resources

You can enter keywords such as "empathy," "authenticity," "assertiveness" and "self-disclosure" in InfoTrac® to find articles such as: Holm, O. (1997). Ratings of empathic communication: Does experience make a difference? *Journal of Psychology, 131,* 6; Oswald, P. A. (1996). The effects of cognitive and affective perspective taking on empathic concern and altruistic helping. *Journal of Social Psychology, 136,* 5; Mitchell, C. G. (1998). Perceptions of empathy and client satisfaction with managed behavioral health care. *Social Work, 43,* 5.

EXERCISES IN RESPONDING AUTHENTICALLY AND ASSERTIVELY

The following exercises will assist you in gaining skill in responding authentically and assertively. Read each situation and client message and formulate a written response as though you are the social worker in the situation presented. Then compare your written responses with the modeled responses provided in the following section, keeping in mind that the modeled responses are only examples of many appropriate responses.

You will find additional exercises that involve authentic and assertive responding under exercises in confrontation in the final portion of Chapter 18 and in exercises concerned with managing relational reactions and resistance in the final section of Chapter 19.

Client Statements and Situations

1. *Marital partner* [*in third conjoint marital therapy session*]: It must be really nice being a marriage counselor—knowing just what to do and not having problems like ours.

2. *Female client, age 23* [*in first session*]: Some of my problems are related to my church's stand on birth control. Tell me, are you a Catholic?

3. *Client* [*fifth session*]: You look like you're having trouble staying awake. [*Social worker is drowsy from having taken an antihistamine for an allergy.*]

4. *Adult group member* [*to social worker in second session; group members have been struggling to determine the agenda for the session*]: I wish you'd tell us what we should talk about. Isn't that a group leader's function? We're just spinning our wheels.

5. *Male client* [*sixth session*]: Say, my wife and I are having a party next Wednesday, and we thought we'd like to have you and your wife come.

6. *Client* [*calls 3 hours before scheduled appointment*]: I've had the flu the past couple of days, but I feel like I'm getting over it. Do you think I should come today?

7. *Client* [*scheduled time for ending appointment has arrived, and social worker has already moved to end session. In previous sessions, client has tended to stay beyond designated ending time*]: What we were talking about reminded me of something I wanted to discuss today but forgot. I'd like to discuss it briefly, if you don't mind.

8. *Client* [*has just completed behavioral rehearsal involving talking with employer and played role beyond expectations of social worker*].

9. *Female client* [*tenth interview*]: I've really felt irritated with you during the week. When I brought up taking the correspondence course in art, all you could talk about was how some correspondence courses are rip-offs and that I could take courses at a college

for less money. I knew that, but I've checked into this correspondence course, and it's well worth the money. You put me down, and I've resented it.

10. *Client* [*seventh session*]: You seem uptight today. Is something bothering you? [*Social worker has been under strain associated with recent death of a parent and assisting surviving parent, who has been distraught.*]

11. *Client* [*sends the following message as the final session of successful therapy draws to a close*]: I really want to thank you for your help. You'll never know just how much help you've been. I felt like a sinking ship before I saw you. Now I feel I've got my head screwed on straight.

12. *Male delinquent on probation, age 15* [*first session*]: Before I tell you much, I need to know what happens to the information. Who else learns about me?

13. *Social worker* [*forgot to enter an appointment in daily schedule and, as a result, failed to keep a scheduled appointment with a client. Realizing this the next day, she telephones her client.*]

Modeled Responses

1. [*Smiling.*] "Well, I must admit, it's helpful. But I want you to know that marriage is no picnic for marriage counselors either. We have our rough spots, too. I have to work like everyone else to keep my marriage alive and growing."

2. "I gather you're wondering what my stand is and if I can understand and accept your feelings. I've worked with many Catholics and have been able to understand their problems. Would it trouble you if I weren't Catholic?"

3. "You're very observant. I have been struggling with drowsiness these past few minutes, and I apologize for that. I had to take an antihistamine before lunch, and a side effect of the drug is drowsiness. I want you to know my drowsiness has nothing to do with you. If I move around a little, the drowsiness passes."

4. "I can sense your frustration and your desire to firm up an agenda. If I made the decision, though, it might not fit for a number of you and I'd be assuming the group's prerogative.

Perhaps it would be helpful if the group followed the decision-by-consensus approach we discussed in our first session."

5. "Thank you for the invitation. I'm complimented you'd ask me. Although a part of me would like to come because it sounds like fun, I must decline your invitation. If I were to socialize with you while you're seeing me professionally, it would dilute my role, and I couldn't be as helpful to you. I hope you can understand my not accepting."

6. "I appreciate your calling to let me know. I think it would be better to change our appointment until you're sure you've recovered. Quite frankly, I don't want to risk being exposed to the flu, which I hope you can understand. I have a time open day after tomorrow. I'll set it aside for you if you'd like in the event you're fully recovered by then."

7. "I'm sorry I don't have the time to discuss the matter today. Let's save it for next week, and I'll make a note that you wanted to discuss it. We'll have to stop here today because I'm scheduled for another appointment."

8. "I want to share with you how impressed I was with how you asserted yourself and came across so positively. If you'd been with your boss, he'd have been impressed too."

9. "I'm glad you shared those feelings with me. And I can see I owe you an apology. You're right, I didn't explore whether you'd checked into the program, and I made some unwarranted assumptions. I guess I was overly concerned about your not being ripped off because I know others who have been by taking correspondence courses. But I can see I goofed because you had already looked into the course."

10. "Thank you for asking. Yes, I have been under some strain this past week. My mother died suddenly, which was a shock, and my father is taking it very hard. It's created a lot of pressure for me, but I think I can keep it from spilling over into our session. If I'm not able to focus on you, I will stop the session. Or if you don't feel I'm fully with you, please let me know. I don't want to shortchange you."

11. "Thank you very much. As we finish, I want you to know how much I've enjoyed working

with you. You've worked hard, and that's the primary reason you've made so much progress. I'm very interested in you and want to hear how your new job works out. Please keep in touch."

12. "Your question is a good one. I'd wonder the same thing if I were in your situation. I keep the information confidential as much as I can. We keep a file on you, of course, but I'm selective about what I put in it, and you have the right to check the file if you wish. I do meet with a supervisor, too, and we discuss how I can be of greatest help to clients. So I might share certain information with her, but she keeps it confidential. If you report violations of the law or the conditions of your probation, I can't assure you I'll keep that confidential. I'm responsible to the court, and part of my responsibility is to see that you meet the conditions of your parole. I have to make reports to the judge about that. Could you share with me your specific concerns about confidentiality?"

13. "Mr. M, I'm very embarrassed calling you because I realized just a few minutes ago I blew it yesterday. I forgot to enter my appointment with you in my schedule book last week and completely forgot about it. I hope you can accept my apology. I want you to know it had nothing to do with you."

SKILL DEVELOPMENT EXERCISES IN EMPATHIC COMMUNICATION

The following exercises, including a wide variety of actual client messages, will assist you in gaining mastery of reciprocal empathic responding (level 3). Read the client message and compose on paper an empathic response that captures the client's surface feelings. You may wish to use the paradigm "You feel _____ about (or because) _____" in organizing your response before phrasing it in typical conversation language. Strive to make your responses fresh, varied, and spontaneous. To expand your repertoire of responses, we strongly encourage you to continue using the lists of affective words and phrases.

After formulating your response, compare it with the modeled response provided at the end of the exercises. Analyze the differences, being particularly aware of the varied forms of responding and the elements that enhance the effectiveness of your own and/or the modeled responses.

Because 29 different exercises are included, we recommend that you not attempt to complete them in one sitting, but space them across several sessions. Consistent practice and careful scrutiny of your responses are essential in gaining mastery of this vital skill.

Client Statements

1. *Father of developmentally disabled child, age 14* [*who is becoming difficult to manage*]: We just don't know what to do with Henry. We've always wanted to take care of him, but we've reached the point where we're not sure it's doing any good for him or for us. He's grown so strong—we just can't restrain him anymore. He beat on my wife last week when she wouldn't take him to the Seven-Eleven late at night—I was out of town—and she's still bruised. She's afraid of him now, and I have to admit I'm getting that way too.

2. *Latino* [*living in urban barrio*]: Our children do better in school if they teach Spanish, not just English. We're afraid our children are behind because they don't understand English so good. And we don't know how to help them. Our people been trying to get a bilingual program, but the school board pay no attention to us.

3. *Female client, age 31:* Since my husband left town with another woman, I get lonely and depressed a lot of the time. And I find myself wondering whether something is wrong with me or whether men just can't be trusted.

4. *Mother* [*to child welfare protective services worker on doorstep during initial home visit*]: Who'd want to make trouble for me by accusing me of not taking care of my kids? [*Tearfully.*] Maybe I'm not the best mother in the world, but I try. There are a lot of kids around here that aren't cared for as well as mine.

5. *Male ninth-grade student* [*to school social worker*]: I feel like I'm a real loser. In sports

I've always had two left feet, and when they choose up sides, I'm always the last one chosen. A couple of times they've actually got into a fight over who doesn't have to choose me.

6. *Member of abused women's group at YWCA:* That last month I was living in mortal fear of Art. He'd get that hateful look in his eyes, and I'd know he was going to let me have it. The last time I was afraid he was going to kill me—and he might have if his brother hadn't dropped in. I'm afraid to go back to him. But what do I do? I can't stay here much longer!

7. *Male, age 34* [*to marital therapist*]: Just once I'd like to show my wife I can accomplish something without her prodding me. That's why I haven't told her I'm coming to see you. If she knew it, she'd try to take charge and call all the shots.

8. *African American man* [*in a group session*]: All I want is to be accepted as a person. When I get hired, I want it to be for what I'm capable of doing—not just because of my skin color. That's as phony and degrading as not being hired because of my skin color. I just want to be accepted for who I am.

9. *Client in a state prison* [*to rehabilitation worker*]: They treat you like an animal in here—herd you around like a damn cow. I know I've got to do my time, but there are some times I feel like I can't stand it any longer—like something's building up in me that's going to explode.

10. *Client* [*to mental health worker*]: I don't have any pleasant memories of my childhood. It seems like just so much empty space. I can remember my father watching television and staring at me with a blank look—as though I didn't exist.

11. *Patient in hospital* [*to medical social worker*]: I know Dr. Brown is a skilled surgeon, and he tells me not to worry—that there's very little risk in this surgery. I know I should feel reassured, but to tell you the truth, I'm just plain panic-stricken.

12. *Female member, age 29* [*in marital therapy group*]: I'd like to know what it's like with the rest of you. Hugh and I get into nasty

fights because I feel he doesn't help me when I really need help. He tells me there's no way he's going to do women's work! That really burns me. I get to feeling like I'm just supposed to be his slave.

13. *Male college student, age 21:* Francine says she's going to call me, but she never does—I have to do all the calling, or I probably wouldn't hear from her at all. It seems so one-sided. If I didn't need her so much I'd ask her what kind of game she's playing. I wonder if she isn't pretty selfish.

14. *White student, age 14* [*to school social worker*]: To be really honest, I don't like the black kids in our school. They pretty much stay to themselves, and they aren't friendly to whites. I don't know what to expect or how to act around them. I'm antsy when they're around and—well, to be honest—I'm scared I'll do something they won't like and they'll jump me.

15. *Single female, age 27* [*to mental health worker*]: I've been taking this class on the joys of womanhood. Last time the subject was how to catch a man. I can see I've been doing a lot of things wrong. But I won't lower myself to playing games with men. If that's what it takes, I guess I'll always be single.

16. *Married male, age 29* [*to marital therapist*]: Sexually, I'm unfulfilled in my marriage. At times I've even had thoughts of trying sex with men. That idea kind of intrigues me. My wife and I can talk about sex all right, but it doesn't get better.

17. *Married female, age 32* [*to family social worker*]: I love my husband and children and I don't know what I'd do without them. Yet on days like last Thursday, I feel I could just climb the walls. I want to run away from all of them and never come back.

18. *Married blind female* [*to other blind group members*]: You know, it really offends me when people praise me or make a fuss over me for doing something routine that anyone else could do. It makes me feel like I'm on exhibition. I want to be recognized for being competent—not for being blind.

19. *Male teacher* [*to mental health social worker*]: I have this thing about not being able to accept compliments. A friend told me about

how much of a positive impact I've had on several students over the years. I couldn't accept that and feel good. My thought was, "You must be mistaken. I've never had that kind of effect on anyone."

20. *Lesbian, age 26* [*to private social worker*]: The girls at the office were talking about lesbians the other day and about how repulsive the very thought of lesbianism was to them. How do you think I felt?

21. *Male member of alcoholics group:* I don't feel like I belong in this group. The rest of you seem to have better educations and better jobs. Hell, I only finished junior high, and I'm just a welder.

22. *Patient* [*to a medical social worker*]: Maybe it doesn't seem important to other people, but I don't like having to share a room with a heavy smoker. When I went through the admissions inteview, I specifically requested that I not be put in a room with a smoker.

23. *Male, age 30* [*to private social worker*]: Sometimes I can't believe how bent out of shape I get over little things. When I lose a chess game, I go into orbit. First, I'm furious with myself for blundering. It's not like me to make rank blunders. I guess I feel humiliated, because I immediately want to start another game and get even with the other guy.

24. *Male client, age 72* [*to medical social worker*]: Since I had my heart attack, I've just had this feeling of foreboding—like my life's over for all practical purposes. I feel like I'm just an invalid—of no use to myself or anyone else.

25. *Male applicant* [*to public assistance worker*]: This is a very hard thing for me to do. I never thought I'd have to turn to welfare for help. But what do you do when you're backed into a corner? I've looked for jobs everywhere, but there's none to be had.

26. *Child, age 15, in foster care* [*to child welfare worker*]: I've had it with them [*the foster parents*]. They want me to work all the time—like I'm a slave or something. If you don't get me out of here, I'm going to run.

27. *Family member, age 13* [*in initial family group session*]: Yeah, I can tell you what I'd like to be different in our family. I'd like to

feel that we care about each other, but it's not that way. Every time I go in the house, Mom nags me, and Dad doesn't say anything—he doesn't seem to care. Sometimes I feel there's no point in going home.

28. *Married woman* [*in initial interview with marital therapist*]: I think this is just a complete waste of time. I didn't want to come and wouldn't be here if my husband hadn't forced me. He's the one who should be here—not me.

29 *Married woman* [*in YWCA adult women's group*]: This past week I've felt really good about how things are going—like I've finally got my act together. I've handled my emotions better, and for the first time in a long time, I've felt like an intelligent human being.

Modeled Responses

1. "So you're really on the horns of a dilemma. You've wanted to keep him at home, but in light of his recent aggressiveness and his strength, you're becoming really frightened and wonder if other arrangements wouldn't be better for both you and him."

2. "I can see you're worried about how your children are doing in school and believe they need a bilingual program."

3. "It's been a real blow—your husband leaving you for another woman—and you've just felt so alone. And you find yourself dwelling on the painful question, 'Is something wrong with me, or is it that you just can't trust men?'"

4. "This is very upsetting for you. You seem to be saying that it's not fair being turned in when you believe you take care of your children. Please understand I'm not accusing you of neglecting your children. But I do have to investigate complaints. It may be I'll be able to turn in a positive report. I hope so. But I do need to talk with you further. May I come in?"

5. "So I gather you feel you really got short-changed as far as athletic talents are concerned. It's humiliating to you to feel so left out and be the last guy chosen."

6. "It sounds as though you lived in terror that last month and literally feared for your life. You

were wise to remove yourself when you did. A number of other women in the group have had similar experiences and are facing the same dilemma about what to do now. As group members, each of us can be helpful to other group members in thinking through what's best to do now. In the meantime, you have a safe place to stay and some time to plan."

7. "Sounds like you get pretty annoyed, thinking about her prodding and trying to take charge. I gather it's important right now that you prove to her and to yourself you can do something on your own."

8. "I gather you're fed up with having people relate to you as a color or a minority, instead of being accepted as an individual—as yourself."

9. "If I understand you, you feel degraded by the way you're treated—as though you're less than a human being. And that really gets to you—sometimes you find yourself seething with resentment that threatens to boil over."

10. "From what you say, I get a picture of you just feeling so all alone as you were growing up—as though you didn't feel very important to anyone, especially your father."

11. "So intellectually, you tell yourself not to worry, that you're in good hands. Still, on another level you have to admit you're terrified of that operation. [*Brief pause.*] Your fear is pretty natural, though. Most people who are honest with themselves experience fear. I'd be interested in hearing more about your fears."

12. "So the two of you get into some real struggles over differences in your views as to what is reasonable of you to expect from Hugh. And you seem to be saying you very much resent his refusal to pitch in—like it's not fair to have to carry that burden alone. Hugh, I'd be interested in hearing your views. Then we can hear how other members deal with this kind of situation."

13. "Sounds like part of you is saying you have a right to expect more from Francine—that you don't feel good about always having to be the one to take the initiative. You also seem to feel you'd like to confront her with what she's doing, but you're uneasy about doing that because you don't want to risk

losing her."

14. "So, you're uncomfortable around them and just don't know how to read them. I gather you kind of walk on eggs when they're around for fear you'll blow it and they'll climb all over you."

15. "There is a lot of conflicting advice around these days about how men and women should relate to each other and it is hard to figure out what to believe. You know you don't want to play games, and yet that is what the class is telling you to do if you don't want to be single."

16. "Things don't get better despite your talks, and you get pretty discouraged. At times you find yourself wondering if you'd get sexual fulfillment with men, and that appeals to you in some ways."

17. "So even though you care deeply for them, there are days when you just feel so overwhelmed you'd like to buy a one-way ticket out of all the responsibility."

18. "Are you saying you feel singled out and demeaned when people flatter you for doing things anyone could do? It ticks you off, and you wish people would recognize you for being competent—not being blind."

19. "In a way you seem to be saying you don't feel comfortable with compliments because you feel you don't really deserve them. It's like you feel you don't do anything worthy of a compliment."

20. "You must have felt extremely uncomfortable and resentful believing that they would condemn you if they knew. It must have been most painful for you."

21. "Ted, you seem to feel uncomfortable, like you don't fit with the other group members. I gather you're feeling the rest of the members are above you, and you're concerned they won't accept you."

22. "I can see you'd be pretty irritated then, ending up with a smoker, especially after making a specific request as you did. I can understand your feelings, and I'll look into having this corrected. Thanks for letting me know."

23. "When you lose, lots of feelings surge through you—anger and disappointment with yourself

for goofing, loss of face, and an urgency to prove you can beat the other guy."

24. "So things look pretty grim to you right now. As though you have nothing to look forward to and are just washed up. And you're apprehensive that things might get worse rather than better."

25. "It sounds like you've struggled hard to make it on your own and that it's been painful to admit to yourself you needed help. I'm sensing you're feeling some embarrassment about having to ask for help."

26. "You sound pretty burned up right now, and I can sense you feel there has to be a change. I'd like to hear more about exactly what has been happening."

27. "Am I getting it right, that you feel picked on by Mom and ignored by Dad? And you'd like to feel they really care about you. You'd like more love shown by family members for each other."

28. "You're feeling pretty angry with your husband for forcing you to come. I gather you're pretty resentful right now at having to be here and just don't see the need for it."

29. "That sounds great. You seem delighted with your progress—like you're really getting on top of things. And most of all you're liking yourself again."

Answers to Exercise in Identifying Surface and Underlying Feelings

1. *Apparent feelings:* unimportant, neglected, disappointed, hurt. *Probably deeper feelings:* rejected, abandoned, forsaken, deprived, lonely, depressed.

2. *Apparent feelings:* unloved, insecure, confused, embarrassed, left out or excluded. *Probable deeper feelings:* hurt, resentful, unvalued, rejected, taken for granted, degraded, doubting own desirability.

3. *Apparent feelings:* chagrined, disappointed in self, discouraged, letting children down, perplexed. *Probable deeper feelings:* guilty, inadequate, crummy, sense of failure, out of control, fear of damaging children.

Answers to Exercises to Discriminate Levels of Empathic Responding

CLIENT STATEMENT	
1	
Response	*Level*
1.	2
2.	1
3.	1
4.	3
5.	2
6.	2
7.	4
8.	1

CLIENT STATEMENT			
2		**3**	
Response	*Level*	*Response*	*Level*
1.	1	1.	1
2.	3	2.	4
3.	1	3.	2
4.	2	4.	2
5.	4	5.	5
6.	1	6.	1
7.	3	7.	2
8.	2	8.	2

Notes

1. In categorizing her husband as a "bump on a log," the wife makes a sweeping generalization that fits her husband's behavior into a mold. Although the social worker chose to keep the focus momentarily on the husband, it is important that he helps the couple to avoid labeling each other. Strategies for intervening when clients use labels are delineated in a later chapter.

CHAPTER 6

Verbal Following, Exploring, and Focusing Skills

CHAPTER OVERVIEW

In this chapter, we introduce verbal following skills and their uses in exploring client concerns and focusing. In addition to work with clients in micro practice, such skills are also useful at the meso level in work on behalf of clients, through advocacy, and in work with colleagues and other professionals.

MAINTAINING PSYCHOLOGICAL CONTACT WITH CLIENTS AND EXPLORING THEIR PROBLEMS

Researchers and theoreticians agree that verbal following by social workers is critical in communication with clients (Finn & Rose, 1982; D. Katz, 1979; Mayadas & O'Brien, 1976; Schinke, Blythe, Gilchrist, & Smith, 1980). Verbal following involves the use of and, at times, blending of discrete skills that enable social workers to maintain psychological contact on a moment-by-moment basis with clients and to covey accurate understanding of their messages. Moreover, embodied in verbal following behavior are two performance variables that are essential to satisfaction and continuance on the part of the client:

1. *Stimulus-response congruence:* the extent to which social workers' responses provide feed-back to clients that their messages are accurately received.

2. *Content relevance:* the extent to which the content of social workers' responses is perceived by clients as relevant to their substantive concerns.

These variables were first conceptualized by A. Rosen (1972), who detailed empirical and theoretical support for their relationship to client continuance. They received further validation as critical social worker behavioral responses in findings of a study by Duehn and Proctor (1977). Analyzing worker-client transactions, these authors found that social workers responded incongruently to clients' messages much more frequently with clients who terminated treatment prematurely than with clients who continued treatment. (Incongruent messages fail to provide immediate feedback to clients that their messages have been received.) Further, social workers gave a lower proportion of responses that matched the content expectations of "discontinuers" than they did with "continuers." These authors concluded that responses that are relevant and accurately attend to client messages gradually increase moment-by-moment client satisfaction with interactions in the interview. On the other hand, continued use of questions and other responses not associated with previous client messages and

139

139

unrelated to the client's substantive concerns contribute to consistent client dissatisfaction. When client content expectations are not fulfilled, clients prematurely discontinue treatment. Effective use of such attending behaviors should facilitate motivational congruence, or the fit between client motivation and social worker goals, which has been shown to be associated with better outcomes in social work effectiveness studies (Reid & Hanrahan, 1982). Employing responses that directly relate to client messages and concerns thus enhances client satisfaction, fosters continuance, and also greatly facilitates the establishment of a viable working relationship.

The importance of explaining the relevance of questions to Asian Americans seen for mental health problems has been emphasized by Tsui and Schultz (1985): The social worker must explicitly educate the client about the purpose of questions regarding clinical history, previous treatment information, family background, and psychosocial stressors. The linkage of these issues to their current symptoms is not clear to many Asians or other clients. Many Asian clients conceive of mental distress as the result of physiological disorder or character flaws. This issue must be dealt with sensitively before any sensible therapeutic work can be effected (pp. 567–568). Similarly, clients who are members of oppressed groups may perceive questions as interrogations not designed to help them with their own concerns, so the rationale for such questions must be explained.

In addition to enabling social workers to maintain close psychological contact with clients, verbal following skills serve two other important functions in the helping process. First, these skills yield rich personal information, allowing social workers to explore clients' problems in depth. Second, these skills enable social workers to focus selectively on components of the clients' experience and on dynamics in the helping process that facilitate positive client change.

In the following pages, we introduce you to skills for verbally following and exploring clients' problems. Several of these skills are easily mastered. Others require more effort to acquire. We provide exercises in the body of the chapter to assist you in acquiring proficiency. Although empathic responding is the most vital skill for verbally following clients' messages, we have not included it in this chapter because it was discussed in the preceding one. Later, however, we discuss the blending of empathic responses with other verbal following skills to advance your ability in focusing upon and fully exploring relevant client problems.

VERBAL FOLLOWING SKILLS

Briefly, the discrete skills highlighted in this chapter include the following types of responses:

1. Furthering
2. Paraphrasing
3. Closed-ended questions
4. Open-ended questions
5. Seeking concreteness
6. Providing and maintaining focus
7. Summarizing

Furthering Responses

Furthering responses indicate social workers are listening attentively and encourage the client to verbalize. They are of two types:

1. *Minimal prompts,* which signal the social worker's attentiveness and encourage the client to continue verbalizing, can be either nonverbal or verbal. *Nonverbal minimal prompts* consist of nodding the head, using facial expressions, or employing gestures that convey receptivity, interest, and commitment to understanding. The nonverbal prompts implicitly convey the message, "I am with you; please continue."

Verbal minimal prompts consist of brief messages that convey interest and encourage or request expanded verbalizations along the lines of the previous expressions by the client. These messages include "Yes," "I see," "But?" "Mm-mmm" (the so-called empathic grunt), "Tell me more," "And then what happened?" "And?" "Please go on," "Tell me more, please," and other similar brief messages that affirm the appropriateness of what the client has been saying and prompt him or her to continue.

2. *Accent responses* (Hackney & Cormier, 1979) involve repeating, in a questioning tone of voice or with emphasis, a word or a short phrase. If, for instance, a client says, "I've really had it with the way my supervisor at work is treating me," the social worker might use the short response, "Had it?" to prompt further elaboration by the client.

Paraphrasing Responses

Paraphrasing involves using fresh words to restate the client's message concisely. Responses that paraphrase are more apt to focus on the cognitive aspects of client messages (i.e., emphasize situations, ideas, objects, persons) than on the client's affective state, although reference may be made to obvious feelings. These are four examples of paraphrasing:

Elder client: I don't want to get into a living situation in which I will not be able to make choices on my own.

Social Worker: So independence is a very important issue for you.

Client: I went to the doctor today for a final checkup, and she said that I was doing fine.

Social worker: She gave you a clean bill of health, then.

Client: I just don't know what to think about the way my girlfriend treats me. Sometimes she seems so warm—like she really likes me—and at other times she acts really cold.

Social worker: Her hot and cold behavior really confuses you.

Managed care utilization reviewer: We don't think that your patient's condition justifies the level of service that you recommend.

Social worker: So you feel that my documentation does not justify the need that I have recommended according to the approval guidelines you are working from.

Note that in the latter example, paraphrasing is used as part of the communication with a person whose opinion is important as it relates to delivering client services, the health insurance care manager (Strom-Gottfried, 1998). When employed sparingly, paraphrases may be interspersed with other facilitative responses to prompt client expression. Used to excess, however, paraphrasing produces a mimicking effect. Paraphrases are helpful, however, when social workers want to bring focus to an idea or situation for client consideration. However, paraphrasing is inappropriate when clients are preoccupied with feelings. In such cases, social workers need to relate with empathic responses that accurately capture clients' affect and assist them to reflect on and sort through feelings. Sometimes social workers may choose to direct discussion away from feelings for therapeutic purposes. For instance, a social worker may believe that a chronically depressed client who habitually expresses discouragement and disillusionment would benefit by focusing less on feelings and more on actions to alleviate distress. When the social worker chooses to deemphasize feelings, paraphrases that reflect content are helpful and appropriate.

Exercise in Paraphrasing

In the following exercise, formulate written responses that paraphrase the messages of clients and other persons. Remember, paraphrases usually reflect the cognitive aspects of messages rather than feelings. Modeled response for these exercises are found at the end of the chapter. Please note that paraphrasing a client's or other person's comments does not mean that you agree with or condone those thoughts.

Client/Colleague Statements

1. *Client:* I can't talk to people. I just completely freeze up in a group.
2. *Wife:* I think that in the last few weeks I've been able to listen much more often to my husband and children.
3. *Client:* Whenever I get into an argument with my mother, I always end up losing. I guess I'm still afraid of her.

4. *Husband:* I just can't decide what to do. If I go ahead with the divorce, I'll probably lose custody of the kids—and I won't be able to see them very much. If I don't, though, I'll have to put up with the same old thing. I don't think my wife is going to change.

5. *Elder client:* It wasn't so difficult to adjust to this place because the people who run it are helpful and friendly and I am able to make contacts easily—I've always been a people person.

6. *Mother* [*speaking about daughter*]: When it comes right down to it, I think I'm to blame for a lot of her problems.

7. *Mother* [*participating in welfare-to-work program*]: I don't know how they can expect me to be a good mother and make school appointments, supervise my kids, and put in all these work hours.

8. *Member of treatment team:* I just don't see where putting in more services in this family makes sense. The mother is not motivated and the kids are better off away from her. This family has been messed up forever.

Closed- and Open-Ended Responding

Generally used to elicit specific information, *closed-ended questions* define a topic and restrict the client's response to a few words or a simple yes or no answer. Typical examples of closed-ended questions are the following:

- "When did you obtain your divorce?"
- "Do you have any sexual difficulties in your marriage?"
- "When did you last have a physical examination?"
- "Is your health insurance Medicare?"

Although closed-ended questions restrict the client and elicit limited information, in many instances these responses are both appropriate and helpful. Later in this chapter we discuss how and when to use this type of response effectively.

In contrast to closed-ended responses, which circumscribe client messages, *open-ended questions* and statements invite expanded expression and leave the client free to express what seems most relevant and important. For example:

Social worker: You've mentioned your daughter. Tell me how she enters into your problem.

Client: I don't know what to do. Sometimes I think she is just pushing me so that she can go live with her father. When I ask her to help around the house, she won't, and says that she doesn't owe me anything. When I try to insist on her helping, it just ends up in an ugly scene without anything being accomplished. It makes me feel so helpless.

In the preceding example, the social worker's open-ended question prompted the client to expand on the details of the problems with her daughter, including a description of her daughter's behavior, her own efforts to cope, and her present sense of defeat. The information contained in the message is typical of the richness of data obtained through open-ended responding.

In other circumstances, such as in the prior example of a telephone conversation with a managed care utilization reviewer, the social worker can use an open-ended question to attempt to explore common ground that can lead to a mutually beneficial resolution.

- *Social worker* [*to managed care utilization reviewer*]: Can you clarify for me how appropriate coverage is determined for situations such as the one I have described?

Some open-ended responses are unstructured, leaving the topic to the client's choosing ("Tell me what you would like to discuss today," or "What else can you tell me about the problems that you're experiencing?"). Other open-ended responses are structured in that the social worker defines the topic to be discussed but leaves clients free to respond in any way they wish ("You've mentioned feeling ashamed about the incident that occurred between you and your son. I'd be interested in hearing more about that.") Still other open-ended responses fall along a continuum between structured and unstructured in that they give the client leeway to answer with a few words or to elaborate with more information ("How willing are you to do this?").

Social workers may formulate open-ended responses either by asking a question or by giving a polite command. For example, when a terminally ill cancer patient said, "The doctor thinks I could live about six or seven months now; it could be less, it could be more; it's just an educated guess is what he told me," the social worker could respond by asking, "How are you feeling about that prognosis?" or "Would you tell me how you are feeling about that prognosis?" Polite commands have the effect of direct questions in requesting information but are less forceful and involve greater finesse. Similar in nature are embedded questions that do not take the form of a question but embody a request for information. Examples of embedded questions are "I'm curious about . . ." "I'm wondering if . . ." and "I'm interested in knowing . . ." Open-ended questions often start with *what* or *how. Why* questions are often unproductive inasmuch as they ask for reasons, motives, or causes that are either obvious, obscure, or unknown to the client. Asking how ("How did that happen?") rather than why ("Why did that happen?") often elicits far richer information regarding client behavior and patterns.

Exercises in Identifying Closed- and Open-Ended Responses

The following exercises will assist you to differentiate between closed- and open-ended messages. Identify each statement with either a C for closed or O for open. Turn to the end of the chapter to check your answers.

1. "Did your mother ask you to see me because of the problem you had with the principal?"

2. "When John says that to you, what do you experience inside?"

3. "You said you're feeling fed up and you're just not sure that pursuing a reconciliation is worth your trouble. Could you elaborate?"

4. "When is your court date?"

Now read the following client messages and respond by writing open-ended responses. Avoid using *why* questions. Examples of open-ended responses to these messages can be found at the end of the chapter.

Client Statements

1. *Client:* Whenever I'm in a group with Ralph, I find myself saying something that will let him know that I am smart too.

2. *Client:* I always have had my parents telephone for me about appointments and other things. I might foul up.

3. *Terminally ill cancer patient:* Some days I am really angry because I'm only forty-six years old and there are so many more things I wanted to do. Other days, I feel kind of defeated, like this is what I get for smoking two packs a day for twenty-five years.

4. *Teenager* [*speaking of a previous probation counselor*]: He sure let me down. And I really trusted him. He knows a lot about me because I spilled my guts.

5. *Group nursing home administrator:* I think that we are going to have to move Gladys to another more suitable kind of living arrangement. We aren't able to provide the kind of care that she needs.

In the following sections, we explain how you can blend open-ended and empathic responses to keep a discussion focused on a specific topic. In preparation for that, respond to the next two client messages by formulating an empathic response followed by an open-ended question that encourages the client to elaborate on the same topic.

6. *Unwed teenage girl seeking abortion* [*brought in by her mother who wishes to discuss birth alternatives*]: I feel like you are all tied up with my mother, trying to talk me out of what I have decided to do.

7. *Client:* Life is such a hassle, and it doesn't seem to have any meaning or make sense. I

just don't know whether I want to try figuring it out any longer.

The difference between closed-ended and open-ended responses may seem obvious to you, particularly if you completed the preceding exercises. It has been our experience, however, that beginning and even seasoned social workers have difficulty in actual sessions in discriminating whether their responses are open- or closed-ended, in observing the differential effect of these two types of responses in yielding rich and relevant data, and in deciding which of the two types of responses is appropriate at a given moment. We recommend, therefore, that as you converse with your associates, you practice drawing them out by employing open-ended responses and noting how they respond. We also recommend that you use the form provided at the end of the chapter to assess both the frequency and the appropriateness of your closed- and open-ended responses in several taped client sessions.

Discriminate Use of Closed- and Open-Ended Questions

Beginning social workers typically ask an excessive number of closed-ended questions, many of which block communication or are inefficient or irrelevant to the helping process. When this occurs, the session tends to take on the flavor of an interrogation, with the social worker bombarding the client with questions and taking responsibility for maintaining verbalization. Notice what happens, for example, in the following excerpt from a recording of a social worker interviewing an institutionalized youth.

Social worker: I met your mother yesterday. Did she come all the way from Colorado to see you?

Client: Yeah.

Social worker: It seems to me that she must really care about you to take the bus and make the trip up here to see you. Don't you think so?

Client: I suppose so.

Social worker: Did the visit with her go all right?

Client: Fine. We had a good time.

Social worker: You had said you were going to talk to her about a possible home visit. Did you do that?

Client: Yes.

When closed-ended responses are used to elicit information in lieu of open-ended responses, as in the preceding example, many more discrete interchanges will occur, but the client's responses will be brief and the information yield markedly lower.

Open-ended responses often elicit the same data as closed-ended questions but in addition draw out much more information and elaboration of the problem from the client. The following two examples contrast open-ended and closed-ended responses that address the same topic with a given client. To appreciate the differences in the richness of information yielded by these contrasting responses, compare the likely client responses elicited by such questions to the closed-ended questions used above.

1. *Closed-ended:* "Did she come all the way from Colorado to see you?"

   Open-ended: "Tell me about your visit with your mother."

2. *Closed-ended:* "Did you talk with her about a possible home visit?"

   Open-ended: "How did you mother respond when you talked about a possible home visit?"

Occasionally, beginning social workers also use closed-ended questions to explore feelings, but responses from clients typically involve minimal self-disclosure, as might be expected. Rather than encourage expanded expression of feelings, closed-ended questions limit responses, as illustrated in the following example:

Social worker: Did you feel rejected when she turned down your invitation?

Client: Yeah.

Social worker: Have there been other times when you've felt rejected that way?

Client: Oh, yeah. Lots of times.

Social worker: When was the first time?

Client: Gee, that's hard to say.

Had the social worker employed empathic and open-ended responses to explore the feelings and thoughts associated with being rejected, the client would likely have revealed much more.

Because open-ended responses elicit more information than closed-ended ones, frequent use of the former increases the efficiency of data gathering. The richness of information revealed by the client, in fact, is directly proportional to the frequency with which open-ended responses are employed. Frequent use of open-ended responses also fosters a smoothly floating session; consistently asking closed-ended questions, by contrast, often results in a fragmented, discontinuous process.

Closed-ended questions are used chiefly to elicit essential factual information. Skillful social workers use closed-ended questions sparingly, since clients usually reveal extensive factual information spontaneously as they unfold their stories, aided by the social worker's open-ended and furthering responses. Employed little during the first part of a session, closed questions are used more extensively later to elicit data that may have been omitted by clients, such as names and ages of children, place of employment, date of marriage, medical facts, and data regarding family or origin.

In obtaining factual data such as the preceding, the social worker can unobtrusively weave into the discussion closed-ended questions that directly pertain to the topic. For example, a client may relate certain marital problems that have existed for many years, and the social worker may ask parenthetically, "And you've been married how many years?" Similarly, a parent may explain that a child began to truant from school when the parent started to work 6 months ago, to which the social worker may respond, "I see. Incidentally, what type of work do you do?" It is vital, of course, to shift the focus back to the problem. If necessary, the social worker can easily maintain focus by using an open-ended response to pick up the thread of the discussion. For example, the social worker may comment, "You mentioned that Ernie began missing school when you started to work. I'd like to hear more about what was happening in your family at that time."

Because open-ended responses generally yield rich information, they are used throughout initial sessions. They are used most heavily, however, in the first portion of sessions to open up communication and to invite clients to reveal problematic aspects of their lives. The following open-ended polite command is a typical opening message: "Could you tell me what it is you wish to discuss, and we can think about it together." Because such responses convey interest in clients as well as respect for clients' abilities to relate their problems in their own way, they also contribute to the development of a working relationship.

As clients disclose certain problem areas, open-ended responses are also extensively employed to elicit additional relevant information. Clients, for example, may disclose difficulties at work or in relationships with other family members. These are typical open-ended responses that will elicit clarifying information:

- "Tell me more about your problems at work."
- "I'd like to hear more about the circumstances when you were mugged coming home with the groceries."

Open-ended responses can be used to enhance communication with collaterals, colleagues, and other professionals. For example, Strom-Gottfried suggests using effective communication skills in negotiation and communication between care providers and utilization reviewers. When a client has not been approved for a kind of service that the social worker recommended, the worker can attempt to join with the reviewer in identifying goals both would embrace and request information in an open-ended fashion.

- "I appreciate your concern that she gets the best available services and that her condition does not get worse. We are concerned with safety as we know you are. Could you tell me more about how this protocol can help us assure her safety?" (Strom-Gottfried, 1998, p. 398).

It may sometimes be necessary to employ closed-ended questions extensively to elicit information if the client is unresponsive and withholds information or has limited conceptual and mental abilities. However, in the former case it is vital to explore the clients' immediate feelings about being in the session, which often are negative and impede verbal expression. Focusing on and resolving negative feelings, which we discuss in Chapter 12, may pave the way to using open-ended responses to good advantage. Using closed-ended messages as a major interviewing tool early in sessions may be appropriate with some children, but the use of open-ended responses should be consistently tested as the relationship develops.

When you incorporate open-ended responses into your repertoire, you will experience a dramatic positive change in interviewing style and confidence level. To assist you to develop skill in blending and balancing open-ended and closed-ended responses, we have provided a recording form that you may wish to use in examining your own interviewing style (see Figure 6-1). Utilizing the form, analyze several recorded individual, conjoint, or group sessions over a period of time to determine changes you are making in employing these two types of responses. The recording form will assist you in determining the extent to which you have used open- and closed-ended responses. In addition, however, you may wish to review your work for the following purposes:

1. To determine when relevant data are missing and whether the information might have been more appropriately obtained through an open- or closed-ended response.

2. To determine when your use of closed-ended questions was irrelevant or ineffective, or distracted from the data-gathering process.

3. To practice formulating open-ended responses you might use in place of closed-ended responses to increase client participation and elicit richer data.

SOCIAL WORKER'S RESPONSE	OPEN-ENDED RESPONSES	CLOSED-ENDED RESPONSES
1.		
2.		
3.		
4.		
5.		
6.		
7.		

Directions: Record your discrete open- and closed-ended responses and place a check in the appropriate column. Agency time constraints will dictate how often you can practice it.

Figure 6-1 Recording Form for Open- and Closed-Ended Responding

Seeking Concreteness

People (including clients and beginning social workers) are inclined to think and talk in generalities and to use words that lack precision when speaking of their experiences. In order to communicate one's feelings and experiences so that they are fully understood, however, a person must be able to respond concretely, that is, with specificity. Responding concretely involves utilizing words that describe in explicit terms specific experiences, behaviors, and feelings. In the following message, the respondent expresses his experiencing in vague and general terms: "I thought you gave a good speech." By contrast, he might have described his experience in precise language: "As you delivered your speech, I was impressed with your relaxed manner and your clear articulation of the issues." To test your comprehension of the concept of concreteness, assess which of the following messages give descriptive information concerning what a client experiences:

1. "I have had a couple of accidents that would not have happened if I had full control of my hands. The results weren't that serious but they could be."

2. "I'm uneasy right now because I don't know what to expect from counseling, and I'm afraid you might think that I really don't need it."

3. "You are a good girl, Susie."

4. "People don't seem to care whether other people have problems."

5. "My previous experience with counselors was lousy."

6. "I really wonder if I'll be able to keep from crying and to find the words to tell my husband that it's all over—that I want a divorce."

7. "You did a good job."

You could probably readily identify which of the preceding messages contained language that increased the specificity of the information conveyed by the client. In developing competency as a social worker, one of your challenges is to consistently recognize clients' messages expressed in abstract and general terms and to assist them to reveal highly specific information related to feelings and experiences. Such information will assist you to make accurate assessments and, in turn, to plan interventions accordingly.

The second challenge is to help clients learn how to respond more concretely in their relationships with others, a task you will not be able to accomplish unless you are able to model the dimension of concreteness yourself.

The third challenge is to describe your own experience in language that is precise and descriptive. It is thus not enough to recognize concrete messages; you must familiarize yourself with and practice responding concretely to the extent that it becomes a natural style of speaking and relating to others. The remainder of our discussion on the skill of seeking concreteness is devoted to assisting you in meeting the three challenges.

Types of Responses That Facilitate Specificity of Expression by Clients

Social workers who fail to move beyond general and abstract messages often have little grasp of the specificity and meaning of a client's problem. Eliciting highly specific information that minimizes errors or misinterpretations, however, is a formidable challenge because clients typically present impressions, views, conclusions, and opinions that, despite efforts to be objective, are biased and distorted to some extent. Further, as we have already mentioned, clients are prone to speak in generalities and to respond with imprecise language, and thus their messages may be interpreted differently by different people. To help you to conceptualize various ways you may assist clients to respond more concretely, in the following sections we have identified, discussed, and illustrated different facets of responses that seek concreteness:

1. Checking out perceptions

2. Clarifying the meaning of vague or unfamiliar terms

3. Exploring the basis of conclusions drawn by clients

4. Assisting clients to personalize their statements

5. Eliciting specific feelings

6. Focusing on the her-and-now, rather than on the distant past

7. Eliciting details related to clients' experiences

8. Eliciting details related to interactional behavior

In addition to discussing the preceding categories, we have included ten skill development exercises, the completion of which will further bring your comprehension of concreteness from the general and abstract to the specific and concrete.

Checking Out Perceptions   Responses that assist social workers to clarify and to "check out" whether they have accurately heard clients' messages (e.g., "Do you mean . . ." or "Are you saying...") are vital in building rapport with clients and in communicating the desire to understand their problems. Such responses also minimize misperceptions or projections in the helping process. Clients benefit from social workers' efforts to understand, in that clarifying responses assist clients in sharpening and reformulating their thinking about feelings and other concerns and thus encourage self-awareness and growth.

At times, perception checking is necessary because clients convey messages that are incomplete, ambiguous, or complex. Occasionally, social workers encounter clients who repetitively communicate in highly abstract or metaphorical styles, or other clients whose thinking is scattered and whose messages often just do not "track" or make sense. In such instances, social workers must sometimes spend an inordinate amount of time sorting through clients' messages and clarifying perceptions.

At other times, the need for clarification is not because of confusing, faulty, or incomplete client messages but because the social worker has simply not fully attended to a client's message or comprehended its meaning. It is important to realize that fully attending moment by moment throughout a session requires intense concentration. Further, it is impossible to full focus on and comprehend the essence of every message in group and family meetings where myriad transactions occur and competing communications bid for the social worker's attention. Thus, it is important that you develop skill in using clarifying responses to elicit ongoing feedback regarding your perceptions and to acknowledge freely your need for clarification when you are confused or uncertain. Rather than reflect personal or professional inadequacy, your efforts to accurately grasp the client's meaning and feelings will most likely be perceived as signs of your genuineness and your commitment to understand.

Perception checking may be accomplished by asking simple questions that seek clarification or by combining your request for clarification with a paraphrase or empathic response that reflects your perception of the client's message (e.g., "I think you were saying _____. Is that right?").

Examples of various clarifying messages include the following:

- "You seem to be really irritated, not only because he didn't respond when you asked him to help but because he seemed to be deliberately trying to hurt you. Is that accurate?"

- "I'm not sure I'm following you. Let me see if I understand the order of the events you described . . ."

- "Would you expand on what you are saying so that I can be sure that I understand what you mean?"

- "Could you go over that again and perhaps give an illustration that might help me to understand?"

- "I'm confused. Let me try to restate what I think you're saying."

- "As a group, you seem to be divided in your approach to this matter. I'd like to summarize what I'm hearing, and I would then appreciate some input regarding whether I understand the various positions that have been expressed."

In addition to clarifying their own perceptions, social workers need to assist clients in conjoint or group sessions to clarify their perceptions of the messages of others who are present. This may be accomplished in any of the following ways:

- *By modeling* clarifying responses, which occurs naturally as social workers seek to check out their own perceptions of clients' messages.

- *By directing* clients to ask for clarification. Consider, for example, the following response by a social worker in a conjoint session: "You [*mother*] had a confused look on your face, and I'm not sure that you understood your daughter's point. Would you repeat back to her what you heard and then ask her if you understood correctly?"

- *By teaching* clients how to clarify perceptions and by reinforcing their efforts to "check out" the messages of others, as illustrated in the following responses:

- [*To group*]: "One of the reasons families have communication problems is that members don't hear accurately what others are trying to say, and therefore, they often respond or react on the basis of incorrect or inadequate information. I would like to encourage all of you to frequently use what I call 'checking out' responses such as, 'I'm not sure what you meant. Were you saying . . .?' to clarify statements of others. As we go along, I'll point out instances in which I notice any of you using this kind of response.

- [*To family*]: "I'm wondering if you all noticed Jim 'checking' out what his dad said. . . . As you may recall, we talked about the importance of these kinds of responses earlier. [*To dad*] I'm wondering, Bob, what you experienced when Jim did that?"

Clarifying the Meaning of Vague or Unfamiliar Terms In expressing themselves, clients often employ terms that have multiple meanings or use terms in idiosyncratic ways. For example, in the message, "My husband is cruel to me," the word *cruel* may have different meanings to social worker and client. Before establishing what this term means to a particular client, a social worker cannot be certain whether the client is re-

ferring to physical abuse, criticism, nagging, withholding affections, or other possibilities. The precise meaning can be clarified by employing one of the following responses:

- "In what way is he cruel?"

- "I'm not sure what you mean by cruel. Could you clarify that for me?"

- "I can tell that is painful for you. Could you give me some examples of times he has been cruel?"

Many other adjectives also lack precision, and it is therefore important to avoid assuming that the client means the same thing you mean when you employ a given term. The terms *oversexed, codependent, irresponsible, selfish, careless,* and other terms conjure up meanings that vary according to the reference points of different persons. Exact meanings are best determined by asking for clarification or for examples of events in which the behavior alluded to actually occurred.

Exploring the Basis of Conclusions Drawn by Clients Clients often present views or conclusions as though they are established facts. For example, the messages "I'm losing my mind," or "My partner doesn't love me anymore," involve views or conclusions that the client has drawn. To accurately assess the client's difficulties, additional information upon which the views or conclusions are based must be elicited. This information is valuable in assessing the thinking patterns of the client, which are powerful determinants of emotions and behavior. For example, a person who believes his or her partner no longer feels loved will behave as though this belief represents reality. The social worker's role, of course, is to unravel distortions and to challenge erroneous conclusions in a facilitative manner.

Responses that would elicit clarification of the basis of views and conclusions embodied in the messages cited earlier include the following:

- "How do you mean, losing your mind?"

- "How have you concluded you're losing your mind?"

- "What leads you to believe your partner no longer loves you?"

It should be noted that entire groups may hold in common erroneous conclusions or biased or distorted information about any variety of subjects, and in such instances, the social worker has the challenging task of assisting members to reflect upon and to analyze their views. The social worker may need to assist group members to assess conclusions or distortions like the following:

- "We can't do anything about our problems. We are helpless and others are in control of our lives."

- "We are innocent victims."

- "People in authority are out to get us."

- "Someone else is responsible for our problems."

- "They (members of another race, religion, group, etc.) are no good."

We further discuss the social worker's role in challenging distortions and erroneous conclusions and identify relevant techniques that may be used for this purpose in several chapters of the book.

Assisting Clients to Personalize Their Statements   The relative concreteness of a specific client message is related in part to the focus or subject of that message. Client messages fall into several different classes of topic focus (Cormier & Cormier, 1979), each of which emphasizes different information and leads into very different areas of discussion:

- *Focus on self,* indicated by the subject "I" (e.g., "I'm disappointed that I wasn't able to keep the appointment").

- *Focus on others,* indicated by subjects such as "they," "people," "someone," or names of specific persons (e.g., "they haven't fulfilled their part of the bargain").

- *Focus on the group or mutual relationship between self and others,* indicated by the subject "we" (e.g., "We would like to do that").

- *Focus on content,* indicated by such subjects as events, institutions, situations, ideas (e.g., "School wasn't easy for me").

Clients are more prone to focus on others or on content, or to speak of themselves as a part of a group rather than to personalize their statements by using "I" or other self-referent pronouns, as illustrated in the following messages: "Things just don't seem to be going right for me," "They don't like me," or "It's not easy for people to talk about their problems." In the last example, the client means that it is not easy for her to talk about her problems; however, in talking about this concern, she uses the term *people,* thus generalizing the problem and obscuring her struggle.

In assisting clients to personalize statements, social workers have a three-part task:

1. To model, to teach, and to coach clients to use self-referent pronouns (*I, me*) in talking about their concerns and their own emotional response to those concerns. For example, in response to a vague client message that focuses on content rather than self ("Everything at home seems to be deteriorating"), the social worker can gently ask the client to reframe the message by starting the response with "I" and giving specific information about what she is experiencing. It is also helpful to teach clients the difference between messages that focus on self ("I think," "I feel," "I want") . . . and messages that are *other-related* ("It . . ." "someone . . .").

2. To teach the difference between self-referent messages and *subject-related* messages (objects, things, ideas, or situations). Although teaching clients to use self-referent pronouns when talking about their concerns is a substantive task, clients derive major benefits, because not owning or taking responsibility for feelings and speaking about problems in generalities and abstractions is perhaps one of the most prevalent causes of problems in communicating.

3. To focus frequently on the client and use the client's name or the pronoun *you*. Beginning social workers are apt to attend to client talk about other people, distant situations, the group at large, various escapades, or other events or content that give little information about self and the relationship between self and situations or people. Notice in the following illustration that the social worker's response focuses on the situation rather than on the client:

- *Client:* My kids want to shut me up in a nursing home.
- *Social worker:* What makes you think that?

In contrast, consider the following message, which personalizes the client's concern and explicitly identifies the feelings she is experiencing:

- *Social worker:* You're really frustrated and disappointed with your children for feeling that you would be better off in a nursing home. You would like to be part of the decision about what would be a safe environment for you.

A social worker may employ various techniques to assist clients to personalize messages; in the preceding example, however, the social worker utilized an empathic response. In this instance, this skill is invaluable to the social worker in helping the client to focus on self. Remember that personalizing feelings is an inherent aspect of the paradigm for responding empathetically ("You feel _____ about/because _____"). Thus, clients can make statements in which there are no self-referent pronouns, and by utilizing empathic responding, the social worker may assist clients to "own" their feelings.

Eliciting Specific Feelings Even when clients personalize their messages and express feelings, social workers often need to elicit information to clarify what they are experiencing, for certain "feeling words" *denote general feeling states rather than specific feelings.* For example, in the message, "I'm really *upset* that I didn't get a raise," the term *upset* helps to clarify the client's general frame of mind but fails to specify the precise feeling. "Upset" in this instance may refer to feeling disappointed, discouraged, unappreciated, devalued, angry, resentful, or even to feeling incompetent or inadequate over not having been granted a raise. The point is that until social workers have elicited additional information, they cannot be sure of how being "upset" is actually experienced by the client. Other feeling words that lack specificity include *frustrated, uneasy, uncomfortable, troubled,* and *bothered.* When clients employ such words, you can pinpoint their feelings by employing responses such as the following:

- "How do you mean, upset?"
- "I'd like to understand more about that feeling. Could you clarify what you mean by frustrated?"
- "Can you say more about in what way you feel bothered?"

Focusing on the Here and Now Still another aspect of concreteness embodies responses that shift the focus from the past to the present, the here and now. Messages that relate to the immediate present are high in concreteness, whereas those that center on the past are low. Some clients (and social workers) are prone to discuss past feelings and events. Precious opportunities for promoting growth and understanding may slip through the fingers of social workers who fail to focus on emotions and experiences that unfold in the immediacy of the interview. Focusing on feelings as they occur will enable you to observe reactions and behavior firsthand, thus eliminating bias and error caused by reporting feelings and experiences after the fact. Furthermore, the helpfulness of your feedback is greatly enhanced when this feedback relates to the client's immediate experience.

An example of concreteness in such situations is provided in the following excerpt:

Client [*choking up*]: When she told me it was all over, that she was in love with another man—well, I just felt—it's happened again. I felt totally alone, like there just wasn't anyone.

Social worker: That must have been terribly painful. [*Client nods; tears well up.*] I wonder if you're not having the same feeling just now—at this moment. [*Client nods agreement.*]

Not only do such instances provide direct access to the client's inner experience, but they may also produce rich benefit as the client shares deep and painful emotions in the context of a warm, accepting, and supportive relationship. Here-and-now experiencing that involves emotions toward the social worker (anger, hurt, disappointment, affectional desires, fears, and the like) is designated as *relational immediacy.* Skills pertinent to relational immediacy warrant separate consideration and are dealt with in Chapter 19.

Focusing on here-and-now experiencing with groups, couples, and families, discussed at length in Chapter 16, is a particularly potent technique for assisting members of these systems to clear the air of pent-up feelings. Further, interventions that focus on the immediacy of feelings bring covert issues to the surface, thus paving the way for the social worker to assist members of these systems to clearly identify and explore their difficulties and (if appropriate) engage in problem solving.

Eliciting Details Related to Clients' Experiences

As we previously mentioned, one of the reasons why concrete responses are essential is that clients often offer vague statements regarding their experiences. For example: "Some people in this group don't want to change bad enough to put forth any effort." Compare this with the following concrete statement in which the client assumes ownership of the problem and fills in details that clarify its nature:

- "I'm concerned because I want to do something to work on my problems in this group, but when I do try to talk about them, you, John, make some sarcastic remark. It seems that then several of you [*gives names*] just laugh about it and someone changes the subject. I really feel ignored then and just go off into my own world."

Aside from assisting clients to personalize their messages and to "own" their feelings and problems, social workers have the task of asking questions that elicit illuminating information concerning the client's experiencing, such as that illustrated in the preceding message. In this regard, questions that start with "how" or "what" are often helpful in assisting the client to give concrete data. To the client message, "Some people in this group don't want to change bad enough to put forth any effort," the social worker might ask, "Specifically what has been happening in the group that leads you to this conclusion?"

Eliciting Details Regarding Interactional Behavior

Concrete responses are also vital in accurately assessing interactional behavior. Such responses pinpoint what actually occurs in interac-

tional events, that is, what circumstances preceded the events, what the participants said and did, what specific thoughts and feelings the client experienced, and what consequences followed the event. In other words, the social worker elicits details of what happened, rather than settling for clients' views and conclusions. An example of a concrete response to a client message follows:

Client: Well, Fred blew his top as usual last night. He really read me the riot act, and I hadn't done one thing to deserve it.

Social worker: Could you recall exactly what happened—what led up to this situation and what each of you said and did? To understand better what went wrong, I'd like to get the details as though I had been there and observed what happened.

In such cases, it is important to keep clients on topic by continuing to assist them to relate the events in question, using responses such as "Then what happened?" "What did you do next?" or "Then who said what?" If dysfunctional patterns become evident after exploring numerous events, social workers have a responsibility to share their observations with clients, to assist them to evaluate the impact of the patterned behavior, and to assess their motivation to change it.

Specificity of Expression by Social Workers

Seeking concreteness applies to the communication of not only clients but social workers as well. In this role, you will frequently explain, clarify, give feedback, and share personal feelings and views with clients. As a budding social worker who has recently entered a formal professional educational program, you, too, may be prone to speak with the vagueness and generality that characterize much of the communication of the lay public. When such vagueness occurs, clients and others may understandably misinterpret, draw erroneous conclusions, or experience confusion about the meaning of your messages. Consider, for example, the lack of specificity in the following actual messages of social workers:

- "You seem to have a lot of pent-up hostility."

- "You really handled yourself well in the group today."
- "I think a lot of your difficulties stem from your self-image."

Vague terms, such as *hostility, handled yourself well,* and *self-image,* tend to leave the client in a quandary as to what the social worker actually means. Moreover, conclusions are presented without supporting information, thus requiring the client to accept them at face value, to reject them as invalid, or to speculate on the basis of the conclusions. Fortunately, some clients are sufficiently perceptive, inquisitive, and assertive to request greater specificity, but many are not.

Contrast the preceding messages with the following in which the social worker responds to the same situations but this time with messages that have a high degree of specificity:

- "I've noticed that you've become easily angered and frustrated several times as we've talked about ways you might work out child custody arrangements with your wife. This appears to be a very painful area for you. I would like to know just what you have been feeling."
- "I noticed that you responded several times in the group tonight, and I thought you offered some very helpful insight to Marjorie when you said. . . . I also noticed you seemed to be more at ease than in previous sessions."
- "We've talked about your tendency to feel inferior to other members of your family and to discount your own feelings and opinions in your contacts with them. I think that observation applies to the problem you're having with your sister that you just described. You've said you didn't want to go on the trip with her and her husband because they fight all the time, and yet you feel you have to go because she is putting pressure on you. As in other instances, you appear to be drawing the conclusion that how you feel about the matter isn't important."

When social workers speak with specificity, clarify meanings, personalize statements, and document the sources of conclusions, clients are much less likely to misinterpret or project their own feelings or thoughts. Clients are clear about what is expected of them and how they are perceived, as well as how and why social workers think and feel as they do about various matters discussed. Equally important, clients vicariously learn to speak with greater specificity as social workers model sending concrete messages.

Both beginning and experienced social workers face the additional challenge of avoiding the inappropriate use of jargon, which has pervaded professional discourse and has become rampant in social work literature and case records. The use of jargon confuses rather than clarifies meanings for clients. The careless use of jargon with colleagues also fosters stereotypical thinking and is therefore antithetical to the cardinal value of individualizing the client. Furthermore, labels tend to conjure up images of clients that vary from one social worker to another, thus injecting a significant source of error into communication. Consider, for example, the lack of specificity in the following messages that are rich in jargon:

- "Mrs. N manifests strong passive-aggressive tendencies."
- "Sean displayed adequate impulse control in the group and tested the leader's authority in a positive manner."
- "Hal needs assistance in gaining greater self-control."
- "The client shows some borderline characteristics."
- "The group members were able to respond to appropriate limits."
- "Ruth appears to be emotionally immature for an eighth-grader."

To accurately convey information about clients to your colleagues, you must explicitly describe their behavior and document the sources of your conclusions. Keeping in mind the preceding vague message, "Ruth appears to be emotionally immature for an eighth-grader," consider how much more accurately another social worker could perceive your client if you conveyed information in the form of a concrete response: "The teacher says Ruth is quiet and stays to herself in school. She doesn't answer any questions in class unless directly called upon, and she often doesn't complete her assignments. She also spends considerable time daydreaming or playing with objects." By describing behavior, you avoid biasing your colleague's perceptions of clients through conveying either vague impressions or erroneous conclusions.

It has been our experience that mastery of the skill of communicating with specificity is gained only through extended and determined effort. The task is complicated by beginning social workers' typical lack of awareness of the vagueness and generality of their communication. We recommend that you carefully and consistently monitor your recorded sessions and your everyday conversations with a view toward identifying instances in which you did or did not communicate with specificity. Such monitoring will enable you to set relevant goals for yourself and to chart your progress. We also recommend that you enlist the assistance of your practicum instructor in providing feedback about your performance level on this vital skill.

Exercises in Seeking Concreteness In the preceding discussion, we identified guidelines for formulating concrete responses. To review, you achieve specificity by the following:

• Checking out perceptions
• Clarifying the meaning of vague or unfamiliar terms
• Exploring the basis of conclusions drawn by clients
• Assisting clients to personalize their statements
• Eliciting specific feelings
• Focusing on the here and now
• Eliciting details related to clients' experiences
• Eliciting details related to interactional behavior

In the following exercises, formulate written responses that will elicit concrete data regarding clients' problems. You may wish to combine your responses with either an empathic response or a paraphrase. A review of the preceding guidelines as you complete the exercise will assist you in formulating effective responses and will help you to clearly conceptualize the various dimensions of this skill as well. After you have finished the exercises, compare your responses with the modeled responses following the last client statement.

CLIENT STATEMENTS

1. *Adolescent* [*speaking of his recent recommitment to a correctional institution*]: It really seems weird to be back here.

2. *Client:* You can't depend on friends; they'll stab you in the back every time.

3. *Client:* He's got a terrible temper—that's the way he is, and he'll never change.

4. *Client:* My supervisor is so insensitive, you can't believe it. All she thinks about is reports and deadlines.

5. *Client:* I was upset after I left your office last week. I felt you really didn't understand what I was saying and didn't care how I felt.

6. *Client:* My dad's fifty-eight years old now, but I swear he still hasn't grown up. He always has a chip on his shoulder.

7. *Elder client:* My rheumatoid arthritis has affected my hands a lot. It gets to be kind of tricky when I'm handling pots and pans in the kitchen.

8. *Client:* I just have this uneasy feeling about going to the doctor. I guess I've really got a hang-up about it.

9. *African American student* [*to African American social worker*]: You ask why I don't talk to my teacher about why I'm late for school. I'll tell you why. Because she's white, that's why. She's got it in for us blacks, and there's just no point talking to her. That's just the way it is.

10. *Client:* John doesn't give a damn about me. I could kick the bucket, and he wouldn't lose a wink of sleep.

MODELED RESPONSES

1. "In what way does it seem weird?"

2. "I gather you feel that your friends have let you down in the past. Could you give me a recent example in which this has happened?"

3. "Could you tell me more about what happens when he loses his temper with you?" or "You sound like you don't have much hope that he'll ever get control of his temper. How have you concluded he will never change?" [*A social worker might explore each aspect of the message separately.*]

4. "Could you give me some examples of how she is insensitive to you?"

5. "Sounds like you've been feeling hurt and disappointed over my reaction last week. I can sense you're struggling with those same feelings right now. Could you tell me what you're feeling at this moment?"

6. "That must make it difficult for you. Could you recall some recent examples of times you've had difficulties with him?"

7. "When you say that handling the pots and pans is kind of tricky, can you tell me about recent examples of what has happened when you are cooking?"

8. "Think of going to the doctor just now. Let your feelings flow naturally. [*Pause.*] What goes on inside you—your thoughts and feelings?"

9. "So you see it as pretty hopeless. You feel pretty strong about Ms. Wright. I'd be interested in hearing what's happened that you've come to the conclusion she's got it in for blacks."

10. "So you feel like you're nothing in his eyes. I'm wondering how you've reached that conclusion?"

FOCUSING: A COMPLEX SKILL

Skills in focusing are critical to effective social work practice for several reasons, the first of which is purely pragmatic. Clients and social workers spend limited time together, and it is critical that they use that time fruitfully by focusing on topics and employing processes that produce maximal yield. Social workers, therefore, are responsible for giving direction to the helping process and avoiding wandering that unnecessarily consumes valuable time. Indeed, one feature that differentiates effective helping relationships from general social relationships is that the former are characterized by sharp focus and continuity, whereas the latter are relatively unstructured.

Another reason why focusing skills are vital is that clients have limited perspectives of their problems and look to professionals for expertise and guidance in concentrating their efforts in areas likely to produce desired results. Moreover, many of use (both clients and social workers) tend to be scattered in our thinking and dissipate energies by rapidly shifting focus from one topic to another. Social workers perform a valuable role by assisting clients to focus on problems in greater depth and to maintain focus until they accomplish desired changes.

Still another reason for developing focusing skills is that families and groups often engage in dysfunctional processes that not only cause interactional difficulties but also hinder groups from focusing effectively on their problems. To enhance family and group functioning, therefore, social workers must be able to refocus the discussion any time interactional processes cause families and groups to prematurely shift away from the topic at hand.

To assist you in learning how to focus effectively, we consider the various functions of focusing skills, which are as follows:

1. Selecting topics for exploration

2. Exploring topics in depth

3. Maintaining focus and keeping on topic

Knowledge of these functions assists you to focus sharply on relevant topics and elicit sufficient data to formulate an accurate problem assessment—a prerequisite for competent practice.

CLIENT MESSAGE	OPEN-ENDED RESPONSES	CLOSED-ENDED RESPONSES	EMPATHIC RESPONSES	LEVEL OF EMPATHY	CONCRETE RESPONSES	SUMMARIZING RESPONSES	OTHER TYPES OF RESPONSES
1.							
2.							
3.							
4.							
5.							
6.							
7.							

Directions: Categorize each of your responses from a recorded session. Where responses involve more than one category (blended responses), record them as a single response, but also check each category embodied in the response. Excluding the responses checked as "other," analyze whether certain types of responses were utilized too frequently or too sparingly. Set tasks for yourself to correct imbalances in future sessions. Retain a copy of the form so that you can monitor your progress in mastering verbal following skills over an extended period of time.

Figure 6-2 Recording Form for Verbal Following Skills

Selecting Topics for Exploration

Areas relevant for exploration vary from situation to situation. However, clients who have contact with social workers in the same setting, such as in nursing homes, group homes, or child welfare agencies, may share many common concerns. Before meeting with clients whose concerns differ from client populations with which you are familiar, you can prepare yourself to conduct an effective exploration by developing (in consultation with your practicum instructor or field supervisor) a list of relevant and promising problem areas to be explored. This preparation will assist you to avoid the tendency of beginning social workers to focus on areas irrelevant to clients' problems and thus to elicit numerous bits of inconsequential information. In initially interviewing an institutionalized youth, for example, you could more effectively select questions and responses if you knew in advance that you might explore the following areas. As the institutionalized youth is an involuntary client, part of this exploration would include the youth's understanding of what parts of his work are nonnegotiable requirements, and what parts could be negotiated or free choices (R. H. Rooney, 1992).

1. Client's own perceptions of problem areas
2. Client's perceived strengths and resources
3. Reasons for being institutionalized and brief history of past problems related to legal authority and to use of drugs and alcohol
4. Details regarding client's relationships with individual family members, both as concerns and sources of support
5. Brief family history
6. School adjustment, including information about grades, problem subjects, areas of interest, and relationships with various teachers
7. Adjustment to institutional life, including relationships with peers and supervisors
8. Peer relationships outside the institution
9. Life goals

10. Reaction to previous experiences with counseling
11. Motivation to engage in counseling relationship and to work on concerns

Similarly, if you plan to interview a self-referred middle-aged woman whose major complaint is depression, the following topical areas could assist you in conducting an initial interview. As she is self-referred, she is likely to be more voluntary than the institutionalized youth. High attention would be paid to identifying the specific concerns that have led her to seek help.

1. Concerns as she sees them, including nature of depressive symptoms such as sleep patterns and appetite changes
2. Client perception of her strengths and resources
3. Health status, date of last physical examination, and medications being taken
4. Onset and duration of depression, previous depressive or manic episodes
5. Life events associated with onset of depression (especially losses)
6. Possible suicidal thoughts, intentions, or plans
7. Dysfunctional thought patterns (self-devaluation, self-recrimination, guilt, worthlessness, helplessness, hopelessness)
8. Previous coping efforts, previous treatment
9. Quality of interpersonal relationships (interpersonal skills and deficiencies, conflicts and supports in marital and parent-child relationships)
10. Reactions of significant others to her depression
11. Support systems (adequacy and availability)
12. Daily activities
13. Sense of mastery vs. feelings of inadequacy
14. Family history of depression or manic behavior

As noted previously, problem areas vary, and outlines of probable topical areas likewise vary accordingly. A list of areas for exploration in an initial session with a couple seeking marriage counseling or with a group of alcoholics will include a number of items that differ from those in the first list. Note, however, that items 1, 2, and 8 through 11 would likely be included in all exploratory interviews with individual clients and would be equally applicable to preparatory interviews with prospective group members.

In using an outline, you should avoid following it rigidly or using it as a crutch, for you may otherwise destroy the spontaneity of sessions and block clients from relating their stories in their own way. Rather, you should encourage clients to discuss their problems freely and play a facilitative role in exploring in greater depth problems that emerge. You must use outlines flexibly, reordering the sequence of topics, modifying, adding, or deleting topics, or abandoning the outline altogether if using it hinders communication.

You should note that you cannot always anticipate fruitful topical areas, for although clients from the same population share many commonalities, their problems also have unique aspects. It is thus important to review tapes of sessions with your practicum instructor or a field supervisor for the purpose of identifying other topical areas you should explore in future sessions.

Exploring Topics in Depth

A major facet of focusing involves centering discussions on relevant topics to assure that exploration moves from generality and superficiality to more depth and meaning. Social workers must have skills that enable them to explore problems thoroughly, for success in the helping process depends on clear and accurate definitions of problems.

Selectively attending to specific topics is challenging for beginning social workers, who often wander in individual or group sessions, repeatedly skipping across the surface of vital areas of content and feelings and eliciting largely superficial and sometimes distorted information. This is illustrated in the following excerpt from a first session with an adolescent in a school setting:

Social worker: Tell me about your family.

Client: My father is ill and my mother is dead, so we live with my sister.

Social worker: How are things with you and your sister?

Client: Good. We get along fine. She treats me pretty good.

Social worker: How about your father?

Client: We get along pretty well. We have our problems, but most of the time things are okay. I don't really see him very much.

Social worker: Tell me about school. How are you getting along here?

Client: Well, I don't like it very well, but my grades are good enough to get me by.

Social worker: I notice you're new to our school this year. How did you do in the last school you attended?

Notice that by focusing superficially on the topics of family and school, the social worker misses opportunities to explore these potential problem areas in the depth necessary to illuminate the client's situation. The exploration thus yielded little information of value, in large part because the social worker failed to employ responses that focus in depth on topical areas. In the following sections, we further delineate skills discussed earlier in the chapter that considerably enhance a social worker's ability to maintain focus on specific areas.

Open-Ended Responses

Social workers may employ open-ended responses throughout individual, conjoint, and group sessions to focus unobtrusively on desired topics. Earlier we noted that some open-ended responses leave clients free to choose their own topics and that others focus on a topic but encourage clients to respond freely to that topic. The following examples, taken from an initial session with a mother of eight children with a complaint of depression, illustrate how social workers can employ open-ended responses to define topical areas that may yield information vital in grasping the dynamics of the client's problems.[1]

- "What have you thought that you might like to accomplish in our work together?"

- "You've discussed many topics in the last few minutes. Could you pick the most important one and tell me more about it?"

- "You've mentioned that your oldest son doesn't come home after school as he did before and help you with the younger children. I would like to hear more about that."

- "Several times as you've mentioned your concern that your husband may leave you, your voice has trembled. I wonder if you could share what you are feeling."

- "You've indicated that your partner doesn't help you enough with the children. You also seem to be saying that you feel overwhelmed and inadequate in managing the children by yourself. Tell me what happens as you try to manage your children."

- "You indicate that you have more problems with your fourteen-year-old daughter than with the other children. Tell me more about Janet and your problems with her."

In the preceding illustrations, the social worker's open-ended questions and responses progressively moved the exploration from the general to the specific. Note also that each response or question defined a new topic for exploration. To encourage in-depth exploration of the topics thus defined, the social worker must blend open-ended questions with other facilitative verbal following responses that focus on and elicit expanded client expressions.

After having defined a topical area by employing an open-ended response, the social worker may deepen exploration by weaving other open-ended responses into the discussion. If the open-ended responses shift the focus to another area, however, the exploration suffers a setback. Note in the following illustration that the social worker's second open-ended response shifts the focus away from the client's message, which involves expression of intense feelings:

Social worker: You've said you're worried about retiring. I'd appreciate your sharing more about your concern. [*Open-ended response.*]

Client: I can't imagine not going to work every day. I feel at loose ends already, and I haven't even quit work. I'm afraid I just won't know what to do with myself.

Social worker: What are your thoughts about doing some traveling? [*Open-ended response.*]

Even though open-ended responses elicit information about clients' problems, they may not facilitate the helping process if they prematurely lead the client in a different direction. If social workers utilize open-ended or other types of responses that frequently change the topic, they will gain information that is disjointed and fragmented. As a result, assessments will suffer from large gaps in the social worker's knowledge concerning clients' problems. As social workers formulate open-ended responses, they must be acutely aware of the direction that responses will take.

Seeking Concreteness

Earlier we discussed and illustrated the various facets of seeking concreteness. Because seeking concreteness enables social workers to move from the general to the specific and to explore topics in depth, it is a key focusing technique. By focusing in depth on topical areas, social workers are able to discern, and to assist clients to discern, dysfunctional thoughts, behavior, and interaction. We illustrate in subsequent sections how social workers can effectively focus on topical areas in exploratory sessions by blending concreteness with other focusing skills. In actuality, the majority of responses that social workers typically employ to establish and maintain focus are blends of various types of discrete responses.

Empathic Responding

Empathic responding serves a critical function by enabling social workers to focus in depth on troubling feelings, as illustrated in the next example:

Client: I can't imagine not going to work every day. I feel at loose ends already, and I haven't even quit work. I'm afraid I just won't know what to do with myself.

Social worker: You seem to be saying, "Even now, I'm apprehensive about retiring. I'm giving up something that has been very important to me, and I don't seem to have anything to replace it." I gather that feeling at loose ends, as you do, you worry that when you retire, you'll feel useless.

Client: I guess that's a large part of my problem. At times I feel useless now. I just didn't take time over the years to develop any hobbies or to pursue any interests. I guess I don't think that I can do anything else.

Social worker: It sounds like you regret not having developed other interests in the past and are afraid that now you may lack the ability to develop in other areas. Maybe you're wondering if it's too late.

Client: Yes, that's right. But it isn't just that. I'm really dreading being at home with time on my hands. I can just see it now. My wife will want to keep me busy doing things around the house for her all the time. I've never liked to do that kind of thing.

Observe in the preceding example that the client's problem continued to unfold as the social worker utilized empathic responding, revealing rich information in the process.

Blending Open-Ended, Empathic, and Concrete Responses to Maintain Focus

After employing open-ended responses to focus on a selected topic, social workers should use other responses to maintain focus on that topic. In the following excerpt, observe how the social worker employs open-ended and empathic responses to explore problems in depth, thereby enabling the client to move to the heart of her struggle. Notice also the richness of the client's responses elicited by the blended messages.

Social worker: As you were speaking about your son, I sensed some pain and reluctance on your part to talk about him. I'd like to understand more about what you're experiencing. Could you share with me what you are experiencing right now? [*Blended empathic and open-ended response that seeks concreteness.*]

Client: I guess I haven't felt too good about coming this morning. I almost called and canceled. I feel I should be able to handle these problems with Jim [*son*] myself. Coming here is like having to admit I'm no longer capable of coping with him.

Social worker: So you've had reservations about coming [*paraphrase*]—you feel you're admitting defeat and that perhaps you've failed or that you're inadequate—and that hurts. [*Empathic response.*]

Client: Well, yes, although I know that I need some help. It's just hard to admit it, I think. My biggest problem in this regard, however, is my husband. He feels much more strongly than I do that we should manage this problem ourselves, and he really disapproves of my coming in.

Social worker: So even though it's painful for you, you're convinced you need some assistance with Jim, but you're torn about coming here because of your husband's attitude. I'd be interested in hearing more about that. [*Blended empathic and open-ended response.*]

In the preceding example, the social worker initiated discussion of the client's here-and-now experiences through a blended open-ended and empathic response, following this with other empathic and blended responses to explore the client's feelings further. With the last response, the social worker narrowed the focus to a potential obstacle to the helping process (the husband's attitude toward therapy), which could also be explored in a similar manner.

Open-ended and empathic responses may also be blended to facilitate and encourage discussion from group members about a defined topic. For instance, after using an open-ended response to solicit group feedback regarding a specified topic ("I'm wondering how you feel about . . ."), the social worker can employ empathic or other facilitative responses to acknowledge the contribution of members who respond to the invitation to comment. Further, by utilizing open-ended responses, the social worker can successfully reach for comments of individual members who have not contributed ("What do you think about _____, Ray?").

In the next example, the social worker blends empathic and concrete responses to facilitate in-depth exploration. Notice how these blended responses yield behavioral referents of the problem. The empathic messages convey sensitive awareness and concern for the client's distress. The open-ended and concrete responses focus on details of a recent event and yield valuable clues that the client's rejections by women may be associated with insensitive and inappropriate social behavior, awareness of which is a prelude to formulating relevant goals. Goals thus formulated are highly relevant to the client.

Single male client, age 20: There has to be something wrong with me, or women wouldn't treat me like a leper. Sometimes I feel like I'm doomed to be alone the rest of my life. I'm not even sure why I came to see you. I think I'm beyond help.

Social worker: You sound like you've about given up on yourself—as though you're utterly hopeless; but apparently part of you still clings to hope and wants to try. [*Empathic response.*]

Client: What else can I do? I can't go on like this, but I don't know how many more times I can get knocked down and get back up.

Social worker: I sense you feel deeply hurt and discouraged at those times. Could you give me a recent example of when you felt you were being knocked down? [*Blended empathic and concrete response.*]

Client: Well, a guy I work with got me a blind date for a dance. I took her, and it was a total disaster. I know I'm no Prince Charming, but you'd think she could at least let me take her home. After we got to the dance, she ignored me the whole night and danced with other guys. Then, to add insult to

injury, she went home with one of them and didn't even have the decency to tell me. There I was, wondering what had happened to her.

Social worker: Besides feeling rejected, you must have been mad as blazes. When did you first feel you weren't hitting it off with her? [*Blended empathic and concrete response.*]

Client: I guess it was when she lit up a cigarette while we were driving to the dance. I kidded her about how she was asking for lung cancer.

Social worker: I see. What was it about her reaction, then, that led you to believe you might not be in her good graces? [*Concrete response.*]

Client: Well, she didn't say anything. She just smoked her cigarette. I guess I really knew then that she was upset at me.

Social Worker: As you look back at it now, what do you think you might have said to repair things at that point? [*Stimulating reflection about problem solving.*]

In the next example, observe how the social worker blends empathic and concrete responses to elicit details of interaction in an initial conjoint session. Such blending is a potent technique for eliciting specific and abundant information that bears directly on clients' problems. Responses that seek concreteness elicit details; empathic responses enable social workers to stay attuned to clients' moment-by-moment experiencing, thereby focusing on feelings that may present obstacles to the exploration.

Social worker: You mentioned having difficulties communicating. I'd like you to give me an example of a time when you felt you weren't communicating effectively, and let's go through it step by step to see if we can understand more clearly what is happening.

Wife: Well, weekends are an example. Usually I want to go out and do something fun with the kids, and John just wants to stay home. He starts criticizing me for wanting to go, go, go.

Social worker: Could you give me a specific example? [*Seeking concreteness.*]

Wife: Okay. Last Saturday I wanted for us all to go out to eat and to a movie, and John wanted to stay home and watch TV.

Social worker: Before we get into what John did, let's stay with you for a moment. There you are, really wanting to go to a movie—tell me exactly what you did. [*Seeking concreteness.*]

Wife: I think I said, "John, let's take the kids out to dinner and a movie."

Social worker: Okay. That's what you said. How did you say it? [*Seeking concreteness.*]

Wife: I expected him to say no, so I might not have said it the way I just did.

Social worker: Turn to John, and say it the way you may have said it then. [*Seeking concreteness.*]

Wife: Okay. [*Turning to husband.*] Couldn't we go out to a movie?

Social worker: There seems to be some doubt in your voice as to whether or not John wants to. [*Focusing observation.*]

Wife: [*interrupting*] I knew he wouldn't want to.

Social worker: So you assumed he wouldn't want to go. It's as though you already knew the answer. [*To husband.*] Does the way your wife asked the question check out with the way you remembered it? [*Huband nods.*]

Social worker: After your wife asked you about going to the movie, what did you do? [*Seeking concreteness.*]

Husband: I said, nope! I wanted to stay home and relax Saturday, and I felt we could do things at home.

Social worker: So your answer was short. Apparently you didn't give her information about why you didn't want to go but just said no. Is that right? [*Focusing observation.*]

Husband: That's right. I didn't think she wanted to go anyway—the way she asked.

Social worker: What were you experiencing when you said no? [*Seeking concreteness.*]

Husband: I guess I was just really tired. I have a lot of pressures from work, and I just need some time to relax. She doesn't understand that.

Social worker: You're saying, then, "I just needed some time to get away from it all," but I take it you had your doubts as to whether she could appreciate your feelings. [*Husband nods.*] [*Turning to wife.*] Now, after your husband said no, what did you do? [*Blended empathic and concrete response.*]

Wife: I think that I started talking to him about the way he just sits around the house.

Social worker: I sense that you felt hurt and somewhat discounted because John didn't respond the way you would have liked. [*Empathic response.*]

Wife [*nods*]: I didn't think he even cared what I wanted to do.

Social worker: Is it fair to conclude, then, that the way in which you handled your feelings was to criticize John rather than to say, "This is what is happening to me?" [*Wife nods.*] [*Seeking concreteness.*]

Social worker: [*to husband*]: Back, then, to our example, what did you do when your wife criticized you? [*Seeking concreteness.*]

Husband: I guess I criticized her back. I told her she needed to stay home once in a while and get some work done.

The social work has asked questions to enable the couple to provide a guide to the sequence of their interaction in a way that elicits key details and provides insight into unspoken assumptions and messages.

Evaluating Use of Focusing and Exploring Skills

The gain mastery of focusing skills and other verbal following and exploring skills, it is important that you "track" the categories of your responses, to determine the extent to which you are exploring problem areas in depth. By examining a portion of a session transcribed in verbatim form, you can diagram the session to identify topical areas, to determine the depth of exploration of each, and to analyze the categories of responses used. In an initial 15-minute session you may find that your first attempts at interviewing take this form:

t1	t2	t3	t4	t5	t6	t7	t8	t9	t10
OER	OER	OER	OER	OER	OER	OER	OER	OER	P
OER	OER	OER	MP	P	MP	OER		OER	
						MP			
						CEQ			

Key: t = Topical area
  CEQ = Closed-ended question
  OER = Open-ended response
  MP = Minimal prompt
  P = Paraphrase

In the preceding diagram, note that the social worker used a limited number of verbal following skills and changed topics frequently, thus exploring subjects only superficially. This type of interviewing explains why beginners sometimes complain that they "just couldn't get anywhere" in sessions or that clients discussed their problems in vague terms. Such difficulties, of course, may also result in part from behaviors of clients that interfere with social workers' efforts to focus, as we discuss later. Often, however, the social worker's interviewing style is largely responsible for the low yield of information and the sketchy picture of the client's situation.

If you use open-ended responses to focus on selected areas and employ verbal following skills to maintain focus on these topics, a profile of a 15-minute segment of an interview would likely resemble the following:

t1	t2	t3	t4	t5
OER	OER	ER/OER	OER	CEQ
MP	ER	CEQ	ER	OER
ER	ER	ER	OER/SC	ER
A	ER	ER	ER	A
ER		ER	ER	ER
SC		MP	CEQ	
ER		P	ER	
SR		SC	A	
			SR	

Key: t = Topical area
  ER = Empathic response
  CEQ = Closed-ended question
  OER = Open-ended response
  MP = Minimal prompt
  P = Paraphrase response
  A = Accent response
  SC = Seeking concreteness
  SR = Summary response

A diagram of an actual initial session, of course, is unlikely to be as tidy as our illustration. Other types of responses (e.g., information-giving responses) might be intermixed with exploring and focusing responses. Further, social workers expend considerable time and effort in sessions on activities such as negotiating goals and contracting.

We recommend that you diagram and analyze segments of actual and simulated sessions many times with the goal of assessing your focusing patterns. Doing so will assist you to make appropriate modifications in style so that you achieve the second type of profile.

Although individual sessions are easier to diagram than group or conjoint sessions, it is possible to diagram the latter to determine the extent to which you focused and assisted members of the group to focus or to refocus on pertinent topics.

Managing Obstacles to Focusing

Occasionally you may find that your efforts to focus selectively and to explore topical areas in depth are unsuccessful in yielding pertinent information. Although you have a responsibility in such instances to assess the effectiveness of your own interviewing style, you should also analyze clients' styles of communicating to determine to what extent their behaviors are interfering with your focusing efforts. As we noted in an earlier chapter, a common reason why clients seek help is that they have, but are not aware of, patterned communications or behaviors that cause difficulties in relationships. In addition, involuntary clients who do not yet perceive the relationship as helping may be included to avoid focusing. Also manifested in their contacts with social workers, these repetitive behaviors can impede communication; the pursuit of practice objectives; and, pertinent to this discussion, exploration of problems. The following list includes common types of client communications that may challenge your efforts to focus in individual, family, and group sessions:

• Responding with "I don't know."

• Changing the subject or avoiding sensitive areas.

• Rambling from topic to topic.

• Intellectualizing or using abstract or general terms.

• Diverting focus from the present to the past.

• Responding to questions with questions.

• Interrupting excessively.

• Failing to express opinions when asked.

• Producing excessive verbal output.

• Using humor or sarcasm to evade topics or issues.

• Verbally dominating the discussion.

You can counter repetitive behaviors and communications that divert the focus from exploring problems by tactfully drawing them to clients' attention and assisting clients to assume behaviors that are compatible with practice objectives. In groups, social workers must assist group members to modify behaviors that repetitively impede effective focusing and communication or the groups will not move to the phase of group development wherein most of the work related to solving problems is accomplished.

Social workers may use a number of different techniques for managing and modifying client obstacles. Some of these techniques include requesting the client to communicate or behave differently; teaching, modeling, and coaching clients to assume more effective communication styles; reinforcing facilitative responses; and selectively attending to functional behaviors.

Intervening to Help Clients Focus or Refocus

Communications that occur in group or conjoint sessions are not only myriad and complex but may also be distractive or irrelevant. Consequently, the social worker's task of assisting members to explore defined topics fully, rather than meander from subject to subject, is a challenging one. Related techniques that social workers can employ are highlighting or clarifying issues or bringing clients' attention to a comment or matter that has been overlooked. In such instances, the objective is not necessarily to explore the topic (although that may subsequently occur) but, rather, to stress or elucidate important content. The social worker thus focuses clients' attention on communications and/or events that occurred earlier in the session or immediately preceded the social worker's focusing response, as illustrated in the following messages:

• [*To son in session with parents*]: "Ray, you made an important point a moment ago that I'm not sure your parents heard. Would you please repeat your comment?"

• [*To individual*]: "I would like to return to a remark made several moments ago when you said _____. I didn't want to interrupt then. I think perhaps the remark was important enough that we should return to it now."

• [*To family*]: "Something happened just a minute ago as we were talking. [*Describes event.*]

We were involved in another discussion then, but I made a mental note of it because of how deeply it seemed to affect all of you at the time. I think we should consider what happened for just a moment."

- [*To group member*]: "John, as you were talking a moment ago, I wasn't sure what you meant by _____. Could you clarify that for me and for others in the group?"

- [*To group*]: "A few minutes ago, we were engrossed in a discussion about _____, yet we have moved away from that discussion to one that doesn't really seem to relate to our purpose for being here. I'm concerned about leaving the other subject hanging because you were working hard to find some solutions and appeared to be close to a breakthrough."

Because of the complexity of communications in group and family sessions, some inefficiency in focusing process is inescapable; however, the social worker can sharpen the group's efforts to focus and encourage more efficient use of time by teaching focusing behavior. We suggest that social workers actually explain the focusing role of the group and identify behaviors, such as attending, active listening, and asking open-ended questions, emphasizing that by utilizing these skills members facilitate exploration of problems. Social workers can also foster use of these skills by giving positive feedback to group or family members when they have adequately focused on a problem, thus reinforcing their efforts.

Although group members usually have difficulty in learning how to focus, they should be able to delve deeply into problems by the third or fourth session, given sufficient guidance and education by social workers. Such efforts by social workers tend to accelerate movement of groups to maturity, a phase in which members achieve maximum therapeutic benefits. A characteristic of a group in this phase, in fact, is that members explore issues in considerable depth rather than skim the surface of many topics.

SUMMARIZING RESPONSES

The technique of summarization embodies four distinct and yet related facets. Although employed at different times and in different ways, each facet serves the common purpose of tying together functionally related elements that occur at different points in the helping process. These four facets include:

1. Highlighting key aspects of discussions of specific problems before changing the focus of the discussion

2. Making connections between relevant aspects of lengthy client messages

3. Reviewing major focal points of a session and tasks clients plan to work on before the next session

4. Recapitulating the highlights of a previous session and reviewing clients' progress on assignments during the week for the purpose of providing focus and continuity between sessions

These facets of summarization are considered in the following sections.

Highlight Key Aspects of Problems

During the phase of an initial session in which problems are explored in moderate depth, summarization can be effectively employed to tie together and highlight essential aspects of a problem before proceeding to explore additional problems. The social worker may summarize how the problem appears to be produced by the interplay of several factors, including external pressures, overt behavioral patterns, unfulfilled needs and wants, and covert thoughts and feelings. Connecting these key elements assists clients in gaining a more accurate and complete perspective of their problems. Employed in this fashion, summarization involves fitting pieces of the problem together to form a coherent whole. Seeing the problem in a fresh and more accurate perspective is beneficial, as it expands clients' awareness and can generate hope and enthusiasm for tackling a problem that has hitherto seemed insurmountable.

Summarization that highlights problems is generally employed at a natural point in the session when the social worker believes that relevant aspects of the problem have been adequately explored and clients appear satisfied in having had the opportunity to express concerns. The following example illustrates this type of summarization:

The client, an 80-year-old widow, has been referred to a Services to Seniors program for exploration of alternative living arrangements because of her failing health, isolation, and recent falls. As the social worker has helped her explore alternative living arrangements, several characteristics that would be important for her in an improved living situation have been identified. Highlighting the salient factors, the social worker summarizes:

• "So it sounds as if you are looking for a situation in which there is social interaction but your privacy is also important to you: you want to maintain your independence."

Summarizing responses of this type serve as a prelude to the process of formulating goals, as goals flow naturally from problem formulations. Moreover, highlighting various dimensions of the problem facilitates the subsequent delineation of subgoals and tasks that must be accomplished to achieve an overall goal. In the preceding situation, to explore an improved living situation, the client would be helped to explore the specific form of privacy (whether living alone or with someone else) and social interaction (how much and what kind of contact with others).

Summarizing salient aspects of problems is a valuable technique in sessions with groups, couples, and families, enabling the social worker at timely moments to highlight the difficulties experienced by each member. In a family session with a pregnant adolescent and her mother, for example, the social worker might say:

• [*To pregnant adolescent*]: "You feel as if deciding what to do about this baby is your decision—it's your body and you have decided that an abortion is the best solution for you. You know that you have the legal right to make this decision

and want to be supported in making it. You feel as if your mother wants to help but can't tell you what decision to make."

• [*To mother*]: "As you spoke, you seemed saddened and very anxious about this decision your daughter is making. You are saying, 'I care about my daughter, but I don't think she is mature enough to make this decision on her own.' As you have noted, women in your family have had a hard time conceiving, and you wish that she would consider other options besides abortion. So you feel a responsibility to your daughter, but also to this unborn baby and the family history of conceiving children."

Such responses synthesize in concise and neutral language the needs, concerns, and problems of each participant for all other members of the session to hear. When summarization of this type is used, it underscores the fact that all participants are struggling with and have responsibility for problems that are occurring, thus counteracting the tendency of families to view one person as the exclusive cause of family problems.

Summarizing Lengthy Messages

Client's messages range from one word or one sentence to lengthy and sometimes rambling monologues. Although the meaning and significance of brief messages are often readily discernible, lengthy messages confront the social worker with the challenge of encapsulating and tying together diverse and complex elements. Linking the elements together often highlights and expands the significance and meaning of the client's message. For this reason, such messages represent one form of additive empathy, a skill discussed in Chapter 18.

Because lengthy client messages typically include emotions, thoughts, and descriptive content, you will need to be perceptive to how these dimensions relate to the focal point of the discussion. To illustrate, consider the following message of a mildly brain-damaged and socially withdrawn 16-year-old female—an only child who is extremely dependent on her overprotective but subtly rejecting mother:

• "Mother tells me she loves me, but I find that hard to believe. Nothing I do ever pleases her; she yells at me when I refuse to wash my hair alone. But I can't do it right without her help. 'When are you going to grow up?' she'll say. And she goes bowling with her friends and leaves me alone in that creaky house. She knows how scared I get when I have to stay home alone. But she says, 'Nancy, I can't just baby-sit you all the time. I've got to do something for myself. Why don't you make some friends or watch TV or play your guitar? You've just got to quit pitying yourself all the time.' Does that sound like someone who loves you? I get so mad at her when she yells at me, it's all I can do to keep from killing her."

Embodied in the preceding message are the following elements:

1. Wanting to be loved by her mother yet feeling insecure and rejected at times

2. Feeling inadequate about performing certain tasks, such as washing her hair

3. Feeling extremely dependent upon her mother for certain services and companionship

4. Feeling afraid when her mother leaves her alone

5. Feeling hurt (implied) and resentful when her mother criticizes her or leaves her alone

6. Feeling intense anger and wanting to lash out when her mother yells at her

The following is a summarizing response that ties these elements together:

• "So you find your feelings toward your mother pulling you in different directions. You want her to love you, but you feel unloved and resent it when she criticizes you or leaves you alone. And you feel really torn because you depend on her in so many ways. Yet at times, you feel so angry you want to hurt her back for yelling at you. You'd like to have a smoother relationship without the strain."

In conjoint interviews or group sessions, summarization can also be used effectively to high-

light and to tie together key elements and dynamics embodied in transactions, as illustrated in the following transaction and summarizing responses of a social worker:

Wife [*to husband*]: You're just never home when I need you. I need your help making decisions about the children. We've got this big activity coming up with Susan this weekend. And where are you going to be? [*Said with animation and sarcasm.*] Deer hunting—of course!

Husband [*bristling and defensive*]: You're damned right! You make it sound like a crime. I suppose you expect me not to go deer hunting just because you can't make a decision. Once a year I get to do something I really enjoy, and you bitch about it. Why shouldn't you make decisions? I didn't marry you to make your decisions for you. Making decisions about the children is your job. Why don't you learn to stand on your own two feet for a change?

Social worker: Let's stop here and think about what each of you is saying. [*To wife.*] You're feeling overwhelmed in coping with the children alone. I gather the bottom line of what you're saying is that your husband is very important to you, and you want to work together as a team in dealing with matters related to the children. [*Wife nods in agreement as husband listens attentively.*] [*To husband.*] And I gather you're reading your wife's message as an attempt to pass the buck to you, no pun intended. You also sounded as though you felt attacked and read her message as an attempt to deny you an opportunity to enjoy yourself. [*He vigorously nods affirmatively.*] [*To both.*] Each of you seems to be feeling a lack of caring and understanding by the other, but these needs get buried under your criticism and attempts to defend yourselves. Let's explore further what each of you is needing from the other.

The social worker's summarization employs additive empathy in identifying needs that underlie the negative and destructive messages exchanged by the spouses. Going beyond the negative surface feelings, the social worker summarizes implied messages and needs, the exploration of which may lead to increased understanding and to positive feelings rather than mutual recriminations.

On occasion, client messages may ramble to the extent that they contain numerous unrelated elements that cannot all be tied together. In such instances, your task is to extract and focus on those elements of the message that are most relevant to the thrust of the session at that point. Utilized in this manner, summarization provides focus and direction to the session and averts aimless wandering. With clients whose thinking is loose or who ramble to avoid having to focus on unpleasant matters, you will need to interrupt on occasion to assure some semblance of focus and continuity. Otherwise, the interview will be disjointed and unproductive. Skills in maintaining focus and continuity are discussed at length later in the chapter and in Chapter 13.

Reviewing Focal Points of a Session

During the course of an individual, conjoint, or group session, it is common to focus on more than one problem and to discuss numerous factors associated with each problem. Toward the end of the first or second session, therefore, depending on the length of the initial exploration, summarization is employed to review key problems that have been explored and to highlight themes and patterns that relate to these problems. Summarizing themes and patterns expands the client's awareness of dysfunctional patterns and his or her role in the difficulties manifested (assuming the client affirms the validity of the summarization). Therefore use of this skill opens up promising avenues for growth and change.

In fact, through summarizing responses, the social worker can review problematic themes and patterns that have emerged in the session and test the client's readiness to consider goals aimed at modifying these dysfunctional pat-terns. The following is an example of such a message:

- "As we explored the stresses that appear to pre-cede your periods of depression, the theme of your discounting yourself by trying so hard to meet unreasonable demands of your family members struck me as very significant, and you seemed to agree. As we begin to consider goals, I wonder what you think about working toward the goal of giving your own needs higher prior-ity and learning to say 'No!' and feeling good about it when others make demands that con-flict with your needs?"

Providing Focus and Continuity

The social worker can also use summarization at the beginning of an individual, group, or con-joint session to review work that clients have ac-complished in the last session(s) and to set the stage for work in the present session. At the same time, the social worker may wish to identify a promising topic for discussion or to refresh clients' minds concerning work they wish to accomplish in that session. In addition, summa-rization can also be employed periodically to synthesize salient points at the conclusion of a discussion or utilized at the end of the session to review the major focal points. In so doing, the social worker will need to place what was accom-plished in the session within the broad perspec-tive of the client's goals. The social worker tries to consider how the salient content and move-ment manifested in each session fit into the larger whole. Only then are the social worker and clients more likely to maintain a sense of direc-tion and to avoid needless delays caused by wan-dering and detours that commonly occur when continuity within or between sessions is weak.

Used as a "wrap-up" when the allotted time for a session is nearly gone, summarization also assists the social worker to draw a session to a natural conclusion. In addition to highlighting and linking together the key points of the session, the social worker reviews with clients plans for performing tasks that they have agreed to accomplish before the next session. Upon concluding the session in such a manner, all participants are clear about where they have been and where they are going in relation to the goals toward which their mutual efforts are directed.

Analyzing Your Verbal Following Skills

After taking frequency counts over a period of time of some of the major verbal following skills (empathy, concreteness, open-ended and closed-ended responses), as suggested in this chapter, you are ready to assess the extent to which you employ, blend, and balance these skills in relation to each other. Employing the form for verbal following (Figure 6-2), categorize each of your responses from a recorded session. As you analyze your relative use and blending of responses alone or with your practicum instructor, determine whether you think certain types of responses were used either too frequently or too sparingly. Further, think of steps that you might take to correct any imbalances in your utilization of skills for future sessions.

Summary

This chapter has helped you learn how to explore, paraphrase, and appropriately use closed- and open-ended responses as a means of better focusing and following in your social work practice. These skills may be applied both with clients and with other persons and colleagues, on behalf of clients. In the next chapter, we will explore some common difficulties experienced by beginning social workers and some ways to overcome them.

Internet Resources

 You can use InfoTrac® to find a useful article about social work with Native Americans: Earle, K. A. (1999). Harvest festival (social work with Native Americans). *Families in Society, 80,* 3. For information and associated sites linked with education organizations such as the Council on Social Work Education (CSWE), you can access *http://www.cswe.org* and the Canadian Association of Schools of Social Work at *http://www.cassw-access.ca*.

Modeled Responses to Exercise in Paraphrasing

1. "You just get so uptight in a group you don't function."
2. "So you've made some real progress in tuning in to your husband and children."
3. "Because your fears really block you when you argue with your mother, you consistently come out on the short side."
4. "So you don't have much confidence in your ability to make calls for yourself. How do you think we might help you feel more confident about trying such calls?"
5. "So you have conflicting feelings of anger and powerlessness. How do you cope with these feelings in working with your treatment team?"
6. "It sounds as if you were disappointed in your previous counselor. How do you think that might affect our working together?"
7. "So you feel that your facility cannot provide what Gladys needs. Can you describe the kind of care you believe she needs?"

8. "So you don't trust that I want to try to help you make what you feel will be the best decision. Can you tell me what I have done that has caused you to think that your mother and I are allies?"

9. "You sound as if you are at a pretty hopeless point right now. When you say you don't know if you want to keep trying to figure it out, can you tell me more about what you mean?"

Answers to Exercise in Identifying Closed- and Open-Ended Responses

STATEMENT	RESPONSE
1	C
2	O
3	O
4	C

Modeled Open-Ended Responses

1. "Could you tell me more about your wanting to impress Ralph?"

2. "What are you afraid you'd do wrong?"

3. "I'm so pleased for you. Tell me more about your job."

4. "So you have mixed feelings of resentment and guilt. Can you tell me more about those feelings?"

5. "It sounds like you feel ganged up on and really resent it. I'd like to understand those feelings better. Could you tell me about when you last felt I took her side?"

6. "Sounds like you're feeling lost and confused about whether you want to try finding yourself. I gather you've been confused about what's been happening to you recently. I'd like to hear more about that."

7. "It sounds as if you feel overloaded with conflicting parenting and work responsibilities."

8. "It sounds as if your experience causes you to doubt whether more services would be helpful. Could you tell me about your feeling that the mother is not motivated."

Notes

1. You will note that several of these messages could also be categorized as seeking concreteness. Messages that seek concreteness and open-ended messages are not mutually exclusive and often overlap considerably.

CHAPTER 7

Eliminating Counterproductive Communication Patterns

CHAPTER OVERVIEW

In this chapter, we explore possible communication difficulties that often appear in the practice of beginning and many experienced social workers and suggest some positive alternatives. By becoming alert to these difficulties, beginning social workers can focus attention on communicating in a positive fashion. In addition to applications in direct practice, communication examples with mesopractice and macropractice will be described.

IMPACTS OF COUNTERPRODUCTIVE COMMUNICATION PATTERNS

As beginning social workers, you bring a desire to learn to be helpful and a commitment to improve. That desire and commitment will not directly translate into flawless skills that help all clients improve and appreciate your abilities. Instead, your learning will include making mistakes that make you wonder if you will ever do it all, or without great effort. Our experience is that even the most successful social workers were once beginners, and learning from mistakes is an integral part of learning.

We focus in this chapter on nonverbal and verbal communication patterns that inhibit the helping process. The communication repertoires of as-

piring social workers usually include halting beginning practice of new skills and some response patterns that inhibit the free flow of information and negatively affect helping relationships. Such responses impede progress each time they occur, eliciting, for example, defensiveness, hostility, or silence. Consistent use of such responses can block growth, precipitate premature terminations, or cause deterioration in clients' functioning. The findings of a research study by Nugent (1992) have documented the inhibitory impact on helping relationships of the types of responses discussed in this chapter. More recently, Nugent and Halvorson (1995) have demonstrated how differently worded active-listening responses may lead to different short-term client affective outcomes.

ELIMINATING NONVERBAL BARRIERS TO EFFECTIVE COMMUNICATION

Nonverbal behaviors strongly influence interactions between people. The importance of this medium of communication is underscored by the fact that counselors' nonverbal interview behavior contributes significantly to ratings of counselor effectiveness. Nonverbal cues, which serve to confirm or to deny messages conveyed verbally, are in large part beyond the conscious awareness of participants. In fact, nonverbal cues may produce "leakage" by transmitting information the sender did not intend to communicate. Facial expressions, such as a blush, a sneer, or a look of shock or dismay, convey much more about the social worker's attitude toward the client than what is said. In fact, if there is a discrepancy between the social worker's verbal and nonverbal communication, the client is more likely to discredit the verbal, for people learn through myriad transactions with others that nonverbal cues more accurately indicate feelings than do spoken words.

Physical Attending

Beginning social workers are often relatively unaware of their nonverbal behaviors, and they may not as yet have learned to consciously use these behaviors to advantage in conveying caring, understanding, and respect. Therefore, mastering physical attending, a basic skill critical to the helping process, is an initial learning task. Physical attentiveness to another person is communicated by receptive behaviors, such as facing the client squarely, leaning forward, maintaining eye contact, and remaining relaxed. Attending also requires social workers to be fully present, that is, to keep in moment-to-moment contact with the client through disciplined attention. Attending in a fully present, relaxed fashion is not to be expected with beginning social workers who are anxious about what to do next, how to help, and how to avoid hurting. Such skill is likely to be attained with experience after considerable observation of expert social workers, role playing, and beginning interviews with clients.

Cultural Nuances of Nonverbal Cues

To consciously use nonverbal behaviors to full advantage in transcultural relationships, social workers must be aware that different cultural groups ascribe varied meanings to certain nonverbal behaviors. Eye-to-eye contact, for example, is expected among communicating persons in mainstream American culture. People who avoid eye-to-eye contact, in fact, may be viewed as untrustworthy or evasive.

Members of some Native American tribes, however, regard direct gazing as an intrusion on privacy. It is important to observe and find out about the norms for gazing before employing eye-to-eye contact with members of some tribes (Gross, 1995).[1]

A social worker's failure to understand the significance of the nonverbal behavior of Asian clients may pose a major barrier to effective communication. Many Asian clients tend to view helping professionals as authorities who can solve their problems (often presented as physical symptoms) by providing advice. Because Asian cultural patterns prescribe deference to authority, the Asian client may speak little unless spoken to by the social worker, who may mistakenly perceive what the client regards as being respectful as being passive, silent, and ingratiating. Consequently, "long gaps of silence may occur as the client waits patiently for the therapist to structure the interview, take charge, and thus provide the solution" (Tsui & Schultz, 1985, p. 565). Such gaps in communication engender anxiety in both parties that may undermine the development of rapport and defeat the helping process. Further, failure to correctly interpret the client's nonverbal behavior may lead the social worker to conclude erroneously that the client has flat affect (i.e., little emotionality). Given these potential hazards, social workers must be more active and directive with Asian clients, and they most focus on role expectations, a matter we discuss at more length in Chapter 12.

Other Nonverbal Behaviors

Barriers that prevent the social worker from staying in psychological contact with the client can be caused by preoccupation with judgments or evaluations about the client or by inner pressures to find immediate solutions to the client's problems. Reduced focus on the client can also result from being preoccupied with oneself while practicing new skills. Further, extraneous noise, a ringing phone, an inadequate interviewing room, or lack of privacy can also interfere with the social worker's being psychologically present.

Lack of concern for the client can also be conveyed by numerous undesirable behaviors and revealing postural cues. For example, staring vacantly, looking out the window, frequently glancing at the clock, yawning, and fidgeting convey inattention; trembling hands or rigid posture may communicate anger or anxiety. These and a host of other behavioral cues that convey messages such as a lack of interest, disapproval, shock, or condemnation are readily perceived by most clients, many of whom are highly sensitive to criticism or rejection in any form.

Taking Inventory of Nonverbal Patterns of Responding

To assist you in taking inventory of your own styles of responding to clients, we have listed de-sirable and undesirable nonverbal behaviors in Table 7-1. You will probably find that you have a mixed repertoire of nonverbal responses, some of which have the potential to enhance helping relationships and foster client progress. Others often indicate beginning social worker nervousness that may block your clients from freely disclosing information and otherwise retard the flow of the helping process. You thus have a threefold task: (1) to assess your repetitive nonverbal behaviors; (2) to eliminate nonverbal styles that hinder effective communication; and (3) to sustain and perhaps increase desirable nonverbal behaviors.

DESIRABLE	UNDESIRABLE
Facial expressions:	
Direct eye contact (except when culturally proscribed)	Avoidance of eye contact
Warmth and concern reflected in facial expression	Staring or fixating on person or object
Eyes at same level as client's	Lifting eyebrow critically
Appropriately varied and animated facial expressions	Eye level higher or lower than client's
Mouth relaxed; occasional smiles	Nodding head excessively
	Yawning
	Frozen or rigid facial expressions
	Inappropriate slight smile
	Pursing or biting lips
Posture:	
Arms and hands moderately expressive; appropriate gestures	Rigid body position; arms tightly folded
Body leaning slightly forward; attentive but relaxed	Body turned at an angle to client
	Fidgeting with hands
	Squirming or rocking in chair
	Slouching or placing feet on desk
	Hand or fingers over mouth
	Pointing finger for emphasis
Voice:	
Clearly audible but not loud	Mumbling or speaking inaudibly
Warmth in tone of voice	Monotonic voice
Voice modulated to reflect nuances of feeling and emotional tone of client messages	Halting speech
	Frequent grammatical errors
Moderate speech tempo	Prolonged silences

Table 7-1 Inventory of Practitioner's Nonverbal Communication   *(continued)*

DESIRABLE	UNDESIRABLE
Voice:	
	Excessively animated speech
	Slow, rapid, or staccato speech
	Nervous laughter
	Consistent clearing of throat
	Speaking loudly
Physical proximity:	
Three to five feet between chairs	Excessive closeness or distance
	Talking across desk or other barrier

Table 7-1 *cont'd*

There is a checklist at the end of this chapter for use in training or supervision to obtain feedback on nonverbal aspects of attending. Given opportunity to review a videotape of your performance in actual or simulated interviews and/or to receive behaviorally specific feedback from supervisors and peers, you can adequately master physical aspects of attending in a relatively brief time. Review of your taped performance may reveal that you are already manifesting many of the desirable physical attending behaviors listed in Table 7-1. Further, you may possess personal nonverbal mannerisms that are particularly helpful to you in establishing relationships with others, such as a friendly grin or a relaxed, easy manner. As you take inventory of your nonverbal behaviors, elicit feedback from others regarding both your desirable and undesirable nonverbal behaviors. When appropriate, increase the frequency of positive behaviors that you have identified and especially cultivate the quality of warmth, which we discussed in Chapter 3.

As you review videotapes, pay particular attention to your nonverbal responses at those moments when you experienced pressure or tension, which will assist you in determining whether your responses were counterproductive. All beginning interviewers experience moments of discomfort in their first contacts with clients, and nonverbal behaviors are an index of their comfort level. As a

way of beginning to develop your self-awareness of your own behavioral patterns, develop a list of your own verbal and nonverbal behaviors when you are under pressure. When you actually review your beginning work, you may notice that under pressure you respond with humor, fidget, change voice inflection, assume a rigid body posture, or manifest other nervous mannerisms. Making an effort to become aware of and to eliminate obvious signs of anxiety is an important step in achieving mastery of your nonverbal responding.

ELIMINATING VERBAL BARRIERS TO COMMUNICATION

Many types of ineffective verbal responses prevent clients from exploring problems and sharing freely with the social worker. We are assisted here by reactance theory, which suggests that clients will act to protect valued freedoms (Brehm & Brehm, 1981). Such freedoms can include the freedom of one's own opinions and inclination to action. When such valued freedoms are threatened, clients will often withdraw, argue, or move to a superficial topic. The following list identifies common verbal barriers that usually have an immediate negative effect upon communications and thus prevent clients from revealing pertinent information and working on problems:

1. Moralizing

2. Advising and giving suggestions or solutions prematurely

3. Trying to convince client about right point of view through logical arguments, lecturing, instructing, and arguing

4. Judging, criticizing, or placing blame

5. Analyzing, diagnosing, making glib or dogmatic interpretations

6. Reassuring, sympathizing, consoling, excusing

7. Using sarcasm or employing humor that is distractive or makes light of clients' problems

8. Threatening, warning, or counterattacking

The negative effect of certain types of responses is not always apparent because the client does not manifest untoward reactions at the time or because the retarding effect upon the helping process cannot be observed in a single transaction.

In order to assess the effect of responses, then, the social worker must determine the frequency of detrimental responses and evaluate the overall impact of such responses on the helping process. Frequent use of some types of responses by the social worker indicates the presence of counterproductive patterns of communication such as the following:

• Using questions inappropriately

• Interrupting inappropriately or excessively

• Dominating interaction

• Fostering safe social interaction

• Responding infrequently

• Parroting or overusing certain phrase or clichés

• Dwelling on the remote past

• Going on fishing expeditions

Individual responses that fall within these patterns may or may not be ineffective when employed singularly; when employed extensively in lieu of varied response patterns, however, such responses inhibit the natural flow of a session and limit the richness of information revealed. Sections that follow expand on each of these verbal barriers and detrimental social worker responses.

Verbal Barriers to Effective Communication

1. Moralizing and Sermonizing by Using "Shoulds" and "Oughts"

• "You shouldn't have done that."

• "You're too young to get into a permanent relationship."

• "You should try to understand your parents' position. They really have your welfare at heart."

• "You ought to pay your bills."

• "If you care about client services, you should grant our application for extended insurance coverage."

Sometimes social workers have strong views about appropriate ways of looking at client problems and resolving them. However, moralizing, sermonizing, admonishing, or otherwise passing judgment is an unethical and ineffective way to be helpful to clients in making choices. Such responses are equally unproductive when communicated to fellow professionals such as managed care eligibility reviewers. "Should" and "ought" messages, which imply that clients have a duty to some vague, external authority, have often been used effectively by significant others in clients' lives to make them feel guilty or obligated. Moralizing responses by social workers have the same effect, eliciting feelings of guilt and resentment. Such messages also communicate lack of trust—"I'll tell you what to do because you're not wise enough to know." When experiencing such criticism and lack of confidence in their ability and judgment, clients are unlikely to be receptive to assessing their own positions or to consider others. We know from reactance theory that such efforts are likely to boomerang as clients act to protect their freedom to think and act by opposing such pressures (Brehm & Brehm, 1981).

Although imposing values is not appropriate, sometimes raising client concerns about an issue can be useful. For example, when a client proposes to act in a way that is illegal, dangerous, or contrary to his or her own goals or values, posing questions is an appropriate ethical response. Asking an inductive or Socratic question can be a more tactful way of raising an issue without imposing a value. For example, "What happens when your bills are not paid on time?" or "How do you think your situation appears from your parents' viewpoint?"

2. Advising and Giving Suggestions or Solutions Prematurely

- "I suggest that you move to a new place because you have had so many difficulties here."

- "I think you need to try a new approach with your daughter. Let me suggest that . . ."

- "I think it would be best for you to try using time-out . . ."

- "Because your partner is such a loser, why don't you try to make some relationships with other people?"

Little is known about actual provision of advice in terms of frequency or circumstances in which it occurs (Jayaratne, Croxton, & Mattison, 1997). Clients often seek advice, and appropriately timed advice can be an important helping tool. However, untimely advice often elicits opposition for reasons similar to the moralizing efforts considered above. Interestingly, even when clients solicit advice in early phases of the helping process, they often react negatively when they receive such advice because recommended solutions based on superficial information often do not address their real needs. Further, because clients often are burdened and preoccupied with little-understood conflicts, feelings, and pressures, they are not ready to take action on their problems. For these reasons, after offering premature advice, social workers may observe clients replying with response such as "Yes, but I've already tried that," or "That won't work." In fact such responses can serve as feedback clues that you may have slipped into premature advice.

Social workers often dispense advice prematurely because they feel pressure to provide quick answers or solutions for clients who unrealistically expect magical answers and instant relief from problems that have plagued them for long periods

of time. Beginning social workers also experience inner pressure to dispense solutions to clients' problems, mistakenly believing that their new role demands that they, like physicians, prescribe a treatment regimen. They thus run the risk of giving advice before they have conducted a thorough exploration of the problem. Instead of dispensing wisdom, however, a major role of social workers is to create and shape processes with clients in which they engage in mutual discovery of problems and solutions, work that will take time and concentrated effort.

In the helping process, the timing and form of recommendations are all-important. Generally, advice should be offered sparingly, only after thoroughly exploring a problem and clients' ideas regarding possible solutions. At that point, social workers may serve as consultants, tentatively sharing ideas regarding solutions to supplement those developed by clients. Pressures from clients to influence social workers to dispense premature knowledge would deprive them of developing effective solutions to these problems. Social workers should also stress clients' roles in helping to discover and to "tailor-make" solutions that fit their unique problems.

Clients may also expect to receive early advice if social workers have not appropriately clarified roles and expectations about mutual participation in generating possible solutions to further the growth and self-confidence of clients. Assuming a position of superiority and quickly providing solutions for problems without encouraging clients to formulate possible courses of action fosters dependency and stifles creative thinking. Freely dispensing advice also minimizes or ignores clients' strengths and potentials, and many clients may be expected to respond with inner resentment. In addition, clients who have not been actively involved in planning their own courses of action may lack motivation to implement the advice given by social workers. Further, when advice does not remedy a problem, as if often doesn't, clients may blame social workers and disown responsibility for an unfavorable outcome.

3. Trying to Convince Client about Right Point of View through Lecturing, Instructing, Arguing

- "Let's look at the facts about drugs."
- "You have to take some responsibility for your life, you know."
- "Running away from home will only get you in more difficulty."
- "That attitude won't get you anywhere."

Clients sometimes consider courses of action that appear to social workers to be unsafe, illegal, or contrary to client goals. However, attempting to convince clients through arguing, instructing, and the like often provokes the kind of boomerang effect described above. According to reactance theory, clients will attempt to defend valued freedoms when these are threatened (Brehm & Brehm, 1981). For some clients (especially adolescents for whom independent thinking is associated with a developmental stage), deferring to or agreeing with social workers is tantamount to giving up individuality or freedom. In vigorously attempting to persuade clients to another point of view, social workers also often foster power struggles, thereby perpetuating dynamics that have previously occurred in clients' personal relationships. By arguing, social workers also ignore feelings and views of clients, focusing instead on "being right," which may engender feelings of resentment, alienation, or hostility. Such efforts are both unethical and ineffective. Persuasion in the sense of helping clients to have accurate information from which to make informed decisions can be an ethical intervention. When clients contemplate actions that are contrary to their own goals, or will endanger themselves or others, then an effort to persuade can be an ethical intervention. Such efforts should not be focused on the one "pet" solution of the social worker, as suggested above, but rather should assist the client in examining the advantages and disadvantages of several options, including those with which the social worker may disagree (R. H. Rooney, 1992). Hence, the effort is not to convince, but rather to assist clients in making informed decisions. So, the social worker might ask whether the client is interested in exploring some factual information about drugs. Similarly, the social worker might ask the client to think about the benefits of running away from home and then to consider the potential drawbacks.

4. Judging, Criticizing, or Placing Blame

- "You're wrong about that."
- "Running away from home was a bad mistake."
- "One of your problems is that you're not willing to consider another point of view."
- "You're not thinking straight."

Responses that evaluate and show disapproval are detrimental to clients and to the helping process. Clients usually respond defensively and sometimes counterattack when they experience criticism by social workers; further, they often cut off any meaningful communication with social workers. Intimidated by a social worker's greater expertise, some clients also accept negative evaluations as accurate reflections of their poor judgment or lack of worth or value. In making such negative judgments about clients, social workers violate the basic social work values of nonjudgmental attitude and acceptance. If the social worker is concerned about danger to the client or others, or law violations, then the social worker may ask a question to raise the client's awareness of consequences and alternatives: for example, "How do you look now at the consequences of running away from home?" or "How would this appear from your partner's point of view?"

5. Analyzing, Diagnosing, Making Glib or Dramatic Interpretations; Labeling Clients' Behavior

- "You're behaving that way because you're angry with your partner."
- "Your attitude may have kept you from giving their ideas a fair chance."
- "You are acting in a passive-aggressive way."
- "You are really hostile today."

Used sparingly and appropriately timed, interpretation of the dynamics of behavior is a potent change-oriented skill (see Chapter 19). However, even accurate interpretations that focus on purposes or meanings of behavior substantially beyond clients' levels of conscious awareness engender client opposition and are doomed to failure. When stated dogmatically (e.g., "I know what's wrong with you," or "how you feel," or "what your real motives are"), interpretations also present a threat to clients, causing them to feel exposed or trapped. When a glib interpretation is thrust upon them, clients often expend their energies disconfirming the interpretation, explaining themselves, or making angry rebuttals rather than working on the problem at hand.

Using social work jargon such as fixation, transference, resistance, reinforcement, repression, passivity, neuroticism, and a host of other terms to describe the behavior of clients in their presence is also destructive to the helping process, often confusing or bewildering clients and creating opposition to change. These terms also oversimplify complex phenomena and psychic mechanisms and stereotype clients, thereby obliterating their uniqueness. In addition, these sweeping generalizations provide no operational definition of clients' problems, nor do they suggest avenues for modification of behavior. If clients accept social workers' restricted definitions of their problems, they may then define themselves in the same terms as those used by social workers (e.g., "I am a passive person," or "I have a schizoid personality"). This type of stereotypic labeling often causes clients to view themselves as "sick" and their situations as hopeless, thus providing them a ready excuse for not working on problems.

6. Reassuring, Sympathizing, Consoling, Excusing

- "You'll feel better tomorrow."

- "Don't worry, things will work out."

- "You probably didn't do anything to aggravate the situation."

- "I really feel sorry for you."

When used selectively and with justification, well-timed reassurance can engender much-needed hope and support.[2] In glibly reassuring clients that "things will work out," "everybody has problems," or "things aren't as bleak as they seem," however, social workers avoid exploring clients' feelings of despair, anger, hopelessness, or helplessness. Situations faced by clients are often grim, with no immediate analgesics or relief at hand. Rather than gloss over clients' feelings and seek to avoid discomfort, it is the task of social workers to explore distressing feelings and to assist clients in acknowledging painful realities.

Reassuring clients prematurely or without genuine basis often serves the purposes of social workers more than of clients and, in fact, may represent efforts by social workers to dissuade clients from their troubling feelings. Such reassurance thus serves to restore the comfort level and equilibrium of social workers rather than to help clients. Rather than foster hope, glib reassurances also convey a lack of understanding of clients' feelings and raise doubts about the authenticity of social workers, causing clients to react with thoughts such as "It's easy for you to say that, but you don't know how very frightened I really am," or "You're just saying that so I'll feel better." In addition, responses that excuse clients (e.g., "You're not to blame") or sympathize with their position (e.g., "I can see exactly why you feel that way; I think I would probably have done the same thing") often have the effect of unwittingly reinforcing inappropriate behavior or reducing clients' anxiety and motivation to work on problems.

7. Using Sarcasm or Employing Humor That Is Distractive or Makes Light of Clients' Problems

- "Did you get up on the wrong side of the bed?"

- "It seems to me that we've been all through this before."

- "You really fell for that line."

- "You think *you* have a problem."

Humor is an important therapeutic tool, bringing relief and sometimes perspective to work that may otherwise be tense and tedious. Pollio (1995) has suggested ways to determine appropriate use of humor. Van Wormer and Boes (1997) also describe ways that humor permits social workers to continue to operate in the face of trauma. Using plays on words or noting a sense of the preposterous or incongruous can help social workers and clients face difficult situations. Similarly, Kane (1995) describes the way humor in group work can facilitate work with persons afflicted with HIV. In group work, T. Caplan (1995) has described how facilitation of humor can create a necessary safety and comfort level in work with men who batter. Excessive use of humor, however, is distracting, keeping the content of the session on a superficial level and interfering with therapeutic objectives. Sarcasm often emanates from unrecognized hostility that tends to provoke counterhostility in clients.

8. Threatening, Warning, or Counterattacking

- "You better . . . or else!"
- "If you don't . . . you'll be sorry."
- "If you know what's good for you, you'll . . ."

Sometimes clients consider actions that would endanger themselves or others or are illegal. In such instances, alerting clients to potential consequences is an ethical and appropriate intervention. However, conveying threats of the sort described above often produces a kind of oppositional behavior that exacerbates an already strained situation. Still, even the most well intentioned social workers may bristle or respond defensively under the pressure of verbal abuse, accusatory or blaming responses, or challenges to their integrity, competence, motives, or authority. Social workers conducting group sessions with adolescents, for instance, can testify that provocative behavior of this client population may defeat even herculean efforts to respond appropriately.

Whatever the dynamics behind provocative behavior, a defensive response by social workers is counterproductive, often duplicating the destruc-

tive pattern of responses that clients have typically elicited and experienced from others. To achieve competence, therefore, it is important that you master your own natural defensive reactions and evolve effective ways of dealing with negative feelings. Empathic communication, for example, produces a cathartic release of negative feelings, defusing a strained situation and permitting a more rational emotional exploration of factors that underlie clients' feelings. For example, to reply to a client, "You have difficult decisions to make, caught between alternatives that you don't consider very attractive. I wish you well in making a decision that you can live with in the future" can convey support and respect for the right to choose.

9. Stacking Questions

In exploring problems, social workers should use facilitative questions that assist clients to reveal detailed information about specific problem areas. However, when social workers ask several questions in succession, they diffuse their focus on specific content areas, confusing and distracting clients, as illustrated in the following messages:

- "When you don't feel you have control of situations, what goes on inside of you? What do you think about? What do you do?"
- "Have you thought about where you are going to live? Is that one of your biggest concerns, or is there another that takes priority?"

Adequately answering even one of the foregoing questions would require an extended response by a client. Rather than focus on one question, however, clients often respond superficially and nonspecifically to the social worker's multiple inquiry, omitting important information in the process. Stacked questions thus have "low yield" and are unproductive and inefficient in gathering relevant information. Slowing down and asking one question at a time is preferable. If you have, however, asked stacked questions (as all social workers have at many points), and the client hesitates in response, you can correct for the problem by repeating your preferred question.

10. Asking Leading Questions

Leading questions are those with hidden or under-the-table agendas designed to induce clients to agree with a particular view or to adopt a solution that social workers deem to be in clients' best interests. For example:

- "Do you think you've really tried to get along with your partner?"

- "You don't really mean that, do you?"

- "Aren't you too young to move out on your own?"

- "Don't you think that arguing with your mother will provoke her to come down on you as she has done in the past?"

In actuality, such leading questions often obscure legitimate concerns that social workers should discuss with clients. Social workers conceal their feelings and opinions about such matters, presenting them obliquely in the form of solutions (e.g., "Don't you think you ought to . . .") in hope that the leading questions will lead clients to desired conclusions. It is an error, however, to assume that clients will not see through such maneuvers. Clients, in fact, often discern the social worker's motives and inwardly resist having views or directives imposed upon them under the guise of leading questions. Nevertheless, to avoid conflict or controversy with the social worker, they may express feeble agreement or may simply divert the discussion to another topic.

By contrast, when social workers authentically assume responsibility for concerns they wish clients to consider, they enhance the likelihood that clients will respond receptively. In addition, they can raise questions that are not slanted to imply the "correct" answer from the social worker's viewpoint. For example, "How have you attempted to come to agreement with your partner?" would not contain the indication of the "right" answer found in the first question above. Similarly, the last question above could be rephrased "I am not clear how you see arguing with your mother as likely to be more successful than it has been in the past."

11. Interrupting Inappropriately or Excessively

Beginning social workers are often excessively worried about covering all items on their and their agency's agenda ("What will I tell my supervisor?"). To ensure focus on relevant problem areas, social workers must at times interrupt clients. To be effective, however, interruptions must be purposive, well timed, and smoothly executed. Interruptions are detrimental to the helping process when they are abrupt or divert clients from exploring pertinent problem areas. Frequent untimely interruptions tend to annoy clients, stifle spontaneous expression, and hinder exploration of problems. Identifying and prioritizing key questions in advance with an outline can assist in avoiding this pattern.

12. Dominating Interaction

At times, social workers may dominate interaction by talking too much or by excessively asking closed-ended questions, thus assuming the initiative for discussions rather than placing this responsibility with clients. Domineering behaviors by social workers also include frequently offering advice, pressuring clients to improve, presenting lengthy arguments to convince clients, frequently interrupting, and so on. Some social workers are also prone to behave as though they are all-knowing, failing to convey respect for clients' points of view or capacities to solve problems. Such dogmatic and authoritarian behavior discourages clients from expressing themselves and fosters a one-up, one-down relationship in which clients feel at a great disadvantage and resent the social worker's supercilious demeanor.

Social workers should monitor the relative distribution of participation by all persons (including themselves) who are involved in individual, family, or group sessions. Although clients naturally vary in their levels of verbal participation and assertiveness, all group members should have equal opportunity to share information, concerns, and views in the helping process. Social workers have a responsibility to ensure this opportunity.

As a general guideline, clients should consume more "speaking time" than social workers in the helping process, although during initial sessions with many Asian American clients, social workers must be more directive than with Anglo clients, as we discussed earlier. Sometimes social workers defeat practice objectives in group or conjoint sessions by dominating interaction through such behaviors as speaking for members, focusing more on some members than others, or giving speeches.

Even social workers who are not particularly verbal may dominate sessions that include reserved or nonassertive clients as a means of averting their own discomfort with silence and passivity. Although it is natural to be more active with reticent or withdrawn clients than with those who are more verbal, social workers must avoid dominating the interaction. Using facilitative responses that draw clients out is an effective method of minimizing silence and passivity.

When review of one of your taped sessions reveals that you have monopolized interaction, it is important that you explore the reasons for your behavior. Identify the specific responses that were authoritarian or domineering and the situations that preceded those responses. Also examine the clients' style of relating for clues regarding your own reactions, and analyze the feelings you were experiencing at the time. Based on your review and assessment of your performance, plan a strategy to modify your own style of relating by substituting facilitative responses for ineffective ones. It may also be necessary to focus on and to explore the passive or nonassertive behavior of clients with the objective of contracting with them to increase their participation in the helping process.

13. Fostering Safe Social Interaction

Channeling or keeping discussions focused on safe topics that exclude feelings and minimize self-disclosures is inimical to the helping process. Social chit-chat about the weather, news, hobbies, mutual interests or acquaintances, and the like tends to foster a social rather than a therapeutic relationship. In contrast to the lighter and more diffuse communication characteristic of a social relationship, helpful, growth-producing relationships are characterized by sharp focus and specificity.

In the main, safe social interaction in the helping process should be avoided. It is important to note two qualifications to this general rule: (1) discussion of safe topics may be utilized to assist children or adolescents to lower defenses and risk increasing openness, thereby assisting social workers to cultivate a quasifriend role with such clients; (2) a brief discussion of conventional topics may be appropriate and helpful as part of the getting acquainted or warm-up period of initial sessions or during early portions of subsequent sessions. A warm-up period is particularly important when engaging clients from ethnic groups for which such informal openings are the cultural norm, as we discussed in Chapter 3.

Even when you try to avoid inappropriate social interaction, however, some clients may resist your attempts to move the discussion to a topic that is relevant to the problems they are experiencing and to the purposes of the helping process. Techniques for managing such situations are found in later chapters of the book. For now, it is sufficient to suggest that it is appropriate for the social worker to bring up the agreed upon agenda for this session within a few minutes of the beginning of the session.

14. Responding Passively

Monitoring the frequency of your responses in individual, conjoint, or group sessions is an important task. As a social worker, you have an ethical responsibility to utilize fully the limited contact time you have with clients in pursuing practice objectives and promoting their general well-being. Relatively inactive social workers, however, usually ignore fruitful moments that could be explored to promote clients' growth and allow the focus of a session to stray to inappropriate or unproductive content. To be maximally helpful, social workers must give structure to the helping process by developing contracts with clients that specify respective responsibilities of both participants, engaging clients in a process of identifying and exploring problems, formulating goals, and delineating tasks to alleviate clients' difficulties. To provide form and direction to the helping process, thereby maximizing change opportunities, you must be consistently active in structuring your work with clients.

Inactivity by social workers contributes to counterproductive processes and failures in problem solving. One deleterious effect, for example, is that clients lose confidence in social workers when social workers fail to intervene by helping them with situations that are destructive to themselves or to others. Confidence is particularly eroded by the failure of social workers to intervene when clients communicate destructively in conjoint or group sessions.

Although social workers' activity per se is important, the quality of their moment-by-moment responses is also critical. Social workers significantly diminish their effectiveness by neglecting to utilize or by underutilizing facilitative responses.

15. Parroting or Overusing Certain Phrases or Clichés

Parroting a message often irritates clients, prompting at times a response of "Well, yes, I just said that." Rather than merely repeating clients' words, it is important that social workers use fresh words that capture the essence of clients' messages and place them in sharper perspective. Social workers generally should also refrain from punctuating their communications with superfluous phrases. The distracting effect of such phrases can be observed in the following message: "You know, a lot of people wouldn't come in for help. It tells me, you know, that you realize that you have a problem, you know, and want to work on it. Do you know what I mean?"

Frequent use of such phrases as "you know," "OK?" ("Let's work on this task, OK?"), and "stuff" ("We went to town, and stuff"), or "that's neat," can be very annoying to some clients (and social workers, for that matter). Further, if used in excess, the same may be said of some of the faddish clichés that have permeated today's language, such as "awesome," "sweet," "cool," "tight," or "dude."

Another mistake social workers sometimes make is to "overrelate" to youth by using adolescent jargon to excess. Adolescents tend to perceive such communication as phony and the social worker as inauthentic, which hinders rather than facilitates the development of a working relationship.

16. Dwelling on the Remote Past

Social workers' verbal responses may focus on the past, present, or future. Helping professionals differ regarding the amount of emphasis they believe should be accorded to gathering historical facts about clients. Focusing largely on the present is vital, however, for clients can change only their present circumstances, behaviors, and feelings. Permitting individuals, groups, couples, or families to dwell on the past may reinforce diversionary tactics employed to avoid dealing with painful aspects of present difficulties and with the need for change. It is important to recognize that often implied in messages about the past are feelings the client is currently experiencing related to the past. For example:

Client [*with trembling voice*]: He used to make me so angry.

Social worker: There was a time when he really infuriated you. As you think about the past, even now it seems to stir up some of the anger and hurt you felt.

Thus, changing a client's statement from past to present tense often yields rich information about clients' present feelings and problems. The same may be said of bringing future-oriented statements of clients to the present (e.g., "How do you feel now about the future event you're describing?"). The point is that it is not only possible but also often productive to shift the focus to the present experiencing of clients even when historical facts are being elicited to illuminate client problems.

17. Going on "Fishing" Expeditions

A danger for beginning (and many experienced) social workers is pursuing content that is tangentially related to client concerns, issues of client and family safety, or legal mandates. Such content may relate to pet theories of social workers or agencies and be puzzling to clients. This may occur if the connection of these theories to the concerns that have brought clients into contact with them is not clear. A first precaution, hence, would be to avoid taking clients into tangential areas if the rationale cannot be readily justified. If the social worker feels that the exploration of new areas is relevant, then an explanation of the purpose of this exploration is called for.

GAUGING THE EFFECTIVENESS OF YOUR RESPONSES

The preceding discussion should assist you in identifying ineffective patterned communications you may have been employing. Because most learners typically ask closed-ended questions excessively, frequently change the subject, and recommend solutions before completing a thorough exploration of clients' problems, you should particularly watch for these patterns. In addition, you will need to monitor your interviewing style for idiosyncratic counterproductive patterns of responding.

The manual that is provided for instructors who use this book contains classroom exercises designed to assist students to recognize and eliminate ineffective responses. Further, because identifying ineffective styles of interviewing requires selective focusing upon the frequency and patterning of responses, you will find it helpful to analyze extended segments of taped sessions using the form "Assessing Verbal Barriers to Communication," found at the conclusion of the chapter.

One way of gauging the effectiveness of your responses is to carefully observe clients' reactions immediately following your response. Because of the number of clients involved in group and family sessions, you will often receive varied and nonverbal cues regarding the relative effectiveness of your responses to engage clients in these systems. As you assess your messages, keep in mind that a response is probably helpful if clients respond in one of the following ways:

- Continue to explore the problem or stay on the topic

- Express pent-up emotions related to the problematic situation
- Engage in deeper self-exploration and self-experiencing
- Volunteer more personally relevant material spontaneously
- Affirm the validity of your response verbally or nonverbally

By contrast, a response may be too confrontational, poorly timed, or off target if clients respond in one of the following ways:

- Disconfirm your response verbally or nonverbally
- Change the subject
- Ignore the message
- Appear mixed up or confused
- Become more superficial, more impersonal, more emotionally detached, or more defensive
- Argue or express anger rather than examine the relevance of the feelings involved

In analyzing social worker–client interactions, it is important to keep in mind that the participants mutually influence each other. Thus, a response by either person in an individual interview affects the following expressions of the other person. In group and conjoint sessions, the communications of each person, including the social worker, also affect the responses of all other participants; in a group situation, however, the influence of messages on subsequent responses of other members is sometimes difficult to detect because of the complexity of the communications.

With respect to the mutual influence process, beginning interviewers often reinforce unproductive client responses through responding indiscriminately or haphazardly or letting pass without comment positive responses that support practice objectives or reflect growth. Novice social workers are also sometimes jolted as they realize the extent to which they have allowed clients to control sessions through dysfunctional or manipulative behaviors. It is extremely important that you, as a beginning social worker, monitor and review your moment-by-moment transactions with clients with a view toward avoiding getting caught in ongoing ineffective or destructive communication perpetuated by yourself and the client.

Although beginning social workers encounter ineffective patterns of communication in individual interviews, they are even more likely to encounter recurring dysfunctional communications in groups or in conjoint sessions with spouses or family members. In fact, orchestrating an effective conjoint interview or group meeting often proves a challenge to even advanced social workers because of clients' rampant use of ineffective communications, which may engender intense anger, defensiveness, and confusion among family or group members.

In summary, you have a twofold task of monitoring, analyzing, and eliminating your own ineffective responses while observing, managing, and modifying ineffective responses by clients—a rather tall order. Although modifying dysfunctional communication of clients requires advanced skill, you can eliminate your own barriers in a relatively short time. You can accelerate your progress by also eliminating ineffective styles of responding and testing out new skills in your private life. It is unfortunate that many social workers compartmentalize and limit their helping skills to work with clients and continue to use ineffective styles with professional colleagues, friends, and families.

It is our experience that social workers who have not fully integrated the helping skills in their private lives do not relate as effectively to their clients as do social workers who have fully implemented and assimilated them as a part of their general style of relating in all situations. It is our conviction, in fact, that to adequately master essential skills and to fully tap their potential in assisting clients, social workers must promote their own interpersonal competence and personality integration, thereby modeling for the client the self-actualized or fully functioning person. Pursuing this personal goal prepares social workers for one of their major tasks or roles: teaching clients new skills of communicating and relating.

THE CHALLENGE OF LEARNING NEW SKILLS

Because of the unique nature of the helping process, establishing and maintaining a therapeutic relationship requires highly disciplined efforts. Moment by moment, transaction by transaction, the social worker must sharply focus on the needs and problems of clients. The success of each transaction is measured by the social worker's adroitness in consciously applying specific skills to move the process toward therapeutic objectives.

Interestingly, one of the major threats to learning new skills emanates from students' fear that in relinquishing old styles of relating they are giving up an intangible, irreplaceable part of themselves. Similarly, students who have previously engaged in social work practice may experience fear related to the fact that they have developed methods or styles of relating that have influenced and "moved" clients in the past; thus, giving up these response patterns may mean surrendering a hardwon feeling of competency. These fears of often exacerbated when the focus of instruction and supervision in the classroom and practicum is predominately upon eliminating errors and ineffective interventions and responses rather than on developing new skills or increasingly employing positive responses or interventions with clients. Learners may thus receive considerable feedback about their errors but receive inadequate input regarding their effective responses or styles of relating. Consequently, they may feel vulnerable and stripped of defenses (just as clients do) and experience more keenly the loss of something familiar.

As a learner, it is important that you develop your capacity to openly and nondefensively consider constructive feedback regarding ineffective or even destructive styles of relating or intervening. However, it is also important that you assume responsibility for eliciting positive feedback from educators and peers regarding the positive moment-by-moment responses you make. Remember that supervision time is limited and that responsibility for utilizing that time effectively and for acquiring

ASSESSING VERBAL BARRIERS TO COMMUNICATION				
Directions: In reviewing each 15-minute sample of taped interviews, tally your use of ineffective responses by placing marks in appropriate cells.				
15-Minute Taped Samples	*1*	*2*	*3*	*4*
1. Moralizing, sermonizing ("shoulds," "oughts")				
2. Advising prematurely				
3. Convincing, lecturing, instructing, arguing, intellectualizing				
4. Judging, criticizing, or blaming				
5. Analyzing, diagnosing, making glib interpretations; labeling behavior				
6. Reassuring, sympathizing, consoling, excusing				
7. Using sarcasm or employing distractive humor				
8. Threatening, warning, counterattacking				
9. Using excessive closed-ended questions				
10. Stacking questions				
11. Asking leading questions				
12. Using phrases repetitively (e.g., "OK," "you know," "that's neat"). List:				
13. Going on "fishing" expeditions				
Other responses that impede communication. List:				

ASSESSING PHYSICAL ATTENDING BEHAVIORS	
	Comments
1. Direct eye contact 0 1 2 3 4	
2. Warmth and concern reflected in facial expression 0 1 2 3 4	
3. Eyes on same level as clients' 0 1 2 3 4	
4. Appropriately varied and animated facial expressions 0 1 2 3 4	
5. Arms and hands moderately expressive; appropriate gestures 0 1 2 3 4	
6. Body leaning slightly forward; attentive but relaxed 0 1 2 3 4	
7. Voice clearly audible but not loud 0 1 2 3 4	
8. Warmth in tone of voice 0 1 2 3 4	
9. Voice modulated to reflect nuances of feelings and emotional tone of client messages 0 1 2 3 4	
10. Moderate tempo of speech 0 1 2 3 4	
11. Absence of distractive behaviors (fidgeting, yawning, gazing out window, looking at watch) 0 1 2 3 4	
12. Other 0 1 2 3 4	

Rating Scale:
0 = Poor, needs marked improvement.
1 = Weak, needs substantial improvement.
2 = Minimally acceptable, room for growth.
3 = Generally high level with few lapses.
4 = Consistently high level.

competency necessarily rests equally with you and your practicum instructor. It is also vital that you take steps to monitor your own growth systematically by reviewing audio- and videotapes, by taking frequency counts of desirable and undesirable responses, and by comparing your responses against guidelines for constructing effective messages contained in the book. Perhaps the single most important requirement for you in furthering your competency is to assume responsibility for advancing your own skill level by consistently monitoring your responses and practicing proven skills.

Most of the skills delineated in this book are not easy to master. Competent social workers have spent years in perfecting their ability to sensitively and fully attune themselves to the inner experiencing of clients, in furthering their capacity to share their own experiencing in an authentic, helpful manner, and in developing a keen sense of timing in employing these and other skills.

In the months ahead, as you forge new patterns of responding and test your skills, you will experience growing pains, that is, a sense of disequilibrium as you struggle to respond in new ways and, at the same time, to relate warmly, naturally, and attentively to your clients. You may also feel at times that your responses are mechanistic and experience a keen sense of transparency, that is, "The client will know that I'm not being real." If you work intensively over several months to master specific skills, however, you awkwardness will gradually diminish, and you will incorporate these skills naturally into your repertoire.

Summary

This chapter has presented a series of nonverbal and verbal barriers to effective communication often experienced by beginning social workers. As you become alert to them and more skilled in applying more productive alternatives, you will become more confident in your progress. We move in Chapter 8 to applying your communication skills to one of the first and most important tasks you will face: conducting a multisystemic assessment.

Internet Resources

 For further information about computer use in social services networks and links to other useful sites, you can access *http://www2.uta/cussn/*.

Notes

1. It is important not to set up artificial dichotomies that do not represent actual behaviors. Emma Gross (1995) argues that too frequently writers have inappropriately generalized across Native American cultures.

2. Reassurance is best directed to clients' capabilities. Appropriate reassurance can be effectively conveyed through the skill of positive feedback described in Chapter 5.

CHAPTER 8

Multidimensional Assessment

Revised and edited by Kim Strom-Gottfried

Chapter Overview

Assessment involves the gathering of information and the formulation of that information into a coherent picture of the client and his or her circumstances. Assessments include our inferences about the nature and causes of clients' difficulties, and thus they serve as the basis for the rest of our work with the client—the goals we set, the interventions we enact, and the progress we evaluate.

This chapter describes the process for conducting assessments and the formal products that result, including diagnostic labels. We will discuss the importance of attending to clients' strengths as well as difficulties and offer a model for incorporating various strengths and assets into assessment processes. The remainder of the chapter describes methods for learning more about clients, important questions to ask, and the meaning that you might ascribe to certain information you gather. The chapter concludes with sample assessments involving child maltreatment and marital difficulties.

Defining Assessment: Process and Product

The word *assessment* can be defined in several ways. First, it refers to a process occurring between practitioner and client in which information is gathered, analyzed, and synthesized to provide a concise picture of the client and his or her needs and strengths. In settings in which social work is the primary profession, the social worker often makes the assessment independently or consults with colleagues or a member of another discipline. Typically, formal assessments may be completed in one or two sessions.

A second use of the term refers to a process whereby potential clients interact with practitioners and organizations to determine if their needs and wants can be appropriately dealt with by the organization (Specht & Specht, 1986a & b). That is, the assessment of potential client concerns often occurs in the context of the organization's goals, capacities, and resources as well as the client's. In this organizational view, assessment begins with a request for service: Does the potential client (whether applicant, referral, or involuntary client) have a need that may be filled by the setting or organization? If such a need is discovered, then the assessment proceeds to exploration of eligibility. In the context of managed health care, this often entails an exploration of the kind of insurance coverage or payment plan available for the potential client. If the potential client is eligible, then an exploration of client resources and ability to make use of agency services follows, aiming toward the development of a contract (Specht & Specht, 1986a & b) (see Figure 8-1).

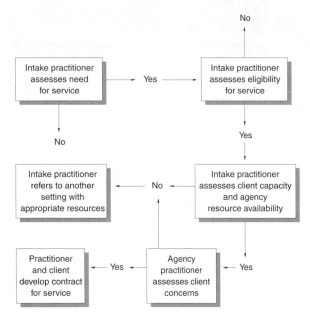

Figure 8-1 The Agency Assessment Sequence

Source: Adapted from Harry and Riva Specht (1986). Social work assessment: route to clienthood. Part 1 (November), 525–532. Part 2 (December), 587-593.

In settings in which social work is not the only or not the primary profession (often called *secondary or host settings)*, the social worker may be a member of a clinical team (e.g., in child guidance, mental health, medical, and correctional settings), and the process of assessment may be a joint effort of a psychiatrist, social worker, psychologist, nurse, teacher, and perhaps members of other disciplines. In such settings, the social worker typically compiles a social history and contributes knowledge related to interpersonal and family dynamics. The process of assessment in such settings may take longer due to the time required for team members to complete individual assessments and to meet as a group to reach a collective assessment.

Social workers engage in the process of assessment from the time of an initial contact with clients to the terminal contact, which may be weeks, months, or even years later. Assessment thus is a fluid and dynamic process that involves receiving, analyzing, and synthesizing new information as it emerges during the entire course of a given case. In

the first session, social workers generally elicit abundant information and must assess its meaning and significance as it unfolds.[1] This moment-by-moment assessment guides the social worker in deciding which information is salient and merits deeper exploration. When they have gathered sufficient information to illuminate the problems, practitioners analyze it and, in collaboration with clients, integrate the data into a tentative formulation of the problem. Many potential clients do not proceed with the social worker beyond this point. If their concerns can be best handled through a referral to other resources, if they do not meet eligibility criteria, or if they choose not to continue, contact often stops here. Specht and Specht (1986b) have emphasized that the relationship in this initial assessment and eligibility process should hence not be considered as necessarily leading to a therapeutic relationship. Communication skills as described in previous chapters are very important in assessment but not necessarily as precursors to a therapeutic relationship.

Should social workers and potential clients move from the exploratory phase to ongoing contact involving a contract for services and full client status, assessment continues, although on a somewhat diminished scale. Clients often disclose new information as problem solving progresses, casting the problems initially presented into a new perspective. Some clients, for example, withhold vital information that they fear may evoke criticism or condemnation from the social worker until they are reasonably confident of the latter's goodwill and helpful intent. Many preliminary assessments thus prove inaccurate and must be discarded or drastically revised.

The process of assessment continues even during the terminal phase of service. During final interviews, the social worker carefully assesses the client's readiness to terminate, assesses the presence of residual difficulties that may cause future difficulties, and identifies possible emotional reactions to termination. The social worker also considers possible strategies to assist the client to maintain improved functioning or to achieve additional progress after formal social work service is concluded.

Finally, assessment refers to the written products that result from these processes. As a product, assessment involves an actual formulation or statement *at a given time* regarding the nature of clients' problems and other related factors. A formal assessment thus involves analysis and synthesis of relevant data into a working definition of the problem that identifies various associated factors and clarifies how they interact to produce and maintain the problem. Because assessments must constantly be updated and revised, it is helpful to think of an assessment as a complex working hypothesis based on the most current data available.

Written assessments may vary from comprehensive psychosocial reports to brief analyses about very specific issues, such as the client's mental status, substance use, or suicidal risk. Assessments may be written to summarize progress on a case or to provide a comprehensive overview of the client to facilitate transfer or termination. The scope and focus of the written product and of the assessment itself will vary depending on the role of the social worker, the setting in which he or she works, and the needs presented by the client. A school social worker's assessment of an elementary school student may focus on the history and pattern of disruptive behaviors in the classroom, and on the classroom environment itself. A social worker in a family services agency seeing the same child may focus more broadly on the child's developmental history and his or her family's dynamics, as well as on the troubling classroom behavior. In another example, a hospital social worker whose focus is discharge planning may evaluate a client's readiness to return home after heart surgery and determine the services and information needed to make the return home successful. A social worker in a community health or mental health agency may assess the impact of the disease and the surgery on the client's emotional well-being and on his or her marital relationship. Further, a social worker in a vocational setting may focus the asssessment on the client's readiness to return to work and the job accommodations that are necessary to facilitate that transition.

While the social worker's setting will lead to focused assessment on particular issues pertinent to that setting, there are priorities in assessment that influence all social work settings. Without prioritization, there is risk that some areas will be explored beyond the need of the situation and the client's interest. Initially, there are three issues that should be assessed in all situations.

1. *What are the problems or concerns as seen by potential clients?* Social work's high priority on client self-determination and a commitment to assisting clients, where legal, ethical, and possible, to reach their own goals means that we explore their concerns in all cases.

2. *What (if any) current or impending legal mandates must the potential client and social worker consider?* Social workers who have a legal mandate to work with a potential client are required to assess those legal concerns in addition to concerns of those potential clients. For example, an adult protection worker must assess the danger of elder abuse, neglect, or other danger, whether or not the elderly person shares those concerns.

3. *What (if any) potentially serious or dangerous health or safety concerns might require the social worker's and potential client's attention?* As described in Chapter 4, an ethical priority of social work is exploring serious dangers to the health and safety of potential clients and their families that represent "serious, foreseeable, and imminent harm" (NASW, 1996, p. 9). Upon exploration, some potential dangers will be discovered to reach a threshold of danger that action is required legally whether or not the potential client considers the concern serious.

These three central foci permit the social worker to proceed to assess additional systems and aspects related to their pertinence to the development of an action plan. Without such a focus, it is possible to gather large amounts of information about elements that are tangential to client concerns, legal mandates, or safety issues. Such unfocused assessment may waste valuable time and lose an impatient potential client in the process.

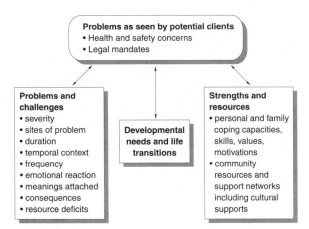

Figure 8-2 Assessment Focus

After exploring these foci, assessment proceeds to include exploration of problems and challenges, strengths and resources, developmental needs and life transitions, and systems impinging on client concerns. The remainder of this chapter will futher delineate how each of these areas is assessed (see Figure 8-2).

ASSESSMENT AND DIAGNOSIS

It is important at this point to clarify the difference between diagnoses and assessments. Diagnoses are labels or terms that may be applied to an individual or his or her situation. The labels provide shorthand desriptions based on specifically defined criteria. They can reflect medical conditions ("end-stage renal disease," "diabetes"), mental disorders ("depression," "agoraphobia"), or other classifications ("mild retardation," "emotionally and behaviorally disturbed," "learning disabled"). Diagnostic labels serve many purposes: They provide a language by which professionals, researchers, and patients can communicate about a commonly understood constellation of symptoms. The use of accepted diagnostic terminology facilitates research on problems, identification of appropriate treatments or medications, and linkages among people with similar problems. For example, diagnosing a set of troubling behaviors as "bipolar disorder" helps the client's

physician and social worker identify necessary medicaton and therapeutic services. The diagnosis may comfort the client by helping "put a name to" the experiences he or she has been having. It may also help the client learn more about the disease, locate support groups, and stay abreast of developments in understanding the disorder.

But diagnoses have their difficulties too. These labels provide an expedient way of describing complex problems, but they never tell the whole story. Diagnoses can become self-fulfilling prophecies, wherein clients, their families, and their helpers begin to define the client only in terms of the diagnostic lable. This distinction is captured in the difference between saying "Joe is a schizophrenic," "Joe has schizophrenia," or "Joe is a person who has schizophrenia." Simiarly, these labels carry a lot of power, and yet they can be erroneous (the result of misdiagnosis or a diagnosis that changes over time), and they may obscure important information about the client's difficulties as well as capacities. Referring to a client as "mildly retarded" may speak only to his or her score on an IQ test, not his or her level of daily functioning, interests, goals, joys, and challenges. This is where assessment comes in. Assessments describe the symptoms that support a particular dianosis, but they go further to help us understand the client's history and background, the effect of the symptoms on the client, the available supports and resources to manage the problem, and so on. In other words, diagnoses may result from assessments, but they tell only part of the story.

EMPHASIZING STRENGTHS IN ASSESSMENTS

Changes in practice have lagged far behind the change in terms from diagnosis to assessment, for social workers persist in formulating assessments that emphasize the pathology and dysfunction of clients—despite the time-honored social work platitude that social workers work with strengths, not weaknesses (Cowger, 1994; Saleeby, 1997).

Saleeby suggests that this focus derives from a historical emphasis on the moral defects of despised, deviant, and often poor clients (Saleeby, 1992, p. 3). In this view, problems were located in the individual and it was the professional's job to "fix" the problem or problem person.

The marked tendency of practitioners to focus on pathology has several important ramifications, the first of which is that to tap client strengths effectively, practitioners must be sensitive to them and skillful in utilizing them in the service of accomplishing case goals. The findings of at least one research study (Maluccio, 1979) strongly suggest that social workers underestimate client strengths. In this study of comparisons between clients' and caseworkers' perceptions of the outcomes of interventions, Maluccio found that the former "presented themselves as proactive, autonomous, human beings . . . able to enhance their functioning and their competence," whereas the latter viewed them as "reactive organisms with continuing problems, underlying weaknesses, and limited potentialities" (p. 399). Given this finding, it is likely that the caseworkers studied focused their efforts extensively on perceived weaknesses.

The findings of this study also revealed that clients were more satisfied with the outcomes of service than were the caseworkers, who manifested concerns about residual pathology, especially with clients who terminated prematurely. These findings have been supported by the findings of Presley (1987) and Toseland (1987). Both found that clients who did not return after one session often terminated service "prematurely" for reasons other than dissatisfaction (often because they felt they had benefited from the session and needed no further help). Presley thus concluded that "therapists may have a more fragile image of the client than appears warranted" (p. 607).

Again, one must wonder if preoccupation with dysfunction reinforced in many settings distorts social workers' perceptions and predisposes them to believe that clients should continue to receive service longer than is necessary. In this regard, Maluccio concluded: "There is a need to shift the focus in social work education and practice from problems or pathology to strengths, resources, and potentialities in human beings and their environments" (p. 401). We strongly concur!

A second ramification of failing to attend to strengths is that selectively attending to pathology impairs a social worker's ability to discern clients' potentials for growth. Although social workers fervently espouse the belief that human beings have the right and opportunity to develop their potentialities, the tendency to focus on pathology undermines that very value commitment. To implement this value fully, social work practitioners must achieve more balanced perceptions of their clients by attuning themselves to strengths and potentialities as well as to dysfunction and pathology. By thus broadening their perspectives of clients, social workers may also enhance the efficacy of their interventive efforts. As Cowger says, "Clinical practice based on empowerment assumes that client power is achieved when clients make choices that give them more control over their presenting problem situations and in turn their own lives" (Cowger, 1994, p. 263). Or, as research on Latino clients has concluded, "In supporting clients' strengths, workers project an honest belief in the clients' ability to deal with problems. This display of belief in the clients' potential strengthens their own belief of the possibilities in the undertaking" (E. Gomez et al., 1985, p. 481).

A third ramification of attending excessively to pathology concerns the fact that a large proportion of clients need help in enhancing their self-esteem. Troubled by self-doubts, feelings of inadequacy, and even feelings of worthlessness, their lack of self-confidence and self-respect underlies many dysfunctional cognitive, emotional, and behavioral patterns, including fears of failure, depression, social withdrawal, alcoholism, and hypersensitivity to criticism—to name just a few. To assist clients to view themselves more positively, social workers and their agencies must first view their clients more positively.

Why does this preoccupation with pathology persist despite increasing exhortations that emphasize strengths? In a study on the implementation of a practice model that focused on client wishes in a public service setting, Bricker-Jenkins (1992) has suggested that supervisors were uncomfortable with the degree to which clients were able to set so much of their own agendas. Similarly, part of the explanation for a preoccupation with pathology is that funding for services, whether through insurance reimbursement or government contracts, may be based on the client's difficulties and level of impairment. Emphasizing clients' strengths in a case report may thus raise questions by utilization reviewers about whether services are needed at all.

Assessing Strengths and Obstacles

Although there may be challenges in employing strengths-based assessments, the advantages of attending to strengths are clear. To assist in emphasizing strengths and empowerment in the assessment process, Cowger (1994, p. 265) suggests that practitioners

1. give preeminence to client understanding of the facts,
2. discover what the client wants, and
3. assess personal and environmental strengths on multiple levels.

Further, Cowger has developed a two-dimensional matrix framework for assessment that can assist social workers in attending to both needs and strengths. On a vertical axis, potential strengths and resources are depicted at one end and potential deficits, challenges, and obstacles at the other. The horizontal axis ranges from environmental (family and community) to individual factors. The framework provides a useful way to press us to move beyond the frequent preoccupation with personal deficits (quadrant 4), to include personal strengths and environmental strengths and obstacles (Cowger, 1992) (see Figure 8-3).

To assist in examining how such a matrix can be helpful in producing a more complete assessment, we will present and examine the following case for points in assessment.

Figure 8-3 Framework for Assessment

Source: Adapted from Charles D. Cowger, *Assessment of Client Strengths* in *The Strengths Perspective in Social Work Practice*, 2/e (Figure 5.2, p. 69) by Dennis Saleebey. Reprinted by permission of Allyn & Bacon.

CASE EXAMPLE

Tom is 20, Caucasian, and has been in the mental health system since he was 9 years old. He was raised by his mother and never knew his father. He had many problems during childhood and was placed in residential facilities on at least three occasions. His primary childhood diagnosis was conduct disorder and he periodically assaulted others during adolescence. Records consistently indicate that Tom and his mother had a very stressful relationship. Tom's maternal grandparents were somewhat involved in his life, and he thinks highly of them. He reports feeling much love and support from them while he was growing up.

Tom was placed in a juvenile facility when he was 17 after hospitalization on a mental health unit where he displayed psychotic behaviors and was, at times, violent. Just prior to turning 18, Tom entered the adult mental health system. At that time he was transferred from a residential juvenile facility to an adult facility where he currently resides.

Tom is hoping to move into an apartment with his significant other (Sarah) in the near future. He currently has several diagnoses including obsessive compul-sive disorder, bipolar disorder, anxiety disorder, and learning disorder. Although medication seems to control his psychotic thoughts, he continues to be easily frustrated and to have verbal outbursts. His overall IQ is 84, and he continues to attend special education classes at his high school, which he can do until his 22nd birthday. He has had considerable difficulty maintaining part-time employment, even when the jobs involved support from his school program. His level of independent living skills is assessed at well below the minimum needed to live independently. He has difficulty completing household tasks, including cooking and cleaning, without much assistance. He has had difficulty in managing his money. Tom has learned to use public transportation, although he is easily frustrated about remembering which bus to take and will sometimes take a cab home despite a lack of funds to pay the fare. Tom has consistently refused assistance in any of these areas, reporting that he does not need assistance.

Tom and Sarah met at a mental health facility and have known each other for about 6 months. Sarah has somewhat better independent living skills and reports that she will help Tom with cooking and taking the bus, among other things. Neither is currently employed, but both plan to get jobs to support themselves. They are now asking for assistance from staff in moving into an apartment together.

To assist in using the assessment framework, the information above has been applied to the matrix. For example, quadrant 4 (individual deficits, challenges, or obstacles) includes the behavioral consequences and difficulties related to his multiple diagnoses. His difficulties with independent living skills and tendencies toward violence are concerns in relation to his living plans. Sarah may be in danger of domestic violence. In addition, without birth control, they may begin a pregnancy soon. His low IQ may impede his learning of necessary independent living skills. The stressful relationship with his mother is of long standing. Finally, Tom is not open to help about these concerns, focusing instead on his desire to move in with Sarah.

Moving to quadrant 3 (environmental, including family and community deficits, obstacles, and challenges), we are alerted to the stressful relationship with his mother and her probable lack of support for his plan. Choosing to live in the community will probably mean that his treatment will be primarily based on medication rather than mental health counseling. In addition, the mental health system is often lacking in resources to support independent living. Employment opportunities commensurate with his skills may be limited.

When we move above the horizontal axis to consider potential strengths and resources, we become alerted to additional factors equally essential to the assessment. In quadrant 1 (potential community resources and strengths), we note that Tom's grandparents have been a valuable source of support in the past and could possibly be again. Sarah supports their joint plan. The high school is able to continue to support him in pursuing his education. Staff in his current facility and vocational services can assist Tom with acquiring more independent living skills. Finally, Tom's mother may be engaged in assisting Tom in making his plans succeed.

In quadrant 2 (potential personal strengths and resources), we are struck by the fact that Tom has a clear goal that he is highly committed to. He has begun work on many independent living skills, is taking the bus, and is motivated to work. Tom has developed a caring relationship with Sarah, one that she is willing to commit to a more permanent relationship. His medication is assisting him in controlling psychotic thoughts.

Cowger's framework for assessment alerts us to the fact that a useful assessment is not limited to either deficits or strengths, and that the environmental dimension is important as well as the personal. Use of the four quadrants provides us with information that can help in pursuing goals, mindful of obstacles and challenges.

To further assist you in perceiving personal strengths, we have identified in the following list a number of strengths often manifested by clients in initial sessions. We urge you to cultivate your sensitivity to these and other manifestations of these crucial client resources:

1. Facing problems and seeking help, rather than denying or otherwise avoiding confronting them

2. Risking by sharing problems with the social worker—a stranger

3. Persevering in attempting to keep a family together under difficult circumstances

4. Expressing feelings and views openly rather than being guarded

5. Exercising resourcefulness and creativity in making the most out of limited resources or managing and surviving upon a meager income

6. Making sacrifices on behalf of children and others

7. Seeking to further knowledge, education, and skills

8. Expressing loving and caring feelings to family members

9. Asserting one's rights rather than submitting to injustice

10. Attempting to meet one's debts and obligations despite financial adversity

11. Seeking to be independent

12. Seeking to understand the needs and feelings of others

13. Demonstrating capacity to be introspective and to shift thinking or realign perceptions when presented with new information or alternate views of situations

14. Owning responsibility for one's own action and showing interest in making changes in self rather than focusing extensively on the changes one thinks others should make

15. Demonstrating capacity for self-control

16. Demonstrating ability to make individual value judgments

17. Manifesting emotional capacity to function effectively in stressful situations

18. Demonstrating ability to abstract and to make connections between causes and effects

19. Demonstrating ability to form close relationships with others

20. Demonstrating ability to consider alternative courses of actions and the needs of others when solving problems

SOURCES OF INFORMATION

Where do social workers get the information on which to base their assessment? Numerous sources can be used individually or in combination. The following are the most common:

1. Background sheets or other forms that clients complete

2. Verbal report by clients (i.e., accounts of problems, expressions of feelings, views, thoughts, events, and the like)

3. Direct observation of nonverbal behavior

4. Direct observation of interaction between marital partners, family members, and group members

5. Collateral information from relatives, friends, physicians, teachers, employers, and other professionals

6. Tests or assessment instruments

7. Personal experiences of the practitioner based on direct interaction with clients

Verbal Report

Of these major sources, client verbal report is generally the primary source of information. Verbal report consists of descriptions of problems, expressions of feelings, reporting of events, presentation of views, and the like. Clients' feelings and reports should always be respected as indicating their understanding of their circumstances. As with other information sources, verbal reports often need to be augmented because of possible faulty recall, biases, and limited self-awareness on the part of clients. As discussed in Chapter 6, your assessment can be strengthened by gathering specific details from clients, through techniques such as focusing in depth and seeking concreteness.

Direct Observation of Nonverbal Behavior

Direct observation of clients' nonverbal behavior adds additional information, for people generally lack awareness of their nonverbal behavior and it is therefore less subject to conscious control than is verbal report. Nonverbal cues are valuable indicators of emotional states and reactions such as anger, hurt, embarrassment, and fear. It is thus vital to develop an acute perceptiveness to nonverbal cues, such as tone of voice, tears, clenched fists, voice tremors, quivering hands, tightened jaws, pursed lips, variations of expression, and gesticulations. The doors to many rich discussions of emotional reactions have been opened by empathic responses directed to nonverbal cues (e.g., "Your eyes are telling me you feel very sad right now. Could you put into words what you're experiencing at this moment?").

Observation of Interaction

Direct observation of interaction between spouses or partners, family members, and group members often is extremely enlightening. Students (as well as seasoned practitioners) frequently are amazed at the striking differences between clients' reports of their relationships and the behaviors they demonstrate in those relationships. A social worker may observe a father interacting with his daughter, impatiently telling her "I know you can do better," yet in an earlier session, the father may have described his behavior to her as "encouraging." Direct observation may reveal that his words are encouraging while his tone is not.

Observation can occur in natural settings (such as viewing a child in the classroom, adults in a group setting, or a family as they answer a worker's question in session). "Enactment" can also be employed by social workers to observe interaction firsthand rather than to rely on verbal report. Use of this technique involves having clients

reenact a conflictual event during a live session. Participants are instructed to recreate the situation exactly as it occurred, using the same words, gestures, and tones of voice as in the actual event. Before giving the instructions, however, it is important to provide an explanation for making the request, such as the following:

- "To understand what produced the difficulties in the event you just described, I'd like you to recreate the situation here in our session. By seeing what both of you do and say and how you do it, I can get an accurate picture of what actually happens. I'd like you to recreate the situation exactly as it happened. Use the same words, gestures, and tone of voice as you did. Now, where were you when it happened, and how did it start?"

Most clients are willing to engage in enactment, but encouragement is sometimes needed. Enactment can also be used in contrived situations to see how a couple or family interact in situations that involve decision making, planning, role negotiation, child discipline, or other like activities. Practitioners will need to exercise their creativity in designing situations likely to generate and clarify the types of interaction the practitioner desires to observe. Another form of enactment involves the use of symbolic interactions, for example through the use of dolls in play therapy or in assessment of possible sexual abuse.

Direct observation of spontaneous behavior or of enacted situations is not without flaws, for clients often understandably attempt to create a favorable impression and behave differently than they have in actual situations. Practitioners can counter this possibility after enacted situations by asking to what extent the behaviors of participants corresponded with their behavior in actual situations. It is wise to elicit views of all participants to ascertain the authenticity of reported discrepancies. Reported discrepancies that are validated by participants are highly informative.

It is also important to recognize that an office setting is not a natural arena for family interaction and that clients' behavior may be strongly influenced by this unnatural environment. As a corrective measure, it is desirable to visit clients in their homes, if possible. In fact, one of the strengths of an emerging form of practice, in-home, family-based services, is the opportunity to observe family difficulties firsthand rather than rely on second-hand accounts (Ronnau & Marlow, 1995). Observations of living conditions, incidentally, may also reveal problems that would otherwise not come to light. Direct observation is also subject to perceptual errors by the observer. Social workers should take care about the conclusions they draw from their observations. A method to compensate for this error is to determine the degree of congruence between observations made independently by different observers and avoid drawing conclusions until more information is available to "complete the picture." These corrective measures, however, require time and may not be feasible in practice. Despite the flaws of direct observation, information gained by this means adds significantly to that gained from verbal report.

Client Self-Monitoring

Client self-monitoring is a potent source of information (Kopp, 1989). Involvement in self-monitoring not only produces rich and quantifiable data but also assists in empowering the client during the assessment process by actively obtaining some of the information considered in treatment planning as a collaborator rather than a passive participant.

Self-monitoring can involve clients in writing descriptions and recording feelings, behaviors, and thoughts associated with occurrences of their targeted problems. The first step in self-monitoring is to recognize the occurrence of the event (e.g., events that lead to anger outbursts, temper tantrums by children, heated disputes, episodes of drinking or overeating). The next step is to chart or graph the information to determine the baseline of the behavior. Using self-anchored rating scales (Jordan & Franklin, 1995) or simple counting measures, clients and/or those around them can keep a record of the frequency of intensity of a

behavior. How often was Joe late for school? How severe was Joan's pain in the morning, at noon, and in the evening? Which nights did Ralph have particular difficulty sleeping? Did this difficulty relate to events during the day, medications, stresses, or anything he ate or drank?

A major advantage of using self-monitoring is that by focusing their attention, clients gain insights about their situations. Moreover, as they discuss their recorded observations they "spontaneously operationalize goals and suggest ideas for change" (Kopp, 1989, p. 278).[2] The targeted behaviors can then be quantified, which assists in monitoring progress.

Collateral Sources of Information

Information sometimes is also provided by relatives, friends, physicians, and others who possess essential information about relevant aspects of clients' lives. Information from such collateral sources is subject to the same limitations as other indirect sources. Nevertheless, persons who are not directly implicated in the problematic situation may provide information that illuminates otherwise obscure dynamics of problematic behavior.

However, it is not necessary or even desirable to contact collateral sources routinely, and you must exercise prudence in deciding when such information is needed. Furthermore, client consent is required, except in the case of bona fide exigencies. It is prudent to obtain written consent from clients with agency "release of information" forms.

Although clients occasionally will request that you contact others to gain their views, you will often need to initiate such discussions. If you explain that you can best serve the client by gaining a well-rounded picture of the problematic situation and that others often can identify factors that may otherwise be overlooked, clients will often consent to and even welcome such collateral contacts.

In weighing the validity of information obtained from collateral sources, it is important to consider the degree to which collateral persons are emotionally involved with clients. Those most emotionally involved, such as members of the immediate family, may be biased in some ways and, hence, less objective. Similarly, persons who have something to gain or to lose from pending case decisions (e.g., custody of a child, property settlement, or the burden of caring for a chronically mentally ill person) may be less credible than persons more emotionally removed from case situations. On the other hand, those who have limited contact with the client (such as other service providers) may have narrowed or otherwise skewed views of the client's situation. As with other sources of information, input from collateral contacts must be critically viewed and weighed in light of other information in the case.

Tests and Assessment Instruments

Still another possible source of information consists of various assessment instruments, including psychological tests, screening instruments, and assessment tools. Some of these tests are administered by professionals (such as psychologists or educators) who are specially trained in the administration and scoring of such assessment tools. In these cases, social workers might receive reports of the testing and incorporate the findings into their psychosocial assessments or treatment plans. Examples of these include intelligence tests such as the WAIS or WISC (Lukas, 1993), tests of neurological functioning such as the Bender Gestalt, or projective tests such as the Rorschach or the TAT (Thematic Apperception Test).

Some instruments are designed for use by social workers and allied professionals. Examples of these include the WALMYR Assessment Scales, which can be used to measure depression, self-esteem, clinical stress, anxiety, alcohol involvement, peer relations, sexual attitudes, homophobia, marital satisfaction, sexual satisfaction, nonphysical abuse of partners, and a variety of other clinical phenomena.[3] Instruments such as the Beck Depression Inventory (Beck, Rush, Shaw & Emery, 1979) and the Beck Scale for Suicidal Ideation (Range & Knott, 1997) have well-established validity and reliability, can be effectively administered and scored by clinicians from a variety of professions, and can

assist practitioners in evaluating the seriousness of a client's condition.

Other tools may be helpful for identifying clients' strengths and needs, when used within the context of an assessment interview (VanHook, Berkman, & Dunkle, 1996). Examples of these include the Primary Care Evaluation of Mental Health Disorders (PRIME-MD), which helps with the identification of mental health problems (Spitzer et al., 1994), and the Older Americans Resources and Services Questionnaire (OARS) (L. George & Fillenbaum, 1990), which provides information about the client's functioning across a variety of domains, including economic and social resources and activities of daily living.

Taking the use of instruments a step further, Nurius and Hudson (1998, 1993a) have reported on the development of a computer-based evaluation tool that includes all of the WALMYR Assessment Scales listed in the preceding section and a Multi Problem Screening Inventory (MPSI).[4] The MPSI scale is a multidimensional self-report measure that helps practitioners to better assess and understand the severity or magnitude of client problems across 27 different areas of personal and social functioning. The completed instrument helps both the client and the social worker evaluate areas of difficulty and the relative severity of difficulties in different life areas. In addition to the advantages for accuracy and efficiency that these and other computerized instruments afford, they also simplify the tracking of results over time and assist in the use of data for tracking case progress.

Tests and screening instruments represent useful and expedient methods of quantifying data and behaviors, and thus they can form an important part of assessments, case planning, and outcome evaluations. To use these tools effectively, however, practitioners must be well grounded in knowledge of test theory and in the characteristics of specific tests. Many tests, for example, have low reliability and validity and should be used with extreme caution, if at all. In the hands of unqualified persons, clinical assessment tools may be grossly misused. Because "a little knowledge is a dangerous thing," social workers should thoroughly understand any instruments they are using or recommending, and seek consultation in the interpretation of tests administered by other professionals. Sources such as Corcoran and Fischer (1999) and Bloom, Fischer, and Orme (1999) can acquaint social workers with both available instruments and their proper use.

Personal Experience Based on Direct Interaction

A final source of information is your own personal experience based on direct interaction with clients. You will react in varying ways to different clients, and your reactions may be useful in understanding how other people react to these clients. For example, you may experience certain clients as withdrawn, personable, dependent, caring, manipulative, seductive, assertive, overbearing, or determined. Client behavior is often influenced by the situation of contact with the practitioner. For example, potential clients referred by others or mandated for service can be expected to behave in a more guarded fashion than persons who have applied for a service. However, some patterns may also occur in their general social relationships. Hence, your own reaction may be a vital clue to understanding their possible difficulties or successes in interpersonal relationships. For example, a client who reports that others take him for granted and make unreasonable demands upon him may make inordinate efforts to please a practitioner and may manifest self-deprecating behavior. The practitioner's experience with the clients provides clues to at least part of the source of their problems.

A caution in the use of this method is required, however. Initial impressions can be misleading and must be supported by additional contacts with clients. Moreover, such impressions are subjective and may be influenced by your own interpersonal patterns and perceptions. Before drawing even tentative conclusions, it is important to scrutinize your reactions to identify possible biases, distorted perceptions, or behavior on your part that may have contributed to clients' behavior. If you tend to be domineering or represent an agency that may

have a reputation (deserved or not) for intrusiveness (such as child protective service), clients may respond with passivity or counteraggressiveness that does not reflect their typical ways of interacting. Similarly, overly challenging or confrontational behavior on your part may produce defensiveness or withdrawn behavior that is in part a natural reaction to your inappropriate behavior.

Your perceptions of and reactions to clients may also be distorted by your own life experiences. For example, if you had painful experiences as a child with a controlling and critical parent, you may react negatively to clients who manifest similar qualities and may have difficulty perceiving their strengths and uniqueness. If you were abused or sexually molested as a child, you may have a tendency to overidentify with victims of child maltreatment and to feel hostile toward perpetrators of abuse. If you had an alcoholic parent, you may also unknowingly experience discomfort or feelings of rejection toward alcoholic clients. There are, of course, many other types of life experience that distort perceptions of and judgments regarding clients. Self-awareness thus is indispensable to drawing valid conclusions about your experiential reactions to clients. Just as part of your role with clients is to assist them to disentangle reaction from reality, you have a similar obligation toward yourself.

THE MULTIDIMENSIONALITY OF ASSESSMENT

Human problems, even those that appear to be simple, often involve a complex interplay of many factors. Rarely do sources of problems reside solely within an individual or within that individual's environment. Rather, reciprocal interaction occurs between a human being and the external world. One acts upon and responds to the external world, and the quality of one's actions affects reactions and vice versa. For example, a parent may complain about poor communication with an adolescent child, attributing the difficulty to the fact that the adolescent is sullen and refuses to talk about most things. The adolescent, however, may complain that it is pointless to talk with the parent because the latter consistently pries, lectures, or criticizes. Each participant's complaint about the other may be accurate, but each unwittingly behaves in ways that have produced and now maintain their dysfunctional interaction. Thus, the behavior of neither person is the sole cause of the breakdown in communication in a simple cause-effect (linear) fashion. Rather, it is their reciprocal interaction that produces the difficulty; the behavior of each is both cause and effect, depending on one's vantage point.

The multidimensionality of human problems is also a consequence of the fact that human beings are social creatures, dependent upon other human beings and upon complex social institutions to meet their needs. Basic needs such as food, housing, clothing, and medical care require adequate economic means and the availability of goods and services. Educational, social, and recreational needs require interface with societal institutions. Needs to feel close to and loved by others, to have companionship, to experience a sense of belonging, and to experience sexual gratification require satisfactory social relationships within one's marriage or partnership, family, social network, and community. The extent to which people experience self-esteem depends on certain individual psychological factors and the quality of feedback from other people.

Beyond an initial focus on client concerns, legal mandates, and safety issues, assessment of the concerns of a client system (individual, couple, or family) thus requires extensive knowledge about that system as well as consideration of the multifarious systems (e.g., economic, legal, educational, medical, religious, social, interpersonal) that impinge upon the client system. Moreover, to assess the functioning of an individual entails evaluating various aspects of that person's functioning. For example, one may need to consider dynamic interactions among the biophysical, cognitive, emotional, cultural, behavioral, and motivational subsystems and the relationships of those interactions to problematic situations. With a couple or family client system, the social

worker finds it useful to attend to communication and interactional patterns as well as to each member of the system. Although not all of the various systems and subsystems cited above are likely to play significant roles in the problems of any given client system, overlooking relevant systems results in assessment that is partial at best and irrelevant or erroneous at worst. Interventions based on incomplete or inaccurate assessments, therefore, are likely to have limited remedial effects, to be ineffective, or even to produce detrimental results. Conversely, interventions that are based on accurate and comprehensive assessments are more likely to be effective.

Choices and priorities in assessment occur given client concerns and agency purpose and resources. To reiterate, one part of assessment is to determine if the potential client can or should receive services from the practitioner and his or her agency. A second part is then to gather information that will assist in the formulation of a contract and treatment plan to deal with identified problems and concerns. To assist you to formulate assessments that consider the many dimensions of human problems, we consider in this chapter the major questions that you will need to answer in formulating an assessment. In the next chapter, we address multidimensional assessment of individuals and of the environment. In Chapter 10, we focus on assessment of interpersonal systems, with particular emphasis upon marriages and families. In Chapter 11, we consider assessment within the context of groups.

Questions to be Answered in Assessment

To assist you in determining whether you have considered all of the factors discussed in the preceding sections, we have encapsulated the factors in the following questions. You can employ these questions as a checklist to ensure you have not overlooked a significant factor in your assessment.

1. What are the concerns and problems of potential clients as they perceive them?

2. What current or impending legal mandates (if any) are relevant to the situation?

3. What serious or imminent health or safety issues are relevant to the situation?

4. What are specific indications or manifestations of the problem(s)?

5. What persons and systems are implicated in the problem(s)?

6. How do the participants and/or systems interact to produce and maintain the problem(s)?

7. What unmet needs and/or wants are involved in the problem(s)?

8. What developmental stage or life transition is entailed in the problem(s)?

9. How severe is the problem and how does it affect the participants?

10. What meanings do clients ascribe to the problem(s)?

11. Where do the problematic behaviors occur?

12. When do the problematic behaviors occur?

13. What is the frequency of the problematic behaviors?

14. What is the duration of the problem(s)?

15. What are the consequences of the problem?

16. Have other issues, such as alcohol or substance abuse, physical or sexual abuse, affected the functioning of the client or family members?

17. What are the clients' emotional reactions to the problem(s)?

18. How have the clients attempted to cope with the problem, and what are the required skills to resolve the problem?

19. What are the skills and strengths of the clients?

20. How do ethnocultural, societal, and social class factors bear on the problem(s)?

21. What support systems exist or need to be created for the clients?

22. What external resources are needed by clients?

Questions 1–3 should serve as preliminary inquiries so that the social worker learns if there are prevailing issues that may guide the direction of the interview. Questions 4–17 pertain to further specification of problems. They do not imply a priority for a problem focus over explorations of strengths and resources that follow in questions 18–22. As suggested in the strengths matrix previously described, assessment of strengths, resources, and limitations or challenges is required for a full assessment.

Getting Started

After opening social amenities and an explanation of the direction and length of the interview, you should begin by exploring the client's concerns. Sometimes this question is as simple and open ended as "Mrs. Smith, what brings you in to see me today?" This allows the client the opportunity to express his or her concerns and helps give direction to the questions that will follow.

At this point, the worker must also be attentive to other issues that may alter the direction of the interview, at least at the outset. If the client's request for service is nonvoluntary, and particularly if it is the result of legal mandate (e.g., part of probation, the result of a child maltreatment complaint) the nature of the mandate, referring information, and the client's perception of the referral will frame the early part of the first interview.

A further consideration at the first interview is whether any danger exits for harm to the client or to others. Some referrals, for example in emergency services, clearly involve the risk for harm, which should be discussed and evaluated at the outset. In other instances, the risk may be more subtle. For example, a client may open an interview saying, "I'm at the end of my rope. . . . I can't take it any longer." The social worker should respond to this opening by probing further. "Can you tell me more . . .?" "When you say you can't take it, what do you mean by that?" If further information raises the social worker's concerns about the danger for suicidal or aggressive behavior, more specific questioning should follow, focused on assessing the lethality of the situation. Whatever the client's presenting problem, if shared information gives rise to safety concerns, the worker must redirect the interview to focus on the degree of danger. If the threats to safety are minor or manageable, the worker may resume the interview's focus on the issues that brought the client in for service. However, if the mini-assessment reveals serious or imminent risk to the client or others, the focus of the session must then be on assuring safety rather than continuing the assessment.

Chapter 9 describes the process for conducting a suicide lethality assessment. Beyond this, sources such as Morrison (1995), Houston-Vega et al. (1997), and Lukas (1993) offer guidelines for interviewing around issues of danger and assessing the degree of risk in various situations. Such texts can be useful resources for learning more about the topic.

Identifying the Problem, Its Manifestations, and Other Critical Concerns

In your initial contacts with potential clients, you take the first step in uncovering the sources of their problems and engaging them in planning appropriate remedial measures. People typically seek help because they have exhausted their coping efforts and/or lack resources required for satisfactory living. They have often found that, despite earnest efforts, their coping efforts are futile or seem to aggravate the problematic situation. In many such instances, applicants have misidentified their problems, so their solutions ironically have become problems in and of themselves. An applicant, for example, may make heroic efforts to please others—a spouse, parent, or employer—to no avail. The problem, however, may not be an inability to please others but rather a pattern of striving excessively to please others. Leaning over backward to win approval of others tends to be self-defeating because one thereby devalues oneself in the eyes of others and invites being taken for granted. Having exhausted their coping efforts, such applicants may turn to a professional person, expecting that the latter will somehow assist them to discover a solution to their problem.

Problem identification takes a somewhat different course when the potential client has been referred or is an involuntary client. Referred clients may approach services willingly, assisted by the referral from a professional, friend, or family member familiar with your own or your agency's services. However, many referred clients acquiesce passively because someone else thinks that they "need help." Their initiation of contact does not necessarily imply willingness to accept services.

Meanwhile, involuntary clients are further down the continuum of voluntarism, reluctantly "seeking help" because of coercion from family members or some official power structure. Involuntary clients often do not perceive themselves as having problems or portray pressure from the referral source as the problem. Typically used by such clients is the following message: "I don't know why I should have to come. My wife is the one with the problems, and she's the one who should be here." When the source of motivation thus lies outside the client, the parameters of the problem are less readily identifiable. In such instances, after attempting to understand and reduce the client's negativism about being pressured to seek help, the social worker engages the client in an exploration of the latter's life situation. The goals are to determine if wants or areas of dissatisfaction on the client's part can be identified and if motivation can be engendered to work toward enhancing the client's satisfaction in pertinent areas. When and if the client acknowledges a problem, the boundaries of the problem become clear, and the exploration then proceeds in a normal fashion.

Early in a session, often after introductions have been made (or after a warm-up period), the social worker should invite potential clients to describe their problems or concerns. Applicants typically respond to such overtures by giving a general account of their problems. The problem identified by clients typically involves a deficiency of something needed (e.g., health care, adequate income or housing, companionship, harmonious family relationships, self-esteem) or an excess of something that is not desired (e.g., fear, guilt, temper outbursts, marital or parent-child conflict, or addiction). In either event, applicants are in a state of disequilibrium and experience both tension and troubled emotions. The emotions thus are often a prominent part of the problem configuration, which is one reason empathic communication is such a vital skill.[5] The presenting problem as viewed by the applicant is highly significant because it reflects his or her immediate perceptions of the problem and is the focal point of the motivation for seeking help.

Those potential clients referred by others sometimes encounter the fact that the referral source (often a doctor, employer, family member, or school official) has a view of the problem and recommendations for a treatment plan. It is important to clarify with referred clients that they can choose to work on problems of concern to them, not necessarily the concerns of the referral source (L. Epstein, 1992).

In the case of involuntary clients under threat of a legal mandate, choices are also available. While the consequences of avoiding a court order or impending legal action may be serious, involuntary clients may choose to do so and accept the consequences. More importantly, involuntary clients frequently have their own views of concerns that do not correspond with their legal pressures and may in fact include "getting them off my back" (R. H. Rooney, 1992). It is frequently possible to engage involuntary clients in contracts that are at least partially voluntary through finding and including their motivation in the contract.

At this point, it is important to call your attention to the difference between the "presenting problem" and the "problem for work." The issues that bring the client and worker together initially may not be the issues that are the focus of goals and interventions later in the relationship. The problem for work may differ from the original or presenting problem for a number of reasons. Clients generally modify their perceptions of their problems as they explore factors of which they previously had little or no awareness. Moreover, potential clients do not always initially reveal their most troubling problems because to do so may be highly embarrassing or may risk condemnation. This does not mean, however, that you should disregard the problems that

brought clients to you in the first place. If you proceed to work exclusively on problems clients do not acknowledge, you may risk losing their motivation. Several reviews of studies of casework effectiveness have suggested that more successful outcomes are associated with motivational congruence, or a fit between practitioner and client views of the problem (Reid & Hanrahan, 1982; Videka-Sherman, 1988).

The presenting problem is also of vital significance because it suggests areas to be explored subsequently. If the presenting problem described by parents involves truancy and rebellious behavior of an adolescent, the exploration will include the family, school, and peer systems. As the exploration proceeds, it may also be useful to explore the marital system if there is some indication that difficulty in the marital relationship is negatively affecting the parent-child relationship. If learning difficulties appear to contribute to the truancy, the cognitive and perceptual subsystems of the adolescent may also need to be assessed as part of the problem. The presenting problem thus identifies systems that are constituent parts of the problem. Finally, it should be noted that truancy and rebellious behavior reflect the presenting problem as seen by parents. If their view alone is accepted, then the adolescent is transformed from potential client to problem bearer or target. While such behavior is likely to be an important focus, it is important also to explore the adolescent's view, to enhance the possibility of collaboration and becoming a client.

The Interaction of Other Persons or Systems

The presenting problem and the exploration that follows usually identify key persons, groups, or organizations that are participants in the client's difficulties. An accurate assessment must consider all the elements and how they interact to produce difficulties. Furthermore, an effective plan of intervention should embody these same elements, even though it is not always feasible to involve everyone who is a participant in a given problematic situation. Some participants, for example, may refuse to become involved.

To understand more fully how the client(s) and other involved systems interact to produce and maintain the problem, you must elicit specific information that pertains to the functioning and interaction of these various systems. Systems with which clients commonly transact include:

1. The family and extended family or clan
2. The social network (friends, neighbors, co-workers, religious leaders and associates, club members, and cultural groups)
3. Public institutions (educational, recreational, law enforcement and protection, mental health, social service, health care, employment, economic security, legal and judicial, and various governmental agencies)
4. Personal service providers (doctor, dentist, barber, or hairdresser, bartender, auto mechanic, landlord, banker, etc.)
5. Religious/spiritual belief system.

To understand how the interaction of participants result in difficulties, it is essential to understand the contributions of each to the problem situation. This requires detailed information about the behavior of all participants, including what they say and do before, during, and after problematic events. This specific information will help you and the client illuminate circumstances associated with the problematic behavior, how each person affects and is affected by others, and consequences of events that tend to perpetuate problematic behavior. It is important to keep in mind that human behavior is purposive and can be understood by analyzing the forces that motivate people to behave as they do. Motivational forces consist of both external events (that is, those that are visible to others) and covert forces (that is, inner thoughts, beliefs, emotions, wishes, and images) as well as physiological and psychological states.

With regard to external events, certain circumstances or behaviors typically precede problematic behavior. One family member may say or do something that precipitates an angry, defensive, or hurt reaction by another. A child's outburst in the class-room may follow certain stimuli. A co-worker's critical comment may precede an episode of self-doubt and recrimination. Events that precede problematic behavior are referred to as antecedents. Antecedents often give valuable clues as to the behavior of one participant that may be provocative or offensive to another, thereby triggering a negative reaction, followed by a counter negative reaction, thus setting the problematic situation in motion.

What each participant does and says during the problematic event must also be determined, for the response of each participant is a stimulus to other participants, and the nature and intensity of these responses tend to intensify, perpetuate, or even mitigate the dysfunctional interaction. One person may blame or insult another, and the latter may respond by yelling, making a counteraccusation, or calling the first party an unprintable name. We examine this interaction and patterns in depth in Chapter 10.

Determining the environmental consequences associated with problematic behaviors also may elucidate factors that perpetuate dysfunctional behaviors. Certain actions or responses increase the frequency of (reinforce) behaviors that precede them, and effective intervention must therefore be aimed at modifying such consequences. Tantrum behavior may be unwittingly perpetuated by parents who yield to their children's demands. Pouting by a marital partner may similarly be reinforced by pleading with the pouter to talk or consistently apologizing even though apologies may not be warranted. Recognizing the dynamic significance (effects) of such response patterns often enables practitioners to assist clients in developing new response patterns that break dysfunctional cycles and gradually reduce the frequency of the problematic behaviors.

Analyzing the antecedents of problematic behavior, describing the behavior in specific terms, and assessing the consequences or effects of the problematic behavior provide a powerful means of identifying factors that motivate dysfunctional behavior and are appropriate targets of interventions. This straightforward approach to analyzing the functional significance of behavior has been designed by numerous authors as the ABC model (A = antecedent, B = behavior, C = consequence). Although it is far less simple than it may seem, the ABC model provides a coherent and practical approach to understanding behavior, particularly when it is supplemented by consideration of cognitive factors.

Assessing Developmental Needs and Wants

As we noted earlier, clients' problems commonly involve unmet needs and wants that derive from lack of goodness of fit between these needs and resources in the environment. (Recall from Table 1-2 in Chapter 1 the close link between individual needs and sources of need gratification in the social milieu or in the environment.) Determining unmet needs, then, is the first step in identifying resources that must be tapped or developed. If resources are available but clients have been unable to avail themselves of the resources, it is important to determine the barriers to resource utilization. Some people, for example, may suffer from loneliness not because of an absence of support systems but because their interpersonal behavior alienates others and leaves them isolated. Still other clients may *appear* to have emotional support available from family or others, but closer exploration may reveal that these potential resources are unresponsive to clients' needs. Reasons for the unresponsiveness typically involve reciprocal unsatisfactory transactions between the participants. The task in such instances is to assess the nature of the dysfunctional transactions and to attempt to modify them to the benefit of the participants—often a complex and difficult task.

Human needs include the universal necessities (adequate nutrition, clothing, housing, and health care). Needs are critical and must be at least partially met for human beings to survive and maintain sound physical and mental health and well-being. As we use the term, *wants* involve strong desires that motivate behavior and that, when fulfilled, enhance satisfaction and well-being. Although fulfillment of wants is not essential to survival, some wants develop a compelling nature,

rivaling needs in their intensity—for example, people who are compelled to seek power, wealth, and prestige or people who are compelled to gain acceptance by others at any price. For illustrative purposes, we provide the following list of examples of typical wants involved in presenting problems.

TYPICAL WANTS INVOLVED IN PRESENTING PROBLEMS

- To have less family conflict
- To feel valued by one's spouse or partner
- To be self-supporting
- To achieve greater companionship in marriage
- To gain more self-confidence
- To have more freedom
- To handle conflict more effectively
- To control one's temper
- To overcome depression
- To get someone or something off one's back
- To have more friends
- To be included in decision making
- To gain release from an institution
- To stay out of trouble
- To make a difficult decision
- To master fear or anxiety
- To cope with children more effectively

In determining clients' unmet needs and wants, it is essential to consider the developmental stage of the individual client, couple, or family. For example, the psychological needs of an adolescent for acceptance by peers, for sufficient freedom to develop increasing independence, for development of a stable identify, including a sexual identity, are markedly different from the typical needs of elderly persons for health care, adequate income, social relationships, and meaningful activities. As with individuals, families go through developmental phases that also include both tasks to be mastered and needs that must be met if the family is to provide a climate conducive to the development and well-being of its members.

Different theorists conceptualize developmental stages for individuals in different ways and use different terms, but the following stages correspond with those generally identified:

Infancy	Late teenage
Preschool	Early adulthood
School age	Middle age
Early teenage	Old age

Families also have discrete stages of development, but we defer discussion of them until Chapter 10, which is concerned with assessment of families. Although knowledge of the needs and tasks associated with each developmental stage is critical, we will not provide a detailed list of needs, for that content is germane to human behavior courses and textbooks.

Although clients' presenting problems often reveal obvious needs and wants (e.g., "Our unemployment benefits have expired and we have no income"), sometimes it is up to the social worker to infer what is lacking. Presenting problems may reveal only what is troubling clients on the surface, and careful exploration and empathic "tuning in" are required to identify unmet needs and wants. Marital partners, for example, may initially complain that they disagree over virtually everything and fight constantly. From this information, one could safely conclude that they want a more harmonious relationship. Exploring their feelings on a deeper level, however, may reveal that their ongoing disputes are actually a manifestation of unmet needs of both partners for expressions of love, caring, appreciation, or increased companionship.

Translating complaints and problems into needs and wants is often helpful to clients, many of whom have dwelled on the troubling behavior of other participants in the problem systems and have not thought in terms of their own specific needs and wants. The presenting problem of one client was that her husband was married to his job and spent little time with her. When the practitioner responded, "I gather then you're feeling left out of his life and want to feel important to him and valued by him," she replied, "You know, I hadn't thought of it that way, but that's exactly what I've been feeling." The practitioner then encouraged her to express this need directly to her husband, which she did. He listened attentively and responded with genuine concern. This was the first time she had expressed her needs directly. Previously, her messages had been complaints and his usual response had been defensive.

Identifying needs and wants also serves as a vital prelude to the process of negotiating goals. Goals, of course, often embody specified changes in problematic behavior on the part of participants that will enhance the degree of need gratification and satisfaction for those who are part of the problem system. Expressing goals in terms that address needs and wants also enhances the motivation of clients to work toward goal attainment, as the payoff for goal-oriented efforts is readily apparent to them.

Although goals generally relate to unmet wants and needs, clients' wants are sometimes unrealistic when assessed against the capacity of the client and/or opportunities in the social environment. (One mildly brain-damaged and slightly retarded young adult, for example, wanted to become a movie producer.) Moreover, wanting to achieve a desired goal is not the same as being willing to expend the time and effort and to endure the discomfort required to attain that goal. These are matters that warrant extensive consideration and, as such, are central topics in Chapter 13.

Stresses Associated with Life Transitions

In addition to developmental stages that typically correspond to age ranges, individuals and families commonly must adapt to other major transitions that are less age specific. Some transitions (e.g., geographical moves and immigrations, divorce, and untimely widowhood) can occur during virtually any stage of development. Many such transitions can be traumatic and the adaptations required may temporarily overwhelm the coping capacities of individuals or families For example, losses or separations from a person, homeland, or familiar role are highly stressful for most persons and often temporarily impair social functioning. Again, the environment plays a crucial role in facilitating people's adaptation to major transitional events. People with strong support networks (e.g., close relationships with family, kin, friends, and neighbors) generally have less difficulty in adapting to traumatic changes than do those who lack strong support systems. Assessments and interventions related to transitional periods, therefore, should consider the availability or lack of essential support systems. The following are major transitions that may beset adults:

ROLE CHANGES

Work, career choices	Retirement
Health impairment	Separation and divorce
Parenthood	Institutionalization
Postparenthood years	Single parenthood
Geographic moves and migrations	Death of a spouse or partner
Marriage or partnership commitment	

In addition to these transitions, others affect specialized groups. For example, gay and lesbian persons have difficult decisions to make about to whom and under what conditions they will reveal their sexual identity (Cain, 1991a & b); further they may need to create procedures and rituals for events (such as marriage, divorce, and end-of-life decisions) from which they are legally excluded because of sexual orientation. The parents and siblings of those with severe illnesses or disabilities may experience repeated "losses" if joyous milestones such as graduations, dating, marriage, and parenthood are not available to their loved one. Retirement may not present a time of release and relaxation if it is accompanied by poverty, poor health, or new responsibilities such as caring for ill family members. Gibson has depicted the mixture of challenges and rewards befalling those grandparents who find themselves responsible for raising their grandchildren at a stage in life when they expected to be free of child care commitments (P. A. Gibson, 1999). Clearly, life transitions can be differentially impacted by individual circumstances, culture, socioeconomic

status, and other factors. Social workers must be sensitive to these differences and take care not to make assumptions about the importance of a transitional event or developmental milestone.

Assessing whether clients are in the throes of a developmental phase or transitional period is vital because clients' presenting problems often involve "being stuck" as a result of failing to master tasks essential to adapting successfully to developmental or transitional periods of life. Practitioners can play a vital role in educating clients about essential tasks and helping them to master the tasks, a role central to the modality of crisis intervention, which we discuss in Chapter 13.

Severity of the Problem

Determining the severity of problems can be useful in determining whether clients have the capacity to continue functioning in the community or whether hospitalization or other strong supportive or protective measures are needed. Moreover, determining the level of stress can assist in determining the frequency of sessions and the need to mobilize support systems. The large majority of clients are able to function adequately so that weekly or even less frequent sessions suffice.

When clients are severely depressed and potentially suicidal, however, hospitalization may be required until they manifest significant improvement. Similarly, people whose functioning is temporarily impaired by extreme anxiety and loss of emotional control, such as people who are experiencing acute posttraumatic stress disorders (Patten, Gatz, Jones, & Thomas, 1989), may require short-term hospitalization.

Acute stress reactions also sometimes occur because of crises in people's lives (such as rape or unexpected loss of a job) that temporarily overwhelm their coping capacities. Relaxation procedures, combined with short-term crisis intervention (see Chapter 14), may enable such clients to regain their equilibrium. Frequent sessions over a short period are commonly employed in such situations.

Exploring the level of stress through interviewing techniques often suffices in evaluating the client's level of stress. You may wish to quantify the level of stress, however, by using a scale devised for this purpose. The Index of Clinical Stress (Hudson, 1992) is a convenient, self-administered scale of proven reliability (Abell, 1991). Other instruments developed to assess depression and suicidal risk are discussed in the next chapter.

Meanings Clients Ascribe to Problems

Despite the utility of the ABC model, assessments of the forces that motivate clients' behaviors are incomplete until the clients' perceptions and definitions of the problem are carefully considered. The meanings people attribute to events ("meaning attributions") are as important as the events themselves, a fact recognized by the ancient Greek stoic philosopher Epictetus (first century A.D.), who asserted, "Men are disturbed not by the things which happen to them but by their opinions about the things." You, your clients, other participants in problems, and external observers thus may view problem situations in widely varying ways. Determining the views of the major actors will enhance your understanding of the motivation of each, for people behave according to the meaning a situation has for them. Moreover, to apply the principle of starting where the client is, you must first know clients' perceptions of the causes of problematic behavior (H. Goldstein, 1983).

Determining meaning attributions is also vital because clients' beliefs about factors that cause problems often represent barriers to changes that must be made if problems are to be ameliorated. Such meaning attributions thus tend to maintain problematic behavior and can also be regarded as targets of change (Hepworth, 1979). Hurvitz (1975, pp. 228–229) has categorized meaning attributions that pose obstacles to change, which in modified form with examples are as follows:

1. *Pseudoscientific explanations:*

   "Our biorhythms don't mesh, and there's nothing we can do about it; we're just not good for each other."

   "Jenny [*an adopted child*] just has bad blood. Her mother was a prostitute."

2. *Psychological labeling:*

   "Mother is a paranoid; I've only lied to her a few times."

   "I think Larry is just hyperactive."

3. *Beliefs that other major actors lack the ability or desire to make essential changes:*

   "I know he says he wants our marriage to work, but I know better. He wants a divorce, and he's trying to provoke me into giving him a reason for it."

   "She'll never change. She never has. I think we're wasting our time and money."

4. *Unchangeable external factors:*

   "There's no point in talking to my teacher. She's got it in for me and doesn't even try to understand."

   "As long as his father's alive, we don't have a chance of making it. His father just seems to have a hold on him."

5. *Misconceptions about innate qualities that cannot be changed:*

   "I was born a loser. There's no point in talking about learning to be a mechanic. I'd just wash out."

   "I know he has a right to expect me to be a better sexual partner. I wish I could be, but I've never had any sexual desires, and I never will."

6. *Unrealistic feelings of helplessness:*

   "There's nothing I can do. Gloria is such a strong person that she defeats me at every turn."

   "What can I do? I'm completely at the mercy of Hal. If I don't settle on his terms, he'll take the children away from me."

7. *Reference to "fixed" religious or philosophical principles, natural laws, or social forces:*

   "Sure, I already have as many children as I want. But I don't really have a choice. The church says that birth control is evil."

"She calls all the shots because that's just how women are. They just see men as someone to bring home a paycheck."

8. *Assertion based upon presumed laws of human nature:*

"All children tell lies at that age. It's just natural. I did when I was a kid."

"Sure, I've had trouble with people in authority. When people get authority, they try to step on others. It's just human nature."

9. *Allegations about limitations of significant others involved in the problem:*

"He's just dense. I've tried every way I know how to get through to him, but he's too dense to understand my feelings."

"I think she must be a little stupid. Anyone with any brains would know how to balance a checkbook."

Fortunately, many clients manifest meaning attributions that are not contrary to change. Some clients are open and even eager to examine the part they play in problematic situations. Others readily acknowledge their parts and desire to modify their behavior. When obstacles such as those listed are encountered, however, it is vital to explore them and to resolve them before attempting to negotiate change-oriented goals or to implement interventions. Until such barriers are removed, clients do not assume responsibility for their part in problems and typically and understandably resist having goals or interventions imposed upon them, for from their vantage point the practitioner is barking up the wrong tree.

To elicit meaning attributions from clients, you must employ appropriate exploratory responses following clients' accounts of their problems. Appropriate responses include the following:

- "What meaning do you make of his behavior?"
- "What were the reasons for your parents grounding you?"
- "What conclusions have you drawn about why your landlord evicted you?"

- "What are your views as to why you didn't get a promotion?"

Sites of Problematic Behavior

Determining where problematic behavior occurs may provide clues to the factors that trigger problematic behavior. Children may throw tantrums in certain locations and not in others. As a result of repeated experiences, they soon discriminate where certain behaviors are tolerated and where they are not. Adults may experience anxiety or depression in certain environmental contexts and not in others. One couple, for example, invariably experienced breakdown in communication in the home of one spouse's parents. Some children manifest problematic behavior at school but not at home, or vice versa. Determining where problematic behavior occurs will assist you in identifying areas that warrant further exploration aimed at pinpointing factors associated with the behavior in question.

Identifying where problematic behavior *does not* occur is also of value in some instances, for as L. Brown and Levitt (1979) explain, such understanding may identify sources available to the client for temporary relief of painful states, such as fear, anxiety, depression, loneliness, and insecurity. One client may be assisted to gain temporary respite from overwhelming anxiety by visiting a cherished aunt. In other instances, clients may actually gain permanent relief from intolerable stress by changing employment, discontinuing college, or moving out of relationships when tension or other unpleasant feeling states are experienced exclusively in these contexts.

The Temporal Context of Problematic Behaviors

Determining when problematic behaviors occur often yields valuable clues to factors that play a critical role in clients' problems. Onsets of depressive episodes, for example, may coincide with the time of year when a loved one died or when a divorce occurred. Family problems may also occur, for example, when one parent returns from work or travel, at bedtime for the children, at mealtimes, or when children are (or should be) getting ready for school. Similarly, couples may experience severe conflict when one partner is working the midnight shift, a few days before the wife's menstrual period, after participation by either spouse in activities that exclude the partner, or when one or both drink at parties. Clues such as these shed light on clients' difficulties, indicate areas for further exploration, and provide insight to helpful interventions.

Frequency of Problematic Behaviors

The frequency of problematic behavior is an index to both the pervasiveness of a problem and its impact on the participants. Clients who constantly nag or criticize family members, who habitually drink too much, or who frequently express anger in violent ways severely impair family functioning by producing tension, conflict, and fear and eroding self-esteem of family members. Services for such clients and their families may need to be more intensive than for clients whose dysfunctional behaviors are less frequent or intermittent. Similarly, clients who report feeling constantly depressed may require more vigorous treatment measures than those who experience episodic periods of depression. Determining the frequency of problematic behaviors thus helps to clarify the degree of dysfunctional behavior and the extent to which it impairs the daily functioning of clients and their families.

Assessing the frequency of problematic behaviors also provides a baseline on behaviors targeted for change. Making subsequent comparisons of the frequency of the targeted behaviors enables you to evaluate the efficacy of your interventions, as we discuss in Chapter 13.

Duration of the Problem

Another important dimension vital to assessing problems relates to the history of the problem. Knowing when the problem developed and under what circumstances assists in further evaluating the degree of the problem, formulating psychosocial dynamic factors associated with the problem,

determining the source of motivation to seek assistance, and planning appropriate interventions. Often significant changes in people's life situations, including even seemingly positive ones, disrupt their equilibrium to the extent that they are unable to adapt to changes. An unplanned pregnancy, loss of employment, job promotion, severe illness, birth of a first child, move to a new city, death of a loved one, divorce, retirement, severe disappointment—these and many other life events may cause severe stresses. Careful exploration of the duration of problems often discloses such antecedents to dysfunctional behavior. These antecedent events often are equally as significant as the immediate problematic situation and warrant careful exploration to determine residual emotions and problems that must be addressed.

Antecedent events that immediately precede decisions to seek help are particularly informative. Sometimes referred to as "precipitating events," these antecedents often give valuable clues to critical stresses that might otherwise be overlooked. Clients often report that their problems have existed longer than a year. Why they chose to ask for help at a particular time is not readily apparent, but knowing why may cast their problems in a somewhat different light. For example, careful exploration revealed that a couple who identified their problem as fighting incessantly for the past 4 years did not decide to seek help until the wife began working outside the home for the first time, just 2 weeks before they called for an appointment. Similarly, a parent who complained about his teenage daughter's longstanding rebelliousness did not seek assistance until he became aware (1 week before calling the agency) that she was engaging in an affectional relationship with a woman 6 years her senior. In both instances, the precipitating events would not have been disclosed had the practitioner not sought to answer the critical question of why they were seeking help at this particular time.

Precipitating events can usually be determined by directly asking clients to identify reasons for seeking assistance at a particular time. In some instances, clients themselves will not be fully aware of their reasons, and it may be necessary to explore what events or emotional experiences were occurring shortly before their decision to seek help.

Determining the duration of problems is also vital in assessing clients' levels of functioning and in planning appropriate interventions. Exploration may reveal that a client's adjustment has been marginal for many years and that the immediate problem is only an exacerbation of long-term multiple problems. In other instances, the onset of a problem may be acute, and clients may have functioned at an adequate or high level for many years. In the first instance, modest goals and long-term intermittent service may be indicated; in the second instance, short-term crisis intervention may be sufficient to restore clients to their previous level of functioning.

Other Issues Affecting Client Functioning

A variety of other circumstances and conditions can affect the problem that the client is presenting and his or her capacity to address it. For this reason, it is often wise to explore specifically the client's use of alcohol or other substances, exposure to abuse or violence, the presence of health problems, depression or other mental health problems, and the use of prescription medication.

Questions to probe into these areas should be a standard element of the initial interview. As such, they can be asked in a straightforward and nonjudgmental fashion. For example, opening questions might include: "Now, I'd like to know about some of your habits. First, in an average month, on how many days do you have at least one drink of alcohol?" "Have you ever used street drugs of any sort?" "Have you had any major illnesses in the past?" "Are you currently experiencing any health problems?" "What medications do you take?" "How do these medications work for you?" "Have you been in situations recently or in the past where you were hurt or where you witnessed others being hurt?"

The answers you receive to these questions will determine what follow-up questions you ask. In some circumstances, you may ask for more specific information, for example to determine the degree of impairment due to drug and alcohol use. At a minimum you will want to learn how the client views these issues in light of the presenting problem. For example, "How has the difficulty sleeping affected your ability to care for your kids?" "What role do you see your alcohol use playing in this marital conflict?" "Did the change of medication occur at the same time these other difficulties began?" "I wonder if the run-in with the bullies has anything to do with you skipping school lately?"

Depending on the setting and purpose of the interview and on the information gathered, the social worker may focus the interview specifically on the client's medical history, abuse, substance use, or mental health. Lukas (1993) and Morrison (1995) offer particularly good resources for conducting these specialized assessments.

Clients' Emotional Reactions to Problems

When people encounter problems in living, they typically experience emotional reactions to those problems. It is important to explore and assess such reactions for three major reasons. First, people often gain relief from expressing troubling emotions related to their problems. Common reactions to typical problem situations are worry, concern, resentment, hurt, fear, and feeling overwhelmed, helpless, or hopeless. Being able to ventilate such emotions in the presence of an understanding and concerned person is a source of great comfort to many persons. Moreover, releasing pent-up feelings often has the effect of relieving oneself of a heavy burden. In fact, ventilating emotions may have a liberating effect for persons who tend to be out of touch with their emotions and have not acknowledged to themselves or others that they even have troubled feelings.

A second reason for exploring and assessing emotional reactions is that, because emotions strongly influence behavior, the emotional reactions of some people impel them to behave in ways that exacerbate or contribute to difficulties.

In some instances, in fact, people create new difficulties as a result of emotionally reactive behavior. In the heat of anger, a noncustodial parent may lash out at a child or former spouse. Burdened by financial concerns, an individual may be impatient and verbally abusive, behaving in ways that frighten, offend, or alienate employers, customers, or family members. An adult experiencing unremitting grief may cut him- or herself off from loved ones who "cannot stand" to see him or her cry. Powerful emotional reactions may thus be an integral part of the overall problem configuration.

The third major reason for assessing emotional responses is that intense reactions often become primary problems, overshadowing the antecedent problematic situation. Some people develop severe depressive reactions associated with problematic situations. A mother may become depressed over an unwed daughter's pregnancy; a man may react with depression to unemployment or retirement; and culturally dislocated persons may become depressed following relocation, even though they may have fled intolerable conditions in their homeland. Other individuals may react to problematic events with feelings of helplessness or panic that cause virtual paralysis. In such instances, interventions must be addressed to the overwhelming emotional reactions as well as to the problematic situation that triggered them.

Coping Efforts and Needed Skills

Perhaps surprisingly, you can also learn more about clients' difficulties by determining how they have attempted to cope with their problems. The coping methods they employ give valuable clues to their levels of stress and of functioning. Exploration may reveal that a client has marked deficits in coping skills, relying upon rigid patterns that often prove dysfunctional. Some clients employ avoidance patterns through immersion in tasks or work, by withdrawing, or by numbing or fortifying themselves with drugs or alcohol. Other clients attempt to cope with interpersonal problems by resorting to aggressive, domineering behavior or by placating or becoming submissive.

Still other clients manifest flexible and effective coping patterns but collapse under unusually high levels of stress that would overwhelm even the strongest persons. By contrast, other clients depend heavily upon others to manage problematic situations for them.

Exploring how clients have attempted to cope with problems sometimes reveals that they have struggled effectively with similar problems in the past but are no longer able to do so. In such instances, it is important to explore carefully what has changed. For example, a person may have been able to cope with the demands of one supervisor but not with a new one who is more critical and aloof.

Changes in clients' levels of functioning also occasionally reduce their capacity to cope. Severely depressed clients commonly overestimate the difficulty of their problems and underestimate their coping abilities. A series of transitions or crises may overwhelm an otherwise healthy individual's coping abilities. Some clients are also able to cope effectively in one setting but not in another. Interestingly, some people slay various and sundry dragons at work with dispatch but find themselves unable to cope with the needs and emotions of family members. Some schoolteachers are able to be firm and consistent with challenging pupils but are at a loss as to how to deal effectively with their own children. And finally, some social workers have marvelous ability to listen to and understand their clients, only to find they simply cannot understand the "irrationality" of their own partners. The point is that by exploring the different circumstances, meaning attributions, and emotional reactions of clients, you will be able to identify subtle differences that account for the varied effectiveness of their coping patterns in different contexts.

Another aspect of assessment is to identify the skills clients must possess to ameliorate their difficulties. Knowledge of needed skills enables you to negotiate appropriate and feasible goals aimed at assisting clients to develop skills not already possessed. To improve parent-child relationships, for example, clients may require the development of listening and negotiating skills. Socially inhibited clients may similarly need to learn skills in approaching others, introducing themselves, and engaging others in conversation. To enhance marital relationships, partners often need to learn communication and conflict management skills. To cope effectively with people who tend to exploit them, still other clients must acquire assertiveness skills.

Cultural, Societal, and Social Class Factors

As we noted in earlier chapters, ethnocultural factors influence the problems that people experience, how they feel about requesting assistance, how they communicate, how they perceive the role of the professional person, and how they view various approaches to solving problems. It is thus vital that you be knowledgeable about these factors and competent in responding accordingly. Your assessment of clients' life situations, needs, and strengths must be viewed through the lens of cultural competence (R. H. Rooney & Bibus, 1995). What does this mean in practice? Some examples follow:

- A client immigrating from Mexico or Eastern Europe may display psychological distress that is directly related to the migration refugee experience. Beyond this, a worker who understands the ramifications of immigration may be sensitive to the special issues that may arise for refugees or others whose immigration was made under forced or dire circumstances (Mayadas et al., 1998–99).

- An interview with an older person experiencing isolation should take into account that hearing difficulties, death or illness of peers, housing and economic status, and other factors may impede the client's ability to partake in social activities.

- Racial and ethnic stereotypes may lead to differences in the way that minority youth and white youth are perceived when accused of juvenile crimes. Similarly, detrimental experiences with authority figures and institutional racism may affect the way these clients interact with the social worker (Bridges & Steen, 1998).

- A young woman is persistently late for appointments, which her social worker interprets as a sign of resistance and poor organizational skills. In fact, the young woman must make child care arrangements and take three bus transfers to reach the mental health clinic. Rather than indicating shortcomings, her arrival at appointments (even late) is a sign of persistence and precise organization.

The following chapter addresses cultural factors at length and offers guidelines for effective assessment across worker and client differences.

External Resources Needed

When clients request services it is essential to determine if the services requested match the functions of the agency and if the staff possesses the skills required to provide high-quality service. Often when clients apply for services from an agency or practitioner, they have made their selection based on knowledge gained from others who have used the services of the agency or practitioner. In either instance, the service requested may match the services available, and external resources may not be needed.

Many clients, however, have inadequate or erroneous information about an agency's functions or eligibility requirements and/or need services in addition to those provided by an agency, such as medication, rehabilitation services, or special education services. Specific service needs of clients also may be better provided by staff members of other agencies that specialize in certain services (e.g., sex therapy, divorce counseling, and rape crisis counseling), and referral may be indicated to ensure that the client receives the highest quality of service. In such instances, the practitioner performs a broker or case manager role. Performing these roles effectively requires knowledge of community resources or at least knowledge of how to obtain relevant essential information. Fortunately, many large communities have community resource information centers that are of great value to both clients and professionals in locating needed resources. To familiarize you with typical resources available in large communities, we have compiled a list (see Table 8-1), which is intended to be illustrative and not comprehensive.

In certain instances, in addition to the public and private resources listed in the table, two other major resources should be considered. The first is self-help groups, which have been extremely helpful to some individuals with personal problems. Eschewing professional leadership, members of these groups look to themselves to help each other, and the rapid expansion of such groups in recent years attests to their value. Self-help groups typically provide emotional support and the opportunity to share with and benefit from others who have had to cope with similar problems.

A second major resource, which is often overlooked, consists of natural support systems that may be tapped to counter isolation and difficulties in coping with disruptions caused by transitional stresses. Natural support systems include the family, relatives, friends, neighbors, co-workers, and close associates from school, church, and other social groups.

NEED	RESOURCES
Income maintenance	Public assistance; Old Age, Survivors, Disability, and Health Insurance (OASDHI); unemployment compensation; workers' compensation; church welfare programs; food stamps
Housing	Special housing programs for the elderly, other low-income persons, and homeless; housing outreach programs; Salvation Army; YMCA, YWCA, migrant housing
Health care	Tax-funded hospitals, local public and private health centers, Shriners' hospitals, veterans' hospitals, Medicare, Medicaid, visiting nursing services, convalescent homes, rehabilitation programs, home health services
Child services	Day care centers, child guidance clinics, child welfare divisions, shelter homes, Children's Service Society, church programs, Head Start program, adoption agencies, school social services, special education and developmentally disabled programs, children's treatment centers, crippled children's services
Vocational guidance and rehabilitation	Job service, public vocational rehabilitation programs, veterans' services, Job Corps, psychosocial rehabilitation programs, "clubhouses" such as Fountain House
Mental health care	Mental health centers, hospitals with psychiatric units, substance abuse centers, private practitioners
Legal services	Legal service societies (United Way), public defender, county attorneys, American Civil Liberties Union
Marital and family therapy	Family service agencies, publicly sponsored family services, spiritual leaders, church-affiliated services, private practitioners, mental health centers
Youth services	YMCA, YWCA, public and private recreational programs, local youth service programs, residential treatment programs, youth group homes, juvenile courts, Youth Authority programs
Recreation	Public and private recreation programs and centers, senior citizens' centers, arts and handicrafts programs
Transportation	Traveler's Aid Society, local governmental programs, volunteers

Table 8-1 Types of Community Resources

Some family therapists have developed innovative ways of tapping support systems collectively through an intervention termed network therapy. These therapists contend that much of the dysfunctional behavior labeled as mental illness derives from feelings of alienation from one's natural social network, which consists of all human relationships that are significant in a person's life, including natural support systems. Employing network therapy, these practitioners mobilize 40 to 50 significant people who are willing to come together in a period of crisis for one or more members of the network. The goal is to unite their efforts in tightening the social network of relationships for the purpose of offering support, reassurance, and solidarity to troubled members and other members of the social network. Mobilizing social networks is in keeping with the best traditions of social work.

In instances of cultural dislocation, natural support systems may be limited to the family, and practitioners may need to mobilize other potential resources in the community (Hulewat, 1996). Assisting refugees poses a challenge, for a cultural reference group may not be available in some communities. The language barrier poses an additional obstacle, and practitioners may need to search for interpreters and other interested parties who can assist these families in locating housing, gaining employment, learning the language, adapting to an alien culture, and developing social support systems.

In still other instances, people's environments may be virtually devoid of natural support systems. Consequently, environmental changes may be necessary to accomplish a better fit between needs and resources, a topic we consider at greater length in the next chapter.

WRITTEN ASSESSMENTS

This chapter ends with two examples of written assessments, incorporating concepts described in this chapter. The first is written in a child protective services setting; the second in a family services agency.

REPORT DATE: 11/1/98

REFERRAL INFORMATION

Edgar Jones is a white, 23-year-old father of three children, ages 6, 3, and 10 months. The family was referred for assessment following a report last evening of child neglect, filed by a neighbor who saw the children playing in the street well after midnight. Police responding to the call found the children in good health and reasonably clean, but distressed and fearful, asking repeatedly for their father. The children were placed in emergency care overnight and officers eventually located Mr. Jones at his place of employment. Mr. Jones was "visibly upset" about the children's situation, but stated that he "had no choice" but to leave the 6-year-old in charge of the others, since he had no child care and could not afford to miss work (Mr. Jones loads trucks at United Parcel Service from 10 P.M. to 6 A.M.).

BACKGROUND INFORMATION

Mr. Jones married his wife Ella after she became pregnant during their junior year of high school. All three children are a product of that relationship. The couple had a fairly tumultuous early marriage. Mr. Jones acknowledges a problem with alcohol use and two convictions for breaking and entering when he was 19 and 20 years old. Mr. Jones attributes those crimes to "getting crazy and partying" and states that he has been sober with the help of AA since 1995. Mr. Jones has been employed at UPS for 2 years and is now in line for transfer to a day shift.

Mr. Jones reports that his wife "got messed up on crack" about a year ago and left the family in September of this year. Her current whereabouts are unknown. Mr. Jones seems annoyed but otherwise unperturbed by his wife's drug use or her disappearance. Since Ella's departure, the children have stayed with a family friend while Mr. Jones is at work. However, that relationship soured a week ago, and since that time, the children have been left alone during his working hours. Mr. Jones reports taking precautions, such as assuring that they are asleep before he leaves for work, and locking the doors and any dangerous items, "so they can't get into trouble if they wake up before I get home."

During the day, the oldest is enrolled in school, and according to school personnel, attends regularly and appears withdrawn, though well cared for. The two youngest are cared for by Mr. Jones, who states that he sleeps during their nap times, and occasionally puts them in the playpen for safety while he sleeps or does errands. In their interactions with their father, the children seem somewhat tentative, though not fearful. They are clearly glad to see him and he appears to be attentive to them and responsive to their needs. He states that "the kids were always Ella's deal" and that he is "figuring out what they need as I go along." He appears open to information and capable of implementing it, but is, at this point, grossly uninformed about the capacities and needs of young children such as his. He does appreciate the gravity of the current situation and is adamant in his contention that it will not happen again.

Mr. Jones appears to have few formal or informal supports to help him with the responsibilities in attending to the daily needs of his family. His primary activities are work and his recovery program, and his social contacts seem confined to those arenas. He has been estranged from his family of origin since the birth of his first child and he describes long-standing friends and acquaintances as "not too trustworthy," implying that they are involved with drug use.

PLAN

Work with Mr. Jones to develop alternative work or child care options and monitor weekly for the next 3 months. Provide client with written material on parenting and child development. Recommend parenting class (optional at this time) to better prepare Mr. Jones to address his children's developmental needs and their reactions to the abrupt loss of their mother.

DATE OF SERVICE: 5/5/99

IDENTIFYING INFORMATION

Jack and Marie Smith presented for service, requesting assistance with recent marital difficulties having to do with Mr. Smith's retirement. This assessment is based on information gathered during the initial interview. The Smiths describe themselves as African American; he is 65, she 53. Mrs. Smith is employed

as an esthetician; Mr. Smith is retired. The couple has two grown children, both of whom are married and live out of state.

ASSESSMENT INFORMATION

The couple presented as well-groomed, polite, and apprehensive. Mrs. Smith reports that she initiated the contact following weeks of "almost constant bickering" and that her husband reluctantly agreed to attend. Mr. Smith retired 4 months ago from a local accounting firm. The retirement had been anticipated, but was precipitated by a merger in which senior employees were offered incentives to retire early. Both Mr. and Mrs. Smith agreed that the retirement was appropriate and timely. Mrs. Smith continues to work, though she states it's "less for the money than the social aspect," as she values the time spent with her co-workers and customers.

Mrs. Smith states that since the date of his retirement, her husband had been "a drag on the system," "moping around the house," "not doing anything to help out," and "spending money like it is going out of style" on televised shopping stations, Internet purchases, and trips to a nearby casino. When asked, she states that they had a satisfying sexual relationship throughout the course of their marriage, but that over the last few months her husband has shown little interest in her and has rejected her attempts at all forms of physical intimacy. She states that she is "afraid this is what the rest of my life will be like" and wants to do what they can to change things now.

Mr. Smith acknowledges that retirement has brought a change from the structure and high pressure of his career. He defends the way he spends his days as relaxation he's earned after his lifetime of work. He maintains that since his wife is at work anyway, it "should be no concern of hers" what he does with his money. He reports that he enjoys the escape of the casino and that he spends only a preallotted amount of money when he goes there. With regard to their sexual relationship, Mr. Smith states that there have been "dry spells" at different points in their marriage, and that this is another of those—one that he is clearly uncomfortable discussing.

During the session, the couple displayed a communication pattern that they say is relatively similar to that which they experience at home. Mrs. Smith sharply voices her discontent and Mr. Smith offers a rejoinder and refuses to discuss the matter further. Mr. Smith states that because he is older, he is more "laid back" and refuses to waste time and energy on disagreements. He notes that this was his style in dealing with workplace conflicts and with difficulties with his children when they were younger. The Smiths agree that this pattern is frustrating and unconstructive, but state that this is always how they've dealt with conflict—each goes his or her own way, to work or friends—and the disagreement blows over; only the frequency of such disagreements is different now.

Both clients report that their health is good and that there are no prevailing financial difficulties or extramarital involvements, nor is there a history of violence or substance abuse.

CONCLUSION

This couple has had a relatively harmonious marriage of almost 30 years. They have successfully raised two children and maintain fruitful and financially rewarding careers. The core issue at this time appears to stem from Mr. Smith's retirement and the role changes that this change has necessitated. Mrs. Smith has continued with her usual activities but appears to have expectations for her husband that have not been well articulated or explored. It may also be that this transition has highlighted and exacerbated the age and developmental differences between the two partners. Mr. Smith appears to be somewhat at sea with his newfound freedom, enjoying the independence from constraints but experiencing some void in the meaningfulness of his activities. The couple appears to have a limited capacity to discuss difficulties and this is sorely tested by their current change in circumstances.

PLAN

Provide conjoint therapy to focus on communication and problem-solving skills, examination and discussion of mutual expectations, and development of common activities. Explore and address particular fears and other concerns as they arise.

Summary

This chapter has introduced you to the knowledge and skills of multidimensional assessment from a social work perspective. We have shown how a psychiatric diagnosis may be part of but is not the same as a social work assessment. We have emphasized strengths and resources in assessments. A framework for prioritizing what must be done in assessment has been presented, as well as the components of the assessment. Finally, two models of assessments have been presented. In the next chapter, we move to assessing interpersonal and environmental systems.

Internet Resources

 You can gain more information on the WALMYR Assessment Scales cited in this chapter at the following Web site: *http://www.syspac.com/~walmyr/*. Using InfoTrac®, you can enter the keywords "social work assessment" to directly access useful articles such as: Berkman, B., Chauncey, S., Holmes, W., Daniels, A., Bonander, E., Sampson, S., & Robinson, M. (1999). Standardized screening of elderly patients' needs for social work assessment in primary care: Use of the SF-36. *Health and Social Work, 24,* 1; Bisman, C. D. (1999). Social work assessment: Case theory construction. *Families in Society, 80,* 3; Cascio, T. (1998). Incorporating spirituality into social work practice: A review of what to do. *Families in Society, 79,* 5.

Notes

1. It is also crucial to engage the client in the helping relationship while eliciting data; otherwise, you may gain data but lose the client in the process.
2. The potency of this method in producing insight and change with a mother who had a severe problem with controlling anger has been reported by Nugent (1991).

3. For more information, consult Hudson, W. W. (1990). WALMYR Assessment Scales, Scoring Manual. WALMYR Publishing Co., PO Box 6229, Tallahassee, FL 32314-6229. (850) 656-2787. E-mail: scales@walmyr.com

4. For more information, consult Hudson W. W. (1990). WALMYR Assessment Scales, Scoring Manual, MPSI & MPSI Scoring manual. WALMYR Publishing Co., PO Box 6229, Tallahassee, FL 32314-6229. (850) 656-2787. E-mail: scales@walmyr.com.

5. The importance of having skills in relating to and identifying the emotions and unmet needs of partners with marital difficulties has been discussed by Denton (1991). Moreover, it is noteworthy that one approach to marital therapy has been denoted Emotionally Focused Therapy (P. James, 1991), attesting to the vital role of emotions in interpersonal problems.

Assessing Intrapersonal and Environmental Systems

Revised and edited by Kim Strom-Gottfried

CHAPTER OVERVIEW

This chapter reviews two more aspects of a comprehensive assessment—those things going on within the client (physically, emotionally, cognitively) and those things in the client's environment (physical and social). We will introduce you to these areas for examination and help you develop an understanding of the difficulties and the assets to consider in these systems. We'll also discuss the impact of culture on intrapersonal systems and offer guidance for understanding these impacts when the worker and client do not share common cultural backgrounds.

THE INTERACTION OF MULTIPLE SYSTEMS IN HUMAN PROBLEMS

Problems, strengths, and resources encountered in direct social work practice result from interaction of intrapersonal, interpersonal, and environmental systems. Difficulties are rarely confined to one of these systems, for functional imbalance in one system typically contributes to imbalance in others. Individual difficulties (e.g., feelings of worthlessness and depression) invariably influence how one relates to other people; interpersonal difficulties (e.g., marital strain) likewise affect individual functioning. Similarly, environmental deficits (e.g., in-adequate housing, hostile working conditions, or social isolation) affect individual and interpersonal functioning.

The reciprocal impacts among the three major systems, of course, are not limited to the negative effects of functional imbalance and system deficits. Assets, strengths, and resources also have reciprocal *positive* effects. A supportive environment may partially compensate for intrapersonal difficulties; similarly, strong interpersonal relationships may provide positive experiences that more than compensate for an otherwise impoverished environment.

To adequately assess the many forces that interact to produce problems, it is essential to be well grounded in knowledge about the three major systems that are typically involved in problems. Therefore, we devote this and the next two chapters to assisting you to grasp more fully the complexities of these systems. This chapter deals with the intrapersonal (within the person) and environmental systems; the next chapter is focused on interpersonal systems (between people), with particular emphasis on marital and family systems.

THE INTRAPERSONAL SYSTEMS

In assessing the social functioning of individuals, social workers often make global judgments, such as "at best, this person's level of functioning is marginal." Such a general statement, however, has limited usefulness, for it fails to specify areas in which the client's functioning is marginal and it emphasizes deficits. We will attempt in this chapter to provide you with models that are more useful by clearly specifying strengths, resources, and challenges. Some individuals, of course, uniformly function at high or low levels; in actuality, most of us experience some variability in our functioning. A comprehensive assessment of the individual considers a variety of elements, including biophysical, cognitive/perceptual, emotional, behavioral, cultural, and motivational factors. However, your assessment and written products may focus on some of these areas more than others, depending on the nature of the client's difficulties, the reason for the assessment, and the setting in which the assessment is being done. It is important to remember, however, that an assessment is really only a "snapshot" of the client system's functioning at any given point in time. Further, the social worker's beliefs and actions and the client's feelings about seeking help may distort the assessment. The collection and synthesis of information in an assessment must be done with care and respect.

BIOPHYSICAL FUNCTIONING

Biophysical functioning is vital to and affects both individuals and families. Biophysical functioning encompasses physical characteristics, health factors, and genetic factors, and we consider each of these factors separately. Because drug and alcohol use and abuse embody biophysical components, we also address assessment of use of these substances, realizing that systems other than biophysical are also implicated.

Physical Characteristics and Presentation

The physical characteristics and appearance of clients may be either assets or liabilities. In Western society, physical attractiveness is highly valued, and unattractive people are disadvantaged

in the realms of social desirability, employment opportunities, and marriageability. Further, the findings of at least one study (Farina, Burns, Austad, Bugglin, & Fischer, 1986) indicate that physical attractiveness facilitates the readjustment of patients who are discharged from psychiatric facilities. It is thus important to be observant of distinguishing physical characteristics that may affect social functioning. Particular attributes that merit attention include body build, posture, facial features, gait, and any physical anomalies that may distort the self-image or pose a social liability.

How clients present themselves is also important. Clients who walk slowly, display stooped posture, talk slowly and without animation, lack spontaneity, and show minimal changes in facial countenance as they talk may be depressed. Dress and grooming often reveal much about a person's morale, values, and lifestyle. While lack of sufficient income is a key issue, people who wear shabby, inappropriate, or neglected clothes, and have disheveled hair, poor grooming, and the like are often considered depressed or mentally ill. By contrast, when clients, despite financial difficulties or other circumstances, are neatly dressed and well groomed, this may reflect positively on their coping, energy, and motivation.

The standard for assessing appearance is generally whether or not the dress is appropriate for the setting. Is the client barefoot in near-freezing weather or wearing a helmet and overcoat in the summer sun? Is the client dressed seductively, in pajamas, or "overdressed" for an appointment with the social worker? Social workers assessing clients' appearance should take care in the conclusions they reach. Westermeyer (1993) notes that our determination of "appropriateness" is greatly influenced by the interviewer's cultural background and values. A "disheveled" appearance may indicate poverty, carelessness, or the latest fashion. Being clothed in bright colors may indicate mania or simply an affiliation with a cultural group that favors that form of dress (Morrison, 1995; Othmer & Othmer, 1989).

Other factors associated with appearance that merit attention include hand tremors, facial tics, rigid or constantly shifting posture, and tense muscles of the face, hands, and arms. Sometimes these characteristics reflect the presence of an illness or physical problem. These physical manifestations may also indicate a high degree of tension or anxiety, warranting exploration by the social worker. It is normal, of course, for clients to experience a certain degree of anxiety, especially in initial sessions. This is especially true for referred and legally mandated clients who have not requested the session and are understandably apprehensive about the social worker's goals and the personal consequences of the session (e.g., assessment of possible child abuse). It is up to the effective social worker to determine in assessment whether the anxiety displayed is typical for the given situation or whether it is excessive and might reveal an area for further discussion.

Physical Health

Ill health can contribute to depression, sexual difficulties, irritability, low energy, restlessness, anxiety, inability to concentrate, and a host of other problems. It is therefore important for social workers to routinely consider state of health as they explore clients' situations. One of the first assessment activities is then to determine if clients are under medical care and, if not, ask when they last had a medical examination. Social workers should rule out medical sources of difficulties by referring clients for physical evaluations, when appropriate, before attributing problems solely to psychosocial factors. Practitioners have occasionally employed psychotherapy to treat dramatic increases in irritability, sudden losses of emotional control, and other personality changes, to discover too late that these changes were caused by brain tumors or other organic ailments. To avoid such tragedies, social workers should be cautious and avoid drawing premature conclusions about the sources of problems when there is even a remote possibility that medical factors may be involved.

A variety of biophysical factors can affect cognitive, behavioral, and emotional functioning in individuals. For example, a history of child malnutrition has been linked to attention deficits, poor social skills, and emotional problems that affect children even after they become adequately nourished (Johnson, 1989). Nutritional deficits can also cause dementia in elderly people; however, some of the cognitive decline may be reversed if treated early enough (Naleppa, 1999). Encephalitis, which has been shown to cause brain damage, can manifest symptoms of ADHD (Johnson, 1989). Hormone levels also affect behavioral and emotional functioning; for example high testosterone levels have been correlated with high levels of aggression.

Assessing the health of clients is especially important with groups known to underutilize medical care. These groups include people who live in poverty, ethnic minority groups, elderly people, immigrants (including refugees), foster children, unwed pregnant adolescents, homeless people, people with AIDS, and persons who lack health insurance. These groups may experience a greater-than-average need for health care due to their health status. They may also experience increased vulnerability to disease due to poor nutrition, dangerous environmental conditions, and the lack of preventive services (Buss & Gillanders, 1997; Ensign, 1998; Jang, Lee, & Woo, 1998; Suarez & Siefert, 1998; Zechetmayr, 1997).

Along with the increased need for health care, persons in particularly vulnerable groups may experience diminished access to care. Access can be limited by a variety of factors: affordability, availability, and acceptability. Whether care is affordable depends on whether the client has health insurance coverage and whether he or she can afford the services not covered by insurance. Approximately 44 million persons in the United States lack basic health insurance. Even those who do have coverage may be unable or reluctant to pursue care, given the cost of medications, deductibles, and co-payments not covered by insurance. The concern about costs may lead people to delay basic care until situations worsen to a dangerous level or to the point where even more expensive interventions are required. Individuals with extensive or chronic health problems, such as persons with AIDS, may find that hospitalization and drug costs outstrip both insurance and income, affecting even those with considerable financial assets and jobs that pay well.

Availability refers not only to the location of health care services but the hours they are available, the transportation needed to reach them, and the adequacy of the facilities and personnel to meet the client's needs (Mokuau and Fong, 1994). If the nearest after-hours health care resource is a hospital emergency room, that may be the facility of choice for a desperate mother, even if the health concern, such as a child's ear infection, might be better addressed in another setting.

Acceptability refers to the extent to which the health services are compatible with the client's cultural values and traditions. New immigrants may have limited knowledge of Western medical care and of the complex health care provider systems in the United States and they may be reticent to seek care because of concerns about their documentation and the fear of deportation (Congress, 1994). The use of indigenous healers or bilingual and bicultural staff can enhance the acceptability of health care.

Social workers should inquire not only about their clients' health status but also about their use of care. Practitioners should also understand the impediments to seeking care, as clients may fail to follow through on referrals for any of the reasons already discussed (Julia, 1996).

Cultural Factors in Illness

An important task in assessment involves determining your clients' views about the causes of illness, physical aberrations, disabling conditions, and mental symptoms. Understanding the client's perceptions of health or illness will inform your assessment of his or her functioning. Further, the client's receptiveness to medical diagnoses and treatment will depend on their credibility from the client's perspective. In modern Western society, despite the increasing acceptance by professionals of the systems perspective, most people continue to attribute illness to physical causes (i.e., infections, toxins, degenerative processes, heredity, improper nutrition, chemical imbalance, lack of exer-

cise, or other unknown physical factors). People thus tend to be receptive to diagnoses and treatments that match their expectations. Most Americans, for example, are familiar with and accept antibiotics, vitamins, hormones, diverse medications, surgical procedures, radiation therapy, chemotherapy, exercise, and proper rest. By contrast, the majority of mainstream Americans may be unfamiliar with acupuncture, herbal therapy, and spiritualistic rituals as legitimate treatments.

Differing from members of the majority culture, many ethnic minority clients espouse markedly different beliefs about the causes of ill health or other physical afflictions. Consequently, their expectations regarding diagnoses and treatment may differ sharply from those presented by Western health care professionals (Yamamoto, Silva, Justice, Chang, & Leong, 1993). In this regard, Low (1984) has noted: "Numerous cases of ethnic differences in expectations of treatment, behavior and compliance can be traced to cultural distinctions embedded in belief systems and norms of culturally appropriate behavior" (p. 13).

When major discrepancies exist between clients' expectations and physicians' diagnoses and recommendations for treatment, clients tend to covertly reject diagnoses and fail to comply with treatment regimens, often producing confusion and consternation for health care professionals who may misunderstand the source of this "resistance." Experienced practitioners in health care settings can attest to many instances of clients' noncompliance with medical recommendations based on clashes between diverse cultural and Western medical beliefs concerning causes of illness and physical afflictions. One of the many case examples reported by Kumabe et al. (1985)[1] highlights the significance of cultural factors:

CASE EXAMPLE

Living in Hawaii after migrating from the Philippine Islands 5 years earlier, the parents of a small child had resisted having surgical repair of their child's cleft lip and palate even though the costs would be paid by insurance. After carefully exploring both the circumstances that preceded the birth of the child and the parents' beliefs regarding the cause of the condition, the social worker learned that the parents attributed the child's condition to punishment from God for their use of withdrawal as a contraceptive measure during sexual intercourse. The father's uncle, who lived with the family, asserted they had interfered with God's will by practicing contraception. The withdrawal method, he claimed, caused deformed babies; because sexual intercourse was never completed, a baby could never be completed either. Fortunately, the practitioner recognized the futility of attempting to dissuade them from their belief and instead referred them for a consultation with a physician of their ethnicity. The Filipino physician readily gained their trust and assisted them to accept that their child's condition was congenital and unrelated to their sexual practices. This consultation paved the way to having the corrective surgery performed and liberated the parents from oppressive guilt.

It is important for all practitioners to be knowledgeable about the significance of folk healers and shamans in diverse cultures throughout the world. As Canda (1983) points out, shamanism exists on every continent and on the islands in the oceans. Beliefs in supernatural forces, such as witchcraft, evil spirits, curses, and hexes are widespread among ethnic minority persons, especially those who are poorly educated, from low socioeconomic levels, and closely tied to cultures whose belief systems are rooted in traditional folkways.[2]

Because of the significance of folk healers and shamans in the lives of many persons of color, social workers should view these indigenous practitioners as resources. As an example, Canda (1983) cites references that report successful informal arrangements between medical professionals and nature healers in the Cook Islands, Nigeria, and Puerto Rico.

Family Factors

Attitudes of key family members should also be considered in assessing health problems. In most cultures, the family decides whether or not a member is ill, the meanings of illnesses, and how family members should cope with illness. Moreover, cultural values and the family lifestyle affect the course of a patient's illness and recovery. The family influences decision making during each phase of a member's illness, beginning with the initial steps involved in seeking medical care, the response to the diagnosis, and the compliance or noncompliance with the treatment recommendations.

Practitioners must also assess how illness of a member affects the functioning of a family. The illness of a member, particularly of a parent, creates imbalance in a family system, often requiring adjustment in role performance by family members. Further, outside resources (e.g., financial aid, homemaking services, or visiting nursing service) may be required to assist families to maintain their equilibrium.[3] The social worker may be called on to facilitate these arrangements, or to help family members organize their social networks for assistance in time of ill health.

Assessment may at times include gathering information about illnesses in the client's family. Many biophysical disorders have genetic roots, including cleft palate, diabetes melitus, spina bifida, congenital scoliosis, hemophilia, Duchenne's muscular dystrophy, Huntington's disease, neurofibromatosis, cystic fibrosis, sickle-cell anemia, and Tay-Sachs disease. While social workers may not provide genetic counseling, they should be aware of specialized resources for this service (Waltman, 1996). Bernhardt and Rauch (1993) offer an informative guide for social workers interested in learning more about the genetic basis for illnesses and about conducting genetic family histories.

ASSESSING USE AND ABUSE OF ALCOHOL AND DRUGS

Effective assessments of a client's biophysical functioning must include information on the client's use of both legal and illicit drugs. First, some conditions may necessitate a referral for evaluation and medication. Health problems such as menopausal difficulty, depression, attention deficit disorders and hyperactivity in children, and tic disorders may respond favorably to medication. Another reason for evaluating drug use is that even beneficial drugs can produce side effects that affect the functioning of various biopsychological systems. Drowsiness, for example, is a side effect of many drugs. Changes in sexual functioning may also result from use of certain medications, such as those used to treat high blood pressure. A jaundiced appearance, rigid gait, zombielike countenance, tongue-thrusting, and various involuntary muscle contractions may result from excessive dosages of major tranquilizing drugs used to treat certain forms of psychosis, and medical evaluation of dosage may be needed. Symptoms of confusion, inertia, and stomach pains may result from inappropriate combinations of prescription drugs.

Alcohol is another form of legal drug, but its abuse can severely impair health, disrupt or destroy family life, and create serious community problems. Conservatively estimated to afflict from 9 to 10 million Americans, alcoholism can occur in any culture, though it may be more prevalent in some than in others. Alcoholism is also associated with high incidence of suicide, homicide, and spouse and child abuse.

Like alcohol abuse, the misuse of illicit drugs may have detrimental consequences for both the user and his or her family. Beyond these effects, other problems may arise from using substances that are banned by law. For example, users may engage in dangerous or illegal activities (such as prostitution or theft) to obtain their supply of drugs. Further, variations in the purity of the drugs used or the methods of administration (i.e., sharing needles) may expose users to risk beyond the drug use itself.

The following sections will introduce you to the areas for concern around alcohol and drug abuse and the strategies for effectively assessing use and dependence.

Alcohol Use and Abuse

Alcoholism, although a part of human life for thousands of years, is still not fully understood by modern professionals. The disease model of alcoholism, which provides the most established and accepted view of alcoholism today, first entered the professional literature through the writings of Benjamin Rush, M.D., in the early 1800s. Although different perspectives and treatments have emerged in recent years, especially dealing with the influences of family, biology, and genetics, there is still no single universally effective treatment for alcohol dependence (Goodwin & Gabrielli, 1997). The true prevalence of alcoholism is not even known; most research places the number of Americans with alcohol dependency between 5 million and 14 million (p. 142). Research indicates that a significant majority of those Americans who suffer from alcoholism are male, with the highest percentage being young, single men who are residents of wet regions along with urban, less educated men of lower socioeconomic status (Winick, 1997). Studies are mixed with regard to differences in ethnicity among those with alcohol problems; however, most studies have shown a higher prevalence in urban African Americans and Native Americans, and a low prevalence in Asian Americans (Goodwin & Gabrielli, 1997).

Alcoholism differs from heavy drinking in that alcoholism causes distress and disruption in the life of the person with alcohol dependency, as well as in the lives of his or her social and support systems (Goodwin & Gabrielli, 1997). It is marked by a preoccupation with making sure the amount of alcohol necessary for intoxication is accessible at all times, which may cause the person to surround him- or herself with heavy drinkers in order to escape observation. As alcoholism advances, the signs tend to become more concealed, as the user hides bottles or other "evidence," drinks alone, and covers up drinking binges. Feelings of guilt and anxiety over the behavior begin to appear, which usually leads to more drinking in order to escape the negative feelings, which in turn leads to an intensification of the negative feelings. This cycle of guilt and escape continues and despondency sets in until the person often "falls to rock bottom" and seeks treatment (1997, pp. 143–144).

Women who drink have patterns more like non-addicted women than men. They are more likely to abuse prescription drugs, to consume them in isolation, and to have had the onset of abuse after a traumatic event such as incest or racial or domestic violence (Nelson-Zlupko, Kauffman, & Dore, 1995). Women who drink are likely to come from families in which drugs and alcohol were used. Women are less likely than men to enter and complete treatment programs. The obstacles to treatment include social stigma associated with alcoholism and lack of available transportation and child care while in treatment (Yaffe et al, 1995). Because guilt and shame tend to be high already among alcohol-abusing women, aggressive confrontation designed to break through denial tends to be counterproductive. Treatment approaches that focus on strengths, including coping tools such as identifying characteristics of an unhealthy environment that has triggered drug usage and familiarizing women with a context of oppression, are recommended for better serving the needs of this population (Nelson-Zlupko, Kauffman & Dore, 1995).

Another serious problem associated with alcohol abuse involves adverse effects on offspring produced by alcohol consumption during pregnancy. The effects range from full-blown fetal alcohol syndrome (FAS) to fetal alcohol effects (FAE). At the extreme end of a range of potential effects of alcohol on a fetus, FAS (found in infants of chronic alcoholic mothers who have four to six drinks per day) involves prenatal and postnatal growth retardation, mental retardation, central nervous system involvement, and abnormalities in shape and size of the head and/or facial features (dysmorphology).

The severity of FAE (found in mothers who are social drinkers) varies according to the amount of alcohol consumed, but the risks associated with two drinks daily include miscarriage, prenatal growth retardation, behavioral deficiencies, and various anomalies. With increased consumption, partial effects of FAS may develop. In addition, some newborns manifest withdrawal effects from alcohol such as irritability, tremulousness, alcohol on the breath, transient seizures, and jitteriness.[4]

Because excessive alcohol consumption can cause potentially severe damage to developing fetuses, social workers should routinely question prospective mothers about their use of alcohol during pregnancy. By taking a history of consumption of beer, wine, and liquor during pregnancy (focusing on frequency, quantity, and variability), practitioners can determine clients' drinking patterns. Numerous screening tools for alcoholism are also available, as we discuss later. It is now recommended that all women avoid drinking during pregnancy. If the prospective mother drinks more than two or three drinks daily or more than five drinks on any occasion, practitioners should strongly encourage involvement in a treatment program.

The Use and Abuse of Other Substances

Because of widespread publicity, the public is aware of the dangers and tragic consequences resulting from drug abuse and overdose. Less well known by the public (but extremely familiar to social workers) are the ravages to individual lives and the disruption and suffering experienced by families of both alcohol and drug abusers.

People abuse many types of drugs. Because immediate care may be essential in instances of acute drug intoxication, and because drug abusers often attempt to conceal their use of drugs, it is important that practitioners know the indications of abuse of commonly used drugs. Table 9-1 lists by category the most commonly abused drugs and their indications.

In addition to those indications of abuse of specific drugs, common general indications include the following:

- Changes in attendance at work or school
- Decrease in normal capabilities (work performance, efficiency, habits, etc.)
- Poor physical appearance, neglect of dress and personal hygiene
- Use of sunglasses to conceal dilated or constricted pupils and to compensate for eyes' reduced ability to adjust to sunlight

TYPE OF DRUG	TYPICAL INDICATIONS
1. Central nervous system depressants (alcohol, Quaalude, Doriden, and various barbiturates)	Intoxicated behavior with/without odor, staggering or stumbling, "nodding off" at work, slurred speech, dilated pupils, difficulty concentrating.
2. Central nervous system stimulants (amphetamines, including methamphetamine or "speed")	Excessively active, irritable, argumentative, nervous, dilated pupils, long periods without eating or sleeping.
3. Cocaine and crack (also CNS)	Energetic, euphoric, fixed and dilated pupils, possible tremors (euphoria quickly replaced by anxiety, irritability, and/or depression, sometimes accompanied by hallucinations and paranoid delusions).
4. Opiods (opium, heroin, morphine)	Scars on arms or backs of hands from injecting codeine drugs, fixed and constricted pupils, frequent scratching, loss of appetite (but frequently eat sweets). May have sniffles, red and watering eyes, and cough until another "fix," lethargic, drowsy, and alternate between dozing and awakening ("nodding").
5. Cannabinols (marijuana, hashish)	In early stages, may be euphoric and appear animated, speaking rapidly and loudly with bursts of laughter; pupils may be dilated and eyes bloodshot; may have distorted perceptions such as increased sense of taste or smell; increased appetite; in later stages, may be drowsy.
6. Hallucinogens (LSD, STP, DOM, mescaline, DTM, DET)	Behavior and mood vary widely, may sit or recline quietly in trancelike state or appear fearful or even terrified; dilated pupils in some cases; may experience nausea, chills, flushes, irregular breathing, sweating, or trembling of hands; may experience changes in sense of sight, hearing, touch, smell, and time.
7. Inhalants and volatile hydrocarbons (chloroform, nail polish remover, metallic paints, carbon tetrachloride, amyl nitrate, butyl, isobutyl, nitrous oxide, lighter fluid, fluoride-based sprays)	Reduced inhibitions, euphoria, dizziness, slurred speech, unsteady gait, giddiness, drowsiness, nystagmus (constant involuntary eye movement).
8. Anabolic and androgenic steroids	Increased muscle strength and reduced body mass; aggression, competitiveness, and combativeness.

Table 9-1 Indications of Abuse of Commonly Used Drugs

Source: *Substance Abuse: A Comparative Textbook* (3rd ed.), by J. H. Lowinson, P. Ruiz, R. B. Millman, and J. G. Langrod (Eds.), 1997, Baltimore, MD: Williams & Wilkins.

- Unusual efforts to cover arm and hide needle marks
- Association with known drug users
- Need to steal or engage in prostitution to raise cash to support drug habit

In assessing the possibility of drug abuse, it is important to elicit information not only from the suspected abuser (who may not be a reliable reporter for a number of reasons) but also from persons who are familiar with the habits and lifestyle of the individual. It is also important to assess problems of drug abuse from a systems perspective. Explorations of family relationships often reveal that drug abusers feel alienated from other family members. Moreover, family members often unwittingly contribute to the problems of both alcoholics and drug abusers. Consequently, many professionals regard problems of drug abuse as manifestations of dysfunction within the family system. Keep in mind that drug abusers affect and are affected by the family system.

Dual Diagnosis: Co-occurring Addictive and Mental Disorders

Because alcohol and other drug abuse problems can co-occur with a variety of health and mental health problems, accurate assessment is important for proper treatment planning. As Lehman (1996) suggests, there are several combinations of factors that must be taken into account. These include (1) the type and extent of the substance use disorder, (2) the type of mental disorder(s) and the related severity and duration, (3) the presence of related medical problems, and (4) co-occurring disability or other social problems resulting from use, such as correctional system involvement, poverty, or homelessness.

Depending on the combination of factors, clients may have particular difficulty seeking out and adhering to treatment programs. Further, an understanding of the interaction of factors may affect the social worker's interventive approach. For example, some psychiatric problems may emerge as a result of substance use (e.g., paranoia or depression). Some co-occurring social problems such as joblessness or incarceration may limit the client's access to needed treatment. Some problems such as personality disorders may impede the development of a trusting and effective treatment relationship. Lehman (1996) suggests that the consistent use of screening devices will help alleviate gaps in assessment and identify service priorities for the social worker and the treatment team. Smyth (1996) goes on to suggest motivational interviewing and the application of "stages of change" as methods for encouraging client participation in treatment of both disorders.

Using Interviewing Skills to Assess Substance Use

Social workers are often involved with substance users before they have actually acknowledged a problem or sought help for it (Barber, 1995b). Griffin (1991) emphasizes the need to manifest nonjudgmental acceptance while interviewing people who may be alcoholic. Doing so can be difficult because the user denies that alcohol use is a problem and may attempt to conceal it by blaming others, lying, arguing, distorting, attempting to intimidate, diverting the interview away from discussion of drinking, or verbally attacking the social worker. Despite these aversive behaviors, the social worker needs to express empathy and sensitivity to the client's feelings, realizing the behaviors are often a subterfuge behind which lie embarrassment, guilt, shame, ambivalence, and anger.

Being direct and seeking concreteness can facilitate exploration and constructive confrontation. When asking about alcohol use, the worker should be forthright in explaining why that line of questioning is being pursued. Asking indirect questions tends to support the client's evasion and yields unproductive responses. The questions listed in Table 9-2 should be asked in a direct and compassionate manner. As indicated, they address the extent and effects of the client's substance use. Because the effects of drugs and alcohol tend to pervade all aspects of a user's life, it is important to explore all of the social systems that play a key role in the client's life.[5]

Conveying Assessment Findings to Clients

When sufficient information has emerged in an interview to enable the social worker to conclude that the client has an alcohol or drug problem, the worker should begin by reviewing details elicited about the impact of the substance-abusing behaviors on the various aspects of the client's life, as reviewed during the interview, and invite the client's views about the extent of the problem. The worker can also describe objective behavioral criteria

---

The first six questions will help guide the direction of your interview, the questions you ask, and your further assessment.

1. Do you—or did you ever—smoke cigarettes? For how long? How many per day?
2. Do you drink?
3. What do you drink? (Beer, wine, liquor?)
4. Do you take any prescription medications regularly? How do they make you feel?
5. Do you use any over-the counter medications regularly? How do they make you feel?
6. Have you ever used any illegal drug?
7. When was the last time you had a drink/used?
8. How much did you have to drink/use?
9. When was the last time before that?
10. How much did you have?
11. Do you always drink/use approximately the same amount? If not, is the amount increasing or decreasing?
12. (If it is increasing) Does that concern you?
13. Do most of your friends drink/use?
14. Do (or did) your parents drink/use?
15. Have you ever been concerned that you might have a drinking/drug problem?
16. Has anyone else ever suggested to you that you have (or had) a drinking/drug problem?
17. How does drinking/using help you?
18. Do other people report that you become more careless, or angry, or out of control when you have been drinking/using?
19. Do you drink/use to "get away from your troubles?"
20. What troubles are you trying to get away from?
21. Are you aware of any way in which drinking/using is interfering with your work?
22. Are you having any difficulties or conflict with your spouse or partner because of drinking/using?
23. Are you having financial difficulties? Are they related in any way to your drinking/using?
24. Have you ever tried to stop drinking/using? How?

Table 9-2 Interviewing for Substance Abuse Potential

Source: From *Where to Start and What to Ask: An Assessment Handbook* by Susan Lukas. Copyright © 1993 by Susan Lukas. Used by permission of W. W. Norton & Company, Inc.

accepted as indicators of alcohol or drug abuse and ask the client how his or her behavior compares with these criteria. Problem drinkers are more likely to respond to feedback conveyed empathically and nonjudgmentally with specific information about how consumption is affecting this person's life. Such feedback is more likely to be accepted when the source is seen as a medical practitioner or specially qualified to assess consequences of use (Barber, 1995b).

The worker should also express forthrightly his or her own conclusions, including an estimate of the severity of the problem. It is also appropriate to explain treatment options and to express guarded optimism that with hard work and persistence the client can overcome the dependency or addiction. It is important not to paint a rosy picture, to explain that the process may be lengthy and painful at times, and to describe the risks and triggers of relapse (Griffin, 1991).

ASSESSING COGNITIVE/ PERCEPTUAL FUNCTIONING

Assessing how clients perceive their worlds is critically important, for people's perceptions of others, themselves, and events largely determine how they feel and respond to life's experiences in general and to their problematic situations in particular. Perceptions, of course, do not exist apart from meanings that are ascribed to them; hence, we have considered perceptual and cognitive functioning as a single entity. The meanings or interpretations of events, rather than the events themselves, motivate human beings to behave as they do. Furthermore, every person's world of experience is unique. Perceptions of identical events or circumstances thus vary widely according to the complex interaction of belief systems, values, attitudes, state of mind, and self-concepts, all of which in turn are highly idiosyncratic. It follows, then, that in order to understand and to influence human behavior you must first be knowledgeable about how people think.

People's thought patterns, of course, are influenced by numerous factors, including intellectual functioning, judgment, reality testing, coherence, cognitive flexibility, values, mistaken beliefs, self-concept, cultural belief system, and dynamic interaction between cognition, emotions, and behavior. In the following sections, we briefly consider these factors.

Intellectual Functioning

Understanding the intellectual capacity of clients is essential for a variety of reasons. Your assessment of intellectual functioning will allow you to adjust your verbal expressions to a level clients can readily comprehend, and it will help you in assessing strengths and difficulties, negotiating goals, and planning tasks commensurate with their capacities. In most instances, a rough estimate of level of intellectual functioning is sufficient. You may want to consider clients' ability to grasp abstract ideas, to express themselves fluently, and to analyze or think logically. Additional criteria include level of educational achievement and vocabulary employed, although these factors must be considered in relationship to the clients' previous educational opportunities and/or possible learning difficulties. Some adults with average or higher intellectual capacity may be unable to read or write because of learning disabilities or poor instruction. It is important to avoid confusing unfamiliarity with the language for non-native speakers with problematic intellectual functioning.

When clients have marked intellectual limitations, it is vital that you employ a vocabulary consisting of easily understood words and avoid abstract explanations. To avoid embarrassment, many of us will pretend we understand when we do not. Therefore, you should use keen observations and actively seek feedback to determine whether the client has grasped your intended meaning. Greater time and patience will be required with those clients who have limited intelligence or life experience. You can also assist them by using multiple, concrete examples to convey complex ideas.

Intellectual capacity, of course, establishes the upper limits of goals that clients can reasonably be expected to accomplish. To encourage clients to pursue goals that exceed their capacities is to risk failure, which can be devastating when they already are painfully aware of their limitations. This caution is particularly relevant to educational and vocational planning. Failures in these ventures may so discourage clients that they lose confidence in their abilities and simply quit trying.

Judgment

Some clients (and nonclients, for that matter) who have adequate or even keen intellect encounter severe difficulties in life because of deficiencies in judgment. Clients with poor judgment may experience more difficulties than those with intellectual deficiencies because the former may get themselves into one jam after another. By contrast, some people with intellectual limitations manifest strengths and live stable and productive lives by exercising prudence in making decisions and governing their behavior. Typical manifestations of deficiencies in judgment involve consistently living beyond one's means, entering get-rich schemes without carefully exploring possible ramifications, quitting jobs impulsively, leaving small children unattended, moving in with a partner with little knowledge of that person, failing to safeguard or maintain personal property, squandering resources, and the like.

Deficiencies in judgment generally come to light as you explore clients' problematic situations and patterns in detail. Often it is apparent that clients act with little forethought, fail to consider probable consequences of their actions, or engage in wishful thinking that things will somehow work out. Other clients manifest repetitive dysfunctional coping patterns that lead predictably to unfavorable outcomes. Failing to profit from past mistakes, these clients appear to be driven by intense impulses that overpower consideration of the consequences of their actions. These impulse-ridden clients may lash out at authority figures, write bad checks, or misuse credit cards, all of which provide immediate gratification but ultimately lead to loss of jobs, arrest, or other adverse consequences.

Reality Testing

Reality testing is a critical index to a person's mental health. Strong functioning on this dimension involves the following:

1. Being properly oriented to time, place, person, and situation
2. Reaching appropriate conclusions about cause-effect relationships
3. Perceiving external events and discerning the intentions of others with reasonable accuracy
4. Differentiating one's own thoughts and feelings from those that emanate from others

Relatively few clients manifest disorientation, but those who do usually are severely mentally disturbed, under the influence of drugs, or suffering from a pathological brain syndrome. Disorientation is usually readily discernible, but when doubt exists, questions about the date, day of the week, current events that are common knowledge, and recent events in the client's life will usually clarify the matter. Clients who are disoriented typically respond inappropriately, sometimes giving bizarre answers. For example, in responding to a question about his daily activities, a recluse reported that he consulted with the White House about foreign policy.

Some clients who do not have thought disorders may still manifest poor reality testing, choosing to blame circumstances and events rather than take personal responsibility for their actions (R. H. Rooney, 1992). For example, one client who stole an automobile externalized actions for his behavior by blaming the owner for leaving the keys in the car. Some clients blame their employers for losing their jobs, even though they habitually missed work for invalid reasons. Still others attribute their difficulties to the fact that fate decreed them to be losers. Whatever the source of these problems with reality testing, they serve as impediments to motivation and meaningful change. It is a welcome strength when clients own responsibility for their actions.

Perceptual patterns that involve *distortions* of external events are fairly common among clients and may cause severe difficulties, particularly in interpersonal relationships. Mild distortions may be associated with stereotypical perceptions (e.g., "All policemen are cruel and punitive" or "The only interest men have in me is sexual"). Moderate distortions often involve marked misinterpretations of the motives of others and may severely impair interpersonal relationships (e.g., "My boss told me I was doing a good job and that there is an opportunity to be promoted to a job in another department; he wants to get rid of me" or "My wife says she wants to take an evening class, but I know what she really wants. She wants to have an affair because she's not satisfied with me"). In instances of extreme distortions, people may manifest delusions that others plan to harm them, and on rare occasions take violent actions to protect themselves from their imagined persecutors. Seemingly random killings of innocent strangers are more often the actions of troubled people attempting to protect themselves from imagined communists, CIA agents, the federal government, or other feared groups.

Dysfunction in reality testing of psychotic proportions is involved when people "hear" voices (auditory hallucinations) telling them to murder, steal, or commit rape or criticizing them for being utter failures. Such persons lack the capacity to distinguish between thoughts and beliefs that emanate from themselves and those that originate from external sources and thus can present a danger to themselves or others when acting in response to such commands. Social workers must be able to recognize such severe cognitive dysfunction and respond with referrals for medication, protection, and/or hospitalization.

Coherence

Social workers occasionally encounter clients who manifest major thought disorders characterized by rambling and incoherent speech. Successive thoughts of these persons may be highly fragmented and disconnected from one another, a phenomenon referred to as *looseness of association* or *derailment* in the thought processes. As J. Morrison puts it, the practitioner "can understand the sequence of the words, but the direction they take seems to be governed not by logic but by rhymes, puns or other rules that might be apparent to the patient but mean nothing to you" (1995, p. 113). Another form of derailment is *flight of ideas*. In this, the client's response seems to "take off" based on a particular word or thought, unrelated to logical progression or the original point of the communication.

These difficulties in coherence may be indicative of mania or thought disorders such as schizophrenia. (Incoherence, of course, may also be produced by acute drug intoxication, and practitioners should be careful to rule out this possibility.)

Cognitive Flexibility

Receptiveness to new ideas and the ability to analyze many facets of problematic situations are conducive not only to effective problem solving but to general adaptability as well. People with cognitive flexibility generally seek to grow, to understand the part they play in their difficulties, and to understand others; such persons also can ask for assistance without believing it is an admission of weakness or failure. Many people, however, are rigid and unyielding in their beliefs, and their inflexibility poses a major obstacle to progress in the helping process.

A common pattern of cognitive inflexibility is thinking in absolute terms (e.g., a person is good or evil, a success or a failure, responsible or irresponsible—there is no in-between). Clients who think this way are prone to be critical of others who fail to measure up to their stringent expectations. Difficult to live with, many such people appear at social agencies because of marital difficulties or problems in parent-child relations. Improvement often requires helping them to examine the destructive impact of their rigidity, to broaden their perspectives of themselves and others, and to "loosen up" in general.

Negative cognitive sets also include biases and stereotypes that render clients unable to relate to members of certain groups (e.g., authority figures, ethnic groups, and the opposite sex) as individuals. Severely depressed clients evince tunnel vision, viewing themselves as helpless and/or worthless and the future as dismal and hopeless. These clients also selectively attend to their own negative attributes, leaving no way to feel good about themselves.

Values

Values are an integral part of the cognitive-perceptual subsystem, because they strongly influence human behavior and often play a key role in the problems presented by clients. For this reason, you should seek to identify clients' values, assess the role they play in their difficulties, and consider ways in which their values can be used to create incentives to modify their problematic behaviors. Further, you have an ethical responsibility to respect the rights of clients to cling to their values and to make choices consistent with them—an obligation that requires awareness of their values.

Many values, of course, are a product of cultural conditioning. Practitioners therefore must have knowledge about the values of clients' cultural reference groups to avoid making errors in assessment. Traditional Native American values, for example, may differ sharply from mainstream values on the following (Native American values are listed first): (1) harmony with nature versus mastery of nature, (2) orientation to the present versus orientation to the present and future, (3) orientation to "being" activity versus orientation to "doing" activity, and (4) primacy of family and group goals versus primacy of individual goals (DuBray, 1985). Gross has suggested that while a traditional value orientation may be preferred by many, there is reason to believe that actual preferences occur on a continuum with considerable diversity among individuals in any given culture with respect to value preferences (Gross, 1995).

Value conflicts often lie at the heart of clients' difficulties, as, for example, being torn between a desire for independence on one hand and a desire to be a homemaker on the other. Other clients may be engaged in a tug-of-war between a desire for liberation from an oppressive spouse and a belief that marriage should be maintained at all costs. Value conflicts may also be central to difficulties between partners. One partner may strongly value having children, whereas the other partner may reject this value. Conflicts between partners over religious values and clashes in beliefs between parents and adolescent children concerning premarital sexual behavior or the importance of education and achievement are also prevalent.

Being aware of clients' values is also prerequisite to employing these values to create incentive for changes in dysfunctional behavior. Clients may express strong commitment to certain values and yet engage in behavior that is in direct opposition to their purported values. When clients are assisted to measure their behavior against the yardstick of values they themselves have identified, they often realize for the first time that their behavior is inconsistent and self-defeating. For example, an adolescent who has protested that his parents should trust him agrees that being trusted is important to him. The practitioner then clarifies that his persistent lying to his parents defeats any possibility of his meriting their trust. Only by changing his behavior can he realistically expect them to trust him.

Awareness of client values is critical to ethical persuasion. Clients are more open to influence around instrumental values (means to ends) than they are around terminal values (ultimate goals) (R. H. Rooney, 1992). *Cognitive dissonance* may result when clients discover inconsistencies between thoughts or values and behaviors. You can determine clients' relevant values by exploring what matters most to them, how they believe spouses should relate to one another, how they think children should be disciplined, and so on. Examples of questions that will clarify clients' values are as follows:

- "You say you believe your parents are old-fashioned about sex; what are your beliefs?"

- "If you could be married to an ideal wife, what would she be like?"

- [*To a couple*]: "What are your beliefs as to how couples should make decisions?"

- "So you feel you're not succeeding in life. To you, what does being successful involve?"

Misconceptions

Clients commonly hold mistaken beliefs about human relationships, sex roles, authority, and countless other facets of life. Increasing emphasis has been accorded to these beliefs, and one prominent school of thought (cognitive theory) posits the tenet that beliefs mediate both emotions and behavior (Ellis, 1962; Lantz, 1996). A central promise in this approach is that mistaken beliefs lie at the heart of human maladjustment. In Table 9-3, we have listed a few common misconceptions as well as contrasting functional beliefs.

MISCONCEPTIONS	FUNCTIONAL BELIEFS
It is a disaster if I displease someone and I must suffer.	I can't be constantly at the mercy of others' reactions to me, or I will be extremely vulnerable to hurt. Pleasing myself is more important than pleasing others.
I am completely at the mercy of circumstances beyond my control and totally powerless.	Although many circumstances are beyond my control, there is much I can do to improve my situation.
The world is a dog-eat-dog place. No one really cares about anyone except themselves.	There are all kinds of people in the world, including those who are ruthless and those who are themselves caring. If I seek the latter, I will find them. The world will be a better place if I strive to be a caring person.
All people in authority use their power to exploit and control others.	People in authority vary widely. Some exploit and control others. Some usurp others' rights; others are benevolent. I must reserve judgment, or I will indiscriminately resent all authority figures.
Men's only interest in women is to dominate them and use them for sexual pleasure.	Men are as different from one another as are women. Healthy men and women are interested in sex but not necessarily to use others for selfish pleasure.
To be worthwhile, a person must be thoroughly competent and successful in every endeavor.	Everyone has a range of talents and will do better in some endeavors than in others. No one is perfect, and disappointments are bound to occur from time to time.
It's disgraceful to lose.	Although it makes me feel good to win, there must be a loser for every winner.
To be worthwhile, one must be the center of attention and admired by everyone.	Self-esteem that depends on constant attention is tenuous. Stable self-esteem comes from within; therefore I must learn to esteem myself.
If I don't put on the perfect holiday celebration, I'm a rotten mother and wife.	I'll do the best I can for the holiday. It will be perfect if my family and I are able to enjoy it. The celebration isn't a referendum on my abilities as a wife and mother.

Table 9-3 Examples of Distorted Conceptions and Functional Beliefs

Because misconceptions lie at the roots of many human problems, it is vital to learn to identify them and to include them in assessments. Goals often involve modifying key misconceptions, thus paving the way to behavioral change.

Self-Concept

Convictions, beliefs, and ideas about the self have been generally recognized as one of the most crucial determinants of human behavior. It is thus a strength and is conducive to mental health to have high self-esteem and to be realistically aware of one's positive attributes, accomplishments, and potentialities as well as one's limitations and deficiencies. A healthy person can accept limitations as a natural part of human fallibility without being distressed or discouraged. People with high self-esteem, in fact, can joke about their limitations and failings.

Many human beings, however, are tormented with feelings of worthlessness, inadequacy, and helplessness. These and other like feelings pervade their functioning in diverse negative ways, including the following:

- Underachieving in life because of imagined deficiencies
- Passing up opportunities because of fears of failing
- Avoiding social relationships because of fears of being rejected
- Permitting oneself to be taken for granted and exploited by others
- Ingratiating oneself to others
- Being self-conscious or retiring in social situations to avoid looking stupid
- Gravitating in social relationships to low-status persons
- Drinking to excess or taking drugs to fortify oneself because of feelings of inadequacy
- Devaluing or discrediting one's worthwhile achievements
- Becoming depressed
- Failing to defend one's rights

Because clients with poor self-concepts often desperately need help in enhancing their self-esteem, it is vital to assess this dimension of their functioning. Often clients will spontaneously discuss how they view themselves. When they do not, an open-ended response, such as "Tell me how you see yourself," will often elicit rich information. Because many people have not actually given much thought to the matter, they will hesitate or reply, "I'm not sure what you mean; what did you have in mind?" Persistence on your part will usually be rewarded. A further response, such as "Just what comes into your head when you think about the sort of person you are?" is usually all that is needed.

Instruments have also been developed to measure self-esteem. The Index of Self-Esteem, one of the WALMYR scales (Hudson, 1992), can be completed by clients in a matter of minutes. It is also easily scored and interpreted.

Interaction Between Cognition, Emotions, and Behavior

As is apparent in the foregoing discussion, cognitive functioning embraces many critical factors that interact with other variables to influence social functioning. Cognition, for example, plays a powerful role in mediating emotional arousal. Cognitive/perceptual sets, particularly the self-concept, influence both emotions and behavior. Because theoreticians and researchers have increasingly realized the significance of cognitive factors, they have in recent years developed and empirically tested a number of cognitive-behavioral interventions that have widespread application. Accordingly, we have devoted portions of Chapters 13 and 14 to these interventions.

ASSESSING EMOTIONAL FUNCTIONING

Emotions powerfully influence behavior and thus are an important area of concern for social workers. Strong emotions or states of feeling often play a central role in the problems of people who seek help. Some persons, for example, are emotionally volatile and engage in violent behavior while in the heat of anger. Others are emotionally unstable, struggling to stay afloat in a turbulent sea of emotion. Some people become emotionally distraught as the result of stress associated with the death of a loved one, divorce, severe disappointment, or another blow to self-esteem. Still others are pulled in different directions by opposing feelings and seek help to resolve their emotional dilemmas. To assist you in assessing emotional functioning, we devote the following sections to vital aspects of this dimension.

Emotional Control

People vary widely in the degree of control they exercise over their emotions, ranging from emotional constriction to emotional excesses. Individuals experiencing constriction may appear unexpressive and withholding in relationships. Out of touch with their emotions, they do not permit themselves to feel joy, hurt, enthusiasm, and other emotions that invest life with zest and meaning. Such persons may be comfortable intellectualizing but retreat from expressing or discussing feelings. They often favorably impress others with their intellectual styles, but sometimes have difficulties maintaining close relationships because their emotional detachment thwarts fulfilling the needs of others for intimacy and emotional stimulation.

Clients who manifest emotional excesses may have a "short fuse" and react intensely to even mild provocations. Clients who physically abuse family members, for example, lose control of anger and express it in violent ways. Others overreact to stress with tears, panic, depression, helplessness, and the like. Still others have difficulties in interpersonal relationships because they are excessively grouchy, irritable, or morose.

Cultural Factors

In considering emotional excesses, cultural factors should be considered, for cultures vary widely in approved patterns of emotional expressiveness. For example, individuals from Jewish, Greek, Lebanese, or Italian cultures may express emotions more freely, particularly within their families, than might those from Scandinavian, English, or east Indian cultures (McGoldrick, Giordano, & Pearce, 1996). Latinos also tend to be emotionally reactive, as Queralt (1984, p. 118) indicates in his description of Cubans: "Uninhibited emotionality and a hedonistic tendency that manifests itself through love of comfort, of life, and of pleasure, sensuality, playfulness, lightness, and gaiety are important Cuban traits." Latinos also vary in emotional expressiveness when they switch from speaking Spanish to English. According to Queralt: Latinos generally offer more carefully weighted, rational, and intellectualized messages in English and more emotional messages in Spanish. . . . Latinos may come across as relatively guarded and businesslike in English, and yet, when switching to Spanish, they frequently become much more open, expansive, in-

formal, jovial, friendly, jocose, explosive, negative, or positive. It is as if two personalities resided in the same person at once. (p. 119)

In assessing cultural factors, however, it is vital to differentiate individual from cultural factors, for a wide range of emotional expressiveness exists among members of specific cultural groups. In addition, client levels of acculturation must also be taken into account in cultural assessments. Individual patterns thus must be weighed against cultural norms.

Emotional health in any culture, however, involves having control over the emotions to the extent that one is not overwhelmed by them. Emotionally healthy persons also enjoy the freedom of experiencing and expressing emotions appropriately. It is also a strength to be able to bear painful emotions when beset by stress without denying or masking feelings or being incapacitated by them. Further, emotionally healthy persons are able to discern the emotional states of others, empathize, and discuss painful emotions openly without feeling unduly uncomfortable—recognizing, of course, that a certain amount of discomfort is natural. Finally, it is a strength to be able to mutually share deeply personal feelings in intimate relationships.

Range of Emotions

Another aspect of emotional functioning involves the ability to experience and to express a wide range of emotions that befit the diversity of situations encountered by human beings. Some people's emotional experiencing is confined to a limited range, which often causes interpersonal difficulties. A marital partner, for example, may have difficulty expressing tender emotions, causing the partner to feel rejected, insecure, or deprived of deserved affection. Some individuals are unable to feel joy or to express many pleasurable emotions, a dysfunction referred to as anhedonia. Still others have been conditioned to block angry feelings, blame themselves, or placate others when friction develops in relationships. Because of the blocking of natural emotions, they often experience extreme tension or physiological symptoms such as asthma, colitis, and headaches when involved in situations that normally would engender anger. Finally, some people, to protect themselves from unbearable emotions, evolved psychic mechanisms early in life that blocked experiencing rejection, loneliness, and hurt. Often such blockage is reflected by a compensatory facade of toughness and indifference, combined with verbal expressions such as "I don't need anyone" and "No one can hurt me."

Emotionally healthy people experience the full gamut of human emotions within normal limits of intensity and duration. It is thus a strength to experience joy, grief, exhilaration, disappointment, and all the rest of the full spectrum of emotions. When clients manifest emotional obstructions that inhibit resolution of the problems they are seeking help with, the practitioner has the task of enabling them to get in touch with the blocked emotions.

Appropriateness of Affect

Direct observation of the affect (emotionality) manifested by clients often discloses valuable information about their emotional functioning. Some anxiety or mild apprehension is natural in initial sessions (especially for involuntary clients and those referred by others), as contrasted to intense apprehension and tension at one extreme or complete relaxation at the other. Spontaneous experiencing and expressing of emotion that befits the content of material being discussed indicates healthy emotional functioning. It is thus a strength to be able to laugh, to cry, to express hurt, discouragement, anger, and pleasure when these feelings match the mood of the session. Such spontaneity indicates that clients are in touch with emotions and can express them appropriately.

Inordinate apprehension manifested through muscle tension, constant postural shifts, handwringing, lip-biting, and other like behaviors usually indicate a client is fearful, suspicious, or exceptionally uncomfortable in unfamiliar interpersonal situations. Such extreme tension may be expected in involuntary situations. In other cases, it may be characteristic of a client's demeanor in other interpersonal situations.

Clients who appear completely relaxed and express themselves freely in a circumstance that would normally suggest apprehension or anxiety may reflect a denial of a problem and may indicate a lack of motivation to engage in the problem-solving process. Further, charming demeanor may be a reflection of skill in projecting a favorable image when it is advantageous to do so. In some situations, as in sales or promotional work, such charm may be an asset; in others it may be a coping style to conceal self-centeredness and manipulation or exploitation of others. Such individuals often engender anxiety in those who are victimized by their manipulation, but they themselves typically lack anxiety that is prerequisite to wanting to change their own behavior.

Emotional blunting or apathy frequently is indicative of severe mental disorder. It is important to consider this possibility when clients discuss in a detached matter-of-fact manner traumatic life events or conditions, such as murder of one parent by another, deprivation, or physical and/or sexual abuse. When such emotional blunting appears in tandem with thought disorder, a strong likelihood exists that the client is psychotic and in need of careful psychiatric evaluation.

Inappropriate affect can also be manifested in other forms, such as laughing when discussing a painful event (gallows laughter) or wearing a constant smile regardless of whatever is being discussed. Elation or euphoria that is incongruent with one's life situation, combined with constant and rapid shifts from one topic to another (flight of ideas), irritability, expansive ideas, and constant motion also suggest mania. Although manic behavior is relatively rare, it is important to recognize manifestations of it, for manic clients urgently need medication and/or hospitalization to safeguard their health or protect them from impulsive and irrational actions, such as squandering resources on foolish investments.

Cultural Factors

In transcultural work, appropriateness of affect must be considered in light of the impact of cultural differences. As Lum (1996) has indicated, minority persons may feel uncomfortable with nonminorities but mask their emotions as a protective measure. Moreover, in the presence of nonminority social workers, minority persons may control painful emotions according to culturally prescribed behavior. An Asian American, for example, may react with politeness, quietness, and friendliness in the face of an overwhelming and threatening situation. A person of Hungarian extraction may display extreme or seemingly exaggerated affect. Persons with Polish cultural backgrounds may appear unmoved or inappropriately angry, when in fact the stoicism or anger may cover fears of dependency and anxiety (McGoldrick et al., 1996).

ASSESSING AFFECTIVE DISORDERS

In an earlier section we referred to DSM-IV, the manual widely employed as a guide for formulating psychiatric diagnoses. The DSM (American Psychiatric Association, 1994) contains extensive information on the criteria for diagnosing affective disorders (i.e., disorders of mood). Of particular importance for this text are bipolar disorders (known formerly as manic-depressive illness) and unipolar/major affective disorders (such as severe depression). Treatment of persons with these diagnoses generally includes medication (often with concurrent cognitive or interpersonal psychotherapy) so that these diagnoses also provide direction in treatment planning. Moreover, these disorders can often be linked to suicidal ideation and other serious risk factors. For these reasons, we discuss diagnosis of the major affective disorders in the following sections.

Bipolar Disorder

The dominant feature of this disorder is the presence of manic episodes (mania) with intervening periods of depression. Among the symptoms of mania are "a distinct period of abnormally and persistently elevated, expansive or irritable mood . . . " (p. 332) and at least three of the following:

• Inflated self-esteem or grandiosity

• Decreased need for sleep

• More talkative than usual or pressure to keep talking

• Flight of ideas or subjective experience that thoughts are racing

• Distractibility

• Increase in goal-directed activity (either socially, at work or school, or sexually) or psychomotor agitation

• Excessive involvement in pleasurable activities which have a high potential for painful consequences, e.g., unrestrained buying sprees, sexual indiscretions, or foolish business investments. (American Psychiatric Association, 1994)

Full-blown manic episodes require that symptoms be sufficiently severe to cause marked impairment in job performance or relationships, or to necessitate hospitalization to protect patients or others from harm.

If exploration seems to indicate a client has the disorder, immediate psychiatric consultation is needed; first, to determine if hospitalization is needed, and second, to determine the need for medication. This disorder is biogenetic, and various compounds containing lithium carbonate produce remarkable results in stabilizing and maintaining these persons. Close medical supervision is required, however, because commonly used medications for this disorder have a relatively narrow margin of safety.

Major Depressive Disorder

Major depressive disorder, in which persons experience recurrent episodes of depressed mood, are far more common than bipolar disorders. Major depression differs from the "blues" in that dysphoria (painful emotions) and the absence of pleasure (anhedonia) are present. The painful emotion commonly is related to anxiety, mental anguish, an extreme sense of guilt (often over what appear to be relatively minor offenses), and restlessness (agitation).

To be assigned a diagnosis of major depressive episode, a person must have evidenced depressed mood and loss of interest or pleasure as well as at least five of the following nine symptoms for at least 2 weeks:

- Depressed mood . . . most of the day, nearly every day
- Markedly diminished interest or pleasure in all, or almost all, activities
- Significant weight loss or weight gain when not dieting . . . or decrease or increase in appetite
- Insomnia or hypersomnia
- Psychomotor agitation or retardation
- Fatigue or loss of energy
- Feelings of worthlessness, or excessive or inappropriate guilt
- Diminished ability to think or concentrate, or indecisiveness
- Recurrent thoughts of death or suicidal ideation or attempts
  (American Psychiatric Association, 1994)

There are a number of scales available to assess the presence and degree of depression. They include the Depression Scale in the WALMYR Scales (Hudson, 1992), the Beck Depression Inventory (Beck, Ward, Mendelson, Mock, & Erbaugh, 1961), and the Zung Self-Rating Depression Scale (Zung, 1965). All of these scales are easy to complete, to score, and to interpret. All are also highly correlated with each other.

When assessment reveals clients are moderately or severely depressed, psychiatric consultation is indicated to determine the need for medication and/or hospitalization. Antidepressant medications have proven to be effective in accelerating recovery from depression and work synergistically with cognitive or interpersonal psychotherapy.

In assessing depression, it is important to identify precipitants of the depressive episode. Commonly an important loss or series of losses have occurred, and clients may need assistance in working through grief associated with these losses and developing compensatory sources of companionship and support. While depression and mourning may share

certain characteristics such as intense sadness and sleep and appetite disturbances, grief reactions generally don't contain the diminished self-esteem and guilt often observed in depression. As Worden notes, "That is, the people who have lost someone do not regard themselves less because of such a loss or if they do, it tends to be only for a brief time. And if the survivors of the deceased experience guilt, it is usually guilt associated with some specific aspect of the loss rather than a general, overall sense of culpability" (1991, p. 30).

Assessing Suicidal Risk

When clients manifest severe depressive symptoms or a sense of hopelessness, it is critical to evaluate suicidal risk so that precautionary measures can be taken when indicated. With adults the following factors are associated with high risk of suicide:

- Feelings of despair and hopelessness
- Previous suicidal attempts
- Concrete, available, and lethal plans to commit suicide (when, where, and how)
- Family history of suicide
- Perseveration about suicide
- Lack of support systems
- Feelings of worthlessness
- Belief others would be better off if one were dead
- Advanced age (especially for white males)
- Substance abuse

When a client indicates, directly or indirectly, that he or she may be considering suicide, it is incumbent on the social worker to address those concerns through careful and direct questioning. The social worker may begin by stating, "You sound pretty hopeless right now, I wonder if you might also be thinking of harming yourself?" or "When you say 'They'll be sorry' when you're gone, I wonder if that means you're thinking of committing suicide?" An affirmative answer to these probes should be followed with a frank and calm discussion of the client's thoughts about suicide. Has the client considered how he or she might do it? When? What means would be used? Are those means accessible? In asking these questions, the social worker is trying to determine not only the lethality of the client's plans but also the specificity. If a client has a very well thought out plan in mind, the risk of suicide is potentially greater. An understanding of the client's history, especially with regard to the risk factors mentioned and previous suicide attempts, will also help the worker decide the degree of danger presented and the level of intervention required. In addition, the following scales can be used to evaluate suicidal risk: the Hopelessness Scale (A. Beck, Resnik, & Lettieri, 1974), the Scale for Suicide Ideation (A. Beck, Kovacs, & Weissman, 1979), and the Suicide Probability Scale (Cull & Gill, 1991).[6] When the factors cited indicate a potentially lethal attempt, it is appropriate to mobilize client support systems and arrange for psychiatric evaluation and/or hospitalization if needed. Such steps provide a measure of security around the client who may feel unable to control his or her impulses or who may become overwhelmed with despair.

Assessing Depression and Suicidal Risk with Children and Adolescents

Children and adolescents, too, may experience depression, and suicide can be a risk with these groups. It is estimated that half a million young people between ages 15 and 24 attempt suicide each year and nearly 5,000 children and youth (age 5 to 24) kill themselves each year. In fact, suicide is the third leading cause of death for those in the 15- to 24-year-old age bracket (Peters & Murphy, 1998). Therefore, it is important to recognize the symptoms of depression in adolescents and the behavioral manifestations that may be reported by peers, siblings, parents, or teachers. Common symptoms of depression in adolescents include the following:

• Anhedonia
• Depressed mood
• Significant weight loss or gain
• Insomnia or hypersomnia

• Psychomotor agitation or retardation
• Fatigue or loss of energy
• Feelings of hopelessness, worthlessness, guilt, and self-reproach
• Indecisiveness or decreased ability to concentrate
• Suicide ideation, threats, attempts
• Recurring thoughts of death

Childhood depression is not markedly different from depression in adolescence; behavior manifestations and intensity of feelings are similar, once developmental differences are taken into consideration (Wenar, 1994). One major difference between childhood and adolescent depression appears when comparing prevalence rates between the sexes. The prevalence of depression is approximately the same in boys as girls in middle childhood, but beginning in adolescence twice as many females suffer from depression as males (Kauffman, 1997). Also, researchers found that adolescent girls diagnosed with depression reported more feelings of anxiety and inadequacy in middle childhood, while adolescent boys reported more aggressive and antisocial feelings (Wenar, 1994).

Because parents, coaches, and friends often do not realize the child or adolescent is depressed, it is important to alert them to the following additional behavioral manifestations (American Association of Suicidology, 1999; M. Gold, 1986):

• Deterioration in personal habits
• Decline in school achievement
• Marked increase in sadness, moodiness, and sudden tearful reactions
• Loss of appetite
• Use of drugs or alcohol
• Talk of death or dying (even in a joking manner)
• Withdrawal from friends and family
• Making final arrangements, such as giving away valued possessions
• Sudden or unexplained departure from past behaviors (from shy to thrill seeking or from outgoing to sullen and withdrawn)

Given the mood swings and tempestuousness typical of adolescence, the above warning signs should be regarded as indications of serious depression only when they persist for 10 days or longer. If a child manifests several of these symptoms, psychiatric consultation is advisable. Suicidal risk is highest when the adolescent, in addition to the listed symptoms of severe depression, manifests feelings of hopelessness, has recently experienced a death of a loved one, had severe conflict with parents, lost a close relationship with a key peer or a sweetheart, and has no support system. Brent et al. indicate that "interpersonal conflict, especially with parents, is one of the most commonly reported precipitants for completed and attempted suicides" (1993, p. 185). Other studies have indicated that moderate to heavy drinking and/or drug abuse were implicated in at least 50% of adolescent suicides (Fowler, Rich, & Young, 1986).

While completed suicides and suicide attempts are more common among adolescents (with adolescent males completing more suicides and adolescent females attempting more suicides), the numbers of younger children completing and attempting suicide is increasing (Kauffman, 1997). Therefore, it is important to be cognizant of depressed behavior and signs of suicide ideation in children as well as adolescents. Warning signs of suicide ideation in younger children are similar to those already discussed for adolescents when translated to the appropriate developmental level.

When faced with a young client who is considering suicide, social workers should use the same lethality assessment questions discussed earlier for work with adults. In addition, assessment tools geared to evaluating suicide risk in children and adolescents are available, such as the Children's Depression Scale (Kovacs, 1992) and the Johns Hopkins Depression Scale (Joshi, Capozzoli, & Coyle, 1990). After the degree of lethality is determined, appropriate interventions can then be put into place, such as making a no-suicide agreement, teaching nonviolent ways to solve problems and

get attention, and reestablishing or creating peer and adult support networks (Kauffman, 1997).

An additional technique for exploring and responding to suicidal ideation in young people is to ask "Who would find you?" The question helps uncover the "child's suicidal fantasies and actions, affects, concepts of death and family circumstances" (Pfeffer, 1986, p. 176) and aids in the assessment of interpersonal conflicts that may have precipitated the suicidal threat. Exploration of the client's responses to such probes as "How would they find you?" "Would you still be alive?" "How would they react?" all help the interviewer to weigh the level of suicidal risk and learn more about the feelings and needs leading to the consideration of suicide. As such, these questions also facilitate the development of curative responses, such as examining how to meet the needs expressed (for love, forgiveness, acceptance) without resorting to self-injurious behaviors (Holman, 1997).

ASSESSING BEHAVIOR FUNCTIONING

In direct practice, change efforts typically are aimed at modifying behavioral patterns that impair the social functioning of clients and others involved in the problem. As you assess behavior, it is important to keep in mind that one person's behavior does not influence another person's behavior in simple linear fashion. Rather the behavior of all participants reciprocally impacts upon and shapes the behavior of others.

Because behavioral change is commonly the target of interventions, you must be skillful in discerning and assessing both dysfunctional and functional patterns of behavior. In individual sessions, you will be able to directly observe certain social and communication patterns of clients, as well as some personal habits and traits. In conjoint interviews and group sessions, you will be able to observe these behavioral patterns and the effects these actions have on others with whom they interact.

In assessing behavior, it is helpful to think of problems as consisting of excesses or deficiencies on the part of clients. With respect to the former, interventions are aimed at the goal of *diminishing* or *eliminating* behavioral excesses, which include temper outbursts, excessive talking, arguing, overachieving, and consummatory excesses (e.g., overeating, immoderate drinking, and excessive sexual indulgence). With regard to deficiencies, interventions are employed to assist clients to *acquire* skills and behaviors needed to function more effectively. The behavioral repertoires of clients, for example, may not include skills in expressing feelings directly, engaging in social conversation, listening to others, solving problems, managing finances, planning nutritional meals, being a responsive sexual partner, handling conflict, and other behaviors that are essential to effective social functioning.

In addition to identifying dysfunctional behavioral patterns, it is important to be aware of those that are effective and represent strengths. To assist you in assessing both dysfunctional and functional patterns of behavior, we have listed, according to major behavioral categories, numerous patterns of behavior (see Table 9-4). Although the list is extensive, it is by no means comprehensive, nor are the categories all-inclusive. We have, however, included those patterns that most frequently create interpersonal difficulties. As you review the list, you may question whether a few patterns are functional or dysfunctional. This determination, of course, depends on the situational context within which the behavior occurs. Aggressive behavior may serve a self-protective function in a prison environment but may be dysfunctional in family relationships or in most groups. When we compiled the list, our frame of reference encompassed typical marital, family, and group contexts.

You will note that the list consists of many adjectives and verbs that are very general and are subject to different interpretations. In assessing behavior, therefore, it is vital to specify actual problem behaviors. For example, rather than assess a client's behavior as "abrasive," a social worker might describe the behaviors leading to

that conclusion, for example, that the client constantly interrupts his fellow workers, insults them by telling them they are misinformed, and boasts about his own knowledge and achievements. When detrimental behavior is thus pinpointed, the changes that must be made become clear.

An adequate assessment of behavior, of course, goes beyond identifying dysfunctional behaviors. You must also determine the antecedents of behaviors—when, where, and how frequently they occur—and specify the consequences of the behaviors as well. Further, you should explore thoughts that precede, accompany, and follow the behavior, as well as the nature of and intensity of emotions associated with the behavior. We identified these factors in the preceding chapter and earlier in this chapter.

We have also limited the dysfunctional behaviors embedded in the list to the individual patterns of behavior. The list does not include dysfunctional patterns of interaction between two or more persons in marital, family, and group contexts. However, we devote the following chapter to this important topic.

ASSESSING MOTIVATION

Evaluating and enhancing the motivation of clients are integral parts of the assessment process. Clients who don't believe that they can influence their environments may manifest a kind of learned helplessness (Gold, 1990, p. 51). When working with family members or groups, social workers are likely to find a range of motivation. In order to assess motivation, the social worker needs to understand the person and his or her perception of the environment. Motivation, of course, is a dynamic force that is strongly influenced by ongoing interaction with practitioners. By relating facilitatively and determining clients' wants and goals, social workers often succeed in engaging clients, increasing motivation and channeling energies effectively. Conversely, clients who initially are adequately motivated may lose that motivation if their encounter with a social worker is negative.

DIMENSIONS OF BEHAVIOR	DYSFUNCTIONAL PATTERNS	FUNCTIONAL PATTERNS (STRENGTHS)
Power/control	Autocratic, overbearing, aggressive, ruthless, demanding, domineering, controlling, passive, submissive; excludes others from decision making.	Democratic, cooperative, assertive; includes others in decision making, stands up for own rights.
Nurturance/support	Self-centered, critical, rejecting, withholding, demeaning, distant, punitive, fault-finding, self-serving; insensitive to or unconcerned about others.	Caring, approving, giving, empathic, encouraging, patient, generous, altruistic, warm, accepting, supportive; interested in others
Responsibility	Undependable, erratic; avoids responsibility, places pleasure before responsibility, externalizes responsibility for problems, neglects maintenance of personal property.	Dependable, steady, consistent, reliable; follows through, accepts responsibility, owns part in problems, maintains personal property.
Social skills	Abrasive, caustic, irritable, insensitive, aloof, seclusive, sarcastic, querulous, withdrawn, self-conscious, ingratiating; lacks social delicacy.	Outgoing, poised, personable, verbally fluent, sociable, witty, courteous, engaging, cooperative, assertive, spontaneous, respectful of others, sensitive to feelings of others; has sense of propriety.
Coping patterns	Rigid, impulsive, rebellious; avoids facing problems, uses alcohol or drugs when under stress, becomes panicky, lashes out at others, sulks.	Flexible; faces problems, considers and weighs alternatives, anticipates consequences, maintains equilibrium, seeks growth, consults others for suggestions, negotiates and compromises.
Personal habits and traits	Disorganized, dilatory, devious, dishonest, compulsive, overly fastidious, impulsive; manifests poor personal hygiene, has consummatory excesses, has irritating mannerisms.	Planful, organized, flexible, clean, efficient, patient, self-disciplined, well-groomed, honest, open, sincere, temperate, considerate, even-dispositioned, punctual.
Communication	Mumbles, complains excessively, nags, talks excessively, interrupts others, tunes others out, stammers, yells when angry, withhold views, defensive, monotonic, argumentative, taciturn, verbally abusive.	Listens attentively, speaks fluently, expresses views, shares feelings, uses feedback, expresses self spontaneously, considers others' viewpoints, speaks audibly and within tolerable limits.
Accomplishment/ independence	Unmotivated, aimless, nonproductive, easily discouraged, easily distracted, underachieving; lacks initiative, seldom completes endeavors, workaholic, slave to work.	Ambitious, industrious, self-starting, independent, resourceful, persevering, successful in endeavors, seeks to advance or to improve situations.
Affectionate/sexual	Unaffectionate, reserved, distant, sexually inhibited, promiscuous, lacking sexual desire, engages in deviant sexual behavior.	Warm, loving, affectionate, demonstrative, sexually responsive (appropriately).

Table 9-4 Behavioral Patterns

As Reid (1978) has pointed out, motivation consists of two critical aspects. The first aspect is the direction of the motivation; that is, toward what goals is the client motivated? Clients are generally motivated to fulfill certain wants or needs. In evaluating the direction of motivation, the central issue concerns whether or not clients' wants are realistic and achievable. Some clients seek to accomplish goals that exceed their capacity (e.g., vocational goals that require aptitude well beyond that possessed by the client). Others express wants that require changes beyond the sphere of influence of the client and/or practitioner (e.g., "I want you to persuade my wife to drop her divorce action and to reconcile with me" or "I want you to get my kids back; they need me and are not happy in that foster home"). In such instances, it is important to tactfully assist clients to recognize the unrealistic nature of their wants and to direct them toward realistic goals that are relevant to their problematic situation (e.g., "Only the judge has the authority to return your children to you, but I'm very willing to assist you in making whatever changes are necessary to meet the conditions he has specified for the return of your children").

The second aspect concerns the strength of motivation. Clients often manifest wants but lack the willingness or current skill to participate actively in planning and implementing remedial actions. Many clients have misconceptions about the helping role, imputing to the practitioner magical power for solving their difficulties. Others are willing to participate but mistakenly perceive their role as compliantly carrying out the social worker's directives. Still others manifest strength and independence by correctly perceiving the practitioner as a partner and facilitator and by assuming responsibility for mutually exploring their problems and for planning and implementing remedial measures.

Precipitating Events and Motivation

All potential clients, both applicants and persons who are referred, are motivated. Their motivation frequently differs, however, from the problems attributed to them by others. By carefully exploring life events that precipitate applicants' decisions to seek service, you can often discern both the direction and strength of their initial motivation. When applicants decide to seek service shortly after critical events and request assistance in modifying behavior or circumstances associated with these events, their motivation is likely to be adequate in both direction and strength.

When potential clients' decisions to seek assistance result from a referral in the form of an ultimatum from a family member or employer, their motivation is likely to be less strong. To differentiate such referred clients from applicants, Rooney has described such clients as nonvoluntary to reflect their response to external, nonlegal pressure and to suggest that they are the "invisible involuntary" because the nonlegal pressure they experience is often hidden or ignored by the practitioner (R. H. Rooney, 1992). For example, though a couple requested marital therapy, the intake practitioner discovered that in fact their request was precipitated by an ultimatum from the husband's mother, with whom they were living, to get help or move out. Further exploration revealed that intense verbal arguments between the couple had precipitated the mother's ultimatum. When nonvoluntary clients lack motivation to work on the problem attributed to them by the referral source, social workers should first clarify available choices. In this case, the couple could choose not to continue with the pressured request for services, to ignore the recommendation of the referral source, or to work on concerns of their own (R. H. Rooney, 1992). Such a clarification focuses attention on problems acknowledged by clients rather than those attributed by others (Reid, 1978). Consequently, it is possible to find problems for which there *is* adequate motivation both in strength and direction if attention is devoted to those problems acknowledged by clients. Frequently nonvoluntary clients will choose to get rid of or reduce the pressure for change. In this case, the couple did not view themselves as in need of marital treatment. They did, however, wish to remain living with the mother for the time being. After assurances that these arguments had not escalated to physical violence, the couple agreed to work on verbal means for reducing conflicts, partly motivated by their wish to avoid eviction from the mother's home.

Meanwhile, mandated clients whose contact with helping professionals is impelled by legal mandate or the threat of such rarely acknowledge the same problems as do the sources of the legal mandate. For example, parents who are alleged to have abused or neglected their children rarely acknowledge child abuse or neglect as their concern. Similarly, mandated clients in correctional institutions rarely acknowledge the same problems as those for which they have been imprisoned. Rooney describes strategies whereby practitioners can seek to discover acknowledged problems with mandated clients and link them to mandated pressures (R. H. Rooney, 1992). We will discuss these strategies in Chapter 12.

ASSESSING CULTURAL FACTORS

In this and previous chapters, we have discussed many cultural factors related to various aspects of the helping process. In this section, we focus on general cultural factors that are relevant to the process of assessment. This section focuses largely on culture as it is related to racial or ethnic groups. Other groups (e.g., gay, lesbian, bisexual, transgendered persons, the hearing impaired, the elderly, and persons in recovery) reflect distinct cultural attributes as well. Aspects of cross-cultural practice with those groups and other cultural factors are discussed throughout other portions of the book.

Cultural Norms

Knowledge of the norms related to a client's culture of origin is indispensable when the client's cultural background is markedly different from your own. Without such knowledge, you may make serious errors in assessing both individual

and interpersonal systems, for cognitive, emotional, behavioral, and interpersonal patterns that are deemed functional in one cultural context may be deemed problematic in another and vice versa. Further, such errors in assessment may lead to selecting interventions that aggravate rather than diminish clients' problems. For example, encouraging relatively unacculturated Latina women to assert themselves to their husbands may subject them to ostracism or negative reactions because such behavior is contrary to cultural norms. Similarly, to suggest that an Asian American youth should stand up to or distance himself from "controlling" parents would be potentially damaging because of the cultural norm that dictates respect for older persons and maintenance of strong family ties (see Lum, 1996, or McGoldrick et al., 1996, for a more extensive discussion of cultural norms and values).

Cultures vary widely in their prescribed patterns of child care, child rearing, adolescent roles, mate selection, marital roles, and care of the aged—to name just a few. In Anglo-American culture, for example, there has been a major trend toward equality of the sexes, resulting in the prevailing view that domineering behavior by husbands is dysfunctional. While there are feminists among American Latinas and in Middle Eastern cultures, autocratic behavior by husbands and dependent behavior by wives is often the norm. Patterns of communication between marital partners also vary widely from culture to culture. Among certain Native American tribes, husbands and wives tend to communicate more with members of their same sex than with each other. Similarly, the extent of communication between parents and children varies substantially from culture to culture.

Differentiating Individual and Culturally Determined Patterns

Although knowledge about the client's culture is vital in transcultural work, practitioners must guard against stereotyping clients on the basis of that knowledge. Considerable variation exists among subgroups of identified ethnic groups, and overgeneralizations about members of these groups may obscure rather than clarify the meanings of individual behavior. For example, there are over 400 different tribal groups of Native Americans in the United States, and these groups speak over 250 distinct languages (E. Edwards, 1983). Comparisons of Plains tribes with Native Americans of the Southwest have revealed sharply contrasting cultural patterns and patterns of individual behavior as well as marked differences in the incidence of certain social problems (May, Hymbaugh, Aase, & Samet, 1983). Cubans, Puerto Ricans, and Mexican American groups also differ widely from one another although they are much more alike than different because of their common Latino heritage (Queralt, 1984). Filipinos also embody diverse cultural groups who speak eight major different languages and 75 or more different dialects (Ponce, 1980). Obviously, Asian Americans also represent many different cultures that share certain characteristics but also differ significantly from one another in language, history, and values.

Within homogeneous cultural groups, wide variations also exist among individuals. Being knowledgeable about the cultural characteristics of a given group is necessary but insufficient for understanding the behavior of individual members of the groups. As with members of the cultural majority, each member of an ethnic minority group is unique. Social workers, therefore, must consider each ethnic minority client as an individual, for dysfunctional or deviant behavior as viewed from the perspective of the cultural majority may be similarly viewed by members of ethnic minority groups. The task confronting practitioners, therefore, is to differentiate between behavior that is culturally mediated and that which is a product of individual personality. Possession of in-depth knowledge about a given cultural group facilitates making such differentiations, but when in doubt, practitioners are advised to consult with well-informed and cooperative members of the ethnic group in question. Kumabe et al. (1985), for example, have reported an instance involving a neglectful Southeast-Asian refugee mother who appeared to be depressed. After making extended and futile efforts to assist this mother, the practitioner consulted with another refugee and learned that the mother (who spoke little English) was mentally retarded rather than depressed. Further, she had manifested child neglect in her native community before coming to the United States.

Degree of Acculturation

In assessing the functioning of ethnic minority clients, it is important to consider the degree to which they have been socialized into the mainstream culture. Ethnic minority clients are actually members of two cultures, and their functioning must be considered in relationship to both their culture of origin and the majority culture. Clients from the same ethnic group may vary widely in the degree of their acculturation, which depends upon a number of factors. Foremost is the number of generations that have passed since the original emigration from the native land. Ordinarily, first generation minority clients adhere closely to their traditional beliefs, values, and patterns of behavior. By the third generation, however, clients have usually internalized many of the patterns of the dominant culture although they typically maintain many traditional patterns of family relationships.

Even when considering the degree of acculturation of an ethnic minority client, social workers can make errors if they fail to attend to a client's uniqueness. For example, although unacculturated Asian Americans are generally regarded as emotionally unexpressive and preferring structure and direction by social workers, S. Sue and Zane (1987) report that "many . . . seemed quite willing to talk about their emotions and to work well with little structure" (p. 39).

Still, the significance of the different generations to Japanese Americans is reflected in the fact that this ethnic group specifies by linguistic terms each generation of descendants from the original immigrant group. The terms *Issei*, *Nisei*, and *Sansei* thus refer to first, second, and third generations, respectively. Mass (1976) has discussed characteristics, patterns, and problems of each of these groups.

Lott (1976) has presented a similar discussion of different generations of Filipino immigrants.

Other factors also affect the degree of "bicultural" socialization and interactions of ethnic minority clients with mainstream society. One writer (De Anda, 1984, p. 102) identified and discussed six such factors:

1. The degree of commonality between the two cultures with regard to norms, values, beliefs, perceptions, and the like

2. The availability of cultural translators, mediators, and models

3. The amount and type (positive or negative) of corrective feedback provided by each culture regarding attempts to produce normative behaviors

4. The conceptual style and problem-solving approach of the minority individual and his or her mesh with the prevalent or valued styles of the majority culture

5. The individual's degree of bilingualism

6. The degree of dissimilarity in physical appearance from the majority culture, such as skin color, facial features, and so forth.

Other authors (Kumabe et al., 1985) have reported that varying degrees of acculturation occur among members of the same family and same generation. These authors also discuss and illustrate the complexities involved in acculturation when parents are from different ethnic minority backgrounds, for example, a Japanese American married to a Filipino American. The socialization of children to such parents is tricultural. Such permutations are not uncommon in truly pluralistic societies such as Hawaii, where people often refer to their ethnic heritage as smorgasbord. Transcultural work is the rule rather than the exception in such communities, and effective practice requires extensive knowledge of the cultures represented.

Biculturalism and Mental Health

Controversy has fermented for many years as to whether policies should encourage minority mem-

bers to retain their cultural roots, assimilate into mainstream society, or both. Many factors, of course, enter into the debate, including whether one adopts the majority or minority perspective. Chau has noted that most cross-cultural change efforts have focused on psychological adaptation of the minority person to the majority culture (Chau, 1990). These efforts often reflect an ethnocentric assumption that the minority person needs to gain from strengths of the majority culture. When the assumptions shift from ethnocentrism to cultural pluralism, change efforts can reflect a two-way interaction in which attention is devoted to strengths different cultures can bring to each other, strengthening both host and minority cultures.

From the standpoint of mental health, one important study sheds some light on the matter. Studying the mental health of Cuban Americans, M. R. Gomez (1990) measured the degree of biculturalism of the study groups and then determined the relationship between the degree of biculturalism and the psychological well-being, self-esteem, marital adjustment, and job satisfaction of the subjects. The findings indicated that the more bicultural the subjects were, the higher their psychological well-being and self-esteem. Further, among married subjects there was a relationship between biculturalism and higher marital adjustment. Findings related to job satisfaction were less impressive.

Others note that members of nondominant groups may experience psychological difficulties as a result of trying to identify with the dominant group while being treated in a prejudiced or racist manner at the hands of the group they aspire to join (Mayadas et al., 1998–99). Other difficulties may emerge from conflicting values between cultures. For example, Jamaicans may experience pressure to identify with African Americans yet have difficulty doing so because of culturally based judgments related to skin color. Amish men or women who choose to leave the faith may find themselves caught between two worlds and accepted in neither (McGoldrick et al., 1996).

These findings further support the need for social workers to assess the biculturalism of clients, to sensitize themselves to minority cultures, to encourage clients to maintain ties to their cultural roots, and to assist them in adapting to mainstream culture. Cultural self-awareness is likewise important for social workers themselves, as that knowledge will help them understand and serve their clients better.

Fluency with the English Language

Social workers should also consider the client's degree of bilingualism when conducting an assessment. Clients whose command of English is very limited often have great difficulty in formulating and explaining their problems in a different language. Even for clients who have a strong command of English, care providers "should be aware that the foundational thought structures through which the client processes the world will likely be in the primary language, with English language interpretations only a rough equivalent of the original. Subtle shifts in meaning can create confusion, frustration and even fear in the client or the client's family (Ratliff, 1996, pp. 170–71). An interpreter may be called in to bridge the language gap, but even when one is used, the social worker should be cognizant that interpretations may be only approximations of what the client is attempting to convey. If an interpreter is not available, it is important to speak in simple terms and to proceed at a slower pace. Clients need ample time to process messages, and practitioners must exercise care in checking out whether clients have grasped the intended meaning of their messages and whether they have truly understood what the client is trying to express.

The use of interpreters is also an important issue to consider when working with deaf clients (Santos, 1995). The primary language used by many deaf people is American Sign Language (ASL), which is a unique and separate language from English, not merely a visual translation of English. Interpreters are often a necessity for deaf clients to communicate effectively with hearing social workers; however social workers should keep in mind that concepts may not be easily transferred from ASL to English and should therefore take time to make sure concepts are being accurately understood on both ends. Social workers working with deaf clients who use ASL should also apply the factors mentioned in the previous paragraph to make sure that language differences are not becoming barriers to effective treatment.

Limited fluency in language can also block ethnic minority clients from access to essential community resources (especially clients isolated from their cultural reference groups). Inability to converse with others and to take advantage of the vast information provided through newspapers, radio, and television thus not only produces social isolation but also deprives people of information essential to locating and utilizing essential resources.

Attitudes Toward Receiving Help

Approaches to problem solving also vary among different cultures. Within the mainstream culture, an analytical cognitive style appears to be the most highly valued approach to defining most problems and searching for solutions to them (De Anda, 1984). Certain ethnic minority groups, however, rely on approaches based on group values about coping with problems that differ from the individually focused style of the mainstream culture. All cultures exert pressures on individuals to follow prescriptive courses of action in given problematic situations. Novel and creative solutions that differ from cultural assumptions are discouraged in such circumstances. Deviation from those culturally prescribed rules may generate anxiety and/or guilt for clients strongly influenced by their cultures.

Variations among cultures are also common with respect to key persons who normally become involved in efforts to solve problems. In most Native American tribal groups, for example, family members actively seek counsel from elderly members of the extended family unit in coping with family problems. The wisdom of elders is highly valued, and elderly members of the tribe are accorded much respect (Hull, 1982). When sought for counsel, elderly Native Americans often pass along their wisdom in the form of storytelling, "which does not insult the intelligence or integrity of the listener because one is always free to ignore unacceptable suggestions" (Hull, 1982, p. 343). Asian Americans similarly look to the extended family for direction in problem-solving situations and value the wisdom of the elderly. Southeast Asian immigrants may seek assistance from clan leaders, shamans, or herbalists, depending on the nature of the difficulty.

Behavior of members of certain ethnic minority groups is strongly influenced by their attitudes toward asking for help and by the type of help needed. Yamashiro and Matsuoka (1997) note that for Asian Americans the underutilization of (or "resistance" to) seeking mental health services may have origins in several cultural themes. For example, an acceptance of "fate" may lead to "quiescence in the face of unpleasant life situations" (p. 178) and the tradition of arranged marriages may mitigate against the pursuit of formal assistance for problems that could reflect poorly on the suitability of a prospective spouse. Given the ways that religion and culture shape the perception of problems and therefore the methods chosen to address them, it is little wonder that Asian Americans and other cultural groups seek help first from "informal" helpers, such as spiritual leaders, community or clan leaders, or traditional healers.

In light of attitudes such as those just reported, clients from various ethnic groups may be expected to manifest shame and apprehension during an initial interview. Practitioners must be sensitive to the causes of such reactions for two important reasons. First, the client's manifest behavior is likely to be atypical, and assessment of the client's functioning without this knowledge could lead the practitioner to draw erroneous conclusions. Second, such untoward emotional reactions about seeking help can be formidable barriers to establishing trust and rapport. Awareness of clients' feelings, however, enables the practitioner to respond to them with empathy and understanding, which enhances the possibility of working through the feelings.

Members of certain ethnic minority groups who have negative experiences with the dominant culture and particularly with the government are disposed to approach helping agencies with skepticism and even hostility. In light of efforts of the federal government first to annihilate Native Americans and then to assimilate them, their distrust of the government is understandable (Diorio, 1992; Hull, 1982). Similarly, skepticism toward Anglo Americans by African Americans, Latinos, and Asian Americans is a natural consequence of their histories of being exploited and victimized by overt racism and/or institutionalized racist practices. Behavior of these individuals in transcultural relationships must be assessed accordingly. Moreover, social workers working transculturally must be prepared to deal with distrust, fear, and even hostility, which may be natural by-products of clients' experiences with majority persons in power who have been unhelpful or who have abused their authority.

Achieving Credibility

Social workers whom clients consider likable, trustworthy, and having the client's best interest at heart are most likely to be perceived by clients as positive sources of influence (Harper & Lantz, 1996; R. H. Rooney, 1992). These factors may be facilitated by cultural similarity between client and practitioner. However, practitioners who are culturally similar to their clients may differ from them in other important ways such as values, education, socioeconomic status, and level of acculturation. In fact, a Southeast Asian child welfare worker reported that his job was easier with Caucasian clients than with Southeast Asian clients who expected that cultural similarity would override professional allegiances and legal mandates. L. E. Davis and Gelsomino (1994) report in a study of cross-cultural contact that Caucasian practitioners were more likely to explore psychological problems and internal difficulties with minority clients than were minority practitioners working with minority clients. The study suggests that minority practitioners were more likely to take structural problems seriously and were less likely to focus exclusively on internal difficulties. Cultural self-awareness is thus important for all social workers, regardless of the status of the social worker or clients served, as this knowledge will help facilitate the social worker–client relationship.

Cross-cultural contact also occurs between minority practitioners and clients from the majority culture. While the minority practitioner is usually more familiar with the majority culture than majority culture practitioners are with minority cultures, clients often challenge the credibility of minority practitioners (Proctor & Davis, 1994). Cultural differences between practitioner and client are often ignored in a color-blind assumption that services are not affected by those differences. Proctor and Davis indicate that trust is enhanced when the practitioner describes the helping process and the rationale for questions in the assessment and addresses the client by terms preferred by the client (e.g., "Mrs. Jones") as a demonstration of respect. In addition, the practitioner should not attempt to hide ignorance of client values, but rather acknowledge differences and take on the learner role. Finally, the social worker should directly ask clients about their experiences with practitioners from a different culture rather than expect clients to raise the issue.

Credibility is also ascribed to a social worker by reason of education, position, role, age, gender, and other factors emphasized in the client's culture: factors over which a practitioner has little control. Credibility can also be achieved, however, when clients have favorable experiences with practitioners who foster respect, confidence, trust, and hope (Harper & Lantz, 1996). Sue and Zane (1987) hypothesize that practitioners gain credibility by following three major guidelines:

1. The practitioner must conceptualize the problem in a manner that is consistent with the client's belief systems. Imposing upon clients problem formulations that are antagonistic to the client's belief systems may block achievement of credibility.

2. Expectations of change efforts to be made by clients must be compatible with their cultural values. For example, encouraging an Asian client to express anger directly to a father would require the client to violate a deeply embedded value and would be perceived by the client as destructive and inappropriate.

3. Treatment goals must be consonant with clients' perceptions of desired objectives. When goals reflect the practitioner's agenda rather than the client's, credibility may not be achieved and clients may disengage from the helping process.

Although these guidelines are applicable to all client groups, they are particularly relevant to ethnic minorities. Prerequisite to adhering to these guidelines, of course, is possessing knowledge about the belief systems and values of a given ethnocultural group.

Providing Immediate Benefits

Sue and Zane (1987) maintain that in addition to establishing credibility, gift giving is also vital in transcultural work. The term "gift giving" is used symbolically rather than literally and refers to enabling clients to experience a direct benefit from treatment, as soon as possible, preferably in the first session. These authors use the term "gift" because "gift giving is a ritual that is frequently a part of interpersonal relationships among Asians" (p. 42). Explanations to clients that benefits of the helping process will be forthcoming in the future are insufficient, according to Sue and Zane. Rather, ethnic minority clients, especially Asians, who tend to be skeptical of Western forms of treatment, need demonstration of the direct relationship between activities in the helping process and the alleviation of problems.

What kind of gifts (immediate benefits) can the practitioner provide? One important gift cited is *normalization* (also denoted as universalization), which refers to "a process by which clients come to realize that their thoughts, feelings, or experiences are common and that many individuals encounter similar difficulties" (p. 42). Use of this supportive technique tends to reduce anxiety associated with the mistaken belief that one's difficulties are strange and different and reflect one's being different and less adequate than others. The social worker can offer other "gifts": stress relief procedures, responsiveness to client's phone calls, concrete assistance, depression relief, clarification of factors producing difficulties, reassurance (when it is reality based), hope, plans for skill training, discussion of promising coping measures, and setting of relevant goals. As with credibility, we believe that "gift giving" is also applicable to nonminority clients but is of particular value in building a meaningful and effective relationship with clients of different cultures.[7]

Social workers should also recognize "gift giving" by minority clients, which often is a sign of acceptance of someone previously seen as an outsider. For example, when an African American client shares family pictures or invites a social worker to look at the client's garden, it shows the social worker that the client is accepting him or her into the client's life.

Cultural Resources

By attending to cultural factors, you may be able to locate or develop indigenous cultural resources that can be tapped to assist clients who are strangers in another culture and who, because of poverty, language barriers, limited experience, and lack of information, do not know what to do or whom to see when confronted with major stress.

Other more experienced and sophisticated members of a given cultural group often are willing to assist such clients to find their way through the maze of bureaucratic structures. Indigenous nonprofessionals have also been employed as staff members to serve as client advocates and to provide direct outreach services to impoverished minority clients (Budner, Chazin, & Young, 1973). Valuable services performed by indigenous nonprofessionals include assuming the role of advocate and interpreter (in both language and policy), assisting people to utilize resources within a given agency, intervening with other social systems to obtain timely

responses to needs of clients, providing direct services (e.g., homemaking, baby-sitting, shopping, and escorting clients to various agencies), discussing problems in times of crisis, and rendering technical assistance (e.g., completing forms, writing letters, and establishing eligibility for services) (Congress, 1994; Harper & Lantz, 1996).

Indigenous nonprofessionals may also organize groups to engage in social action, such as tenant groups among impoverished minority members to obtain essential repairs of facilities and to use legal means of assuring that landlords comply with housing laws. Participating in such groups not only results in improved living conditions but also counters the sense of helplessness and creates cultural reference groups that combat the social isolation commonly experienced by poverty-stricken minority persons.

Extended family members are also an important resource to be considered in work with ethnic minority clients. Filipinos, for example, have a strong sense of loyalty that extends far beyond the nuclear family, and thus, they have an extensive network of people to whom they can turn for support and assistance in crisis situations (Ponce, 1980). The same is true of Native Americans (Jilek, 1982), African Americans (R. Jones, 1983; Mwanza, 1990), Asian Americans (D. Sue, 1981), Hawaiians (Kumabe et al., 1985), Samoans (Wong, 1983), and Hispanics (Sotomayer, 1991). The availability of kinship networks for ethnic minority families, of course, varies according to the number of generations a given family is removed from the original family of immigration. That availability is also influenced by geographic distance, placing heavy demands on long-distance telephone conversations and occasional reunions.

The Role of Religion and Spirituality

In addition to understanding culturally derived beliefs, resources, and experiences, social workers must also understand their clients' religious and spiritual backgrounds. Canda differentiates between spirituality and religion; spirituality is the totality of the human experience that cannot be broken into individual components and religion is the socially sanctioned institution based upon those spiritual practices and beliefs (1997). Sherwood also suggests a distinction between spirituality and religion, wherein the former reflects the "human search for transcendence, meaning and connectedness beyond the self" and "religion refers to a more formal embodiment of spirituality into relatively specific belief systems, organizations and structures" (1998, p. 80). He cites a typology by Ressler (1998) wherein persons may fall into one of four categories; spiritual and nonreligious, religious and disspirited; disspirited and nonreligious, and spiritual and religious. A "spiritual assessment," then, may help the worker to better understand the client's belief system and resources. Questions such as "What are your sources of strength and hope?" "How do you express your spirituality?" "Do you identify with a particular religion or faith?" and "Is your religious faith helpful to you?" can begin to elicit information as the foundation to seeking further understanding about the client's beliefs. Authors such as Sherwood (1998) and Ellor et al. (1999) offer a variety of guides for gathering information about both clients' spiritual beliefs and religious affiliations.

Why is it important to understand the role of religion and spirituality in the lives of your clients? As Ratliff notes in discussing health care settings,

> Religious beliefs may dictate food choices, clothing styles, customs of birthing and dying, etiquette in the sick room, use of modern conveniences, invasive procedures, organ donation, reception, use of blood products, certain diagnostic tests, gynecological procedures, spiritual influences on or control of sickness and healing, the wearing of protective devices or tattoos, and the need for prayers and rituals performed by various religious specialists. (1996, p. 171)

At times, religious issues may be central to the presenting problems clients bring to service. For example, parents may disagree about the spiritual upbringing of their children; couples may be at odds over the proper roles of women and men; families may be in conflict about behaviors pro-

scribed by certain religions, such as premarital sex, contraceptive use, alcohol use, divorce, or homosexuality (Meystedt, 1984).

As Thibalt et al., conceptualize it, spirituality involves three relevant areas—cognitive (the meaning given to past, current, and personal events), affective (one's inner life and sense of connectedness to a larger reality), and behavioral (the way in which beliefs are affirmed, e.g. through group worship or individual prayer) (1991). Thus, spiritual beliefs may affect the client's response to adversity, the coping methods employed, the sources of support available (e.g., the faith community may form a helpful social network), and the array of appropriate interventions available. Particularly when clients have experienced disaster or unimaginable traumas, the exploration of suffering, good and evil, shame and guilt, and forgiveness can be a central part of the change process. As Ellon et al. (1999) and others suggest, social workers must be aware of their own spiritual journey and understand the appropriate handling of spiritual content, depending on the setting, focus, and client population involved. Social workers are also advised to involve clergy or other leaders of faith communities to work jointly in addressing the personal and spiritual crises faced by clients (Grame et al., 1999).

ASSESSING ENVIRONMENTAL SYSTEMS

The environment was a central concern of pioneers in social work in the late 1800s and early 1900s, but receded into the background of social work theory by the 1920s, having been overshadowed by the impact of evolving theories related to individual functioning, most notable of which was Freudian psychoanalysis. Emphasis on the individual continued to the 1960s and 1970s, when it was supplemented by interactional and systems theory (including theories of family therapy). Although theoreticians did not exclude the environment from their formulations, they accorded it minor significance. The emphasis on the person, and to a lesser extent on interpersonal transactions, undoubtedly was a consequence of the fact that theories pertaining to individual and interpersonal functioning were far more developed than theories pertaining to the environment.

A strong resurgence of interest in the environment commenced in the early 1970s. Greatly influence by ecological and systems theories, and by the increased emphasis placed on the environment by prominent ego psychologists, Germain (1973), Meyer (1970), and Siporin (1975) advocated a perspective of social work practice that revolved around systems theory and ecological theory. These theorists incorporated this perspective in their practice textbooks, and acceptance of the ecological perspective has steadily expanded. Coinciding with this change, milieu treatments came into prominence in many residential and institutional settings.

The ecological perspective does not represent a swing of the pendulum from primary focus on the person to the other extreme of primary focus on the environment. Rather, assessment focuses on the transactions between the two, and problem-solving efforts may be directed toward assisting people to adapt to their environments (e.g., training them in interpersonal skills), altering environments to meet the needs of clients more adequately (e.g., enhancing both the attractiveness of a nursing home and the quality of its activities), or a combination of the two (e.g., enhancing the interpersonal skills of a withdrawn, chronically ill person and moving the person to a more stimulating environment).

In assessing client's environments, attention should be limited to those aspects of the environment that are salient to the problem situation. Relevant factors vary according to the needs of specific clients, which in turn are determined by clients' personalities, states of health, stages of development, interests, aspirations, and other related factors. You should thus tailor your assessments of clients' environments to their varied life situations, weighing clients' unique needs against the availability of essential resources and opportunities within their environments. Remember,

however, that it is easy to focus exclusively on the limitations or problems posed by inadequate physical or social environments. When social workers do so they may overlook the strengths at play in the client's life—the importance of a stable, accessible, affordable residence or the value of a support system that mobilizes in times of trouble.

Health and Safety Factors

In this context, we are considering not the personal factors that influence health and safety but rather the environmental factors. A safe environment can refer to one that is free of threats such as personal or property crimes. Persons who live where violence and crime are concerns may confine themselves to their homes because of these fears. Often such persons need assistance in moving to safer areas, but it is difficult for some to leave familiar neighborhoods, friends, and living arrangements to which they have become attached. In some instances, social workers have organized neighborhoods to increase the security of residents by forming "block watch" groups and by organizing elderly groups to check up on each other and to develop strategies for notifying the police when a threat to security appears. Organizing residents in this way serves an empowering function that counters feelings of helplessness.

Assessing health and safety factors includes considering sanitation, space, and heat. Large families may be crammed into small homes or apartments without adequate beds and bedding, homes may not be designed for running water or indoor toilets, or access to water may be broken or shut off. Inadequate heat or air conditioning can exacerbate existing health conditions and can lead to danger during periods of bad weather. Further, families may take steps to heat their residences (such as with ovens or makeshift fires) that can lead to further health dangers. Homes may have insect or rodent infestations that threaten residents' health and safety or they may be located in areas with exposure to toxic materials or poor air quality. In other instances, landlords may be negligent in conforming to building standards and in maintaining plumbing, so that sanitation is compromised.

For an elderly client, an environmental assessment should also look at the client's living situation and whether or not the situation meets the client's health and safety needs. Issues to consider include: If an elderly client lives alone, does the home have adequate resources for the client to meet his or her functional needs? Can the client use bathroom and kitchen appliances to conduct his or her daily activities? Is the home a safe environment for the client to be in, or are there aspects of the building (such as stairs or loose carpeting) that could pose a danger to less mobile clients? Does the client have outside social contacts (such as family members, neighbors, or Meals-on-Wheels workers) who can periodically check in with the client to make sure the client is safe and still able to meet his or her health needs and perform basic living tasks? Tools designed to assess functional ability provide objective information that can be used to screen for and address risk factors, as well as evaluate progress at a later date. Instruments such as the Older American Resources and Services questionnaire (OARS) utilize information gathered from the client, from collaterals such as family members, and from interviewer impressions regarding different aspects of the client's life, including activities of daily living (ADLs) and the client's environment, to assess functioning (Van Hook et al., 1996).

When environment poses dangers to clients or exacerbates other problems, steps must be taken to improve living conditions, often a difficult challenge given the scarcity of adequate low-cost housing. Some groups, such as the elderly, may qualify for government-subsidized housing facilities, which provide not only adequate housing but social opportunities as well. You may also help clients to access home improvement, heating assistance, and other programs to improve their living conditions. Further, when others are responsible for detrimental environmental conditions, social workers should assist clients in advocacy actions to address such problems.

Environmental Resources Universally Needed

Beyond an adequate physical environment, all people need a range of resources within their social environment. We have therefore compiled the following list of basic environmental needs, which you can employ in evaluating the adequacy of clients' environments. The list, of course, must be individualized to each client.

1. Adequate social support systems (e.g., family, relatives, friends, neighbors, organized groups)
2. Access to specialized health care services (e.g., physicians, dentists, physical therapists, hospitals, nursing homes)
3. Access to day care services (for working mothers and single-parent families, as well as for seniors and impaired clients)
4. Access to recreational facilities
5. Mobility to socialize, utilize resources, and exercise rights as a citizen
6. Adequate housing that provides ample space, sanitation, privacy, and safety from hazards and pollution (both air and noise)
7. Adequate police and fire protection and a reasonable degree of security
8. Safe and healthful work conditions
9. Adequate financial resources to purchase essential resources
10. Adequate nutritional intake
11. Predictable living arrangements with caring others (especially for children)
12. Opportunities for education and self-fulfillment
13. Access to legal resources
14. Access to religious organizations
15. Employment opportunities

Identifying Relevant Social Systems

Embodied in the preceding list of resources are a number of social systems that provide needed goods and services. Diverse social systems either are part of the problem configuration or represent resources needed to improve the goodness of fit between personal and family needs on one hand and environmental resources on the other. To enable you to identify pertinent social systems, we have constructed a diagram (see Figure 9-1) that depicts interrelationships between individuals and families and other systems (A. Hartman, 1994).

Systems that are central in a person's life are in the center of the diagram. These systems typically play key roles as both sources of difficulties and as resources that may be tapped or modified in problem solving. Moving from the center to the periphery in the areas encompassed by the concentric circles are systems that are progressively more removed from individuals and their families. There

Figure 9-1 Diagram of Ecological Social Systems

are exceptions, of course, as when an individual feels closer to an intimate friend or a pastor than to family members. Moreover, as clients' situations require frequent contacts with institutions or organizations (e.g., child protective services, income maintenance programs, and judicial systems), those institutions no longer occupy a peripheral position because of the intense impact they have upon individuals and families at such times. Reciprocal interactions thus change across time, and diagrammatic representation of such interactions should be viewed as snapshots that are accurate only within limited time frames. The challenge in formulating such ecological diagrams of your clients' social networks is to include the salient boundaries of the clients' situation and to specify how the systems interact, fail to interact, or are needed to interact in response to clients' needs.

The nature of positive interactions, negative interactions, or needed resources can be depicted by using different colored lines to connect the individual or other family members to pertinent systems, where specified colors represent positive, negative, or needed connections and interactions with those systems. If colored lines do not appeal to you, different types of lines—single, double, broken, wavy, dotted, or cross-hatched—can be used.

Social Support Systems (SSSs)

Social support systems (SSSs) are increasingly recognized as playing a crucial role in determining the level of social functioning of human beings, especially in consideration of the changing role of the government in providing social services. Theorists, of course, have long recognized the critical importance of a nurturing environment to healthy development of infants and children. In recent years, however, it has become clear that adults, too, have vital needs that can be met only through a nurturant environment. What benefits accrue from involvement with SSSs?

1. Attachment, provided by close affectional relationships that give a sense of security and sense of belonging.

2. Social integration, provided by memberships in a network of persons that share interests and values.

3. The opportunity to nurture others (usually children), which provides incentive to endure in the face of adversity.

4. Physical care when persons are unable to care for themselves due to illness, incapacity, or severe disability.

5. Validation of personal worth (which promotes self-esteem), provided by family and colleagues.

6. A sense of reliable alliance, provided primarily by kin.

7. Guidance, child care, financial aid, and other assistance in coping with difficulties as well as crises.

It is thus apparent that, at best, absence of adequate SSSs renders people vulnerable to major maladaptation to external stress and, at worst, is itself a primary source of stress, as with people who are socially isolated or feel alienated from society. By contrast, the presence of adequate SSSs tends to reduce the impact of stressful situations and facilitates successful adaptation. SSSs thus represent a vital resource that practitioners should consider as they assess problems of living. Moreover, social workers increasingly employ interventions that tap the potential of dormant SSSs and mobilize new SSSs in assisting clients to cope with life's stresses.

A variety of groups may have particular need for enhanced SSSs, or may be especially vulnerable due to limited or blocked SSSs. These include the elderly (Berkman et al. 1999), abused or neglected children (Brissette-Chapman, 1997), teenage mothers and parents (Barth & Schinke, 1984; Brindis, Barth, & Loomis, 1987; De Anda & Becerra, 1984), persons with AIDS (Indyk, Belville, Lachapelle, Gordon, & Dewart, 1993), widows and widowers (Lieberman & Videka-Sherman, 1986), persons with severe mental illness, and their families (Zipple & Spaniol, 1987; Rapp, 1998), the terminally ill (Arnowitz, Brunswick, & Kaplan, 1983), persons with disabilities (Hill,

Rotegard, & Bruininks, 1984; Mackelprang & Hepworth, 1987), transients (Breton, 1984), and people who experience geographical and/or cultural dislocation as refugees and immigrants (Hulewat, 1996). The reasons for diminished social supports may vary by group, and each presents challenging opportunities to social workers in collaborating to develop natural support networks and to plan service delivery systems that are responsive to the individual's unique needs.

To this point, we have highlighted the positive aspects of SSSs. The presence of certain types of SSSs, however, may foster and sustain dysfunctional behavior, and social workers must be alert to this possibility as they assess problem systems. For example, families with overprotective parents thwart the development of autonomy and personal responsibility in their children. Children from such families often fail to develop social skills, problem-solving skills, and the ability to relate in a mature give-and-take manner. Unrealistic expectations of others and excessive dependency are typical manifestations of people reared in such cloistered environments. Urban gangs and other antisocial peer groups exemplify social supports that may foster destructive behaviors such as violence and criminality. An SSS that ridicules or undermines a client's efforts to further her education and pursue a secure career is another example of a negative SSS.

Social workers must be aware of the various social networks at play in a client's life, and assess the role that such SSSs play in the client's difficulties, or in the client's ability to overcome such problems. A negative support system can, at times, be counteracted by the development of prosocial or positive networks. At other times, the system itself may be the focus of intervention, as the social worker strives to make the members aware of their role in the client's problems and progress.

Assessing Reciprocal Interactions Between Individuals and SSSs

In formulating assessments, practitioners must consider the reciprocal interaction between individuals and their SSSs. The responsiveness of SSS members to individuals and families under stress depends in great measure on the nature of previous interactions between these systems. For example, people who have been warm, sensitive, and generous in responding to the needs of others are far more likely to receive nurturant social support in times of distress than are people who typically relate to others in a complaining, aggressive, or withholding manner. Further, people vary widely in their perceptions of the adequacy of social support, and in the actual social support available in times of adversity.

A number of instruments have been developed to assess the personal SSSs of clients. One such instrument is the Interview Schedule for Social Interaction (Henderson, Duncan-Jones, Byrne, & Scott, 1980). Others include the Social Support Network Inventory (Flaherty, Gaviria, & Pathak, 1983), and the Perceived Social Support Network Inventory (Oritt, Paul, & Behrman, 1985). An instrument that is especially practical for social workers is the Social Network Grid (Tracy & Whittaker, 1990). This instrument yields the following information:

1. Key persons in clients' social networks
2. Areas of life in which the support occurs
3. Specified types of support provided by each person
4. The degree to which support persons are critical
5. Whether the support is reciprocal or unidirectional
6. The degree of personal closeness
7. The frequency of contacts
8. Length of the relationship

Completion of the grid, for which Tracy and Whittaker provide explicit instruction, yields rich information for both the practitioner and the client. Students who have used it report favorable reactions from clients, who describe feeling more positive as they gain expanded awareness of the social support they receive or can tap when needed.[8]

Summary

In the preceding sections, we discussed assessment of physical, cognitive/perceptual, emotional, and behavioral functioning, as well as motivation and cultural and environmental factors. Although we presented each of these factors as discrete entities, we again emphasize that these factors are neither independent nor static. Rather, the various functions and factors interact dynamically over time, and from the initial contact, the practitioner is a part of that dynamic interaction. Each of the factors is therefore subject to change, and the social worker's tasks are not only to assess the dynamic interplay of these multiple factors but also to instigate changes that are feasible and consonant with clients' goals.

We also reemphasize that assessment involves synthesizing relevant factors into a working hypothesis about the nature of problems and their contributory causes. You thus need not be concerned in every case with assessing all the dimensions identified thus far. Indeed, an assessment should be a concise statement that embodies only pertinent factors.

We also remind you that the scope of this chapter was limited to intrapersonal and environmental dimensions. We purposely excluded marital, family, and group systems, not because they are not important components of people's social environments but because they generally are the hub of people's social environments. To work effectively with interpersonal systems, however, requires an extensive body of knowledge about these systems. Therefore, we devote the next two chapters to assessing marital and family systems and growth-oriented groups.

Internet Resources

- You can access information about co-existing psychiatric disorders at *http://text.nlm.nih.gov/ftrs/pick?ftrsK=54359&cd=1&t=909932608&collect=tip&dbName=tip9/* and information on schizophrenia at *http://www.mhsource.*

com/narsad/. You can find out about addiction research at *http://www.arf.org/.* Using InfoTrac®, you can search keywords "dual diagnosis," "alcohol abuse assessment," "drug abuse assessment," "affective disorders," "suicide assessment," "social support systems" or you can access this article: Berg-Weger, M., McGartland, D., & Tebb, S. (2000). Depression as a mediator: Viewing caregiver well-being and strain in a different light. *Families in Society, 81, 2.*

Notes

1. For a more comprehensive list of questions and a discussion on assessing for substance use, see Lukas (1993).

2. A shaman is a sacred specialist who utilizes a technique of ecstatic trance to communicate with spirits and other powerful forces, natural and supernatural. The shaman acquires sacred power from the spiritual realm to heal and to enhance the harmony between the human community and the nonhuman environment (Canda, 1983). Lake (1983) lists the cosmic laws as identified by a Yurok shaman, and we recommend this article to those interested in learning more about Native American medical beliefs and practices. Delgado (1977) has presented eight recommendations that can be extremely useful to practitioners in working with clients who believe in the efficacy of spiritualist folk healing.

3. Kumabe et al. (1985) have extensively discussed cultural nuances involved in the reciprocal effects of illness and disability and family functioning.

4. See G. Steinmetz (1992) for an article about FAS, including photographs comparing a normal fetus with one damaged by excessive alcohol consumption by the mother. Detailed information about FAS and FAE has been presented in articles by Giunta and Streissguth (1988) and Anderson and Grant (1984). Anderson and Grant have discussed such treatment programs, and Giunta and Streissguth have discussed the needs of caregivers of children with FAS, as well as related family needs and community services and resources.

5. For a more comprehensive list of questions and a discussion on assessing for substance use, see Lukas (1993).

6. Range and Knott (1997) offer a comprehensive evaluation of these and 17 other suicide assessment instruments.

7. In the preceding, we have highlighted major ethnic and cultural factors that are salient to the process of assessment. Space limitations, however, preclude dealing comprehensively with this important topic. Other authors (Devore & Schlesinger, 1981; Green, 1982; Julia, 1996; McGoldrick, et al., 1996; Sue & Moore, 1984; Wright, Saleeby, Watts, & Lecca, 1983) have devoted entire books to ethnocultural factors.

8. With respect to issues involved in the measure of social support, evaluation of eight related instruments, and guidelines for practitioners, we recommend an article by Streeter and Franklin (1992).

CHAPTER 10

Assessing Family Functioning in Diverse Family and Cultural Contexts

Revised and edited by Glenda Dewberry Rooney

CHAPTER OVERVIEW

Chapter 10 focuses on family dimensions of the assessment phase of the helping process. It is intended to assist social workers in developing skill in family assessment and in adopting both a "cultural variant" and a "family variant" perspective, allowing them to assess families within their own idiosyncratic context. It also discusses a systems framework for assessing families. Within this framework, family is defined as a social system in which each of its parts or elements interact with each other in a predictable organized fashion. Within the family system, personal dimensions of the individual are given consideration as well as the social context of the family unit.

THE EVOLUTION OF FAMILY SYSTEMS

Social work from its professional beginning has been concerned with the family as a unit and as a focus of intervention. Nichols and Schwartz (1998) trace social work's contributions to work with families to the friendly visitors of the Charity Organization Societies and to family casework. The profession's focus on the person and the environment, according to Nichols and Schwartz, anticipated "family therapy's ecological approach,

long before systems theory was introduced" (p. 25). The rationale for conceptualizing the family as a system was clarified by Mary Richmond's classic text *Social Diagnosis* in 1917, in which the family is conceptualized as a system and treatment for the family as a unit was introduced (Nichols & Swartz, 1998).

The family has the highest significance among the various systems of concern to social work. The family, consisting of people who share both history and future, performs essential functions of "meeting the social, educational and health care needs of its constituent members" (A. Hartman, 1981, p. 10). It is largely through the family that character is formed, vital roles are learned, and members are socialized for participation in the larger society.

Social workers practice with families in a variety of settings and with a range of problems. In some instances their practice involves formally designated family interventions designed to have an impact on family structure and processes (see Chapter 16). In many other instances, social workers practice with family members related to a specific concern and agency function. For example, social workers in health and elderly care settings often focus on health, safety, and independence issues of the elderly or infirm as a part of an interdisciplinary team. In child welfare settings, they focus on the health and safety of children and the preservation of families. The family therapy literature provides a rich, informative resource for work with families. However, elements from that perspective must be used selectively when therapy is not the agency function, the concern of the family, or a family need (Kilpatrick & Holland, 1999; Nichols & Schwartz, 1998; W. Reid, 1985).

FAMILY STRESSORS

Families served by social workers frequently encounter a hostile or indifferent environment with major deficits in health care and day or after school care, insufficient income, and unsafe neighborhoods and schools. Tensions between work and family created by inflexible workplace policies affect family functioning and, in some cases, the ability to carry out family roles and responsibilities. Another source of tension is the denial of comparable family benefits for domestic partners. Conflicts are created for families who are deemed not to meet the image of the traditional family. The "family values" movement, which emerged during the 1992 presidential campaign, along with the call for personal responsibility for parents during the latter part of the last decade, shaped social policies that emphasized trimming welfare costs. Pressured families, often the most vulnerable, were required to seek work without sustainable compensation and requisite benefits such as health care or child care. Moreover, child welfare and family services have been almost exclusively devoted to the problems of child abuse and neglect; the majority of those affected are poor, minority women and their children. In working with families, social workers must be aware of the extent to which policies support or burden family well-being and inhibit access to resources (Vosler, 1990; Zimmerman, 1995). Finally, extreme stress can occur in minority or culturally diverse families whose composition, values, or beliefs clash with those of the dominant culture.

DEFINING FAMILY

Now more than ever, social workers come in contact with families for whom influences of culture, race, and lifestyle shape how family is defined. Social workers face the challenge of assessing families during the evolution of the "traditional family" into other more accommodating forms. "It is a phenomenon of our times that people have discovered so many ways to come together as family," observes Meyer (1990). She asserts that many social workers and others have not fully recognized these new family forms as "permanent features of the American landscape" (p. 4). Applying a broader "lens" to how family is defined, Carter and McGoldrick (1999b) include extended kin, the community, and the cultural group as composing the family. Broader definitions of family along with marked growth in diverse populations in the United States present challenges for social workers in assessing family functioning.

Given the nature of modern families, how then can social workers meet this challenging task? Meyer (1990), in advocating for a less standardized view of what constitutes family, urges social workers to free themselves of personal and professional biases that force families into preformed nuclear patterns, thus creating the illusion of clinical pathology. Rather, social workers can usefully conceptualize the modern "family" as two or more people who are joined together by bonds of sharing and intimacy. (Meyer, 1990, p. 16). This flexible "no-fault definition" will aid social workers to meet clients on their own turf, in their own terms, within their own self-definition. Because family needs and circumstances are varied, assessing families through the lenses of their particular level of functioning, strengths, migratory status, and the life cycle are important factors as well (Hernandez & McGoldrick, 1999; Kilpatrick & Holland, 1999). This approach with families allows for more collaborative practice in which strengths and cultural, racial, and lifestyles differences can be explored in the context of change and problem solving. McGoldrick (1998) reminds us that the increased multiculturalism that has occurred in the United States indicates the need to be more inclusive in our understanding of emotional and social connectedness in our work with families. This framework has broad implications for families in general, yet guides social workers to reflect upon those indigenous patterns and perceptions that influence help-seeking behavior within diverse groups. (Green, 1999; Hirayama, Hirayama, & Cetingok, 1993).

A SYSTEMS FRAMEWORK FOR ASSESSING FAMILY FUNCTIONING

In keeping with our earlier discussion of families, we ask that readers keep in mind the various ways in which family membership is achieved. Members may enter the family system through marriage or commitment, birth or adoption. You should consider also informal arrangements that extend family relationships beyond the immediate household. Such connections may involve friends, intergenerational networks, and community (Hardy, 1997; Hines & Boyd-Franklin, 1996) or, as described by Weston (1991), the "family of creation."

As we introduced in Chapter 1, a primary characteristic of any system is that all of it is parts are in transaction. There is interdependence between systems and their component parts, which means that whatever affects that system, whether internal or external, to some degree affects the whole. In general systems terms, the system as a whole is greater than the sum of its parts. Systems are in constant exchange with other systems. They manage inputs from other systems through boundary maintenance. When faced with inputs, a system may seek to ensure stability or equilibrium, change, or remain in a steady state (P. Y. Martin & O'Connor, 1989).

The systems framework is useful for assessing families in that the focus may be on the internal family systems; yet that framework can also include larger systems' influence on the family.

Assessment of internal family functioning, family history, or relationships is aided by completion of a genogram. Similarly, the eco-map enables you to focus on the interactions between the family and the larger society. You will also find the culturagram (Congress, 1994) a useful tool for assessing family dimensions in the context of culture, because Green (1999) asserts, "The systems view limits important cultural considerations" (p. 8). The family assessment wheel is yet another tool that will aid you in examining the sociopolitical and cultural context of the family experience (Mailick & Vigilante, 1997).

Families, like other systems, are differentiated into subsystems, such as parents, siblings, and kin, who join together to perform various family functions. Members of the family system influence and are influenced by every other member, creating a system with properties of its own, governed by implicit and explicit rules that specify roles, power structures, forms of communication, and ways of problem solving and negotiating. Roles, power structure, and communication patterns are the dynamic processes of the system and its interrelated and interdependent component parts.[1]

Because the family is a unique system, using the systems framework will enable social workers to analyze and assess the context of the ongoing operations of the family as well as external influences. This chapter discusses concepts that will assist you in viewing the family as a system and prepares you for family assessment. In the interest of addressing the importance of family assessment in which formal family therapy is neither requested nor the function of the agency, family assessment concepts are illustrated through application in a case study in a health care setting.[2]

CASE EXAMPLE

Carlos Diaz, 66, lives with his 16-year-old son, John, in a subsidized apartment on the second floor of a three-story building. Mr. Diaz is diabetic, is visually impaired but not legally blind, and has a history of heavy alcohol use, though has been abstinent for 7 years. Mr. Diaz's companion of 18 years, Ann Mercy, recently died of a massive stroke. Ann Mercy provided emotional support, gave Mr. Diaz his insulin injections, and managed the household. Mr. Diaz has difficulty walking, has fallen several times in the past year, and is now hesitant to leave his apartment. In addition to John, Mr. Diaz has eight children from an earlier marriage who live in nearby suburbs, though only one, Maria, calls him regularly. Mr. Diaz's physician considers his current living arrangement dangerous because of the stair climbing and is concerned about his capacity to administer his own insulin. A medical social worker convenes a family meeting with Mr. Diaz, his son John, his daughter Maria, and his stepdaughter Anita.

SYSTEMS IMPINGING UPON FAMILY FUNCTIONING

Problems occur in a person or family and situation context. In this case, the problems occur in part because of the living situation of Mr. Diaz, his access to alternative living environments, and the availability of a continuum of care that might include in-home supports. Mr. Diaz's income and health insurance coverage will also influence alternatives available to the family. Such systems factors should always be accorded prominence to avoid assumptions that problems are caused by factors internal to the family system and resolved by interventions addressed to those internal factors. Both internal and external factors may impinge upon and disrupt family functioning. In this section, we discuss two case examples, the Diaz and the Barkley families, to apply systems concepts that may be utilized in the assessment of internal family system dynamics and processes.

FAMILY HOMEOSTASIS

Homeostasis is a systems function that attempts to maintain or preserve balance. When faced with a disruption, it is the tendency of the system to regulate and maintain cohesion in response to, for example, transitions in the life cycle or stressors

associated with acculturation or environmental events. As systems, families develop mechanisms to maintain balance or homeostasis in their structure and operations. They may restrict the interactional repertoires of members to a limited range of familiar behaviors and develop mechanisms for restoring equilibrium whenever it is threatened (in much the same way that the thermostat of a heating system governs the temperature of a home). The death of a family member, in this case, Mrs. Diaz, is one of the factors that have disrupted the family equilibrium. In effect, previously established patterns and expectations—for example, Mr. Diaz as the head of the family—are called into question along with his ability to care for himself and John because of his physical condition. Atchey (1991) notes, "It is common for the elderly to feel a lower of power as a result of social limitations imposed by other's perceptions of physical conditions as well as the limitations of the condition itself" (p. 79). As observed in the Diaz case, intergenerational conflicts may also occur around issues of care taking, dependency, and loss or health declines, especially when there is a loss of a spouse. Mr. Diaz may be seen as attempting to restore family equilibrium in the family system by asserting his independence and protecting his role. Minuchin (1974) speaks of this tendency of families to maintain preferred patterns as long as possible and to offer resistance to change beyond a certain range of specific behaviors:

> *Alternative patterns are available within the system. But any deviation that goes beyond the system's threshold of tolerance elicits mechanisms, which reestablish the accustomed range. When situations of system disequilibrium arise, it is common for family members to feel that other members are not fulfilling their obligations. Calls for family loyalty and guilt-producing maneuvers then appear. (p. 52)*

When the medical social workers convenes the Diaz family, she recognizes that the previous equilibrium in Mr. Diaz's life and health care has been disrupted by the death of Ann Mercy. Maria is concerned about Mr. Diaz's capacity to care for himself and his son John. Ann's daughter Anita from a previous marriage has taken Ann's possessions, including a washing machine, without Mr. Diaz's knowledge or approval. Mr. Diaz fears that his children want to place him in a nursing home and take John out of his care. He states emphatically that he can administer his own insulin and can cook, clean, and vacuum, though he has not done these tasks for many years. Mr. Diaz's wishes can be seen as an effort to protect his independence and restore as much of the family equilibrium as possible. Meanwhile, family members (except son John) and the doctor doubt his capacity to assume these duties. These dynamics, including those stemming from family rules, play a decisive role in the family's interactions.

FAMILY RULES

Family homeostasis is maintained to the extent that all members of the family adhere to a limited number of rules or implicit agreements that prescribe the rights, duties, and range of appropriate behaviors within the family. Rules are formulas for relationships or guides for conduct and action in the family. Unwritten and covert, rules represent a set of prescriptions for behavior that define relations and organize the ways in which family members interact. Since rules are implicit (i.e., unwritten laws governing behavior that are often beyond the participants' level of awareness), they must be inferred from observing family interaction and communication. Examples of implicit rules that dictate the behavior of members in relation to family issues include: "Father has the final word," "It's OK to talk about sex in front of everyone but Mother," "Don't say what you really feel," and "It is important to respect the personal property and privacy of other family members."

Families do, of course, formulate rules that are openly recognized and explicitly stated, such as "Teenagers are to be in the house by ten at night," "Children are limited to two hours of TV a day," "There will be no swearing in this house," and "Children don't talk back to parents." In assessing family systems, the social worker is most interested in implicit rules that guide a family's actions because, to the extent these rules are dysfunctional, they may have insidious effects on the family (e.g., inflicting severe emotional damage on members, limiting the family's ability to accommodate to changing circumstances, and restricting choices and opportunities for growth). Because rules are implicit, their damaging impact on the lives of families often goes unrecognized, and members become caught in situations in which their behavior is dictated by forces of which they are unaware. By thus adhering to dysfunctional "rules," family members often perpetuate and reinforce the very problematic behavior of which they complain.

Although rules govern the processes of families from any cultural origin, they differ drastically from one culture to another. In some cultures, for example, major rules governing family processes are similar to the following:

- Do not bring attention to yourself.
- Respect your elders.
- Avoid shaming your family at all costs.
- Bring honor to your family.
- The duty of children is to listen and obey.
- Share what you have with your relatives.
- A wife's duty is to her husband.
- Always defer to authority.

You probably recognize that these rules may differ significantly from typical rules of families in Western society, for Western culture tends to stress competitiveness, assertiveness, and individualism and limits obligations beyond the nuclear family. No doubt, you will recognize some of these rules in your own family. Two of these rules, however, appear to be acting in the Latino Diaz family: (1) Respect your elders and (2) the duty of children is to listen and obey. Mr. Diaz appears to perceive a threat to his autonomy both physically and as head of the family. Reactions to these rules on the part of the various family members contributes to the family dynamics as well as impedes attempts by the practitioner to move the family toward problem consensus and problem solving.

Functional and Dysfunction Rules

With respect to the preceding discussion, it is vital to recognize that the implicit rules or "norms" found in a family system may be either functional or dysfunctional in a cultural or situational context. Rules that may be considered to have consequences for families include the following:

- "Dad can express his needs and wants, but other members of the family can't express theirs unless they are consistent with those of Dad."

- "Be careful what you say around Mom. She might get upset."

- "Self-control is evidence of strength. Don't let people see your weaknesses."

- "Avoid serious discussions of family problems."

- "Don't take responsibility for your own behavior. Always put the blame on someone else."

- "Don't be different from other family members."

- "It is important to win all arguments."

If rules are functional, however, they enable the family to respond flexibly to environmental stress, to individual needs, and to the needs of the family unit. From a Western perspective, functional rules are those that provide the family with opportunities to explore solutions and thus contribute to the development of capable, adaptive, and healthy family members within the family system. In assessing family rules, keep in mind that rules in which there is family consensus and that permit the system to respond to the needs of family members are optimal. Examples of functional rules that are considered to be optimal from a Western point of view may include the following:

- "In this family everyone's ideas and feedback are important."

- "It is acceptable to be different; family members don't always have to agree or like the same things."

- "It is desirable to talk about any feelings—disappointments, fears, hurts, anger, criticisms, joys, or achievements."

- "It is important to work out disagreements with other family members."

- "It is OK to admit mistakes and to apologize; other family members will understand and provide with support."

The extent to which these types of rules apply or vary by race, culture, or class is an important element of the assessment process. As you observe family processes, then, keep in mind that all families have rules that are functional and facilitative as well as rules that are dysfunctional. Identifying both types of rules is critical to making a balanced assessment of family functioning. Remember also that family systems are operated by a relatively small set of rules governing relationships that are influenced by race, class, culture, and status. Your understanding of families' rules and their relevance to the family enhances the assessment of the family system. Inasmuch as families are rule governed, many behaviors or communications you observe will likely be stylized or patterned. Be alert to repetitive sequences of behavior in all areas of family life; behaviors that are crucial to the operations of the family will appear over and over. You thus will have many opportunities to observe stylized behavior that is an integral part of the family's functioning.[3]

In the Diaz family, the medical social worker observed that the rules "Dad has the final say" and "respect your elders" pose difficulties for problem solving. Others in the family may contribute ideas that could be functional rules if those contributions are focused on helpful solutions that support his independence. The role of the social worker in this case may be to establish a climate in which members may express their concerns without blaming and defensive or polarizing positions. For this to occur, the neutrality of the social worker is important.

Perceptions of whether rules are dysfunctional deserve a word of caution. In this particular case situation, the rules observed by Mr. Diaz form the basis on the norms in which parents are to be obeyed or have status. His assertion of his parental status coupled with his capacity to care for himself and John, although in conflict with one of the daughters, may be a cultural factor. Her unwillingness to honor this family rule results in conflict. The basis for this tension may be intergenerational tension between traditional norms and the degree of acculturation of various family members (McAdoo, 1993, p. 11). In this situation, it could be assumed that cultural norms are dysfunctional. Therefore, what may be considered dysfunctional in certain racial or cultural groups should be explored in the context of cultural expectations and origins of the family. Because it is almost impossible to be attentive to all the nuances of race and culture without generalizations, asking the client about the role of culture or race may be the "most direct and accurate information about cultural realities" (Caple, Salcido, & diCeco, 1995, p. 162; McAdoo, 1993).

Violation of Rules

When rules are violated and new behaviors are introduced into its system, a family may employ habitual models of restoring conditions to a previous state of equilibrium, thereby keeping the system "on track." These modes often take the form of negative feedback to members, filled with "shoulds," "oughts," and "don'ts" intended to modify or eliminate behaviors that deviate from the norm. Family members, through anger, depression, silence, guilt induction, or other such forms of behavior, may also counteract irregularities in the system. To help grasp the potency of a system in limiting or eliminating proscribed behaviors, note in the following example the pressure exerted by Mr. Diaz on his stepdaughter to adhere to the rule of "Dad has the final say."

Anita: I have taken Mom's things including the washing machine because they were hers, she bought them. I want things to remember her by, and she said I could have them.

Mr. Diaz: You have no right to come in here and take things that belonged to your mother and me. You show no respect for your stepfather.

Anita: You were often a burden to Mom with your drinking and providing for your insulin. It is clear that you can't take care of John and something has to be done.

Mr. Diaz: You cannot come into this house and take things and decide how things will be done.

Anita: If you don't agree, I can go to court to get custody of John.

In the preceding scene, Anita and Mr. Diaz do not agree on the rule that "Dad has the final say" because Anita does not consider Mr. Diaz to be her father. If the family has a rule that anger may not be expressed overtly (for example, in a physically or verbally aggressive manner), family members may stop speaking and ignore an offending member until the latter offers an apology. If the family's rule is that all members should have a sense of humor about negative things that happen to them, other family members may kid a member who fails to see the irony of his situation until he laughs. Further, if the family abides by the rule "the family comes first and friends and activities second," other family members may make guilt-inducing remarks if a member plans an activity that excludes the family on "family" days (such as "Don't you want to be with us on our day?").

The previous examples of rules may remind you of incidents in your own nuclear or extended family in which your behavior was regulated, reinforced, or extinguished by the behaviors of other members of those systems. As you contemplate your own experiences, perhaps you can begin to appreciate more fully the potent influence of the family in shaping and continuing to influence the lives, behaviors, and problems of clients, even years after they have physically departed from their families of origin.

Flexibility of Rules

The opportunity to influence rules or to develop new rules varies widely from family to family. Optimally, families have rules that permit the system to respond flexibly to change and to evolve new rules compatible with changing needs of family members. On the other hand, rigid rules prevent members from modifying their behavior over time in response to changing circumstances and pressures, thus crystallizing relationships and stereotyping roles.

With respect to flexibility of rules, Becvar and Becvar (2000b) discuss the concepts of morphostasis and morphogenesis. Morphostasis describes a system's tendency toward stability, a state of dynamic equilibrium. Morphogenesis refers to the system-enhancing behavior that allows for growth, creativity, innovation, and change (p. 68). In order for a system to find and maintain balance, it must be able to remain stable in the context of change and change in the context of stability (Becvar and Becvar, 2000b). Optimally, system rules allow for a change when such change is needed to meet individual and family needs. As you assess family systems, then, you must not only identify a family's rules and operations, but also determine the degree of flexibility (or rigidity) of the rules and of the system itself. This may be observed in part by assessing the degree of difficulty a family has in adjusting and maintaining a dynamic state of balance in response to potentially disruptive developments that occur during its life cycle, such as individual maturation, emancipation of adolescents, marriage, birth, aging, and death (as in the case of Ann Mercy).

Strains on families often occur when a first child is born, a grandparent comes to live with the family, an adolescent reaches puberty, the last child is launched, a wife returns to work, or an individual retires. Pressures on families are also caused by ongoing developmental changes of children who press for redefinition of family rules and often pursue interests and values alien to those embraced traditionally by the family. These pressures, write Goldenberg and Goldenberg (1991), cause "disequilibrium within the family system, a sense of loss, and perhaps a feeling of strangeness until new transactional patterns restore family balance" (p. 40). In addition to assessing the stresses on rules caused by developmental changes and internal events (inner forces), you must also assess the extent to which a family's rules allow the system to respond flexibly to dynamic societal stresses (outer forces), such as those that may occur with the loss of a job, concerns about neighborhood safety, relocation of the family, the occurrence of a natural disaster that affects the family, or the uprooting of the family experienced by immigrants or refugees. Adding to the complexity of these dynamics are stresses incurred by new immigrant families, who must also face vast contrasts between themselves and the Western culture. The process of immigration and cultural transition requires a large number of life changes over a short period of time, including material, economic, educational, and role changes, and the loss of extended family, familiar environments, and support systems (Green, 1999; Hirayama, Hirayama & Cetingok, 1993).

Responding successfully to inner and outer stresses requires constant transformation of the rules and behaviors of family members to accommodate to necessary changes while maintaining family continuity. Families often seek help because of an accumulation of events that have strained the coping ability of the entire family or of individual members. The family is a vulnerable system that may break down under accumulated stress that may occur as a result of life-change patterns or transitions. Ironically, even when the changes are for the better they may, if significant, overwhelm the coping mechanisms of individual members or an entire family system.

It appears that most families have some maladaptive behaviors and rules that do not allow the system to respond readily to dynamic inner and outer forces. The normal family in our society thus probably has some maladaptive features, and the optimally functioning family may actually be an atypical phenomenon. The Diaz family may fall in the midrange of this continuum, because they have both rigid and more flexible rules. The rule that "Dad has the final say" is a rigid rule with his biological children. However, the rule that "Taking care of family members is a primary obligation" is functional in the sense that it has meant that both Maria and John, two of his biological children, wish to assist him to continue independently in a manner safe for his health and well-being. Maria offers to help him find a first-floor apartment near her and to learn, with John, how to administer his insulin.

Content and Process Levels of Interaction

To make adequate family assessments and to identify important rules and behaviors, it is also vital to grasp the concepts of content and process levels of interaction. Pretend for a moment that the following brief scenario occurs in your office in a family agency as you conduct an initial interview with Mr. and Mrs. Barkley. In response to your inquiry as to the problems they are experiencing, Mr. B glances at his wife and then indicates that she has been depressed and "sick" for some time, and they have come to the agency seeking help for "her" problem. As you look at Mrs. B, she nods her assent. You are concerned at this moment with what the couple is saying to you (the content of the discussion); however, you are also keenly interested in assessing the underlying intent or meaning of messages and in observing the manner in which the spouses are relating or behaving as they talk about their problems. In other words, you are also observant of the process that occurs as the couple discusses content. You therefore make a mental note of the fact that the husband served as spokesman for his wife (with her tacit approval) and that the problem as defined by both spouses resides with the wife. Both spouses thus disregarded any impact of the problem on the husband, any possible part he might play in reinforcing or exacerbating the wife's depression or other problematic behavior, or any problems the

husband might be experiencing. Essentially, with respect to roles, the couple has presented the wife as the "problem person," and the husband as the social worker's "consultant." Several important interactional behaviors thus occurred at the process level in the opening gambits of the session, revealing information about the manner in which the spouses define their problem and how they relate, and pointing to promising avenues for exploration in assessing their problems.

Families' rules are often revealed at the process level—a level often ignored by beginning social workers as they selectively attend to what clients are "saying." Learning to sharpen one's observational skills to attend to what people are doing as they discuss problems is crucial to assessing and intervening effectively in family systems. Otherwise, the social worker can easily get caught up at the content level and, for example, continue to explore the etiology of Mrs. B's "depression" (with the husband as information-giver and Mrs. B as the passive identified patient) while ignoring stylized behaviors of the couple that play a vital part in their problems.

Family relationships form reciprocal repetitive patterns and have circular rather than linear motion. Carter and McGoldrick (199b) caution social workers against cause-and-effect thinking, which asks why and looks for someone to blame. Instead they suggest that "identifying patterns and tracing their flow" are useful, because family patterns "once established, are perpetuated by everyone involved in them, although not all have equal power or influence" (p. 437).

Sequences of Interaction

In order to assess family rules adequately, social workers must also pay attention to sequences of interaction that occur between members. All families play out scenarios or a series of transactions in which they manifest redundancies in behavior and communication. Analysis of interactional sequences may reveal functional or dysfunctional coping patterns utilized by members or by the entire family system. In troubled families, however, the scenarios are often destructive, serving to reinforce maladaptive behavior and dysfunctional rules. Observation of these destructive interactional sequences yields rich information concerning communication styles and dysfunctional behavior of individuals and the manner in which all family members reinforce dysfunctional interactions.

The following excerpt is taken from the first minutes of a first session with the Diaz family. This example, with Mr. Diaz, daughter Maria, son John, and stepdaughter Anita, illustrates habituated sequential behaviors that have a powerful impact on the system. The medical social worker, as described, has convened the family to consider health and safety alternatives for Mr. Diaz.

Anita [*to social worker*]: Carlos can't maintain himself or John. John runs wild, with no appropriate adult supervision, and Carlos can't take care of himself now that Mother has died. [*Anita looks earnestly at the social worker while Mr. Diaz sits stolidly, arms folded, glowering straight ahead.*]

Maria [*to social worker*]: Dad is having trouble with John and hasn't taken care of himself all these years with Ann Mercy doing the cooking and cleaning and injecting his insulin. [*To Mr. Diaz:*] Dad, I respect you and want to help you in any way, but things just can't continue like they are.

Mr. Diaz [*to social worker*]: These children "no tienen respeto," they don't give me the respect they should give the father of this family. They want to put me in a nursing home and take John away from me.

Anita: Maybe that would be for the best, since you can't take care of yourself or John.

Maria [*to social worker*]: Dad is used to having his own way and we do respect him, at least I do, but he won't listen to how some things have to change.

Mr. Diaz: Maria, you have been a good daughter, and I am surprised at your behavior. I would think that you would stick by your father if anyone would.

John: Dad, you know I stick by you. And I can help with some things too. I want to stay with you. We have been getting along OK and I want to be a good son and take care of you.

Anita: John, you have been running the streets, in trouble with the law, taking money from your father. You are no help to him, and he can't be a good parent to you.

Maria: John, I know you want to help, and you are close to your dad. But you have made a lot of problems for him and I too wonder if you can take care of him or he of you.

In this example, the family plays out discordant thematic interaction that, with slight variation, can be observed over and over in the family's transactions.[4] It is as though the family is involved in a screenplay, and once the curtain is raised, all members participate in the scenario according to the family script. It is important to understand that the family script has no beginning or end; that is, anyone may initiate the scenario by enacting his or her "lines." The rest of the members almost invariably follow their habituated styles of relating, editing their individual scripts slightly to fit different versions of the scene being acted out by the family. In the scenes, the subjects discussed will vary, but the roles taken by individual members and the dysfunctional styles of communicating and behaving that perpetuate the scenario fluctuate very little.

In the preceding scenarios, notice the sequencing of the transactions that took place:

- Anita speaks forthrightly about her concerns about John and Mr. Diaz's capacity for parenting him because of his medical condition. Responding nonverbally (folding his arms and glowering straight ahead), Mr. Diaz declines to participate openly.

- Maria affirms some of Anita's concerns but also speaks directly to her father, affirming her respect for him as father and head of the family.

- Mr. Diaz asserts that his children "*no tienen respeto*" and that their motivation is to put him away.

- Anita does not deny that a nursing home might be the best solution.

- Maria reasserts her respect for her father, yet notes that some things will have to change.

- Mr. Diaz addresses Maria and questions whether she is in fact showing proper respect for him as her father.

- John joins the fray and tries to identify himself as a good son with *respeto*, which adds another dimension to the transactions.

- Anita puts John in his place by doubting whether he has acted as a good son or whether Mr. Diaz can be a good parent to him.

- Maria supports John's desire to be a good son but agrees that there are problems with Mr. Diaz and his care of John that remain.

In observing this and other similar scenarios of the Diaz family, the social worker may identify patterned behaviors and "rules" governing family interaction that may not be apparent when observing single transactions. For example:

1. Anita, perhaps because she is a stepdaughter, does not acknowledge the family rule of *respeto* and challenges Mr. Diaz's wishes and capabilities.

2. Maria does acknowledge Mr. Diaz's place in the family and tries to show appropriate respect while acknowledging that problems do exist.

3. John attempts to present a strong coalition with Mr. Diaz by identifying his wishes to maintain the current situation.

4. Mr. Diaz addresses the social worker and Maria, ignoring Anita, who has violated a family rule.

5. Anita and Mr. Diaz invariably disagree.

6. Maria attempts to mediate, affirming Mr. Diaz's position and the rule, while acknowledging problems.

Sifting out the habituated interactional responses in family processes enables the social worker to focus interventions strategically on the family's limited number of destructive processes. By analyzing the rules and patterns involved in the interaction, the social worker has many entry points for intervening in the family processes to assist the family incoming to a decision. Despite the agreement between the stepsisters (Maria and Anita) that Mr. Diaz cannot continue to live his life as he has and that change is required, Mr. Diaz's role is not altogether clear at this point. Mr. Diaz and John appear to be allied as the two males in the family, protective of one another. It is important to recognize that there are many family situations such as the Diaz family in which family rules and patterns are significant; however, the function of the agency is not family treatment nor is this the client's request. Nonetheless, family rules and patterns are playing a part in the problem and its potential resolution.

Employing "Circular" Explanations of Behavior

In our previous discussion, we viewed the behavior of the Diaz family from a systems framework, establishing the repetitive nature of interactional behavior and the reciprocal influence of all actors on the behaviors of other family members. In so doing, we applied a circular concept of causality to the Diaz family, demonstrating that each member's behavior becomes a stimulus to all other involved members of the system. Further, interactions with the environment including the neighborhood and the availability of a continuum of services, play a part in the maintenance of problems. This may be contrasted to a linear explanation of the causes of behavior in which A event causes B event; B event causes C, and so forth. To illustrate the difference between these two conceptual frameworks for viewing the causality of behavior, we turn once again to the Diaz family. Employing a linear explanation of behavior, one would say, "When Anita attacks Mr. Diaz, he defends himself." A circular explanation of behavior would involve the following: "When Anita attacks Mr. Diaz, he defends himself, and Maria acts to mediate, both supporting Mr. Diaz and Anita. The mediation is not accepted and the charges and countercharges between Anita and Mr. Diaz continue with John attempting to ally with his father. Also, consider the extent that the problem is influenced or maintained by a lack of resources to resolve the difficulties. Further assessment in this case could include a focus on potential resources and family strengths that may allow Mr. Diaz to remain in his home and care for John (Cowger, 1994).

Nichols and Schwartz (1998) underscore that circular and linear concepts of causality reflect contrasting approaches employed by social workers in assessing and intervening in family processes. The circular explanation is systemic and is utilized by systems-oriented social workers, not only because it offers a more adequate description of behavior but also because it offers more alternatives for intervention. In the preceding example, for instance, a social worker who operated from a linear orientation might intervene to stop Anita from attacking Mr. Diaz, whereas a social worker who employed a circular explanation of the causes of behavior might target the entire circular pattern for intervention. Further, as a social worker sensitive to the role of the external factors (for example, the level of insurance coverage), you would also assist family members in examining environmental constraints and solutions.

Tomm (1981), emphasizing that a preference for circularity influences the social worker's interviewing style in the assessment (and intervention) process, notes that three types of differences may be usefully explored in family assessment. These include differences between individuals (e.g., "Who gets angry the most?"), differences between relationships (e.g., "What is the difference between the way Mr. Diaz treats Anita compared with how he treats Maria?"), and differences between time periods (e.g., "How did she get along with Mr. Diaz last year as compared with now?"). By orienting the assessment to solicit information regarding differences, Tomm points out, the social worker elicits more relevant data and does so

more efficiently than would occur by obtaining linear descriptions.

Beginning social workers tend to employ linear rather than circular perspectives when explaining behavior and view interactional processes as "action-reaction" cycles, often assigning responsibility or blame for problems to one or more members whose problematic behavior is conspicuous. When not attuned to the repetitive nature of dysfunctional interactions, however, social workers sharply reduce their ability to help family members, who often need the help of an expert in removing themselves from destructive interactional patterns. They also often ignore the role of the larger environment in maintaining and resolving problems.

Not unlike beginning social workers, family members also tend to explain behavior using a linear orientation, often assigning arbitrary beginnings and endings to sequences of interaction in ways that define other members as villains and themselves as victims. Mr. Diaz, for instance, viewed himself as an innocent victim of Anita's disrespectful behavior and defined her as the person in the family who needed to change. In this situation, it is useful for the social worker to counteract the linear perspective of one person as the initiator, the other as the reactor, by explaining systems concepts about the responsibility of all family members, emotional interactions, reciprocity, and the role of all family members in maintaining dysfunctional interactions and problem solving. The goal is to create a climate in which thoughtful rather than reactive responses becomes the norm.

Assessing Problems Employing a Systems Framework

The utilization of a systems view of family problems has implications for gathering relevant data in the assessment process. Many clients, even those designated as troubled by other family members, see themselves as victims of the actions of significant others or of external forces over which they have no control. Most often they initially seek help prepared to "complain" about those who are "causing" their problems, rather than to engage in efforts to change themselves. Because of their selective perception of the "causes" of events, they often do not offer information that assists social workers to formulate a clear picture of how these problems may be reinforced and exacerbated either by the client or by significant others in the family system. It is important that social workers have an appropriate conceptual framework and accompanying skills to identify themes within the family's processes and to elicit relevant data about the family system. Otherwise, social workers may unwittingly adopt clients' definitions of "who has the problem," focus interventions on changing the behavior of these selected persons, and neglect the influence of other significant family members upon the problems in the systems.

It should be noted that although systemic patterns that restrict and mold clients' behavior are woven throughout the fabric of many client problems, social workers often do not have the opportunity of observing these firsthand. Family members, for instance, may refuse service or be unavailable because of geographical location. In this case, a family member who lived at a distance (Anita) was available briefly. It was unclear whether she would be involved with the family beyond this session as a participant in problem solving. At other times, it may not be expedient to involve key actors who play significant roles in the problems of clients. It is vital to remember when clients describe problems, however, that they often talk extensively about difficulties they are experiencing in relationships with family members or with significant others who are not present. Thus, when you cannot directly observe interactional processes, you have the important task of eliciting highly specific information from clients that will aid you in assessing the interpersonal patterns and rules of the family system. This is best accomplished by carefully exploring a number of critical incidents that illustrate problematic behav-

iors manifested in the family system. In order to identify underlying family patterns, you must elicit descriptive information about the behaviors and communications of all involved actors and establish the sequencing of discrete transactions and events that occurred before, during, and after the identified incident. Inasmuch as clients tend to summarize critical incidents, thereby omitting critical details, it is helpful to explain to them that you are searching for family styles of relating and to underscore the importance of carefully identifying each discrete event or transaction that occurred in any critical incident targeted for exploration.

We recommend that you request clients to give a descriptive account of an event so that you see what happened as clearly as if you had been present. Even when clients define their problems as involving some members of a family and not others, it is critical to explore family relationships to the extent that you can identify key interaction patterns and the nature of alignments among various subsystems of the family. In such explorations, it is not uncommon to discover that other persons besides parents (e.g., sibling, stepfather, grandparents) play significant roles in contributing to the problem behaviors of a child brought to an agency. Based on information gained in exploring family affiliative ties and rules, you will often need to "redefine" and expand the problem system to include more actors than originally identified by clients.

In assisting clients to understand the need for an overall assessment of family relationships when they initially believe that only one or two members are involved in problems, it is helpful to explain that the family is a "system" and to stress that the entire family is affected by, and may even exacerbate, problems experienced by one member. Further, you should stress that the causes of problems usually reside largely in interactions that involve various members of the family rather than with individual family members. As underscored by Nichols and Schwartz (1998), "there may sometimes be parts of family members that fear change, but the parts of them that want relief often can be activated without having to confront the fearful parts" (p. 466). In other words, as Wile (1978) emphasized, "family members are as likely to be relived and grateful as they are to be threatened and resistant when a problem they had attributed to the 'identified patient' is redefined as a general family problem" (p. 16). Both Nichols and Schwartz and Wile stress, however, that this approach holds only to the extent that the social worker's approach is nonaccusatory and that the social worker clarifies for the whole family how all involved members are caught in difficult conflicts or dilemmas related to the problematic family situation.

DIMENSIONS OF FAMILY ASSESSMENT

In explicating integral concepts of a systems framework for viewing family functioning in our earlier discussion, we have set the stage for family assessment. In this section, we present dimensions of assessment that represent guidelines for exploring and organizing the massive data you will gather in working with family systems. These dimensions will also assist you in bringing patterned interaction into bold relief and will prepare you to evaluate functional and dysfunctional aspects of family operations, a critical preliminary step to planning interventions to assist a family in problem solving.

The following list contains the dimensions that we consider at length in the chapter.

1. Family context
2. Family strengths
3. Boundaries and boundary maintenance
4. Family power structure
5. Family decision-making process
6. Family goals
7. Family myths and cognitive patterns
8. Family roles

9. Communication styles of family members
10. Family life cycle

In employing these dimensions to formulate assessments and plan interventions, we recommend you utilize the following format:

1. *Identify the dimensions that are most relevant to your clients.* Although the dimensions apply to the processes of all couples and families, some may not be pertinent when viewed in the perspective of the presenting complaint and the nature of the help requested by the family. For example, a family may seek help because of stress caused by the advanced senility of an aged relative living in the home. Initial exploration may reveal no major deficits in functioning (e.g., ineffective style of decision making) that are contributing to the family's problem. Thus, the social worker would narrow the assessment to an exploration of factors that contribute to the specific problem identified by the family.

2. *Utilize the dimensions to guide your exploration of family behavior.* After the first session, review the dimensions and develop relevant questions to further your exploration in subsequent sessions.

3. *Utilize the dimensions as guidelines for compressing new data into themes and patterns.* Determine the family's or couple's rules or habitual ways of relating in relation to *each* relevant dimensions. For example, ask yourself what the family's rules are in relation to decision making, communicating, and the other dimensions. Refer to appropriate discussions in the book for guidelines that will help you pinpoint specific rules.

4. *Based on the relevant dimensions, develop a written profile of functional and dysfunctional behaviors of individual members of the system.* For example, with respect to the dimension of communication, a family member may often paraphrase messages of others and personalize statements (functional behaviors). The same family member may be prone to interrupt and to talk excessively, thus monopolizing the session at times

(dysfunctional behaviors). Developing a profile of these two types of behavior for each family member will serve as a conceptual framework not only for assessing behaviors but for planning interventions as well.

5. *Employ the dimensions to assess relevant behaviors of the entire family, developing a profile of salient functional and dysfunctional behaviors that are manifested by the system itself.* Again, utilizing the dimension of communication, functional behaviors of a family may include occasional listening responses and responses that acknowledge the contributions of others (e.g., "You did a good job"). In contrast, dysfunctional responses manifested by the same family may include labeling of members (e.g., "You're dumb") and frequent expressions of anger directed toward others.

Family Context

Factors involved in assessing family context include culture, race, family form, sexual orientation, basic resources, and the experience of oppression and discrimination. Recall also the discussion on family stressors in an earlier section of this chapter. The extent to which each of these factors influences family functioning or impinges on the family system is an essential part of the assessment process. Families learn to live in a context, often coping with situations that over time may lead to disruptions within the family system that diminish family well-being.

An assessment dimension of family context involves the extent to which the family has access to basic resources, such as food, health care, housing, financial aid, or job training, and their ability to secure such resources (Kilpatrick & Holland, 1999; Vosler, 1990). Assisting families to meet their survival needs must often take precedence, in fact, over interventions to change family dynamics or to teach communication or parenting skills (Kilpatrick & Holland, 1999). Such interventions are simply not relevant to families who are in dire need of basic sustenance.

Paramount to gathering data and assessing families is the task of accurately viewing the family within the context of its cultural milieu, sexual orientation, and family form. The social worker's challenge in even deciding who make sup the family is illustrated by McPhatter (1991), who observed that in exploring the structure of a family, the worker should not make assumptions about family composition and type based on traditional definitions of family. Family form has changed from the postwar 1950 ideal of the two-parent, one–wage earner unit. While this image projected the ideal, it is important to note that in a majority of poor and minority families, women almost always worked outside of the home.

In the latter part of the 20th century, as discussed in the beginning section of this chapter, evolving family constellations include single-parent households, same-sex parents, informal kin networks, ancestors and descendants, extended family members, and families formed through friendship or community who are committed to each other. The fact that the definition of "family" differs greatly from culture to culture adds even more complexity to the social worker's assessment task. Although the dominant American definition focuses on the intact nuclear family, for Italians there is no such thing as the "nuclear" family, observes McGoldrick (1982a). "To them family means a strong tightly knit three-or four-generational family, which also includes godparents and old friends. The Chinese go beyond this and include in their definition of family all their ancestors and all their descendants" (p. 10).

Though the contexts of families differ dramatically, external systems of the dominant culture have considerable influence on family functioning. Carter and McGoldrick (1999b) note, for example, that gay and lesbian couples experience harassment, violence, and the denial of "key legal protections and entitlements" (p. 352). This lack of protection, along with the lack of roles and language for gay or lesbian families, are not only stressors; these families also are "vulnerable to intrusion and invalidation" (Slater, 1995).[5]

Minorities who are gay or lesbian face additional difficulties of racial discrimination and may have fewer resources as a result of the stigma of their sexual orientation in their communities. Moreover, there is limited social support for gay and lesbian youth and in many instances these young people experience family as well as social isolation (Morrow, 1993).

Despite the differences in how family is defined, it is commonplace for practitioners to commence, maintain, and terminate treatment without having the slightest appreciation, knowledge, or respect for the larger contextual issues (e.g., race, culture, gender, sexual orientation) that subsequently impact treatment. This practice is often the result of agency goals that focus on individual and internal family concerns. This oversight often results in . . . a 'neglect of context' that is replete throughout the field of family therapy" (Hardy, 1989, pp. 17–18). The consequence to families is that practitioners "may filter out their inner resources, values, intelligence, spirituality, and wisdom; and most importantly, [they] may underestimate the influence of the social settings in which they live" (Saba, Karrer, & Hardy, 1989, p. 2).

It is vital, then, that social workers have a working knowledge of the family in its own reality. This includes culture, biculturalism, ethnic status, language, social class, customs, history, and sexual orientation as these factors affect families and the problems they experience. In engaging families to filter out the extent to which these factors are important, you can employ what Norton (1978) and McPhatter (1991) call a "dual perspective." This perspective involves "the conscious and systematic process of perceiving, understanding and comparing simultaneously the values, attitudes of the larger societal system with those of the client's immediate family and community system," a vital aspect in assessing the social context of a family's presenting problems (McPhatter, 1991, pp. 14–15).

Kilpatrick and Holland (1999), in the context of ethnic or diverse families, suggest that the "dual perspective fosters problem resolution in tune with distinct values and community customs" (pp. 40–41). Further, they suggest that this perspective recognizes that families are members of two systems, one of which "is dominant or sustaining and the other, the nurturing system. Attention to the influence of both systems is important" (pp. 40–41).

Utilizing the "dual perspective" helps to identify the points of conflict between the family and larger systems. This can be seen, for example, in the assessment of same-sex couples. Such couples live in the context of "homophobia" in the larger culture, "defined operationally as the fear and hatred of same-sex intimacy, love, sexuality, and relationships, and of those individuals and institutions that participate in, affirm, and support same sex relating." As a consequence, these couples risk jobs, freedom, custody of children, and homes if identified in the larger culture (Dahlheimer & Feigal, 1991; Slater, 1995).

A "dual perspective" is an absolute must in assessing the rich variety of family cultures, for family behavior makes sense "only in the larger cultural context in which it is embedded" (McGoldrick, 1982a, p. 4). Such a perspective also aids social workers to avoid relying on broad generalizations about particular groups or considering behavior patterns or lifestyles as indicators of dysfunction (Green, 1999; McAdoo, 1993). They must also avoid being "triggered" by ethnic characteristics they may have regarded negatively or caught in an ethnocentric view that their group values are more "right" or "true" than others (McGoldrick, 1982a, p. 25). Utilizing a dual perspective, social workers can view the functionality of a family's behavior within the context of what is "normal" for that particular family's culture, for what is dysfunctional in one culture may not be in another.

Numerous authors have offered cautions against social workers imposing their own cultural perceptions on the families they serve. Such errors may cause social workers to intervene in ways that are actually disruptive to the family system. Terms such as *enmeshment, fusion,* and *undifferentiated ego mass* may be inappropriate when describing the interdependence observed in some families (Berg & Jaya, 1993; Bernal & Flores-Ortiz, 1982; Boyd-Franklin, 1989b; Flores & Carey, 2000). Similarly, although women have a shared history of discrimination, gender when combined with race or ethnicity may not be assumed to be the most important factor for women of color because their lives are also shaped by other realities of oppression (Boyd-Franklin & Garcia-Preto, 1995; Brown, 1990).

Limited definitions of family or personal bias present difficulties for social workers working with gay or lesbian families without an understanding that family means caring, committed, and intimate relationships over time (Dahlheimer & Feigal, 1991). Effects of poverty, discrimination, culture, and "remembered history" have shaped Native American "attitudes toward child welfare, social workers and other professionals." In many Native American families, the extended family structure has been important to economic, social, and spiritual survival. Not understanding the practice of, for example, consulting about important decisions with the family and reliance on family input for a course of action can cause further alienation between the social worker and the family (Horesji, Hevy Runner, & Pablo 1991). In not understanding cultural factors, social workers can punish families for acting normally (Red Horse, Lewis, Feit, & Decker, 1978).

Because of perceptions of mental illness and the negative connotation for self and the family, Southeast Asian families may respond to assistance that focuses on the cognitive rather than the emotional aspects of family difficulties (Hirayama et al., 1994). Finally, the principle of self-determination may have a different meaning for some cultural or ethnic groups. In exploring self-determination as a concept, Ewalt and Mokou (1995) suggest that the term may have greater meaning for interests and obligation to entire groups rather than in the traditional sense of individualism commonly observed in dominant Western culture.

It is not possible for social workers to understand the cultural nuances and their implications in every diverse family. Ironically, applying acquired knowledge of various groups may lead to the danger of stereotyping. As a practitioner you may feel caught between wanting to be sensitive, yet experiencing resentment when you are lectured to about the importance of understanding racial and cultural differences. At the risk of adding to this tension, we feel that it is important to discuss aspects of culture and race that are important considerations in the assessment and overall helping process.

It is important for social workers to recognize that members of various groups, in particular minority group members, may differ considerably from profiles or descriptions of typical behaviors. Within groups designated as racial or ethnic minorities there are vast differences in race, language, and culture (Green, 1999). Spanish-speaking people, for example, share some aspects of Hispanic or Latino heritage and similar language, but they nonetheless belong to diverse cultures, social class, and nationalities and vary in many respects. McAdoo (1993), Hirayama et al. (1994), and Cople, Salcido, and di Cecco (1995) are among the writers who inform us that formative values of a minority group are not necessarily embraced by all group members. Accordingly, differences may also be observed along intergenerational lines (as in the case of family rules in the Diaz family) and the evolving degree of acculturation. Children may adapt to new cultures at a much more rapid pace than their parents because of their exposure to the dominant culture through school, and perhaps because they have fewer years of experience with the culture of origin (Cople et al., 1995; Hirayama et al., 1994). Furthermore, because the values of cultural groups are not fixed but are always evolving and depending on the acculturation process, there may be variations within families. McAdoo (1993) suggests using acquired knowledge in formulating a hypothesis and exploring the extent to which this information is relevant in a particular situation. The implications of these observations are critical to social workers, for each family system is unique, and social workers must be able to individualize each family within its cultural context.

As social workers assess the processes of families from various cultural groups, they must also be aware of the extent to which a family may struggle with efforts to maintain values and norms of their country of origin while adapting selectively to aspects of American society. All ethnic minority groups in the United States who have migrated or come as refugees face issues related to acculturation. The problems immigrants or refugees face in acculturating to mainstream society are extreme and plainly visible to social workers. However, as McGoldrick, Giordano, and Pearce (1996) observe, family values and identity may be retained for several generations after the migration experience and continue to influence the family's outlook, life cycle, and development.

In assessing the functioning of families of immigrants, social workers must gain information concerning the family's migration and look for the continuing stresses on the family of accommodating to two (and sometimes more) cultures. The amount of disruption to immigrants or refugee families from Southeast Asia or Africa or from other regions who have been uprooted from their homelands and have suffered losses in all aspects of their lives is particularly extreme. Immigrants from some countries will have better educations and financial situations. The experience, however, causes family disruption as these families face the related tasks of finding work, clothing, and shelter and learning a new language. This often preempts the completion of family developmental tasks, and "requires the reconstruction of social networks," including families, friends, and community (Kilpatrick and Holland, 1999, pp. 170–172). Social workers can help by exploring the family's relative effectiveness in coping with its situation and rejuvenating its connectedness or roots with its historical and cultural reference group (Congress, 1994).

G. D. Rooney (1997) emphasizes the dilemma that immigrant families may face in a society that can be both welcoming and hostile. As the work-force becomes more diverse, workplace policies, seldom responsive to family concerns, often become additional stressors for diverse families and their ability to fulfill traditional role obligations. Pressure to conform may distract or delay finding employment, resulting in stress in the family system. Language is another source of conflict for families, as reflected in societal indifference to bilingualism and antipluralistic public policy. In the latter part of the last decade, several states passed legislation that made English the official language. In addition, society expects immigrants to act, speak, and dress like the majority population. Tensions exist in the interactions between majority and immigrant groups, and between racial minority and immigrant groups as well (p. 316).

In working with families who are ethnically or racially diverse, Green (1999) suggests that a basic dimension of cultural competence is identifying what is salient about a client's culture and honestly addressing this factor (p. 37). Green presents a case situation by R. H. Rooney and Bibus (1996) as an example concerning a Native American family (p. 43). Lum (1996) and Chau (1990) have developed practice assessment dimensions in which psychosocial and socioenvironmental factors impact clients (for example, oppression and powerlessness). Lum (1996) also includes the spiritual dimension as important (p. 223). These dimensions may be integrated into helping social workers become ethnically sensitive throughout the helping process. In working with diverse families, social workers are reminded to consider the influence of race, ethnicity, gender, and sexual orientation in the problems that a family may experience.

The essence of systems thinking consists of seeing patterns. Over time, practice with families has encouraged using a systems approach and defining the family in a broader context. In presenting this view, we agree with others who have urged consideration of both internal and external forces that impact the family system, shape family dynamics, and affect the relationship with the larger social environment. External issues such as racism, classism, poverty, work pressures, and homophobia may be referred to as "extrafamilial obstacles" (Nichols & Schwartz, 1998, p. 135). Although all families experience obstacles in their transactions with the other social systems, obstacles may disproportionately affect diverse families, add stressors, and affect the resources available to them. We hope that our discussion of these issues has given you a better understanding of the role played by external factors in the experiences of families and their relevance in the assessment process.

Family Strengths

Almost all families, even those that function marginally, have a range of individual and group strengths that you should identify during the assessment process. However, because of the deeply entrenched focus on pathology in the helping professions, social workers sometimes must revise their perceptual sets in order to discern family strengths that are not evident at first glance. Highlighting what is going right and what is working in troubled families is difficult because members of these families usually dwell on problems and troubles. Thus, in assessments that involve families or couples, observing and accrediting the strengths inherent in the system requires deliberate and disciplined effort on your part.

In assessment, you also need to pay particular attention to the strengths of families from various cultural groups. Many of these groups have suffered discrimination or, as political refugees, have suffered extreme losses, including the loss of identity along with homeland, reference and support groups, and social and vocational roles. Often demoralized by discrimination, crippled by family disruption, and handicapped by difficulties with language, lack of education or job skills, and lack of resources or knowledge of how to obtain them, many minority families feel powerless to cope with overwhelming circumstances. Yet these families have many strengths, and it is vital that social workers identify strengths and use them in the

treatment process to empower families to accomplish desired changes. Assessment questions that explore family strengths and resources focus on family traditions, patterns of help-seeking behavior, individuals or institutions that the family may utilize in times of difficulty, as well as family hopes, dreams, or aspirations. Although the questions are useful with all families, they may have particular relevance to minority groups as a means to identify and observe strengths.

Boundaries and Boundary Maintenance of Family Systems

Boundaries, a central concept in family systems theories, utilize abstract dividers between and among other systems or subsystems within the family or between the family and the environment. These boundaries may change over time as the system experiences various developmental levels. In adapting Bertalanffy's general systems theory, Martin and O'Connor (1989) conclude that all systems are open and interdependent with their environment. The extent to which a system permits or screens inputs in the form of information, people, or events is a function of boundary maintenance.

As open systems that are part of still larger systems, families necessarily have diverse transactions with the environment. Families differ widely, however, in the degree to which they are open to transactions with other systems and in the flexibility of their boundaries. By flexibility, we mean the extent to which outsiders are permitted or invited to enter the family system, members of the family are allowed to invest emotionally and to engage in relationships outside the family, and information and materials are exchanged with the environment. Those who hold authority in families perform the bounding functions in such a way that they create discrete family space that exists apart from the larger space of the neighborhood and community.

The family system with thick boundaries thus is characterized by strict regulation that limits transactions with the external environment and restricts incoming and outgoing people, objects, information, and ideas. Typical features are locked doors, tight parental control over input from the media, supervised excursions, close scrutiny of strangers, trespass prohibitions, high fences, and unlisted telephones. Tight boundaries serve the function of preserving territoriality, protecting the family from undesired intrusions, safeguarding privacy, and even fostering secretiveness. Authorities in the family maintain tight control of traffic at the family's perimeter, and the bounding function is never relinquished or shared with outsiders or even with family members who have not been assigned the role of performing bounding functions.

In families where the bounding movements are flexible, family territory extends into the larger community spaces and external culture comes into the family space. Individuals are permitted the freedom to regulate their own incoming and outgoing traffic to the extent that they do not adversely affect other family members or violate the family norms. Features of this family system include having guests in the home, visiting with friends, participating in external activities, belonging to outside groups, participating in community affairs, and permitting free information exchange with minimal censorship of the media. Examining system boundaries and the boundary maintenance of families helps us to assess the extent to which the family is an included system, specifically its connection to other kin, the community, and other groups. All family systems selectively respond, accepting or rejecting external influences. Boundary maintenance functions to maintain equilibrium in the family system and may take the form of rules that limit the interaction of family members.

In assessing the bounding patterns of families, consideration of the family's unique style, strengths, and needs are important. Families may have more flexible boundaries with extended family members that may include well-defined obligations and responsibilities to each other. They may on the other hand appear less flexible when it appears that external influences may intrude upon family traditions and values, become a source of conflict or disruption to the family system. Still, at other times the family can change to accommodate new inputs over the course of the life cycle. Immigrant families are often open to new information as they transition into a new society. On the other hand, they may erect boundaries in an effort to screen out what they deem as undesirable aspects of the new culture.

Knowledge of the boundary and boundary maintenance function of family structure and processes as discussed in the preceding sections should assist you in identifying the bounding patterns of families you encounter in practice. Bear in mind that these are only prototypes and that the actual bounding patterns of families may include aspects of all these types of structures. No living system is every truly closed. It is vital, therefore, to assess each family's unique style of transacting with the environment. Optimally, family system boundary maintenance should not be too permeable or too rigid.

Internal Boundaries and Family Subsystems

Assessing the bounding patterns in stepfamilies may prove particularly difficult, as frequently there is lack of agreement between stepfamily members as to who is in the household. "As a result, there is boundary ambiguity in many parts of the stepfamily—between households and between parenting adults, as well as within households where intergenerational boundaries may be problematic and personal space a complicated matter" (Visher & Visher, 1988, p. 203). We found this to be the case in the Diaz family earlier, as there was not agreement about the stepdaughter Anita's role in the ongoing decisions of the family about her brother John and stepfather.

Use of family genograms, in which the social worker pictorially diagrams a family's history and constellation over several generations, can provide important data on bounding patterns when working with any type of family (Kilpatrick & Holland, 1999). Visher and Visher (1988) particularly recommend the use of a genogram in work with stepfamilies, as it provides information about previous marriages, the length of the single-parent household phases, and details about the shifts in the living arrangements of the children. It also "gives a picture of where family members have been and the direction in which they need to go" (p. 32).

All families develop networks of coexisting subsystems formed on the basis of gender, interest, generation, or functions that must be performed for the family's survival (Minuchin, 1974).[6] Members of a family may simultaneously belong to a number of subsystems, entering into separate and reciprocal relationships with other members of the nuclear family, depending on the subsystems they share in common (e.g., husband/wife, mother/daughter, brother/sister, father/son) or with the extended family (e.g., grandmother/ granddaughter, uncle/nephew, mother/son-in-law). Each subsystem can be thought of as a natural coalition between participating members. Many of the coalitions or alliances that families form are situation related and temporary in nature. A teenager may be able to enlist her mother's support in asking her father's permission for a special privilege or for new clothing. A grandmother living in a home may voice disagreement with her daughter and son-in-law regarding a particular decision involving one of their children, thus temporarily forming a coalition with the affected child. Such passing alliances are characteristic of temporary subsystems (Goldenberg & Goldenberg, 1991). We noticed this in the situational alliance of the Diaz stepsisters.

Other subsystems, particularly the spouse, parental, and sibling subsystems, are more enduring in nature. According to Minuchin (1974), the formation of stable, well-defined coalitions between members of these vital subsystems is, in fact, critical to the well-being and health of the family. Unless there is a strong and enduring coalition between husband and wife, for instance, conflict reverberates throughout a family, and children are often co-opted into one faction or

another as parents struggle for power and control. For optimal family functioning, according to Minuchin, the boundaries of these three subsystems must be clear and defined well enough to allow members sufficient differentiation to carry out functions without undue interference but permeable enough to allow contact and exchange of resources between members of the subsystem. Minuchin, in fact, points out that the clarity of the subsystem boundaries is of far more significance in determining family functioning than the composition of the family's subsystem. A parental subsystem that includes a grandmother or a parental child may for instance function quite adequately, if the roles and the lines of responsibility are clearly defined.

The relative integrity of the boundaries of the spouse, parental, and sibling subsystems is determined by related rules of the family. A mother clearly defines the boundary of a parental subsystem, for instance, in telling her oldest child not to interfere when she is talking to a younger child about assigned chores that the child has left undone. The message, or "rule," then, is that children are not allowed to assume parenting roles with the other children in the family. The mother, however, may delegate responsibility for parenting to her oldest child when she leaves the home. Nevertheless, the "rules" regarding who does the parenting and under what circumstances clearly delineate the boundaries of the parental and sibling subsystems.

Culture also plays a determining role in family subsystems. For example, traditionally, many Native American tribes did not consider people to be functional adults until they were in their mid-fifties or a grandparent. For this reason grandparents were assigned the child-rearing responsibilities and thus the parenting subsystem included grandparents and grandchildren, rather than parents and their own children (Tafoya, 1989). Similar arrangements may be found in other minority group families whereby a variety of adults may function as parental or kin subsystems, and in which there is a distribution of family tasks and functions (Boyd-Franklin, 1989a; Carter & McGoldrick, 1999b; McAdoo, 1993).

The clarity of boundaries within a family is a useful parameter for evaluating family functioning. Minuchin (1974) conceives of all families as falling somewhere along a continuum of extremes in boundary functioning, the opposite poles of which are disengagement (diffuse boundaries) and enmeshment (inappropriately rigid boundaries). Family closeness in an enmeshed family system is defined as everyone thinking and feeling alike. Membership in such families requires a major sacrifice of autonomy, thereby discouraging members from exploration, independent action, and problem solving. Members of disengaged families, on the other hand, tolerate a wide range of individual variations by members but are apt to lack feelings of family solidarity, loyalty, and a sense of belonging. Members of such families find it difficult to give or to get support from other family members. Family organization in such systems is unstable and chaotic, and may become factionalized, with leadership often shifting moment to moment. Family members often develop individual bounding patterns or become disengaged. In disengaged families, only high-level stresses upon one family member appreciably affect other members or activate the family's supportive systems. These systems, in fact, tend not to respond when a response is appropriate (parents may not worry when their adolescent child stays out all night). At the enmeshed end of the continuum, one member's behavior immediately affects others, reverberating throughout the family system. Members tend to respond to any variations from the accustomed with excessive speed and intensity; parents become very angry, for instance, if a child does not eat everything on his plate.

Enmeshment and disengagement as processes are not necessarily dysfunctional and may hold little to no relevance for some cultural or racial groups. According to Minuchin (1974), every family experiences some enmeshment or disengagement in its subsystems as a family goes through developmental phases. During a family's early developmental years, mother and young children may represent an enmeshed subsystem, with father in a peripheral position. Adolescents gradually disengage from the parental-child subsystem, as they get ready to leave home. But continued operations by a family at either extreme of the continuum may signal the presence of maladaptive patterns and rules that hinder the growth needs of members. Many relatively dysfunctional and highly intractable coalitions between members occur in families who adopt enmeshed styles of relating. Mother and child in a highly enmeshed subsystem may form a coalition against father. In another instance, a mother may relinquish many of her parenting functions to become a member of a sibling subsystem as manifested by a mother's descriptive message: "I treat my daughter just like my sister." A "parental" child may join an executive subsystem, forming a destructive coalition with the parents against other children in the family. Or a woman may "parent" both her grown daughter and the daughter's children, thus interfering with her own offspring's parental functioning. An entire family may also shun one member whose behavior deviates from the family's prescribed norms.

In disengaged families, by contrast, coalitions may be formed between some members, but these alliances are apt to be fragile and transitory, based on immediate gratification of the needs of family members who abandon the alliance once their needs are temporarily satisfied or the coalition no longer serves their purposes. In such families, it is the relative lack of opportunity to form stable alliances that is detrimental to the growth needs of individuals. The resulting "disconnectedness" of this transactional family style leaves members isolated and alienated from each other and unable to utilize family resources. In assessing the various structural arrangements of a family, attend to the alignments between family members and outsiders that tug at family loyalties and cause acute family stress. For example, a grandparent living outside the home may take the side of children in family disputes and provide a refuge for them, which may interfere with parents and children working out their difficulties. A 15-year-old girl may begin to keep company with an older man and, despite her parents' objections, may continue to see him surreptitiously. Ignoring his wife's protests, a husband may also keep late hours and spend an inordinate amount of time with a "best friend," going to bars, playing poker, and the like. Even social workers may form inappropriate alliances with clients that interfere with family members working together on their problems.

Family Power Structure

Aspects of power may be defined as psychological, economic, and social. The focus of this discussion deals primarily with power as a dynamic process within the family system. In keeping with the systems framework, we remind the reader that the family as a system interacts with and is influenced by other systems. In working with families, social workers must be aware of the extent to which policies support or burden family well-being and inhibit access to resources (Vosler, 1990; Zimmerman, 1995). Zimmerman (1995), for example, points to the differences in male and female power and the consequences in policies and programs that do not favor women. J. A. Miller (1994) calls our attention to historical events that influence family structure, gender roles, even courtship and marriage. Further, Miller asserts, "the family's construction of power is shaped in a context of neighborhood and community," (p. 224). The relevance of context is that factors such as political processes, occupational opportunities, social class, race and ethnicity, and policies can "differentially affect the fortunes of families" (Miller, 1994, p. 224).

Families may experience a lack of power as a result of classism, homophobia, prejudice, discrimination, or historical oppression that has been institutionalized into the formal and informal fabric of society. Examples are social policies that define family. Lack of power can take the form of denial of basic resources, access to socioeconomic, health, and housing opportunities. The social worker and

the politician, and indeed the social welfare organization, that define family needs or functioning constitute a power system that has the capacity to determine the level of services a family may receive. In assessing power as it relates to families, we believe that the issue of power external to the family is an important dimension of the assessment. These external vestiges of power influence family functioning and well-being irrespective of power differentiation in the family structure.

Having alerted you to some of the external issues around power, we now turn our attention to an exploration of power within the family system. All families develop a power structure. It is through this structure that the family system is able to maintain the behaviors of individuals with acceptable limits and to provide leadership to assure that maintenance functions of the family are carried out. Parental subsystems, for example, use the power vested in their roles to socialize, establish rules, and shape the behaviors of their children.

Another dimension of power relates to the capacity of a dominant family members to impose their preferred interpretations or viewpoints on other members, in effect denying a meaning or reality other than those they hold (Kilpatrick & Holland, 1999, p. 29). In this regard, power may have disruptive consequences for the family and members may feel pressured to feel, speak, or react to events or situations in the manner preferred by the dominant member. Providing an opportunity for family members to tell their story is a way to explore the extent that this dynamic exists in the family. In some families, customs or tradition may be enforced despite the fact that some members may question their value. They may cooperate, however, to avoid conflict, allowing the family to maintain a perception of balance. This type of power may be viewed as a source of conflict where the family rule may be to respect elders and consult the family before making a decision. Power may also be leveraged in the form of scapegoating because this dynamic forces the attention and energy of the family on a particular member.

Dominant family members may also determine the bounding patterns in the family system in situations of family violence or child abuse.

Power in the family may be held covertly as well as overtly. For instance, one partner may be formally acknowledged as the central figure in the family and thus have more power in family decision making. In traditional Western culture, at one point in time, this status may have been associated with the economic resources of the male. Even so, other less visible members or subsystems held significant power in the family.

Distribution and Balance of Power

Families are often viewed as having a single monolithic power structure. What we know about modern families is that one partner may be the primary decision maker in some situation and in others all members of the family may participate equally. While it may be that on the surface in some cultures the male may be the central figure in the family, social workers should explore the extent that this is true to avoid making premature decisions about the family. It is important to also keep in mind that power may shift depending on the situation or family structure. As families are more diverse both in form and structure, traditional roles have become eroded and others have evolved. There are other sources of power within the family, for instance, family coalitions or the power within subsystems. A strong alliance may exist between a child and grandparents or a parent and a child. Extended kin, family networks, or connections may also be factors. The extent, for example, to which children are able to influence decisions made by the parental subsystem or assume the decider role illustrates that they also play a part in the family's power structure. Parental subsystems exert appropriate influence over their children. Yet, a parent may also delegate authority to an older child when the parent is absent. Where language is an issue, a child may interpret for parents. This form of power is temporary and must not be construed as the child exercising power beyond this particular situation.

Shifts in power may occur as the result of inner and outer forces; for example, loss of employment, threatening changes in the family's condition, life cycle changes, or the opposition to family rules. Shifts in power often occur when new stepfamilies are formed. Factors associated with adults holding more power are having custody of the children; being older; being male; being better educated; having a higher income; providing more financial support of children/stepchildren, and having interpersonal alliances—any of which may change in a new marriage. Finally, children in stepfamilies may acquire more power than in their nuclear family, where both parents were in one household. As a result, these children acquire a standing in the hierarchy that is greater than that of at least one (or more) of the adults (Visher & Visher, 1988).

Although almost all cultures view the male as the central power figure in the family, social workers are advised to refrain from making this generalization. Many cultures are male oriented and females may appear to lack power in the traditional sense. In the preceding discussion, the question of who holds power and under what circumstances was explored and caution was advised about making assumptions. This caution may be particularly advisable with racial or ethnic groups. For instance, diverse groups may differ in their gender role definitions, expectations, and responsibilities, yet these roles may not be uniformly constructed as lacking in power. Women, grandparents, and other significant individuals included in the family system have powerful roles in the family. For example, in some Latino, Asian American, and African American families, the voice of elders is important. In some Latino families male dominance and female subordination as a cultural ideal ignores the norm of *hembrismo* or *marianismo*, which emphasizes the status of the mother (Hines, Garcia-Preto, McGoldrick, Almeida, & Weltman, 1992). Culture may play a decisive role in who holds power in the family. The covert power held by women in some cultures, despite what is defined as their subservient status, is referred to by Rotunno and McGoldrick (1982) as a paradox simply because what may be observed as a cultural script for women does not diminish the powerful role they play in the family system.

Because of many complex factors, including industrialization, the higher level of education of women and their entrance into the workforce, the contributions of the feminist perspective, and the equal rights movement, families in Western society are moving toward more egalitarian definitions of male-female roles. Many families, however, continue to suffer stress because of the difficulty in resolving discrepancies between traditional and new egalitarian definitions of male-female roles. As immigrant families enter the United States, they too face resolution of the same issues.

Families encounter many stressful situations (e.g., loss of a job, reduced copy capacity caused by mental illness, debilitation resulting from an accident) that may challenge the balance of power and cause realignments in the power base of the family. In fact, the emotional impact of these stressors and the upheaval caused as family members struggle for power and control in a transitional situation may play a key role in a family's difficulties. In a single-parent family system for example, conflict may arise when the parent initiates his or her role with children of the opposite gender. In assessing family systems, therefore, you must not only determine how power has been distributed in the family but also whether changing conditions of the family are "threatening" the established power base. You must also assess the extent to which the family's "rules" allow the system to reallocate power flexibly and to adjust roles to meet the demands of the family's changing circumstances. Finally, you must assess how we view the relative vestment of power in the family, for even if power is unequally distributed, the family may be well satisfied with the arrangement. Thus, unless power dynamics play a significant role in family problems, it is not appropriate to seek to make adjustments in this area.

Assessing Power

A number of factors, then, must be addressed in assessing with families the power base and the manner in which power is distributed. This may include who holds the "balance of power"; who, if anyone, is the formally designated leader; to what extent power is covertly held by members who have aligned to form a power bloc; and to what extent covert power accrues to individual members who are manifesting extreme symptoms in the family. The role of a family's culture in determining the distribution of power, of course, must also be considered.

Keep in mind that family struggles over power issues and the resulting destructive coalitions that are formed are manifested in families' processes. Observation of family interaction often reveals an affect-laden process in which coalitions are being proposed, accepted, modified, locked, tested, qualified, broken, rejected, and betrayed in a constant flowing process. All families must address power issues and allocate power in some manner. It is the functionality of the power structure in meeting individual psychological needs and promoting the health of the system that must be determined in assessing this dimension of family functioning. Assessment questions that address the functionality of the power structure include:

1. Is the family's power structure stable, allowing the system to carry out its maintenance functions in an orderly manner, or does the power base shift as members compete for power?

2. Does the power base reside within the executive subsystem or within covert coalitions in the family?

3. Are members of the family satisfied with the relative distribution of power?

Family Decision-Making Processes

Closely tied to issues of power is the family's style of decision making. Families range in extremes from leaderless groups in which no one has enough power to determine and direct activities or to organize decision-making processes to families in which virtually absolute power to make decisions is rigidly held by one member. Although effective deliberation and decision making are considered to be important in determining the well-being of the system, most families do not consciously select a modus operandi for making family decisions. Rather, the family's style of decision making usually evolves in the formative stages of development of the system and is often patterned after decision-making approaches modeled by parents in the families of origin. In some instances, persistent family conflicts can often be traced largely to the inability to resolve, at a covert level, incompatible expectations (emanating from their role models) regarding the distribution of power and the manner in which decisions should be made in the family. As children are added to the system, they too may be pulled into the situation, as neither parent is fully successful in wresting power from the other.

Approaches in decision making may change over the course of the family life cycle. Young children, for example, have fewer opportunities in the decider role. As they become adolescents and young adults, they may have more input into family decisions, with the parental subsystem retaining the right of final decision. For some families, decision making may extend beyond the immediate family, which may be a reflection of family tradition, race, or culture. A tradition observed in the traditional Hmong community, for example, about matters related to health and Western medicine is not a decision that may reside solely with the immediate family. Given the variants of culture and in consideration of the distribution of power that may exist in a family and understanding the similar to power, decision making may shift on a situation basis, or be influenced by external forces. In the assessment of decision making in the family, the overall goal is to determine the extent to which decisions facilitate family well-being, disrupt the family system, or cause conflict. Prolonged or unresolved conflict may factionalize

the family unit and cause some members to disengage. In order to assess the decision-making processes found in families, it is important to understand vital ingredients that are inherent in effective problem solving with family systems. We offer the following guidelines:

1. *Effective decision making requires open feedback and self-expression among members, compromise, agreeing to disagree, or taking turns to negotiate and resolve differences.* Members can say what they think and feel without fear of destroying themselves or others in the system. In systems that do not allow feedback regarding feelings, preferences, and opinions, members are stifled, pressured to ignore their own needs and wishes and to conform, without complaint, to maladaptive processes in the system. Without open feedback and self-expression, decision-making processes are not responsive to needs of individual members that emerge as the system goes through transitional developmental phases that demand adaptation to inner and outer stresses and crises.

2. *Effective decision making requires a philosophical or attitudinal set on the part of each family member that all members of the system "count,"* that is, that each member's needs will be taken into consideration in decision making that will affect that member. Satir (1967) identified four exhaustive solutions to what she calls the four "self-other" dilemmas in relationships that apply to decision-making processes in families:

   a. In the first position, the person discounts the wants of self ("I count myself out"). Operating form this position, people handle differences by submitting, agreeing, placating, apologizing, or in other ways discounting their own needs (regardless of how they really feel) when negotiating with others.

   b. In the second position, a person discounts the wants of the "other" ("I count you out"). In this position, persons may behave by finding fault, blaming, and disagreeing with others, thus leaving no room for negotiating differences.

c. In the third position, the person discounts the wants of both ("Let's count us both out"). Operating from this position, persons may exclude both themselves and others by being irrelevant, changing the subject, leaving the situation, or behaving in other ways that make it impossible to negotiate differences openly with others.

d. In the fourth position, a person takes into account the wants of other parties involved ("I count myself in but try to make room for others"). In this position, a person openly and clearly negotiates differences with others and permits or invites others to do the same.

Satir describes the fourth position as the "only growth-producing" solution to negotiation of differences between self and others. This alternative allows individual members to flourish while remaining a part of the system—and vitalizes and energizes the system itself. By contrast, the other three positions may promote individual survival at the expense of others in the family and cause conflict, intrigue, and resentment in the system that divert energies from productive tasks and block the family's developmental progress.

These positions can be viewed as interpersonal patterns or styles of individual family members that are consistently expressed in the family. In decision making (as well as other interpersonal events), individual family members and the family as a unit may "count in" some members and "count out" others. Before a family may become an optimally nurturing environment for individual growth, all members must be "counted in" in the sense that their needs are considered when important decisions affecting them are made in the family. Members of the family are likely to contribute productively when they know that every member "counts" and that needs, rather than power, are at issue in the decision-making process.

In traditional patriarchal families, the issue of the wife's feeling "counted in" in the decision-making process (even if both spouses agree that the husband should have the final say) is of obvious importance. Further, although children should have considerably less power than parents in a family and often should not be vested with decision-making authority in problem-solving processes, they should have the opportunity to express themselves or to give feedback in relation to decisions that affect them. Examples of such decisions include activities in which the family engages, responsibilities assigned them in the home, and personal leisure time activities in which they engage.

3. *Effective decision making requires members of a family system to think in terms of needs rather than solutions.* Members of families are often conditioned by life experiences to see solutions in terms of dichotomies—"either we do things your way or mine; one of us has to lose"—a narrow approach to problem solving that centers on competing solutions, preventing negotiation and compromise. "Do what I want, think what I think, feel what I feel"—in other words, "Do things my way"—is often the position taken by individual family members as they attempt to coerce or coax others to adopt their solutions to life's problems. They operate from the principle that love and total agreement go together. Needs include basic conditions (e.g., to be trusted, to be considered) that must be addressed in order to arrive at a satisfactory solution.

Effective decision making requires the ability of family members to generate alternatives, which is closely parallel to group brainstorming in which members generate options, no matter how farfetched, without criticism or censorship. Individuals manifest this skill when they draw from a repertoire of ideas; not merely variations on a single theme but rather different categories of solutions or alternatives to a given problem. In the assessment process, then, one of your tasks may be to determine to what extent families identify alternatives in contrast to quarreling over competing solutions.

4. *Effective decision making requires ability on the part of family members to weigh alternatives.*

Decisions may be made in families after gathering information, input by members, and deliberation; or decisions may be made impulsively without gathering or weighing relevant information or without considering the needs of family members in relation to possible solutions. Effective decision making also requires that the family organize to carry out decisions through assignments to individual members. Planning to implement a decision is just as important as making the decision initially. Some systems are so disorganized and chaotic that members have great difficulty in either making a decision or implementing it. In other systems, members lack motivation to carry out decisions because their input was not elicited or considered in the decision-making process. Thus, even when decisions have been made in the system, the process may break down at the point of implementation. Ascertaining the extent to which families can implement as well as make decisions is a key task in assessing family functioning.

5. *Effective decision making also requires the system to allow for negotiation and adjustment of earlier decisions* based on new information and emerging individual and family needs. Some systems, of course, are much more responsive and flexible in relation to this item than others.

6. *In assessing the family's decision-making style, then, you should elicit information and view the processes you observe in relation to the preceding guidelines.* Keep in mind that you are looking for functional as well as dysfunctional patterns in each of these areas. In addition, keep in mind that the decision-making skills we have described encourage optimal family functioning as it is perceived in Western culture. These decision-making skills may be lacking in some families and may not be fully developed even in the best-functioning families in Western culture.

7. *Decision making, a key to autonomous functioning of the family unit, may not be ideal or desirable for all families.* Such skills may not be considered important in families from different ethnic backgrounds, for many cultural groups have no frame of reference for "joint decision making," and, in fact, espouse cultural values prescribing behavior that is in direct contradiction to the methods of decision making we discuss here and in Chapter 13. Including family members in decision making and assuring that the needs of all are satisfied is a Western culture ideal advocated by helping professionals and social scientists. Although we espouse the need for families to learn skills in decision making, social workers must assess whether introducing these skills to family members will facilitate family functioning or cause family disruption by disturbing patterns that are deeply engrained and culturally sanctioned. Hence, collaboration with families in the assessment process is essential.

Consider the case of a young Somali woman living with her parents. In assessing resources, she describes a family situation in which she and other family members are expected to contribute a portion of their earnings to family members still living in Somalia. The social worker in case consultation describes this situation as dysfunctional because, in her view, this family prohibits the young woman from moving out and living independently. Examining this situation through Western values of autonomy and independence, she asserts the right of the young woman to manage her own money. Intervention in this situation by the social worker without consideration for cultural values and norms has the potential to be disruptive to this family system.

McAdoo (1993) asserts that there are few differences between the decision-making responses of African Americans and their white counterparts of similar socioeconomic status. The study results did reveal, however, that African Americans "with limited resources tend to be more cooperative than other groups in their relationships and decision-making patterns." Thus, McAdoo stresses the importance of understanding the context in which ethnic families function, their decision making and broader relation patterns, and that cooperation as a value may be the result of helping each other to "survive and thrive within the American community" (p. 119). This value or sense of obligation may also be evident in other ethnic or racial groups.

Family Goals

The family is a social group in which members typically cooperate and coordinate their efforts in order to achieve certain goals. While family members may talk to each other about goals, and children may express a preference, as with decision-making and power, family goals are generally established by the parental subsystem. Families may establish goals in one of two ways. First, families to some extent may adopt and have in common goals established by society; that is, socializing children, transferring major cultural patterns, and meeting certain personal, nurturing, and safety needs of family members. Second, partners may bring individual goals with them into the family, perhaps based on preferences of their family or origin.

Goals that families espouse may be openly recognized or embraced by the family or they may be covert and beyond the family's awareness. "We want to put all the kids through college" or "It is important for children to remember the old ways" are examples of explicit goals. Covert or unrecognized goals may also have a profound influence on a family system. In a competitive society, a covert goal drives a family's striving toward being at the top of the social ladder and, while unspoken, influences the individual efforts of the family. At the same time, families who are new arrivals to Western culture may want their children to maximize opportunities, yet maintain connections with their traditional roots. The first goal related to opportunities may be explicit; the other, unspoken yet though to be understood.

When families are in crisis, the system's goals and their ordering often become more apparent, for at these times families may be forced to choose between competing goals and values. For example, a wide variety of responses would be observed if one were to study a number of families confronted with a sudden and drastic reduction in

income. A family with limited financial resources may give priority to maintaining an adequate diet for the children. In a study that examined definitions of child neglect, the mothers reported that when faced with limited finances, they would choose food and clothing. Their reasoning had to do with avoiding potential intervention by child protection. As a result, they would sacrifice other things, for example, a bed with a frame (G. D. Rooney, Neathery, & Suzek, 1997).

Family goals may also conflict with societal and social worker expectations in other ways. Consider the case of a single mother who wishes to move the family to a better neighborhood. To accomplish this goal, she holds two jobs, one of which is the evening shift in a convenience store adjacent to the apartment building in which the family lives. The 12-year-old is delegated the responsibility of caring for the younger siblings, ages 6 and 8. A neighbor's report to the authorities that the children are home alone at night results in an intervention from child protective services. The mother is devastated, angry, and confused. Such actions may at first seem irresponsible or irrational, but they are comprehensible when the goals and aspirations of the family are understood in the context in which they were developed.

In most families, members vary in regard to the goals each considers important and the value each attaches to common goals. Parents may have a goal of educating their children well. As in any organization, a family functions best when there is a high degree of consensus concerning the majority of family goals. Provision within the system to negotiate and to take into consideration the unique needs, aims, and wishes of individuals is also important. Because goals often are not explicit, however, differences among family members in relation to major goals and expectations may not be worked through, creating dissension and disappointment within the group. Further, because of pressures from the most powerful or influential members of the group, the family may give lip service to particular goals, although several or the majority of the members may not agree in principle with them. While family goals may vary and may break down in times of crisis, family goals are a strength that may be used as a resource in problem solving. Many patterns of interaction in families evolve in part to achieve goals. If social workers examine the family's interactions without considering the goals of the system, they may miss the meaning of patterns they identify. To illustrate this and other points that we have discussed throughout this section, consider the following case example of a covertly held goal around which family energies are extensively organized.

CASE EXAMPLE

In the White family, an overriding goal was to "keep the house clean," a goal set and maintained by Mrs. White, who felt constant inner pressure to keep her house tidy in order to avoid criticism from her own mother and other relatives. The inability to maintain this goal caused Mrs. White to feel depressed. Although she participated only infrequently in the housecleaning, she kept constant pressure on her younger daughters, ages 14 and 16, to keep the house clean and orderly. To her two older girls, attending school and holding down part-time jobs, however, she gave permission to participate only minimally in housecleaning chores because "they're tired when they come home and need time to relax and study." Seeing the older girls often excused from housecleaning (even when they left messes), the two younger girls were extremely resentful and often complained bitterly to their father about the situation. Further, they attacked the older girls with accusations such as "You don't act like you're members of the family" or "You don't care about anybody around here." Assuming the role of their absent mother, they monitored the older sisters, pointing out the messes they had created and ordering them to clean them up, which the older girls always refused to do. The older daughters, who felt mistreated and misunderstood, defended themselves and counterattacked by name-calling and threatening. Trying to maintain peace, Mr. White consistently served as a mediator between the warring factions and often picked up or cleaned the house to avoid the inevitable disputes

that would arise when chores were assigned to his daughters. Whenever his wife intermittently emerged from her room, Mr. White also felt compelled to serve as mediator between her and the daughters because she usually found something out of order and would angrily blame one of the younger daughters for "not doing her job."

In this illustration, the entire White family attempted to adhere to the mother's goal of keeping the house clean. Because the younger girls experienced much more pressure than the older girls, however, more of their energies were invested in carrying out or in persuading other members of the family to implement this goal. The unequal distribution of pressure in the family had shaped the alliances that were in place at the time this family initially sought therapy. Only as the social worker carefully explored and clarified the family goal and rules associated with it were family members able to recognize the extent to which their behaviors revolved around this goal.

In summary, then, we offer the following questions to assist you in assessing family goals for both strengths and difficulties:

1. To what extent do clear goals guide the family group?
2. To what extent are members aware of the overriding goals of the family?
3. To what extent is there shared consensus among members regarding major goals and the priority assigned to these goals?
4. To what extent is family conflict caused by the lack of consensus regarding primary goals of individual family members?
5. How functional are commonly held goals in meeting the needs of individual members and promoting the well-being of the group as a whole?
6. To what extent are patterns of interaction related to covert goals espoused by the family?

To the extent that goals are clear, that consensus exists regarding major goals, and that goals serve the needs and interests of the individual members and of the group, families manifest key strengths on this dimension of family functioning. We reiterate what has been a recurring theme throughout this chapter, namely that social workers must view the family's goals in the family's cultural context and avoid the hazard of assessing family goals against those deemed desirable in Western culture. Also, to avoid biased evaluations, it is important not to view a family as deficient because the means to achieve its goals may not conform to the resources of the mainstream. Rather it is important to determine the goals of families and to assess them in the context of their cultural reference groups and the resources available to them.

Family Myths and Cognitive Patterns

Earlier in this chapter, we discussed family rules and emphasized how they pervade all aspects of family life. Rules have both a behavioral and a cognitive component; that is, the behaviors manifested by family members flow from and are inextricably related to shared perceptions or myths about each other, the family unit, and the world at large. These shared perceptions may be congruent with the views of neutral outside observers or may be distortions of reality, that is, ill-founded, self-deceptive, well-systematized beliefs uncritically held by members. Such distortions are often part of the beliefs or myths subscribed to by the family that help shape, maintain, and justify interactional patterns and relationships, as the following case illustrates.

Over the past 4 years, 10-year-old Jeffrey has been in constant difficulty with his teachers at school because of open defiance of classroom rules, argumentative behavior, and physical skirmishes with other children. As a result of these problems, his parents have changed Jeffrey's enrollment from one school to another several times during the past 3 years. Sharing the cognitive set that "the teachers do not try to understand Jeffrey," they regard each school contact as a battleground in which they must argue, protest their

rights, and defend their son. Continually bombastic, they alienate school personnel, pushing them to take extreme stands on issues that might otherwise be mutually negotiated if the parents were amenable. Further, the parents' constant negative and angry comments at home regarding Jeffrey's teachers and his school may reinforce and foster Jeffrey's classroom behavior.

In the preceding example, the behaviors and cognitive processes of the family are mutually reinforcing. The myths determine the behavior, which predictably elicits negative responses from school personnel. In turn, the family's negative encounters with the school reinforce and confirm their perceptions of the world as dangerous and their view that authoritarian figures cannot be trusted and are out to get them.

Other myths may also prevail in family systems, shaping the behavior and interactions among family members or with outsiders, including the following:

- "Things are permanent and unchangeable in our family. No matter what we do, we are powerless to change our circumstances. We are victims of fate."

- "Mother doesn't care about the kids; Dad does."

- "Problems in the family will take care of themselves."

- "It's a sign of weakness to apologize."

- "It's important to get even with people who hurt you."

Social cognitions also play a role in how individuals and families may interpret, remember information, and categorize internal and external events. These thematically organized categories are referred to as "cognitive schemas" (Berlin & Marsh, 1993, p. 5). In a general sense, schemas are generalizations that may be utilized to process information about attributes, guide perceptions, and influence memory. Imagine, for example, the cognitions that may be held about people with certain attributes. People of certain groups are on welfare. Certain groups are very smart. Seeing a group of youths with certain characteristics cues us to perceive them as members of a violent gang. The stored memory from schemas may also be an integral part of the shared experience of families from homogeneous groups. For example, it may be difficult for an African American who shares a history of racial discrimination and oppression to distinguish when race is not a concern in social situations and encounters with the police. Berlin and Marsh (1993) maintain that the cognitions associated with schemas may persist long after a particular event or episode has occurred. Not all schemas are problematic. The important thing to remember is that they operate as a heuristic device that involves taking a shortcut in the processing of information. When these cognitions are challenged, they cause cognitive dissonance and thus are not easily replaced. They may function as both internal and external bounding patterns observed in the family.

Potentially damaging to development are the persistent beliefs within a family that single out one member as being different or deviant from the group. Assigned labels such as sick, bad, crazy, or lazy, a family member often becomes the scapegoat for the family, carrying the blame for problems and obscuring the fact that other members also carry responsibility for difficult transactions and communications. In many families, members may carry permanent labels, such as "black sheep of the family," "intellectual one," "baby of the family," "strict parent," "family pet," "clown," "good child," or "dumb." It should be noted that labels such as talented, handsome, or bright may separate and estrange a member of the family from others and cause others to resent the inordinate amount of attention, praise, and recognition accorded to the individual. Labels stereotype roles of family members, causing other members to relate to them on the basis of a presumed single characteristic and to overlook a wide range of attributes, attitudes, and feelings, limiting their range of behavioral options.

Family Roles

Family roles may be thought of as complementary and reciprocal, and family members are differentiated into social roles within the family system. Role theory when applied to the family system suggests that each person in a family carries many roles that are integrated into the family's structure and represent certain expected, permitted, and forbidden behaviors. According to Nichols and Schwartz (1999), family roles are not independent of each other, and role behavior involves two or more persons in reciprocal transactions. Roles within the family system may be assigned on the basis of legal or chronological status or cultural and societal scripts. In many cultures, including our own, many roles are gender based, despite the fact that changes over the past several decades have shaped our thinking about the differences between male and female roles. Yet, in almost all families, including those that are diverse racially and ethnically, exposure to changing political and social environments has had an influence on women's role within the family system. As in our previous discussion on power and decision making, roles may be flexible and diffused.

Roles and role expectations are learned in the process of social interactions. Earlier, we mentioned that roles could be accorded on the basis of status. The role of parent, for example, is both accrued and learned. Similarly, the various roles that exist between couples in a relationship are learned as a result of interactions over time. Satisfaction with respective role behavior between individuals indicates a level of harmony in interpersonal relationships. Janzen and Harris (1997) refer to "harmonized" interpersonal roles as independent-dependent relationships. Roles may be either complementary or symmetrical. An example of a complementary independent-dependent role is the relationship between parents and children in which the needs of both are fulfilled. In contrast, symmetrical relationships are equal and may be characterized by a couple in which each shares family chores, decision making, and child rearing.

Roles for the most part are not static and often defy traditional stereotypical behaviors. In actuality, roles in most families operate along a continuum and may be characterized as complementary, quid pro quo, symmetrical, and double bind (Nichols and Schwartz, 1998, p. 41).

Life transitions often demands changes, flexibility, and modifications in role behavior. Families may experience role transition difficulties in making the necessary adjustments. Elderly parents, for example, may experience difficulties in adjusting to becoming dependent on an adult child. Another significant change that may pose difficulties for some parents in the adjustment to the void when children leave the home.

Conflict in the family may occur when individuals are dissatisfied with their roles, when there is disagreement about roles, or when roles become overburdened. Parents for example, may disagree about discipline. One parent may overdiscipline, while the other may have a more permissive style. Interrole conflict occurs as a result of competing multiple role obligations, especially when two or more roles are incompatible. In exploring the concerns of employed women, G. D. Rooney (1997) found that women, single or married, experienced difficulties with their management of multiple roles. Excessive role demands as described by the women in this study amounted to feeling caught by juggling multiple roles, for example, wife or partner, mother, daughter, employee, and often caretaker for an elderly parent. Multiple role taking or compliance to gender role and time pressures were complicated by factors such as the separate of work and family, unresponsive workplace policies, and time for self. They also reported feeling interpersonal conflict, diminished physical stamina, and concerns for their physical health and impact on their job performance. Minority women experienced similarly arranged gender divisions of labor. In addition, gender, role division carried the adjoining weight of strong cultural norms explicit to gender role expectancies. For single-parent women, the absence of another parent meant that they fulfilled both male and female roles in the family system. Also, single, never-married women reported being expected to be the primary caretakers of elderly individuals in the family. The stresses upon women in particular in today's world were further discussed by Larsen (1991) in *I'm a Day Late and a Dollar Short and It's Okay! A Woman's Survival Guide for the 90's.* A point to consider with minority families is that interrole conflict may occur in their transactions with the larger community.

Intrarole tensions may emerge in the family when there are contradictions between role performance. Imagine a child who has been delegated responsibility for younger siblings, yet is expected to be obedient. Consider two individuals who contribute to the economic interest of the family but are not equal participants in deciding how the family spends money. The latter example may be considered complementary, but, unless both partners are satisfied with the arrangement, tensions can occur.

Understanding the distribution of roles within the family, the way in which these roles are defined, and role conflict are important assessment dimensions in planning the intervention strategy. Because each culture or family structure may have its own definition of roles, social workers must also determine and assess the goodness of fit with the needs of family members. Assessment then must also include the extent to which families are amendable to changing determined roles that adversely affect individuals and the functioning of the family system.

Communication Styles of Family Members

One theme that cuts across many cultural groups is that of patterns discouraging the open expression of feelings. Although Western culture espouses the value that openness and honesty are the best policies, the reality is that most people have considerable difficulty in asserting themselves or in confronting others, particularly in ways that are facilitative rather than destructive.

Because of strongly embedded norms, people in many other cultures are much less open than even those in Western society. In Asian culture, for example, free participation and exchange of opinions contradict Asian values of humility and modesty (Ho, 1987). In Hawaiian culture, "it is totally unacceptable to resolve conflicts openly and through confrontation" (Young, 1980, p. 14). The Irish, too, have communication patterns that differ from the Western ideal, as McGoldrick (1982b) observes:

> The Irish often fear being pinned down and may use their language and manner to avoid it. The affinity of the Irish for verbal innuendo, ambiguity, and metaphor have led the English to coin the phrase "talking Irish" to describe the Irish style of both communicating and not communicating at the same time. (p. 315)

Problems experienced by some families, then, may partially arise because of cultural prohibitions against openness. In some instances, social workers can assist clients to understand their cultural norms and make decisions as to whether they are willing to change communication patterns and styles that negatively affect relationships. In other instances, social workers may need to work more subtly to bring about enough openness in the system to promote the growth of family members. Falicov (1982) describes such an indirect approach in working with Mexican Americans:

> When feelings are subtly elicited by the therapist, Mexican Americans respond much more openly than when they are asked to describe and explain their feelings and reactions. An experiential communication approach with emphasis on "telling it like it is" or "baring one's soul" or interpretations about nonverbal behavior will be threatening insofar as it challenges inhibitions about personal disclosure and supports symmetrical interactions. (p. 148)

Whether or not family communication patterns are culturally influenced or otherwise determined, they may be faulty, causing significant problems and pain for family members. Social workers thus must be prepared to assess the impact of a family's communication styles upon the problems of members. To do so, they must be aware of the complexities of communication and prepared to assess the function of members' communication styles across a number of dimensions, as illustrated in the following discussion.

Congruence and Clarity of Communication

Family members convey messages through verbal and nonverbal channels and qualify those messages through other verbal and nonverbal messages. A task for social workers, therefore, is to assess the *congruency* of communications, that is, whether there is correspondence between the various verbal and nonverbal elements of messages. According to Satir (1967) and other communication theorists, messages may be qualified at any one of three communication levels:

1. *Verbal level:* When people explain the intent of their messages, they are speaking at a metacommunication level. For example: "I was trying to see if you agreed with me." "I thought you were feeling bad, and I was trying to comfort you." Contradictory communications occur when two or more oppositional messages are sent in sequence via the same verbal channel: "I love you … I hate you." "You should follow my advice…You need to make your own decisions."

2. *Nonverbal level:* People qualify their communications through many nonverbal modes, including gesture, facial expressions, tone of voice, posture, intensity of eye contact, and the like. Nonverbal messages may:

   a. Reinforce verbal messages.

      A mother smiles at her child and says, "I love you."

      A husband says to his wife that he is pleased that she has found a new job, and his countenance conveys his genuine pleasure.

   b. Contradict or modify verbal expressions.

      A lover says, "Come closer," and then stiffens.

With a bored look on his face, a friend says, "Of course I'm interested in what you've been doing lately."

c. Contradict or modify nonverbal expressions.

A person behaves in a seductive manner, but pulls back when the other person responds.

A visitor puts on his coat to leave, but lingers in the doorway.

3. *Contextual level:* The situation in which communication occurs also reinforces or disqualifies the verbal and nonverbal expressions of a speaker. For example, a mother leans over to her misbehaving child during church services and threatens, "If you don't stop that, I'm going to spank you *right now!*" The context or situation in which she sends the message, then, inherently disqualifies her verbal expression, as it is unlikely that she will spank the child in church.

Functional communicators identify discrepancies between levels of communication and seek clarification when a person's words and expressions are disparate. They also are receptive to feedback and clarify their own communications when they have sent incongruent messages. Vital to assessment, then, is the task of ascertaining the extent to which there is congruence between the *verbal, nonverbal,* and *contextual* levels of messages on the part of individuals in a family system. The more distressed the system and the more symptomatic the behavior, the more likely that surface messages are contradicted by other communications that leave family members bewildered, angry, hurt, and in binds from which they see no way of extricating themselves.

In addition to considering the congruence of communications, it is important to assess the *clarity* of messages. Laing (1965) uses the term *mystification* to describe how some families befuddle or mask communications and obscure the nature and source of disagreements and conflicts in their relationships. Mystification of communications can be accomplished by myriad kinds of maneuvers, including disqualifying another person's experience

("You must be crazy if you think that"), addressing responses to no one in particular when the intent of the speaker is to relay a message to a certain person, employing evasive responses that effectively obscure knowledge of the speaker, or utilizing sarcastic responses that have multiple meanings and are hard to decipher (J. Lewis, Beavers, Gossett, & Phillips, 1976). A more exhaustive listing of response categories that represent obstacles to communication and may serve to cloud communications is provided and delineated in the following section.

Barriers to Communication

In Chapter 7, we identified a number of barriers to communication that, when utilized by social workers, block client communication and impeded therapeutic progress. Likewise, clients often repetitively respond with these and other similarly destructive responses in their communications with others, preventing meaningful exchanges and creating conflict and tension in relationships. In the following list, we include examples of categorical responses that obstruct open communication and prevent genuine encounters in relationships:

1. Prematurely shifting the subject or avoiding topics
2. Asking excessive questions, verbally dominating interactions
3. Sympathizing, excusing, or giving reassurance or advice
4. "Mind reading," diagnosing, interpreting, overgeneralizing
5. Dwelling on negative historical events in a relationship
6. Negatively evaluating, blaming, name-calling, or criticizing
7. Directing, threatening, admonishing
8. Using caustic humor, excessive kidding, or teasing

Assessment of problematic communication of couples and families must also include behaviors on a nonverbal level including, for instance, glaring, turning away from a family member, fidgeting, shifting posture, pointing a finger, raising the voice, and looking with menacing expressions or with expressions of disgust or disdain. As we emphasized in the previous section, the social worker also needs to be aware of discrepancies between verbal and nonverbal levels of communication.

All families have communication barriers within their conversational repertoires. Members of some families, however, monitor their own communications and adjust their manner of responding when they have had a negative impact on another person. Indeed, such families have "rules" that prevent many kinds of negative communications, for example, "We do not yell or call people names in our family," or "It is important to listen attentively when someone is talking to you." Other families have destructive entrenched styles of communication that pervade many of their exchanges, and members manifest little awareness of their aversive styles. Further, members of these families tend to assume little responsibility for the negative impact of their communications upon others and resist giving up destructive modes of communication in favor of others that are more facilitative. As you observe the communication styles of families, then, it is important to assess (1) the presence of patterned negative communication, (2) the pervasiveness of such negative patterns, and (3) the relative ability of individual members of the system to modify habituated communication styles.

In addition to assessing the preceding factors, it is also vital to ascertain the various combinations of styles that occur repetitively as individual members of the system relate and react. For instance, in a marital relationship, one partner may frequently dominate, criticize, or accuse the other, whereas the other may defend, apologize, placate, or agree, as adapted from the following exchange between two marital partners (Larsen, 1982):

Wife: You never spend time with Jody [*their child*]. It's more important to you to surf the Internet with your computer and talk to people you don't even know.

Husband: I do spend time with her [*gives examples*]. You just don't ever notice.

Wife: I do notice. You spend precious little time with her. You can hardly wait to get back to your computer.

Husband: Last Saturday I spent several hours with her. [*Further elaborates on how he spent the time.*]

In the preceding exchange, the wife continues to attack the husband, who continues to defend his position, thus manifesting a "fault-defend" pattern of marital communication identified by E. Thomas (1977). Such patterns that involve exchanges of different types of behavior have been designated complementary patterns. In such instances, the conflict issues or content discussed changes, but the stylized categories of communication of each partner and the manner in which they orchestrate their scenario remains unchanged. Further, repetitions of the same type of partner-to-partner interchanges will be manifested across many other areas of the couple's interaction.

The thematic configurations that occur in marital communication are limited in number and vary from couple to couple. For instance, rather than the fault-defend pattern just illustrated, spouses may engage in reciprocal or symmetrical patterns in which each attacks, blames, and continually finds fault with the other, that is, a fault-fault pattern. Another marital pair may "collude" by talking only about superficial matters or matters extraneous to the relationship, thereby consistently avoiding disagreements or openly sharing feelings or complaints.

Assessing the communications of entire families is much more complex than assessing couple communication because of the greater number of relationships involved. Each person in the family has stylized ways of communicating that interface in patterned ways with the thematic communications of other family members. For example, a father may continually serve as a spokesperson or "mind reader" for others in the family (e.g., "You don't really feel that way" or "Randy, you're not hungry: You just like to eat"). Stylized reactions of family members to the father's patterned behavior may range from objections to the mind-reading activity ("That's not how I feel!") to nonverbal withdrawal (e.g., turning away from the father, slumping in chair), or tacit approval ("We always see eye to eye").

Receiver Skills

A third critical dimension of communication is the degree of receptivity or openness of family members to the inner thoughts and feelings of other members in the system. Receptivity is manifested by the use of certain receiving skills, which we will discuss shortly. These skills are decidedly Western, and therefore may be inconsistent with some minority or ethnic families. Before considering these, however, it should be stressed that a majority of families operate along a continuum with respect to their skills in verbal and nonverbal responses. Social workers may observe response patterns in some families that convey understanding and demonstrate respect for the sender's message. In others, the reactions of members can take the form of ridicule, negative evaluation, or depreciation of character, or punish or invalidate the expression of personal thoughts and feelings of members. In such families, members also engage frequently in "dual monologues"; that is, they communicate simultaneously without acknowledging the responses of others. In contrast, it is desirable that members invite, welcome, and acknowledge the views and perceptions of each other. Members also feel free to express agreement or disagreement openly, knowing that even though doing so may sometimes spark conflict or argument, their rights to varying perceptions of events are protected within the system. Facilitative responses that convey understanding and acceptance are as follows:

1. Physical attending (direct eye contact, receptive body posture, attentive facial expressions)
2. "Listening" or paraphrasing responses by family members that restate in fresh words the essence of a speaker's message ("You seem to be saying that. . ." or "I sense you're feeling. . .")
3. Responses by receivers of messages that elicit clarification of messages ("I'm not sure what you meant. Will you tell me again?" "Am I right in assuming you meant. . . ?)
4. Brief responses that prompt further elaboration by the speaker ("Oh," "I see," "Tell me more.")

In assessing communication styles of families, you must gauge the extent to which individual members (and the group at large) utilize the facilitative categories of communication identified in the preceding list. Many distressed families almost entirely lack these response categories in their communication repertoires. Fortunately, educative interventions can be employed to assist members to develop these communication skills.

Sender Skills

A fourth critical dimension of communication is the extent to which members of families can share their inner thoughts and feelings with others in the system. Becvar and Becvar (2000) refer to this quality as the ability of individual family members to express themselves clearly as feeling, thinking, acting, valuable, and separate individuals and to take responsibility for thoughts, feelings, and actions. Operationalized, "I-ness" involves messages in the first person (commonly referred to as "I" messages) that openly and congruently reveal either pleasant or unpleasant feelings, thoughts, or reactions experienced by the speaker—"I (feel, think, want)—because—" In working families, social workers may focus on helping them to create a family climate in which members are candid, open, and congruent. This climate is in sharp contrast to families where communications are characteristically indirect, vague, and guarded, and individuals fail to take responsibility for feelings, thoughts, or their own participation in events. Rather than "I" messages, family members are likely to use "you" messages that obscure or deny responsibility or attribute responsibility for the feelings to others (e.g., "You've got me so rattled, I forgot"). Such messages are barriers to communication, and are often replete in injunctions (shoulds and oughts) concerning another's behavior or negatively evaluate the receiver of the message (e.g., "You're really lazy, Jenny" or "You shouldn't feel that way").

Responses That Acknowledge Strength and Achievement and Accredit Growth

Critical to the development of high self-esteem in individual family members are messages from others that consistently validate a person's worth and potential. Social workers can intervene to alter patterns in which the communication repertoires are characterized by constant negative messages that, for example, put down, attack, criticize, or otherwise humiliate or invalidate the experiences of the members. Family members may be caught in a cycle, but when given the opportunity to do otherwise will put more emphasis upon positive attributes of members and what they can become rather than on their deficiencies. To a certain extent, most families are able to accredit the strengths, growth, and positive actions of the members of the system, although the capacity of even these families to observe and to give positive feedback on these vital areas is often strained or underdeveloped. The family's capacity to acknowledge strengths and achievements and create an atmosphere conducive to growth may in fact depend on family context, in particular, family transitions or internal and external stressors.

The Family Life Cycle

The last criterion for assessing families involves the developmental stages through which families as a whole must pass. Based on the seminal work of Duvall (1977) and other theorists, Carter and McGoldrick (1988) offer a conceptual framework of the life cycle of the middle-class American family. This model, involving the entire three- or four-generational system as it moves through time, includes both predictable development events (e.g.,

birth, marriage, retirement), and those unpredictable events that may disrupt the life cycle process (e.g., untimely death, birth of a handicapped child, divorce, chronic illness, war).

Carter and McGoldrick (1988) identified six stages of family development, all of which address nodal events related to the comings and goings of family members over time. These stages include "the unattached young adult," "the new couple," "the family with young children," "the family with adolescents," "the family which is launching children," and "the family in later life." To master these stages, families must successfully complete certain tasks. The "unattached young adult," for example, must differentiate from the family of origin and become a "self" before joining with another to form a new family system. The "new couple" and the families of origin must renegotiate their relationships with each other. The "family with young children" must find the delicate balance between over- and underparenting. In all the stages, problems are most likely to appear when there is an interruption or dislocation in the unfolding family life cycle, signaling that the family is "stuck" and having difficulty moving through the transition to its next phase.

Variations in life cycle are, of course, likely to occur in today's world, particularly in the lives of reconstituted families. As Meyer (1990) notes:

> The ground rules have changed as far as the timing and sequence of events are concerned. Education, work, love, marriage, childbirth, retirement are now out of synch. There is no expectation that one phase follows another in linear fashion. In this world, life events are not preordained. They are more likely atomistic, mixed-and matched, responses to self-definition and opportunity. (p. 12)

Variations also occur in the family life cycle among cultures. Every culture marks off stages of living, each with its appropriate expectations, defining what it means to be a man or woman, to be young, to grow up and leave home, to get married and have children, and to grow old and die.

Exploring the meanings of the life cycle with diverse families is particularly critical in order to determine important milestones. Cultural variants that have a negative connotation in Western society include the age for marriage, responsibilities and roles for children, and responsibilities to the family. Immigrants in particular often experience reactions to practices common in their country of origin. Recall the earlier case example of the young Somali woman in which the social worker felt that her family obligation prevented her from living independently, and thus showed a dysfunctional family dynamic. Carter and McGoldrick (1999b) emphasize that culture plays an important role in family progression and life cycle expectations. Therefore, culture is an essential dimension in the assessment of family development, functioning, and the life cycle.

Summary

In this chapter we have discussed and illustrated through case examples dimensions of assessing family functioning. This chapter also discussed systems concepts that will aid you in the assessment process. Families, irrespective of form, composition, class, race, or ethnicity play an important role in meeting the needs of constituent members. The task of assessing family functioning has never been more challenging, for over the past several decades, the definition of family has changed, and there has been a marked growth in the diversity of racial and ethnic groups in the United States. Families operate as systems in which members influence and are influenced by every other member, creating their own implicit rules, power structure, forms of communication, negotiation, and problem solving. Families are not made up of equals, nor do they reflect in their totality the preferred norms of functioning. Therefore, it is vitally important that we as practitioners respect family variants and cultural variants in family leadership, hierarchy, decision making, and communication styles.

As a final note, we want to emphasize that for the most part the dimensions of assessment discussed in this chapter have evolved from a Western perspective with regard to the family system and family functioning. The extent to which all aspects of these dimensions may be observed as prominent for diverse groups is not well documented in the literature. As such, family context may be one of the more salient factors in the assessment process, for it is this factor that may determine to a large extent family rules, roles, bounding, or communication patterns as well as the family's experience with other social systems.

Internet Resources

You can use the worldwide net resources for social workers site at *http://www.nyu.edu/socialwork/wwwrsw/* to seek family sites by choosing "social work," then "practice," then "families" or "diversity." For example, one such site is *http://www.priory.com/psych/family.htm*. Using InfoTrac®, you can enter 'family strengths' as keywords and find the following article to read and/or download: Early, T. J., & GlenMaye, L. F. (2000). Valuing family strengths: Social work practice with families from a strengths perspective. *Social Work, 45*, 2.

Notes

1. Although our discussion centers largely on families, the concepts presented are pertinent to couples as well.

2. The social worker in this case was Marilyn Luptak, MSW and Ph.D. student at the University of Minnesota.

3. Note that clients may discuss an endless variety of topics or content issues, but their processes contain only a limited number of rules or stylized behaviors.

4. Although families may engage in destructive sequences of interaction such as the preceding as they first begin to discuss problems, it is vital that social workers actively intervene early in sessions to prevent these scenarios from being played out and to assist family members to assume more facilitative ways of communicating about their problems.

5. For an expansion of information on role issues faced by same-sex couples, see Card (1990) and Barret and Robinson (1990). E. F. Levy (1992) and Cain (1991a) also ad dimension to the subject of role issues of lesbians and gay men.

6. Information in this section was drawn in part from a discussion by Goldenberg and Goldenberg (1991) of Minuchin's structural approach.

CHAPTER 11

Forming and Assessing Social Work Groups

CHAPTER OVERVIEW

Social workers who plan and lead groups do so now in a variety of new contexts and with new populations. This chapter describes essential processes in developing the purpose, forming, and conducting appropriate assessment with a variety of groups.[1]

Social workers frequently practice with groups. Toseland and Rivas define group work as "goal-directed activity with small groups of people aimed at meeting socio-emotional needs and accomplishing tasks. This activity is directed to individual members of a group and as a whole within a system of service delivery" (Toseland & Rivas, 2001, p. 12). This definition suggests that all social work practice with groups is aimed at reaching specific goals. Those goals may focus on helping individuals to make changes. They may also focus on the group as a whole as a unit of change or the group as a mechanism for influencing the environment. Among the former are *treatment groups* aimed at enhancing the socioemotional well-being of members through provision of social skills, education, and therapy using the vehicle of group process. Among the latter are *task groups* focused on completion of a project or development of a product. Social workers in task groups work with other professionals in formats such as consultation

groups and collaborative teams to facilitate client service.

Competent group leaders of both kinds of groups have a threefold task: (1) to create effective groups that serve the purposes for which they were designed; (2) to accurately assess individual and group dynamics; and (3) to intervene effectively to modify processes central to the achievement of the group's goals.

Skillfully conceiving a group and formulating a group's purpose, structure, and composition must precede all else, as these processes lay the groundwork for both effective assessment and intervention and the ultimate success of the group. Without careful forethought in creating group structure and atmosphere, all assessment and intervention efforts are for naught, for there is no solid foundation to support them. Accurate assessment of group processes also precedes and undergirds effective interventions.

This chapter provides a framework that will enable group leaders to effectively form groups and accurately assess group processes. Ultimately, this chapter lays the foundation for effective group interventions, the subject of Chapter 17.

Before focusing on these objectives, we briefly discuss the types of groups that social workers create and lead in practice settings.

CLASSIFICATION OF GROUPS

The groups with which social workers are often associated fall into two categories: treatment groups and task groups, each with several subtypes, which we will consider. Treatment groups have the broad purpose of increasing the satisfaction of member's socioemotional needs. Task groups, on the other hand, are established to accomplish a task, produce a product, or carry out a mandate (Toseland & Rivas, 2001, p. 15). Treatment and task groups can be contrasted in a number of basic ways. In treatment groups, communications are open and members are encouraged to actively interact. In task groups, on the other hand, communications are focused on the discussion of a particular task. Roles in treatment groups evolve as a result of interaction, but they may be assigned in task groups. Procedures in treatment groups are flexible or formal, depending on the group, whereas in task groups there are usually formal agendas and rules.

Treatment and task groups further differ with respect to self-disclosure, confidentiality, and evaluation. In treatment groups self-disclosure is expected to be high, proceedings are kept within the group, and success is based on members' success in meeting treatment goals. By contrast, in task groups self-disclosure is low, proceedings may be private or open to the public, and the success of the group is based on members' accomplishing a task or mandate, or producing a product.

Toseland and Rivas (2001) further refine their classification of treatment groups by employing subtypes determined by the following five primary purposes served by such groups:

1. *Support groups* help members cope with life stresses by revitalizing coping skills to more effectively adapt to future life events (e.g., schoolchildren meeting to discuss the effect of divorce or persons with cancer discussing the effects of the disease and how to cope with it) (Magen & Glajchen, 1999).

2. *Educational groups* have the primary purpose of helping members learn about themselves and their society (e.g., an adolescent sexuality group).

3. *Growth groups* stress self-improvement, offering members opportunities to expand their capabilities and self-awareness and make personal changes (e.g., a marital enhancement group for married couples). Growth groups focus on promoting socioemotional health rather than remediating socioemotional illness.

4. *Therapy groups* help members change their behavior, cope with or ameliorate their personal problems, or rehabilitate themselves after a social or health trauma (e.g., a drug addiction group). While support is emphasized in therapy groups, they focus on remediation and rehabilitation.

5. *Socialization groups* are designed to facilitate transitions through developmental stages, from one role or environment to another, through improved interpersonal relationships or social skills. Such groups often employ program activities, structured exercises, role plays, and the like (e.g., a social club for formerly institutionalized persons).

These group purposes are met in a variety of public and private settings serving both voluntary and involuntary clients. For example, social workers now are exploring connections with clients who cannot meet in the same physical place through the use of telephone and computer groups (Meier, 1997; Schopler, Galinsky, & Abell, 1997). Social workers also find that groups are useful for supporting disempowered groups such as people of color and gays and lesbians (D. B. Miller, 1997; Peters, 1997; Saulnier, 1997; Schopler, Galinsky, Davis, & Despard, 1996). Meanwhile, involuntary clients are served with populations such as perpetrators of domestic violence and adolescents in correctional settings (Goodman, 1997; Thomas & Caplan, 1997). Some groups are designed to meet multiple purposes. For example, Bradshaw describes therapy groups for persons with schizophrenia that provide therapy, have a major educational component, and simultaneously provide support (Bradshaw, 1996).

Self-help groups can be distinguished from treatment and task groups by the fact that they have central shared concerns such as coping with addiction, cancer, or obesity. Although a social worker might have aided in establishing a self-help group, the group itself is led by nonprofessionals who are struggling with the same issues as members of the group. The emphasis of such groups is on interpersonal support and creating an environment in which individuals may once again take charge of their lives. Such groups offer support for such shared problems as addictions, aggressive behavior, mental illness, disability, death of children, gambling, weight control, family violence, sexual orientation, and AIDS, among others. It is the social worker's task to offer support and consultation to such groups without taking them over.

Toseland and Rivas (2001) emphasize that in actual practice much overlap exists in the functions and objectives of the different types of groups. There are also underlying principles that apply to all forms of group work practice. We will begin with the creation and assessment of treatment groups before proceeding to task groups.

FORMATION OF TREATMENT GROUPS

The success or failure of a treatment group rests to a large extent on the thoughtful creation of groups and the careful selection and preparation of members for the group experience. Approaches to achieve the initial conditions essential to positive group outcome are presented in this section.

Establishing Group Purpose

Clarifying the overall purpose(s) of a group is vital, for the group's objective(s) influence all the processes that follow. Further, as Levine (1967) underscores: "Clarity about the purpose for which the group is formed provides a framework for observation, assessment, and action [and] provides a base for the group members to develop a bond and a means for attaining this common goals"

(p. 2). Thus, clearly delineating the basic purpose of a group provides the base upon which specific goals and objectives may be constructed. Kurland and Salmon (1998) describe several common problems in developing an appropriate group purpose.

1. Group purposes are promoted without adequate consideration of client need. That is, the purpose may make sense to the prospective leaders or agency but not to the potential clients. For example, clients may be assembled because they share a status such as person with serious and persistent illness living in the community. From the viewpoint of these potential clients, a purpose that relates to a commonly perceived need such as recreation or socializing may be more attractive than grouping by status.

2. The purpose of the group is confused with the content. For example, the group's purpose is described in terms of what the members will do in the group—their activities—rather than the outcome toward which those activities are directed.

3. The purpose of the group may be stated at such a high level of generality that it is vague and meaningless to potential members and provides little direction to prospective leaders.

4. Leaders may be reluctant to share their perceptions about the purpose, leaving members to grapple with the issue alone.

5. On the other hand, a group may be formed with a "public" purpose that conflicts with its actual hidden purpose. For example, prospective members may not know the basis on which they were contacted to become part of a group. For example, potential clients may be invited on the basis of the fact that they overuse prescription drugs, yet this commonality is not shared with them.

6. Group purposes may be understood as static rather than dynamic (adjusting to the evolving desires and needs of the members).

General group purposes may include overarching goals such as the following:

- To provide a forum for discussion and education whereby divorced women with small children who live in a rural area may explore and seek solutions to common problems, such as a sense of alienation, scarcity of resources, and lack of opportunities for adult companionship.

- To provide an opportunity for lesbians with problems of alcoholism to explore their marginalization and environmental context as a means for creating coping responses to alcoholism (Saulnier, 1997).

- To participate in decision making that affects the quality of life in a nursing home by establishing a governing council for residents.

- To assist incarcerated adolescents to seek release by making behavioral changes such as improvements in school performance, behavior toward peers and staff, and the like.

The overall purpose of a planned group should be established by the social worker in consultation with agency administrators and potential clients prior to forming the group. Goals subsequently negotiated by the group should reflect the perspectives of the agency, the client(s), and the social worker.

The Agency's and Social Worker's Perspectives

Because of the agency's key role in determining and/or influencing purpose, social workers must assure that agency objectives are reflected in the group's overall purpose. However, the agency and social worker may not always share a common perspective regarding desired goals for a new group. Differences between the views of the agency and social worker may occur, for instance, because of the latter's personal or professional orientation or because of preferences of either the agency or the social worker for particular theories, ideologies, or techniques not espoused by the other. For example, one of the authors was asked to form a group of women in an outpatient mental health setting who were perceived to overuse tranquilizers. Rather than focus on the negative

identity of drug abuser, the author formed a women's growth group. That growth was defined as including reduction of inappropriate use of drugs.

In the preformation period, then, social workers must be clear about their own objectives for a proposed group and must engage in dialogue with administrators and staff *and potential clients* for the purpose of eliciting their views concerning group purpose. In cases where agency and social workers' goals differ, social workers must address such disparities with administrators and bargain for a general group purpose that is agreeable to both parties.

The Client's Perspective

The potential member of a group wants to know: Why should I join this group? What is in it for me? What will it do for me? Will it help me? (Kurland & Salmon, 1998, p. 8). The potential voluntary group member wants to know this before deciding whether to join a group and, later, whether to continue attending. The potential member who is mandated or pressured to attend also wants to know the answer to these questions even if the consequences of failure to join or attend are often more punishing than for the voluntary client.

At the point of entry to a group, the client's goals may differ considerably from those of either the agency or the social worker. This is particularly true when potential members have been referred by others or are mandated to participate in the group (R. H. Rooney, 1992). Schopler and Galinsky (1974) emphasize that the client's goals may be influenced by many internal or external forces.

> *The expectations held by significant others (e.g., husband, mother, teacher) for the client may...influence the client's perspectives of his problem and his motivation to do something about it. His [or her] capabilities provide resources and define limits for work on his problems and his contributions to the group. Further, as he enters the group, each client has some idea,*

however vague, of what the worker, agency, and group will be like . . . based on personal experiences from school, work, and friendship groups and from reports of others. Thus, various factors determine what goals the client sees as relevant and what goals he thinks are attainable. (p. 128)

The social worker must then carefully explore clients' expectations of the group and help them to develop individual and collective goals that are realistically achievable. The social worker must further work to negotiate between individual, group, and agency purposes. For example, in an alternative to prostitution group for which potential members make a constrained choice to participate or risk prosecution, it is important to acknowledge members' goal of avoiding prosecution as central while recognizing that exploring alternative lifestyles is a nonnegotiable condition for participation in the group (R. H. Rooney, 1992). Other perspectives in voluntary groups must not supersede clients' goals, as clients are the consumers of the service offered. The need to highlight and preserve clients' goals is reflected in the findings of H. Levinson (1973). Levinson identified several common patterns concerning the consequences of agreement or disagreement of purpose between the social worker and group members. When the purposes of social workers and members were in accord or when the purposes of the two diverged but the social worker went along with the group's purpose, groups tended to operate optimally. However, when the social worker advocated purposes that were rejected by members, groups prematurely dissolved.

Establishing Specific Individual and Group Goals

After having established an overall purpose for the group and convened the group, the social worker engages members in formulating specific goals at both individual and group levels. Individual goals embody the hopes and objectives of members as they enter the group. Group goals, on the other hand, "are the emergent product of the interaction of all participants together, the organizer and the members, as they express their ideas and feelings about the reasons for the existence of the group and its anticipated outcomes. Group goals include, therefore, rationale, expectations and objectives toward which the group puts its collective efforts" (Hartford, 1971, p. 139).

The following list contains examples of specific goals that may be formulated at either individual or group levels:

1. To discern strengths and incremental growth in one's self and in others and to give and receive positive feedback in relation to the same.
2. To expand awareness of one's own behavior (or the group's processes).
3. To identify one's own self-defeating behaviors and to replace these with more functional behaviors.
4. To develop problem-solving skills that enhance decision making in both individual and group contexts and to apply them to specific problems.
5. To relate to others with increased authenticity.
6. To become more liberated from external imperatives, that is, "shoulds," "oughts," and "musts."
7. To learn employment skills that will assist in becoming employed.
8. To learn how to hear accurately the messages of others and to convey one's understanding of these messages to others.
9. To grow in self-acceptance and to explore hidden potentials and creativity.
10. To increase one's capacity to care for others and to manifest that caring.
11. To learn to express thoughts, feelings, needs, and ideas to others.
12. To develop trust in one's own judgment.
13. To learn and practice skills in making friends.

Conducting a Preliminary Interview

Before convening a group, social workers often meet individually with potential group members for the purpose of establishing rapport, exploring relevant concerns, and formulating initial contracts with those motivated to join the group, and clarifying constrained choices for involuntary clients. Conducting individual interviews is essential to composing a group carefully, which entails selecting members according to predetermined criteria and including those who have specific behavioral or personality attributes thought to be beneficial for the purposes of the group. Further, when composing a group of involuntary clients (e.g., delinquents, court-referred parents, or felons), having an individual interview is a vital first step in assisting potential members to identify acknowledged as well as attributed problems and to clarify constrained choices.

Pregroup meetings with potential members assist social workers to gain essential information that may be of substantial value in selecting and directing interventions to those members in early sessions. (Because of the time limitations in regular group sessions, such vital information may not otherwise emerge for several weeks.) Further, conducting preliminary interviews enables social workers to enter initial group sessions with a previously established relationship with each member, a distinct advantage given the fact that leaders must attend to multiple communication processes at both individual and group levels. In addition, previous knowledge about individual members facilitates grasping the meaning of the behavior of those members in the group, thus enabling social workers to focus more fully on group processes and the task of assisting members to develop relationships with each other. Establishing rapport with the leader prior to initial sessions also enables members to feel more at ease and to open up more readily in the first meeting.

Objectives that social workers may wish to accomplish in preliminary interviews include the following:

1. *Orienting potential members to proposed goals and purposes of the group,* its content and structure, the philosophy and style of the leader in managing group processes, and the respective roles of the leader and group members. It is important with involuntary groups to distinguish between nonnegotiable rules and policies, such as attendance expectations and general themes to be discussed, and negotiable norms and procedures, such as arrangements for breaks, food, and selection of particular topics and their order. The social worker should elicit the client's reactions and suggestions that would enable the group to better serve the client's needs. Orientation should also include a sharing of the time, place of meetings, length of sessions, and the like. In addition, the social worker may wish to emphasize commonalities that the client may share with other persons considering group membership, such as problems, interests, concerns, or objectives.

2. *Eliciting the client's view of prior group experiences,* including the nature of the client's relationship with the leader and other members, the client's style of relating in the previous group, the goals that the client accomplished, and the personal growth that was achieved. Social workers should anticipate negative reactions from involuntary group members, recognize them as expectable, and yet emphasize ways they can make use of their decision to participate in the group to reach their own goals as well as mandated goals.

3. *Eliciting, exploring, and clarifying clients' problems,* and identifying those that are appropriate for the proposed group. In some instances, either because clients are reluctant to participate in the group or because their problems appear to be more appropriately handled through other treatment modalities or community agencies, you may need to refer them to other resources. With respect to treatment approaches, Garvin (1981) emphasizes that "the client's choice of individual, group, or family services should be an informed one based on information regarding different

forms of interpersonal helping and what they are like." He suggests employing media aids such as films, tapes, or even comic books to portray what happens in the agency's groups (p. 75). Garvin also emphasizes that some clients' problems are better addressed within a family than a group context. To determine which modality is mutually preferable, Garvin identifies the following three criteria (p. 74):

a. Is the problem maintained by processes operating in the family as a system? (See Chapter 10.)

b. How will the family respond to changes the individual may choose to make, and will these responses support or retard such changes?

c. Does the individual wish to involve the family, and is the family amenable to such involvement?

4. *Exploring the client's hopes, aspirations, and expectations* regarding the proposed group (e.g., "What would you like to be different in your life as a result of your attending this group?").

5. *Identifying specific goals that the client wishes to accomplish,* discussing whether these goals can be attained through the proposed group, and determining the client's views as to whether the group is an appropriate vehicle for resolving personal problems. It is critical, of course, to respect a client's right not to participate in a voluntary group. Garvin, Reid, and Epstein (1976) emphasize the need to put "high priority on the client's autonomy, particularly his right to freedom from imposed or deceptive treatment." These authors recommend employing a specific contract that protects each client from "help for a condition he may not wish to change or from treatment for an unacknowledged problem" (pp. 242–243). With involuntary groups, sharing personal goals that prior members have chosen such as going back to school in addition to mandated goals such as seeking alternatives to prostitution can assist in enhancing the attractiveness of the group.

6. *Mutually developing a profile of the client's attributes* and determining any that the client might like to enhance through work in the group.

7. *Identifying and exploring potential obstacles* that might prevent clients from participating in or receiving desired benefits from the group, including reservations they may have about attending the group. Other obstacles may include shyness or nonassertiveness in group situations, opposition from significant others about entering the group, a heavy schedule that would likely preclude attending all group meetings, or problems in finding baby-sitters. After exploring obstacles, it is appropriate to assist clients in generating possible alternatives that might obviate these obstacles. In some cases, obstacles may preclude clients from group participation.

8. *Ensuring that the screening for the group is a two-way process.* Potential members of voluntary groups should have the opportunity to interview the group leader and to determine whether the group is appropriate for their problems and interests.

Group Composition

In most instances, an overriding factor in selecting group members is whether a candidate is motivated to make changes and is willing to expend the necessary effort to be a productive group member. Another factor is the likelihood of a person's compatibility with other members in the group. Social workers also usually address the following in determining the composition of groups: sex, age, marital status, intellectual ability, education, socioeconomic status, ego strength, and type of problem (Flapan & Fenchal, 1987).

Homogeneity versus heterogeneity of these characteristics is a vital issue in composing a group. Significant homogeneity in personal characteristics and purpose for being in the group is necessary to facilitate communication and group cohesion. Without such homogeneity, members will have little basis for interacting with each other. Toseland and Rivas (2001), for example, identify levels of education, cultural background, degree of expertise relative to the group task, and communication ability as characteristics vital to creating group homogeneity.

On the other hand, some diversity among members with respect to coping skills, life experience, and levels of expertise fosters learning and introduces members to differing viewpoints, lifestyles, ways of communicating, and problem solving. To attain the end product of providing "multiple opportunities for support, mutual aid, and learning," a treatment group, for example, might be composed of members from different cultures, social classes, occupations, or geographic areas. Heterogeneity is a vital variable in the membership of task groups that ensures sufficient resources to provide for an efficient division of labor when dealing with complex tasks (Toseland & Rivas, 2001). The challenge is to attain a workable balance between homogeneity and heterogeneity.

G. Corey (1990) cautions against including members in voluntary groups whose behavior or pathology is extreme, inasmuch as some people reduce the available energy of the group for productive work and interfere significantly in the development of group cohesion. This is particularly true of individuals who have a need to monopolize and dominate, of hostile people or aggressive people with a need to act out, and of people who are extremely self-centered and who seek a group as an audience. However, such oppositional behavior may be a common denominator in some groups such as those addressed to domestic violence and drug addition (Milgram & Rubin, 1992). Others who should generally be excluded from most groups are people who are in a state of extreme crisis, who are suicidal, who have sociopathic personalities, who are highly suspicious, or who are lacking in ego strength and are prone to fragmented and bizarre behavior (p. 89).

A decision to include or exclude a client has much to do with the purposes of the group. For example, an alcoholic might be excluded from a personal growth group but appropriately included in a homogeneous group of individuals who suffer from various types of addictions. Similarly, angry clients are expected in a domestic violence group.

Garvin (1987) warns against including in a treatment group a member who is very different from others, for the danger is that this person: "will be perceived as undesirable or, in sociological terms, deviant by the other members. When the difference is based on some attribute such as age or race, the members may avoid communicating with this person, thus creating a group isolate. When the difference is based on a behavior such as topics discussed, personal disclosure, or social skills, the members may become critical of the individual and then scapegoat the person, who will then develop negative feelings toward the group, avoid its influence, and eventually drop out" (p. 64).

When there is the likelihood that group composition will lead to creating a deviant member, Garvin recommends enrolling another member who "is either similar to the person in question or who is somewhere in the 'middle,' thus creating a continuum of member characteristics" (p. 65). Speaking of gender, and of ethnic groups that may be oppressed economically or socially such as blacks, Asians and Pacific Islanders, Latinos, or Native Americans, Garvin also cautions against composing a group in which a person, by virtue of such gender or ethnicity, represents a small minority of one or two within the group. These persons may experience considerable discomfort and have little in common with the rest of the group. For example, some agencies have found that there are advantages to creating groups for women who have chemical dependencies, as their issues often differ from men (Nelson-Zlupko, Kaufman, & Dore, 1995).

Open Versus Closed Groups

Groups may have either an open format, in which the group remains open to new members, or a closed format in which no new members are added once the group gets under way. Open-ended groups are used for helping clients cope with transitions and crises, providing support, acting as a means for assessment, and facilitating outreach (Schopler & Galinsky, 1981). Having open-ended groups ensures that a group is immediately available at a time of crisis. An open format itself presents different models (M. Henry, 1988; K. E. Reid, 1991), including the drop-in (or drop-out) model in which members are self-selecting, entry criteria are very broad, and members attend whenever they wish for an indefinite period. Another is the replacement model, in which the leader immediately identifies someone to fill a group vacancy, and a third is the re-formed model, in which group members contract for a set period of time, during which no new members are added but original members may drop out. At the end of the contract period, a new group is formed consisting of some old and some new members.

The choice of format depends on the purpose of the group, the setting, and the population served. An open format provides the opportunity for new members to bring fresh perspectives to the group and offers immediate support for those in need, who can stay as long as they choose. At the same time, the instability of such a format discourages members from developing the trust and confidence to openly share and explore their problems, a strong feature of the closed-ended group. Frequent changes of membership may also disrupt the work of the open-ended group. Leaders of open-ended groups hence need to be attuned to clients being at different places in the group process and to be able to work with core members to carry forth group traditions (Schopler & Galinsky, 1981). Advantages associated with a closed group include higher group morale, more predictability of role behaviors, and an increased sense of cooperation among members. A disadvantage, however, is that if too many members drop out, the group process is drastically affected by the high attrition.

Group Size

The size of the group depends in large part on the purpose, the age of clients, the type of problems to be explored, and the needs of members. Five to 12 members is usually an optimum number for a group with an emphasis on close relationships (K. E. Reid, 1991). Bertcher and Maple (1985) observe: "In general, the group should be small enough to allow it to accomplish its purpose, yet large enough to permit members to have a satisfying experience."

Frequency and Duration of Meetings

Closed groups benefit from having a termination date at the outset, which encourages productive work. Regarding the possible lifespan of a group, G. Corey (1990) notes: "The duration varies from group to group, depending on the type of group and the population. The group should be long enough to allow for cohesion and productive work yet not so long that the group seems to drag on interminably" (p. 92). For a time-limited therapy group, K. E. Reid (1991) recommends approximately 20 sessions, stating that this length provides adequate time for cohesiveness and a sense of trust to develop. Reid recommends the use of time limits, noting that if the leader errs in estimating the length of time needed, "there is an end point in which the group can be reformulated as opposed to it going on indefinitely" (p. 189).

Formulating Group Guidelines

Developing consensus concerning guidelines for behavior (e.g., staying on task) among group members is a vital aspect of contracting in the initial phase with voluntary clients. Some group guidelines, especially when clients are involuntary, cannot be determined by consensus. Wherever possible, voluntary agreement should be sought on as many group guidelines as possible. In formulating guidelines with the group, the social worker takes the first step in shaping the group's evolving processes to create a "working group" capable of achieving specific objectives. Attempts to formulate guidelines often fail to achieve this intended effect for three major reasons.

First, a social worker may establish parameters *for* the group, merely informing members of behavioral expectations to which they are expected to adhere. While nonnegotiable requirements such as attendance are often part of involuntary groups, overemphasis on such control may convey the message "This is my group, and this is how I expect you to behave in it." Such an emphasis may negate later actions by the social worker to encourage members to assume responsibility for the group. Without consensus among members concerning desirable group guidelines, power struggles and disagreements may ensue as to the appropriateness of certain behaviors. Further, members may not feel bound by what they consider the "leader's rules" and may, in fact, deliberately test them, creating a counterproductive scenario. Members may thus cast the social worker in the role of "authoritarian parent" and assume the role of "errant children."

Second, the social worker may discuss group guidelines only superficially and neglect either to identify or to obtain commitment to guidelines. Such neglect by a group leader is unfortunate, for the extent to which members delineate specific and functional parameters greatly influences the extent to which they will modify their behavior in future sessions to conform to adopted guidelines or to achieve stated group objectives.

Third, even when the group adopts viable guidelines for behavior within the group, the social worker may erroneously assume that members will subsequently conform to these guidelines. To the contrary, there is often little relationship between contracted behaviors and actual behaviors. Establishing group guidelines merely sets guideposts against which members may measure their current behavior. Social workers must consistently intervene to assist members to adhere to guidelines and to consider discrepancies between contracted and actual behaviors before negotiated behaviors actually become normative.

Because formulating guidelines is a critical process that substantially influences the success of a group, we offer the following suggestions to assist you.

1. If there are nonnegotiable agency rules (e.g., adolescents often are not allowed to smoke in correctional settings), you should present the rules, explain their rationale, and encourage discussion of them (Behroozi, 1992). Confidentiality is often a nonnegotiable rule. The rationale for ensuring that issues discussed in the group will not be shared outside the group should be explained.

2. Introduce the group to the concept of *decision by consensus* on all negotiable items (explained later in this section), and solicit agreement concerning adoption of this modus operandi for making decisions *prior* to formulating group guidelines.

3. Ask group members to share their vision of the kind of group they would like to have by responding to the following statement: "I would like this group to be a place where I could. . ." Reach for responses from all members, and once this has been achieved, summarize the collective thinking of the group. Offer your own views of supportive group structure that assists members to work on individual problems or to achieve group objectives.

4. Ask members to identify guidelines for behavior in the group that will assist them to achieve the kind of group structure and atmosphere they desire. You may wish to brainstorm possible guidelines at this point, adding your suggestions. Then, through group consensus, choose those that seem most appropriate.

Depending on the setting and purpose of your group, you may need to develop guidelines that pertain to the following group behaviors. Guidelines adopted by many groups regarding these behaviors have proven conducive to achieving individual and group objectives.

Group Format

Pursuing ill-defined objectives within a structure that provides few guidelines for efficient use of time can defeat the best-intentioned leader or group. Developing a group structure during the initial phase that embodies the following activities, however, assists leaders and members to focus their energies on therapeutic objectives actively and efficiently.

1. Define group and individual goals in behavioral terms and rank them according to priority.

2. Develop an overall plan that organizes the work to be done within the number of sessions allocated by the group to achieve its goals.

3. Specify behavioral tasks to be accomplished outside the group each week that will assist individuals to make desired changes.

4. Achieve agreement among members concerning weekly format and agenda, that is, how time will be allocated each week to achieve goals. For instance, a group might allocate its weekly 2 hours to the format in Table 11-1.

15 MIN.	1½ HOURS	15 MIN.
Reviewing and monitoring tasks	Focusing on relevant content and formulating tasks	Sessional endings Evaluating group sessions

Table 11-1

Other than nonnegotiable policies in involuntary groups, avoid imposing structure upon a group; rather, assist the group to evolve a format that will facilitate achieving the group's proposed objectives. The structure adopted by your group should also be flexible enough to accommodate to group processes and to the needs of members. To ensure its continued functionality, review the format periodically throughout the life of the group.

We are not recommending that your group attempt to adopt all of the preceding suggestions, but we stress the need for a clearly conceptualized format that provides the means for evaluating the ongoing process of group members. Our position is based on a conviction that, regardless of the treatment modality utilized, clients have a right to receive help within a format that provides for accountability in the form of continuing and concrete feedback concerning their progress.

Group Decision Making

Effective deliberation and decision making are critical in determining the productivity and success of a group. To achieve its objectives, every group ultimately develops methods of making decisions. Left to their own devices, however, groups may evolve counterproductive decision-making processes. Some groups, for example, permit the power for making decisions to be vested in a few members, "counting in" some members and "counting out" others. This modus operandi perpetuates conflict and intrigue in the group, causing unrest and resentments that divert energies from productive tasks and block developmental progress.

Members of newly formed groups have varying styles of making decisions and do not know how to make decisions effectively as a group. As a result, most treatment groups learn problem solving through extended trial-and-error processes, gradually gaining from their mistakes (we hope). Most groups, however, can quickly learn to adopt a model of decision by consensus, given effective leadership in educating the group. Further, equipping groups with an effective decision-making model in the early stages of development can expedite group process and assist groups in more readily achieving an advanced level of group functioning. Our decision-by-consensus method can be taught early in the first group session according to the following sequence:

1. Explaining that groups need a decision-making method that gives each person an equal vote and "counts everyone in"

2. Gaining group acceptance of this method of making decisions

3. Explaining steps for effective decision making (these steps are discussed in Chapter 14)

4. Identifying the leader's function in assisting the group to make decisions that meet the needs of all members

5. Using the decision-by-consensus approach in setting up the initial contract and focusing explicitly on the process to enhance group awareness of the use of this approach

Additional Group Issues to Address

In the paragraphs that follow, we will suggest guidelines for ten issues that are pertinent to treatment groups, though their applicability depends on the specific focus of the group.

1. *Help-Giving/Help-Seeking Roles.* Groups formed to assist individuals with personal problems benefit from clarification of what might be termed *help-giving* and *help-seeking* roles. Although the two terms are self-explanatory, you may wish to assist the group to operationalize these roles by considering behaviors embodied in them. The help-seeking role, for example, incorporates such behaviors as making direct requests for help, authentically sharing one's feelings, being open to feedback, and demonstrating willingness to test new approaches to problems. The help-giving role involves such behaviors as listening attentively, refraining from criticism, clarifying perceptions, summarizing, maintaining focus on the problem, and pinpointing strengths and incremental growth. A critical aspect of the help-giving role you should clarify for group members is the necessity of exploring personal problems of fellow members carefully before attempting to solve them. Otherwise, groups tend to move quickly to giving advice and offering evaluative suggestions about what a member "ought" or "ought not" to do. You can further help the group to adopt these two roles by highlighting instances in which members have performed in either of these helping roles, accrediting them accordingly.

2. *Visitors.* A group convened for treatment purposes should develop explicit guidelines specifying whether and under what conditions visitors may attend group meetings. If the group has an open format, allowing frequent changes in membership, the presence of a visitor will have little impact. However, in closed groups (i.e., ones that do not usually add members once the group has convened), visitors can have a devastating effect on group processes. The presence of visitors can cause members to refrain from sharing feelings and problems openly and create resentments toward the member (or social worker) who invited the visitor and thereby violated the integrity of the group. Anticipating with members the possible impact of visitors upon the group and establishing procedures and conditions under which visitors may attend sessions can avert group turmoil as well as embarrassment for individual members.

3. *New Members.* Procedures for adding and orienting new members may also need to be established. In some cases, the group leader may reserve the prerogative of selecting members. In other instances, the leader may permit the group to choose new members, with the understanding that choices should be based on certain criteria and that the group should achieve consensus regarding potential members. In either case, procedures for adding new members and the importance of the group's role in orienting them should be clarified. As mentioned above, adding new members in an open-ended group should occur in a planned way, considering the stage of development of the group.

4. *Individual Contacts with the Social Worker.* Whether you encourage or discourage individual contacts with members outside thee group depends on the purpose of the group and the anticipated consequences or benefits of such contacts. In some cases, individual contacts serve to promote group objectives. For example, in a correctional setting, planned meetings with an adolescent between sessions provide opportunities to focus on the youth's problematic behaviors in the group and

to develop an individual contact with the youth to modify them and support strengths. In the case of marital therapy groups, however, individual contacts initiated by one spouse may be a bid for an alliance with the social worker against the other partner or may be perceived as such by the other spouse. If you have questions regarding the advisability of having individual contacts outside the group, you should thoroughly discuss these questions with members and mutually develop guidelines pertaining to this matter.

5. *Cleanup*. Making group decisions regarding cleanup before having to contend with a messy room is an effective strategy that encourages members to assume responsibility for themselves and for the group. Resentments fester, and subgroupings destructive to group cohesiveness tend to form when some members consistently stay to help with cleanup and others do not.

6. *Use of Recorder*. The social worker should always gain the group's permission before recording a group session. Further, before asking for a decision you should provide information concerning the manner in which the recording is to be utilized outside the session. Reservations regarding recording the session should be thoroughly aired, and the group's wishes should be respected.

7. *Use of Profanity*. Some social workers believe that group members should be allowed to use whatever language they choose in expressing themselves. However, profanity may be offensive to some members, including the social workers, and the group may wish to develop guidelines concerning this matter. For some groups, the social workers might be the only ones offended, and imposition of the social workers' preferences might inhibit the group.

8. *Attendance*. Discussing the problems that irregular attendance can pose for a group before the fact and soliciting commitment from members to attend regularly can do much to solidify group attendance in future group sessions. Involuntary groups often have attendance policies permitting a limited number of absences and late arrivals.

Further, late arrivals and early departures by group members can be minimized if the group develops relevant guidelines in advance. Allowances on an individual basis are needed, of course, to accommodate the schedules of members in special instances with the understanding that these situations should be rare. To expedite adherence to a group contract regarding a time frame, you should start and end meetings promptly and extend meetings only after the group has made the decision to do so. Although you may sometimes feel the press of unfinished business at the end of a meeting, holding group members beyond the scheduled time without their consent violates the group contract and may create resentment.

9. *Eating, Drinking, Smoking*. Opinions vary among group leaders concerning these activities in groups. Some groups and leaders believe these activities distract from group process; others regard them as relaxing and actually beneficial to group operation. You may wish to elicit views from members concerning these activities and develop guidelines with the group that meet member needs and facilitate group progress.

10. *Programming*. At times, group formats include activities or exercises. For example, there is much psychoeducational programming in the operation of domestic abuse and chemical abuse groups. Unfortunately, however, such programming does not always directly relate to the group's purpose; further, the activities or exercises in which the group participate may not be discussed by members for the purpose of learning from the experience or relating it to behavioral changes members wish to achieve. Thus, when programming is utilized, social workers need to discuss with members how such activities can be best utilized to meet specified objectives and to plan with them ways of evaluating and generalizing the group's experience.

Remember that guidelines are helpful only to the extent that they expedite the development of the group and should be reviewed periodically to assess their functionality in relationship to the group's stage of development. Outdated guidelines, of course, should be discarded or reformulated. Further, when a group's behavior is incompatible with group guidelines, it may be advisable to describe what is happening in the group (or request that members do so) and, after thoroughly reviewing the situation, ask the group to consider whether the guideline in question is still viable. If used judiciously, this strategy not only helps the group to reassess guidelines but also places responsibility for monitoring adherence to guidelines with the group, where it belongs. Leaders who unwittingly assume the role of "enforcer" place themselves in an untenable position, for group members tend to struggle against what they perceive as authoritarian control on the leader's part.

ASSESSING GROUP PROCESSES

In group assessment, social workers must attend to processes that occur at both the individual and group levels, including emerging themes or patterns they must necessarily consider as they intervene to enhance the functioning of individuals and the group as a whole. In the following section, procedures for making accurate assessment of the processes of both individuals and groups are delineated. Such assessments must be set within a systems framework that allows social workers to see the patterning of individual and group behaviors. Social work researchers have recently made strides in measuring group processes in ways that monitor the quality of the process and assist in predicting the outcome. For example, Macgowan (1997) has developed a groupwork engagement measure (GEM) that combines measures of attendance, satisfaction, perceived group helpfulness, group cohesion, and interaction. Magen and Glajchen report that members of 12 different cancer support groups ranked cohesion, hope, and altruism as important factors in their satisfaction with the group process (Magen & Glajchen, 1999).

A Systems Framework for Assessing Groups

Like families, groups are social systems characterized by repetitive patterns. The operations within all social systems share an important principle, namely, that persons who compose a given system gradually limit their behaviors to a relatively narrow range of patterned responses as they interact with others within that system. Groups thus evolve implicit rules or norms that govern behaviors, shape patterns, and regulate internal operations. Employing a systems framework in assessing the processes of groups, leaders attend to the patterned interactions of members, infer rules that govern those interactions, and weigh the functionality of the rules and patterns.

Knowledge that group processes can be conceptualized and organized into response patterns enables leaders to make systematic, ongoing, and relevant assessments. This knowledge can be comforting to inexperienced group leaders, who often feel they are floundering in group sessions. Some beginning group leaders, in fact, are greatly relieved and gain considerable confidence as they realize it is possible to "make sense" out of group process.

As leaders observe groups to discern patterned behaviors, they must concurrently attend to behavior manifested by individuals and by the group itself. Observing processes at both levels is difficult, however, and leaders sometimes become discouraged when they realize they attended more to individual dynamics than to group dynamics (or the converse), causing their formulations of individual and/or group patterns to be vague or incomplete. We thus discuss strategies for accurately assessing both individual and group patterns in the remainder of the chapter.

Assessing Patterned Behaviors of Individuals

Some of the patterned behaviors group members manifest are *functional,* that is, enhance the well-being of individual members and the quality of relationships. Other patterned behaviors are dysfunctional in that they erode the self-esteem of members and are destructive to relationships. Many members of growth groups, in fact, join such groups because certain of their patterned dysfunctional behaviors produce distress in interpersonal relationships for themselves and others. Often, of course, these members are not aware of the patterned nature of their behavior nor of the fact that some of these entrenched behaviors cause interpersonal problems. Rather, group members often regard other persons as the source of their difficulties.

A major role of leaders in growth groups, then, is to aid members to become aware of their patterned behavioral responses, to determine the impact of these responses on themselves and others, and to choose whether to change such responses. To carry out this role, leaders must formulate a profile of the recurring responses of each member.

Understanding Content and Process

To formulate accurate assessment of individual behavioral responses, you must apply the concepts of *content and process,* which we discussed in the preceding chapter. To refresh your memory, content refers to verbal statements and related topics that members discuss, whereas process involves the ways members relate or behave as they interact in the group and discuss content. To expand your understanding of the concept of group process, consider for a moment the following description of a member's behavior in two initial group sessions:

In the first group meeting, John moved his chair close to the leader's. Several times when the leader made statements, John expressed agreement. In the second group meeting, John again sat next to the leader and used the pronoun *we* several times, referring to opinions he thought were jointly held by himself and the leader. Later, John tried to initiate a conversation with the leader concerning what he regarded as negative

behavior of another group member in front of that member and the rest of the group.

This example describes how John is behaving and communicating rather than what he is saying, and thus it deals with process rather than content.

It is at the process level that leaders discover many of the patterned behavioral responses of individuals. The preceding example reveals John's possible patterned or thematic behaviors. For example, we might infer that John is jockeying to establish an exclusive relationship with the leader and bidding for an informal position of co-leader in the group. Viewed alone, none of the discrete behaviors in the preceding excerpt provides sufficient information to justify drawing a conclusion as to a possible response pattern. Viewed collectively, however, the repetitive responses warrant inferring that a pattern does, in fact, exist.

Identifying Roles of Group Members

In identifying patterned responses of individuals, leaders also need to attend to various roles members assume in the group. Members, for example, may assume *leadership* roles that are formal (explicitly sanctioned by the group) or informal (emerge as a result of group needs). Further, a group may have several leaders who serve different functions or who head rival subgroups.

Some members may assume *task-related roles* that facilitate the group's efforts to define problems, to implement problem-solving strategies, and to carry out tasks. These members may propose goals or actions, suggest procedures, request pertinent facts, clarify issues, or offer an alternative or conclusion for the group to consider. Other members may adopt *maintenance* roles that are oriented to altering, maintaining, and strengthening the group's functioning. Members who take on such roles may offer compromises, encourage and support the contributions of others, or suggest group standards. Some members of involuntary groups often emerge as spokespersons around concerns of the group. Rather than confront such a person as a negative influence, it is often useful to explore whether, in fact, that person is bringing to the fore issues that have been discussed outside of the group. In short, that person may in fact be acting as an informal group leader who can be joined in wishing to make the group succeed (Breton, 1985). Still other members may assume self-serving roles by seeking to meet their own needs at the expense of the group. Such members attack the group or its values, stubbornly resist the group's wishes, continually disagree with or interrupt others, assert authority or superiority, display lack of involvement, pursue extraneous subjects, or find various ways to call attention to themselves.

Members may also carry labels assigned by other members, such as "clown," "uncommitted," "lazy," "dumb," "silent one," "rebel," "overreactor," or "good mother." Such labeling stereotypes members, making it difficult for them to relinquish the set of expected behaviors or to change their way of relating to the group. Hartford (1971) elaborates:

> For instance, the person who has become the clown may not be able to make a serious and substantial contribution to the group because, regardless of what he says, everyone laughs. If one person has established a high status as the initiator, others may not be able to initiate for fear of threatening his position. If one has established himself in a dependency role in a pair or subgroup, he may not be able to function freely until he gets cues from his subgroup partner. (p. 218)

One or more members may also be assigned the role of scapegoat, bearing the burden of responsibility for the group's problems and the brunt of consistent negative responses from other members. Such individuals may attract the scapegoating role because they are socially awkward and repeatedly make social blunders in futile attempts to elicit positive responses from others (Balgopal & Vassil, 1983; Klein, 1970). Or they may foster the role because they fail to recognize nonverbal cues that facilitate interaction in the group and thus behave without regard to the sub-

tle nuances that govern the behavior of other members (Balgopal & Vassil, 1983; A. Beck, 1974). Individuals may also unknowingly perpetuate the scapegoating role they have assumed in their nuclear families. Although group scapegoats manifest repetitive dysfunctional behaviors that attract the hostility of the group, the presence of the scapegoating role signals a group phenomenon (and pattern), the maintenance of which requires the tacit cooperation of all members.

Individuals may also assume the role of an isolate, the characteristics of which Hartford (1971) described:

> The social isolate is the person who is present but generally ignored by the others. He does not seem to reach out to others or her reaches out but is rejected. His lack of affiliation with others in the group may be due to lack of capacity on his part to get along with others, or he may differ in values, beliefs, and lifestyle from others enough to be deviant. He is not generally the scapegoat for if he were, he would be getting attention, however negative. The true isolate is ignored, his contributions go unnoted, his opinions are not asked for. (p. 208)

It is important to identify roles that members assume because such roles profoundly affect the group's capacity to respond to the individual needs of members and its ability to fulfill treatment objectives. Further, identifying roles is vital because members tend to play out in treatment groups the same roles that they assume in other social contexts. Members need to understand the impact of enacting dysfunctional roles on themselves and others. Some members, of course, assume roles that strengthen relationships and are conducive to group functioning. By highlighting these positive behaviors, leaders enhance members' self-esteem and also place the spotlight on behaviors other members may emulate.

Developing Profiles of Individual Behavior

In assessment, group leaders need to develop accurate behavioral profiles of each individual. To carry out this function, leaders record functional and dysfunctional responses of members manifested in initial sessions. Operating from a strengths perspective, it is important to record and acknowledge such functional behaviors as the following.

FUNCTIONAL BEHAVIORS

1. Expresses caring for group members or significant others.
2. Demonstrates organizational or leadership ability.
3. Expresses self clearly.
4. Cooperates with and supports others.
5. Assists in maintaining focus and helping the group accomplish its purposes.
6. Expresses feelings openly and congruently.
7. Accurately perceives what others say (beyond surface meanings) and conveys understanding to them.
8. Responds openly and positively to constructive feedback.
9. Works within guidelines established by the group.
10. "Owns" responsibility for behavior.
11. Risks and works to change self.
12. Counts in others by considering their opinions, including them in decision making, or valuing their differences.
13. Participate in discussions and assists others to join in.
14. Gives positive feedback to other concerning their strengths and growth.
15. Accredits own strengths and growth.
16. Expresses humor facilitatively.
17. Supports others nonverbally.

DYSFUNCTIONAL BEHAVIORS

1. Interrupts, speaks for others, rejects others' ideas.
2. Placates, patronizes.
3. Belittles, criticizes, or expresses sarcasm.
4. Argues, blames, attacks, engages in name-calling.
5. Verbally dominates group "air time."
6. Gives advice prematurely.
7. Expresses disgust and disapproval nonverbally.
8. Talks too much, too loudly, or whispers.
9. Withdraws, assumes role of spectator, ignores, shows disinterest.
10. Talks about tangential topics or sidetracks in other ways.
11. Manifests distractive physical movements.
12. Is physically aggressive or "horses" around.
13. Clowns, mimics, or makes fun of others.
14. Aligns with others to form destructive subgroups.
15. Intellectualizes or diagnoses (e.g., "I know what's wrong with you").
16. Avoids focusing on self or withholds feelings and concerns pertinent to personal problems.

Table 11-2 is a record of a women's support group that illustrates how leaders can develop accurate behavioral profiles of each member by keeping track of the functional and dysfunctional behaviors manifested by members in initial sessions. The profile of group members' behaviors in Table 11-2 identifies specific responses manifested by individuals in the group but does not necessarily identify their *patterned or stylized* behaviors. Recording specific responses of individuals at each session, however, aids in identifying recurring behaviors and roles members are assuming. With regard to roles, for example, a glance at the preceding profiles suggests that Dixie is vulnerable to becoming an isolate in the group.

Identifying Growth of Individuals

Because growth occurs in subtle and diverse forms, a major role of leaders is to document (and to assist the group to document) the incremental growth of each member. To sharpen your ability to observe growth of individuals, we suggest that you develop a record-keeping format that provides a column for notations concerning the growth members make from one session to the next or across several sessions. Without such a recording system, it is easy to overlook significant changes and thus miss vital opportunities to substantiate the direct relationship between their efforts to change and the positive results they attain.

The Impact of Culture

Assessment of individual functioning, of course, must be tempered by the individual's cultural background. Tsui and Schultz (1988) stress that "the group norms comprising the so-called therapeutic milieu are actually Caucasian group norms that, in themselves, resist intrusion and disruption from minority cultures: (p. 137). Individuals from other cultures living amidst a majority culture different from their own are influenced by that majority culture in unique ways. That is, they range on a continuum of acculturation. Further, the behavior of a minority group member might be significantly negatively influenced by a group composed largely of Caucasians who try to assimilate the minority member into what they see as the therapeutic milieu. Chau suggests that needs assessments with groups unfortunately often relegate sociocultural reality to a place of secondary concern (Chau, 1993). Further, the problems faced by people of color are often defined in terms of psychological dysfunction, with the individual targeted for change. Chau notes that many of the supposed symptoms of "dysfunctional" behavior may be attempts to influence others in their environment; to cope with the stress and strain of adaptation. That is, their responses may be adaptive to problems of prejudice and discrimination (p. 54).

Gaining Information from Other Sources

In addition to direct observation, information concerning the behavioral styles of members can be obtained from many other sources.

In the formation phase of the group, for example, leaders can elicit pertinent data in preliminary interviews with the prospective member or from family members, agency records, or social workers who have referred members to the group. Within the group, leaders may also glean substantial data concerning patterned behavior of members by carefully attuning to and exploring members' descriptions of their problems and interactions with others.

Assessing Cognitive Patterns of Individuals

Just as group members develop patterned ways of behaving, they develop patterned cognitions, that is, typical or habituated ways of perceiving and thinking about themselves, other persons, and the world around them. Such patterned cognitions are manifested in the form of silent mental speech or internal dialogue that individuals utilize to make meaning of life events. To use an analogy, it is as though various types of events in a person's life trigger a tape recording in his or her mind that automatically repeats the same messages over and over, coloring the person's perceptions of events and determining his or her reality. Examples of negative internal dialogue that tend to create problems for group members include repeated messages such as "I'm a failure," "I'll never be able to succeed," and "Other people are better than I am."

Patterned cognitions and behavior are inextricably related and reciprocally reinforce each other. The following example of a group member's problem illustrates the marriage between cognitions and behavior and the insidious effect that negative cognitions may have on a client's life:

Jean, a 25-year-old dental assistant, entered an adult support group because of problems at work that were jeopardizing her position. As Jean reported her problems to the group, the following situation unfolded: Jean was experiencing severe negative reactions toward her employer, Dr. A. An attractive young dentist, Dr. A was the "darling"

NAME	DESCRIPTIVE ATTRIBUTES	FUNCTIONAL BEHAVIOR	DYSFUNCTIONAL BEHAVIOR
June	35 years old Legal secretary 8-year-old son Divorced five years	Gave positive feedback several times Expressed feelings clearly Outgoing and spontaneous Adds energy to group	Ruminated several times about the past Sometimes interrupted others and dominated discussion
Raye	29 years old Homemaker Three children	Articulate Sharp at summarizing feelings of group Expressed ambivalence about attending group	Seemed to have self-doubt concerting validity of own opinions
Janet	34 years old Clerical supervisor Divorced one year	Initiated group discussion of several topics	Was dogmatic and unyielding about several of her opinions Became angry several times during session; appears to have short fuse
Pam	35 years old Truck driver Six children Divorced three years	Joined in discussions Accredited self for several strengths	Responses indicate she labels and puts down her children Twice challenged the comments of others
Dixie	30 years old Homemaker Two children Divorce in progress	Stated she came to group despite considerable apprehension Artist; exhibits paintings	Very quiet in session Acts intimidated by group Sat in chair slightly outside circle
Rachael	30 years old Unmarried	Readily shared problems Responsive to others Able to describe feelings Articulate	Seemed to pull the group toward feeling sorry for her through constant story-telling
Karen	31 years old Homemaker Three children Divorced one year	Seemed eager to work on problems Talked about self introspectively	Several times appeared to appease others rather than expressing how she really felt about issues
Elaine	45 years old Cafeteria worker Two teenagers Divorce in progress	Listened attentively to others Nodded approvingly when others spoke	Did not speak up in group

Table 11-2   Examples of Behavioral Profiles of Group Members

of the large dental organization for which Jean worked. Watching Dr. A, who was single, pursue other young women in the office, Jean concluded that he was disinterested and "bored" with her and that she was doing an inadequate job. As Jean worked daily with Dr. A, she made repeated statements to herself such as "He doesn't like me," "He'd rather have someone else as an assistant," and "There's something wrong with me." Jean worked at hiding her growing resentment toward Dr. A but ultimately could not contain her feelings. Defensive and easily riled because of what she constantly said to herself, Jean repeatedly snapped at Dr. A in front of patients. Angered and confused by Jean's irritable behavior, Dr. A began to grow annoyed himself and to relate to Jean more and more coolly. Jean interpreted Dr. A's behavior as evidence that she was correct in her conclusion and that he did not like her and that she was inadequate not only as an assistant but as a person as well.

Because patterned behavioral and cognitive responses are inextricably interwoven and perpetuate each other, leaders must be able to intervene in groups to modify dysfunctional cognitions. Preliminary to intervening, however, leaders must fine-tune their perceptual focus to identify the thematic cognitions that are manifested in members' verbal statements. The following statements, for example, revel conclusions members have drawn about themselves and others:

- **Husband** [*about wife's behavior*]: She doesn't allow me to smoke in the house. (My wife is in charge of me.)

- I can't tell how I feel. (If I do, they'll reject me or I will hurt them.)

- **Member of alcoholics group:** If I can't trust my wife, how can I stop drinking? (My fate rests in the hands of someone else.)

In the same manner that group leaders observe and record functional and problematic behavioral responses of members, they can record the cognitive themes or patterns of members. Returning to the example of the women's support group cited earlier, note the cognitive responses of several members recorded by the leader in the same session, as illustrated in Table 11-3.

Leaders can help group members identify cognitive patterns during problem exploration by asking questions such as "When that happened, what did you say to yourself?" "What conclusions do

NAME	FUNCTIONAL COGNITIONS	PROBLEMATIC COGNITIONS
June	It's OK to risk talking about feelings. Other people will usually treat those feelings with respect and be responsive. I can do things to make myself feel better. I can get help from this group.	I've been hurt by the past. I don't think I'll ever get over it. I will always blame myself for what happened. I can't stop myself from talking so much. I always do that when I get anxious.
Raye	I care about other people. I want to help them. I'm willing to risk by staying in this group because I know I need help.	Other people's opinions are more important than mine. If I express my opinion, other people may disagree with me and/or think I'm not very bright. People in this group may not like me.
Janet	I have personal strengths. There are some good things about me. I'm a survivor. I can take care of myself.	My ideas, beliefs, positions are right; those of other people are wrong. I have to be right (or others won't respect me). You can't trust other people; they will hurt you if they can. The less you disclose about yourself, the better.

Table 11-3 Examples of Behavioral Profiles of Group Members

you draw about others under those circumstances?" or "What kind of self-talk did you use to make yourself depressed when that happened?" Leaders can also teach groups to recognize manifestations of patterned cognitions. As the group grasps the significance of internal dialogue and attends to cognitive patterns manifested by members, leaders should accredit the group's growth by giving members descriptive feedback concerning their accomplishments.

Identifying Patterned Group Behavior

To heighten your awareness of functional and dysfunctional patterned behaviors that may occur in groups, we provide contrasting examples of such behavior in Table 11-4.

The functional behaviors in the table are characteristic of a mature therapeutic group. However, note that facilitative group behaviors may emerge in the initial stages of development. These behaviors are usually fleeting, for the group must accomplish a number of developmental tasks, such as building trust and defining common interests and goals, before attaining the supportive and productive behaviors of the group's working stages. Brief or short-lived positive behaviors manifested early in groups include behaviors such as the following:

- The group "faces up to" a problem and makes a necessary modification or adjustment.

- The group responds positively the first time a member takes a risk by revealing a personal problem.

- Members of the group are supportive toward other members or manifest investment in the group.

- The group moves in a positive direction without the leader's guidance or intervention.

- The group works harmoniously for a period of time.

- Members effectively make a decision together.

- Members adhere to specific group guidelines such as maintaining focus on work to be accomplished.

- Members give positive feedback to another member or observe positive ways the group has worked together.

- The group responsibly confronts a member who is dominating interaction or interfering in some way with the group's accomplishing its task.

- Members pitch in to clean up after a group session.

The preceding list of positive behaviors, of course, is by no means exhaustive. Once social workers fine-tune their observational skills to register positive group behavior, they will catch glimpses of many newly developing behaviors that enhance a group's functioning. Social workers can then intervene to facilitate the group's adoption of such functional behaviors. Their challenge, of course, is to focus on these fleeting behaviors before the moment is lost by authentically disclosing positive feelings and by documenting in behavioral terms the positive movement they have observed (Larsen, 1980).

The group may also manifest transitory negative behaviors in initial sessions. As we noted, many of these behaviors can also be seen as expectable in the early phases of group development. These behaviors may signal evolving group patterns that are not firmly "set" in the group's interactional repertoire. Counterproductive behaviors that may evolve into patterns include any of the examples of dysfunctional behavior listed in Table 11-4.

Just as we have suggested that you employ a record-keeping system for recording the functional and dysfunctional responses of individual members, we also recommend using the same type of system for recording the functional and dysfunctional behaviors of the group itself, adding a column to record the growth or changes that

PROBLEMATIC GROUP BEHAVIOR	FUNCTIONAL GROUP BEHAVIOR
• Members talk on a superficial level and are cautious about revealing their feelings and opinions.	• Members openly communicate personal feelings and attitudes and anticipate that other members will be helpful.
• Members are readily critical and evaluative of each other; they rarely acknowledge or listen to contributions from others.	• Members listen carefully to each other and give all ideas a hearing.
• Dominant members count out other members in decision making; members make decisions prematurely without identifying or weighing possible alternatives.	• Decisions are reached through group consensus after considering everyone's views and feelings. Members make efforts to incorporate the views of dissenters rather than to dominate or override these views.
• Members focus heavily on negatives and rarely accredit positive behaviors of others.	• Members recognize and give feedback regarding strengths and growth of other members.
• Members are critical of differences in others, viewing them as a threat.	• Members recognize the uniqueness of each individual and encourage participation in different and complementary ways.
• Members compete for the chance to speak, often interrupting each other.	• Members take turns speaking. Members use "I" messages to speak for themselves, readily owning their own feelings and positions on matters.
• Members do not personalize their messages but instead use indirect forms of communication to express their feelings and positions.	• Members encourage others to speak for themselves. Members adhere to guidelines or behavior established in initial sessions.
• Members speak for others.	
• Members display disruptive behavior incompatible with group guidelines. Members resist talking about the here and now or addressing personal or group problems. Distractive behaviors may include maneuvers such as fingering objects, whispering, and throwing spitballs.	• The group is concerned about its own operations and addresses obstacles that prevent members from fully participating or the group from achieving its objectives.
• Members show unwillingness to accept responsibility for themselves or the success of the group and tend to blame the leader when things are not going well.	• Members assume responsibility for the group's functioning and success.
• Members dwell on past exploits and experiences and talk about issues extraneous to group purpose. Members also focus on others rather than themselves.	• The group manifests commitment by staying on task, assuming group assignments, or working out problems that impair group functioning.
• Members show little awareness of the needs and feelings of others; emotional investment in others is limited.	• Members concentrate on the present and what they can do to change themselves.
	• Members are sensitive to the needs and feelings of others and readily give emotional support.
	• Members also express their caring for others.

Table 11-4   Examples of Group Behavior

you note in the group's behavior. For example, using the categories that you wish to track, develop a chart such as depicted for individuals on Table 11-2.

Identifying Group Alliances

As members of new groups find other members with compatible attitudes, interests, and responses, they develop patterns of affiliation and relationship with these members. As Hartford (1971) points out, subgroup formations that evolve include pairs, triads, and foursomes. Foursomes generally divide into two pairs but sometimes shift to three and one. Groups as large as five may operate as a total unit, but generally these groups begin to develop subdivisions influencing "who addresses whom, who sits together, who comes and leaves together, and even who may meet or talk together outside of the group" (Hartford, 1971, p. 204).

Subgroupings that invariably develop do not necessarily impair group functioning. Group members, in fact, often derive strength and support from subgroups that enhance their participation and investment in the larger group. Further, it is through the process of establishing subgroups, or natural coalitions, that group members (like family members) achieve true intimacy. Problems arise in groups, however, when members develop exclusive subgroups that disallow intimate relationships with other group members or inhibit members from supporting the goals of the larger group. Competing factions can often impede or destroy a group.

To work effectively with groups, leaders must be skilled in identifying subdivisions and assessing their impact on a group. To recognize these subdivisions, leaders may wish to construct a sociogram of group alignments. Credited to Moreno and Jennings (Jennings, 1950), a sociogram graphically depicts patterned affiliations and relationships between group members by using symbols for people and interactions. Hartford (1971, p. 196) illustrates a sociogram that captures the attractions and repulsions among group members (see Figure 11-1).

Sociograms are representations of alliances in a group at a given point, because alliances do shift and change, particularly in early stages of group development. Charting the transitory bondings that occur early in group life can be invaluable to leaders in deciding where and when to intervene to modify, enhance, or stabilize relationships between members.

We suggest you construct a sociogram of members' interactions after every session until you are confident that group relationships have stabilized in positive ways that support the group's therapeutic objectives. Be creative with your sociograms. You may wish to use different colors to show attractions, repulsions, or strength of relationships or to place members closer together or farther apart to convey emotional closeness or distance. Avoid trying to capture in a single sociogram the exact nature of relationships each member has with every other one in the group, as the drawing will become overly complicated. Rather, depict only the major subgroupings in the group and identify the relationships in which major attractions or repulsions are occurring.

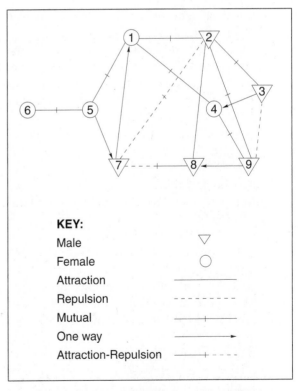

Figure 11-1 Sociogram Capturing the Attractions and Repulsions among Group Members

Source: From *Groups in Social Work* by Margaret Hartford. (New York: Columbia University Press, 1971, p. 196.) Reprinted by permission of the author.

Identifying Power and Decision-Making Styles

Groups as well as families develop ways of distributing power among members. To ensure their needs are not discounted, some members may make bids for power and discount other members. Others tend to discount themselves and permit more aggressive members to dominate the group. Still others value power and actively pursue it as an end in itself. Involved in power struggles, groups may initially fail to make decisions on an "I count you count" basis. Further, subgroups may try to eliminate opposing factions from the group or align themselves with other members or subgroups to increase their power. Groups, in fact, are sometimes torn apart and meet their demise because unresolved power issues prevent the group from meeting the needs of some members.

Power struggles that arise in groups are often caused by members aggressively competing over solutions to a problem. Interested members or factions may vigorously advocate opposing solutions that they are not willing to relinquish. Given these conditions, some members will win and some will lose because ultimately only one of the competing factions can prevail.

As in assessing families, when social workers assess groups they need to identify the current capacity of members to share power and resources equally among themselves and to implement problem-solving steps that ensure "win-win" solutions (see Chapter 13). Increased ability of the group to "count in" all members must necessarily occur for the group to advance through stages of development into maturity. Members are more committed to implementing decisions if they think they have had a fair say in making those decisions. Leaders can thus accelerate the group's progress through the various stages by assuming a facilitative role in teaching and modeling facilitative decision making and assisting members to adopt explicit guidelines for making decision in initial sessions.

Group Norms, Values, and Cohesion

Of central importance to group assessment are *group norms,* a term that reers to implicit expectations and beliefs shared by members concerning how they or others should behave under given circumstances. Norms are regulatory mechanisms that give groups a measure of stability and predictability by providing members with information concerning what they can expect from each other. Norms may define *specific* behaviors of individuals that are appropriate or permissible or define the *range* of behaviors that are acceptable in the group. Group norms are thus similar to the family "rules" discussed in the previous chapter.

Just as families have processes for dealing with rule violations, groups also develop sanctions to reduce behaviors that are considered deviant and to return the system to its prior equilibrium (Lieberman, 1980). For example, an implicit group norm may be that the opinions of the informal leader are not to be challenged by other group members. If a new group member treads on this norm by questioning the opinion of the informal leader, other members may side with the informal leader against the "upstart," pressuring him or her to back away.

People often learn about the norms of particular groups by observing situations in which norms have been violated. Speaking of group members, Toseland and Rivas (2001) note that, as members watch the behavior of others, they reward some behavior and punish others. Once members realize that sanctions are applied to certain behaviors, they usually attempt to adapt their behavior to avoid disapproval or punishment. Sanctions are powerful regulators of behavior, as Lieberman (1980, p. 501) has observed: "Ordinarily, sanctions do not need to be exerted frequently or vigorously; rather, the anticipation of sanctions is often as effective in controlling deviant behavior as is aactual application."

The extent to which members adhere to norms often varies. Some norms are flexible, and the psychological "costs" to members of violation are low or nonexistent. In other instances, the group's investment in norms is signficant and group reaction is severe when members violate such norms. The relative status of members, that is, the evaluation or ranking of each member's position in the group relative to the others, also determines the extent to which members adhere to norms. Toseland and Rivas (2001) observe that low-status members are the least likely to conform to group norms because they have little to lose by deviating. This is less likely if they have hopes of gaining a higher status. Medium-status group members tend to conform to group norms so that they can retain their status and perhaps gain a higher status. High-status members perform many valued services for the group and generally conform to valued group norms when they are establishing their position. However, because of their position, high-status members have more freedom to deviate form accepted norms.

Norms may or may not support the treatment objectives of a group and should be viewed as to whether they are beneficial or detrimental to the well-being of members and the overall treatment objectives of the group. Examples of norms that may be functional and problematic are presented in Table 11-5.

All groups develop norms, and once certain norms are adopted, they influence the group's response to situations and determine the extent to which the group offers its members therapeutic experiences. A major leader's role, therefore, is to identify evolving group norms and influence them in ways that create a positive ambience for change. Discerning them is often difficult, however, inasmuch as such norms are subtly embedded in the group process and can be inferred only from the behavior occurring in the group. Leaders may be able to identify norms by asking themselves key questions such as the following:

1. What subjects can and cannot be talked about in the group?

2. What kinds of emotional expressions are allowed in the group?

3. What is the group's pattern with regard to working on problems or staying on task?

FUNCTIONAL	PROBLEMATIC
• Risk by spontaneously revealing personal content about yourself.	• Keep the discussion centered on superficial topics; avoid risking or self-disclosing.
• Treat the leader with respect and seriously consider the leader's input.	• Play the game "Let's get the leader." Harass, criticize, or complain about the leader whenever the opportunity arises.
• Focus on working out personal problems.	• Spend time complaining about problems and don't commit the energy necessary to work them out.
• Allow members equal opportunity to participate in group discussions or to become the focus of the group.	• Let aggressive members dominate the group.
• Talk about any subject pertinent to your problem. Communicate directly to other group members.	• Don't talk about emotionally charged or delicate subjects.
• Talk about obstacles that get in the way of achieving the group's goals.	• Direct comments to the leader.
	• Ignore obstacles and avoid talking about group problems.

Table 11-5   Examples of Group Norms

4. Do group members consider it their own responsibility or the leader's to make the group's experience successful?

5. What is the group's stance toward the leader?

6. What is the group's attitude toward feedback?

7. How does the group view the contributions of individual members? What kind of labels and roles is the group assigning to them?

Asking such questions also enables leaders to increase their observations of redundant or patterned behavior of members. This is a vital point, for patterned behaviors are always undergirded by supporting norms. Another strategy for identifying norms is to explain the concept of norms to group members and to ask them to identify the guiding "rules" that influence their behavior in the group. This strategy enables members to bring to a conscious level the group norms that are developing and to make choices concerning norms that will increase therapeutic possibilities.

In addition to norms, every treatment group will create a set of values held in common by all or most of the group's members that include ideas, beliefs, ideologies, or theories about the truth, right or wrong, good or bad, and beautiful or ugly or inappropriate (Hartford, 1971). Examples of such values include the following:

• This is a "good" group and worth our commitment and investment of time. (Or, this is a "dumb" group. We're not going to get anything out of it.)

• It is "bad" to betray confidences to outsiders.

• People who belong to different groups (e.g., authorities, persons, of a different race, religion, status) are "bad" or inferior.

• It is undesirable to show feelings in the group. It is fun to try to outwit authority figures (particularly applicable to groups of juvenile or adult offenders).

Just as the group's "choice" of norms significantly affects its capacity to offer a therapeutic milieu, so does the group's "choice" of values.

Similar to norms, values can be categorized as functional or dysfunctional when viewed in light of the group's therapeutic objectives. Values that encourage work on personal problems or self-disclosure, acceptance of others, and a positive attitude toward the group, for example, are functional to the group's development. By contrast, values that discourage self-disclosure, create barriers in relationships or negative attitudes toward the group, or prevent members from working on problems are obviously dysfunctional.

In initial phases, leaders must also assess and foster the development of cohesion in groups. Defined as the degree to which members are attracted to each other, cohesion is correlated, under certain conditions, to productivity, participation in and out of the group, self-disclosure, risk taking, attendance, and other vital concerns (S. D. Rose, 1989; Stokes, 1983). Cohesion in groups positively affects members' satisfaction and personal adjustment. Further cohesiveness leads to increased self-esteem, more willingness to listen to others, freer expression of feeling, better reality testing, greater self-confidence, and the effective use of other members' evaluations in enhancing a member's own development (Toseland & Rivas, 2001; Yalom, 1985).

Cohesion is inextricably linked to norm development in a beginning group. Norms that interfere with both group formation and cohesion include, for example, irregular attendance, frequent tardiness, pairing off, excessive interpersonal aggression, excessive dependence on the leader, dominance of interaction by a few members, and general passivity in the interaction (Rose, 1989). The presence of such norms, which indicate low levels of cohesion, requires the attention of the group and group leader, for to ignore such variables is to discourage group development and, indeed, to jeopardize the very group itself.

TASK GROUPS

We move now from consideration of treatment groups to task groups. Although many of the same issues considered with treatment groups also apply to task groups, we will focus on planning and beginning task groups in this chapter. Task groups are organized to meet client, organizational, and community needs (Toseland & Rivas, 2001, p. 29). Among task groups are teams, treatment conferences, and staff development groups. Other task groups are formed to meet organizational needs such as committees, cabinets, and boards of directors. Finally, task groups to meet community needs include social action groups, coalitions, and delegate councils (Toseland & Rivas, 2001). Task groups focus on producing products, developing policies, and making decisions rather than on the personal growth of members (Ephross & Vassil, 1988). Social workers can often act to enhance the quality of client services through focusing treatment conferences on client concerns and emphasizing client strengths and resources (Toseland, Ivanoff, & Rose, 1987). Too frequently, such groups do not include clients and family members and hence focus on professional consensus while ignoring the potential of mutual involvement of clients and family members (p. 91).

Important early tasks in forming and assessing task groups are planning for the group and structuring initial sessions to address the purpose of the group.

Planning for Task Groups

Although members of treatment groups are recruited for the specific purpose of the group, membership in task groups may be constrained by organizational bylaws or dictated by organizational structure (Toseland & Rivas, 2001). For example, members of a delegate council may be elected by constituents and an organization may decide by role who should participate in a treatment conference. However constituted, task groups are assisted by a clear focus on the goals of the group. For example, a treatment conference may have the purpose of coordinating efforts of members of a team to assist consumers in safely reaching their goals. The purpose of a task group may be originally generated by social workers,

agency staff, or members. For example, a staff member might propose a delegate council in a half-way house, the director of an agency might propose a committee to generate alternate sources of funding for the agency, or residents of a housing development might suggest a social action group to deal with poor housing conditions.

Members of a task group should have the interest, information, skills, and power needed to accomplish the purpose of the group. The specific purpose suggests sources for the group. For example, a group formed to study the impact of managed care on service delivery might include consumers, providers, and representatives from insurance groups. Membership should be large enough and sufficiently diverse to represent constituencies affected by the focus of the group and possess adequate skills and knowledge for addressing the purposes.

Quality planning in this stage is reflected by transmitting a clear message about the purposes of the group to prospective members. That clarity is then associated with whether those prospective members decide to attend and, later, how well they perform the functions of the group.

Beginning the Task Group

The agenda for a beginning session of a task group is similar to that of a treatment group. That agenda includes facilitating introductions, clarifying the purpose of the group, discussing ground rules, helping members feel a part of the group, setting goals, and anticipating obstacles (Toseland & Rivas, 2001). An opening statement, including the agency's function and mission as it relates to the group purpose, should be shared in order for members to understand why they have been called together. Members can then be assisted to find out commonalities in their concerns and experiences and shared goals for group participation. Some members may know each other from previous roles and have positive or negative preconceptions from that past. They can be asked to pair up with someone they do not know to share their interests and perspective on the purpose of the group. In sharing after such pairing, a list of potential resources and perspectives for addressing the group purpose can be generated.

Developing group rules then follows, including the importance of confidentiality. For example, premature release of information can hinder work of the group. Such rules in task groups usually include proceeding with formal written agendas developed prior to the group.

Members can be encouraged to submit formal items to be included in future agendas. Such agendas usually include approval of minutes, reports from committees and administrators, work on current business, and new business. Items can be further classified into three categories: information, discussion, and action. Such agendas should be given to team members several days prior to the session with sufficient information for members to be able to adequately discuss items.

Task groups then proceed to goal setting. Such goals include those mandated by the external purpose of the group, such as reviewing managed care arrangements in the agency. In addition, the group may generate its own goals, which might include generating a list of best practices that meet consumer, provider, and funder needs and a detailed description of situations that are most problematic for meeting the needs of any of these groups. Individual goals might then include interviewing members of these constituent groups prior to the next session.

Summary

This chapter has presented guidelines for assessing and beginning treatment groups and task groups. We move now in Chapter 12 to considerations of how we build on our assessment knowledge from the previous chapters to construct workable contracts with individuals. We will return to consideration of groups in Chapter 17.

Internet Resources

 You can find many useful group work sources at the site of the Association for the Advancement of Social Work with Groups, *http://www.aaswg.org.*
Using InfoTrac®, you can search keywords "group norms," "group cohesion," and "group leadership." You can also find out about on-line support groups in the care of cancer patients at *http://www.noah.cuny.edu/illness/cancer/ cancercare/services/support_groups/online.html* and at *http://www.noah.cuny.edu/illness/cancer/cancercare/ professional/evaluate.html.*

Notes

1. For new developments in social group work, you can contact the Association for the Advancement of Social Work with Groups, University of Akron, Ohio, 44325-8050. You can also contact them at (800) 807-0793 or at jhramey@uakron.edu.

Negotiating Goals and Formulating a Contract

Revised and edited by Glenda Dewberry Rooney

CHAPTER OVERVIEW

We move, in this chapter, to the point in the helping process in which the stage is set for the work to be completed between the practitioner and the client. Essential elements of this stage are developing goals, establishing procedures for measuring progress, and formulating the contract. To develop goals and use contracts to their maximal advantage, you must be aware of their components and be skilled in their application. The purpose of this chapter is to assist you to gain this knowledge and skill. The first section of the chapter discusses development and measurement of goals. The remainder of the chapter is committed to other components of the contract and the actual process of mutually formulating a contract between you and the client. We referred in Chapter 8 to assessment as both product and process. Similarly in this chapter, we emphasize goals and the contract as products of assessment, essential to achieving desired outcomes and measurement as a part of that process.

GOALS

The importance of formulating goals has been emphasized in social work literature for many years. Marked advances in formulating goals oc-

curred as a result of research studies that extended from the mid-1960s to the late 1970s. Based on a landmark research study, Reid (1970) concluded that practitioners were overly general in specifying goals, leading to "unrealistic aspirations and to repeated shifts in direction" (p. 145). K. Wood (1978), Dillon (1994), and Kazdin, Stolar and Marciano (1995) have drawn similar conclusions. Dillon (1994) cautions against setting goals to "transform clients." In establishing goals, specificity is also important as goals that are too vague might unreasonably subject clients to cruel and destructive experiences, disappointments, or frustrations, and erode their confidence in their own capacities. When goals were set in advance without consulting clients, poor outcomes, including the risk of dropping out, could well have resulted from the fact that the clients and practitioners were working toward different ends (I. K. Berg & Hopwood, 1991; Pardeck, Murphy, & Chung, 1995). Jackson (1995) suggests that racial and ethnic groups as well as gay men and lesbian women often drop out of the helping process because of conflict in setting goals and because of their experiences of prejudice with majority culture.

In some instances, it may be important for social workers to examine their own values, cultural, political, or religious beliefs, and biases. Goal setting is an opportunity to empower clients and enhance their self-efficacy. Goal development and negotiation is further enhanced by the social worker's skill in exploring goals in the context of the client's value system and reality. In many minority communities, individuals and families experience being referred to seek help, often under pressure and in some instances because of mandates. This creates an atmosphere of suspicion, which may be heightened when the practitioner or agency has predetermined goals for the problem or concerns. Goals established by referral sources should not be accepted as necessarily reflecting the client's will, especially when they might be based on perceived deficits assigned on the basis of status, such as culture, gender, or family form.

Some clients from minority communities may also want to involve extended family networks in establishing goals. It has been our experience as social workers that clients value being able to work on problems and set goals that include their own reality. In determining goals, we also urge consideration of environmental conditions, such as racism, classism, and discrimination.

The Purpose of Goals

Goals specify what clients wish to accomplish and are utilized as a means to facilitate the desired outcomes. They are formulated around situations, statuses, behaviors, or attitudes that are the target of change. Inherent in goals are desired changes in clients' life situations that correspond to wants and needs identified when problems were explored and assessed. Goals thus are inextricably connected with and flow directly from the assessment process. Indeed, as you explore clients' wants and needs, you are engaging in preliminary goal selection work. When clients are involuntary, some goals may be agreed to as ways of satisfying a legal mandate. Goals serve the following valuable functions in the helping process:

1. Ensure that practitioners and clients are in agreement, where possible, about objectives to be achieved.

2. Provide direction and continuity to the helping process and prevent needless wandering.

3. Facilitate the development and selection of appropriate strategies and interventions.

4. Assist practitioners and clients in monitoring their progress.

5. Serve as outcome criteria in evaluating the effectiveness of specific interventions and of the helping process.

Utilizing goals to perform the preceding functions requires knowledge of the types of goals, criteria for selecting them, and knowledge of and skill in negotiating goals, each of which we consider in the following sections.

Types of Goals

The systems of subsystems that will be the focus for change are another factor that determines the type of goal. With individual clients, this focus typically involves intrapersonal subsystems as well as the client's interaction with the social and physical environment. Goals with individual clients commonly involve changes in both overt and covert behaviors. Common examples include changes in *cognitive functioning* (e.g., reducing the incidence of self-depreciating thoughts); changes in *emotional functioning* (e.g., reducing the frequency and intensity of depressive feelings); or *behavioral changes* (e.g., reducing or eliminating consumption of alcohol). Goals may also include changes in interpersonal behavior (e.g., asking someone for a date or engaging others in conversation).

When the target system is a couple, family, or group, goals typically embody changes on the part of all relevant participants in the system. In these larger systems, goals may be held in common by members of the system (shared goals) or may involve agreed-upon exchanges of different behavior (reciprocal goals). Examples of *shared* goals include marital partners agreeing to listen to one another without interrupting or to adopt a certain strategy of decision making. Family members and group members may agree to pursue a shared goal of supplanting critical, demeaning messages to others with positive, emotionally supportive messages. The distinguishing feature of shared goals is that all members are committed to change their behaviors in essentially the same way.

With *reciprocal* goals, members of a system seek to solve interactional problems by exchanging different behaviors. For example, a couple may seek help because they communicate infrequently and are becoming increasingly distant emotionally. The wife may complain that her husband seldom talks with her, and he may counter that he gradually stopped talking with her because she seldom listened and instead criticized him and ridiculed his points of view. After exploring their problem, the couple may agree to a shared goal of increasing their verbal exchanges and further agree to reciprocal individual subgoals that include attentive listening by the wife and increased verbal sharing by the husband. A parent may agree to stop yelling at a child, if the child responds to the first request to wash the dishes. Reciprocal goals thus tend to be quid pro quo in nature; that is, each person agrees to modify personal behavior contingent upon corresponding changes by the other.

GUIDELINES FOR SELECTING AND DEFINING GOALS

Because goals serve several vital functions (listed earlier), it is important to select and define them with care. The following guidelines will assist you in advancing your proficiency in formulating goals.

Goals Must Relate to the Desired End Results Sought by Voluntary Clients

To be adequately motivated, voluntary clients must believe that accomplishing selected goals will enhance their life situations by resolving or mitigating their problems. Clients are thus likely to pursue only those goals in which they are emotionally invested. Therefore, practitioners who define goals unilaterally or attempt to impose goals

on clients are unlikely to enlist their cooperation. In fact, clients are likely to respond by agreeing superficially or by terminating prematurely. In negotiating goals, you should have no hidden agendas and should accord the voluntary client the final decision in selecting appropriate goals. This does not mean that you should assume a passive role in negotiating goals. To the contrary, clients will look to you for guidance in selecting goals, and you have a responsibility to share your expertise in this regard. We discuss your role in negotiating goals in a later section.

Goals for Involuntary Clients Should Include Motivational Congruence

Work on problems on which there is motivational congruence, that is, aimed toward personally meaningful goals, is more likely to succeed and result in longer-lasting change than motivation that is primarily devoted to escaping punishments or gaining rewards (R. H. Rooney, 1992). Consequently, practitioners should seek to limit involuntary goals to legal mandates and include goals perceived by involuntary clients. Involuntary clients often express their own views of problems or situations that resulted in the mandated referral. Typically their views diverge from those of the legal authority or person(s) who mandated the referral. The *agreeable mandate* strategy in such instances is to search for common ground that bridges the differing views. Reframing the definition of the problem to adequately address the concerns of the client as well as the referral source reduces reactance and makes a workable agreement possible. This strategy occurred in a case involving a husband whose wife threatened to "call it quits" if he didn't seek professional help. The client could not accept that he was the sole cause of the problem, but through skillful handling did acknowledge that the relationship was "rocky" and that he was "uptight." He was receptive to entering marital therapy rather than individual therapy if his wife would participate. Another example would be reframing the problem of a rebellious adolescent referred by the parents as a family problem that requires participation of other family members.

Bargaining can also be used through a *let's make a deal* strategy in which the private concerns of the involuntary client can be included with the problem that precipitated the referral. For example, a patient in a mental institution may reject the view that he has problems with sexual impulses, but may express concerns over being inhibited in social situations. The practitioner may agree to focus on the latter if the patient will agree to explore the former. The potency of this strategy derives from being able to offer a payoff to a client (create an incentive).

With some involuntary clients, none of the preceding strategies is viable and the only recourse left to the practitioner is to appeal to clients' desire to be free of the restraints imposed by the mandating referral source. In such a strategy, a goal of *getting rid of the mandate or outside pressure* is included (R. H. Rooney, 1992). For example, some involuntary clients are motivated to "get child protection out of my hair," to escape what they consider an adversarial or oppressive presence. If the overall goal is return of the children to the home, incremental strategies may be developed with the client that would satisfy both the mandate and the client's desire to be rid of child protection.

Goals Should Be Defined in Explicit and Measurable Terms

To provide direction in the helping process, goals must specifically define the desired end results so that all participants are clear about changes to be accomplished within the problem system. In other words, each actor should be able to specify what she or he will be doing differently or what environmental factors will be changed. Goals should thus be defined in specific rather than general terms. Yet some goals defined by practitioners have been so nebulous (e.g., "to improve the Youngs' marital relationship," or "to increase the solidarity of the Williams family") that "drift" (W. Reid, 1970) or wandering in the helping process occurs and a substantial number of clients report being unclear about what a practitioner has been seeking to assist them to accomplish. Recording goals and their progression in the record is important to focus as well as evaluation of the outcome.

Appropriately stated, goals specify both overt and covert changes to be accomplished and should be measurable. Overt behavioral changes (e.g., "Jimmy will complete his homework each evening before watching television") can be observed by others, making precise measurement possible. Covert changes (e.g., curtailing derogatory thoughts about oneself) are also measurable, but only by the client. Measures of covert behavior thus are more subject to error as a result of inconsistent self-monitoring, the effects of self-monitoring on the target behavior, and other factors.

The lists presented in Table 12-1 will further assist you in discriminating between global and explicit goals. Included in the lists are goals that involve both overt and covert behaviors. Notice that explicit goals refer to specific behaviors or environmental changes that suggest the nature of corresponding remedial interventions.

Goals can be expressed at various levels of abstraction. Because clients and practitioners tend to define goals generally, you will need to practice defining goals with increased specificity. Goals should be considered the desired end product of a change effort. For example, completing an academic program with a GED is a specific goal. It is important to distinguish a goal (the desired outcome of intervention efforts) from general tasks (the instrumental strategies used to attempt to reach those goals) (W. Reid, 1992). Goals are listed in Table 12-1 in the left column and general tasks are described in the right column. For example, a parent may want to set a goal of reducing tantrum behavior from three times to once a day. Using time-outs would be a general task toward this goal. Using time-outs is not in itself a goal

GOALS	GENERAL TASKS
1. Gain increased control over emotions	1. Reduce frequency and intensity of anger outbursts by discerning cues that elicit anger, using internal dialogue that quells anger, and employing relaxation procedures that counter anger
2. Improve social relations	2. Approach others and initiate and maintain conversation by employing listening skills and furthering responses
3. Enhance social environment	3. Explore living arrangements in a center for elderly persons that provides social activities
4. Enhance self-esteem	4. Arrest habitual negative self-statements by engaging in self-dialogue about their destructive consequences; align performance expectations with realistic criteria; attend to strengths and positive qualities; silently express self-approval when merited
5. Improve quality of parenting	5. Demonstrate competence and responsibility in assuring continuous child care, planning and preparing nutritious meals, and maintaining adequate sanitary and hygienic conditions
6. Increase social participation in a group context	6. Resolve fears of "looking stupid," initiate discussion of personal views, ask questions, and participate in group exploring and problem-solving activities
7. Improve marital communication	7. Express needs and wants to each other, listen without interrupting and check out meaning attributions, increase frequency of positive messages, avoid competitive interaction, reduce critical and blaming messages
8. Relate more comfortably with desired romantic partners	8. Explore and resolve fears of rejection, introduce self and initiate conversations, ask for date, engage in appropriate activities

Table 12-1   Goals and General Tasks

because it is valued primarily as a way of reaching the client goal.

General tasks may also be categorized in a broad sense as *discrete*, on the one hand, and *ongoing* or continuous, on the other. Discrete general tasks consist of one-time actions or changes that resolve or ameliorate problems. Examples include obtaining a needed resource (e.g., public as-

sistance, housing, or medical care); making a major decision (e.g., deciding whether to keep an unborn infant or place it for adoption); or making a change in one's environment (e.g., changing living arrangements). Ongoing general tasks, in contrast, involve actions that are continuous and repetitive, and progress toward such goals is therefore incremental. Examples of ongoing general tasks include managing conflict effectively, expressing feelings openly, asserting one's rights, setting limits with children, controlling anger, and participating in group discussions.

Another aspect of defining a goal explicitly involves specifying essential behavioral changes of all persons in the target system with respect to shared or reciprocal goals. Observing this guideline ensures that all participants are clear about the part they play in accomplishing the overarching goal that relates to the broader system. For example, if a global or *ultimate* goal in family therapy is to reduce conflict and to achieve closer and more harmonious family relationships, family members must be clear about their individual goals in relationship to the larger system. The same principle applies in marital therapy and other small groups.

A final aspect of defining goals explicitly is to specify the degree or extent of change desired by clients that matches their situation. With goals that involve ongoing behavior, growth is potentially infinite, and it is desirable, therefore, to determine the extent of change sought by the client. The advantage of specifying desired levels of change is that practitioners and clients mutually agree to the ends sought by the latter. For example, clients who seek to enhance their social skills and to expand their social participation commonly aspire to varying levels of goal accomplishment. One client may be satisfied with being able to engage minimally in occasional conversations limited to co-workers and relatives, whereas another may aspire to engage openly and actively in a broad array of social situations. Marital partners who seek to reduce the frequency and intensity of conflict likewise differ in their definitions of acceptable levels of goal attainment. Some couples seek total elimination of intense conflicts that involve yelling, name-calling, and other destructive behaviors. Other couples seek only to reduce the frequency of aversive interactions.

Goals Must Be Feasible

Selecting unachievable goals sets up clients for failure that may produce discouragement, disillu-

sionment, and a sense of defeat. Therefore, it is vital to consider both the capacity of clients for accomplishing goals and possible environmental constraints that militate against goal accomplishment. In most instances, clients possess the capacity to accomplish goals they set for themselves, and it is desirable to affirm the validity of their goals and to express belief in their capacity to attain them. Occasionally, you will encounter clients who are grandiose or who deny personal limitations that are obvious to others. In these instances, you can perform a valuable service by sensitively and tactfully assisting them to lower their aim to the upper range of what is realistically achievable. Sometimes agency or funding priorities establish the range of goals. For example, assisting clients to return to a level of functioning or reside in a less restrictive setting may be an agency program goal.

In cases involving involuntary clients, you may encounter agencies and judges who have grandiose expectations about what clients can accomplish in a short time period. Some practitioners seeking to mollify other agencies and courts have been inclined to develop "kitchen sink" contracts, often including everything but the kitchen sink, committing the client to simultaneous treatment and support groups, training programs, and work expectations. It is unethical to set up clients to fail. Prioritizing goals for a particular contract period with focus on legal mandates and items of greatest significance to the presenting problem can enable the involuntary client to have a reasonable opportunity to develop and demonstrate skill and capacity (R. H. Rooney, 1992).

With respect to environmental constraints, it is important to weigh opportunities, the receptiveness and capacity of significant others to change along desired lines, economic and employment conditions, group and community attitudes, and other related factors. The following example illustrates the importance of considering environmental opportunities. A client may wish to move from a convalescent facility to the residence of relatives, but the latter may be unwilling or unable to provide the accommodations and care needed. Practitioners may agree to help the client attempt to secure the assistance and support of key outside resources and agents needed to reach goals. If such support is critical to the success of the goal and cannot be attained, then agreeing to the goal would be unethical and setting up the client to fail.

Goals Should Be Commensurate with the Knowledge and Skill of the Practitioner

You should agree to join clients in working toward only those goals for which you have or can gain requisite knowledge and skill. Certain problems and goals require high levels of expertise that you may not yet have attained, and it is your responsibility to clients, the profession, and yourself not to undertake interventions for which you lack competence. Certain problems also require specialized knowledge in particular areas, for example, family therapy, child sexual abuse, sex therapy or behavior modification, emotional disorders, and treatment techniques.

If you are receiving supervision from a person who possesses the requisite competence, it can be ethical to contract for goals beyond your competence, for you have access to the guidance needed to enable you to tender the essential service. Otherwise, you are ethically bound to undertake only goals commensurate with your competence and to refer clients who require service beyond your competence to other qualified professionals. What course of action should one follow if qualified professionals are not available? This often occurs in rural areas.

Under these circumstances, the choice may be between no service or less than optimal service. In our judgment, practitioners are justified in extending service in such cases under two provisions. First, practitioners are obligated to explain their limitations with regard to the goals in question, enabling the client to decide on an informed basis whether to proceed. Second, the practitioner

should be confident that undertaking the goals does not place clients or others at risk. With severely depressed clients, for example, the risk of suicide may preclude undertaking treatment without medical consultation and without arranging precautionary measures with significant others. A similar risk may exist when clients have a history of violent behavior that poses a threat to others. Consultation and hospitalization should be considered before undertaking treatment in such instances. In some situations, a practitioner may seek supervision or consultation from another qualified professional.

Goals Should Be Stated in Positive Terms That Emphasize Growth

Defining goals in ways that stress growth highlights beneficial changes or gains that will accrue in the lives of clients as a result of attaining goals. In formulating goal statements, stipulating negative behaviors that must be eliminated tends to draw attention to what clients must give up. Even though clients ordinarily welcome relinquishing dysfunctional behavior (e.g., tearing themselves down, fighting, and eating or drinking to excess), they may feel a sense of impending loss, for even though such behaviors produce stress or difficulties; they are nonetheless accustomed to living with those problems. Psychologically defining goals in terms of gains rather than losses tends to enhance motivation and to mitigate opposition to change. Examples of contrasting negative and positive goal statements are included in Table 12-2.

Avoid Agreeing to Goals About Which You Have Major Reservations

Sometimes it is neither ethical nor wise to enter into agreements to pursue certain goals. Clients may request your assistance in pursuing goals that are incompatible with your values. Values, of course, are highly individual, but many practitioners have serious reservations about working with clients whose life philosophies, moral values, or sexual practices diverge markedly from their own. For example, because of deeply held religious or moral beliefs, some practitioners may not work effectively with people who are considering abortions, or who may not meet the goals that will allow them to be reunified with their children. If clients pose goals about which you have strong reservations, it is generally wise to refer them to another professional person or agency that is comfortable in working toward such goals, if such a resource is available. It is important to explain your reason for making the referral, being careful to safeguard the client's self-esteem. For example: "I'm sorry I can't join you in working toward that goal. My values are different, and my concern is that this difference would get in the way of giving you the help you're seeking. I'm not faulting you for being different from me. We're all different, and that's how it should be. Because I do want to help you to obtain the service you need, we can explore together an alternative resource, and I would be willing to make a referral." In cases in which a referral cannot be made, reservations about the kind of help you may be able to provide should be shared up front. Continuing to work with a client under these circumstances is a delicate balance between client's rights to self-determination and the social worker's own values. In the final analysis, in instances where another resource is unavailable, practitioners must rely on the professional nature of the client-practitioner relationship, which means that client goals are primary, and that goals embedded in our own values or resources should not intrude upon our work with clients.

Occasionally, you may also have reservations about clients' goals that appear to be potentially harmful to the physical or mental well-being of themselves or others. An adult may have a goal of using devious means to regain custody of children in foster placement. A pregnant adolescent may seek to enlist your assistance in planning to entrap an unwary male into marrying her. In these and similar situations, you would be justified in declining to assist clients. In such instances, it is appropriate to candidly but tactfully explain the basis of your misgiving while expressing your willingness to consider other goals.

Goals Must Be Consistent with the Functions of the Agency

Explorations of problems and clients' wants sometimes disclose desired changes that are incompatible with the functions of the agency. For example, after exploring a couple's problems in a family service agency, it may be apparent that the couple's primary need relates to vocational counseling, a service not provided by the agency. Similarly, in

NEGATIVE	POSITIVE
1. To reduce the frequency of criticism among family members	To increase the family members' awareness of each other's strengths and to increase the frequency of positive messages
2. To eliminate pouting between marital partners	To deal with disagreements openly, promptly, and constructively
3. To eliminate subgroupings and nonparticipatory behavior by group members	To unite efforts of group in working collectively and to draw each member into participation
4. To eliminate or reduce the frequency of drinking binges	To achieve ever-increasing periods of sobriety, taking one day at a time
5. To eliminate yelling at the children and resorting to physical punishment	To consistently apply new ways of influencing and disciplining children, such as utilizing 'time-out' procedures, increasing feedback, and employing a problem-solving approach with them

Table 12-2   Negative and Positive Goal Statements

hospital settings, clients often manifest problems that require services beyond the scope of the hospital's function, such as marital therapy, mental health services, or financial assistance. In such instances, it is appropriate to assist the client to secure the needed services through referral to another agency. You may want to ensure the linkage to the referral agency by making the call with the client or a follow-up call to make sure the client is satisfied with the referral.

THE PROCESS OF MUTUALLY SELECTING AND DEFINING GOALS

Having considered the rationale of employing goals and delineating criteria for selecting and defining them, we are now ready to consider the actual process of negotiating goals. This process consists of several activities that may be implemented in the following sequence, adapting the sequence to the circumstances of each case.

1. Determine clients' readiness to negotiate goals.
2. Explain the purpose of selecting and defining goals.
3. Elicit goals from clients, suggest other potential goals, and then mutually select those that are appropriate.
4. Include mandated goals with involuntary clients.
5. Define the goals explicitly and specify the extent of change desired by clients.
6. Determine the feasibility of targeted goals and discuss potential benefits and risks associated with them.
7. Assist clients in making a choice about committing themselves to specific goals. When involuntary clients have mandated goals, make sure they have given informed consent about the consequences of not working on those goals.
8. Rank goals according to clients' priorities. Also prioritize any mandated goals.

To clarify how to implement these steps, we will briefly discuss each one in the following sections.

Determine Clients' Readiness

When you believe you have explored clients' problems sufficiently, it is appropriate to determine if your clients concur with your opinion and are ready to negotiate goals.[1] A message similar to the following may be used to assess clients' readiness: "You've provided a good description of your problems and situation, and I feel I have a pretty good grasp of them." At this point, you may summarize your understanding of what the client has said. If this summarization leads to agreement, you would then move the exploration of goals: "I wonder if you feel ready to talk about some specific goals at this point or if you feel we need to discuss some additional information first." If the client conveys readiness, you can advance to the next step. This step of checking with the client conveys to the client that you are attentive and that he or she is continually involved in the process of setting goals.

Explain the Purpose of Goals

Explaining the purposes of goals increases clients' receptivity to the process and fosters their participation. It has been our experience that clients respond positively to such explanations and they understand and appreciate the significance of goals in the problem-solving process. Usually a brief explanation is all that is needed. Your explanation, of course, should be consistent with the functions of goals listed early in this chapter and should emphasize the importance of clients' participation and ultimate authority in selecting voluntary goals. An example of such an explanation follows:

- "We've been exploring your problems at some length, and you've indicated a number of things you'd like to be different in your life [or marriage or family]. I'd like to think with you now about some specific goals you'd like to accomplish. Selecting goals assures that we're all trying to accomplish the same results. They also provide a sense of direction and serve as guideposts to make sure we stay on track. With goals, we can also evaluate your progress and determine how successful we've been in our work together. It's important that the goals represent the changes that are most important to you. Although I have some ideas about goals, I'd like to hear from you about the goals you regard as most important."

When the client is involuntary, the statement might include something similar to the following:

• "As we have been talking about the problems we have been legally mandated to work on and your own views of those problems as well as your own concerns, it would help us focus our efforts if we can spell out what we are trying to accomplish. As you know, participation in a parent training group as well as an assessment of your parenting after you complete the program are part of your court order. You can choose between different programs from an approved list."

Goals that are set as a part of a mandate may be vague and clients may be confused about what is expected of them. Therefore, it is important for you to have clarity with respect to the changes that are required. It is important to explain the intent of the goal. For example, "the parent training group will help you set limits with your children." Explaining the intent of goals to clients provides specificity and demonstrates for them that they are able to retain some control over their lives. Finally, you will want to share with the client the importance of demonstrating progress toward the mandate as a measure to avoid further action from the court.

The setting of goals with involuntary clients may also include a goal that the client has identified. Returning to a summary of goals that emerged during the negotiation, you might proceed with a statement that focuses attention on a goal identified by the client. "In addition, you have discussed your desire to return to school. This is not a mandated goal and we can decide together the best way to approach this goal."

If a client appears to be confused or manifests misgivings about proceeding further, you will need to explore those feelings and perhaps clarify further

the function of goals. If the client responds positively, you are ready to advance to the next step.

Jointly Select Appropriate Goals

Although involuntary clients have some mandated goals, the practitioner can help them as well as voluntary clients in identifying goals they would like to achieve. An effective way of assisting them is to employ messages similar to the following:

• "If we succeed in our work together, how will you think and behave differently?"

• "If your family could be the way you would like it to be, what would you as family members be doing differently?"

• "It's been very evident in our session so far that both of you want to improve your marriage. I'd like to hear from each of you as to specific improvements you'd like to achieve."

• "Now the court would like to see changes in your parenting as we have discussed. What kinds of changes do you want to see on your own, regardless of the court?"

Notice that each message requests clients to identify specific changes desired, which paves the way to the next step. If clients have difficulty identifying goals, you can prompt them by making reference to problems and wants identified during the exploratory process and suggest they consider changes related to those problems and wants. The following is an example of such a prompting message. In Chapter 10, Mr. Diaz reported wanting to maintain some independence in his living arrangements and medical regimen: "As you talked about your feeling that your family wanted to infringe on your freedom, you mentioned that you thought you could be capable of administering your own medication with your son's help. I wonder if you might like to work toward getting the kind of help necessary for you and your son to administer the medication?"

With a little encouragement, most clients will identify key goals. We recommend that as they define goals you write them down, explaining that because goals are extremely important, you are keeping a record of them. As clients verbalize goals, you may need to interject comments that seek clarification or to suggest rewording a goal to clarify its meaning or enhance its specificity. It is important, however, not to take liberties with clients' goals but to gain their approval of rewordings. It has been our experience that if you offer suggestions tentatively and respectfully, clients welcome them. Giving the client a copy of the goals that have been developed also encourages attentiveness. Some practitioners provide clients with a folder that will help them keep track of goals and progress made between sessions.

Clients often identify most or all of the goals and general tasks that must be accomplished to resolve their problems. Frequently, however, because of your external vantage point, general task strategies will occur to you that clients have overlooked or omitted. Consequently, you have a responsibility to introduce these methods for reaching client goals for clients' consideration. In introducing such general tasks, it is important to offer them as suggestions and to explain your reason for offering them, referring to related information revealed earlier in the session.

Define the Goals Explicitly

After mutually selecting goals, you are ready to refine them by defining them explicitly and determining the extent of change desired by the client or required by legal mandate. If you were successful in the previous step, this task may require little or no further attention. If the goals were expressed in somewhat general terms, however, you will need to increase their specificity. Examples of messages you can employ to enhance the specificity of goals were presented in the preceding section. You may need to supplement these messages with suggestions of your own as to pertinent behavioral changes that would operationalize general goals.

In determining the desired extent of changes, you can employ messages similar to the following:

- "You say you want to improve your housekeeping. What standards do you want to achieve?"

- "You have set decreasing your anxiety as a goal. What would be signs for you that you have achieved that?"

- [*To elderly client*]: "You have said that you want to maintain your independence in any kind of new living arrangement. What level of independence do you want to ensure in a new place?"

- [*To family members*]: "You have agreed upon a goal of wanting to do more things together as a family. What are some activities that the family could do together?"

Determine the Feasibility of Goals and Discuss Their Potential Benefits and Risks

Before settling upon goals, it is important to ascertain their feasibility and to assess the benefits and risks associated with them. To assist clients in evaluating the feasibility of questionable goals, you can employ responses similar to the following:

- "What obstacles do you foresee that might block the family from doing activities together?"

- "That sounds like a very ambitious goal. I can sense how you'd like to accomplish it, but I'd hate to see you struggle for a goal that may be out of reach. Let's think about what you'd have to do to accomplish your goal."

Discussing benefits that will derive from attaining goals tends to enhance clients' commitment to exerting vigorous efforts to achieve them. A response similar to the following assists in identifying such benefits:

- "What benefits do you expect to reap by achieving this goal?"

- [*To marital partners*]: "How will your marriage be enhanced by achieving this goal?"

- [*To family members*]: "In what ways will your family life improve by successfully accomplishing this goal?"

You also have an obligation to ensure that clients weigh possible risks associated with attaining goals. Enhanced functioning sometimes entails growth pains and negative as well as positive consequences. Examples of the former include losing a job by being assertive with an unjust employer, being rejected when making social overtures, experiencing increased pressure and family conflict by going to work, and suffering from anxiety and discomfort by exposing painful emotions to family and group members.

Clients have a right to be aware of potential risks, and you may be vulnerable to lawsuits if you neglect your obligation in this regard. Because clients may lack awareness of certain risks, you may need to draw their attention to them. Clients may also be aware of risks you have overlooked, and it is therefore important to inquire as to risks they may anticipate.

Assist Clients to Choose Specific Goals

After discussing the benefits and risks of pursuing specific goals, the next step is to weigh these potential consequences and to reach a decision about making a commitment to strive to attain the goals in question. In most instances, benefits are likely to outweigh risks, and clients will manifest adequate readiness to contract to work toward the goals. A simple but effective means we have employed to assess clients' readiness is to ask them to rate this factor on a scale from 1 to 10, where 1 represents "extremely uncertain and not at all ready" and 10 represents "optimistic, eager to start, and totally committed." Most clients report their readiness in the range of 6 to 8, which usually indicates sufficient willingness to proceed with the contracting process. When clients rate their readiness at 5 or lower, they usually are unready to proceed. Should this occur, it is useful to ask the client to visualize which of the goals would bring immediate relief.

Occasionally, clients manifest marked ambivalence, indicating the need to explore their reservations further. Should this occur, we recommend that you accept their misgivings and avoid attempting to convince them to proceed further. It is important, of course, to determine if their misgivings are realistic

or are based on irrational fears (e.g., a parent may be hesitant to pursue a goal of setting consistent limits for a child because of fears of losing the child's love, or an immigrant family may fear that moving away from the community will result in a lost of cultural ties). When you encounter fears, you should assist the client to realize that the fears may be an important dynamic in the problem and that it would be unfortunate to decide against working to accomplish a worthwhile goal on the basis of fears. Rather, the client may choose to pursue the goal to explore or resolve the fears as an intermediate goal before moving on. Negotiating an intermediate goal reduces the threat to the primary goal and enhances the readiness of the client to enter a working contract.

With involuntary clients, commitment to mandated goals might be expected not to be in the highest range. While the practitioner can empathize with the feeling of pressure to work on a goal that has been imposed, you can emphasize that clients have the freedom to choose or approach the goal in their own way. It is also their choice to avoid working on the goal and risk legal consequences (R. H. Rooney, 1992).

When voluntary clients manifest continued ambivalence, it is appropriate to suggest that they may desire additional time to think about a decision. We recommend that you express your willingness to think with them further about the matter inasmuch as discussing feelings and concerns with another person often serves to clarify issues and to resolve feelings. Again, we emphasize the importance of not exerting pressure upon voluntary clients to continue. It has been our experience that voluntary clients who reluctantly submit to pressure often fail to return for scheduled sessions. Voluntary clients thus tend to exercise their right to self-determination when practitioners unwittingly fail to fully respect this right.

Rank Goals According to Clients' Priorities

After clients have established goals and have committed themselves to working toward them, the final step in goal negotiation is to assign priorities to the goals. (Usually clients select from two to five goals.) The purpose of this step is to ensure that beginning joint-change efforts are directed to the goal that is most important to clients. When mandated goals are included, these can also be prioritized because simultaneous efforts on all may not be possible and some contain greater consequences than others. This step further ensures maximal responsibility and participation in the process by clients, thereby enhancing their motivation to work on goal attainment. As a lead-in to the ranking process, we recommend a message similar to the following: "Now that you've settled upon these goals, it's important to rank them according to priority. I suggest you start with the goal most important to you, then you can rank the others as you see fit. We'll get to all of them in time but we want to be sure to start with the most important one."

With involuntary clients, this message might be: "While we are coming to agreement about the priority of those goals most important to you, we also need to consider the priority of those goals that are mandated. Your court order states that you must complete a chemical dependency evaluation immediately, so this one is a top priority. Exploring educational and employment possibilities might be delayed a bit until this has begun, and you can choose which one of those you want to explore first." There may be instances in which a mandated goal and a client's own goals can be worked toward simultaneously as is illustrated in the following case example.

William, 16, repeatedly truant from school, recently became involved with a group of other truants who were caught stealing from the local convenience store. Because this was a first offense, the judge ordered William to attend school. Failure to attend school would result in his being sent to a juvenile detention center for 90 days. During the initial session with the practitioner, William indicated that he was unlikely to attend school, as he thought school was stupid and uninteresting. When asked about his interests, he indicated that he would like to learn how to play the guitar. This

goal, of course, was inconsistent with the mandate. The practitioner was, however, able to find a music teacher at the school who was willing to give William guitar lessons, but William had to be in school on a regular basis. The practitioner and William negotiated a goal plan that would ensure that he attended school, and in which he could also learn to play the guitar. The importance of this intermediary or transitional goal—that of learning to play the guitar—is that William was more amenable to attending school.

When the target system involves more than one person, different members may accord different priorities to goals. Further, members may have individual goals as well as shared or reciprocal goals. If the target system is a couple, a group, or a family it is desirable to have goals that pertain both to individuals and to the larger system. With larger systems, it is desirable to have lists of goals for both individuals and the system and to rank the goals for each person and the system. Where differences exist in ranking goals for a system, your help is needed to assist members to negotiate rankings.

BASELINE MEASUREMENT AND EVALUATION

As we discussed in Chapters 1 and 3, evaluation of the outcomes of treatment with clients is an important component of direct practice. Demands from funding sources and administrators for accountability have increasingly required service providers to furnish evidence of the efficacy of their work with clients. Until recent years, direct practitioners have tended to resist these demands, with the effect that a small percentage of social workers actually evaluated their practice (Bailey-Dempsey & Reid, 1996; Gingerich, 1984). The intervening years, however, reveal marked improvement, perhaps resulting from a combination of even more strident demands for accountability and an increasing number of social work graduates who possess the competency and inclination to employ evaluation procedures (Penka & Kirk, 1991). Although the majority of practitioners are engaged in evaluation with their clients, their evaluations have not tended to be systematic. We support the position that evaluation is a component of practice that is necessary to inform practitioners about the effectiveness of intervention strategies and in order to document change or outcomes in client conditions (Bloom, Fischer, & Orme, 1999; Corcoran & Gingerich, 1994).

In this section of the chapter, we provide an overview of both quantitative and qualitative methods that may be used to measure progress and to evaluate outcomes. We consider the following as fundamental to this process:

1. identification of the specific problem or behavior to be changed
2. specific, measurable, and feasible goals
3. a match between the goal and measurement procedures
4. maintaining a systematic record of relevant information

A discussion of the first three factors has occurred previously in this chapter. At this point, we want to stress the importance of recording systematic data in the case record. This information allows both the practitioner and the client to track progress or lack thereof over the course of the contract. In the latter case, goals may be reviewed or renegotiated as indicated.

Available Resources

Computerized information systems are available to assist direct service practitioners with collecting and analyzing practice evaluation information (Nurius & Hudson, 1993b). Many human service organizations have computerized management information systems in which practitioners record case plans and client progress toward goals. These systems may also be utilized to provide evidence of program effectiveness.

A number of standardized instruments are also available, some of which utilize computers to track progress over time (Hudson, 1991; 1992). A limitation of standardized instruments is the fact that for the most part they focus on problems rather than strengths, resources, or specific client situations (Berlin & Marsh, 1993; Vosler, 1990). A notable exception is a set of instruments developed by Gilgun (1999) that assesses risks and assets in families. Standardized instruments, even with established reliability and validity, may not be desirable with certain populations or directly related to the goals of a specific client concern. In this case, the practitioner and client may agree upon and develop their own scales or measures that are tailored to the specific condition (Collins, Kayser, & Platt, 1994; Jordan & Franklin, 1995). One example is illustrated in Figure 12-1. This example represents a goal and task form developed by a client and practitioner that allows for the tracking of progress toward the desired outcome. Task forms, although tailored to an individual client situation, may also be summarized to demonstrate program effectiveness. In choosing resources for measuring progress and evaluating outcomes, the practitioner should be sure to match the methods used with the client situation and need.

The goal and task summary form provides both client and practitioner a means to review and monitor progress toward identified goals as well as an overall summary of what has been accomplished. Potential barriers and benefits to goal achievement are also discussed. A significant number of barriers that pose a threat outside of client or practitioner control may mean that a goal should be revised. This form may be used for each identified target concern and goal and is especially useful as a review in the termination phase. Once goals and tasks have been identified with the client, we recommend providing them with a copy for their records. Tasks and their utility for goal achievement are discussed in greater detail in Chapter 13.

Name: _____

Statement of Problem/Condition to Be Changed: _____

_____

Goal

Statement: _____

Barriers: _____   _____   _____   _____

Benefits: _____   _____   _____   _____

General

Task: _____

_____

Tasks (steps to be taken to achieve goal):

	Completion Date	Review Date	Outcome Code
1. _____	_____	_____	_____
2. _____	_____	_____	_____
3. _____	_____	_____	_____

Outcome Codes

Tasks & Goal Status [ ] C (completed) [ ] P (partially completed) [ ] NC (not completed)

Figure 12-1   Sample Goal and Task Form

Quantitative Baseline Measurement

The process of evaluation described in this section is essentially a form of single-subject or single-system evaluation. This basic approach can also be used for research purposes, including testing the effectiveness of specific interventions and comparing the effectiveness of different interventions. Proctor (1990) has discussed issues related to the purpose and design of single-system research (some of the information is based on her article). When the approach is used strictly for research purposes, stringent guidelines should be followed, and doing so may conflict with delivering services in an optimal fashion (Gambrill & Barth, 1980; E. Thomas, 1978). Further, rigorous research employing single-subject design requires knowledge beyond the scope of this book.[2]

Quantitative evaluation embodies the use of procedures that measure the frequency and/or severity of target problems. Measurements taken before implementing change-oriented interventions are termed *baseline* measures because they provide a baseline against which measures of progress and measures at termination and follow-up can be compared. These comparisons thus provide quantitative data that make it possible to evaluate the efficacy of work with clients.

Measuring Overt Behavior

Baseline measures can be of either overt or covert behaviors. Overt behaviors are observable and, as such, lend themselves to frequency counts. For example, if family members negotiated a shared goal of increasing the frequency of positive messages sent to each other, you might instruct them to keep a daily tally of the number of such messages they convey for a period of 1 week. The daily average thus would serve as a baseline against which progress could be measured. Similar baselines can be determined for behaviors that involve eliminating temper tantrums, overeating, speaking up in social situations, expressing troubling feelings, listening to one's children, and a myriad of other possible target behaviors. Such measures quantify problem behaviors and make it possible to ascertain both weekly progress and ultimate outcomes of change efforts. In addition, clients are enabled to discern small incremental changes that might otherwise escape detection, which often sustains and enhances their motivation.

Frequency counts may be made by clients, by observers, or by practitioners themselves (when the target behavior occurs in conjoint or group sessions). Because it is convenient, practitioners often have clients record personal behaviors that occur outside the therapeutic sessions. Baselines obtained through self-monitoring, however, are not true measurements of behavior under "no treatment" conditions, for self-monitoring itself often produces therapeutic effects. For example, monitoring the rate of a desired behavior may influence a client to increase the frequency of that behavior. Similarly, measuring the rate of negative behavior may influence a client to reduce its frequency. These effects of self-monitoring on the behavior being monitored are termed *reactive effects*. Viewed by a researcher, reactive effects are a source of contamination that confounds the ef-

fects of interventions being tested. From a clinician's viewpoint, however, self-monitoring may be employed to advantage *as an intervention* precisely because reactive effects tend to increase or decrease certain target behaviors.[3] Although desired changes may result from self-monitoring of either positive or negative behaviors, selecting positive behaviors is preferable because doing so focuses on strengths related to goals.

When baseline measures of current overt behaviors are taken, repeated frequency counts across specified time intervals are typically employed. The time intervals selected should be those during which the highest incidence of behavioral excesses occur or times in which positive behaviors are desired. It is also important to obtain measures under relatively consistent conditions. Otherwise, the measure may not be representative and reflect the true picture accurately (Proctor, 1990).

Retrospective Estimates of Baseline Behavior

Baseline measurements are obtained before change-oriented interventions are implemented; either by having clients makes retrospective estimates of the incidence of behaviors targeted for change or by obtaining data before the following session. Although less accurate, the former method often is employed because change-oriented efforts need not be deferred pending the gathering of baseline data. This is a key advantage, for acute problems often demand immediate attention and delaying intervention for even 1 week may not be justifiable. On the other hand, delaying interventions for 1 week while gathering baseline data often does not create undue difficulty, and the resultant data are likely to be far more reliable than mere estimates.

When determining the baseline of target behavior by retrospective estimates, it is common practice to ask the client to estimate the incidence of the behavior across a specified time interval that may range from a few minutes to 1 day, depending on the usual frequency of the target behaviors. Time intervals selected for frequent behaviors, such as nervous mannerisms, should be relatively short (e.g., 15-minute intervals). For relatively infrequent behaviors, such as temper tantrums, intervals may consist of several hours.

Measuring Covert Behaviors

Baseline data can also be obtained for covert behaviors, such as troubling thoughts or feelings (e.g., irrational fears, depressed states, or self-depreciating thoughts). Clients may make frequency counts of targeted thoughts or rate degrees of emotional states. Where goals involve altering feelings, such as anger, depression, loneliness, and anxiety, it is desirable to construct self-anchoring scales (Bloom, 1975) that denote various levels of an internal state. To do this, employ a five- or seven-point scale that represents varying levels of internal states ranging from absence of the troubling feeling or thought on one end to maximal intensity on the other. To "anchor" such scales, ask clients to imagine themselves experiencing the extreme degrees of the given internal state and to describe what they experience. You can then use the descriptions to define at least the extremes and the midpoint of the scale. Developing scales in this manner quantifies internal states uniquely for each client. In constructing self-anchoring scales, it is important to avoid mixing different types of internal states, for even though emotions such as "happy" and "sad" appear to belong on the same continuum, they are qualitatively different, and mixing them will result in confusion. Figure 12-2 depicts a seven-point anchored scale.

1	2	3	4	5	6	7
Least anxious (calm, relaxed, serene)		Moderately anxious (tense, uptight, but still functioning with effort)			Most anxious (muscles taut, can't concentrate or sit still; could climb the wall)	

Figure 12-2   Sample of Self-Anchored Scale

Clients can employ self-anchoring scales to record the extent of troubling internal states across specified time intervals (e.g., three times daily for 7 days) in a manner similar to that of making frequency counts of overt behaviors. In both instances, clients keep tallies on the target behaviors. A minimum of ten separate measures is generally necessary to discern patterns of data, but urgent needs for intervention sometimes require practitioners to settle for less.

Guidelines to Obtaining Baseline Measures

To employ baseline measures, it is vital to maximize the reliability and validity of your measurements (Berlin & Marsh, 1993). Otherwise, your baseline measures and subsequent comparisons with measures will be flawed. Adhering to the following guidelines will assist you in maximizing reliability and validity:

1. **Define the target of measurement in clear and operational terms.** Reliability is enhanced when behavior (overt or covert) that is targeted for change is specifically defined. Global descriptions and sloppy specifications of behaviors block accurate measurement.

2. **Be sure your measures relate directly and specifically to the goals targeted for change.** Otherwise, the validity of your measurements at baseline and subsequent points will be highly suspect. For example, when clients' problems embody low self-esteem, measures designed to tap self-esteem should be employed. If a mother's child care and organization of household tasks are deficient, measures should be devised that directly specify behavioral changes that are deemed essential. Similarly, measures of violent behavior and alcohol abuse should correspond to frequency of angry outbursts (or control of anger in provocative situations) and consumption of alcohol (or periods of abstinence), respectively.

3. **You will often need to use multiple measures.** Because clients typically present more than one problem and because individual problems

may embody several dimensions (e.g., depressed affect, low self-esteem, and low assertiveness are frequently components of depression).

4. **Measures should be obtained under relatively consistent conditions.** Otherwise, changes may reflect differences in conditions rather than in goal-related behaviors.

5. **Baseline measures are not feasible with discrete goals,** for evaluating the efficacy of helping efforts in such instances is a clear-cut matter; either clients accomplish a goal or they do not. By contrast, progress toward ongoing goals is incremental and not subject to fixed limits. Employing baseline measures and periodic measures, therefore, effectively enables both practitioners and clients to discern incremental changes that might otherwise be overlooked.

Measuring with Self-Administered Scales

Self-administered scales are also useful for obtaining baseline data. Many psychological scales are available, but the WALMYR assessment scales (Hudson, 1992) are especially useful for social workers. Designed by Hudson and fellow social workers, the 22 separate scales (most of which we listed in Chapter 8) tap many of the dimensions relevant to social workers. Ease of administration, scoring, and interpretation, as well as acceptable reliability and validity, are among the advantages of these scales.[4] Self-administered scales also quantify measurement of target problems, and although they are subjective and less precise than behavioral counts, they are particularly useful in measuring covert behavioral states (e.g., anxiety, depression, self-esteem, and clinical stress) and perceptions of clients about their interpersonal relationships. As with measures of overt behaviors, selected scales can be administered before implementing treatment and thereafter at periodic intervals to monitor progress and to assess outcomes at termination and follow-up. It is interesting to note that unlike behavioral self-monitoring (i.e., counting behaviors or thoughts),

subjective self-report through self-administered instruments such as those just discussed are less likely to produce reactive effects (Applegate, 1992).

Receptivity of Clients to Measurement

Some practitioners may be hesitant to ask clients to engage in self-monitoring or to complete self-report instruments because they are concerned that clients will resist or react negatively. Research studies by Applegate (1992) and Campbell (1990) indicate such concerns are not justified. These researchers found that clients generally were receptive to formal evaluation procedures, and Campbell found, in fact, that clients preferred being involved in evaluation to having evaluations limited to practitioner's opinions. Moreover, Campbell found that practitioners were able to estimate accurately their clients' feelings about different types of evaluation procedures.

Monitoring Progress

After obtaining baseline measures of targets of change, the next step is to transfer the data to a graph on which the horizontal axis denotes time intervals (days or weeks) and the vertical axis denotes frequency or severity of target behaviors. Simple to construct, such a graph makes it possible to evaluate the progress of clients and the efficacy of interventions. Figure 12-3 is an example of such a graph, which depicts the incidence of anxiety before and during the implementation of change.

Note that the baseline period was 7 days and the time interval selected for self-monitoring was 1 day. Interventions were employed over a period of 4 weeks. From the graph, it is apparent that the client experienced some ups and downs (as usually occurs), but achieved marked progress.

In monitoring progress through repeated measures, it is critical to employ the same procedures and instruments employed in obtaining baseline measures. Otherwise, meaningful comparisons cannot be made. It is also important to continue to adhere to the guidelines listed in the preceding

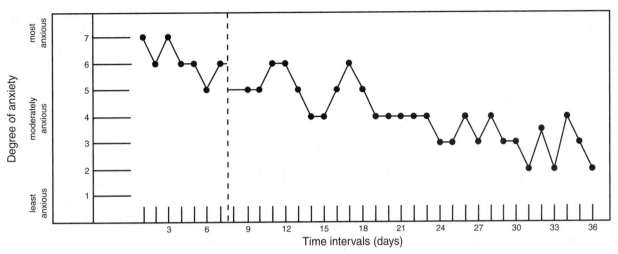

Figure 12-3   Sample of Graph Recording Extent of Anxiety during Baseline and Intervention Periods

section. Repeated measurement of the same behavior at equal intervals enables practitioners not only to assess progress but also to determine variability in clients' behavior and to assess the impact of changes in the clients' life situation. For example, by charting measures of depression and self-esteem from week to week it is possible to discern either positive or negative change that corresponds to concurrent stressful or positive life events. Visible representation on graphs of measured changes thus not only enables clients to view discernible evidence of progress but also to gain awareness of how specific life events affect their emotional states or behavior.

QUALITATIVE MEASURES

Within the last several years, qualitative methods have emerged as a viable option for practice evaluation. There is a limited amount of information in the literature; nevertheless, we think that it is important to acquaint you with the information that is available.

Qualitative methods are different in their "philosophical, theoretical and stylistic orientation from quantitative methods" (Jordan & Franklin, 1995, p. 97). The process of data collection is more open ended and allows clients to express their reality and experience. In the assessment process, the aim is to explore the client's frame of reference, beliefs, values, and cultural realities, as he or she is considered the key informant or expert regarding his or her own problem (Crabtree & Miller, 1992; Jordan & Franklin, 1995). Gilgun has suggested that this focus on client perception makes a good fit with social work values emphasizing self-determination (Gilgun, 1994).

The aim of qualitative methods in evaluating progress or assessing outcomes is to understand the *clients' experience and the meaning that experience holds for them* (S. Witkin, 1993). In this sense, information obtained from clients provides us with context as well as the dynamic dimensions of their concerns, which may not be assessable with standardized instruments. In addition, qualitative methods provide insight into the interaction or combination of factors that contribute to a desired change. Descriptive in nature, this information relies on words, pictures, diagrams, and narratives. For example, symbols used in the structural approach to work with families provided a visual map of underlining family structure. In a situation where the intervention goal is to realign relationships between family members, this process could be graphically illustrated and observed over time. The family narrative, which would include the experience and meaning as well as the quality of change associated with the desired goal, becomes an important element in the evaluation of the change. Systematic observation and multiple points of observation or triangulation may include, for example, client self-reports, the observations of the practitioner, and other relevant systems. This replication serves the purpose of establishing the credibility of information as well as guarding against bias.

The following are examples of qualitative methods that have been used to demonstrate change or the achievement of goals, providing descriptive information regarding the process of change or reduction of symptoms.

Logical Analysis Effects

Reid (1990) describes logical analysis effects as establishing a linkage among context, intervention, and change. The case of William, the truant, will be used to illustrate the use of this method. William was ordered by the court to attend school to avoid being placed in a juvenile detention center. He thought school was stupid and uninteresting. He continued to miss a significant number of days, or he would go to school but not attend classes. The social worker working with William arranged for him to begin working on his goal of learning to play the guitar. The music teacher agreed to give William guitar lessons provided that he was a student. After several weeks, William reported that he had missed fewer days in school, and the majority of his absences were excused. In William's case the intervention was arranging for him to have guitar lessons. To track this change, we would need to establish that improved school attendance was the result of this intervention. This information could be graphically illustrated as pre and post data, recording the number of

days missed prior to and following the intervention. This information would be combined with William's report about school attendance and with information from the school attendance record.

Informative Events or Critical Incidences

Clients and practitioners are often able to identify a "turning point" associated with a particular event or intervention that contributed to a reduction in the target problem (I. P. Davis & Reid, 1988; Reid, 1990). They may also be asked to describe the intervention or task completed as the most and least helpful. Greater weight may be assigned to those activities in which the client and the practitioner agree. Completion of a certain task toward a particular goal may be defined as contributing to change and a particular outcome. This method may also be used to evaluate program effectiveness. For example, focus group participants evaluating a family reunification and preservation program were asked to identify the particular intervention that marked a change in their ability to move toward reunification.

Existing assessment tools such as the eco-map may be utilized to measure progress or change in the target problem. The eco-map is used to examine the relationship between a family and other social systems, identifying resources and areas of tension. For evaluation purposes, this tool may be used in a pre-post fashion to graphically demonstrate change in the areas indicated as target concerns for the family or individuals. In Figure 12-4, the family has identified the goal of paying off credit card debt so that they can afford to move to a different neighborhood.

ADVANTAGES OF MONITORING PROGRESS

Whether practitioners utilize qualitative or quantitative measures, or a combination of both, monitoring progress has numerous advantages.

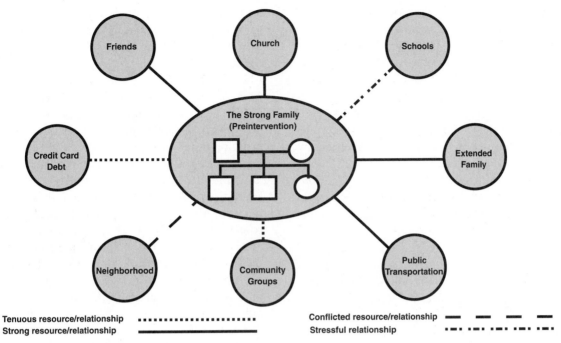

Figure 12-4a   Eco-map

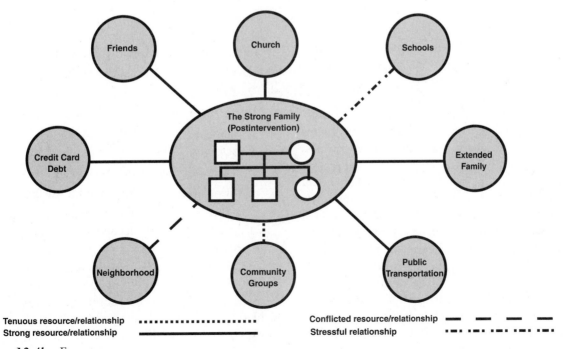

Figure 12-4b   Eco-map

Quantitative measures provide descriptive information in relationship to the process of change or reduction of symptoms. Qualitative methods afford both practitioner and client the opportunity to assess the meaning of the desired change, adding the richness of client experience.

Measures afford guidelines to both client and practitioner as to when treatment can be terminated. For example, when the observable behaviors of neglectful parents improve to the degree that they conform to explicit criteria, termination is justified. Similarly, when measurements of a client's depression drop to the range of nonclinical depression, termination may be indicated. Results of monitoring can provide evidence of progress for third-party payers to justify continued coverage. A final advantage is that if interventions are not achieving measurable results after a reasonable trial period, the practitioner can explore possible reasons for this lack of progress and negotiate the use of different interventions when indicated.

CONTRACTS

In the first portion of this chapter, we outlined the purpose of goals and utility of goals and also the various components involved in their development. We now turn our attention to the contract. If problems are explored sufficiently and agreement is reached as to the nature of the problems and the systems involved and the appropriateness of the practitioner and agency for addressing those problems, the practitioner and client(s) are ready to formulate a *contract*. Contracting is the natural culmination of the first major phase and the introduction of the change-oriented (goal attainment) phase—the heart of the helping process. Contracts specify goals to be accomplished and the means of accomplishing them, clarify the roles of the participants, and establish the conditions under which assistance is provided. An initial contract thus is an agreement that guides practitioners and clients in their joint ef-

forts to achieve specified objectives. While most appropriate with voluntary clients, semivoluntary contracts can also be negotiated with involuntary clients (R. H. Rooney, 1992).

Research findings attest to the value of social work contracts. Wood (1978) reviewed numerous outcome studies of direct practice and reported that in a substantial number of those reporting negative outcomes, practitioners did not employ explicit contracts. Studies that reported positive outcomes typically utilized contracts. Reid and Hanrahan (1982) have suggested that the contracts in the studies with more successful outcomes were characterized by motivational congruence (the fit between client motivation and what the practitioner attempts to provide). To use contracts to maximal advantage, you must be aware of their component parts and be skillful in systematically negotiating them. The purpose of this section is to assist you to gain knowledge and skill in utilizing contracts effectively.

Formulating a Contract

When you have completed the process of negotiating goals with clients, you are ready to formulate a *contract*. Practitioners generally agree that a contract should include the following elements:

1. Goals to be accomplished (ranked by priority)
2. Roles of the participants
3. Interventions or techniques to be employed
4. Time frame and frequency and length of sessions
5. Means of monitoring progress
6. Stipulations for renegotiating the contract
7. Housekeeping items, such as beginning date, provisions for canceling or changing scheduled sessions, and financial arrangements

Although it is the final discrete activity of the first phase of the helping process, contracting continues throughout the entire course of the helping venture. Goals are fluid and should be expanded or modified as situations change and new information comes to light. Hence, goals are not to be set aside at the time of contracting only to be returned to at termination; they provide a focus for work in ongoing sessions. Time limits, types of intervention employed, frequency of sessions, and participants in the helping process may be altered according to the changing circumstances of each case. It is for these reasons that item 6, "stipulations for renegotiating the contract," is included as an essential element of the contracting process. Ongoing explicit understandings between practitioners and clients are vital. Keeping the contract updated also conveys continuing respect for the client and enhances ongoing motivation and cooperation. The initial contract thus is only preliminary and must be tailored to fit the changing circumstances of each case.

Practitioners construct contracts with varying degrees of formality. Public agencies often require signed service agreements. Such *written contracts* specify each of the items listed and provide space for entering details. The clients and practitioners sign the contract, giving it much the same form as a legal contract. The rationale for using a written contract is that it emphasizes the commitments both clients and practitioners make and minimizes the possibility of misunderstandings. The document, of course, is not legally binding, and this should be clarified verbally or stipulated in the written contract. Otherwise clients may believe they are justified in filing suit for malpractice if they do not achieve the goals of the contract. Some practitioners prefer *verbal contracts*, which include all of the same provisions but without the sterility and finality of a written contract. A third solution is to include a partially verbal and partially written contract with the latter including the basics of problems and goals identified, role expectations, time limits, and provisions for revision. If a written contract is not used, questions of informed consent arise. You or your agency may choose not to use written contracts. Nonetheless, goals and their priority should be recorded in the case record, along with your notes of progress, which makes them available for review during

each session with the client. Whether verbal or written, we recommend that a copy of the goals to be accomplished be made available to the client. We now consider elements 2 through 7 in greater depth. Item 1 (goals) was considered earlier in this chapter.

Roles of Participants

We reviewed the verbal process of socialization to client and practitioner roles in Chapter 5. Those should be reviewed in the contracting process and, in the case of mandated clients or public agency practice, specified in writing. The written contract provides an opportunity for such clients to model the mutual accountability of all parties. The practitioner should spell out what he or she and the agency are committing themselves to providing. For example, the agency may agree to provide child care during sessions or transportation to certain appointments. Similarly, if the client has agreed to participate in a parenting group, that would be specified.

Interventions or Techniques to Be Employed

This aspect of the contract involves specifying interventions and techniques that will be implemented to accomplish goals. During initial contracting it is often possible to specify interventions only on a somewhat global level, such as individual, conjoint, or family sessions or a mixture of them. You can, however, specify that you will be discussing problematic situations and considering alternate remedial courses of action, which is common to virtually all problem-solving efforts.

In some instances, depending on your assessment, you can discuss interventions with greater specificity. You may thus specify such interventions as relaxation training; identifying and eliminating irrational thoughts, beliefs, and fears (cognitive restructuring); role playing and behavioral rehearsal; self-management techniques; and developing skills (e.g., communication, assertiveness, problem solving, and conflict resolution). Whenever you consider implementing interventions, it is vital to discuss them with clients, to present a brief overview of the intervention, to elicit clients' reactions, and to gain their consent. Bear in mind that contracting is ongoing.

Temporal Conditions

Another integral aspect of the contract involves the duration of the helping process and the frequency and length of sessions. With respect to duration, there are basically two patterns: time limited service (also known as planned short-term service) and open-ended service. The former pattern involves a specified maximum number of sessions (usually within a limited time frame), whereas the latter pattern does not specify time limits. Both patterns have existed in social work for many decades. The open-ended pattern is historically tied to the diagnostic school of casework, which developed from roots in Freudian psychoanalytic theory. Time limits were introduced by Otto Rank, a contemporary of Freud, and were adopted by the functional school of social work, which emerged in the 1930s.

Time limits were incorporated as a major component of the task-centered system of social work, a model of practice that emerged in 1972 (Reid & Epstein, 1972). This model, which has gained wide acceptance, was developed as a result of compelling research evidence. Reid and Shyne conducted a study designed to compare the efficacy of time-limited casework with open-ended casework, and the results indicated that clients who received service under the former method achieved results that equaled (and sometimes exceeded) those achieved under the latter pattern. Moreover, the results were as durable, measured 6 months following termination of service (Reid & Shyne, 1969). More recent reviews of the research support the use of tasks and time limits in the helping process (Corcoran & Gingerich, 1994; Reid, 1997a; 1997b).

The use of time limits is supported by grounds other than the research cited above. From a strictly logical standpoint, it can be persuasively argued that most humans tend to intensify their efforts to accomplish a given task when a deadline exists, as, for example, last-minute cramming that students do before an examination. Time-limited service thus employs time as a dynamic to counter the human tendency to procrastinate.

Still another argument supportive of time limits is that even in planned long-term treatment, most of the gains are achieved early in treatment (i.e., by the fifth or sixth session). Moreover, whatever the intended length, most treatments turn out to be relatively brief, as indicated by the findings of several studies, some of them national in scope. The National Center for Health Statistics, for example, reported in 1966 an average of fewer than five contacts for the almost 1 million psychiatric patients seen during that year. Even more impressive is the fact that if only those patients who actually began treatment are considered, the median duration of treatment is between five and six sessions.

The advantages of time-limited interventions have far-reaching implications for practitioners, including the following:

1. Time-limited service is cost-effective. Results equal to those of open-ended service can be achieved at much less cost.

2. More clients can be served under time-limited patterns. The problem of waiting lists can be reduced appreciably when agencies adopt time-limited services as the primary pattern of service delivery (as many have).

3. Time limits foster clients' optimism when practitioners express confidence that improvement is possible in a short time.

4. Time-limited service facilitates the process of termination by introducing it during the preliminary contracting phase.

5. Time limits sharply demarcate the problem-solving process into the beginning, middle, and ending phases.

6. Funding sources are more willing to approve and pay for time-limited than open-ended

treatment because of the specificity of goals and the limitation of time (Corcoran & Vandiver, 1996).

In addition to the preceding implications, two others warrant discussion. First, by adopting skilled time-limited intervention as the primary mode of service delivery, an agency can accommodate more clients over a span of time, which enhances the likelihood of being able to provide service when it is needed most, as delays in providing service may negatively affect results. The second implication concerns the matter of employing time-limited service with disadvantaged clients, who represent the major population served by social workers. Based on research findings, Lorion (1978) and W. Reid (1978) concluded that working-class clients better utilize and prefer structured and time-limited interventions. Indeed, both the earlier research that provided the impetus for developing the task-centered system and later research that involved subsequent refinements of the system have been conducted largely with working-class clients.

Time limits, of course, are not appropriate for all client populations or situations. For clients whose goals involve or whose problems are related to deeply ingrained personality dysfunction, long-term therapy may be essential. In addition, problems correlated with poverty, such as chronic neglect, require longer-range investment of agency resources and advocacy than short-term treatment provides. Time limits with institutionalized mentally ill patients or chronically mentally ill outpatients for whom practitioners have ongoing responsibility are impractical, except when circumscribed problems of living are defined as goals. For example, the latter may involve multiple short-term contracts related to specific problems and episodes. Similarly, time limits with assigned clients who are legally confined to correctional institutions or who are on probation or parole for extended periods of time are also inappropriate. Even in these instances, however, time limits may be used selectively to assist clients to achieve circumscribed goals.

Are time limits effective with racial and ethnic minority clients? Based on a previously cited outcome study of mental health services provided to Chicano clients, Gomez et al. (1985) concluded: "the short-term casework services provided had a positive effect on the problems of Chicano clients and . . . clients were highly satisfied with the services" (p. 482). Some theorists, however, believe that time limits are inconsistent with perspectives on time held by some minority groups (Devore & Schlesinger, 1999; Logan, Freeman & McRoy, 1990; Green, 1990).

The lengths of time limits vary across different theories or models of social work, counseling, and psychotherapy. Because of the extensive use of and substantial research with the task-centered system, a social work model, we recommend following the time limits commonly employed under this system. Most task-centered contracts specify from 6 to 12 sessions over a time span from 2 to 4 months (Reid, 1987). Given this flexibility, you can negotiate with the client for the specific number of sessions. Both clients' preferences and your best estimate of the number of sessions required should be considered. The advantage of determining clients' preferences, of course, is that mutuality in contracting is enhanced and clients are more likely to react positively to time limits when they have participated in selecting them.

Another aspect of time structuring pertains to the frequency of sessions. In social work, weekly sessions are the norm (except in instances cited below), although more frequent sessions may be employed in cases that require intensive support and monitoring. Provision can also be made in contracts for spacing sessions further apart during the termination phase of the helping process.

To enhance mutuality in contracting, it is generally desirable to elicit clients' preferences related to the frequency of sessions. Occasionally, clients may request more frequent sessions than appear justified, and you will need to express your recommendations. It has been our experience that most clients look to the practitioner for recommendations and readily agree to them.

When intensive home-based family preservation service (see Chapter 16) or intensive outpatient crisis stabilization is the intervention selected, marked divergence from usual patterns of service delivery occurs. In such instances, service is intensive with each family, and practitioners may have a caseload of six or fewer cases. Many hours weekly are spent with each family and the practitioner is on call on a 24-hour basis. The period of intensive service, however, is generally limited to a few weeks.

A final time factor concerns the length of each session. Research offers no solid guidelines as to superior arrangements. A 50-minute session for individuals is the prevailing norm, but more time (usually 1½ to 2 hours) is frequently allotted to intake sessions and to regular family and group sessions. Because some children, adolescents, and elderly clients have difficulty tolerating 50-minute sessions, shorter but more frequent sessions are a common variation. Finally, requirements in schools, hospitals, and other settings often influence the length of sessions. For example, contacts in a hospital setting may last 15 or 20 minutes, depending on the condition of the patient and the goals to be achieved.

Means of Monitoring Progress

Stipulating in the contract how progress will be monitored serves the vital function of fostering an action-oriented mind-set that is conducive to change. Maintaining an expectancy of change enhances motivation and actualizes a positive self-fulfilling prophecy. When baseline measures on target problems have been obtained, the preferred method of monitoring progress is to use the same measuring devices at specified intervals, as we noted in an earlier section. If baseline data are not available, a crude method of attempting to quantify progress is to ask clients to rate their progress on a scale of 1 to 10 where 1 represents no progress and 10 denotes complete achievement of a given goal. Comparing their ratings from one time to the next gives a rough estimate of clients' progress.

Another method of assessing progress is to depict it graphically. Calibrated drawings of thermometers with a scale from 1 to 10 can be employed for each goal, and clients can color in the thermometers to reflect their progress. This method is particularly appealing to children and developmentally disabled adults, who derive satisfaction in coloring in the units as they achieve progress. The dramatic effect is further enhanced when accompanied by recognition from the practitioner and significant others.

The frequency of monitoring sessions should be negotiated. We find that clients often ask for recommendations and that spending a few minutes every other session to evaluate progress works out well. Some clients may prefer to take a few minutes each session, whereas others may prefer to discuss progress less frequently. We recommend that you be flexible but not allow more than three sessions between discussions of progress. Less frequent monitoring dilutes the benefits achieved by highlighting growth and by maintaining focus on desired changes.

Stipulations for Renegotiating the Contract

Because contracting continues during the entire helping process, it is important to clarify for clients that conditions in the contract are subject to renegotiation at any time. Circumstances change, new facts emerge, assessment evolves, and progress occurs. These and other changing factors require that the contract be constantly updated to maintain its relevance and fit. We therefore recommend that you explain that any participant in the helping process (including you) may request modifications in the contract at any time. Such an explanation further highlights the expectancy of change and enhances mutuality in the helping process. When contracting with involuntary clients, any circumstances such as evidence of new legal violations that would cause a unilateral change in the contract should be specified.

Housekeeping Items

The final element involved in formulating a contract includes establishing a beginning date, clarifying provisions for canceling or changing scheduled sessions, and firming financial arrangements (when fees are required). With respect to changes in appointments, it is important to stress that clients are responsible for time that has been set aside for them. Should legitimate circumstances warrant changing or canceling an appointment, they should generally provide advance notice of at least 24 hours so that the time can be rescheduled for another client. Ordinarily, it is desirable (and indeed often essential) to charge clients for appointments they fail to keep, inasmuch as the time was allocated for them. Explicitly discussing these matters emphasizes the importance of attending sessions, tends to avoid misunderstandings, and reduces the frequency of changes, cancellations, and failed appointments.

Discussing financial arrangements is painful for many practitioners, who are often uncomfortable in discussing payment for their services for a variety of reasons. One concern is that a discussion about fees may interfere with the client-practitioner relationship. Still, agencies have fee policies that require payment for services, which include sliding fee scales, and the majority of clients expect to pay for services.

Practitioners should bear in mind that part of competency is being able to handle financial arrangements effectively, which requires openly discussing fees, without apology. Recognizing that clients expect to discuss fees may assist you in dealing with this matter more comfortably. Your responsibility, of course, does not end after negotiating the contract. Notification from the business office that a client has failed to pay fees according to the contract should be explored promptly and in a respectful manner. Failure to pay fees may signal additional difficulties in a client's life, such as financial strain or negative feelings toward the practitioner; either merits immediate attention. In some instances of nonpayment of fees, where the client has been given ample opportunity to rectify the situation, termination of the professional relationship may be indicated. According to Houston-Vega, Nuehring and Daguio (1997), "a practitioner can end the service relationship for nonpayment of fees if the client's or another's welfare is not in jeopardy" (p. 82). When services are terminated for this reason, they advise documentation of efforts to remedy the situation in the case record.

Sample Contract

To assist you in developing contracts, we have included a sample contract (see Figure 12-5 on pages 354–355) that includes most of the components discussed in preceding sections. Elements of the sample contract were adapted from Houston-Vega, Nuehring, and Daguio (1997). This informative resource includes sample contracts for individuals, families, and groups as well as guidelines for practitioners on ethical practice and managing malpractice risks.

Summary

In this chapter we have focused on goals and the service contract as essential elements of the goal achievement and change process. It may be useful to think of goals as global, whereas tasks are akin to objectives that you develop in field contracts. In case, general tasks and objectives represent the measurable relationship between what is desired and the manner in which the outcome will be achieved. We have focused on the knowledge and

Agreement for Professional Services

Name(s) of Client(s)   _____

_____

_____

I. **Problem/Concern:** I (we) have discussed my (our) situation with _____, and have identified and
agreed upon the statement(s) of concerns listed below:

1 _____

2 _____

3 _____

4 _____

5 _____

II. **Goals:** I (we) hereby agree to work collaboratively in achieving certain goals that will enable me (us) to resolve
the statement of concerns listed above to improve (my) our situation. I (we) agree that to achieve these goals I
(we) will share my (our) experiences, life events, and reactions to the goals. I (we) agree that I (we) will actively
participate in planning and carrying out actions or steps that are mutually planned for the purpose of achieving
goals. The initial goals that we have agreed upon in order of priority are as follows:

1 _____

2 _____

3 _____

4 _____

5 _____

I (we) understand that goals may be added, revised, or changed in the course of our work together. I (we)
also understand that there may be time limits, which may influence the rate at which goals may need to be
accomplished or where significant progress toward goals may need to be documented.

III. **Sessions:** I (we) agree to meet with _____ on a _____ basis, for a total number of

_____ sessions, and that these meetings will last _____.
                                                                      (duration)

I (we) agree that the format of session will be: _____ Individual _____ Conjoint or Family

_____ Group or Combination.

I (we) have discussed the fee for professional service and agree to the fee of _____ per session

which I (we) will pay _____ (specify arrangement).

Figure 12-5   Sample Contract

IV. Evaluation:

    a) I (we) agree to participate in the evaluation of my (our) progress each session by reviewing the goal plan and the steps taken to achieve goals.

    b) I (we) also agree to participate in a final evaluation session after we have completed our work together.

    c) I (we) agree that I (we) will participate in follow-up evaluation after we have completed our work together.

V. Records & Reports:

    a) I (we) understand and give consent for release of information or reports about my (our) service plan and progress to others (e.g., court, third-party payer) with whom _____ is required to share about my family or me.

    b) I (we) understand that in all other instances, I (we) will be asked to sign a consent form to release information about my family or me.

    c) I (we) understand that _____ will maintain a confidential case record on me (us) and that I (we) have access to this record.

    d) I (we) understand that _____ is by law mandated to report abuse or neglect of children or vulnerable adults; and actions by me (us) in instances where I (we) are in danger or I (we) pose a threat or place someone else in danger, or when a court of law orders disclosure.

VI. Agreement:

Family/Client

    a) I (we) have discussed and reviewed the above terms of this agreement and on this date agree to abide by them in my (our) work with _____ .

    b) I (we) understand that this agreement can be renegotiated at any time.

Family Signature(s): _____   _____

                         _____   _____

                         _____   _____

Practitioner:

    a) I agree to work collaboratively with _____ to achieve the goals outlined in this plan.

    b) I agree to adhere to the conduct that XYZ agency expects of its staff, and to abide by the regulatory laws and ethical codes that govern my professional conduct.

    c) I have explained and provided a copy of agency information about the rights of program participants, agency services to the family/client, and information about XYZ agency.

    d) I have read the above terms of the agreement and pledge to do my best to assist the family (client) to achieve the goals listed and others that we may subsequently agree upon.

Practitioner Signature: _____

Date: _____

skills that will assist you in the development of goals and means of measuring progress. The negotiation and development of goals must be undertaken in the context of the clients' value systems and reality, and their involvement in this process is an important factor in their participation.

Measurement requires systematic observation and multiple points of observation. This chapter has included examples of both qualitative and quantitative measurement procedures to assist you in this process. As a final note, we want to emphasize that goals relate directly and specifically to the target concern and that measures are consistent with goal-related behaviors or conditions.

Internet Resources

 You can find out more about solution-focused treatment including links and further sources with this article: Rymarchyk, G. K., Solution-focused therapy for child welfare at the following site: *http://trochim.human.cornell.edu/ gallery/rymar/rymar.htm/*. Additional resources on solution-focused treatment are available at *http://www.ollusa.edu/CLASSES/psyc8357/sft. htm/* and at *http://www.socwel.ukans.edu/syllabi/ Fall99/sw855/855summer.html/*. You can explore

more about qualitative research at *http://don. ratcliff.net/qual/expql.html/*. Finally, you can connect to social work research centers at *http:// webdb.nyu.edu/sociallinks/menu.cgi?cid=503/*. You can also use InfoTrac® with the keywords "solution-focused treatment" and "qualitative research."

Notes

1. The time required for an adequate exploration varies but usually ranges from 45 minutes to 90 minutes. Initial conjoint interviews typically require about 30 minutes more than individual interviews.

2. For those interested in studying single-subject research, Bloom and Fischer (1982), Jayaratne and Levy (1979), and Tipodi and Epstein (1980) have written informative texts. Bloom, Fischer, and Orme (1999), and Corcoran, Fischer, (1999) have most informative texts on a wide variety of methods that may be used to evaluate practice.

3. In fact, Paquin (1981) has written about using self-monitoring for this purpose in marital and family therapy.

4. Many others scales, of course, are also available, a number of which are described in the book by Corcoran and Fischer (1999).

PART 3

The Change-Oriented Phase

After formulating a contract, the participants enter phase two of the problem-solving process—the goal attainment or change-oriented phase. In this phase, social workers and clients plan and implement strategies to accomplish the goals selected. Implementing these strategies involves employing interventions and techniques specified in the contract and contracting to use others as changing circumstances dictate. Before considering these factors further, however, a preview of Part 3 is in order.

A Preview of Part 3

Chapter 13 begins with a discussion of planning goal-attainment strategies, followed by a section on a general social work practice model, namely the task-centered system. We next consider crisis intervention; a practice model related to the task-centered system but applied in somewhat more specific situations. The chapter concludes with a focus on cognitive restructuring, a cognitive behavioral intervention procedure that is useful in addressing the cognitive component of diverse problems and is often combined with other interventions (see Chapter 14). In subsequent chapters of Part 3, we explicate a number of widely used interventions, many of them empirically grounded. Chapter 14 is devoted to widely used interventions employed to increase clients' vital coping skills in independent problem solving, interpersonal relationships, assertiveness, and managing stress. Chapter 15 focuses on macro level interventions including social planning. In Chapter 16, we delineate process and structural intervention strategies employed to enhance functioning of families. Chapter 17 then focuses on group interventions. Techniques employed to expand self-awareness and to pave the way to change (additive empathy, interpretation, and confrontation) are considered in Chapter 18. Part 3 concludes with Chapter 19, which is concerned with skills in managing barriers to change of individuals, families, and groups.

CHAPTER  13

Planning and Implementing Change-Oriented Strategies

Revised and edited by Glenda Dewberry Rooney

CHAPTER OVERVIEW

The "helping process," as conceptualized in this book, is divided into three distinct phases. Each of these phases requires skills and knowledge to complete the dimensions or processes of assessment, the development of goals, and the evaluation of progress and outcomes. In this and the chapters that follow, we focus your attention on goal attainment and intervention strategies that may be used to affect the target concern as identified during the assessment and goal development phase.

Effective intervention strategies must flow from the assessment of the problem and must be the most relevant and promising means of achieving the goals identified in the contract. Often beginning social workers have a conceptual understanding of models, theories, or practice principles, yet wonder what they should do next. This chapter is devoted to three goal attainment strategies that may be used in collaboration with clients. The three approaches, Task-Centered System, Crisis Intervention, and Cognitive Restructuring, each have advantages but are not useful with every client in all situations. The models have the advantage of adapting to various theories of human behavior, need, and lifestyle as well as adhering to the principle of individual capacity to change and grow. They are also com-

patible with social learning and systems theories. Perhaps the most salient characteristic of each is their emphasis on increasing the power of clients to participate in and influence change in their lives. Each also lends itself tooth qualitative and quantitative methods to assess outcomes. We begin this chapter with a discussion of goal attainment principles that will assist you in preparing for and selecting the most appropriate strategy. To avoid a mismatch between interventions on one hand and problems and goals on the other, it is important that interventions be relevant to the target system or subsystems and to clients' specific problems.[1]

PLANNING GOAL ATTAINMENT STRATEGIES

Goal attainment strategies as presented in this book focus on mobilizing individuals and families toward positive action that demonstrates that change can occur. Within this context, we also emphasize strengths rather than deficits and strategies that assist clients in achieving an increased sense of self-efficacy and empowerment. Empowerment makes use of resources within the client system and actively encourages their participation in taking control over their lives (Gutierrez, Parsons, & Cox 1998; Saleeby, 1997).

As we emphasized in Chapter 12, it is vital to include clients in planning strategies to accomplish goals. Besides safeguarding clients' rights to self-determination, including clients in selecting interventions enhances the likelihood of their cooperation. This is also true with involuntary clients, even when choices are constrained. For example, a court order to secure a chemical dependency assessment may be nonnegotiable. However, choices are available in selecting the particular program from which an assessment will be secured. Clients who do not understand an intervention and its relevance to their problems and goals are unlikely to be invested in the change effort and may cooperate in a halfhearted fashion or not at all. To achieve cooperative participation, *interventions must make sense to the client.* Involving clients in planning strategies, of course, does not mean discussing strategies in detail or even identifying all strategies that will be employed. Clients are generally satisfied with a brief explanation of the rationale for and descriptions of strategies.

MATCHING INTERVENTIONS TO TARGET SYSTEMS

To achieve effective outcomes, interventions must be directed to the systems implicated in problems and must be appropriate for those systems. To accomplish this is no small task, for one must be knowledgeable about the broad array of interventions and techniques and skillful in selecting and employing them. Many of these interventions are appropriate only for individual problems, some are appropriate for modifying dysfunctional interactions in families and groups, and still others relate to modifying the environment. It is important, therefore, to select and employ interventions that match systems targeted for change. Mismatches tend to lead to negative outcomes, often in the form of premature terminations by clients. For example, if a client's depression appears to be caused by social isolation associated with an impoverished physical and social environment, employing an intervention aimed at enhancing the client's self-awareness (i.e., an insight-oriented therapy) is inappropriate. Similarly, planning separate sessions for marital partners when their marital problems are largely the product of dysfunctional communication and interaction makes little sense unless there are compelling reasons for not seeing the partners conjointly. And finally, implementing an intervention aimed solely at assisting a child-abusing parent to gain emotional control when that parent's loss of control appears to be triggered by overwhelming stresses associated with inadequate finances, poor housing, responsibilities for many children, lack of support systems, and severe marital conflict is tantamount to prescribing an aspirin for severe bacterial infection. Matching the appropriate intervention strategy to the problem or condition presented by the client also embodies the principles of ethical social work practice.

MATCHING INTERVENTIONS TO PROBLEMS

It is also vital in treatment planning to match interventions to problems, a task that is facilitated when empirical evidence has proven that a certain intervention is effective with a specified problem. Unfortunately, we are still a long way from possessing comprehensive empirical knowledge to guide treatment selection. Significant progress has been made in recent years, however, and even more rapid progress is likely to occur with increasing numbers of social workers engaging in practice research. In this and other chapters, we delineate certain interventions and cite empirical support for their use with certain problems. For example, cognitive therapy is known to be effective in treating depression, and certain behavioral skills training programs have proven to be effective in treating people whose problems derive from deficiencies in basic interpersonal and problem-solving skills (see Chapter 19).[2]

MATCHING INTERVENTIONS TO DEVELOPMENTAL PHASES

Because clients vary in levels of achieved maturity, it is vital to match interventions to their developmental phases. Young children typically lack the capacity to think abstractly, so play therapy, structured group activities (with leaders employing behavior modification techniques), mutual storytelling directed at enhancing coping skills and teaching moral principles, and skill development groups are commonly employed. When parent-child interactional difficulties appear to underlie rebelliousness, truanting, substance abuse, antisocial behavior, and other related problems, family therapy may be the treatment of choice. Parent training groups are also increasingly employed to assist parents to enhance their skills in communicating, setting limits, negotiating, and problem solving. Assisting a parent to establish a bedtime routine may mean that the times will vary with the age of the children. In some instances, severe family problems associated with children and adolescents require interventions involving environmental changes. Residential treatment, inpatient psychiatric treatment, confinement in correctional facilities, and other such programs may be required. Severe problems of child neglect/abuse may necessitate temporary or permanent removal of a child to a safe environment.

We will not attempt to discuss interventions appropriate for all developmental and life cycle phases. It is sufficient to reemphasize that you should carefully consider the development stages of individuals and families in planning interventions.

MATCHING INTERVENTIONS TO STRESSFUL TRANSITIONS

As we indicated in Chapter 8, clients' problems are often associated with overwhelming stresses precipitated by major life transitions or situational events. Stress is common in everyday life; however, prolonged stress or dramatic events such as a natural disaster can diminish the coping capacity. The ability to cope may depend on a number of factors, for example, adaptability and the adequacy of resources both social and institutional. In families, cohesion, communication patterns, and commitment among members may be deciding factors as well as the extent of the family's links to networks beyond the family system. Events that naturally occur in the various stages of the family life cycle may also produce stress. These transitions may involve death, marriage, or the birth of a child, relocating to a new home, or changes in role. Minority families may experience situational stress as a result of their interactions with the larger social environment. Public policy, and the extent to which policies support family life and family transitions can also affect the stress level within families. Examples are the recent policies that promote welfare-to-work and child welfare laws, both of which have created stressful transitions for poor women and their children.

Crisis intervention and the task-centered system, which we discuss in this chapter, are models that have general application to transition problems. In recent years support groups have also been used extensively to cope with transition problems. These groups include divorce groups, rape crisis groups, groups for parents whose children have died, groups for farm families in crisis (Van Hook, 1987), groups for wives who learn their husbands are gay or bisexual (Auerback & Moser, 1987), and groups for widows and widowers (Lieberman & Videka-Sherman, 1986), to mention just a few. We also want to note that different cultures may react differently to the importance assigned to situational crisis, for example, death. For some groups, death is a time of celebration, while for others it is a time of great mourning and rituals (Hines, Preto, McGoldrick, Almeida & Weltman, 1999).

MATCHING INTERVENTIONS TO ETHNOCULTURAL GROUPS

As we have stressed in previous chapters, accurate assessment of the problems of ethnic minority persons requires knowledge of their culture, their degree of acculturation, as well as the psychosocial and socioenvironmental aspects of problems within the minority experience. The same is true when planning interventions. In planning intervention strategies, factors such as race, class, gender, sexual orientation, and the accompanying issues of oppression and powerlessness must be considered (Boyd-Franklin, 1989b; Carter & McGoldrick, 1999b; Green, 1999; Lum, 1996). Carter and McGoldrick (1999b) provide an example of an African American female who is depressed as a result of her lack of progress on her job. Further questioning by the therapist revealed that the racist attitude of the woman's supervisor was significant to her lack of job advancement. The relevant point of this illustration is that without the persistence of the therapist, the intervention employed may have included medication along with the exploration of her family of origin without recognition of discrimination as the reason for her poor job performance (p. 21).

A useful guideline to planning interventions with ethnic minority persons (and other clients, for that matter) is to solicit their views as to what needs to be done to remedy their difficulties. Their suggestions will be in harmony with their beliefs, values, and spirituality. Moreover, their views about essential changes are often on target; they lack only the "know-how" required to accomplish the changes. Deficiencies in the latter are often associated with limited knowledge about available resources and about the complexities of our service delivery systems. Determining clients' views enables the practitioner to suggest interventions that clients will perceive as relevant and to couch the rationale for selecting them in terms that make sense to clients. Including clients in the planning of intervention strategies enhances their cooperation, as we noted previously.

Another important factor to consider in planning interventions with ethnic minority clients is the importance in some cultures of family ties and the extended family. Family ties and relationships have tended to be a source of emotional and concrete support for diverse groups and as such their inclusion may be critical to goal attainment. Extended family, along with the church, are potential sources of resilience and strength available to clients. Citing the fact that in Mexican American culture the family is the primary source of identity and of support in times of crisis, Rothman, Gant, and Hnat (1985) and De Las Fuentes (2000) recommend that family therapy including the extended family or *familiar* should be considered regularly. Of course, the inclusion of family members or other resources requires the agreement of the client or family. Because of the family structure of some groups and the esteemed position of elders, we recommend exploring the involvement of extended family elders in treatment, according them due respect.

THE TASK-CENTERED SYSTEM

Task-centered is a social work model of practice that emphasizes the use of tasks and time limits to reduce or alter the target problem identified by the client. It attempts to "reduce problems in living," including those related to interpersonal conflicts, difficulties in social relations or role performance, reactive emotional distress, inadequate resources, or difficulties with organizations (Epstein, 1992). A central theme of the model is that people are capable of solving their problems. Client identification and prioritization of concerns and the collaborative nature of the client-practitioner relationship are empowering aspects of the model. Similarly, in a concrete and functional manner, the use of tasks to achieve goals functions to increase a sense of self-efficacy. In their evaluation of models of practice, Devore and Schlesinger (1999) conclude that the basic principles of the task-centered model represent a "major thrust" in ethnic sensitive practice (p. 121).

The task-centered approach to attaining goals is both systematic and efficient. The approach is based on advances in methods that have resulted from the advent of short-term interventions over the past 40 years and particularly the task-centered system, which has evolved over the past 30 years. Prior to the 1960s, open-ended, long-term interventions (for intrapersonal and interpersonal problems) were the prevailing norm in social work practice and in allied disciplines. Practice theories posited the belief that attempts to produce change are opposed by countervailing forces, including unconscious resistance, inertia, fear of the unknown, and vicissitudes in the helping relationships. Resistance to change was viewed as a powerful force that required an extended time to resolve.

In the 1960s, authors began to challenge the prevailing views of resistance and advocated that the lengthy time often required for successful treatment could result from defective treatment methods. Masserman (1965) took the position that resistance may be a healthy response to poor treatment technique. Wolberg (1965) specifically criticized the practice in long-term therapy of "permitting the patient to wallow in resistance until he somehow muddles through," noting that "where time is of no object the therapist can settle back comfortably and let the patient pick his way through the lush jungles of his psyche" (p. 235), Wolberg further faulted long-term therapists for their passivity and their failure to provide direction.

Recognizing that the sources of resistance included defects in the helping process was a theoretical milestone, for it opened the door to major changes in the process that held promise of accelerating the rate of clients' progress. Short-term therapies subsequently evolved rapidly, achieving in the 1960s a strong momentum that has continued to the present. Numerous research studies also disclosed with unanticipated consistency that brief therapies were as effective as long-term therapies and, in some instances, more effective (Wells, 1994; R. A. Wells & Gianetti, 1990).

Early short-term therapies, however, were not systematic and provided few guidelines to practitioners (with the exception of time limits) as to how they should provide direction to the helping process. Wolberg (1965) acknowledged this dilemma when he lamented, "The most pressing problem that confronts us today in short-term therapy is that we do not possess an adequate methodology. We apply the same tactics that we find useful in prolonged treatment" (p. 128). The development of the task-centered system, a social work method characterized by highly specified tactics of intervention, was a tailor-made solution to this problem. This system has the key advantage of providing a framework that accommodates interventions and techniques from many practice models.

The task-centered system has been adapted to many of the settings in which social workers practice, and its efficacy has been empirically established with many different client populations (W. J. Reid, 1987, 1997a, 1997b). The use of tasks as noted by Devore and Schlesinger (1999) and Boyd-Franklin (1989b) may be attractive to minority clients, as they are perceived as a useful distinction between talking and actual change. Nevertheless, we are not recommending wholesale adoption of the system. Indeed, time limits, which are central to the system, are not feasible for certain types of clients or groups and problematic situations, as we noted in Chapter 12. However, many of the tactics of the system can be employed to increase the efficiency of other types of interventions. Progress can often be accelerated in open-ended interventions, for example, by maintaining sharp focus and continuity—another key aspect of the system. In fact, *the major components of task accomplishment—preparation, implementation, and follow-up—are found in all of the more specific change-oriented interventions.* The ongoing development and utilization of tasks toward a particular goal provides immediate feedback and actively involves clients in the monitoring and evaluation process.

Developing General Tasks

Although the distinction between goals and tasks was discussed at length in Chapter 12, this information is emphasized in this section as a reminder that general tasks as described by W. J. Reid (1992) and Epstein (1992) are those strategies planned to reduce problems and reach goals. General tasks are, therefore, sets of discrete actions to be undertaken by the client and, in some instances, by the practitioner to reduce or alter the target concern and achieve the desired goal. They may be covert as well as overt. Cognitive tasks may include dismissing irrational fears of being ridiculed when one expresses a view or reminding oneself that it is not a disaster to make ordinary mistakes inasmuch as all humans occasionally make mistakes.

Partializing Goals

Partializing goals is not a new technique in social work practice; indeed, partialization has long been a basic tenet of practice theory (Perlman, 1957, pp. 147–149). Yet, in reviewing seven outcome studies of intensive services rendered to welfare recipients by public agency workers, K. Wood (1978, p. 443) noted that social workers in successful projects were apparently more skilled in partializing problems and goals than were workers in unsuccessful projects. It thus appears that partialization is underutilized by at least some practitioners.

Even goals formulated with a high level of specificity often are complex and involve multiple actions that must be completed in proper sequence. Because of this complexity, many clients feel overwhelmed and are unable to break their ultimate goals into constituent parts that are less intimidating. As they dissect them into bite-sized portions, guided by practitioners, they gain a sense of efficacy to undertake discrete corrective actions (tasks), which leads to goal accomplishment. This process is hence consistent with social work values reflecting commitment to empowerment in facilitating client capacity and ability to make decisions and effecting events in their lives.

Partializing thus involves developing goals and then dissecting them into general tasks that specify explicit actions prerequisite to goal accomplishment. To illustrate this process, we consider three varied goals and identify general tasks associated with them.

1. The ultimate goal of a single mother is to regain custody of children removed from her custody because of neglect. As the practitioner and the mother explore conditions that must be met to regain custody, they develop the following general tasks:
   a. *Improve conditions in the home* by developing and following a housekeeping schedule developed in collaboration with the practitioner.
   b. *Institute acceptable hygienic and nutritional standards* (enlist services of a public health nurse to provide instruction and temporary supervision).
   c. *Improve parenting effectiveness* by participating in a parenting class and in a parents' group.
   d. *Explore and develop support systems* that will make child care available, thereby freeing time to socialize in the evenings.

2. The ultimate goal of a couple is to reduce the incidence and severity of marital conflict. The goal is partialized into the following general tasks:
   a. *Reduce criticism and put-downs* that provoke defensiveness and recriminations.
   b. *Avoid venting anger on one another;* express ourselves without antagonizing each other; to explain that one is angry but not express raw anger; identify and express feelings underlying anger, such as hurt or disappointment, or feeling discounted.
   c. *Identify sources of anger* and learn and apply effective conflict resolution skills.
   d. *Work together in identifying problems* and employing problem-solving strategies.

e. Increase positive, supportive messages (compliments, approval, affection, and appreciation).

3. The goal is to improve sanitation in an apartment house by bringing pressure to bear on a recalcitrant landlord to fulfill his obligations. General tasks include the following:

   a. Talk with other tenants and mobilize an action group.

   b. Plan meetings of the tenants to enlist leaders and develop strategies.

   c. Explore legal resources and obtain legal counsel.

   d. Present a formal grievance to the landlord and express intention of resorting to legal means to force him, if necessary, to make needed improvements.

   e. File a complaint with the health department and initiate court action, if necessary.

From these examples, it is apparent that general tasks may involve actions on the part of the client, the practitioner, or both. In the first illustration, for example, the practitioner may assume responsibility for enlisting the services of a public health nurse. In the third example, the practitioner may explore possible legal resources, subsequently involving the client or representatives of the tenants' group in talking with legal counsel.

Partializing Group Goals

The same processes also pertain to a family or a treatment group. In such cases, the entire group may engage in formulating relevant general tasks to accomplish an identified group objective. For example, to achieve a group goal of preparing for discharge from a psychiatric hospital, a group of adult men and women may decide on the following courses of action:

1. Visit the halfway house to which they will be discharged and discuss facets of the program, such as daily schedule, living arrangements, rules concerning behavior, and the format of the biweekly group therapy sessions.

2. Investigate leisure time community resources, such as theaters, restaurants, and facilities for recreation.

3. Invite several discharged patients who are successfully living in the community to share their experiences with the group.

4. Plan several activities in the community, such as shopping or going out to dinner, and discuss the reactions of group members upon return to the hospital.

After partializing goals into general tasks, the next step is to order the general tasks so that they flow from one to another in a natural sequence, as was done in the preceding example of the goal of improving sanitation.

General tasks sometimes tend to be disconnected, however, and do not fall into logical sequence, as is true in the preceding illustration of assisting a mother to regain custody of her children. In such instances, you must determine which subgoal is of most immediate concern to the client and focus your beginning change efforts on that subgoal. For example, depending on the single parent's own priorities, actions in developing support systems to make child care available might be tabled or, if free time was an urgent desire, might become a priority. However, you should note one caution: It is important to settle upon a specific task that poses excellent chances for successful accomplishment by the client. Success with one general task engenders confidence and courage to tackle another; failure produces discouragement and undermines confidence in the helping process.

Formulating Specific Tasks

Even general tasks can prove to be overwhelming to hard-pressed clients. The key to the task-centered system is then to divide general tasks into specific agreements about client and practitioner actions to attempt between one session and the next. A general task such as "seek employment" must be cut into specific tasks such as "develop a resume" and "contact employment service." For example, the single mother may be unable to begin work on all of these general tasks in the first week. She might agree to draft a housekeeping schedule to share with the practitioner in the following week. The practitioner might then agree to contact the public health nurse to arrange a first home visit. The practitioner might also bring in descriptions of parenting classes and available groups for the following session, at which time the client would decide which ones to contact first. Specific tasks may consist of either behavioral or cognitive actions that require effort (and often discomfort) on the client's part. The following lists illustrate both behavioral and cognitive forms of specific tasks.

BEHAVIORAL TASKS

a. Phone for information about a rehabilitation program.

b. Convey feelings of hurt to a significant person.

c. Study each day for a specified length of time.

d. Follow a schedule for completing household tasks.

e. Give positive feedback to a family member at least three times daily.

COGNITIVE TASKS

a. Meditate for 30 minutes daily.

b. Engage in cognitive rehearsal involving talking to an employer.

c. Keep a daily tally of self-demeaning thoughts over three 1-hour intervals.

d. Recognize manifestations of anger arousal before they mount out of control.

e. Spend 15 minutes in the morning anticipating difficulties that may develop at work and mentally rehearse coping responses.

Essential tasks are sometimes readily apparent. Further, clients themselves sometimes propose tasks, and if such tasks are realistic, it makes good sense to endorse them because clients are likely to be committed to tasks they themselves identify. In many instances, however, tasks are less readily apparent, and it becomes necessary to explore alternate ways of accomplishing a general task. The challenge is to select a promising alternative that optimally fits a particular client.[3]

An effective way of identifying alternatives is to brainstorm with clients. Brainstorming involves the creative process of mutually focusing efforts on generating a broad range of possible options from which clients can choose. (We discuss brainstorming at greater length in the next chapter.) Although useful in any context, brainstorming is particularly fruitful in yielding alternatives in work with groups or families. If clients overlook options, it is important to suggest additional ones to ensure a broad range of alternatives. We have found that practitioners often need to assume the initiative, as many clients fail to generate alternatives. Keep in mind that if clients were able to formulate detailed and effective remedial courses of action, they likely would not have needed assistance in the first place. Clients generally are receptive to suggested tasks, and research indicates little difference in the rate with which they accomplish tasks suggested by practitioners as compared with those they propose themselves (W. Reid, 1978, p. 251).

It is important that you be sensitive to clients' reactions to tasks that you propose, for further research (W. Reid, 1978) indicates, "the degree of the client's apparent commitment or expressed willingness to work on the task was positively related to task progress" (p. 250). Although clients may be just as committed to tasks you introduce as to their own, if you attempt to "assign" tasks, thereby failing to enlist their commitment, it is unlikely they will expend their best efforts in implementing tasks, if indeed they undertake such tasks at all. Reactance theory suggests that clients may be inclined to protect valued freedoms when they perceive little choice (Brehm & Brehm, 1981). The same principle applies in working with groups or families. Persons in these systems may be quick to come up with tasks they think other individual members should assume. Thus, it is important for the group leader to protect individual members' right to choose—without pressure—which tasks they will undertake and, indeed, whether they will undertake any tasks. A common mistake of beginning practitioners is to conclude erroneously that clients oppose change when, in fact, they oppose tasks imposed upon them. such opposition often manifests a healthy assertion of individuality.

To demonstrate how specific tasks flow from general tasks, we return to one of the examples we cited earlier. Don and Jean identified a goal of reducing their marital conflict by communicating more effectively. By exploring the specific ways they would communicate differently if they accomplished their goal, the practitioner assisted them to break the goal down into several general tasks, one of which was, "We will express ourselves without antagonizing each other." Further exploration of how they antagonized each other revealed that in discussing various topics, Jean often felt her husband demeaned her by invalidating her opinion, which "gets my hackles up." Don agreed her complaint was legitimate and expressed a desire to avoid putting her on the defensive. He explained, however, that he had been very unhappy at work, where he was deriving little satisfaction and sense of accomplishment. Jean acknowledged his difficulties, complaining that; "He often comes home from work looking very glum, which tends to cast a dark cloud over the family." He agreed this was true, adding he didn't feel very important to anyone. He explained further, "I need strokes, and if she would give me some strokes I would have a brighter attitude and be less inclined to put her down." Jean said if this would help she would be happy to give him some strokes, which wouldn't be difficult because of his many good qualities.

The practitioner observed that each was giving the other valuable information that, if acted upon, could assist them in achieving their general task of expressing themselves without antagonizing each other. After exploring their feelings and ascertaining that both were receptive to making changes in line with the discussion, the practitioner and the clients formulated the following reciprocal tasks:

1. When Jean expresses her opinions, Don will listen attentively without criticizing or belittling her. He will also endeavor to be more positive when he comes home after work.

2. Jean will be more attentive and supportive of Don, expressing affection and greater interest and concern over his frustrations at work.

Both Jean and Don agreed to keep daily tallies of the number of times they performed the actions inherent in their respective tasks, willingly committing themselves to increase the frequency of these actions to at least twice daily during the first week. To illustrate further, let us consider another general task—to talk with other tenants and mobilize an action group—taken from a preceding example. This general task already embodies an action strategy but can be partialized still further by developing plans for contacting specific tenants, including setting a time frame for accomplishing the tasks and preparing the presentation to be made to other tenants. Specified at this level, both the practitioner and clients are clear about the task to be accomplished before the next session (assuming the clients manifest commitment to the task).

Notice that the preceding tasks have been formulated in terms of positive behaviors that clients are to perform rather than behaviors from which they are to refrain. Positively framed tasks that specify undertaking desired behaviors highlight growth and gains that clients will achieve. By contrast, tasks that specify eliminating negative behaviors focus exclusively on what clients are to give up. Clients tend to be more enthusiastic about tasks oriented to growth and achievement, and accomplishing such tasks often motivates them to undertake even further changes.

Certain situations present opportunities for combining tasks that involve decreasing the frequency of dysfunctional behaviors and increasing the frequency of related functional behaviors. A parent, for example, may agree to implement tasks that involve decreased nagging and increased expressions of approval when a child performs assigned duties. Similarly, a client may agree to dismiss negative thoughts about a spouse and to increase the frequency of thoughts about the spouse's positive attributes. Still another example may involve reducing time spent brooding over disappointments and increasing time spent in recreational activities with friends.

The process of partializing goals into general tasks and ultimately into specific tasks occupies a substantial portion of the time in the early portion of the change-oriented phase. Much time is also spent in preparing to accomplish one or more tasks before the next scheduled session. We clarify the rationale for this in later sections of this chapter.

Although it is often appropriate to identify more than one task, it is important to identify and carefully plan implementation of at least one before concluding a session. In fact, many clients ask for "homework assignments." Mutually identifying tasks and planning implementation of them in each session sharpen the focus on change and facilitate progress by maintaining action-oriented involvement of clients between sessions. Without such actions, sessions become primarily verbal, and little or no change may occur between them. The ongoing focus upon task accomplishment, by contrast, concentrates, intensifies, and accelerates the helping process.

Planning Task Accomplishment

After settling upon one or more tasks, the next step is to assist clients in preparing to implement each task. Skillfully executed, this process augments clients' motivation for undertaking tasks and substantially enhances the probability of successful outcomes. A systematic approach termed the task implementation sequence or TIS has been described by Reid (1975), who reported research findings to the effect that clients were more successful in accomplishing tasks when TIS was employed than when it was not.

Task Implementation Sequence (TIS)

The TIS involves a sequence of discrete steps that encompass major ingredients generally associated with successful change efforts. Although Reid recommends that the TIS be applied systematically, he also cautions practitioners to be sufficiently flexible to permit adaptation to the circumstances of each case. Reid's caution, of course, also applies to modifying the TIS to fit a group format. The TIS thus embodies the following steps:

1. Enhance clients' commitment to carry out a specific task.
2. Plan the details of carrying out the task.
3. Analyze and resolve obstacles that may be encountered.
4. Have clients rehearse or practice the behaviors involved in carrying out the task.
5. Summarize the plan of task implementation and convey both encouragement and an expectation that the client will carry out the task.

Before considering each of the preceding steps, it is important to recognize that the accomplishment of a task often poses a formidable challenge to clients. It would be simplistic to assume that merely agreeing to carry out a task assures that the client has the knowledge, courage, interpersonal skill, and emotional readiness to implement a task successfully. Clients who possess these ingredients are unlikely to need the assistance of the practitioner in the first place. Moreover, if a client is ill prepared to undertake a task, the probable outcome will be failure either to attempt the task or to complete it successfully. Either outcome is likely to cause the client to feel discouraged and to experience lowered self-esteem and subsequent difficulty in facing the practitioner. Opposition can thus become an issue, which might be manifested by not keeping the next appointment or by diverting attention from the pertinent task. Having clarified the challenges inherent in tasks, let us consider each step in more detail.

Enhancing Client Commitment to Carry Out a Task   Directly aimed at enhancing motivation to carry out a task, this step involves clarifying the relevance of tasks to clients' goals and identifying benefits that will result from carrying out tasks. The rationale of this step is that to follow through with tasks, clients must perceive gains that outweigh potential costs (including anxiety and fear) associated with risking new behavior. Because change is difficult, involving apprehension, discomfort, and uncertainty, this step is especially critical when clients' motivation to carry out a given task is questionable.

In many instances, the potential gains of carrying out a task are obvious, and it would be pointless to dwell on this step. The potential gains of applying for a job interview or securing essential information about eligibility for financial assistance are self-evident. The benefits of other tasks, however, are less apparent, and a discussion of them may be essential for the client to grasp the relationship between the task and the goals. Benefits of the following a medical regimen may not be clear if a client's physician has not explained the need for the regimen and the consequences of not following it. Similarly, the benefits of keeping a daily log on self-defeating thoughts may be unclear to a client who does not see the connection between this task and an ultimate goal of overcoming depression.

It is preferable to begin implementing step 1 by asking clients to identify benefits they will gain by successfully accomplishing a task. Clients are usually able to identify obvious benefits but may overlook others that are less apparent. Consequently, you may need to bring these benefits to their awareness.

To illustrate this process, we consider an actual case situation involving a male client in his early twenties who was distressed over the fact that when he took his girlfriend on a date they frequently encountered some of her friends, and she often left him standing for lengthy intervals while she conversed with them in a foreign language

that he neither spoke nor understood. After exploring his reactions of feeling left out, less important to her than her friends, and frankly irritated over her insensitivity to his feelings, he agreed to work on the task of directly but tactfully expressing his feelings to her.

When asked what benefits he would gain by carrying out the task, he replied that he would feel better about dealing with her rather than just feel irritated and left out. The practitioner agreed, adding he would also feel stronger and experience more self-respect for facing the problem rather than avoiding it. Furthermore, his girlfriend would also likely respect him more, and they would gain experience in dealing with relationship problems. Last, he would be taking an important step toward accomplishing one of his ultimate goals—to resolve his mixed feelings toward his girlfriend.

Just as it is important to identify benefits, it is also essential to consider possible risks of carrying out tasks. (Recall our making this same point in the last chapter with respect to the process of selecting goals.) Again, we recommend you ask clients to identify risks, and then add others that occur to you. In the case situation discussed in the foregoing paragraph, the client expressed concern that his girlfriend might take offense and construe his expressing his feelings as an attempt to control her. He described her as independent and somewhat domineering. Further discussion, however, led him to conclude this was not a real risk because he needed to learn to stand up to her in any event. Otherwise, he might be inviting being dominated, and that was unacceptable to him. He definitely wished to carry out the task even though it might introduce some strain in the relationship.

In work with groups, practitioners can use group process to good advantage in assisting individual members to weigh the benefits and risks of individual goals. In using group process, it is important to elicit expressions from other group members. Preferably, this should take place after a member considering a potential change has had an opportunity individually to contemplate the relative benefits and risks in assuming a task. As "outside consultants" who often share many of the same situations and dilemmas as the person contemplating the task, other members often make a penetrating analysis of the costs and rewards involved.

In enhancing motivation to change ingrained behaviors, it is sometimes essential to create immediate incentives by planning tangible rewards for carrying out planned actions. One client had a long-established pattern of going on eating binges, during which she would consume large quantities of food, to her later chagrin. She initially viewed herself as helpless to control her impulses to gorge herself, attributing her difficulties to "lack of willpower." Careful assessment had led the practitioner to disagree with her explanation, imputing her problem instead to (1) mistaken and demeaning beliefs about herself and (2) the habituated use of eating as a substitute for gratification she was not gaining through more appropriate modes of behavior.

To enable her to experience success in exercising self-control, the practitioner suggested that she identify something she wanted badly and earn the privilege of acquiring it by modifying her eating habits during the week. (Her previous longest time of maintaining control of her eating was 4 days.) With a smile, she responded that she had wanted to purchase a pair of leather boots for several months but had not done so because it seemed extravagant. She and the practitioner then negotiated an agreement whereby she could reward herself by buying the boots if she ate only at mealtimes and consumed average portions of food over the week's time. She could also have one small snack each day but only by making a conscious choice to do so and then eating it while sitting at the dining room table. On the other hand, if she indulged in a binge, she would forfeit the right to purchase the boots for at least 4 months. She appeared excited about the challenge and agreed to share it with her husband, whose knowledge of it would create additional incentive. (He

had earlier encouraged her to buy the boots.) If she successfully implemented her task, she was to reward herself further by expressing silent approval and to remind herself she had consciously made decisions to exercise self-control. Further, she was to think of herself as capable of increasing self-control week by week.

In her session 1 week later, the client's success was mirrored in her countenance as she greeted the practitioner. With obvious pride, she described how she had constantly reminded herself she could exercise self-control, and her success over the week's time gave substance to her thoughts. She described how pleased her husband was with her success and how they had planned to celebrate by going together to purchase the boots. The initial success was the first of a series of similar successes that led to increased self-confidence and to eventual mastery of her excessive eating.

Rewarding oneself (self-reinforcement) to enhance the incentives for completing a task is particularly relevant when changes sought involve yielding pleasures or excesses or carrying out essential activities that may be perceived as aversive (e.g., studying, cleaning the house, mowing the lawn, doing the dishes, or planning and preparing regular meals). Possible rewards should be considered in light of each client's uniqueness, but the following are typical examples: going to a special movie or artistic production; allocating time to engage in special activities, such as reading a novel, swimming, or bowling; visiting or shopping with a special friend; or purchasing a desired item.

Rewards can also be utilized to create incentives for children to complete tasks, such as completing homework assignments, showing caring behaviors to siblings, picking up after themselves, or doing household chores. In addition to negotiating tasks with children, practitioners often establish complementary tasks with parents or other significant persons for the purpose of assisting children in carrying out their tasks or modifying dysfunctional behavioral patterns that involve both children and parents. When rewards are used to create incentives for children, it is important during the early stages of change to provide rewards immediately after children perform desired behaviors. It is also important to reward small changes; otherwise, children may become discouraged and give up, believing they cannot meet the standards expected by parents. Naïve parents and practitioners mistakenly assume that elaborate long-range rewards (e.g., get a bicycle in June) will motivate children to make changes. In actuality, even for older children, smaller rewards given soon after the behavior tend to be far more effective motivators.

In setting up tasks with accompanying rewards for children and parents (or significant others, such as teachers), the following guidelines are helpful:

a. Frame tasks so that what children and parents are to do and when they are to do it are explicitly defined. For example, with an 8-year-old child who frequently argues and complains when parents make requests of him, a task can be formulated so that the child will carry out the requested actions immediately. The task also specifies what the parent is to do in a given circumstance (e.g., make the request in a calm and cheerful manner). And finally, the task specifies the time frame and conditions under which the task is to be performed (e.g., every 2 hours, twice daily, each Wednesday, for the next 4 days).

b. Designate points that children can earn for performing specified target behaviors, and establish a method of keeping track of the points (e.g., each time the child responds appropriately to requests, the parent will enter a mark on a chart constructed conjointly by the parents and the children).

c. Establish a reward for earning a specified number of points for specified periods of time (e.g., if the child earns five points by 8 o'-clock each night, he or she will have a choice of playing a short game or having a parent read a story). Whenever possible, it is important to offer "relationship" rewards, as contrasted with ones that are monetary or material. Relationship rewards involve time spent in an attractive activity with a parent or other significant person. It is also important to involve children in decisions about the type of reward they wish to earn, because they will choose rewards that have maximal value as incentives.

d. Give a bonus for consistent achievements of tasks over an extended period of time (e.g., if the child achieves a quota of five points each day for 7 consecutive days, he or she and the involved parent will celebrate by going out for a favorite meal).

e. Teach parents or others to give consistent positive feedback regarding the child's progress, and negotiate tasks related to expressing encouragement and approval as the child engages in task-related efforts.

Tasks buoyed by creative rewards can do much to reduce parent-child tensions, motivating both adults and children to focus on developing positive behaviors. One parent, who was consistently embarrassed in restaurants by the disruptive behavior of her five children, readily consented to a task of monitoring her children's positive behaviors during the meal. Also giving her children the task of reporting to her their positive actions, the mother gave them credit by recording one point for each positive action. At the end of the meal, each child had earned enough points (at the rate of a penny a point) to redeem them for an after-dinner treat (something they usually received anyway). Although the mother spent more time recording points than eating, she was ecstatic about the successful outcome of the activity and particularly about the sharp increase in caring behaviors manifested by her children toward each other and toward her during the evening, which, incidentally, generalized to other situations throughout the week. She also reported experiencing more positive feelings toward her children.

Plan the Details of Carrying Out the Task

Planning is vital in assisting clients to prepare

themselves for all the actions inherent in a task. Most tasks consist of a series of actions to be carried out sequentially, including both cognitive and behavioral subtasks. For example, before carrying out an overt action, such as asking a boss for a raise, requesting repairs from a landlord, or submitting to a painful medical examination, clients often benefit by preparing themselves psychologically. This may involve reviewing potential benefits, dismissing needless fears by reminding themselves of reality factors, mustering courage by accrediting themselves for past successes, recalling the encouragement of the practitioner, and praying for strength if they are religiously inclined. By planning such cognitive strategies, clients are better able to cope with the inevitable ambivalence and trepidation associated with implementing new actions.[4]

Planning overt actions involves considering details of actual required behaviors. For example, in the first case cited under step 1, the client would need to consider when he would talk with his girlfriend, and how he would introduce the topic, express his feelings, and cope with possible reactions on her part. The more detailed the plans, the greater the likelihood of success. Moreover, by discussing discrete actions, you increase opportunities to elicit cues to misgivings, fears, or skill lacks that must be remedied if clients are to complete tasks successfully.

Task planning may also involve practitioner tasks that must be coordinated with the client's actions. For example, an unemployed and unskilled young adult may be interested in obtaining vocational guidance. A task may be to take tests that assess aptitudes and interests. Task planning may involve telephone calls by the practitioner to locate an appropriate resource and to convey information to the client, as well as subsequent actions by the client to arrange to take the tests and have the results interpreted. Subsequent tasks may involve exploring and arranging appropriate vocational training, locating financial resources, and the like. Practitioner tasks should be undertaken when the practitioner has access to resources or

information that will facilitate client work. If the client could benefit from eventually being able to carry out the practitioner task on his or her own, it is useful to walk through the steps together. In other instances, practitioners may accompany or arrange for someone else to accompany the client in performance of a task. In group contexts, a group or family member might also informally assist a designated person in planning and carrying out actions outside the group.

In many instances, it is important to specify carefully the conditions under which the task will be carried out. For example, a sixth-grade boy who constantly disturbs his peers and irritates his teacher through boisterous talk and teasing behavior may accept a task of listening attentively when the teacher is speaking during the 1-hour arithmetic class and raise his hand three times to answer questions during that time. He is to carry out this task each day for the next 5 days. A grandmother who is living with her son and daughter-in-law and whose specialty is monitoring and critically reporting to the parents all of their children's negative behaviors may be asked during a family therapy session to assume a task of reporting *positive* behaviors directly to the children and to the parents. This grandmother may agree to work on this task extensively during the upcoming weekend, a time when all of the children are at home. It has been our experience that if the time for implementing tasks is left indefinite, clients (and practitioners) tend to procrastinate until it is too late to implement requisite actions effectively. Although we have not subjected our impression to empirical testing, we are convinced that clients implement tasks at a higher rate when specific times are stipulated than when they are left indefinite. In determining a time frame, it is also important to elicit feedback from clients regarding the amount of time they feel is needed to accomplish a specific objective rather than to set a time frame arbitrarily.

In selecting and planning tasks pertaining to *ongoing* goals, you should observe an additional caution. Because progress on such goals is incremental, it is vital to begin with relatively simple tasks that are within the clients' capacity to achieve. The chances of clients undertaking more difficult tasks later are much enhanced if they achieve success on initial tasks. Conversely, if they experience failure on initial tasks, their confidence and courage may decline, and they may be reluctant to undertake additional ones. It is thus preferable to have the first task be too easy than too difficult.

Analyze and Resolve Obstacles This step is aimed at countering the inevitable forces that counter the client's thrust for change.[5] Implementing it involves anticipating and analyzing obstacles that may be encountered as the client seeks to accomplish a task. Employed effectively, this step is a powerful technique for enhancing task accomplishment and for accelerating change.

With commonplace tasks, obstacles are generally minor and can often be readily identified by asking clients what difficulties, if any, they expect to encounter. Included in such tasks are those requiring simple actions, such as telephoning a community agency that the client and the practitioner have just discovered, which holds promise of providing needed assistance. A caveat should be observed, however: what is a simple action for most people may be difficult for a few. Making a telephone call was an overwhelming task for one client. Mildly brain damaged and overprotected by his parents for all his 19 years, the client had depended on them to make telephone calls for him because he feared he would "foul up and sound stupid." In such instances, fears may pose formidable barriers to accomplishing a task and may require careful exploration and working through before they are overcome.

When tasks are complex, obstacles likewise tend to be complex and difficult to identify and resolve. Tasks that involve changes in patterns of interpersonal relationships tend to be multifaceted, encompassing subsidiary but prerequisite intrapersonal tasks as well as a mastery of certain interpersonal skills. Successfully resisting unwanted

sexual advances, for example, may involve overcoming powerful fears that refusal to submit will result in utter rejection. The irrational belief that one has nothing to offer other than sex must be supplanted by a belief about oneself that is aligned with reality. The client must also master new behaviors that tactfully but firmly set limits with predatory males.

Clients vary widely in their capacity to anticipate obstacles. Consequently, it is vital to elicit from them (and from members in a group context) possible obstacles to achieving their planned course of action. The practitioner may also make observations regarding obstacles. In introducing the possibility of relevant obstacles, it is vital to safeguard the client's self-esteem by explaining that obstacles are common to many people. An example of an obstacle that had to be identified involved a withdrawn, late adolescent client whose goal was to mingle socially with others. She was embarrassed and hesitant to reveal that she was afraid of accepting an invitation to visit a friend in her neighborhood because her legs might become rubbery and she might vomit on the neighbor's rug. Similarly, a musically talented male client who wished to play the organ for others was afraid to display his talents because others might perceive him as weird.

As these examples imply, psychological barriers to accomplishing tasks are often encountered regardless of the nature of the target problem. Overlooking such barriers may in some instances cause needless difficulties in the accomplishment of tasks and, in others, result in outright failure. Applying for a job, submitting to a medical examination, talking to a schoolteacher, expressing tender feelings—these and a host of other seemingly everyday tasks are charged with strong emotionality for some people and may be threatening.

Prerequisite to the successful accomplishment of a task, therefore, may be a subsidiary task of neutralizing untoward emotions. This can be accomplished often in a brief time by eliciting and clarifying the apprehension, rationally analyzing it, and modeling and rehearsing the behavior required to implement the task successfully. In other instances, more extensive efforts are required. Whatever time and effort are invested is likely to be rewarded by achieving a higher rate of success in accomplishing tasks. An economy of time is also affected, because failures in implementing tasks further extend the time required for successfully implementing them.

Other cues and techniques may also facilitate identifying obstacles. In discussing plans for implementing a task, you should be alert to nonverbal cues that indicate apprehension on the client's part about undertaking the task. Such cues include looking away from you, speaking diffidently and unenthusiastically about the task, changing the topic, fidgeting atypically, and tightening facial and body muscles. If you detect such reactions, you should further explore the presence of undisclosed barriers or work further on resolving obstacles already identified.

Vital to successful task implementation is the client's readiness to tackle the mutually negotiated task. Such readiness, however, should not be confused with feeling comfortable; it is neither realistic nor desirable to expect clients to feel altogether comfortable with the task. A certain amount of tension and anxiety is to be expected and may positively motivate the client to risk the new behavior embodied in the task. Inordinate anxiety, by contrast, may be a major deterrent to undertaking the task or may impair the client's effectiveness upon attempting it. Obviously, when clients report that they did not carry out a task, you should consider the possibility that the task was premature and that unresolved barriers remain. Another possibility is that the client was inadequately committed to the task, an important factor to be discussed later.

A simple yet effective way to gauge readiness for undertaking tasks is to ask clients to rate their readiness on a scale from 1 to 10, with 1 representing total unreadiness and 10 complete readiness. It is important to explain first that a certain amount of apprehension is natural and should not deter the client from trying out new behaviors; indeed, relative freedom from apprehension is not achieved before implementing the task but is rather a by-product of successful implementation. This explanation is important because many clients are overly hesitant to risk themselves and needlessly postpone taking actions.

When clients rate their readiness at 7 or higher, you can assume a sufficient degree of readiness and suggest that they appear prepared to undertake the task. Also provide support by expressing restrained confidence that the client can successfully implement the task and by conveying an expectation that the planned actions will be carried out. Exploring the reasons why clients rate themselves at 7 rather than 10 on the readiness scale will often give you vital information concerning potential obstacles to change, including reservations they may have about completing the task.

After identifying barriers to change, you must next assist the client in overcoming them. Barriers encountered most frequently include *deficiencies in social skills and misconceptions and irrational fears* associated with performing tasks. The former is a formidable barrier that must be overcome, for one may lack the skill and experience to know how to carry out a task. In such instances, clients commonly fear bungling a task and appearing ridiculous as a result. Undertaking the task thus is perceived as placing one's self-esteem in jeopardy.

Modeling and behavioral rehearsal in sessions may assist clients to gain the courage and skills necessary to carry out interpersonal tasks. In some instances, however, more intensive interventions may be required, such as personal effectiveness training and assertiveness training.

The second major type of barrier to task accomplishment involves misconceptions and irrational fears that embrace misunderstandings of the self, stereotypic perceptions of others, and intense apprehensions based on distorted and dreaded consequences of actions. Cognitive theorists present a compelling case to the effect that the quality and intensity of emotions experienced in a given situation is largely determined by the perceptions and attributions of meaning associated with that situation. Inordinate fear and apprehension are thus cues that something is amiss in the client's patterns of thought. Your task is to elicit the problematic emotions, to identify their cognitive sources, and to assist clients in aligning their thoughts and feelings with reality. Removing this barrier usually enables clients to move several points higher on the readiness scale.

Resolving misconceptions, perceptual distortions, and irrational fears was once believed to require a lengthy expedition into the unconscious to discover the genesis of such inhibiting forces. In recent years, however, new techniques (see Chapter 14) have been used successfully in eliminating fears and misconceptions rapidly without shifting the focus to the remote past.

Have Clients Rehearse or Practice Behaviors Involved in Carrying Out Tasks   Certain tasks involve skills clients lack or behaviors with which they have had little or no experience. Step 4 is thus aimed at assisting clients to gain experience and mastery in performing behaviors essential to task accomplishment. Successful experience, even in simulated situations, fosters belief in having the ability to carry out a task effectively. Having an expectancy of success is vital, for as Bandura (1977) has indicated, "The strength of people's convictions in their own effectiveness is likely to affect whether they will even try to cope with given situations" (p. 193). Bandura builds a strong case, documented by research evidence, to the effect that the degree of positive expectation that clients have in their ability to perform tasks effectively determines how much effort they will expend in attempting tasks and how long they will persist in the face of obstacles or aversive circumstances. It follows that a major goal of the helping process is to enhance clients' sense of self-efficacy wit respect to the tasks they select.

Research evidence cited by Bandura (1977, p. 195) indicates that, once established, self-efficacy and skills tend to be transferred by clients to other situations that they previously avoided. According to Bandura, people receive information about self-efficacy from four sources: (1) performance accomplishments, (2) vicarious experience, (3) verbal persuasion, and (4) emotional arousal. Of these four sources, performance accomplishment is especially influential because it is based on personal mastery experience.

Major methods of increasing self-efficacy through performance accomplishment include assisting clients to master essential behaviors through modeling, behavior rehearsal, and guided practice, all of which we discuss at length later in this chapter. An example of performance accomplishment would be assisting family members to master certain communication skills during actual sessions.

Vicarious experiences gained by observing others demonstrate target behaviors or perform threatening activities without adverse consequences can also generate expectations in clients that they too can master the target behaviors. Efficacy expectations based on observing the practitioner or others model desired behaviors, however, are likely to be weaker and more vulnerable to change than expectations based on performance accomplishment. Information about one's capabilities based on assumptions that one can perform comparably to a model is hardly as persuasive as direct evidence of personal accomplishment.

Attempting to reassure or convince clients that they can perform new behaviors has limitations as an enduring source of personal self-efficacy. Nevertheless, it can and does contribute to successful performance when accompanied by measures that equip clients for effective action. Verbal persuasion contributes by raising *outcome expectations* rather than enhancing self-efficacy per se.

The fourth source of information about self-efficacy, emotional arousal, is based on the fact that the perceived level of emotional arousal affects how people perform. Clients who are extremely anxious or fearful about performing a new behavior are unlikely to have sufficient confidence that they can perform the behavior competently. Many interventions are therefore directed to reducing anxiety or fear or to influencing clients to *believe* they are not fearful or anxious. Evidence cited by Bandura indicates that to be effective, reductions in emotional arousal must be genuine and not based on deceptive feedback aimed at assuring clients they are not anxious when they are anxious. Emotional arousal obviously is an undependable source of self-efficacy because it too is not related to actual evidence of capability. Perceived self-competence tends to reduce emotional arousal rather than the converse.

Having defined the sources of information about self-efficacy, we return to the topic of behavioral rehearsal. As employed in actual sessions, behavioral rehearsal assists clients to practice new coping patterns under the tutelage of the practitioner. Indications for using behavioral rehearsal include situations that clients feel inadequately prepared to confront. When clients manifest strong uneasiness or appear overwhelmed by the prospects of carrying out a given task, behavioral rehearsal is an effective way of developing requisite skills and reducing the threat posed by the action. Such tasks usually involve interacting with significant other people with whom strain already exists or is expected to develop as a result of the planned actions. Typical examples include asserting one's rights to an authority figure; expressing feelings of hurt or rejection to one's spouse; or making a social overture to a member of the other sex.

Role playing is the most common mode of behavioral rehearsal. Before engaging clients in rehearsal of desired behaviors, however, practitioners can use role playing to have clients demonstrate their initial levels of skills, thus enabling practitioners to model skills that build on clients' extant skills. Practitioners frequently model behavior that clients are expected to perform before actually having them rehearse the behavior. Used particularly when the requisite behavior is unfamiliar to the client, modeling has been amply documented as an effective means of enabling clients to learn new modes of coping behavior vicariously, as we noted earlier.

In employing modeling, ask the client to play the role of the other person involved in the real-life difficulty and, in doing so, to simulate as accurately as possible the anticipated behavior to be encountered in the actual situation. The role playing thus enables you to model appropriate responses to behavior that has previously overwhelmed the client. After the role playing, it is productive to discuss what happened, focusing on the client's reactions and on questions and concerns as well. It is also beneficial to explain your rationale for particular responses and to share difficulties you may have experienced. It has been our experience that in assuming the role of clients, we often gain new insights and fuller appreciation of the difficulties they encounter.

If your coping in the modeling situation falls short of being effective, it is appropriate and even helpful to acknowledge the difficulties you experienced and to consider mutually other possible coping responses. Indeed, it is desirable to model imperfect *coping efforts* rather than *mastery,* for research indicates that clients benefit more from observing a "coping model" (Kazdin, 1979; Meichenbaum, 1977). A coping model manifests the struggles that a person might expect to experience in performing the behavior or activity, including expressing anxiety and hesitation and making errors. Clients identify more easily with and are less threatened by a coping model than one who performs flawlessly.

Modeling need not be limited to overt behaviors, for clients may also benefit from modeling of covert coping with cognitive barriers to task accomplishment. Covert modeling involves expressing aloud thoughts and feelings associated with manifest difficulties and demonstrating appropriate ways of coping with related problematic thoughts and feelings. As with modeling of overt behavior, covert modeling should demonstrate coping rather than mastery.

After completing a modeling exercise, the next step is to reverse the roles so that the client rehearses the actual target behavior and you assume the role of the other significant person. In so doing, it is important that you attempt to approximate the anticipated behavior of the other person, including tone of voice, facial expressions, gestures, choice of words, and provocative behavior as modeled earlier by the client. The responses of the client to your simulated behavior provide an opportunity for corrective suggestions and for identifying need for additional practice, as well as for reinforcement and encouragement. Moreover, clients' readiness to tackle situations in real life can best be assessed by observing their behavior in rehearsal. Most important, clients' confidence to carry out tasks is enhanced by practice. You can further enhance clients' self-efficacy by expressing confidence in their ability to carry out the planned task successfully, if your support and encouragement are genuine.

As clients mobilize the strength and courage gained through behavioral rehearsal and face problems head-on rather than avoid them, their previous greatly feared consequences dwindle into realistic perspective. Clients have affirmed the effectiveness of modeling and behavioral rehearsal numerous times for the authors by reporting that their practice during sessions was the single most important factor in assisting them to accomplish their tasks. Behavioral rehearsal, incidentally, need not be confined to sessions. It is often productive to encourage clients to continue rehearsing target behaviors outside the interviews by pretending to engage in real-life encounters.

Modeling and behavioral rehearsal need not be confined to relationships between practitioners and individual clients. Often, a client in a group or family session may be able to provide effective and realistic coping modeling for another group member. Indeed, a rule of thumb in conducting group role playing sessions is to tap group resources for coping models whenever possible. This enhances the help-giving role of group members.

Closely related to behavioral rehearsal, *guided practice* is another form of performance accomplishment, which differs from behavioral rehearsal in that it consists of *in vivo* rather than simulated behavior. Using guided practice as a mode of intervention, you assist clients to gain mastery of target behaviors by coaching them as they actually attempt to perform the target behaviors. For example, in conjoint marital sessions, you may assist clients to master skills in solving problems or resolving conflicts by instructing them as they deal with actual problems or conflict situations. Guided practice is particularly relevant to family and group contexts. Skills in brainstorming, active listening, assertiveness, and control of anger—to name just a few—can be effectively learned through guided practice in groups.

Guided practice is an especially potent method of inducing change. The practitioner can observe live behavior and provide immediate corrective feedback as well as encouragement and approval. Observing behavior directly is especially valuable in marital and family sessions, for opportunities exist to intervene immediately when dysfunctional behavior occurs. Such on-the-spot interventions enable you to clarify what is going wrong, to explain more effective ways of coping, and to coach clients in employing more competent behavior.

Summarize the Plan of Task Implementation
This final step involves reviewing the various actions clients are to carry out in accomplishing a task. Implementing this step, which is done in the concluding segment of an individual or group session, enables clients to emerge from the session with a clear understanding of what they are to do and in what sequence. To enable clients to gain maximum benefit from this step, we recommend that you ask them to review details of their plan for implementing the task, including strategies for coping with obstacles that may be encountered. By eliciting clients' descriptions of their plans, you can assess whether certain aspects of the plan need to be further clarified. It is often useful to begin by describing your own plans for practitioner tasks: "I have agreed to do x-y-z by our meeting next week," followed by a request for a review of client plans: "What is it that you plan to do by next week?" Many clients find it beneficial to have a written list of agreed-upon tasks. Some clients prefer to write their own lists, and in other cases, the social worker can write down the tasks, keeping a

carbon copy for his or her own records. To counter procrastination, it is advantageous to specify the time frame for implementing the plan.

After summarizing the plan of task implementation, it is appropriate to terminate the session. An effective way of closing the session is to express approval of clients' plans and expectations that they implement them. Because results cannot be accurately predicted, however, it is desirable to convey restrained optimism. We recommend you also express interest in hearing about their experience at the beginning of the next session.

Maintaining Focus and Continuity

The strength of the task-centered system lies in its focus on change through task accomplishment and its systematic format that promotes continuity of change efforts. Individual sessions are sharply focused, and continuity is maintained from one session to the next. Each session begins with a review of clients' experiences in implementing tasks that were agreed upon during the previous session. There are two major objectives and benefits of discussing clients' experiences in implementing tasks. First, both clients and practitioners can identify ways in which clients can further improve their effectiveness in performing newly developed behaviors. This discussion may further enhance clients' comfort in coping with problematic situations and suggest additional activities in the session to refine their skills. A second benefit is that the practitioner can explore clients' perceptions of their impact on others and their feelings as they implemented the tasks. This discussion provides an opportunity to identify additional work to be done and prepares the ground for mutually planning future tasks.

Still another benefit of reviewing task implementation is that you can reinforce clients for carrying out planned tasks. When clients report successes, it is appropriate to express your delight, to accredit their strength and progress, and briefly to share in savoring their successes. Your own way of conveying your positive feelings is best, but the following is a typical message:

- "I'm delighted with how well you did. As I listened to you describe how you talked with your teacher, I was impressed with how clearly you expressed your feelings. Your teacher must have been impressed too, because you showed a part of yourself she hasn't seen before. How do you feel about it?"

In reviewing task accomplishments, it is critical to elicit details of actions or behaviors that assisted clients in achieving a task. Even when tasks have been only partially completed, it is important focus on results clients achieved as a consequence of their efforts. In so doing, it is important to connect clients' efforts with the results that they attained, underscoring that in accomplishing specified tasks, they demonstrated ability to shape their own lives. Establishing that clients have more control than they had previously realized is a powerful force for countering feelings of helplessness, hopelessness, or depression that many clients experience.

Although they may report improvements in problem situations discussed in previous sessions, some clients attribute the reasons for these changes to circumstances beyond themselves. Through careful exploration, practitioners often are able to establish that changes occurred (at least in part) through clients' efforts. Establishing such cause-effect relationships is critical to successful outcomes, for clients are thereby enabled to view themselves as actors who have the potential to solve their problems and to enhance their life situations. The same goal and task form illustrated in Figure 12-1 (see Chapter 12) is a useful guide for developing tasks as well as for recording the status of goals at the beginning of each session with clients. Copies of the completed forms are given to clients to help them to remain focused, and also provide them with evidence of what has been accomplished. In addition to recording tasks to be undertaken to achieve goals, the form is a resource for ongoing monitoring and a summary of outcomes during the termination and evaluation phase. The goal and task form has in our experience proven to be a useful tool.

After completing a review of task implementation, you mutually plan additional tasks that enable clients to progress closer to their focal goals. In addition to following the steps previously delineated for defining tasks, it is important in working toward accomplishment of *ongoing goals* to plan tasks that involve incremental changes and build on one another. Planning tasks that are graded in difficulty enhances chances of successful accomplishment and tends to increase clients' motivation to exert greater efforts in the change process.

To illustrate gradual progression in developing tasks, we consider an extremely self-conscious, socially inhibited client in his early twenties who negotiated a goal of being able to socialize with his fellow workers in the shipping department of a large wholesale supply firm . He rarely engaged in discussions with co-workers, his conversations being limited to job-related topics. To accomplish his goal, the following tasks were mutually negotiated and accomplished sequentially as listed:

1. Smile at workers and look them in the eyes upon arriving at work.

2. Verbally greet co-workers each morning and when leaving work say "see you tomorrow." (Expect startled reactions from co-workers.)

3. Greet co-workers and ask, "How are you doing, [person's name]?"

4. Ask if he can join co-workers at lunch.

5. Listen to co-workers at lunch and "shut off" thoughts about possible negative impressions they may have of him.

6. Make at least one comment or ask one question at lunch.

7. Make at least three comments at lunch.

8. Make overtures to initiate conversation at other times by picking up on topics discussed at lunch.

9. Share at least one personal view or experience during luncheon discussion.

10. Ask a co-worker to join him for a cold drink at break time.

Extensive planning, including modeling, behavioral rehearsal, and discussion of problematic feelings, was involved in preparing to execute each of the preceding tasks. As the client successfully accomplished the tasks, he decided to risk himself in social relationships away from work and formulated a new goal of asking a woman out on a date. To accomplish this goal, progressive tasks building on those previously listed were negotiated.

In actual practice, progress is rarely as smooth as the preceding implies. Not infrequently, clients fail to carry out tasks or to achieve the desired results when they do. Occasionally, unforeseen circumstances such as illness, crowded schedules, and unavailability of others involved in tasks preclude task accomplishment between sessions, necessitating carrying them over to the next week.

Clients may also fail to carry out tasks because of weak commitment to them, emergence of more pressing problems, negative reactions to the practitioner or to the group, or inadequate preparation. In any event, it is vital to explore the reasons carefully, attempting to resolve factors that have blocked implementation if both you and the clients agree the task remains valid. If you determine the task is not valid, it is important to shift your focus to more relevant tasks, as we discuss later. The importance of commitment to the task has been documented by W. Reid (1977), who cited this factor as "the only consistent statistically significant predictor of task progress" (p. 69).

A lack of commitment is not to be confused with a lack of readiness. In the former, the willingness to change is absent; in the latter, clients possess the willingness but are blocked from acting by other barriers. One frequent cause of a lack of commitment to undertake interpersonal tasks is a covert unwillingness to own one's part of a problem. A spouse or parent may pay lip service to carrying out a specific task but subsequently report feeble excuses for not doing so. Unwilling clients often blame others for their difficulties and passively wait for others to initiate corrective actions. In such instances, it is important to explore further the interactions between clients and other actors and to clarify which part of the difficulty is owned by each. Confrontation may also be used to help clients recognize their responsibility for maintaining the undesired status quo by waiting for others to change. If clients exhibit a continued unwillingness to work on tasks, it is appropriate to question their willingness to change.

A lack of commitment to carry out specific tasks is also frequently associated with the efforts of involuntary clients. In these instances, it is the practitioner's responsibility to engage such clients by creating an incentive for change, as we discussed in Chapter 12. Persistent failure to carry out tasks, however, belies expressed intentions. Inaction certainly speaks louder than words, and in such instances, the advisability of continuing should be carefully weighted.

In some instances, what may appear to be clients' lack of commitment to tasks may actually be a reflection of other more pressing concerns. Clients with multiple problems and limited coping skills may be best between sessions with difficulties that supersede the focal problem. Such situations require judicious handling, for the practitioner and clients are faced with a difficult decision. On one hand, it is important to be flexible and to shift focus when emerging problems demand immediate attention. On the other hand, some clients are constantly besieged with "crises," and they should be made aware of the consequences of making little progress with any one when there is too much shifting form one to another.

Although you should be flexible in shifting focus, you must avoid letting crises dictate change efforts. Some clients who live from crisis to crisis benefit in the long run by seeing individual tasks through to completion, taking brief detours only to "apply Band-Aids" as needed. By successfully completing individual tasks, they gain increments of positive coping strengths they can apply to other crises. Clients may not implement tasks in other situations because of overriding problems they have not as yet revealed. Some clients disclose only relatively minor difficulties during initial interviews and defer revealing more burden-

some problems until they feel more comfortable in sharing them. Tasks agreed upon initially thus may not be valid in that they do not relate to the clients' paramount concerns. When this occurs, it is proper to shift the focus to more burdensome difficulties and to formulate new goals and tasks accordingly. It is important, however, to be satisfied that you are shifting focus for valid reasons and not reinforcing a pattern of avoidance.

Frequently tasks fail because they have been inadequately specified: The client did not understand what to do. In other cases, they may be based on adverse beliefs. For example, some parents are hesitant to utilize reward systems, believing that parents should not be bartering with children (R. H. Rooney, 1992, p. 241).

A variety of other reasons may be responsible for task failure. In marital therapy, individual spouses often renege on their commitments to carry out tasks because each does not trust the other partner to carry out his or her part of the bargain. Further, during the week, one or both partners may gather "evidence" that the other spouse is uncommitted to the agreed-upon task, thus justifying his or her own noncompletion of it. Adequate preparation for an initial task in marital therapy thus entails exploration of the trust issue and establishment of a contract that each partner will strictly monitor his or her own task regardless of whether the other person does or does not.

When a client's problems involve the family system, it is important to include relevant members of the family in the sessions. Practitioners often defeat their client's objectives (and their own) by limiting their contacts to the individual client when the behaviors of other persons in a system impinge greatly on identified problems. Although at times families will accommodate an individual member who steadfastly achieves and maintains changes in the system, in many instances families defeat the individual's change efforts. Some families are so disorganized or insensitive to individual change efforts that they discourage any positive efforts of individual family members to modify behavior. Further, other families have dysfunctional interactional patterns that are so pervasive and intractable that it is extremely difficult for members to make needed behavioral changes without great cost unless adjustments are made in the entire system. In such situations, it is vital to involve all family members in sessions to assess individual needs as well as family dynamics and to include them in goal and task planning.

A factor that practitioners must consider in assisting groups to assume tasks is the group's stage of development. Group members have difficulty accomplishing significant change-oriented tasks in the first two stages of group development. In these stages, members tentatively test out the practitioner, other group members, and the group itself, at the same time attempting to find their own positions. Thus, they sometimes have little psychic energy or commitment to accomplish individual or group tasks. For this reason, tasks should be kept simple, and accomplishing them should not require an inordinate amount of investment by members. For instance, asking a newly formed group of delinquent adolescents in a correctional facility to make changes in their behavior toward staff or peers before they are "emotionally committed" to the purposes of the group is doomed to failure. On the other hand, asking members to assume small tasks during the week so that the group might participate in an attractive activity may have greater appeal.

Failure to carry out tasks occurs for a variety of reasons. Negative reactions to the practitioner may block task accomplishment. Such reactions often result when the practitioner assigns tasks unilaterally. Assigning tasks in such a manner tends to activate negative feelings in clients akin to those experienced in childhood toward a parent when unpleasant chores were assigned. Another factor that may block task accomplishment is failure on the practitioner's part to follow up on task implementation. If practitioners neglect to review the client's experience in implementing a task, the client (or practitioner) may shift the focus to other topics before actually seeing previous efforts through to completion. Such shifts disrupt the continuity of change efforts and foster "drift," which dilutes and prolongs the helping process. For this reason, it is vital to review progress in implementing tasks, preferably at or close to the beginning of each session. Use of a written task sheet facilitates such a review.

A final factor sometimes involved in failures either to attempt or to implement tasks successfully involves inadequate preparation. A practitioner may overestimate the coping skills of clients or may not devote sufficient time and effort to the task implementation sequence, leaving clients ill prepared to cope with tasks' demands. Actually, it is preferable for clients not to attempt tasks rather than to attempt them and fail because they are not adequately prepared. In the former instance, blows to self-esteem are usually minimal, and additional efforts can be made to prepare a client more adequately. Failure, by contrast, may damage self-esteem and undermine confidence in the helping process.

Even when preparation has been adequate, successful outcomes of task efforts are not ensured. Unanticipated reactions of others, ineffectual task performance, panic reactions, inappropriate task selection based on inaccurate assessment, and adverse circumstances may block goal attainment. To avoid or minimize undue discouragement by clients when results are negative, it is helpful to interpret such results not as failures but as indications of the need for additional information and task planning. Negative results, in fact, sometimes serve a constructive purpose in further elucidating dynamics of problems, thereby enabling clients and practitioners to sharpen their assessment, goals, and tasks.

Evaluating Progress

A final mode of maintaining focus and continuity is to evaluate progress toward goal attainment regularly. We discussed this process in the previous chapter, but here we add the following objectives served by systematically monitoring progress.

1. By eliciting clients' views of their progress or by comparing latest rates of target behavior

with the baseline, you maintain focus on goals and enhance continuity of change efforts.

2. Clients gain perspective not only in determining where they stand in relationship to ultimate goals but also to their pretreatment level of functioning. Discerning incremental progress toward goals tends to sustain motivation and to enhance confidence in the helping process and in the practitioner.

3. Eliciting clients' feelings and views regarding progress enables practitioners to detect and to work through feelings of disappointment and discouragement that may impede future progress and lead to premature discontinuance.

4. Practitioners can evaluate the efficacy of their interventions and change strategies. If a given approach fails to yield positive results within a reasonable time, more of the same is unlikely to produce different results. We recommend you apply the maxim, "If what you're doing isn't working, try something different."

5. Indications of marked progress toward goal attainment alert practitioners to possible readiness by clients to shift the focus to another goal or to consider planning for termination if all goals have been substantially achieved.

Evaluation of progress should be conducted in accordance with the agreement negotiated in the contracting process. Progress should be monitored every two or three sessions at a minimum. Methods of assessing progress should also be those negotiated in the contract.

CRISIS INTERVENTION (CI)

Crisis intervention (CI) is another widely employed general intervention strategy or modality. This modality shares much in common with task-centered casework. Crisis intervention (1) is time limited, (2) focuses on problems of living rather than psychopathology, (3) is oriented to the here and now, (4) involves a high level of activity by the practitioner, (5) employs tasks as a primary tactic of change efforts, and (6) is an eclectic framework that can accommodate various practice theories and interventions. Because crisis intervention addresses urgent crisis situations precipitated by stressful events, maturational crises, and acute transitional situations, its potential use is somewhat more limited than that of task-centered casework.

CI methods were used during the Gulf War to provide immediate responses to traumatic events. Critical response teams using crisis intervention strategies are used in the workplace and schools in instances where individuals or groups experience trauma following a dramatic event. The interventions range from single session, telephone intervention to intervention with groups (Gilbar, 1992; West, Mercer, & Altheimer, 1993). Social workers are thought to be especially qualified to take a leadership role in the organization of such traumatic event debriefing (Bell, 1995). On a more local scale, social workers have taken the lead in developing post interventions in the public schools to assist family members and the school community in dealing with the grief caused by student suicide (Komar, 1994).

Tenets of Crisis Intervention Theory

Basic to CI theory is the concept that when people are beset by a crisis, a potential exists for them to cope in ways that are either adaptive or maladaptive. Stress occurs when an individual or family experiences a situation that is beyond their capacity to handle. Prolonged stress exceeds the ability of the family or individual to effectively handle the stressors, and the usual ways of coping are unlikely to work. According to CI theorists, most crisis situations are limited to a period of 4 to 8 weeks, during which time people manage to achieve a degree of equilibrium, which may be equivalent to, lower than, or higher than the precrisis level of functioning. The amount of time required before a crisis is resolved depends on the stress; persons coping with cancer surgery are reported to need from 4 weeks to 5 years in adjustment, and rape victims often require 6 months to several years to recover (Barth, 1988, p. 92). Life crises can thus be viewed as presenting potential threats that can permanently impair people's level of functioning or as painful challenges that embody opportunities for growth in personal strength and coping capacity. CI theory emphasizes the importance of intervening immediately to assist clients who are overwhelmed by crises. Timely intervention is critical not only to prevent deterioration in functioning but also to reach people when their defenses are low and their receptiveness to therapeutic interventions is greatest, as occurs during acute periods of crisis.

Most CI theorists accept Caplan's (1964) definition of a crisis as an upset in a steady state (state of equilibrium) that poses an obstacle, usually important to the fulfillment of important life goals or to vital need satisfaction, and that the individual (or family) cannot overcome through usual methods of problem solving. A crisis thus is stressful and disruptive and can adversely affect biological, psychological, and social functioning and can produce disturbed emotions, impair motor functioning, and negatively affect ongoing behavior. Crisis situations have a subjective element, for people's perceptions and coping capacities vary widely. What is severely stressful and overwhelming for one person or family may be stressful but manageable for others. Gilliland and James (1993) acknowledge that individual reactions to the same traumatic situation may differ. They describe this process as "crisis in perception of an event or situation as an intolerable difficulty that exceeds the resources and coping mechanisms of the person" (p. 3). Nevertheless, although crisis situations or events (denoted as hazardous events) are diverse, most people would agree that natural disasters, death of a loved one, disabling or life-threatening illness or injury, cultural dislocation, rape, out-of-wedlock pregnancy, and other like events usually pose a crisis to those involved.

Hazardous events can be experienced as a threat, challenge, or loss. A threat (e.g., possibility of losing a job, spouse, home, or valued status, or removal of a child from the home by authorities) may involve anticipated loss of an individual's sense of integrity or autonomy. A threat thus involves high anxiety and apprehension about a possible dreaded event. A challenge involves anxiety over the possibility of failure in the immediate future, as, for example, not performing adequately on a new job or failing an examination crucial to one's future. Challenge, of course, also involves motivation to succeed and hope of success. Loss, by contrast, involves an acute sense of deprivation resulting from an event that has already occurred, such as a death, divorce, or move from one's homeland. Loss, therefore, produces depressed affect associated with the grieving process.

CI theory posits that people's reactions to crises typically involve going through different stages. Theorists differ as to whether three or four stages are involved. Our description involves a synthesis of stages identified by various authors. The first stage involves an initial rise in tension accompanied by shock and perhaps even denial of the crisis-provoking event. To reduce the tension, persons resort to their usual emergency problem-solving skills, and when these fail to alleviate the tension, heightened tension ensues. At this point, the person or family enters the second stage, which is characterized by tension so severe that the person feels confused, overwhelmed, helpless, angry, or perhaps acutely depressed. The length of this phase varies according to the nature of the hazardous event, the strengths and coping capacities of the person, and the degree of responsiveness from social support systems. After the crisis experience, people need immediate support so that they are able to stabilize and begin the process of adapting or coping.

As people move from stage 2 to stage 3, they resort to different coping tactics, the outcome of which depends on whether these tactics are adaptive or maladaptive. If the tactics arc maladaptive, tension may continue to escalate and the person may suffer a mental breakdown or, in extreme instances, attempt suicide. If the efforts are adaptive, the person regains equilibrium and perhaps achieves a higher level of functioning.

According to CI theory, crisis periods are time limited and people achieve a degree of equilibrium for better or for worse during this time. Consequently, immediate intervention aimed at restoring clients to their precrisis level of functioning or better is crucial. Departures from the traditional weekly 50-minute sessions are common, and some clients may even be seen daily during acute periods of crisis.

Time limits (generally 6 to 8 weeks) are employed in CI, although some clients require even shorter periods of time. Practitioners assume an active role and deliberately employ their authority and expertise to inspire the hope and confidence so badly needed by clients. The temporal focus of CI is on the here and now, and goals are limited to alleviating distress and enabling clients to regain equilibrium. No attempt is made to deal either with precrisis personality dysfunction or intrapsychic conflict, although even minor changes effected through CI may provide the impetus for enhanced personal and interpersonal functioning as well as improved transactions with social support systems.

The heart of CI involves delineating tasks that clients can perform to achieve a new state of equilibrium. Although practitioners are active and directive in defining tasks, clients should be encouraged to participate to the extent of their capability, for their active participation fosters autonomy. Obviously, clients' abilities to participate actively are limited during periods of severe emotional distress but increase as the distress subsides.

After completion of the essential tasks, CI moves into the final major activity, which consists of anticipatory guidance. This activity, which has preventive implications, involves assisting clients to anticipate future crisis situations and to plan coping strategies that prepare them to face future stresses.

Having reviewed the essential concepts of CI, we now turn to procedures for implementing the modality.

The Initial Phase of Crisis Intervention

During the initial phase of CI, the practitioner's objectives are (1) to relieve the client's emotional distress, (2) to complete an assessment, and (3) to plan the strategy of intervention, focusing on relevant tasks the client must perform. The following sections briefly focus on each of these processes.

Relieving Emotional Distress

Drawing out clients' emotions and responding empathically to them often assist clients to unburden themselves of painful and sometimes overwhelming emotions. Practitioners can also provide needed emotional support as they encourage clients to ventilate pent-up emotions by reassuring them that their emotions are a natural reaction to an extremely distressing situation.

When clients in an acute crisis are immobilized by tension and anxiety, deep breathing and progressive muscle relaxation procedures (see Chapter 14) can be helpful in alleviating tension and in assisting clients to gain composure. Practitioners should also consider the need for antianxiety or antidepressant medications in extreme instances.

Use of social support systems may also reduce emotional distress for some clients. Friends and loved ones may provide comfort and compassion that clients sorely need to buffer the devastating impact of certain crises. Clients' religious affiliations can also be a source of great emotional support. Local church leaders can often provide solace and guidance and rally the support of church members. Moreover, support groups for diverse crises are available in many communities. Practitioners may need to develop such resources in others.

Assessment

Because of the short time involved in CI, practitioners concurrently assess and alleviate clients' emotional distress. Objectives of the assessment involve determining the nature of the crisis situation, its significance to and impact on the clients(s), factors or events that precipitated the crisis, adaptive capacities of the client, and resources that can be tapped to alleviate the crisis situation. These factors are crucial to formulating tasks that must subsequently be accomplished. A. R. Roberts (1990), Parad and Parad (1990), and R. A. Wells and Giannetti (1990) provide a review of crisis assessment and intervention models that have been used in numerous settings and individual and family situations.

The nature of a crisis, of course, provides valuable clues to the sources of clients' distress. Losses, for example, leave people bereft of vital sources of emotional supplies and typically produce grieving reactions. The meanings people attach to losses of close kin vary considerably, however, leading to differing emotional reactions. A client who has been extremely dependent on a spouse may react to the spouse's death not only with grief but also with feelings of helplessness and hopelessness concerning ability to manage independently. A client whose relationship to a decreased spouse or parent was ambivalent and conflictual may react to the death with feelings of guilt, hostility, or even relief. Practitioners, therefore, must determine the unique meaning of crisis situations to each client. Determining the meaning and significance of precipitating events can be highly therapeutic to clients. Through exploring precipitating events and other factors that bear on clients' reactions, practitioners enable clients to view their situation in a new perspective, which can foster hope. Many clients, in fact, improve dramatically as they gain expanded understanding of the complex forces involved in their crisis situations and their reactions to them.

Assessing clients' capacities for adaptive coping involves not only determining their current level of functioning but also their precrisis level. Obviously, to restore clients to their previous level of functioning, one must first ascertain that level. Knowledge of adaptive capacity is also essential to formulating relevant tasks and selecting appropriate intervention techniques. Practitioners, therefore, must rapidly assess individuals' and families' precrisis functioning.

Cultural Factors and CI

Cultural factors are also vital in understanding and assessing clients' reactions to crisis situations. Situations deemed as crises vary widely from one culture to another, as do the reactions to them. Divorce or unwed pregnancy, for example, requires considerable adaptation in most cultures but may pose an extreme crisis to first-generation Asian Americans because of the social ostracism, loss of face, and shame involved for persons in Asian cultures. In some instances, a crisis for a family or individual may become heightened because of a lack of understanding of culture or language. De Las Fuentes (2000) points to studies that demonstrate crisis intervention programs with Hispanic children and adolescents when cultural awareness is an element of the treatment plan. Extended family, religious institutions, and informal networks often prove to be useful resources to tap into in implementing crisis intervention strategies with diverse groups.

Refugees from nations that are torn by war and/or political upheaval suffer multiple losses and are especially in need of CI services. Many arrive in the United States stripped of social, economic, psychological, and religious supports. Some are physically ill. Moreover, most are ill equipped to adapt to American patterns of life such as shopping, transportation, banking, food preparation, use of home appliances, health care systems, and bureaucratic structures. Limited language proficiency as well as the experience of a foreign culture act to further compound overwhelming stressors. Weiss and Parish (1989) have written about the need to adapt crisis intervention to these most vulnerable groups.

CI with Marginally Functioning Persons It is important to note, as Lukton (1982) and others have stressed, that use of CI need not be limited to people who ordinarily are psychologically intact. Target groups for CI have been extended to include marginally functioning people with chronic problems. Moreover, even acutely psychotic people can be helped. A psychotic break, in fact, may be viewed as a way of responding to a crisis state and as an opportunity for developing more effective coping mechanisms and interpersonal skills (Lukton, 1982, p. 277). (With clients whose precrisis functioning was marginal, case management services may be needed to link them with other needed resources.) Crisis teams have also been employed in the public sector (e.g., in hospital emergency rooms, youth service centers, and mental health centers) to provide immediate assistance aimed at stabilizing people and their families and preventing relapses of psychiatric patients.

Assessing Support Systems

Another aspect of assessment in CI is to determine clients' social support systems, for "interventions that enhance the natural helping network can be enormously helpful in crisis intervention" (Lukton, 1982, p. 280). Practitioners can enhance natural helping networks by mobilizing family, friends, neighbors, the clergy, or cultural reference groups. Another valuable resource is self-help groups, which consist of people with similar problems. Members of self-help groups provide mutual support and assistance to each other in solving problems. You will recall we discussed assessment of support systems in Chapter 9. We also discuss support systems at greater length in Chapter 15.

Contracting and Planning

Contracting in CI involves basically the same elements as those described in Chapter 12. The overall goal, to restore equilibrium, is applicable to all cases, but general and specific tasks vary according to the nature of the crisis situation and the unique characteristics of each person and/or family. Similar crisis situations, of course, involve similar tasks that must be accomplished, and the literature contains many articles that identify tasks relevant to specific crisis situations such as rape (Holmes, 1981; Koss & Harvey, 1991); having AIDS (Gambe & Getzel, 1989); out-of-wedlock pregnancy (Chesler & Davis, 1980); and cultural dislocation (Golan & Gruschka, 1971). Lukton (1982) has cautioned, however, that in addressing

the same types of crisis situations, different writers often identify different tasks. Moreover, the sequence of accomplishing tasks may vary from client to client. Practitioners, therefore, can benefit from available knowledge in determining and negotiating essential tasks but must consider the individuality of each client situation.

In negotiating time limits, it is important to involve clients (thereby increasing their autonomy) by soliciting their views as to how long they believe they will need to "get back on an even keel." Many will suggest just a few weeks, which is the time ordinarily required. Some clients will suggest only 2 to 3 weeks and will, in fact, require no more. When clients are reluctant to commit themselves, practitioners can suggest that from 4 to 8 weeks are usually sufficient and ask the client to select a limit, recognizing that fewer sessions may prove ample.

Problems of Transition   An exception to the use of the usual time limits involves clients in certain states of transition, such as adapting to the death of a spouse, domestic partner, or child, single-parent status following divorce, isolation from family, retirement, and a new country and culture. Golan (1980, 1981), Lukton (1982), and others argue persuasively that traditional CI is not appropriate for such transition states that require "identity transformation and role change that continues long after the acute phase of disorganization is overcome" (Golan, 1981, p. 264). With respect to loss of a child, research cited by Videka-Sherman (1987) indicates that "grief after a child dies lasts a very long time and may actually intensify over the first 1–2 years following the child's death. Social workers must be very careful not to impose unrealistic expectations that acute grief will end in 6 months or even in 1 or 2 years" (p. 109). R. Weiss and Parkes (1983) report similar findings regarding the time required for spouses to adapt following the death of a mate. In such instances, principles of CI are relevant to the acute phase of disorganization, but extended service is required for clients to adapt to new roles and to develop new sources of emotional supplies. The phases of crisis resolution thus are far longer for this group than earlier believed.

Task Implementation

In facilitating clients' accomplishment of tasks deemed essential to mastery of crisis situations, practitioners should observe the guidelines to task implementation delineated earlier in this chapter. Practitioners assume an active and directive role and give advice to a greater extent than when using other approaches. Still, it is important to foster client autonomy by involving clients in planning for task implementation and by encouraging and reinforcing independent actions whenever feasible.

Anticipatory Guidance

During the concluding phase of CI (after the crisis has subsided), practitioners engage in anticipatory guidance, an activity of major preventive significance. This activity is a strong feature of CI, and we urge practitioners to include it in the terminal phase of any practice model. Anticipatory guidance involves assisting clients to anticipate future crises that might develop and to plan effective coping strategies (based on knowledge gained during the preceding period of problem solving) that they can employ to avoid being overwhelmed in the future. Relevant strategies might include analyzing sources of distress, recalling and accrediting successful efforts in coping with past crisis situations, anticipating needs, identifying and utilizing support systems and other potential resources, and formulating and implementing essential tasks. It is important, however, not to convey an expectation that clients should be able to manage all problem situations independently in the future. Indeed, during the process of termination, practitioners should express continuing interest, reassure clients that the door is open should they need future help, and explain that the practitioner will be contacting them soon to check on their continued progress.[6]

COGNITIVE RESTRUCTURING

Cognitive restructuring is a therapeutic process derived from cognitive behavioral therapy. Intervention techniques are designed to help individuals modify beliefs, faulty thought patterns or perceptions, and destructive verbalizations, thus leading to changed behavior. An assumption of cognitive therapy is that people often manifest cognitive distortions, irrational thoughts, or thoughts derived from negative schema that lead to unrealistic interpretations of people, events, or circumstances. The goal of cognitive therapy is to restructure or change the thoughts, feelings, or overt behaviors that maintain problem behavior. Sessions are structured on the here-and-now, and goals focus on increasing the client's cognitive and behavioral skills in order to enhance functioning.

Theories of social work, counseling, and psychotherapy acknowledge the central role of cognition in human behavior and the problems of cognitive dysfunction. Over four decades ago, however, Ellis's (1962) book, *Reason and Emotion in Psychotherapy*, posited the theory of rational-emotive therapy (RET). This work proved to be seminal, and since that time, particularly in the past 25 years, cognitive therapy has burgeoned. Numerous books and articles have been published delineating the significance of mistaken beliefs and faulty patterns of thought in diverse emotional and behavioral problems ranging from childhood and adolescence (Weisz, Weiss, Wasserman, & Rintoul, 1987) to old age (Lam, Brewin, Woods, & Bebbington, 1987). Many of these same publications also describe the application of cognitive therapy (CT) to widely varying disorders. Perhaps the most significant of these publications is *The Cognitive Therapy of Depression* (A. Beck, Rush, Shaw, & Emery, 1979), a book widely recognized as the definitive work on treatment of depression. Further, research studies have documented that cognitive/behavioral therapy is one of the two major psychotherapeutic approaches that produces outcomes equivalent to those produced by antidepressant medication (Elkin, Shea, Watkins, & Collins, 1986). A number of treatment manuals provide practitioners with systematic guidelines for working with clients to resolve problems related to depression, stress, personality disorders, and substance abuse (Barkley, 1997; A. Beck & Freeman, 1990; A. Beck, Wright, Newman & Liese, 1993; Linehan, 1993; Meichenbaum, 1977).

In social work, CT has been a major treatment modality. Examples include B. Cohen (1985), who has reported on the use of CT with criminals; Barth (1985) has described cognitive/behavioral treatment of depression in mothers who maltreat children; and T. K. Marshall and Mazie (1987) have delineated a cognitive approach to treating depression. Cognitive behavioral interventions are also a major component of treatment programs for reducing the anger of parents at risk of abusing children (Nugent, 1991; Whiteman, Fanshel, & Grundy, 1987) and for treating male spouse batterers (Eisikovits & Edleson, 1989). Schrodt and Fitzgerald (1987) present a rationale for using CT in work with adolescents.

Advantages of cognitive therapy are evidence of strong empirical support, the focus on the here and now (unless history plays a role in the presenting problem), and a time-limited framework for resolution of the presenting problem. Techniques used in cognitive therapy can be utilized with other models or approaches to problem solving. To be maximally effective, practitioners must become proficient in assessing cognitive functioning and in applying appropriate interventions to enhance cognitive functioning. (We focused on assessing cognitive functioning in Chapters 9 and 11.)

Uses of Cognitive Restructuring

Cognitive restructuring is particularly useful in assisting clients to gain awareness of dysfunctional and self-defeating thoughts and misconceptions that impair personal functioning and to replace them with beliefs and behaviors that are aligned with reality and lead to enhanced functioning. Cognitive restructuring techniques are particularly relevant for problems associated with low self-esteem; distorted perceptions in interpersonal relations; unrealistic expectations of self, others, and life in general; irrational fears, anxiety, and depression; inadequate control of anger and other impulses; and lack of assertiveness. Practitioners have found cognitive restructuring to be especially useful in assisting people with problems of impulse control manifested in child abuse. Cognitive restructuring is often blended with other interventions (e.g., modeling, behavioral rehearsal, relaxation training, assertiveness training, drug therapy, and desensitization) because combinations of interventions are sometimes more potent in producing change than are single interventions.

Cautions

Although cognitive theorists attribute most dysfunctional emotional and behavioral patterns to mistaken beliefs, they are by no means the only causes. Dysfunction may be produced by various biophysical problems, including brain tissue damage, neurological disorders, thyroid imbalance, blood sugar imbalance, circulatory disorders associated with aging, ingestion of toxic substances, malnutrition, and other forms of chemical imbalance in the body (Lantz, 1978). Consequently, these possibilities should be considered before undertaking cognitive restructuring.

Tenets of Cognitive Therapy

A major tenet of CT is that thinking is a basic determinant of behavior. Thinking consists of statements that people say to themselves, and it is this inner dialogue, rather than unconscious forces, that is the key to understanding behavior.

To grasp this first major tenet accurately, practitioners must clearly differentiate thinking from feeling. Clients (and practitioners, too) often confuse feelings and thoughts, which tends to foster confusion in communication and hinders successful implementation of cognitive restructuring techniques. The confusion is manifested in messages such as, "I feel our marriage is on the rocks," or "I feel nobody cares about me." The word *feel* is used incorrectly in these messages, which do not involve feelings but rather views, thoughts, or beliefs. Thoughts per se are devoid of feelings, although they are often accompanied by and tend to generate feelings or emotions. Feelings involve emotions such as sadness, joy, disappointment, exhilaration, and any of the hundreds of feelings listed in the "Affective Words and Phrases" found in Chapter 5.

To assist clients to differentiate between feelings and cognitions, it is helpful to explain the difference and to provide several examples of both. Thereafter, it is important to intervene when clients fail to distinguish between these functions. It is critical that clients be able to make these distinctions, for self-monitoring of cognitions (discussed later) requires this ability. J. S. Beck (1995) has emphasized the use of *Socratic questioning* as basic to cognitive therapy. For example, in a situation where a client complains about workplace difficulties, a practitioner might pose the question, "Does your use of alcohol contribute to the difficulties you are experiencing at work?" rather than say, "I think that your use of alcohol is the reason that you are having work difficulties."

A second major tenet of cognitive therapy is that the past is important only in identifying the origins of faulty thinking. It is the present faulty thinking, not the past, that motivates behavior. Furthermore, new patterns of thinking can be learned and problems resolved without determining the origins of faulty thinking. Therefore, the focus of cognitive therapy is largely on the present and the future. Clients are not permitted to use the past as an excuse for present difficulties.

Still another major tenet of cognitive therapy is that to make constructive changes, people must realize that their misconceptions may produce or contribute to many of their problems, and they must assume responsibility for modifying these misconceptions. In our view, this assumption must be tempered with the recognition that many factors contribute to the problems of clients, including inadequate resources and adverse environmental conditions. Still, with clients whose problems are rooted in misconceptions and faulty

logic, this tenet is valid. The thrust of this tenet is that as practitioners we must assist clients to assume maximal responsibilities for themselves.

Steps in Cognitive Restructuring

In the assessment phase, cognitive theorists view symptoms as learned responses that may be involuntary, learned, or acquired. Learning new skills as well as the capacity to change is emphasized as means to alter responses to situations, people, or various life circumstances. Several discrete steps are involved in cognitive restructuring. Different authors vary slightly in their definitions of these steps, as well as their application to specific target concerns. The similarities are far greater than the differences. We have combined general steps as identified in the works of Goldfried (1977), Cormier and Cormier (1979), A. R. Roberts (1990), and Parad and Parad (1990) to be the most useful. These steps together with guidelines for implementing them are as follows:

1. Assist clients in accepting that their self-statements, assumptions, and beliefs largely mediate (i.e., determine or govern) their emotional reactions to life's events. Assisting clients to accept this explanation is vital, for clients are unlikely to commit themselves to procedures that they view skeptically or reject. To enhance their acceptance, we recommend that you present the rationale for cognitive restructuring and also demonstrate its relevance by citing common life experiences that document how cognitions mediate emotions. Draw examples from your own experiences, if possible, because they will be most meaningful to you. To guide you in assisting clients to accept the rationale, we offer the following example of an explanation provided to a client who was severely inhibited in social situations by feelings of inadequacy and social incompetence.

"For you to achieve your goal of expressing yourself more openly with others, we first need to determine what happens inside you that maintains your fears. That will involve your becoming aware of thoughts you experience in social situations—in other words, what you say to yourself before, during, and after social situations. Generally, such thoughts occur automatically, and you won't be fully aware of many of them. We also want to discover assumptions and beliefs you have about social situations—beliefs you may have had much of your life. Becoming aware of self-defeating thoughts, assumptions, and beliefs is an extremely important first step in discarding them in favor of others that serve you better.

"What you think determine in large measure what you feel and do. For example, if a friend tells me I'm stupid because I bought a new car instead of a used one, I can make various meanings or self-statements related to that message, each of which results in different feelings and actions. Consider, for instance, the different ways I might think about this:

1. *He's probably right; he's a bright guy, and I respect his judgment. Why didn't I think of buying a used car? He must really think I'm a clod.* If I think that, I'll feel crummy about myself, probably regret buying a new car, and won't enjoy it as much as I might.

2. *Who does he think he is calling me stupid? He's the one who's stupid. What a jerk!* If I think that, I'll feel angry and defensive. I may get in a heated argument over the merits of a new car or a used one.

3. *It's apparent that we have different ideas on that subject. He's entitled to his opinion, although I certainly don't agree with him and do feel good about what I did. I don't like his referring to my decision as stupid, though. No point getting upset over it, but I think I'll let him know I don't feel good about his putting me down that way.* If I think these thoughts, I'm not going to experience negative feelings. I'll feel good about my actions despite the other person's difference of opinion and I won't be unduly influenced by his insensitivity.

"There are other meanings we could make, of course, but these should make the point. To en-

able you to master your fears, we'll explore together statements you make to yourself and how they affect your feelings and behavior. After we've identified thoughts and beliefs that are causing difficulties, we'll begin working on developing others that are realistic and consistent with your goal of expressing yourself more openly in social situations."

When the rationale is presented in a simple, straightforward manner, the majority of clients respond positively. Nevertheless, it is important to elicit clients' reactions to your explanation and to invite discussion. It is important not to proceed with cognitive restructuring until clients manifest receptivity and commitment to implementing the intervention. Clients, indeed, tend to resist changing their beliefs if they feel they are being coerced to adopt the beliefs of someone else.

2. Assist clients in identifying dysfunctional beliefs and patterns of thoughts that underlie their problems. Once clients accept the proposition that thoughts and beliefs mediate emotional reactions, the next task is to assist them to examine personal thoughts and beliefs that pertain to their difficulties. This step involves detailed exploration of events related to problematic situations, with particular emphasis upon cognitions that accompany distressing emotions. For example, some clients attribute their problems to factors such as fate, inherent personal inadequacy or unlovability, and various forces beyond their control. In identifying key misconceptions, it is vital that you and your client agree as to what beliefs need to be changed. Although there are a number of ways of reaching agreement, the preferred way is to involve clients so that they feel they are actively participating and contributing.

You can begin the process of exploration by focusing on problematic events that occurred during the preceding week or on events surrounding a problem the client has targeted for change. As you mutually explore these events, it is important to elicit specific details regarding overt behavior, cognitions (i.e., self-statements and images), and emotional reactions. Focusing on all three aspects of behavior enables you to assist the client to see the connections between them and to grasp the role of cognitions in mediating feeling and behavior. As clients identify their self-statements and beliefs, they become increasingly aware that automatic thoughts and beliefs they have not subjected to critical analysis are powerful determinants of their behavior. This, in turn, increases their receptivity and motivation to work on tasks involving liberating themselves from these dysfunctional thoughts and beliefs.

As you engage in explorations, it is important to identify thoughts and feelings that occur before, during, and after events. To elicit such self-statements, ask clients to recreate the situation just as it unfolded, recalling exactly what they thought, felt, and actually did. If clients experience difficulty, it may be helpful to have them close their eyes and "run a movie" of the problematic event, including thoughts and feelings that preceded, accompanied, and followed the event.

Identifying self-statements and assumptions that precede events makes it possible to pinpoint cognitive sets that predispose clients to experience certain emotions and to behave in predictable ways. For example, our socially inhibited client, cited earlier, disclosed that he made the following self-statements in anticipation of a disappointing discussion with co-workers in the lunchroom:

1. "I'm not sure I want to join the others. If I do, I'll just sit there and feel left out."

2. "I'll bet they'd rather that I didn't join them. They will probably think that I'm a real bore."

3. "I'd better join them, I guess. If I don't, they'll ask me where I was, and I'll have to come up with some excuse."

Given these self-statements, the client felt uneasy and apprehensive about joining his coworkers. As typically occurred, these thoughts predisposed him to enter the situation programmed for defeat. Moreover, he was tense and preoccupied with himself as he engaged in self-debate and finally decided to eat with his fellow workers. Such preoccupation is self-defeating because it limits involvement by dominating thinking with fears and worries about making mistakes.

Exploration of self-statements during events reveals that dysfunctional thoughts maintain self-defeating feelings and behavior and drastically reduce personal effectiveness. For example, clients who dwell on worries and are hypervigilant to the possible negative reactions of others are unable to "tune in" fully to discussions and to express themselves in positive ways that create favorable impressions. In other words, it is difficult for them to be fully present and involved because of self-consciousness and fears of exposing their imagined personal inadequacies. To illustrate the destructive impact of such dysfunctional thoughts, let us again consider the self-statements of our socially inhibited client during lunch with co-workers:

1. "Well, here I am again, and it's just like it's always been. I'm just out of it."

2. "I wish I had something interesting to say, but my life's such a drag. They couldn't possibly be interested in anything I might say."

3. "They're probably wondering why I even join them. I sure don't add anything to the group. I wish I could just disappear."

It is apparent from these and other like self-statements that the client dwells on self-demeaning thoughts. He thinks of himself as having little or nothing to offer, behaves accordingly, and feels unwanted and unworthy to participate actively. His preoccupation with these thoughts and assumptions about himself block him from engaging in ongoing interaction with his peers.

Clients' self-statements and feelings following events reveal the impact of earlier thoughts and behaviors on subsequent feelings, thereby highlighting further the mediating function of cognitions. Moreover, the conclusions clients draw about the outcomes of events indicate further whether they are able to focus on positive aspects of their behavior and to identify challenges for further growth or whether they merely perceive an event as the latest in a long series of failures caused by their personal inadequacies. The meanings clients make of events, of course, are powerful in shaping their attitudes and feelings toward similar future events, as illustrated by the thoughts and feelings of our familiar client:

1. "I blew it again. I might as well quit trying. No use kidding myself, I just can't talk with others."

2. "They didn't really try to include me. It's obvious they could care less about me. They'd probably be pleased if I didn't join them tomorrow."

3. "I think I won't eat lunch with them anymore. I don't enjoy it, and I'm sure they don't either. Tomorrow I'll just eat by myself."

Clearly, this client's thoughts lead to feelings of utter failure. Without intervention into his circular self-defeating patterns of thought, he will tend to withdraw even further socially. It could be expected that he would experience further self-demeaning thoughts accompanied by depressed feelings.

As you mutually identify self-statements, it is important to assist clients to assess the degree of rationality of these self-statements. Through guided practice in critically analyzing the validity of their thoughts, clients gain experience that prepares them to engage in a similar process outside the sessions. Clients, however, may not acknowledge the irrationality of certain beliefs, especially those that are deeply embedded in their belief systems. Indeed, clients can cling tenaciously to key misconceptions and argue persuasively about their validity. Practitioners must, therefore, be prepared to challenge or dispute such irrational beliefs and to persist in assisting clients to recognize the costs or disadvantages associated with not relinquishing these beliefs.[7]

Techniques that challenge clients to assess the rationality of their beliefs and self-statements include:

1. Asking them how they reached certain conclusions.

2. Challenging them to present evidence supporting dysfunctional views or beliefs.

3. Challenging the logic of beliefs that magnify feared consequences of certain actions.

To illustrate the applications of these techniques, we have provided three self-statements, or beliefs, followed by responses that direct clients to analyze their validity.

1. *Self-statement:* "I've got to study every available moment. If I don't get the highest score on that test, it will be just awful."

   Response 1: "Let's just suppose for a moment you really bombed out on that test. What would it really mean?"

   Response 2: "So if you're not number one, it will be a catastrophe. I can agree it's nice to be number one, but why is it such a disaster if you were to be number two?"

2. *Self-statement:* "I don't want to tend her children, but if I don't she'll be furious. I don't dare risk displeasing her."

   Response 1: "How have you concluded she'd be furious?"

   Response 2: "Suppose you did risk turning her down and she became furious. Perhaps a question you should answer is whether you are going to let possible unreasonable reactions on her part dictate your behavior."

3. *Self-statement:* "There's no point in my taking a time-out when my wife starts ragging on me. She would see me as trying to escape, and there's no way she would see that I am trying to avoid a potentially violent situation."

   Response 1: "What evidence do you have that she wouldn't believe you?"

   Response 2: "Sounds like you've convinced yourself that she would not understand what you are trying to do. Have you explained to her what we are working on and what you are attempting to change?"

Clusters of misconceptions are commonly associated with dysfunctional behavior. Often it is possible to discern such patterns of thoughts even by the end of one session. By closely following feelings and eliciting accompanying thoughts, you can identify such clusters early. Dysfunctional thoughts typically include the following clusters of misconceptions:

1. About oneself
2. About others' perceptions and expectations of oneself
3. Expectations of oneself
4. Expectations of others

For illustrative purposes we have provided our conception of a cluster of beliefs associated with having unreasonable self-expectations:

1. "I must be the best in everything I do."
2. "It is terrible if I am unsuccessful in any venture."
3. "I am worthwhile as a person only if I am constantly working."
4. "I never quite achieve the level of excellence I should."
5. "When I compare myself with others, I never quite measure up."
6. "I should be able to succeed in any endeavor; if I don't, it's because I'm incompetent."
7. "I should be able to accept numerous assignments and perform all at a high level."
8. "I don't really deserve praise for my accomplishments because they're not that significant."
9. "If I'm not perfect in everything I do, it is terrible, and I'm a failure."

By identifying clusters or patterns of misconceptions, you can direct your efforts to the theme common to all of them, rather than deal with each as a separate entity. Common to the cluster identified in the preceding is the theme of setting unrealistic expectations for oneself. By focusing on this central theme, you can conserve efforts, for the related misconceptions are merely derivatives of the central one and lose their potency when the core misconception is resolved.

By gaining practice in identifying and assessing the validity of self-statements and beliefs during sessions, clients achieve readiness to engage in self-monitoring *between* sessions. After the session in which you introduce clients to cognitive restructuring and mutually explore cognitions related to their difficulties, it is timely to negotiate a task that involves self-monitoring of thoughts and beliefs related to problematic events that occur between sessions. Through self-monitoring, clients become increasingly aware of the pervasive nature of their dysfunctional thoughts and recognize the need to cope actively with them. Self-monitoring thus expands self-awareness and paves the way for later coping efforts. Moreover, self-monitoring alone often enables clients to nip self-defeating thoughts in the bud as they realize the irrational nature and destructive impact of these thoughts.

To facilitate self-monitoring, we recommend that you ask clients to keep daily logs to record information in columns, as illustrated in Figure 13-1.[8]

Date: Tuesday, September 22		
Situation or Event	**Feelings (rate intensity from 1–10)**	**Beliefs or Self-Statements (rate rationality from 1–10)**
1. Asked boss for a day off	Scared (7)	He'll be annoyed and critical of me (4)
2. Clerk at store gave me incorrect change; I did not say anything	Annoyed (4); afraid to tell clerk (8); disgusted with self (7)	I ought to tell the clerk (9); she'll be displeased and I'd feel embarrassed (2); it is not worth the hassle (3)

Figure 13-1   Sample Daily Log

Daily logs are valuable because they focus clients' efforts between sessions; clarify further the connections between cognitions and feelings; and provide valuable information to the practitioner about the prevalence and intensity of dysfunctional thoughts, images, and feelings. Moreover, they stimulate clients to engage in logical analysis of their thoughts. To prevent clients from feeling overwhelmed by the task of keeping a log, suggest they begin by limiting their recording to events related to those identified during the session and that they record only about three such events each day. Otherwise, clients tend to experience the task as unduly burdensome because of the host of troubling thoughts they may have during a given day. As other dysfunctional patterns of thoughts emerge during sessions, the focus of self-monitoring can be shifted as necessary.

In the preceding discussion, we have made passing references to images as an integral part of cognitions. Explorations of cognitions and self-monitoring should include images, for they may also play a key role in mediating emotions. Some clients are, however, immobilized by terrifying images that may involve imagined rape, violence, or actual events that have left a permanent imprint upon their minds. Using images requires skill, particularly when a client has experienced a traumatic event firsthand. Further, the use of images in these situations is not advisable in other than very controlled circumstances.

3. Assist clients in identifying situations that engender dysfunctional cognitions. As practitioners and clients review completed log sheets and continue to identify problematic feelings and cognitions associated with stressful events, it is important to note recurring situations and themes. Pinpointing the place where stressful events occur, key persons involved in them, situations that involve tearing oneself down for failing to fulfill self-expectations, and the like enables you and your clients to develop tasks and coping strategies tailor-made for those specific situations. Clients who have difficulties controlling anger

may discover that certain situations or types of persons consistently trigger their anger. Other clients may experience depression after having disputes with their spouses or with certain children. Still others may feel inadequate and demean themselves severely after interactions that have involved the slightest hint of criticism by others. Again, awareness of their areas of vulnerability often lowers clients' susceptibility to dysfunctional thoughts and feelings.

4. Assist clients in substituting functional self-statements in place of self-defeating cognitions. As clients gain expanded awareness of their dysfunctional thoughts, beliefs, and images and recognize how these produce negative emotional reactions, they generally welcome efforts to learn new coping patterns. These coping strategies consist of employing self-statements that are both realistic and effective in eliminating negative emotional reactions and self-defeating behaviors. Although functional self-statements foster courage and facilitate active coping efforts, they are not idealistic and do not ignore the struggles inherent in shifting from habitual, ingrained patterns of thinking, feeling, and behaving to new patterns. In fact, as with coping modeling, coping self-statements embody recognition of the difficulties and anxiety inherent in risking new behavior. To introduce clients to coping self-statements, we recommend an explanation similar to the following:

- "Now that you've identified many of your key self-defeating beliefs and thoughts, we're going to focus on how to replace them with new self-statements. It will take a lot of hard work on your part, but as you practice new coping self-statements, you'll find that they will become more and more natural to you until they finally crowd out the old ones."

After providing such an explanation, it is desirable to model coping self-statements that can be substituted for self-defeating thoughts and beliefs. In modeling, it is helpful to explain that you are going to assume the role of the client and are going to think aloud as the client might when coping with a target situation. To illustrate the process, we return to our socially inhibited client and model coping self-statements he might substitute for self-defeating ones before joining his co-workers in the lunchroom.

1. "I know a part of me wants to avoid the discomfort of socializing, but it's not going to get any better by not becoming involved."

2. "I don't have to say a lot to be part of the group. If I listen to the others and get my mind off myself, I can involve myself more."

3. "I can't expect them to draw me into the conversations. It would be nice if they did, but if I'm going to be included, I'll have to be responsible for including myself. I can do it even though it's going to take courage and strong effort. It's better than withdrawing and feeling out of it."

Notice in these self-statements that the practitioner models the struggle going on within the client rather than modeling "mastery" self-statements. This is important because coping self-statements lie close to clients' actual experience, whereas mastery self-statements do not. Moreover, the former convey empathy for and understanding of the client's struggle, which in turn inspires greater confidence in the process and in the practitioner.

After modeling coping self-statements, it is appropriate to ask if the client feels ready to practice similar behavior. With a little encouragement, most clients agree to engage in guided practice. To enhance the effectiveness of this practice, we recommend suggesting that clients close their eyes and picture themselves in the exact situation they will be in before engaging in the targeted behavior. When they report they have succeeded in capturing this situation, ask them to think aloud the thoughts they typically experience when contemplating the targeted behavior. Then ask them to substitute coping thoughts and coach them as needed. Give positive feedback as they produce functional statements independently and provide

encouragement as they struggle with conflicting thoughts. Expect your clients to express doubt and uncertainty about their ability to master new patterns of thinking and explain that most people experience misgivings as they experiment with new ways of thinking. Continue to practice with them until they feel relatively comfortable in their ability to generate coping self-statements. When clients demonstrate increased confidence in employing coping self-statements before entering a target situation, you can shift to a strategy for the *during* stage. Again, model coping self-statements, of which the following are examples with our same client:

1. "Okay, so I'm feeling anxious. That's to be expected. I can still pay attention and show interest in the others. That's it, look at the others and smile. What they're talking about is interesting. Ask them for clarification if I want to know more. That'll show them I'm interested."

2. "I have some thoughts on the subject they're discussing. My opinions are worth as much as theirs. Go ahead, take a chance and express them, but look at others as I talk."

After modeling, ask how the client is feeling about what has happened so far. This is important, for if clients are overly anxious, uncomfortable, or skeptical, you must first deal with these feelings before proceeding further. If they continue to respond positively, you may then ask them to rehearse coping self-statements, following essentially the same format as for the preceding phase.

When clients have demonstrated beginning ability to generate coping self-statements in the during phase, they are ready to enter the *after* phase. Again, it is important to model coping self-statements, of which the following are examples:

1. "Well, I did it. I stuck it out and even said a couple of things. That's a step in the right direction."

2. "No one looked down their nose when I expressed myself. They appeared genuinely interested. Maybe I'm not so bad after all."

3. "Even though it was sweaty, it went pretty well, even better than I expected. I handled it, and that's an accomplishment. I'll join them again tomorrow and maybe do even better."

After modeling self-statements, you should again explore the clients' reactions and feelings. If they indicate they are ready, you can then proceed to having them rehearse more coping self-statements. To assist clients to apply coping statements in actual life situations, it is beneficial to negotiate tasks that they can tackle between sessions. It is important, of course, not to rush clients, for undue pressure may threaten or discourage them. Again, we suggest using the readiness scale, as defined earlier in this chapter, to gauge their readiness.

Continued self-monitoring by clients is essential as clients implement step 4. Maintaining a daily log, employing the format suggested earlier (but augmented with a fourth column headed with the caption "Rational or Coping Self-Statements"), facilitates active ongoing efforts by clients and requires them to attempt to place situations and events in realistic perspective by identifying coping self-statements they can substitute for self-defeating ones. Furthermore, maintaining a log and implementing tasks foster independent action by clients.

Substituting coping self-statements for self-defeating thoughts or misconceptions is the heart of cognitive restructuring. Because they tend to be automatic and deeply embedded, however, dysfunctional thoughts tend to persist and clients sometimes become discouraged when they do not achieve quick mastery of them. It is important to recognize that step 4 extends across a number of weeks. When clients express discouragement, we find they are reassured when we explain that change is only gradual and that it takes most people several weeks at least before they achieve a satisfactory degree of mastery.

Nevertheless, we stress that they can hasten the process by planning at the beginning of each day to anticipate situations they will encounter that present opportunities for using their newly discovered coping skills.

Another technique that equips clients to cope with automatic dysfunctional self-statements is to encourage them at first awareness of such thoughts to nip them in the bud. We explain to clients that their first awareness of such thoughts is a flashing signal that they need to apply coping techniques. One way of coping is "to have a talk with oneself," reminding oneself that it is vital to *make a choice* not to continue thinking dysfunctional thoughts. Permitting such thoughts to continue leads to predictable undesired emotional reactions and reinforces the dysfunctional pattern. By contrast, stopping negative self-statements averts negative reactions and adds another increment of growth in the quest for mastery.

Assist clients in rewarding themselves for successful coping efforts. For clients who attend only to their failures and shortcomings and rarely, if ever, give themselves a pat on the back, this step is especially important. Aimed at reinforcing coping efforts, this step also assists clients in savoring their progress in learning still another new and functional cognitive pattern.

In implementing this step, it is desirable to explain the rationale of giving oneself credit for progress. The following is an example of such an explanation:

• "Louise, now that you've experienced some success in substituting coping self-statements for self-defeating ones, it's important to learn to give yourself credit for your well-deserved accomplishment. By giving yourself a pat on the back, you savor your success and encourage yourself to continue with your efforts. It's also an important way of learning to feel good about yourself. I'm going to help you learn to reward yourself by pretending I'm you and thinking aloud self-statements you might make after a successful coping experience."

After providing such an explanation, you then model several laudatory self-statements of which the following are typical examples:

1. "You weren't sure you could do it, but you did."

2. "You didn't back off. You were able to dismiss those negative thoughts."

3. "That was a big step. You are making progress and you've made a really good start, and it feels just great."

As with step 4, you should elicit the client's reactions to your explanation and modeling. If clients appear receptive, instruct them to recreated a recent success and practice making approving self-statements by expressing them aloud. Because positive self-statements are alien to many clients, initially they may feel awkward or self-conscious. Empathic understanding and encouragement on your part will usually prompt them to begin, and they may actually enjoy the experience. Indeed, it is vital to give consistent positive feedback, identifying the small and often-subtle increments of growth clients achieve.

To facilitate the transfer of coping skills form sessions to real life, it is important to negotiate tasks with clients that involve making positive self-statements about their progress and about other accomplishments in daily living. Self-monitoring is again a valuable tool. We recommend asking clients to record in their logs all their daily successes, including small ones they may be inclined to overlook, and to record self-statements that give themselves credit for the achievements. This approach can be a powerful means of eliminating patterns of attending selectively to shortcomings, failures, and negative experiences.

Limitations of Cognitive Restructuring

In assisting clients to make changes, practitioners must not mistakenly assume that clients can perform new behaviors solely as a result of cognitive changes. Often clients lack social skills and require instruction and practice before they can effectively perform new behaviors, such as making social overtures, expressing personal feelings, engaging in problem solving, and asserting themselves. Cognitive restructuring removes cognitive barriers to change and fosters willingness to risk new behaviors but does not equip clients with requisite skills. In the next chapter, we focus on behavioral interventions that enable clients to learn requisite coping skills. In actual practice, combining these skills with cognitive structuring produces a potent package for effecting desired changes.

Summary

The goal attainment strategies discussed in this chapter may be used with clients in a variety of situations. The three approaches are empirically based, time limited, and emphasize the capacity to change and grow. They represent systematic processes for achieving desired changes as a result of the collaborative actions taken by the client or practitioner. This aspect, along with an emphasis on increasing the power of clients to participate in and influence change in their lives, are perhaps the most salient characteristics of each approach.

As we noted in the beginning of this chapter, intervention begins with a clear description of goals. For the intervention to be effective, it is critical that the goal attainment strategy selected is consistent with the problem or behavior agreed upon with the client. It has been our experience as practitioners that people who come in contact with social workers are seeking relief. Often, they are overwhelmed and may be immobilized by the complexity and longevity of their problems. The very act of setting goals, taking action, and being able to see movement is in and of itself an empowering experience. They are energized and motivated when they are able to see progress toward a desired outcome.

Internet Resources

 Useful information on crisis intervention is available at *http://www.vcsun.org/ ~sharbet/433/433crisis.html/* and *http:// www.cmrg.com/*. You can also access resources about cognitive therapy, brief therapy, and the task-centered approach at *http://www.cognitivetherapy.com/*; *http://www. brief-therapy.org/hottips.htm*; and *http://www.task-centered.com/*. You can also use InfoTrac® with the keywords "crisis intervention," "task-centered practice," and "cognitive therapy."

Notes

1. The importance of careful planning in direct practice has been emphasized by A. Rosen, Proctor, and Livne (1985). For a discussion of components that practitioners should consider in planning treatment strategies, you will find this article useful.

2. To adequately discuss the integration of treatments with diverse clinical problems, however, would require writing a separate volume. In the field of clinical psychology, Beutler and Clarkin (1990) have done just that, and we highly recommend their book. O'Hare (1991) has written a useful article for social workers that provides a framework for integrating research and practice.

3. W. J. Reid (1992) has elaborated specific task strategies to address a great variety of client problems and situations.

4. A series of videotapes depicting individual and family practice using the task-centered approach is available from Ronald Rooney at the University of Minnesota.

5. Much of the information in this section is taken from Hepworth (1979).

6. Of necessity, the preceding discussion of CI has been brief. For more extensive expositions of CI, we recommend as resources the works of A. R. Roberts (1990), Parad and Parad (1990), and Wells and Giannetti (1990).

7. Walen, DiGiuseppe, and Wessler (1980) present and illustrate comprehensive strategies for disputing beliefs, and we strongly recommend this reference.

8. We wish to acknowledge that this schema is based on one developed by Aaron Beck and colleagues as presented in *Cognitive Therapy of Depression* (A. Beck et al., 1979, Appendix).

CHAPTER 14

Enhancing Clients' Problem Solving, Social, Assertiveness, and Stress Management Skills

CHAPTER OVERVIEW

This chapter builds on previous skills in communicating with clients, assessing their concerns, and developing useful contracts to equip you with skills to enhance problem solving, social skills, assertiveness and stress management.

Humans constantly encounter situations, events, and problems that require coping responses. Effective coping with the diverse demands of daily living requires skills in making decisions, communicating, solving problems, resolving conflicts, and managing stresses. Increasing evidence from research studies suggests that these and other coping skills are essential to sound mental health and behavioral adjustment. Ineffective coping in problematic situations, in fact, can lead to emotional and behavioral disorders that have a severe impact on functioning.

Clients seek professional help when their coping efforts have failed to remedy problematic situations. Some clients possess meager coping skills and others have rich coping repertoires that have been temporarily overwhelmed by virtually insuperable stresses. It is the former group, however, that most frequently comes to the attention of social workers.

Over the past 30 years, human service social workers and researchers have increasingly devoted attention to ways of increasing clients' coping capacities by assessing strengths and resources as well as deficits or challenges (as we described in Chapter 8). Training programs have been developed to assist clients in developing many skills. Four areas of skills training that have broad application—problem solving, social skills, assertiveness, and stress management—are the topics of this chapter. Chapter 16 focuses on other interpersonal skills that are vital in families, groups, and other social contexts.

PROBLEM-SOLVING SKILLS

Teaching clients problem-solving skills can equip them to cope more effectively with the myriad difficulties they will encounter in the future. A major advantage of learning problem solving is that the principles can be readily transferred from one situation to another. At this point, some clarification is in order. We have previously made repeated reference to the problem-solving process, and you may be confused as to why clients need additional assistance in learning to apply problem-solving strategies. After all, clients and social workers engage in problem solving, so isn't it logical to assume they learn the process? The answer is that most clients probably do learn something about the problem-solving process, but what they usually learn is likely to be incomplete. In fact, many social workers have difficulty delineating precisely the elements of independent problem solving. Utilizing problem solving to assist clients in coping with discrete problems and teaching them the principles in preparation for coping independently with future problems are different processes. We propose that social workers engage in both processes, thereby seeking not only to remedy immediate problems but also to enhance clients' future coping capacities.

Our proposal is not new. About 30 years ago, behaviorally oriented psychologists (D'Zurilla & Goldfried, 1971) advocated that social workers assist clients to enhance their problem-solving skills. These authors maintained that much of what was viewed as abnormal or disturbed behavior could be viewed as resulting from ineffective behavior that fails to solve life's challenging problems and leads to undesired effects such as anxiety and depression. Support for their view came from the research of Spivack, Platt, and Shure (1976), who reported two major findings. First, deviant or abnormal people manifested inferior skills in problem solving compared with "normal" people. The former group (1) generated fewer possible solutions to hypothetical problem situations than the latter, (2) suggested solutions that often were antisocial, and (3) had very inaccurate expectations about probable consequences of alternate solutions. Other researchers similarly found deficiencies in problem-solving skills among conflicted marriages as compared with nonconflicted marriages (Vincent, Weiss, & Birchler, 1976). Subsequent studies have extended the findings to conduct-disordered adolescents (Tisdelle & St. Lawrence, 1988), antisocial children (Kazdin, Esveldt-Dawson, French, & Unis, 1987), depressed children (Weisz et al., 1987), Vietnam veterans with posttraumatic stress disorder (Nezu & Carnevale, 1987), suicidal psychiatric patients (Schotte & Clum, 1987), people with alcoholism (Jacob, Ritchey, Cvitkovic, & Blane, 1981), and people with schizophrenia (Kelly & Lamparski, 1985).

The second major finding of Spivack et al. (1976) was that promising results were obtained in several projects in which youth received systematic training in problem solving. Of particular relevance have been similar results indicating that instruction in and practice of problem-solving skills assist children with antisocial behavioral patterns (Kazdin et al., 1987), nondelinquent early adolescents (LeCroy & Rose, 1986), predelinquent youth (Kifer, Lewis, Green, & Phillips, 1974), and delinquent adolescents (Tisdelle & St. Lawrence, 1988) to deal with conflictual situations more effectively. Other findings indicate that training in problem solving also assists families to function more harmoniously (Blechman, 1974; Blechman, Olson, Schornagel, Halsdorf, & Turner, 1976).

Still another study (Nezu, 1985) found that self-appraised effective problem solvers reported less depression, less anxiety, a greater sense of internal control, fewer problems, and less distress than those who appraised themselves as ineffective problem solvers.

It is thus clear that many of the most vexing problems encountered in social work involve clients whose capacities for coping with problems of living are inadequate. The research findings that systematic efforts to remedy these deficiencies have produced higher levels of functioning are most promising.

By mastering a systematic approach to making decisions and solving problems, clients gain the following benefits:

- Learn a process that promotes collaboration, cohesiveness, and mutual respect among family or group members.
- Prevent interpersonal conflicts produced by dysfunctional modes of reaching decisions or solving problems.
- Reduce tension, anxiety, and depression by solving stress-producing problems effectively.
- Generate a wider range of options for coping, thereby enhancing chances of selecting maximally effective decisions or solutions.

- Enhance the likelihood that family and group members will commit themselves to implementing options that are selected.

- Increase confidence, self-efficacy, and self-esteem by acquiring a mode of problem solving that can be employed in future problematic situations.

- Prevent children from developing dysfunctional coping patterns by including them in effective problem-solving efforts and by teaching and guiding them in employing such efforts.

Embedded in the preceding benefits and central to the rationale for independent problem solving is the preventive function of this intervention. Clients gradually achieve mastery of skills that they can transfer to the real world. Their dependence on social workers gradually decreases, and their self-reliance increases.

Before delineating problem-solving strategies and methods of assisting clients to learn them, we wish to clarify that theory related to making decisions and solving problems is not limited to the helping professions. Because of the importance of decision making in business management, governmental policy formulation, public administration, and other phases of life, numerous articles and entire books have been devoted to this topic. Across fields, authors agree that effective problem solving involves a systematic approach consisting of several discrete phases, and their views of the basic elements involved in problem solving are similar. The strategy we delineate is a synthesis of our own ideas with those of several authors, most notably Janis and Mann (1977), T. Gordon (1970), and Jacobson and Margolin (1979). We have adapted this strategy particularly for interpersonal situations typically encountered in families and groups.

Preparing Clients to Learn Problem-Solving Skills

Before delineating the steps involved in problem solving, we first discuss conditions prerequisite to introducing this intervention. Preparing clients is critical, for unless they are receptive (1) to learning the process and (2) to engaging in collaborative efforts with the social worker and with each other, employing this intervention is likely to be futile. Early in the helping process, clients often meet neither of these conditions, and social workers therefore face the challenges of enlisting their willingness to engage in the process and of fostering a collaborative set.

Several strategies can be employed to influence clients to adopt a collaborative set, including the following:

- Lay groundwork during the initial contracting process.

- Demonstrate the need to learn problem solving by focusing on the destructive impact of self-defeating interaction.

- Enhance use of capacities by intervening to increase positive and collaborate interactions.

- Accredit collaborative efforts and highlight the connections between these efforts and positive outcomes.

- Define problems as belonging to a system rather than to any one person.

In the following sections, we consider the preceding strategies in greater detail.

Lay Groundwork During the Initial Contracting Process

We consider the learning of problem-solving skills a vital component of most contracts established by the social worker with couples, families, or groups. As you may recall, in Chapter 1 we encouraged social workers to develop a contract with new groups to the effect that all members will be "accounted in" in decision making and also stressed the need for social workers to teach decision-making steps to groups in initial sessions. In Chapter 10, we also emphasized that many families have both dysfunctional interactional patterns and ineffective styles of decision making that discount the needs of some or all members—which perpetuates resentment, unrest, and conflict. Thus, opportunities to negotiate the goal of learning to apply effective problem-solving methods often occur when clients are seen in conjoint sessions. For example, we have worked with many couples and families with presenting problems similar to the following:

- "Our ideas about child-rearing are totally different, which creates constant friction between use and confuses our children."

- "We bicker constantly in our family about who should do the dishes, vacuum the rugs, and cut the grass. We just can't seem to work together on anything."

Common to each of the preceding presenting complaints is failure of the participants to work collaboratively in solving problems related to carrying out vital functions within a family. By reflecting these complaints in terms of wants, you focus on the necessity for collaborative problem solving and thus pave the way to negotiating a goal of learning mutual problem solving, as illustrated in the following responses to the problems:

- "You seem to be saying you're working at cross purposes in rearing your children, which causes divisiveness between you and is hard on your children. I gather you're feeling a need to resolve your differences and *to learn to work together as partners.*"

- [*To family member*]: "Sounds like the constant bickering creates a strain and leads nowhere. I'm sensing that learning ways of working together as a family in planning to get things done could improve things in your family."

Clients generally respond affirmatively to such messages, indicating some degree of receptivity to learning collaborative problem solving. The social worker can then suggest that later in the session they may want to consider a goal of learning a problem-solving process that has proven effective in resolving difficulties similar to their own. Subsequently, during the contracting process, clients themselves may select as goals learning to make decisions or to cope with marital or family difficulties without excessive conflict. If clients do

not identify such goals, you may make reference to the difficulties they described earlier and again suggest that seeking to develop effective problem-solving strategies may be an effective way of remedying identified problems and of averting similar problems in the future.

Demonstrate the Need to Learn the Problem-Solving Process

This strategy can be employed in tandem with the preceding strategy or can be introduced later at an expedient time. Implementing the strategy in the former instance involves providing an expanded explanation of the benefits of learning to collaborate in problem solving. In the latter instance, after observing clients engage in competitive, unproductive interaction that produces stain, the social worker capitalizes on their obvious frustration by emphasizing the destructive impact of the interaction, drawing attention to how each participant contributes to the dysfunctional behavior and presenting a case for learning effective problem solving strategies. Executed well, such a timely intervention often motivates clients to welcome modifying their contract to include a goal of learning problem-solving strategies. The following illustrates application of this intervention strategy in the third interview with Rose and Gary Wilson, a couple who sought help with difficulties involving intense conflicts in many aspects of their marriage. The social worker intervenes following a heated interchange between the partners involving Rose's criticism of Gary's handling of their 8-year-old son, Danny:

Social worker: You're both pretty angry with each other right now, and if you continue along the same lines, you're likely to get even angrier. Let's stop a moment and consider what's happening between you.

Gary: You're damn right I'm mad. She always thinks she has the answers. It's like my opinion couldn't possibly be worth anything.

Rose: That's not true, and you know it. It's just that you expect too much of Danny.

Gary [*shakes head in disgust*]: What's the use? I can't get through to her.

Social worker: Wait a minute! I know that you both have some strong feelings right now and it is hard to disengage, but it is very important that we look at what's going wrong. Are you willing to do that now? [*They agree.*] Both of you have your ideas about what you need to do with Danny—right? [*Each nods.*] What's happening is that each of you believes you're right and you're trying to convince the other. Then each of you gets uptight because the other doesn't listen and puts your ideas down. So you end up arguing. Am I right? [*They concede this happens.*] You get into a battle of "Who's right," and both of you only lose when you get caught up in that. You get mad at each other, and your communication breaks down just as it did a few moments ago.

Rose: Well, I think you've describe it pretty well. But what do we do about it?

Social worker [*smiling*]: I thought you'd never ask. All kidding aside, what I'd like to suggest is that the two of you consider working toward a goal of learning a method of solving problems that avoids getting into hassles. It involves working together, seeking to understand each other's views, and searching together for solutions that are acceptable to both of you, rather than struggling over who's right. The advantage of learning this method is that you learn to work *with* rather than against each other.

Gary: That'd be different for a change.

Social worker: Then I take it the idea has some appeal to you. [*Both nod in agreement.*] Do you feel it might be a goal you'd like to tackle, then?

Rose: I'm game. I think it might really help us. What we're doing now isn't working—that's for sure. How about you, Gary?

Gary: Let's do it.

Obtaining a commitment to work collaboratively is a crucial step in achieving a climate conducive to the change process, but it would be naïve to assume that commitment alone is sufficient. Persistent effort is required to break established patterns of interaction. The same applies to formed groups, for members bring with them patterns of communication they habitually employ in other contexts. Furthermore, people can employ only those skills they already possess. Therefore, for some clients, learning to solve problems collaboratively may entail learning a new set of skills. Consequently, the next two strategies are essential in assisting contentious members of systems to achieve a collaborative set.

Intervene to Produce Collaborative Interactions

Tactics involved in this strategy are twofold. First, the social worker actively intervenes to arrest negative, competitive, and other destructive patterns of interaction. Interrupting such dysfunctional interaction, the social worker translates or redefines negative, blaming messages into expressions of needs or wants or requests for change. The second tactic involves inducing collaborative interaction by recognizing constructive patterns and teaching clients to express their needs, to listen attentively, to personalize their feelings, and to give positive feedback. The potency of collaborative interaction derives from the fact that enabling clients to engage in such interactions assists them to learn new modes of behavior and to experience the benefits of them. Experiencing the benefits of collaborating enables clients to gain a measure of success and satisfaction from this different mode of relating, which in turn encourages additional efforts to collaborate with other members of the system and with the social worker. Implementation of the preceding techniques is illustrated in the following excerpt involving parents and an adolescent daughter.

Daughter [*to parents*]: You're on my back all the time. Why don't you get off my case for a change? [*Attacking, blaming message.*]

Father: We wouldn't be on your case if you'd get in at night when you're supposed to. [*Counterattacking message.*]

Daughter: Well, if you'd quit bugging me, maybe I'd feel more like getting in. Besides, you expect me to be home before any of the other kids, and it isn't fair. [*More of same.*]

Mother: I don't think eleven o'clock is unreasonable. [*Defensive response.*]

Social worker: I'd like to stop and see if we can understand better just what's troubling everyone here. Each of you has some needs that aren't being met, and let's begin by seeing if we can identify what those needs are. I'd like each of you just to listen and try to understand the other person's needs. You may not agree with each other, but I would like to ask you to hold your disagreement for a while. Just try to understand. Let's begin with you, Betty. From what you were saying, I sensed you're wanting more room to move around. You'd like more freedom, am I right?

Notice the destructive interaction among the family members characterized by verbal attacks, blaming messages, defensiveness, and counterattacks. The social worker intervenes and begins to translate the blaming messages into needs. The social worker further requests the participants to listen to and attempt to understand each other's needs. We now pick up the interaction where we left off.

Daughter: Yeah! That's right. I get tired of being nagged all the time.

Social worker: OK. But let's stay with what you want. Would you tell your parents specifically what positive changes you'd like? Tell them what you'd like them to do, not what you feel they're doing wrong. [*Maintaining focus on her want; suggesting she request positive changes.*]

Daughter: I'll try. Well, I'd like you to give me more freedom. I feel you're trying to control me, and I'm able to run my own life. You act like you don't trust me.

Social worker [*to parents*]: So she's telling you she wants more freedom and wants to be treated as an adult. Was that the message you got? [*Still*

focusing on her wants; checking out meaning attribution with parents.]

Father: Yeah, but ...

Social worker: I would appreciate it if we could save the "but" for later. Right now I think it's important to work on understanding your needs. [*To parents*] Let's turn to your needs now. What positive changes would each of you like to see happen?

In this last response, the social worker assertively intervened to avert sidetracking that would likely follow father's "but." The social worker maintains focus on the participants' needs, shifting to the parents' needs. Now return to the interaction.

Mother: I'd like Betty to get in earlier. I worry when she stays out late.

Social worker: That tells me you have some fears. Can you tell Betty what those fears are?

Mother: Betty, I know you're basically a good kid. But I do worry. Even the best of kids can get into trouble when they spend too much time together late at night.

Social worker [*to Betty*]: Betty, I hope you're hearing what your mother is telling you. She's expressing a concern for you—not distrust or wanting to control you. [*To mother*] Why all the concern? Please tell Betty. I'll tell you in a minute why I ask.

In the last response, notice how the social worker facilitates understanding and positive interaction by clarifying that mother's fears emanate from positive concern, not from distrust or a desire to control Betty. In the last question, the social worker seeks to elicit further positive feelings, as reflected in the continuation of the interaction.

Mother: Well, Betty, it's because we—well—you're our only daughter. We love you. We don't want anything bad to happen.

Social worker: I'll tell you now why I asked. I sensed you were concerned because Betty's so important to you. But I'm not sure that message had gotten through to Betty. [*To Betty*] What you've thought is that your parents have wanted to control you. Do you hear that underneath all of their negative messages is love and concern for you? [*Clarifying further the parents' positive concerns and facilitating positive feedback.*]

Daughter: I do right now. But that isn't what I've been hearing lately. No way!

Social worker: But you hear it now. How does that make you feel right now? Can you tell your parents? [*Maintaining focus on positive feedback.*]

Daughter: Good. Real good. Like maybe they're not so bad after all.

Social worker: Well, maybe you're beginning to understand each other a little better. [*To father*] We didn't hear from you, dad. Could you let us know your needs or wants? [*Drawing father into discussion of needs and wants.*]

Father: My wife expressed them pretty well. Not much I could add.

Social worker: Nevertheless, I'd like Betty to hear it from you. Could you tell Betty your feelings?

Notice in the preceding excerpts that the social worker identified the needs of each participant, an important step in problem solving discussed at length later in the chapter. Further, the social worker actively intervened each time the participants began to revert to negative messages. By being attuned to the concerns and underlying love inherent in the mother's statement, the social worker rechanneled the interaction in positive directions. The social worker thus elicited feelings of caring, and what began as typical dysfunctional interaction was converted into an embryonic form of collaborative communication. This strategy incidentally provides participants with an initial "success" experience in communicating in a positive manner about problems.

We cannot emphasize too strongly your responsibility as a social worker in converting negative interaction to positive interaction. Except for making an initial assessment, no constructive purpose

is served by passively permitting clients to engage in destructive patterns of communication, whether the target system be a couple, family, or group.

Accredit Collaborative Efforts

This strategy is employed to reinforce spontaneous collaborative behavior on the part of clients and to enhance their awareness of consequent beneficial effects by highlighting connections between positive behavioral change and its beneficial effects. Although collaborative behavior tends to be self-reinforcing because it produces positive results, expressing recognition and approval of collaborative efforts further reinforces such behavior. Moreover, assisting clients to discern the association between their collaborative behavior and its favorable results further enables them to make choices to interact collaboratively, as illustrated in the following:

Social worker [*to group*]: I'd like to point out something that just happened that pleased me a great deal. You'll recall in our first session you agreed as members to assist one another to understand each other's problems better and to work cooperatively in searching for solutions. I know we struggled in our last session with interruptions and with members trying to talk at the same time. Well, what pleases me is that during these past minutes as Julie shared her problems we really began to work as a group. Everyone listened, no one interrupted, and several of you supported Julie in her struggle to express herself. As a result, Julie appeared to open up and shared more with us. I was really impressed with how you pitched in as a group. Julie, I'd like to hear how it felt to you.

Julie: Well, it was hard at first, but like you said, it got easier. I really felt everyone was behind me. It felt great.

Define Problems as Belonging to the System

When a client reveals a problem, significant others tend to see the problem as residing solely with that person and to disclaim any part in it. From the standpoint of systems theory, however, problems of one member are problems of the system, and other members share responsibility for working out solutions. Moreover, solutions are far more likely to be efficacious if contributions of all members to the problem are considered and if all participate in planning corrective measures. In formed groups, the situation is somewhat different, for members have not contributed to the preexisting problems of others. In becoming part of the new system, however, each makes a commitment to assist other members, and each member shares responsibility for contributing to the effective functioning of the group. Further, as groups evolve, all participants contribute in some manner to dysfunctional group processes and all have capacities to escape them.

The following are typical examples of how participants mutually contribute to problematic situations:

- Mrs. Adams complains that her husband spends little time with her. He agrees but explains he spends increasing time away from home because she nags and badgers him constantly.

- Mr. Sharp expresses a desire for his wife to make sexual overtures. She explains that she has desires to do so but when she has made overtures in the past he has rebuffed her. To avoid the resultant hurt, she decided not to take the risk.

- Parents of 15-year-old Alan complain he seldom talks to them about his daily activities. He agrees but explains that when he has shared in the past his parents criticized him or gave him lectures.

It is apparent in the preceding examples that all of the participants play a part in the problems. Your task is to assist all parties to recognize their respective parts and to agree to make behavioral changes accordingly. This is not easy, for people tend to be more aware of and to focus more on the distressing behaviors of others than on their own; hence, their tendency is to define solutions in terms of changes *others* need to make. However, by intervening and guiding clients to

interact collaboratively, you assist them not only to reveal their respective perceptions of problematic situations but also to listen attentively to others' views. You can further enhance their receptivity to owning their respective parts by explaining that successful change results from each person working to change his or her own behavior, not from trying to change others.

Perhaps the most effective strategy of assisting people to define problems as mutually owned is to appeal to their self-interest. If they can see a payoff for themselves, they will be inclined to participate in seeking a solution. For example, if a husband is helped to consider how his wife's depression or unhappiness negatively affects him, dampening his interaction with her and reducing his own satisfaction and happiness, he is likely to be receptive in helping her to overcome her depression. Through this involvement, he may also be helped to see how he has contributed to her depression. Similarly, if you assist family members to recognize that improved functioning of one person enhances relationships and solidarity within the system, they will be more likely to accept responsibility for participating actively in problem solving.

By defining problems as mutually owned and clarifying the part each participant plays in maintaining them, you enhance the likelihood that participants will be willing to initiate positive behavioral changes. Manifest willingness on the part of one person tends to foster reciprocal willingness by others. No one loses face because no one is defined as the sole cause of the problems. Moreover, impasses tend to dissolve as each person becomes aware that others care enough to acknowledge their parts and to commit themselves to making changes.

Introducing the Problem-Solving Process

After clients have begun to engage in collaborative interactions, have demonstrated beginning awareness of behaviors entailed in such interactions, and have contracted to learn the problem-solving process, it is appropriate to introduce them to the process and then to guide them in applying it to some of their problems. Before defining the formal process, however, it is vital to explain conditions prerequisite to using it effectively. Carefully explaining these conditions and the rationale behind them further enhances receptivity and prepares clients to implement the process successfully.

Introducing clients to the process begins by clarifying its nature with an explanation similar to the following:

> "Let's begin by clarifying what the problem-solving process is all about. Basically, it's an approach that will enable you to collaborate in solving problems or in reaching decisions effectively. It involves a number of steps that will assist you to define problems accurately and to generate several possible solutions so that you can select the best possible one. The best option is the one that meets your needs best, so another step involves helping you to identify and understand each other's needs. There are also guidelines that will assist you to work together and to avoid needless and unproductive hassles."

It is also critical to clarify that the process is *effective* and that clients can succeed in applying it, but only if they commit themselves to following the steps and guidelines. However strong their good intentions, they will tend to revert to habitual patterns of interaction, and if they permit this to happen, they will likely end up arguing, blaming, or playing "who wins." For this reason, it is vital to differentiate problem solving from other interactions. Clients must understand that when they agree to engage in problem solving they commit themselves to follow the structured pattern of interaction. In sessions, the social worker will guide them in adhering to these steps and guidelines. Outside the sessions, they must practice carefully to avoid falling into habitual patterns of interaction.

Managing Interaction During Problem Solving

Before teaching the actual steps of the problem-solving process, it is important to be prepared to manage clients' interaction and to guide them so that they adhere to the steps and thereby achieve successful results. Toward this end, the social worker should assist clients to observe the following guidelines:

- Be specific in relating problems.
- Focus on the present problem rather than on past difficulties.
- Focus on only one problem at a time.
- Listen attentively to others who are sharing problems.
- Share problems in a positive and constructive manner.

In the following sections we delineate each of these guidelines.

Guideline 1. Be Specific in Relating Problems

To define a problem accurately, it is essential to express it so that others can determine the specific nature of one's concerns or needs. Further, specifying problems with precision avoids the confusion and misunderstanding that may result from expressing them in vague and general terms. You can utilize the skill of seeking concreteness to elicit specific details of clients' problems. Keep in mind that when clients express problems globally, you will need to press for details and clarify the importance of pinpointing difficulties.

Guideline 2. Focus on the Present Problem Rather Than on Past Difficulties

As you help clients to define problems, it is important to maintain focus on the present. Needless and fruitless arguments over circumstances and details tend to ensue when clients dredge up numerous examples of problematic behavior from the past. Details of recent difficulties do help in pinpointing problematic behavior at times, but more than a few examples amount to overkill. We therefore recommend that you develop a contract with clients specifying the need to focus on present problems and that you intervene to refocus the process when clients begin to employ lengthy recitations of past events as verbal ammunition against others.

Guideline 3. Focus on Only One Problem at a Time

Clients often have a tendency to bring up a problem and then rapidly shift to another, which diffuses their effort and impairs the helping process. Shifts in focus (*sidetracking*) may result from deliberate diversionary tactics or occur because some people have difficulty staying on one topic for any length of time.

When clients sidetrack, it is important to intervene and bring them back to the original problem. It is also important to assist them to discern sidetracking by labeling it and clarifying how it blocks problem-solving efforts. You can further assist clients to cope independently by intervening when sidetracking occurs, asking them to identify what they are doing. They will usually correctly identify their shift in focus. An effective method of assisting clients to reduce sidetracking is to negotiate tasks with them to monitor their interaction between sessions, attempting to avoid sidetracking, gently drawing the attention of others to the fact they are sidetracking, and refocusing on the original topic.

Guideline 4. Listen Attentively to Others Who Are Sharing Problems

Implementing this guideline means that others must suspend judgment about the validity of a person's concerns and feelings and hold in check the natural tendency to express contrary views or to advise the person as to what she or he should do to resolve the problem. To ascertain that one fully understands what the other person is saying, it is important to check out perceptions by giving feedback. Summarizing what one has heard is an effective means of providing feedback that enables the person who has shared the problem to determine if others have accurately understood the intended message.

This guideline is critical, for how others respond to the sharing of a problem determines whether a positive and collaborative climate will evolve or whether defensiveness will ensue. Although providing feedback may seem artificial and mechanical, it is a powerful way of enhancing collaborative communication.

You can facilitate clients' implementation of this guideline by instructing those who are to be recipients of a problem-sharing message to listen carefully and attempt to understand the sender's message and feelings. Ask clients to attempt to shut off their own thoughts and to put themselves in the shoes of other persons so that they can be fully attuned to those persons. After they have received the message, ask them to check out with the sender what they have heard; be prepared to intervene should the recipient of the message respond negatively. Coach them in using feedback until both sender and receiver agree upon the intended meaning of the message.

Guideline 5. Share Problems in a Positive and Constructive Manner

The way in which a person presents a problem sets a tone that tends to elicit either concern and collaboration or defensiveness from other participants. In presenting a problem or concern that involves the behavior of another participant, it is important to express the concern without blaming or attacking the other person. Expressing problems in the form of accusations, such as "You're insensitive to my feelings," "You never notice how hard I work," or "You've been staying out too late," tends to engender defensiveness or countercriticism, undermining the process almost before it starts. It is thus important that the person presenting the problem begin by expressing positive intent and by owning personal feelings rather than focusing on what another person is doing wrong. An effective way of introducing concerns is to send a positive, caring message before bringing up a concern. For example, contrast the following two messages of a pregnant, unwed adolescent and consider the likely impact upon a recipient:

- "Mom, you are a good mother and I know you care for me. I don't always show it, but I appreciate that. But I feel like it is my decision whether or not to have this baby, and I need support, not pressure, in making it."

- "Mom, you are always getting into my business, and now especially I need you to butt out because this is my baby and my decision."

Clients usually require help in expressing problems without blaming or attacking. When they express their problem or concerns in a negative manner, it is important to intervene immediately to avert destructive interaction. Explaining how blaming messages cause others to bristle or asking recipients of blaming messages to express their reactions assists clients to differentiate between positive messages that involve ownership of feelings and negative, accusatory messages. After making this clarification, coach the client in couching the concern or problem in a positive manner. During the course of subsequent interactions, you will likely need to intervene many times, for the *pull of* habituated patterns of communication is strong and clients revert to these patterns frequently.

In sharing problems, some clients also need help in learning to avoid making overgeneralized or absolute types of statements, such as "You *never* clean up after yourself" or "I *always* have to remind you to do your chores." Overgeneralizations have a negative effect on communication not only because they are accusatory but also because they are generally inaccurate. Recipients of such messages typically counterattack, seeking to disprove the validity of the accusation. Arguments then ensure and disputes tend to escalate.

When clients send overgeneralized messages, immediate interventions are indicated. We recommend that you stop the interaction, label the message as an overgeneralization (defining what that means), and clarify the destructive impact of such messages. You can then request the sender of the message to send an accurate and positively phrased message, coaching the person as needed.

Steps for Problem Solving

In the following sections, we delineate the steps of the problem-solving process and present techniques in assisting clients to master each step. To assist clients in grasping and applying this process, we recommend that you provide them with a reference sheet that lists the steps.

Before discussing the process with clients, explain that implementing the process does not *ensure* that resultant decisions and solutions will always produce desired results, for outcomes cannot always be predicted with accuracy. Employing the process avoids discord, however, and substantially enhances the chances of achieving favorable outcomes. Realistically, this is all that can be expected, for outcomes are usually determined by the interplay of many factors, some of which cannot be anticipated.

The steps of the problem-solving process are as follows:

- Acknowledge the problem.
- Analyze the problem and identify the needs of participants.
- Employ brainstorming to generate possible solutions.
- Evaluate each option, considering the needs of participants.
- Implement the option selected.
- Evaluate the outcome of problem-solving efforts.

We consider each of these steps in the following sections.

Step 1. Acknowledge the Problem

People often do not face problems until they become so severe that they can be ignored no longer. Furthermore, because facing problems often produces discomfort, some people attempt to rationalize their problems away or to ignore them in the hope they will disappear. Although it is true that some problems do clear up without planned corrective action, more often they worsen and expand, sometimes leaving in their wake irreparable damage, great expense, and mental anguish.

Explain this step to clients in a straightforward fashion, emphasizing that in their early stages problems usually are manageable. If ignored, however, problems may escalate severely.

Step 2. Analyze the Problem and Identify the Needs of Participants

This step is crucial, for participants in a problem situation often are prone to prematurely consider solutions before they have accurately analyzed the problem. Consequently, their solutions may be misdirected, resulting in wasted time and energy and causing discouragement. Moreover, clients' ensuing interaction may be adversarial, centering around whose proposed solution should be adopted. In fact, clients often start their "problem solving" with arguments over incompatible solutions rather than first assessing needs and then developing creative solutions that meet the needs of all concerned.

As you assist clients to analyze problems, it is important not to dwell on their problem at length or to engage in deep probing aimed at discovering the root causes of difficulties. The objective is not to search for causes, for doing so often leads to unproductive speculation. Rather, the purpose in analyzing problems is to discover factors that produce clients' difficulties and to identify the needs of participants that must be met in order to solve the problem to the satisfaction of all persons involved. To define problems accurately, clients must learn to adhere to the following guidelines:

- Pinpoint problematic behaviors and explicitly express feelings related to them (e.g., "When you go to a bar after work, I resent it and feel unimportant to you").

- Analyze who owns what part of the problems.
- Specify needs of the participants germane to the problematic situation.

Earlier we discussed the first two guidelines at length and need not elaborate further on them. The third guideline, however, merits elaboration. Specifying the needs of participants in problem situations is critical for two reasons. First, to be acceptable, any solution must satisfactorily meet the needs of all participants. Therefore, it is logical to identify the needs in advance so that clients can employ them as criteria for assessing possible solutions. Second, by sharing personal needs, clients are far more likely to be listened to receptively by other participants than by complaining about what others are doing. Identifying needs in problem solving further enhances collaboration because mutually seeking to determine and to understand each other's needs fosters mutual caring and respect. Equally important, identifying needs paves the way for arriving at a solution that best meets the needs of all concerned—the hallmark of effective problem solving.

The following are examples of messages that identify the needs of clients:

- "I don't like your going to the bar with your buddies several nights in a row. I feel unimportant to you when you spend so little time with me. I'd like to share more evenings with you."

- "It humiliates me when you get on my case in front of my friends. I would like to feel I can bring my friends home without fear of being embarrassed."

Notice that in the preceding messages the sender specifies the problematic behavior, the situational context, the emotional reaction to the behavior, and the unmet needs or wants. In addition, the senders own their own feelings, avoid accusatory comments, and focus on the immediate present.

Identifying needs of participants requires careful structuring of processes and active intervention, particularly in family sessions, for clients are quick to move from needs to accusations and criticisms of others. To avert defensive responses, it is often necessary to help clients reframe negative messages by modeling "I" messages for them and coaching them to alter parts of their subsequent messages so that they accurately identify and own their feelings and express their needs. Further, it is often necessary to guide recipients of "problem" messages to assume an "understanding" stance by using feedback to ascertain if they have grasped the intended meaning of the initial message.

To structure processes in a manner that assists clients to identify and to value the needs of each other, we recommend that you implement the following sequence of actions:

- Explain that the most effective solution to a problem is the one that best meets the needs of everyone concerned.

- Clarify that the needs of every person are important and that no one will be counted out in the problem-solving process. All persons will be asked in turn to identify their needs, and others will be asked to listen attentively and to seek to understand, seeking clarification as needed.

- Ask for a volunteer to write down needs as they are identified. If no one volunteers, you may request that a person serve as a recorder or do it yourself.

- Ask each person in succession to identify his or her personal needs, encouraging open discussion and requesting clarification when expressed needs are vague or confusing. Begin with the person who initially identified a problem. Ensure that needs are recorded, and have the recorder check with participants to ascertain that their needs are accurately worded and that none is omitted.

Before participants identify their needs, it is important to ask them not to challenge the needs identified by other participants or to debate whose needs are of highest priority when potential conflicts are apparent. Stress that identifying needs should be limited to just that. Further, clarify that assigning priorities and resolving conflicts come later in the problem-solving process. It is also vital to intervene to stop criticism or arguments, should either occur during discussion of needs.

Although identifying needs is important in problem solving with couples, families, and groups, we have chosen a family system to illustrate this process. The Taylor family has had frequent family squabbles about use of the family automobile. The social worker sees this as an opportunity to assist the family in learning problem-solving skills, and the parents and their two teenage children, Bert and Renee, both of whom drive, are receptive to learning this process.

The parents define the problem as heated arguments among family members over who will use their automobile on frequent occasions. They say that the children make excessive requests for the car, creating difficulties for them in meeting their obligations. The children mildly protest that they need a car for special activities. The social worker intervenes, explaining that all the family members have needs and that the objective is to seek a solution that best meets all their needs. Mr. Taylor nods with understanding and assures Bert and Renee that their needs are important and that they will work together to develop a solution to their liking. The social worker than explains the importance of recording the needs, and Renee volunteers to serve as recorder. In the ensuing discussion, the following needs are identified:

- *Bert:* Transportation for dates and for going to athletic events held at other schools.

- *Renee:* Transportation to sorority meetings and to go to a drive-in movie or to engage in other recreation with friends.

- *Mrs. T:* Transportation to the hairdresser's once a week and to the grocery store; also needs to visit her widowed mother several times a week and take her on errands.

- *Mr. T:* Transportation for bowling on Tuesday and for usual dinner date on Friday night with Mrs. T; also needs the car to drive to work.

Having identified their needs, the Taylors are ready to advance to step 3. We will rejoin them in step 4.

Step 3. Employ Brainstorming to Generate Possible Solutions

To reach sound decisions, participants need to consider a number of possible alternatives. Otherwise, they may limit their deliberations to one or two obvious options and overlook more promising alternatives. Brainstorming produces a wide range of possibilities through freewheeling discussion aimed at generating many possible solutions. Therefore, request all participants to stretch their thinking in identifying several creative solutions. If participants are hesitant or unable to suggest many alternatives, it is appropriate for you to offer additional possible solutions. The goal of effective decision making is to arrive at the best possible solution, not one that is merely satisfactory.

To maximize the productivity of brainstorming, it is essential that participants foster a climate of openness and receptivity to each other's ideas. Therefore, you should request that all participants refrain from criticizing or ridiculing suggestions, however impractical or absurd they may seem. Otherwise, participants will be hesitant to share their ideas for fear they will be rejected as stupid or silly. This step encourages the family or group norm that everyone is important and that criticism is detrimental to the system's process.

Brainstorming should be open, spontaneous, and freewheeling. Encourage participants to contribute their ideas, and give them positive feedback when they do so. The goal is to promote enthusiastic participation without evaluating any of the proposed solutions. To facilitate the subsequent process of evaluation, it is desirable to ask the recorder to list each proposed solution on a sheet of paper or on a chalkboard, leaving room on one side to enter ratings, as we illustrate later.

Step 4. Evaluate Each Option, Considering the Needs of Participants

This step is the heart of the decision-making process. If participants satisfactorily complete the preliminary steps, they enter step 4 with a cooperative frame of mind, ready to measure solutions generated in the preceding step against the needs of each participant. The objective of step 4 is to carefully weigh the pros and cons of each solution and to select the one that best meets the needs of all participants. Evaluating solutions in this manner avoids needless and unproductive hassles and employs the decision-by-consensus principle. Because the problem-solving method thus averts power struggles, it has been termed a no-lose method. The final solution has maximal fit for all participants, and each person, in effect, "wins."

To implement this step, guide the participants in evaluating each proposed solution generated. Ask the recorder to read each proposed alternative, and guide the participants in turn to rate the solution as to whether or not it meets their needs. Ratings can be assigned by using a plus to indicate an acceptable solution, a minus for an unacceptable solution, and a neutral rating (zero) for a solution that meets needs only marginally. An alternative method of rating is to ask participants to assign ratings based on a scale from 1 to 10, where 1 represents "totally fails to meet my needs" and 10 represents "completely meets my needs."

To illustrate this process, we return to the hypothetical case of the Taylor family, listing each alternative generated by the family and rating it according to whether or not it meets the needs of family members, as shown in the following illustration:

Having the family inspect the ratings of alternative solutions reveals that proposals 1 and 2 fail to meet the needs of most family members; after discussion, therefore, the family members eliminate these alternatives from further consideration. Proposals 3, 4, 5, and 6, however, appear to be promising alternatives, because all family members

POSSIBLE SOLUTIONS	RATINGS			
	Father	Mother	Bert	Renee
1. Buy a second car	−	−	+	+
2. Reduce social and recreational activities that require driving	0	−	−	−
3. Reduce need for car by walking and catching bus when feasible	+	+	+	+
4. Attempt to form car pools for various events	+	+	+	+
5. Double-date more frequently, reducing the times a family car is required	+	+	+	+
6. Meet as a family at the beginning of each month and week to determine members' needs for car and to plan schedule according to priorities negotiated by family	+	+	+	+

rate them as pluses. The family members conclude these solutions are not in conflict with one another and may be combined to resolve the problem adequately.

As they consider solution number 3, Mr. T indicates he could catch the bus to work instead of driving, except on Wednesdays when he needs the car. Mrs. T volunteers to curtail driving to the grocery store by planning needs for the week and limiting her shopping to weekly visits. She also believes she could reduce trips to her mother's apartment by combining shopping trips with social visits and compensate by phoning her mother more frequently.

With respect to proposed solution number 4, Mr. T expresses his intention to suggest to other members of his bowling team that they form a car pool for bowling nights. Renee and Bert follow suit by volunteering to explore car pools to attend sorority meetings and athletic events. Bert also agrees to comply with solution number 5 by double-dating more often. All agree that proposal number 6 would prevent arguing and result in decisions fair to all family members.

Pleased with the results of their deliberations, the Taylors believe they will be able to meet the transportation needs of each family member. Equally important, they emerge from the problem solving with mutual respect and high family morale.

Choosing an alternative often does not proceed as smoothly as it did for the Taylors, and the stakes are sometimes much higher. Furthermore, two or more alternatives may receive an equal number of plus ratings, and the participants may be forced to choose only one of them. When this occurs, you will need to assist the participants to analyze further the acceptable alternatives. This is best done by having participants identify the pros and cons of each option and assign weights according to the relative importance of each factor. To enhance this process, have the recorder list the pros and cons so that comparisons can be made readily and objectively.

In weighing pros and cons, it is critical to guide participants in considering the likely consequences of each acceptable alternative, keeping in mind the following: "Is a certain decision likely to produce lasting beneficial results by getting to the core of a problem, or is it merely relieving pressure temporarily and postponing an inevitable course of action that will be more difficult later?" "How is a decision likely to affect relationships among the participants?" "Has sufficient information been gained to assess the probable effects of a given solution?" "Have all likely obstacles to the given solution been anticipated?" "Are personal biases producing favoritism for one alternative over another?" You can play an active and vital role by encouraging participants to share their ideas and by supplementing their discussion by pointing out consequences they may have overlooked. Your role in this regard is vital, for clients learn from your modeling. Modeling related to considering consequences of decisions is particularly beneficial, as many clients tend to be impulsive and fail to anticipate probable consequences of their actions.

After participants have weighed the pros and cons of acceptable solutions, ask them to reassess these proposed solutions, employing the scale from 1 to 10 described earlier. (Because all the remaining solutions are acceptable, the "plus-minus" scale is no longer applicable.) On the basis of the new ratings, guide the members in selecting the solution that they have given the highest overall ratings.

Step 5. Implement the Option Selected

After the participants have selected an option, explain that the next step is to implement it with enthusiasm and confidence. After all, they have done their best to reach a sound decision, and they will enhance the chances of achieving a successful outcome by wholeheartedly applying themselves to implementing it. It is important to emphasize this point because some people tend to dwell on uncertainties and to delay actions because of lingering doubts. Others carry out solutions in a half-hearted manner, which sabotages the chances of successfully solving the problem. Many well-conceived solutions fail not because they are defective but because of defective execution, which may result from hesitation, doubt, and fears of bungling.

Step 6. Evaluate the Outcome of Problem-Solving Efforts

Effective problem solving does not end after participants have implemented an alternative. Because of human fallibility and life's vicissitudes, even carefully chosen and well-executed solutions sometimes fail to achieve desired results. Consequently, it is vital that participants systematically monitor the effects of their chosen course of action.

Keeping records based on careful and consistent observations assists them in making thorough and objective evaluations and thus determining early on if their solution is working as planned.

To assist clients in evaluating outcomes of solutions, it is important to explain the value of monitoring and to guide participants in developing a mutually acceptable strategy of monitoring. Appropriate strategies may involve keeping daily logs that record the incidence of desired behaviors or, in the case of the Taylor family, maintaining records to determine if the incidence of family squabbles over the car decreased. Similarly, parents who have implemented a strategy to reduce the frequency of a child's temper tantrums can evaluate the effectiveness of their strategy by recording daily over several weeks the frequency of the tantrums.

A less rigorous method of monitoring is to hold regularly scheduled meetings in which participants share their views as to how solutions are working. Groups, for example, may agree to review over a course of several weeks whether strategies developed by members to keep the group on task are indeed proving effective. Scheduled meetings of couples and families also have the advantage of promoting sustained collaborative efforts by participants.

When a solution has not produced positive results over a reasonable trial period, participants can safely conclude their solution is ineffective. This need not cause alarm, as they likely have not assessed the problem accurately or anticipated all the obstacles. Further efforts may identify a more efficacious solution. To assist participants to develop a more effective solution, have them return to step 2 and repeat the process. It is possible their first solution failed because their problem formulation was inaccurate. When participants are confident of their problem formulation, however, ask them to return to step 3 and carefully review other alternate solutions or generate additional ones. Assisting them to follow the guidelines and steps presented earlier will expedite their devising an effective and timely solution to their problem.

Expediting the Development of Clients' Problem-Solving Skills

Although couples and families may select the development of problem-solving skills as a goal in initial sessions (with the social worker's help), the social worker may not actually *teach* members these skills until a later date. With respect to groups, an important aspect of the social worker's role in an initial session is to assist the group to agree to use a decision-by-consensus method of solving problems and to teach steps for decision-making members. The problem-solving method can be taught to groups, families, or couples using a structured learning experience to facilitate the learning of the steps. Actual practice of the steps, however, should occur in an informal manner that provides for maximum interaction among members. An ultimate goal of the social worker, in fact, is to help clients learn to apply problem-solving steps spontaneously in their relationships with others.

Clients can be expected to struggle in adhering to the steps and guidelines at first. Even in couple, family, and group sessions you will need to intervene actively when participants get off track or begin to engage in dysfunctional interactions. By intervening and clarifying the destructive nature of their interaction, you can guide clients to achieve positive outcomes. Gradually, you can give them increasing responsibility for getting back on track by asking family or group members to identify what is going wrong and by challenging them to take corrective action. You can also anticipate with them how they will encounter similar obstacles outside of sessions and participate with them in planning corrective strategies.

When evaluating clients' efforts to employ problem solving, keep in mind that the hard-won ability to make decisions collaboratively with others is a reflection of substantial growth in a number of areas. Clients may falter in their first tentative efforts to apply the problem-solving process because implementation of a decision-by-consensus approach requires extensive adjustments in the in-dividual styles of many members. For example, many families must alter crystallized dysfunctional patterns in order for members to count each other in and to acknowledge and address the needs of members through problem solving. It is also difficult for a newly formed group to orchestrate a problem-solving process that effectively meets the needs of all concerned when members are strangers with no previous experience in mutual problem solving. The ability of formed groups to solve problems consistently in a facilitative manner, in fact, is a sure sign that such groups have achieved the working stage of development.

The following statements illustrate the social worker's role in facilitating development of problem-solving skills early in initial or group sessions:

- "As we make this decision, let's consider members' needs first and then develop a number of possible solutions before we decide on a course of action."

- "The experience we just had is an example of decision by consensus. What did you observe as we went through this process?"

- "I'm really pleased with the way the group approached this problem; everyone's needs were considered. We chose our solution from several alternatives, and everyone seems satisfied with the decision."

Thus, by intervening to guide groups through problem solving (message number 1), assisting them to discuss their efforts to make decisions collaboratively (message number 2), and accrediting their increments of growth and success (message number 3), you can assist members in assuming increasing responsibility for self-directed problem solving.

Applying Problem Solving with Individuals

Although our preceding discussion and examples of problem solving related to couples, families, and groups, the steps are equally applicable to work with individuals. Individuals function within an interpersonal context and need to learn skills that apply to that broader arena of life. In enabling individual clients to solve problems, you must also guide them through essentially the same steps as outlined in this chapter.

The step concerned with generating numerous alternatives is particularly vital in working with individual clients. Clients can learn to engage in individual brainstorming, thereby expanding their range of options and avoiding impulsive actions. With clients who tend to act impetuously, learning to generate alternatives, to assess their pros and cons, and to weigh possible consequences of actions may significantly enhance their social functioning by equipping them with new and more effective coping patterns.

Facilitating Transfer of Problem-Solving Skills

Enabling clients to apply problem-solving processes in the real world is a challenging task. Because the process embodies a number of discrete concepts and skills and requires both commitment and self-discipline, mastering it requires persistent and determined effort. The benefits more than justify the efforts, and it is important to emphasize to clients the benefits that will gradually accrue if they persevere until they achieve mastery.

As you guide clients through the steps, they gain rudimentary skills in applying the process. These "in-session" activities are merely a means to an end. The ultimate benefit lies in whether clients succeed in applying the process outside the session.

You can assist clients to expand and to transfer their problem-solving facility by negotiating tasks of applying the process to problems that emerge between sessions. Suggest to clients that they agree to assist each other to adhere to the steps and guidelines by gently drawing deviations to their attention and facilitatively suggesting they get back on course. By applying the process independently, they will gain additional practice and will experience rough spots that can be explored and ironed out in their next session.

Applying the process under your tutelage provides additional opportunity for them to refine their skills. As you observe them effectively following the steps and guidelines, you can accredit their progress, thereby enhancing their confidence and reinforcing their efforts.

You will further enhance transfer of the skills to the real world by intervening less frequently and giving less direction as clients demonstrate increasing mastery of the process. By giving them increasing responsibility to monitor their own behavior and to make their own "interventions" when their efforts go awry, you are preparing them for successful independent problem solving. You will, of course, need to continue making timely interventions and to coach them until they are better able to stand on their own feet. Always bear in mind that you achieve ultimate success with clients when they are able to function effectively without your services.

SOCIAL SKILLS TRAINING (SST)

Training in social skills has expanded over the past two decades with many articles and evaluations of SST programs. SST programs have been employed to teach a wide variety of skills for both primary prevention and remediation. SST assists clients by providing them with the opportunity to learn skills needed to function effectively in their current environment, and in anticipated roles, relationships, and life cycle stages. In this section, we explain the rationale of SST for prevention and remediation, identify target groups, enumerate various skills, and describe a format that can be employed for teaching various skills.

Rationale for and Uses of SST

Beginning with Rapoport (1961) 40 years ago, prominent social workers have increasingly promoted the development of primary preventive programs in social work. The rationale for preventive programs is that efforts to prevent social dysfunction by equipping people with coping skills reduces the possibilities of later maladjustment, unhappiness, failure to develop potentials, and loss of productivity. Moreover, preventive programs cost much less than remedial programs such as mental health treatment, foster care, substance abuse treatment programs, public assistance, and correctional institutions, to name just a few.

Many research studies document the importance of adequate socialization during childhood and adolescence to adequate adjustment. Children who are deprived of adequate socialization fail to learn certain vital social skills and are at risk to experience a variety of personal and interpersonal difficulties. For example, a study (Weisz et al., 1987) revealed that perceived personal incompetence by children is linked with depression in childhood. Other research studies (summarized in LeCroy, 1983) have documented the importance of skills in forming peer relationships to the healthy socialization of children. As a consequence of these findings, social workers have developed preventive skill training programs (LeCroy & Rose, 1986), including one that uses a game format (LeCroy, 1987).

(Moote, Smyth, and Wodarski 1999) recently summarized the research on social skills training with young people in youth settings. Fourteen of the 25 studies they found that had been published since 1985 reported beneficial effects. Benefits included outcomes such as reduced absenteeism and tardiness, fewer disciplinary referrals, and increased social and relaxation skills. These authors suggest that the amount of research on this intervention approaches what is needed to call it an empirically validated treatment.

The rationale for SST in remediation programs is similar to that just discussed. Social dysfunction is commonly associated with a lack of social skills essential to achieving self-esteem, forming satisfying interpersonal relationships, and performing various social roles effectively. Limited social skills contribute to difficulties involving loneliness and depression, marital dysfunction, parent-child problems, family breakdown, employment problems, various mental health problems, and other difficulties. As a consequence, SST programs are often included in services provided in diverse practice settings. For example, a training program in social skills aimed at expanding social support for mothers at risk of child maltreatment has been developed by Lovell and Richey (1991). Another program has been developed to assist transient women in learning skills essential for daily functioning (Breton, 1984).

Skills selected for remedial SST are diverse and vary according to the setting and the target problems of clients typically served. Among the more common skills are various parenting skills, assertiveness, listening to others and sending clear messages, personalizing feelings, making requests, initiating and maintaining conversation, making friends, managing anger, and solving problems. With clients who lack many social skills, skills may include personal grooming, using public transportation, ordering meals, making telephone calls, and initiating conversation, to name just a few.

Use with Persons with Disabilities

Skill building is especially relevant for developmentally and mentally disabled persons, for these groups often lack social skills and other coping skills. Vital preventive work can be accomplished by enhancing the parenting skills of developmentally disabled parents. Whitman, Graves, and Accardo (1989) have described such a program for mentally retarded parents. Another parenting skills program has been developed and tested (with promising results) for normal parents of children with developmental disabilities (Gammon & Rose, 1991). Still another program has been designed to enable developmentally disabled persons to develop skills requisite to utilizing transportation they need to secure essential resources (Taylor, 1988). In another study, a social skills training package was administered to two groups of developmentally disabled adults using a multiple baseline design. Participants demonstrated improved performance on a role play test, but in vivo assessment showed little change (Hall, Schlesinger, & Dineen, 1997). Participants practiced skills such as making introductions, small talk, asking for help, differing from others, and handling criticism. While they were able to demonstrate the skills in role plays, actual practice proved difficult.

Assessing Skill Deficits

The first step in employing SST is to determine the skills targeted for training. When deficits are readily apparent this is a simple task. Adolescents who are easily provoked to anger and discharge anger in violent and destructive ways, for example, lack skills in coping with provocation and controlling anger. Socially inhibited people commonly lack skills in making social overtures, maintaining conversation, and asserting themselves. Certain clients will themselves identify problems and request assistance in learning certain social behaviors, for example, accepting compliments or overcoming extreme sensitivity to criticism.

With other clients, however, as with those who lack many skills or those whose deficits are more subtle, assessment is more complex. Parent-child difficulties, for example, may involve a lack of parental skill in providing encouragement and approval, expressing expectations, setting limits, managing demands or tantrums, being firm and consistent, being flexible, or listening to children without lecturing or being critical. Clients with schizophrenia may have many skill limitations that require extensive SST. To identify specific skill deficits of persons with schizophrenia, Curran et al. (1985) recommend administering a scale that covers major areas of psychosocial functioning and identifies stressors to which patients have not adapted adequately. Various other instruments have also been developed by behaviorally oriented marital and family therapists to assess skills of partners in performing various marital roles.[1]

Identifying Components of Social Skills

After selecting a social skill for training, the next step is to break down the skill into its discrete components or subskills. This process is essentially the same as that of dissecting tasks into behavioral units, as discussed in Chapter 13. As with dissecting tasks, the analysis should consider cognitive and emotional components as well as specific behaviors, for fears and uncertainties often must be mastered before clients can effectively perform requisite actions. We will illustrate this process later in this chapter in the section on assertiveness training.

Format for Training

SST can be conducted in sessions with individuals or in a group context. We have chosen to focus on the group context; however, you can follow essentially the same format in sessions with individuals because the principles and steps are virtually identical. It is important, of course, to prepare members for the group, as we discussed in Chapter 11. Once the group has been formed, the following steps are typically followed.

1. **Discuss the Rationale and Describe the Skill.** This first step is critical to successfully engaging members in learning a selected skill. Participants must believe that developing the skill will benefit them. To enhance the relevance for participants we recommend you briefly introduce the skill, alluding in general to situations in which it is applicable, and then elicit from participants specific relevant social situations that have posed difficulties for them and have led to adverse outcomes because of ineffectual coping. For example, if the selected skill is assertively resisting peer pressure you might use a message similar to the following: "Learning to say 'No!' with firmness and not giving in to pressure from other kids can help you avoid doing things you don't really want to do and things that can get you into trouble. Probably a number of you can recall times you gave in to pressure and later regretted it. I know I can (gives an example). How about the rest of you? Could you share times when you wished you had been able to say 'No'?" As participants share experiences, commend them for risking with the group. After a

number of participants have shared experiences, you can further attempt to enhance their motivation by asking if they can think of several benefits of learning the skill. Initiate the discussion by listing an advantage on a chalkboard (e.g., "don't get started on drugs" and "have higher self-respect"). Compliment persons who identify advantages and list the advantages on the chalkboard, elaborating on advantages when clarification is needed.

2. **Identify the Components of the Skill.** Explain that the skill involves a number of different components. Then list each component on the chalkboard, explaining its significance to successfully employing the skill. It is helpful as you do so to involve participants by asking if they have had difficulties with the component being discussed (e.g., the cognitive/emotional component—fearing the reactions of peers if one refuses to participate in a certain problematic activity). Explain that the group will discuss and practice each component.

3. **Model the Skill.** Recall from an earlier chapter that vicarious learning is the second most potent source of self-efficacy. To tap this source, you can model the component of the skill (using *coping* modeling rather than mastery) or ask if a member of the group will volunteer to model the skill. A critique or discussion by participants regarding their observations of the modeling is often fruitful in highlighting aspects of the target component that contribute to effective and ineffective performance.

4. **Role-Play Use of Each Component.** Explain that the most effective way of learning a skill is to practice until one feels confident in applying the skill. Therefore, participants will take turns practicing each component and will give feedback to each other to assist in further developing the skill. Ask for volunteers to begin roll playing and set the stage by prescribing roles they are to play. (You will need to prepare for this step by identifying problematic situations typical of those that participants commonly encounter.

You can also enlist the aid of participants in identifying relevant situations.) It is desirable to begin with less difficult situations and, as participants demonstrate the ability to apply the skills, move to more challenging situations. Before beginning the role playing, ask participants to observe carefully so that they can provide feedback to each other.

5. **Evaluate the Role Play.** After each episode of role playing, invite participants to provide feedback. To foster a climate that is conducive to openness, encourage participants to give positive feedback initially. You may wish to initiate the process or add feedback about positive aspects of the participant's role play that may have been overlooked.

For maximum benefit, feedback should be addressed to both verbal and nonverbal behaviors. For example, a participant may employ appropriate words but may speak hesitantly with a subdued tone of voice or may avoid eye-to-eye contact with the other protagonist. When such nonassertive behaviors are evident, it is beneficial to have the participant engage in further practice, seeking to modify the behaviors in question. Again, positive feedback should be given for even slight improvements. Participants should be requested to evaluate their own performance, focusing on both positive and negative aspects, and to share feelings experienced during the role play. Discussion of feelings that inhibit performance can be valuable in identifying common barriers to implementing the skill effectively.

6. **Combine the Components in Role Play.** After participants have role-played and demonstrated adequate mastery of the various components, have them take turns role-playing the skill itself. Continue to have members give feedback to each other and continue practicing until they manifest self-efficacy with respect to the skill. A simple way of assessing the self-efficacy of participants is to have them rate their readiness to perform the skill in real-life situations on a scale from 1 to 10, where 1 represents a total lack of

confidence and 10 represents complete confidence. Ratings of 7 or higher generally indicate adequate mastery.

7. **Apply the Skill in Real-Life Situations.** This step entails applying the skill in actual social situations, the ultimate test of the skill training efforts. Preparing participants adequately for this crucial step begins with eliciting situations that are likely to occur during the forthcoming week and obtaining the commitment of participants to apply the newly gained skills in these situations. Reviewing components of the skill and practicing application of them further prepares participants. Anticipating difficulties that will likely arise and preparing to surmount them through rehearsing appropriate thoughts and behaviors produces maximal preparation and self-efficacy.

Subsequent debriefing sessions provide opportunities to discuss and analyze the experiences of participants in applying the skill. The social worker should encourage participants to accredit successes, enthusiastically drawing attention to specific behaviors and cognitions that resulted in successful outcomes. Such focusing draws the attention of participants to their mastery of components targeted for learning and further enhances their self-efficacy.

Not all participants report successes, of course, and even those who achieve successful outcomes may report aspects of their performance that were flawed. Debriefing sessions thus provide opportunities for additional practice in enhancing and refining skills. Step 7 thus may be extended for several weeks, depending upon the needs of participants and the feasibility of doing so.

GAME FORMATS FOR LEARNING SKILLS

Another format for assisting people to learn problem solving and social skills is the use of games specifically developed for those purposes. Use of a game format has a number of advantages, including the following cited by Rabin, Blechman, Kahn, & Carel, (1985):

- Many participants are receptive to this approach because games are expected to be fun.
- Experimentation with new forms of behavior is natural in the context of a game.
- Games with easily understood rules exert powerful control over the behavior of players.
- Well-designed rules promote learning at participants' own pace with a minimum of failures.
- Skill-training games foster adaptive interdependence of players and minimize the need for a third party.

Because the game format is a recent innovation, empirical support for this approach is scanty. Nevertheless, the rationale for the format appears sound and preliminary findings are promising. Rabin et al. (1985) describe the Marriage Contract Game, which was designed to teach marital partners the skills of successful problem solving and of warm and open communication. Outcome findings of the use of the game with four distressed couples who had requested treatment for a child and were averse to marital therapy indicated these couples learned to solve problems and to communicate positive feelings along the dimensions targeted by the game.

The game format appears particularly promising for work with children because of the high appeal of games to children. LeCroy (1987) has reported that the use of a board game designed to teach social skills that are components of social competence produced results that were equivalent to but not superior to results achieved using a standard social skills group. The game format had been designed partly as a response to difficulties encountered by social workers in involving children in formal skills groups. According to the group leaders who employed the game, children responded positively to the game and group attractiveness and cohesion increased.

Based on the limited experimentation described in the preceding, it appears that expanded use of and testing of the game format are warranted. This format offers a new approach to teaching skills to children and adults who might otherwise be hesitant to participate in formal skills development programs.

ASSERTIVENESS TRAINING (AT)

Lack of assertiveness pervades many aspects of interpersonal difficulties, and assertiveness training (AT) as a clinical intervention has been applied in diverse settings to almost every major diagnostic classification or behavioral disorder. Particularly relevant for both battered wives and their abusive husbands, AT achieved popularity with the publication in 1970 of *Your Perfect Right: A Guide to Assertive Behavior* (Alberti & Emmons, 1970, 1974) and has since become a widespread movement in the United States. At least one study has shown that assertiveness by social workers in the place of employment was associated with greater job satisfaction (Rabin & Zelner, 1992). The construct of assertiveness has been defined in various ways. Our definition, which synthesizes some of these definitions and adds our own interpretation, is that assertiveness embodies specific components of behavior that enable individuals to express their opinions, feelings, wants, and preferences in a manner that respects the rights and feelings of others even when such expressions risk aversive consequences such as criticism, disapproval, or punishment. Assertiveness is not a unitary construct, as revealed by Bucell (1979), who empirically studied behaviors embodied in various assertiveness inventories. Bucell identified the following relatively distinct types of assertive behaviors or response classes: (1) refuse requests, (2) express unpopular opinions, (3) admit personal shortcomings, (4) accept compliments, (5) express positive feelings, (6) make requests for changes in behavior, and (7) initiate and maintain conversations.

The first step in AT, therefore, is to identify the response class in which training is needed. After doing so you can prepare the client(s) for training by following the guidelines and steps delineated earlier in the section on skills training. Training can be implemented either with individuals or in a group context. As with training in other social skills, modeling, behavioral rehearsal, and guided practice are crucial aspects of AT. To avoid redundancy we will not delineate steps involved in AT but refer you to a chapter by Schroeder and Black (1985) that describes in detail AT aimed at teaching conversational behavior.

Cultural Factors

Before discussing assertiveness further, we should say that assertiveness training may not be appropriate for clients whose culturally prescribed roles prohibit assertive behavior. Asian American cultures, for example, prescribe deference to authority. Similarly, women from traditional Latino and Asian cultural backgrounds are often expected to be submissive to their husbands. Assertiveness training could compound rather than resolve difficulties for such clients. Nevertheless, ethnic minority clients need to learn to assert their legal rights to resources to which they are entitled. Social workers, therefore, often must assume an advocacy role in assisting them to gain assertiveness in dealing with bureaucratic structures.

Differentiating Assertiveness from Other Response Styles

In preparing clients for AT, it is important to differentiate assertiveness from the response styles of *nonassertiveness* and *aggressiveness*. We have previously defined assertiveness but add that the basic message relayed by persons who are relating assertively is that they "count" and that their ideas, perceptions, and opinions are important. By contrast, nonassertiveness involves the violation of one's own rights "by failing to express honest feelings, thoughts, and beliefs and consequently permitting others to violate oneself, or expressing one's thoughts and feelings in such an apologetic, diffident, self-effacing manner that others can easily disregard them" (Lange & Jakubowski, 1976, p. 9). Persons who relate nonassertively attempt to appease others and to avoid conflict, conveying through their behavior that their needs, wants, and opinions are not important and that others are superior to them.

The third response style, *aggression*, as defined by Lange and Jakubowski (1976), involves "directly standing up for personal rights and expressing thoughts, feelings, and beliefs in a way which ... violates the rights of the other person" (p. 10). Persons who relate aggressively seek to dominate others, ignoring their needs, wants, and feelings.

The idea of relating assertively has had immense popular appeal to the lay public. Many people have problems with nonassertiveness or timidity, frequently permitting themselves to be pushed aside or discounted by others. Unable to express themselves effectively in a wide variety of situations, such persons often feel unappreciated, taken for granted, and exploited by others. Many other persons, who relate aggressively, often suffer the loss of significant relationships because others weary of their abrasive, debasing response styles. Still other persons vacillate between aggressive and nonassertive or passive behavior, failing to develop an effective and comfortable style of relating to others.

Clients often seek (or are coerced to seek) professional assistance because of problems that can be traced to habitual styles of relating aggressively or passively. Experienced over long periods of time, such difficulties may cause or contribute to low self-esteem, depression, or marked anxiety in interpersonal situations.

Congruence Between Verbal and Nonverbal Behavior

Nonverbal components of messages may either strengthen and complement an assertive statement or contradict it. Persons who wring their hands, look at the floor, or stammer, for instance, do not appear assertive no matter how assertive the verbal content of their message. Social workers must thus observe clients' nonverbal behaviors to determine whether these behaviors convey assertiveness, aggressiveness, or nonassertiveness. Common nonverbal behaviors associated with as-

sertive relating and the other two response styles include the following:

ASSERTIVENESS	AGGRESSIVENESS	NONASSERTIVENESS
Relaxed posture	Rigid body posture	Clammy hands
Direct eye contact	Glares	Evasive or fleeting eye contact
Firm and moderate tone of voice	Sarcastic or belittling tone of voice	Soft, whiny, or pleading voice
Fluent speech pattern	Loud speech	Hesitant speech
Appropriately varied facial expressions	Clenched jaws, pursed lips	Nervous laughter or throat clearing
Moderately expressive gestures	Tightened fists	Nervous gestures
	Finger pointing	

Cognitive/Perceptual Obstacles to Assertiveness

Developing assertiveness is not easy for social workers or clients. Clients often experience extreme tension and paralyzing emotions that block them from asserting themselves despite strong desires to do so. These powerful emotions are generally a product of deeply embedded mistaken beliefs, of which clients usually have limited or vague awareness. Consequently, social workers need to assist clients to expand their awareness of these irrational beliefs and to replace them with realistic conceptions.

Common misconceptions that inhibit assertiveness include (1) beliefs that one's obligations to others far outweigh one's own wants or rights, (2) extreme concern with pleasing or impressing others favorably, and (3) extreme fears about the consequences of asserting oneself with others. With respect to beliefs, many clients were conditioned as children to believe that it is bad or selfish to accord equal significance to personal wants and needs as compared with responding to the needs or wants (and sometimes demands) of others. To feel they are "good" persons (or, rather, not *bad* persons), such individuals develop keen sensitivity to the wants of others, sometimes going to extremes to please them, often at great expense to themselves. Saying no (and sometimes even thinking it) automatically triggers feelings of guilt and badness. Sadly, these individuals are so governed by the wants and expectations of others that they are often out of touch with their own needs and wants.

The second and third types of misconceptions are linked with the first. Having an inordinate need to please or impress others derives from the mistaken belief that one's worth as a person is directly proportional to the extent that one gains the approval of others. Often rooted in early life experiences in which parental love and approval were not expressed generously and were contingent upon pleasing the parents, such beliefs link self-esteem the reactions of others.

Self-esteem, under such circumstances, is tenuous at best, and it is overwhelming to such persons to risk incurring the displeasure of others. The tacit motto of these persons is "I am of value only as I win approval from others." The irony in this motto is that persons who seek excessively to please others tend to attain the opposite effect, for others often devalue them. Such persons need to adopt instead the realistic belief that people tend to value those who value themselves and are assertive.

The third type of misconception involves fearing disastrous consequences if one asserts one's rights, wants, or feelings. Some people, who were severely punished as children for not conforming to parental demands, experience vague fears of being physically or verbally abused if they assert themselves. Others have conscious fears of being rejected or literally abandoned (as they feared in childhood) if they assert themselves. These feared reactions are of catastrophic proportions, and it is understandable that these people are extremely threatened by the prospects of asserting themselves.

Assisting clients to surmount the obstacles described in the preceding involves an approach that combines cognitive restructuring (see Chapter 13), behavior rehearsal, and stress management (the topic of the next section).

STRESS MANAGEMENT

Stress management is a broad term that refers to varied approaches that share the common objective of enabling people to cope more effectively with the tensions and stresses associated with problems of living. These approaches are employed to assist people to use coping skills that prevent excessive reactions to stressful events and situations. For example, stress management skills enable people to avoid being immobilized by extreme tensions or losing control of emotions or impulses and expressing them in violent ways that can be damaging to others or to themselves. Training in stress management skills thus is widely employed with people who react to stress with excessive anxiety or anger. For example, de Anda (1998) reports an experimental evaluation of a stress management program for middle school adolescents. Adolescents in the experimental group reported a significant increase in the use of cognitive control strategies and adaptive rather than maladaptive strategies, and significantly lower stress than participants in the control group. They also reported a 67% reduction in muscle tension following use of relaxation procedures.

Not all methods for assistance related to stress are carried out in person. Meier (1997) has reported the development and preliminary testing of an innovative online support group for assisting social workers in the management of stress. Social workers participating in the study found that by using e-mails and mailing lists, they could receive assistance despite their busy schedules because they could send or respond to e-mails at their own discretion. In addition, confidentiality could be preserved because participants could conceal their identities with aliases. Meier found that the messages posted became complex over time. The leader served to post summaries of themes discussed. While questions of access remain, it is clear that use of e-mail, the Web, and Internet for new purposes including relief of stress will only continue to expand.

The stress management approach we delineate has been denoted as stress inoculation (Meichenbaum, 1977), a multidimensional approach that embodies skills directed to biophysical, cognitive/perceptual, and behavioral components of clients' reactions to stressful situations. We focus first on relaxation training, an integral part of stress inoculation that addresses the biophysical component. Relaxation training, however, is also employed as an intervention in its own right to assist people to reduce anxiety and to keep emotions within manageable limits. To the best of our knowledge, Vattano (1978) was the first social work author to describe muscle relaxation procedures and to recommend this intervention for stress management.

RELAXATION TRAINING

Two major physiological components of excessive tension and anger are rapid breathing and tightening of the muscles. Relaxation training targets both of these components through deep breathing and muscle-relaxing exercises. Numerous studies have reported that relaxation training has been used successfully to assist clients with problems related to various stress-related physical symptoms (e.g., high blood pressure, tension headaches, insomnia, and anxiety). It has also been effectively employed to reduce the extreme emotional reactions of people in crisis situations, to reduce tension associated with performance anxiety (e.g., before giving talks or taking examinations), and to reduce anger in provocative situations. Arnette (1997) has reported the development of a psychophysiological intervention with couples experiencing marital conflict. Relaxation therapy with biofeedback assistance is used along

with counseling to address the marital discord. Relaxation training also occupies a central role in the Lamaze (1958) method of childbirth.

Social workers may employ relaxation training to particular advantage when clients

- are chronically tense and anxious,
- are acutely anxious as a result of a crisis situation,
- are anxious and fearful about various anticipated events or situations,
- have tension headaches, migraines, tightness of the chest, breathing difficulties, and other psychophysiological reactions when medical causes have been ruled out,
- suffer with insomnia,
- have difficulty controlling anger,
- are moderately depressed.

A major advantage of relaxation training is the fact that it is a simple procedure that clients can readily learn and can practice at home, which enables them to master the procedure in a few weeks' time. Another advantage is that clients can employ abbreviated forms of muscle relaxation in diverse stressful situations, thereby reducing tension and enhancing coping efforts.

Cautions

Although relaxation training can be employed in diverse situations, it is important to employ this procedure with discrimination, for there are limitations and contraindications associated with this modality. For example, although relaxation training is useful in assisting people to regain emotional control following a crisis, it should not be employed as a substitute for coping with situations that have created or contributed to the crisis. If a crisis is precipitated by sudden loss of a job, family disruption, loss of housing, unplanned pregnancy, or other stress, to achieve *enduring* benefit you must implement other interventions that address the sources of the crisis. When clients are distraught, panicky, or otherwise overwhelmed by intense emotionality, however, muscle relaxation serves as a useful adjunct in assisting them to regain equilibrium, thereby enabling them to begin exploring their problems.

Another caution relates to clients with motor disorders (e.g., cerebral palsy) or muscular or skeletal disorders. These clients should not engage in muscle relaxation exercises without clearance from a physician.

Implementing Relaxation Training

While instructing clients in relaxation, it is important to observe the guidelines spelled out in the following sections.

Explaining the Rationale of the Procedure and Gaining Consent

To gain maximal cooperation of clients, social workers should explain the purpose of muscle relaxation and obtain their consent. It has been our experience that clients readily and willingly agree to participate in the procedure, for they typically are highly motivated to gain alleviation from the discomfort produced by excessive tension, anxiety, or fear. In explaining the rationale, we recommend you include the following factors:

- The causes and adverse effects of excessive tension

- The beneficial effects of muscle relaxation

- The diverse uses of muscle relaxation

- The need to develop a "muscle sense"; that is, to recognize the presence of excessive tension

- The need to practice to gain mastery of the procedure

The following is an example of an explanation of the rationale of the procedure:

Life gets pretty hectic at times, causing people to become tense. At such times we often breathe rapidly and tighten our muscles, sometimes without even being aware of it. On occasions being tense and uptight for an extended time can produce muscle spasms, headache, and even gastrointestinal difficulties caused by involuntary contractions of the smooth muscles in the stomach and the intestines.

When people are chronically tense, they may experience other physical reactions such as elevation in blood pressure and heart rate, headaches, and nervous stomach. Excessive muscle tension also burns up energy rapidly and can produce fatigue. Muscle tension can also interfere with sleep. By learning to relax the skeletal muscles, you can counter all of these negative effects.

Muscle relaxation first involves developing awareness of the sensation of tension in your muscles. The procedure heightens awareness of the sensations of tension in various muscle groups, and you'll become keenly aware of the difference between tension and relaxation. You're also going to learn how to instruct your muscles to relax so that when you're aware of tension you can consciously reduce it.

I'm going to instruct you in a procedure that you can practice in your home. By practicing each day, you'll become more and more skillful so that you won't need to relax all of the muscle groups separately. Some people, in fact, learn to relax in a matter of a few seconds but only after much practice. I'll tell you more about how to practice later.

Clarifying Conditions Conducive to Relaxation

Optimal conditions for relaxation training include a comfortable and quiet environment. Further, furniture that permits relaxed posture should be employed, such as a reclining chair or padded chaise lounge. When instructing a group, you may use padded floor mats or blankets if appropriate furniture is not available.

Clients should wear loose-fitting clothing that permits freedom of movement. We recommend that you explain to clients that tight-fitting clothing restricts movements and produces discomfort that may be distracting. It is also desirable to suggest that clients make these same arrangements for comfort when they practice relaxation training at home. As they gain facility in relaxing their muscles, the environment becomes less important.

Indeed, their ultimate goal is to learn to relax in stress-producing situations.

Guidelines for Instructing Clients

To assist you in instructing clients in muscle relaxation, we offer the following guidelines, which involve a synthesis of procedures developed by E. Jacobson (1929), D. Bernstein and Borkovec (1973), and ourselves. We recommend that you study these guidelines until you have memorized them and that you practice instructing friends, relatives, or student colleagues in muscle relaxation before applying the procedures with individual clients or groups.

- Allow sufficient time to apply the procedure. Preliminary discussion, implementation of the procedure, and subsequent discussion and planning usually consume the largest part of a 50-minute session.

- Explain that when you ask clients to tighten a group of muscles, you do not mean for them to tense the muscles as hard as they can. Tightening muscles to the extreme can strain a muscle; tightening them to the point of uncomfortable tension is sufficient.

- Explain that to enhance muscle relaxation, clients should breathe deeply, exhaling all the air, and think the word *relax* when you instruct them to relax. (Deep breathing facilitates relaxation, as does thinking the word *relax*.) Ask them to practice with you. Model taking three or four deep breaths and exhaling completely. Ask them to do the same, concentrating on the word *relax*. Explain that you will remind them of this procedure with the first two muscle groups, but thereafter you want them to continue this breathing procedure without further reminders.

- Explain that as clients relax their muscles they may experience warm, heavy, or tingling sensations. They should not be alarmed, because these sensations are merely indications that they are succeeding in achieving relaxation.

- Explain that you will be practicing muscle relaxation along with them. Practicing in concert with clients enhances timing in giving instruction and models appropriate behaviors. Moreover, clients are less likely to feel awkward and self-conscious if you participate with them in applying the procedure.

- Speak with a relaxing and soothing tone of voice but avoid being dramatic. When you use the word *relax*, express it slowly and softly in a manner that fosters relaxation.

Instructing Clients in Applying the Procedure

After you have completed the foregoing procedures, you are ready to instruct clients in applying relaxation training.

Instructing clients involves five discrete activities (Bernstein & Borkovec, 1973) in the following sequence:

- Draw the client's attention to the appropriate muscle group.

- Instruct the client to tense the muscle group (we will list the muscle groups and provide directions for tensing them later).

- Ask the client to hold the tension (for 5 to 7 seconds) and to be aware of the sensations in the affected muscles.

- Instruct the client to relax.

- Instruct the client to be aware of the pleasant feeling of relaxation as contrasted to the discomfort associated with tension (relaxation interval lasts about 10 seconds).

To enhance clients' awareness of varying degrees of muscle tension, we instruct them to tense and to relax each group of muscles three times, reducing the degree of tension during the second and third contractions. We also emphasize the importance of being aware of the sensations of tension and contrasting them with the feelings of relaxation, as we illustrate in the following instructions to clients.

Before actually engaging in muscle relaxation, ask clients to get into a comfortable position. Then explain that you are going to teach them to relax 16 different muscle groups. Ask them to listen closely and to follow your instructions carefully. You are now ready to begin with the muscle groups, which should be relaxed in the sequence listed. (Different authors suggest lists of muscle groups that vary slightly. The list below is the one we have found most useful.) To assist you in giving instructions, we have provided a verbatim example for the first muscle group and partial instructions for the third and fifth muscle groups. We have also listed the remaining muscle groups together with methods of tensing them. Instructions for the remaining muscle groups are essentially the same as for those we have illustrated.

- *Fingers and hands.* "We're going to begin with your finger and hand muscles. Clench both of your fists tightly as I'm doing, but not too tightly. Keep them clenched and be aware of the tension in your fingers, the back of your hand, and your forearm. [*After 7 seconds.*] Now r-e-l-a-x. Tell yourself to relax, take a deep breath, and exhale all the air. Let your hand be limp and be aware of the pleasant feelings. [*After 10 seconds.*] Now I want you to make a fist again, but tense your muscles just half as tight as last time. Be aware of where you feel the tension. [*Pause for a few seconds.*] Now relax, breathe deeply, and think the word *relax*. Let the tension flow out of your fingertips and enjoy the relaxation. [*After 10 seconds.*] Make a fist again, but this time tighten your fingers very lightly so that you can barely feel the tension. Hold your hand in this position and be aware that you can still feel the tension in the same places. [*Brief pause.*] Now relax, take a deep breath, and think the word *relax*. Just savor the exhilarating feeling of relaxation for a few moments."

- *Wrist and lower arm.* "Bend your wrists forward toward your head and point your fingers toward the ceiling so that you feel tension in the muscles in the back of your hand and forearm." [*Repeat procedure described with first muscle group, but explain that clients will need to remember to breathe deeply and think the word relax.*]

- *Upper arm and biceps.* "Now we're going to work with your upper arm muscles. Make your hands into fists and bring them toward your shoulders, tightening your biceps. Hold the muscles tightly and be aware of the tension in your upper arm. [*After 5 to 7 seconds.*] Now relax and let all the tension drain out of your arms and fingers. Be aware of the pleasurable feeling of relaxation, and just enjoy it for a few moments." [*Repeat procedure after pauses, using reduced degrees of tension as indicated for the first group.*]

- *Shoulders.* "Shrug both of your shoulders, bringing them close to your ears."

- *Forehead and eyebrows.* "Now that you've relaxed your shoulders, you should have a refreshing relaxed feeling down both of your arms. Notice the pleasant feeling when your arms are free of tension. Now we'll work on relaxing the muscles of the face. First, wrinkle your brow tightly. Make it furrow as though you are scowling and be aware of the tension in your forehead and eyebrows. [*Pause.*] Now relax. Smooth out your forehead until the muscles are loose. Be aware of the feeling of relaxation and enjoy it a few moments." [*Pause for 10 seconds.*] [*Repeat the preceding twice, tensing the muscles only half as tightly the second time and very lightly the third time as illustrated for the first group. Vary your words to avoid being monotonous.*]

- *Eyes.* "Close your eyes tightly and be aware of the tension around your eyes."

- *Jaws.* "Clench your jaws together and study the tension and discomfort in your jaws, cheeks, and temples." [*With clients who wear dentures, you may use alternate exercises of having them push their tongue against the roof of the mouth or thrust their lower jaw forward.*]

- *Lips.* "Now press your lips together tightly and be aware of the tension all around your mouth."

- *Back neck muscles.* "Push your head backward into the chair. Be aware of the tension in the back of your neck and in the upper part of your back."

- *Front neck muscles.* "Now, we're going to work with your front neck muscles. Tilt your head forward so that your chin is tight against your chest. Concentrate on the tension in the front of your neck."

- *Back.* [*Advise clients who have lower back pain or spinal difficulties to avoid straining their back.*] "Now, turn your attention to your upper back. Arch your back by sticking out your chest and stomach. Study the tension and discomfort in your back."

- *Chest.* [*Many clients complain of tightness in the chest when they are tense and anxious.*] "Take a deep breath and hold it, thrusting your chest forward. Be aware of the tension in your chest and upper abdomen. [*Pause.*] Now exhale completely and just relax. Enjoy the pleasant feeling of relaxation."

- *Abdomen.* "Now focus on your stomach area. Pull in your stomach and tighten the muscles of your abdomen so that they feel like a knot."

- *Upper leg.* [*Take one leg at a time.*] "Lift your right leg and hold it. Get in touch with the tension in your upper leg." [*Repeat with left leg after alternately raising and lowering right leg three times.*]

- *Lower leg.* "Direct your attention to your lower leg. Now flex your ankle and point your toes at your head. Be aware of the tension in your lower leg."

- *Feet and toes.* "Arch your foot by tightening your toes and pushing them against the floor. Experience the tension in your toes and in the ball of your foot."

After tensing and relaxing each muscle group three times, the next step is to review each muscle group and to instruct the client to dispel residual tension. To accomplish this, draw attention to each muscle group as follows:

- "Now we're going to go over all the muscle groups again. As I name each group, be aware of any tension remaining in those muscles. If you feel tension, focus on those muscles, breathe

deeply, and instruct them to relax. Think of the tension draining completely from your body. Let's being with the toes and feet. If you feel any tension, let it drain out." [*5-second pause*]

Then repeat the procedure with each muscle group, moving from the muscle groups in the legs to the abdomen, lower back, chest, shoulder, upper arms, lower arms, hands, neck, and ending with the facial muscles. After relaxing the facial muscles, instruct the client to remain relaxed from head to toes and to sit quietly and enjoy being relaxed for a few moments. Note that you instruct the client to relax each group once in the review.

To evaluate the extent of relaxation achieved, ask clients to relate their degree of relaxation on a scale from 1 to 10, where 1 represents complete relaxation and 10 extreme tension. If the client reports an uncomfortable level of tension, you may wish to suggest implementing an additional procedure to deepen the degree of relaxation. Akin to self-hypnosis (Lechnyr, 1980a), this procedure involves instructing the client to take 10 deep breaths as follows:

- "Listen very carefully to me, and shut off all other thoughts. Breathe deeply and easily [*model deep breathing*]—that's right. Now I'm going to count to ten slowly. With each number, you will become more and more relaxed. By the tenth breath, you will be very relaxed and sleepy. Now, one [*pause*], you're becoming more relaxed. Two [*shorter pause*] *still* more relaxed." [*Continue counting slowly with a soft, soothing voice, suggesting deeper relaxation with each count.*]

When you have finished counting, your client should be deeply relaxed and may be in a light hypnotic trance. Instruct the client to remain relaxed for a few moments and enjoy it fully. After a pause of about 20 seconds, instruct the client as follows:

- "I'm going to count backwards from five, and with each count, you will feel more alert. When I reach one you will be fully alert and will feel refreshed and relaxed."

When you have finished and the client is alert, explain that in the future the client can employ this procedure independently by breathing easily and deeply and counting from 1 to 10, becoming increasingly relaxed with each count. You may explain that this is a form of self-hypnosis that many people use to relax or to go to sleep.

Posttraining Follow-up

After you complete the preceding relaxation training procedure, it is important to emphasize again that learning to relax, like any other skill, requires considerable practice. To master the skill, therefore, the client should practice 20 to 30 minutes daily under the conditions specified earlier. After practicing each day, the client should rate the degree of relaxation achieved, using the scale described earlier, thereby making it possible to assess progress.

After clients have consistently practiced relaxing the 16 muscle groups for a week or two and report satisfactory progress in achieving relaxation, they are ready to advance to more streamlined forms of muscle relaxation. One such form involves reducing the number of muscle groups from 16 to 4 by combining the muscle groups into major anatomical parts of the body, which include the following:

• Fingers, hands, lower arms, and upper arms

• Face and neck muscles

• Shoulders, back, chest, and abdominal muscles

• Upper legs, lower legs, feet, and toes

The instructions for relaxing these four muscle groups are similar to those outlined earlier. Instruct the client to tighten and relax each of the muscle groups three different times, decreasing the degree of tension the second and third time according to the pattern described earlier. Taking a deep breath while simultaneously thinking the word *relax,* is also part of the procedure. Counting to 10 while breathing deeply after relaxing all four muscle groups is optional according to the degree of relaxation reported by the client. After completing this procedure, you should again

instruct the client to practice relaxing the four muscle groups daily for one week.

When the client reports success in relaxing the four muscle groups, you may employ a still more advanced procedure termed *recall* (D. Bernstein & Borkovec, 1973). Employing this procedure, the client relaxes the four muscle groups without first tensing them, focusing instead upon recall of the sensations experienced during the previous procedure. In introducing the client to the recall procedure, you can use an explanation similar to the following:

• "Now we're going to increase your skills in relaxing your muscles without the need to tighten them first. Relax the muscles in your hands and lower and upper arms, and contrast the feeling of relaxation with your memory of what it was like to release the tension in these same muscles as you practiced during the week. Just relax now and enjoy it. If any tension remains, send the message 'relax' to the muscles and let the tension flow out of them."

Because muscles are not tightened in the recall procedure, muscle groups are relaxed only once. Counting to ten while breathing easily and deeply is again optional according to the degree of relaxation the client reports.

When clients have mastered the recall procedure, they are ready to begin applying relaxation procedures as a means of coping with daily stresses. Explain to them that as they become aware of being excessively tense, they can take deep and easy breaths, think the word *relax,* and consciously relax tense muscles that are not needed in given situations (e.g., the facial, chest, and abdominal muscles). By consciously practicing and employing muscle relaxation, they are developing a valuable coping tool they can use all their lives. Situations in which clients can employ this skill include the following: driving under nerve-wracking conditions, waiting up for children who stay out late, taking an examination, delivering a talk, managing an aversive social situation, talking to a supervisor, overcoming sexual fears, reducing self-consciousness, keeping anger under control, and mastering various types of irrational fears.

Abbreviated Muscle Relaxation Training for Crisis Situations

The procedures described in the preceding sections commonly extend across 2 to 6 weeks. When clients are overwhelmed by crisis situations, however, abbreviated muscle relaxation training often provides temporary relief from extreme tension and enables clients to reestablish emotional equilibrium. In such instances, social workers can assist clients to achieve relaxation during a session by having them practice taking deep breaths, visualize pleasant and tranquil scenes, relax the four major muscle groups, and think appropriate cue words such as *calm, relax,* and *peaceful.* Should extreme tension recur between sessions, clients can implement these same procedures. Researchers have experimented with modifications of relaxation procedures including tape-recorded instructions, brief procedures (Marks, 1975), and use of biofeedback in tandem with muscle relaxation. Based on a review of this research, Borkovec and Sides (1979) have concluded that taped relaxation instructions are less effective than therapist-directed instructions. Lehrer (1982) has also concluded that brief procedures (often employing hypnosis) are not as effective as a full course of relaxation training and that biofeedback does not enhance the efficacy of relaxation training.

STRESS INOCULATION TRAINING (SIT)

This intervention involves combining relaxation training, cognitive coping skills, and behavioral rehearsal skills discussed in this chapter and the preceding chapter. Stress inoculation (SIT), like medical inoculation, strengthens clients' coping skills for stressful situations and then exposes them to stress strong enough to arouse their coping defenses without overwhelming them. As clients progress in mastering coping skills, they are exposed to increasing increments of threat that require greater coping capacity. The potency of the "inoculation" thus increases gradually according to the degree of mastery attained. Numerous and successful applications of SIT have been reported in the literature, the most common of which are reducing tension and fear in anxiety-producing situations, managing anger in provocative situations, and coping with pain associated with physical conditions. In our opinion, SIT can be adapted for effective use in virtually all situations in which reduction of tension and fear and management of emotions and impulses are indicated. For example, SIT can be used to good effect with child or spouse abusers. Wertkin (1985) even has demonstrated that SIT is effective in reducing stress associated with the rigors of graduate social work education.

SIT consists of three major phases: (1) educational, (2) rehearsal, and (3) application. In the following sections, we delineate each of these phases. For illustrative purposes, we consider SIT as employed in anger control.

Educational Phase

The purposes of this phase are to provide a rationale for SIT and to present a conceptual framework in lay terms that enables clients to understand their reactions to stressful events. Ordinarily this phase lasts for only one session, and because it consists primarily of instruction, you can employ it in a group context. It is critical to provide a plausible explanation of SIT because clients will not engage wholeheartedly in the procedure unless they understand and accept its logic.

In presenting the rationale for SIT, emphasize that emotional reactions are more than just single phase reactions. Moreover, mastery of emotions involves being aware of what triggers them, recognizing indications of emotional arousal, and developing new ways of coping with stressful situations that permit appropriate expressions of emotions. The following is an example of such a rationale:

- "You've been having difficulty in controlling anger (fear, anxiety, tension) in certain situations. To learn to control your anger, you need to understand it more fully, what triggers it, indications your anger is being aroused, and what you say to yourself and actually do when you're angry. You also need to learn new ways of coping with situations that trigger anger so that you can keep it from mounting out of control. Stress inoculation training is designed to accomplish these various tasks. Our first session will involve exploring all these matters further. Do you have any questions?"

If clients accept the rationale and appear receptive, you can proceed with presenting the conceptual framework. If they raise questions or manifest misgivings, it is important to focus on them, as favorable results depend on gaining willing and active participation by clients. The conceptual framework you present depends on the nature of the stressor causing difficulties. If you are seeking to inoculate clients against fears of public speaking, for example, your conceptual framework will be very different from one relevant to inoculating against stressors that arouse intense anger.[2] Novaco (1975)[3] conceptualizes anger as an emotional response to stress that is shaped by three subresponses—namely, *cognitive, somatic-affective,* and *behavioral*. To grasp how each of these components relates to their anger responses, clients must first grasp the general meaning of the concepts and then discover how these concepts apply to their individual experiences.

The cognitive component relates to self-statements that clients make in the face of provocative situations. These self-statements involve appraising a situation, which includes predicting the behavior of others by gauging their intentions and motives; evaluating one's own self-expectations, personal intentions, and images; weighing the magnitude of a situation; and assessing possible outcomes. Some clients, however, exclude some of the preceding types of self-statements, which contributes to deficient anger control. Failing to consider

their own intentions or the magnitude of a situation, some clients lash out wildly and impulsively when confronted with provocative situations. Such clients do not ask themselves, "How can I work this situation *out?*" or "What will be the consequences if I blow my stack?" What clients do *not* say to themselves is often equally important as self-statements they *do* make.

To assist clients to appreciate the importance of self-statements in provocative situations, it is helpful to provide examples of contrasting self-statements that lead predictably to increasing anger or to maintaining self-control. The following are examples you may wish to use:

DESTRUCTIVE SELF-STATEMENTS:

- "What does that rotten SOB think he's trying to pull off? I'll show him."
- "Look at that smirk on her face. She really thinks she put me down. I'll get even with her."
- "That arrogant bastard must think he can call all the shots. I'll show him a thing or two."

CONSTRUCTIVE SELF-STATEMENTS:

- "She's really acting like a jerk. I'll have to keep my cool, or it could really get out of hand."
- "He's doing everything he can to get my goat. But I can cope. Take deep breaths. That's right, don't let him get to you."
- "Boy, this really is sweaty. He's totally unreasonable. But I can handle it. If I lose my cool, it'll be an awful mess."

By discussing examples similar to these, clients usually readily grasp the significance of self-statements. For many clients it is a revelation, as they spontaneously realize for the first time that they make self-statements.

After illustrating the cognitive component of anger arousal, explain the somatic-affective dimension. (You should complete the explanation of general concepts before assisting clients to apply them to themselves.) This component involves the physiological and emotional manifestations of anger arousal. To assist clients to grasp the significance of this component, we recommend you explain that physical and emotional manifestations of anger serve as signals of the need to employ coping skills. By recognizing these signals, they can head off anger before it reaches unmanageable proportions. It is important to clarify further that the somatic-affective component is important also because mounting tension and emotion tend to increase the intensity of the anger response.

Physiological manifestations of anger arousal include body tension, sweaty palms, increased heart rate, rapid breathing, clenched jaws, pursed lips, gastric upset, and the like. Because people experience tension in somewhat different ways, clients need to develop awareness of their own "signals." Early emotional reactions include irritation, agitation, and feelings of resentment.

The behavioral component of anger arousal may involve withdrawal or antagonistic and aggressive behavior, either of which may produce negative consequences. For example, a person may repeatedly withdraw when a spouse makes verbal attacks, letting resentments fester and accumulate until finally even a minor provocation may trigger a violent and destructive outburst of anger. Other persons may respond aggressively to provocations by counterattacking (e.g., name-calling, or counteraccusations), thereby fostering escalation of anger by both participants and culminating in heated interaction and even violence.

Phase 1 culminates with having clients identify their individual patterns of anger arousal and analyze situations that provoke strong anger responses. More specifically, the social worker guides clients to determine exact aspects of situations that trigger anger, focusing particularly on self-statements and feelings that are experienced in such situations.[4] An effective way of assisting clients to pinpoint their individual patterns of anger arousal is to have them close their eyes, as though running a movie of provocative events, reporting thoughts, feelings, and reactions they experience. At the conclusion of this first session, clients are asked to carry out tasks of (1) monitor-

ing their self-statements when angry, (2) further analyzing aspects of stressful situations that provoke anger, and (3) listing anger-provoking situations on index cards and ranking them according to the intensity of anger they provoke. These tasks facilitate consolidation of the concepts presented in the session and also set the stage for phase 2.

Rehearsal Phase

Whereas the educational phase can be conducted in a group context, subsequent phases are generally implemented individually. The rehearsal phase consists of assisting clients to develop coping skills that involve direct action and cognitive restructuring with special emphasis on self-dialogue. Direct action involves two different aspects: (1) obtaining information about objects or situations that engender fear, pain, or anger; and (2) relaxation training. Before engaging in these activities, it is important to explain the rationale for them and to gain cooperation.

In the case of inoculation against losing control of anger, obtaining information involves analyzing the nature of stressors that provoke anger, building on the preliminary work begun in phase 1. As clients report on their task related to analyzing situations that provoke anger, further analysis and discussion occur. The social worker expands their awareness by assisting them to identify unrealistic appraisals of situations that may lead to unwarranted defensiveness and aggressiveness. According to Novaco (1975), clients' negative self-statements often reveal intolerance of mistakes by others, unrealistic self-expectations about the necessity of success, excessive expectations of others, hypersensitivity to criticism, and a belief that retaliation is essential when one is wronged. The social worker emphasizes meanings clients attribute to situations where they perceive a threat to their self-worth, which in turn often are followed by aggressive or defensive behavior that escalates the degree of negative emotionality. You should also assist clients to analyze other options that are available (e.g., assertive but nonaggressive behavior). Obtaining information and analyzing it thus tends to neutralize the provocative potential of stressful situations.

The second aspect of direct action, relaxation training, proceeds along the lines discussed earlier in this chapter. Before beginning relaxation training, it is important to explain that you are teaching them the procedure because relaxation is incompatible with tension and anger. Thus, when they anticipate confronting a provocative situation or recognize anger arousal manifestations, they can employ deep breathing and muscle relaxation to mitigate anger.

The cognitive restructuring component of phase 2 consists of assisting clients (1) to substitute positive self-statements for their habitual negative, anger-generating self-statements; and (2) to confront provocative situations constructively. Novaco (1975) and Meichenbaum (1977) concur that self-dialogue related to provocation and anger reactions should be viewed in four stages as follows:

- Preparing for the provocation whenever possible
- The impact and confrontation
- Coping with arousal
- Subsequent reflection when conflict was resolved successfully or when conflict was unresolved (Meichenbaum, 1977, p. 165).

Numerous positive, stress-reducing self-statements for each of these stages are listed by Meichenbaum and Turk (1976, pp. 6–9). We recommend that you become familiar with these self-statements. In the following, for illustrative purposes, we provide a few examples of self-statements for each of the four stages in stress inoculation for controlling anger:

PREPARING FOR PROVOCATION:

- "This is going to be upsetting, but I can handle it."
- "If I work out a plan, I'll be prepared and won't lose my cool."
- "I've learned to how to manage my anger—no need to push the panic button."

- "Remember, deep breaths and relax. Don't let it get to you."

IMPACT AND CONFRONTATION:

- "Nothing gained by getting mad. It just makes it worse."
- "It's too bad he acts like this. I'm pleased I'm staying in control. Whatever he says doesn't matter. What really matters is that I control myself."
- "I'm staying on top of this situation by keeping under control."

COPING WITH AROUSAL:

- "I can feel I'm getting tense. Need to breathe deeply and slow things down."
- "I have a right to be irritated but must keep my feelings under control."
- "Even though he's making a fool of himself, treat him with respect."
- "It takes two to have a fight, and I'm not going to let it happen."
- "Don't let him push you around. Express your views, but don't blow it by losing your cool."
- "He's really trying to get to me, but I won't let him. I'm in control of the situation."

REFLECTING ON THE PROVOCATION:

a. *When coping is successful and conflict is resolved*

- "Chalk that up as a success."
- "It paid off."
- "I actually got through it without blowing my top. It sure feels good."
- "I did better than I thought I could. I really can learn to control my anger."

b. *When conflict is unresolved*

- "Even though it wasn't a total success, it was not a lost cause. It takes time to work out sticky problems."
- "Don't dwell on it. That only makes it worse. It could have gone a lot worse."

- "You can't expect success every time. You did the best you could. Simmer down, don't let it eat at you. Relax, take a deep breath."

Note that in the last stage, self-statements are included for both successful and unsuccessful outcomes. It is important to recognize the possibility of the latter and to inoculate the client for that possibility. After all, despite the best laid plans, people do not always cope successfully; moreover, forces beyond one's control (e.g., refractory behavior by another person) may produce undesired outcomes. By assisting clients to view unsuccessful outcomes as sometimes unavoidable and to construe the same as evidence of the need to persist, rather than as ultimate failure, you inoculate them against being unduly discouraged or overwhelmed by life's occasional disappointments.

After learning the coping skills discussed in the preceding, clients rehearse employing these skills by imagining themselves in the stressful situations they earlier listed on the index cards after completing their first session. They begin with the situation they ranked as least stressful, instructing themselves with coping self-statements, breathing deeply, and relaxing their muscles. The social worker guides them as necessary. As they gain confidence in their ability to cope successfully with one situation, they advance to the next, thereby gradually increasing the potency of their inocula-tion. During this process, it is important for the social worker to express approval of their progress and to encourage them to make reinforcing self-statements also. Clients continue this process until they complete the hierarchy of stressful situations. Homework assignments involving practice of the skills with the imagined stressful situation continue between sessions. Phase 2 thus extends across approximately three weekly sessions.

Application Phase

In this phase, clients apply their newly won coping skills to actual life situations and other imagined stressful situations or engage in simulated stressful situations with the social worker playing the role of other protagonists. In this last activity, the social worker should play the role "to the hilt," being sufficiently provocative to challenge the coping skills of clients without overwhelming them. The ultimate proof of effectiveness of the coping skills is coping successfully *in vivo,* and clients' confidence increases as they discover they can indeed cope with situations that previously overwhelmed them.

SIT concludes with instructions to the client to continue practicing the skills indefinitely, thereby maintaining and further enhancing the potency of the inoculation. Ordinarily SIT extends across five or six sessions, although a longer time can be taken if deemed necessary.

Summary

This chapter has assisted you in developing skills for helping clients with a variety of common concerns including problem solving, enhancing social skills, increasing assertiveness, relaxation and managing stress. We move in Chapter 15 to assisting you to develop your skills in helping clients in macro practice areas of empowerment, resource development, and organizing.

Internet Resources

You can gather additional information on the topics of this chapter by entering the keywords "social skills" and "children" in InfoTrac®. In so doing, you will find articles such as: Evans, S. A., & Sapia, J. (2000). Effective school-based mental health interventions: Advancing the social skills training paradigm. *Journal of School Health, 70,* 5. If you enter "assertiveness" as a keyword, you can find articles such as: Thompson, K. L., Bundy, K. A., & Wolfe, W. R. (1996). Social skills training for young adolescents: Cognitive and performance components. *Adolescence, 31* (123); Yoshioka, M. (2000). Substantive differences in the assertiveness of low-income African American, Hispanic, and Caucasian women. *Journal of Psychology, 134* (3); Niikura, R. (1999). Assertiveness among Japanese, Malaysian, Filipino, and U.S. white-collar workers. *Journal of Social Psychology, 139* (6). Entering "stress management," you can access: Wijnberg, M. H., & Reding, K. M. (1999). Reclaiming a stress focus: The hassles of rural, poor single mothers. *Families in Society, 80* (5). Entering "problem-solving in therapy" you can access: Mecca, W. F., Rivera, A., & Esposito, A. J. (2000). Instituting an outcomes assessment effort: Lessons from the field. *Families in Society, 81* (1).

Notes

1. These and related instruments are described in the *Handbook of Measurements for Marriage and Family Therapy* (Fredman & Sherman, 1987).

2. For discussion of conceptual frameworks that pertain to several types of stressors, we refer you to Meichenbaum (1977).

3. We wish to acknowledge that much of the material in this section is based on this reference.

4. If situations that provoke anger responses usually involve family members, relatives, or others with whom clients have frequent contacts, you should also make efforts to involve these significant others to assist them in modifying their provocative behavior.

CHAPTER 15

Developing Resources, Planning, and Advocacy as Intervention Strategies

Revised and edited by Glenda Dewberry Rooney

CHAPTER OVERVIEW

This chapter builds on the previous chapters, focusing on direct practice roles to present social work action in macro practice. Interventions designed to enhance social work's empowerment goals are explored through developing resources, planning, and advocacy. The chapter contains guidelines and case studies to assist you in incorporating macro practice and case management skills into your repertoire.

Social work has focused throughout its history on social reform, social justice, equality, and improving social conditions. The NASW Code of Ethics has consistently included, as primary obligation, enhancing the welfare of individuals, including improving social conditions through resource development, planning, and social action (NASW, 1996). Promotion of social and economic justice and improving social conditions also includes a context of social work practice with populations at risk as outlined in the Curriculum Policy Standards of the Council on Social Work Education, which emphasizes a commitment "to enhancement of human well-being and to the alleviation of oppression" (CSWE, 1995, p. 97). Social work programs must also "present theoretical and practice content about patterns, dynamics and consequences of discrimination, economic deprivation and oppression, and provide students

with the skill to promote social change as well as content about people of color, women, gay and lesbian persons." (pp. 101–102).

Macro level intervention strategies help us approach these goals. Interventions with individuals or families may be necessary to help them reach these goals, but intervening at a systems level is equally important. As noted by Netting, Kettner, and McMurtry (1993), social workers regardless of their specializations will at some time "engage in macro-level interventions as the appropriate response to a need or problem" (p. 5). By definition, macro practice has as its focus problem solving around situations or problems at the systems rather than the individual level. Parsons, Jorgensen, and Hernandez (1988) frame social problems as targets, and professional social workers use a variety of social work roles to hit them. These roles include educator, enabler, mediator, advocate, resource developer, and broker. Macro level intervention strategies make use of the same skills and processes introduced earlier in the helping process, beginning with a multidimensional assessment of the condition or situation to be changed, goal development, selection of the intervention strategy, and evaluation. Many different forms of macro level interventions to alter conditions, improve environments, and respond to a particular need may be found within groups or communities. Limited space precludes discussing the various strategies in depth, but we discuss selected general strategies using examples in this chapter that emphasize the following:

1. Developing and supplementing resources
2. Utilizing and enhancing support systems
3. Employing advocacy and social action
4. Social planning and organizing
5. Improving institutional environments
6. Collaboration and coordinating services

Throughout this chapter, we emphasize macro strategies in the context of empowerment. At the conclusion of the chapter we offer some general guidelines to assist in evaluating outcomes of macro level intervention strategies.

WHY THE FOCUS ON EMPOWERMENT?

By *empowerment* we mean enabling groups or communities to gain or regain the capacity to interact with the environment in ways that enhance resources to meet their needs, contribute to their well-being and potential, give their life satisfaction, and provide control over their lives to the extent possible. Further, as practitioners we act in a manner that responds to needs and interests as identified by groups and communities and that will assist them to realize their hopes, dreams, aspirations, and strengths. We believe that macro level intervention strategies when combined with empowerment foster the principle of collaboration as an integral part of social work practice.

Constituents of social work often include individuals, groups, and entire communities who lack power. An empowerment perspective assumes that issues of power and powerlessness are inextricably linked to the experience of racial and ethnic minority communities and other oppressed groups. Embedded in the experiences of these groups is a history of discrimination, stigma, and oppression, the results of which are a limited sense of individual and collective self-efficacy or a pervasive sense

of powerlessness to alter their circumstances (Gutierrez, 1994). Certain vulnerable groups are unable to cope effectively with stressful situations and to avail themselves of essential environmental resources because of a sense of powerlessness and hopelessness. To gain a sense of power, of course, requires that essential resources are available in the environment. Moreover, a sense of power is closely linked to competence, self-efficacy, support systems, and the belief that individual actions or actions in concert with others can alter or improve situations. Gutierrez (1994) suggests that in addition to increasing self-efficacy and developing new skills, empowerment includes the development of a critical consciousness about the causes of injustice and powerlessness. It is important to keep in mind that these groups or communities who experience a lack of fit between themselves, their needs, and the social environment have strengths that may be temporarily eroded by oppressive and discriminatory forces. Valuing their definition of the problem, building on existing strengths, and defining the helping relationship as collaborative are critical aspects of the empowerment process (Gutierrez & Lewis, 1999). In essence, the social work role, in the empowerment process is to "help individuals develop the capacity to change their situations" (Gutierrez & Ortega, 1991, p. 25).

In this chapter we will draw upon a number of examples in which social workers acting as change agents develop resources and support systems, plan programs, and utilize advocacy or social action as collaborators of empowerment.

OPPORTUNITIES AND CHALLENGES

The social environment, with which groups and communities interact, also exerts influence over their lives and contains both challenges and opportunities. Most of us who live in the United States enjoy a standard of living that provides for safety and protection, regulatory agencies, governmental welfare services, and public education.

Because of demographic characteristics such as race, sex, class, ethnicity, and culture, what some citizens experience as opportunities may be challenges for members of other groups. Minority communities, particularly those in the urban core, are often unable to take advantage of job opportunities because of limited transportation systems to areas where jobs are located. Earned income does not ensure a living wage. Many families who work live in poverty or may be homeless because of a lack of affordable housing. Gaps in income based on racial groups and gender still exist. Economic trends in the global economy have meant a loss of jobs in the United States. Minimum wage and service jobs, many of which are part-time and lack health care benefits, also contribute to poverty. Although some states stipulate that companies using state tax dollars are required to offer a living wage, Congress has continually resisted raising the minimum wage. There is an obvious discrepancy in arguing that the primary goal of projects in urban centers is not job creation (thus employers using state or city funding can avoid meeting a living wage requirement), while prisons, the most expansive growth industry, are being built in some smaller communities to create economic opportunities for residents.

Many families, and indeed entire communities, experience chronic stressors in their everyday lives without minimum standards or resources to meet basic needs (Tolan & Gorman-Smith, 1997). Poverty continues to play a role in social problems, child development, family stability, and access to resources (Brooks-Gunn & Duncan, 1997; Ewalt, 1994; Halpern, 1990; McLoyd, 1997). Opportunities for macro level intervention strategies exist in educational systems where significant numbers of children of color are characterized as underachievers. This results in "enormous social costs to individuals and society" and "sustains class, economic and social inequities" (L. F. Williams, 1990, p. 236). Public school systems, reacting to violence, stylized urban dress and behavior, and fear of the unfamiliar have become zones of zero tolerance in which the application of

policies are perceived by minority communities as disproportionately affecting children of color.

A study conducted by Rank and Hirschl (1999) traces poverty over the life span and suggests that minorities, in particular poor African Americans, are likely to remain so throughout their lifetime. Brooks-Gunn and Duncan (1997) discuss the incidence of poverty through third-generation minority and immigrant groups. Poor and minority families struggle with obstacles and challenges that may indeed be institutionalized, further exacerbating their marginal status in the social environment. These challenges affect entire communities, the majority of which are racially or ethnically diverse and female, and those who are segregated by geographical location with limited access to alternatives. In Chapter 10, we referred to extrafamilial obstacles to describe situations that are faced by families who are different because of race, class, or sexual orientation.

In his vivid portrayal of the ecological realities of inner city life, *There Are No Children Here*, Alex Kotlowitz (1991) described a situation in which 1,000 new appliances were found waterlogged and rodent infested in the storage area of a housing project despite the fact that a majority of the residents were without adequate appliances. Although this story focuses on one family, they are representative of groups of families—indeed, entire communities—who live, cope, and survive in circumstances beyond their control. The harmful effects of prolonged exposure to poverty and stressful life events on child and adolescent development are well documented in the literature (Freeman, & Dyers, 1993; Icard, Longres & Spenser, 1999; Jose, Cafasso & D'Anna, 1994; McLoyd, 1997; Mosley & Lex, 1999; C. Smith & Carlson, 1997).

Social services continue to be directed toward individuals. Because the various organizations have their own mission, structure, and service goals for which they receive funding, clients with multiple concerns may experience a service system that is fragmented, segmented, and lacking coordination. The Personal Responsibility and Work Opportunity Reconciliation Act of 1996, which reformed welfare, and the Adoption and Safe Family Act of 1997 are examples of both segmentation and limited coordination. The former requires the head of the family receiving welfare assistance to become employed within 2 years and sets a 5-year lifetime limit on assistance. At the same time, the Safe Family and Adoption Act emphasizes greater scrutiny of often poor families and their ability to care for their children. This law does not sufficiently account for the removal of some of the safeguards that were diminished by welfare reform. Further, it does not consider as pertinent those conditions that have plagued poor families in contact with child welfare, such as insufficient living wages, lack of adequate jobs, and lack of child care. We are not suggesting that welfare and child welfare reform were not needed. However, there has been an unexamined impact of these two pieces of legislation on families who now often face multiple, competing deadlines for child welfare, for welfare, and for chemical dependency treatment (Courtney, 1999).

On another level, rules, policies, and procedures (RPPs), legislative mandates, and managed care directives, rather than professional orientation, increasingly frame the context in which social welfare services are delivered. The effects of this context limit professional discretion and in some instances pose ethical dilemmas for social workers and other professionals. It is important for social workers to remain grounded in the historical roots of the profession, by promoting social and economic justice and social change to address inadequate resources and deal with policies that adversely impact well-being. Understanding the ecological systems nature of social problems calls for social workers to emphasize macro level interventions in concert with other intervention strategies. Before proceeding further, we wish to note that because client concerns are multidimensional and involve reciprocal interactions among multiple systems, interventions aimed exclusively at the environment or the individual or family may ignore critical dimensions. At the same time, multiple interventions may be employed simultane-

ously to address both individual and environmental concerns.

In the preceding discussion, we have identified conditions, trends, and patterns that demand the attention of social work and its focus on problem solving at various systems levels. Constituents served by social workers benefit from all levels of practice. In many cases, concerns of clients involve micro, mezzo, and macro issues. It is entirely possible that macro level situations may be generalized to the groups to which clients belong and with which social workers interact on a daily basis. In many instances, opportunities to employ macro level strategies evolve from caseloads. For example, a social work practitioner works in a low-income community neighborhood health clinic. As a member of an interdisciplinary community-based health team, her caseload consists primarily of young mothers and their children. In reviewing her case records, the social worker notes that a common theme among the families that she sees individually is running out of food near the end of the month. She also notes that it is during this time that the mothers and their children are more likely to miss clinic appointments. When a member of the team raises a concern about families missing appointments, the social worker suggests exploration of this concern in the context of a larger group issue. At the suggestion of the social worker the team agrees to sponsor a series of focus groups with young mothers in the community to explore resource and service needs.

In this situation, the social worker effectively moved from a micro level focus on a specific problem to a strategy that has the potential to address the issue of running out of food as a representative condition of a larger group. Although the interdisciplinary team is a joint effort to assist individuals or families in the community with health care, the social worker brings a unique systems perspective to the various theoretical and professional orientations represented on the team (Long & Holle, 1997). The use of the focus group is an example of empowerment because the discussion among the mothers is sufficiently open-ended that it allows them to define and prioritize their concerns and experiences, using their own frame of reference, and evaluate the services they are currently receiving.

DEVELOPING AND SUPPLEMENTING RESOURCES

Social workers are in a strategic position to identify resource needs of people living in impoverished conditions because of our contact with individuals, families, and groups on a daily basis. Within the context of our work, resource development includes educating and alerting policy makers, civic groups, and social welfare organizations to clients' conditions and also advocating on their behalf. By augmenting or developing resources for groups and communities, it is also possible to meet the needs of individuals and families. Vosler (1990) notes that resource needs are often missed, perhaps in large part because of the structure of social welfare services in which the primary focus tends to be on individual treatment. Because of this focus, aggregate information about whole groups or populations may not be as obvious.

Mobilizing Community Resources

Resources for addressing concrete needs may vary depending on the community. Rural communities, for example, may have fewer formal resources, but informal networks may exist. Many low-income individuals living in suburban communities may lack access to adequate services because of the assumption of affluence that leads to the invisibility of the poor. Resource development may involve special assistance or helping clients to secure essential items on an individual basis. In other instances, social workers may need to become involved in the development of programs to assist groups of people with extensive needs.

Organizing to develop or supplement resources is indicated when a significant number of people within given ecological boundaries (e.g., neighborhoods, communities, institutions) or populations who share certain characteristics have needs for which matching resources are unavailable. Moreover, as physical environments, technological advances, and political and social circumstances relentlessly change, social workers are constantly confronted with the need to organize resources in response to both old and evolving needs.

The role of enabler and the principles of empowerment may be particularly important for social workers in macro practice situations who organize and develop resources. The earlier case example of the community-based health clinic and the young mothers illustrates how the social worker sought information from the mothers so that resources were developed with *rather than for* them. Results from the focus group discussions revealed that among other things, the mothers were frustrated by the inability to use the local park with their children because of drug traffic, police harassment, and "johns" soliciting prostitutes. Community safety was another concern that emerged. Also, the women, the majority of whom were single parents, asked for assistance in developing alternative child care options.

Encouraged by the social worker, a number of the mothers began to attend local community organization meetings that involved members from area churches and businesses to discuss their concerns about the park. She and a group of mothers also visited several of the large churches in the neighborhood to explore options for evening child care that would allow the mothers to have time away from their children. Many of the women had used the food shelves provided by the churches but were skeptical of the churches' interest in their situation. As a result they were reluctant to approach the churches. In talking to the churches, the social worker found that they were interested in becoming more involved in the community, especially with children, and that they too had concerns about community safety. It was arranged for a group of the mothers to meet with church officials. Although concerns about the use of the parks remained, the women gained a greater sense of their ability to effect change in their community and for themselves as a result of their involvement with the churches and the community organization. The community organization whose meetings previously had not been well attended was also revitalized and provided an additional opportunity to become mobilized around their concerns.

Following a series of meetings between the mothers' group, church officials, and area business owners, several of the churches agreed to use existing space for a mother's night out child care program staffed by the mothers and community volunteers. In addition, the social worker helped the women to establish a child care cooperative, which enabled the mothers to do laundry or other errands. Developing and mobilizing community resources in this example illustrates the potential for partnerships between various groups who may not routinely interact, yet share common concerns like community safety. In working with the women, the social worker also met with church members, the majority of whom did not live in the community, to educate them about the community as well as respond to their concerns about safety and the additional traffic in the churches by nonmembers.

Supplementing Existing Resources

Resource needs vary according to a particular concern and vary substantially from one community to another. In some instances, existing resources may be inadequate for the level of need. Stigma and dominant culture values and beliefs often clash with the realities and may unintentionally reinforce oppression and access to needed resources.

Views that, for example, characterize homeless individuals as lazy, immoral, or otherwise depraved in many respects resemble 19th century thought (McChesney, 1995). More recently, the homeless have been characterized as having mental illness, addiction or substance abuse problems, lack of personal responsibility, and low job skills. These views ignore poverty as a primary reason for homelessness, the increase in homeless families and the influence of available and accessible substantial institutional supports on the likelihood of

a family's exit from this status (McChesney, 1995; Piliavin, Wright, Mare, & Westerfelt, 1996).

Poverty is a primary factor in homelessness, which extends to the ability to find and maintain affordable housing. Many families have exhausted or overextended informal networks and have few alternatives (McChesney, 1995). Limited and aging housing stock in inner cities, the resistance of suburban communities to allow low income housing, and the phasing out of governmental programs to develop and subsidize affordable housing all compound this very real social problem. Although the homeless are a homogenous group because they share a need for shelter and food, they vary in many ways.

The demographics of the homeless differ in both composition and geography. Studies have established that the majority of homeless in urban areas are families rather than individuals, and the majority are African American. In rural and suburban areas, the issue has not been sufficiently acknowledged or discussed, making it difficult to determine the composition of this geographical group (Gerstel, Bogard, McConnell, & Schwartz, 1996; McChesney, 1995). Youth leaving their homes for a variety of reasons increasingly represent yet another significant portion of the homeless population (Nord & Luloff, 1995). Kurtz, Jarvis, and Kurtz (1991) have reported on a regional research study conducted in the southeastern states. Most of the youth in the study lacked stable, supportive families and were victims of a fragmented child welfare system. Homeless youth are a highly vulnerable population that presents a wide range of problems and needs. Among the homeless are individuals who often need health or mental health services, employment counseling, or rehabilitation and social support.

Living arrangements for the homeless are also varied. Being homeless may mean frequent transitions between shelters and transitional housing facilities. Some may be living on the streets, others in shelters, or with family or friends. Irrespective of the various entry points into homeless status, the resources for this population are inadequate and contribute to further problems. Homeless families, for example, are also at risk for intervention by child protective services.

Social workers working with communities and homeless groups have been instrumental in mobilizing resources to respond to the needs of this population as well as taking an active role in developing legislative and policy initiatives as illustrated by the following example. The example also illustrates the fact that although community, civic, or church groups may be instrumental in the development of resources, there are often unanticipated difficulties.

CASE EXAMPLE OF SUPPLEMENTING RESOURCES

Social workers and residents of a homeless shelter convened a group of religious and business leaders to explore the possibility of expanding available shelter beds to accommodate increasing demands. The proposal involved the use of churches throughout the city for bed-only space in the evenings. Many of the large, old urban churches had large gymnasiums, recreational centers, and dining halls, which had served the recreational and social needs of members who had once lived in the city. Although several churches agreed and there was minimal opposition from the business community, the proposal to expand resources by creating a coordinated effort was not without difficulties in one community. Not only did the implementation of the proposal require city permits and significant financial and human resources, it also needed the goodwill of the neighborhoods in which the churches were located. Believing that they had involved all of the critical stakeholders, the social workers were unprepared for the most vocal opposition from parents at a day care center that rented space in one of the churches. Parental concerns centered on child safety and reservations about the presence of homeless men in the community. In conceptualizing change, it is important to explore potential barriers such as ideological conflicts, fears, and value conflicts that community members may have (Kettner, Netting, & McMurtry, 1993). Unfortunately, in this situation day care center parents and staff were not involved in the initial discus-

sion and therefore their concerns were not adequately addressed.

Both of the previous examples emphasize the need for social workers to work closely with community leaders, civic or religious groups, elected officials, and organized task and informal groups that include vulnerable people and their advocates. Managing and coordinating these various groups calls for being a broker, a mediator, and an enabler. In both situations the need for long-range solutions, requiring social planning efforts at the federal, state, and local levels, were also necessary. Providing food and shelter for the homeless population is vital. The social workers recognized that additional shelter space was an interim solution. Intermediary efforts are by no means a substitute for long-range planning and action when a particular issue affects a significant number of people or a community. Toward this end, the social worker in the shelter was also involved in lobbying and educating elected officials about the plight of the homeless and active in groups that focused on larger systemic issues, for example, advocating for affordable housing, living wage jobs opportunities, and job transportation services.

Many times, expanding or developing resources requires problem analysis and interventions from a micro to macro perspective. This dual focus as presented in the situations previously discussed promotes change and growth for individual and environmental systems. The challenges of developing or expanding resources may require advocacy, social action, brokering, educating, and enabling.

UTILIZING AND ENHANCING SUPPORT SYSTEMS

In the assessment phase of the helping process, the whole person is explored along with his or her concerns. This assessment is most comprehensive and inclusive when it examines the ecology of the client's identified problem, the systems involved, strengths, resilience, and support systems. Social supports or kinship networks exist in almost all groups and communities. Many groups and communities, despite chronic stressors and life events, also demonstrate a tremendous amount of re-silience, coping, and the capacity to help in times of need. Mobilized relatives, neighbors, and con-gregations are natural ecological structures and as such may offer resources needed by a variety of groups. Support networks were common in prein-dustrial communities but are virtually an untapped resource in postindustrial Western society, espe-cially with the advent of more formal social wel-fare systems. In exploring the dynamics of help, Bertha Reynolds (1951), stressed, "people seem to look upon taking and giving help as they do any other activity of life" (p. 16).

Community Support Systems and Networks

Although modern social welfare services have tended to remove or substitute for natural helping that sustained people over time, there is a rich his-tory of Jewish, Catholic, Protestant, fraternal, and civic groups that have provided mutual aid and support for individuals and families.

Among historically oppressed groups, reliance on indigenous networks and community supports were critical to economic and social survival. In ad-dition, members of minority groups have been re-luctant to seek assistance from resources outside of their communities because of demeaning, imper-sonal, or negative experiences with formal social welfare organizations or because services were not available to them as a result of discriminatory prac-tices (Green, 1999). Horejsi, Heavy Runner, and Pablo (1992) note that persistent poverty among Native Americans has resulted in a norm of sharing concrete resources. In African American commu-nities the strength and survival of families and groups were often dependent on strong kinship ties, flexibility in family membership, and connec-tions to the church as a social and economic re-source. African American mutual aid societies and civic and church groups traditionally provided as-sistance to the community. This legacy also ex-tended to building institutions of higher educa-tion, caring for orphaned children and widows,

and establishing insurance societies. In other com-munities of color there is a long history of human services, for example, Buddhist mutual aid associa-tions in the Asian community. Associations for Southeast Asians may be found in many parts of the country (Canda & Phaobtong, 1992).

In recent years social workers have increasingly relied on interventions that tap both formal and in-formal support networks and have developed new ones that provide vitally needed resources to spe-cific populations. Relatives, friends, neighbors or neighborhoods, and organizations located in com-munities are natural support systems that can act in times of adversity. The move to identify and utilize support systems is both warranted and welcomed by groups and communities. Empowerment in spirit and practice means that community residents are experts in identifying and solving concerns. In this regard, community residents are also experts in mobilizing or employing support systems in ways that are relevant to them. Such support systems are not only valuable but virtually essential because so-cial workers and other professional helpers can spend only limited time with clients. Members of support systems can often be available when a crisis occurs and give the ongoing support that profes-sionals cannot provide.

Natural support systems consisting of friends, relatives or neighbors can assist social workers in supporting families at risk for child abuse and ne-glect. The child care cooperative and the "mother's night out program" organized with neighborhood mothers in the earlier example provided much-needed respite for overburdened mothers and their children. Research has shown that feeling lonely and isolated are risk factors for parental neglect and abuse. Parents who are abusive or neglectful are often less skilled in the use of support networks (Beeman, 1993). Mothers in a research group where the focus was to define neglect agreed that "sometimes the best thing that you can do for somebody is to be their friend" (Rooney, Neathery, & Zuzek, 1997, p. 19). Other examples of natural support and advocacy groups include Alzheimer's groups for caretakers; groups such as Parents,

Family and Friends of Lesbians and Gays, an organization founded by a parent of a gay man; and the National Alliance for the Mentally Ill, which is made up of family members and consumers of mental health services. Kinship care and support systems such as the church, neighborhood groups, and networks also serve as community level protective factors (Brookins, Peterson, & Brooks, 1997; P. A. Gibson, 1999; Haight, 1998; Jackson, 1998; Tracey & Whittaker, 1990).

Developing Support and Networks

For some groups or communities, sustained support may be indicated, and resources for supportive networks may need to be developed. For example, homebound persons and refugee or immigrant groups who have been disconnected from their homeland may lack support besides their immediate family. There are also individuals who lack social connections or who are isolated because of weak kinship or neighborhood ties. Often experiences of single-parent, low-income families cause them to feel disconnected from mainstream society. Isolation from support systems can also result from living in sparsely populated areas. For example, new arrivals in urban communities, such as Native Americans who leave the reservation or individuals who relocate from other communities in search of better job or educational opportunities, may experience such isolation. Stigma as a result of AIDS or severe and persistent mental illness or disability is also a reason for isolation. An innovative method for countering isolation in rural areas, described by Galinsky and Stern (1991), involved bringing a support group into the homes of people with AIDS in rural areas through teleconferencing. This procedure can, of course, be used with other groups. Advancing technology provides opportunities for social workers to create innovative strategies to connect people who share a common situation.

Organizations can also act as support systems, particularly for people who are in transition. The American Red Cross is an example of a formal organization that assists communities in times of disaster. Transitional housing, shelters for battered women, and work environments that have policies responsive to work and family demands, that provide classes for individuals for whom English is a second language, or that promote health and wellness programs for employees are other examples of supportive environments.

CASE EXAMPLE OF DEVELOPING SUPPORTS AND NETWORKS

An innovative residential reunification and permanency program for youth placed outside of the home illustrates how one human services organization built support into its program design. The target group was African American males who had experienced multiple out-of-home placements. The agency was concerned about the significant numbers of African American males between the ages of 12 and 17 who had repeat stays in its shelter system and who seemed destined to remain adrift or cycle through various placements or institutions. The goal of the program was to move the youth toward permanency, either through reunification with the family, living with a relative, or independent living in the community. In the development of the program, a group of youth in the shelter were interviewed to obtain their view of their situation and to determine the resource needs and supports that would achieve the goal of reunification and permanency.

Evaluation sessions were conducted with youth, parents, and relatives after the first complete year of the program. Among the factors identified by both youth and family members as being the most helpful were respite and home visits. Home visits facilitated gradual reentry into the family system as well as transition into the community. Families were also involved in activities hosted by the agency in the residential program. In recognition of the fact that the transition from institution to home environment potentially posed some difficulties for families, respite became a central program feature that was both supportive and preventive. In addition to residential beds, the agency maintained respite beds that could be used for up to 72 hours by the youth and family in times of crisis. As an alternative, the youth could reside for a brief period with kin or a member of the community network. During the respite period, kin or community members were involved in the effort to resolve the difficulty in order to avoid another out-of-home placement. At a focus group designed to evaluate the program's effectiveness, the comment of one parent on the support the agency provided was particularly poignant: "The staff held our family's hand until we could go it alone."

This innovative program illustrates how the utilization of support and networks can be incorporated into and facilitate agency program goals. It is also an example of a macro level intervention strategy designed to alter the situation of a particular group. The agency determined form its experience as a short-term shelter that a significant number of minority youth continued to cycle throughout the system. The response addressed a system level issue intended to reverse the trend of the youth remaining disconnected from their families and communities. In developing the program, the agency viewed the support provided by the agency along with that of relatives, mentors, and the community as natural support systems critical to the ultimate program goal of permanency. This shift in the agency's program focus required providing information about the lack of permanency for youth in the shelter system. Statistical data compiled by the agency, including a profile of the youth in the shelter system, were used in advocating for a different approach and convincing other organization funders and the community of the program's potential as well as in training for staff.

Immigrant and Refugee Groups

Immigrant or refugee groups have particular needs for social support and resources. Geographic relocation in and of itself is traumatic. We include in this group individuals who are categorized by the Immigration and Naturalization Service (INS) as undocumented aliens. Although formal organizations (civic, social, and governmental) offer assistance and respond to the basic needs of recognized immigrant or refugee groups, these services cannot make up for the cultural isolation and discontinuity, the grief and guilt, or occupational concerns. In addition, some groups may be unfamiliar with formal services or assistance from the government

and therefore may not seek the services to which they are entitled. Undocumented individuals are of course not eligible for government programs and may be underserved by civic groups or churches. They have needs particular to their status including fear of deportation and being exploited as cheap labor. A case in point occurred when a group of hotel employees consisting of both legal and undocumented individuals attempted to join the local union. The management retaliated by calling the INS. This action mobilized numerous community and professional groups and the issue was successfully resolved. Increasingly, social workers will be involved in the workplace as organizations seek to meet the demands for a viable labor force. The current demand for labor is similar to that which occurred during the turn of the century, often referred to as welfare capitalism, in which social workers had an active role in developing resources and advocating for immigrants (Brandes, 1976).

Children are often included within the group of the undocumented, but some are born in the United States and therefore entitled to services. Yet their families are reluctant to seek or utilize services for these children to avoid calling attention to themselves, particularly in instances where there are children or other family members who are undocumented. A case of a social worker who sought consultation is an illustration of this point. In this situation, a widowed mother had two children born in the United States. The mother and a third child, the eldest, were undocumented. The mother understood that the eldest child required medical attention but was fearful of the family being deported. Assuring the mother of confidentiality and receiving her permission to act, the social worker approached the development officer of a local private children's hospital. A pediatrician on staff agreed to provide medical care for the child. In exploring resource options for this family, the social worker learned that the hospital board viewed outreach to this particular community as a part of the hospital's mission. The result of this effort was an additional resource for the community. Also, the social worker became a member of a hospital and community task group charged with making a recommendation regarding prenatal and infant care programs and infant loss support groups, a need that had been identified by the community.

Limitations of Social Support

Although social work has acknowledged the strengths and resources found in chronically impoverished communities, many social workers believe that we have yet to fully exploit the opportunities for networks and social support systems. Building on the natural helping systems in communities or groups recognizes strengths. Assisting or engaging groups or communities to deal with concerns utilizes strengths as a strategy toward empowerment to change circumstances (Gutierrez & Ortega, 1991). At the same time, agencies that include support or utilize networks as an integral part of their programs are responsive in their approach to client concerns.

Caution is advised, however. Utilizing or developing social support should not favor one type over the other. For example, groups or communities may act in some instances as supplemental resources instead of more formal services to which people may be entitled. At times, informal resources that are utilized or developed should not be strained or exhausted or cause a hardship. As mentioned earlier in this chapter, many homeless families have lived with relatives prior to becoming homeless. The availability of support networks as resources cannot suffice for long-term efforts that address the issue of homelessness and other persistent social problems. Coordination between formal and informal resources may be the preferred approach. This dual focus requires the various social work roles and an approach that promotes growth or resolves concerns for the individual and environmental systems (Parsons, Jorgenson, & Hernandez, 1994).

In developing or supplementing supportive systems or networks within a community, you must become familiar with cultural nuances, values and norms, and the political orientation of various groups. The tendency to generalize information about certain groups may lead to potential conflicts because all groups have status and power, clan or religious differences even though they may share the same country of origin.

Many non-Western cultures are often emphasized as valuing interdependence and collectivism over the more Western postindustrial influence of independence (Greenfield, 1994; Ogbu, 1987). This would suggest that resources are more readily available in immigrant or refugee communities. In some cases, this is a useful framework for understanding cultural influences or pressures and social and economic arrangements. It should be stressed that length of stay and the extent of acculturation within group power structures and kinship ties may ultimately influence social support systems. For example, a social worker seeking assistance for immigrant women who were abused by their husbands found that the community was sympathetic to the issue. Fear of the husband's role of leadership in the community and relationships between clans were sufficient enough to prevent providing a safe haven for these women. Moreover, perceptions of what constituted an abusive relationship in this community were not the same as in Western society. In another situation, a social worker urged a woman to seek assistance from a shelter rather than rely on the family and clan to help resolve a marital conflict. This resulted in the woman becoming isolated from her community. Intervention strategies must always be informed by and sensitive to how particular communities resolve situations, and wherever possible, those strategies should be supported.

These examples, as well as those provided by Hirayama, Hirayama, and Citengok (1993) and Green (1999), point to the fact that various groups differ in their definition of the problem and therefore may not respond to resources developed to address a particular concern. Hirayama, Hirayama, and Citengok (1992) note, for example, that although many Southeast Asian refugees experience reactive depression, they may not access mental health services because of a negative perception of a mental illness label. In many cases, mental status may be more appropriately framed in the context of stress intervention strategies rather than the more traditional approaches. Cultural differences and perceptions of mental illness may also influence the extent to which some Latinos access mental health services (Green, 1999, p. 261). Reluctance to articulate concerns may also be influenced by the larger society's stigma or negative perceptions of the community, especially in individuals or groups who already feel marginalized.

The institutionalized are a group of people for whom social support is needed yet may be difficult to develop. Persons in controlled therapeutic environments or institutional placements are psychologically and in some cases geographically isolated from the community. In the best of situations, contact with relatives, neighbors, or friends remains grossly inadequate. Although the objective is often to return to the community, connections to the community are rarely an integral part of services. Institutional placements provide social workers with opportunities to explore social support through connections with the community as well as within the institutions. Finally, within some groups such as undocumented individuals, the development of social support and networks are critically important.

EMPLOYING ADVOCACY AND SOCIAL ACTION

The social work profession has a proud tradition of advocacy and social action leading to social reform. Indeed, P. H. Stuart (1999) characterizes the focus on the person and the environment as "linking of clients and social policy, and as a distinctive contribution of the social work profession" (p. 335). Haynes and Mickelson (2000) trace the involvement of social workers during the development of some of the more enlightened and humane social policies in both the 19th and 20th centuries. Within the African American community, community practice that involved advocacy and social action, concern for the "private troubles of individu-

als and the larger policy issues that affected them," were at the forefront of early African American social work pioneers (Carlton-LaNey, 1999). Social workers were also active in social action, often in concert with grassroots or minority civic groups. For example, support of the United Farm Workers, the Equal Rights Amendment, National Welfare Rights Organization, and civil rights movement have involved social workers and professional organizations in providing advocacy, including expert testimony on a variety of social issues.

Despite this rich history, social work has not always been attentive to the sociopolitical and historical mandates of the profession. Franklin (1990) traces the "cycles of social work practice" and concludes, as do many others in the field, that the profession has changed and that the focus has tended to reflect the dominant views and ideologies of the times. In their book *Unfaithful Angels*, Specht and Courtney (1994) ignited a debate about the profession's goals with regard to the role of social workers as advocates and initiators of change. This argument has roots in the "emergence of two separate and interacting movements" from which the profession evolved, the charity organization societies and the settlement houses, and the perception that social work has failed to maintain a leadership role in social reform efforts (Haynes & Mickelson, 2000). More recently, both the Council on Social Work Education and the National Association of Social Workers have reaffirmed support for the prominent inclusion of social action and social advocacy in social work education and professional standards. For a more comprehensive review of the profession's involvement with advocacy and social action we refer you to the 1999 Centennial Issue 2 of *Social Work* (Volume 44, 4).

Earlier in this chapter we discussed social conditions, trends, and patterns that frame the essence of macro practice. We now call your attention to policy and legislative initiatives that influence social work practice, the resources available to clients, and the extent to which they are affected by environmental and social conditions. Sometimes social workers, agencies, and funding sources distinguish between direct and indirect practice. This distinction is no doubt influenced by the emphasis on "billable hours" for direct client contact. We take the position that this distinction is at best artificial and fails to acknowledge the systemic integration or relationship between clients, the larger social environment, and social work practice.

On a day-to-day basis, social workers along with their clients are confronted with an array of issues for which advocacy and social action is indicated. Policies and legislative initiatives during the final decades of the 20th century have had a profound and adverse effect on significant segments of the population. Beginning with the Reagan era, the federal government has increasingly taken an aggressive stance against both the philosophy and funding of social programs. Cuts or reductions in social programs, the results of political ideology transformed into social policy, have fueled a movement toward personal responsibility, welfare-to-work, and an ambiguous notion of family values. Those adversely affected are disproportionately women, minorities, and children. The new policies largely ignore the social and economic supports needed by the working poor. Few opposing voices emerged to counter criticism of the War on Poverty as the goals that gave rise to important social and economic programs were replaced by the Contract with America. As noted by Haynes and Mickelson (2000), "blaming the poor took on new meaning," (p. 17), reflective of the ideological political negativism and activism of the times. Programs or policies that took aim at resolving social conditions with sustainable wages, housing, and health care essentially became peripheral to political agendas, and those affected were further marginalized.

Within the legislative policy arena of the final period of the 20th century, crime became a central focus, as did family structure, despite the acknowledged relationship between poverty and the incidence of crime, and in spite of the cost of incarceration. Comprehensive legislation such as the Personal Responsibility and Work Opportunity

Act of 1996 not only changed the welfare system but also implemented drastic changes in child care, the food stamp program, Supplemental Security Income (SSI), benefits for legal immigrants, and nutrition programs, and health, education, and welfare funding to the states were all modified (Schneider & Netting, 1999; Haynes & Mickelson, 2000, p. 16). In addition, these authors stress that human rights and basic dignity, both of which are values important to social work, were eroded. Withorn (1998) questioned the ethics of welfare reform and the lack of discussion among both liberal and conservative politicians about the consequences of the mandates of federal entitlement programs. Further ethical questions emerge because the new welfare legislation appears to have as a goal the reduction of caseloads rather than the reduction of poverty. Questions that might be posed are, for example:

1. Have people actually left poverty?
2. Are children, for whom welfare was actually intended, living healthier lives?

This review of social work history and of legislation over the final decades of the 20th century provides a rationale for the importance of the role of social workers as change agents. Although minorities will be disproportionately affected, the changes in social policy influence the lives of all people who are poor, many of whom hold several low-wage jobs with few benefits like health care. The fact is that these laws and public policies influence and regulate social work and agency practice, the conditions that clients experience, and the services that are provided.

Case and Class Advocacy

We define *advocacy* and social action as the process of effecting or initiating change. This process involves working with and/or on behalf of clients (1) to obtain services or resources that would not otherwise be provided, (2) to modify or influence policies, procedures, or practices that adversely affect groups or communities, or (3) to promote legislation or policies that will result in the provision of much-needed resources or services. Agency goals and functions strongly influence the amount of job-related advocacy by social workers, and that advocacy tends to be focused on individual cases (Ezell, 1994). Yet social workers are often involved in class advocacy in their private lives and through professional associations, for example, the Child Welfare League of America and the National Association of Social Worker's PACE Committee. In addition, there are some national organizations such as Family Service of America in which local agencies have advocacy units that work with citizen groups on the local level.

Advocacy embodies two separate yet related facets. The first facet is *case advocacy*, which involves working with and on behalf of individuals or families to assure that they receive benefits and services to which they are entitled and that the services are delivered in ways that safeguard their dignity. Because this aspect of advocacy is on behalf of an individual or family, it is denoted case advocacy, corresponding closely to one dictionary definition of an advocate as "one who pleads the cause of another." Individual or case advocates may act with or on behalf of battered women, rape victims, and homeless youth.

The second facet of advocacy involves acting to effect changes in policy, practice, or laws that affect all persons in a specific class or group; hence this type is denoted *class advocacy*. Organizations such as the Children's Defense Fund, the Jewish Defense League, the National Association for the Advancement of Colored People, the National Organization for Women, and the National Center for Lesbian Rights are examples of advocates on behalf of a segment of the population. They are involved in policy advocacy and have the ability to mobilize around concerns that affect a particular group. The American Civil Liberties Union has, for example, taken up the cause of racial profiling, which involves the indiscriminate stop and search of minority males by the police. Research may also be used as a tool for class advocacy. A. H. Rice (1998) reports on the use of focus groups with welfare participants to discuss their experiences

and experiences with the newly enacted welfare reform legislation. Data from the focus groups were provided to the state legislature.

Class advocacy is much broader in scope and, in essence, is a form of social action and may lead to other macro level interventions such as community organizing or influencing legislation. Hyde (1996), in discussing feminist community intervention strategies, describes several examples in which class advocacy and social action were combined to achieve the desired result. Social action as defined by Barker (1995, p. 217) is "a coordinated effort to achieve institutional change to meet a need, solve a social problem, correct any injustices or enhance the quality of life." Class advocacy is inherently political. Policy models for political advocacy are defined and discussed by Haynes and Mickelson (2000). They stress that models are important because they guide the intervention and ensure a match between the problem and the strategy employed. We refer you to this resource as an informative guide.

Although the two types of advocacy are different, they are also highly interrelated. Advocacy action on behalf of an individual client or family may result in a precedent that leads to a change that benefits others in the same position. Class advocacy as illustrated by the following example may be an extension of case advocacy.

CASE EXAMPLE OF CLASS ADVOCACY

A social worker in a child protection unit was assigned to complete a child safety assessment in a situation in which a young child had opened the door of her home and walked about 3 blocks to the home of a relative while the father, a single parent, was asleep on the couch. The police report described the father as a drunken Indian because of his speech pattern. The assessment of the situation showed no indication that the child was in danger and therefore the social worker advocated for the return of the child to the home. In talking to the father and other family members, the social worker learned that Native Americans often experience encounters with the police and helping professionals who are influenced by the perception held by the police officer in this situation. The speech pattern that caused the police officer to determine that the father was drunk was in fact the manner in which he pronounced or enunciated words. From this situation, the social worker with the support of her agency and permission of the community organized a meeting between Native Americans in the community and the police. The intent of the meeting was to educate the police about the experience of the community and through this process curtail discriminatory practices, thereby avoiding further adverse situations. This situation is an example of participatory empowerment practice (Gutierrez & Lewis, 1999). Participatory empowerment practice involves working collaboratively within a community to confront issues of concern. A key element is using one's own power to develop the power and build the capacity of others.

Indications for Advocacy or Social Action

Class advocacy and social action may be appropriately employed in numerous situations, including the following:

1. When services or benefits to which people are entitled are denied to a group or community

2. When services or practices are dehumanizing, confrontational, or coercive

3. When discriminatory practices or policies occur because of race, gender, sexual orientation, religion, culture, family form, or other factors

4. When gaps in services or benefits cause undue hardship or contribute to dysfunction

5. When people lack representation or participation in decisions that affect their lives

6. When governmental or agency policies and procedures, or community or workplace practices, adversely affect or target groups of people

7. When a significant group of people have common needs for which resources are unavailable

8. When clients are denied civil or legal rights

Special circumstances for which advocacy or social action may be indicated involve situations in which clients are unable to act effectively on their own behalf. Included in this group may be persons who are institutionalized, children in need of protection, or those who have a need for immediate services or benefits because of a crisis situation or their legal status.

Competence and Skills

The overall goal of macro level advocacy or social action is system change. Targets of advocacy or social action may be individuals, communities, organizations, public officials, policy-making bodies, courts, legislatures, and divisions of government. Approaches to situations vary considerably according to the target system and involve a thorough understanding of how organizations or communities are structured and how they function, the legislative and rule-making processes, and "an appreciation for organizational politics" (Rothman, 1991). Advocacy can also involve different levels of assertive intensity ranging from discussion and education to a high level of social action and organizing. Sosin and Caulum (1983) developed a useful typology of advocacy that assists practitioners in planning appropriate advocacy actions. This typology along with the models discussed by Haynes and Mickelson (2000) can help determine the context of the advocacy action, the opportunities that exist, and techniques or strategies to be used and at what level.

Skills required in advocacy or social action include policy analysis, group facilitation, interviewing, and the ability to gather and analyze multidimensional and systematic information in much the same way as with individuals and families. Group facilitation and organizing techniques are useful in coalition building. Information that documents the problem and the extent to which groups or communities are affected is also important. Recall the earlier example in which the agency compiled statistical information that demonstrated the pervasive problem of minority youth remaining in the shelter system. Both advocacy and social action assume a wide range of social work roles, knowledge of the problem-solving process, and the values and ethics of the profession. Still another requirement of advocacy and social action is gathering information and assessing the situation. It is prudent to assess the situation and the systems involved carefully, thereby avoiding the drawing of premature and erroneous conclusions that may lead to undesired or embarrassing consequences.

Values and principles of the profession guide advocacy and social action. Ethical principles for the most part help social workers in the context of agency practice at the micro and mezzo levels. Netting, Kettner, and McMurtry (1993) discuss the principles of autonomy, beneficence, and justice as considerations to guide macro practice along with the ethical dilemmas that the social worker may face in initiating change efforts (pp. 57–61). As we discussed earlier in this chapter, strengths and empowerment are important elements in macro practice. Strengths as a focus allow for the mobilization of the positive capacities of people, bringing into focus their resources, hopes, talents, and aspirations in the change process (Weick, 1992, p. 24). Strengths as a perspective also embody the process and outcome of empowerment as outlined by Gutierrez and Lewis (1999) and Gutierrez (1994), moving from the individual to entire groups or communities. In considering advocacy and social action as interventions, social workers must also bear in mind the principle of self-determination. In some instances clients may not wish to assert their rights; thus social workers are ethically bound to respect their position. In pursuing an action, practitioners must also be certain that the focus is on what the client has defined as important, as illustrated in the earlier example of the group of mothers participating in the focus groups. Moreover, practitioners should go no farther in advocacy or social action activities that the client group wishes to go. The sense of empowerment that people gain through identifying their own concerns and participating in the solutions may be more significant than the changes themselves.

Practitioners also have the responsibility to discuss with clients the barriers and possible adversarial or negative consequences to advocacy and social action activities. Weighing the likelihood of success, securing resources, organizing groups and coalitions, and following a strategic plan are important steps in the change process. Yet implementing advocacy and social action typically involves a certain amount of strain and tension; moreover, a positive outcome cannot be assured. However, discussing possible consequences or barriers not only allows for the planning of alternative strategies; it is important to involve clients in the pros and cons, leaving the final decision to them.

Techniques of Advocacy and Social Action

There are many techniques of advocacy and social action. Deciding which techniques to employ depends on the nature of the problem, the wishes of the group or community, the nature of the actions, the political climate, and the extent to which the practitioner's agency will support advocacy and social action as interventions. In a given situation, several strategies may be indicated, but as a rule of thumb, no more are required than necessary to achieve a given objective. Although militant action may be required in some instances, it should be utilized with discretion, for accomplishing certain gains through militant action may be more than offset by ills or negative images. Techniques and methods of advocacy and social action often involve building coalitions and organizing, with the practitioner assuming the role of enabler, mediator, broker, and educator. The following techniques include those most often employed in class advocacy and social action.

Conferring with Other Agencies

When problems involve denial of resources or dehumanizing treatment, case conferences may be held with appropriate staff persons or with administrators to present the grievance. Information about the concern should be well documented. In some cases, it may be advantageous to have clients accompany you, as they gain strength from learning to deal head-on with such situations. It is generally prudent to present the client's case in a firm and professional manner. If the other parties appear indifferent or otherwise are unwilling to take appropriate remedial measures, it may be necessary to serve notice of intention to pursue the grievance further by contacting higher authorities or initiating other more vigorous measures.

Appeals to Review Boards

Client satisfaction surveys are increasingly used as a form of outcome evaluation. Such surveys sometimes provide information suggesting that clients have been denied services or benefits inappropriately. Most agencies and governmental bodies have appeal procedures for clients who believe they have been unjustly denied services or benefits. Often successful appeals result in changes in procedures and policies.

Initiating Legal Action

When clients' rights are violated and the preceding interventions fail to achieve redress, filing a legal suit may be an appropriate alternative. However, clients often lack the resources to hire a private lawyer, and it may be necessary to engage a legal service agency or legal services provided through public funds. There may also be an opportunity to develop a resource from the private sector, and many law schools have legal services staffed by students. Of course, clients must be willing to testify in court, and practitioners can assist in their preparation.

Forming Interagency Committees or Coalitions

When individual agencies are unsuccessful in effecting essential changes, a coalition of agencies may combine their efforts in addressing common problems or filling a service gap. Membership from affected groups or communities is an essential consideration. The advantage of forming an agency coalition is twofold. First, a group of agencies that are committed to a specific objective present a united front and thus significantly influence decision makers. Second, when agencies join a common effort, no one agency is vulnerable to attack. It is entirely possible that membership in a coalition may involve community or civic groups who may not be directly concerned about a particular issue but have concerns that overlap or intersect.

Providing Expert Testimony

Social workers may exert a powerful force in influencing the development of public policies or developing resources by speaking forcefully about clients' problems and needs in the political and public arenas. With the support of the social worker, client groups may also serve in this capacity.

Gathering Information Through Studies and Surveys

The impact of testifying in public is much enhanced when concrete data are provided to support a position. Conducting studies and surveys and reviewing the literature thus arm the social worker with information that can be employed in responding to the penetrating and sometimes hostile questions that may be raised in public hearings and in direct contacts with public officials and legislators.

Educating Relevant Segments of the Community

Often the strongest enemy of developing progressive policies and programs is the ignorance of the public and decision makers about the issues. To educate the public in general and decision makers in particular, all forms of media should be considered, including press campaigns; telephone contacts; local television programs concerned with public issues; panel discussions at local, state, and national conventions; exhibits; and speeches at meetings of influential civic organizations. Other ways of informing or influencing public opinion are letter writing campaigns, position papers, letters to the editor, newspaper commentaries, and using the Internet or electronic mail. Another method, which is useful in both educating and involving the community, is petitions. This activity may be used to call attention of decision makers to an issue or to exert pressure by expressing the voice of a constituency.

Contacting Public Officials and Legislators

This contact can be a powerful way of promoting needed policies and programs. Social workers may contact legislators and public officials directly or may appear at committee meetings to present information those legislators need to make informed judgments. To be effective in these endeavors, social workers must be knowledgeable about how special interest groups influence legislators and the role or status of the legislator involved (Haynes & Mickleson, 2000; Netting, Kettner, & McMurtry, 1993). Technical and political information is a significant influence to which legislators respond. Obviously, social workers who aspire to influence legislators must first do their homework. Influence's, an organization of social work educators whose stated mission is to assist and train faculty and students to effectively influence the formation, implementation, and evaluation of state-level policy and legislation. This organization is an important resource for developing skills in this area.

Organizing Client Groups

This intervention involves forming action groups for social change that consist of consumers who have a mutual problem. The social worker of an agency initiates formation of the group, stimulates it to take action, and serves a consultative role in assisting it to obtain information, gain access to selected people, and act in concert with other community groups. Organizing client groups is especially appropriate for minority groups, who often feel impotent from a political standpoint. Lum (1992, p. 202) has reported a vignette illustrating the successful work of a practitioner in organizing African Americans to advocate for rights that had been violated in a public housing project.

Making Persistent Demands

This technique involves going beyond the usual appeal process by bombarding officials with continuous letters and telephone calls. Although this intervention stays within the law, it approximates the use of harassment as a pressure tactic and can cause a rebound effect.

As is apparent, the foregoing techniques involve both advocacy and social action. Effective social action and advocacy requires a rational, planned approach that consists of the following steps:

1. Define the problem.
2. Systematically gather information and an analysis of the people, structure, or system to be changed.
3. Assess both the driving forces that may promote change and the resistance forces that may conceivably retard it.
4. Identify specific goals, eliciting a broad range of viewpoints.
5. Carefully match techniques or strategies of social action and advocacy with a model and the goal desired.
6. Make a feasible schedule for implementing the plan of action.
7. Incorporate in the plan a feedback process for evaluating the changes that the action stimulates.

In addition to these steps and the skills and competence areas we discussed previously, certain ingredients are required for effective social action and class advocacy. These ingredients include having a *genuine* concern for that cause, the ability to keep the cause in *focus*, and *tenacity*. It is interesting to note that John Gardner, a leader of the Common Cause organization, concluded: "The first requirement for effective citizen action is stamina." Successful advocates really understand how their government and service systems are organized and changed. Blind emotion may work a few times, but successful, sustained stamina requires know-how. Finally, to make a real difference in any major cause there is a need for people in real numbers. Politicians, administrators, and the public have learned to look behind angry shouts and disruptions. We also want to emphasize that there are risks and limitations to advocacy and social action. Rothman (1999) cautions community practitioners about the potential for opposition and obstacles to social action and organizing activities, including "institutions that block needed improvements in education, housing, employment and law enforcement." He further states that "change advocates have to keep in mind that elites will lash out when they perceive that their interests are challenged," and thus advocates should "calculate" their ability to sustain, remain focused, and defend themselves against counterattacks (p. 10). The earlier example of an innovative agency program providing support for youth reunified with their families was in some ways a form of social action and advocacy. The agency initially encountered considerable opposition from other agencies involved in shelter services, and this opposition effectively derailed the program for a period.

SOCIAL PLANNING/COMMUNITY ORGANIZATION

A macro approach to enhancing environments and improving social conditions, the practice method of social planning/community organization (SP/CO) goes beyond typical direct practice activities in that the focal units with which practitioners engage are larger systems such as neighborhoods, citizens' groups, representatives of organizations, agency executives, and governmental leaders. The joint efforts of the participants are typically directed to solving social problems ranging in scope from those of various resident groups on one end of the continuum to international problems on the other end. Policies and programs of national scope that have emerged over the past 30 years as a result of intensive planning aimed at social problems include the Community Health Act (1963), the Economic Opportunity Act (1964), the Model Cities Program (1967), the Housing and Community Development Act (1974), the Jobs Training Partnership Act (1983), the Title XX amendments to the Social Security Act (1974), VISTA (Volunteers in Service to America, under the direction of a social worker) and the Peace Corps, servicing national and international communities, to name just a few. More recently, AmeriCorps was initiated as a way to involve

youth in some of the more pressing problems facing communities.

Emerging trends and funding patterns discussed earlier in this chapter are evidence of an "increasing inequality in our society" (Gutierrez, 1999, p. 375). They also provide opportunities for community organizing and building broad-based community participation. Current problems on which planners are or should be focusing include homelessness, welfare reform, child welfare legislation, child and spouse abuse, substance abuse, affordable housing, adolescent runaways, poverty, high rates of unemployment of urban and some rural communities, transportation, and education. Many of these issues, particularly in cities, are being addressed by the development of economic empowerment zones. According to Gutierrez (1999), these empowerment zones may support corporate projects but may not result in the creation of job opportunities. Another trend identified by Gutierrez as significant for community organizers is "the increasingly multicultural composition of our society," and whether community will be defined as separate, where services are aimed at a particular segment of the community, rather than a more holistic approach that brings resources and people together without regard to race or ethnicity (p. 375). Although such services evolved in response to community concerns and needs, there are risks involved. In many respects efforts to create minority agencies within an agency is reminiscent of the old separate but equal formula that existed in education prior to *Brown v. Board of Education* (1955). In other respects, this practice risks competition among minority groups for scarce resources. Finally, as with all services, this practice should be evaluated for effectiveness.

Although practitioners with expertise in SP/CO typically perform planning roles in urban centers and even larger systems, direct practitioners may need to engage in SP/CO activities in rural areas, where experts in planning usually are not available. In rural areas, practitioners may join with community leaders in planning to remedy problems associated with lack of transportation for residents with health care needs, needs for child care, problems of child neglect and/or maltreatment, needs for recreational programs, isolation of the elderly, and other such problems. It is important, therefore, for all practitioners to have at least rudimentary knowledge of the principles and skills involved in SP/CO. Strategies of community practice along with their basic means of influence are described by Rothman, Erlich, and Tropman (1995, p. 234). The strategies are social action, social planning, and policy and locality development. These strategies may overlap or be employed simultaneously. Hyde (1996) cites a number of examples in which feminists have successfully mixed SP/CO strategies.

Unlike planning and policy development that tends to emphasize the technical process of problem solving conducted by expert professionals, locality development aims to involve the community in defining a problem and determining goals. Defined by Cnaan and Rothman (1986), locality development seeks to build relationships within the community and foster community integration. Within the last several years, funders such as the United Way have urged agencies to include citizens and consumers in the development of agency programs or services. Focus groups are also used with increasing frequency to involve communities and client groups in the development of services and funding priorities.

Community living rooms are also mechanisms for the building and integration of communities. Farmer and Walsh (1999) report on the use of a community living room in a homeless shelter. Community living rooms, as one social worker found, can serve the purpose of bringing the community together to exert pressure on public officials around city services, police brutality, and housing code violations as well as for community networks and celebrations. In one community, a supportive network that evolved from a community living room consisted of a group of women who had previously been homeless. These women compiled a booklet of tips on locating housing, questions to ask landlords, and properties to avoid, for women who were homeless or in transitional housing. The community social worker as-

sisted the women in this effort by securing the funds to print and distribute the information.

Locality development should not replace other strategies that may be preferable depending on the issues at hand. It is a viable option for including community participation and for developing resources or support networks as illustrated by the previous examples. Irrespective of strategy, inclusion of community participants in advocacy or social action is preferable and consistent with the principles of social work practice.

As with direct practice, the problem-solving process is central to practice involving SP/CO. However, the problem-solving process at the macro level differs widely from that at the micro level, and social workers in SP/CO "seem to have more in common with professionals in other fields who are engaged in the same type of efforts, such as trade unionists, politicians, and city and regional planners" (Gilbert & Specht, 1987, p. 610). Before implementing the problem-solving process, planner-organizers must identify and recruit people who will provide funding and other support to undertake a SP/CO effort, identify a problem to which the planning or organizing efforts will be directed, or agree to work on a problem that has previously been identified. The next step is to select goals and to develop a plan that brings together and mobilizes those who have been recruited, organizational and political support, funding sources, and community support essential to attainment of the goals.

STRATEGIES AND SKILLS OF COMMUNITY INTERVENTION

Theorists conceptualize the problem-solving process in SP/CO in different ways, defining different numbers of stages that vary according to the levels of elaboration of relevant tasks. Rothman, Erlich, Tropman, (1995, p. 16) and Rothman (1999) use a six-phase process developed by Garrison in 1983 that consists of (1) identification of a need problem, (2) definition and clarification of the need or problem, (3) a systematic process of obtaining information, (4) analysis of the information, (5) development and implementation of a plan of action, and (6) terminal actions that include evaluation of outcome or effects.

For our purposes, we use the general four-phase process identified by Gilbert and Specht (1987, p. 613), which consists of (1) identification and analysis of the problem, (2) development of a plan of action, (3) implementation of the plan, and (4) evaluation of its outcome. At this level of abstraction, the process is similar to that of the problem-solving process of direct practice. The process may not be entirely linear, as new information may require alternative action, including a new start or the reframing of strategies and tactics (Rothman, Erlich, Tropman, & Cox, 1999). As we mentioned earlier, however, focus is important in the change process and this schema of activities assists in this regard. Implementing these activities requires some of the same skills employed in direct practice, for example, interviewing skills and the ability to facilitate group development by applying knowledge of interpersonal relationships and group dynamics. Other skills required include those embodied in policy analysis and program evaluation, research methods, management of data, and sociopolitical processes. As Homan (1999) points out, we should keep in mind that organizing or planning to promote change "involves more than just fixing a specific problem. Productive organizing includes the intent to increase the capability of people to respond meaningfully and effectively in the face of future challenges" (p. 160). In this regard, the practitioners work collaboratively with communities, facilitating the process by engaging in the roles of enabler, educator, and mediator.

Problem or Need Identification

The first task in identifying and analyzing the problem is to assess the state of the target system (e.g., neighborhood, community, county, or state). Although conceptual approaches to problem analysis vary, common elements in the frameworks of prominent experts include "the need to identify which social values are threatened by the situation, to carry out a detailed analysis of who is affected

and the scale of the problem, and to delineate the etiology of the problem" (Moroney, 1987, p. 598). Further, the analysis also addresses the political environment, assessing the readiness of the target system to deal with the problem and to allocate resources to remedy or mitigate the problem.

Identifying the causes of the problem is central to problem analysis. Although founded in the scientific method, this process varies according to the theoretical premises and values of the problem analysts, as attested to by the varying explanations offered as to the causes of poverty, crime, adolescent pregnancy, and other social problems. Approaches to identifying causes of problems often begin by compiling data regarding the incidence and distribution of the social problems in terms of age, sex, race, income levels, severity, duration, and so on. After the data are analyzed, inferences are made concerning causes of the problem.

Another useful method employed in problem analysis entails applying techniques that produce information used to predict demands for services and fiscal resources. These techniques, which include social surveys, estimates of future populations, and compositions of the same, as well as trend and probability analyses, are beyond the scope of this book.

Needs assessment is another form of problem analysis that follows the steps described in the preceding paragraphs. Needs assessment is used to estimate from the focal system the numbers of people at risk and in need or remedial measures. Defining needs, however, is an elusive task because need is a complex concept that can be stated as normative, perceived, expressed, and relative. Netting, Kettner, and McMurtry (1993, pp. 96–97) define four ways to identify community and also use Mallow's hierarchical framework as a means of rank ordering and assessing community needs. Needs can be assessed by utilizing professional judgment and social surveys (normative needs), by holding public forums (perceived needs), by determining the number and profile of people who seek a service (expressed needs), and by assessing relative need by measuring "differences in levels of services in different geographical areas, weighting each area's statistics to account for differences in population and social pathology" (Moroney, 1987, p. 599). Because each approach deals with a different aspect of need, comprehensive needs assessments employ all four different approaches.

Developing a Plan of Action

After identifying and analyzing a problem, the next phase of SP/CO entails developing a plan of action. Ideally, the concept of rationality is embedded in the process of developing a plan of action. Adhering to this concept, planners objectively use information they have gained to describe, to understand, and to make predictions about phenomena in question. Economic rationality requires determining the single or "best" remedy for the focal problem. Ideally, selecting a remedy thus entails identifying all reasonable strategies (for example, bargaining and negotiating), assessing the likely consequences of each strategy, and evaluating each set of consequences. Evaluating the cost-effectiveness of each alternative is also part of the process. This task involves determining which alternative will generate the most favorable ratio between valued input and valued output, or in other words, seeking to achieve maximal return for the least investment.

In fact, planning and organizing based exclusively on the concept of rationality are generally impractical, and decisions about alternatives typically must consider complex factors that include political realities in the focal system, limited funding, and the possible impact of special interest groups. Because of the magnitude of these and other realities, "The technical aspects of designing the 'best' programmatic solutions are de-emphasized in favor of sociopolitical behavior that seeks the agreement of relevant interest groups. From this perspective, interactional tasks such as bargaining, exchange, compromise, and building consensus emerge as the predominant features of the problem-solving process" (Gilbert & Specht, 1987, pp. 614–615). Less than ideal, this approach has been called "incremental decision making" because it seeks to improve upon the shortcomings of present policies

rather than to select superior courses of action that are likely to be rejected. In this regard, findings of one research study (Gilbert & Specht, 1979) revealed that mobilization of strong political support correlated highest with positive outcomes of Title XX allocations of resources for the aged. So much for the idealism of rational planning!

Implementation of the Plan

After plans have been accepted, support mobilized, and funding allocated, implementation of the plan commences. Where the change effort resulted in a program, activities involve performing internal administrative tasks including selecting, training, and supervising staff; providing for intra-organizational communication and quality control, and establishing policies and procedures that serve the interests of both consumers and staff. Other tasks entail managing external relations with other service organizations, funding sources, consumer groups, governmental entities, employee unions, and so forth. Maintaining positive relationships with these various entities is crucial, for their support is indispensable if a new program is to flourish. Managing external relations thus is a primary activity required of planners and organizers.

Evaluation of Outcome

Evaluation seeks to assess the extent to which the change effort, whether it involved a program, policy, or practice, was successful and also to identify areas for improvement. Evaluation thus involves ongoing systematic monitoring of the impact, which requires development and implementation of techniques of data management. Systematic analysis of data enables planners to determine, for example, if the program is functioning effectively and accomplishing the goals for which it was planned. Evaluation also enables planners and organizers to determine which strategies were the most effective, under which conditions, and with which populations.

Methods utilized for evaluation require expertise in research design, techniques of measurement, and analysis of data. Techniques involved in these processes, however, require much greater detail and therefore are beyond the scope of this book. The requisite knowledge needed to implement these processes is commonly embodied in research courses. In the final section we discuss in a general way methods that may be used for evaluating macro practice interventions.

We should also like to draw your attention to innovative approaches that hold promise for enhancing the effectiveness of planning community programs. The first approach consists of applying developmental research (E. Thomas, 1989), which is a rigorous, systematic, and distinctive methodology consisting of many techniques and methods taken from other fields and disciplines. Its sophisticated methodology relates to social research and development and model development.

Far less systematic, the second approach has been implemented in Quebec (Gulati & Guest, 1990). This approach places emphasis on natural helping networks, involves lay citizens in analyzing problems and planning remedial measures, deals with users of service not as client consumers but as partners in the provision of services, facilitates integration and coordination of local programs and services by having them housed in close proximity, focuses on prevention, uses multidisciplinary teams extensively, fosters flexibility in organizational structure, and decentralizes administration so that local communities can develop programs that are responsive to their unique needs. This approach is closer to grassroots community planning than are planning approaches in the United States.

IMPROVING INSTITUTIONAL ENVIRONMENTS

Social welfare organizations are organized to provide a service, information, benefits, or goods. They are formal social systems with multiple constituents, the dynamic arenas in which client eligibility for services is determined and the resources vital to the organization's existence are distributed. The culture of an organization includes the core values of the organization, often described in a mission statement: leadership, assumptions, and rituals. Schein (1985) describes organizational culture as follows:

A pattern of basic assumptions—invented, discovered, or developed by a given group as it learns to cope with its problems of external adaptation and internal integration—that has worked well enough to be considered valid and therefore to be taught to new members as the correct way to perceive, think and feel in relation to those problems. (p. 9)

Change strategies in organizations require an understanding and analysis of organizational structure, function, culture, and resource environment. Martin and O'Connor (1989, p. 181) analyze the social welfare organization using systems theory. Conceptualizing them as open systems, Martin and O'Connor offer a conceptual scheme for understanding social welfare organizations that involves (1) the organization's relations with the environment, (2) internal structures and processes, and (3) dilemmas associated with a conflictual, sometimes hostile, social, cultural, and political-economic environment. Netting, Kettner, and McMurtry (1993) provide guidelines for analyzing change effort in social welfare organizations, and we refer you to this resource for further elaboration of this process. Similar to the other strategies for macro level interventions, the process begins with identification of the goal or problem to be changed.

We have previously referred to institutions such as residential centers, nursing homes, or group homes in which social supports, community networks, and resources developed by social workers were considered measures that could enhance the quality of life for residents. The quality of the environment as experienced by clients is an important aspect of service delivery. In this section we briefly consider ways of enhancing three major facets of institutional environments—namely staff, policies and procedures and programs. Institutional environments as discussed include those of residential facilities and agencies.

Staff

Staffs, of course, are the heart of an institutional environment. They are a major input into the social system. In this mix there are professional staff who have routine contact with clients, support staff, and administrative personnel (supervisors and management), all of whom are key to organizational operations, vision, and purpose in the organization's highly interdependent environment. To a certain extent, staff behavior is governed by professional orientations, ethical codes and standards, licensing or regulatory boards, union contracts, funding sources, the media, and the public. All represent powerful constituents of the organization.

When staffs are dedicated and caring, responsive to client's needs, and congenial with each other, the institutional or agency environment tends to be conducive to the growth and well-being of all concerned. To be optimally effective staffs require empowerment and a sense of commitment to deliver high-quality service while operating in their particular domains. Among the factors that mark a healthy organizational culture and climate are open communication, a willingness to deal with conflict, flexibility and risk taking, a sense of interdependence and cohesiveness, yet a respect for boundaries. The creation of this environment is the responsibility of all staffing levels.

Hackman and Oldham (1976, 1980) have conceptualized the most elaborate and widely accepted theories of job design and motivation as contributing to the overall psychological states of meaningfulness, employee responses, and morale and job satisfaction. The five core characteristics are task identity, task significance, skill variety, job feedback, and autonomy. Task identity, task significance, and skill variety all lead to feeling the meaningfulness of work. Feedback with regard to performance provides information on the results achieved. Autonomy elicits a sense of responsibility for one's own work outcomes or those of a team. Empowerment, implicit in autonomy, is much the same as self-determination is for clients. As clients may drop out when their interest and need are ig-

nored, the lack of staff empowerment affects job performance and productivity and contributes to turnover. The extent to which staff feel empowered, for example by participating in decisions that affect their work, may depend on the structure of the organization. One social worker, for example, recounted how attempts to address concerns in his organization resulted in a manager stating, "If staff are involved in decision-making, there would not be a reason for upper management." Thus when staff input was solicited about ways to decrease indirect service expenditures, they showed little interest in the problem. We would like to stress that most organizations provide a climate conductive to change by encouraging staff to identify needed changes and having in place mechanisms whereby proposals for change can be initiated. Many human organizations are moving to such arrangements as total quality management teams as a means to ensure quality and involve staff in organizational decision making (Martin, 1993).

Areas of tension for staff include conflict between professional orientations, competing ideologies, diversity, values controversies, rules and regulations, workloads, and decision making. In addition, staff may be faced with issues related to co-workers, for example, the impaired professional or colleagues who fail to observe clients' right to be treated with dignity and worth or other concerns that impact clients. Expectations about clients, constraints around providing services or resources for clients, and the "magnitude of the problems" are yet other areas of conflict, the results of which are stressful and frustrating for staff (Kirk & Koeske, 1995). We raise this discussion in the context of how organization structure, climate, and culture affect staff morale, performance, and job satisfaction as well as the relationship between these factors and services to clients.

Although practitioners may be very adept in advocating for clients, developing resources or support networks, and organizing, they often feel an inability to exert influence or propose changes within their own organizations. The skills and competencies used in direct practice with clients, along with many of the macro practice strategies previously discussed, may also be employed in organizational change. In some instances, practitioners tend to identify organizational concerns in a linear fashion and in doing so conclude that changes or resolutions reside in the domain of management. Depending on the organizational structure and design, this may be the case, and we acknowledge that some organizational operations indeed fall within the responsibility of management irrespective of structure and design. We encourage practitioners nonetheless to assess situations and present their concerns in a systematic manner and to become active participants in change efforts. Assuming responsibility for alerting others in the organization to the potential for change as well a participating in the resolution of problems is consistent with the ethical principle of the profession of social work.

Netting, Kettner, and McMurtry (1993) suggest two types of macro level changes in organizations: to improve resources provided to clients and to enhance the organization's working environment so that personnel can perform more efficiently and effectively, thus improving services to clients. Brager and Holloway (1978) have outlined organizational change as focusing on three areas: people-focused change, technological change, and structural change. Changes may take the form of a policy, program, or project (Kettner, Daley, & Nichols, 1985).

Knowledge and Skills

To perform the roles of organizational diagnostician and facilitator/expediter effectively, practitioners must also be armed with knowledge and skills that will enable them to analyze the organization as well as the risks and benefits of the proposed change. G. A. Frey (1990) has developed a useful framework for direct practitioners to assess organizational opposition. The change strategy requires the practitioner to assume various social work roles and begins with the identification of the problem area. In assessing the potential benefits of a proposal, it is important to consider the input and impact of four different groups:

1. Clients (the extent to which the proposed change directly benefits this group will effectively alter and enhance the services they receive)

2. Administrators who ultimately have legitimate authority for accepting the proposal and providing the resources for implementation

3. Supervisors or staff who will have responsibility for planning and/or overseeing implementation

4. Staff persons who ultimately carry out the change or are affected by it once it is implemented

By considering the impact of the potential change on each group, practitioners can weigh benefits against detrimental effects and can plan strategies to counter resistance when the former clearly and substantially outweigh the latter.

Risks and Benefits

Promoting change in organizations is a complex process, and organizational opposition to change is perhaps as common as is opposition to change by families, individuals, and groups. Central to the change proposal is the documentation of need and the questions of who is affected, in what way, and who benefits. Frey (1990) identifies three types of high-risk proposals, including (1) proposals that involve substantial costs (e.g., purchasing expensive equipment or creating new units), (2) proposals that must be adopted in their entirety rather than implemented in stages, and (3) proposals that are radical or in conflict with the dominant values of the organization, its members, or the public. Finally, proposals that call for changes that exceed the capacity of the organization to implement because of resources or ideological differences and those that would significantly change the organization are at risk for opposition. Extending agency hours of operation may be considered to be a peripheral change, because it does not alter the basic goals and objectives of the organization. In contrast, programmatic changes, which alter ways that policies or programs are implemented, have greater organizational depth.

A CASE EXAMPLE OF EFFORTS TO IMPROVE ORGANIZATIONAL ENVIRONMENT

A successful proposal for a programmatic change initiated by a social worker resulted in weekly scheduled classes for individuals for whom English was their second language. The social worker documented the time required for individual staff to assist individuals or families to complete financial assistance eligibility forms. Follow-up meetings were often necessary because incomplete forms resulted in the need for clients to schedule an additional appointment. The classes as envisioned by the social worker would not only respond to this concern by eliminating duplication of effort but also an additional benefit for clients was the development of a social network.

In general, proposals that fit with the ideology of an organization, its resource capacity, or potential, as well as those that have the support of a significant number of members, are more likely to succeed. In response to some initial resistance to the proposal, the social worker was able to document the cost-benefit ratio to the organization as staff time was freed for other tasks, the proposal did not radically alter the goals of the organization, and she had the support of a number of co-workers whose schedules were overburdened by the need to reschedule appointments with clients for the purpose of completing the eligibility forms. Finally, this change effort illustrates that groups within organizations act favorably to proposals that they perceive to benefit them.

Policies and Procedures

Because practitioners in agency or institutional operations deliver services in face-to-face contacts with clients, they are in critical positions to evaluate the impact of policies, procedures, and practice on service delivery. When certain organizational practices or policies impede service delivery or block the agency from fulfilling its mission in an optimal fashion, staff are in a position to identify the impediments and proposed changes. In doing so they perform the roles of organizational diagnostician/facilitator, mediator, expediter, and advocate.

The extent to which organizational policies and practice promote social justice, support client self-determination, and adhere to the principles of empowerment and strengths are other lenses by which practitioners may examine agency policies and practices. G. D. Rooney (2000) has developed an exercise for students designed to examine the values and ethics reflected in organizational policy decisions. Policies or practices that lend themselves to assessment include eligibility for services, rules that govern client's behavior in residential or institutional settings, rules related to access to services, and procedures for developing treatment plans. Points for assessing a policy or practice as outlined by Rooney (pp. 52–53) include:

1. What origin, ideology, and values appear to have influenced the policy?

2. What are intended and unintended consequences of the policy's application?

3. To what extent is the policy and its expectations of clients influenced by societal ideology (for example, the worthy and unworthy poor, social control or compliance)?

4. What image of clients and practitioners is portrayed by the policy?

5. What does the policy or practice demand of clients and practitioners?

6. What are client reactions to the practice or policy?

7. To what extent do the policy and its procedures support or constrain social work values, ethics, and social justice concerns?

Attainment of clients' goals often requires services provided by social agencies and other community organizations and institutions that are vital strands in the network of resource systems. Unfortunately, helping organizations sometimes have policies or engage in practices that in effect are barriers to fully and effectively delivering services and resources. Social workers are in a strategic position to identify ways in which these organizations can enhance their responsiveness to clients' needs. In discharging this responsibility, social workers sometimes play the roles of mediator and advocate in

- increasing accessibility of services
- promoting service delivery in ways that enhance clients' dignity
- ensuring equal access and quality of services to *all* people eligible to receive them

Increasing Accessibility of Services

Social workers have a responsibility to work with administrators within their own agency or with responsible staff of other organizations when services are not accessible to clients. Agencies that offer services only from 8 A.M. to 5 P.M. may make it virtually impossible for working adults to avail themselves of their services. Adopting flexible scheduling practices in agencies that serve families may result in involving increased numbers of working parents, which in turn may produce better outcomes. Providing staff coverage on weekends also makes it possible to respond to clients' crises when they occur, rather than waiting until the following week. Timely intervention provides support when people need it most and are optimally receptive to services.

Another example involves modifying scheduling procedures in health care centers so that patients do not have to wait several hours to be seen. Some clients' conditions or circumstances are such that they are unable to wait for long periods of time. Others become disgusted and leave, failing to receive treatment they vitally need. Services are not accessible to other people because agencies are not located in proximity to them. Difficulties in arranging transportation and child care may make such services virtually inaccessible to many clients. For these reasons, many family service agencies and community mental health centers have located satellite offices in communities rather than having only a central office.

Providing for home visits to large families may circumvent problems of child care, although young children in the home can make it nearly impossible to conduct a productive interview. Some agencies have tried to solve the problem by locating an office in the heart of the area served and providing space for children to play while they wait for their parents. In locating offices that serve the elderly, as well as other groups who are physically frail, it is important not to place them in areas without consideration for their safety.

Promoting Service Delivery in Ways That Enhance Clients' Dignity

It is unfortunate that some people who need services decline to use them because they have been degraded or humiliated by the actions of staff persons, by breaches of confidentiality, or by demeaning procedures. An example is inadequate provisions for privacy, so that interviews are conducted in view of or within earshot of others. Even worse, some staff persons may be either openly or subtly judgmental of clients, making remarks about their morality, veracity, character, or worthiness to receive assistance. Still other staff members may be brusque or rude or intrude unjustifiably into deeply personal aspects of clients' lives, thereby needlessly subjecting them to embarrassment and humiliation. Such behaviors are not only inhumane but unethical, and practitioners who become aware of such behavior by staff persons respond according to the ethical standards of social work practice, which includes discussing the concern with the staff person and/or the organization's administration and, if necessary, filing a complaint with the appropriate licensing board and professional organization.

Another circumstance that strips clients of their dignity may involve requiring them to go to unreasonable lengths to establish eligibility for concrete aid or services. A vignette entitled "Four Pennies to My Name" is a powerful illustration of a client's perspective and experience as she attempts to respond to eligibility requirements for financial assistance (Compton & Galaway, 1989, pp. 259–269). Clients' dignity may also be hurt if practitioners are habitually tardy for appointments, cancel or change scheduled appointments frequently, or don't extend common courtesies.

Concerns for safety and threats of violence have prompted both public and private organizations to employ private security personnel or off-duty police. In responding to this very real concern, organizations must also be aware of the image and effect that this practice has on clients and the organizational climate. A recent visit to a local Social Security office by one of the authors on behalf of a client was a demeaning experience. She was required to let officers examine the contents of her purse and briefcase and pass through a metal detector. While this may be an essential practice for organizations, they should be aware of the client's experience and the implications for social justice and equality, and formulate policies that ensure client dignity. Although questions have been raised about the legitimacy and authority of security guards, and some view it as another form of oppression and social control, this practice is unlikely to go away. Social workers can play an additional role in this area by providing interpersonal and human relations skills for officers and security guards and also by developing criteria for the selection and hiring of these individuals. When security procedures result in clients being treated unfairly and without regard for their dignity, social workers must act as advocates.

Ensuring Equal Access to and Equal Quality of Services to Eligible Persons

People may be denied resources to which they are entitled or receive services that are of lesser quality than others receive for at least seven different reasons: (1) institutional racism, (2) discrimination by socioeconomic level, age, or ethnicity, (3) arbitrary decisions of practitioners, (4) inability to assert rights, (5) lack of knowledge of resources, (6) failure of authorities to develop resources mandated by laws, and (7) dysfunctional policies and procedures. In the following sections, we consider each of these factors.

Institutional Racism   Embedded in the fabric of our society to the extent that many people fail to recognize it, institutional racism often affects service delivery and availability of resources and opportunities in subtle ways. It is therefore vital that practitioners be sensitized to its manifestations so that they can liberate themselves and others

from its pernicious effects. The effects of institutional racism range across the entire developmental span beginning with prenatal care and ending with care of the elderly and even burial arrangements. Racism pervades our educational, legal, economic, and political institutions as well as employment opportunities and health care services.

Social workers have an ethical responsibility to work toward obliterating institutional racism in organizational policies and practices and enhancing cultural competence; both are worthy but formidable challenges. The first step toward meeting this challenge begins with developing awareness of possible traces of racist attitudes within oneself. Practitioners must also analyze policies, procedures, and practices of social agencies and other organizations to assure that all people are treated equitably. Wolf (1991), for example, describes problems encountered by African Americans in mental health settings using standardized diagnostic manuals. In analyzing the relationship between race and diagnostic and social labels, Longres and Torrecilha (1991) conclude that minority children all too often are labeled irrespective of need. In school settings, subtle evidence of institutional racism, including a disproportionate number of suspensions of black children and frequent assignments of children to instructional groups based on skills, has a direct effect on the self-efficacy and confidence of minority children (L. F. Williams, 1990). The failure of child welfare practices to act upon the relationship between parenting and poverty and people of color has resulted in the out-of-home placement of a disproportionate number of minority children. The continuing trend bolstered by the enactment of the Adoption and Safe Family Act (1997), gives rise to an ethical question: Are a larger proportion of minority parents dysfunctional, or are they coping with conditions both personal and environmental that act as risks rather than protective factors? (Halpern, 1991).

Much of the attention related to cultural competence has focused on culturally sensitive interventions in recognition that "traditional forms of practice were often ineffective with and sometimes oppressive to ethnic minority clients" (Rodgers & Potocky, 1997, p. 391). Cultural sensitivity and competence, to be effective, must also be supported and embraced by the organization and evident in organizational policies and practices. To assist organizations in this process, the Child Welfare League of American (1993) has developed a Cultural Competence Self-Assessment Instrument, which enables organizations to assess and develop cultural competence at all levels of the organization. Strom-Gottfried and Morrissey (2000) have developed an organizational audit that enables social workers to assess agency policies and practices as well as organizational strengths and effectiveness with respect to diversity. Cross, Bazron, Dennis, and Issacs (1989) describe a continuum of cultural competence at the organizational level. At a midpoint on this continuum is the practice of implementing policies that could be described as "color-blind" and lacking sensitivity to the effects on minorities. Below this level on the continuum are agencies that carry out culturally destructive policies. As an example of a destructive practice they describe the boarding school policies enforced on Native American families and children earlier in this century that had the express purpose of eliminating Native American culture. Above this midpoint is culturally sensitive and culturally competent practice. These levels require that the agency examine policies for their differential impact on populations served and proactive development of culturally sensitive policies.

Agencies have also attempted to accommodate diverse needs and interests by hiring professionals or community staff who represent a targeted ethnic group. The assumption is that these individuals are more likely to identify with those they represent and the nature of the group experience. This trend, while useful on one level, in effect creates the ethnic agency within an agency. There are other difficulties with the practice. In essence the representative is responsible for all clients in a particular category and therefore rarely works with other clients. This practice may also enable other staff to ignore or to have limited responsibility for clients who are different from themselves. One Hmong social worker spoke of his frustration with being called each time a Southeast Asian family was seen at intake and with being assigned only cases for this group. This practice also limits the organization's ability to promote diversity with nonminority clients. Cultural competence is not only a matter of representative staff or bilingual printed materials; it requires the commitment, competence, and effort of the entire organization. Indeed, representative staff, whether assigned to a targeted group because of race or culture or sexual orientation, are often overwhelmed by the volume of work that includes responding to the demands and representing the community.

The issue of cultural competence is one that must be addressed in both the practice and educational levels. At this time, many agencies rely on the utilization of targeted group representatives or community staff because there are not enough professionals and/or students in professional programs to hire at representative levels. Community staff representing specific ethnic groups and acting as cultural consultants are an important resource. At the same time, their skills and utilization should not be defined solely in terms of culture or race. Moreover, where is the responsibility of the agency and social work to those individuals with respect to becoming professionals? The concern is that when funding priorities change, these individuals who hold positions created for a singular purpose are in jeopardy.

To adapt service delivery systems to the needs of ethnic minority clients, administrators should include representatives of ethnic groups in the process of shaping policies, procedures, and staffing to the unique needs of ethnic minority persons. Moreover, they should develop systems of feedback that assure ongoing input from the ethnic groups they serve by having representatives of ethnic groups on agency boards and by employing periodic follow-up contacts with clients to assess the impact of agency policies and of the service provided. Enlisting volunteers from ethnic groups to serve as interpreters, facilitators, case finders, and investigators can also reduce barriers to service delivery and maintain liaison with ethnic groups.

Arbitrary Decisions to Deny Resources to People   This is another factor that restricts the access of some people to resources for which they are eligible. It is an unfortunate reality that some organizations allow staff to be punitive and wield their authority to the detriment of certain clients. Recent revisions of the public welfare system will at best support some recipients in making a transition to work. At worst, needed benefits will be unavailable as we undergo a period in which policies become increasingly punitive to the poor. When clients are arbitrarily denied services or resources, practitioners have a responsibility to serve as an advocate for the client in securing those resources.

Clients' Lack of Ability or Skills to Assert Their Rights   Some clients lack the physical and/or mental ability to assert their rights and therefore have unequal access to benefits and services. Because they are at a distinct disadvantage in asserting their rights, many such individuals tend to acquiesce to injustices that deprive them of badly needed resources. Persons with disabilities (particularly those who are homebound) are also likely to need special advocacy services to obtain resources to which they are entitled. Many people with disabilities cannot stand in lines, move from office to office, fill out multiple forms, and engage in other activities typically required to gain services from public clinics or offices. Moreover, homebound persons usually lack access to communication networks that provide inside information about how to remedy some of these problems. Still another obstacle for many persons with disabilities is that they lack clout and find it difficult to disagree with professionals concerning their rights. In these situations social workers can make remedial interventions.

Immigrants and minorities also typically are limited in their ability to assert their rights and historically have tended to submit to injustices rather than to risk becoming embroiled in difficulties. When non-English-speaking people attempt to locate services, they often end their search in anger and frustration. From the client's point of view, concrete difficulties interfere with their gaining access to services from agencies: arbitrary denial of services; institutional inflexibility; red tape with long delays and silences; undignified or callous treatment; complex forms and procedures of eligibility; long waiting lists; inaccessibility by telephone or in person; a runaround from agency to agency; lack of simple, clear directions and explanations. To assist immigrants to cope with the difficulties, agencies should translate documents, provide assistance in completing forms, provide information about and make referrals to social service programs, and mediate problems between clients and other agencies. The role of the social worker within the organization is that of an enabler or an advocate. Drachman (1992) has also delineated the many needs of refugees and discussed ways that social workers with the support of agency practices and policies can respond to these needs.

Lack of Knowledge About or Failure to Use Available Resources   This factor obviously precludes clients from receiving services they need. Immigrants and minority group members who do not speak English are at a particular disadvantage in this regard, as they are not privy to information about services that tends to circulate by means of formal and informal networks in broader society. By no means are these the only groups who lack access to information about resources. People who live in rural or geographically isolated areas or have limited reading skills or visual or hearing impairments are also at a distinct disadvantage.

To enhance the accessibility of resources to all persons, both public and private human service organizations often engage in outreach efforts aimed at people who are unaware of or do not voluntarily seek services or resources that could improve their life situations. Outreach aimed at promoting an awareness of resources or services is also a means through which organizations can build relationships with targeted groups. Effective outreach as a means of building relationships between agencies and communities may require personal interactions in order to dispel perceptions or discomfort related to the minority experience. In both rural and urban areas, outreach efforts may also be directed to key community informants, indigenous caregivers, and local officials.

Failure of Authorities to Develop Resources Mandated by Law Sosin (1979) has written a cogent article in which he points out that enactment of new legislation or regulations does not ensure implementation of the same. Ignoring new laws, in fact, is a widespread phenomenon. In addition, the flexibility given to states and discretion allowed state agencies in the administration of welfare legislation may result in unequal availability and distribution of resources (Brodkin, 1997). It is important for social workers to be aware of the effects of legislation on their clients. Indeed, there may be a need for advocacy and social action even after new laws are enacted. Because new mandates that involve social and child welfare have altered social priorities, those who bear responsibility for implementing the mandates may minimize social change by ignoring, evading, or subverting a new law, thus denying benefits intended by the law to potential beneficiaries.

Dysfunctional Policies and Practice Rigid, outdated, and otherwise dysfunctional policies and practice may also have the unintended effects of limiting access to resources for some clients. For example, clients who are illiterate, have limited reading skills, or use English as their second language are at a decided disadvantage when they must complete numerous forms and procedures to qualify for services or benefits. The obvious implications are that organizations should reduce red tape to a minimum, simplify forms, and provide aid in completing forms to clients who lack skills. Other practices that limit accessibility include the requirement that clients visit the organization. Rural clients who must travel long distances to agency offices, parents with small children, those with limited and costly public transportation options, and those who may feel intimidated by com-

ing to the agency have severely limited accessibility. For clients who are handicapped or bedridden, the problem is even more severe. To accommodate such persons, either home visits or telephone applications for service or benefits are essential.

Policies may also altogether exclude some needy persons from obtaining resources—for example, the requirement that homeless persons have an address in order to receive benefits. Other examples include (1) the requirement that welfare recipients be work ready, but without child care subsidies, (2) denial of food stamps to migrants because they could not verify their incomes, and (3) policies of food shelves that limit the number of times a family may use this resource. Many times, policies are put in place so that organizations are able to manage limited resources and ensure their distribution to those in need. Policies may be considered dysfunctional when the intent to eliminate cheating takes precedence over providing service. Obviously, more flexible policies are needed to remedy these situations, along with advocacy.

Institutional Programs

At this point we consider programs, the third facet of improving of the institutional or organizational environment. The program of an institution is crucial to the effective functioning of clients. Stimulating, constructive, and growth-promoting programs tend to enhance the functioning, whereas custodial care that fosters idleness produces the opposite effects. The introduction in the 1950s of socioenvironmental programs in mental institutions contributed to the dramatic results in eliminating wards populated by regressed patients, most of whom were regarded as hopeless.

An important factor in institutional programming involves the extent to which residents can exercise choice and control in their daily living. When people have little control over what happens to them, they tend to become helpless, hopeless, and depressed. To enhance choice and control, progressive institutions foster democratic participation in governance of the institution to the extent that such is feasible. Social work students involved in a cooperative study experience in Taiwan were surprised to observe the relative unimportance of rules that governed the behavior of children and adolescents living in a group situation. They found the facility (in which they also resided along with Taiwanese social workers) to be noisy. Although the children had study and quiet periods, after school they were able to engage in activities of their choice, often with staff joining them. In response to a question about rules, the U.S.-educated Taiwanese social worker explained that "this is the children's home, and therefore they are allowed to behave as if this is so." Another program feature allowed the children to remain connected to the community because they attended community schools and were involved in community activities.

Mental hospitals and correctional institutions often have ward or unit councils through which residents have input into decision-making processes. Even some nursing homes have resident councils that foster choice. Mercer and Kane (1979), in fact, have reported a study indicating that nursing home patients in an experimental group who were given choices in caring for a plant and participating in a resident council improved more than a control group in reduction of hopelessness, increased physical activity, and psychosocial functioning.

Other aspects of institutional programs should involve education for youth, intellectual stimulation for adults, training opportunities for prisoners, social skill development programs for residents with deficiencies, and opportunities for social intervention. Art, music, and dance therapies have also been described by numerous authors as methods of fostering expression and creativity in institutions. For ambulatory residents, a leisure room with television and various games fosters social interaction and constructive activity. Likewise, facilities that permit vigorous physical activity are essential in correctional institutions. In nursing homes and hospitals, it is desirable for residents to have contact with the outside world. When people share rooms, they should be permitted to choose roommates with whom they are compatible. Few things can be more demoralizing than occupying limited space with people who wear on one's nerves.

Obviously, many other factors come into play in ensuring that programs provide opportunities for social interaction and a sense of mastery and connectedness. Still, practitioners should be sensitive to patients' needs and should be patients' advocates when factors within a program adversely affect their well-being. Empowerment, self-determination, and a sense of self-efficacy are important factors in residential programs. Certain vulnerable groups of clients unable to cope effectively with stressful situations and avail themselves of essential environmental resources because of a sense of powerlessness or helplessness need the assistance of social workers as advocates and brokers. In other situations, social workers should strive to ensure that residential programs allow residents to exercise control over their lives and their environment to the fullest extent possible. For example, a resident complained to the social worker that he did not like to have his cigarettes and money rationed to him by staff. Another common complaint among institutional residents, particularly adolescents, is the point system in which they lose points or privileges for certain behaviors and have limited choices about activities. In many instances, failure to respond to complaints of this nature provokes more assertive or aggressive behaviors on the part of clients, resulting in staff reactance.

Policies or practices are best when they empower clients by including them in decisions that affect their lives and that enable them to gain or regain the capacity to interact with the environment in ways that enhance their needs gratification, well-being, and satisfaction. To gain a sense of power, of course, requires that essential resources be available in the environment. Moreover, a sense of power is closely liked to competence, self-esteem, support systems, and belief that individual actions or actions in concert with others can lead to improvement in one's life situation. These attributes or factors, however, are reciprocally influenced by the quality of the environment. Nurturant environments that produce strong goodness of fit between people's needs and corresponding resources foster these positive attributes. Conversely, poor goodness of fit caused by major environmental deficiencies and inflexibility tends to foster powerlessness, helplessness, low self-esteem, and depression.

SERVICE COORDINATION AND INTERORGANIZATIONAL COLLABORATION

Social welfare organizations have always interacted with each other through referrals, purchase of service agreements, and in some cases sharing space in a central community service center. These networks may be described as cooperative and the content of the relationship as discretionary, whereby the patterns of interaction are ad hoc or as needed, and each organization maintains its own resources, capabilities, goals, and mission. Cooperation as defined by Graham and Barter (1999) "facilitates support and assistance for meeting goals that are specific to the individual stakeholders" (p. 7).

Within the last several years concerns related to service fragmentation, duplication, complex social problems, and an environment influenced by managed care have led to more formal interorganizational relationships. In addition, concerns for improving the quality and availability of services have resulted in an increased demand for interdependence between social welfare organizations beyond that previously described. Funding initiatives and formal mandates from both local and federal agencies have also served as an impetus for more formal linkages between agencies in the form of coordination or collaborations. Much of the thinking behind this movement has been that effective relationships between organizations are often needed to enhance aspects of the environment of a group of clients who share a common condition.

The experience of clients as illustrated in Figure 15-1 is perhaps the most telling with regard to service fragmentation and duplication. The family involved is composed of the mother, who is developmentally delayed, and three daughters. The father is deceased. The family was referred for services soon after the father died. This referral led to others and eventually the family was involved with 12 service providers.

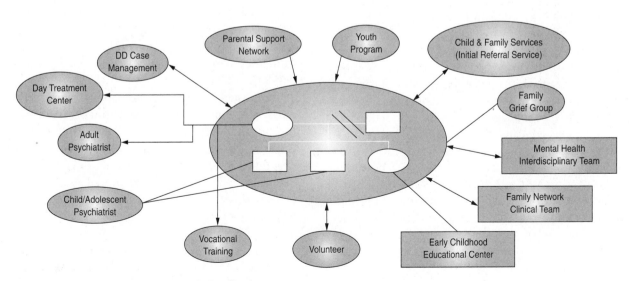

Figure 15-1 Service Fragmentation & Duplication

In this situation, each of the service agencies involved with this family had goals, many of which were contradictory or competing, adding stress to the family system. Note, for instance, that two agencies are providing parent support or parenting services. Parenting support was also the reason the volunteer became involved with the family. Family treatment teams from two different agencies were providing services to the family. In addition, individual members have their own therapist and are involved with other service providers as a result of referrals. In addition to the overwhelming involvement of the various providers in this family, the lack of coordination and duplication fragments the family system. A crisis developed for the family when the condition of their housing required that they relocate. This particular family, far more representative than we would like to admit, was spending more than 50 hours per week in appointments with the various agencies involved. When the mother cancelled appointments in order to look for housing, several of the service agencies reported that she was resistant to change or lacked initiative to make progress; some threatened to withdraw their services. Instead of providing support to the family for their problem-solving efforts, the actions of the providers inhibited independent thought and action. A social worker involved in this situation was extremely frustrated, as was the family, by the lack of responsiveness on the part of the service providers to the family's housing crisis.

Types of coordination and collaboration between organizations include interdisciplinary or multidisciplinary teams, joint planning or programming, and case management. Many school districts, for example, are using interdisciplinary teams to address school truancy. Membership of these teams consists of staff from a group of organizations that have an interest in this issue. Multidisciplinary teams staffed by mental health and medical professionals are yet another form of collaborative practice. The use of teams as a form of collaborative practice is beyond the scope of this book. We refer you to the literature (see, for example, Glisson, 1994; Lim & Adleman, 1997; Rothman, 1994) for

resources on this topic. In addition, we refer you to Congress (1999) and Reamer (1998b) for an articulation of the ethical standards and dilemmas related to interdisciplinary collaboration for social workers who are members of interdisciplinary teams (Reamer, 1998b).

In this section, we focus on interorganizational service coordination, which includes case management and interorganizational collaboration as macro practice strategies because they involve the development and coordination of resources and services as system level interventions to address complex social issues or target groups.

Interorganizational Service Coordination

Interorganizational coordination has as its basic intent to improve service to clients, address community or target population concerns by offering a range of services, bridge service gaps, or implement policies that are too big for one agency to achieve alone (Alexander, 1991; Beatrice, 1990). Within this context, the collective behavior of the organizations involved may be conceptualized as a social action system, in which interdependent processes, tasks, and functions emerge through a division of labor between the members of the coordinated effort. It is important to remember that although organizations may join together in a coordinated effort with compatible goals and mission, they continue to function in relative independence of each other.

Interorganizational coordination provides a range of options for the coordination of services: an individual coordinator, a coordinating unit, or an organization that may act as the coordinating lead. The function of this individual, unit, or agency is to "coordinate the decisions, activities of an interorganizational system with respect to a given area, issue, problem or program" (Alexander, 1991, p. 217). The intent of this management of services or resources is to provide a better, more integrated mix of services for groups or communities. A critical issue in service coordination is that the agencies involved share a common priority, for example, "to strengthen family shelter and transitional housing capacity in the state" (Beatrice, 1990). This arrangement requires that each organization contribute the elements necessary to achieve the joint goal (Rothman, 1994).

Case Management

Case management, a type of interorganizational service coordination, is not a unitary type of service, and the literature contains varied conceptualizations of case management (see, for example, C. D. Austin, 1990; S. T. Moore, 1990; Patterson & Lee, 1998; Roberts-DeGennaro, 1987; Rose, 1992; Rothman, 1994; P. Solomon & Draine, 1996; and Walsh, 2000). In health care settings, additional case management functions include utilization review or management as well as locating and coordinating a defined group of services for a defined group of people. Loomis (1992) and Capitman, MacAdam, and Yee (1988) in their evaluation of case management in health care have identified program types and models of case management in health care settings. All models, however, share the basic premise that central to case management is the function of linking clients with essential resources and services.

The case management function of locating, organizing, coordinating, and monitoring services may be carried out by an individual practitioner in the role of a case manager or by an administrative unit. Large state agencies often have units in which staff act in an administrative function that coordinates services for a target group. This function involves purchasing service contracts, providing clients with information about services, and allocating funds to community based agencies. Rarely are these administrative units involved with clients directly and hence they have a relationship with the service delivery agency. Although case management may vary in goals and settings, Kane, Penrod, Davidson, Moscovice, and Rich (1991) articulate a consensus that case management involves (1) screening, (2) multidimensional assessment, (3) care planning, (4) implementation, (5) monitoring progress and adequacy of services, and (6) reassessment at fixed intervals.

Case Managers

Practitioners perform their case management roles somewhat differently according to the type of setting and role definitions within specific agencies. This role may involve acting as an advocate, broker, and mediator. In some instances they may be involved in direct practice. The case manager role, more than any other, entails work at the interface between clients and their environments. Case management, in fact, moved to the forefront of direct social work practice with expanded recognition that the needs of increasing numbers of clients with major disabilities (e.g., frail elderly, and developmentally and mentally disabled persons) were not being met because these people could not negotiate the complex and often uncoordinated human service delivery systems (Austin, 1990). Social workers are well qualified to serve as case managers because of their knowledge of community resources, their skills in communication and advocacy, and the purposes and objectives of the profession as defined in Chapter 1. To refresh your memory, the central objectives include (1) helping people to obtain resources, (2) facilitating interactions between individuals and others in their environment, and (3) making organizations and society as a whole responsive to people. Serving as case manager thus is consonant with the spirit of social work. Knowledge of resources, skills in connecting clients with resources (as delineated in Chapter 3), and skills in following up to ensure that clients receive services and resources in a timely fashion thus are common to all case management roles.

Some have asked how case management differs from traditional social work practice. The answer is that all social workers engage in case management in varying degrees, and, as Moore (1990) has aptly put it, "case management is just old-fashioned social work wearing new clothes" (p. 444). *Case management* in a strict sense entails "generalist" practice, but in another sense case managers are resource "specialists" who possess knowledge about community resources (in areas of practice defined by the populations they serve) and employ skills in utilizing community resources to benefit their clients.

An Empirically Based Model

In carrying out their roles, case managers do much more than perform the broker role in connecting clients with resources. They must also be competent in implementing all aspects of the problem-solving process. Recognizing that case management cuts across many human service fields and that "nobody quite knows what case management is" (Rothman, 1991, p. 520), Rothman developed an empirically grounded model of case management based on a review of 132 pertinent articles and a survey of 48 case managers. We list the steps of *case management* (as identified by Rothman) and briefly discuss the steps. We do not presume to do justice to Rothman's article and hope our brief discussion will stimulate you to read this resource.

1. *Access to agency.* Case managers need to facilitate clients' access to the system by being receptive and by arranging appointments as quickly as possible when people are referred to the organization. Outreach efforts may also be required to encourage people in need of case management service to enter the system (e.g., homeless, mentally disabled, and frail elderly people).

2. *Intake.* This step involves exploring clients' problems and needs and determining their eligibility for services and financial resources. Information about the services of the organization is provided and forms are completed as needed. Skills in fostering rapport and eliciting information are employed. Some preliminary planning may be initiated.

3. *Assessment.* Problems are defined more explicitly, and additional collateral information is obtained when needed. The family of the client is carefully assessed to determine their capability in coping with a disabled client and their potential as a support system that can be tapped. Accurate assessment may require collaboration of different professionals from different disciplines in the agency.

4. *Goal setting.* Objectives are determined by obtaining the client's perception of areas needing improvement and the case manager's perceptions. Both short-term and long-term goals are formulated, as, for example, treating acute physical and mental symptoms and securing housing versus engaging in a rehabilitation program and building self-esteem. Goals must be realistically geared to the capacities of clients (which often are very limited).

5. *Planning intervention or identifying and indexing resources.* This step is dual in nature because planning interventions (e.g., counseling or therapy and planning services) is inextricably connected to linking clients with resources. Necessary resources may not be available at a given time and access to services changes according to the demands made on external agencies at a given time. Identifying resources may entail telephone or personal contacts with agencies. Case managers may have files on available resources and may use them in locating resources. As with assessment, clients should be involved in planning interventions to the fullest possible extent.

6. *Linking clients.* As expected, respondents contacted by Rothman indicated that linking clients with resources was a very common activity. As we suggested in Chapter 3, connecting clients with resources is active and facilitative. As Rothman states, "Preparing the client for linkage involves providing detailed information, anticipating difficulties, role playing, and accompanying clients on the first visit" (p. 524).

7. *Monitoring and reassessment.* This is a vital process aimed at determining if the arrangements implemented are adequately maintaining the client in the community. Adequate monitoring requires a substantial allotment of time, which is used to telephone agencies and staff and to phone and visit clients. Crisis situations are expected, and careful monitoring enables case managers to implement timely remedial measures. In the context of long-term continuing care, ongoing reassessment is essential. Reassessment can be formal or informal but should be done at periodic intervals.

Clients should be actively involved in reassessment, which may entail use of instruments employed in the initial assessment phase to obtain baseline measures on specified aspects of the client's problem situation.

8. *Outcome evaluation.* Where it is appropriate, outcome evaluation entails determining the extent to which goals have been attained (e.g., locating housing, securing medical care, or attaining the capacity to live independently). When baseline measures were employed during the assessment phase, they will be employed again as part of outcome evaluation.

Other Case Management Functions

Embodied in the preceding steps are a number of other common functions performed by case managers, as identified by Rothman's (1991) research. This function includes interagency service coordination and entails developing effective working relationships with agencies that will enhance the linkage function. Policies or agreements, either formal or informal, are often formulated to foster mutual understanding and to define procedures for service coordination. Advocacy and empowerment are embodied in the function of case management. Although some critics suggest that case management is not necessarily a form of client empowerment, Cnaan (1994) believes that empowerment is a valued goal and within the function of the case manager. Advocacy in case management may be intermittently employed to assist a client to receive services. Both empowerment and advocacy as elements of the helping process assist clients with securing needed resources or services while enabling them to manage their own affairs to the extent of their capabilities.

Vulnerable Populations and Service Coordination

Vulnerable groups in need of case management typically require extensive services and resources, including those provided by systems of health care, mental health, rehabilitation, education, child protection, housing, employment, and other related systems. Because of the pervasive needs of these clients, it is vital that one of the service providers be designated to perform a service coordination function. Such an arrangement affixes responsibility for planning and orchestrating the delivery of services in a systematic and timely manner, arranging meetings, and communicating with other agencies to identify additional needed services and to avoid duplication and working at cross-purposes.

Although the needs of vulnerable groups served by case managers are generally pervasive, they vary from one group to another and even within broad client groups. (Recall, for example, that homeless people are a heterogeneous population with widely varying needs.) Space limitations preclude discussing the needs of each group, but in the following we identify some vulnerable groups and relevant references: people with AIDS (Gillman, 1991); severely psychiatrically disabled adults (Bush, Langford, Rosen, & Gott, 1990), developmentally disabled children (Fiene & Taylor, 1991); mental health adult patients sexually abused as children (Rose, Peabody, & Stratigeas, 1991); elderly homeless persons (Kutza & Keigher, 1991); developmentally disabled adults (Kaplan, 1992); refugees and immigrants (Drachman, 1992). Resources needed by the vulnerable groups just listed are not always available, especially in rural communities. Case managers or service coordinators, therefore, must (or should) sometimes serve still another function—that of resource developer as discussed earlier in this chapter.

Interorganizational Collaboration

Although the terms *cooperation, coordination,* and *collaboration* are often used interchangeably to denote formal relationships between organizations, collaboration involves a much more elaborate process and planning. A more recent term used to denote this relationship is *wrap around services.* Three models of interorganizational collaboration are described by Reitan (1998), with a rationale for the formation of agency relationship within each model. In this discussion, collaboration is both a process and product of the collaborative arrangement.

Unlike service coordination, in which the goals and mission of the organizations remain separate, collaboration involves creating a shared vision and the developing new goals. Mission and authority are determined by the members involved. Ownership and control of the project is balanced; risks and benefits are shared and mutual. Interorganizational collaboration as defined by Mattesisch and Monsey (1992) as:

> *a mutually beneficial well defined relationship entered into by two or more organizations to achieve common goals. This relationship includes a commitment to: a definition of mutual relationships and goals; a jointly developed structure and shared responsibility; mutual authority and accountability for success; and sharing of resources and rewards. (p. 7)*

Similar to coordination, interorganizational collaboration draws upon the collective strength, knowledge, and expertise of each member organization to achieve through joint effort that which is not possible by a single organization. Other assumptions of collaboration include efficient and effective services, a reduction in staff costs, and the ability to address the total needs of a client group. In this respect, interorganizational collaboration is consistent with the trends described earlier in this chapter as well as the emergence of a more holistic framework in human services.

Collaboration can also involve the development of innovative approaches utilizing intervention and practice research (Galinsky, Turnbull, Meglin, & Wilner, 1993; Hasenfeld & Furman, 1994) case management to improve the flow and form of services clients receive (Rothman, 1994) the development of social policy (Beatrice, 1990) and coordination between researchers and practitioners in the development of practice knowledge (Hess & Mullen, 1995).

Graham and Barter (1999, pp. 9–10) have identified four phases of collaboration, which we summarize:

1. Problem setting in which stakeholders within a domain are identified with mutual acknowledgment and common definition of issues.

2. Agreement on direction and common values that guide individual pursuits and purposes including expectations of outcome.

3. Implementation of the plan and skills, for example, conferring, consulting, cooperating as well as understanding the interdependence between the various professional orientations involved.

4. Creation of a long-term structure that enables the collaboration to sustain, evaluate, and nurture the collaborative effort over time.

Several resources in the literature outline the antecedents, conditions, and factors that facilitate successful interorganizational collaboration (Bruner, 1991; Graham & Barter, 1999; Reitan, 1998; Sandfort, 1999). Collaborative practice between professionals as discussed in the team literature, or social worker to client, or agency to agency, focuses on micro practice. Meanwhile interorganizational collaboration refers to the macro level. Interorganizational collaboration requires a blending of resources, a relational system in which joint goals are created, joint decision-making, and the creation of a new structure to accomplish the mutually determined goals (Alexander, 1991; Graham & Barter, 1999; Reitan, 1998; Sandfort, 1999). It means that organizations are willing to relinquish old ways of conducting business and redefines roles: "Collaboration assumes the inevitability of conflicting ideas and differential power relationships as well as the necessity for compromise, continued advocacy for a position, and the knowledge and skills to differentiate between the two" (Graham & Barter, 1999, p. 10). The dynamics of creating and sustaining the collaborative relationship are illustrated in the following case example.

COLLABORATION: A CASE EXAMPLE

Staff from a community youth service agency considered that there were mutual benefits for exploring collaboration with a group of county probation officers. Both organizations were interested in addressing the recidivism rate of youth offenders. Resources to ensure the development of the newly created organization combined budgetary allocations from both the agency and the county. Staff and managers were responsible for the development of the organization's mission and goals, developing joint interventions strategies and case plans for youth.

Although members of the collaboration had a shared vision, actually coming together posed some difficulties. Concerns centered upon trust among staff as well as trust within the community because of community perceptions of probation officers. In particular, staff from the community agency had a working relationship with families that tended to be more family and community centered than was common with the probation officers. Their role as advocates for youth often resulted in an adversarial relationship with probation officers. Another level of concern had to do with loss of autonomy, decision making, and communication. Probation officers, for example, were reluctant to relinquish their authority over case plans and decisions about expectations for the youth. Differences in salaries, actual and perceived, were also factors.

Resolutions of the factors illustrated in this example are among those identified by Mattesisch and Monsey (1992), Meyers (1993), and Sandfort (1999) as influencing a successful collaboration. Many of the concerns were resolved over time as the two groups worked to refine their vision, problem-solving skills, and relationships. They also used an outside consultant who worked with them around team and consensus building.

The social and political climate also influences service coordination and interorganizational collaboration. Critical to creating and sustaining interorganizational efforts is the communication and problem-solving process participants use to establish goals, objectives, agreed upon roles, decision-making, and conflict resolution. Sandfort (1999), in describing the structural impediments that affected the collaboration between a private and public agency, suggests that the culture of each organization as well as the beliefs and prior relationships between staff play an important part in the extent to which frontline staff are able to work together.

Although there is no one model for coordination or collaboration, the importance of a shared vision about service delivery, the outcomes participants wish to achieve, and the dynamics involved in forging a relationship should not be underestimated. Social workers can play an important role in both the development and implementation process. First, social workers through their contact with client groups can identify opportunities where new initiatives are needed. Second, in the implementation process, social workers can play a valuable role in problem solving and facilitating group process. Social workers can also ensure that client rights and confidentiality are maintained. For example, tensions that often arise in coordination and collaborative arrangements stem from the extent to which member organizations share information. Finally, social workers can use their skills to manage the collective actions and beliefs that organizations may have about each other. These skills are especially needed in the resolution of philosophical differences about how clients are viewed or treated. In this role, the social worker acts as a mediator and advocate.

MACRO PRACTICE EVALUATION

Evaluation is important to all levels of social work practice. Each of the macro level strategies we have discussed in this chapter lends itself to a variety of procedures for which outcomes may be assessed. In general, evaluation is an ongoing process and it is important to establish indicators at the beginning to the intervention. The overall intent of the evaluation process is to assess whether the desired goals have been achieved, whether change in the target problem has occurred, and the extent to which the strategies employed were effective. For example, the social workers involved in the effort to expand the number of beds for the homeless would determine how many new beds are available. The focus of this evaluation is on the overall outcome. Because evaluation also involves process, another aspect of the evaluation is to examine how the outcome was achieved. In this regard they may also examine the strategies used to recruit additional churches. Soliciting feedback from the church groups and participants is one way to obtain this information. A pre and post rating scale in conjunction with interviews could be used with the community group discussed in an earlier example to determine the effect of the community-police buddy system initiated by the neighborhood group. In this way the evaluation process makes use of summative and formative information and includes both qualitative and quantitative data. Evaluation in whatever form requires clearly specified goals and objectives in measurable terms.

In keeping with the empowerment theme stressed throughout this chapter, we wish to advocate the importance of including client groups in the evaluation process. They should be involved in establishing success indicators as well as evaluating the outcomes. Gutierrez, Parsons, and Cox (1998) report several examples of facilitating empowerment through evaluation.

Summary

In this chapter we have emphasized the range of roles for social workers as well as the social, economic, demographic, and political trends that present opportunities for action and intervention at the macro practice level. In talking to social workers in preparation for writing this chapter, we were impressed with the breadth and depth of macro practice strategies they used. Many of their efforts were discussed in this chapter. The social workers saw their practice as holistic and were comfortable employing a range of strategies to help people resolve or change conditions. As one social worker stated, "It would be difficult to ask people to change without also addressing the circumstances and conditions which contribute to their situations."[1] The person and environment focus frames the essence and foundation of macro practice.

Internet Resources

 You can learn about mental health outreach for older adults through the following site: *http://www.wiche.edu/ MentalHealth/ElderBroch/index.htm/*. You can find out about community-building tools at *http://www.acosa.org* and a community toolbox is available at *http://ctb.ukans.edu/*. Using InfoTrac®, you can also gather additional information on the topics of this chapter by entering the keywords "social reform," "advocacy," and "resource development."

Notes

1. The authors wish to thank the many social workers and agencies that provided the rich examples of macro level intervention strategies discussed in this chapter.

CHAPTER 16

Enhancing Family Relationships

Revised and edited by Glenda Dewberry Rooney

CHAPTER OVERVIEW

This chapter builds on the skills you learned in Chapter 10 on family assessment to include skills in enhancing family relationships. You will learn how to engage families, plan initial contacts, improve communications, and practice in a culturally sensitive manner.

APPROACHES TO WORK WITH FAMILIES

Social workers are involved with families in a variety of settings and for diverse purposes. As Reid expresses it, "social workers may work with . . . a family in preparation for the discharge of a family member from an institution, may help a mother take action to secure the return of her child from foster care, may have crisis-oriented interviews with distraught parents who have brought their injured child to an emergency room, may help mediate conflict between a family and a manager of a housing project" (W. Reid, 1985, p. 7). Reid's definition suggests that social work practice with families encompasses a range of interventions, including therapy and home and community based services. Recurring emphasis in the various approaches to work with families has been to consider the family as a social unit. As conceptualized by Mary Richmond

in the late 19th century, the family was a social system and focus for intervention (Nichols & Schwartz, 1998). The family as a social system is influenced by interactions with larger social systems in the environment. Thus, there are approaches to families that view working with families in an integrative, ecological, or multisystems context (Boyd-Franklin, 1989b; Henggeler, Schoenwald, Bourduin, Rowland, & Cunningham, 1998; Kilpatrick & Holland, 1999). In this chapter, we will emphasize family as a social unit, examining the continuous interaction and relationship patterns internal to the family that influence family functioning.

Family relationship and interactions are often punctuated and strained by numerous factors. Family life transitions, structural arrangements, patterns of communication, roles, including definition overload and strain, and unrealistic expectations or standards are but a few sources of strain that contribute to family relational dynamics. Therapeutic intervention strategies and goals, whether the focus is on family structure or family processes, have as their primary aim to alter relationship and interaction patterns in order to provide growth and development of all family members. Concepts related to family structure are rooted in family transaction patterns, interpersonal boundaries, and arrangements between subsystems and interpersonal boundaries. Process-oriented approaches conversely focus on the nature of family dynamics, their patterned interaction, and circularity and the cause and effect sequences. In the following section, we discuss intervention strategies that delineate both process and structural approaches to work with families.

The cognitive behavioral approach to families, for example, involves helping individuals and the family learn new behaviors and altering circular or reciprocal sequences of behavior (Becvar & Becvar, 2000). Regulating communication and altering communicational styles is another strategy that may be used to promote positive interactions and family relationships. Virginia Satir, as noted by Janzen and Harris (1997), was the first social work family therapist to examine and alter faulty communications processes through direct intervention. The family systems approach seeks to reduce anxiety and symptoms by emphasizing unresolved multigenerational issues that intrude upon an individual's ability to balance emotional and intellectual functioning, intimacy and autonomy and interpersonal relations (Goldenberg & Goldenberg, 2000). Conversely, the focus of the structural approach is to strengthen family relationships, interactions, and transactional patterns. More recently, approaches to work with families have tended to rethink past assumptions about what constitutes healthy or normal family development and functioning. This rethinking has been inspired by the feminist critique, loss of faith in truth and objectivity, an increased interest in diversity and pluralism well as the practitioner as an expert. Newer approaches such as the Solution Focused approach, a brief treatment model, place emphasis on the here and now and problem solving. Similarly, narrative and social constructionists seek to draw out the family or individual's interpretation of experiences; and in doing so, emphasize a more collaborative and conversational approach to work with families. The goal is to help individuals and families create a new meaning and viewpoints by exploring the effects that problems have on the family. This exploration includes family context, for example, culture in relationship to the problem (Nichols & Schwartz, 1998).

In this chapter we draw from a number of family practice approaches, interventions, and techniques you can employ to enhance the interactions between clients and significant others. These interventions and techniques are of course employed upon completion of the multidimensional assessment phase of the helping process. Mastering the content of this chapter and practicing relevant skills will advance your competence in the following ways:

1. Engaging families (voluntary, referred, or mandated) in the helping process and initial sessions
2. Assisting families to enhance their interactions by increasing positive feedback
3. Modifying dysfunctional patterns of interactions
4. Modifying misconceptions and distorted cognitions that impair interactions
5. Modifying dysfunctional family alignments

Though the interventions and techniques that are discussed in this chapter are applied to couples and families, most are also relevant to interventions in treatment groups, a topic discussed in Chapter 17.

Family, as we defined earlier in Chapter 10, includes traditional family forms, same-sex couples, or guardians. This definition reflects social or cultural arrangements in which family extends to kin, friends, and informal and formal intergenerational relationships, and provides the flexibility for the family to define the relevant members of the family system. Because the family system interacts with larger systems, factors external to the family affect family interactions and family functioning. Societal pressures and the accompanying stress on nontraditional families, for example lesbian, single-parent, or low-income families, are capable of influencing internal family interaction patterns. Family processes and structure may also be embedded in cultural values and norms, and therefore conventional concepts and themes used to assess and intervene with families may not match the needs of diverse families. We highlight some of these issues later in this chapter as well as discuss ecologically based concerns that influence family functioning. You may also want to review Chapter 10 for the discussion related to family rules, boundaries, and communication styles that frame family interaction patterns. Prior to presentation of intervention strategies, we begin by focusing on the initial contact with families and the skills that will facilitate engaging the family in the helping process.

INITIAL CONTACTS WITH COUPLES AND FAMILIES

To enhance the functioning of couples and family systems, social workers must be skilled in engaging members of these systems and in focusing on the family systems as a whole. Because clients generally do not think from a systems perspective, it is important to manage initial contacts in ways that encourage work with relevant members of the family system rather than settle prematurely on an individual request for service. In this section, then, we describe ways of handling initial contacts that lay the groundwork for implementing the systems-oriented interventions in this chapter.

Request for Service

The initial request for service often may involve only one member of the family. Depending on the practice setting or the nature of the referral, initial contact may occur in the home, in a school or hospital setting, over the telephone, or in the social worker's office. If the family has previously been screened for a family approach during a telephone intake, all that the social worker may need to do in the initial contact is to work out details related to the appointment.[1] If there has been no previous contact with the caller, the social worker may need to accomplish several other vital objectives, one of which is to determine whether intervening at a family level may be appropriate. Social workers can generally explore a family approach when the initial contact deals with difficulties that

involve immediate family members or other persons living under the same roof, such as a relative, friend, or live-in partner. When problems involve persons less intimately involved with the caller (e.g., employer, parents who live elsewhere), the social worker usually makes an initial appointment with the individual who initiated the contact.

Other critical objectives of the initial contact include reaching an agreement as to who will attend the first session and establishing rapport with the potential client who initiated the request for service. Striking a balance between conveying empathy for the client and establishing expectations regarding the initial contact is sometimes difficult, but as we demonstrate shortly, skills delineated in earlier chapters aid in this task. O. L. Wright and Anderson (1998) emphasize attachment skills that involve "connecting" to clients and ensuring that they are heard and their experience is validated. Even so, the initial contact should be kept short and focused on relevant objectives to avoid becoming entangled in individual perception of the family problems. To this end, we suggest the following guidelines:

1. Ask the client to describe the problem briefly, and empathically respond to the client's messages. This is a strategy that not only helps establish rapport but also elicits information that will help you determine who else is involved in the problem. When you believe you have established beginning rapport and have heard the presenting complaint, summarize the client's view of the problem and relevant feelings and emphasize the client's needs or wants.

2. In the instance of referred or mandated contact, the social worker should share the outlines of the circumstances of the referral, including the source and expressed purpose of the referral. The social worker should make clear what choices the potential client may make, including whether to meet at all (in the case of referred contact) or what might be addressed. Any mandates that might affect potential client choices should be shared (R. H. Rooney, 1992). Social workers should also review any applicable time limits.

3. If your exploration reveals that family involvement is appropriate, introduce the client to the "family approach," using a message such as the following: "In helping people with the kinds of problems you've described, it is often helpful to have other family members come for sessions also. It has been my experience that when members of the family affect and influence each other's problems other members also experience stress and discomfort. Equally important, changes in one member require changes and adjustments in other family members as well. People accomplish the kinds of changes you're wanting more rapidly when all family members work together. For this reason, it will be important that other members of the family be involved in the helping process."

4. Specify which family members you want to see in the initial session. Social workers who espouse a family systems orientation differ in their views as to whether the entire family should be included in the initial session. Some strongly advocate involving all members from the beginning. Because inexperienced social workers commonly encounter difficulties managing initial contacts with entire families (which requires advanced skills), we recommend a less ambitious approach. If a parent identifies a child-related problem, request that parents or the parent attend the first session *without* the child (or children) unless there are strong objections or unusual contraindications (e.g., a child threatening suicide). We also recommend that you include in this session any other adult who serves a parental or executive function in the home (e.g., live-in partner or grandmother). When you make this request, however, convey that you may wish to involve other members of the family in future interviews.

When a caller complains of problems involving a spouse or partner, ask that this individual be included in the initial session. Respond, however, to any preference of a caller to be seen alone in a first session by agreeing to this but indicating that a usual next step would be to schedule an individual interview for the other partner, thus giving that person "equal time" and providing the social worker with a balanced view of the problem. Some clients comply with requests to bring specific family members to the initial session, but others offer explanations such as, "My husband has to work," "She won't come," or "He's not the one with the problem." These messages often reflect the caller's reluctance to include other members as well as the reluctance of others to participate in family sessions.

Despite the advantage of seeing partners, a parent, or other specified family members together, you must respond sensitively to a caller's reactions to your requests. When clients openly state they do not want to involve other family members, it is important to explore their reasons thoroughly, if not on the phone, then in the first session. You should stress during the exploration that other family members can play an important role in helping to find solutions to problems. If clients do not subsequently modify their position, however, you should "begin where they are" by arranging to see those they are willing to bring. Although the emphasis is on the family system and the potential contribution of each member to the problem solution, not all family members may need to be present in all family sessions. For example, children may be excluded from family sessions if the focus is on the relationship between the parents. Furthermore, insisting that all family members are involved may undermine the helping process and the initial contact may in fact be the last (Janzen and Harris, 1997). When clients maintain that other family members are unwilling to attend sessions, ask their permission to contact those persons directly. If you gain permission (as will usually happen), you may wish to utilize a telephone approach similar to the following example after introducing yourself and stating the purpose of the call:

- "As you know, _____ has contacted me concerning problems involving your family. I understand that you are quite busy but I thought I would give you a personal call to ask you to come. Your participation would be extremely helpful because I am interested in your perspective on the problem the family is experiencing and it may even aid in the resolution. Would you be available for an appointment, say, at four P.M. next Wednesday?"

After conveying this message, you should explore this individual's reactions. Although you may wish to reiterate your views that participation in *at least one* session is very important, you should respect a decision not to participate. Exerting pressure tends to alienate the client and may destroy future opportunities for involvement. With skillful handling of their contacts with families, social workers are sometimes able to dissipate strong opposition, thereby making it possible to involve key family members in the helping process.

MANAGING INITIAL CONTACTS WITH PARENTS

Earlier we recommended that initial sessions involve parents or another family member who performs the executive parental function, and include children in subsequent sessions. This strategy gives social workers more time to become acquainted with the problems of the family and, on the basis of known information, to plan strategies with instructors or supervisors for engaging other members. Having an initial session with parents also provides the opportunity to establish rapport with them, enhancing the potential to influence the parents in later sessions involving children. Social workers also have an opportunity to assess whether modifications by the parents are needed *before* they meet with children. Some parents, for example, manifest such unproductive styles of relating to their children that initial attempts to see the entire family would be disastrous. Further, having an initial session with parents enables social workers to clarify the systemic nature of problems and to emphasize where indicated the need for parents to concentrate on changing their own behaviors.

When meeting with parents or others who serve this function in initial sessions, social workers can begin to delabel children who are identified as problem bearers. They may also clarify that although the

parents may believe that one child is responsible for the family's difficulties, entering the family session in this frame of mind will cause the identified problem bearer to feel defensive and to oppose becoming involved in the helping process. Social workers can further emphasize that even though one person may cause significant strain in the family, all family members are usually involved in the problem and need to make some changes. Social workers can thus inform the parents that they will be working in family sessions "to take some heat off" one member of the family and to engage all members in a discussion of changes they would like to make to alleviate family problems. Social workers may need to reassure the parents that they will also be helping the child to change, but they should stress that change is less difficult if the child does not believe that other family members expect him or her to make changes expressly to accommodate them. (A similar strategy is appropriate when an adult has been designated as the problem.)

Interviewing parents in an initial session also makes it possible to plan how best to bring an identified child into the helping process. Rather than see a child individually, for example, a social worker may wish to interview all the children together or to see the "problem child" with a sibling near his or her age. Seeing the child with others reinforces the message that the social worker views the problem as residing in the system rather than in a particular individual. By interviewing parents first, social workers can also help them to plan how to explain to their children why they are seeking professional help and can coach them in preparing a child. The parents' explanation should clarify that the *family* is having problems (not that the family is having problems *with the child*). The parents should also give children a general explanation of what to expect when the children meet with a social worker and should listen carefully to reservations they may have about coming to the sessions.

Social workers can also coach parents to behave constructively when children attend sessions. For example, a social worker may suggest that parents create a climate conducive to open communication by withholding blaming messages, focusing on positive behaviors of their children, and listening attentively to their concerns. Further, the social worker can ask each parent to refrain from engaging in dysfunctional communications. Coaching parents to relate in positive ways to their children in initial sessions is critically important, for a key role of social workers is to foster positive interactions among family members. If parents do bring the "problem child" to an initial session, a social worker should seek permission to interview the child first, giving the child a chance to "tell his story" without the social worker having been biased (as the child perceives it) by information provided by the parents. At the same time, the social worker must avoid subordinating the executive function of the parent or giving the impression of forming an alliance with the child. Thus the rationale for a request to see the child first should be carefully explained to both the parents and the child. Even so, in some cultures, separating the child from the parents could be problematic. After interviewing the child, the social worker should then interview the parents, reserving the latter part of the session for seeing all participants. At this time, the social worker will want to emphasize the systemic nature of the family problem, assist members to share individual goals with each other, and formulate family goals.

ORCHESTRATING THE INITIAL FAMILY SESSION

The goal of bringing the family together is to identify the problem concern by eliciting the viewpoint of the various family members. The initial session, whether it occurs in the office or in the home, is referred to as the *social* or *joining* stage (Nichols & Schwartz, 1998; Boyd-Franklin, 1989b). It is important in this session to establish rapport and build an alliance with the family. It is useful to restate the reason for the contact and gather information about the family in addition to their viewpoints about the family problem. In facilitating this process, listening is particularly important so that all members feel understood and accepted. Adopting a stance of "what can I learn from and about this family that will help me work with them" is a means of facilitating entry into the family system. The social worker also facilitates this process by ensuring that members are able to speak without interruptions from other family members.

Clients' experiences during this session are crucial in determining whether they will engage in the helping process and contract to work toward specific goals or whether they will decide against proceeding further. Moreover, clients perceive the initial session as a prototype of the helping process. To lay a solid foundation for future work with families, it is important that social workers accomplish a number of objectives. We briefly discuss each of these objectives in this section, but first we list them for use as a guide in both planning for and evaluating initial sessions:

1. Establish a personal relationship with individual members and an alliance with the family as a group.
2. Clarify expectations and explore reservations about the helping process.
3. Clarify roles and the nature of the helping process.
4. Clarify choices about participation in the helping process.
5. Elicit the family's perception of the problem(s).
6. Identify needs and wants of family members.
7. Define the problem as a family problem and begin to delabel any identified patients.
8. Begin highlighting individual and family strengths.
9. Ask questions to elicit information about the patterned behaviors of the family.
10. Begin drawing repetitive problematic communications to the attention of family members and discuss whether they wish to change these patterns.
11. Begin helping members to relate to one another in more positive ways.

12. Communicate hope that the family can change.

13. Establish individual and family goals.

14. Gauge motivation of family members to return for future sessions and negotiate a contract.

15. Negotiate tasks to be accomplished during the week.

16. End the session by summarizing problems discussed, goals formulated, and progress achieved.

You will note these objectives are essentially the same as those identified in earlier chapters of the book. In the following sections, however, we explain how to accomplish these objectives specifically in work with families. The following discussion will also assist you in consolidating knowledge and skills that have been presented earlier.

1. *Establish a personal relationship with individual members and an alliance with the family as a group.* In working with families (or groups), social workers have a twofold task of establishing personal relationships with each individual while developing a "connectedness" with the family as a unit. To cultivate relationships with family members, social workers can employ several techniques. The technique of *socializing* involves the use of social chitchat and is used briefly by social workers at the beginning of the session to reduce tension.

Social workers can also employ joining or coupling techniques (Minuchin, 1974) to expedite their entrance into the family system. One way social workers "join" the family is to respect family rules (for example, allowing a husband to be spokesperson for the family), even though they may intervene later to change such rules. Social workers also convey their acceptance of the family by highlighting strengths or offering support to threatened members. The social worker uses the family's language and idioms and consciously makes statements that establish similarities or parallels between themselves and clients (e.g., "Oh, I had a dog almost like that").

A third technique, *facilitating,* involves the use of empathic responses to establish emotional linkages with individual members. Empathic responding can be particularly useful in developing rela-tionships with reserved family members. For instance, when members do not respond spontaneously to new topics of discussion, a social worker can solicit a response (e.g., "Tamiko, I don't think you've said what you experienced when you learned you were coming here. Could you tell us how you felt?"). The social worker can then respond empathically to what that member says or does (e.g., "Yes, I can understand why you would feel this way"). In reaching for the responses of reticent or less assertive members, the social worker encourages them to become involved but does not press the point. Empathic responses and genuine interest on the part of practitioners demonstrated through verbal and nonverbal messages often cause some family members to become more active participants.

In addition to the preceding strategy, social workers should also endeavor to distribute time and attention somewhat equally among members, to highlight individual strengths, and to intervene when one member speaks for another or when one member is the target of blaming or put-down messages (techniques are discussed later in the chapter). Through such interventions, social workers demonstrate positive regard for individuals and the value they place on the unique contributions of each family member.

Social workers also develop rapport with members by addressing observations and questions to the *family.* For example: "From what you've said, it appears that all of you would like others in the family to listen when you speak." Such responses not only facilitate developing a "connectedness" to family members at a group level but also serve to heighten their awareness that their family often functions as a unit, and that as members of this unit, they have common aspirations, goals, and (at times) shared emotions. Effectively connecting with families may also require that the social worker demonstrate an understanding of the sociopolitical and cultural context of the family as well as their strengths and competencies. Often, it is the latter that have enabled the family to function in spite of these factors.

2. *Clarify expectations and explore reservations about the helping process.* Family members have varying and often distorted perceptions of the helping process and may have misgivings about participating in sessions. To identify obstacles to full participation in these areas (which is prerequisite to establishing a viable contract), it is helpful to elicit the responses of all family members to questions such as the following:

- "What were your concerns about meeting with me?"
- "What do you hope might happen in our meetings together?"
- "What are your fears about what might happen?"

Although questions of a more general nature are preferable, in some cases, it may be useful to help family members articulate their concerns as illustrated in the following examples:

- "Are you concerned that your family might be judged?"
- "Does seeking help from someone outside of your family make you feel uncomfortable?"
- "In what way do you think that I can be of help to your family?"

As you elicit reservations, concerns, and hopes from individual family members, you can broaden the focus to the family by asking, "I'm wondering if others share the same concerns as . . ." As members acknowledge similar feelings, they often begin to realize that despite feeling some degree of alienation from others in the family, they share certain common concerns, a realization that tends to draw members together as a unit. Exploring reservations about participating in the helping process often diminishes negative feelings or enables clients to move on in the process. Social workers will also want to be sensitive to cultural norms related to expressions of feelings and the fact that some clients may be baffled by questions that explore feelings. In any case, in exploring expectations or reservations about the helping process, you will want to gauge questions about feelings, as questions of this nature may also result

in a strong reaction or no reaction. If certain clients continue to manifest strong opposition to participating, you can address their reluctance by asking them one or both of the following questions and exploring their subsequent responses:

- "What (if anything) would make you feel better about participating?"
- "Given your concerns, are you willing to stay for the remainder of the session and decide at the conclusion as to whether to continue?"

Willingness to negotiate the terms under which clients participate and acknowledging their right to make a choice often reduces negativism to the point that they will agree to continue for the remainder of the interview and, at times, to return for further sessions. In instances where the family has been referred, they may not have an idea about the reason for the contact. Adolescents, for example, may be reluctant to be actively involved. A social worker might employ a paradoxical directive, a technique from strategic approaches, as a means of engaging the reluctant member. This may include a request to attend sessions, while being under no obligation to participate. The paradoxical technique of telling the member not to talk, to read a book, or just be present in the session, places no direct pressure on the person to contribute.

Reluctance to participate may occur when an individual is viewed as the problem. Reluctance may also be viewed as a protective function rather than as opposition to change. Families may fear "what might happen" if their problems are brought out into the open (Nichols & Schwartz, 1998, p. 132). Boyd-Franklin (1989), citing the historical experience of minority families who are often pathologized and viewed as unhealthy, suggests that they may attempt to hide their problems until they escalate to the point of crisis. Also, members of some minority families may adhere to the unspoken cultural or community rule of keeping family secrets and the value of privacy, or there may be a sense of shame in involving someone from outside of the community in family matters. Flores and Carey (2000) note, for instance, that the comfort level of

Hispanic families is increased when they do not feel the need to be defensive about their culture. Social workers are thus encouraged to acknowledge the protective function of reluctance whether in a family member or the family system and create a nonblaming atmosphere where the family and individual member feel safe and affirmed. Reluctance to attend or participate in family sessions may be a particular issue among ethnic minority families in which some members may be undocumented or residing illegally in the United States (Falicov, 1996; Fong, 1997; Pierce & Elisme, 1997). Poor families and gay or lesbian families may have good reason to experience apprehension and anxiety about the helping process. O. L. Wright and Anderson (1998) suggest that in actively tuning in to the family, a social worker might pose the question, "What is it like [*for me*] being with the client, especially during the initial portion of the interaction?" allowing the social worker to evaluate whether reactions to clients will enter into the helping process (p. 202). We add an additional question, "What is it like to be this client?" as a means to focus sensitively and to understand the client's experience in seeking help.

3. *Clarify roles and the nature of the helping process.* In exploring misgivings and reservations, social workers must often explain the nature of the helping process and also clarify both their own and clients' roles. When an explanation is not necessary early in the session, however, social workers often defer it until they engage clients in negotiating a contract, an activity that takes place toward the end of the initial meeting. A primary role of the social worker is to create an atmosphere and structure where problem solving can take place. Toward this end, the social worker assumes a facilitative role, gaining the participation of family members by assisting them to talk about their lives and their concerns (Janzen & Harris, 1997).

4. *Clarify choices about participation in the helping process.* In the instance of referred contact, the social worker can clarify again the message conveyed in telephone contact that the potential client is free to decide whether further contact meets his or her

needs and, if so, what to work on, regardless of the concerns of the referring source. If contact is mandated, it is necessary to clarify what the social worker is required to do (such as submit a report) and the parameters of required contact for clients. In addition to mandated concerns, clients may be advised that they can choose to deal with other problems of concern to them. For some families expansive arrays of problems are a major fact of life. Therefore to focus concerns on family structure or dynamics to the exclusion of their realities, for example adequate housing, food, or shelter, may mean a missed opportunity to "join" the family in the helping process (Boyd-Franklin, 1989b).

5. *Elicit the family's perception of the problems.* In initiating discussion of problems, social workers ask questions such as "Why did you decide to seek help?" (in the case of voluntary contact), "What changes do you want to achieve?" or "How could things be better in the family?" Eliciting the client view of the problem is equally important in involuntary or referred contacts. In such cases, the nature of the referral is summarized, but family members are encouraged to tell their story.

Janzen and Harris (1997) discuss the social worker's role in structuring initial discussion of the family's problems. Because each person has his or her own viewpoint of preference about both the problem and the solution, it is important to elicit the support of each member in the process of problem consensus. During this time, the social worker will want to be aware of differences in interpretation, various roles within the family, and socialization with respect to issues of gender, power, and boundaries. Rosenblatt (1994) urges social workers to pay attention to the language and the use of metaphors. In particular, how individual family members express their views reflects their culture, their realities, and meaning of the family experience. The family experience includes exploring the role of spirituality and religion in the life of the family (Anderson & Worthen, 1997). By the end of the session, the opinions of all family members should have been elicited, as well as their opinions about efforts to solve the problem.

Although the focus may be to move the family toward a consensus with regard to their concerns, it is the strength of the family rather than the problem that will ultimately enable them to resolve their concerns. By exploring how the family has coped or handled previous difficulties, their experiences with positive episodes or past successes, and future hopes and dreams for family life, the social worker can activate family strengths and a greater commitment to goals and problem solving (Weick & Saleeby, 1995).

6. *Identify needs and wants of family members.* As social workers engage the family in a discussion of problems, they listen for needs that are inherent in their messages and can inform clients that they are doing just that, as illustrated in the following explanation:

• "You're here because some of your wants or needs are not being met in the family. As we discuss the family's problems, therefore, I'm going to ask you to help me identify those needs and wants. In turn, we will consider them as we formulate goals and plan our change efforts."

Even early in the session, the social worker explores the needs of participants through empathic responses, as illustrated in the following excerpt from a family session:

Marcos, 16 years old [*to parents*]: You don't ever let me do anything with my friends. [*Feels resentful, wants more autonomy and freedom.*]

Social worker: It sounds to me, Marcos, as though you want to be more independent—you'd like more freedom to move around and more trust from your parents. Am I hearing your needs correctly?

Other family members, perhaps uneasy about where the discussion may lead, may interrupt such messages or in some way discount them. For example, Marcos's father (Mr. Gonzalez) might respond:

Mr. Gonzalez: We're just not about to let you run around wherever you want, particularly with that friend who's been coming to the house lately. You'd just get into trouble.

The social worker, however, can prevent family members from sidetracking an exploration of needs by using the technique of temporarily "putting clients on hold." This technique involves blending an empathic response that addresses the participant's feelings with a focusing response that restructures the interpersonal interaction to achieve the immediate objective. As illustrated in the following excerpt, the social worker works to enable members to listen and acknowledge each others' needs and perceptions:

• "I hear your concern about your son—you don't want him to just run loose. I also know you want to have your views heard and I'd like to hear your views in a minute. But first, I'd like to ask you to hear Marcos's point of view. I would also ask that you listen to him describe his needs or wants."

In initial discussions of needs, the social worker also corrects misperceptions often held by some members that a discussion of the needs of one person means that the social worker will support that person's position. In the following message, for example, the social worker allays Mr. Gonzalez's fear that the social worker may support his son's desire for independence and that Marcos's want is preferable to his concern as a parent.

• "Identifying needs and the conflict surrounding various viewpoints precedes problem solving. When we get to the point of considering solutions, we'll identify options that might help you and Marcos with problems you've pinpointed and select ones that meet *both* your needs."

When one person, such as Marcos in this situation, is perceived as the problem, the social worker will want to challenge this linear thinking by asking others about their role in creating or maintaining the problem. In the life cycle and family systems approach, Marcos's desire for greater independence is to be expected as he moves toward age appropriate autonomy and differentiation. Changes in the bonds between adolescents seeking greater autonomy are consistent with adolescent development but may require changes in parenting behavior and communication patterns (Baer, 1999). At the same time, the father feels responsible as a parent and is making certain demands consistent with this role. This concern often results in parents establishing protective boundaries that may include anxieties about peers, the neighborhood, and intense monitoring. Baer's (1999) study of family relations and parenting in three ethnic groups found that while monitoring was "significant" for all ethnic groups as a deterrence to deviance, monitoring was heightened in some families because of real or perceived dangers (p. 282). Low-income African American parents, for example, may initiate intense monitoring of adolescents in order to minimize dangers in neighborhoods and the outright hostility of society toward minority male youth (Jarrett, 1995). In some cultures, Marcos's desire for greater autonomy may signal an attempt to reconcile acculturation and traditional values.

While considering the influence of relevant cultural or ethnic factors, the goal is to encourage family members to talk among themselves and get beyond the stage of criticism and blaming to talk directly about what they feel, their anxieties, what they want, and their part in the unproductive interaction patterns. In our illustration below, we pick up at the point where the social worker returns to the father's needs. Notice that the social worker works to establish *common* needs of father and son:

Social worker: You probably noticed that I kept the discussion focused on Marcos's needs. I did so because it is critical for me to understand what each of you would like to change. I'd like you to help me to identify *your* needs now. You were saying, "I can't go along with Marcos's just running around. That worries me."[2] What would you like to change?

Mr. Gonzalez: I guess I need to know where he's going—after all, I'm responsible for him. And I need to know he's not getting in trouble when he's gone.

Social worker: Marcos, could you hear what your father said?

Marcos: He said, he needs to know where I am and what I'm doing.

Social worker: Good. I am pleased that you could hear your father so readily. Now, I'm going to try filling in your dad's message. I think he's also saying, "I need to know because I care very much about my son and I am afraid of what might happen to him." Is that accurate, Mr. Gonzalez? [*Father nods.*][3]

Social worker: I'd like you to talk directly to Marcos.

Mr. Gonzalez: I do care and I am anxious about your going out with people that I don't know. [*Hesitates.*] I also feel that we don't do things together anymore.

Marcos: I didn't know you felt that way. I haven't ever heard you talk like that before.

Social worker: See if you can tell your dad how you feel.

Marcos: I feel bad. I'd like to do things with him also, but I can't talk to him. All he does is bad-mouth my friends. He's always critical of what I'm doing.

Social worker: Try to talk directly to your dad rather than to me, and tell him what you need from him.[4]

Marcos: I'd like for us to do things together and be with my friends. I'd also like to be able to talk to you without always ending up in an argument over my friends.

By identifying and highlighting common needs, the social worker is able to focus the intervention on the similarities rather than the differences between father and son and to formulate goals they can mutually achieve to improve their relationship. Both Marcos and his father have expressed a desire to spend time together. The social worker can also assist the two of them to communicate and negotiate their concerns directly, thereby relieving some of the tension in their relationship. Negotiating their concerns would of course lead to the development of a plan that would allow Marcos to have the freedom he is seeking and the father to function in his parental role.

7. Define the problem as a family problem and relabel problem individuals or problem situations. Relabeling in essence changes the label attached to a person or situation from negative to positive, altering the emotional or conceptual context so as to effect a different perception of the person or problem. Earlier in the chapter, we modeled the type of message you can use in clarifying the systemic nature of problems. Continue to maintain that stance throughout the family session, emphasizing that every member's perspective is important; that family members can do much to support the change efforts of other family members; that all members will need to make adjustments to alleviate stress upon the family; and that the family can do much to increase the quality of relationships and the support that each member receives from others.

Despite efforts to influence members to define problems as belonging to the family, you will often encounter a persistent tendency of some members to blame others as the problem. Your consequent task is twofold: First, you must *monitor* your own performance to ensure that you do not collude with some family members in labeling others as problems, and thus responsible for the family's difficulties. It is essential to model the circular orientation to causality of behavior and to emphasize that family members reciprocally influence each other in ways that perpetuate patterns of interaction. A useful rule of thumb when you become aware that you are viewing one or more members as responsible for family problems is to consciously pull back from the immediate interaction in order to gain perspective on how other family members may be contributing to the behavior of the person(s) in question.

Your second task is to *relabel the identified problem individual* and engage members in assuming appropriate ownership for the part they play in the

family's problems. One vital strategy for accomplishing these objectives is to explore relationships *between* family members in lieu of focusing on the behavior of individual members. For example, you may center on a dyad (brother/brother), then move to a triad (father/son/son), and finally explore interrelationships involving all four family members (mother/father/son/son). It is also vital to plan interventions to change the relationships among these various subsystems, a subject upon which we elaborate later in this chapter.

Another key strategy for relabeling is to focus initially on the role of blamers (or plaintiffs) in the difficulties about which they complain. This strategy counteracts the tendency of these family members to attribute blame to others and highlights the fact that they, too, are contributing to the problem. To illustrate this strategy, consider the example of a mother of a young man with mental illness who has decided to live independently with his girlfriend rather than remain in the group home. Rather than turn to the son, the social worker utilizes such questions as the following to focus on the mother's participation in the problematic situation:

- "You've said that your son doesn't listen to you about your concerns related to his plans. When you want to discuss these concerns with him, how do you approach him?"

- "When he says he doesn't want to talk to you, how do you respond? How does his reluctance to talk to you affect you and your relationship with him?"

After first posing questions to the mother, the social worker can then divide responses between mother and son and determine the son's participation in the identified problem by asking questions such as the following:

- "How does your mother approach you when she wants to discuss her concerns?"

- "What is your reaction to her approach?"

- "What might she do differently that would make you feel more like talking to her?"

This line of inquiry emphasizes the reciprocal nature of the problem. Further, the last question enables the social worker to set the stage for identifying positive behaviors each participant would like from the other. If both are receptive, the social worker can help them formulate a reciprocal task that each can work on during the week to improve their relationship. Another way in which social workers can maintain focus on a plaintiff is to ask that person to change a complaint to a request, as illustrated in the following transaction:

Daughter [*to invalid mother*]: I can hardly go out at night because you drink all that coffee and wet the bed and I have to change the sheets.

Social worker: Carol, I'd like you to tell your mother what you'd like her to do differently.

This strategy helps to divert focus from an identified individual as the problem and therefore decreases reactance. In addition, such interventions influence plaintiffs to consider behavior they *would like* and provide valuable information to others concerning desired changes. When parents complain about children (or for that matter, when a teacher complains about a child), it is important to stress the value of completing a multidimensional assessment of the situation or behavior (Henggeler et al., 1998). This inquiry examines interaction patterns between parent and child and between the child and influences external to the family system (e.g., peers or other adults) as well as the way the parents work together. Such exploration often reveals disagreements between parents as to how they manage (or should manage) the child, ways in which they may be working at cross-purposes, dysfunctional communication patterns that block them from effectively discussing the problem, and ways in which they may use the child as a pawn in their relationship.

Parents may be particularly sensitive about questions raised with regard to their own relationships and a child's behavior. When such questions are raised (e.g., "I don't see how talking about our relationship relates to our child's problem"), the social worker should fully explore the parent's view and elicit concerns the other parent may have. In easing parental anxiety it may be useful to emphasize the systemic nature of a child's behavior as being affected by how the family interacts as a whole as well as other influences that may be external to the family system. This strategy serves the purpose of shifting focus from the identified problem bearer and assisting other family members to assume responsibility for making changes. Questions posed in this regard might include, "What would you like to change in your way of relating (or coping) that might encourage your child (or another person) to change . . . ?"

In helping family members to take responsibility for change (rather than wait for others to change), it is critical to emphasize that members can change the dynamics of a situation by concentrating on changing their own behavior or response.

8. *Begin emphasizing individual and family strengths.* In work with families, social workers highlight family strengths at two levels—the strengths of individual members and of the family itself. At the individual level, the social worker observes the strengths and resources of members, drawing them to the attention of the family (e.g., "I really like your sense of humor"). At the family level, the social worker reports the strengths she or he observes in the way members operate as a group (e.g., "In your family, I sense that even though there are problems, you seem to have a strong sense of loyalty to each other." "The way that your family observes traditional ways seems to connect the family"). Family strengths may also be utilized to communicate a focus on the future. In particular, what hopes and dreams, talents or capabilities of individual members and the family unit energize the family to resolve current difficulties?

9. *Ask questions such as the following to elicit information about the patterned behaviors and structure of the family.*

- What brought the family here? Who made the decision and what was the process of deciding?

- How are decisions usually made in the family?

- Who is most likely to argue in the family? least likely? with whom?
- Who is the most likely to help with chores? the least likely?

Base your questions about family patterns and structure on the dimensions of assessment. In cases where the culture of the social worker varies from that of the family, asking questions such as the following can assist you in understanding the family.

- What are the traditional ways in which families in your culture have approached this issue?
- How do families in your culture express anger?
- How do families show affection?
- Who is involved in making decisions in your family?

Asking questions such as these aids social workers in entering the family's cultural frame of reference and allows the family to articulate the extent to which their culture or ethnicity is a critical element in the family's experience.

10. *Begin drawing repetitive problematic communications to the attention of family members* and discuss whether they wish to change these patterns. If problematic communications occur during the initial session (as they frequently do), social workers often intervene to counteract their influence without focusing on the problematic communication per se. For example, a social worker can translate a blaming message into a neutral one by empathically reflecting the feelings and wants of the sender of the message. When one client speaks for another, the social worker can intervene to elicit the personal views of the latter. As the session proceeds, the social worker begins to draw dysfunctional communications to the family's attention through responses such as the following:

- "I observed [*describes behavior and situation*] occurring between family members. How do you see the situation?"
- "Did you notice a reaction from other family members as you talked about ... ?"

Questions such as these help clients to become aware of problematic patterned communications. However, the social worker also needs to stimulate participants to analyze their behaviors further and to consider whether they wish to modify such communications. This can be accomplished by asking clients questions similar to the following:

- "How would you like to address these concerns?" "How would you like to solve these problems?"
- "How would you like to relate differently?"
- "How would behaving differently change your relationship?"
- "Given the problem the behavior creates in the relationship, how important is it to you to change the behavior?"

Utilizing this line of exploration in initial and subsequent sessions, you can assist family members to define for themselves the relative functionality of behavior and to make choices as to whether they wish to change it. If they choose to modify their behavior, you can negotiate relevant goals that will guide their efforts (and yours) in the helping process.

11. *Begin helping members to relate to each other in more positive ways.* We discuss strategies for accomplishing this objective later in this chapter.

12. *Communicate hope that the family can change.* Although we discussed this topic at length in Chapter 12, we remind you that you can engender significant hope in a family by assisting individual members to see how they can make changes that will reduce pressures. When family members mistakenly believe that the only hope for alleviating their problem involves changes by others (who choose not to change), they feel powerless and helpless—and thus defeated.

13. *Establish individual and family goals based on your earlier exploration of wants and needs.* Goals that flow from this exploration should include individual goals, goals for the entire family, and goals that pertain to subsystems (e.g., "Mr. Gonzalez and Marcos, you indicated you wanted to explore ways of spending time together"). The identification of goals can be facilitated during an initial in-

terview by posing and exploring answers to the "miracle question" utilized by de Shazer (1988, p. 5): "Suppose that one night, while you were asleep, there was a miracle and your marriage (family) became perfect—just the way you wanted. When you woke up in the morning how would the marriage (family) be different?"

When asked this question, even the most troubled couples or families are able to describe a "new" miracle relationship. This vision and other desired conditions that they identify can then become goal statements, guiding efforts of both the family and the social worker.

14. *Gauge interest of family members in returning for future sessions and negotiate a contract.* Because family members may not always reveal their feelings openly, never assume that all members want to return for another session (even if you were successful in engaging members and sparking their interest in working on problems). You will also want to assess the difference between the attitudes of participants at the beginning and end of the session. Ask about reservations that participants may still have about engaging in the helping process, and after exploration, if reluctant members decide to return for another session, indicate that you will continue in future sessions to check on their concerns about continuing. It is important to stress that it may take a number of sessions before any family member decides to participate fully or to commit to making changes. If family members are sufficiently motivated to return for another session, specify the time of the next session and who will be involved, and negotiate other elements of a contract as delineated in Chapter 12. Other important elements of the contract are a discussion of the duration of the contact with the family as well as any time limits that are consistent with a referral source, third-party payer, or legal mandate. Although the duration of the contract may depend on a number of factors, research findings show that contracts with families for 20 or fewer sessions have resulted in positive outcomes (Goldenberg & Goldenberg, 2000; Nichols & Schwartz, 1998). Also emphasized by

Nichols and Schwartz (1998) is the fact that positive outcomes are more likely when the problem is clearly specified in the contract and when the problem has clear implications for family relationships.

If a member is not willing to meet with the family, determine whether it would be useful to contract to see that person individually on a limited basis. During your meeting(s), endeavor to establish a relationship that provides a positive emotional experience, and use the time to explore and resolve obstacles to participating in family sessions. Paralleling this work, help other family members to identify and modify problematic processes that may discourage the participation of the absent member, and generally prepare them for the return of that person. If some members decide not to participate in person in sessions, help them consider ways they can support other family members or at least not block their efforts.

15. *Negotiate tasks to be accomplished during the week.* Although tasks were discussed at length in Chapter 13, we reemphasize that tasks should directly relate to goals identified by individual members or by the family system. Assisting the family to explore and decide upon steps that can be taken during the week aids in focusing their attention on problem resolution.

16. *End the session by summarizing the problems discussed and goals, tasks, and progress achieved.* Wrapping up the session by summarizing major topics, goals, and tasks accomplished in the session tends to engender hope and increases the momentum of change efforts.

INTERVENING IN FAMILIES: CULTURAL AND ECOLOGICAL PERSPECTIVES

In intervening with clients of a different ethnicity, social workers, of course, must strive to be "culturally sensitive" in their approach, modifying expectations espoused as universal norms for family functioning. Social workers must also be aware of the potential intrusion of their own bias. A general conclusion drawn from a study by Lavee (1997), for example, revealed "noticeable differences" between the ways social workers and clients defined a healthy marriage. Social workers tended to focus more on process indicators, for example, cooperation and communication, whereas clients tended to place greater emphasis on love, understanding, cohesion, and family cohesion. Different emphasis on the quality of family life, marital relationships, or problem definition may be a function of cultural and class differences between social workers and clients.

Cultural sensitivity and competence is an ongoing learning process. While certain factors may be germane to various ethnic or cultural groups, it is important to clarify specific cultural content and its relevance to a particular family's culture or subculture. Goldenberg and Goldenberg (2000) suggest that learning about specific cultures requires social workers to assess the extent to which families identify with their ethnic or cultural background and to ascertain what role background plays in the presenting family concern. Toward this end, the "therapist must try to distinguish family patterns that are universal (common to a wide variety of families), culture-specific (common to a particular group) or idiosyncratic (unique to this particular family)" (p. 52). "Cultural dimensions" to explore can include respect, heroes, roles of men and women, perceptions of destiny, fate, and power, language, opinion molders, elders, rituals, and spirituality and religion.[5]

Patterns in family interactions with regard to culture may of course vary, and social workers' understanding of this fact essentially avoids the tendency to formulate generalizations about family dynamics. Identity with culture or ethnicity may be peripheral for some families. In other instances, it may be useful to help families determine culturally specific behavior from family of origin concerns (Flores & Carey, 2000). At the same time, culture should not be used to minimize or overlook family behavior or relationships that are damaging or harmful to the family or individuals. With these words of caution in mind, in the following

discussion we highlight factors that may be considerations in initiating interventions with families who are diverse with respect to culture, race, and family form.

1. *Differences in communication styles.* There are differences in the speech patterns among nonnative English speakers; thus in many situations it may be more important to focus on process rather than content. In many Native American tribes, for example, there may be a "pause time," the signaling of when one person finishes and another can begin speaking. Discomfort with the silence may result in a social worker interrupting the Native American speaker. Individuals from other groups may be more demonstrative in both verbal and nonverbal communication, while others unaccustomed to seeking outside help may appear to be passive because of a sense of shame or suspicion in their encounter with professional helpers (Berg & Jaya 1993; Boyd-Franklin, 1989; Fong, 1997; Pierce & Elisme, 1997). Studies of ethnic differences in resolving conflict, emotional expression, and coping with stress by Mackey and O'Brien (1998) and Choi (1997) show differences in communication styles based on gender and ethnicity. It is also important to examine our own communication style and how it stems from majority culture preferences. In facilitating communication styles and differences, contributions of postmodern family practice models may be considered. For example, the narrative or social constructionist approaches emphasize a more conversational, collaborative approach allowing a more meaningful dialogue between client and social worker to occur (Laird, 1993).

2. *Hierarchical considerations.* For example, because of age-sex hierarchies in the Chinese culture, E. Lee (1989) advises that social workers address questions to the father first, then the mother, then to other adults, and finally to the older and younger children. Also, in immigrant families where a child who has greater proficiency in language interprets, the social worker should be sensitive to the fact that this may undermine traditional roles in the family and result in tensions be-

tween parents and their children (Ho, 1987; Pierce & Elisme, 1997). Coming from a culture in which chronological age and familial hierarchy play a significant role, Asian Indian and African American families, for example, may view open dialogue between parents and children as insolent or disrespectful (Carter & McGoldrick, 1999; Segal, 1991). It is also of note that what may appear to be a rigid hierarchical role definition in the family may instead by complementary. Flores and Carey (2000), in counteracting the popular notion of machismo dominance in Hispanic families, emphasize this point. Specifically, fathers function as the protective figure in the family while the mother's role is complementary in being expressive, caring, and nurturing.

3. *Authority of the social worker.* Many Asian/Pacific Americans, for example, do not understand the social worker's role and may confuse him or her with a physician. Nevertheless, observes Ho (1987), they will perceive the social worker as a knowledgeable expert who will guide them in the proper course of action, requiring that social workers take a more directive rather than a more passive role. Social workers should not hesitate to discuss their professional background, for these clients need assurance that the social worker is more powerful than their illnesses or family problem and will "cure" them with competence and the necessary know-how. At the same time, social workers should be aware of the fact that writing and documenting, while necessary for case notes, may reinforce perceptions of power differences between the social worker and the family (Flores & Carey, 2000; Boyd-Franklin, 1989). It is hence useful for the social worker to explain the purpose of case notes and confidentiality as well as requirements for information that may involve an identified third party.

The authority of a social worker also relates to the use of first names with families and social distance. When working with African American clients, J. B. Robinson (1989, p. 328) recommends that social workers use last names until invited by the client to do otherwise: "The racial importance

of first names is magnified for the black client because of the historical tradition of calling black people by their first names in situations in which first names would not be permitted if both participants were white." In working with Asian Americans, Berg and Jaya (1993) note that addressing elders by the first name may inhibit establishing a positive therapeutic alliance. An informal and egalitarian approach, second nature to many Americans, is actually considered improper in many cultures, including that of Mexican American clients, whose initial encounters may tend to be formal, polite, and reserved, with the expectation that the social worker take the initiative in solving the family's problem (Janzen & Harris, 1997). Further, "direct questioning, informal use of language and expectations of full disclosure may increase suspicions and sharpen defenses" (Falicov, 1982, p. 148). Passivity among immigrants may stem from their social and political status in the United States and distrust of helpers, along with fears about expressing their true feelings to figures of authority (Pierce & Elisme, 1997). Aponte (1982) perhaps summarizes the issue of authority and power best in his assertion that power and authority is a critical element of the relationship between client or family and social worker, especially for ethnic or racial groups. A family or individual perceives the social worker in his or her professional role as a representative of majority society that symbolizes societal power, values, and standards.

4. *Engaging the family.* Techniques for engaging or joining are particularly crucial in involving diverse families. Listening in context, specifically allowing the family to present their story, and being mindful of process such as differences in communication styles, the cultural context of seeking help outside of the family, and the perceived authority of the social worker and the agency are also considerations. Although there is no guarantee that knowledge of culture provides a social worker an advantage with a family, exploring the relevance of cultural meanings of particular groups may aid the process of engagement (Janzen & Harris, 1997). As for African

Americans and Asian Americans, the use of last names is appropriate in the introductory stage with Mexicans (Flores & Corey, 2000). Engaging the family may also include extended family members in the process of joining whether or not they participate in family sessions. Boyd-Franklin (1989), while stressing the importance of the joining stage with African American families, also points to the fact that a crucial factor is the link between engagement and problem solving, which enables the social worker to establish credibility and trust with the family.

Families of diverse backgrounds may feel more welcomed in agencies where objects and symbols of their culture are visible in offices and waiting rooms (Bernal & Flores-Ortiz, 1982). Home visits may be invaluable to social workers in the engagement stage with some families because they afford an opportunity to observe and assess a family in its natural environment (I. K. Berg, 1994). Visits to the home may also allow social workers to learn and observe the cultural practices of families, meet important members of the family network, and convey interest in the family by inquiring about portraits, cultural objects, and other items of interest. In visits to the home, "remember that you are on the client's home turf," caution Boyd-Franklin and Bry (2000); observe flexibility and deference to the rules and structure of the family and the order of the household (p. 39). Even so, some family members may resist involvement in the initial session. Culture may be used as a defense against joining (Flores & Carey, 2000). In instances where the family has been referred, members may be angry and resentful of this intrusion. Social workers who encounter this situation should avoid personalizing this experience and move quickly to acknowledge, accept, and validate these feelings (I. K. Berg, 1994; R. H. Rooney, 1992).

Engaging families is facilitated when the social worker understands the cultural relevance of terminology describing family dynamics and structure. Autonomy and self-differentiation, when considered in a sociopolitical or cultural context, may not be desirable or the expected norm in some cultures.

5. *Utilizing an ecological approach with families.* Culture and race are but two factors in the ecological schema of practice with families. Others include gender, poverty, class, family status, and work and family concerns. Sensitivity to multisystem influences and their relationship to family concerns means that social workers must focus on family environmental interactions and assess the extent to which they affect family relationships and interaction patterns. Work and family pressures may intrude upon parental ability to fulfill role functions within the family, producing role overload, conflict, and strain (Marlow, 1993; G. D. Rooney, 1997). For some poor families, immediate survival and resource needs may take precedence over more insight-oriented approaches (Kilpatrick & Holland, 1999). Thus, the family-environmental interaction may include intervening to address problems of housing, public assistance, and unresponsive social institutions and working with the extended family or other key people to reduce dysfunctional interaction and to increase concrete support to the family. Pinderhughes (1982, p. 91), in fact, warns that failure of social workers to focus on family-environmental interaction "may lead to a distorted understanding of family functioning and to interventions that may be pathogenic." Dysfunctional interactions may emerge in immigrant families in their attempt to cope with problems of adjustment. For example, Fong (1997) advises that Chinese immigrants experience problems that may contribute to spousal or child abuse.

Flores and Carey (2000) note that many well-established approaches to work with families are "silent" on issues of social justice, oppression, and the marginalization of the minority experience. Until recently, the same was true for women. In gaining a fuller understanding of families, social workers must be sensitive to gender. Goldenberg and Goldenberg (2000) summarize gender sensitivity as not merely being nonsexist. Instead, they suggest that gender-sensitive practice is proactive and deliberate in helping women move beyond limitations imposed by social and political barriers (pp. 50–51). For minority women, gender when combined with race or culture often adds yet another dimension to social and political barriers.

Although the ideal of egalitarian roles is becoming more evident in both rural and urban families in many cultures, women for the most part still manage multiple roles of wife, daughter, mother, parent, and employee (Marlow, 1993; G. D. Rooney, 1997). Acculturation may mean that gender roles are in transition yet become a source of tension in much the same way that parent-child conflicts result in stressors in the family system.

Negative societal attitudes and conditions can also pose environmental threats to families and thus influence the family system. Single-parent families are almost always viewed by society from a point of pathology rather than their strength as a viable family form. Lesbian families, for example, are largely ignored as a viable family form. Noting that internal family stress is a given for lesbian couples because of a hostile environment, Janzen and Harris (1997) conclude that an assessment of gay or lesbian family concerns should explore both internal and external factors. Concerns voiced among lesbian mothers, as a case in point, related to reactions from the community toward their children and protecting them from harm (Hare, 1994). In addition, Hare found that while these families may find acceptance in their family of origin, they experienced tensions similar to those found in the larger community toward their family within the nonparent lesbian community.

The preceding examples are but a few of the variables to which social workers must attend in assessing family functioning and relational dynamics. Fitting practice and intervention strategies to the ecology of a particular family is, of course, a complicated process that requires a multidimensional assessment that includes examination of the interrelated factors that shape family life. Social workers are thus urged to use their knowledge of culture, race, gender, sexual orientation, and socioeconomic issues as a lens to view families. Considerable diversity among families may mean that some factors have more relevance than others. For some families, culture or race may be peripheral to their identity, yet they may retain essential attributes that guide their family life. Acquiring sensitivity to the importance of gender, sexual orientation, and racial and cultural influences may be achieved by facilitating the family narratives and taking an active, genuine, and collaborative interest in their story.

FOCUSING ON CHANGE

Families are often overwhelmed, frustrated and perhaps saturated with their problems. As social workers meet with families, they are charged with the responsibility of creating and structuring an atmosphere of hope and a therapeutic climate, which alleviate stress and guide the family toward change. One major obstacle to change is the propensity of couples or families to focus on what they don't have or what isn't working rather than on what they would like *in the future*. The Solution-Focused approach provides social workers with techniques that move away from a focus on the problem to focus on solutions (Nichols & Schwartz, 1998). Using this approach, the social worker might pose the miracle question: "What can you do about this in the future?" or "How would you know, what would you feel, if you woke up one morning and the family was all together?" In addition, *scaling questions* can be used to rate the level of the potential goal. For example, "When you called for an appointment with me, you felt depressed. Imagine how you might feel on a scale of one to ten after you have achieved your goal." Such questions are useful in helping families to reframe and feel more in control of their lives. Berg and Jaya (1993) and Boyd-Franklin (1989b) emphasize that establishing a tone in which the focus is on solutions rather than on feelings is preferable to Asian American and African American families. Focusing on change and "opting for the future" as a guiding principle in the helping process for clients and social workers can be utilized, for example, in the following manner:

- A discussion of an argument can lead quickly to consideration of what each person is willing to do to prevent a recurrence of that argument *in the future.*

- A complaint or criticism can be translated into information about what changes in others might help *in the future.* Recipients can also give information such as "This is what you could do *in the future* that would aid me in giving you the changes you want."

- A breakdown in communication can be analyzed from this point of view: "What can we learn from what just happened that we can apply *in the future?*"

- Conflicts of interest can alert clients to the need to apply "win-win" problem solving: "How can we resolve this problem right now so we can feel good about it *in the future?*"

"Opting for the future," adopted as a philosophy and guideline by clients and social workers, takes the blame out of relating. It is the future, not the past, that is relevant and the future is fresh, hopeful, and untainted by tensions or stressors. Opting for the future, of course, requires that each client commit to attending only to what he or she is going to do in the future, rather than monitor the activities of the other person in that regard. The question each client must answer moment by moment is "How can I improve on my performance?" Opting for the future also requires that clients monitor and accredit their successes: "What did we do well that gave us the closeness we just enjoyed?" "How can we repeat that in the future?"

Clients monitor their successes rather than their failures. Each client acknowledges the changes he or she sees in the other. Each participant focuses on what is possible and changeable, rather than on what is impossible and intractable. This puts clients on the same team, as advocates rather than adversaries, as they move in concert to create the positive conditions they opt for in their relationship. Social workers, of course, help create a hopeful future through their own vision of what is possible and their frequent interventions to remind clients to approach any particular complaint or problem from a futuristic perspective. Social workers can increase clients' focus on the future by always starting sessions with a question regarding what successes clients have had in achieving goals or tasks, or in creating fresh, positive ways of relating.

Clients are often reluctant at first to focus on solutions, for their orientation is to talk about problems. In addition, clients have been socialized in their encounters with human services to articulate problems. In setting the tone for the future, if social workers persevere, even repeatedly putting "problem talk" on hold until clients have spent significant time acknowledging and savoring even small changes, over time clients will often adopt a social worker's vision and initiate "change talk" themselves. One possible goal social workers can encourage clients to adopt, in fact, is that of opting for the future in their transactions at home and counting their successes in that regard each time they return for another session.

Complementing this approach, Weiner-Davis (1992) teaches clients to focus on the "exceptional times" to determine what's working and why, and then encourages them to turn productive behaviors into habits. Focusing on exceptions diminishes problems, she notes, because identifying what they can do is infinitely more hopeful and empowering to clients than noting what they can't do. Focusing on exceptions also demonstrates to clients that they are changeable and that seemingly fixed traits are fluid. Finally, focusing on exceptions supplies clients with a blueprint for describing exactly what they need to do the next time a particular situation occurs.

"Opting for the future," as a guiding philosophy for enhancing relationships, encourages clients to increase their positive feedback to others, a vital therapeutic goal in the change process. Positive feedback from significant others (i.e., expressions of caring, approval, encouragement, affection, appreciation, and other forms of positive attention), of course, is a vital source of nourishment for self-esteem, high morale, emotional security, confidence, and feeling valued by others.

Thus, aiding clients to increase positive feedback fosters the well-being of individuals and harmonious relationships with others as well. To enable clients to increase positive feedback, social workers must be skilled in

1. engaging clients in assessing the extent to which they give and receive positive feedback
2. educating clients as to the vital role of positive feedback
3. cultivating positive cognitive sets
4. enabling clients to give and receive positive feedback

In the following sections, we focus on each of the skills that will facilitate this process.

Engaging Clients in Assessing the Extent to Which They Give and Receive Positive Feedback

When relationships become strained, destructive patterns are often the result and the family system becomes unbalanced. Communication theorists view the family as a functional system that depends on two processes of negative and positive feedback. They also believe that all behavior is communication; thus the social worker's goal is to help the family change the process of family interactions. Social workers can assist families and individual members to directly explore dimensions of communication by assessing how often and in what manner they convey positive feedback to significant others. Questions you might ask in couple or family sessions to achieve this end include the following:

• "How do you send messages that let family members (or your partner) know that you care about them?"
• "How frequently do you send such messages?"
• "How often do you give feedback to others concerning their positive actions?"

In instances of severe marital or family breakdown, clients commonly acknowledge they send positive messages infrequently or not at all. In some instances, they may actually experience only weak positive feelings, but usually they experience more than they express. Besides exploring how couples or family members convey positive feedback, you can also explore their desires to receive increased feedback from each other. Discussing how clients send positive messages or to what extent they desire increased positive feedback often opens channels for positive communication and enhances relationships that have been stuck as a result of repetitive arguments, criticisms, blaming messages, and put-downs.

Educating Clients as to the Vital Role of Positive Feedback

As clients communicate about their needs to receive positive feedback, they begin to appreciate the significance of this dimension in interpersonal relationships. You can expand their awareness of the significance of positive feedback and enhance their motivation to increase the same by further explaining why this dimension is crucial. The logic behind increasing positive feedback is straightforward, and clients generally grasp it readily because it rings true in terms of their own needs and experiences. Explanations vary according to whether the unit of concern involves parent-child, marital, family, or other interpersonal relationships. Teaching clients to express their needs involves assisting them to send personalized messages in which they own their feelings and wants. The following are examples of messages that explicitly express needs for positive feedback:

Partner: When we were talking about plans for my mother, I didn't interrupt you. I wish you would notice when I do something different.

Adolescent: I felt dissed when I showed you my report card yesterday. I really worked hard this term, and the only thing you noticed was the one B I got. It didn't seem to matter that the rest were As. Sometimes I wonder if I can please you at all. I need to know that you respect how well I'm doing in most classes.

In earlier chapters, we discussed how to assist clients to personalize messages. We also illustrated how, through on-the-spot interventions, you can coach clients to formulate clear messages that express their feelings and needs. Reviewing that discussion will assist you in helping clients to express their needs for positive feedback, as will reading the following illustration.

Ruth [*to husband*]: I worked really hard at picking up the house before our guests arrived, but the only thing you noticed was what I had not done, like the comment you made about fingerprints on the bathroom door.

Carl: Well, let's face it, the fact is, the fingerprints were on the door and you admitted it.

Social worker: Carl, Ruth was expressing what is important to her in the relationship, and I don't want this to get lost in an argument. Ruth, think for a moment about what you said. What is it you are asking of Carl?

Ruth [*Pause*]: Do you mean his not noticing what I do?

Social worker: In a way, yes. Would you like for Carl to let you know you're appreciated for what you had done?

In this scenario, Ruth has shared something that's very important, the need to feel valued. People require getting positive feedback for what they are and what they do. Continuous interactions in which the focus is negative results in feeling discouraged and insecure, and as a consequence relationships suffer. In instructing Ruth and Carl about the importance of positive feedback, the social worker can use this opportunity to allow them to practice communicating in a different manner as illustrated in the following example.

Social worker: Ruth, I'd like you to start over and express your need for positive feedback to Carl. This time, however, send an "I" message to clarify what you need from Carl.

Ruth: I hope that I can. Carl, I need to hear from you about the things that I do well and not only about what is wrong.

Initially clients may feel timid about expressing their feeling clearly. The second part of helping clients to express their needs is enhancing sensitivity to the needs of others by assisting them to listen attentively. Asking Carl to repeat what he heard in Ruth's message is a way to emphasize listening for content. Because others may not always express needs openly and clearly, family members may need to go beyond just listening. They may also need help with becoming attuned to needs expressed in the form of complaints, questions, and the attitudes of others. Tuning in may also involve alerting clients to nonverbal messages and what those messages communicate about how people are feeling. Because it is difficult for clients to attune to the needs inherent in the messages of others, it is important that you take full advantage of "teachable moments" to help them to learn this skill, as presented in the preceding excerpt.

Note that the social worker focused sharply on Ruth's needs and played a facilitative role in prompting her to express herself directly to Carl. The social worker could likewise use the opportunity to advantage by having Carl provide feedback to Ruth, thus performing a vital role in facilitating positive interaction between the partners. This is a crucial point, for by serving as catalysts, social workers enable clients to learn by actually engaging in positive interaction, a much more effective mode of learning than merely having clients talk about what they need to do. The social worker should also address the need for learning skills to both partners. By not singling out one partner, the social worker avoids appearing to take sides with one over the other. The social worker could further stress the needs of both participants for positive feedback by centering the exploration on Carl to identify how often and in what ways he receives positive feedback from his wife and then negotiating a mutual task with partners to increase such feedback during the coming week.

Cultivating Positive Cognitive Sets

Before clients can provide positive feedback, they must first be aware of the strengths, positive attributes, and actions of others. Some clients, of course, have cognitions that are attuned to the positive attributes and behaviors of others, but some habitually perceive weaknesses and flaws in the personalities and actions of others. Cognitive sets may involve distorted assumptions or automatic thoughts from other relationships; schemas that result in negative thoughts that are not reality based, however, sustain dysfunctional relationships (Berlin & Marsh, 1993; Collins, Kayser, & Platt, 1994). Recognizing that attitudes, thoughts, and expectations are recognized as intertwined with emotions, the cognitive behaviorist attempts to improve family interactions by helping individual family members alter cognitive distortions and learn new behaviors (Nichols & Schwartz, 1998). The social worker has the responsibility of bringing negative cognitive sets that influence thoughts, feelings, and actions to the attention of clients and helping them learn to focus on positive behaviors. Strategies for accomplishing these tasks are delineated in the following subsections.

Sensitizing Couples to Positives

As alluded to earlier, social workers can set the stage for helping families and couples to develop positive cognitive sets by negotiating a contingency contract. The contingency contract establishes desirable behavior change between two parties and explicit rules for interaction, specifying that the parties involved agree to exchange positive rewarding behavior with each other (Becvar & Becvar, 2000). Using the contingency contract as a process, the social worker actively intervenes in the early stages of the helping process to highlight strengths and growth and to help clients to incorporate "attention to positives" as part of their normative behavior. As discussed by Collins et al. (1994), social workers may assist clients to develop their own set of positive indicators for desirable behavior change. Social workers then include a review of these indicators with the family (or couple) each week until members themselves spontaneously report incidents that involve positive behaviors of other members, thus indicating

the family has internalized the value of focusing on positives.

Reviewing Progress and Accrediting Incremental Growth

Social workers may also increase a family's sensitivity to positives by engaging members in briefly reviewing at each session's end the work that has been accomplished, including incremental growth achieved by individuals or by a family. Increments of growth are often manifested very subtly in the helping process, and social workers must therefore make a concerted effort to focus the attention of clients on indicators of progress. To highlight incremental growth, social workers may also wish to ask members to contrast their current functioning with their functioning at an earlier time, as illustrated in the following message:

• [*To family*]: "This is your fourth session. Let's see if you can identify any changes you've made in the way you communicate by contrasting how you related today with the way you related in the first session. I have some observations about that, but first I would like to hear from you."

Employing Tasks to Enhance Cognitive Sets. Social workers can also assist clients to develop positive cognitive sets by negotiating tasks that clients can implement between sessions. For example, they can further expand partners' awareness of the frequency with which they provide positive feedback by negotiating the task of having them keep a daily tally of the number of positive messages they send their partners over a period of 1 week. Clients (and social workers) thus not only gain a clear picture of their performance on this dimension but also develop a baseline against which they can later assess their progress. Monitoring also provides advantages because, without explicitly planning to do so, clients often begin to increase the frequency of the desired behavior.

Another task that assists persons to view their partners more positively is to have them compile lists of their partners' positive qualities. Social workers may ask partners to begin by writing down at least ten positive qualities and, without discussing their lists, bring them to the following session. In the session, the social worker asks the spouses to read their lists to each other. This activity is beneficial in affording practice to spouses both in giving and in receiving positive feedback. After having clients read their lists to each other, social workers may ask them to discuss their reactions to hearing the positive feedback. Social workers can further negotiate tasks of having the partners review their lists daily, with the objective of expanding them on an ongoing basis. A related task is to ask partners to focus not only on their partners' positive attributes but on those of others as well, especially when they find themselves thinking negative thoughts about others. By systematically focusing on the positive attributes of others, clients can gradually achieve more positive cognitive sets.

Enabling Clients to Give and to Receive Positive Feedback

To assist clients in learning to convey positive feedback, social workers can teach them to personalize messages and guide them in practicing giving positive feedback to others. Social workers should ask clients to base their practice messages on recent situations during which they experienced positive feelings but did not share them with others. Timely use of this educative intervention assists clients to conceptualize the elements of positive messages and to develop skill in authentically sharing their positive experiencing. Social workers may also need to assist some clients to learn how to accept as well as to give positive feedback. Be deflecting positive feedback, in fact, these clients discredit information that could significantly increase their self-esteem.

After completing the activities previously delineated, clients are ready to work on the ultimate goal of increasing their rates of positive feedback. Social workers can assist them by negotiating tasks that specify providing positive feedback at higher levels. Clients, of course, must consent to such tasks and determine the rate of positive feedback they seek to achieve. We recommend that social workers have clients review their baseline obtained earlier and encourage them to set a daily rate that "stretches" their usual level but not to an unrealistic extent. For example, a husband whose mean baseline daily rate in giving positive feedback to his wife is 0.8 might select a beginning level of giving positive feedback twice daily. The client could then gradually increase the number of daily responses until reaching a self-selected optimal rate of five times daily. As some clients implement the task of increasing positive feedback, they may inappropriately employ insincere positive expressions. Social workers should caution against this, as such expressions have a hollow ring and create discomfort for both sender and receiver. Social workers can stress, however, that as clients practice attuning to positives, and they will gradually gain a natural facility for perceiving actions or qualities that warrant positive feedback.

In planning with clients to implement this task, it is important to adhere to the task-implementation sequence. In part, this involves anticipating obstacles, two of which are by far the most common. First, clients who have been inhibited in expressing feelings report discomfort with expressing caring messages, explaining, "It just doesn't come naturally to me." Social workers should respond empathically to clients' discomfort but explain that engaging in new behaviors is bound to be uncomfortable and that if clients will risk themselves and endure the discomfort, they will gradually gain facility and comfort in expressing positive feedback.

The second common obstacle is that others may not respond favorably to clients' increased level of positive feedback and, instead, may question their sincerity. Because some clients have given virtually no positive feedback previously, the skepticism of others is understandable. Social workers can assist clients to deal with others' skepticism by modeling and having clients rehearse appropriate coping behavior (including asserting the sincerity of their efforts) and by emphasizing the necessity of persisting in their efforts despite obstacles. As with all tasks, it is vital to review clients' experiences in succeeding sessions. Clients may have experienced difficulties that warrant exploration, may continue to struggle with awkwardness or discomfort, or may report highly favorable reactions from others. Reviewing outcomes is vitally important, for social workers can then give encouragement and positive feedback to clients, enable them to savor their successes, and, if warranted, point to the need for additional effort.

As clients implement tasks to increase their rates of positive feedback, they will need to continue keeping tallies of instances in which they give such responses. Through monitoring, they not only maintain an ongoing record of their progress but also reinforce themselves each time they record a tally. Of course, the ultimate reinforcement derives from improved interactions with others. By giving positive feedback to others, clients increase the likelihood of receiving the same in return.

Tasks for Couples

One of many techniques you can employ to increase positive interactions or increasing mutual demonstrations of caring between marital partners involves a cognitive development strategy discussed by Stuart (1980) and Collins et al. (1994). Both partners are asked to identify actions or behaviors that communicate caring on the part of the other partner. By asking each partner, "Exactly what would you like your partner to do as a means of showing that he or she cares for you?" you assist each partner to identify desired actions that become a resource to the other. As each partner identifies caring behaviors, the other writes them down. You then ask each partner to assume the task of carrying out a specified number of caring behaviors identified by the other, using his or her respective list of positive actions as a resource. Another basic aspect of this activity involves each partner's expressing positive feedback in the form of appreciation when the other partner performs one of the actions from the list.

Tasks and Activities for Families and Couples

An exercise that cultivates positive feedback among family members involves the activity or game of "Guess Who?" In this game, family members sit in a circle and a parent presents each member with a slip of paper and a pencil. A parent then instructs members of the family to write down something they like about the person sitting on the member's right. (Family members who are unable to write may ask another member to write for them.) The slips are then folded, put into a hat, and mixed up. In succession, each family member draws a slip from the hat and reads it aloud, and members guess which person matches the written description. Family members then shift positions in the circle and repeat the procedure until they have had the opportunity to write about every other family member. This game assists you in centering the attention of family members on the positive attributes of each member about strengths and attributes as perceived by other family members. This exercise may be especially useful for parents in conflicted relationships with teens.

An exercise that promotes positive feedback among family and group members (which is appropriate in groups only after members have become well acquainted) involves asking the family or group to "spotlight" each member in turn. Other members then give positive feedback about the strengths of the person in the spotlight. If it is necessary to prime the group, you may initiate positive feedback regarding strengths or growth of a member each time the spotlight shifts.

Tasks for Parents

Preliminary to negotiating tasks with parents to increase positive feedback to their children, you can request that parents list functional and dysfunctional behaviors of each child. You then ask parents to choose the three behaviors they would most like to change. The next step is to negotiate a task that involves parents giving positive feedback at opportune times during the week when the specified behavior is not occurring (e.g., when the child is *not* fighting with a sibling). Further instruct the parents to give positive feedback when children manifest behaviors the parents would like them to assume in place of the targeted behaviors (e.g., when the child *has* told the truth or *did* follow through on an assigned task). Parents are understandably handicapped in using this strategy if children's usual behaviors do not include the behaviors that are desired. For instance, children may never pick up their clothes or do their homework until specifically asked or only after continual nagging. In such instances, you will first need to motivate children by establishing an agreement that they may earn certain rewards in exchange for specified behavior.

Because parental attention to children's behavior is a potent force for modifying or reinforcing behavior, it is vital that you work intensively with parents so that they master the skill of positive feedback and learn to reward their children's positive behaviors systematically. We thus ask parents to reinforce the positive behaviors of children that they earlier identified, incrementally increasing the number of positive responses over a period of time. For example, a child may sometimes relate to siblings or other family members in a caring way or take a responsibility seriously. Parents, unfortunately, often take such behaviors for granted. But children need to know what they are *already* doing that pleases parents. Used consistently by parents, messages such as these have a significant effect in shaping and cultivating desired behavior. If parents want their children to assume particular behaviors, they must give them positive feedback when those behaviors occur. Note the reinforcing property of the following parental messages:

- "I really appreciate your taking the time to visit your grandmother. It really adds joy to her day."

- "When I asked you if you had pushed your little brother down just a minute ago, you said yes. I appreciated your telling me the truth. I know it was hard for you to do that, knowing that I was angry when I asked. Being honest is very important to me, and I'm glad that you made the choice to tell the truth."

In addition to providing positive messages that reinforce desired behavior, parents can also enhance learning by providing tangible rewards.

Parents must also be aware of their own behavior as it relates to vicarious learning and modeling. Children by observing other people and events are able to learn the consequences of behavior. Incremental change and subsequent reinforcement may be a particularly useful strategy with young children. This process, referred to as successive approximation, is a shaping process that divides the desired behavior into subparts, providing contingencies and rewards until the whole of the desired behavior is achieved. "Thus, if having a child sit quietly at her desk, paying attention to the teacher, raise her hand, and wait to be called upon before speaking is the target behavior, one might initially reward 'sitting' as the first subpart of the whole" (Becvar & Becvar, 2000, p. 262).

STRATEGIES TO MODIFY DYSFUNCTIONAL INTERACTION

Interactional difficulties that clients commonly present include repetitive heated arguments; struggles over power and authority; conflict over issues related to dependence, independence, or interdependence; dissension in making decisions; friction associated with discrepant role perceptions and/or fulfillments; and other forms of defective communication. Interpersonal conflicts tend to be redundant. That is, in relations with others, individuals repeat over and over again various types of dysfunctional interaction that predictably lead to the same negative consequences. To assist you in helping clients to evolve more functional patterns of communication and interaction, we delineate guidelines and techniques that you can employ in modifying dysfunctional interaction as you work with marital partners, families, groups, and other types of relationships. Note that teaching communication skills to clients is a vital aspect of modifying dysfunctional communications.

Metacommunication

To modify dysfunctional communication, participants must discuss such communication, analyzing their behaviors and emotional reactions as well as the impact of the interaction on their relationship. Such discussions are termed *metacommunication,* for they involve communication about communication. When social workers discuss with clients communication that has just occurred, they too are engaging in metacommunication. Indeed, much of couple, family, and group therapy involves metacommunication. Likewise, when social workers discuss relational reactions that occur in the context of the helping relationship, they are clarifying the meanings of messages and actions. Still other examples of metacommunication are messages that clarify intentions (e.g., "I'm teasing you" or "I want to talk with you because I feel bad about the strain between us") or messages that "check out" or seek clarification of others' messages that are vague or ambiguous (e.g., "I'm not sure what you mean by that" or "Let me see if I understood what you were saying"). Metacommunications also contain both verbal and nonverbal content. The content of a message is established through the tone of voice and body language, further shaping and defining the intent of the message and the relationship between those involved.

Skills in metacommunications play a vital role in effective communications because they avoid needless misunderstandings (by checking out the meanings of messages) and provide feedback that enables others to make choices about modifying ways of communicating that are offensive or abrasive. Moreover, conflicts in relationships are kept at a minimum level of antagonism or disruption. A major role of social workers, therefore, is to assist clients to learn to metacommunicate effectively.

Although skills in assisting people to metacommunicate are important with all client systems, they are especially critical in working with families that manifest dysfunctional patterns of communication, including frequent use of incongruent and double bind messages. Families that extensively employ these forms of communication seldom clarify meanings or attend to the effect their messages have on each other. It is thus crucial to intervene in these dysfunctional processes and to teach family

members to communicate effectively. The following excerpt illustrates use of metacommunication to enhance communication between Anne, age 14, and her mother, Ms. T, who acts as a spokesperson for Anne and sends disconfirming messages.

Social worker: Anne, could you tell me how you've been doing in your gym class? I know you were having a rough time in gym.

Ms. T: It's been *really* rough for her, having to change clothes and shower in front of all the other girls. She feels like she's in a goldfish bowl. I mean—I know what it's like because I went through it when I was in junior high. [*Anne lowers her head and looks at the floor.*]

Social worker: Excuse me, Ms. T, but you were speaking for Anne. Anne, I'd like to hear from you what it has been like. [*Intervening to counter Ms. T's acting as Anne's spokesperson.*]

Anne [*looking up slightly*]: Well, it has been going a little better, I think. The gym teacher hasn't been after me. In fact she was pretty friendly this last week. And I ... [*Ms. T. interrupts.*]

Ms. T: But is hasn't been going better, Anne. [*Disconfirming Anne as a separate person.*] When you shower, you just feel everyone's eyes are glued on you.

Social worker [*to mother*]: I'd like to hear from Anne herself about how she feels about showering. [*To Anne.*] I know your mother's view, but I don't know what your experience has been.

Anne: Actually, it hasn't been like my mother said. It was bad until the past couple of weeks, but I've made friends with a couple of girls, and we shower together. It isn't nearly as bad now.

Ms. T: But you were saying . . . [*social worker interrupts to avert another disconfirming message.*]

Social worker: Anne, when your mother spoke for you the first time, you looked at the floor as if you were distressed. I wonder if you could tell your mother how you feel when she speaks for you. [*Encouraging metacommunication.*]

Anne: I don't mind, sometimes. But, Mother, you don't always know how I feel. You get your feelings mixed up with mine, and it confuses me. I want to speak for myself.

Ms. T: But, darling, I was just trying to help. I know how hard it's been for you. I mean, you understand that, don't you?

Anne: I guess so, but I wish you wouldn't do it so much.

Social worker [*to mother*]: I know you're trying to help, Ms. T. But what do you hear Anne telling you? [*Using metacommunication to check out Ms. T's perception.*]

Ms. T: That she doesn't want me to say how she feels?

Social worker: Yes. I think Anne's saying that she wants to be her own person. Is that right, Anne? [*Using metacommunication to check out meaning attribution.*]

Anne: I don't want to be a little girl anymore. [*Ms. T squirms.*]

Social worker [*to both*]: What we've been talking about is very important in improving your communication as well as helping Anne to grow up. [*To Ms. T.*] Though you're meaning to help, your assumptions about Anne's feelings are sometimes inaccurate. If you want to understand Anne, you'll need to ask how she feels rather than assume you know. [*To Anne.*] If you want to help your mother understand, you'll need to remind her not to speak for you when she does. And you'll also need to tell her your real feelings rather than just keeping them inside. I was very impressed with how you did that with your mother just now. I know that was difficult for you.

Notice that in the preceding excerpt the social worker assertively intervened to prevent the interaction from following its usual destructive course. By not permitting Ms. T to act as Anne's spokesperson, by involving the participants in metacommunicating about the impact on Anne of Ms. T's behavior, and by defining how both can modify their dysfunc-

tional pattern of communication, the social worker initiated corrective processes. Of course, many such interventions over a period of time are required to produce enduring changes.

Modifying Dysfunctional Family Rules

Dysfunctional family rules can also severely impair the functioning of family members. Because family rules are often covert, it follows that changes can occur only by bringing them into the open. The social worker thus assists family members through metacommunication to acknowledge and consider the impact of rules on family interaction. Openly discussing rules suggests options for replacing them with other processes that better serve the needs of all family members. Social workers prepare families to consider rules by introducing them to the concept, as illustrated in the following message:

- "As we begin work on problems the family is experiencing, we need to know more about how your family operates. Every family has some rules or understandings about how members are to behave. Sometimes these rules are easy to spot. 'Each person is to clear his own plate when leaving the table' is a rule that all members of a family might be expected to follow. This is an apparent rule because every member of the family could easily tell me what is expected of them at the end of the meal. But the family's behavior is also governed by other rules that are less easy to identify because they are hidden. Even though members follow these rules, they are often unaware that they exist. In the next few minutes, I'm going to ask you some questions that will help you to understand these two kinds of rules better and to identify some of the ones that operate in your family."

The social worker can then ask the family to list some apparent rules and coach the family, if needed, by asking questions such as "What are your rules about bedtime?" (or watching television or getting the work done around the house).

Once family members have identified some of their common and readily apparent rules, the social worker can then lead them into a discussion of implicit rules by asking them to identify guidelines they follow with regard to any of the dimensions of assessment listed in Chapter 10. For example, the social worker might ask family members to identify family rules about showing anger or positive feelings or to explore facets of decision making or power (e.g., "Whom do the kids go to in the family when they want something?"). Rather than engage the family in a lengthy exploration, social workers should use the discussion to illustrate the presence of hidden rules that significantly influence their behavior. In the discussion, social workers should stress that certain rules may undermine opportunities for members to achieve their maximum potential and, in fact, may be destructive to the growth and well-being of both individuals and the family itself.

After explaining the concept of rules to the family, social workers can utilize this concept in assisting members to identify their patterned ways of interacting. Consider the social worker's role in this regard in the following excerpt from a third session with Mr. and Mrs. Johnson and their three daughters:

Martha, age 14: You took the red jersey again, right out of my closet—and you didn't ask. That really gripes me.

Cynthia, age 15: You took the CD last week, and you still have it. What's up with that?

Father: In this family, we share and you girls need to understand this.

Social worker: What does that mean in this family?

Father: It means that we buy things for the girls to use together and no one person owns the things we buy. The girls are expected to share because they are so close in age and like similar things.

Social worker: What happens when there is a disagreement about a particular item?

Martha: I told Cynthia I was mad at her.

Social worker [*To Cynthia*]: Then what did you do?

Cynthia: I told Martha she didn't have any right to complain because she wasn't sharing things either.

Social worker: The two of you then were engaged in what is referred to as blaming messages. Do you see it the same way? [*Girls nod. To father.*] I wonder if you observed what you did when your daughters were involved in their argument?

Father: I was trying to get them to stop arguing and blaming each other, and remind them of how we operate in this family.

Social worker: We may have the makings of a hidden family rule. Let's explore a little more to find out for sure. [*To family.*] While I'm asking a few questions, let's see if you can figure out what the rule is. [*To 13-year-old Jennifer.*] You weren't involved in this argument. Do you argue with anyone in the family?

Jennifer [*laughing*]: My mother and my sisters.

Social worker: When you get in an argument with your mother, what happens?

Jennifer: If my dad is there, he tries to stop it. Sometimes he tells my mother to go upstairs, and he'll talk to me.

Social worker [*to mother*]: When your husband does that, what do you do?

Mother: Sometimes I let him handle the problem with Jennifer or one of the other girls. But when he gets involved like that, it makes me so furious that sometimes he and I end up in a fight as well.

Social worker: We need to do a lot more work to understand what happens in such situations, but for the moment, let's see, father, if you can put your finger on the rule.

Father: I guess I'm always trying to stop everyone from fighting and arguing in the family.

Social worker: It does appear that you are the family's mediator. I would think that would be a very difficult role to play.

Father: Well, there are no rewards for it, I can tell you that!

Social worker: There's more to the rule. Who lets father be the mediator?

Martha: We do.

Social worker: That's right. It isn't father's rule; it's the family rule. It takes the rest of the family to argue and father to break up the fights.

There are many avenues that could be explored in this scenario, but the social worker chose to narrow the focus by assisting the family to identify one of its major rules. After further exploring specific patterned interactions of the family, the social worker can introduce questions such as the following that will help the family to weigh whether or not they wish to continue relating under the old rule.

TO FATHER:

- "How effective are you in actually stopping family members from fighting?"
- "What are your worst fears about what might occur in the family if you didn't play that role?"
- "Would you like to free yourself from the role of being the family mediator?"

TO OTHER FAMILY MEMBERS:

- "Do you want father to continue to be the third party in your arguments?"
- "What are the risks to your relationship if he discontinues playing the role of mediator?"
- "Do you want to work out your own disputes?"

Questions of this nature focus on the participation of all members in the patterned interaction and assist the social worker and members to determine the *function* of the behavior in the system. To assist the family to modify their rule, the social worker will need to teach family members new skills for resolving disagreements. The social worker will also need to coach the father in declining the role of mediator and to coach others in requesting that he let them manage their own conflicts.

On-the-Spot Interventions

On-the-spot interventions are a potent form of metacommunication used to modify dysfunctional patterns of interaction by intervening immediately when such communication occurs between spouses or family members. On-the-spot interventions are appropriate when clients send fuzzy or abrasive messages; when receivers distort meanings of or fail to respond appropriately to important messages; when actors imply but do not explicitly express wants, needs, or feelings; and when destructive interaction occurs. In implementing on-the-spot interventions, social workers focus on the destructive impact of the preceding communication (labeling the type of communication so that clients themselves can subsequently identify their dysfunctional behavior) and facilitatively teach and guide participants to implement more effective ways of communication. This technique is illustrated in the next excerpt, which depicts a social worker intervening into a "blind alley" argument, one that cannot be resolved because neither party can be proved right or wrong.

Husband: I distinctly remember telling you to buy some deodorant when you went to the store.

Wife: You may have thought you did, but you didn't. I'd have remembered if you said anything about it.

Husband: But you didn't remember. I told you for sure, and you're shifting the blame.

Wife [*with obvious irritation*]: Like hell you did! You're the one who forgot to tell me, and I don't appreciate your telling me I forgot.

Social worker: Let's stop for a moment and consider what's happening between you. Each of you has a different recollection of what happened, and there's no way of determining who's right or wrong. You were involved in what I call a blind alley argument because you can't resolve it. You just end up arguing over who's right and feeling resentful because you're convinced the other is wrong. This doesn't help you solve your problem but only creates distance in your relationship.

Let's go back and start over, and I'll show you a more effective way of dealing with the situation.

After labeling the dysfunctional interaction and guiding clients to communicate constructively, social workers often subsequently intervene into related dysfunctional interactions but challenge clients themselves to identify their dysfunctional behavior and to modify it accordingly. For example, a social worker may interrupt interaction, exclaiming, "Wait a minute! Think about what you're doing just now and where it's going to lead you if you continue." If clients fail to discern the nature of their behavior, the social worker can again label the dysfunctional process and review with them more effective processes. In modifying dysfunctional patterns, the intermediate objective is for clients to arrest their dysfunctional behavior by recognizing it, metacommunicating about it, and substituting newly gained communication skills. The ultimate goal, of course, is for them to eliminate the dysfunctional processes through concentrated efforts between sessions.

Guidelines for Making On-the-Spot Interventions

1. *Focus on process rather than content.* Social workers can be infinitely more helpful to clients in enhancing interaction by focusing on interaction processes rather than on the content of conflicts. Conflicts typically are manifested over content issues, but how clients interact in dealing with the focal point of a conflict is far more important than the focal point itself. As we illustrated in the preceding excerpt, the issue of who is right in a given dispute is usually trivial when compared to the destructive effects of dysfunctional processes such as belittling, dominating, name-calling, threatening, arguing bitterly, or resorting to violence.

You should usually ignore topics of disputes, focusing instead on assisting clients to learn to listen attentively and respectfully, to employ effective decision making, to own feelings, to examine their own parts in problems, to increase positive feedback and reduce negative feedback, to compro-

mise, to disengage from competitive interaction, and to implement effective conflict resolution tactics. Clients, of course, will confront countless potentially conflictive situations but will manage them without damaging their relationships if they master effective patterns of communication that preserve mutual respect and self-esteem. Indeed, well-adjusted families differ from poorly adjusted families not in the sheer number of conflictive events but in the fact that the former manage conflict effectively, whereas the latter do not.

2. *Give feedback that is descriptive and neutral rather than general and/or evaluative.* As you intervene, it is important to present feedback in a neutral manner that does not fault clients and that enables them to pinpoint specific behavior that produces difficulties. Feedback that evaluates their behavior produces defensiveness; general feedback fails to focus on behavior that needs to be changed. To illustrate, consider a situation in which a marital partner glares at his spouse and says: "I've had it with going to your parents' house. You spend all the time there visiting with your mother and I do not feel included or welcomed in the conversation. You can go by yourself in the future." A general and evaluative message would be:

- "Garth, that message was an example of poor communication. Try again to send a better one."

Contrast the preceding message with the following one, which is neutral and behaviorally specific:

- "Garth, I noticed that when you just spoke to Barbara, you glared at her and sent a 'you' messages that focused on what you thought she was doing wrong. I watched Barbara as you spoke and noticed that she frowned and seemed to be angry. I'd like you to get some feedback from Barbara about how your message affected her. Barbara, would you share with Garth what you experienced as he talked?"

In the last message, the social worker implies the client's message was dysfunctional but avoids making an evaluative judgment, as the social worker did in the first example. Moreover, by describing specific behavior and eliciting feedback about its impact, the social worker enhances the possibility that the client will be receptive to examining his behavior and to modifying it. Note that this message also highlights the interaction of *both* participants, as specified in the following guideline.

3. *Balance interventions to divide responsibility.* Because more than one client is involved in conjoint sessions, social workers must avoid singling out one person as being the sole cause of interpersonal difficulties. Otherwise, that person may feel the social worker and others are taking sides and placing the blame on him or her. By focusing on all relevant actors, the social worker distributes responsibility, models fairness, and avoids alienating one person. Moreover, although one person may contribute more to problems than others, all members of a system generally contribute to difficulties in some degree. The following excerpt illustrates the technique of balancing as an intervention in a lesbian couple therapy session:

Partner at home: It makes me furious that you won't come home and take care of the baby. You agreed for me to go back to work part-time and now you won't get off work to take care of him. You think your own career is more important than caring for our child and letting me go back to work.

Partner at work: I'm new at this job and I just can't take time off now. You know that. Besides, I told you we weren't ready to have a baby now. I really can't get involved in taking care of Charley on work time now.

Social worker: Both of you seem to have some feelings and concerns that are legitimate, but for some reason you seem to be stuck and unable to work things out. [*To partner at home.*] You resent her not playing a more full part in child care so you can go ahead with the plan you agreed to about going back to work part-time. [*To partner at work.*] You feel that because you are on a new job, now is not the time to ask for time off for child care. I'd like to explore what both of you can do to make things better for each other.

In the preceding excerpt, the social worker responds empathically to the feelings of the participants, thus validating the feelings of each. In so doing, the social worker remains neutral rather than side with or against either of the participants. The empathic responses also soften the impact of the participants' attacking messages. When dysfunctional interactions such as the preceding occur, social workers may need to address interventions to three or four persons or even the entire family.

4. *Balance interventions to distribute time and focus equitably.* As diverse interactions occur among family members, social workers must make choices about intervening in processes so that all members have opportunities to focus on their concerns. When intervening in such situations, remember that although it appears that some members of a family are monopolizing the interaction, exploration of the situation usually reveals that less aggressive members are contributing to the problem through their own inactivity. Thus, social workers must address the responsibility all participants have in maintaining the status quo, highlight inaction as well as action in their interventions.

5. *Direct messages from participants to each other.* Because spouses and family members need to learn to communicate effectively with each other, social workers must facilitate effective communication between them rather than act as an intermediary. Clients often complain or express feelings to a social worker that concern a spouse or other family members, and it is easy in such instances to fall into the pattern of communicating with individual members rather than directing them to talk to each other. But clients do not gain essential skill in communicating with each other by talking through the social worker. Therefore, social workers should often redirect messages to the parties whom they concern, which is accomplished by utilizing a message such as "Would you tell your partner, please?"

Sometimes social workers err by asking members to express directly to others messages that are hostile, blaming, or critical. Such messages may exacerbate an already strained situation and lead to arguing or fighting among participants. Before redirecting messages, then, you must consider the likely consequences of the ensuing interaction. When redirecting messages, actively intervene to facilitate positive interaction by coaching clients to own feelings, to translate complaints to expressions of needs or requests for change, to metacommunicate by clarifying positive intentions, and to avoid harsh tones of voice or hostile facial expressions. In some instances, when clients begin to talk but do not face one another or maintain eye contact, you may need to interrupt and direct them to face one another and to look each other in the eye, as illustrated in the following message: "Margaret, please stop for just a moment. You were talking to me, not to Helen. Will you please start again, but this time talk and look directly at her?"

Assisting Clients to Disengage from Conflict

One of the most common (and destructive) types of dysfunctional interaction involves arguments that quickly escalate, producing anger and resentment between participants and perhaps involving other family members. Intense competitiveness in which neither person is willing to let the other be one-up by winning the argument may be a contributing factor. Thus the content issues involved are secondary to the fact that on a process level each participant is struggling to avoid being one-down, which would mean losing face or yielding power to the other.

To assist clients to avoid competitive struggles, you can use metacommunication about the dysfunctional process, emphasizing that all participants lose competitive arguments because of the negative feelings and emotional estrangement that ensue. It is also vital to stress that far more important than winning an argument is safeguarding mutual respect. As found by Mackey and O'Brien (1998), there are differences in responses related to gender and ethnicity in conflict situations. Their findings suggest a need for practitioners to be cognizant of these differences in the selection of intervention strategies. Berg and Jaya (1993) note, for example,

that in Asian families, concerns are viewed as "our problems," emphasizing the interdependence between family members. Assisting families to explore the family narrative regarding how conflict is managed in their culture as well as the attached meanings or feelings is essential to formulating an effective intervention strategy.

Within this context, the concept of disengaging from conflicts simply means that participants avoid escalating arguments by declining to argue further. A graceful way that spouses or family members can disengage is by making a comment similar to the following: "Listen, it doesn't really matter who's right. If we argue, we just get mad at each other, and I don't want that to happen." Where appropriate, a culturally sensitive approach might include encouraging parties to think about the effects on the entire family system.

You can further assist clients to avoid arguing between sessions by teaching them to employ code words that signal the need to disengage. We recommend that you encourage family members or partners to develop their own code words, an activity that most clients enjoy. Although the process of disengagement is easy to learn, it is not simple for many clients to apply because of their virtually reflexive pattern of responding competitively. You will thus need to intervene frequently at first, gradually transferring responsibility to them for recognizing and disengaging from competitive struggles. Negotiating tasks of applying disengagement in their interaction between sessions is essential in transferring use of this process to their daily lives.

Modifying Dysfunctional Complementary Interaction

Relationships, as described by communication theorists and without attributing a value, are either symmetrical or complementary (Becvar & Becvar, 2000). Symmetrical relationships are thought to be a more egalitarian arrangement. The converse is true of complementary relationships, in which parties have developed an exchange as a means for avoiding conflict, resolving differences, and creating a workable relationship. Preferences or relationship patterns may be culturally derived and therefore considered to be a functional division of roles and responsibilities. Social workers must avoid using a lens that would characterize these patterns as being dysfunctional unless the family has indicated otherwise. A complementary type of relationship may prove to be dysfunctional to one or both partners. Sources of frustrations may stem from role overload or strain, limitations imposed by role expectations, and disagreements related to decision making. One partner may grow to resent what he or she perceives as dominance, in which case the relationship becomes asymmetrical, and may engage in passive resistance or openly challenge the other partner. Moreover, one partner, weary of assuming the exchange, may devalue the other partner, resenting his or her lack of involvement. In either event, destructive interactions are likely to occur, culminating in their seeking relationship therapy.

In modifying dysfunctional complementary relationships, it is vital to work with both partners so that you can assist each in adapting to changes that bring the relationship more into balance (assuming the partners have chosen that goal). The submissive partner will need assistance in becoming more assertive, and the dominant partner will need assistance in learning to share power and to encourage and reinforce assertiveness by the submissive partner. By relating to the partners as a system, you avoid the pitfall of severely disrupting the relationship by assisting one partner to make changes that are threatening or unacceptable to the other.

Negotiating Agreements for Reciprocal Changes

During the course of marital and family therapy, a client will sometimes spontaneously propose to make a specific change in behavior if another person will agree to make a reciprocal change. Such conditional proposals reflect the fact that people unconsciously attempt to maintain balance in relationships, a phenomenon described by Janzen and Harris (1997) as the *quid pro quo*. For example, a marital partner may agree to be more affectionate

if the spouse will agree to be less sexually demanding. Parents may agree to permit their children to watch a favorite television program if the children complete their homework by a specified time. The reasons clients are more receptive to making changes when other parties agree to make reciprocal changes are twofold. First, people are more prone to give when they know they are getting something in return. Second, when all involved parties agree to make changes, no single person loses face by appearing to be the sole cause of an interactional problem.

Contracting for reciprocal changes can be a powerful way of inducing change. A particular advantage of reciprocal contracting is that it counters the tendency of many clients to wait for others to initiate changes. Another advantage is that in working on reciprocal tasks, clients are mutually involved in a change venture. This mutual involvement may spark collaboration in other dimensions of relationships, an important gain for couples whose interactions have been largely competitive rather than collaborative.

Clients are unlikely to implement reciprocal contracts if they have not moved beyond competitive bickering and blaming each other for their problems. We thus recommend deferring use of this technique (unless clients spontaneously begin to negotiate) until you have assisted them to listen to each other attentively and to express their needs and wants. It is also essential that they demonstrate a commitment to wanting to improve their relationship. This latter condition is especially crucial, for as Becvar and Becvar (2000) have pointed out, if clients view change (their own or others) as emanating primarily from meeting stipulations of an agreement, rather than the importance of the relationship, they are likely to devalue the changes. Therefore, we strongly recommend you have clients explicitly clarify that caring for the other person is the primary factor motivating willingness to make changes (when such appears to be the case). Social workers can employ reciprocal contracts to enhance interaction in diverse problematic situations, as illustrated in the following:

- Husband agrees to visit wife's parents if wife agrees to talk with her mother about refraining from interfering in the discipline of the children.

- Parents agree to allow a child to hang out with friends if the child agrees to observe curfew.

- Wife agrees to host a family reunion meal if the husband agrees to help clean up afterwards.

- Partner agrees to express feelings more if the other partner agrees to listen without interrupting.

In employing reciprocal contracting, it is wise to place maximal responsibility on clients for making proposals. By so doing, you enhance the investment of clients in proposed changes. Moreover, clients often generate innovative and constructive proposals that might not occur to a social worker. To engage clients in making proposals, you can use a message such as "It's clear both of you are unhappy with the situation. I'd be interested in hearing each of you make proposals as to what you could do to make it better." With some encouragement, most clients make proposals, but you may need to prompt them by suggesting possible reciprocal actions. As you mutually consider proposals, it is important to guard against encouraging clients to undertake overly ambitious actions. Clients (and social workers as well) are prone to want to effect major changes immediately, which is commendable but unrealistic. Bear in mind that people change by increments and that encouraging them to attempt overly difficult tasks sets them up for failure and disappointment. Moreover, failure in implementing tasks tends to cause clients to lose confidence in the helping process. It is vital, therefore, to encourage modest tasks that are commensurate with clients' capacities and motivation. By successfully accomplishing small reciprocal changes, clients experience the benefits of both giving and getting, which enhances their motivation to attempt additional reciprocal tasks.

Initial task exchanges should be relatively simple and likely to succeed. When intense conflict has marked the interaction, initial tasks may include reciprocal exchanges that do not require face-to-face contact. For example, a child agrees to clean up his room. The mother agrees to purchase the child's favorite brand of cereal. Another caution you should observe in negotiating reciprocal contracts is that clients should avoid undertaking multiple changes at the same time. Multiple tasks dilute efforts and reduce chances for successful accomplishment. Single changes, by contrast, foster concentrated efforts and enhance the likelihood of successful results.

As clients discuss proposals, you should attend carefully to nonverbal messages that suggest misgivings, apprehension, or opposition to carrying out the contract. Clients are sometimes hesitant to express their opposition and may agree to a contract to which they are not actually committed and have no intention of fulfilling. This is particularly true in relationships that include persons with different levels of power such as parent and child. Empathic responsiveness to nonverbal cues, however, may encourage them to disclose misgivings. By exploring the nature and source of misgivings, you may be able to assist clients to resolve them. If they prove unreceptive to the proposed changes, you can encourage them to identify changes they are willing to make. Our point is that it is critical to avoid contracts and tasks that clients are unlikely to accomplish successfully.

After eliciting or offering one or more feasible proposals for a reciprocal contract and determining that clients are willing to carry out the contract, you assist them to reach an explicit agreement. This agreement specifies tasks clients are to implement before the next session. It is important to plan with clients for implementing the task by following the steps of the task-implementation sequence, delineated in Chapter 13. As you plan with clients for task implementation, it is also vital to stress that each person must exercise *good faith* in carrying out his or her part of the contract, as illustrated in the following message:

- "I am pleased that you have both agreed to make the changes we've discussed because the changes can make things better for both of you. To carry out these changes successfully, however, each of you will need to carry out your part no matter what the other does. If you wait for your partner to carry out his or her part first, you may both be waiting for the other to make the first move by the time of our next session. Remember, failure by the other person to keep the contract should be no excuse for you to do likewise. If your partner doesn't keep the agreement, you can take satisfaction in knowing you did your part."

Emphasizing the individual responsibility of all participants in the helping process to fulfill their respective commitments, as in the preceding message, counters the tendency of clients to justify their inaction in subsequent sessions by asserting, "He (or she) didn't carry out his part. I knew this would happen, so I didn't do my part either." During the next session, it is vital to follow up on clients' experience in implementing their agreement. If results have been favorable, discussion of their reactions often results in further expressions of positive feedback between participants and leads to discussion of other ways of achieving further positive interaction. If one or more clients have not fulfilled their agreement, you can explore their interactions of the previous week, focusing on obstacles that prevented them from doing so.

Teaching Clients to Make Requests

Most clients have difficulty identifying what they need from others and expressing those needs clearly and fully to others. Many times when communication breaks down it is because clients demand, rather than invite, others to respond to their wishes. Social workers can make extensive headway in modifying destructive processes of clients by encouraging them to make clear requests to others when they want changes. Almost always underutilized by clients, requesting is a simple but powerful skill that social workers can quickly teach clients by introducing them to the following concepts:

- On the flip side of any complaint is an unmet need or want. Ask for what you need, then, in-

stead of complaining about what you are not getting.

- Avoid canceling out positive requests with negative riders: "I know you won't want to do this, but . . ."

- Treat your request as a favor others can grant you, not as something to which you are entitled, using language such as "Would you be willing . . . ?" or "I'd appreciate . . ."

- Agree that each party has the right to make any request, but each also has the right to turn down a request. Also agree, because parties are on the same team, that no one will just emphatically say "no" to requests that don't appeal, make counterproposals ("What if I did this instead?"), or ask for others ("Could you propose another avenue for solving the problem?").

- Teaching clients how to make clear requests is a form of empowerment, equipping them with an on-the-spot skill to negotiate their differences with others.

Helping Families to Give Up the Past

No relationship over time escapes the accumulation of past hurts. Often hurts are recycled by couples and families, and thus provide an ongoing fertile field for fights and arguments. Dwelling on the past, in fact, is one of the most common and destructive problems families encounter as they attempt to communicate. Social workers can aid clients in giving up their habitual focus on the past by asking them not to talk about any problem more than 24 hours old. Declaring a moratorium on the past brings many of the destructive communications of clients to a screeching halt. Social workers can also ask clients to save their "problem talk" for therapy sessions until they have acquired effective problem-solving strategies, pointing out that it is fruitless to continue in wheel-spinning conflict. In later stages of therapy, social workers might also consider engaging clients in a "past hurts" exercise. In this exercise, clients make individual lists of all the past hurts they still carry with them, no matter how long ago the injuries occurred or how ridiculous they feel about harboring them. Clients then rate their "hurts" on a scale of 1 to 10 (1 = low; 10 = high-intensive hurt) and negotiate together over which past hurts they would be willing to forget or "trade."

MODIFYING MISCONCEPTIONS AND DISTORTED PERCEPTIONS

Clients' cognitions often embody erroneous beliefs that produce dissatisfaction in marital and family relationships, engender resentments toward others, and contribute to dysfunctional interaction. Three common examples of mistaken beliefs manifested in couples, families, and groups are the following:

1. It's important to get even with people who hurt you or take advantage of you.

2. All people in authority (especially police) exploit their authority to the detriment of others.

3. We must conceal the fact that we have conflict in our family; otherwise, people will think badly of us.

Unrealistic expectations of others and myths are two other forms of misconceptions that contribute to interaction problems. As with rules, myths and unrealistic expectations often are not readily apparent, and social workers must sometimes infer them by exploring clients' expectations of each other, of marriage, and of family relationships. Myths are also similar to rules in that they govern family operations by shaping beliefs and expectations of spouses, family members, and other relatives. Goldenberg and Goldenberg (1992) identified numerous myths and unrealistic expectations that can profoundly influence interactions in couple and family relationships. Common examples of such myths include the following:

- Family members should meet all their emotional needs within their family.

- Partners should know without being told their partners' needs, feelings, and wants.

- If partners are well matched and love one another, a successful relationship will evolve without effort.

To eliminate misconceptions and dispel myths, draw them to the awareness of clients, gently assist clients to accept the error in the misconceptions, and focus on how they affect couple, family, and group interactions. Because misconceptions and myths commonly protect clients from having to face certain unpleasant realities and to make changes that are perceived as threatening, clients often do not relinquish them without a struggle. To facilitate their making essential changes, you must recognize that making changes entails resolving fears and risking the consequences of learning and implementing new behavior. Responding empathically to these fears and providing emotional support to clients as they struggle with their ambivalence toward change often supply the impetus that clients need to change their patterns of interaction.

To illustrate this process, we consider a family in which an adolescent, age 17, experiences extreme tension and anxiety. During family sessions, it has become apparent that the parents have exerted intense pressure on him to perform well academically and have made it clear they expect him to become a doctor. It has also been apparent that they mistakenly believe the myth that by trying hard enough anyone can become anything he wants. In an effort to reduce the pressure on the son by dispelling the myth and modifying the parents' expectation, the social worker arranges to meet separately with the parents. The following excerpt is taken from that session.

Social worker: I've been very concerned that Gary has been making an almost superhuman effort to do well in chemistry and physics but still is floundering in these subjects. I get the impression he believes he has to become a doctor at any price and that one reason he's so uptight is that he realizes he isn't cutting it despite his efforts. It's terribly important to him to meet your expectations, and he's falling short even though he drives himself.

Father: I know he's working hard, but it'll come. He can become a doctor if he really wants to. I could have been a doctor if I had applied myself, but I didn't. I goofed off too much. I don't want Gary to make that mistake. He has opportunities that neither his mother nor I had.

Social worker: I can sense your concern for Gary. Still, my impression is that both of you convey to your children the belief that they can become anything they want and that Gary is blaming himself because he's not making it, no matter how hard he tries.

Mother: Don't you think anyone can succeed in anything if they try hard enough?

Social worker: That belief doesn't square with what we now about differences between people. People have different aptitudes, talents, and learning styles. Some are able to handle types of work that require finger dexterity. Others are able to visualize spatial relationships. Everyone has certain aptitudes and certain limitations. What's important in career planning is discovering what our aptitudes are and making choices that match them. I wonder if each of you is able to identify talents and limitations that you have.

Note that in seeking to dispel the family myth, the social worker focused on the destructive impact of the myth on Gary. This tactic switched the focus from the abstract to the concrete and provided an opportunity to review their belief. The social worker then further attempted to invalidate the myth by asking them to apply it to themselves.

Social workers also frequently encounter clients who have distorted perceptions of one another that contribute to dysfunctional interactions. As you will recall from Chapter 10, labeling others is a common form of such perceptual distortions. The effect of labeling is tantamount to that of wearing blinders, for labels obscure perceptions of others' strengths, limitations, feelings, beliefs, interests, goals, attitudes, hopes, and the like. Instead, one's perceptions are limited to attributes and behaviors that are inherent in the label. When social workers observe the process of labeling (e.g., "You're lazy," "stupid," "frigid,"

"rigid," or "undependable"), it is important to intervene, highlighting the negative impact of labeling on the person (labeling produces defensiveness and resentment) and the fact that labeling limits awareness of the other person, causing that person to disengage. In focusing on the destructive impact of labeling, the social worker must be careful to label the process and not the client. Moreover, it is important to respond empathically to the frustrations the client experiences and assist the client to explore the feelings and cognitions associated with being labeled and to make specific requests for change.

MODIFYING DYSFUNCTIONAL FAMILY ALIGNMENTS

As we emphasized in Chapter 10, all families develop patterns of affiliation between members that either enhance or impair opportunities for individual growth or the family's ability to carry out operations vital to its survival. The functional structure, that is, the invisible or covert set of demands or codes that reflect and regulate family functioning, determines transactional patterns (Minuchin, 1974). In this section, we draw from techniques in the Structural Approach to guide intervention strategies when family functioning is impaired. The Structural Approach, as noted by Goldenberg and Goldenberg (2000), maintains, that "well functioning families are hierarchically organized which means a cohesive executive parental subsystem and age appropriate roles and responsibilities and privileges for children" (p. 199). Interventions to modify alignments are generally indicated:

1. When bonds are weak between spouses, other individuals who form the parental subsystem, or other family members.

2. When there are enmeshed alliances, rigid or overly restrictive boundaries between members that limit appropriate bonds with other members (or outsiders).

3. When two members of a family attempt to cope with dissatisfaction or conflict in their

relationship by forming a coalition with a third family member. This phenomenon, referred to as *triangulation,* most frequently involves marital partners who use a child as a pawn in their struggles.

4. When family members are disengaged or alienated from one another, tending to go their own ways, with little reliance on each other for emotional support.

5. When members of the family have formed alliances with persons outside the immediate family (e.g., friends and relatives) that interfere with performing appropriate family roles or providing appropriate emotional support to other family members.

In intervening to modify alignments, *structural mapping,* a technique from the Structural Approach, may be used to delineate family boundaries and highlight and modify interactions and transactional patterns:

- *To develop alliances,* which involves cultivating new alliances or strengthening relationships that are underdeveloped. A social worker can thus assist a new stepfather and stepson in exploring ways they can develop a relationship, or can work with siblings who have been estranged to strengthen their emotional bonds.

- *To reinforce an alliance,* which involves acting to maintain the alliance or to amplify its scope and/or strength. For instance, a social worker may enable parents to increase their ability to operate as an effective executive subsystem.

- *To differentiate individuals and subsystems,* which involves helping members who heretofore have been enmeshed to reinvest some of their emotional energy in others.

- *To increase family interactions* in disengaged families to make boundaries more permeable by changing the way in which members relate to each other.

- *To help family members accommodate changing circumstances or transitions* by decreasing rigid structures that are no longer functional.

As can be surmised from the above examples, structural problems may arise when the family structure is unable to adequately adjust to changing circumstances that are the results of external environmental forces or stressful transitions or interactions within the family. Before social workers intervene, they should understand that structural change is unique to the family situation and the nature of the structural dysfunction. Thus, they should involve the family in determining whether and in what ways such changes should take place. The social worker's first task in this respect is to assist family members to observe the nature of their alignments. This may be accomplished by asking questions that stimulate family members to consider their alignments:

- "If you had a difficult problem and needed help, whom would you seek out in the family?"

- "Sometimes members of a family feel closer to some members than to others and may pair up or group together. Which members of your family, if any, group together?"

- "In most families, members argue to some extent. With whom do you argue? With whom do other members argue?"

The social worker can also bring alignments and coalitions to the family's attention as they are manifested in the session. For example:

- [*To partner*]: "It seems that you're the hub of the family. Most of the conversation seems to be directed through you, while you [*other partner*] appear to be an observer or onlooker to the family's discussion."

- [*To family member*]: "Whom did you speak to before making a decision?"

As family members become aware of their alignments, the social worker must assist them in considering whether they wish to become closer to others and to identify obstacles that could prevent that from happening. Family alignments may in fact involve configurations described by Boyd-Franklin (1989b, p. 124) as "complex extended patterns," involving clan or tribal members, extended kin, friends, or clergy who are involved in family decisions.

Yet another strategy for assisting family members to analyze their family structure is to involve them in family sculpting (Nichols & Schwartz, 1998). *Family sculpting,* a technique used in experiential models, is an avenue for enabling family members to observe their alliances and to make decisions concerning possible changes. This technique allows family members to nonverbally communicate spatial relationships in the family system in a tableau to help families to discern problematic family alignments and to recognize the need to realign their relationships.

Members are instructed to use rectangles in their drawing to represent each person in the family. Rectangles can be of any size and located any place on the paper. Social workers coach family members to position the rectangles in ways that depict relative closeness and distance among family members as well as perceptions of power. After family members have completed their drawings, the social worker asks them to draw relationships as they would *like* them to be on the other side of the paper. In a subsequent discussion, the social worker asks members in turn to share their drawings of existing family relationships and then assists the family to formulate conclusions concerning the nature of alignments and the emotional closeness and distance that members experience in their relationships with others (e.g., "It appears, then, that father and Jeff feel quite close to each other, but that you, Mike, don't feel as close to your father as Jeff does"). The social worker then asks members to explain their second drawings that show how they would like family relationships to be. During the discussion, the social worker highlights the desires of members to increase their closeness to others and assists them to formulate goals that reflect changes they would like to make.

Social workers' actions to engage the family in discussions related to their family structures often stimulate family members to begin changing the nature of their alignments. Social workers can also assist members to modify various alignments by employing one or more of the following interventions.

Strengthening Parental Coalitions and Marking Generational Boundaries

In optimally functioning families, strong parental coalitions exist, and generational boundaries are clearly demarcated so that parents neither triangulate children nor permit them to intrude into the parental systems. In working with families that manifest weak parental coalitions, therefore, social workers face the challenge of assisting partners to strengthen their relationships and to present a united front in their interactions with their children. Otherwise, children learn to relate primarily to the most permissive parent and turn to that parent with requests for privileges, emotional support, and affection. Some such children become adept at playing one parent against the other, which fosters parental divisiveness and produces strain between children and the "excluded" parent. The hazards for the development of such an inimical family climate are especially great in stepfamilies with older children because loyalties and emotional bonding between parents and stepchildren may be lacking. The difficult challenge that confronts such families is to develop unity and cohesiveness when two families have joined together. Hare (1994) urges social workers to recognize that "problems faced by heterosexual stepfamilies, such as differences in parenting styles and custody difficulties also exist for lesbian families" (p. 34).

Strategies for strengthening marital coalitions may include negotiating agreements that parents will present a united form in parent-child transactions requiring decision making and/or disciplinary actions, unless, of course, the other partner is truly hurtful or abusive to the child. Strengthening boundaries is a quest for most families and couples and may be an issue through the entire course of the helping process. Social workers can aid clients in restructuring boundaries and dismantling dysfunctional political alliances with on-the-spot interventions that show the relevance of the preceding decision rules for relating.

Formulating Tasks That Strengthen Relationships or Encourage Rearrangements in Alignments

Social workers can modify various alignments by asking various groupings of family members to assume relevant tasks. For example, when bonds are strong between a father and one son and weak between the father and another son, it is important to preserve the strong bonding in the first relationship while strengthening the bonding in the second. The social worker may thus formulate a task with the father to spend a specified amount of time daily with *each* son and plan activities involving both sons at least once a week. In another situation, a social worker may seek to modify a parent-child coalition that is maintained by the mother's encouraging the child to tattle on another child who is excluded from the coalition. To dismantle the coalition, the social worker can ask the favored child to assume a task of reporting to the mother the positive behaviors of the other child during the week. In turn, the social worker can negotiate with the mother the task of refraining from accepting negative feedback (e.g., "I don't need to know about that. Thank you anyway") and rewarding the favored child for conveying positive information about the other.

KEEPING FAMILIES TOGETHER

In preceding sections, we discussed significant interventions to modify the processes of families and to enhance the functioning of members. At times, however, the stresses on families are so great that traditional ways of treating families are ineffective. When severely disrupted families are beset with violence or physical or sexual abuse, or children have become emotionally disturbed or delinquent, children are often removed from families.

In response to a rise in the number of children being removed from their families, family preservation services have emerged as an alternative to immediate out-of-home placement for children and families. Intensive services are provided in crisis at a point when removal of the child is imminent (Maluccio, 1990, p. 17). Such services have a strong congruence with the values underlying this book: the belief that people can change, considering clients as colleagues, a commitment to facilitating empowerment for families, and a view that it is the social worker's responsibility to instill hope (p. 20). In addition, the time-limited, crisis-focused nature of the work with an emphasis on tangible, mutually agreed upon goals is consistent with our perspective (Cole & Duva, 1990). Intensive family preservation services include assessment, contracting, organizing linkages to other resource providers and support networks, and counseling. Assessment includes recognition of the multilayered risks and opportunities in the family's social and cultural context. Examples of matters to be explored include parenting style as linked to quality of life; family stressors within a neighborhood; truancy in the context of the home, school environment, or neighborhood (Henngeler et al., 1998; D. Collins, Jordan, & Coleman, 1999).

The approach has been adapted for use with many populations, including first-generation immigrant families and lesbian households (Faria, 1991; Sandau-Beckler & Salcido, 1991). In addition, home-based services enable the social worker to observe family relationships and interactions in a familiar environment providing perhaps a more accurate assessment of family functioning (Boyd-Franklin & Bry, 2000; D. Collins et al., 1999). Among the strategies that are emphasized in home-based services is teaching "families and children technical skills that promote new behaviors and create more effective methods of managing family relationships" (D. Collins et al., 1999, p. 11). While intensive family preservation services appear to prevent the placement of some children for some period of time, differences in rates compared with control groups who have not received intensive services appears to diminish over time. Rather than perceive intensive home-based services as a panacea for problems of children and families, it is perhaps better to see such services as an important alternative that must be available when problems occur and placement is considered (K. Wells & Biegel, 1991, pp. 242–249).

Summary

In this chapter we focused on intervention techniques and strategies that may be used to strengthen family or couple relationships. Employing these techniques as a beginning social worker may appear to be daunting and we urge you to seek supervision and consultation as well as more comprehensive knowledge of the various approaches as a means of enhancing your skills. In employing these strategies, we urge caution to avoid making inappropriate assumptions about normal family functioning that are not congruent with the cultural and social class backgrounds of families you serve. In Chapter 13, we discussed at length the importance of matching intervention strategies to goals and the client system. We restate this point here to exemplify its importance in work with families as well as the need for problem specificity and multidimensional assessment. Research findings as summarized by Nichols and Schwartz (1998) point to positive outcomes where specific problems are treated in a systematic manner.

Internet Resources

With InfoTrac®, you can enter the keywords "family therapy" and "solution-focused therapy" to access articles such as Mumm, A. M., Olsen, L. J., & Allen, D. (1996). Families affected by substance abuse: Implications for generalist social work practice. *Families in Society, 79* (4). You can explore divorce mediation and download articles such as: Imbrogno, A. R., & Imbrogno, S. (2000). Mediation in court cases of domestic violence. *Families in Society, 81* (4); Gentry, D. B. (1997). Including children in divorce mediation and education: Potential benefits and cautions. *Families in Society, 78* (3); Gentry, D. B. (1997). Facilitating parent-child communication during divorce mediation. *Families in Society, 78* (3). You can also find out more about single-parent families at *http://users.aol.com/LIFT516/parents/sparents.htm/* You can explore use of therapeutic paradox at *http://www.mckergow.com/interview.htm/* and about the resistance concept in work with families at *http://www.albany.net/~deavila/existft.html/*.

Notes

1. Because of the complexity of family issues and processes, practitioners may initially meet with families for sessions of an hour and a half.

2. The practitioner picked up from where she left off with the father by utilizing an empathic response that reflected the father's feelings.

3. In this instance, the practitioner employed an additive empathetic response to reach for the positive feelings inherent in the client's message, a potent technique for highlighting caring feelings of participants and for facilitating more positive interactions.

4. The practitioner persisted in getting Marcos to talk to his father by repeating her instructions. Clients often require extensive coaching in learning to talk directly to significant others.

5. Cultural dimensions and concepts listed were in part excerpted from the keynote address by Dr. Joseph L. White, The New Community Professional Conference, Pillsbury Neighborhood Service, Minneapolis, MN, June 6, 2000.

CHAPTER 17

Intervening in Social Work Groups

CHAPTER OVERVIEW

This chapter builds on the skills you developed in Chapter 11 in forming and composing task, treatment, and support groups. Critical knowledge in effective intervention with groups comes from knowledge of stages of group development and social worker skills in enhancing those stages.

As we noted in Chapter 11, social workers operate in a variety of group formats including task, treatment, and support groups. In any group with social work goals, it is the task of the leader to intervene facilitatively to further that group's progress toward goal achievement. In treatment groups, a leader's role is particularly challenging, requiring in-depth, balanced interventions to facilitate growth of both individuals and the group. To add to the complexity of the role, a leader must be astute in sorting through the maze of multilevel communication to bring meaning to the group's experience, to shape the group's therapeutic character, and to provide direction and focus to the group's processes at critical moments. Finally, the leader must formulate all interventions within the context of the stages of development through which a group progresses to reach full maturity. Similarly, in a task group, the leader plays a variety of facilitative roles in assisting the group in meeting its objectives. This chapter focuses primarily on treatment groups with additional content on task groups in the final section.

It is toward the achievement of such ends that we dedicate this chapter. Because the leader's interventions are inextricably related to a group's stages of development, we begin at that point.

STAGES OF GROUP DEVELOPMENT

All groups go through natural stages of development in their progression toward full maturity, varying only in tempo and in the complexity of issues in each stage. Understanding these stages of group development is paramount, assisting leaders to anticipate the thematic behaviors characteristic of each stage and to recognize the significance of behaviors that occur in the group. Comprehension of stages also allows a leader to intervene in appropriate ways to encourage the group's development and the normative behaviors that support its treatment objectives. In addition, the leader is able to remove obstacles that impair the development of the group or the individuals within it and to make tempered choices regarding the level of leader activity necessary at any one time across the lifespan of a group.

Without knowledge of stages, leaders are prone to make errors, such as expecting group members to begin in-depth explorations in initial sessions or concluding that they have failed in their role when groups manifest the turmoil and discord typical of early development. Leaders may also ignore rather than encourage fleeting positive behaviors that herald the group's approaching a more mature stage of development. Further, they may not intervene at critical periods in a group's development to assist groups, for example, to "stay on task," to "count in" all members in decision making, to foster free expression of feelings, or to adopt many other behaviors that are hallmarks of a seasoned group.

Various models of group development provide social workers frameworks for organizing a large body of observations and group properties and identifying thematic group behaviors. All the models identify progressive steps in group development, although they may organize these steps into four, five, or even six stages. In recent years, social group work theorists have come to question certain aspects of the original model for stages of development. For example, Schiller (1997) has suggested that groups composed of women may emphasize intimacy for a longer period and come to power and control later in the group's history. Berman-Rossi and Kelly suggest that stages of group development are influenced by many variables, including but not restricted to gender of the members. For example, attendance patterns of members, worker skills, member characteristics, and the content of the group all influence stages of development (Berman-Rossi & Kelly, 2000). They further maintain that both women and men are concerned about both power and control and intimacy. While we will use the model developed by Garland, Jones, and Kolodny (1965), which delineates five stages, we will comment on recent developments such as the foregoing that influence stages of any particular group.[1] The five stages are

1. Preaffiliation
2. Power and control
3. Intimacy
4. Differentiation
5. Separation

Stage 1. Preaffiliation—Approach and Avoidance Behavior

The frame of reference used by Garland et al. to describe the group's initial stage is that of *approach-avoidance* behavior of members, whose tentativeness toward involvement in the group is reflected in their vacillating willingness to assume responsibility, to interact with others, and to support program activities and events. Hesitancy to participate is also shown by tentative speech, and silence is common as members operate as separate individuals and are preoccupied with their own problems and feelings of uneasiness and apprehension that emanate from their first encounter with the group. Often fearful and suspicious, members tend to be apprehensive regarding the responses of others to their expressions, fearing possible domination, aggression, isolation, rejection, and hostility. Thus, behavior is wary, sometimes even provocative, as members assess possible social threats and attempt to discern the kinds of behaviors the group wants and expects. Members also tend to identify each other by status and roles and engage in social rituals, stereotyped introductions, and detailed intellectual discussions. They are uncertain as to how the group will benefit them, and their understanding of the group's purpose is fuzzy. At times, members employ testing operations to "size up" other members, to test the group's limits, to find out how competent the leader is, and to determine to what extent the leader will safeguard the rights of members and protect them from feared hurt and humiliation. Members also move tentatively toward the group at times as they seek to define common ground with other members, search for viable roles, and seek approval, acceptance, and respect. Much of the initial communication in the group is also directed toward the leader, and some members may openly demand that the social worker assume a "take charge" approach by forcefully making decisions regarding group issues and structure and by issuing prompt directives to control the behavior of members. As noted above, Schiller (1997) suggests that groups composed entirely of women experience a longer preaffiliation phase as they explore empathic identification with others and differences. Berman-Rossi and Kelly (2000) suggest that groups tend to move from dealing with safer material to more difficult.

Stage 2. Power and Control—A Time of Transition

The first stage merges imperceptibly into the second as members, having determined that the group experience is potentially safe and rewarding and worth preliminary emotional investment, shift their concerns to matters related to autonomy, power, and control. The frame of reference for this stage is that of *transition* in that members must endure the ambiguity and turmoil of change from a nonintimate to an intimate system of relationships while they try to establish a frame of reference whereby the new situation becomes understandable and predictable. Moving from a struggle of whether they "belong" in the group, members now become preoccupied with how they "rank" in relation to other members. Turning to others like themselves for support and protection, members evolve subgroups and a hierarchy of statuses, or social pecking order. Gradually, the processes of the group become stylized as various factions emerge and relationships solidify. Conflicts between opposing subgroups often occur in this stage, and members may team together in expressing anger toward the leader, other authority figures, or outsiders. Disenchantment with the group may show itself in hostilities, withdrawal, or in confusion about the group's purposes. Verbal abuse, attacks, and rejection of lower-status members may also occur, and isolated members of the group who do not have the protection of a subgroup may discontinue coming to sessions. Attrition in membership may also take place as individuals find outside pursuits more attractive than the conflicted group experience; depleted membership, indeed, may put the group's very survival in jeopardy. Schiller (1997) suggests that groups composed of women may have to learn that constructive conflict is possible

and not to be avoided. Berman-Rossi and Kelly (2000) suggest that both male and female groups are concerned with intimacy and power and control. Further, passage of particular groups through stages depends on factors such as group attendance, thematic focus of the group, power, and worker skill.

Stage 3. Intimacy—Developing a Familial Frame of Reference

Having clarified and resolved many of the issues related to personal autonomy, initiative, and power, the group moves from the "preintimate" power and control stage to that of intimacy. As the group enters this stage, conflicts fade, personal involvement between members intensifies, and there is growing recognition of the significance of the group experience. Members also experience an increase in morale and "we-ness," a deepening commitment to the group's purpose, and heightened motivation to carry out plans and tasks that support the group's objectives. Mutual trust also increases as members begin to acknowledge each other's uniqueness, spontaneously disclose feelings and problems, and seek the opinion of the group. In order to achieve desired intimacy, however, members may suppress negative feelings that could produce conflict between themselves and others. In contrast to earlier sessions, members express genuine concern for absent members and may reach out to invite them to return to the group.

During this period of development, a group "character" also emerges as the group evolves culture, style, and a set of values. Clear norms are established, based on personal interests, affection, and other positive forces. Roles also take on form as members find ways of contributing to the group, and leadership patterns become firmly settled. The frame of reference for members is a familial one as members liken their experience to that of their own nuclear families, occasionally referring to other members as siblings or to the leader as the "mother" or "father" of the group.

How groups experience this stage depends on factors such as regularity of attendance and whether or not the group is open or closed (Berman-Rossi & Kelly, 2000). In groups with frequent member turnover, such as open-ended groups, they suggest that barriers to development are created. In such groups, it is important to develop rituals to help the group move to later stages.

Stage 4. Differentiation— Developing Group Identity and an Internal Frame of Reference

The fourth stage is marked by tight group cohesion and harmony as members come to terms with intimacy and make choices to draw closer to others in the group. In this stage, group-centered operations are achieved and a dynamic balance between individual and group needs evolves. Members, who participate in different and complementary ways, experience greater freedom of personal expression and come to feel genuinely accepted and valued as their feelings and ideas are validated by others in the group. Gradually, the group becomes a mutual-aid system in which members spontaneously give emotional supplies in proportion to the needs of each individual.

In experiencing newfound freedom and intimacy, members begin to perceive the group experience as unique, and as the group creates its own mores and structure, in a sense it becomes its own frame of reference. Customs and traditional ways of operating emerge, and the group may adopt a "club" name or insignia that accurately reflects the group's purpose. The group's energy is now channeled into carrying out purposes and tasks that are clearly understood and accepted. New roles, more flexible and functional than before, are developed to support the group's activity, and organizational structures (e.g., officers, dues, attendance expectations, rules) may evolve. Status hierarchies also tend to be less rigid, and members may assume leadership roles spontaneously as the need for particular expertise or abilities arises.

By the time the group reaches the differentiation stage, members have accumulated experience in "working through problems" and have gained skill in analyzing their own feelings and those of others in communicating their needs and positions effectively, in offering support to others, and in grasping the complex interrelationships that have developed in the group. Having become self-conscious about their own operations, groups bring conflict out into the open and identify obstacles that impede their progress. All decisions are ultimately the unanimous reflection of the group and are rigidly respected. Disagreements are not suppressed or overridden by premature group action, but rather the group carefully considers the position of any dissenters and attempts to resolve differences and to achieve consensus among members. New entrants serve as catalysts and may express their amazement at the insight shared by older members, who in turn become increasingly convinced of the value of the group. Members may now publicize their group meetings among peers, whereas previously membership in the group may have been linked with secret feelings of shame. Secure in their roles and relationships in the group, members may become interested in meeting with other groups or in bringing in outside culture.

Stage 5. Separation—A Time of Breaking Away

During the last phase, members begin to separate, loosening the intense bonds often established with other members and with the leader, and searching for new resources and ties to satisfy needs. Group members are likely to experience a broad range of feelings about leaving the group, and the approach of group termination may set off a number of reactions, the diversity of which is reminiscent of the approach-avoidance maneuvers displayed in Stage 1. Members may feel anxiety again, this time in relation to moving apart and breaking bonds that have been formed. There may be outbursts of anger against the leader and others at the thought of the group ending, the reappearance of quarrels that were previously settled, and an increase of dependence on the leader. Denial of the positive meaning of the group experience is not uncommon. These separation reactions may appear in flashes or clusters as members attempt to square their positive feelings about the group with their subconscious feelings of abandonment, rejection, and apprehension over the group's ending.

Termination is also a time of evaluation, of contemplation of the work achieved, and of consolidation of learning. It is a time of finishing unfinished business; of getting and giving focused feedback; and of savoring the good times and the close relationships gained in the group.[2] Members, who have often begun to pull back their group investments and to put more energy into outside interests, speak of fears, hopes, and concerns about the future and about one another. There is often focus on how to apply what has been learned in the group to other situations and talk of reunions or follow-up meetings.

STAGES OF GROUP DEVELOPMENT AND LEADER ROLE

As suggested earlier, the role of the leader shifts and changes with the evolution of the group. Referring to earlier work by Lang (1972), S. Henry (1992) conceptualizes the leader as enacting certain roles and occupying different locations throughout the group's life span. The shifting *role* of leader is cast along a continuum from primary to variable to facilitative, depending on the needs, capacities, and characteristics of the group's membership and its stage of development. Likewise, the leader occupies a *location* in the group that may be cast along a continuum ranging from central to pivotal to peripheral, depending again on the same variables.

The leader's role—a primary one at the outset of the group is to select candidates for the group. The leader is also in a central location in gathering the people who will compose the group. The leader continues to retain this primacy and centrality during the preconvening phase of the group as he or she brings structure to the group, plans its nature and function, conducts pregroup interviews, and negotiates reciprocal contracts with each prospective member. This set of role and location conditions prevails throughout the beginning phase of the group as the leader initiates and directs group discussion, encourages participation, and begins blending the reciprocal contracts with members into a mutual group contract.

As the group evolves to a new level of connectedness, the leader intentionally takes a variable role and occupies a pivotal location with respect to the group. According to S. Henry (1992):

> As the worker steps back from the central location and primary role, the members begin to supplant some of what the worker has been doing. In the vernacular of cinematography, the worker fades out as the group system comes up. However, because the group's (internal and external) systems are not yet stabilized at full functioning capacity, the worker needs to let the process run at its own speed and sometimes needs to move back in to help keep the system afloat. This is why the worker's role is referred to as variable, and the worker's location as pivotal. This role and location will be part of the mutual contract that is being negotiated at this time. (p. 34)

Henry notes that the leader's variable role and pivotal location continues in the group during the conflict/disequilibrium stage (the Power and Control stage in Garland, Jones, and Kolodny's terminology). When the group enters its maintenance or working phase (the Intimacy and Differentiation stages), the leader assumes a facilitative role and occupies a peripheral location. Inasmuch as the group has achieved full capacity to govern itself, the leader is in a resource role rather than a primary role. "He or she will be at the boundary of the system," observes Henry, "because the group is maintaining itself, internal and external systems are 'go,' it conceives of itself as an entity, and it is functioning in a self-directed way" (p. 34).

As the group moves into its separation or termination phase, Henry notes, the leader once again returns to a primary role and central location to supplant the divesting of members, who are launching their own independent courses. In this role the leader aids the group in working through any regression to earlier stages of development and assures the successful ending of the group.

The shifts in role and location can be inferred by studying Table 17-1, which illustrates the evolution of the leader's focus as a group advances through stages of development. Information contained in the table comes from a variety of sources, including Garland, Jones, and Kolodny (1965), S. D. Rose (1989), S. Henry (1992), and Corey and Corey (1992).

INTERVENTION INTO STRUCTURAL ELEMENTS OF A GROUP

The primacy of the leader's role and the centrality of the leader's location is related at one level to the ability of members to assume responsibility for the treatment functions of the group. At another level, these leader positions are related to the relative need to intervene to shape the group's therapeutic character, thereby creating a vehicle for the change process of individuals. In that respect, across stages of group development, the leader pays particular attention to the shaping of the following group elements:

- Cohesion
- Normative structure
- Role structure
- Subgroup structure
- Leadership structure

It is, in fact, the evolution of these structures over time that encompasses the phenomenon of group development (Rose, 1989; Yalom, 1985). Because of their importance in determining the relative therapeutic nature and impact of the group, these elements are considered successively in sections that follow.

Cohesion

Because the presence of cohesion in a group plays such a central role, leaders must encourage the development of this positive force in groups. In so doing, the leader forges connections between people who are unrelated to each other and tries to expand the interpersonal network of subgroups of people in the group who are too closely related. Further, the leader encourages cohesive behaviors by "pointing out who is present and who is absent . . . , by making reference to 'we' and 'us' and 'our,' and by including the groups as a whole in his or her remarks in group sessions" (S. Henry, 1992, p. 167).

Leaders also encourage the development of cohesion by commenting on and thus reinforcing manifestations of the same. Henry identifies signs of cohesiveness that leaders might highlight:

> *When members return to the group sessions after absence following conflict or disequilibrium, it is a sign of their attraction to the group, to other members, and to what the group does. When the members regroup and reformulate their configuration and stay with that piece of work, it is a sign of their attraction to what the group is doing. When members notice the presence or absence of other members and ask the worker for information about others, it is a sign of their attraction to other members. When people act to take others into account, seeking to be in their shoes when decisions are taken, it is a sign of their attraction to the group. When members take more and more responsibility for what the group does and where it is going and how it is getting there, it is a sign of the attraction that the experience holds for them. (p. 167)*

Although these indicators of cohesion are earmarks of advanced stages of group development, they often make fleeting appearances early in a group.

Leaders also increase the attractiveness and cohesion in groups by developing high levels of interaction; by aiding members to successfully achieve goals, fulfill expectations, and meet needs; and by providing opportunities for prestige and access to rewards and resources that individual members alone could not obtain (Toseland & Rivas, 2001).

Ironically, although throughout the group experience leaders seek to increase cohesiveness, they may work to reverse this process during the termination phase, as Garvin (1987) notes:

> Members must be helped to become less attracted to the group and, when appropriate, more attracted to alternative relationships. The worker, therefore, also reverses the application of principles for attaining group cohesion. For example, instead of increasing the frequency with which members have contact with one another, this may be reduced by having meetings less often and/or for a shorter time. . . . The worker may place less emphasis on resolving conflicts within the group and may not call attention to commonalities of experiences or attitudes except as those relate to ways of coping with termination. This may not be true in group psychotherapy, when this type of process is maintained until the very end. (p. 222)

Normative Structure

As a group develops, norms may not evolve to support its treatment objectives. A group, for example, may split into several self-serving factions or subgroups that compete for control. Further, members may develop a habit of socializing rather than focusing on legitimate group tasks. Some members may also repeatedly scapegoat other vulnerable members, harassing those members and blaming them for various group ills. In these and myriad other ways, groups may develop redundant behaviors that undermine the ability of members to aid each other in alleviating problems.

As described in Chapter 11, a vital role of leaders is that of observing evolving group behavior and assessing whether emerging patterns of behavior undermine or support the treatment purposes of the group. Once leaders have determined the impact of emerging patterns, they then intervene to nurture functional group behaviors and to assist the group to modify behaviors destructive to individuals or to the group.

The leader sets the stage for a therapeutic atmosphere and a "working group" by establishing an explicit contract with members in initial sessions that include normative "guideposts" for the group. Guidelines to promote therapeutic behavior such as the following may be generated and recorded in initial sessions and then reviewed in later sessions to assess the group's success in adopting them. These may include:

- Adhering to a decision-by-consensus method of solving problems
- Personalizing statements and feelings by speaking from an "I" position, for example, "I (think) (feel) (want) . . ."
- Keeping the group's focus on the task and mission of the group
- Keeping group discussion focused primarily on the present rather than on the past
- Focusing extensively on individual and group strengths and progress
- Avoiding "gossiping," that is, talking about someone in front of that person
- Agreeing that the group will "stop action" when there is a breakdown in communication or other problems that interfere with the group's doing its work

Setting the stage for intervention, the leader emphasizes that it is his or her role in numerous ways to aid the group to observe these contractual guidelines over time, recognizing that adherence to a contract is a process, not an event, and that compliance will occur gradually as the group matures. Significant adherence to these guidelines is a mark, in fact, that the group has achieved full maturity.

STAGE	DYNAMICS	LEADER FOCUS
Preaffiliation	Arms-length exploration Approach/avoidance Issues of trust, preliminary commitment Intellectualization of problems Interaction based on superficial attributes or experiences Protection of self; low-risk behavior Milling around Sizing up of leader and other members Formulation of individual and group goals Leader viewed as responsible for group Member evaluation as to whether group is safe and meets needs Fear of self-disclosure, rejection Uncertainty regarding group purpose Little commitment to goals or group	Observes and assesses Clarifies group objectives Establishes group guidelines Encourages development of personal goals Clarifies aspirations and expectations of members Encourages discussion of fears, ambivalence Gently invites trust Gives support; allows distance Facilitates exploration Provides group structure Contracts for help-seeking, help-giving roles Facilitates linkages among members Models careful listening Focuses on resistance Assures opportunities for participation
Power and Control	Rebellion; power struggles Political alignments forged to increase power Issues of status, ranking, and influence Complaints regarding group structure, process Challenges to leader's role Emergence of informal leadership, factional leaders Individual autonomy; everybody for him/herself Dysfunctional group roles Normative and membership crisis; drop-out danger high Testing of leader; other group members Dependence on leader Group experimentation in managing own affairs Program breakdown at times; low planning Feedback highly critical	Protects safety of individuals and property Clarifies power struggle Turns issues back to group Encourages expression and acceptance of differences Facilitates clear, direct, unabrasive communication Examines nonproductive group processes Examines cognitive distortions Facilitates member evaluation of dissident subgroups Holds group accountable for decision by consensus Clarifies that conflict, power struggles are normal Encourages norms consistent with therapeutic group aims Consistently acknowledges strengths, accomplishments Nondefensively deals with challenges to leadership Focuses on "here and now"

Table 17-1 Stages, Dynamics, and Leader Focus

STAGE	DYNAMICS	LEADER FOCUS
Intimacy	Intensified personal involvement Sharing of self, materials Striving to meet others' needs Awareness of significance of the group experience Personality growth and change Mutual revelation, risking Beginning commitment to decision by consensus Beginning work on cognitive restructuring Importance of goals verbalized Growing ability to govern group independently Dissipation of emotional turmoil Member initiation of topics Feedback constructive	Encourages leadership Assumes flexible role as group vacillates Aids sharper focus on individual goals Encourages deeper-level exploration, feedback Encourages acknowledgment, support, of differences Guides work of group Encourages experimentation with different roles Encourages use of new skills inside and outside group Assists members to assume responsibility for change Gives consistent feedback regarding successes Reduces own activity
Differentiation	Here-and-now focus High level of trust, cohesion Free expression of feelings Mutual aid Full acceptance of differences Group viewed as unique Clarity of group purpose Feelings of security; belonging; "we" spirit Differentiated roles Group self-directed Intensive work on cognitions Goal-oriented behavior Work outside of group to achieve personal goals Members feel empowered Communication open, spontaneous Self-confrontation	Emphasizes achievement of goals, exchange of skills Supports group's self-governance Promotes behaviors that increase cohesion Provides balance between support, confrontation Encourages conversion of insight into action Interprets; explores common themes Universalizes themes Encourages deeper-level exploration of problems Assures review of goals, task completion Stimulates individual and group growth Supports application of new behaviors outside group
Separation	Review and evaluation Development of outlets outside group Stabilizing and generalizing Projecting toward future Recognition of personal, interpersonal growth Sadness and anxiety over reality of separation Expression of fears, hopes, anxiety for self and others Some denial, regression Moving apart, distancing Less intense interaction Plans as to how to continue progress outside group Talk of reunions, follow-up	Prepares for letting go Facilitates evaluation and feelings about termination Reviews individual and group progress Redirects energy of individuals away from group and toward selfing process Enables individuals to disconnect Encourages resolution of unfinished business Reinforces changes made by individuals Administers evaluation instruments

Table 17-1 Stages, Dynamics, and Leader Focus *(continued)*

In addition to generating structural guidelines that pave the way for the adoption of therapeutic norms, leaders aid members in adopting the following personal guidelines, adapted from Corey and Corey (1992):

- Help establish trust. Initiate discussion of trust issues rather than wait for some other person to take the first risk or to make some gesture of trust.

- Express persistent feelings. Rather than shroud feelings of boredom, anger, or disappointment, air persistent feelings related to the group process.

- Decide how much to disclose. You are in charge of what, how much, and when you share personal issues.

- Be an active participant, not an observer. Share reactions to what others are saying in the group rather than remain an unknown entity and thus a possible object of others' flawed observations.

- Listen closely and discriminately. Do not accept others' feedback wholesale or reject it outright, but decide for yourself what does and doesn't apply to you.

- Pay attention to consistent feedback. If a message has been received from a variety of sources, it is likely to have a degree of validity.

- Focus on self. Talk about your role in problems; also avoid focusing on extraneous situations or people outside of the group.

Leaders, of course, often intervene to articulate the need for, or to acknowledge the presence of, the personal normative behaviors that they desire individual members to adopt.

Role Structure

Roles are closely related to norms, as Toseland and Rivas (2001) explain:

> *Whereas norms are shared expectations held, to some extent, by everyone in the group, roles are shared expectations about the functions of individuals in the group. Unlike norms, which define behavior in a wide range of situations, roles de-*
> *fine behavior in relation to a specific function or task that the group member is expected to perform. (p. 68)*

Within the group, role dimensions consist of who occupies formal positions (such as chairperson or secretary) and who fills informal positions created through group interactions (such as mediator, clown, rebel, or scapegoat). Leaders may utilize formal group roles in the service of furthering treatment aims such as increasing leadership or other skills. Leaders must also address antitherapeutic roles that evolve in a group, as, for example, focusing on instances in which members criticize other members, manifest excessive dependence on the leader, adopt a "therapist's role," or remain aloof from the group.

Garvin (1986) notes that in later phases of the group, members may become locked into dysfunctional roles. For instance:

> *The "clown" may wish to behave more seriously, the "mediator" to take sides, and passive people to function assertively. The worker, being cognizant of roles that are created out of group interactions, will attend to those that impede either the attainment of individual goals or the creation of an effective group. (p. 112)*

Dysfunctional role performance is a critical choice point for intervention. One means of intervening is to use a technique developed by Garvin (1986) to identify informal roles occupied by members. Leaders administer a questionnaire asking members to "vote" on whom, if anyone, fulfills group roles such as referee, humorist, nurturer, spokesperson, and "devil's advocate." A subsequent group discussion of results has significant potential for effecting changes in group processes. Another manner of intervening is to simply describe a specific role a member seems to have assumed and to ask that member for observations regarding the accuracy of input. Inquiring as to whether the member would like group feedback preliminary to any moves in that direction reduces defensiveness and gives the member appropriate control over the situation. The strategy of asking members' permission regarding group feedback is potent in instances in which a member might gain from such input.

Another aspect of role performance is aiding members to achieve role attainment, i.e., to fulfill the requirements of roles that they aspire to or are already in, such as student, parent, spouse, employee, friend, or retired person. This may be accomplished by aiding members to assess their own interactions, to practice, and then to apply new ways of interacting and approaching their roles. In this regard, Garvin (1987) suggests steps by which groups can aid members to role-play or in other ways simulate the behaviors they seek to possess. Leaders may also draw from Chapter 14 to obtain strategies to enable members to change behavior through behavioral rehearsal and other skill training.

Subgroup Structure

Subgroups inevitably emerge and exist in groups, affecting them in numerous ways, at times facilitating, at other times hindering group processes. Negative subgroups can raise issues of loyalty and exclusion in the group, challenge the leader's authority, and fragment communication as members of a subgroup talk among themselves. The leader, who must intervene in ways to modify the impact of such subgroups, can do so by utilizing strategies such as the following:

1. Initiate discussion of the reasons for dissident subgroupings and their impact on the group as a whole. "Talking about reasons for the subgroup's formation can help the whole group by revealing difficulties in group goal-setting, communication, interaction, interaction, and decision making," as Toseland and Rivas (2001) indicate.

2. Neutralize the effects of negative subgroups through programming or structuring. The leader, for example, might challenge dissident subgroups to work toward a common goal, change seating arrangements, use a "round-robin" approach to get feedback from all members, assign members from different subgroups to work on common group tasks, or use programming materials or exercises to separate subgroup members.

3. Create safe positions or roles for marginal members of the group that require minimal activity but at the same time involve such members in group activity (Balgopal & Vassil, 1983).

4. Enable powerful subgroups or individuals to relinquish power or to use it sparingly in the interest of other members. This may be accomplished by encouraging concern for others in the group and also enabling members to grasp that domination of others can be destructive to themselves (Garvin, 1987).

5. Appoint powerless members to roles that carry power, such as arranging for group activities, securing resources for the group, or fulfilling significant roles, for example, as observer, chairperson, or secretary.

6. Find means to "connect" with dissident subgroups and to demonstrate a concern for their wants (Garvin, 1987).

7. Provide ways for such subgroups to attain legitimate power by creating useful roles and tasks in the group.

Leadership Structure

The leader's role in a group can be described as a set of behaviors that facilitate the attainment of group and individual goals and ensure the maintenance of the group.

> It is the leader's role in the long run to facilitate the distribution of those behaviors associated with group leadership so that at least some of the rewards and control of leadership accrue to all members. Thus, an important function of the group leader is to gradually eliminate the central leadership role while continuing to maintain focus on the work of the group. The group leader must maintain sufficient responsibility until the members themselves are able to provide guidance to the group. (S. D. Rose, 1989, p. 260)

Aiding members to assume leadership behaviors is vital for three reasons, according to Rose. First, members develop vital skills that transfer to other social groups, where leadership is usually highly valued. Second, the more that members exercise leadership, the more likely they are to invest in the group. Third, performance of leadership activities enhances the perceived power or self-efficacy of members, who often experience powerlessness in a wide variety of social situations.

Leaders should expedite the sharing of power with members and the group as a whole. They may do this by (1) encouraging member-to-member rather than member-to-leader communications, (2) asking for members' input into the agenda for the meeting and the direction the group should take in future meetings, (3) supporting indigenous leadership when members make their first tentative attempts at exerting their own influence on the group, and (4) encouraging attempts at mutual sharing and mutual aid among group members during the first meeting (Shulman, 1984).

Group leadership problems occur when a member of the group or vying subgroups attempt to usurp the reins of power. Challenges to leadership (or lack of it) are, in fact, an inherent part of the group's struggle over control, division of responsibility, and decision making (Corey & Corey, 1992). It is important not to label such members because their efforts may be interpreted as attempting to help the group succeed by focusing it on personally meaningful roles (Hurley, 1984). These authors give examples of messages that illustrate control issues:

- "I don't want to talk just because you want me to talk. I learn just as much by listening and observing."

- "There are several people in here who always get the attention. No matter what I do, I just don't seem to get recognized, especially by the leaders."

- "You should pay more attention to Paul. He's been crying several times, and you haven't been taking care of him."

In response to a challenge of leadership, a leader might immediately explore a member's statement through empathic responding, eliciting feedback from other members regarding leadership style, and asking for input (e.g., "What would you have me do differently?"). Another choice, that of authentic responding, is encouraged by Corey and Corey (1992), who emphasize the need of leaders to become aware of their own reactions to a personal challenge as well as to other obstacles manifested by a "resistant group." Leaders, say these authors, often make the mistake of focusing on "problem members" or difficult situations, rather than on how they are affected personally when group processes go awry:

> *Typically, leaders have a range of feelings: being threatened by what they perceive as a challenge to their leadership role; anger over the members' lack of cooperation and enthusiasm; feelings of inadequacy to the point of wondering if they are qualified to lead groups; resentment toward several of the members, whom they label as some type of problem; and anxiety over the slow pace of the group, with a desire to stir things up so that there is some action. (p. 155)*

By ignoring their reactions, leaders leave themselves out of the interactions that occur in the group. Instead, Corey and Corey urge leaders to model

> *a "direct" style of dealing with conflict and resistance, rather than bypassing. Your own thoughts, feelings and observations can be the most powerful resource you have in dealing with defensive behavior. When you share what you are feeling and thinking about what is going on in the group—in such a way as not to blame and criticize the members for deficiencies—you are letting the members experience an honest and constructive interaction with you. (p. 155)*

By consistently responding authentically, even when challenged or under attack, the leader encourages the group's eventual wholesale adoption of this mode of representing self, one that is vital to members' dealing effectively with the inevitable differences they encounter among themselves.

LEADER INTERVENTIONS ACROSS STAGES OF GROUP DEVELOPMENT

As previously mentioned, a leader's role must always be pursued within the framework of the group's stages of development. Here, in more detail, key aspects of the leader's role are explicated across the Garland, Jones, and Kolodny (1965) model.

Preaffiliation Stage

Conducting individual interviews to orient potential members to a group experience, as discussed in Chapter 11, is but the beginning of the leader's efforts to prepare members to make effective use of a group. In many ways, in initial sessions the leader can prepare members for the experience to come by articulating the basics of group process. These include, for example, the stages of development through which the group will pass; ways in which to create a therapeutic working environment; behaviors and attitudes characteristic of an effective working group; the vital need to establish and adhere to clear group guidelines that lend structure and purpose to the group, and the importance of committing to win-win decisions regarding group matters. Research, in fact, suggests that direct instruction or teaching regarding group processes tends to facilitate a group's development during early stages (Corey & Corey, 1992; Dies, 1983).

Leaders must also intervene to address initial concerns of members. In early sessions members will be tentative about what it is they hope to get from the group. Most also experience fear and apprehension regarding the group experience. They worry about how they will be received by other members; whether they will be pressured to talk; whether they will be misunderstood or look foolish; whether they are at risk of verbal attack; and whether they indeed want to go through a change process. The leader may aid in explicating and allaying these anxieties by asking all members to share their feelings about coming to the initial group session. One method is to ask members to rate their feelings about being present in the group at that moment on a scale of 1 to 10 in which 1 represents "I don't want to be here" and 10 represents "I'm completely at ease with being in the group." The leader may then ask members to explain the reasons for their ratings.

In focusing on members' fears, leaders need to draw out the feelings and reactions of all members, to validate the importance of their fully disclosing feelings, and to emphasize the need for the group to be a safe place in which such issues can be expressed. Finally, leaders may elicit suggestions for group structuring that address member fears, out of which may flow the formulation of relevant group guidelines.

Leaders can measure the progress of a new group in addressing initial member concerns by administering a questionnaire developed by S. D. Rose (1989) containing items to which members can respond by circling a point on a scale. Examples of items include: How useful was today's session for you? Describe your involvement in today's session. Rate the extent of your self-disclosure of relevant information about yourself or your problem. How important to you were the problems or situations you discussed (others discussed) in the group today? Circle all the words that best describe you at today's session (e.g., excited, bored, depressed, interested, comfortable). How satisfied were you with today's session?

In initial sessions, leaders must review basic information several times regarding the group's purpose, the manner in which the group will be conducted, and its ground rules. K. E. Reid (1991, p. 205) emphasizes that none of this information should surprise members. However, reiteration is necessary because "in the beginning, members are often so preoccupied that they do not comprehend the group's purpose, their particular role, the worker's role, and what will be expected of them." If the leader does not make these issues clear early in the group's development, they will come back to haunt the group and hinder its progress.

In preliminary interviews, members contract with the leader for general goals they would like to achieve. In initial sessions the leader must then blend individual and group goals. The binding contract thus is expanded from a reciprocal one between leader and individuals to a mutual contract between individuals and group. In the first meeting, S. Henry (1992, p. 80) notes, the leader engages "all persons present in a discussion that establishes a group way of functioning yet allows each person's initial objectives to be addressed." Henry, who views finding common ground as "an unfolding process," utilizes what she calls a "Goal Questionnaire" to facilitate formulation of the mutual contract. On this questionnaire are two questions to which members respond in writing: (1) "Why do you think all of you are here together?" and (2) "What are you going to try to accomplish together?" Discussion of responses gives the group a beginning point from which to proceed (pp. 83–88).

In the ongoing contractual process in initial sessions, leaders also aid members to refine their general goals. Corey and Corey (1992, pp. 121–122) use examples to illustrate the role of the leader in clarifying global goals:

- *Member:* I want to get in touch with my feelings.
- *Leader:* What kind of feelings are you having difficulty with?
- *Member:* I want to work on my anger.
- *Leader:* With whom in your life are you angry? What do you most want to say?

The leader thus uses the skill of concreteness explicated in Chapter 6 to further the creation of clear and specific goals. The leader also keeps accomplishment of goals at the forefront of the group. G. Corey (1990, p. 94) encourages "reading, reflecting, and writing" to aid members to focus on their own themes. He suggests selected books and also asks members to keep a journal, which allows them to record the spontaneous reactions they have during and between sessions. Members are also encouraged to bring to the group the gist of their journal entries, which teaches the value of continuing work between sessions.

Maximizing member productivity and satisfaction requires that leaders attend to how they open and close meetings. Corey and Corey (1992) encourage leaders to draw from the following procedures in opening meetings:

- Give members a brief opportunity to say what they want from the upcoming session.
- Enable members to share accomplishments since the last session.
- Elicit feedback regarding the group's last session and give any reflections you have of the session.

To bring meetings to closure, Corey and Corey (1992) emphasize the need to summarize and integrate the group experience and recommend procedures such as the following:

- Ask members what it was like for them to be in the group today.
- Ask members to identify briefly what they're learning about themselves through their experience in the group. Are they getting what they want? If not, what would they be willing to do to get it?
- Ask members whether there are any topics, questions, or problems they would like to explore in the next session.
- Ask members to indicate what they would be willing to do outside of the session to practice new skills.
- Ask members to give one another feedback, especially regarding positive observations, and relate them to leader reactions and observations.

Developing skills in opening and closing sessions increases the possibility of continuity from meeting to meeting. Such continuity heightens the transfer of insights and new behaviors from the group into daily life.

Power and Control Stage

In the Power and Control stage, the group enters a period in which the group's dynamics, tone, and atmosphere are often conflict ridden. As noted by

Schiller (1997), some female groups may need to be encouraged here that it is not always helpful to "be nice"; that conflict can occur in a way that produces growth. Groups are beset with divisions among individuals and subgroups, complaints and unrest over group goals, process and structure, and challenges to leadership. At the same time, the group is trying out its capacity to manage its own affairs. It is the leader's role to bring the group intact through this stormy period with emerging capacity to cope with individual differences and to manage its own governance. The following are strategies that leaders can employ to discharge this responsibility.

Minimize Changes

During the Power and Control stage, groups with a closed format are particularly susceptible to inner and outer stressors such as a change of leader, moving to a new meeting place, addition or loss of members, or change in meeting time. Traumatic events such as a runaway, a death, an incidence of physical violence in an institutional setting, or acutely disturbing political or natural events at the community or national level may also affect a group.

Such changes or events bring stress to a group at any stage of development. However, they are particularly difficult to manage in the Power and Control stage because members have not yet invested to an appreciable extent in the group and thus become easily disenchanted. Adding new members or changing the group's leader is particularly stressful, causing members to raise their defenses because there are risks involved in revealing themselves when either the leader or member is an unknown entity. The loss of a leader can also be inordinately traumatic to members who have difficulty investing in relationships, affirming their stance that investing in others brings disappointment.

In addition, significant change in group structure without group involvement may cause members to conclude that the leader or agency has disregard for the impact of decisions on the group and that the group is not important to either.

Though changes are sometimes unavoidable, it thus behooves leaders to keep changes to a minimum, to prepare members in advance whenever possible, and to aid them to "work through" their feelings in any regard.

Encourage Balanced Feedback

In the Power and Control stage, leaders must emphasize the need for balanced positive and negative feedback. As they observe that group members are tentatively moving into their first authentic encounters, leaders should intervene in negative interactions to draw the group's attention to providing balanced feedback. They thus remind members of the provision in the contract for focusing on positives as well as negatives, as illustrated in the following excerpt from an early group session with adult members.

Gary [*to Wayne, in irritated voice*]: When you keep zapping me with questions like that, I feel like I'm being interrogated.

Wayne: I didn't know I was coming across like that. Frankly, I just wanted to get to know you better.

Leader [*to Wayne*]: You said in the first session that you'd like to use the group as a way of getting feedback about how you come across to others. I'm wondering if this might be a time for this. Are you game?

Wayne: Yeah. I don't know what's coming, but I really think I do need to know more about how other people perceive me. I was really surprised at what Gary said.

Leader [*to Wayne*]: Good. I can understand you may have reservations, but I'm also pleased that you're willing to take a risk this early in the group. [*To group.*] Because this is the group's first experience in giving feedback to members, I'd like to remind you of the contract not only to help members identify problems but also to share positive observations you may have. As you do so, I'd like you to personalize your statements. I'll help you do this.

The group's first experiences in giving feedback to members are crucial in setting the tone for all that follows. By intervening to guide the group's first tentative efforts to drop facades and to engage at an intimate level, the leader enables the group to have a successful experience and to incorporate attention to positives as a part of its character. As members gain confidence that a group will attend to positives as well as negatives, they will often increase their level of participation and take initiative in soliciting group feedback.

In addition to aiding a group to give positive feedback to individuals, leaders can elicit feedback concerning positive behaviors that have supported the group's accomplishing its task during a session. Such behaviors may include, for example, willingness by members to participate in discussions, to answer questions, and to risk revealing themselves; support shown members; members speaking in turn; the group's giving full attention to the task at hand; acceptance of differing values, beliefs, and opinions; or significant accomplishments by the group or individuals.

If there has been an absence of destructive behaviors that have previously retarded the group's progress in other sessions, leaders might highlight the change. Destructive behaviors absent in an adolescent group, for instance, might include whispering, getting out of one's seat, not attending to the person speaking, verbally and physically "hassling" others, playing with objects, introducing tangential subjects, arguing, interrupting, or the like.

Among the leader's roles is that of aiding members to acknowledge and accept positive feedback, as illustrated in the following:

Kim [*to Pat*]: I know you get discouraged sometimes, but I admire the fact you can manage four children by yourself and still work. I don't think I could ever manage that in a million years.

Pat: I don't always manage it. Actually, I don't do near enough for my children.

Leader: I hear you saying, Pat, that you feel inadequate as a mother—and I'll ask you in a moment whether you'd like to return to those feelings—but right now would you reflect on what you just did?

Pat: I guess I didn't acknowledge Kim's compliment. I didn't feel I deserved it.

Leader: I wonder if others of you have experienced the same feeling when someone has given you positive feedback.

The last response broadens the focus to include the experience of other group members, which may lead into a discussion of the difficulties individuals sometimes encounter in accepting positive feedback.

The leader may wish to help individuals or the entire group to identify dysfunctional cognitive patterns that underlie such discomfort in receiving positive messages (e.g., "I have to do things perfectly" or "Nothing I do can be very good"). The leader may emphasize that the preceding experience illustrates how the group experience can enhance responsiveness to positive feedback.

Increase Effective Communication

Intervening moment by moment to increase the chances of effective communication is particularly vital in the Power and Control stage. Previous chapters have explicated five basic relationship skills that, when possessed by clients, significantly increase their personal efficacy and ability to create satisfying relationships. These skills include (1) positive feedback, (2) empathic listening (the receiver skill), (3) authentic responding (the sender skill), (4) problem solving and decision making, and (5) requesting (a skill for expressing one's needs). In addition, other facets of communication enable members to relate facilitatively as a group, such as taking turns in talking; learning how to explore problems before offering solutions; speaking for themselves, not others; and speaking directly to a person for whom a message is intended. Finally, members benefit from learning to distinguish between effective and noneffective ways of responding and from formulating personal goals to eliminate negative stylistic responses from their communication repertoires, a matter discussed in depth in Chapter 7.

Leaders increase the probability of members adopting effective communications by heavily utilizing and modeling these skills themselves. In addition, leaders aid acquisition of skills by adopting the role of "coach" and intervening to shape the playout of communications in the group, as illustrated in the following:

- [*Eliminating negative communications*] "I'd like you to shy away from labeling, judging, lecturing, criticism, sarcasm, 'shoulds' and 'oughts,' and the words 'always' and 'never.' As per our group contract, try to give self-reports rather than indirect messages that put down, judge, or otherwise focus on another person."

- [*Personalizing messages*] "That was an example of a 'you' message. I'd like you to try again, this time by starting out with the pronoun 'I.' Try to identify your feelings, or what you want or need."

- [*Talking in turn*] "Right now several of you are speaking at the same time. Try to hold to the guideline that we all speak in turn. Your observations are too important to miss."

- [*Speaking directly to each other*] "Right now you're speaking to the group but I think your message is meant for _____. If so, then it would be better to talk directly to him."

- [*Exploratory questions*] "Switching from closed- to open-ended questions right now could help Liz to tell her story in her own way." (Leader explains difference between these two modes of questioning.)

- [*Listening*] "Try to listen carefully to what she's saying. Help her to let out her feelings and to get to the source of the problem."

- [*Problem exploration vs. problem solving*] "When the group offers advice too quickly, members aren't able to share their deeper-level feelings or to reveal a problem in its entirety. We may need to allow Richard five to ten minutes to share his concerns before the group offers any observations. The timing of advice is critical as we try to help members share and solve problems."

- [*Authenticity*] "Could you risk and tell the group what you're feeling at this very moment? I can see you choking up and I think it would be good for the group to know what you're experiencing."

- [*Requesting*] "You've just made a complaint about the group. On the flip side of any complaint is a request. Tell the group what would help. Make a request."

Intervening moment by moment to shape the communications of members, as in the instances illustrated above, increases the therapeutic potential of a group.

Create Therapeutic Norms

As explicated earlier, leaders must be concerned about the nature of the norms that evolve in the group. It is in the Power and Control stage of a group that many of the group patterns are forming and that the leader can intervene to shape the power structure, the stylistic communications of the group, and ways the group "chooses" to negotiate and solve problems.

In shaping the group's therapeutic norms, leaders need to intervene, for example, in the following instances:

- Distractive behavior substantially interferes with the group's task.

- One or more members monopolize the group's airtime.

- One or more members are "out of step" with the group process and/or experience strong feelings such as hurt, anger, disgust, disappointment, or disapproval.

- Several members or the entire group begin to talk about one member.

- Behavior of members is incompatible with the governing guidelines set by the group.

- Socializing interferes with the task of the group.

- Members intellectualize about emotionally loaded material.

- One or more members manifest hostility in the form of caustic remarks, jokes, sarcasm, or criticism.

- One or more members or the group begin interrogating or ganging up on someone.
- The group offers advice or suggestions to a member without first encouraging that member to fully explore a problem.
- Members ramble or participate in lengthy recitations that ignore self-disclosure of current problems, feelings, thoughts, or reactions.
- There is silence or withdrawal by one or more members or the group itself seems to be "shut down."
- A member adopts a "co-leader" role.
- The group scapegoats one of its members, blaming that member for group problems.
- One member attacks another, who reacts by defending, attacking, or withdrawing.

When members manifest obstacles such as the preceding, it is the leader's role to focus the group's attention on what is occurring in the "here and now." Leaders may simply document what they see by describing specific behaviors or the progression of events that have occurred and then request group input. Once the group focuses on the problem, it is the task of leaders to facilitate discussion and problem solving rather than to take decisive action themselves. The responsibility for resolution needs to rest with the group.

S. Henry (1992) supports the vital function of leaders in the Power and Control stage in turning issues back to the group, observing:

> When the members are vying for ownership of the group, the wisest intervention for the worker is to join their struggle and to put issues and decisions back to them. The worker does not wholly give up her or his power, but holds back from what had previously been a more directive and active performance (p. 148)

However, Henry notes, at the end of a particularly conflict-filled episode or session, leaders need to intervene with a proposal to process what has occurred and to lead that processing. In such instances, leaders do not turn issues back to the group but opt, in the interest of closure and resolution, to "clarify what information people carry away from the confrontation, and to see what level of discomfort people are experiencing" (p. 151).

Although leaders need to avoid premature closure on heated issues in a group, they must intervene immediately to refocus process when group members begin to criticize, label, "cut down" others, or argue among themselves. Leaders may make the assumption that letting members verbally "fight it out" when they have conflicts is cathartic or helpful. To the contrary, ample research indicates that aggression begets aggression and that not intervening in conflict only encourages members to continue in the same mode of venting their anger. A leader's passive stance could lead to conflict escalating to the point that it breaks out into physical fighting. In instances of serious disruption, a leader's lack of intervention may "prove" to members who are scrutinizing the leader's behavior that it is dangerous to take risks in the group because the leader will not protect them.

It is vital that leaders intervene assertively when dysfunctional group processes warrant such interventions. Otherwise, the leader is in a "one-down" position in the group and loses his or her ability to effect change. Leaders must thus be willing to respond decisively when significant group disruption occurs, if necessary by clapping their hands loudly, standing up, speaking louder than group members, or putting themselves between members who are arguing.

In intervening in group-as-a-whole matters (as contrasted to focusing on individual attitudes or behaviors), leaders increase the effectiveness of their interventions by focusing on a pair, a trio, a foursome, or the group, thus avoiding the singling out of one person or inadvertently getting caught in "siding." In fact, rarely does the destructive or self-defeating behavior of one member or a subgroup not directly affect other members. Rather, such behavior not only affects the group but may also be fostered or reinforced by the group. Intervening to place responsibility on the group for owning its part in maintaining dysfunctional behavior by members or by the group as a whole serves the best interest of all parties.

Consider, for instance, the following leader intervention in an adolescent group: "Mark and Jeannie, you're whispering again and interrupting the group. We need your attention." This message places the responsibility for the distractive behavior solely upon the two members and does not take into account what is happening with the group. As a consequence, the leader's message is more likely to reinforce negative behavior than to encourage positive change for the following reasons:

- It may polarize the group by aligning the leader with members who are irritated by this behavior ("the good guys") and against the two offending members ("the bad guys").

- The leader's solution ("we need your attention") circumvents group handling or problem solving of the matter.

- The leader's blunt intervention fails to attend to the message inherent in the distractible behavior that "this group does not meet our needs at the moment"—a view that may be shared but not expressed by other members.

A guideline to formulating interventions that confront dysfunctional behavior is that the behavior must be analyzed in the context of the group process, with the leader considering how such behavior affects and is affected by group members. This is illustrated by the following message to the same situation:

- "I'm concerned about what is happening right now—several of you are not participating; some of you are whispering; one of you is writing notes; a few of you are involved in the discussion. As individuals, you appear to be at different places with the group and I'd like to check out what each of you is experiencing right now."

The preceding message focuses on all group members, neutrally describes behavior that is occurring, and encourages the group process. By not imposing a solution on the group, the leader assumes a facilitative rather than an authoritarian role, the latter being the "kiss of death" to productive group discussion.

Intimacy and Differentiation Stages

The Intimacy and Differentiation stages of a group constitute its working phase. In initial stages of a group's evolution, critical issues at stake were those of trust versus mistrust, the struggle of power, and self-focus versus focus on others. In the working phase, however, issues shift to those of disclosure versus anonymity, honesty versus game playing, spontaneity versus control, acceptance versus rejection, cohesion versus fragmentation, and responsibility versus blaming (Corey & Corey, 1992).

In the working phase, the leader continues to promote conditions that aid members to make healthy choices in resolving issues such as the preceding, for example, by straightforwardly addressing and resolving conflict, openly disclosing personal problems, taking responsibility for their problems, and making pro-group choices.

In the relaxed stance of the working phase, leaders have more opportunities to intensify therapeutic group conditions. Leaders may focus on refining feedback processes, coaching members to give immediate feedback, to make such feedback specific rather than global, to render feedback in nonjudgmental ways, and to give feedback regrading strengths as well as problem behaviors (Corey & Corey, 1992).

Leaders can also enhance individual and group growth by focusing on the universality of underlying issues, feelings, and needs that members seem to share, as Corey and Corey indicate:

> *The circumstances leading to hurt and disappointment may be very different from person to person or from culture to culture. But the resulting emotions have a universal quality. Although we may not speak the same language or come from the same society, we are connected through our feelings of joy and pain. It is when group members no longer get lost in the details of daily experiences and instead share their deeper struggles with these universal human themes that a group is most cohesive. (p. 209)*

Common themes identified by Corey and Corey include

fears of rejection, feelings of loneliness and abandonment, feeling of inferiority and failure to live up to others' expectations, painful memories, guilt and remorse over what they have and have not done, discovery that their worst enemy lives within them, need for and fear of intimacy, feelings about sexual identity and sexual performance, and unfinished business with their parents. (p. 210)

This list is not exhaustive, note Corey and Corey, but "merely a sample of the universal human issues that participants recognize and explore with each other as the group progresses" (p. 210).

In the working phase leaders also support a continuing trend toward differentiation, in which members establish their uniqueness and separateness from others. Leaders do not create these expressions of differences but rather stimulate or advance them, for example, noting when a member reveals

a heretofore hidden talent, or access to a resource that was previously believed inaccessible, or possession of a needed skill or perspective. A member may articulate a previously unspoken need, or offer an interpretation not thought of by the others, or pose a question that catalyzes or synthesizes a piece of the group's work. (Henry, 1992, p. 183)

The working phase is a time of intensive focus on achieving members' goals. Much of the group's work during this phase is devoted to carrying out contracts developed in initial sessions. Toseland and Rivas (2001) emphasize that leaders should not assume that members continue to be aware of their goals as the group progresses. Rather, a major role of leaders is to confirm goals periodically and promote organized and systematic efforts to work on them, thus assuring that individuals and leader remain focused on the same issues.

The leader assumes the ongoing responsibility of monitoring the time allocated to each member to work on goals. Toseland and Rivas suggest that the leader help each member to work in turn. Should a

group spend considerable time aiding one member to achieve goals, leaders should generalize concepts to other members so that everyone benefits. They should also encourage members to share relevant personal experiences with the member receiving help, thus establishing a norm for mutual aid. In addition, they should check on the progress of members who did not receive due attention and encourage their participation in the next session. These authors state, "This helps to prevent repeated and prolonged attention to a few members and reduces the possibilities that some members will avoid working on their contracts" (p. 202).

Finally, leaders should establish a systematic method of monitoring treatment goals and tasks in sessions. Without such procedures, monitoring may be haphazard and focused on those who are more assertive and highly involved; those who are less assertive or resistant will not receive the same attention. Without systematic monitoring, tasks to be completed between sessions do not receive the proper followup. As Toseland and Rivas (2001) suggest, members are frustrated when they have completed a task between sessions and have no opportunity to report on the results. The expectation of a weekly progress report helps members' motivation to work toward goals between sessions, reduces the necessity of reminding them of their contract agreements, and aids them in gaining a sense of independence and accomplishment.

In the working phase leaders also intensify efforts to aid members to analyze the rationality of thoughts and beliefs that maintain or exacerbate dysfunctional behavior. Group members, say Toseland and Rivas (2001), may

(1) overgeneralize from an event, (2) selectively focus on portions of an event, (3) take too much responsibility for events that are beyond their control, (4) think of the worst possible consequence of future events, (5) engage in either/or dichotomous thinking, and (6) assume that because certain events have led to particular consequences in the past they will automatically lead to

the same consequences if they reoccur in the future. (p. 288)[3]

Termination

Termination is a difficult stage for members who have invested heavily in the group; have experienced intensive (and often unheralded) support, encouragement, and understanding; and have received effective aid for problems. Leaders must be astute in sensitively employing interventions to aid members to successfully complete the termination stage, which Mahler (1969) has called a "commencement." To this end we refer you to Chapter 20, which identifies significant termination issues and also change-maintenance strategies that may be utilized with clients in facilitating termination and generalizing changes to the outside world. Here, however, we address aspects of the leader's role that are specific to facilitating planned endings in groups. Leaders may aid groups to complete their "commencement" proceedings by adopting strategies such as the following:

- Ensure that the issues and concerns worked on by the group are representative of those that members encounter outside the group. Also assure that the group is a place where members get honest feedback about how their behavior is likely to be received outside the group and a setting where they may get help in coping with those reactions (Toseland & Rivas, 2001).

- Use a variety of different situations and settings throughout the group experience to aid members to practice and acquire skills, thus better preparing them for the multifaceted situations they encounter outside the group (Toseland & Rivas, 2001).

- Aid members during the last few group sessions to discuss how they will respond to possible setbacks in an unsympathetic environment. Build member confidence in existing coping skills and abilities to solve problems independently. Also teach therapeutic principles that underlie interventive methods, such as those inherent in as-

sertiveness, effective communication, or problem solving (Toseland & Rivas, 2001).

- Share leader reactions to endings as a way of helping members to identify their own conflicted feelings and any sense of abandonment, anger, sadness, or loss.

- Reinforce positive feelings of members regarding themselves and the group, including the potency that comes from realizing they are capable of accomplishing goals and assuming responsibility for their own lives; the sense of satisfaction, pride, and usefulness in being able to help others; and the sense of growth and of accomplishment in successfully completing the group experience (Lieberman & Borman, 1979; Toseland & Rivas, 2001).

- Aid review and integration of learning by helping members to put into words what has transpired between themselves and the group from the first to the final session and what they have learned about themselves and others. Also solicit what members were satisfied and unsatisfied with in the group and ways in which sessions could have had greater impact. Finally, ask members to spontaneously recall moments of conflict and pain as well as moments of closeness, warmth, humor, and joy in the group (Corey & Corey, 1992).

- Suggest to members several sessions before termination that they consider using the remaining time to complete their own agenda. Leaders may ask the question, "If this were the last session, how would you feel about what you have done, and what would you wish you had done differently?" (Corey & Corey, 1992, p. 229).

- Facilitate the finishing of unfinished business between members by utilizing an exercise suggested by S. Henry (1992, p. 124) in which each person, in turn, says in a few short phrases, "What I really liked was the way you . . . (supply a specific behavior exchanged between the persons, such as 'always gave me positive strokes when I could finally say something that was hard for me to say')," and then, "But I wish we . . . (supplying a specific wish for a behavioral exchange between the two persons that did not occur, such as 'had made more opportunity to talk to each other more directly')." Use this exercise, Henry recommends, not to generate new issues but to bring closure to the present situation.

- Solicit feedback from the group regarding areas in which members could productively focus once they leave the group. Consider asking members to formulate their own individual change contracts, which may be referred to once the group ends, and request that each member review these contracts with the group (Corey & Corey, 1992).

- Engage individual members in relating how they have perceived themselves in the group, what the group has meant to them, and what growth they have made. Ask remaining members to give feedback regarding how they have perceived and felt about that person, including measured feedback that helps members strengthen the perceptions that they gained during the course of the group (e.g., "One of the things I like best about you is . . . " "One way I see you blocking your strengths is . . . " "A few things that I hope you'll remember are . . . ") (G. Corey, 1990, p. 512).

- Utilize evaluative measures to determine the success of the group and the leader's interventions. Such measures have the following benefits: (1) address the leader's professional concerns about the specific effects of interventions; (2) help leaders improve their leadership skills; (3) demonstrate to agencies or funding sources the efficacy of the group; (4) help leaders assess the member and group progress in accomplishing agreed-upon objectives; (5) allow members to express their satisfactions and dissatisfactions with the group; and (6) give leaders the opportunity to develop knowledge that can be shared with others who are using group methods for

similar purposes and in similar situations (K. E. Reid, 1991; Toseland & Rivas, 2001).

NEW DEVELOPMENTS IN SOCIAL WORK WITH GROUPS

There is increased interest in the use of social work groups for empowerment. For example, E. Lewis (1991) notes the influences of feminist theory and liberation theology as resources for an empowerment-focused social group work. Feminist theory is egalitarian, participatory, and validates each person's life experience in context. On the other hand, liberation theology focuses on the participation in economic and political action by those persons most vulnerable to injustice (E. Lewis, 1991). For example, Cox has described how women welfare recipients have learned to advocate for themselves with social services and other agencies through participation in empowerment-oriented groups (Cox, 1991). Meanwhile, other writers are focusing on the special needs of persons of color and immigrant client groups (Congress & Lynn, 1994). Finally, Tolman and Molidor have shown in a review of the research on social work with groups in the decade of the 1980s that cognitive behavioral groups dominated this research with many programs addressing the social skills of children (Tolman & Molidor, 1994).

As described in Chapter 11, social workers are beginning to explore the potentials of technology to enhance the delivery of service to clients through groups. Persons who are home bound or find attendance at agency settings difficult may yet be able to experience the support and benefit of groups through the medium of telephone, e-mail, or Web. Leaders have to be more active in guiding process and drawing out implications for feelings and tone that are masked by the medium of communication. This may include development of conventions or signals for indicating emotions in content (Schopler, Galinsky, & Abell, 1997). As access to such media increases for populations served by social workers, it behooves social workers to take advantage of the media to reach groups who cannot be reached by conventional means. In other cases, issues about relative advantage or disadvantage to groups will be addressed according to their access to media.

WORK WITH TASK GROUPS

As described in Chapter 11, a significant aspect of professional social work practice involves performance in task and work groups. In contrast to treatment groups, task groups try to accomplish a purpose, produce a product, or develop policies (Ephross & Vassil, 1988). Hence you are likely to experience participation in task groups throughout your career, starting with academic task groups as students and continuing as staff members and eventually leaders of such groups in your practice. Effective participation in task groups is not solely reliant on the skills of the formal leaders of the group. For example, social workers have often been effective participants in interdisciplinary teams through their knowledge of group processes. Social workers can assist task groups particularly in identifying problems to focus on, getting members involved, paying attention to stages of development, and managing conflict.

Problem Identification

Leaders can help groups effectively identify problems that the group is capable of solving, that are within the group's domain, and that, among many to choose from, would provide a meaningful focus (Toseland & Rivas, 2001). It is useful in this process to help the group avoid responding prematurely with solutions before the problem is well defined. In defining appropriate problems and goals, the group can be helped through techniques such as brainstorming and nominal group techniques to consider an array of possibilities before selecting a focus. Brainstorming includes expression of a variety of opinions without evaluating them. The nominal group technique is one in which members privately list potential problems and rank them (Toseland & Rivas, 2001). The

group then proceeds to take one potential problem from each member until all are listed, before proceeding to evaluate and rank them as a group.

Getting Members Involved

All members of the group need to have a clear understanding of the functions of the group, to have input into the agenda and decision making. Roles can be assigned such that members will have to depend on each other to get the work of the group accomplished (Toseland & Rivas, 2001). Background papers often need to be circulated to get all members to the appropriate level of information. It is often helpful to conduct the preceding suggested brainstorming exercises in small groups that facilitate member interaction. Recognition of the particular skills, experiences, and perspectives that different members bring can also facilitate more confident sharing by new members.

Awareness of Stages of Development

The stages of group development also occur in task groups though not unidirectionally, as some issues will recur, taking the group back to revisit earlier stages. In the preaffiliation stage, individuals enter with varying hopes for the group because common goals have not yet been established. Early development of identity with the group may be influenced by the fact that frequently some members of the group know and work with each other in other capacities. For example, some members of task groups may be colleagues from the same unit or may have worked together on other projects in the past.

The power and control phase in task groups often occurs around competition for which programs or ideas the group will adopt. Conflict about ideas is to be expected, as it is necessary to well-developed discussions and products and hence should not be avoided. Too often, task groups avoid conflict by evasion, even tabling an issue when enough facts are available to make a decision. Establishing norms at this stage in which differing options are sought and evaluated on their own merits aids the group in accomplishing its objectives.

Leaders should attempt, in fact, to stimulate a conflict of ideas while managing and controlling conflict of persons and personalities. Failure to achieve this results in a diminution of the potential contribution of members and a less complete product. Without such healthy conflict, there is danger of "group think," a condition in which alternative views or options are not expressed or taken seriously. Leaders (and members) can assist other members in expressing the reasons behind conflicting opinions, clarifying what information needs to be developed to answer questions raised in the conflicts. Group leaders and members can hence use communication skills described earlier in this book to reframe communications, making them understandable to all parties, reflecting, probing, and making summarizing statements. Group leaders can contribute to a productive working atmosphere by conveying that each member has something to contribute and maintaining civility by not allowing anyone or his or her ideas to be degraded (Toseland & Rivas, 2001).

Summary

This chapter has focused on knowledge and skill you will need in effectively intervening in social groups for a variety of purposes. By applying your knowledge of stages of development, leadership, norms, and power structures, you will be able to help groups reach their goals more effectively. In the next chapter, we move to enhancing your knowledge and skills in managing obstacles to growth with individuals.

Internet Resources

You can find useful resources with InfoTrac® by entering the keywords "group problem solving" to access Friedman, M. J. (1996). Facilitating productive meetings. (Training 101). *Training & Development, 50* (10). There are additional useful connections and information at the website for the Association for the Advancement of Group Work at *http://www.aaswg.org/*.

Notes

1. We also refer you to Hartford (1971), S. Henry (1992), and Corey and Corey (1992), sources from which we have drawn information on filling in the Garland, Jones, and Kolodny model.

2. K. E. Reid (1991) has reviewed procedures for evaluating outcome in groups, including group testimonials, content analysis of audio- or videotapes, several forms of sociometric analysis, self-rating instruments, and other subjective measures. We refer you to Reid (1991) and to G. Corey (1990) for further discussion of such vital evaluative measures.

3. Though it is beyond the scope of this chapter to provide details, techniques abound in the literature to address the preceding issues and other self-defeating client attitudes, including those found in Meichenbaum (1977), Mahoney (1974), and Burns (1980). Both Toseland and Rivas (2001) and S. D. Rose (1989) offer specific ways of altering cognitions within a group context.

CHAPTER 18

Additive Empathy, Interpretation, and Confrontation

CHAPTER OVERVIEW

This chapter builds on the skills introduced in Chapters 5 and 6 to assist clients in deeper understanding of their own behavior, that of others, and their options in exploring change. In this regard, appropriate timing for and uses of confrontation are presented as a means of gaining greater self-knowledge and assisting clients in making decisions informed about their potential consequences.

THE MEANING AND SIGNIFICANCE OF CLIENT SELF-AWARENESS

Self-awareness is a priceless ingredient generally acknowledged as essential to sound mental health. Humans have long known of the profound importance of self-awareness, as reflected by Socrates, the ancient Greek philosopher, in his often-quoted admonition, "Know thyself." Self-awareness is often sought by voluntary clients and is indispensable to the helping process they seek, particularly during the change-oriented phase. People's efforts to solve problems and to change are effective only if they are properly directed, which in turn depends on accurate awareness of behaviors and circumstances that need to be changed. Indeed, many people experience incessant problems in

daily living related to their lack of awareness of forces that produce these problems.

As we employ the term, *self-awareness* refers largely to awareness of forces operating in the present. Social workers thus assist clients to expand their awareness of needs or wants, motives, emotions, beliefs, dysfunctional behaviors, and of their impact on other people. We do *not* use self-awareness to refer to insight into the etiology of problems, for, as we have noted in earlier chapters, people can and do change without this type of insight. On occasion, brief excursions into the past may be productive and enlightening, for example, to determine what qualities attracted marital partners to each other, to identify factors that have contributed to sexual dysfunction, to assess the chronicity of problems, to highlight previous successes, and the like. It is important in making such brief excursions, however, to relate elicited information to *present* work and *present* problems, emphasizing to clients that they can change the present, altering current effects of history but not history itself.

Social workers have numerous tools to assist clients to gain expanded self-awareness, of which additive empathy, interpretation, and confrontation are probably employed most extensively. In this chapter, we define these techniques, specify indications for their use, present guidelines for employing them effectively, and finally, provide skill development exercises.

ADDITIVE EMPATHY AND INTERPRETATION

By now you are aware that empathy on the social worker's part is critical to the helping process. In earlier chapters, we explained various uses of empathy in the initial phase of the helping process. During the action-oriented phase, additive levels of empathy are used to expand clients' self-awareness, to cushion the impact of confrontations (discussed later in this chapter), and to explore and resolve relational reactions and other obstacles to change (which we discuss at length in Chapter 19). Bear in mind that social workers also continue to use reciprocal levels of empathy during the goal attainment phase because the purposes of empathy in the initial phase continue throughout the helping process. The difference is that additive levels of empathy are employed sparingly in the initial phase but occupy a prominent position during the action-oriented phase.

Additive empathic responses go somewhat beyond what clients have expressed and therefore require some degree of inference by social workers. For this reason, these responses are moderately interpretive because they interpret to clients forces operating to produce feelings, cognitions, reactions, and behavioral patterns. Indeed, after an exhaustive study of research involving psychoanalysis, Luborsky and Spence (1978) concluded that interpretation, as employed by psychoanalysts, is basically the same as empathic communication. Insight through *interpretation*, it should be noted, is the "supreme agent" in the hierarchy of therapeutic principles that are basic to psychoanalysis and closely related therapies.

Proponents of several other theories (most notably, client centered, Gestalt, and certain existential theories) have avoided the use of interpretation. Still others (Claiborn, 1982; L. Levy, 1963) maintain that interpretation is essential to the counseling process, regardless of theoretical orientation, and that many behaviors of social workers (whether intentional or not) perform interpretive functions. Semantic and conceptual confusion has contributed to the divergence in views, but recent writings have tended to sharpen concepts and to reduce vagueness and confusion.

Based on Levy's (1963) conceptualization, Claiborn (1982) posits that interpretation, whatever the theoretical orientation, "presents the client with a viewpoint discrepant from the client's own, the function of which is to prepare or induce the client to change in accordance with that viewpoint" (p. 442). Viewed in this light, interpretation assists clients to view their problems from a different perspective, the desired effect of which is to open up new possibilities for remedial courses of action. This generic view, which emphasizes a *discrepant viewpoint*, is sufficiently broad to encompass many change-oriented techniques identified in different theories, including refraining (Watzlawick, Weakland, & Fisch, 1974); relabeling (Barton & Alexander, 1981); positive connotation (Selvini-Palazzoli, Boscolo, Cecchin, & Prata, 1974); positive reinterpretation (Hammond et al., 1977); additive empathy, and traditional psychoanalytic interpretations. The content of interpretations concerning the same clinical situation thus can be expected to vary according to the theoretical allegiances of social workers; however, research (summarized by Claiborn, 1982) indicates that "interpretations differing greatly in content seem to have a similar impact on clients" (p. 450).

Levy (1963) classifies interpretations in two categories, *semantic* and *propositional*. Semantic interpretations describe clients' experiences according to the *social worker's* conceptual vocabulary (e.g., "By 'frustrated,' I gather you mean you're feeling hurt and disillusioned"). Semantic interpretations thus are closely related to additive empathic responses. Propositional interpretations involve the social worker's notions or explanations that assert causal relationships among factors involved in clients' problem situations (e.g., "When you try so hard to avoid displeasing others, you displease yourself and end up resenting others for taking advantage of you").[1]

Social workers should avoid making interpretations or additive empathic responses (we are using the terms interchangeably) that are far removed from the awareness of clients. Research (Speisman, 1959) has indicated that moderate interpretations (those that reflect feelings that lie at the margin of the client's experiencing) facilitate self-exploration and self-awareness, whereas deep interpretations engender resistance. Because the latter are remote from clients' experiencing, they appear illogical and irrelevant to clients, who therefore tend to reject them despite the fact that such interpretations may be accurate. The following is an example of such an inept, deep interpretation:

Client: My boss is a real tyrant. He never gives anyone credit, except for Fran. She can do no wrong in his eyes. He just seems to have it in for me. Sometimes I'd like to punch his lights out.

Social worker: Your boss seems to activate the same feelings you had toward your father. You feel he favors Fran, who symbolizes your favored sister. It's your father who you feel was the real tyrant, and you're reliving your resentment toward him. Your boss is merely a symbol of him.

Understandably, the client would likely reject and perhaps resent this interpretation. Though the social worker may be accurate (the determination of which is purely speculative), the client is struggling with feelings toward his boss. To shift the focus to feelings toward his father misses the mark entirely from the client's perspective.

The following interpretation, made in response to the same client message, would be less likely to create opposition because it is linked to recent experiences of the client:

• "So you really resent your boss because he seems impossible to please and shows partiality toward Fran. [*Reciprocal empathy*.] Those feelings reminded me of similar ones you expressed about two weeks ago. You were talking about how, when your parents spent a week with you on their vacation, your father seemed to find fault with everything you did but raved about how well your sister was doing. You'd previously mentioned he'd always seemed to favor your sister and that nothing you did seemed to please him. I'm wondering if those feelings might be connected with the feelings you're experiencing at work."

In the preceding message, notice that the social worker carefully documented the rationale of the interpretation and offered it tentatively, a matter we discuss later under "Guidelines for Employing Interpretation and Additive Empathy."

Because we discussed, illustrated, and provided exercises related to additive empathy in Chapter 5, we shall not deal with these topics in this chapter. Rather, we limit our discussion to uses of interpretation and additive empathy in expanding clients' self-awareness of (1) deeper feelings, (2) underlying meanings of feelings, thoughts, and behavior, (3) wants and goals, (4) hidden purposes of behavior, and (5) unrealized strengths and potentialities.

DEEPER FEELINGS

Clients often have limited awareness of certain emotions, perceiving them only dimly if at all. Moreover, emotional reactions often involve multiple emotions, but clients may experience only the dominant or surface feelings. Further, some clients experience only negative emotions, such as anger, and are out of touch with more tender feelings including hurt, disappointment, compassion, loneliness, fears, caring, and the like. Additive empathic responses (semantic interpretations) thus assist clients to become aware of emotions that lie at the edge of awareness, enabling them to experience these feelings more sharply and fully, to become more aware of their humanness (including the full spectrum of emotions), and to integrate emerging emotions into the totality of their experience.

Social workers frequently employ additive empathic responses directed at expanding clients' awareness of feelings for several purposes, which we identify and illustrate in the following examples:

1. TO IDENTIFY FEELINGS THAT ARE ONLY IMPLIED OR HINTED AT IN CLIENTS' VERBAL MESSAGES

Client [*in sixth session*]: I wonder if you feel we're making any progress. [*Clients frequently ask questions that embody feelings.*]

Social worker: It sounds as though you're not satisfied with your progress. I wonder if you're feeling discouraged about how it's been going.

2. TO IDENTIFY FEELINGS THAT UNDERLIE SURFACE EMOTIONS

Client: I've just felt so bored in the evenings with so little to do. I went down to the bowling alley and watched people bowl, but that didn't seem to help. Life's just a drag.

Social worker: I'm getting the impression you're feeling empty and pretty depressed. I wonder if you're feeling lonely and wishing you had some friends to fill that emptiness.

3. TO ADD INTENSITY TO FEELINGS CLIENTS HAVE MINIMIZED

Client, 30-year-old mildly retarded, socially isolated woman: It was a little disappointing that Jana [*her childhood friend from another state*] couldn't come to visit. She lost her job and had to cancel her plane reservations.

Social worker: I can see how terribly disappointed you were. In fact, you seem really down even now. You'd looked forward to her visit and made plans. It has been a real blow to you.

4. TO CLARIFY THE NATURE OF FEELINGS CLIENTS EXPERIENCE ONLY VAGUELY

Client: When Ben told me he wanted a divorce so he could marry another woman, I just turned numb. I've been walking around in a daze ever since, telling myself, "This can't be happening."

Social worker: It has been a crushing blow to you. You were so unprepared. It hurts so much it's hard to admit it's really happening.

5. TO IDENTIFY FEELINGS MANIFESTED ONLY NONVERBALLY

Client: My sister asked me to tend her kids while she's on vacation, and I will, of course. [*Frowns and sighs.*]

Social worker: But your sigh tells me you don't feel good about it. Right now the message I get from you is that it seems an unfair and heavy burden to you and that you resent it.

Underlying Meanings of Feelings, Thoughts, and Behavior

Used for this purpose, additive empathy or interpretation assists clients to conceptualize or make meaning of feelings, thoughts, and behavior. Social workers thus assist clients in understanding what motivates them to feel, think, and behave as they do; to grasp how their behavior bears on their problems and goals; and to discern themes and patterns in their thinking, feelings, and behavior. As clients discern similarities, parallels, and themes in their behavior and experiences, their self-awareness gradually expands in much the same way as single pieces of a puzzle fit together, gradually forming discrete entities and eventually coalescing into a coherent whole. The previous interpretation made to the client who resented his boss for favoring a co-worker is an example of this type of additive empathic response (which also fits into the category of a propositional interpretation).

In a more concrete sense, then, social workers may employ this type of interpretation or additive empathy to assist clients to discern that they experience troublesome feelings in the presence of a certain type of person or in certain circumstances. For example, clients may feel depressed in the presence of critical people or feel extremely anxious in situations wherein they must perform (e.g., when expected to give a talk or take a test). Social workers may thus use additive empathy to identify negative perceptual sets and other dysfunctional cognitive patterns that can be modified by employing cognitive restructuring. Clients may attend exclusively to trivial indications of their imperfections and completely overlook abundant evidence of competent and successful performance. Similarly, a social worker may assist a client to discern a pattern of anticipating negative outcomes of relatively minor events and dreading (and avoiding) the events because of perceiving any of the negative outcomes as probable absolute disasters. One client dreaded visiting a lifelong friend who had recently sustained a severe fall, leaving her partially paralyzed. When the social worker explored possible negative events that the client feared might occur if she were to visit the friend, she identified the following:

- "What if I cry when I see her?"
- "What if I stare at her?"
- "What if I say the wrong thing?"

Using an additive empathic response, the social worker replied, "And if you did one of those things, it would be a total disaster?" The client readily agreed. The social worker then further employed cognitive restructuring to assist her to view the situation in realistic perspective by discussing each feared reaction, clarifying that anyone might react as she feared reacting and that if she were to react in any of the feared ways it would be uncomfortable but certainly not a disaster. They discussed the situation further, concluding that she had a certain amount of control over how she reacted rather than being totally at the mercy of circumstances. Following behavioral rehearsal, her fears of disaster gradually dwindled to manageable proportions.

Social workers may also employ this type of additive empathy to enhance clients' awareness of perceptual distortions that adversely affect interpersonal relationships. Parents may reject children because they perceive characteristics in them that they abhor. Previous exploration, however, may have disclosed that parents abhor the same qualities in themselves and project their self-hatred onto their children. By assisting clients to recognize how self-perceptions (which may also be distorted) warp their perceptions of their children, social workers enable them to make discriminations and to perceive and accept their children as unique individuals different from themselves.

Similar perceptual distortions may occur between marital partners, causing spouses to perceive and to respond inappropriately to each other as a result of unresolved and troublesome feelings that derive from earlier relationships with parents of the opposite sex.

Wants and Goals

Another important use of additive empathy is to assist clients to become aware of wants and goals that they imply in their messages but do not fully recognize. Beset by difficulties, people often tend to think in terms of problems and relief from them rather than in terms of growth and change; yet the latter two processes are often implied in the former. When they become more aware of the thrust toward growth implied in their messages, clients often welcome the prospect and indeed may wax enthusiastic. This type of additive empathy not only expands self-awareness, but it also may enhance motivation, as illustrated in the next interchange.

As is apparent in the following excerpt, additive empathic messages that highlight implied wants and goals often result in formulating explicit goals and pave the way to change-oriented actions. Moreover, such messages also play a critical role in arousing hope in dispirited clients who feel overwhelmed by problems and have been unable to discern positive desires for growth manifested in their struggles. This type of message thus plays a key role in the first phase of the helping process and in the change-oriented phase as well.

Client: I'm so sick of always being imposed upon. All of my family just take me for granted. You know, "Good old Ella, you can always depend on her." I'm so fed up with it all I could just chew nails.

Social worker: Just thinking about it gets your hackles up. Ella, it seems to me that what you're saying adds up to an urgent desire on your part to be your own person—to feel in charge of yourself rather than being at the mercy of others' requests or demands.

Client: I hadn't thought of it that way but you're right. That's exactly what I want. If I could just be my own person.

Social worker: Maybe that's a goal you'd like to set for yourself. It seems to fit, and accomplishing it would liberate you from the oppressive feelings you've described.

Client: Yes, yes! I'd like very much to set that goal. Do you really think I could accomplish it?

Expanding Awareness of Motives Underlying Behavior

Social workers sometimes employ interpretations to assist clients to become more fully aware of basic motivations that underlie dysfunctional patterns of behavior. Other people may misinterpret clients' motives, and they themselves may have only a dim awareness of them because of the obscuring effect of their dysfunctional behaviors. Prominent among these motives are the following: to protect tenuous self-esteem (e.g., by avoiding situations that involve any risk of failing), to avoid anxiety-producing situations, and to compensate for feelings of impotency or inadequacy. The following are typical examples of surface behavior and hidden purposes served by the behavior.

1. Underachieving students may exert little effort in school (a) because they can justify failing on the basis of not having really tried (rather than having to face their fears of being inadequate) or (b) because they are seeking to punish parents who withhold approval and love when they fall short of their expectations.

2. Clients may present a facade of bravado to conceal from themselves and others underlying fears and feelings of inadequacy.

3. Clients may set themselves up for physical or emotional pain to expiate for deep-seated feelings of guilt.

4. Clients may engage in self-defeating behavior to validate myths that they are destined to be losers, or to live out life scripts determined by circumstances beyond their control.

5. Clients may avoid relating closely to others to protect against fears of being dominated or controlled.

6. Clients may behave aggressively and/or abrasively because they thereby avoid risking rejection by keeping others at a distance.

Interpretations must be based on substantial supporting information that clients have disclosed previously. Without supporting information, interpretations are little more than speculations that clients are unlikely to accept. Indeed, such speculations often emanate from social workers' projections and are most often inaccurate. Social workers who engage in deep and unfounded psychodynamic interpretations might be best described as "armchair psychoanalysts." Their inept interpretations often are calculated to impress others with their erudition, but the actual effect is often quite the opposite. Clients may regard their interpretations as offensive or may question their competence. The following example illustrates appropriate use of interpretations to expand awareness of underlying motives.

The client, Mr. R, age 33, together with his wife, entered marital therapy largely at his wife's instigation. She complained about a lack of closeness in the relationship and felt rejected because her husband seldom initiated affectional overtures. When she initiated overtures, he typically rebuffed her by pulling back. Mr. R had revealed in the exploratory interviews that his mother had been (and still was) extremely dominating and controlling. He had little warmth for his mother and saw her no more than was absolutely necessary. The following excerpt from an individual session with Mr. R focuses on an event that occurred during the week when the Rs went to a movie. Mrs. R reached over to hold his hand. He abruptly withdrew it, and Mrs. R later expressed her feelings of hurt and rejection. Their ensuing discussion was unproductive, and their communication strained. Mr. R discusses the event that occurred in the theater:

Client: I know Carol was hurt when I didn't hold her hand. I don't know why, but it really turned me off.

Social worker: So you're wondering why you turn off when she reaches for some affectional contact. I wonder what was happening inside of you at that moment. What were you thinking and feeling?

Client: Gee, let me think. I guess I was anticipating she'd do it, and I just wanted to be left alone to enjoy the movie. I guess I resented her taking my hand. Gee, that doesn't make sense when I think about it. Why should I resent holding hands with the woman I love?

Social worker: Jim, I think you're asking an awfully good question—one that's a key to many of the difficulties in your marriage. Let me share an idea with you that may shed some light on why you respond as you do. You mentioned you felt resentful when Carol took your hand. Based on the feelings you just expressed, I'm wondering if perhaps you feel you're submitting to her if you respond positively when she takes the initiative and pull back to be sure you're not letting yourself be dominated by her [*the hidden purpose*]. Another reason for suggesting that is that as you were growing up you felt dominated by your mother and resented her for being that way. Even now you avoid seeing her any more than you have to. I'm wondering if, as a result of your relationship with her, you could have developed a supersensitivity to being controlled by a female so that you resent any behavior on Carol's part that even suggests her being in control. [*The latter part of the response provides the rationale for the interpretation.*]

Unrealized Strengths and Potentialities

Another vital purpose served by interpretation and additive empathy is to expand clients' awareness of their strengths and undeveloped potentialities. Clients' strengths are manifested in varied ways, and it behooves social workers to sensitize themselves to these often subtle manifestations by consciously cultivating a positive perceptual set. This objective is vital, for clients are often preoccupied with their weaknesses. Moreover, becoming aware of strengths tends to arouse clients' hopes and to generate courage to undertake making changes.

Drawing clients' awareness to strengths tends to enhance self-esteem and to foster courage to undertake tasks that involve risking new behaviors. With conscious effort, social workers can become increasingly aware of clients' strengths, even

with clients who possess marked limitations. A mildly mentally retarded and brain-damaged client, for example, lamented to one of the authors that she felt she was a total "zero." In addition to being brain-damaged, she was plagued by numerous phobias, including a fear of leaving home. She commented it had been a major effort for her to canvass the neighborhood soliciting donations for the heart fund. She believed this was a worthy cause, however, and it gave her satisfaction despite the tension and anxiety she experienced. The social worker replied that her action was evidence of an important strength—namely, her caring about other people to the extent she would make such an effort on behalf of unknown others. He added that caring about others is a precious quality that many people lack and that she certainly was not a "zero" in light of this apparent strength. She beamed and guessed maybe she did have some good qualities. This case is but one of the countless examples that could be cited for clients' strengths manifested as they report seemingly mundane events.

GUIDELINES FOR EMPLOYING INTERPRETATION AND ADDITIVE EMPATHY

Considerable finesse is required to employ these skills effectively. The following guidelines will assist you in acquiring this finesse.

1. *Use additive empathy sparingly until a sound working relationship has evolved.* Because these responses go somewhat beyond clients' awareness of self, clients may misinterpret the motives of a social worker and respond defensively. When clients demonstrate they are confident of a social worker's goodwill, they are able to tolerate and often to benefit from additive empathic and interpretative responses. The exceptions to this guideline involve messages that identify (1) wants and goals and (2) strengths and potentialities, both of which are also appropriate in the initial phase of the helping process. Social workers must avoid

identifying strengths excessively in the initial phase, however, for some clients interpret such messages as insincere flattery.

2. *Employ these responses only when clients are engaged in self-exploration or have manifested readiness for the same.* Clients or groups that are not ready to engage in self-exploration are likely to resist social workers' interpretive efforts and may interpret such efforts as unwarranted attempts by social workers to impose their formulations upon them. Exceptions to this guideline are the same as those cited in the preceding guideline.

3. *Pitch these responses to the edge of the client's awareness, and avoid attempting to foster awareness that is remote from clients' current awareness or experiencing.* Clients generally are receptive to responses that closely relate to their experiencing but resist those that emanate from the social worker's unfounded conjectures. It is poor practice to attempt to push clients into rapidly acquiring new insights, for many deep interpretations prove to be inaccurate and produce negative effects, including reducing clients' confidence in social workers, conveying lack of understanding, or engendering resistance. Social workers should not employ interpretive responses until they have amassed sufficient information to be reasonably confident their responses are accurate and should share the supportive information upon which the interpretation is based.

4. *Avoid making several additive empathic responses in succession.* Because interpretation responses require time to think through, digest, and assimilate, a series of such responses tends to bewilder clients.

5. *Phrase interpretive responses in tentative terms.* Because these responses involve a certain degree of inference, there is always the possibility of being in error. Tentative phrasing openly acknowledges that possibility and invites clients to agree or disagree. If social workers present interpretations in an authoritarian or dogmatic manner, however, clients may not feel free to offer candid feedback and may outwardly agree while actually covertly

rejecting interpretations. Tentative phrases include "I wonder if . . . ," "Could it be that your feelings may be related to . . . ?" and "Perhaps you're feeling this way because . . . "

6. *To determine the accuracy of an interpretive response, carefully note clients' reactions after offering the interpretation.* When responses are on target, clients affirm their validity, continue self-exploration by bringing up additional relevant material, or respond emotionally in a manner that matches the moment (e.g., ventilate relevant feelings). When interpretations are inaccurate or are premature, clients tend to disconfirm them (verbally or nonverbally), change the subject, withdraw emotionally, argue or become defensive, or simply ignore the interpretation.

7. *If the client responds negatively to an interpretative response, acknowledge your probable error, respond empathically to the client's reaction, and continue your discussion of the topic under consideration.* To assist you in expanding your skill in formulating interpretive and additive empathic responses, we have provided a number of exercises, together with modeled responses, at the end of the chapter.

CONFRONTATION

Similar to interpretation and additive empathy in that it is a tool to enhance clients' self-awareness and to promote change, confrontation involves facing clients with some aspect of their thoughts, feelings, or behavior that is contributing to or maintaining their difficulties. Social workers, perhaps more than the social workers of other helping professions, have to struggle with a dual focus on both individual rights and social justice. In fact, some argue that the ability to juggle these demands is an essential strength of the profession (Regehr & Angle, 1997). Meanwhile others argue that "there are some activities people can do that put them outside any entitlement to respect . . . some people called clients are not much respected

(Ryder & Tepley, 1993, p. 146). For example, persons who act to harm or endanger others such as the perpetrators of domestic violence or sexual abuse challenge this dual commitment and the ethical obligation described in Chapter 4 of respecting the inherent worth and dignity of all individuals regardless of the acts they may have committed.

In this context, when is confrontation appropriate? With whom? Under what conditions? Is confrontation a skill or a style of practice? In some settings, confrontation became a style of practice rather than a selective skill. As a style of practice, it has been the belief that some clients are so well defended with denial, rationalization, and refusal to accept responsibility that only repeated confrontations will succeed. For example, in work with batterers some have claimed that "almost every word they [batterers] utter is either victim blaming or justification for their violence. So I have to start confronting all of that stuff right from the beginning and it gets very intense" (Pence & Paymar, 1993, p. 21). It was believed that only when the offender admitted responsibility for the behavior and accepted the label of offender could meaningful change occur. If the clients did not accept the label, if they defended themselves, they were labeled as in denial and resistant (W. R. Miller & Sovereign, 1989). Hence, confronting them in an authoritarian and aggressive style (W. R. Miller & Rollnick, 1991) was considered necessary to achieve an admission of guilt, admission that they had a problem and were not in control of their behavior. In short, the clients were expected to give up their own view of the situation and to accept the view of those who had the power to confront them. It was hence assumed that disempowered persons, with no motivation owned by them, incapable of making their own decisions and controlling their behavior, would then accept the formulation of the problem by the social workers and/or group and were expected to cooperate with that formulation (Kear-Colwell & Pollock 1997). If they reacted by showing disagreement and resistance, they were

seen as persisting in denial, lacking motivation, often reflecting pathological personality patterns. This view too often leads to an interactive cycle of confrontation and denial in which the person acts to protect his or her self-esteem by denying charges (W. R. Miller & Sovereign, 1989).

Social workers and theorists in fields such as treatment of domestic abuse perpetrators, persons with addictions, and sexual offenders are questioning whether this style is effective or ethical (Fearing, 1996; Kear-Colwell & Pollock, 1997; Miller & Sovereign, 1989; C. M. Murphy & Baxter, 1997). They are questioning whether intense confrontation of defenses is helpful or whether it may unwittingly reinforce the belief that relationships are based on coercive influences (Murphy & Baxter, 1997). A supportive and collaborative working alliance is more likely to increase motivation in clients. Motivational interviewing is more likely to create dissonance and encourage offenders to own the process. Even in the use of interventions with addicted persons, new approaches acknowledge the importance of developing a positive, respectful approach toward the person receiving the intervention (Fearing, 1996).

Instead of all-purpose confrontation at any time, it is now suggested that it is more useful to be aware of the stage of change the person is at regarding the problematic behavior. Prochaska, DiClemente, and Norcross (1992) have proposed a six-stage process (see Table 18-1) beginning with precontemplation, in which the person has not considered the behavior a problem. In the motivational interviewing approach, it is the social worker's responsibility to pursue a positive atmosphere for change based on accurate empathic understanding, mutual trust, acceptance, and understanding of the world from the offenders' perspective (Kear-Colwell & Pollock, 1997). In this exploration, the focus is on the offending behavior and its effects and origins, not on the person of the offender (Kear-Colwell & Pollock, 1997). The effort is to be persuasive by creating an awareness that the person's problem behavior is dissonant with personal goals. By engaging in a risk-benefit analysis, the social worker assists the client in

STAGE	CHARACTERISTIC BEHAVIOR	SOCIAL WORKER TASK
Precontemplation	Client does not believe that he or she has a problem; considered unmotivated by others	Raise awareness of concerns held by others; stimulate dissonance with risk-reward analysis
Contemplation	Aware of existence of problem but not moved to action; appears ambivalent; shows awareness, then discounts it	Attempt to tip decisional balance by exploring reasons to change; strengthen confidence in change as a possibility
Preparation	Recognizes problem; asks what can be done to change; appears motivated	Help client plan appropriate course of action
Action	Implements plan of action	Develop plan to implement action; plan details to make it possible (e.g., transportation, child care)
Maintenance	Sustains change through consistent application of strategies	Identify strategies to prevent lapses and relapse
Relapse	Slips into problematic behavior and may return to precontemplation stage	Attempt to return to contemplation without becoming stuck or demoralized; reinforce achievement; treat with respect

Table 18-1 Stages of Change Model
Source: Adapted from Kear-Colwell and Pollock (1997) and Prochaska, DiClemente, & Norcross (1992).

deciding whether it makes sense to explore a change in order to better reach his or her own goals. The goal would then be to assist the client to make a decision. Once a client has decided to act, then the form of influence can move to helping him or her decide what action to take. For example, having decided to deal with a domestic violence problem, he can be helped to consider alternatives about how to go about it. When a decision has been made, then efforts need to be aimed at planning useful action to reach the goal. When a change has occurred, efforts are aimed at exploring in detail the contingencies and triggers that have been associated with the behavior. With such knowledge, alternatives can be planned and practiced for avoiding a relapse into the offending behavior.

Confrontation is most likely to be heard when it comes from a source liked and respected by the client. Consequently, confrontations that occur early in contact are often not accurately heard or heeded. Nevertheless, social workers sometimes have responsibilities to confront clients with law violations and dangers to themselves and others before a helping relationship has developed. Such confrontations should be sparing, given the likelihood that they will not be heeded so early in contact (R. H. Rooney, 1992).

In the middle phase of work, social workers employ confrontation to assist clients to achieve awareness of forces blocking progress toward growth and goal attainment and to enhance their motivation to implement efforts toward change. Confrontation is particularly relevant when clients manifest blind spots to discrepancies or inconsistencies in their thoughts, beliefs, emotions, and behavior that tend to produce or to perpetuate dysfunctional behavior. Of course, blind spots in self-awareness are universal among human beings because all humans suffer from the limitation of being unable to step out of their perceptual fields and look at themselves objectively.

Additive empathy and confrontation have much in common. Skillful confrontations embody consideration of clients' feelings that underlie obstacles to change. Because fears are often involved in obstacles to change, skill in relating with high levels of empathy is prerequisite to using confrontation effectively. Indeed, effective confrontation is an extension of empathic communication because the focus on discrepancies and inconsistencies derive from a deep understanding of clients' feelings, experiences, and behavior.

It is important for social workers to have a range of confrontation skills and not to confront primarily to vent their frustration with lack of progress. Social workers do better to consider confrontation on a continuum ranging from fostering *self-confrontation* at the lower end of the continuum to assertive confrontation at the higher end (R. H. Rooney, 1992). That is, clients can often be engaged quickly in self-confrontation by asking them questions that cause them to reflect on the relation between their behaviors and their own values. Skillfully designed intake forms can serve a similar function, asking potential clients to reflect on concerns and their perceptions of the causes. Such confrontations are subtle, respectful, and rarely engender strong client opposition. As clients gain expanded awareness of themselves and their problems through self-exploration, they tend to become aware of and to confront discrepancies and inconsistencies themselves. Self-confrontation is generally preferable to social worker–initiated confrontation because the former is less risky and because clients' resistance to integrating insights is not an obstacle when they initiate confrontations themselves. Clients vary widely in the degree to which they engage in self-confrontation. Emotionally mature, introspective persons engage in self-confrontations frequently, whereas persons who are out of touch with their emotions, who lack aware-

ness of their impact on others, and who blame others or circumstances for their difficulties are least likely to engage in self-confrontation.

Inductive questioning can be a form of confrontation that is more active on the social worker's part but still conveyed in a respectful manner. The social worker asks questions that lead the client to consider potential discrepancies between thoughts, values, beliefs, and actions. Also, when the therapist asks a question that relates to facts rather than one that requires the client to label himself or herself, the question is more likely to be effective. For example, asking a client with a chemical dependency problem "Are you powerless over alcohol?" would require the client to essentially label himself an alcoholic. On the other hand, "Do you ever have blackouts? Do you find it easier to bring up a problem with another person when you have had something to drink? Do you ever find that once you begin drinking you can't easily stop?" are questions that, taken together, raise the possibility that drinking is a problem that might need attention (Citron, 1978).

When a danger is imminent, the social worker may not be able to rely on the tactful self-confrontation facilitated by inductive questioning, but rather must engage in a more assertive confrontation in which the connection between troubling thoughts, plans, values, and beliefs must be stated in declarative form, connecting them for the client. Such assertive confrontation is a more high-risk technique because clients may interpret confrontations as criticisms, put-downs, or rejections. Paradoxically, the risk of these reactions is greatest among the groups of clients who must be confronted most often because they rarely engage in self-confrontation. These clients tend to have weak self-concepts and are therefore prone to read criticism into messages when none is intended. Moreover, ill-timed and poorly executed confrontations may be perceived by clients as verbal assaults and may seriously damage helping relationships. Using confrontations therefore requires keen timing and finesse. Social workers must make special efforts to convey helpful intent and goodwill as they employ confrontations. Otherwise, they may engender hostility or offend and alienate clients.

Effective assertive confrontations embody four elements: (1) expression of concern; (2) a description of the client's purported goal, belief, or commitment; (3) the behavior (or absence of behavior) that is inconsistent or discrepant with the goal, belief, or commitment; and (4) the probable negative outcomes of the discrepant behavior. The format of a confrontive response may be depicted as follows:

I'm concerned because you (want)
(believe)
(are striving to)

_____
(describe desired outcome)

but your _____
(describe discrepant action, behavior, or inaction)

is likely to produce _____
(describe probable negative consequence)

This format is purely illustrative. You may organize these elements in varying ways, and we encourage you to be innovative and to develop your own style. For example, you may challenge clients to analyze the effects of behavior that is incongruous with purported goals or values, as illustrated in the following:

- [*To male on parole*]: "Al, I know the last thing you want is to have to return to prison. I want you to stay out too, and I think you sense that. But I have to level with you. You're starting to hang out with the same bunch you got in trouble with before you went to prison. You're heading in the same direction you were before, and we both know where that leads."

Notice that in the preceding confrontation the social worker begins by making reference to the client's purported goal (remaining out of prison) and expresses a like commitment to the goal. The social worker next introduces concern about the client's behavior (hanging out with the same bunch the client got in trouble with before) that is discrepant with that goal. The social worker concludes the confrontation by focusing on the possible negative consequence of the discrepant behavior (getting into trouble and returning to prison). Notice these same elements in the following additional examples of confrontive responses.

- [*To father in family session*]: "Mr. D, I'd like you to stop for a moment and examine what you're doing. I know you want the children not to be afraid of you and to talk with you more openly. Right? [*Father agrees.*] OK, let's think about what you just did with Steve. He began to tell you about what he did after the school assembly, and you cut him off and got on his case. Did you notice how he clammed up immediately?"

- [*To mother in child welfare system*]: I have a concern I need to share with you. You've expressed your goal of regaining custody of Pete, and we agreed that attending the parents' group was part of the plan to accomplish that goal. This week is the second time in a row you've missed the meeting because you overslept. I'm very concerned you may be defeating yourself in accomplishing your goal."

Because employing assertive confrontation runs the risk of putting clients on the defensive or alienating them, expressing concern and helpful intent is a critical element because it reduces the possibility that clients will misconstrue the motive behind the confrontation. The tone of voice is also vital in conveying helpful intent. If the social worker conveys the confrontation in a warm, concerned tone of voice, the client will be much less likely to feel attacked. If the social worker uses a critical tone of voice, verbal reassurance that criticism was not intended is likely to fall on deaf ears. Keep in mind that people tend to attach more credence to nonverbal aspects of messages than to verbal aspects.

Guidelines for Employing Confrontation

To assist you in employing confrontation effectively, we offer the following guidelines:

1. *When a law violation or imminent danger to self or others is involved, a confrontation must occur no matter how early in the working relationship.* Such confrontations may impede the development of the relationship, but the risk of harm to self and

others is more important than the immediate effect on the relationship.

2. *Whenever possible, avoid confrontation until an effective working relationship has evolved.* This can occur when a client is contemplating action (or inaction) that impedes his or her own goals but is not an imminent danger to self or others. Employing empathic responsiveness in early contacts conveys understanding, fosters rapport, and enhances confidence in the perceptiveness and expertise of the social worker. When a foundation of trust and confidence has been established, clients are more receptive to confrontations and, in some instances, even welcome them.

3. *Use confrontation sparingly.* Keep in mind that confrontation is a potent technique that generally should be employed only when clients' blind spots are refractory to other less risky methods. Some social workers use confrontation frequently, professing it to be a "high-yield" technique. Research by Lieberman, Yalom, and Miles (1973) involving groups refutes this argument. Their findings indicate that destructive group leaders tend to be highly confrontive and challenging persons who frequently attack members and pressure them for immediate change. Based on their findings, these authors concluded that this type of leadership is associated with negative outcomes. Indeed, poorly timed and excessive confrontations can inflict psychological damage on clients. Another reason to employ confrontation judiciously is that some clients may yield to forceful confrontation for reasons that are counterproductive. Seeking to please social workers (or to avoid displeasing them), they may temporarily modify their behavior. But changing merely to comply with expectations of a social worker fosters passivity and dependence, both of which are anathema to actual growth. Some clients already are excessively passive, and pressuring them for compliance only reinforces their dysfunctional behavior.

4. *Deliver confrontations in an atmosphere of warmth, caring, and concern.* As we have previously emphasized, if social workers employ confrontations in a cold, impersonal, or critical way, clients are likely to feel they are being attacked. By contrast, if social workers preface confrontations with genuine empathic concern (as recommended in the paradigm presented earlier), clients are more likely to perceive the helpfulness intended in the confrontation.

5. *Whenever possible, encourage self-confrontations.* Recall from the previous discussion that self-confrontations have decided advantages over social worker–initiated confrontations. Learning by self-discovery fosters independence and enhances the likelihood that clients will act upon newly gained self-awareness. Social workers can encourage self-confrontation by drawing the attention of clients to issues, behaviors, or inconsistencies they may have overlooked and by encouraging them to analyze the situation further. For example, the social worker may directly intervene into dysfunctional interaction and challenge individuals, couples, families, or groups to identify what they are doing. Responses that encourage self-confrontation in such a context include the following:

- "Let's stop and look at what you just did."
- "What did you just do?"

Other inductive question responses that highlight inconsistencies and foster self-confrontation are as follows:

- "I'm having trouble seeing how what you just said (or did) fits with . . . "
- "I can understand how you felt, but how did (describe behavior) make it better for you?"
- "What you're saying seems inconsistent with what you want to achieve. How do you see it?"

Still another technique is useful when clients overlook the dynamic significance of their own revealing expressions or when their manifest feelings fail to match their reported feelings. This technique involves asking them to repeat a message, to listen carefully to themselves, and to consider the meaning of the message. Examples of this technique follow:

- "I want to be sure you realize the significance of what you just said. Repeat it, but this time listen carefully to yourself, and tell me what it means to you."

- [*To marital partner in conjoint interview*]: "Joan just told you something terribly important, and I'm not sure you really grasped it. Could you repeat it, Joan, and I want you to listen very carefully, Bob, and check with Joan as to whether you grasped what she said."

- [*To group member*]: "You just told the group you're feeling better about yourself, but it didn't come through that way. Please say it again, but get in touch with your feelings and listen to yourself."

6. *Avoid using confrontation when clients are experiencing extreme emotional strain.* Confrontations tend to mobilize anxiety, and when clients are under heavy strain, supportive techniques rather than confrontation are indicated. Clients who are overwhelmed with anxiety and/or guilt generally are not receptive to confrontation and do not benefit from it. Rather, confrontations may be detrimental, adding to tension that is already excessive. Confrontation is appropriate for clients who experience minimal inner conflict or anxiety when such reactions would be appropriate in light of their problematic behavior as perceived by others. Self-satisfied and typically insensitive to the feelings and needs of others (whom they cause to be anxious), such clients, popularly referred to as having character disorders, often lack the anxiety needed to engender and maintain adequate motivation. Confrontation, combined with the facilitative conditions, may mobilize the anxiety they need to examine their own behavior and to consider making constructive changes.

7. *Follow confrontations with emphatic responsiveness.* Because clients may take offense to even skillful confrontations, it is vital to be sensitive to their reactions. Clients often do not express their reactions verbally, so you will need to be especially perceptive of nonverbal cues that suggest hurt, anger, confusion, discomfort, embarrassment, or resentment. If clients manifest these or other unfavorable reactions, it is important to explore their reactions and to respond empathically to their feelings. Discussing such reactions provides opportunities for clients to ventilate their feelings and for social workers to clarify their helpful intent and to assist clients to work through negative feelings. If social workers fail to sense negative feelings or clients withhold expressions of them, the feelings may fester and adversely affect the helping relationship.

8. *Expect that clients will respond to confrontations with a certain degree of anxiety.* Indeed, confrontations are employed to produce a temporary sense of disequilibrium that is essential to break an impasse. The anxiety or disequilibrium thus serves a therapeutic purpose in impelling the client to make constructive changes that eliminate the discrepancy that prompted the social worker's confrontation. Empathic responsiveness following confrontations thus is not aimed at diluting this anxiety but rather at resolving untoward reactions that may derive from negative interpretations of the social worker's motives for making the confrontation.

9. *Don't expect immediate change after confrontations.* Although awareness paves the way to change, clients rarely succeed in making changes immediately following acquisition of insight. Even when clients fully accept confrontations, corresponding changes ordinarily occur by increments. Known as working through, this change process involves repeatedly reviewing the same conflicts and the client's typical reactions to them, gradually broadening the perspective to encompass more and more situations to which the changes are applicable. Unfortunately, some naïve social workers press for immediate change, sometimes inflicting psychological damage on their clients, as we noted earlier.

Indications for Assertive Confrontation

As we have previously indicated, confrontations are appropriate (1) when law violations or imminent threats to the welfare and safety of self or others are involved, (2) when discrepancies, inconsistencies, and dysfunctional behaviors (overt or covert) block progress or create difficulties, and (3) when efforts at self-confrontation and inductive questioning have been ineffective in fostering clients' awareness of these behaviors and/or attempts to make corresponding changes. Discrepancies may reside in cognitive/perceptual, emotional, or behavioral functions or may involve interactions between these functions. A comprehensive analysis of types of discrepancies and inconsistencies has been presented elsewhere (Hammond et al., 1977, pp. 286–318); therefore, we merely highlight some of those that most commonly occur.

Cognitive/Perceptual Discrepancies

Many clients manifest dysfunctional behavior that is a product of inaccurate, erroneous, or incomplete information, and confrontations may assist them in modifying their behavior. For example, clients may lack accurate information about indicators of alcoholism, normal sexual functioning, or reasonable expectations of children according to stages of development. Even more common are misconceptions about the self, the most common of which, in the authors' experience, involve self-demeaning perceptions. Even talented and attractive persons may view themselves as inferior, worthless, inadequate, unattractive, stupid, and the like. Such perceptions are often deeply embedded and do not yield to change without extensive working through. Still, confronting with strengths, or raising awareness of other areas of competence, can be helpful in challenging the self-deprecating view. Other cognitive/perceptual discrepancies include interpersonal perceptual distortions, irrational fears, dichotomous or stereotypical thinking, denial of problems, placing responsibility for one's difficulties outside of oneself, failing to discern available alternate solutions to difficulties, and failing to consider consequences of actions. We focused on these categories of dysfunction in Chapter 9.

Affective Discrepancies

Discrepancies in the emotional realm are inextricably linked to the cognitive/perceptual processes, as emotions are shaped by cognitive meanings clients attribute to situations, events, and memories. For example, one may experience intense anger that emanates from a conclusion that another person has intentionally insulted, slighted, or betrayed one. The conclusion is based on a meaning attribution that may involve a grossly distorted perception of another person's intentions. In such instances, social workers assist clients to explore their feelings, to provide relevant detailed factual information, to consider alternate meanings, and to realign their emotions with reality.

Affective discrepancies that social workers commonly encounter include denying or minimizing actual feelings, being out of touch with painful emotions, expressing feelings that are contrary to purported feelings (e.g., claiming to love a spouse or child but expressing only critical or otherwise negative feelings), or verbally expressing a feeling that contradicts feelings expressed nonverbally (e.g., "No, I'm not disappointed," said with a quivering voice and tears in the eyes). Gentle confrontations aimed at emotional discrepancies often pave the way to ventilation of troubling emotions, and many clients appreciate social workers' sensitivity in recognizing their suppressed or unexpressed emotions. If a client appears unready to face painful emotions, the social worker should proceed cautiously and may be wise to defer further exploration of them. Confronting the client vigorously may elicit overwhelming emotions and engender consequent resentment toward the social worker.

Behavioral Discrepancies

Clients may manifest many dysfunctional behavioral patterns or lifestyles that create difficulties for themselves and others. Even though these patterns may be conspicuous to others, clients themselves may have blind spots to their patterns or to the impact of the same on others. Therefore, confrontation may be required to expand their awareness of these patterns and their pernicious effects. In Chapter 9 (Table 9-3), we enumerated many of the myriad dysfunctional patterns that social workers encounter. We will not repeat them here but will highlight certain pervasive categories of dysfunctional behavior.

Irresponsible behavior tends to spawn serious interpersonal difficulties for clients as well as problems with broader society. Neglect of children, weak efforts to secure and maintain employment, undependability in fulfilling assignments, failure to maintain property—these and other like derelictions often result in severe financial, legal, and interpersonal entanglements that may culminate in loss of employment; estrangement from others; and loss of property, child custody, self-respect, and even personal freedom. Irresponsible behavior often pervades the helping process as well, being manifested by tardiness, unwillingness to acknowledge problems, and failure to keep appointments or pay fees. Effective confrontations with such clients require a firm approach couched in expressions of goodwill and concern about wanting to assist the client to avoid adverse consequences of not assuming responsibilities. It is a disservice to clients to permit them to rationalize, deny, and evade responsibility for their actions or inaction. Further, the social worker must counter their tendency to blame others or circumstances for their difficulties by assisting them to recognize that *only they* can reduce the pressures that beset them.

Other common behavioral discrepancies involve repeated actions that are incongruous with purported goals or values. Adolescents may describe ambitious goals that require extensive training or education but make little effort in school, truant frequently, and otherwise behave in ways entirely inconsistent with their goals. Spouses or parents may similarly espouse goals of improving their marital or family life but persistently behave in abrasive ways that further erode their relationships. Confrontations often must be used to assist them to desist from self-defeating behaviors. In some instances, therapeutic binds (a special form of confrontation discussed in Chapter 19) may be employed to supply additional needed leverage to motivate clients to relinquish destructive and unusually persistent patterns of behavior.

Three other common categories of discrepancies or dysfunctional behavior that warrant confrontation are manipulative behavior, dysfunctional communication, and resistance to change. In groups, certain members may attempt to dominate the group, bait group members, play one person against the other, undermine the leader, or engage in other destructive ploys. The price of permitting members to engage in such behaviors may be loss of certain group members, dilution of the group's effectiveness, or premature dissolution of the group. To avert such undesired consequences, the leader may elicit reactions of other members to such behavior and may assist members to confront manipulators with their destructive tactics. Such confrontations should adhere to the guidelines delineated earlier, and the leader should encourage members to invite offending members to join with them in constructively seeking to accomplish the purposes of the group.

Because dysfunctional communication frequently occurs in individual, conjoint, and group sessions, social workers encounter abundant opportunities to employ confrontation to good effect. Intervening during or immediately following dysfunctional communication is a powerful means of enabling clients to experience firsthand the negative effect of their dysfunctional behavior (e.g., interrupting, attacking, claiming, or criticizing). By shifting the focus to the negative reactions of recipients of dysfunctional messages, social workers enable clients to receive direct feedback as to how their behavior offends, alienates, or engenders defensiveness in others, thereby producing effects contrary to their purported goals.

Summary

This chapter has presented confrontation as a vital tool in working through clients' opposition both to change and to relating openly in the helping relationship. If individual clients are left to struggle alone with negative feelings about the helping process or the social worker, their feelings may mount to the extent that they resolve them by discontinuing their sessions. If family members or groups are permitted to oppose change by engaging in distractive, irrelevant, or otherwise dysfunctional behavior, they may likewise lose both confidence in the social workers (for valid reasons) and motivation to continue. For these reasons, social workers must accord highest priority to being helpful to clients who encounter obstacles or may be opposed to change. The next chapter will assist you with the skills for addressing opposition to change.

Internet Resources

Articles related to the content in this chapter can be read and/or downloaded through InfoTrac®, including the following: Witkin, S. (1999). Questions [factors affecting social workers' questions]. *Social Work, 44* (3); Henry, J. (1999). Changing conscious experience: Comparing clinical approaches, practices, and outcomes. *British Journal of Psychology, 90* (4).

SKILL DEVELOPMENT EXERCISES IN ADDITIVE EMPATHY AND INTERPRETATION

To assist you to advance your skill in responding with interpretation and additive empathy, we provide the following exercises. Read each client message, determine the type of response called for, and formulate a written response you would employ if you were in an actual session with the client. As you formulate your responses, keep in mind the guidelines for employing interpretive additive empathic responses. Compare your responses with the modeled responses provided at the end of the exercises.

CLIENT STATEMENTS

1. *White female client* [*to African American male social worker*]: You seem to be accepting of white people, at least you have been of me. But somehow I still feel uneasy with you. I guess it's just me. I haven't really known many black people very well.

2. *Married woman, age 28:* I feel I don't have a life of my own. My life is controlled by *his* work, *his* hours, and *his* demands. It's like I don't have an identity of my own.

3. *Prison inmate, age 31* [*one week before date of scheduled parole, which was canceled the preceding week*]: Man, what the hell's going on with me? Here I've been on good behavior for three years and finally got a parole date. You'd think I'd be damned glad to get out of here. So I get all uptight and get in a brawl in the mess hall. I mean I really blew it, man. Who knows when they'll give me another date?

4. *Male, age 18:* What's the point in talking about going to Trade Tech? I didn't make it in high school, and I won't make it there either. You may as well give up on me—I'm just a dropout in life.

5. *Widow, age 54:* It was Mother's Day last Sunday, and neither of my kids did as much as send me a card. You'd think they could at least acknowledge I'm alive.

6. *Female secretary, age 21:* I don't have any trouble typing when I'm working alone. But if the boss or anyone else is looking over my shoulder, it's like I'm all thumbs. I just seem to tighten up.

7. *Married female, age 26, who is 5 pounds overweight:* When I make a batch of cookies or a cake on the weekend, Terry [*husband*] looks at me with that condemning expression, as though I'm not really trying to keep my weight down. I don't think it's fair just because he doesn't like sweets. I like sweets, but the only time I eat any is on the

weekend, and I don't eat much then. I feel I deserve to eat dessert on the weekend at least.

8. *Disabled male recipient of public assistance (with a back condition caused by recent industrial accident):* This lying around is really getting to me. I see my kids needing things I can't afford to get them, and I just feel—I don't know—kind of useless. There's got to be a way of making a living.

9. *Depressed male, age 53:* Yeah, I know I do all right in my work. But that doesn't amount to much. Anyone could do that. That's how I feel about everything I've ever done. Nothing's really amounted to anything.

10. *Mother, age 29, who has neglected her children:* I don't know. I'm just so confused. I look at my kids sometimes, and I want to be a better mother. But after they've been fighting, or throwing tantrums, or whining and I lose my cool, I feel like I'd just like to go somewhere—anywhere—and never come back. The kids deserve a better mother.

MODELED RESPONSES FOR INTERPRETATION AND ADDITIVE EMPATHY

1. [*To clarify feelings experienced only vaguely*]: "So I gather even though you can't put your finger on why, you're still somewhat uncomfortable with me. You haven't related closely to that many African Americans, and you're still not altogether sure how much you can trust me."

2. [*Implied wants and goals*]: "Sounds like you feel you're just an extension of your husband and that part of you is wanting to find yourself and be a person in your own right."

3. [*Hidden purpose of behavior, underlying feelings*]: "So you're pretty confused about what's happened. Fighting in the mess hall when you did just doesn't make sense to you. You know, Carl, about your getting uptight—I guess I'm wondering if you were worried about getting out—worried about whether you could make it outside. I'm wondering if you might have fouled up last week to avoid taking that risk."

4. [*Underlying belief about self*]: "Sounds like you feel defeated before you give yourself a chance. Like it's hopeless to even try. Jay, that concerns me because when you think that way about yourself, you are defeated—not because you lack ability but because you think of yourself as destined to fail. That belief is your real enemy."

5. [*Deeper feelings*]: "You must have felt terribly hurt and resentful they didn't as much as call you. In fact, you seem to be experiencing those feelings now. It just hurts so much."

6. [*Underlying thoughts and feelings*]: "I wonder if, in light of your tightening up, you get feeling scared, as though you're afraid you won't measure up to their expectations."

7. [*Unrealized strengths*]: "Paula, I'm impressed with what you just said. It strikes me you're exercising a lot of control by limiting dessert to weekends and using moderation then. In fact, your self-control seems greater than that of most people. You and Terry have a legitimate difference concerning sweets. But it's exactly that—a difference. Neither view is right or wrong, and you're entitled to your preference as much as he's entitled to his."

8. [*Unrealized strength and implied want*]: "Steve, I can hear the frustration you're feeling, and I want you to know it reflects some real strength on your part. You want to be self-supporting and be able to provide better for your family. Given that desire, we can explore opportunities for learning new skills that won't require physical strength."

9. [*Underlying pattern of thought*]: "Kent, I get the feeling that it wouldn't matter what you did. You could set a world record, and you wouldn't feel it amounted to much. I'm wondering if your difficulty lies more in long-time feelings you've had about yourself that you somehow just don't measure up. I'd be interested in hearing more about how you've viewed yourself."

10. [*Underlying feelings and implied wants*]: "So your feelings tear you and pull you in different directions. You'd like to be a better mother, and you feel crummy when you lose your cool. But sometimes you just feel so overwhelmed and inadequate in coping with the children. Part of you would like to learn to manage the children better, but another part would like to get away from it."

SKILL DEVELOPMENT EXERCISES IN CONFRONTATION

The following exercises involve discrepancies and dysfunctional behavior in all three experiential domains—cognitive/perceptual, emotional, and behavioral. After reading the brief summary of the situation involved and the verbatim exchanges between the client(s) and social worker, identify the type of discrepancy involved and formulate your next response (observing the guidelines presented earlier) as though you are the social worker in a real-life situation. Next, compare your response with the modeled one, keeping in mind that the latter is only one of many possible appropriate responses. Carefully analyze how your response is similar to or differs from the modeled response and whether you adhered to the guidelines.

SITUATIONS AND DIALOGUE

1. You have been working with Mr. Lyon for several weeks, following his referral by the court after being convicted for sexually molesting his teenage daughter. Mr. Lyon has been 15 minutes late for his last two appointments, and today he is 20 minutes late. During his sessions he has explored and worked on problems only superficially.

Client: Sorry to be late today. Traffic was sure heavy. You know how that goes.

2. The clients are marital partners whom you have seen conjointly five times. One of their goals is to reduce marital conflict by avoiding getting into arguments that create mutual resentments.

Mrs. J: This week has been just awful. I've tried to look nice and have his meals on time—like he said he wanted, and I've just felt so discouraged. He got on my back Tuesday and . . . [*Husband interrupts.*]

Mr. J [*angrily*]: Just a minute. You're only telling half the story. You left out what you did Monday. [*She interrupts.*]

Mrs. J: Oh, forget it. What's the use? He doesn't care about me. He couldn't, the way he treats me.

Mr. J [*Shakes head in disgust.*]

3. The client is a slightly retarded young adult who was referred by a rehabilitation agency because of social and emotional problems. The client has manifested a strong interest in dating young women and has been vigorously pursuing a clerk (Sue) in a local supermarket. She has registered no interest in him and obviously has attempted to discourage him from further efforts. The following excerpt occurs in the seventh session.

Client: I went through Sue's checkstand this morning. I told her I'd like to take her to see a movie.

Social worker: Oh, and what did she say?

Client: She said she was too busy. I'll wait a couple of weeks and ask her again.

4. Tony, age 16, is a member of a therapy group in a youth correctional institution. In the preceding session, he appeared to gain a sense of power and satisfaction from provoking other members to react angrily and defensively, which tended to disrupt group process. Tony directs the following message to a group member early in the fourth session.

Tony: I noticed you trying to get with Maggie at the dance Wednesday. You think you're pretty hot stuff, don't you?

5. The client is a mother, age 26, who keeps feelings inside until they mount out of control, at which time she discharges anger explosively.

Client: I can't believe my neighbor. She sends her kids over to play with Sandra at lunchtime and disappears. It's obvious her kids haven't had lunch, and I end up feeding them, even though she's better off financially than I am.

Social worker: What do you feel when she does that?

Client: Oh, not much, I guess. But I think it's a rotten thing to do.

6. You have been working for several weeks with a family that includes the parents and four children ranging in age from 10 to 17. The mother is a domineering person who acts as spokesperson for the family, and the father is passive and soft-spoken. A teenage daughter, Tina, expresses herself in the following excerpt.

Tina: We always seem to have a hassle when we visit our grandparents. Grandma's so bossy. I don't like going there.

Mother: Tina, that's not true. You've always enjoyed going to her house. You and your grandmother have always been close.

7. Group members in their fifth session have been intently discussing difficulties of the members in social interaction. One of the members takes the group off on a tangent by describing humorous idiosyncrasies of a person she met while on vacation, and the other group members follow suit by sharing humorous anecdotes about "oddballs" they have encountered.

8. The client is an attractive, personable, and intelligent woman who has been married for 3 years to a self-centered, critical man. In the fourth session (an individual interview), she tearfully says:

Client: I've done everything he's asked of me. I've lost ten pounds. I support him in his work. I golf with him. I even changed my religion to please him. And he's still not happy with me. There's just something wrong with me.

9. The clients are a married couple in their early thirties. The following excerpt occurs in the initial interview.

Wife: We just seem to fight over the smallest things. When he gets really mad, he loses his temper and knocks me around.

Husband: The real problem is that she puts her parents ahead of me. She's the one who needs help, not me. If she'd get straightened around, I wouldn't lose my temper. Tell her where her first responsibility is. I've tried, and she won't listen to me.

10. The clients are a family consisting of the parents and two children. Terry, age 15, has been truanting and smoking marijuana. Angie, age 16, is a model student and is obviously her parents' favorite. The family was referred by the school when Terry was expelled for several days. The father, a highly successful businessman, entered family therapy with obvious reluctance, which has continued to this, the fourth session.

Mother: Things haven't been much different this week. Everyone's been busy, and we really haven't seen much of each other.

Father: I think we'd better plan to skip the next three weeks. Things have been going pretty well, and I have an audit in process at the office that's going to put me in a time bind.

Modeled Responses for Confrontation

1. [*Irresponsible behavior by the client*]: "Ted, I'm concerned you're late today. This is the third time you've been late in a row, and it shortens the time available to us. But my concerns go beyond that. I know you don't like having to come here and that you'd like to be out from under the court's jurisdiction. But the way you're going about things won't accomplish that. I can't be helpful to you and can't write a favorable report to the court if you just go through the motions of coming here for help. Apparently it's uncomfortable for you to come. I'd be interested in hearing just what you're feeling about coming."

2. [*Discrepancy between purported goal and behavior, as well as dysfunctional communication*]: "Let's stop and look at what you're doing right now. I'm concerned because each of you wants to feel closer to the other, but what you're both doing just makes each other defensive." [*To husband.*] "Mr. J, she was sharing some important feelings with you, and you cut her off." [*To wife.*] "And you did the same thing, Mrs. J, when he was talking. I know you may not agree, but it's important to hear each other out and to try to understand. If you keep interrupting and trying to blame each other, as you've both been doing, you're going to stay at square one, and I don't want that to happen. Let's go back and start over, but this time put yourself in the shoes of the other and try to understand. Check out with the other if you really understood. Then you can express your own views."

3. [*Dysfunctional, self-defeating behavior*]: "Pete, I know how much you think of Sue and how you'd like to date her. I'm concerned that you keep asking her out, though, because she never accepts and doesn't appear to want to go out with you. My concern is that you're setting yourself up for hurt and disappointment. I'd like to see you get a

girlfriend, but your chances of getting a date are probably a lot better with persons other than Sue."

4. [*Abrasive, provocative behavior*]: "Hold on a minute, guys. I'm feeling uncomfortable and concerned right now about what Tony just said. It comes across as a real put-down, and we agreed earlier one of our rules was to support and help each other. Tony, would you like some feedback from other members about how you're coming across to the group?"

5. [*Discrepancy between expressed and actual feeling*]: "I agree. But I'm concerned about your saying you don't feel much. I should think you'd be ticked off and want to change the situation. Let's see if you can get in touch with your feelings. Picture yourself at home at noon and your neighbor's kids knock on the door while you're fixing lunch. Can you picture it? What are you feeling in your body and thinking just now?"

6. [*Dysfunctional communication, disconfirming Tina's feelings and experiences*]: "What did you just do, Mrs. Black? Stop and think for a moment about how you responded to Tina's message. It may help you to understand why she doesn't share more with you." [*or*] "Tina, could you tell your mother what you're feeling right now about what she just said? I'd like her to get some feedback that could help her communicate better with you."

7. [*Discrepancy between goals and behavior, getting off topic*]: "I'm concerned about what the group's doing right now. What do you think is happening?"

8. [*Misconception about the self, cognitive/perceptual discrepancy*]: "Jan, I'm concerned about what you just said because you're putting yourself down and leaving no room to feel good about yourself. You're assuming that you own the problem and that you're deficient in some way. I'm not at all sure that's the problem. You're married to a man who seems impossible to please, and that is more likely the problem. As we agreed earlier, you have tasks of feeling good about yourself, standing up for yourself, and letting his problem be his. As long as your feelings about yourself depend on his approval, you're going to feel down on yourself."

9. [*Manipulative behavior*]: "I don't know the two of you well enough to presume to know what's causing your problems." [*To husband*] "If you're expecting me to tell your wife to shape up,

you'll be disappointed. My job is to help each of you to see your part in the difficulties and to make appropriate changes. If I did what you asked, I'd be doing both of you a gross disservice. Things don't get better that way."

10. [*Discrepancy between behavior and purported goals*]: "What you do, of course, is up to you. I am concerned, however, because you all agreed you wanted to relate more closely as family members and give each other more support. To accomplish that means you have to work at it steadily, or things aren't likely to change much." [*To father.*] "My impression is that you're backing off. I know your business is important, but I guess you have to decide whether you're really committed to the goals you set for yourselves."

Notes

1. Claiborn (1982) presents numerous examples of both types of interpretation as well as a comprehensive discussion of this important topic. Other researchers (J. Beck & Strong, 1982; Claiborn, Crawford, & Hackman, 1983; Dowd & Boroto, 1982; Feldman, Strong, & Danser, 1982; Milne & Dowd, 1983) have also reported findings comparing the effects of different types of interpretations.

CHAPTER 19

Managing Individual and Family Barriers to Change

CHAPTER OVERVIEW

Clients with the best of intentions cannot easily overcome the obstacles they face. Those obstacles may occur within the individual, representing conflicting wants and needs, with the environment, and with combinations of the two. In addition, social workers' own behaviors can both contribute to resolution of those barriers and inadvertently aggravate them. This chapter will include guidelines for being self-aware about your own role in assisting clients in removing barriers to change.

BARRIERS TO CHANGE

Progress toward goal attainment is rarely smooth; rather, the change process is characterized by rapid spurts of growth, plateaus and impasses, and sometimes brief periods of retrogression. Even getting started can be a formidable challenge with involuntary clients and families, such as those with problems of child maltreatment or spouse abuse. The degree and rate of change vary widely, being affected by many variables. The most critical of these are variations in the motivation and strengths of clients, the severity and duration of problems, vicissitudes in the helping relationship, environmental forces that support or militate against change, and the responsiveness (or lack thereof) of institutions in providing needed resources. In this chapter we focus on these

potential barriers to change and ways of managing them so that they do not unduly impede progress or precipitate premature termination by clients.

First we address the topic of relational reactions and discuss potential barriers that derive from clients, social workers, transracial and transcultural relationships, and sexual attractions toward clients. Then we focus on managing opposition to change by individuals and families. The chapter concludes with skill development exercises related to managing relational reactions.

RELATIONAL REACTIONS

The social worker–client relationship is the vehicle that animates the helping process, especially for voluntary clients. Indeed, the quality of the helping relationship critically determines both the client's moment-to-moment receptiveness to the influence and intervention of the social worker and the ultimate outcome of the helping process. Further, the helping relationship per se may be a source of positive change for many clients, who gain self-respect and feelings of worth in positive helping relationships. For clients whose previous life experiences have been void of sustained caring relationships, the helping relationship may be a corrective emotional experience in the sense of compensating for emotional deprivation experienced in earlier life.

Because of the profound importance of the helping relationship, it is critical that social workers be skillful in both cultivating relationships and keeping them in repair. In earlier chapters, we discussed qualities and skills in cultivating sound relationships.

Skills in maintaining relationships are equally vital, as feelings that influence the relationship for better or worse constantly flow back and forth between participants in the helping process. Therefore, to maintain positive helping relationships, you must be alert to threats to such relationships and be skillful in managing them. In the following sections, we discuss these factors at length.

RECOGNIZING AND MANAGING THREATS TO HELPING RELATIONSHIPS

Helping relationships that are characterized by reciprocal positive feelings between social worker and clients are conducive to personal growth and successful problem solving. Social workers strive to develop positive helping relationships by relating in a facilitative fashion with high levels of warmth, acceptance, unconditional caring, empathy, genuineness, and spontaneity, as we discussed earlier. Despite these efforts, however, some clients do not respond positively for a number of reasons that we discuss later. Social workers, too, may have difficulty responding positively to clients with certain personality attributes and types of problems. Even when a positive relationship evolves, various events and moment-by-moment transactions may pose threats to the continuing viability of the relationship. Social workers must be vigilant to manifestations that something is going awry in the relationship. Failure to perceive these manifestations and to manage them effectively may result in needless impasses or, even worse, premature termination. In the following discussion, we focus on threats to the relationship that emanate from the client, from the social worker, and from dynamic mixes of both.

Under- and Overinvolvement of Social Workers with Clients

Social workers desire to be attuned and helpful to their clients as often as possible. However, it is not unusual for there to be circumstances in which contact is less than facilitative. If clients experience a negative emotional reaction during the course of sessions that create a temporary breach in a helping relationship, and if social workers fail to recognize and handle them skillfully, the reactions may expand into major obstacles in the helping process. Raines has suggested that such reactions can be classified as overinvolvement or underinvolvement. Such levels can also be classified according to the social worker's general viewpoint or attitude toward the client. While we strive to maintain a balanced attitude, appreciative of strengths and aware of obstacles, we sometimes tip more to one side or the other, generally favorable or unfavorable to the client. Table 19-1 presents an adaptation of Raines's schema for classifying involvement (Raines, 1996).

When the social worker is underinvolved and has a negative attitude toward the client, it can be reflected in lack of attention or empathy, tuning out, having memory lapses, and the like. All (or most) social workers, certainly including the authors, have had bad sessions and even bad days in which their attentiveness was less than desirable. Cell 1 of Table 19-1 alerts us to circumstances in which such underinvolvement becomes associated with your services to a particular client. Such social worker behaviors are a signal that the cause of the behavior must be examined. Hence, part of professional behavior is the capacity for self-observation and correction. If you note one of these patterns, examination of their cause in supervision and/or consultation with peers can assist in developing plans for rectifying the behavior.

Underinvolvement when there is a positive social worker attitude can also occur when the social worker withholds assistance in an overassessment of the client's current capacity and need for help. For

	SOCIAL WORKER WITH UNFAVORABLE ATTITUDE TOWARD THE CLIENT	SOCIAL WORKER WITH FAVORABLE ATTITUDE TOWARD CLIENT
Underinvolvement	• difficult to empathize with the client • inattentive or "tuning out" client • has lapses of memory about important information previously revealed by clients • drowsy or preoccupied • dreads sessions, comes late, cancels sessions inappropriately • off the mark with interpretations • client perceives feedback as put-downs • fails to acknowledge client growth • never thinks about client outside of sessions	• withholds empathy inappropriately because of belief in client's strength • refrains from interpretation to promote insight • reflects or reframes excessively without answering • never considers self-disclosure • gives advice or tasks that clients feel incapable of carrying out
Overinvolvement	• has unreasonable dislike • argumentative • provocative • gives excessive advice • employs inept or poorly timed confrontations • disapproves of a client's planned course of action inappropriately • appears to take sides against a client (or subgroup) or actually does so • dominates discussions or frequently interrupts clients • utilizes power with involuntary clients to interfere in lifestyle areas beyond the range of legal mandates • competes intellectually • has violent thoughts or dreams	• overly emotional or sympathetic • provides extra time inappropriately • fantasizes brilliant interpretations • unusually sensitive to criticisms • has sexual thoughts or dreams • seeks nonprofessional contact

Table 19-1 Social Worker Under- and Overinvolvement with Clients

Source: Adapted from J. C. Raines (1996). Self-disclosure in clinical social work. *Clinical Social Work Journal, 24*(4): 357–375. Reprinted by permission of Kluwer Academic/Plenum Publishers and the author.

example, a client who has been making good progress but encounters a setback might need more support than usual, but the social worker could show a lack of expressed empathy. Similarly, settling on tasks that the client feels incapable of

can be a sign of positive underinvolvement. As in negative underinvolvement, such occurrences may happen with particular clients on a special occasion. However, patterns of repeated positive underinvolvement call for examination and correction.

Once again, reflection on the pattern with peers and supervisors can assist in finding ways to adjust the involvement level. Hence, while generally focusing on client strengths and having a positive attitude toward clients is consistent with social work values, this cell alerts us to ways that attention to strengths could be exaggerated and not fully helpful in some circumstances.

Overinvolvement with a negative social worker attitude then refers to attention, but negative attention, such that clients feel punished or in combat with the social worker. Patterns of arguing, acting provocative in an inappropriate fashion, arbitrary use of power, and the like can signal negative overinvolvement. It should be noted that if the social worker is operating under a legal mandate to provide, for example, services to persons who have neglected their children, power and authority may be used appropriately in some instances. Such overinvolvement with a negative social worker attitude can refer to those times when use of power becomes personal and punishing rather than appropriate to the circumstances and safety of children. This behavior is contrary to social work values described in Chapter 4 but does occur. It might be expected to be overrepresented in high-stress settings in which social workers have close contact with clients who have been harmed and others who have either harmed them or not acted fully to prevent the harm. Social workers in such settings, and their supervisors, should take special precautions to avoid stereotyping clients and ignoring client strengths and values.

Finally, *overinvolvement with a positive social worker attitude* refers to excessive preoccupation with a particular client such that the client dominates the social worker's thoughts and dreams, including sexual fantasies. In the most extreme cases, that positive overinvolvement can lead to more serious consequences, including boundary violations such as sexual contact with clients. Because of the seriousness of this issue, it will be discussed later in greater detail.

Although most of the preceding events or circumstances involve mistakes by social workers, others may involve misperceptions by clients. Whatever their source, it is vital to sense and to discuss clients' feelings and thoughts as they are manifested and thus prevent them from escalating. Often clients will not initiate discussion of their negative reactions, and if you are not sensitive to nonverbal cues, the feelings and cognitions will linger and fester. To avert such a development, it is crucial to be perceptive of indicators of negative reactions including the following nonverbal cues: frowning, fidgeting, sighing, appearing startled, grimacing, changing the subject, becoming silent, clearing the throat, blushing, and tightening the muscles. When you discern these or related cues, it is important to shift the focus of the session to the clients' here-and-now feelings and cognitions. You should do this tentatively, checking out whether your perception is accurate. If accurate, proceed sensitively, manifesting genuine concern for the client's discomfort and conveying your desire to understand what the client is experiencing at the moment. Examples of responses that facilitate discussion of troubling feelings and thoughts are the following:

- "I'm sensing you're reacting to what I just said. Could you share with me what it meant to you and what you're thinking and feeling at this moment?"

- "You appear distressed right now. I'd like to understand just what you're experiencing and if I may have said or done something that caused your troubled thoughts and feelings."

- "You are quiet right now, looking away from me. I am wondering if you have some feelings about the draft of the progress report I just shared with you."

Keep in mind that discussing negative feelings and cognitions toward a social worker is extremely difficult for many clients. You can reduce the threat by being warmly attentive and accepting of clients, even though their thoughts and feelings may be entirely unrealistic. By eliciting the client's feelings and thoughts, you have the opportunity to correct a misunderstanding, clarify your intention, rectify a blunder, or identify a dysfunctional belief or pattern of thought. Indeed, some clients benefit from observing a model who can acknowledge imperfections and apologize for errors without appearing humiliated. Moreover, clients may gain self-esteem by realizing that social workers value them sufficiently to be concerned about their thoughts and feelings and to rectify errors of omission or commission. After productive discussions of here-and-now thoughts and feelings, most clients regain positive feelings and resume working on their problems.

On occasions, however, clients may succeed in concealing negative thoughts and feelings, or you may overlook nonverbal manifestations of them. The feelings may thus fester until it becomes obvious that the client is relating atypically by holding back, being overly formal, responding defensively, or manifesting other forms of opposition enumerated later in this chapter. Again, it is vital to accord priority to the relationship by shifting focus to what is bothering the client and responding as we recommended earlier. After you have worked through the negative reaction of the client, it is helpful to negotiate a "minicontract" related to discussing troublesome feelings and thoughts as they occur. The objective of this renegotiation is to avert similar recurrences in the future and to convey your openness to discussing negative reactions toward you. Learning to express negative feelings and thoughts can be a milestone for clients who typically withhold such reactions to the detriment of themselves and others. The following is an example of a message aimed at negotiating an appropriate minicontract:

- "I'm pleased that you shared your hurt with me today. That helped me to understand what you've been thinking and feeling and gave me a chance to explain what I really meant last week. For us to work well together, it is important for both of us to put negative reactions on the table so that we can prevent strains from developing between us. I wonder how you'd feel about our updating our contract to include discussing immediately any troubling thoughts

and feelings that might present obstacles in our relationship so that we can explore them together and work them out."

"Pathological" or Inept Social Workers

Although all social workers commit rectifiable errors from time to time, some social workers blunder repeatedly, causing irreparable damage to helping relationships and inflicting psychological damage upon their clients. Gottesfeld and Lieberman (1979) refer to such social workers as *pathological* and point out, "It is possible to have therapists who suffer from as many unresolved problems as do clients" (p. 388). We agree, based on knowledge of social workers who are abrasive, egotistical, controlling, judgmental, demeaning, rigid, habitually tardy for appointments, sexually promiscuous, patronizing, detached, and who create additional difficulties for clients or foster unhealthy dependency, to mention just a few "pathogenic" attributes. Social workers with these attributes tend to lose clients prematurely. The majority of voluntary clients discern these attributes and have the good sense to "vote with their feet" by terminating such contacts. Mandated clients suffer greater consequences for deciding to terminate unilaterally. They may be more likely to evade contact or attempt to be transferred to another social worker. Supervisors should hence be alert when there are several requests for transfer from the same social worker.

These social workers are injurious to their clients, their agencies, and the profession. Consequently, other social workers face a difficult situation in knowing what steps to take when they become aware of injurious social workers. As Gottesfeld and Lieberman (1979) note: "It is painful to be a helpless observer of a situation that seems to be antitherapeutic for a client. Yet it is also painful and difficult to render a judgment about a professional colleague's competence" (p. 392).

Clearly, both individual social workers and agencies have a responsibility to protect clients from pathological social workers. Gottesfeld and

Lieberman encapsulate this responsibility in their assertion that "agencies organized to help clients should not accept employee pathology that defeats the system's purpose" (p. 392). Actions to rectify such situations, however, must safeguard the rights of social workers as well as clients, for unfair judgments may result from biased or inaccurate reports of social workers' behavior. To protect clients' rights, "a professional's behavior must be open for review through consultation, supervision, or a peer review process" (Gottesfeld & Lieberman, 1979, p. 392). When peer review appears justified, a referral to the closest chapter of the professional organization (NASW) or state licensing or certification board may be in order. Chapters and boards have committees formed to investigate complaints of unethical and unprofessional behavior.

Racial and Transcultural Barriers

Clients may also experience adverse reactions in transracial or transcultural relationships with social workers who either lack knowledge of the client's culture or lack experience in working with members of a given race or minority group. Foster (1998) suggests that treatment has often included goals such as achieving separation from others and autonomy that are bounded by assumptions in certain Western cultures. Those goals may not be shared by persons from cultures that place greater value on connectedness and merging with the cosmos. In cross-cultural contexts, it is hence important to understand the person from the viewpoint of the lifestyles and standards for well-being of their reference group. Similarly, social workers who are members of ethnic minority groups are more likely to be familiar with values of majority group clients than those clients are accustomed to having minority social workers. As Proctor and Davis note, Caucasian social workers tend to know little about the realities of other cultures. Such transcultural conflicts are negatively charged, with both sides uncomfortable discussing racial and ethnic differences. Caucasian social workers fear rejection and clients of color distrust representatives of systems considered oppressive (Proctor & Davis, 1994).

Hence participants in transcultural relationships may experience a mutual strangeness based on limited interaction with members of each others' culture. In such instances, "the void may be filled by stereotyped 'knowledge' and preconception, but the essential unknownness remains" (Gitterman & Schaeffer, 1972). Given these circumstances, mutual defensiveness and guardedness become an obstacle to effective communication. Too often, differences of race and culture are ignored in a form of "color blind" practice designed to avoid conflict (Proctor & Davis, 1994, p. 316).

Empathic communication is a basic skill that tends to bridge the gap often present in transracial and transcultural relationships. Empathically confronting clients' anger and suspiciousness tends to neutralize these negative feelings by demonstrating acceptance and understanding, as we have pointed out previously. Based on modest research evidence, several authors (Banks, 1971; Cimbolic, 1972; Santa Cruz & Hepworth, 1975) recommend that in preparing students to work across racial or ethnic lines, educators should train them to attain high levels of skill in the facilitative conditions of empathy, respect, and genuineness.

Even relating with high levels of the facilitative conditions may be insufficient to bridge the racial gap with certain clients. In analyzing sources of nondisclosure of African American clients, Ridley (1984) has developed a useful typology that identifies "cultural paranoia" as a major barrier to transracial work involving Caucasian social workers. Some African American clients distrust Caucasians to a degree that effective communication may not be possible; same-race social workers may be preferable in such instances. Of course, cultural paranoia frequently overlaps with involuntary status such that involuntary clients with high levels of distrust often have limited access to same-race social workers.

Another source of negative reactions by African American clients to Caucasian social workers may be a lack of awareness by the latter of the duality of their feelings toward African Americans. On one hand, as a result of a lack of adequate awareness of the effects of discrimination and oppression upon blacks, social workers may be insensitive to African American resentment, fear, distrust, and sense of powerlessness. Such social workers may stereotype African Americans and have a limited capacity for empathizing with them. On the other hand, some Caucasian social workers may overidentify with African Americans, losing sight of clients' individual problems and erroneously attributing them to racial factors. When this occurs, as Cooper (1973) aptly puts it, "clients tend to lose their individual richness and complexity; there is the danger of no longer treating people—only culture carriers" (p. 76). Clearly then, Caucasian social workers must empathize with African American clients but not to the extent of overidentifying with them.

Given the potential obstacles that may emerge in transracial and transcultural relationships, one may well wonder if the solution is to match clients with social workers of the same race or ethnic group. This solution is often not practicable, however, nor is there evidence that matching always works to the clients' advantage. Research studies have indicated that traditional mental health services rendered by Anglo social workers to Asian Americans and Latino are markedly underutilized (Sue & Zane, 1987) and that "regardless of utilization rates, all of the ethnic-minority groups had significantly higher drop-out rates than whites" (p. 37). Further, Sue and McKinney (1975) reported dramatic increases in utilization rates by Asian Americans when a counseling center was established specifically for this ethnic group and culturally relevant services were provided by bilingual therapists. These findings clearly illustrate that it is advantageous to match clients with social workers of the same race or ethnicity. However, rigorous studies comparing treatment outcomes of racially and ethnically matching helping relationships with transcultural counterparts have not been reported. Moreover, several studies suggest that social workers have been able to help clients of different races and ethnicity. Whether therapists of the same race or ethnicity could have been more helpful cannot be inferred because these studies lacked control or comparison groups. Based on the dearth of solid information, the most that can be concluded is that client and social worker racial and ethnic homogeneity promote utilization of services by minority clients and that practitioners who engage in transcultural work, at a minimum, should be knowledgeable about the cultures of their clients and competent in relating with high levels of the facilitative conditions.

Because racial and cultural matching is often not possible, it becomes part of the social worker's responsibility to become better educated about working with persons who are different culturally and racially from the social worker. This education includes becoming informed about the history of the groups one works with, both nationally and locally, including the ways such groups have been oppressed and the consequences of that oppression. The education also includes becoming appreciative of the cultural strengths of the groups through becoming familiar with literature, art, and films that accurately portray culture. Finally, it includes a professional education with reviewing journal articles geared toward working with members of a particular culture and participating in staff training aimed at ethnically sensitive practice.

Difficulties in Trusting and Transference Reactions

Clients vary widely in their capacity to trust. Those whose self-esteem and levels of interpersonal functioning are high may plunge into exploring their problems after only a few moments of checking out the social worker. Yet despite the latter's goodwill and skills in imparting warmth, caring, and empathy, other clients may be guarded and test a social worker for weeks or even months before letting down their defenses. As noted in previous chapters, involuntary clients who have not sought a helping relationship should not be expected to readily come to trust social workers. Attempting to persuade such clients of one's helpful intent is usually counterproductive. Many distrustful clients trust actions before words. That is, social workers who fulfill commitments or social worker tasks they have agreed to are more likely eventually to be perceived as trustworthy.

With such clients, social workers must exercise patience and persistence. Pushing for self-disclosure before trust and a positive relationship are established may alienate them, prolong the period of testing, or precipitate discontinuance of the helping relationship. Because these clients do not enter helping relationships readily and hence often disclose their problems only superficially during early sessions, setting time limits on the duration of the helping process is inappropriate. In fact, it may be necessary to reach out to these clients to maintain their involvement in the helping process. Often they cancel or miss appointments, and unless the social worker reaches out by phoning them, making a home visit, or writing a letter (the last is the *least* effective), they often do not return. It is important to recognize that many of these clients urgently need help and that their failure to keep appointments may emanate more from a pattern of avoidance than from lack of motivation. Assisting them to come to terms with fears behind their avoidance behavior thus may be therapeutic, whereas letting them terminate by default contributes to perpetuation of their avoidance behavior.

Unrealistic perceptions of and reactions to a social worker are known as *transference reactions,* that is, the client transfers to the social worker wishes, fears, and other feelings that are rooted in past experiences with others (usually parents, parental substitutes, and siblings). Transference reactions may not only impede progress in the helping process but also may create difficulties in other interpersonal relationships. A male may have difficulty trusting all women because he felt rejected and/or abused by his mother or stepmother; similarly, some people resent and rebel against all people in positions of authority, mistakenly perceiving all such people as they perceived an overbearing, punitive, controlling, and exploitative parent.

Transference reactions thus involve overgeneralized and distorted perceptions that create difficulties in interpersonal relationships. Besides being a possible impediment to progress, transference reactions in therapeutic relationships also represent an opportunity for growth. Because the therapeutic relationship is, in effect, a social microcosm wherein clients' interpersonal behavior and conditioned patterns of perceiving and feeling are manifested, in this context clients often recreate here-and-now interactions that are virtually identical to those that plague and defeat them in other relationships. The consequent challenge and opportunity for the social worker is to assist such clients to recognize their distorted perceptions and to develop finer interpersonal perceptual discriminations so that they can differentiate and deal with the social worker and others as unique individuals rather than as overgeneralized projections of mental images, beliefs, or attitudes.

The extent to which transference reactions occur during the course of the helping process varies considerably. In time-limited, task-focused forms of intervention, the likelihood of transference reactions is minimal. When treatment extends over a lengthy period of time, focuses on the past, and involves in-depth analysis of intrapsychic processes, transference may play a pivotal role in the helping process. Psychoanalytically oriented therapy and other long-term, insight-oriented therapies, in fact, tend to foster transference, whereas task-centered, behavioral, and crisis interventions do not. Similarly, working with marital partners conjointly tends to discourage transference reactions, whereas working with only one partner may foster transference by the client and overidentification on the social worker's part. V. G. Smith and Hepworth (1967) have written about ways of avoiding pitfalls in working with one marital partner. As for groups:

> *Multiple transference reactions may also emerge in groups. An individual can be experienced as a mother by one member, as a father by another, and as a sibling by still another. Similarly, that individual often "finds" parents and siblings in the group. Usually the leader is experienced as a mother or father. As the individual*

sees how he distorts perceptions in the group, he can begin to appreciate how he distorts other interpersonal relationships. (Strean, 1979, p. 194)

Kinds of clients served also are a significant factor that determines the incidence of transference reactions. In public assistance, child welfare, and correctional settings, for example, many clients come from emotionally deprived backgrounds and have histories of ambivalent involvement with social agencies that predispose them to view social workers with fear and distrust, to react with humiliation and resentment, and to view themselves as helpless. Given these feelings, such clients are caught in a paradoxical situation, for, on the one hand, they have limited coping skills, desire to be assisted with their problems, and have dependency longings; but on the other hand, their fears and negative feelings are powerful deterrents to risking involving themselves with helping professionals. Consequently, many of these clients openly oppose helping efforts or tend to relate in passive, dependent ways that block growth toward competency and independence. To counter these inimical reactions, social workers confront the challenge of having clients accept them and their offer of assistance.

Managing Transference Reactions

Whatever the agency setting and the intervention, you will occasionally encounter transference reactions and must be prepared to cope with them. For example, the authors have encountered the following:

1. A client who had great difficulty revealing her problems because the social worker resembled her brother in appearance.

2. A client (whose father was a harsh and domineering person) who resisted becoming involved in marital therapy because she resented anyone telling her what to do. (The social worker earlier had clarified that was not his role.)

3. A client who wanted the social worker to embrace her because it was important to know he cared for her.

4. A client to whom it was important to be the social worker's favorite.

5. A client who was sure the social worker couldn't possibly have a genuine interest in her and saw her only because it was his job.

6. A client who misinterpreted a message of the social worker and almost terminated as a result of feeling put down.

7. A client who accused the social worker of being in collusion with her husband when the social worker, in fact, viewed the husband as the major contributor to their marital difficulties.

It is evident that although such reactions derive from the past, they are manifested in the here and now. The question can be raised as to whether transference reactions can best be resolved by focusing on the past to enable clients to gain insight into their origin. We maintain that reactions that derive from past experiences are played out in the present and can usually be resolved by focusing on the inaccurate and distorted perceptions of the present. Some clients, of course, will bring up hurtful experiences and circumstances from the past. Brief excursions into the past provide opportunities for emotional catharsis and facilitate understanding of the origin of dysfunctional patterns of thinking, feeling, and behaving.

When it appears clients have experienced traumatic stresses in childhood, such as physical or sexual abuse, gentle probing and exploration of these past experiences may be vital to gaining understanding of and recovery from the detrimental effects of those experiences (Rosenthal, 1988; Wartel, 1991). Focusing on past traumatic experiences of adulthood (such as rape and horrible events in war) may also be essential to healing from the psychic wounds of those experiences.

Except for the circumstances just cited, it is counterproductive to focus extensively on the past, as so doing diverts efforts from problem solving in the present and unnecessarily prolongs treatment. Further, there is no evidence that focusing on the remote origin of unrealistic feelings, perceptions, and beliefs is more effective in modifying them than scrutinizing their validity in the here and now.

To manage transference reactions you must first be aware of their manifestations, of which the following are typical:

1. Relating to the social worker in a clinging, dependent way or excessively seeking praise and reassurance.

2. Attempting to please the social worker by excessive compliments and praise or by ingratiating behavior.

3. Asking many personal questions about the social worker.

4. Behaving provocatively by arguing with or baiting the social worker.

5. Questioning the interest of the social worker.

6. Seeking special considerations, such as frequent changes in scheduled appointments for trivial reasons.

7. Attempting to engage social workers socially by inviting them to lunch, parties, and the like.

8. Having dreams or fantasies about the social worker.

9. Responding defensively, feeling rejected, or expecting criticism or punishment without realistic cause.

10. Offering personal favors or presenting gifts.

11. Behaving seductively by flirting, wearing revealing clothing, or making affectionate gestures.

12. Regressing or behaving in destructive ways when the social worker must cancel or miss sessions.

13. Being unusually silent, inattentive, or drowsy in sessions.

14. Being tardy for appointments or striving to stay beyond the designated ending time.

15. Dressing or behaving in ways that diverge markedly from the client's usual style.

When clients manifest the preceding behaviors or other possible indications of transference reactions, it is vital to shift focus to their here-and-now feelings, for such reactions generally cause clients to disengage from productive work and may undermine the helping process. To assist you in managing transference reactions, we offer the following guidelines:

1. *Be open to the possibility that the client's reaction is not unrealistic* and may be produced by your behavior. If through discussion and introspection you determine the client's behavior is realistic, respond authentically by owning responsibility for your behavior.

2. *When clients appear to expect you to respond in antitherapeutic ways, as significant others have in the past, it is important to respond differently,* thereby disconfirming the expectations. Responses that contrast sharply from expectations produce temporary disequilibrium and force the client to differentiate the social worker from past figures. The client must thus deal with the social worker as a unique and real person rather than perpetuate fictional expectations based on past experiences.

3. *Assist the client to determine the immediate source of distorted perceptions* by exploring how and when the feelings emerged. Carefully explore antecedents and meaning attributions associated with the feelings. Avoid attempting to correct distorted perceptions by immediately revealing your actual feelings. By first exploring how and when problematic feelings emerged, you assist clients to expand their awareness of their patterns of overgeneralizing and making both faulty meaning attributions and unwarranted assumptions based on past experience. This awareness can enable them in the future to discriminate between feelings that emanate from conditioned perceptual sets and reality-based feelings and reactions.

4. *After clients have discerned the unrealistic nature of their feelings and manifested awareness of the distortions that produced these feelings, share your actual feelings.* This can be a source of reassurance to clients who have felt offended, hurt, resentful, rejected, or the like.

5. *After you have examined problematic feelings, assist clients to determine whether they have experienced*

similar reactions in other relationships. You may thus assist clients to discern patterns of distortions that create difficulties in other relationships.

The application of these guidelines is illustrated in the following excerpt taken from an actual session (the eighth) of one of the authors with a 25-year-old female who had sought help because of loneliness and discouragement in finding a marital partner.

Client: Boy, the weeks sure go by fast. [*Long pause.*] I don't have much to talk about today.

Social worker [*sensing the client is struggling with something*]: I gather you didn't really feel ready for your appointment today. [*Empathic response.*] How did you feel about coming? [*Open-ended probing response.*]

Client: I didn't want to come, but I thought I should. Actually it has been an eventful week. But I haven't felt I wanted to tell you about what has been happening. [*Indication of a possible transference reaction.*]

Social worker: Sounds like you've had some misgivings about confiding certain things in me. [*Paraphrasing response.*] Could you share with me some of your thoughts about confiding these things in me? [*Open-ended probing response/polite command.*]

Client: OK. I've wanted to keep them to myself until I find out how things turn out. I've wanted to wait until it really develops into something. Then I would tell you.

Social worker: So you haven't wanted to risk it turning out bad and worrying about how I would feel if it *did.* [*Additive empathy interpretation.*]

Client: I guess I've wanted to impress you. I had a date with the fellow we talked about last week. It was wonderful. He's just the opposite of the other creep I told you about. He either has a real line or he's a super guy. I couldn't believe how considerate he was.

Social worker: You can't be sure yet what he's really like, and you want to be sure he's for real before you tell me about him? [*Additive empathy/ interpretation.*]

Client [*with an embarrassed smile*]: Yes! And if it really developed into something, then I could tell you.

Social worker: And that way you could be sure I'd be favorably impressed? [*Additive empathy/interpretation.*]

Client: Yes! I've felt I wanted you to know someone really good could be attracted to me.

Social worker: Hmm. Sounds like you've felt I've doubted you have much to offer a man and wanted to prove to me you do have something to offer. [*Additive empathy/interpretation.*]

Client: Yes, that's true. I have wanted you to think of me as a desirable person.

Social worker: I'd like to explore where those doubts or fears that I don't see you as a desirable person come from. I'm wondering how you've concluded I don't see you as having much to offer a man. Have I done or said something that conveyed that to you? [*Probing.*]

Client [*thinks for a moment*]: Well—no. Nothing that I can think of.

Social worker: Yet I gather those feelings have been very real to you. I wonder when you first became aware of those feelings.

Client [*after a pause*]: Well, I think it was when we began to talk about my feelings that guys are just interested in me for what they can get. I guess I wondered if you thought I was a real dud. I wanted you to know it wasn't so, that a desirable person could be attracted to me.

Social worker: You know, when we were discussing your feelings toward your mother two or three weeks ago you said essentially the same thing. [*Using summarization to make a connection between separate but related events.*]

Client: I'm not sure what you mean.

Social worker: You had said you felt your mother doubted you would ever marry because you were so cold you couldn't attract a man.

Client [*smiles pensively and nods affirmatively*]: You know I never wanted to elope. I always wanted to marry in my hometown and have a big wedding. When I had my ring on my finger, I would turn to mother and say, "See, you were wrong!"

Social worker: So you've felt you needed to prove to her someone could love you. And that's also what you wanted to prove to me. [*Additive empathy/interpretation.*]

Client: [*Nods affirmatively.*]

Social worker: I'm interested you've thought maybe I, too, didn't see you as lovable. Could you share with me how you reached that conclusion? [*Social worker continues to explore the unrealistic nature of her perception and how it pervades other relationships.*]

By sensitively exploring the client's reluctance to attend the session, the social worker not only resolved an emerging obstacle to productive work but also assisted her to explore further her doubts as to her lovability and to expand her awareness of how these doubts distorted her perceptions of how others viewed her—in this instance, the social worker. As a result of the exploration, she was able to identify a basic misconception that pervaded her relationships with others and to relate more comfortably with the social worker.

Countertransference Reactions

Social workers may also experience adverse relational reactions that can damage helping relationships if not recognized and managed effectively. Just as with clients, these feelings may be realistic or unrealistic. The latter type of reaction, which we discuss first, is the counterpart of transference and is denoted *countertransference*. This phenomenon involves feelings, wishes, and unconscious defensive patterns of the social worker that derive from past relationships, interfere with objective perception, and block productive interaction with clients. Countertransference contaminates helping relationships by producing distorted perceptions, blind spots, wishes, and antitherapeutic emotional reactions and behavior. Social workers who have failed to integrate anger into their own personali-

ties, for example, may be unduly uncomfortable when clients express anger and divert them from expressing such feelings. Other social workers who have not resolved feelings of rejection by parents may have difficulty relating warmly to clients who are cool and aloof. Still other social workers who have failed to resolve resentful feelings toward authoritarian parents may overidentify with rebellious adolescents and experience feelings of condemnation for their parents. Marital therapists whose spouses have been unfaithful, controlling, or sexually withholding may also overidentify with clients who have similar problems and be blind to the part these clients play in the marital difficulties they describe. Finally, some social workers who have excessive needs to be loved and admired may behave seductively or strive to impress their clients. Selective self-disclosure can be potentially beneficial as a form of empathic responsiveness, because clients can be aware of traumatic events in the life of the therapist consciously or unconsciously (E. G. Goldstein, 1997). Raines suggests that self-disclosure decisions can be considered within a range of over- and underinvolvement. Personal sharing should be based on rational grounds related to the current relationship (Raines, 1996).

Before discussing how to manage countertransference reactions, it is first important to identify typical ways they are manifested, which include the following:

1. Being unduly concerned about a client
2. Having persistent erotic fantasies or dreams about a client
3. Dreading or pleasurably anticipating sessions with clients
4. Being consistently tardy or forgetting appointments with certain clients
5. Feeling protective of or uncomfortable about discussing certain problems with a client
6. Feeling hostile toward or unable to empathize with a client
7. Blaming others exclusively for a client's difficulties

8. Feeling persistently bored or drowsy or tuning out a client

9. Consistently ending sessions early or permitting them to extend beyond designated ending points

10. Trying to impress or being unduly impressed by clients

11. Being overly concerned about losing a client

12. Arguing with or feeling defensive or hurt by a client's criticisms or accusations

13. Being overly solicitous and performing tasks for clients that they are capable of performing

14. Being unusually curious about a client's sex life

15. Having difficulties accepting or liking certain types of clients (which may also be reality based)

The reader should note the similarity in this list to reactions described as over- and underinvolvement. Becoming aware of unrealistic feelings toward a client or of reactions such as those just listed are signals that a social worker should immediately take appropriate corrective measures. Otherwise, the countertransference will limit the social worker's potential helpfulness, create an impasse, contribute to the client's dysfunction, or otherwise impair the effectiveness of the helping relationship. Ordinarily, the first step in resolving countertransference (and often all that is needed) is to engage in introspection. Introspection involves analytical dialogue with oneself aimed at discovering sources of feelings, reactions, cognitions, and behavior. Examples of questions that facilitate introspection include the following:

• "Why am I feeling uncomfortable with this client? What is going on inside me that I'm not able to relate more freely?"

• "Why do I dislike (or feel bored, impatient, or irritated) with this client? Are my feelings rational or does this client remind me of someone from the past?"

• "What is happening inside of me that I don't face certain problems with this client? Am I afraid of a negative reaction on the client's part?"

• "What purpose was served by arguing with this client? Was I feeling defensive or threatened?"

• "Why did I talk so much or give so much advice? Did I feel a need to give something to the client?"

• "What's happening inside me that I'm fantasizing or dreaming about this client?"

• "Why am I constantly taking sides with _____? Am I overlooking the partner's (or parent's or child's) feelings because I'm overidentifying with _____? Could my own similar feelings from the past be blocking my objectivity?"

Introspection often assists social workers to achieve or regain a realistic perspective in their relationships with clients. Discussion of such topics should also be part of consultation with colleagues and supervisors, enabling you to explore your feelings and to gain fresh input. Just as clients are sometimes too close to their problems to perceive them objectively and thus benefit from seeing them from the vantage point of a social worker, the latter can likewise benefit from stepping out of the relationship and viewing it from the unbiased perspective of an uninvolved colleague, consultant, or supervisor.

Social workers who repeatedly become enmeshed in countertransference reactions usually have long-standing and unresolved emotional conflicts that continue to pervade their interpersonal relationships. As such, their range of effectiveness is limited and they may cause or contribute to dysfunction in their clients. Some such "pathological" social workers are able to work through their difficulties by obtaining professional help for themselves. Others are not suited for the profession and for the benefit of themselves, their clients, and the profession should consider making an occupational change.

Realistic Social Worker Reactions

Not all negative feelings toward certain clients involve countertransference reactions. Some clients are abrasive, arrogant, or obnoxious, have irritating mannerisms, or are exploitative of and cruel to others. Even the most accepting social worker may have difficulty developing positive feelings toward such clients. Social workers, after all, are human beings and are not immune to disliking others or feeling irritated and impatient at times. Still, repulsive clients are entitled to service and, in fact, often desperately need help because their offensive behavior alienates others, leaving them isolated and confused as to what creates their difficulties.

When social workers look beyond the offensive qualities of certain clients, they often discover that beneath the façade of arrogance and toughness are desirable, indeed admirable qualities that others rarely, if ever, see. Further, when they gain access to the private worlds of these individuals, social workers often find persons who endured severe emotional deprivation, physical abuse, and other severe stresses as children and who had little opportunity to learn social skills. Being warmly accepted in spite of their annoying behavior often provides a corrective emotional experience for these clients.

Abrasive clients need far more than acceptance, however. They need feedback about how certain aspects of their behavior are offensive to others, encouragement to risk new behaviors, and opportunities to learn and practice the same. Feedback can be extremely helpful if it is conveyed sensitively and imparted in the context of goodwill. In providing such feedback, you must be careful to avoid evaluative or blaming comments that tend to elicit defensiveness. Examples of such comments are "You boast too much and dominate conversation" or "You're insensitive to other people's feelings and say hurtful things." Clients are far more likely to be receptive to messages that describe and document their behavior and personalize the social worker's response to it. An example of a descriptive message that embodies ownership of feelings is "When you sneered at me just now, I began to feel defensive and resentful. You've done that several times before, and I find myself backing away each time. I don't like feeling distant from you, and I'm concerned because I suspect that's how you come across to others." This message, of course, is highly authentic and would not

be appropriate until a sound working relationship has been established.

Sexual Attraction Toward Clients

Romantic and sexual feelings toward clients can be especially hazardous, although such feelings are by no means uncommon. Research findings (Pope, Keith-Spiegel, & Tabachnick, 1986), based on a survey of 585 psychotherapists (psychologists), revealed that only 77 (13%) had never been attracted to any client. The majority (82%), however, had never seriously considered sexual involvement with a client and of the remaining 18%, 87% had considered becoming involved only once or twice. Of the 585 respondents, about 6% had engaged in sexual intimacies with clients. Strom-Gottfried (1999) found in a study of ethics complaints reported to NASW that 29% involved boundary violations, almost three-quarters of which involved some form of sexual violation. She notes that "even a small incidence warrants the attention of the profession, particularly supervisors and educators to assure that any measures available to reduce the incidence further are fully pursued" (p. 448). Social workers need to be informed about appropriate professional behaviors and exposed to good modeling. They should explore challenging situations and use critical thinking skills in such examination. When setting, location, or population exposes the social worker to particular risk such as in rural areas; close religious, cultural, and ethnic communities; or substance abuse treatment settings, potential dilemmas must be explored. Raines suggests that self-disclosure decisions can be considered within a range of over- and underinvolvement, as considered previously. Personal sharing should be based on rational grounds related to the current relationship (Raines, 1996).

Most social workers can thus expect at some point in their careers to experience sexual attraction toward a client. Managing such attraction appropriately, however, is critical. Fortunately, the data indicate that the majority of therapists manage their attractions successfully. Although 83% of those in the cited study who experienced attraction believed the attraction was mutual, 71% believed that the client was not aware of their attraction. When such was the case they believed the attraction did not have a harmful impact on the helping process. By contrast, therapists who believed clients were aware of their attraction thought the impact was detrimental to the helping process. Although only 6% of those surveyed had engaged in sexual activities with clients, this percentage is alarming, for sexual involvement usually leads to grievous consequences for clients, who often suffer confusion and intense guilt and thereafter have great difficulty trusting professional persons. The consequences of sexual involvement may be devastating for social workers as well. When discovered, they may suffer disgrace, suit for unethical practice, and ejection from the profession. The NASW Code of Ethics on this point is unequivocal: "The social worker should under no circumstances engage in sexual activities or sexual contact with current clients, whether such contact is consensual or forced" (Section 1.09 a). Consequently, sexual attraction to clients is normal; acting on that attraction is unethical in a professional relationship.

Effectively managing sexual attractions for clients involves taking the corrective measures identified earlier in relationship to unrealistic feelings and reactions—namely, engaging in introspection and consulting with your supervisor. In this regard, it is noteworthy that in the survey previously cited, 57% of the therapists sought consultation or supervision when they were attracted to a client. We cannot recommend too strongly that you take the same measures under similar circumstances. If allowed to mount unchecked, sexual attraction can lead to the disastrous consequences earlier discussed. Social workers who frequently experience erotic fantasies about clients are particularly vulnerable to becoming sexually involved and should consider receiving treatment themselves.

A few social workers have justified engaging in sexual activities with clients on the basis of assisting them to feel loved or helping them to overcome sexual problems. Such explanations are gen-

erally thinly disguised and feeble rationalizations for exploiting clients. Typically, such sexual activities are limited to persons considered attractive and relatively youthful. Social workers who engage in sexual activities with clients not only render them a grave disservice but also damage the public image of the profession.

MANAGING OPPOSITION TO CHANGE

Social workers and other helping professionals have been inclined to label client behaviors that oppose the direction in which the social worker wishes to go as *resistance*. Resistance has been defined as "holding back, disengaging, or in some way subverting change efforts whether knowingly or not without open discussion" (J. Nelson, 1975, p. 587), or "as any action or attitude that impedes the course of therapeutic work" (Strean, 1979, p. 70). The resistance concept has tended to be used in a fashion that holds the client responsible for the opposition. The first step in avoiding such blaming is to recognize opposition to change as a universal phenomenon, as anyone knows who has attempted to break long-established habits such as being unduly modest, eating excessively, smoking, talking too much or too little, being tardy, or spending freely. The pull of habits is relentless; changing, moreover, often means yielding gratifications or having to cope head-on with situations that are frightening or aversive. Making changes also often involves risking new behavior in the face of unknown consequences. Although the status quo may cause pain and distress, it at least is familiar, and the consequences of habitual dysfunctional behavior are predictable. Further, it is not uncommon to have mixed feelings about change, both desiring it and having hesitance or ambivalence about it. Opposing feelings coexist; part of the client is motivated to change and another part strives to maintain the status quo (Leader, 1958).

Recognizing clients' ambivalent feelings about changing enables social workers to assist them to explore their feelings and to weigh advantages and disadvantages of making changes. Indeed, as clients think through their feelings and reassess the implications of maintaining the status quo, the scales often tilt in favor of change. Further, by accepting clients in spite of their opposition to change and by championing their right to self-determination, social workers may similarly tilt the scales, because clients experience no pressure from the social worker to change and are therefore free to make up their own minds. This factor is crucial, for pressure by the social worker often engenders an opposing force or resistance from the client. Viewed in this light, recognizing and accepting oppositional feelings to change prevent such feelings from going underground where they can subtly undermine the helping process. Recognizing, openly discussing, and accepting oppositional feelings thus can liberate a desire and willingness to change.

As described in earlier chapters, reactance theory provides a fruitful perspective for considering opposition to change. Rather than blame clients for oppositional behavior, reactance theory leads the social worker to anticipate objectively the range of responses to be expected when valued freedoms are threatened (Brehm, 1976). For example, some try to regain their freedom directly by attempting to take back what has been threatened. A frequent response is to restore freedom by implication or "find the loophole" by superficial compliance while violating the spirit of requirements. Third, threatened behaviors and beliefs may be more valued than ever before. Finally, the client may respond to the person or source of the threat with hostility or aggression (R. H. Rooney, 1992, p. 130).

Further, reactance theory lends itself to proactive strategies designed to reduce the opposition. For example, clients who perceive global pressure to change their lifestyle are likely to experience less reactance if those pressures are narrowed in scope with emphasis on behaviors that remain free. Second, reactance is likely to be reduced if the client perceives at least constrained choices (R. H. Rooney, 1992). Understanding the client's

perspective on the situation and avoiding labeling also reduces reactance (p. 135).

Preventing Opposition to Change

Opposition to change may emanate from sources other than ambivalence about changing. Clients may misunderstand the nature of service or of a specific intervention and may therefore be reluctant to cooperate fully. Should this occur, it is vital to explain fully the nature of the service or intervention, exploring what is required and where there is room for choice. This should include clarifying roles of the participants and permitting voluntary clients free choice as to whether or not to proceed. The best way of preventing this type of opposition is to be thorough in formulating contracts, clarifying roles, providing a rationale for specific interventions, inviting questions, eliciting and discussing misgivings, and fostering self-determination.

Other sources include apprehension or fear associated with engaging in behavior that is alien to one's usual functioning or having to face a situation that appears overwhelming. Such fears may be so intense that clients resist carrying out essential actions. Their difficulties may then be compounded by embarrassment over failure to implement the actions, which may produce resistance to seeing the social worker or discussing the problematic situation further. Again, these forms of opposition can be prevented by anticipating and exploring the fears and preparing the client to carry out the actions through modeling, behavioral rehearsal, and guided practice. Because we discussed these strategies of resolving obstacles to change in Chapter 13 and because Hepworth (1979) has discussed this topic at length elsewhere, we will not discuss them further here.

Transference Resistance

Some clients become enmeshed in major transference reactions that pose an obstacle to progress. A client may idealize the social worker and attempt to use the helping relationship as a substitute for dependency gratifications that should be obtained elsewhere; such a client may be preoccupied with fantasies about the social worker rather than focused on goal attainment. Other clients may be disappointed and resentful because a social worker does not meet their unrealistic expectations. Perceiving the social worker as uncaring, withholding, and rejecting (as they likewise perceived their parents), these clients may struggle with angry feelings (negative transference) toward the social worker, which divert them from working productively on their problems. Unless social workers recognize and assist such clients to resolve these feelings by discussing them, accepting them, and placing them in realistic perspective, these clients may prematurely terminate, convinced their perceptions and feelings are accurate.

Again we emphasize that transference reactions are relatively infrequent in short-term, task-centered therapies where the social worker takes an active role, which tends to minimize the possibility of projections. Moreover, time limits and focus on task accomplishment militate against dependency and strong emotional attachment. Long-term and insight-oriented therapies, by contrast, may tend to foster dependency and transference.

Manifestations of Opposition to Change

Opposition to change takes many forms, and the frequency with which clients manifest different forms varies according to the type of setting, the personality of the client, and the ethnicity and socioeconomic levels of clients. The following can be manifestations of opposition:

1. Mental blocking (mind going blank)
2. Lengthy periods of silence
3. Inattention or mind wandering
4. Rambling on at length or dwelling on unimportant details
5. Restlessness or fidgeting
6. Discussing superficialities or irrelevant matters
7. Lying or deliberately misrepresenting facts
8. Intellectualizing (avoiding feelings and problems by focusing on abstract ideas)

9. Changing the subject
10. Forgetting details of distressing events or of content of previous sessions
11. Being tardy for or forgetting, changing, or canceling appointments
12. Minimizing problems or claiming miraculous improvement
13. Bringing up important material at the end of a session
14. Not paying fees for service
15. Not applying knowledge and skills gained in sessions in daily life
16. Assuming a stance of helplessness
17. Using various verbal ploys to justify not taking corrective action, including
    - *"I couldn't do that; it just wouldn't be me."*
    - *"I just can't!"*
    - *"I've tried that, and it doesn't work."*
    - *"I understand what you're saying, but . . ."*
    - *"I'm not so different; isn't everyone . . . ?"*

Many of the preceding phenomena do not necessarily indicate client opposition to change. If the client continues to work productively, the phenomenon may not warrant special handling. If, however, the client appears to have reached an impasse, it is safe to conclude that opposition is involved and to shift the focus to exploring factors that underlie the opposition.

Opposition may also emerge in family and group sessions. Individual members may manifest any of the preceding phenomena. In addition, members may form subgroups and not invest themselves in the total group process. Other manifestations of resistance in groups include scapegoating individual members, isolating oneself and not participating, attempting to force the leader to assume responsibility that belongs with the group, engaging in social banter, failing to stay on topic, and struggling for power rather than working cooperatively. It is also important to bear in mind that one family or group member opposing change may be presenting a concern that others also feel (Nelson, 1975, p. 591). As with individuals, it is critical when impasses are reached to shift the focus of the group to the dysfunctional processes so that the group does not dissipate its energies in counterproductive activities.[1]

Managing Opposition to Change

Because opposition to change is a universal phenomenon, it is not necessary to become alarmed about every possible manifestation of it. Moreover, focusing on trivial opposition may elicit adverse reactions from clients, such as feeling the social worker is attempting to scrutinize and analyze their every minute behavior. Ironically, then, overreacting to presumed manifestations of opposition may needlessly engender it. A rule of thumb is that if opposition is not strong enough to impede progress, it is best ignored. Still, opposition can impede progress and, in some instances, damage helping relationships. When clients manifest opposition that blocks progress, it is imperative to grant highest priority to resolving it. When clients are left to struggle with opposition alone, they often resolve it by withdrawing from the helping process.

The first step in managing potential opposition to change is to bring it into the light of discussion by focusing on here-and-now feelings that underlie it. Sensitive and skillful handling is essential because personal feelings toward the social worker are commonly associated with such opposition, and clients find it difficult to risk sharing these feelings. (Otherwise, they would have shared them already.) Empathy, warmth, and acceptance play a critical role in eliciting clients' untoward feelings because these ingredients foster a nonthreatening interpersonal climate.

In exploring sources of opposition, it is important not to focus on the manifestation per se but rather to cite it as an indication that the client is experiencing troubling thoughts and feelings toward the social worker or toward what is happening in the helping process. An authentic response that conveys the social worker's goodwill and concern that progress has bogged down also reaffirms the social worker's helpful intent and desire to work out whatever difficulties have arisen. At times, there may be cues as to the sources of difficulties based on the content discussed in a preceding session. For example, the client may have discussed extremely painful material, disclosed personal feelings that involved shame or guilt, or bristled in response to being confronted with personal contributions to a problematic situation. In such instances the social worker may open discussion of the feelings, as illustrated in the following: "You appear awfully quiet today, as though you're struggling with some troubling feelings. I know our last session was upsetting to you. Could you share with me what you're feeling about it just now?"

Discussing sources of opposition often reveals fears of where exploring certain personal feelings might lead. Some clients mistakenly fear they are losing their minds and that if they share certain thoughts and feelings, the social worker will initiate steps to admit them to a mental hospital. Other clients fear the social worker will condemn them if they disclose hostile feelings toward a child or discuss extramarital affairs. Still other clients fear the social worker will pressure them to obtain a divorce if they reveal their lack of love for a spouse. With respect to feelings toward the social worker, some clients fear the former will be hurt or offended if they share negative feelings or that the social worker will see them as ridiculous and reject them if they share warm and affectionate feelings.

As social workers initiate exploration of the source of opposition, some clients manifest marked hesitancy about revealing relevant feelings. When this occurs, a technique often successful in cutting through the reluctance is to focus empathically on here-and-now fears about disclosing other troublesome feelings. The social worker's sensitivity, empathy, and genuineness may well pave the way for the client to risk opening up more. The following illustrates such an empathic response:

- "I'm sensing that you're very uncomfortable about discussing your feelings. I may be wrong, but I get the impression you're afraid I would react negatively if you shared those feelings. I can't say for sure how I'd respond, but I want you to know I'd do my best to understand your feelings. Could you share with me what you're feeling at this moment?"

When clients do risk sharing their feelings, it is often therapeutic to accredit their strength for risking and to express reassurance. Such positive responses further cultivate a climate conducive to reciprocal openness, obliterate the feared consequences, and reinforce the client for disclosing risky feelings. The following is an example of such a response:

- "I'm very pleased you expressed the anger that has been building up inside you. That took some courage on your part. It's a lot safer to keep those feelings inside, but then they eat at you and create distance in our relationship. I can accept your anger, and your sharing it with me gives both of us an opportunity to talk things out. I'd feel bad if those feelings continued to build and I didn't even know it."

Positive Connotation

This is another technique that is useful in reducing threat and enabling clients to save face, thereby protecting their self-esteem after risking revealing problematic feelings. Positive connotation involves attributing positive intentions to what would be otherwise regarded as a client's undesirable or negative behavior. In using this technique, the social worker recognizes that the meaning ascribed to behavior can be viewed both positively and negatively, depending on one's vantage point. Viewed as an obstacle to progress, opposition takes on a negative meaning. Viewed from the client's perspective, however, the same behavior may have positive intentions. The following examples clarify this point:

- A client cancels an appointment and holds back in the following session. Exploration reveals she resented the social worker's "pressuring her" to follow a certain course of action. The social

worker empathizes with her feelings as evidence of her determination to be her own person.

- A client has been preoccupied with romantic fantasies about the social worker and has digressed from working on problems. The social worker interprets this romantic feeling as evidence he is moving away from his self-imposed isolation and is permitting himself to experience feelings of closeness that he can gradually risk in social relationships.

- After an extended period of silence and exploration of feelings related to it, a spouse launches into a tirade over how the social worker took sides with the partner in the previous session. The social worker labels the client's response as a legitimate effort to be understood and to ensure that the social worker does not make the marriage worse by drawing erroneous conclusions.

The goal of positive connotation is not to condone the client's opposition or to reinforce distorted perceptions. Rather, the objectives are to minimize clients' needs to defend themselves and to safeguard their already precarious self-esteem and act consistent with a strengths perspective. When using this technique, it is important to assist clients to recognize that their untoward reactions derived from distorted perceptions (if, in fact, they did) and to encourage them to express their feelings directly in the future.

Redefining Problems as Opportunities for Growth

This technique is a close relative of positive connotation because it too involves a form of relabeling. Both clients and social workers tend to view problems negatively. Moreover, clients often view remedial courses of action as "necessary evils," dwelling on the threat involved in risking new behaviors. Therefore, it is often helpful to reformulate problems and essential tasks as opportunities for growth and challenges to gain liberation from stifling and self-defeating behaviors. Relabeling thus emphasizes the positives; that is, the benefits of change rather than the discomfort, fear, and other costs. In using this technique, it is important not to convey an unrealistically positive attitude, for the fears and threats are very real to clients, and being unduly optimistic may simply convey a lack of understanding on your part. Relabeling does not minimize clients' problems or ignore fears in risking new behaviors. It does enable clients to view their difficulties in a fuller perspective that embodies positive as well as negative factors. The following are examples of relabeling problem situations as opportunities for growth:

- A teenage foster child who has run away because the foster parent insisted he adhere to certain deadlines in getting in at night does not want to return to the foster home because the foster parents "are unreasonable." The social worker describes returning as a challenge to deal with a problem head-on and to work it out rather than run away from it, which has been the client's pattern.

- A female client participating in a workfare program resists seeing a doctor because she fears she has cancer. The social worker empathizes with her fears but describes having a checkup as also being an opportunity to rule out that frightening possibility or to receive treatment before the disease progresses, should she have cancer.

- A mildly brain-damaged, socially inhibited young adult expresses fear about seeing a counselor for vocational testing and counseling. The social worker accepts the discomfort but depicts the situation as an opportunity to learn more about his aptitudes and to expand choices in planning his future.

- A wife expresses intense apprehension about refusing to submit to her husband's kinky and excessive sexual demands. The social worker empathizes with her fear but also sees an opportunity for her to gain in strength and self-respect and to present herself as a person to be reckoned with.

Confronting Patterns of Opposition

In some instances, clients fail to progress toward their goals because of the persistence of pervasive dysfunctional patterns of behavior. A client may intellectualize extensively to avoid having to experience painful emotions such as loneliness or depression. Other clients relate in a distant, aloof manner or in aggressive ways to protect against becoming close to others and risking painful rejection. Still others may consistently place responsibility on others or on circumstances for their difficulties, failing to examine or acknowledge their part in them. Because such patterns of behavior often create impasses, social workers must recognize and handle them. Confronting clients with discrepancies between expressed goals and behavior that defeats accomplishment of those goals is often needed to break such impasses. Because we discussed confrontation at length in Chapter 18 we limit our discussion to a special case of confrontation, namely therapeutic binds.

Using Therapeutic Binds

Occasionally, social workers encounter clients who stubbornly cling to self-defeating behaviors despite awareness that these behaviors perpetuate their difficulties. In such instances, placing clients in a therapeutic bind may provide the impetus needed to modify the problematic behaviors. Using a therapeutic bind involves confronting people with their self-defeating behaviors in such a way that they must either modify their behaviors or own responsibility for choosing to perpetuate their difficulties despite their expressed intentions to the contrary (Lovern & Zohn, 1982). The only way out of a therapeutic bind, unless one chooses to acknowledge no intention of changing, is to make constructive changes. The following are examples of situations in which the authors have successfully employed therapeutic binds:

- Despite intensive efforts to resolve fears of being rejected in relationships with others, a client continues to decline social invitations and makes no effort to reach out to others. The social worker asks her about her apparent choice to perpetuate her social isolation rather than to risk relating to others.

- A husband who, with his wife, seeks marital therapy because of severe marital conflict that persists in making decisions unilaterally, despite repeated feedback from his spouse and the social worker that doing so engenders resentment and alienates her. The social worker asks him whether he has decided it is more important to him to wield power than to improve his marital relationship.

- An adolescent persists in truanting, violating family rules, and engaging in antisocial acts despite her assertion that she wants maximal freedom. The social worker counters that she appears unready to use freedom wisely, because being a law unto herself will only result in the court placing controls on her until she demonstrates a capacity to set limits for herself.

- A wife constantly harps on her husband's previous infidelity despite seeking marital therapy to strengthen their relationship. His response to her constant reminders is to withdraw and dis-

engage from the relationship. The social worker faces her with the contradiction in her behavior, stressing that it is apparently more important to her to punish her husband than to enhance their relationship.

In using therapeutic binds, it is vital to observe the guidelines for confrontation, thereby avoiding "clobbering" and alienating the client. Hence asking a question about the apparent contradiction or conclusion can be experienced as a more respectful form of confrontation leading to self-reflection. A therapeutic bind is a potent but high-risk technique, and social workers should use it sparingly, being careful to temper its jarring effect with empathy, concern, and sensitive exploration of the dynamics behind the self-defeating patterns. Above all, social workers should be sure they are employing the technique to assist the client and not to act out their own frustrations about the client's opposition.

Summary

This chapter has presented barriers to change with individuals, including relational reactions, over- and underinvolvement, racial and transcultural barriers, transference and countertransference, sexual attraction toward clients, managing opposition to change, and therapeutic binds. In the next chapter, we move to final consideration of evaluation and termination.

Internet Resources

Through InfoTrac®, you can read two articles pertinent to this chapter: Bower, B. (1997). Therapy bonds and the bottle (establishment of therapeutic alliance linked to higher success rate in treatment of alcoholics). *Science News, 152* (8). Handmaker,

N. S., Miller, W. R., & Manicke, M. (1999). Findings of a pilot study of motivational interviewing with pregnant drinkers. *Journal of Studies on Alcohol, 60* (2).

SKILL DEVELOPMENT EXERCISES IN MANAGING RELATIONAL REACTIONS AND OPPOSITION

The following exercises will assist you in expanding your skills in responding appropriately to relational reactions and opposition to change. Study each client message and determine whether a relational reaction or opposition to change might be involved. Then write the response you would give if you were the social worker. Compare your response with the modeled response provided at the end of the exercises. Bear in mind that the modeled response is only one of many possible appropriate responses.

CLIENT STATEMENTS

1. *Male client who has been discussing feelings of rejection and self-doubt after his partner broke up with him* [*suddenly looks down, sighs, then looks up*]: Say, did I tell you I got promoted at work?

2. *Female client, age 23* [*to male social worker, age 25*]: I've been feeling very close to you these past weeks. I was wondering if you could hold me in your arms for just a moment.

3. *Male client, age 27* [*with irritation*]: I've been coming to see you for eight weeks, and things haven't changed a bit. I'm beginning to question your competence.

4. *Delinquent on probation, age 16:* I think it's ridiculous to have to come here every week. You don't have to worry about me. I'm not getting into any trouble.

5. *Female welfare recipient:* Sure, you say you want to help me. All you social workers are just alike. You don't understand the pressure I have to get a good job in the time I have left on welfare. If you really want to help, you would increase the time I have left.

6. *Client, age 27* [*to male social worker*]: I've just never been able to trust men. My old man was alcoholic, and the only thing you could depend on with him was that he'd be drunk when you needed him most.

7. *Male client* [*to female mental health social worker*]: Sometimes I really felt I was cheated in life, you know, with parents who didn't give a damn what happened to me. I think about you—how warm and caring you are, and—I know it sounds crazy but I wish I'd had you for a mother. Sometimes I even daydream about it.

8. *Client, after an emotion-laden previous session* [*yawns, looks out the window, and comments*]: Not much to talk about today. Nothing much has happened this week.

9. *Male client, age 24* [*in fifth interview*]: I have this thing where people never measure up to my expectations. I know I expect too much, and I always end up feeling let down.

10. *Middle-aged Native American:* It's important to me that you do not think of me according to the usual stereotype. I'm ambitious and want to do right by my family. I just need a job right now.

MODELED RESPONSES

1. "No, but before you do, I'd like to know more about what you were feeling just a moment ago when you were discussing your breakup with your partner. I was sensing that was painful for you to talk about. Could you share what you feel as you think about it?"

2. "I'm complimented you would want me to hold you and pleased you could share those feelings with me. I want you to know I feel close to you too, but if I were to let myself feel romantic toward you, I'd be letting you down. I couldn't be helpful to you if I were involved in that way. I hope you can understand."

3. "I can see you're anxious to get things worked out, and that's a plus." [*Positive connotation.*] "But you're pretty ticked off with me, as though I haven't been doing my job. I'd like to understand those feelings more. What do you feel I should be doing different?" [*Exploring feelings and expectations.*]

4. "You sound pretty angry about having to report to me each week. I can't blame you for that. Still, the judge ordered it, and neither of us really has any choice. How do you suggest we make the best of the situation?"

5. "I'm sorry you feel I'm not really interested in helping you. I gather you've had some bad experiences with other caseworkers, and I hope our relationship can be better. I sense your frustration at working under this time pressure and anxiety about what will occur if you don't succeed in the time available. I will work with you to make the best use of the time to get a job you feel good about. Sometimes as we come to the end of the time frame there are some possibilities for extension but that can't be guaranteed. I wonder if the best use of our time might be to do the best we can to get the kind of job you want in the time available."

6. "I can understand then that you might find it difficult to trust me—wondering if I'm really dependable."

7. [*With a warm smile*]: "Thank you for the compliment. I gather you've been experiencing my care for you and find yourself longing for the love and care you didn't receive as a child. I can sense your feelings keenly and appreciate your sharing them."

8. "Somehow that doesn't fit with what we talked about last week. You expressed some very deep feelings about yourself and your marriage. I'd like to hear what you've been feeling about what we discussed last time."

9. "I wonder if that's what you're feeling just now in our relationship—that I haven't measured up to your expectations in some way. Could you share with me what you've been feeling in that regard?"

10. "I appreciate your sharing those feelings with me. I gather you've wondered how I do see you. I see you as an ambitious and responsible person, and I want you to know I appreciate those qualities in you."

Notes

1. In some instances, manifestations of group behaviors that may appear at first to be opposition consist of adjustment reactions of members to excessive changes (e.g., loss of members, canceled sessions, or a move to another meeting place), which tend to frustrate and discourage group members.

PART 4

The Termination Phase

The third and final phase of the helping process involves the final evaluation of progress and termination of the helping relationship. Although it has received less attention in the literature than the beginning and middle phases, the final phase is nevertheless vital, for the manner in which the helping relationship and process are concluded strongly influences whether clients maintain the progress they have achieved and continue to grow following formal termination. It is important that social workers understand how to evaluate their practice and how to sensitively and skillfully conclude their work with the client.

CHAPTER 20

The Final Phase: Termination

Revised and edited by Kim Strom-Gottfried

CHAPTER OVERVIEW

In this chapter we review methods for evaluating case progress, describe various factors that impact the termination process, identify relevant tasks for both social workers and clients, and discuss skills essential to managing termination effectively.

EVALUATION

Evaluating outcomes of the helping process has assumed ever-increasing significance in direct practice; indeed, the majority of direct social workers engage in some form of evaluation, as we noted in Chapter 12. If you have systematically obtained baseline measures, clients will be prepared for evaluation at termination. You can further enhance their cooperation by again reviewing the rationale and actively involving them in the process. Examples for introducing this to the client include:

- "An important part of termination is to assess the results we have achieved and to identify what helped you most and least during our work together."

- "As an agency, we're committed to improving the quality of our services. Your honest feedback will help us to know how we're doing."

- "Our evaluation measures will help you and me see how your symptoms have changed since we began working together."

Evaluation consists of three different dimensions: (1) outcomes, (2) process, and (3) the social worker.

Outcomes

Evaluation of outcomes involves assessing the results achieved against the goals that were formulated during the contracting phase of work. As described in Chapters 8 and 12, the methods utilized during the assessment and goal-setting phase will, in part, determine what outcomes you measure.

If the initial goals for work were vague or unmeasurable, or if no baseline measures were taken, you will need to use an interview or questionnaire to determine your clients' views and can then compare their sense of progress against your own observations. The difficulty with these recollections, of course, is that they may be highly selective and may be affected by a number of factors such as the client's desire to please (or punish) the worker, the client's interest in concluding service, or the hope that problems *are* resolved and that further services are not necessary. Although it is unwise to challenge clients' perceptions, subjectivity can be reduced by asking clients to provide actual examples of recent events that illustrate their attainment of goals. Discussing such events briefly also provides an opportunity for the social worker to reaffirm the client's accomplishments, which tends to heighten confidence and satisfaction. In addition to clients' perceptions of their progress, evaluation should include other criteria where practicable. For example, feedback from collateral contacts, such as family members, teachers, other helpers, or fellow clients (in groups or group settings) may provide additional perspectives on client progress.

Process

Another aspect of evaluation relates to clients' perceptions of aspects of the helping process that were useful or detrimental. Feedback about techniques and incidents that enhanced or blocked progress enables social workers to hone certain skills, eliminate others, and use techniques with greater discrimination. Such "formative evaluation" methods also help organizations to determine which elements of their programs were effective in bringing about the desired change. A technique that is useful with an assertive client, for example, may produce an opposite effect with a depressed client. Likewise a family intervention may be most effective if structured in a particular way. A social worker may have attributed a positive outcome to a masterfully executed technique only to find the client was helped far more by the worker's willingness to reach out and maintain hope when the latter had virtually given up (McCollum & Beer, 1995).

The Social Worker

Some settings facilitate formal feedback by sending out written client feedback forms that not only address satisfaction with the social worker's service but also evaluate structural issues such as appropriateness of the waiting room, convenience of parking, time elapsed between request and first appointment, friendliness of reception staff, and so on (Ackley, 1997; Corcoran & Vandiver, 1996).

TERMINATION

Termination refers to the process of formally ending the individual worker-client relationship and is a feature of practice with a variety of client systems, from individuals and families to task groups, coalitions, and communities.[1] Terminations can occur when goals are met, when clients are transitioned to other services, when time-limited services are concluded, and when workers or clients leave the helping relationship.

Successful termination involves preparing clients adequately for separation from the social worker and/or group and accomplishing other tasks that enhance the transition from being a client to being on one's own. These tasks include:

1. Evaluating the service provided and the extent to which goals were accomplished

2. Determining when to implement termination

3. Mutually resolving emotional reactions experienced during the process of ending

4. Planning to maintain gains achieved and to achieve continued growth

The significance of these tasks and the extent to which they can be successfully accomplished are determined in great measure by the context in which the helping relationship takes place. Factors such as whether the contact is voluntary, the type of client system involved, and the nature of the intervention all may affect the intensity of the termination process. Emotional reactions will vary depending on the nature and length of the helping relationship: involuntary clients and those with more structured and time limited services will likely experience less loss at termination than those who have had longer and more voluntary relationships with the social worker. For example, termination of a time-limited educational group may be less intense and require less preparation of members than would the ending of an ongoing interpersonal support group.[2] Termination from brief crisis intervention, case management, or discharge planning relationships may differ in intensity depending on the nature of the needs met and the length of service. Termination from family sessions may be less difficult than from individual work, in that most of the client system will continue to work and be together, albeit without the benefit of the social worker's involvement. Other interactions between the tasks of termination and the types of termination will be evident in the following sections.

Types of Termination

Terminations generally fall into two categories—unplanned and planned, though there are subsets of each that are worthy of examination. Unplanned terminations occur when the clients withdraw prematurely from services, or when social workers leave the helping relationship due to illness, job change, or other circumstances. Planned terminations can occur when clients' goals are achieved, when transfer or referral is necessary, or when service is concluded due to the time-limited nature of the setting (such as hospitals or schools) or due to the treatment modality used (such as brief treatment or fixed-length groups).

Planned Terminations

As noted, planned terminations can take many forms. The nature of the setting, interventive method, or funding source can all impose external pressures to terminate within a specific period of time. Other planned endings emerge from the helping relationship itself, as clients achieve their goals and move on to independence from the social worker.

In organizations or agencies whose function involves providing service according to fixed time intervals, termination must be planned accordingly. In school settings, for example, services are generally discontinued at the conclusion of an academic year. In hospitals and other institutional settings, the duration of service is determined by the length of hospitalization, confinement, or insurance coverage. Some service models, such as time-limited groups or fixed-length residential programs, are clearly designed to pace and conclude services

within a specific time frame. Some treatment programs are organized such that clients progress from one program (and one set of workers) to another as their needs change. Depending on the context of treatment, then, services may thus extend from several days to several months. Temporal factors are also central in termination when service is provided by social work students, who leave a given practicum setting at the completion of an academic year. "Simultaneous termination" offers the advantage of mutually shared, powerful experiences of ending and it focuses the time and attention devoted to termination tasks (A. S. Joyce, Duncan, Duncan, Kipnes, & Piper, 1996).

Termination under these circumstances involves certain factors peculiar to these settings. First, the ending of a school year or of a training period for students is a predetermined time for termination, which reduces the possibility that clients will (1) interpret time limits as being arbitrarily imposed or (2) perceive the social worker's leaving as desertion or abandonment. Knowing the termination date well in advance also provides ample time to resolve feelings about separation. Nevertheless, this means that in school settings student clients may lose many supports all at one time.

Another factor common to termination determined by temporal constraints related to agency function is that clients' problems may not have been adequately resolved by the ending of a fixed time interval. The predetermined ending may thus prove to be untimely for some clients; consequently, clients may react intensely to losing service and ending the helping relationship in midstream (Weiner, 1984). Social workers are therefore confronted with the dual tasks of working through feelings associated with untimely separation and referring clients for additional services when indicated. We discuss both of these matters in later sections.

Predetermined endings imposed by the close of a school year or a fixed length of service do not necessarily convey the same expectations of a positive outcome as do time limits that are imposed by social workers. In other words, to say "I will see you for eight sessions because that is sufficient time to achieve your goals" conveys a far more positive expectation than "I will see you for eight sessions because that is all the available time before you will be discharged." Still, social workers should not assume that time-limited work leads to less than satisfactory outcomes. Clients can enjoy a fruitful relationship with students and other practitioners even if termination results in referral for further services. For example, one of the authors worked with a client with serious, long-term mental health problems. During the time allotted for her field placement, she was able to help him through a crisis and help build his social supports so that future crises would not result in rehospitalization. In termination, they reviewed the accomplishments of the year and the client met his new worker, who would meet with him on a less-intensive basis for support and maintenance of gains.

When terminations are not predetermined by agency setting or by form of service, how do the worker and client know when to end? When services are highly goal directed, the approach of termination may be clear as goals are reached and changes are sustained. When goals are amorphous or ongoing, however, determining a proper ending point can be more difficult. Theoretically, humans can grow indefinitely, and determining when clients have achieved optimal growth is no simple task. Ordinarily it is appropriate to introduce termination when the client has reached the point of diminishing returns, that is, when the gains from sessions taper off to the point of being minor in significance. The client may indicate through words or actions that he or she is ready to discontinue services, or the social worker may initiate such discussion.

Planned Terminations with Unsuccessful Outcomes

Sometimes termination occurs in a planned manner, but the endings are not marked by successful achievement of service goals. This may occur when clients are hopelessly stalemated despite vigorous and persistent efforts to surmount their difficulties. Groups also occasionally end with unsuccessful results, and members may be frustrated, disappointed, or angry with the leader or with other members. When the helping process ends unsuccessfully, termination should include discussion of (1) factors that prevented achieving more favorable results and (2) clients' feelings about seeking additional help in the future. To successfully work through negative feelings, social workers will need to maintain focus on the feelings until clients are able to move beyond them.

Understanding and Responding to Termination Reactions

Inherent in termination is separation from the social worker (and other clients, in the case of groups or communal settings). Separation typically involves mixed feelings, for both the social worker and the client, which vary in intensity according to the degree of success achieved, the intensity of the attachment, the type of termination, the cultural orientation of the client, and his or her previous experiences with separations from significant others (Dorfman, 1996). When clients successfully accomplish their goals, they experience a certain degree of pride and satisfaction as the helping process draws to a close. If they have grown in strength and self-esteem, they optimistically view the future as a challenge for continued growth.

Most clients in individual, conjoint, family, and group therapy experience positive emotions in termination. Benefits of the gains achieved usually far outweigh the impact of the loss of the helping relationship. Clients may reflect on the experience, saying, "I was such a wreck when I first came to see you—I'm surprised I didn't scare you away," or "You helped me get my thinking straight, so I could see the options I had before me," or "Even if things didn't change that much with my son, it helped me a lot to be in the group and know I'm not alone."

Clients and social workers alike commonly experience a sense of loss during the terminal process. Indeed, sadness is a common element of many of the endings that are a part of life itself (e.g., leaving parents to attend school, advancing from one grade to another, graduating, moving from one home to another, and losing loved ones). This loss may be a deeply moving experience involving the "sweet sorrow" generally associated with parting from a person whom one has grown to value. Adept social workers help clients to give voice to these ambivalent feelings, acknowledging that transitions can be difficult but that successfully handling good times and difficult ones is a necessary part of growth.

Because termination can evoke feelings associated with past losses and endings, clients may respond to it in a variety of ways (and in any of these ways to varying degrees). These reactions may include:

1. *Anger.* Clients may experience anger at termination, especially when termination occurs because the social worker leaves the agency. Because the termination is not planned and occurs with little forewarning, reactions are sometimes similar to those that involve other types of sudden crises. The social worker may need to reach for the feelings evoked by his or her departure, as clients may have difficulty expressing negative emotions while they are also experiencing sadness or anxiety about the impending loss. It is important that the social worker encourage the expression of emotions and respond empathically to them. It is vital, however, not to empathize to the extent of overidentifying and losing the capacity to assist the client with negative feelings and to engage in constructive planning.

2. *Denial.* Clients may contend that they were unaware of the impending termination or time limits on service and behave as if termination is not imminent. Others may avoid endings by failing to appear for concluding sessions with the worker (Dorfman, 1996). A client may thus respond by shutting off thoughts of the impending loss (denial) and relate as though nothing has happened. It is a mistake to interpret the client's business-as-usual demeanor as an indication the client is taking the termination in stride, for the unruffled exterior may represent the calm before the storm. The client's temporary denial of feelings is an attempt to ward off psychic pain associated with a distressing reality that must be faced.

To assist clients in getting in touch with their emotions, it is helpful to reintroduce the topic of termination and to express your desire to assist them in formulating plans to continue working toward their goals after your departure. As you bring up the topic of termination, it is critical to be sensitive to nonverbal cues that manifest emotional reactions. We also recommend employing empathic communication that conveys understanding of and elicits the hurt, resentment, and rejection clients commonly experience when a valued person leaves.

3. *Avoidance.* Occasionally, clients express their anger and hurt over a social worker's leaving by "rejecting the worker before the latter can reject them." As such, they may fail to appear for sessions as termination approaches. Others may ignore the social worker or profess that they no longer need him or her, in effect, employing the strategy that the best defense is a good offense. When clients act in this fashion, it is critical to reach out to them; otherwise, they tend to interpret the failure to do so as evidence the social worker never really cared about them at all. In reaching out, a personal contact by telephone or home visit is essential, for there must be an opportunity for interaction in which the social worker can reaffirm his or her concern and care and convey empathy and understanding of the client's emotional reaction.

4. *Reporting Recurrence of Old Problems.* Some clients tend to panic as treatment approaches closure and experience a return of difficulties that have been under control for some time (H. Levinson, 1977). Other clients whose best functioning is submarginal may manifest more severe reactions by engaging in self-destructive or suicidal acts.

5. *Introducing New Problems.* In an effort to continue the helping relationship, some clients introduce new stresses and problems during the terminal sessions and even during the final scheduled session. Further, clients who normally communicate minimally may suddenly open up, and other

clients may reveal confidential information they have previously withheld. Although the social worker should not minimize the importance of new problems, information, or "doorknob confessions," it is vital not to grasp the bait without first exploring feelings about termination. Placed in context, new information and problems often are relatively insignificant.

At times, it may make sense for you and the client to reconsider a planned ending. Limited extensions of service can be made to accomplish agreed-upon tasks if it appears that additional time would make it possible for the client to achieve decisive progress. There may be legitimate reasons for recontracting for additional sessions, such as not identifying key problems until late in the helping process, returning to problems that were identified earlier but had to be set aside in favor of more pressing problems, or anticipating transitional events that bear on the clients' problems (e.g., getting married, being discharged from an institution, regaining custody of a child). In these instances, continuing the working relationships may be warranted, especially if the client achieved substantial progress on other problems during the initial contract period.

6. *Attempting to Prolong Contact.* Sometimes, rather than reveal new or renewed problems, clients may more directly seek continued contact with the worker by suggesting a social or business relationship with the worker following termination. For example, the client may suggest meeting for coffee on occasion or exchanging cards or letters, or may propose joining a training program that will put him or her in regular contact with the worker. This phenomenon is also evident when groups decide to continue meeting after the agency's involvement has concluded. Unfortunately, the security brought by such plans is only fleeting and the negative effects of continued contact can be serious. Clearly, some requests for continued contact would be inappropriate, given the profession's ethical proscriptions against dual relationships. Other forms of contact, while not prohibited, may still be unwise in that they may undo the work done in the help-

ing relationship and may undermine the client's confidence in the ability to function without the worker. Further, continued, informal involvement may constrain the client from investing in other rewarding relationships (Bostic, Shadid, & Blotcky, 1996). This is not to say that planned follow-up phone calls, appointments, and "booster sessions" are inappropriate. To the contrary, such plans are made within the goals of the helping process with a clear therapeutic purpose, not simply to avoid the inevitability of ending.

Finally, from a pragmatic standpoint, few workers or group members can keep up therapeutic relationships indefinitely.

7. *Finding Substitutes for the Social Worker.* Although finding one or more persons to replace the social worker may be a constructive way of developing social resources, it may also be a way of locating a person on whom the client can become dependent, thereby compensating for the loss of the social worker.

Group members may also seek to compensate for losses of group support by affiliating with other groups and never actually developing enduring social support systems.

Social Workers' Reactions to Termination

Clients are not the only ones to manifest reactions to termination. Social workers' responses can include guilt (at letting the client down or failing to sufficiently help the client), avoidance (delaying announcement of termination to avoid the feelings or reaction evoked), relief (at ending involvement with a difficult or challenging client), and prolonging service (because of financial or emotional fulfillment experienced by the clinician) (Dorfman, 1996; Joyce et al., 1996; B. C. Murphy & Dillon, 1998). In settings where premature terminations are the norm, workers may experience burnout and decreased sensitivity to clients after repeatedly working on cases where closure is not possible and treatment is ended before interventions are carried out (Resnick & Dziegielewski, 1996). Self-understanding and good supervision are the essential elements by which even seasoned social workers can recognize the reactions at play in terminations. As these reactions negatively impact the client, identifying and managing them is crucial.

CONSOLIDATING GAINS AND PLANNING MAINTENANCE STRATEGIES

In addition to managing the emotional and behavioral reactions to ending, another task of termination involves summarizing and stabilizing the changes achieved and developing a plan to sustain those changes. A similar aim in work with groups is not only to assist members to interact successfully within the group context but also to transfer their newly developed interpersonal skills to the broad arena of social relationships.

Failure to maintain gains has been attributed to various factors, including the following:

1. A natural tendency to revert to habitual response patterns (e.g., use of alcohol or drugs, aggressive or withdrawn behavior)
2. Personal and environmental stressors (e.g., family conflicts, pressures from landlords, personal rejection, loss of job, health problems, and deaths of loved ones)
3. Lack of opportunities in the environment for social and leisure activities
4. Absence of positive support systems
5. Inadequate social skills
6. Lack of reinforcement for functional behaviors
7. Inadequate preparation for environmental changes
8. Inability to resist peer pressures
9. Return to dysfunctional family environments
10. Inadequately established new behaviors

It follows that in planning maintenance strategies, you must anticipate such forces and prepare clients for coping with them. A monitoring phase may be useful for some clients. In this, the number and frequency of sessions decrease while support systems are called on to assist the client with new concerns. This technique, in effect, "weans" the client from the social worker's support, yet allows a transitional period to try out new skills and supports while gradually concluding the helping relationship.

Social workers may also encourage clients to return for additional help should problems appear to be mounting out of control. Although it is important to express confidence in clients' ability to cope independently with their problems, it is equally important to convey your continued interest in them and to invite them to return should they need to do so.[3]

Follow-Up Sessions

Posttermination follow-up sessions are another important technique in successful termination and change maintenance. Follow-up sessions benefit both clients and workers.[4] Many clients continue to progress after termination, and follow up sessions provide the opportunity to accredit such gains and encourage them to continue their efforts. These sessions also provide the worker the opportunity to provide brief additional assistance for residual difficulties. Follow-up sessions also enable social workers to assess the durability of changes; that is, to determine whether clients maintain gains beyond the immediate influence of the helping relationship. An additional benefit of planned follow-up sessions is that they may soften the impact of termination.

By introducing the notion of the follow-up session as an integral part of the helping process, social workers can avoid the pitfalls of clients later viewing the follow-up session as an intrusion into their private lives or as an attempt to satisfy the social worker's curiosity. Wells recommends that in arranging for the follow-up session, social workers not set a specific date but rather explain they will contact the client after a designated interval (R. A. Wells, 1994). This interval offers the client an opportunity to test out and further consolidate the learning and change achieved during the formal helping period.

In the follow-up session, the social worker generally relates more informally than during the period of intervention. After appropriate social amenities, the social worker guides the conversation to the clients' progress and obtains postintervention measures when appropriate. The follow-up session also provides an excellent opportunity for further evaluation of the social worker's efforts during the period of intervention. In retrospect, what was most helpful? What was least helpful? Further efforts can also be made to consolidate gains. What was gained from treatment that the client can continue to use in coping with life? Finally, the social worker can contract for further, formalized, help if this appears necessary. Follow-up sessions thus enable social workers to arrange for timely assistance that may arrest deterioration in functioning.[5]

One caution in the use of follow-up sessions is that they may not allow the client to make a "clean break" from services. Clients who had difficulty separating during termination may use follow-up sessions as an opportunity to prolong contact with the worker. This continued attachment is detrimental to the change process and it inhibits the client from establishing appropriate attachments with social networks and with other helping professionals. Social workers should be alert to this possibility in proposing follow-up sessions and assure that clients understand the specific purpose and focus of such sessions.

Ending Rituals

In many settings, termination may be concluded by a form of celebration or ritual that symbolically marks the goals achieved and the relationship's conclusion (Murphy & Dillon, 1998). For example, in residential programs and some treatment groups, termination may be acknowledged in "graduation" ceremonies, where other residents or members may comment on the departing member's growth and offer good wishes for the future. Certificates, collages, cards, or "memory books" (Elbow, 1987) are but a few of the symbolic gifts that terminating clients may receive from staff or fellow clients. In individual and family work, social workers may choose to mark termination with small gifts such as a book, a plant, a framed inspirational quote, or some other token that is representative of the working relationship.

The decision to use rituals to mark termination should be based on an understanding of the client, the appropriateness of such actions for the agency or setting, and the meaning that the client may give such actions. For example, giving the client a personal greeting card may be misinterpreted as a gesture of intimate friendship by some clients, whereas for other clients, such as a child leaving foster care for a permanent placement, it may be a source of comfort and continuity. A gift that is too lavish may cause discomfort if the client feels the need to reciprocate in some way. "Goodbye parties" may reinforce feelings of accomplishment and confidence, or they may obviate the feelings of sadness or ambivalence that must also be addressed as part of closure (Shulman, 1992). Graduation ceremonies may recreate past disappointments and lead to further setbacks if, for example, family members refuse to attend and acknowledge the changes the client has achieved (D. M. Jones, 1996).

Dorfman (1996) suggests asking the client how he or she would like to mark the final session and offering options if the client seems unsure what to suggest. Useful and meaningful ending rituals are numerous. For example, if the final session of the "Banana Splits" group for children of families undergoing divorce or separation, the final session involves making and eating banana splits (McGonagle, 1986). Clients may ask the worker to create a "diploma" indicating what they have achieved and ask to have a photo taken together (Dorfman, 1996). Graduation ceremonies and other events to mark group terminations can facilitate the tasks of termination and model meaningful rituals in a way that clients might not have experienced previously (D. M. Jones, 1996). These endings can also help to motivate other clients toward the achievements being celebrated by fellow group or residence members.

Case Example

"Horizons" is a halfway house for youth whose behavioral problems have resulted in hospitalization or incarceration. The intent of the program is to help teenagers readjust to community life and get social supports in place so that they can return to their homes or move successfully into independent living. Given this focus, the length of stay for any individual resident varies considerably. Some youth encounter difficulties or re-offend and are returned to jail or to inpatient settings or simply "drop out of sight." These endings can be difficult for staff as they deal with disappointment in the client's failure to "make it" this time around and perhaps question what they might have done to prevent this outcome. It is also disturbing for other clients as they worry about their own challenges and their ability to successfully move on to the next step.

When residents terminate prematurely from the program, they are asked to attend a community meeting, where they can process with the group their experiences in the program and the things they learned that can be of use in the future. Staff and other residents are also invited to share their observations and feelings, with the intention of giving supportive and constructive feedback from a caring community—one to which the resident might someday return. When clients quit the program and drop out of sight, such sessions are still held, as residents and staff process their feelings about the departure and discern lessons they can take away from it.

When residents have met their goals and are ready to move on to a more permanent living situation, staff discuss the plan and timeline for departure and they are alert to the difficulties that can arise at termination. The staff make a point of discussing, in groups or individual sessions, the fears that can arise in moving from some place "comfortable" to the unknown. Sometimes, alumni of the program will come to talk about their experiences and offer advice and encouragement. At this time, goals are reviewed, progress is charted, and the client's views are sought on what aspects of the program facilitated change. Clients and staff work together to anticipate the challenges ahead and put in place the strategies necessary to address them.

During a resident's final days the "Horizons" staff and residents create a "graduation" ceremony, and each resident offers the one who is leaving symbolic gifts to take on "the journey." These may be inspirational quotes, reminders of inside jokes or shared experiences, and more tangible gifts, such as towels or pots and pans to help get established in the new setting. Family members, teachers, and workers from other agencies are encouraged to attend, and at the ceremony are asked to support the client in the next steps ahead. These ceremonies are often tearful and moving events, where the emphasis is on achievement and on hope for the future.

Summary

Social workers are well aware of the importance of engagement with clients and the skills and attitudes needed to build an effective working relationship. Unfortunately, when, for whatever reason, the relationship concludes, workers may not be as astute about "taking the relationship apart." Effective evaluation and termination leave both the worker and client with a shared sense of the accomplishments achieved in their work together. It affords the opportunity to model ending a relationship in a way that is not hurtful or damaging to the client. Effective termination equips the client with the skills and knowledge necessary to sustain gains or to seek further help as needed in the future.

Internet Resources

You can access many resources related to evaluation by accessing *http:// www.nyu.edu/socialwork/wwwrsw/* and choosing "social work practice" and then clicking on "evaluation." You can also use the keyword "termination" in InfoTrac® to access Medquest Communications (1997). Treatment drop-outs explained. *Behavioral Health Management,* 17 (3). You can access a useful article on evaluation through InfoTrac®: Gardner, F. (2000). Design evaluation: Illuminating social work practice for better outcomes. *Social Work,* 45 (2).

Notes

1. For information on the concepts and steps of termination as they apply to macropractice, we suggest Harrigan, Fauri, and Netting (1998).

2. For an excellent source on the considerations and strategies in using time-limited group treatments, see McKenzie (1996).

3. Brownell, Marlatt, Lichenstein, and Wilson (1986), Daley (1987, 1991), Marlatt and Gordon (1985), and Catalano, Wells, Jenson, & Hawkins (1989) have authored articles and books that identify various factors that contribute to relapse, discuss beliefs and myths associated with addictions, and delineate models for relapse education and treatment with addicted and impulse-disordered clients.

4. We wish to acknowledge that the content of this section is based largely on Richard A. Wells, who discusses this subject in Wells (1994).

5. For additional guidelines to conducting follow-up interviews, we recommend an article by Bernard (1985) about follow-up interviews with psychotherapy patients.

References

A

Abell, N. (1991). The index of clinical stress: A brief measure of subjective stress for practice and research. *Social Work Research and Abstracts, 27* (2), 12–15.

Abramson, J. (1988). Participation of elderly patients in discharge planning: Is self-determination a reality? *Social Work, 33* (5), 443–448.

Abramson, M. (1985). The autonomy-paternalism dilemma in social work. *Social Work, 27,* 422–427.

Ackley, D. C. (1997). *Breaking free of managed care.* Orlando, FL: Guilford.

Aguilar, I. (1972). Initial contact with Mexican American families. *Social Work, 20,* 379–382.

Aguilar, M. (1983). *Patterns of health care utilization of Mexican American women.* Unpublished doctoral dissertation, University of Illinois, Urbana-Champaign.

Aguilera, D., & Messick, J. (1982). *Crisis intervention: Theory and methodology* (4th ed.). St. Louis: Mosby.

Akabas, H., Fine, M., & Yasser, R. (1982). Putting secondary prevention to the test: A study of an early intervention strategy with disabled workers. *Journal of Primary Prevention, 2,* 165–187.

Albert, R. (1983). Social advocacy in the regulatory process. *Social Casework, 64,* 473–481.

Alberti, R., & Emmons, M. (1970, 1974). *Your perfect right: A guide to assertive behavior.* San Luis Obispo, CA: Impact.

Alcabes, A. A., & Jones, J. A. (1985). Structural determinants of clienthood. *Social Work, 30,* 49–55.

Alcalay, R., Ghee, A., & Scrimshaw, S. (1993). Designing prenatal care messages for low-income Mexican women. *Public Health Reports, 108* (3), 354–362.

Alexander, E. (1991). Sharing power among organizations: Coordination models to link theory and practice. In J. M. Bryson & R. C. Einsweiler (Eds.), *Shared power, What is it? How does it work? How can we make it work better?* (pp. 213–247). Lanham, MD: University Press of America.

Allen-Meares, P., & Lane, B. A. (1987). Grounding social work practice in theory: Ecosystems. *Social Casework, 68,* 515–521.

Altman, H. (1982). Collaborative discharge planning. *Social Work, 27,* 422–427.

American Psychiatric Association. (1987). *Diagnostic and statistical manual of mental disorders* (3rd ed., rev.), Spitzer, R. L. et al. (Eds.). Washington, DC: American Psychiatric Press.

American Psychiatric Association. (1994). *Diagnostic and statistical manual for mental disorders* (4th ed.). Washington, DC: Author.

Anastas, J. W., Gibeau, J. L., & Larson, P. J. (1990). Working families and eldercare: A national perspective in an aging America. *Social Work, 35* (5), 405–411.

Anderson, D. A., & Worthen, D. (1997). Exploring a fourth dimension: Spirituality as a resource for the couple therapist. *Journal of Marital and Family Therapy, 23* (1), 3–12.

Anderson, S., & Grant, J. (1984). Pregnant women and alcohol: Implications for social work. *Social Casework, 65,* 3–10.

Anderson, S., & Mandell, D. (1989). The use of self-disclosure by professional social workers. *Social Casework, 70* (5), 259–267.

Aponte, H. J. (1977). Anatomy of a therapist. In P. Papp (Ed.), *Family therapy—Full length case studies.* New York: Gardner Press.

Aponte, H. J. (1982, March-April). The person of the therapist: The cornerstone of therapy. *Family Therapy Network, 21,* 19–21, 46.

Aponte, H. J., & Van Deusen, J. (1981). Structural family therapy. In A. Gurman & D. Kniskern (Eds.), *Handbook of family therapy* (pp. 310–360). New York: Brunner/Mazel.

Applegate, J. S. (1992). The impact of subjective measures on nonbehavioral practice research: Outcome vs. process. *Families in Society, 73* (2), 100–108.

Arnette, K. J. (1997). A psychophysiological intervention for marital discord. *Journal of Family Psychotherapy, 8* (2), 3–16.

Arnowitz, E., Brunswick, L., & Kaplan, B. (1983). Group therapy with patients in the waiting room of an oncology clinic. *Social Work, 28,* 395–397.

Aronson, H., & Overall, B. (1966). Treatment expectations of patients in two social classes. *Social Work, 11,* 35–41.

Associated Press (1991). Tempe *Daily News Tribune.* (January 9, 1991).

Atchey, R. C. (1991). *Social forces and aging* (6th ed.). Springfield, IL: Charles G. Thomas.

Attneave, C. (1982). American Indians and Alaska native families. In M. McGoldrick, J. Pearce, & J. Giordano (Eds.), *Ethnicity and family therapy* (pp. 55–83). New York: Guilford Press.

Auerback, S., & Moser, C. (1987). Groups for the wives of gay and bisexual men. *Social Work, 32,* 321–325.

Auslander, G. K., & Litwin, H. (1987). The parameters of network intervention: A social work application. *Social Service Review, 61,* 26–29.

Austin, C. D. (1990). Case management: Myths and realities. *Families in Society, 71* (7), 398–405.

Austin, K. M., Moline, M. E., & Williams, G. T. (1990). *Confronting malpractice: Legal and ethical dilemmas in psychotherapy.* Newbury Park, CA: Sage.

B

Baer, J. (1999). Family relationships, parenting behavior, and adolescent deviance in three ethnic groups. *Families in Society, 80* (3), 279–285.

Bagarozzi, D., & Anderson, S. A. (1989). *Personal, marital, and family myths.* New York: Norton.

Bagarozzi, D., & Kurtz, L. F. (1983). Administrators' perspectives on case management. *Arete, 8,* 13–21.

Bahou, C., & Gralnick, M. (1989). High-risk conversations: A response to Reamer. *Social Work, 34* (3), 262–264.

Bailey-Dempsey, C., & Reid, W. J. (1995, March). *Paradigm shifting: Preparing social work students for interdisciplinary practice*. Council on Social Work Education. Annual Program Meeting, San Diego, CA.

Bailey-Dempsey, C., & Reid, W. J. (1996). Intervention design and development: A case study. *Research on Social Work Practice, 6* (2), 208–228.

Balgopal, P., & Vassil, T. (1983). *Groups in social work: An ecological perspective*. New York: Macmillan.

Ballew, J. (1985). Role of natural helpers in preventing child abuse and neglect. *Social Work, 30,* 37–41.

Bandura, A. (1977). Self-efficacy: Toward a unifying theory of behavioral change. *Psychological Review, 84,* 191–215.

Bandura, A., Lipsher, D., & Miller, P. (1960). Psychotherapists' approach-avoidance reactions to patients' expressions of hostility. *Journal of Consulting Psychology, 24,* 1–8.

Banks, G. (1971). The effects of race on one-to-one helping interviews. *Social Service Review, 45,* 137–144.

Banks, G., Berenson, B., & Carkhuff, R. (1967). The effects of counselor race and training upon Negro clients in initial interviews. *Journal of Clinical Psychology, 23,* 70–72.

Barber, J. G. (1995a). Politically progressive casework. *Families in Society: The Journal of Contemporary Human Services, 76* (1), 30–37.

Barber, J. G. (1995b). Working with resistant drug abusers. *Social Work, 40* (1), 17–23.

Barbero, S. L. (1989). Community-based, day treatment for mentally retarded adults. *Social Work, 37* (6), 545–548.

Barker, P. (1981). *Basic family therapy*. Baltimore: University Park Press.

Barker, R. L. (1995). *The social work dictionary* (3rd ed.). Washington, DC: NASW Press.

Barkley, R. A. (1997). *Defiant children: A clinician's manual for parent training*. New York: Guilford Press.

Barozzi, R., & Engel, J. (1985). A survey of attitudes about family life education. *Social Casework, 66,* 106–110.

Barret, R. L., & Robinson, B. E. (1990). *Gay Fathers*. Lexington, MA: Lexington Books.

Barth, R. P. (1985). Beating the blues: Cognitive-behavioral treatment for depression in child-maltreating mothers. *Clinical Social Work Journal, 13,* 317–328.

Barth, R. (1988). Theories guiding home-based intensive family preservation services. In J. K. Whittaker, J. Kinney, E. M. Tracy, & C. Booth (Eds.), *Improving practice technology for work with high risk families—Lessons from the "Homebuilders" social work education project* (pp. 91–113). Seattle: Center for Social Welfare Research, School of Social Work, University of Washington.

Barth, R. P., & Berry, M. (1987). Outcomes of child welfare services under permanency planning. *Social Service Review, 61,* 71–92.

Barth, R. P., & Derezotes, D. (1990). *Preventing adolescent abuse: Effective intervention strategies and techniques*. Lexington, MA: Lexington Books.

Barth, R., & Schinke, S. (1984). Enhancing the supports of teenage mothers. *Social Casework, 65,* 523–531.

Bartlett, H. (1970). *The common base of social work practice*. New York: National Association of Social Workers.

Barton, C., & Alexander, J. (1981). Functional family therapy. In A. Gurman & D. Kniskern (Eds.), *Handbook of family therapy* (pp. 403–443). New York: Brunner/Mazel.

Barusch, A. (1991). *Elder care: Family training and support*. Newbury Park, CA: Sage.

Bassuk, E. L., Rubin, L., & Lauriat, A. S. (1986). Characteristics of sheltered homeless families. *American Journal of Public Health, 76,* 1097–1101.

Bates, M. (1983). Using the environment to help the male skid row alcoholic. *Social Casework, 64,* 276–282.

Bauman, M. (1981). Involving resistant family members in therapy. In A. S. Gutman (Ed.), *Questions and answers in the practice of family therapy* (pp. 16–19). New York: Brunner/Mazel.

Bean, G. J., Stefl, M. E., & Howe, S. R. (1987). Mental health and homelessness: Issues and findings. *Social Work, 32,* 411–416.

Beatrice, D. F. (1990). Inter-agency coordination: A practitioner's guide to a strategy for effective social policy. *Administration in Social Work, 14* (4), 45–60.

Beavers, W. (1977). *Psychotherapy and growth: Family Systems perspective*. New York: Brunner/Mazel.

Beck, A. (1974). Phases in the development of structure in therapy and encounter groups. In D. Wexler & L. Rice (Eds.), *Innovations in client-centered therapy*. New York: Wiley.

Beck, A., & Freeman, A. (1990). *Cognitive therapy and depression*. New York: Guilford Press.

Beck, A., Kovacs, M., & Weissman, A. (1979). Assessment of suicidal intention. *Journal of Consulting and Clinical Psychology, 47,* 343–352.

Beck, A., Resnik, H., & Lettieri, D. (Eds.). (1974). *The prediction of suicide*. Bowie, MD: Charles Press.

Beck, A., Rush, A., Shaw, B., & Emery, G. (1979). *Cognitive therapy of depression*. New York: Guilford Press.

Beck, A., Ward, C., Mendelson, M., Mock, J., & Erbaugh, J. (1961). An inventory for measuring depression. *Archives of General Psychiatry, 4,* 561–571.

Beck, A., Wright, F. D., Newman, C. F., & Liese, B. S. (1993). *Cognitive therapy of substance abuse*. New York: Guilford Press.

Beck, J. S. (1995). *Cognitive therapy: Basic and beyond*. New York: Guilford Press.

Beck, J., & Strong, S. (1982). Stimulating therapeutic change with interpretations: A comparison of positive and negative connotation. *Journal of Counseling Psychology, 29,* 551–559.

Becvar, D. S., & Becvar, R. J. (1988). *Family therapy: A systemic integration*. Boston: Allyn & Bacon.

Becvar, D. S., & Becvar, R. J. (2000a). Family relationships, parenting behavior, and adolescent deviance in three ethnic groups. *Families in Society, 80* (3), 279–285.

Becvar, D. S., & Becvar, R. J. (2000b). *Family therapy: A systemic integration* (4th ed.). Boston: Allyn & Bacon.

Beeman, S. (1993). *Social network structure and interaction among neglecting and nonneglecting mothers*. Unpublished doctoral dissertation, University of Chicago.

Behroozi, C. S. (1992). A model for work with involuntary applicants in groups. *Social Work with Groups, 15* (2/3), 223–238.

Belcher, J. (1988). Rights versus needs of homeless mentally ill persons. *Social Work, 33* (5), 398–402.

Belcher, J., & Ephross, P. (1989). Toward an effective practice model for the homeless mentally ill. *Social Casework, 70* (7), 421–427.

Bell, J. L. (1995). Traumatic event debriefing: service delivery designs and the role of social work. *Social Work, 40* (1), 36–43.

Bendick, M. (1980). Failure to enroll in public assistance programs. *Social Work, 25,* 268–274.

Bendick, M., & Cantu, M. (1978). The literacy of welfare clients. *Social Service Review, 52,* 56–68.

Bennett, C. J., Legon, J., & Zilberfein, F. (1989). The significance of empathy in current hospital based practice. *Social Work in Health Care, 14* (2), 27–41.

Berenson, B., & Mitchell, K. (1974). *Confrontation: For better or worse!* Amherst, MA: Human Resource Development Press.

Berg, I. K. (1994). *Family-based services: A solution-focused approach.* New York: W. W. Norton.

Berg, I. K., & Hopwood, L. (1991). Doing very little: Treatment of homeless substance abusers. *Journal of Independent Social Work, 5* (3/4), 109–119.

Berg, I. K., & Jaya, A. (1993). Different and same: Family therapy with Asian-American families. *Journal of Marital and Family Therapy, 19* (1), 31–38.

Berg-Weger, M., McGartland, D., & Tebb, S. (2000). Depression as a mediator: Viewing caregiver well-being and strain in a different light. *Families in Society, 81* (2), 162–173.

Berg, R. A., Franzen, M. D., & Wedding, D. (1987). *Screening for brain impairment: A manual for mental health practice.* New York: Springer.

Berlin, S. B., and Marsh, J. C. (1993). *Informing practice decisions.* New York: Macmillan.

Berman-Rossi, T., & Kelly, T. B. (2000, February). Teaching students to understand and utilize the changing paradigm of stage of group development theory. Paper presented at the 46th annual program meeting of the Council on Social Work Education, New York, NY.

Bernal, G., & Flores-Ortiz, Y. (1982). Latino families in therapy: Engagement and evaluation. *Journal of Marriage and Family Therapy, 8,* 357–365.

Bernard, H. S. (1985). Follow-up interviews with psychotherapy patients. *Psychotherapy, 22,* 22–27.

Bernhardt, B., & Rauch, J. (1993). Genetic family histories: An aid to social work assessment. *Families in Society, 74,* 195–205.

Bernier, J. C. (1990). Parental adjustment to a disabled child: A family-systems perspective. *Families in Society, 71* (10), 589–596.

Bernstein, A. (1972). The fear of compassion. In B. B. Wolman (Ed.), *Success and failure in psychoanalysis and psychotherapy* (pp. 160–176). New York: Macmillan.

Bernstein, A. G. (1981). *Case managers: Who are they and are they making any difference in mental health service delivery?* Unpublished doctoral dissertation, University of Georgia, Athens.

Bernstein, B. (1977). Privileged social work practice. *Social Casework, 66,* 387–393.

Bernstein, D., & Borkovec, T. (1973). *Progressive relaxation training: A manual for the helping professions.* Champaign, IL: Research Press.

Berry, M. (1988). A review of parent training programs in child welfare. *Social Service Review, 62,* 302–323.

Bertcher, H., & Maple, F. (1985). Elements and issues in group composition. In P. Glasser, R. Sarri, & R. Vinter (Eds.), *Individual change through small groups* (pp. 180–202). New York: Free Press.

Berwick, D. (1980). Nonorganic failure to thrive. *Pediatrics in Review, 1,* 265–270.

Besharov, D. (1990). *Recognizing child abuse.* New York: Free Press.

Beutler, L, E. (1983). *Eclectic psychotherapy: A systematic approach.* New York: Pergamon Press.

Beutler, L. E., & Clarkin, J. *(1990). Systematic treatment selection: Toward targeted therapeutic interventions.* New York: Brunner/Mazel.

Biegel, D., & Naparsteck, A. (Eds.). (1982). *Community support systems and mental health.* New York: Springer.

Biegel, D. E., Sales, E., & Schulz, R. (1991). *Family caregiving in chronic illness.* Newbury Park, CA: Sage.

Biesteck, F. (1957). *The casework relationship. Chicago:* Loyola University Press.

Biggs, D. A., & Blocher, D. H. (1987). *Foundations of ethical counseling.* New York: Springer.

Bisman, C.D. (1999). Social work assessment: Case theory construction. *Families in Society, 80* (3), 240–246.

Blankertz, L. E., Cnaan, R. A., White, K., Fox, J., & Messinger, K. (1990). Outreach efforts with dually diagnosed homeless persons. *Families in Society, 71* (7), 387–395.

Blechman, E. (1974). The family contract game: A tool to teach interpersonal problem solving. *Family Coordinator, 23,* 269–281.

Blechman, E., Olson, D., Schornagel, C., Halsdorf, M., & Turner, A. (1976). The family contract game: Technique and case study. *Journal of Consulting and Clinical Psychology, 44,* 449–455.

Bloom, M. (1975). The *paradox of helping. Introduction to the philosophy of scientific practice.* New York: Wiley, 231–232.

Bloom, M., & Fischer, J. (1982*). Evaluating practice: Guidelines for the accountable professional.* Englewood Cliffs, NJ: Prentice Hall.

Bloom, M., Fischer, J., & Orme, J. G. (1999). *Evaluating practice: Guidelines for the accountable professional* (3rd ed.). Allyn & Bacon.

Blum, K. (1991*). Alcohol and the addictive brain: New hope for alcoholics from biogenetic research.* New York: Free Press.

Blythe, B. J., & Tripodi, T. (1989). *Measurement in direct practice.* Newbury Park, CA: Sage.

Bolton, F., & Bolton, S. (1987). *Working with violent families.* Newbury Park, CA: Sage.

Bolton, F., Morris, L., & MacEachron, A. (1989). *Males at risk: The other side of child abuse.* Newbury Park, CA: Sage.

Bonkowski, S., Bequette, S., & Boomhower, S. (1984). A group design to help children adjust to parental divorce. *Social Casework, 65,* 131–137.

Borden, W. (1991). Stress, coping, and adaptation in spouses of older adults with chronic dementia. *Social Work Research and Abstracts, 27* (1), 14–21.

Borkovec, T., & Sides, J. (1979). Critical procedural variables related to the physiological effects of relaxation: A review. *Behavior Research and Therapy, 17,* 119–125.

Borys, D. S., & Pope, K. S. (1989). Dual relationships between therapist and client: A national study of psychologists, psychiatrists, and social workers. *Professional Psychology: Research and Practice, 20,* 283–293.

Bostic, J. Q., Shadid, L. G., & Blotcky, M. J. (1996). Our time is up: Forced terminations during psychotherapy. *American Journal of Psychotherapy, 50,* 347–359.

Boszormenyi-Nagy, I., & Spark, G. (1973). *Invisible loyalties: Reciprocity in intergenerational therapy.* New York: Harper & Row.

Bowen, G. L. (1987). Single fathers in the Air Force. *Social Casework, 68,* 339–344.

Bower, B. (1997). Therapy bonds and the bottle (establishment of therapeutic alliance linked to higher success rate in treatment of alcoholics). *Science News, 152* (8), p. 122.

Boyd-Franklin, N. (1989). *Black families in therapy: A multisystems approach.* New York: Guilford Press.

Boyd-Franklin, N. (1989). Major family approaches and their relevance to the treatment of black families. In N. Boyd-Franklin, *Black families in therapy: A multisystems approach* (pp. 121–132). New York: Guilford Press.

Boyd-Franklin, N., & Bry, B. H. (2000). *Reaching out in family therapy: Home-based school and community interventions.* New York: The Guilford Press.

Bozett, F. W. (1987). *Gay and lesbian parents.* Westport, CT: Praeger.

Bradshaw, W. (1996). Structured group work for individuals with schizophrenia: a coping skills approach. *Research on social work practice, 6* (2). 139–154.

Brager, G., & Holloway, S. (1978). *Changing human service organizations: Politics and practice.* New York: Free Press.

Brandes, S. D. (1976). *American welfare capitalism, 1880–1940.* Chicago: University of Chicago Press.

Breda, C. S., & Bickman, L. (1997). Termination of mental health services for children. *Journal of Child and Family Studies, 61* (1), 69–87.

Brehm, S. S. (1976). *The application of social psychology to clinical practice.* New York: Wiley.

Brehm, S. S., & Brehm, J. W. (1981). *Psychological reactance: A theory of freedom and control.* New York: Academic Press.

Breton, M. (1984) A drop-in program for transient women: Promoting competence through the environment. *Social Work, 29,* 542–546.

Breton, M. (1985). Reaching and engaging people: Issues and practice principles. *Social Work with Groups, 8* (3); 7–21.

Briar, S. (1964). The family as an organization: An approach to family diagnosis and treatment. *Social Service Review, 38,* 247–255.

Bricker-Jenkins, M. (1992). Building a strengths model of practice in the public social services. In D. Saleeby, (Ed.), *The strengths perspective in social work practice* (pp. 122–135). New York: Longman.

Brickner, P. W., Scharer, L. K., Conanan, B., Elvy, A., & Savarese, M. (1985). *Health care of homeless people.* New York: Springer.

Bridges, G. S., & Steen, S. (1998). Racial disparities in official assessments of juvenile offenders: Attributional stereotypes as mediating mechanisms. *American Sociological Review, 63,* 554–570.

Briere, J. (1989). *Therapy for adults molested as children.* New York: Springer.

Brill, C. K. (1990). *The impact on social work practice of the social injustice content in the NASW Code of Ethics.* Doctoral dissertation, Brandeis University.

Brindis, C., Barth, R. P., & Loomis, A. B. (1987). Continuous counseling: Case management with teenage parents. *Social Casework, 68,* 164–172.

Brisette-Chapman S. (1997). Child protection risk assessment and African American children: Cultural ramifications for families and communities. *Child Welfare, 76,* 45–63.

Brodkin, E. Z. (1997). Inside the welfare contract: Discretion and accountability in state welfare administration. *Social Service Review, 71* (1), 1–33.

Brookins, G. K., Peterson, A. C., & Brooks, L. M. (1997). Youth and families in the inner city: Influencing positive outcomes. In H. J. Walberg, O. Reyes, & R. P. Weissberg (Eds.), *Children and youth: Interdisciplinary perspectives* (pp. 45–66). Thousand Oaks, CA: Sage.

Brooks-Gunn, J., & Duncan, G. J. (1997). The effects of poverty on children: The future of children. *Children and poverty, 7* (2), 55–71.

Brown, G. (1982). Issues in the resettlement of Indochinese refugees. *Social Casework, 63,* 155–159.

Brown, J. L. (1988). Domestic hunger is no accident [Guest editorial]. *Social Work, 33,* 99–100.

Brown, L., & Levitt, J. (1979). A methodology for problem-system identification. *Social Casework, 60,* 408–415.

Brown, L., & Root, M. (1990). *Diversity and complexity in feminist theory.* New York: Haworth Press.

Brown, L., & Zimmer, D. (1986). An introduction to therapy issues of lesbian and gay male couples. In N. Jacobson & A. Gurman (Eds.), *Clinical handbook of marital therapy.* New York: Guilford Press.

Brownell, K., Marlatt, G., Lichenstein, E., & Wilson, G. T. (1986). Understanding and preventing relapse. *American Psychologist, 41* (7), 765–782.

Bruckner, D. F., & Johnson, P. E. (1987). Treatment for adult male victims of childhood sexual abuse. *Social Casework, 68,* 81–87.

Bruner, C., (1991). *Thinking collaboration: Ten questions and answers to help policy makers improve childrens' services.* Washington, DC: Education and Human Services Consortium.

Bryer, J. B., Nelson, B. A., Miller, J. B., & Krol, P. A. (1987). Childhood sexual and physical abuse as a factor in adult psychiatric illness. *American Journal of Psychiatry, 44,* 1426–1430.

Bucell, M. (1979). *An empirically derived self-report inventory for the assessment of assertive behavior.* Unpublished doctoral dissertation, Kent State University, Kent, OH.

Budner, S., Chazin, R., & Young, H. (1973). The indigenous nonprofessional in a multiservice center. *Social Casework, 54,* 354–359.

Burman, S., & Allen-Meares, P. (1991). Criteria for selecting practice theories: Working with alcoholic women. *Families in Society, 72,* 387–393.

Burns, D. (1980). *Feeling good.* New York: Avon Books.

Bush, C. T., Langford, M. W., Rosen, P., & Gott, W. (1990). Operation outreach: Intensive case management for severely psychiatrically disabled adults. *Hospital and Community Psychiatry, 41* (6), 647–649.

Buss, T. F., & Gillanders, W. R. (1997). Worry about health status among the elderly: Patient management and health policy implications. *Journal of Health and Social Policy, 8* (4), 53–66.

Butcher, J., & Koss, M. (1978). Research on brief and crisis-oriented psychotherapies. In S. Garfield & A. Bergin (Eds.), *Handbook of psychotherapy and behavior change* (pp. 725–767). New York: Wiley.

Butler, R. (1975). *Why service? Being old in America.* New York: Harper & Row.

Butz, R. A. (1985). Reporting child abuse and confidentiality in counseling. *Social Casework, 66,* 83–90.

C

Caesar, P. L., & Hamberger, L. K. (1989). *Treating men who batter: Theory, practice and programs.* New York: Springer.

Cain, R. (1991a). Relational contexts and information management among gay men. *Families in Society, 72* (6), 344–352.

Cain, R. (1991b). Stigma management and gay identity development. *Social Work. 36* (1), 67–71.

Camayd-Freixas, Y., & Amato, H. (1984). *The measurement of Hispanic bilingualism and biculturality in the workplace.* Boston: Massachusetts Department of Social Services, Office of Human Resources.

Cameron, J., & Talavera, E. (1976). An advocacy program for Spanish-speaking people. *Social Casework, 57,* 427–431.

Campbell, J. A. (1990). Ability of practitioners to estimate client acceptance of single-subject evaluation procedures. *Social Work, 35* (1), 9–14.

Canda, E. (1983). General implications of Shamanism for clinical social work. *International Social Work, 26,* 14–22.

Canda, E., & Phaobtong, T. (1992). Buddhism as a support system for Southeast Asian refugees. *Social Work, 37* (l), 61–67.

Canda, E. R. (Ed.) (1998). *Spirituality in social work: New directions.* New York: Haworth Pastoral Press.

Capitman, J., MacAdam, M., & Yee, D. (1988). Hospital-based managed care. *Generations, 12* (5), 62–65.

Caplan, G. (1964). *Principles of preventive psychiatry.* New York: Basic Books.

Caplan, T. (1995). Safety and comfort, content and process: facilitating open group work with men who batter. *Social Work with Groups, 18* (2/3), 33–51.

Caple, F. S., Salcido, R. M., & di Cecco, J. (1995). Engaging effectively with culturally diverse families and children. *Social Work in Education, 17* (3), 159–169.

Caputo, R. (1988). Managing domestic violence in two urban police districts. *Social Casework, 69* (8), 498–504.

Card, D. (1990). *Counseling same-sex couples.* New York: Norton.

Carkhuff, R. (1969). *Helping and human relations: Practice and research.* New York: Holt, Rinehart & Winston.

Carlton-LaNey, I. (1999). African American social work pioneers' response to need. *Social Work, 44* (4), 311–321.

Carrillo, D. F., & Thyer, B. A. (1994). Advanced standing and two-year program MSW students: An empirical investigation of foundation interviewing skills. *Journal of Social Work Education. 30* (3), 377–387.

Carter, B., & McGoldrick, M. (Eds.) (1988). *The changing life cycle: A framework for family therapy* (2nd ed.). New York: Gardner Press.

Carter, B., & McGoldrick, M. (1991). Overview: The expanded family life cycle. In B. Carter and M. McGoldrick (Eds.), *The expanded family life cycle: individual, family, and social perspectives* (2nd ed.). Needham Heights, MA: Allyn & Bacon.

Carter, B., & McGoldrick, M. (1999a). Coaching at various stages of the life cycle. In B. Carter & M. McGoldrick (Eds.), *The expanded family life cycle: Individual, family, and social perspectives* (3rd ed.) (pp. 436–454). Boston: Allyn & Bacon.

Carter, B., & McGoldrick, M. (Eds.) (1999b). *The expanded family life cycle: Individual, family, and social perspectives* (3rd ed.). Boston: Allyn & Bacon.

Cascio, T. (1998). Incorporating spirituality into social work practice: A review of what to do. *Families in Society, 79* (5), 523–531.

Catalano, R., Wells, E. A., Jenson, J. M., & Hawkins, J. D. (1989). Aftercare services for drug-using institutionalized delinquents. *Social Service Review, 63* (4), 553–577.

Cates, J. A., Graham, L. L., Boeglin, D., & Tielker, S. (1990). The effect of AIDS on the family system. *Families in Society, 71* (4), 195–201.

Chandler, S. (1985). Mediation: Conjoint problem solving. *Social Work, 30,* 346–349.

Chau, K. L. (1990). A model for teaching cross-cultural practice in social work. *Journal of Social Work Education, 26* (2), 124–133.

Chau, K. L. (1993). Needs assessment for group work with people of color: A conceptual formulation. *Social Work with Groups, 15* (2/3), 53–66.

Chelune, G. J. (1979). Measuring openness in interpersonal communication. In G. Chelune & Associates (Eds.), *Self-disclosure.* San Francisco: Jossey-Bass.

Cherbosque, J. (1987). Differential effects of counselor self-disclosure statements on perception of the counselor and willingness to disclose: A cross-cultural study. *Psychotherapy, 24,* 434–437.

Chesler, J., & Davis. S., (1980). Problem pregnancy and abortion counseling with teenagers. *Social Casework, 61,* 173–179.

Choi, G. (1997). Acculturative stress, social support, and depression in Korean American families. *Journal of Family Social Work, 2* (1), 81–89.

Cimbolic, P. (1972). Counselor race and experience effects on black clients. *Journal of Consulting and Clinical Psychology, 39,* 328–332.

Cingolani, J. (1984, September-October). Social conflict perspective on work with involuntary clients. *Social Work, 29,* pp. 442–446.

Citron, P. (1978). Group work with alcoholic poly-drug involved adolescents with deviant behavior syndrome. *Social Work with Groups, 1* (1), 39–52.

Claiborn, C. (1982). Interpretation and change in counseling. *Journal of Counseling Psychology, 29,* 439–453.

Claiborn, C., Crawford, J., & Hackman, H. (1983). Effects of intervention discrepancy in counseling for negative emotions. *Journal of Counseling Psychology, 30,* 164–171.

Cnaan, R. A. (1994). The new American social work gospel: Case management of the chronically mentally ill. *British Journal of Social Work, 24* (5), 533–557.

Cnaan, R. A., & Rothman, J. (1986). Conceptualizing community intervention: An empirical test of three models of community organization. *Administration in Social Work, 10* (3), 41–55.

Cohen, B. Z. (1985). A cognitive approach to the treatment of offenders. *British journal of Social Work, 15,* 619–633.

Cohen, B. (1999). Intervention and supervision in strengths-based social work practice. *Families in Society, 80* (5), 450–459.

Cohen, C., & Adler, A. (1986). Assessing the role of social network interventions with an inner-city population. *American Journal of Psychiatry, 56,* 278–288.

Cohen, M. B. (1989). Social work practice with homeless mentally ill people: Engaging the client. *Social Work, 34* (6), 505–509.

Cohn, A. H. (1979). Effective treatment of child abuse and neglect. *Social Work, 24,* 513–519.

Cole, E., & Duva, J. (1990). *Family preservation: An orientation for administrators and practitioners.* Washington, DC: Child Welfare League of America.

Collins, D., Jordan, C., & Coleman, H. (1999). *An introduction to family social work.* Itasca, IL: F. E. Peacock.

Collins, P. M., Kayser, K., & Platt, S. (1994). Conjoint marital therapy: A social worker's approach to single-system evaluation. *Families in Society, 71* (8), 461–470.

Commission on Accreditation, Council on Social Work Education. (1995). *Handbook of accreditation standards* (1995, 5th ed.). Alexandria, VA: Author.

Compher, J. (1983). Home services to families to prevent child placement. *Social Work, 28,* 360–364.

Compton, B. R., & Galaway, B. (1989). *Social work processes* (4th ed.). Belmont, CA: Wadsworth.

Compton, B. R., & Galaway, B. (1999). *Social work processes* (6th ed.). Pacific Grove, CA: Brooks/Cole.

Congress, E. (1994). The use of culturagrams to assess and empower culturally diverse families. *Families in Society, 75,* 531–540.

Congress, E. P. (1999). Ethical dilemmas in interdisciplinary collaboration. In E. Congress (Ed.), *Social work values and ethics: Identifying and resolving professional dilemmas* (pp. 117–128). Chicago, IL: Nelson Hall.

Congress, E. P., & Lynn, M. (1994). Group work programs in public schools: Ethical dilemmas and cultural diversity. *Social Work in Education, 16* (2), 107–114.

Congress, E. P. & Lynn, M. (1997). Group work practice in the community: Navigating the slippery slope of ethical dilemmas. *Social Work with Groups, 20* (3) 61–74.

Conklin, C. (1980). Rural care-givers. *Social Work, 25,* 495–496.

Connell, S. (1987). Homelessness. In *Encyclopedia of Social Work* (Vol. 1, pp. 789–795). Silver Spring, MD: National Association of Social Workers.

Constantine, L. (1978). Family sculpture and relationship mapping techniques. *Journal of Marriage and Family Counseling, 4,* 19–25.

Cook, R. (1988). Trends and needs in programming for independent living. *Child Welfare, 67,* 497–514.

Cooley, R., Ostendorf, D., & Bickerton, D. (1979). Outreach services for Native Americans. *Social Work, 24,* 151–153.

Cooper, S. (1973). A look at the effect of racism on clinical work. *Social Casework, 54,* 76–84.

Coplon, J., & Strull, J. (1983). Roles of the professional in mutual aid groups. *Social Casework, 64,* 259–266.

Corcoran, K., & Fischer, J. (1999). *Measures for clinical practice* (3rd ed.). New York: Free Press.

Corcoran, K., & Gingerich, W. J. (1994). Practice evaluation in the context of managed care: Case recording methods for quality assurance reviews. *Research on Social Work Practice, 4* (3), 326–337.

Corcoran, K., & Vandiver, V. (1996). *Maneuvering the maze of managed care: Skills for mental health practitioners.* New York: Free Press.

Corcoran, K., & Winslade, W. J. (1994). Eavesdropping on the 50-minute hour: Managed mental health care and confidentiality. *Behavioral Sciences and the Law, 12,* 351–365.

Corey, G. (1990). *Theory and practice of group counseling.* Pacific Grove, CA: Brooks/Cole.

Corey, G., Corey, M. S., & Callanan, P. (1998). *Issues and ethics in the helping professions.* Pacific Grove, CA: Brooks/Cole.

Corey, M. S., & Corey, G. (1992). *Groups: Process and practice* (4th ed.). Pacific Grove, CA: Brooks/Cole.

Cormier, W., & Cormier, L. (1979). *Interviewing strategies for helpers: A guide to assessment, treatment, and evaluation.* Pacific Grove, CA: Brooks/Cole.

Coudroglou, A., & Poole, D. (1984). *Disability, work, and social policy.* New York: Springer.

Coulton, C. (1979). A study of the person-environment fit among the chronically ill. *Social Work in Health Care, 5,* 5–17.

Coulton, C. (1981). Person-environment fit as the focus in health care. *Social Work, 26,* 26–35.

Council on Social Work Education, *Accreditation standards and self-study guides.* (1995).

Council on Social Work Education. *Community Care Corporation Accreditation Standards and Self-Study Guides* (1995).

Council on Social Work Education. Curriculum Policy Statement. (1995).

Couper, D. P. (1989). *Aging and our families: Handbook for care-givers.* New York: Human Sciences Press.

Courtney, M. (1999). Challenges and opportunities posed by the reform era. Presented at the "Reconciling welfare reform with child welfare" conference. Center for Advanced Studies in Child Welfare, University of Minnesota, February 26.

Courtois, C. A. (1988). *Healing the incest wound: Adult survivors in therapy.* New York: Norton.

Cowan, B., Currie, M., Krol, K., & Richardson, J. (1969). Holding unwilling clients in treatment. *Social Casework, 14,* 146–151.

Cowger, C. D. (1992), Assessment of client strengths. In D. Saleeby (Ed.), *The strengths perspective in social work practice* (pp. 139–147). New York: Longman.

Cowger, C. D. (1994). Assessing client strengths: Clinical assessment for client empowerment. *Social Work, 39* (3), 262–267.

Cox, E. O. (1991). The critical role of social action in empowerment oriented groups. *Social Work with Groups, 14* (3–4), 77–90.

Crabtree, B. F., & Miller, W. L. (1992). *Doing qualitative research.* Newbury Park, CA: Sage.

Cross, T. L., Bazron, B. J., Dennis, K., & Issacs, M. R. (1989). *Toward a culturally competent system of care.* Washington, DC: Georgetown University Child Development Center.

Crotty, P., & Kulys, R. (1985). Social support networks: The views of schizophrenic clients and their significant others. *Social Work, 30,* 301–309.

Cruz, V. K., Price-Williams, D., & Andron, L. (1988). Developmentally disabled women who were molested as children. *Social Casework, 69* (7), 411–419.

Cueller, I., Harris, L. C., & Jasso, R. (1980). An acculturation scale for Mexican American normal and clinical populations. *Hispanic Journal of Behavioral Sciences, 2* (3), 199–217.

Cull, J. G., & Gill, W. S. (1991). *Suicide Probability Scale (SPS).* Los Angeles: Western Psychological Services.

Culp, R. E., Heide, J., & Richardson, M. T. (1987). Maltreated children's developmental scores: Treatment versus nontreatment. *Child Abuse and Neglect, 11* (1), 29–34.

Cummings, N. A. (1991). Brief intermittent therapy throughout the life cycle. In C. S. Austad & W. H. Berman (Eds.), *Psychotherapy in managed health care: The optimal use of time and resources* (pp. 35–45). Washington, DC: American Psychological Association.

Curran, J. P., Sutton, R. G., Faraone, S. V., & Guenette, S. (1985). Inpatient approaches. In M. Hersen & A. S. Bellack (Eds.), *Handbook of clinical behavior therapy with adults* (pp. 445–483). New York: Plenum Press.

Cutler, D., & Madore, E. (1980). Community-family network therapy in a rural setting. *Community Mental Health Journal, 16,* 144–155.

D

Dahl, A. S., Cowgill, K. M., & Asmundsson, R. (1987). Life in remarriage families. *Social Work, 32,* 40–44.

Dahlheimer, D., & Feigal, J. (1991). Bridging the gap. *Networker.* January/February.

Daley, D. C. (1987). Relapse prevention with substance abusers: Clinical issues and myths. *Social Work, 32,* 138–142.

Daley, D. C. (1991). *Kicking addictive habits once and for all: A relapse prevention guide.* New York: Lexington.

Dane, B. O. (1989). New beginnings for AIDS patients. *Social Casework, 70* (5), 305–309.

Dane, B. O. (1991). Anticipatory mourning of middle-aged parents of adult children with AIDS. *Families in Society, 72* (2), 108–115.

Dane, B. O., & Simon, B. L. (1991, May). Resident guests: Social workers in host settings. *Social Work, 36* (3), 208–213.

Dane, E. (1985). *Professional and lay advocacy in the education of handicapped children.* New York: Routledge & Kegan Paul.

Danish, J., D'Augelli, A., & Hauer, A. (1980). *Helping skills: A basic training program.* New York: Human Sciences Press.

Daro, D. (1988). *Confronting child abuse: Research for effective program designs.* New York: Free Press.

Davenport, J., & Reims, N. (1978). Theoretical orientation and attitudes toward women. *Social Work, 23,* 307–309.

Davidson, J. R., & Davidson, T. (1996). Confidentiality and managed care: Ethical and legal concerns. *Health and Social Work, 21* (3), 208–215.

Davies, D. (1991). Interventions with male toddlers who have witnessed parental violence. *Families in Society, 72* (9), 515–524.

Davis, I. P., & Reid, W. J. (1988). Event analysis in clinical practice and process research. *Social Casework, 69* (5), 298–306.

Davis, L. E., & Gelsomino, J. (1994). An assessment of practitioner cross-racial treatment experiences. *Social Work, 39* (1), 116–123.

Davis, L. V. (1987). Battered women: The transformation of a social problem. *Social Work, 32,* 306–311.

Davis, L. V. (1991). Violence and families. *Social Work, 37* (5), 371–373.

Davis, L. V., & Hagen, J. L. (1992). The problem of wife abuse: The interrelationship of social policy and social work practice. *Social Work, 37* (17), 15–20.

Dawson, R. (1986). Fathers anonymous—A group treatment program for sexual offenders. In B. Schlesinger (Ed.), *Sexual abuse of children in the 1980s. Ten essays and an annotated bibliography* (pp. 70–79). Toronto: University of Toronto Press.

De Anda, D. (1984). Bicultural socialization: Factors affecting the minority experience. *Social Work, 29,* 101–107.

De Anda, D. (1998). The evaluation of a stress management program for middle school adolescents. *Child and Adolescent Social Work Journal, 15* (1), 73–85.

De Anda, D., & Becerra, R. (1984). Support networks for adolescent mothers. *Social Casework, 65,* 172–181.

De Anda, D., Bradley, M., Collada, C., Dunn, L., Kubota, J., Hollister, V., Miltenberger, J., Pulley, J., Susskind, A, Thompson, L. A., & Wadsworth, T. (1997). A study of stress, stressors, and coping strategies among middle school adolescents. *Social Work in Education, 19* (2), 87–98.

DeAngelis, D. (2000). Licensing really is about protection. *ASWB Association News, 10* (2) 11.

De Las Fuentes, C. (2000). Group psychotherapy: Adolescent Latinos. In M. T. Flores & G. Carey, *Family therapy with Hispanics: Toward approaching diversity* (pp. 151–156). Boston: Allyn & Bacon.

Delgado, M. (1977). Puerto Rican spiritualism and the social work profession. *Social Casework, 58,* 451–458.

Denton, R. (1989, March). *The religious fundamentalist family: Training for assessment and treatment.* Paper presented to the Annual Program Meeting of the Council on Social Work Education, Chicago.

Denton, W. (1991). The role of affect in marital therapy. *Journal of Marital and Family Therapy, 17* (3), 257–261.

DeShazer, S. (1988). *Clues: Investigating solutions in brief therapy.* New York: Norton.

Devore, W., & Schlesinger, E. G. (1999). *Ethnic-sensitive social work practice* (5th ed.). Boston: Allyn & Bacon.

Devore, W., & Schlesinger, E. (1981). *Ethnic-sensitive social work practice.* St. Louis: Mosby.

Dickson, D. T. (1998). *Confidentiality and privacy in social work.* New York: Free Press.

Dies, R. R. (1983). Clinical implications of research on leadership in short-term group psychotherapy. In R. R. Dies & R. MacKenzie (Eds.), *Advances in group psychotherapy: Integrating research and practice* (American Group Psychotherapy Association Monograph Series) (pp. 27–28). New York: International Universities Press.

Dillon, D. (1994). Understanding and assessment of intragroup dynamics in foster family care: African American families. *Child Welfare, 73* (2), 129–139.

Diorio, W. D. (1992). Parental perceptions of the authority of public child welfare caseworkers. *Families in Society: The Journal of Contemporary Human Services, 73* (4), 222–235.

Donovan, D., & Marlatt, G. A. (1988). *Assessment of addictive behaviors.* New York: Guilford Press.

Dore, M. M. (1993). The practice-teaching parallel in educating the micropractitioner. *Journal of Social Work Education, 29* (2), 181–190.

Dore, M. M., & Durnois, A. O. (1990). Cultural differences in the meaning of adolescent pregnancy. *Families in Society, 71* (2), 93–101.

Dorfman, R. A. (1996). *Clinical social work: Definition, practice, and vision.* New York: Brunner/Mazel.

Doster, J., & Nesbitt, J. (1979). Psychotherapy and self-disclosure. In G. Chelune & Associates (Eds.), *Self-disclosure* (pp. 177–224). San Francisco: Jossey-Bass.

Doster, J., Surratt, F., & Webster, T. (1975, March). *Interpersonal variables affecting psychological communications of hospitalized psychiatric patients.* Paper presented at meeting of Southeastern Psychological Association, Atlanta.

Dougherty, A. M. (1990). *Consultation: Practice and perspectives.* Pacific Grove, CA: Brooks/Cole.

Douglas, H. (1991). Assessing violent couples. *Families in Society, 72* (9), 525–533.

Dowd, E., & Boroto, D. (1982). Differential effects of counselor self-disclosure, self-involving statements, and interpretation. *Journal of Counseling Psychology, 29,* 8–13.

Drachman, D. (1992). A stage-of-migration framework for service to immigrant populations. *Social Work, 37* (1), 61–67.

DuBray, W. (1985). American Indian values: Critical factors in casework. *Social Casework, 66,* 30–37.

Dudley, J. R. (1987). Speaking for themselves: People who are labeled as developmentally disabled. *Social Work, 32,* 80–82.

Duehn, W., & Proctor, E. (1977). Initial clinical interactions and premature discontinuance in treatment. *American Journal of Orthopsychiatry, 47,* 284–290.

Duvall, E. (1977). *Marriage and family development* (5th ed.). Philadelphia: Lippincott.

Dyer, W. (1969). Congruence and control. *Journal of Applied Behavioral Science, 5,* 161–173.

D'Zurilla, T., & Goldfried, M. (1971). Problem solving and behavior modification. *Journal of Abnormal Psychology, 78,* 107–126.

E

Earle, K. A. (1999). Harvest festival (social work with Native Americans). *Families in Society, 80* (3), 213–215.

Early, T. J. & GlenMaye, L. F. (2000). Valuing family strengths: Social work practice with families from a strengths perspective. *Social Work, 45* (2), 118–130.

Edleson, J. (1984). Working with men who batter. *Social Work, 29,* 237–242.

Edleson, J., & Frank, M. D. (1991). Rural interventions in woman battering: One state's strategies. *Families in Society, 72* (9), 543–551.

Edleson, J., & Syers, M. (1990). Relative effectiveness of group treatment for men who batter. *Social Work Research and Abstracts, 26* (2), 10–17.

Edwards, A. (1982). The consequences of error in selecting treatment for blacks. *Social Casework, 63,* 429–433.

Edwards, E. (1983). Native-American elders: Current issues and social policy implications. In R. McNeely & J. Colen (Eds.), *Aging in minority groups.* Beverly Hills, CA: Sage.

Ehrlich, E. J., & Moore, P. A. (1990). Delivery of AIDS services: The New York State response. *Social Work, 35* (2), 175–177.

Eisikovits, Z. C., & Edleson, J. L. (1989). Intervening with men who batter: A critical review of the literature. *Social Services Review, 63* (3), 384–414.

Elbow, M. (1987). The memory books: Facilitating termination with children. *Social Casework, 68,* 180–183.

Elbow, M., & Mayfield, J. (1991). Mothers of incest victims: Villains, victims, or protectors? *Families in Society, 72* (2), 78–85.

Elkin, I., Shea, T., Watkins, J., & Collins, J. (1986). *Comparative treatment outcome findings.* Presentation of the NIMH Treatment of Depression Collaborative Research Program. Paper presented at the annual meeting of the American Psychiatric Association.

Ellis, A. (1962). *Reason and emotion in psychotherapy.* New York: Lyle Stuart.

Ely, A. (1985). Long-term group treatment for young male schizopaths. *Social Work, 30,* 5–10.

Ensign, J. (1998). Health issues of homeless youth. *Journal of Social Distress and the Homeless, 7* (3), 159–174.

Ephross, P. H., & Vassil, T. V. (1988). *Groups that work: Structure and process.* New York: Columbia University Press.

Epstein, L. (1985). *Talking and listening: A guide to interviewing.* Columbus, OH: Merrill.

Epstein, L. (1988). *Brief treatment. A task-centered approach.* New York: McGraw-Hill.

Epstein, L. (1992). *Brief treatment and a new look at the task-centered approach* (3rd ed.). Boston: Allyn & Bacon.

Epstein, R. S., & Simon, R. I. (1990). The exploitation index: An early warning indicator of boundary violations in psychotherapy. *Bulletin of the Menninger Clinic, 54* (4), 450–465.

Epstein, R. S., Simon, R. I., & Kay, G. G. (1992). Assessing boundary violations in psychotherapy: Survey results with the Exploitation Index. *Bulletin of the Menninger Foundation, 56* (2), 150–166.

Erera, P. I. (1997). Empathy training for helping professionals: Model and evaluation. *Journal of Social Work Education, 33* (2), 245–260.

Erickson, S. (1988). *Family mediation casebook.* New York: Brunner/Mazel.

Evans, S. W., Axelrod, J. L., & Sapia , J. L. (2000). Effective school-based mental health interventions: Advancing the social skills training paradigm. *Journal of School Health, 70* (5), 191–194.

Ewalt, P. (1994). Poverty matters. *Social Work, 39* (2), 149–151.

Ewalt, P. L. (1994, September). Wefare—how much reform? *Social Work, 39* (5), 485–486.

Ewalt, P. L., & Mlkua, N. (1995). Self-determination from a Pacific perspective. In P. L. Ewalt, E. M. Freeman, S. A. Kirk, & D. L. Poole (Eds.), *Multicultural issues in social work* (pp. 255–268). Washington, DC: NASW Press.

Ezell, M. (1994). Advocacy practice of social workers. *Families in Society, 75,* (1), 36–46.

F

Falicov, C. (1996). Mexican families. In M. McGoldrick, J. Pearce, & J. Giordano (Eds.), *Ethnicity and family therapy* (pp. 169–182). New York: Guilford Press.

Faller, K. (1989). Decision making in cases of intrafamilial child sexual abuse. *American Journal of Orthopsychiatry, 58,* 121–128.

Faller, K. (1990). *Understanding child sexual treatment.* Newbury Park, CA: Sage.

Faria, G. (1991). Educating students for family-based practice with lesbian families. In *Empowering families* (pp. 15–21). Proceedings of the Fifth Annual Conference on Family Based Services: National Association for Family Based Services, Cedar Rapids, IA.

Faria, G. (1994). Training for family preservation practice with lesbian families. *Families in Society, 75* (7), 416–422.

Farina, A., Burns, G. L., Austad, C., Bugglin, C., & Fischer, E. H. (1986). The role of physical attractiveness in the readjustment of discharged psychiatric patients. *Journal of Abnormal Psychology, 95,* 139–143.

Farmer, R., & Walsh, J. (1999). Living room assessment. *Journal of Community Practice, 6* (4), 79–94.

Fatout, M. (1990). Consequences of abuse on relationships of children. *Families in Society, 71* (2), 76–81.

Fauri, D. P., & Bradford, J. B. (1986). Practice with the frail elderly in the private sector. *Social Casework, 67,* 259–265.

Fearing, James (1996). The changing face of intervention. *Behavioral Health Management, 16* (Sept./Oct.), 35–37.

Fein, E., & Staff, I. (1991). Implementing reunification services. *Families in Society, 72* (6), 335–343.

Feinstein, B., & Cavanaugh, C. (1976). *The new volunteerism: A community connection.* Cambridge, MA: Schenkman.

Feld, S., & Radin, N. (1982). *Social psychology for social work and the mental health professions.* New York: Columbia University Press.

Feldman, D., Strong, S., & Danser, D. (1982). A comparison of paradoxical and nonparadoxical interpretations and directives. *Journal of Counseling Psychology, 29,* 572–579.

Fernandez, L. M. (1997). Running an effective task group: The five C's. *The New Social Worker, 4* (1), 14–15.

Fiene, J., & Taylor, P. (1991). Serving rural families of developmentally disabled children: A case management model. *Social Work, 36* (4), 323–327.

Filinson, R., & Ingman, S. (Eds.). (1989). *Elder abuse: Practice and policy.* New York: Human Sciences Press.

Fine, M., Akabas, S., & Bellinger, S. (1982). Cultures of drinking: A workplace perspective. *Social Work, 27,* 436–440.

Finkelhor, D. (Ed.) (1984). *Child sexual abuse: New theory and research.* New York: Free Press.

Finkelhor, D., & Associates (1986). *A sourcebook on child sexual abuse.* Newbury Park, CA: Sage.

Finkelhor, D., & Browne, A. (1986). Initial and long-term effects: A conceptual framework. In D. Finkelhor, S. Araji, L. Baron, A. Browne, S. D. Peters, & G. E. Wyatt (Eds.), *A sourcebook on child sexual abuse* (pp. 186–187). Newbury Park, CA: Sage.

Finkelstein, N. (1980). Family-centered group care. *Child Welfare, 59,* 33–41.

Finn, J., & Rose, S. (1982). Development and validation of the interview skills role-play test. *Social Work Research and Abstracts, 18,* 21–27.

First, R. J., Roth, D., & Arewa, B. D. (1988). Homelessness: Understanding the dimensions of the problem for minorities. *Social Work, 33,* 120–124.

Fisch, R., Weakland, J., & Segal, L. (1982). *The tactics of change: Doing therapy briefly.* San Francisco: Jossey-Bass.

Fischer, J. (1976). *The effectiveness of social casework.* Springfield, IL: Charles C. Thomas.

Fischer, J. (1978). *Effective casework practice: An eclectic approach.* New York: McGraw-Hill.

Fischer, J., & Corcoran, K. (1994). *Measures for clinical practice* (2nd ed.). New York: Free Press.

Flaherty, J. A., Gaviria, F. M., & Pathak, D. S. (1983). The measurement of social support: The Social Support Network Inventory. *Comprehensive Psychiatry, 24,* 521–529.

Flapan, D., & Fenchal, G. (1987). *The developing ego and the emerging self in group therapy.* Northvale, NJ: Jason Aronson.

Flores, M. T. (2000). La familia latina. In M. T. Flores & G. Carey, *Family therapy with Hispanics: Toward appreciating diversity* (pp. 3–28). Boston: Allyn & Bacon.

Flores, M. T., & Carey, G. (2000). *Family therapy with Hispanics: Toward appreciating diversity.* New York: Allyn & Bacon.

Folberg, J., & Milne, A. (1988). *Divorce mediation: Theory and practice.* New York: Guilford Press.

Fong, R. (1997). Child welfare practice with Chinese families: Assessment issues for immigrants from the People's Republic of China. *Journal of Family Social Work, 2* (1), 33–47.

Forte, J. A. (1998). Power and role-taking: A review of theory, research and practice. *Journal of Human Behavior in the Social Environment, 1* (4), 27–56.

Fortune, A. E. (1985a). Treatment groups. In A. E. Fortune (Ed.), *Task-centered practice with families and groups* (pp. 33–44). New York: Springer.

Fortune, A. E. (1985b). *Task-centered practice with families and groups.* New York: Springer.

Fortune, A. E. (1985c). Planning duration and termination of treatment. *Social Service Review, 59* (4), 647–661.

Fortune, A. E. (1987). Grief only? Client and social worker reactions to termination. *Clinical Social Work Journal, 15* (2), 159–171.

Fortune, A. E., Pearlingi, B., & Rochelle, C. D. (1991), Criteria for terminating treatment. *Families in Society, 72* (6), 366–370.

Fortune, A., Pearlingi, B., & Rochelle, C. D. (1992), Reactions to termination of individual treatment. *Social Work, 37* (2), 171–178.

Foster, R. P. (1988). The clinician's cultural countertransference: The psychodynamics of culturally competent practice. *Clinical Social Work Journal, 26* (3), 253–270.

Fowler, R. C., Rich, C. L., & Young, D. C. (1986). San Diego suicide study, II: Substance abuse in young cases. *Archives of General Psychiatry, 43,* 962–965.

Frank, P. B., & Golden, G. K. (1992). Blaming by naming: Battered women and the epidemic of co-dependence. *Social Work, 37* (l), 5–6.

Frankel, A. J. (1991). The dynamics of day care. *Families in Society, 72* (1), 3–10.

Frankle, H., & Gordon, V. (1983). Helping Selma: A report on a therapist-volunteer relationship. *Social Casework, 64,* 291–299.

Franklin, D. L. (1990). The cycles of social work practice: Social action vs. individual interest. *Journal of Progressive Human Services, 1* (2), 59–80.

Fraser, M., & Hawkins, J. (1984). Social network analysis and drug misuse. *Social Service Review, 58,* 81–87.

Fraser, M. W., Pecora, P. J., & Haapala, D. A. (1991). *Families in crisis: The impact of intensive family preservation services.* Hawthorne, NY: Aldine de Gruyter.

Fredman, N., & Sherman, R. (1987). *Handbook of measurements for marriage and family therapy.* New York: Brunner/Mazel.

Freed, A. (1978). Clients' rights and casework records. *Social Casework, 59,* 458–464.

Freed, A. (1988). Interviewing through an interpreter. *Social Work, 33,* 315–319.

Freeman, E. M., & Dyers, L. (1993). High risk children and adolescents: Families and community environments. *Families in Society, 74* (7), 422–431.

Frey, C. (1987). Minimarathon group sessions with incest offenders. *Social Work, 32,* 534–535.

Frey, G. A. (1990). A framework for promoting organizational change. *Families in Society, 71* (3), 142–147.

Friedlander, M. L., & Schwartz, G. S. (1985). Toward a theory of strategic self-presentation in counseling and psychotherapy. *Journal of Counseling Psychology, 32,* 485.

Friedman, D., & Friedman, S. (1982). Day care as a setting for intervention in family systems. *Social Casework, 63,* 291–295.

Friedman, M. J. (1996). Facilitating productive meetings. *Training and Development, 50* (10), 11–13.

Friedrich, W. (1990). *Psychotherapy of sexually abused children and their families.* New York: Norton.

Froland, C., Pancoast, D., Chapman, N., & Kimboko, P. (1981). *Helping networks and human services.* Beverly Hills, CA: Sage.

G

Gabbard, G. O. (1996). Lessons to be learned from the study of sexual boundary violations. *American Journal of Psychotherapy, 50* (3), 311–322.

Gagliano, C. K. (1987). Group treatment for sexually abused girls. *Social Casework, 68,* 102–108.

Galambos, C. M. (1998). Preserving end-of-life autonomy: the Patient Self-Determination Act and the Uniform Health Care Decisions Act. *Health and Social Work, 23* (4), 275–281.

Galinsky, M. J., Turnbull, J. E., Meglin, D. E., & Wilner, M. E. (1993). Confronting the reality of collaborative practice research: Issues of practice, design, measurement, and team development. *Social Work, 38* (4), 440–449.

Gallo, F. (1982). The effects of social support networks in the health of the elderly. *Social Work in Health Care, 8,* 65–74.

Gambe, R., & Getzel, G. S. (1989). Group work with gay men with AIDS. *Social Casework, 70* (37), 172–179.

Gambrill, E., & Barth, R. (1980). Single-case study designs revisited. *Social Work Research and Abstracts, 16,* 15–20.

Gammon, E. A., & Rose, S. (1991). The coping skills training program for parents of children with developmental disabilities. *Research on Social Work Practice, 1* (3), 244–256.

Garbarino, J., & Ebata, A. (1983). The significance of ethnic and cultural differences in child maltreatment. *Journal of Marriage and the Family, 45* (4), 773–783.

Garbarino, J., Stocking, S., & Associates (1980). *Protecting children from abuse and neglect.* San Francisco: Jossey-Bass.

Gardner, F. (2000). Design Evaluation: Illuminating Social Work Practice for Better Outcomes. *Social Work, 45* (2), 176–182.

Gardner, R. A. (1971). *Therapeutic communication with children.* New York: Science House Press.

Garfield, R. (1981). Convening the family: Guidelines for the initial contact with a family member. In A. Gutman (Ed.), *Questions and answers in the practice of family therapy* (pp. 5–9). New York: Brunner/Mazel.

Garfinkel, I., & McLanahan, S. S. (1986). *Single mothers and their children.* Washington, DC: Urban Institute Press.

Garland, J., Jones, H., & Kolodny, R. (1965). A model for stages in the development of social work groups. In S. Bernstein (Ed.), *Explorations in group work.* Boston: Milford House.

Gartrell, N. K. (1992). Boundaries in lesbian therapy relationships. *Women and Therapy, 12* (3), 29–50.

Garvin, C. (1981). *Contemporary group work.* Englewood Cliffs, NJ: Prentice Hall.

Garvin, C. (1985). Practice with task-centered groups. In A. E. Fortune (Ed.), *Task-centered practice with families and groups* (pp. 45–57). New York: Springer.

Garvin, C. (1986). Assessment and change of group conditions in social work practice. In P. H. Glasser & N. S. Mayadas (Eds.), *Group workers at work: Theory and practice in the 80's.* Totowa, NJ: Rowman & Lillifield.

Garvin, C. (1987). *Contemporary group work* (2nd ed.). Englewood Cliffs, NJ: Prentice Hall.

Garvin, C., Reid, W., & Epstein, L. (1976). A task-oriented approach. In R. Roberts & H. Northern (Eds.), *Theories of social work with groups.* New York: Columbia University Press.

Gaylord, M. (1979). Relocation and the corporate family: Unexplored issues. *Social Work, 24,* 186–191.

Gazda, G. M. (1989). *Group counseling: A developmental approach* (4th ed.). Boston: Allyn & Bacon.

Gelles, R., & Cornell, C. P. (1990). *Intimate violence in families.* Newbury Park, CA: Sage.

Gendlin, E. (1967). Therapeutic procedures in dealing with schizophrenics. In C. Rogers, E. Gendlin, D. Kesler, & C. Truax (Eds.), *The therapeutic relationship and its impact: A study of psychotherapy with schizophrenics.* Madison: University of Wisconsin Press.

Gendlin, E. (1974). Client-centered and experiential psychotherapy. In D. Wexler & L. Rice (Eds.), *Innovations in client-centered therapy.* New York: Wiley.

Gentry, D. B. (1997a). Including children in divorce mediation and education: potential benefits and cautions. *Families in Society, 78* (3), 307–315.

Gentry, D. B. (1997b). Facilitating parent-child communication during divorce mediation. *Families in Society, 78* (3), 316–321.

George, L., & Fillenbaum, G. (1990). OARS methodology: A decade of experience in geriatric assessment. *Journal of the American Geriatrics Society, 33,* 607–615.

George, R. M. (1990). The reunification process in substitute care. *Social Service Review, 64* (3), 422–457.

Germain, C. (1973). An ecological perspective in casework practice. *Social Casework, 54,* 323–330.

Germain, C. (1977). An ecological perspective on social work practice in health care. *Social Work in Health Care, 3,* 67–76.

Germain, C. (1979). Ecology and social work. In C. Germain (Ed.), *Social work practice: People and environments* (pp. 1–2). New York: Columbia University Press.

Germain, C. (1981). The ecological approach to people-environmental transactions. *Social Casework, 62,* 323–331.

Germain, C., & Gitterman, A. (1980). *The life model of social work practice.* New York: Columbia University Press.

Gerstel, N., Bogard, C. J., McConnell, J. J., & Schwartz, M. (1996). The therapeutic incarceration of homeless families. *Social Service Review, 70* (4), 542–572.

Getzel, G. S. (1991). Survival modes for people with AIDS in groups. *Social Work, 36* (1), 711.

Ghali, S. (1982). Understanding Puerto Rican traditions. *Social Work, 27,* 98–102.

Giannandrea, V., & Murphy, K. (1973). Similarity of self-disclosure and return for a second interview. *Journal of Counseling Psychology, 20,* 545–548.

Gibbons, J., Bow, I., & Butter, J. (1979). Clients' reactions to task-centered casework: A follow-up study. *British Journal of Social Work, 9,* 203–215.

Gibbs, L., & Gambrill, E. (1996). *Critical thinking for social workers.* Thousand Oaks, CA: Pine Forge Press.

Gibson, J., & Gutierrez, L. (1991). A service program for safe-home children. *Families in Society, 72* (9), 554–562.

Gibson, P. A. (1999). African American grandmothers: New mothers again. *Affilia, 14* (3), 329–343.

Gil, E. (1991). *The healing power of play: Working with abused children.* New York: Guilford Press.

Gilbar, O. (1992). Workers' sick fund (kupat holim) hotline therapeutic first intervention: A model developed in the Gulf War. *Social Work in Health Care, 17* (4), 45–57.

Gilbert, N. (1977). The search for professional identity. *Social Work, 22,* 401–406.

Gilbert, N., & Specht, H. (1976). Advocacy and professional ethics. *Social Work, 21,* 288–293.

Gilbert, N., & Specht, H. (1979). Title XX planning by area agencies on aging: Effects, outcomes, and policy implications. *Gerontologist, 19,* 264–274.

Gilbert, N., & Specht, H. (1987). Social planning and community organizations. *Encyclopedia of social work* (Vol. 2, pp. 602–619). Silver Spring, MD: National Association of Social Workers.

Gilgun, J. F. (1994). Hand to glove: The grounded theory approach and social work practice research. In L. Sherman & W. J. Reid (Eds.), *Qualitative research in social work* (pp. 115–125). New York: Columbia University Press.

Gilgun, J. G. (1999). CASPARS: New tools for assessing client risks and strengths. *Families in Society, 80* (5), 450–458.

Gillian, C. B., & James, R. K. (1993). *Crisis intervention strategies* (2nd ed.). Pacific Grove, CA: Brooks/Cole.

Gillman, R. (1991). From resistance to rewards: Social workers' experiences and attitudes toward AIDS. *Families in Society, 72* (10), 593–601.

Gingerich, W. J. (1984). Generalizing single-case evaluation from classroom to practice setting. *Journal of Education for Social Work, 20,* 74–82.

Giovannoni, J., & Billingsley, A. (1970). Child neglect among the poor: A study of parental adequacy in families of three ethnic groups. *Child Welfare, 49,* 196–204.

Gitterman, A. (1996). Ecological perspectives: Response to Professor Jerry Wakefield. *Social Service Review, 70* (3), 472–476.

Gitterman, A., & Schaeffer, A. (1972). The white professional and the black client. *Social Casework, 53,* 280–291.

Giunta, C. T., & Streissguth, A. P. (1988). Patients with fetal alcohol syndrome and their caretakers. *Social Casework, 69* (7), 453–459.

Glick, I., & Kessler, D. (1974). *Marital and family therapy.* New York: Grime & Stratton.

Glisson, C. (1994). The effects of service coordination teams on outcomes for children in state custody. *Administration in Social Work, 18* (4), 1–25.

Golan, N. (1978). *Treatment in crisis situations.* New York: Free Press.

Golan, N. (1980). Intervention at times of transition: Sources and forms of help. *Social Casework, 61,* 259–266.

Golan, N. (1981). *Passing through transitions: A guide for the practitioner.* New York: Free Press.

Golan, N., & Gruschka, R. (1971). Integrating the new immigrant: A model for social work practice in transitional states. *Social Work, 16,* 82–87.

Gold, M. (1986, November). (As quoted by Earl Ubell.) Is that child bad or depressed? *Parade Magazine, 2,* 10.

Gold, N. (1990). Motivation: The crucial but unexplored component of social work practice. *Social Work, 35,* 49–56.

Golden, G. K. (1991). Volunteer counselors: An innovative, economic response to mental health service gaps. *Social Work, 36* (3), 230–232.

Goldenberg, I., & Goldenberg, H. (1991). *Family therapy: An overview* (3rd ed.). Pacific Grove, CA: Brooks/Cole.

Goldenberg, I., & Goldenberg, H. (2000). *Family therapy: An overview* (5th ed.). Pacific Grove, CA: Brooks/Cole.

Goldfried, M. (1977). The use of relaxation and cognitive relabeling as coping skills. In R. Stuart (Ed.), *Behavioral self-management* (pp. 82–116). New York: Brunner/Mazel.

Goldstein, E. G. (1983). Issues in developing systematic research and theory. In A. Rosenblatt & D. Waldfogel (Eds.), *Handbook of clinical social work.* San Francisco: Jossey-Bass.

Goldstein, E. G. (1997). To tell or not to tell: The disclosure of events in the therapist's life to the patient. *Clinical Social Work Journal, 25* (1), 41–58.

Goldstein, H. (1983). Starting where the client is. *Social Casework, 64,* 267–275.

Gomes-Schwartz, B., Horowitz, J., & Cardarell, A. (1990). *Child sexual abuse.* Newbury Park, CA: Sage.

Gomez, E., Zurcher, L. A., Farris, B. E., & Becker, R. E. (1985). A study of psychosocial casework with Chicanos. *Social Work, 30,* 477–482.

Gomez, M. R. (1990). Biculturalism and subjective mental health among Cuban Americans. *Social Service Review, 64* (3), 375–389.

Goodman, H. (1997). Social group work in community corrections. *Social Work with Groups, 20* (1), 51–64.

Goodwin, D. W., & Gabrielli, W. F. (1997). Alcohol: Clinical aspects. In J. H. Lowinson, P. Ruiz, R. B. Millman, & J. G. Langrod (Eds.), *Substance abuse: A comparative textbook* (3rd ed.). (pp. 142–148). Baltimore, MD: Williams & Wilkins.

Gordon, J. (1978). Group homes: Alternative to institutions. *Social Work, 23,* 300–305.

Gordon, T. (1970). *Parent effectiveness training.* New York: P. H. Wyden.

Gordon, W. (1962). A critique of the working definition. *Social Work, 7,* 3–13.

Gordon, W. (1965). Toward a social work frame of reference. *Journal of Education for Social Work, 1,* 19–26.

Gordon, W., & Schutz, M. (1977). A natural basis for social work specializations. *Social Work, 22,* 422–426.

Gorey, K. M., Thyer, B. A., & Pawluck, D. E. (1998). Differential effectiveness of prevalent social work practice models: A meta-analysis. *Social Work, 43* (3), 269–278.

Gottesfeld, M., & Lieberman, F. (1979). The pathological therapist. *Social Casework, 60,* 387–393.

Gottlieb, B. (Ed.) (1981). *Social networks and social support.* Beverly Hills, CA: Sage.

Gottlieb, B. (1985). Assessing and strengthening the impact of social support on mental health. *Social Work, 30,* 293–300.

Gottlieb, B. (Ed.) (1988). *Marshaling social support.* Newbury Park, CA: Sage.

Gould, K. (1988). Asian and Pacific islanders: Myth and reality. *Social Work, 33,* 142–147.

Graham, J. R., & Barter, K. (1999). Collaboration: A social work practice method. *Families in Society, 80* (1), 6–13.

Grant, G. B., & Grobman, L. M. (1998). *The social worker's internet handbook*. Harrisburg, PA. White Hat Communications.

Graves, B., & Accardo, P. J. (1989). Training in parenting skills for adults with mental retardation. *Social Work, 34* (5), 431–434.

Green, J. W. (1999). *Cultural awareness in the human services: A multi-ethnic approach*. Boston: Allyn & Bacon.

Greenbaum, L., & Holmes, I. (1983). The use of folktales in social work practice. *Social Casework, 64*, 414–418.

Greenfield, P. M. (1994). Independence and interdependence as developmental scripts: Implications for theory, research and practice. In P. M. Greenfield & R. R. Cocking (Eds.), *Cross-cultural roots of minority child development* (pp. 1–24). Hillsdale, NJ: Lawrence Erlbaum Associates.

Greif, G. L. (1985). *Single fathers*. Lexington, MA: Heath.

Griffin, R. E. (1991). Assessing the drug-involved client. *Families in Society, 72* (2), 87–94.

Grinnell, R., & Kyte, N. (1974). Modifying the environment. *Social Work, 19*, 477–483.

Gross, E. (1995). Deconstructing politically correct practice literature: The American Indian case. *Social Work, 40* (2), 206–213.

Grunebaum, H. (1986). Harmful psychotherapy experience. *American Journal of Psychotherapy, 40*, 165–176.

Guendalman, S. (1983). Developing responsiveness to the health care needs of Hispanic children and families. *Social Work in Health Care, 8*, 1–15.

Gulati, P., & Guest, G. (1990). The community-centered model: A garden variety approach or a radical transformation of community practice? *Social Work, 35* (1), 63–68.

Gurman, A. (1977). The patient's perception of the therapeutic relationship. In A. Gutman & A. Razin (Eds.), *Effective psychotherapy: A handbook of research. New* York: Pergamon Press.

Gutheil, I. A. (1993). Rituals and termination procedures. *Smith College Studies in Social Work, 63* (2), 163–176.

Gutierrez, L. M. (1990). Working with women of color: An empowerment perspective. *Social Work, 35* (2), 149–153.

Gutierrez, L. M. (1994). Beyond coping: an empowerment perspective on stressful life events. *Journal of Sociology and Social Welfare, 21* (3), 201–219.

Gutierrez, L. M. (1999). Current, emerging and future trends for community organization practice. In J. Rothman (Ed.), *Reflections on community organization: Enduring themes and critical issues* (pp. 367–380). Itasca, IL: F. E. Peacock.

Gutierrez, L. M. & Lewis, E. A. (1999). Strengthing communities through groups: A multicultural perspective. In H. Bertcher, L. F. Kurtz, & A. Lamont (Eds.), *Rebuilding communities: Challenges for group work* (pp. 5–16). New York: Haworth Press.

Gutierrez, L. M., & Ortega, R. (1991). Developing methods to empower Latinos: The importance of groups. *Social Work with Groups, 14* (2), 23–43.

Gutierrez, L. M., Parsons, R. J., & Cox, E. O. (1998). *Empowerment in social work practice: A sourcebook*. Pacific Grove, CA: Brooks/Cole.

Gwyn, F., & Kilpatrick, A. (1981). Family therapy with low-income blacks: A tool or turn-off? *Social Casework, 62*, 259–266.

H

Hackman, J. R., & Oldham, G. R. (1976). Motivation through the design of work: Test of a theory. *Organizational Behavior and Human Performance, 16*, 250–279.

Hackman, J. R., & Oldham, G. R. (1980). *Work design*. Reading, MA: Addison-Wesley.

Hackney, H., & Cormier, L. (1979). *Counseling strategies and objectives* (2nd ed.), Englewood Cliffs, NJ: Prentice Hall.

Haeuser, A., & Schwartz, F. (1980). Developing social work skills for work with volunteers. *Social Casework, 61*, 595–601.

Hagen, J. L. (1987a). The heterogeneity of homelessness. *Social Casework, 68*, 451–457.

Hagen, J. L. (1987b). Gender and homelessness. *Social Work, 32*, 312–316.

Hagen, J. L. (1998). The new welfare law: "Tough on work." *Families in Society, 79* (6), 596–605.

Haight, W. L. (1998). Gathering the spirit at First Baptist Church: Spirituality as a protective factor in the lives of African American children. *Social Work, 43* (3), 213–221.

Haley, J. (1963). *Strategies of psychotherapy*. New York: Grune & Stratton.

Hall, J. A., Schlesinger, D. J., & Dineen, J. P. (1997). Social skills training in groups with developmentally disabled adults. *Research on Social Work Practice, 7* (2): 187–201.

Hall, M. (1978). Lesbian families: Cultural and clinical issues. *Social Work, 23*, 380–385.

Halpern, R. (1990). Poverty and early childhood parenting: Toward a framework for intervention. *American Journal of Orthopsychiatry, 60* (1), 6–18.

Hamlin, E. R. (1991). Community-based spouse abuse protection and family preservation teams. *Social Work, 36* (5), 402–406.

Hammond, D., Hepworth, D., & Smith, V. (1977). *Improving therapeutic communication*. San Francisco: Jossey-Bass.

Hampton, R. L. (1990). *Black family violence: Current theory and research*. Lexington, MA: Lexington Books.

Handmaker, N. S., Miller, W. R., & Manicke, M. (1999). Findings of a pilot study of motivational interviewing with pregnant drinkers. *Journal of Studies on Alcohol, 60* (2), 285–287.

Haney, M., & Rabin, B. (1984). Modifying attitudes toward disabled persons. *Archives of Physical Medicine and Rehabilitation, 65*, 431–436.

Haney, P. (1988). Providing empowerment to the person with AIDS. *Social Work, 33*, 251–253.

Hardy, K. (1989). The theoretical myth of sameness: A critical issue in family therapy and treatment. In G. W Saba, B. M. Karrer, & K. Hardy (Eds.), *Minorities and family therapy* (pp. 17–33). New York: Hawthorne Press.

Hardy, K. V. (1997). Steps toward becoming culturally competent. *Family Therapy News, 28* (2), 13, 19.

Hare, J. (1994). Concerns and issues faced by families headed by a lesbian couple. *Families in Society, 75* (1), 27–35.

Harper, K. V., & Lantz, J. (1996). *Cross-cultural practice*. Chicago, IL: Lyceum Books.

Harrigan, M. P., Favri, D. P., & Netting, F. E. (1998). Termination: Extending the concept for macro social work practice. *Journal of Sociology and Social Welfare, 25* (4), 61–80.

Harris, M., & Bergman, H. C. (1987). Case management with the chronically ill. *American Journal of Orthopsychiatry, 57*, 296–302.

Hartford, M. (1971). *Groups in social work*. New York: Columbia University Press.

Hartman, A. (1981). The family: A central focus for practice. *Social Work, 26,* 7–13.

Hartman, A. (1993). The professional is political. *Social Work, 38* (4), 365, 366, 504.

Hartman, A. (1994). Diagrammatic assessment of family relationships. In B. R. Compton & B. Galaway (Eds.), *Social work processes* (5th ed) (pp. 153–165). Pacific Grove, CA: Brooks/Cole.

Hartman, A., & Laird, J. (1983). *Family centered social work practice.* New York: Free Press.

Hartman, C., & Reynolds, D. (1987). Resistant clients: Confrontation, interpretation and alliance. *Social Casework, 68,* 205–213.

Harvey, Y., & Chung, S. (1980). The Koreans. In J. McDermott, Jr., W. Tseng, & T. Maretzki (Eds.), *People and cultures of Hawaii* (pp. 135–154). Honolulu: University of Hawaii Press.

Hasenfeld, Y., & Furman, W. M. (1994). Intervention research as an interorganizational exchange. In J. Rothman & E. Thomas (Eds.), *Intervention research: Design for human services* (pp. 297–313). New York: Haworth Press.

Haslett, D. C. (1997). The education task group: Teaching proposal writing to social work students. *Social Work with Groups, 20* (4), 55–67.

Haynes, K. S., & Mickelson, J. S. (2000). *Affecting change: Social workers in the political arena* (4th ed.). Boston: Allyn and Bacon.

Hegar, R. L. (1989). Empowerment-based practice with children. *Social Service Review, 63* (3), 372–383.

Henderson, S. (1982). The significance of social relationships in the etiology of neurosis. In C. M. Parkes & J. Stevenson-Hinde (Eds.), *The place of attachment in human behavior* (pp. 205–231). New York: Basic Books.

Henderson, S., Duncan-Jones, P., Byrne, D., & Scott, R. (1980). Measuring social relationships: The interview schedule for social interaction. *Psychological Medicine 10,* 723–734.

Henggeler, S. W., Schoenwald, S. K., Bourduin, C. M., Rowland, M. D., & Cunningham, P. B. (1998). *Multisystemic treatment of antisocial behavior in children and adolescents.* New York: Guilford Press.

Henry, J. (1999). Changing conscious experience: Comparing clinical approaches, practice, and outcomes. *British Journal of Psychology, 90* (4), 587–609.

Henry, M. (1988). Revisiting open groups. *Groupwork, 1,* 215–228.

Henry, S. (1992). *Group skills in four-dimensional approach* (2nd ed.). Pacific Grove, CA: Brooks/Cole.

Hepworth, D. (1964). The clinical implications of perceptual distortion in forced marriages. *Social Casework, 45,* 579–585.

Hepworth, D. (1979). Early removal of resistance in task-centered casework. *Social Work, 24,* 317–323.

Hepworth, D. H. (1993). Managing manipulative behavior in the helping relationship. *Social Work, 38* (6), 674–684.

Hepworth, D. H., Farley, O. W., & Griffiths, J. K. (1988). Clinical work with suicidal adolescents and their families. *Social Casework, 69,* 195–203.

Hernandez, M., & McGoldrick, M. (1999). Migration and the life cycle. In B. Carter & M. McGoldrick (Eds.), *The expanded family life cycle: Individual, family, and social perspectives* (3rd ed.) (pp. 169–184). Boston: Allyn & Bacon.

Herz, F., & Rosen, E. (1982). Jewish families. In M. McGoldrick, J. Pearce, & J. Giordano (Eds.), *Ethnicity and family therapy* (pp. 364–392). New York: Guilford Press.

Hess, P. (1982). Parent-child attachment concept: Crucial for permanency planning. *Social Casework, 63,* 46–53.

Hess, P. M., & Mullen, E. J. (1995). Bridging the gap: Collaborative considerations in practitioner-researcher knowledge-building partnerships. In P. M. Hess & E. J. Mullen (Eds.), *Practitioner-researcher partnerships* (pp. 1–30). Washington, DC: NASW Press.

Hill, B., Rotegard, L., & Bruininks, R. (1984). The quality of life of mentally retarded people in residential care. *Social Work, 29,* 275–281.

Hines, P., & Boyd-Franklin, N. (1996). African American families. In M. McGoldrick, J. Giordana, & J. Pearce (Eds.), *Ethnicity and family therapy* (2nd. ed.) (pp. 68–84). New York: Guilford Press.

Hines, P. M., Garcia-Preto, N., McGoldrick, M., Almeida, R., & Weltman, S. (1992). Intergenerational relationships across cultures. *Families in Society, 73* (3), 323–338.

Hines, P. H., Preto, N. G., McGoldrick, M., Almeida, R., & Weltman, S. (1999). Culture and the family life cycle: In B. Carter and M. McGoldrick (Eds.), *The expanded family life cycle: individual, family and social perspectives* (3rd ed.). Needham Heights, MA, Allyn Bacon.

Hirayama, H., & Cetingok, M. (1988). Empowerment: A social work approach for Asian immigrants. *Social Casework, 69,* 41–47.

Hirayama, K. K., Hirayama, H., & Cetingok, M. (1993). Mental health promotion for South East Asian refugees in the USA. *International Social Work, 36* (2), 119–129.

Ho, M. (1976). Social work with Asian Americans. *Social Casework, 57,* 195–201.

Ho, M. K. (1987). *Family therapy with ethnic minorities.* Newbury Park, CA: Sage.

Hochschild, A. (1989). *Second shift.* New York: Viking Penguin.

Hoehn-Saric, R., Frank, J., Imber, S., Nash, E., Stone, A., & Battle, C. (1964). Systematic preparation of patients for psychotherapy—I. Effects on therapy behavior and outcome. *Journal of Psychiatric Research, 2,* 267–281.

Hogarty, G. (1989). Meta-analysis of the effects of practice with the chronically mentally ill: A critique and reappraisal of the literature. *Social Work, 34* (4), 363–372.

Holm, O. (1997). Ratings of empathic communication: does experience make a difference? *Journal of Psychology, 131* (6), 680–682.

Holman, W. D. (1997). Who would find you?: A question for working with suicidal children and adolescents. *Child and Adolescent Social Work Journal, 14* (2), 129–137.

Holmes, K. (1981). Services for victims of rape: a dualistic practice model. *Social Casework, 62,* 30–39.

Holmes, T., & Rahe, R. (1967). The social readjustment rating scale. *Journal of Psychosomatic Research, 11,* 213–218.

Homan, M. S. (1999). *Promoting community change: Making it happen in the real world* (2nd ed.). Brooks/Cole.

Homma-True, R. (1976). Characteristics of contrasting Chinatowns: 2. Oakland, California. *Social Casework, 57,* 155–159.

Honey, E. (1988). AIDS and the inner city: Critical issues. *Social Casework, 69,* 365–370.

Horesji, C., Heavy, Runner B., & Pablo, C. J. (1992). Reactions by Native American parents to child protection agencies: Cultural and community factors. *Child Welfare, 71* (4), 329–342.

Horton, A. L., Johnson, B. L., Roundy, L. M., & Williams, D. (Eds.) (1989). *The incest perpetrator: A family member no one wants to treat.* Newbury Park, CA: Sage.

Houston-Vega, M. K., Nuehring, E. M., & Daguio, E. R. (1997). *Prudent practice: A guide for managing malpractice risk.* Washington, DC: NASW Press.

Howing, P. T., Wodarski, J. S., Gaudin, J. M., & Kurtz, P. D. (1989). Effective interventions to ameliorate the incidence of child maltreatment: The empirical base. *Social Work, 34,* 330–338.

Hudson, W. W. (1991). *The computer assisted social services.* Tempe, AZ: Walmyr.

Hudson, W. (1982). *The clinical measurement package.* Homewood, IL: Dorsey.

Hudson, W. (1992). *Walmyr assessment scales.* Tempe, AZ: Walmyr.

Hudson, W., & Ricketts, W. A. (1980). A strategy for the measurement of homophobia. *Journal of Homosexuality, 5,* 357–371.

Hulewat, P. (1996). Resettlement: A cultural and psychological crisis. *Social Work, 41* (2), 129–135.

Hull, G., Jr. (1982). Child welfare services to Native Americans. *Social Casework, 63,* 340–347.

Hunt, G., & Paschall, N. (1984). *Volunteers forming effective citizen groups.* Lanham, MD: University Press of America.

Hunter, M. (1990). *The sexually abused male: Vol. 2. Application of treatment strategies.* Lexington, MA: Lexington Books.

Hurley, D. J. (1984). Resistance and work in adolescent groups. *Social Work with Groups, 1,* 71–81.

Hurst, C. E. (1992). *Social inequality: Forms, causes and consequences.* Boston: Allyn & Bacon.

Hurvitz, N. (1975). Interactions hypothesis in marriage counseling. In A. Gutman & D. Rice (Eds.), *Couples in conflict* (pp. 225–240). New York: Jason Aronson.

Hutchings, N. (1988). *The violent family: Victimization of women, children and elders.* New York: Human Sciences Press.

Hutchinson, E. D. (1987). Use of authority in direct social work practice with mandated clients. *Social Service Review, 61,* 581–598.

Hutchinson, J., Lloyd, J., Landsman, M. J., Nelson, K. & Bryce, M. (1983). *Family-centered social services: A model for child welfare agencies.* Oakdale, IA: National Resource Center on Family Based Services, University of Iowa.

Hutchinson, W., Searight, P., & Stretch, J. (1986). Multidimensional networking: A response to the needs of homeless families. *Social Work, 31,* 427–430.

Hyde, C. (1996). A feminist's response to Rothman's "The interweaving of community intervention approaches." *Journal of Community Practice, 3* (3/4), 127–145.

Hystad, N. (1989). *The Alcohol Use Profile.* Two Harbors, MN: Chemical Dependency Publications.

I

Icard, L. D., Longres, J. F., & Spenser, M. (1999). Racial minority status and distress among children and adolescents. *Journal of Social Service Research, 25* (1/2), 19–40.

Imbrogno, A. R., & Imbrogno, S. (2000). Mediation in court cases of domestic violence. *Families in Society, 81* (4), 392–401.

Indyk, D., Belville, R., Lachapelle, S. S., Gordon, G., & Dewart, T. (1993). A community-based approach to HIV case management: Systematizing the unmanageable. *Social Work, 38* (4), 380–387.

Ingersoll, S. L., & Patton, S. O. (1990). *Treating perpetrators of sexual abuse.* Lexington, MA: Lexington Books.

Ivanoff, A., Blythe, B. J., & Briar, S. (1987). The empirical clinical practice debate. *Social Casework, 68,* 290–298.

Ivanoff, A. M., Blythe, B. J., & Tripodi T. (1994). *Involuntary clients in social work practice: A research-based approach.* New York: Aldine de Gruyter.

J

Jackson, A. (1995). Diversity and oppression. In C. H. Meyer & M. A. Mattiani (Eds.), *The foundation of social work practice* (pp. 42–58). Washington, DC: NASW Press.

Jackson, A. P. (1998). The role of social support in parenting for low-income, single, black mothers. *Social Service Review, 72* (3), 365–378.

Jacob, T., Ritchey, D., Cvitkovic, J., & Blane, H. (1981). Communication styles of alcoholic and nonalcoholic families when drinking and not drinking. *Journal of Studies on Alcohol, 42,* 466–482.

Jacobson, E. (1929). *Progressive relaxation.* Chicago: University of Chicago Press.

Jacobson, N. (1978). A stimulus control model of change in behavioral couples' therapy: Implications for contingency contracting. *Journal of Marriage and Family Counseling, 4,* 29–35.

Jacobson, N., & Margolin, G. (1979). *Marital therapy.* New York: Brunner/Mazel.

Jacobson, N., Schmaling, K., & Holtzworth-Munroe, A. (1987). Component analysis of behavioral marital therapy: 2–year follow-up and prediction of relapse. *Journal of Marital and Family Therapy, 13* (2), 187–195.

Jaffe, P., Wolfe, D., & Wilson, S. K. (1990). *Children of battered women.* Newbury Park, CA: Sage.

James, B. (1989). *Treating traumatized children: New insights and creative interventions.* Lexington, MA: Lexington Books.

James, K., & MacKinnon, L. (1990). The "incestuous family" revisited: A critical analysis of family therapy myths. *Journal of Marital and Family Therapy, 16* (1), 71–88.

James, P. (1991). Effects of a communication training component added to an emotionally focused couples therapy. *Journal of Marital and Family Therapy, 17* (3), 263–275.

Jang, M., Lee, K., & Woo, K. (1998). Income, language, and citizenship status: Factors affecting the health care access and utilization of Chinese Americans. *Health and Social Work, 23* (2), 136–145.

Janis, I., & Mann, L. (1977). *Decision making:. A psychosocial analysis of conflict, choice, and commitment.* New York: Free Press.

Janzen , C., & Harris, O. (1997). *Family treatment in social work practice* (3rd ed.). Itasca, IL: F. E. Peacock.

Jarrett, R. L. (1995). Growing up poor: The family experience of socially mobile youth in low-income African American neighborhoods. *Journal of Adolescent Research, 10* (1), 111–135.

Jason, L. A., & Burrows, B. (1983). Transition training for high school seniors. *Cognitive Therapy and Research, 7,* 79–92.

Jayaratne, S., Croxton, T., & Mattison, D. (1997). Social work professional standards: An exploratory study. *Social Work, 42* (2), 187–199.

Jayaratne, S., & Levy, R. (1979). *Empirical clinical practice*. New York: Columbia University Press.

Jefferson, C. (1978). Some notes on the use of family sculpture in therapy. *Family Process, 17,* 69–75.

Jenkins, S. (1981). *The ethnic dilemma in social services*. New York: Free Press.

Jennings, H. (1950). *Leadership and isolation*. New York: Longmans Green.

Jilek, W. (1982). *Indian healing: Shamanic ceremonialism in the Pacific Northwest today*. Laine, WA: Hancock House.

Johnson, A. K., & Kreuger, L. W. (1989). Towards a better understanding of homeless women. *Social Work, 34* (6), 537–540.

Johnson, H. C. (1989). Disruptive children: Biological factors in attention deficit disorder and antisocial disorders. *Social Work, 34* (2), 137–144.

Johnson, P., & Rubin, A. (1983). Case management in mental health: A social work domain. *Social Work, 28,* 49–55.

Jones, D. M. (1996). Termination from drug treatment: Dangers and opportunities for clients of the graduation ceremony. *Social Work with Groups, 19* (3/4), 105–115.

Jones, L. (1990). Unemployment and child abuse. *Families in Society, 17* (10), 579–586.

Jones, R. (1983). Increasing staff sensitivity to the black client. *Social Casework, 64,* 419–425.

Jordan, C., & Franklin, C. (1995). *Clinical assessment for social workers: Quantative and qualitative methods*. Chicago: Lyceum Books.

Jose, P. E., Cafasso, L. L., & D'Anna, C. A. (1994). Ethnic group differences in children's coping strategies. *Sociological Studies of Children, 6,* 25–53.

Joseph, M., & Conrad, A. (1980). A parish neighborhood model for social work practice. *Social Casework, 61,* 423–432.

Joshi, P. T., Capozzoli, J. A., & Coyle, J. T. (1990). The Johns Hopkins Depression Scale: Normative data and validation in child psychiatry patients. *Journal of the American Academy of Child and Adolescent Psychiatry, 29* (2), 283–288.

Joyce, A. S., Duncan, S. C., Duncan, A., Kipnes, D., & Piper, W. E. (1996). Limiting time-unlimited group therapy. *International Journal of Group Psychotherapy, 46* (6), 61–79.

Joyce, K., Diffenbacher, G., Greene, J., & Sorakin, Y. (1983). Internal and external barriers to obtaining prenatal care. *Social Work and Health Care, 9,* 89–93.

Julia, M. C. (1996). *Multicultural Awareness in the health care professions*. Needham Heights, MA: Allyn and Bacon.

Jung, M. (1976). Characteristics of contrasting Chinatowns: 1. Philadelphia, Pennsylvania. *Social Casework, 57,* 149–154.

K

Kadushin, A. (1977). *Consultation in social work*. New York: Columbia University Press.

Kadushin, A., & Martin, J. A. (1981). *Child abuse: An interactional event*. New York: Columbia University Press.

Kadushin, A., & Martin, J. A. (1988). *Child welfare services*. New York: Macmillan.

Kadushin, G., & Kulys, R. (1993). Discharge planning revisited: What do social workers actually do in discharge planning? *Social Work, 38* (6), 713–726.

Kagan, R., & Schlosberg, S. (1989). *Families in perpetual crisis*. New York: Norton.

Kane, N. (1995). Looking at the lite side: "I feed more cats, than I have T-Cells." *Reflections, 1* (2), 26–36.

Kane, R. A., & Kane, R. L. (1981). *Assessing the elderly: A practical guide to measurement*. Lexington, MA: Lexington Books.

Kane, R. A., Penrod, J. D., Davidson, G., Moscovice, I., & Rich, E. (1991). What cost case management in long-term care? *Social Service Review, 65* (2), 281–303.

Kantor, D., & Lehr, W. (1975). *Inside the family: Toward a theory of family process*. San Francisco: Jossey-Bass.

Kaplan, K. (1992). Linking the developmentally disabled client to needed resources: Adult protective services case management. In B. S. Vourlekis & R. R. Greene (Eds.), *Social work case management*. Hawthorne, NY: Aldine de Gruyter.

Kardas, E. (1999). *Psychology Resources on the World Wide Web*. Pacific Grove, CA: Brooks/Cole.

Karttunen, F. (1996). Between worlds: Interpreters, guides, and survivors. *Frontiers, 17* (3), 31–33.

Katz, D. (1979). Laboratory training to enhance interviewing skills. In F. Clark, M. Arkava, & Associates (Eds.), *The pursuit of competence in social work* (pp. 205–226). San Francisco: Jossey-Bass.

Katz, L. (1990). Effective permanency planning for children in foster care. *Social Work, 35* (3), 220–226.

Kauffman, J. M. (1997). *Characteristics of emotional and behavioral disorders of children and youth* (6th ed.). Upper Saddle River, NJ: Prentice-Hall.

Kazdin, A. (1979). Imagery elaboration and self-efficacy in the covert modeling treatment of unassertive behavior. *Journal of Consulting and Clinical Psychology, 47,* 725–733.

Kazdin, A., Esveldt-Dawson, K., French, N. H., & Unis, A. S. (1987). Problem-solving skills training and relationship therapy in the treatment of antisocial child behavior. *Journal of Consulting and Clinical Psychology, 55,* 76–85.

Kazdin, A. E., Stolar, M. J., & Marciano, P. L. (1995). Risk factors for dropping out of treatment among white and black families. *Journal of Family Psychology, 9* (4), 402–419.

Kear-Colwell, J. & Pollock, P. (1997). Motivation or confrontation: Which approach to the child sex offender? *Criminal Justice and Behavior, 24,* 20–33.

Keefe, T. (1978). The economic context of empathy. *Social Work, 23* (6), 460–465.

Kelen, J. (1980). *The effects of poetry on elderly nursing home residents*. Unpublished doctoral dissertation, University of Utah, Salt Lake City.

Kelly, J. A., & Lamparski, D. (1985). Outpatient treatment of schizophrenics: Social skills and problem-solving training. In M. Hersen & A. S. Bellock (Eds.), *Handbook of clinical behavior therapy with adults* (pp. 485–506). New York: Plenum Press.

Kelly, J., & Sykes, P. (1989). Helping the helpers: A support group for family members of persons with AIDS. *Social Work, 34* (3), 239–242.

Kennard, W., & Shilman, R. (1979). Group services with the homebound. *Social Work, 24,* 330–332.

Kettner, P. M., Daley, J. M., & Nichols, A. W. (1985). *Initiating change in organizations and communities*. Monterey, CA: Brooks/Cole.

Kifer, R., Lewis, M., Green, D., & Phillips, E. (1974). Training predelinquent youths and their parents to negotiate conflict situations. *Journal of Applied Behavior Analysis, 7,* 357–364.

Kilgore, L. C. (1988). Effect of early childhood sexual abuse on self and ego development. *Social Casework, 69* (4), 224–230.

Kilpatrick, A. C., & Holland, T. (1999). *Working with families: An integrative model by level of need* (2nd ed.). Boston: Allyn & Bacon.

Kinney, J., Haapala, D., & Booth, C. (1991). *Keeping families together: The homebuilders model.* Hawthorne, NY: Aldine de Gruyter.

Kiresuk, T. J., & Garwick, G. (1979). Basic goal attainment procedures. In B. R. Compton & B. Galway (Eds.), *social work. processes* (2nd ed.) (pp. 412–421). Homewood, IL: Dorsey Press.

Kirk, S. A., & Koeske, G. F. (1995). The fate of optimism: A longitudinal study of case managers' hopefulness and subsequent morale. *Research on Social Work Practice, 5* (1), 47–61.

Kirk, S. A., & Kutchins, H. (1988). Deliberate misdiagnosis in mental health practice. *Social Service Review, 62,* 225–237.

Kissman, K. (1991). Feminist-based social work with single-parent families. *Families in Society, 72* (1), 23–28.

Klein, A. (1970). *Social work through group process.* Albany, NY: School of Social Welfare, State University of New York at Albany.

Klier, J., Fein, E., & Gencro, C. (1984). Are written or verbal contracts more effective in family therapy? *Social Work, 29,* 298–299.

Komar, Arne A. (1994). Adolescent school crises: Structures, issues and techniques for postventions. *International Journal of Adolescence and Youth, 5* (1/2), 35–46.

Kooden, H. (1994). The gay male therapist as an agent of socialization. *Journal of Gay and Lesbian Psychotherapy, 2* (2), 39–64.

Kopp, J. (1989). Self-observation: An empowerment strategy in assessment. *Social Casework, 70* (5), 276–284.

Koroloff, N. M., & Anderson, S. C. (1989). Alcohol-free living centers: Hope for homeless alcoholics. *Social Work, 34* (6), 497–504.

Koss, M. P., & Harvey, M. R. (1991). *The rape victim: Clinical and community interventions* (2nd ed.). Newbury Park, CA: Sage.

Kotlowitz, A. (1991). *There are no children here.* New York: Doubleday.

Kovacs, M. (1992). *Children's depression inventory manual.* Los Angeles: Western Psychological Services.

Kratochvil, M. S., & Devereux, S. A. (1988). Counseling needs of parents of handicapped children. *Social Casework, 69* (7), 420–426.

Krona, D. (1980). Parents as treatment partners in residential care. *Child Welfare, 59,* 91–96.

Kruger, L., Moore, D., Schmidt, P., & Wiens, R. (1979). Group work with abusive parents. *Social Work, 24,* 337–338.

Kuhn, D. R. (1990). The normative crises of families confronting dementia. *Families in Society, 71* (8), 451–459.

Kumabe, K., Nishida, C., & Hepworth, D. (1985). *Bridging ethnocultural diversity in social work and health.* Honolulu: University of Hawaii Press.

Kurland, R., & Salmon, R. (1998). Purpose: a misunderstood and misused keystone of group work practice. *Social Work with Groups, 21* (3), 5–17.

Kurtz, P. D., Jarvis, S. V., & Kurtz, G. L. (1991). Problems of homeless youths: Empirical findings and human services issues. *Social Work, 36* (4), 309–314.

Kutchins, H. (1991). The fiduciary relationship: The legal basis for social workers' responsibilities to clients. *Social Work, 36* (2), 106–113.

Kutchins, H., & Kirk, S. A. (1988). The business of diagnosis: DSM-III and clinical social work. *Social Work, 33,* 215–220.

Kutchins, H., & Kirk, S. (1995). Should DSM be the basis for teaching social work practice? No! *Journal of Social Work Education, 31* (2), 159–165.

Kutchins, H., & Kutchins, S. (1978). Advocacy in social work. In G. Weber & G. McCall (Eds.), *Social scientists as advocates* (pp. 13–48). Beverly Hills, CA: Sage.

Kutza, E. A., & Keigher, S. M. (1991). The elderly "new homeless": An emerging population at risk. *Social Work, 36* (4), 288–293.

L

Laing, K (1965). Mystification, confusion, and conflict. In I. Boszormenyi-Nagy & J. Framo (Eds.), *Intensive family therapy: Theoretical and practical aspects.* New York: Harper & Row.

Laird, J. (1993). Family-centered practice: Cultural and constructionist reflections. *Journal of Teaching in Social Work, 8* (1/2), 77–109.

Lake, R., Jr. (1983). Shamanism in Northwestern California: A female perspective on sickness, healing and health. *White Cloud Journal of American Indian Mental Health, 3,* 31–42.

Lam, D. H., Brewin, C. R., Woods, R. T., & Bebbington, P. E. (1987). Cognition and social adversity in the depressed elderly. *Journal of Abnormal Psychology, 96,* 23–26.

Lamaze, F. (1958). *Painless childbirth: Psychoprophylactic method.* London: Burke.

Lamb, H. (1982). *Treating the long-term mentally ill.* San Francisco: Jossey-Bass.

Lamb, S. (1986). Treating sexually abused children: Issues of blame and responsibility. *American Journal of Orthopsychiatry, 56,* 303–307.

Land, H. (1988). The impact of licensing on social work practice: Values, ethics and choices. *Journal of Independent Social Work, 2* (4), 87–96.

Land, H., & Harangody, G. (1990). A support group for partners of persons with AIDS. *Families in Society, 71* (8), 471–481.

Lane, E. J., Daugherty, T. K., & Nyman, S. J. (1998). Feedback on ability in counseling, self-efficacy, and persistence on task. *Psychological Reports, 83* (3, Pt 1), 1113–1114.

Lane, F. E. (1986). Utilizing physician empathy with violent patients. *American Journal of Psychotherapy, 40,* 448–456.

Lang, N. (1972). A broad range model of practice in the social work group. *Social Service Review, 46,* 76–89.

Lange, A., & Jakubowski, P. (1976). *Responsible assertive behavior.* Champaign, IL: Research Press.

Langley, P. A. (1991). Family violence: Toward a family-oriented public policy. *Families in Society, 72* (9), 574–576.

Lantz, J. (1978). Cognitive theory and social casework. *Social Work, 23,* 361–366.

Lantz, J. (1996). Cognitive theory in social work treatment. In F. Turner (Ed.), *Social work treatment: Interlocking theoretical approaches* (4th ed.) (pp. 94–115). New York: Free Press.

Larsen, J. (1975). *A comparative study of traditional and competency-based methods of teaching interpersonal skills in social work education*. Unpublished doctoral dissertation, University of Utah, Salt Lake City.

Larsen, J. (1980). Accelerating group development and productivity: An effective leader approach. *Social Work with Groups, 3,* 25–39.

Larsen, J. (1982). Remedying dysfunctional marital communication. *Social Casework, 63,* 15–23.

Larsen, J. (1991). *I'm a day late and a dollar short and it's okay: A woman's survival guide for the 90's*. Salt Lake City: Deseret Books.

Larsen, J., & Hepworth, D. (1978). Skill development through competency-based education. *Journal of Education for Social Work, 14,* 73–8 1.

Larsen, J., & Mitchell, C. (1980). Task-centered, strength-oriented group work with delinquents. *Social Casework, 61,* 154–163.

Lavee, Y. (1997). The components of healthy marriages: Perceptions of Israeli social workers and their clients. *Journal of Family Social Work, 2* (1), 1–14.

Lazarus, A. A. (1994). How certain boundaries and ethics diminish therapeutic effectiveness. *Ethics and Behavior, 4* (3), 255–261.

Leader, A. (1958). The problem of resistance in social work. *Social Work, 3,* 19–23.

Lebow, G., & Kane, B. (1992). Assessment: Private case management with the elderly. In B. S. Vourlekis & R. R. Greene (Eds.), *Social work case management*. Hawthorne, NY: Aldine de Gruyter.

Lechnyr, R. (1980a). Hypnosis as an adjunct in crisis intervention. *Behavioral Medicine, 7,* 41–44.

Lechnyr, R. (1980b). Tuning-in patients: Biofeedback instrumentation in clinical practice. *Behavioral Medicine, 7,* 13–23.

LeCroy, C. W. (Ed.). (1983). *Social skills training for children and youth*. New York: Haworth Press.

LeCroy, C. W. (1987). Teaching children social skills: A game format. *Social Work, 32,* 440–442.

LeCroy, C. W., & Rose, S. (1986). Evaluation of preventive interventions for enhancing social competence in adolescents. *Social Work Research and Abstracts, 22,* 8–16.

Lederer, W., & Jackson, D. (1968). *The mirages of marriage*. New York: Norton.

Lee, E. (1989). Assessment and treatment of Chinese American immigrant families. In G. Saba, B. Karrer, & K. Hardy (Eds.), *Minorities and family therapy* (pp. 99–120). New York: Hawthorne Press.

Lee, K., & McGill, C. (1991). Confronting the lack of resources for patients with AIDS dementia complex. *Social Work, 36* (6), 473–475.

Lehman, A. F. (1996). Heterogeneity of person and place: Assessing co-occuring addictive and mental disorders. *American Journal of Orthopsychiatry, 66* (1), 32–41.

Lehrer, P. (1982). How to relax and how not to relax: A reevaluation of the work of Jacobson. *Behaviour Research and Therapy, 20,* 417–425.

Lemmon, J. A. (1985). *Family mediation practice*. New York: Free Press.

Leslie, D. R., Holzhalb, C. M., & Holland, T. P. (1998). Measuring staff empowerment: Development of a worker empowerment scale. *Research on Social Work Practice, 8* (2), 212–222.

Lester, L. (1982). The special needs of the female alcoholic. *Social Casework, 63,* 451–456.

Levick, K. (1981). Privileged communication: Does it really exist? *Social Casework, 62,* 235–239.

Levine, B. (1967). *Fundamentals of group treatment*. Chicago: Whitehall.

Levinson, D. (1989). *Family violence in cross-cultural perspective*. Newbury Park, CA: Sage.

Levinson, H. (1973). Use and misuse of groups. *Social Work, 18,* 66–73.

Levinson, H. (1977). Termination of psychotherapy: Some salient issues. *Social Casework, 58,* 480–489.

Levy, C. (1973). The value base of social work. *Journal of Education for Social Work, 9,* 34–42.

Levy, C. (1979). *Values and ethics for social work practice*. Washington, DC: National Association of Social Workers.

Levy, E. F. (1992). Strengthening the coping resources of lesbian families. *Families in Society, 73* (1), 23–31.

Levy, L. (1963). *Psychological interpretation*. New York: Holt, Rinehart & Winston.

Lewis, B. (1985). The Wife Abuse Inventory: A screening device for the identification of abused women. *Social Work, 30* (1), 32–35.

Lewis, E. (1991). Social change and citizen action: A philosophical exploration for modern social group work. *Social Work with Groups, 14,* 3–4, 23–34.

Lewis, J., Beavers, W., Gossett, J., & Phillips, V. (1976). *No single thread: Psychological health in family systems*. New York: Brunner/Mazel.

Lewis, K. (1980). Children of lesbians: Their point of view. *Social Work, 25,* 198–203.

Lewis, R., & Ho, M. (1975). Social work with Native Americans. *Social Work, 20,* 379–382.

Lie, G-Y, & Inman, A. (1991). The use of anatomical dolls as assessment and evidentiary tools. *Social Work, 36* (5), 396–399.

Lieberman, M. (1980). Group methods. In F. Kanfer & A. Goldstein (Eds.), *Helping people change* (pp. 470–536). New York: Pergamon Press.

Lieberman, M., & Borman, L. (Eds.) (1979). *Self-help groups for coping with crisis*. San Francisco, CA: Jossey-Bass.

Lieberman, M., & Videka-Sherman, L. (1986). The impact of self-help groups on the mental health of widows and widowers. *American Journal of Orthopsychiatry, 56,* 435–449.

Lieberman, M., Yalom, I., & Miles, M. (1973). *Encounter groups: Firstfacts*. New York: Basic Books.

Lim, C., & Adelman, H. S. (1997). Establishing a school-based collaborative team to coordinate resources: A case study. *Journal of Social Work in Education, 19* (4), 266–277.

Linehan, M. (1993). *Skills training manual for treating borderline personality disorder*. New York: Guilford Press.

Linzer, N. (1999). *Resolving ethical dilemmas in social work practice*. Boston: Allyn & Bacon.

Lister, L. (1987). Contemporary direct practice roles. *Social Work, 32,* 384–391.

Lockhart, L. L., & Wodarski, J. S. (1989). Facing the unknown: Children and adolescents with AIDS. *Social Work, 34* (3), 215–221.

Long, D. D., & Holle, M. C. (1997). *Macro systems in the social environment*. Itasca, IL: F. E. Peacock.

Long, K. A. (1986). Cultural considerations in the assessment and treatment of intrafamilial abuse. *American Journal of Orthopsychiatry, 56,* 131–136.

Longres, J. F. (1991) Toward a status model of ethnic sensitive practice. *Journal of Multi-Cultural Social Work, 1* (1), 41–56.

Longres, J. F., & Torrecilha, R. S. (1992). Race and the diagnosis, placement and exit status of children and youth in a mental health and disability system. *Journal of Social Service Research, 15* (3/4), 43–63.

Lopez, D., & Getzel, G. S. (1987). Strategies for volunteers caring for persons with AIDS. *Social Casework, 68,* 47–53.

Lorion, R. (1978). Research on psychotherapy and behavior change with the disadvantaged. In S. Garfield & A. Bergin (Eds.), *Handbook of psychotherapy and behavior change* (pp. 903–938). New York: Wiley.

Lott, J. (1976). Migration of a mentality: The Filipino community. *Social Casework, 3,* 165–172.

Lovell, M. L., Reid, K., & Richey, C. A. (1992). Social support training for abusive mothers. *Social Work with Groups, 15* (2/3), 95–107.

Lovell, M. L., & Richey, C. A. (1991). Implementing agency-based social-support skill training. *Families in Society, 72* (9), 563–572.

Lovern, J. D., & Zohn, J. (1982). Utilization and indirect suggestion in multiple-family group therapy with alcoholics. *Journal of Marital and Family Therapy, 8* (3), 325–333.

Low, S. (1984). The cultural basis of health, illness, and disease. *Social Work in Health Care, 9,* 13–23.

Lowinson, J. H., Ruiz, P., Millman, R. B., & Langrod, J. G. (Eds) (1997). *Substance abuse: A comprehensive textbook* (3rd ed.). Baltimore, MD: Williams & Wilkins.

Luborsky, L., & Spence, D. (1978). Quantitative research on psychoanalytic therapy. In S. Garfield & A. Bergin (Eds.), *Handbook of psychotherapy and behavior change* (pp. 331–368). New York: Wiley.

Lukas, S. (1993) *Where to start and what to ask: An assessment handbook.* New York, NY: W.W. Norton.

Lukton, R. (1982). Myths and realities of crisis intervention. *Social Casework, 63,* 275–285.

Lum, D. (1982). Toward a framework for social work practice with minorities. *Social Work, 27,* 244–249.

Lum, D. (1996). *Social work practice and people of color: A process-stage approach* (3rd ed.). Pacific Grove, CA: Brooks/Cole.

M

MacFarlane, K., Waterman, J., et al. (1986). *Sexual abuse of young children: Evaluation and treatment.* New York: Guilford Press.

Macgowan, M. J. (1997). A measure of engagement for social group work: the groupwork engagement measure (GEM). *Journal of Social Service Research, 23* (2), 17–37.

Mailick, M. D., & Vigilante, F. W. (1997). The family assessment wheel: A social constructionist perspective. *Families in Society, 80* (1), 361–369.

Mackelprang, R., & Hepworth, D. H. (1987). Ecological factors in rehabilitation of patients with severe spinal cord injuries. *Social Work in Health Care, 13,* 23–38.

Mackey, R. A., & O'Brian, B. A. (1998). Marital conflict management: Gender and ethnic differences. *Social Work, 43* (2), 128–141.

Magen, R. H., & Glajchen, M. (1999). Cancer support groups: client outcome and the context of group process. *Research on Social Work Practice, 9* (5), 541–554.

Mahler, C. (1969). *Group counseling in the schools.* Boston: Houghton Mifflin.

Mahoney, M. J. (1974). *Cognition and behavior modification.* Cambridge, MA: Ballinger.

Malchiodi, C. (1990). *Art therapy with children from violent homes.* New York: Brunner/Mazel.

Malekoff, A., Johnson, H., & Klappersack, B. (1991). Parent-professional collaboration on behalf of children with disabilities. *Families in Society, 72* (7), 416–424.

Maletzky, B. M., & McGovern, K. B. (1990). *Treating the sexual offender.* Newbury Park, CA: Sage.

Maluccio, A. (1979). Perspectives of social workers and clients on treatment outcome. *Social Casework, 60,* 394–401.

Maluccio, A. N. (1990). Family preservation: An overview. In A. L. Sallee & J. C. Lloyd, (Eds.), *Family preservation: Papers from the Institute for Social Work Educators.* Riverdale, IL: National Association for Family-Based Services.

Maluccio, A. N., Fein, E., & Inger, D. (1995). Family reunification: Research findings, issues and directions. *Child Welfare, 73,* 489–504.

Maluccio, A. N., Fein, E., & Olmstead, K. (1986). *Permanency planning for children: Concepts and methods.* New York: Tavistock.

Mandell, J. G., & Damon, L. (1989). *Group treatment of sexually abused children.* New York: Guilford Press.

Mann, B., & Murphy, K. (1975). Timing of self disclosure, reciprocity of self-disclosure, and reactions to an initial interview. *Journal of Counseling Psychology, 22,* 304–308.

Marburg, G. (1983). Mental health and Native Americans: Responding to the biopsychosocial model. *White Cloud Journal of American Indian Mental Health, 3,* 43–51.

Marckworth, P. (1990). Practice skills and knowledge: Views from the field. In A. L. Sallee & J. C. Lloyd (Eds.), *Family preservation: Papers from the Institute for Social Work Educators* (pp. 29–31). Riverdale, IL: National Association for Family-Based Services.

Maretzki, T., & McDermott, J. (1980). The Caucasians. In J. McDermott, W. Tseng, & T. Maretzki (Eds.), *People and cultures of Hawaii* (pp. 23–52). Honolulu: University of Hawaii Press.

Marks, I. (1975). Behavioral treatments of phobic and obsessive-compulsive disorders: A critical appraisal. In M. Hersen, R. Eisler, & P. Miller (Eds.), *Progress in behavior modification* (pp. 65–158). Newbury Park, CA: Sage.

Marlatt, G. A. (1988). Matching clients to treatment: Treatment models and stages of change. In D. M. Donovan & G. A. Marlatt (Eds.), *Assessment of addictive behaviors* (pp. 474–483). New York: Guilford Press.

Marlatt, G. A., & Gordon, J. R. (1985). *Relapse prevention: Maintenance strategies in the treatment of addictive behaviors.* New York: Guilford Press.

Marlatt, G. A., & Miller, W. R. (1984). *Comprehensive Drinking Profile.* Odessa, FL: Psychological Assessment Resources.

Marlow, C. (1993). Coping with multiple roles: Family configuration and the need for workplace services. *Affilia, 8* (1), 40–55.

Marshall, N. L. (1991). The changing lives of young children: Infant child care as a normative experience. *Families in Society, 72* (8), 496–501.

Marshall, N. L., & Marx, F. (1991). The affordability of child care for the working poor. *Families in Society, 72* (4), 202–211.

Marshall, T. K., & Mazie, A. S. (1987). A cognitive approach to treating depression. *Social Casework, 68,* 540–545.

Martin, L. L (1993). *Total quality management in human service organizations.* Thousand Oaks, CA: Sage.

Martin, P. Y., & O'Connor, G. G. (1989). *The social environment: Open systems applications.* New York: Longman.

Mass, A. (1976). Asians as individuals: The Japanese community. *Social Casework, 57, 160–164.*

Masserman, J. (1965). Historical-comparative and experimental roots of short-term therapy. In L. Wolberg *(Ed.), Short-term psychotherapy* (pp. 44–66). New York: Grune & Stratton.

Masson, H., & O'Byrne, P. (1984). *Applying family therapy.* New York: Pergamon Press.

Mattaini, M. A., & Kirk, S. A. (1991). Assessing assessment in social work. *Social Work, 36* (3), 260–266.

Mattesisch, P. W., & Monsey, B. R. (1992). *Collaboration: What makes it work.* Saint Paul, MN: Amherst Wilder Research Center.

May, P., Hymbaugh, K., Aase, J., & Samet, J. (1983). The epidemiology of fetal alcohol syndrome among American Indians of the Southwest. *Social Biology, 30,* 374–387.

Mayadas, N. (1983). Psycho-social welfare of refugees: An expanding service area for social work. *International Social Work, 26,* 47–55.

Mayadas, N., & O'Brien, D. (1976). Teaching casework skills in the laboratory: Methods and techniques. In *Teaching for competence in the delivery of direct services* (pp. 72–82). New York: Council on Social Work Education.

Mayadas, N. S., Ramanthan, C. S., & Suarez, Z. (1988–1989). Mental health, social context, refugees, and immigrants: A cultural interface. *The Journal of Intergroup Relations, 25* (4), 3–14.

Mayer, J., & Timms, N. (1969). Clash in perspective between worker and client. *Social Casework, 50,* 32–40.

McAdoo, J. L. (1993). Decision making and marital satisfaction in African American families. In H. P. McAdoo (Ed.), *Family ethnicity: Strength in diversity* (pp. 109–118). Thousand Oaks, CA: Sage.

McCarty, P., & Betz, N. (1978). Differential effects of self-disclosing versus self-involving counselor statements. *Journal of Counseling Psychology, 25,* 251–256.

McChesney, K. Y. (1995). Urban homeless families. *Social service Review, 69* (3), 428–460.

McCollum, E. E., & Beer, J. (1995). The view from the other chair. *Family Therapy Networker, 19* (2), 59–62.

McCown, W., & Johnson, J. (1992). *Therapy with resistant families: A consultation-crisis model.* Binghamton, NY: Haworth Press.

McCreath, J. (1984). The new generation of chronic psychiatric patients. *Social Work, 29,* 436–441.

McDermott, C. J. (1989). Empowering the elderly nursing home resident: The resident rights campaign. *Social Work, 34* (2), 155–157.

McDonald, T., & Marks, J. (1991). A review of risk factors assessed in child protective services. *Social Service Review, 65* (1), 112–132.

McGoldrick, M. (1982a). Ethnicity and family therapy. In M. McGoldrick, J. Pearce, & J. Giordano (Eds.), *Ethnicity and family therapy* (pp. 3–30). New York: Guilford Press.

McGoldrick, M. (1982b). Irish families. In M. McGoldrick, J. Pearce, & J. Giordano (Eds.), *Ethnicity and family therapy* (pp. 310–339). New York: Guilford Press.

McGoldrick, M. (1998). Belonging and liberation: Finding a place called "home". In M. McGoldrick (Ed.), *Revisioning family therapy: Culture, class, race, and gender* (pp. 215–228). New York: Guilford Press.

McGoldrick, M., & Gerson, R. (1985). *Genograms in family assessment.* New York: Norton.

McGoldrick, M., Giordano, J., & Pearce, J. K. (Eds.) (1996). *Ethnicity and family therapy.* New York: Guilford Press.

McGonagle, E. (1986). *Banana splits: A peer support group for children of transitional families.* Ballston Spa, NY: Author.

McIntyre, E. L. G. (1986). Social networks: Potential for practice. *Social Work, 31,* 421–426.

McKenzie, K. R. (1996). Time limited group psychotherapy. *International Journal of Group Psychotherapy, 46* (1), 41–60.

McLoyd, V. (1997). The impact of poverty and low socioeconomic status on the socioemotional functioning of African-American children and adolescents. In R. W. Taylor & M. C. Wang (Eds.), *Social and emotional adjustment and family relations in ethnic minority families* (pp. 2–34). Mahwah, NJ: Lawrence Erlbaum Associates.

McNeely, R., & Badami, M. (1984). Interracial communication in school social work. *Social Work, 29,* 22–25.

McPhatter, A. (1991). Assessment revisited: A comprehensive approach to understanding family dynamics. *Families in Society, 72,* 11–2 1.

Mecca; W. F., Rivera, A., & Esposito, A. J. (2000). Instituting an Outcomes Assessment Effort: Lessons From the Field. *Families in Society, 81* (1), 85–89.

Medquest Communications, (1997). Treatment drop-outs explained. *Behavioral Health Management, 17* (3), 36–37.

Meenaghan, T. M. (1987). Macro practice: Current trends and issues. In *Encyclopedia of social work* (18th ed.) (pp. 82–89). Silver Spring, MD: National Association of Social Workers.

Meichenbaum, D. (1977). *Cognitive-behavior modification.* New York: Plenum Press.

Meichenbaum, D. (1994). *A clinical handbook/practical therapist manual for assessing and treating adults with post-traumatic stress disorder (PTSD).* Waterloo, ON: University of Waterloo, Institute Press.

Meichenbaum, D., & Turk, D. (1976). The cognitive behavioral management of anxiety, anger, and pain. In P. Davison (Ed.), *The cognitive-behavioral management of anxiety, anger, and pain* (pp. 1–34). New York: Brunner/Mazel.

Meichenbaum, D. C., & Turk, D. C. (1987). *Facilitating treatment adherence: A practitioner's guidebook.* New York: Plenum.

Meier, A. (1997). Inventing new models of social support groups: A feasibility study of an online stress management support group for social workers. *Social Work with Groups, 20* (4), 35–53.

Mercer, S., & Kane, R. (1979). Helplessness and hopelessness among the institutionalized aged. *Health and Social Work, 4,* 90–116.

Merton, R. (1957). *Social theory and social structure.* Glencoe, IL: Free Press.

Meyer, C. (1970). *Social work practice: A response to the urban crisis.* New York: Free Press.

Meyer, C. (Ed.) *(1983). Clinical social work in the eco-systems perspective.* New York: Columbia University Press.

Meyer, C. (1990, April 11). *Can social work keep up with the changing family?* [Monograph]. The fifth annual Robert J. O'Leary Memorial Lecture. Columbus: The Ohio State University College of Social Work, 1–24.

Meyers, M. K. (1993). Organizational factors in the integration of services for children. *Social Service Review, 67* (4), 547–571.

Meystedt, D. M. (1984). Religion and the rural population: Implications for social work. *Social Casework, 65* (4), 219–226.

Milgram, D., & Rubin, J. S. (1992). Resisting resistance; Involuntary substance abuse group therapy. *Social Work with Groups, 15* (1), 95–110.

Miller, D. B. (1997). Parenting against the odds: African-American parents in the child welfare system—a group approach. *Social Work with Groups, 20* (1), 5–18.

Miller, J. A. (1994). A family's sense of power in their community: Theoretical and research issues. *Smith College Studies in Social Work, 64* (3), 221–241.

Miller, J. L., & Whittaker, J. K. (1988). Social services and social support: Blended programs for families at risk of child maltreatment. *Child Welfare, 67,* 161–174.

Miller, K., Fein, E., Howe, G., Gaudio, C., & Bishop, G. (1984). Time-limited, goal-focused parent aide service. *Social Casework, 65,* 472–477.

Miller, W. R. (1983). Motivational interviewing with problem drinkers. *Behavioral Psychology, 11,* 147–172.

Miller, W. R., & Rollnick, S. (1991). *Motivational interviewing: Preparing people to change addictive behavior.* New York: Guilford Press.

Miller, W. R., & Sovereign, R. G. (1989). The check-up: A model for early intervention in addictive behaviors. In T. Loberg, W. R. Miller, P. E. Nathan, & G. A. Marlatt (Eds.), *Addictive behaviors: Prevention and early intervention* (pp. 219–231). Amsterdam: Swets and Zeitlinger.

Mills, C., & Ota, H. (1989). Homeless women with minor children in the Detroit metropolitan area. *Social Work, 34* (6), 485–489.

Milne, C., & Dowd, E. (1983). Effect of interpretation style and counselor social influence. *Journal of Counseling Psychology, 30,* 603–606.

Milner, J. S., Halsey, L. B., & Fultz, J. (1995). Empathetic responsiveness and effective reactivity to infant stimuli in high-risk and low-risk for physical child-abuse mothers. *Child Abuse and Neglect, 19* (6), 767–780.

Milofsky, C. (1980). Serving the needs of disabled clients: A task-structured approach. *Social Work, 25,* 149–152.

Mindel, C. H., Habenstein, R. H., & Wright, R. (1988). *Ethnic families in America.* New York: Elsevier.

Minuchin, S. (1974). *Families and family therapy.* Cambridge, MA: Harvard University Press.

Mitchell, C. G. (1998). Perceptions of empathy and client satisfaction with managed behavioral health care. *Social Work, 43* (5), 404–411.

Mitchell, M. (1986). Utilizing volunteers to enhance informal social networks. *Social Casework, 67,* 290–298.

Mizio, E. (1974). Impact of external systems on the Puerto Rican family. *Social Casework, 55,* 76–83.

Mokuau, N., & Fong, R. (1994). Assessing the responsiveness of health services to ethnic minorities of color. *Social Work in Health Care, 28* (1), 23–34.

Montero, D., & Dieppa, I. (1982). Resettling Vietnamese refugees: The service agency's role. *Social Work, 27,* 74–81.

Montiel, M. (1973). The Chicano family: A review of research. *Social Work, 18,* 22–29.

Moore, C. (1986). *The mediation process.* San Francisco: Jossey-Bass.

Moore, J. (1983). The experience of sponsoring a parents anonymous group. *Social Casework, 64,* 585–592.

Moore, S. T. (1990). A social work practice model of case management: The case management grid. *Social Work, 35* (5), 444–448.

Moote, G. T., Jr., Smyth, N. J., & Wodarski, J. S. (1999). Social skills training with youth in school settings: a review. *Research on Social Work Practice, 9* (4), 427–465.

Morgan, K. (1961). Is it scientific to be optimistic? *Social Work, 6,* 12–21.

Moroney, R. M. (1987). Social planning. In *Encyclopedia of social work, II* (pp. 593–602). Silver Spring, MD: National Association of Social Workers.

Moroz, K., & Allen-Meares, P. (1991). Assessing adolescent parents and their infants: Individualized family service planning. *Families in Society, 72* (8), 461–468.

Morrison, B. (1983). Physical health and the minority aged. In R. McNeely & J. Colen (Eds.), *Aging in minority groups.* Beverly Hills, CA: Sage.

Morrison, J. (1995). *The first interview: Revised for DSM-IV.* New York: Guilford Press.

Morrissette, P., & McIntyre. S. (1989). Homeless young people in residential care. *Social Casework, 70* (10), 603–610.

Morrow, D. F. (1993). Social work with gay and lesbian adolescents. *Social Work, 38* (6), 655–660.

Mosley, J. C., & Lex, A. (1990). Identification of potentially stressful life events experienced by a population of urban minority youth. *Journal of Multicultural Counseling and Development, 18* (3), 118–125.

Moxley, D. P. (1989). *The practice of case management.* Newbury Park, CA: Sage.

Moynihan, R., Christ, G., & Silver, L. G. (1988). AIDS and terminal illness. *Social Casework, 69,* 380–387.

Mudrick, N. R. (1991). An underdeveloped role for occupational social work: Facilitating the employment of people with disabilities. *Social Work, 36* (6), 490–495.

Mulinski, P. (1989). Dual diagnosis in alcoholic clients: Clinical implications. *Social Casework, 70* (6), 333–339.

Mullen, E. J., & Dumpson, J. R. (Eds). (1972). *Evaluation of social intervention.* San Francisco: Jossey-Bass.

Mumm, A. M., Olsen, L. J., & Allen, D. (1998). Families affected by substance abuse: Implications for generalist social work practice. *Families in Society, 79* (4), 384–394.

Murdach, A. D. (1996). Beneficence re-examined: Protective intervention in mental health. *Social Work, 41,* 26–32

Murphy, B. C., & Dillon, C. (1998). *Interviewing in action.* Pacific Grove, CA: Brooks/Cole.

Murphy, C. M., & Baxter, V. A. (1997). Motivating batterers to change in the treatment context. *Journal of Interpersonal Violence, 12* (4), 607–619.

Mwanza (1990). *Afrikan naturalism.* Columbus, OH: Pan Afrikan Publications.

Myers, L. I., & Thyer, B. A. (1997). Should social work clients have the right to effective treatment? *Social Work, 42* (3), 288–298.

N

Napier, A. (1991). Heroism, men and marriage. *Journal of Marital and Family Therapy, 17* (1), 9–16.

National Association of Social Workers. (1973). *Standards for social service manpower.* New York: Author.

National Association of Social Workers. (1977). 1977 delegate assembly policy statement—Volunteers and the social service systems. *NASW News, 22,* 39.

National Association of Social Workers. (1980). NASW code of ethics. *NASW News, 25,* 24–25.

National Association of Social Workers. (1981). NASW working statement on the purpose of social work. *Social Work, 26,* 6.

National Association of Social Workers. (1991). *NASW News, 36 (10),* 13.

National Association of Social Workers. (1996). *Code of Ethics.* Washington, DC: Author.

National Committee for Prevention of Child Abuse. (1990, March). *Child abuse fatalities continue to rise: The results of the 1989 annual fifty-state survey.* Chicago: Author.

Nelson, J. (1975). Dealing with resistance in social work practice. *Social Casework, 56,* 587–592.

Nelson, M. (1991). Empowerment of incest survivors: Speaking out. *Families in Society, 72* (10), 618–624.

Nelson, T., & Trepper, T. S. (1992). *101 interventions in family therapy.* Binghamton, NY: Haworth Press.

Nelson-Zlupko, L., Kauffman, E., & Dore, M. M. (1995). Gender differences in drug addiction and treatment: implications for social work intervention with substance abusing women. *Social Work, 40,* 1, 45–54.

Nerdrum, P., & Lundquist, K. (1995). Does participation in communication skills training increase student levels of communicated empathy? A controlled outcome study. *Journal of Teaching in Social Work, 12* (1/2), 139–157.

Netting, F., Kettner, P., & McMurtry, S. (1993). *Social work macro practice.* New York: Longman.

Neumann, D. (1989). *Divorce mediation: How to cut the cost.* New York: Holt.

New York Victim Services Agency. (1982). *Experiences of women with services for abused spouses in New York City.* New York: Author.

Nezu, A. M. (1985). Differences in psychological distress between effective and ineffective problem solvers. *Journal of Counseling Psychology, 32,* 135–138.

Nezu, A. M., & Carnevale, G. J. (1987). Interpersonal problem solving and coping reactions of Vietnam. veterans with posttraumatic stress syndrome. *Journal of Abnormal Psychology, 96,* 155–157.

Nichols, M. P., & Schwartz, R. C. (1998). *Family therapy: Concepts and methods* (4th ed.). Boston: Allyn & Bacon.

Nicholson, B., & Matross, G. (1989). Facing reduced decision-making capacity in health care: Methods for maintaining client self-determination. *Social Work, 34* (3), 234–238.

Nikura, R. (1999). Assertiveness among Japanese, Malaysian, Filipino, and US white-collar workers. *Journal of Social Psychology, 139* (6), 690–699.

Nord, M., & Luloff, A. E. (1995). Homeless children and their families in New Hampshire: A rural perspective. *Social Service Review, 69* (3), 461–478.

Northen, Helen (1998). Ethical dilemmas in social work with groups. *Social Work with Groups, 21* (1/2), 5–17.

Norton, D. G. (1978). *The dual perspective: Inclusion of ethnic minority content in the social work curriculum.* New York: Council on Social Work Education.

Novaco, R. (1975). *Anger control: The development and evaluation of an experimental treatment.* Lexington, MA: Heath.

Nugent, W. (1991). An experimental and qualitative analysis of a cognitive-behavioral intervention for anger. *Social Work Research and Abstracts, 27* (3), 3–8.

Nugent, W. (1992). The effective impact of a clinical social worker's interviewing style: A series of single-case experiments. *Research on Social Work Practice, 2* (1), 6–27.

Nugent, W. R., & Halvorson, H. (1995). Testing the effects of active listening. *Research on Social Work Practice, 5* (2), 152–75.

Nulman, E. (1983). Family therapy and advocacy: Directions for the future. *Social Work, 28,* 19–22.

Nurius, P. S., & Hudson, W. W. (1988). Computer-based practice: Future dream or current technology. *Social Work, 33,* 357–362.

Nurius, P. S., & Hudson, W. (1993a). *Computer assisted practice: Theory, methods, and software.* Belmont, CA: Wadsworth.

Nurius, P. S., & Hudson, W. (1993b). *Human services: Practice, evaluation, and computers.* Pacific Grove, CA: Brooks/Cole.

O

O'Connell B. (1978). From service to advocacy to empowerment. *Social Casework, 59,* 195–202.

Office of Policy Development. (1988). *Report to the president on the family.* Washington, DC: The White House.

O'Hare, T. (1991). Integrating research and practice: A framework for implementation. *Social Work, 36* (3), 220–223.

O'Hare, T. (1996). Court-ordered versus voluntary clients: Problem differences and readiness for change. *Social Work, 41* (4), 417–422.

O'Leary, K., Shore, M., & Wieder, S. (1984). Contacting pregnant adolescents: Are we missing cues? *Social Casework, 65,* 297–306.

Oritt, E., Paul, S., & Behrman, J. (1985). The perceived Support Network Inventory. *American Journal of Community Psychology, 13* (5), 565–582.

Orlinsky, D., & Howard, K. (1978). The relationship of process to outcome in psychotherapy. In S. Garfield & A. Bergin (Eds.), *Handbook of psychotherapy and behavior change* (pp. 283–329). New York: Wiley.

Orten, J. D., & Rich, L. L. (1988). A model for assessment of incestuous families. *Social Casework, 69* (10), 611–619.

Oswald, P. A. (1996). The effects of cognitive and affective perspective taking on empathic concern and altruistic helping. *The Journal of Social Psychology, 136,* 5.

Othmer, E., & Othmer, S. C. (1989). *The clinical interview using DSM-III-R*. Washington DC: American Psychiatric Press.

P

Palmer, B., & Pablo, S. (1978). Community development possibilities for effective Indian reservation child abuse and neglect efforts. In M. Lauderdale, R. Anderson, & S. Cramer (Eds.), *Child abuse and neglect: Issues on innovation and implementation* (pp. 98–116). Washington, DC: U.S. Department of Health, Education and Welfare.

Panitch, A. (1974). Advocacy in practice. *Social Work, 19,* 326–332.

Panzer, B., Wiesner, L., & Dickson, W. (1978). Program for developmentally disabled children. *Social Work, 23,* 406–411.

Papp, P. (1976). Family choreography. In P. Guerin (Ed.), *Family therapy* (pp. 465–479). New York: Gardner Press.

Paquin, M. (1981). Self-monitoring of marital communication in family therapy. *Social Casework, 62,* 267–272.

Parad, H., & Parad, L. (1968). A study of crisis-oriented planned short-term treatment. *Social Casework, 49,* 346–355.

Parad, H. J., & Parad, L. G. (Eds.). (1990). *Crisis intervention: Book 2.* Milwaukee, WI: Family Service America.

Pardeck, J. T. (1990). Bibliotherapy with abused children. *Families in Society, 71* (4), 229–235.

Pardeck, J. T., Murphy, J. W., & Chung, W. S. (1995). An exploration of factors associated with clients prematurely exiting psychiatric treatment: Implication for the community mental health center act. *Journal of Health Social Policy, 7* (1), 87–96.

Parlee, M. (1979). Conversational politics. *Psychology Today, 12,* 48–56.

Parloff, M., Waskow, I., & Wolfe, B. (1978). Research on therapist variables in relation to process and outcome. In S. Garfield & A. Bergin (Eds.), *Handbook of psychotherapy and behavior change* (pp. 233–282). New York: Wiley.

Parsonnet, L., & O'Hare, J. (1990). A group orientation program for families of newly admitted cancer patients. *Social Work, 35* (1), 37–40.

Parsons, R. J. (1991). The mediator role in social work practice. *Social Work, 36* (6), 483–487.

Parsons, R. J., & Cox, E. O. (1989). Family mediation in elder caregiving decisions: An empowerment intervention. *Social Work, 34* (2), 122–126.

Parsons, R. J., Jorgensen, J. D., & Hernandez, S. H. (1988). Integrative practice approach: A framework for problem solving. *Social Work, 35* (5), 417–421.

Parsons, R. J., Jorgensen, J. D., & Hernandez, S. H. (1994). *The integration of social work practice.* Pacific Grove, CA: Brooks/Cole.

Patten, S. B., Gatz, Y. K., Jones, B., & Thomas, D. L. (1989). Posttraumatic stress disorder and the treatment of sexual abuse. *Social Work, 34* (3), 197–202.

Patterson, D., & Hepworth, D. (1989). *A comparative study of multiple personality disordered and borderline personality disordered inpatients.* Unpublished study. Salt Lake City: University of Utah, Graduate School of Social Work.

Patterson, D. A., & Lee, M. (1998). Intensive case management and rehospitalization: A survival analysis. *Research on Social Work Practice, 8* (2), 152–171.

Patterson, S. L., Germain, C. B., Brennan, E. M., & Mem Mott, J. (1988). Effectiveness of rural natural helpers. *Social Casework, 69,* 272–279.

Patti, R. J. (1974). Organizational resistance and change. *Social Service Review, 48,* 367–383.

Patton, M. Q. (1991). *Family sexual abuse: Frontline research and evaluation.* Newbury Park, CA: Sage.

Pearlman, M., & Edwards, M. (1982). Enabling in the eighties: The client advocacy group. *Social Casework, 63,* 532–539.

Pence, E., & Paymar, M. (1993). *Education groups for men who batter: The Duluth model.* New York: Springer.

Penka, C. E., & Kirk, S. (1991). Practitioner involvement in clinical evaluation. *Social Work, 36* (6), 513–518.

Perlman, G. (1988). Mastering the law of privileged communication: A guide for social workers. *Social Work, 33* (5), 425–429.

Perlman, H. (1957). *Social casework: A problem-solving process.* Chicago: University of Chicago Press.

Perlman, H. (1968). *Persona: Social role and responsibility.* Chicago: University of Chicago Press.

Peters, A. J. (1997). Themes in group work with lesbian and gay adolescents. *Social Work with Groups, 20* (2), 51–69.

Peters, K. D., & Murphy, S. L. (1998). *Deaths: Final data for 1996. National Vital Statistics Report, 47* (9). Hyattsville, MD: National Center for Health Statistics.

Peterson, C., Patrick, S., & Rissmeyer, D. (1990). Social work's contribution to psychosocial rehabilitation. *Social Work, 35* (5), 468–472.

Pfeffer, R. C. (1986). *The suicidal child.* New York: Guilford Press.

Phillips, M. H., DeChillo, N., Kronenfeld, D., & Middleton-Jeter, V. (1988). Homeless families: Services make a difference. *Social Casework, 69,* 48–53.

Pierce, W. J., & Elisme, E. (1997). Understanding and working with Haitian immigrant families. *Journal of Family Social Work, 2* (1), 49–65.

Piliavin, I., Wright, B. R. W., Mare, R. D., & Westerfelt, A. H. (1996). Exits from and returns to homelessness. *Social Service Review, 70* (1), 33–57.

Pilisuk, M., & Parks, S. H. (1988). Caregiving: Where families need help. *Social Work, 33* (5), 436–440.

Pillemer, K. A., & Wolf, R. S. (Eds.). (1986). *Elder abuse: Conflict in the family.* Westport, CT: Auburn House.

Pincus, A., & Minahan, A. (1973). *Social work practice: Model and method.* Itasca, IL: Peacock.

Pinderhughes, E. (1982). Afro-American families and the victim system. In M. McGoldrick, J. Pearce, & J. Giordano (Eds.), *Ethnicity and family therapy* (pp. 109–122). New York: Guilford Press.

Pinderhughes, E. (1983). Empowerment for our clients and ourselves. *Social Casework, 64,* 331–338.

Pines, B., Krieger, R., & Maluccio, A. (1993). *Together again: Family reunification in foster care.* Washington, DC: Child Welfare League of America.

Pirog-Good, M., & Stets, J. (Eds.). (1989). *Violence in dating relationships: Emerging social issues.* Westport. CT: Praeger.

Pittman, F. (1987). *Turning points: Treating families.* New York: Norton.

Pittman, F. (1991). The secret passions of men. *Journal of Marital and Family Therapy, 17* (1), 17–23.

Polansky, N. A., Ammons, P. W., & Gaudin, J. M., Jr. (1985). Loneliness and isolation in child neglect. *Social Casework, 66,* 38–47.

Pollio, D. E. (1995). Use of humor in crisis intervention. *Families in Society, 76* (6), 376–846.

Polowy, C. I. & Gilbertson, J. (1997). *Social workers and subpoenas: Office of General Counsel law notes.* Washington, DC: NASW.

Ponce, D. (1980). The Filipinos: The Philippine background. In J. McDermott, Jr., W. Tseng, & T. Maretski (Eds.), *People and cultures of Hawaii* (pp. 155–163). Honolulu: University of Hawaii Press.

Pope, K. S., Keith-Spiegel, P., & Tabachnick, B. G. (1986). Sexual attraction to clients. *American Psychologist, 41,* 147–158.

Pope, K. S., Sonne, J. L., & Holroyd, J. (1993). *Sexual feelings in psychotherapy: Explorations for therapists and therapists in training.* Washington DC: American Psychological Association.

Potter-Efron, R., & Potter-Efron, P. (1992). *Anger, alcoholism and addiction: Treating anger in a chemical dependency setting.* New York: Norton.

Prager, E. (1980). Evaluation in mental health: Enter the consumer. *Social Work Research and Abstracts, 16,* 5–10.

Presley, J. H. (1987). The clinical dropout: A view from the client's perspective. *Social Casework, 68,* 603–608.

Pridgen, N. H. (1991). Community-based counseling services for deaf and hard-of-hearing individuals. *Families in Society, 72* (3), 174–176.

Prochaska, J., DiClemente, C. C., & Norcross, J. C. (1992). Transtheoretical therapy: Toward a more integrative model of change. *Psychotherapy: Theory, research, and practice, 19,* 276–288.

Proctor, E. (1990). Evaluating clinical practice: Issues of purpose and design. *Social Work Research and Abstracts, 26* (1), 32–40.

Proctor, E., Vosler, N., & Sirles, E. (1993). The social environmental context of child clients: An empirical exploration. *Social Work, 38* (3), 256–262.

Proctor, E. K., & and Davis, L. E. (1994). The challenge of racial difference: Skills for clinical practice. *Social Work, 39* (3), 314–323.

Prunty, H., Singer, T., & Thomas, L. (1977). Confronting racism in inner-city schools. *Social Work, 22,* 190–194.

Puryear, D. (1979). *Helping people in crisis.* San Francisco: Jossey-Bass.

Q

Queralt, M. (1984). Understanding Cuban immigrants: A cultural perspective. *Social Work, 29,* 115–12 1.

Quinn, M. J., & Tomita, S. K. (1986). *Elder abuse and neglect.* New York: Springer.

R

Rabin, C., Blechman, E. A., Kahn, D., & Carel, C. A. (1985). Refocusing from child to marital problems using the Marriage Contract Game. *Journal of Marital and Family Therapy, 11,* 75–85.

Rabin, C., & Zelner, D. (1992). The role of assertiveness in clarifying roles and strengthening job satisfaction of social workers in multi-disciplinary mental health settings. *The British Journal of Social Work, 22* (1), 17–32.

Raimy, V. (1975). *Misunderstandings of the self.* San Francisco: Jossey-Bass.

Raines, J. C. (1996). Self-disclosure in clinical social work. *Clinical Social Work Journal, 24* (4), 357–375.

Range, L. M., & Knott, E. C. (1997). Twenty suicide assessment instruments: Evaluation and recommendations. *Death Studies, 21,* 25–58.

Rank, M. R., & Hirschl, T. A. (1999). The likelihood of poverty across the American adult life span. *Social Work, 44* (3), 201–208.

Rapoport, L. (1961). The concept of prevention in social work. *Social Work, 6,* 3–12.

Rapp, C. (1982). Effect of the availability of family support services and decisions about child placement. *Social Work Research and Abstracts, 18,* 21–27.

Rapp, C. A. (1998). *The strengths model: Case management with people suffering from severe and persistent mental illness.* New York: Oxford University Press.

Rapp, C. A., & Chamberlain, R. (1985). Case management services for the chronically mentally ill. *Social Work, 30,* 417–422.

Ratliff, S. S. (1996). The multicultural challenge to health care. In M. C. Julia, *Multicultural awareness in the health care professions.* Needham Heights, MA: Allyn & Bacon.

Rauch, J. B. (1988). Social work and the genetics revolution: Genetic services. *Social Work, 33* (5), 389–395.

Rauch, J. B., Sarno, C., & Simpson, S. (1991). Screening for affective disorders. *Families in Society, 72* (10), 602–609.

Raw, S. D. (1998). Who is to define effective treatment for social work clients? *Social Work, 43* (1), 81–86.

Raymond, G. T., Teare, R. J., & Atherton, C. R. (1996). Is "field of practice" a relevant organizing principle for the MSW curriculum? *Journal of Social Work Education, 32* (1), 19–30.

Reamer, F. (1988). AIDS and ethics: The agenda for social workers. *Social Work, 33* (5), 460–464.

Reamer, F. (1989). *Ethical dilemmas in social service* (2nd ed.). New York: Columbia University Press.

Reamer, F. (1992). *AIDS and ethics.* New York: Columbia University Press.

Reamer, F. G. (1994). *Social work malpractice and liability: Strategies for prevention.* New York: Columbia University Press.

Reamer, F. G. (1995). Malpractice claims against social workers: First facts. *Social Work, 40* (5), 595–601.

Reamer, F. G. (1998a). *Ethical standards in social work: A critical review of the NASW Code of Ethics.* Washington, DC: NASW Press.

Reamer, F. G. (1998b). The evolution of social work ethics. *Social Work, 43* (6), 488–500.

Red Horse, J., Lewis, R., Feit, M., & Decker, J. (1978). Family behavior of urban American Indians. *Social Casework, 59,* 67–72.

Regehr, C., & Angle, B. (1997). Coercive influences: Informed consent in court-mandated social work practice. *Social Work, 42* (3), 300–306.

Register of clinical social workers, Vol. 1. (1976). Washington, DC: National Association of Social Workers.

Reid, K. E. (1991). *Social work practice with groups: A clinical perspective.* Pacific Grove, CA: Brooks/Cole.

Reid, W. (1970). Implications of research for the goals of casework. *Smith College Studies in Social Work, 40,* 140–154.

Reid, W. (1975). A test of the task-centered approach. *Social Work, 22,* 3–9.

Reid, W. (1977). Process and outcome in the treatment of family problems. In W. Reid & L. Epstein (Eds.), *Task-centered practice. Self-help groups and human service agencies: How they work together.* Milwaukee, WI: Family Service of America.

Reid, W. (1978). *The task-centered system*. New York: Columbia University Press.

Reid, W. (1985). *Family problem solving*. New York: Columbia University Press.

Reid, W. (1987). Task-centered research. In *Encyclopedia of social work* (Vol. 2, pp. 757–764). Silver Spring, MD: National Association of Social Workers.

Reid, W. J. (1990). Change-process research: A new paradigm. In L. Videka-Sherman & W. J. Reid (Eds.), *Advances in clinical social work research* (pp. 130–148). Silver Spring, MD: NASW Press.

Reid, W. J. (1992). *Task strategies*. New York: Columbia University Press.

Reid, W. J. (1994). The empirical practice movement. *Social Service Review, 68* (2), 165–184.

Reid, W. J. (1997a). Research on task-centered practice. *Social Work, 21* (3), 131–137.

Reid, W. J. (1997b). Long-term trends in clinical social work. *Social Service Review, 71* (2), 200–213.

Reid, W. J. (2000). *The task planner*. New York: Columbia University Press.

Reid, W. J., & Epstein, L. (1972). *Task-centered casework*. New York: Columbia University Press.

Reid, W., & Hanrahan, P. (1982). Recent evaluations of social work: Grounds for optimism. *Social Work, 27*, 328–340.

Reid, W., & Shyne, A. (1969). *Brief and extended casework*. New York: Columbia University Press.

Reitan, T. C. (1998). Theories of interorganizational relations in the human services. *Social Service Review, 72* (3), 285–309.

Remine, D., Rice, R. M., & Ross, J. (1984). Management as a practice model. *Social Casework, 68*, 466–470.

Resnick, C., & Dziegielewski, S. F. (1996). The relationship between therapeutic termination and job satisfaction among medical social workers. *Social Work in Health Care, 23* (3), 17–33.

Reynolds, B. C. (1951). Must it hurt to be helped? In B. C. Reynolds, *Social work and social living: Exploration in philosophy and practice*. New York: Citadel Press.

Reynolds, C., & Fischer, C. (1983). Personal versus professional evaluations of self-disclosing and self-involving counselors. *Journal of Counseling Psychology, 30*, 451–454.

Rhoades, E. R. (Ed.). (1990). *Minority aging. Essential curricula content for selected health and allied health professionals*. Health Resources and Service Administration, Department of Health and Human Services. DHHS Publication No. HRS (P-DU-90-4). Washington, DC: U.S. Government Printing Office.

Rhodes, M. L. (1986). *Ethical dilemmas in social work practice*. London: Routledge & Kegan Paul.

Rhodes, S. (1977). Contract negotiation in the initial stage of casework. *Social Service Review, 51*, 125–140.

Rice, A. H. (1998). *Focusing on strengths: Focus group research on the impact of welfare reform*. A paper presented for the XX Symposium Association for the Advancement of Social Work with Groups, October, 1998, Miami, Florida.

Rice, C. A. (1996). Premature termination of group therapy: A clinical perspective. *International Journal of Group Psychotherapy, 46* (1), 5–23.

Richmond, M. (1917). *Social Diagnosis*. New York: Sage.

Ridley, R. (1984). Clinical treatment of the nondisclosing black client: A therapeutic paradox. *American Psychologist, 39*, 1234–1244.

Roberts, A. R. (1990). *Crisis intervention handbook: Assessment, treatment, and research*. Belmont, CA: Wadsworth.

Roberts, C. S., Severinsen, C., Kuehn, C., Straker, D., & Fritz, C. J. (1992). Obstacles to effective case management with AIDS patients: The clinician's perspective. *Social Work in Health Care, 17* (2), 27–40.

Roberts-DeGennaro, M. (1987). *Developing case*. New York: Columbia University Press.

Robinson, J. B. (1989). Clinical treatment of Black families: Issues and strategies. *Social Work, 34*, 323–29.

Robinson, V. (1930). *A changing psychology in social work*. Chapel Hill: University of North Carolina Press.

Rodgers, A. Y., & Potocky, M. (1997). Evaluating culturally sensitive practice through single-system design: Methodological issues and strategies. *Research on Social Work Practice, 7* (3), 391–401.

Rogers, C. (1957). The necessary and sufficient conditions of therapeutic personality change. *Journal of Consulting Psychology, 22*, 95–103.

Rogler, L. H., Malgady, R. G., Costantino, G., & Blumenthal, R. (1987). What do culturally sensitive mental health services mean? The case of Hispanics. *American Psychologist, 42*, 565–570.

Ronnau, J. P., & Marlow, C. R- (1995). Family preservation: Poverty and the value of diversity. *Families in Society, 74* (9), 538–544.

Rooney, G. D. (1997). Concerns of employed women: Issues for employee assistance programs. In A. Daly (Ed.), *Work force diversity: Issues and perspectives in the world of work* (pp. 314–330). Washington, DC: NASW Press.

Rooney, G. D. (2000). Examining the values and ethics reflected in policy decisions. In K. Strom-Gottfried (Ed.), *Social work practice: Cases, activities and exercises* (pp.50–54). Thousand Oaks, CA: Pine Forge Press.

Rooney, G. D., Neathery, K., & Suzek, M. (1997). *Defining child neglect: A community perspective*. Minneapolis, MN: Minneapolis Human Services Network Research Report.

Rooney, R. H. (1988). Socialization strategies for involuntary clients. *Social Casework, 69*, 131–140.

Rooney, R. H. (1992). *Strategies for work with involuntary clients*. New York: Columbia University Press.

Rooney, R. H., & Bibus, A. A. (1995). Multiple lenses: Ethnically sensitive practice with involuntary clients who are having difficulties with drugs or alcohol. *Journal of Multicultural Social Work, 4* (2), 59–73.

Rose, S. D. (1989). *Working with adults in groups: Integrating cognitive-behavioral and small group strategies*. San Francisco: Jossey-Bass.

Rose, S. M. (Ed.). (1992). *Case management and social work practice*. White Plains, NY: Longman.

Rose, S. M., & Black, B. (1985). *Advocacy and empowerment. Mental health care in the community*. New York: Routledge & Kegan Paul.

Rose, S. M., Peabody, C., & Stratigeas, B. (1991). Responding to hidden abuse: A role for social work in reforming mental health systems. *Social Work, 36* (5), 408–413.

Rosen, A. (1972). The treatment relationship: A conceptualization. *Journal of Clinical Psychology, 38,* 329–337.

Rosen, A., Proctor, E. K., & Livne, S. (1985). Planning and direct practice. *Social Service Review, 59,* 161–177.

Rosen, P., Peterson, L., & Walsh, B. (1980). A community residence for severely disturbed adolescents: A cognitive-behavioral approach. *Child Welfare, 59,* 15–25.

Rosenblatt, E. (1994). *Metaphor of family systems theory.* New York: Guilford Press.

Rosenfeld, J. (1983). The domain and expertise of social work: A conceptualization. *Social Work, 28,* 186–191.

Rosenstein, P. (1978). Family outreach: A program for the prevention of child neglect and abuse. *Child Welfare, 57,* 519–525.

Rosenthal, K. (1988). The inanimate self in adult victims of child abuse and neglect. *Social Casework, 69* (8), 505–510.

Roth, W. (1987). Disabilities: Physical, In *Encyclopedia of social work* (Vol. 1, pp. 434–438). Silver Spring, MD: National Association of Social Workers.

Rothman, J. (1989). Client self-determination: Untangling the knot. *Social Service Review, 59* (4), 598–612.

Rothman, J. (1991). A model of case management: Toward empirically based practice. *Social Work, 36* (6), 521–528.

Rothman, J. (1994). *Practice with highly vulnerable clients: Case management and community-based service.* Englewood Cliffs, NJ: Prentice Hall.

Rothman, J. (1995). Approaches to community intervention. In J. Rothman, J. L. Erlich, & J. E. Tropman (Eds.), *Strategies of community intervention* (5th ed.) (pp. 26–63). Itasca, IL: F. E. Peacock.

Rothman, J. (1999). Intent and content. In J. Rothman (Ed.), *Reflections on community organization: Enduring themes and critical issues* (pp. 3–26). Itasca, IL: F. E. Peacock.

Rothman, J., Gant, L. M., & Hnat, S. A. (1985). Mexican-American family culture. *Social Service Review, 59,* 197–215.

Rotunno, M., & McGoldrick, M. (1982). Italian families. In M. McGoldrick, J. Pearce, & J. Giordano (Eds.), *Ethnicity and family therapy* (pp. 340–363). New York: Guilford Press.

Rounds, K. A. (1988). AIDS in rural areas: Challenges to providing care. *Social Work, 33,* 257–261.

Rounds, K. A., Galinsky, M. H., & Stevens, L. S. (1991). Linking people with AIDS in rural communities: The telephone group. *Social Work, 36* (1), 13–18.

Rowe, W., & Savage, S. (1988). Sex therapy with female incest survivors. *Social Casework, 69* (5), 265–271.

Royfe, E. (1960). The role of the social worker in a big brother agency. *Social Casework, 41,* 139–144.

Rubenstein, D., & Timmins, J. (1978). Depressive dyadic and triadic relationships. *Journal of Marriage and Family Counseling, 4,* 13–24.

Rubin, A. (1985). Practice effectiveness: More grounds for optimism. *Social Work, 30,* 469–476.

Rubin, B. (1982). Refugee settlement: A unique role for family service. *Social Casework, 63,* 301–304.

Rubin, S. (1978). Parents' group in a psychiatric hospital for children. *Social Work, 23,* 416–417.

Rueveni, U. (1979). *Networking families in crisis.* New York: Human Sciences Press.

Ryan, N., Puig-Antich, J., Ambrosini, P., Rabinovich, H., Robinson, D., Nelson, B., Ivengar, S., & Twomey, J. (1987). The clinical picture of major depression in children and adolescents. *Archives of General Psychiatry, 44* (11), 854–861.

Ryder, R., & Tepley, R. (1993). No more Mr. Nice Guy: Informed consent and benevolence in marital family therapy. *Family Relations, 42,* 145–147.

Rzepnicki, T. L. (1991, March). Enhancing the durability of intervention gains: A challenge for the 1990s. *Social Service Review, 65* (1), 92–111.

S

Saba, G. W., Karrer, B. M., & Hardy, K. (Eds.). (1989). *Minorities and family therapy.* New York: Hawthorne Press.

Sager, C., Brayboy, T., & Waxenburg, B. (1970). *Black ghetto family in therapy: A laboratory experience.* New York: Grove Press.

Sakai, C. E. (1991). Group intervention strategies with domestic abusers. *Families in Society, 72* (9), 536–542.

Saleeby, D. (Ed.). (1992). *The strengths perspective in social work practice.* New York: Longman.

Saleeby, D. (Ed.). (1997). *The strengths perspective in social work practice* (2nd ed.). Needham Heights, MA: Allyn & Bacon.

Salter, A. C. (1988). *Treating child sex offenders and victims.* Newbury Park, CA: Sage.

Saltzman, A. (1986). Reporting child abuse and protecting substance abusers. *Social Work, 31,* 474–476.

Sandau-Beckler, P. A., & Salcido, R. (1991). Family preservation services for first-generation Hispanic families in an international border community. In *Empowering families* (pp. 119–129). Proceedings of the Fifth Annual Conference on Family Based Services: National Association for Family Based Services, Cedar Rapids, IA.

Sander, F. (1976). Aspects of sexual counseling with the aged. *Social Casework, 58,* 504–510.

Sandfort, J. (1999). The structural impediments to human services collaboration: Examining welfare reform at the front lines. *Social Service Review, 73* (3), 314–339.

Sands, R. G. (1989). The social worker joins the team: a look at the socialization process. *Social Work in Health Care, 14* (2), 1–14.

Sands, R. G. (1990). Ethnographic research: A qualitative approach to study of the interdisciplinary team. *Social Work in Health Care, 15* (1), 115–129.

Sands, R. G., Stafford. J., & McClelland, M. (1990). "I beg to differ": Conflict in the interdisciplinary team. *Social Work in Health Care, 14* (3), 55–72.

Santa Cruz, L., & Hepworth, D. (1975). Effects of cultural orientation on casework. *Social Casework, 56,* 52–57.

Santos, D. (1995). Deafness. In *Encyclopedia of Social Work,* Vol. 19 (685–703). Washington, DC: NASW Press.

Sarri, R. (1987). Administration in social welfare. In *Encyclopedia of social work* (Vol. 1, pp. 27–40). Silver Spring, MD: National Association of Social Workers.

Satir, V. (1967). *Conjoint family therapy.* Palo Alto, CA: Science & Behavior Books.

Sauer, W. J., & Coward, R. T. (1985). *Social support networks and the care of the elderly.* New York: Springer.

Saulnier, C. F. (1997). Alcohol problems and marginalization: Social group work with lesbians. *Social Work with Groups, 20* (3), 37–59.

Saunders, D. (1977). Marital violence: Dimensions of the problem and modes of intervention. *Journal of Marriage and Family Counseling, 3,* 43–54.

Schiller, L. Y. (1997). Rethinking stages of development in women's groups: Implications for practice. *Social Work with Groups, 20* (3), 3–19.

Schilling, R. F. (1987). Limitations of social support. *Social Service Review, 61,* 26–29.

Schilling, R. F., Schinke, S. P., & Weatherly, R. A. (1988). Service trends in a conservative era: Social workers rediscover the past. *Social Work, 33,* 5–9.

Schein, E. H. (1985). *Organizational culture and leadership.* San Francisco: Jossey-Bass.

Schinke, S. P., Blythe, B. J., & Gilchrist, L. D. (1981). Cognitive-behavioral prevention of adolescent pregnancy. *Journal of Counseling Psychology, 28,* 451–454.

Schinke, S., Blythe, B., Gilchrist, L., & Smith, E. (1980). Developing intake-interviewing skills. *Social Work Research and Abstracts, 16,* 29–34.

Schneider, L., & Struening, E. (1983). SLOF: A behavioral rating scale for assessing the mentally ill. *Social Work Research and Abstracts, 19,* 9–21.

Schneider, R. L., & Netting, F. E. (1999). Influencing social policy in a time of devolution: Upholding social work's great tradition. *Social Work, 44* (4), 349–357.

Schofield, W. (1964). *Psychotherapy: The purchase of friendship.* Englewood Cliffs, NJ: Prentice Hall.

Schopler, J., & Galinsky, M. (1974). Goals in social group work practice: Formulation, implementation, and evaluation. In P. Glasser, R. Sarri, & R. Vinter (Eds.), *Individual change through small groups.* New York: Free Press.

Schopler, J. H., & Galinsky, M. J. (1981). Meeting practice needs: Conceptualizing the open-ended group. *Social Work with Groups, 7* (2), 3–21.

Schopler, J. H., Galinsky, M. J., & Abell, M. (1997). Creating community through telephone and computer groups: Theoretical and practice perspectives. *Social Work with Groups, 20* (4), 19–34.

Schopler, J. H., Galinsky, M. J., Davis, L. E., & Despard, M. (1996). The RAP model: assessing a framework for leading multicultural groups. *Social Work with Groups, 19* (3/4), 21–39.

Schotte, D. E., & Clum, G. A. (1987). Problem-solving skills in suicidal psychiatric patients. *Journal of Consulting and Clinical Psychology, 55,* 49–54.

Schrier, C. (1980). Guidelines for record-keeping under privacy and open-access laws. *Social Work, 25,* 452–457.

Schrodt, G. R., & Fitzgerald, B. A. (1987). Cognitive therapy with adolescents. *American Journal of Psychotherapy, 41,* 402–408.

Schroeder, H. E., & Black, M. J. (1985). Unassertiveness. In M. Hersen & A. S. Bellack (Eds.), *Handbook of clinical behavior therapy with adults* (pp. 509–530). New York: Plenum Press.

Schwartz, F. (1984). *Voluntarism and social work practice: A growing collaboration.* New York: University Press of America.

Schwartz, G. (1989). Confidentiality revisited. *Social Works, 34* (3), 223–226.

Seagull, E. A. (1987). Social support and child maltreatment: A review of the evidence. *Child Abuse and Neglect, 11,* 41–52.

Segal, U. A. (1991). Cultural variables in Asian Indian families. *Families in Society, 72,* 233–244.

Seligman, M. E. P. (1975). *Hopelessness: On depression, development, and death.* San Francisco: W. H. Freeman.

Seligman, M. (1991). Grandparents of disabled grandchildren: Hopes, fears, and adaptation. *Families in Society, 72* (3), 147–152.

Seltzer, M. M., & Bloksberg, L. M. (1987). Permanency planning and its effects on foster children. *Social Work, 32,* 65–68.

Selvini-Palazzoli, M., Boscolo, L., Cecchin, G., & Prata, G. (1974). The treatment of children through brief therapy of their parents. *Family Process, 13,* 429–442.

Selzer, M. L. (1971). The Michigan Alcoholism Screening Test: The quest for a new diagnostic instrument. *American Journal of Psychiatry, 127,* 1653–1658.

Sheafor, B., Horejsi, C. R., and Horejsi, G. A. (1994). *Techniques and guidelines for social work practice* (3rd ed.). Boston: Allyn & Bacon.

Shelby, R. (1992). *If a partner has AIDS: Guide to clinical intervention for relationships in crisis.* Binghamton, NY: Haworth Press.

Shernoff, M. (1990). Why every social worker should be challenged by AIDS. *Social Work, 35* (1), 5–8.

Sherwood, D. A. (1998). Spiritual assessment as a normal part of social work practice: Power to help and power to harm. *Social Work and Christianity, 25* (2), 80–90.

Shimkunas, A. (1972). Demand for intimate self-disclosure and pathological verbalization in schizophrenia. *Journal of Abnormal Psychology, 80,* 197–205.

Shulman, L. (1984). *The skills of helping individuals and groups* (2nd ed.). Itasca, IL: Peacock.

Shulman, L. (1992). *The skills of helping individuals and groups* (3rd ed.). Itasca, IL: Peacock.

Siegel, M., & Roberts, M. (1989). Recruiting foster families for disabled children. *Social Work, 34* (6), 551–553.

Simon, C. E., McNeil, J. S., Franklin, C., & Cooperman, A. (1991). The family and schizophrenia: Toward a psychoeducational approach. *Families in Society, 72* (6), 323–333.

Simonson, N. (1976). The impact of therapist disclosure on patient disclosure. *Journal of Transpersonal Psychology, 23,* 3–6.

Sims, A. R. (1988). Independent living services for youths in foster care. *Social Work, 33* (6), 539–542.

Siporin, M. (1975). *Introduction to social work practice.* New York: Macmillan.

Siporin, M. (1979). Practice theory for clinical social work. *Clinical Social Work Journal, 7,* 75–89.

Siporin, M. (1980). Ecological systems theory in social work. *Journal of Sociology and Social Welfare, 7,* 507–532.

Sistler, A. (1989). Adaptive care of older caregiving spouses. *Social Work, 34* (5), 415–420.

Skinner, H. A. (1982). The Drug Abuse Screening Test. *Addictive Behaviors, 7,* 363–371.

Slater, J., & Depue, R. (1981). The contribution of environmental events and social support to serious suicide attempts in primary depressive disorder. *Journal of Abnormal Psychology, 90,* 275–285.

Slater, S. (1995). *The lesbian lifecycle.* New York: Free Press.

Sluzki, C. (1975). The coalitionary process in initiating family therapy. *Family Process, 14,* 67–77.

Smaldino, A. (1975). The importance of hope in the case work relationship. *Social Casework, 56,* 328–333.

Smith, C., & Carlson, B. E. (1997). Stress, coping, and resilience in children and youth. *Social Service Review, 71* (2), 231–256.

Smith, V. (1979). How interest groups influence legislators. *Social Work, 24,* 234–239.

Smith, V. G., & Hepworth, D. (1967). Marriage counseling with one marital partner: Rationale and clinical implications. *Social Casework, 48,* 352–359.

Smyth, N. J. (1996). Motivating others with dual disorders: A stage approach. *Families in Society, 77* (10), 605–614.

Solomon, B. (1976). *Black empowerment: Social work in oppressed communities.* New York: Columbia University Press.

Solomon, P., & Draine, J. (1996). Service delivery differences between consumer and nonconsumer case managers in mental health. *Research on Social Work Practice, 6* (2), 193–207.

Sosin, M. (1979). Social work advocacy and the implementation of legal mandates. *Social Casework, 60,* 265–273.

Sosin, M., & Caulum, S. (1983). Advocacy: A conceptualization for social work practice. *Social Work, 28,* 12–17.

Sotomayor, M. (1991). Introduction. In M. Sotomayor (Ed.), *Empowering Hispanic Families: A Critical Issue for the 90s* (pp. xi–xxiii). Milwaukee, WI: Family Service America.

Specht, H., & Courtney, M. E. (1994). *Unfaithful angels: How social work abandoned its mission.* Toronto: Maxwell Macmillan Canada.

Specht, H., & Specht, R. (1986a). Social work assessment: Route to clienthood (Part I). *Social Casework, 67,* 525–532.

Specht, H., & Specht, R. (1986b). Social work assessment: Route to clienthood (Part II). *Social Casework, 67,* 587–593.

Speisman, J. (1959). Depth of interpretation and verbal resistance in psychotherapy. *Journal of Consulting Psychology, 23,* 93–99.

Spitzer, R., Williams, J., Kroenke, K., Linzer, M., DeGruy, F., III, Hahn, S., Brody, D., & Johnson, J. (1994). Utility of a new procedure for diagnosing mental disorders in primary care: The PRIME-MD 1000 study. *Journal of the American Medical Association, 272,* 1749–1756.

Spivack, G., Platt, J., & Shure, M. (1976). *The problem solving approach to adjustment.* San Francisco: Jossey-Bass.

Spungen, C., Jensen, S., Finkelstein, N., & Satinsky, F. (1989). Child personal safety: Model program for prevention of child sexual abuse. *Social Work, 34* (2), 127–131.

Steinmetz, G. (1992). Fetal alcohol syndrome. *National Geographic, 181* (2), 36–39.

Steinmetz, S. K. (1988). *Duty bound elder abuse and family care.* Newbury Park, CA: Sage.

Stempler, B., & Stempler, H. (1981). Extending the client connection: Using homemaker-caseworker teams. *Social Casework, 62,* 149–158.

Stith, S. M., Williams, M. B., & Rosen, K. (1990). *Violence hits home: Comprehensive treatment approaches to domestic violence.* New York: Springer.

Stokes, J. P. (1983). Components of group cohesion: Intermember attraction, instrumental value, and risk taking. *Small Group Behavior, 14,* 163–173.

Stordeur, R. A., & Stille, R. (1989). *Ending men's violence against their partners.* Newbury Park, CA: Sage.

Strean, H. (1979). *Psychoanalytic theory and social work practice.* New York: Free Press.

Streeter, C. L., & Franklin, C. (1992). Defining and measuring social support: Guidelines for social work practitioners. *Research on Social Work Practice, 2* (1), 81–98.

Strom, K. (1992, September). Reimbursement demands and treatment decisions: A growing dilemma for social workers. *Social Work, 37* (5), 398–403.

Strom-Gottfried, K. (1998). Applying a conflict resolution framework in managed care. *Social Work, 43* (5), 393–401.

Strom-Gottfried, K. (1999). Professional boundaries: An analysis of violations by social workers. *Families in Society, 80,* 439–448.

Strom-Gottfried, K., & Morrissey, M. (2000). The organizational diversity audit. In K. Strom-Gottfried (Ed.), *Social work practice: Cases, activities, and exercises* (pp. 168–172). Thousand Oaks, CA: Pine Forge Press.

Stuart, P. H. (1999). Linking clients and policy: Social work's distinctive contribution. *Social Work, 44* (4), 335–347.

Stuart, R. (1980). *Helping couples change.* New York: Guilford Press.

Stuntzner-Gibson, D., Koren, P. E., & DeChillo, N. (1995). The youth satisfaction questionnaire: What kids think of service. *Families in Society, 76* (12), 616–624.

Suarez, Z. E., & Siefert, H. (1998). Latinas and sexually transmitted diseases: Implications of recent research for prevention. *Social Work in Health Care, 28* (1), 1–19.

Sue, D. (1981). *Counseling the culturally different: Theory and practice.* New York: Wiley.

Sue, S., & McKinney, H. (1975). Asian Americans in the community mental health care system. *American Journal of Orthopsychiatry, 45,* 111–118.

Sue, S., & Moore, T. (1984). *The pluralistic society: A community mental health perspective.* New York: Human Sciences Press.

Sue, S., & Zane, N. (1987). The role of culture and cultural techniques in psychotherapy. *American Psychologist, 42,* 37–45.

Sunley, R. (1997). Advocacy in the new world of managed care. *Families in Society, 78* (1), 84–94.

Surber, R. W., Dwyer, E., Ryan, K. J., Goldfinger, S. M., & Kelley, J. T. (1988). Medical and psychiatric needs of the homeless—A preliminary response. *Social Work, 33,* 116–119.

Swenson, C. (1995). Clinical social work. In *Encyclopedia of social work.* (19th edition). (pp. 502–513). Washington, DC: NASW Press.

Swenson, C. (1998). Clinical social work's contribution to a social justice perspective. *Social Work, 43* (6), 527–537.

T

Tafoya, T. (1989). Circles and cedar: Native Americans and family therapy. In G. A. Saba, B. M. Kerrer, & K. Hardy (Eds.), *Minorities and family therapy* (pp. 71–94). New York: Hawthorne Press.

Taft, J. (1937). The relation of function to process in social casework. *Journal of Social Work Process, 1* (1), 1–18.

Taube, P. A., & Barrett, S. A. (Eds.) (1983). (DHHS Publication No. ADM 83–1275). Washington, DC: U.S. Government Printing Office.

Taussig, I. M. (1987). Comparative responses of Mexican-Americans and Anglo-Americans to early goal setting in a public mental health clinic. *Journal of Counseling Psychology, 34,* 214–217.

Taylor, B. (1988). Social skills travel training in social work practice. *Social Casework, 69* (4), 248–252.

Taylor, J. W. (1990). The use of nonverbal expression with incestuous clients. *Families in Society, 71* (10), 597–601.

Therapy Privilege Upheld. (1996). *NASW News,* p. 7.

Thibault, J., Ellor, J., & Netting, F. (1991). A conceptual framework for assessing the spiritual functioning and fulfillment of older adults in long-term care settings. *Journal of Religious Gerontology, 7* (4), 29–46.

Thomas, E. (1977). *Marital communication and decision making: Analysis, assessment, and change.* New York: Free Press.

Thomas, E. (1978). Research and service in single-case experimentation: Conflicts and choices. *Social Work Research and Abstracts, 14,* 20–31.

Thomas, E. (1989). Advances in developmental research. *Social Service Review, 63,* 578–597.

Thomas, H., & Caplan, T. (1997). Client, therapist, and context: Addressing resistance in group work. *Social Worker, 65* (3), 27–36.

Thomlison, R. (1984). Something works: Evidence from practice effectiveness studies. *Social Work, 29,* 51–56.

Thompson, T., & Hupp, S. C. (1991). *Saving children at risk: Poverty and disabilities.* Newbury Park, CA: Sage.

Thompson, K. L., Bundy, K. A., & Wolfe, W. R. (1996). Social skills training for young adolescents: cognitive and performance components. *Adolescence, 31* (123), 505–521.

Timberlake, E., & Cook, K. (1984). Social work and the Vietnamese refugee. *Social Work, 29,* 108–114.

Timberlake, E. M., Sababatino, C. A., & Martin, J. A. (1997). Advanced practitioners in clinical social work: A profile. *Social Work, 42* (4), 374–385.

Tisdelle, D. A., & St. Lawrence, J. S. (1988). Adolescent interpersonal problem-solving skill training: Social validation and generalization. *Behavior Therapy, 19,* 171–182.

Tolan, P. H., & Gorman-Smith D. (1997). Families and the development of urban children. In H. J. Walberg, O. Reyes, & R. P. Weissberg (Eds.), *Children and youth: Interdisciplinary perspectives* (pp. 67–91). Thousand Oaks, CA: Sage.

Tolman, R. M., & Molidor, C. E. (1994). A decade of social group work research: Trends in methodology, theory and program development. *Research on Social Work Practice, 4* (2), 142–159.

Tomm, K. (1981). Circularity: A preferred orientation for family assessment. In A. Gurman (Ed.), *Questions and answers in the practice of family therapy* (pp. 84–87). New York: Brunner/Mazel.

Toseland, R. (1977). A problem-solving group workshop for older persons. *Social Work, 22,* 325–326.

Toseland, R. (1981). Increasing access: Outreach methods in social work practice. *Social Casework, 62,* 227–234.

Toseland, R. (1987). Treatment discontinuance: Grounds for optimism. *Social Casework, 68,* 195–204.

Toseland, R., Ivanoff, A., & Rose, S. R. (1987). Treatment conferences: Task groups in action. Working effectively with administrative groups. *Social Work with Groups, 2,* 79–93.

Toseland, R., & Rivas, R. (1984). *An introduction to group work practice.* New York: Macmillan.

Toseland, R. W., & Rivas, R. S. (2001). *An introduction to group work practice* (3rd ed.). Boston: Allyn & Bacon.

Toseland, R., Rossiter, C., Peak, T., & Smith, G. C. (1990). Comparative effectiveness of individual and group interventions to support family caregivers. *Social Work, 35* (3), 209–217.

Tracy, E. M., & Whittaker, J. K. (1990). The Social Network Map: Assessing social support in clinical practice. *Families in Society, 71* (8), 461–470.

Tracy, E. M., & Whittaker, J. K. (1990). *Social Treatment: An introduction to interpersonal helping in social work practice.* New York: Aldine de Gruyter

Tripodi, T., & Epstein, I. *(1980). Research techniques for clinical social workers.* New York: Columbia University Press.

Truax, C., & Carkhuff, R. (1964). For better or for worse: The process of psychotherapeutic personality change. In *Recent advances in the study of behavior change.* (pp. 118–163) Montreal: McGill University Press.

Truax, C., & Carkhuff, R. (1967). *Toward effective counseling and psychotherapy: Training and practice. Chicago:* Aldine-Atherton.

Truax, C., & Mitchell, K. (1971). Research on certain therapist interpersonal skills in relation to process and outcome. In A. Bergin & S. Garfield (Eds.), *Handbook of psychotherapy and behavior change* (pp. 299–344). New York: Wiley.

Tsui, P., & Schultz, G. L. (1985). Failure of rapport: Why psychotherapeutic engagement fails in the treatment of Asian clients. *American Journal of Orthopsychiatry, 55,* 561–569.

Tsui, P., & Schultz, G. L. (1988). Ethnic factors in group process: Cultural dynamics in multi-ethnic therapy groups. *American Journal of Orthopsychiatry, 58,* 136–142.

Turnbull, J. E. (1988). Primary and secondary alcoholic women. *Social Casework, 69* (5), 290–297.

Turnbull, J. E. (1989). Treatment issues for alcoholic women. *Social Casework, 70* (6), 364–369.

Turner, F. J. (Ed.) (1996). *Social work treatment: Interlocking theoretical approaches* (4th ed.). New York: Free Press.

Turner, J. (1984). Reuniting children in foster care with their biological parents. *Social Work, 29* (6), 501–506.

U

Umbreit, M. S. (1993). Crime victims and offenders in mediation: An emerging area of social work practice. *Social Work, 38* (1), 69–73.

U.S. Department of Justice. (1986). *Preventing domestic violence against women.* Washington, DC: Bureau of Justice Statistics.

U.S. Federal Bureau of Investigation. (1988). *Uniform crime reports.* Washington, DC: Author.

V

VandeCreek, L., Knapp, S., & Herzog, C. (1988). Privileged communication for social workers. *Social Casework, 69,* 28–34.

Van Hook, M. P. (1987). Harvest of despair: The ABCX model for farm families in crisis. *Social Casework, 69,* 273–278.

Van Hook, M.P., Berkman, B., & Dunkle, R. (1996). Assessment tools for general health care settings: PRIME-MD, OARS and SF-36. *Health and Social Work, 21* (3), 230–235.

Van Wormer, K., & Boes, J. M. (1997). Humor in the emergency room: A social work perspective. *Health and Social Work, 22* (2), 87–92.

Vattano, A. (1972). Power to the people: Self-help groups. *Social Work, 17,* 7–15.

Vattano, A. (1978). Self-management procedures for coping with stress. *Social Work, 23,* 113–119.

Vernon, R., & Lynch, D. (2000). *Social Work and the Web.* Belmont, CA: Wadsworth.

Videka-Sherman, L. (1987). Research on the effect of parental bereavement: Implications for social work intervention. *Social Service Review, 61,* 102–116.

Videka-Sherman, L. (1988). Meta-analysis of research on social work practice in mental health. *Social Work, 33* (4), 325–338.

Vigilante, F. W., & Mailick, M. D. (1988). Needs-resource evaluation in the assessment process. *Social Work, 33,* 101–104.

Vincent, J., Weiss, R., & Birchlcr, G. (1976). A behavioral analysis of problem solving in distressed and nondistressed married and stranger dyads. *Behavior Therapy, 6,* 475–487.

Visher, E. B., & Visher, J. S. (1988). *Old loyalties, new ties.* New York: Brunner/Mazel.

Vogel, E., & Bell, N. (1960). The emotionally disturbed child as the family scapegoat. In N. Bell & E. Vogel (Eds.), *A modern introduction to the family.* New York: Free Press.

Vosler, N. R. (1990). Assessing family access to basis resources: An essential component of social work practice. *Social Work, 35* (5), 434–441.

Vourlekis, B. S., & Greene, R. R. (1992). *Social work case management.* Hawthorne, NY: Aldine de Gruyter.

Voydanoff, P., & Donnelly, B. M. (1990). *Adolescent sexuality and pregnancy.* Newbury Park, CA: Sage.

W

Wakefield, J. C. (1996a). Does social work need the ecosystems perspective? Part 1. Is the perspective clinically useful? *Social Service Review, 70* (1), 1–32.

Wakefield, J. C. (1996b). Does social work need the ecosystems perspective? Part 2. Does the perspective save social work from incoherence? *Social Service Review, 70* (2), 183–213.

Wakefield, J. C. (1996c). Does social work need the ecological perspective? Reply to Alex Gitterman. *Social Service Review, 70* (3), 476–481.

Walen, S., DiGiuseppe, R., & Wessler, R. (1980). A *practitioner's guide to* RET. New York: Oxford University Press.

Wallace, J. (1989). A biopsychosocial model of alcoholism. *Social Casework, 70* (6), 325–332.

Walsh, J. (2000). *Clinical case management with persons having mental illness: A relationship-based approach.* Pacific Grove, CA: Brooks/Cole.

Waltman, G. H. (1996). Amish health care beliefs and practices. In M. C. Julia, *Multicultural Awareness in the Health Care Professions.* Needham Heights, MA: Allyn & Bacon.

Waltz, T., & Groze, V. (1991). The mission of social work revisited: An agenda for the 1990's. *Social Work, 36* (6), 500–504.

Warren, K., Franklin, C., & Streeter, C. L. (1998). New directions in systems theory: Chaos and complexity. *Social Work, 43* (4), 357–372.

Wartel, S. (1991). Clinical considerations for adults abused as children. *Families in Society, 72* (3), 157–163.

Watson, H., & Levine, M. (1989). Psychotherapy and mandated reporting of child abuse. *American Journal of Orthopsychiatry.*

Watzlawick, P., Weakland, J., & Fisch, R. (1974). *Change: Principles of problem formulation.* New York: Norton.

Weaver, D. (1982). Empowering treatment skills for helping black families. *Social Casework, 63,* 100–105.

Webb, N. B. (1985). A crisis intervention perspective on the termination process. *Clinical Social Work Journal, 13,* 329–340.

Webber, H. S. (1995). The failure of health-care reform: An essay review. *Social Service Review, 69* (2), 309–322.

Weick, A. (1992). Building a strengths perspective for social work. In D. Saleeby, *The strengths perspective in social work practice* (pp. 18–26). White Plains, N.Y.: Longman.

Weick, A., & Pope, L. (1988). Knowing what's best: A new look at self-determination. *Social Casework, 69,* 10–16.

Weick, A., & Saleeby, D. (1995). Supporting family strengths: Orienting policy and practice in the 21st century. *Families in Society, 76,* 141–149.

Weinberg, N. (1983). Social equity and the physically disabled. *Social Work, 28,* 365–369.

Weiner, M. F. (1984). *Techniques of group psychotherapy.* Washington, DC: American Psychiatric Press.

Weiner-Davis (1992). *Divorce-busting.* New York: Summit Books.

Weinman, M. L. (1989). Joint case management planning for pregnant teenagers in school. *School Social Work Journal, 14* (1), 1–8.

Weiss, B. S., & Parish, B. (1989). Culturally appropriate crisis counseling: Adapting an American method for use with Indochinese refugees. *Social Work, 34* (3), 252–254.

Weiss, R. (1974). The provisions of social relationships. In L. Rubin (Ed.), *Doing unto others* (pp. 17–26). Englewood Cliffs, NJ: Prentice Hall.

Weiss, R., & Parkes, C. (1983). *Recovery from bereavement.* New York: Basic Books.

Weissman, A. (1976). *Industrial social services: Linkage of problem formulation and problem resolution.* New York: Norton.

Weissman, H. H., Epstein, I., & Savage, A. (1983). *Agency-based social work: Neglected aspects of clinical practice.* Philadelphia: Temple University Press.

Weissman, H. H., Epstein, I., & Savage, A. (1987). Exploring the role repertoire of clinicians. *Social Casework, 68,* 150–155.

Weisz, J. R., Weiss, B., Wasserman, A. A., & Rintoul, B. (1987). Control-related beliefs and depression among clinic-referred children and adolescents. *Journal of Abnormal Psychology, 96,* 58–63.

Wells, C. C., & Masch, M. K. (1986). *Social work ethics day to day.* White Plains, NY: Longman.

Wells, K., & Biegel, D. E. (Eds.). (1991). *Family preservation services: Research and evaluation.* Newbury Park, CA: Sage.

Wells, R. (1975). Training in facilitative skills. *Social Work, 20,* 242–243.

Wells, R. A. (1994). *Planned short-term treatment* (2nd ed.). New York: Free Press.

Wells, R. A., & Gianetti, V. J. (Eds.) (1990). *Handbook of the brief psychotherapies.* New York: Plenum Press.

Wenar, C. (1994). *Developmental psychopathology from infancy through adolescence* (3rd ed.). New York: McGraw-Hill.

Wertkin, R. A. (1985). Stress-inoculation training: Principles and application. *Social Casework, 66,* 611–616.

Wesley, C.A. (1996). Social work and end-of-life decisions: Self-determination and the common good. *Health and Social Work, 21* (2), 115–121.

West, L., Mercer, S. O., & Altheimer, E. (1993). Operation Desert Storm: The response of a social work outreach team. *Social Work in Health Care, 19* (2), 81–98.

Weston, K. (1991). *Families we choose: Lesbians, gays, and kinship.* New York: Columbia University Press.

Westermeyer, J. J. (1993). Cross-cultural psychiatric assessment. In A. C. Gaw (Ed.), *Culture, ethnicity and mental illness* (pp. 125–146). Washington, DC: American Psychiatric Press.

Whitman, B. Y., Graves, B., & Accardo, P. J. (1989). Training in parenting skills for adults with mental retardation. *Social Work, 34* (5), 431–434.

Whitman, B. Y., & Webb, N. B. (1991). *Play therapy with children in crisis.* New York: Guilford Press.

Whitman, C. (1995). Heading toward normal: Deinstitutionalization for the mentally retarded client. *Marriage and Family Review, 21* (1/2), 51–64.

Whiteman, M., Fanshel, D., & Grundy, J. (1987). Cognitive-behavioral interventions aimed at anger of parents at risk of child abuse. *Social Work, 32* (6), 469–474.

Whitsett, D., & Land, H. (1992). Role strain, coping, and marital satisfaction of stepparents. *Families in Society, 73* (2), 79–92.

Whittaker, J. *(1979). Caring for troubled children.* San Francisco: Jossey-Bass.

Whittaker, J., Garbarino, J., & Associates (1983). *Social support networks. Informal helping in the human services.* Hawthorne, NY: Aldine.

Whittaker, J. K., & Tracy, E. M. (1989). *Social treatment: An introduction to interpersonal helping in social work practice.* New York: Aldine de Gruyter.

Wiehe, V. R. (1990). *Sibling abuse: Hidden physical, emotional and sexual trauma.* Lexington, MA: Lexington Books.

Wijnberg, M. H., & Reding, K.M. (1999). Reclaiming a stress focus: the hassles of rural, poor single mothers. *Families in Society, 80* (5), 506–515.

Wile, D. (1978). Is a confrontational tone necessary in conjoint therapy? *Journal of Marriage and Family Counseling, (4),* 11–18.

Williams, L. F. (1990). The challenge of education to social work: The case for minority children. *Social Work, 35* (3), 236–242.

Williams, O. J. (1994). Group work with African American men who batter: Toward more ethnically sensitive practice. *Journal of Comparative Family Studies, 25* (1), 91–103.

Wilson, J. (1987). Women and poverty: A demographic overview. *Woman and Health, 12,* 21–40.

Wilson, S. K, Cameron, S., Jaffe, P., & Wolfe, D. (1989). Children exposed to wife abuse: An intervention model. *Social Casework, 70* (3), 180–184.

Wilson, V. (1990). The consequences of elderly wives caring for disabled husbands. *Social Work, 35* (5), 417–421.

Winick, C. (1997). Epidemiology. In J. H. Lowinson, P. Ruiz, R. B. Millman, & J. G. Langrod (Eds.), *Substance abuse: A comparative textbook.* (3rd ed.). (pp. 10–16). Baltimore, MD: Williams & Wilkins.

Wiseman, J. C. (1990). *Mediation therapy: Short-term decision making for couples and families in crisis.* New York: Lexington Books.

Wisniewski, J. J., & Toomey, B. G. (1987). Are social workers homophobic? *Social Work, 32,* 454–455.

Withey, V., Anderson, R., & Lauderdale, M. (1980). Volunteers as mentors for abusing parents: A natural helping relationship. *Child Welfare, 59,* 637–644.

Withorn, A. (1998). No win . . . facing the ethical perils of welfare reform. *Families in Society, 79* (3), 277–287.

Witkin, L. (1973). Student volunteers in a guidance clinic. *Social Work, 18,* 53–57.

Witkin, S. (1991). Empirical clinical practice: A critical analysis. *Social Work, 36* (2), 158–163.

Witkin, S. (1993). A human rights approach to social work research and evaluation. In J. Laird (Ed.), *Revisioning social work education: A social constructionist approach.* Binghamton, NY: Haworth Press.

Witkin, S. L. (1998). The right to effective treatment and the effective treatment of rights: Rhetorical empiricism and the politics of research. *Social Work, 43* (1), 75–80.

Witkin, S. (1999). Questions. *Social Work, 44* (3), 197–200.

Wolberg, L. (1965). The technique of short-term psychotherapy. In L. Wolberg (Ed.), *Short-term psychotherapy* (pp. 127–200). New York: Grune & Stratton.

Wolf, K. T. (1991). The diagnostic and statistical manual and the misdiagnosis of African-Americans: An historical perspective. *Social Work Perspectives, 10* (1), 33–38.

Wolff, J. M. (1990). Bite marks: Recognizing child abuse and identifying abusers. *Families in Society, 71* (8), 493–499.

Wong, W. (1983). *Present-day American Samoan family life: A training resource.* University of Hawaii School of Social Work.

Wood, K. (1978). Casework effectiveness: A new look at the research evidence. *Social Work, 23,* 437–458.

Wood, K., & Geismar, L. L. (1989). *Families at risk: Treating the multiproblem family.* New York: Human Services Press.

Wood, W. N. L. (1987). Homosexuality in the family: Lesbian and gay issues. *Social Work, 32,* 143–148.

Worden, J. W. (1991). *Grief counseling and grief therapy: A handbook for the mental health practitioner.* New York: Springer.

Wright, O. L. Jr., & Anderson, J. P. (1998). Clinical social work practice with urban African American families. *Families in Society, 79* (2), 197–205.

Wright, R., Saleeby, D., Watts, T., & Lecca, P. (1983). *Transcultural perspectives in the human services: Organizational issues and trends.* Springfield, IL: Charles C. Thomas.

Wyatt, G. E., & Powell, G. J. (1988). *Lasting effects of child abuse.* Newbury Park, CA: Sage.

Wyers, N. L. (1987). Homosexuality in the family: Lesbian and gay issues. *Social Work, 32,* 143–148.

Y

Yaffe, J., Jenson, J. M., & Howard, M. O. (1995). Woman and substance abuse: Implications for treatment. *Alcoholism-Treatment Quarterly, 13* (2), 1–15.

Yalom, I. (1980). *Existential psychotherapy.* New York: Basic Books.

Yalom, I. (1985). *The theory and practice of group psychotherapy* (2nd ed.). New York: Basic Books.

Yalom, I., & Lieberman, M. (1971). A study of encounter group casualties. *Archives of General Psychiatry, 25,* 16–30.

Yamamoto, J., Silva, J. A., Justice, L. R., Chang, C. Y., & Leong, G. B. (1993). Cross-cultural psychotherapy. In A. C. Gaw (Ed.), *Culture, ethnicity, and mental illness* (pp. 101–124). Washington, DC: American Psychiatric Press.

Yamashiro, G., & Matsuoka, J. (1997). *Helpseeking among Asian and Pacific Americans: A multi-perspective analysis.* National Association of Social Workers.

Yankelovich, D. (1981). New rules in American life: Searching for self-fulfillment in a world turned upsidedown. *Psychology Today, 15,* 35–91.

Yoshioka, M. (2000). Substantive differences in the assertiveness of low-income African American, Hispanic, and Caucasian women. *Journal of Psychology, 134* (3), 243–259.

Young, B. (1980). The Hawaiians. In J. McDermott, W. Tseng, & T. Maretzki (Eds.), *People and cultures of Hawaii* (pp. 5–24). Honolulu: University of Hawaii Press.

Yuker, H. E. (Ed.) (1988). *Attitudes toward persons with disabilities.* New York: Springer.

Z

Zastrow, C. (1987). *Social work with groups.* Chicago: Nelson-Hall.

Zastrow, C., & Kirst-Ashman, K. (1990). *Understanding human behavior and the social environment* (2nd ed.). Chicago: Nelson-Hall.

Zborowski, M., & Herzog, E. (1952). *Life is with people: The culture of the shtetl.* New York: Schocken.

Zechetmayr, M. (1997). Native Americans: A neglected health care crisis and a solution. *Journal of Health and Social Policy, 9* (2), 29–47.

Zeiss, A., Lewinsohn, P., & Munoz, R. (1979). Nonspecific improvements effects in depression using interpersonal skills training, pleasant activities schedules, or cognitive training. *Journal of Consulting and Clinical Psychology, 47,* 427–439.

Zimmerman, S. L. (1995). *Understanding family policy: Theories and applications* (2nd ed.). Thousand Oaks, CA: Sage Publications.

Zingale, D. P. (1985). The importance of empathic responding in the psychotherapeutic interview. *International Social Work, 28,* 35–39.

Zipple, M., & Spaniol, L. (1987). Current educational and supportive models of family intervention. In A. B. Hatfield & H. P. Lefley (Eds.), *Families of the mentally ill.* New York: Guilford Press.

Zung, W. (1965). A self-rating depression scale. *Archives of General Psychiatry, 12,* 63–70.

Zwick, R., & Atkinson, C. C. (1985). Effectiveness of a client pretherapy orientation videotape. *Journal of Counseling Psychology, 32,* 514–524.

Author Index

Subject Index

Derailment, 231
Developmental phases, 361
Developmental stages, 205
Diagnosis, 177–178
    assessment and, 190
Differentiation, 522
Difficulties, anticipating, 91
Directing, 149
Directives
    advance, 68
    giving, 128
    managed, 440
Direct practice, 25, 27–28
    philosophy of, 28–29
Direct practitioners, 29–34
Direct social workers, 35–36
Disconfirming messages, 503
Discouragement, 64
Discrepancies
    affective, 557
    behavioral, 557–558
    categories of, 558
    cognitive/perceptual, 557
Disseminator of information, 30
Distorted conceptions, 233
Do-gooders, 62
Domain, 25–26
Dramatic interpretations,
    177–178
Drugs
    abuse of, 225–227
    assessing use, 223–229
DSM-IV, 237
Dual diagnosis, 227
Dual perspective, 274
Durable power of attorney, 68
Dysfunction
    behaviors, 315, 558
    beliefs, 390–394
    cognitions, 394
    complementary interaction,
        509–510
    interaction, 502–513
    preoccupation with, 191
    processes, 129

Ecological factors
    assessment of, 39
    social systems, 254
    systems model, 17–22
    systems perspective, 19
Eco-map, 347
Economic justice, promoting, 8
Educational groups, 300
Educator, 30
Elder abuse, suspicion of, 73–74
Emotions, 545-546
    assessing function, 52–53,
        234–237, 328
    control of, 234–235
    cultural factors and, 235
    interactions with cognition
        and behavior, 234
    range of, 235–236
Empathic communication,
    92–94
    scale, 100–103
    skills, 111–112, 134–138
    uses of, 107–112
Empathic responding, 51,
    159–160. See also
    Reciprocal empathy
    discriminating levels,
        103–104
    employing, 106–107
    high level, 102–103
    interchangeable, 102
    leads for, 106
    levels, 138
    low level, 101
    moderately high, 102
    moderately low level,
        101–102
    reciprocal level, 102
Empathy
    with client situations, 94
    conveying, 99–103
Empowerment, 438
English language fluency, 347
Enmeshment, 274
Environmental resources, 253

Environmental systems assess-
    ment, 219, 251–256
Equifinality, 20
Ethical decision making, laws
    and, 67
Ethics, 11–12
    boundary provisions, 70–71
    dilemmas of, 77–80
    key principles, 67–75
    laws and, 66–67
    values as, 66–67
Ethnic minority clients, 465
Ethnocultural groups, 362
Evaluation, 339–345
    in macro practice, 475–476
Excusing behavior, 178
Expectations, 51
Expediter, 32
Experiences
    details of, 152
    validity of, 62
Expert testimony, 453
Exploration
    evaluation of use, 162–163
    skills, 139
    topic selections, 157–158
Expression, 152–154

Facilitative conditions, 92
Facilitator, 32
Fact sheets, 70
FAE. See Fetal alcohol effects
False hope, 64
Families
    alignments, 514–517
    approaches to working with,
        477–479
    assessment, 261, 272–273,
        288, 294–295
    boundaries, 280. See also
        Family systems
    bounding patterns of,
        278
    change focus, 495–502
    cognitive patterns, 289–290

Helping relationships
  attitude toward, 247–248
  threats to, 566
Hidden messages, 51
Hidden purpose, 549
Historical facts, 182
Homelessness, 442
Hostile clients, 110
Host settings, 188
Human behavior, 13
Human beings
  capacity to change, 63–66
  intrinsic worth and dignity,
    59–61
  needs and resources, 7
  uniqueness and individuality,
    61–63
Human problems
  assessments, 18
  dimensions, 199
  multiple systems interaction,
    219
Humor, 178–179

Identifiable potential victim, 73
Illness, 222–223
Immigrant families, 276
Immigrant groups, 446–447
Immigration and
  Naturalization Service
  (INS), 446
Impact, confrontation and, 433
Implementation, 41–43
Individual behavior, 312–316
Individuality, 62
  patterns, vs. cultural,
    244–245
  rights, 9
  well-being, 58–59
Information
  collateral sources, 196–197
  disseminator, 30
  eliciting essential, 52
  gathering, 453
  sources, 194–198, 316

Informative events, 346
Informed consent, 69–70
INS. See Immigration and
  Naturalization Service
Institutional environments
  benefits, 461
  improving, 459–469
  policies, 462–467
  procedures, 462–467
  programs, 467–469
  risks, 461
  staff, 460–461
Instructing, 177
Intake, 472
Intellectual functioning, 229
Intelligence test, 197
Interactions, 198
  domination of, 180–181
  managing during problem
    solving, 407–409
  observation of, 195–196
  persons or systems, 202–204
Interagency committees, 453
Interface, 6
Interpretation, 543–545
  guidelines, 549–550
  modeled responses, 560
  skill development, 559–560
Interpreters, 50
Interruptions, 180
  managing, 128–129
Interventions, 27
  balancing, 508
  client view, 360
  criteria, 21–22
  evaluating, 41
  guidelines, 507–509
  matching to ethnocultural
    groups, 362
  matching phases, 361
  matching to problems, 360
  matching to stressful transi-
    tions, 361
  matching to target systems,
    360

on-the-spot, 506
  planning, 472
  strategies, 437–439
  time and focus, 508
Interviewing process
  conducive conditions, 45
  emotional assessment, 52–53
  end, 54
  exploration, 50–52
  focus, 52
  initial contact, 46–50
  outlines, 52
  physical conditions, 45–50
  rapport, 46–50
  skills, 50–52
  structure and skills, 45–55
Intimacy, 521–522, 537–538
Intrapersonal assessments, 219
Intrapersonal systems, 219–220
Intra-role tensions, 291
Involuntary clients, 23
  assessing, 201–202
  goals and, 329–330
  motivation and, 49

Jaffee v. Redmond, 74
Jargon, 153
Joining stage, 482
Joint decision-making, 286
Judgments, 177, 229–230
  withholding, 60

Kinship networks, 443

Labeling, 177–178, 290
Laws
  ethics and, 66–67
  medical power of attorney,
    68
  privilege, 74
Leadership. See also Group
  leaders
  interventions, 531–540
  structure, 529–530
Leakage, 172

TO THE OWNER OF THIS BOOK:

We hope that you have found *Direct Social Work Practice: Theory and Skills,* 6th Edition, useful. So that this book can be improved in a future edition, would you take the time to complete this sheet and return it? Thank you.

School and address: _____

Department: _____

Instructor's name: _____

1. What I like most about this book is: _____

_____

_____

2. What I like least about this book is: _____

_____

_____

3. My general reaction to this book is: _____

_____

4. The name of the course in which I used this book is: _____

_____

5. Were all of the chapters of the book assigned for you to read? _____

   If not, which ones weren't? _____

6. In the space below, or on a separate sheet of paper, please write specific suggestions for improving this book and anything else you'd care to share about your experience in using the book.

_____

_____

_____

_____

_____

BUSINESS REPLY MAIL

FIRST CLASS   PERMIT NO. 358   PACIFIC GROVE, CA

POSTAGE WILL BE PAID BY ADDRESSEE

ATT: *Dean H. Hepworth, Ronald H. Rooney, & Jo Ann Larsen*

Brooks/Cole Publishing Company
511 Forest Lodge Road
Pacific Grove, California 93950-9968

Attention Professors:

Brooks/Cole is dedicated to publishing quality publications for education in the social work, counseling, and human services fields. If you are interested in learning more about our publications, please fill in your name and address and request our latest catalogue, using this prepaid mailer. Please choose one of the following:

☐ social work   ☐ counseling   ☐ human services

Name: _____

Street Address: _____

City, State, and Zip: _____

FOLD HERE

BUSINESS REPLY MAIL

FIRST CLASS   PERMIT NO. 358   PACIFIC GROVE, CA

POSTAGE WILL BE PAID BY ADDRESSEE

ATT: *Marketing*

The Wadsworth Group
10 Davis Drive
Belmont, CA 94002

FOLD HERE

IN-BOOK SURVEY

At Brooks/Cole, we are excited about creating new types of learning materials that are interactive, three-dimensional, and fun to use. To guide us in our publishing/development process, we hope that you'll take just a few moments to fill out the survey below. Your answers can help us make decisions that will allow us to produce a wide variety of videos, CD-ROMs, and Internet-based learning systems to complement standard textbooks. If you're interested in working with us as a student Beta-tester, be sure to fill in your name, telephone number, and address. We look forward to hearing from you!

In addition to books, which of the following learning tools do you currently use in your counseling/human services/social work courses?

_____ **Video** _____ in class _____ school library _____ own VCR

_____ **CD-ROM** _____ in class _____ in lab _____ own computer

_____ **Macintosh disks** _____ in class _____ in lab _____ own computer

_____ **Windows disks** _____ in class _____ in lab _____ own computer

_____ **Internet** _____ in class _____ in lab _____ own computer

How often do you access the Internet? _____

My own home computer is a:

_____

The computer I use in class for counseling/human services/social work courses is a:

_____

If you are NOT currently using multimedia materials in your counseling/human services/social work courses, but can see ways that video, CD-ROM, Internet, or other technologies could enhance your learning, please comment below:

_____

_____

_____

Other comments (optional): _____

_____

Name _____ Telephone _____

Address _____

School _____

Professor/Course_____

You can fax this form to us at (650) 592-9081 or detach, fold, secure, and mail.